The Supreme Court at Work

The Supreme Court at Work

SECOND EDITION

JOAN BISKUPIC and ELDER WITT

CONGRESSIONAL QUARTERLY INC.
WASHINGTON, D.C.

Copyright © 1997 Congressional Quarterly Inc.
1414 22nd Street, N.W., Washington, D.C. 20037

Book design and production by Kachergis Book Design,
Pittsboro, North Carolina

Printed and bound in the United States of America

The paper used in this publication meets the minimum requirements of the American National Standard for Information Science—Permanence of Paper for Printed Library Materials, ANSI z39.48-1984.

Acknowledgments: Lee Epstein and Thomas G. Walker contributed their research on natural courts, which is part of Appendix B. This research was published previously in their book *Constitutional Law for a Changing America: Institutional Powers and Constraints,* Second Edition (Washington, D.C.: CQ Press, 1995), 617. Lee Epstein, Jeffrey A. Segal, Harold J. Spaeth, and Thomas G. Walker provided the map of the federal court system, which is part of Appendix B. The map was published previously in their book *The Supreme Court Compendium: Data, Decisions, and Developments,* Second Edition (Washington, D.C.: Congressional Quarterly, 1996), 651.

LIBRARY OF CONGRESS CATALOGING-IN-PUBLICATION DATA
Biskupic, Joan.
    The Supreme Court at work.—2nd ed. / Joan Biskupic and
Elder Witt.
        p.   cm.
    Rev. ed. of: The Supreme Court at work. c 1990.
    Includes bibliographical references and index.
    ISBN 1-56802-323-5
    1. United States.   Supreme Court.   2. Courts of last resort—
United States.   I. Witt, Elder.   II. Supreme Court at work.
III. Title.
KF8742.S912   1996
347.73'26—dc20
[347.30735]   96-29102

Table of Contents

Preface

The vast power wielded by the modern Supreme Court could hardly have been imagined when the Court convened for the first time on February 1, 1790. Only three of the justices actually attended the opening day's session in New York City. The term lasted just nine days. No cases were argued or decided.

When the national government moved to Washington in 1801, the Court was still such an insignificant part of the national government that those who planned the new capital city forgot to provide a place for it to meet. Well over a century would pass before the Court had its own building.

This book tells the story of how the Court grew from those modest beginnings to a singularly powerful court of justice. Chapters 1 to 3 contain narrative essays, tracing the people, problems, events, and decisions of the Court's history from the first term in 1790 through its term that ended in July 1996.

Chapter 1 considers the Court's first century—the establishment of the power of judicial review during the tenure of John Marshall, the self-inflicted wound of the Dred Scott decision preceding (and some would say precipitating) the Civil War,

and the rebalancing of state and federal power in the wake of war. Chapter 2 examines the Court's second century—during the first half of which the Court resisted change, and during the last half of which it initiated change. Chapter 3 tells the story of the first years of the Court's third century, now less than a decade old. For those who wish more detail about particular decisions during the Court's history, summaries of more than four hundred major decisions are included in Appendix B of the Reference Materials section.

Chapter 4 reviews the history of the Court's operations and traditions. Chapter 5 tells of the growth of the role of chief justice and that of the associate justices, as well as the various supporting personnel of the Court. Chapter 6 recounts the various meeting places of the Court until it moved into its current building in 1935. Chapter 7 examines the 108 members of the Court, and chapter 8 contains brief biographies of each of the justices. Appendixes A and B contain relevant documents, texts, tables, lists, and a selected bibliography.

Joan Biskupic and Elder Witt

The Supreme Court at Work

CHAPTER 1

The First Century: Origins of Power

W E MUST NEVER FORGET that it is a constitution we are expounding," Chief Justice John Marshall admonished his fellow justices in 1819.[1] To modern ears, Marshall's words may seem at first a truism, yet through them rings with clarity the mission that gives the Supreme Court such a significant role in American life and government. The Court's unique role in the United States is a direct outgrowth of the new meaning the word *constitution* assumed in the American experiment.

In 1789 every government had a constitution. The word simply referred to whatever principles and assumptions underlay the existing system. But in the new nation called the United States the word was invested with added significance.

"A Constitution, in the American sense of the word," Justice Samuel Miller would write a century later, "is a written instrument by which the fundamental powers of the government are established, limited, and defined, and by which these powers are distributed among several departments, for their more safe and useful exercise for the benefit of the body politic."

In the U.S. Constitution, Miller continued, "the people themselves have undertaken to frame an organic law governing the relations of the whole people, as well as of the individual states, to the federal government, and to prescribe in many cases the limits and rules of private and personal rights. It is the fundamental law pursuant to which the government is permanently organized and conducted."[2]

In the United States, then, the Constitution is far more than a description of the existing system. It is an active instrument, the charter of the national system, the source of power and of the limits of power.

But the Constitution of the United States is hardly self-enforcing. Chief Justice Marshall described it as a document whose "great outlines should be marked, its important objects designated, and the minor ingredients which compose those objects be deduced from the nature of the objects themselves."[3]

The next question was obvious. Who would undertake these all-important deductions? Who would implement the limits the Constitution set? Who would fill in the broad outlines of the powers it granted? The answer was not long in doubt. The Supreme Court would serve this function, it declared in *Marbury v. Madison*. The "weakest branch" of the new system would assume this critical responsibility; the Court would be "the particular guardian of the terms of the written constitution."[4]

In the ensuing two centuries, the Supreme Court—by virtue of its exercise of this responsibility—has become the most powerful court the world has ever known. It can override the will of the majority expressed in an act of Congress. It can remind a president that in the United States all persons are subject to the rule of law. It can require the redistribution of political power in every state. And it can persuade the nation's citizens that the fabric of their society must be rewoven into new patterns.

There have been mistakes and contradictions along the way. Constitutional development in the United States follows no tidy pattern. The Court does not initiate cases or solicit issues; it must take them as they come. When it decides cases, it often seems tentative and hesitant, zigging and zagging from case to case within a particular issue. The pattern is quintessentially human. For all its remoteness, the Court is the most human of government institutions. It is nine individuals, men and women whose names and faces and histories are publicly known. Issues come to the Court when individuals disagree. Black and white, merchant and consumer, prisoner and warden, president and pauper—they come before the Court to seek resolution of their disputes.

The justices who decide these cases are neither monks nor oracles. They respond to the same concerns and influences as their fellow citizens. They hear the arguments; then they meet, talk, and vote. The Court has decided. The justices write, comment, edit. The opinions are signed. The decision is announced. The dispute is resolved—and the role of the Court in the continuing development of the American system is once again affirmed.

The Court is the nation's balance wheel. Justice Robert H. Jackson explained:

In a society in which rapid changes tend to upset all equilibrium, the Court, without exceeding its own limited powers, must strive to maintain the great system of balances upon which our free government is based. Whether these balances and checks are essential to liberty elsewhere in the world is beside the point; they are indispensable to the society we know. Chief of these balances are: first, between the Executive and Congress; second, between the central government and the States; third, between state and state; fourth, between authority, be it state or national, and the liberty of the citizen, or between the rule of the majority and the rights of the individual.[5]

This is the story of that Court and those balances.

The Foundations

The contrast in the amount of detail is striking. Articles I and II of the Constitution set out in considerable length the powers and prerogatives of Congress and the executive branch. Article III simply sketches the outline of a federal judiciary.

One scholar, Julius Goebel Jr., suggests that at least for some delegates to the Constitutional Convention, "provision for a national judiciary was a matter of theoretical compulsion rather than of practical necessity . . . more in deference to the maxim of separation [of powers] than in response to clearly formulated ideas about the role of a national judicial system and its indispensability."[6]

At any rate, with little discussion and less debate, the convention approved language that declared:

The judicial Power of the United States, shall be vested in one supreme Court, and in such inferior Courts as the Congress may from time to time ordain and establish.

Section 1 provides that federal judges will hold their posts during good behavior and that their salaries may not be diminished during their terms in office.

Article II already provided that the members of the Supreme Court would be appointed by the president by and with the advice and consent of the Senate—and that judges, along with all other civil officers of the new national government, "shall be removed from office on Impeachment for, and Conviction of, Treason, Bribery, or other high Crimes and Misdemeanors."

Section 2 of Article III describes the reach of federal judicial power. Some cases were included because of their subject—"all Cases, in Law and Equity, arising under this Constitution, the Laws of the United States, and Treaties made, or which shall be made, under their Authority . . . all Cases of admiralty and maritime Jurisdiction." Other cases were included because of the parties involved—"all Cases affecting Ambassadors, other public Ministers and Consuls; . . . Controversies to which the United States shall be a Party; . . . Controversies between two or more States."

The Supreme Court would have original jurisdiction—the power to hear the initial arguments—in cases involving foreign dignitaries and those involving states. In all other cases, the Court's jurisdiction was appellate—it would hear appeals from rulings of lower courts.

There ended the Constitution's description of the nation's judicial branch. The remaining sections of Article III dealt with jury trials, the place of trials, and the crime of treason.

The brevity of the constitutional description left to Congress and the Court itself the task of filling in much of the substance and all of the details of the new judicial system. One early observer commented, "The convention has only crayoned in the outlines. It is left to Congress to fill up and colour the canvas."[7]

AN INDEPENDENT BRANCH

Although the Articles of Confederation had not provided for a system of national courts, the concept of a separate and relatively independent judiciary was generally accepted by the delegates to the Constitutional Convention. At the time of the adoption of Article III, six of the original thirteen states had such judicial branches.[8]

There was some debate over the need for any inferior federal courts. Some delegates argued that state courts were adequate to handle all judicial business other than that which the Supreme Court would consider. That debate was resolved by leaving the final decision to Congress.

Delegates also disagreed over whether Congress or the president should appoint the members of the Supreme Court—and whether the Court should try impeachments. A compromise resulted in giving the president the power to name the Court's members with the advice and consent of the Senate, the same body given the power to try impeachments.

To safeguard judicial independence, the "good behavior" and salary provisions were added. Alexander Hamilton wrote in *The Federalist Papers:*

The standard of good behavior for the continuance in office of the judicial magistracy is certainly one of the most valuable of the modern improvements in the practice of government. In a monarchy it is an excellent barrier to the despotism of the prince; in a republic it is a no less excellent barrier to the encroachments and oppressions of the representative body. And it is the best expedient which can be devised in any government to secure a steady, upright, and impartial administration of the laws.[9]

By providing for impeachment of judges, Hamilton wrote, the Constitution ensured their responsible conduct.[10]

FEDERAL SUPREMACY

Neither the separateness nor the independence of the Supreme Court is truly unique. The most notable and peculiar of its characteristics is its power of judicial review, the power to review and nullify state and federal laws that collide with the Constitution.

The need for judicial review grew out of the convention's adoption, in Article VI, of the declaration that

This Constitution, and the Laws of the United States which shall be made in Pursuance thereof; and all Treaties made, or which shall be made, under the Authority of the United States, shall be the supreme Law of the Land; and the Judges in every State shall be bound thereby, any Thing in the Constitution or Laws of any State to the Contrary notwithstanding.

Article VI also states that all officials of the national and state governments were to take an oath to support the Constitution. Left unsaid—again—was who would enforce the provisions and prescriptions of the Constitution if some officials chose to ignore that oath.

Insofar as state actions were concerned, Congress remedied that omission in the Judiciary Act of 1789. This act gave the Supreme Court the power to review rulings of state courts rejecting claims that state laws or actions conflict with the U.S. Constitution, federal laws, or treaties. It also specified that the Supreme Court would consist of a chief justice and five associate justices, meeting twice each year, in February and in August.

This provision for judicial review of state rulings was contained in the famous Section 25 of the Judiciary Act, the subject of much criticism and many repeal efforts over the next three decades.

JUDICIAL REVIEW

Congress did not grant the Supreme Court the power of judicial review over acts of Congress, the power to measure challenged federal laws against constitutional standards. Nor does the Constitution address this aspect of the Court's power.

In 1803 the Court simply claimed this role. In *Marbury v. Madison* the Court struck down a portion of the same Judiciary Act that granted it the power to review state court rulings. The offending section, wrote Chief Justice Marshall, purported to enlarge the original jurisdiction of the Court—something Congress had no power to do.

Marbury v. Madison sparked a long scholarly debate over whether the Court was undertaking a role the Framers intended it to fill or was usurping power it was never intended to possess. Despite its sporadic intensity, the debate is irrelevant. The Court's power to review acts of Congress is firmly established and has never been seriously challenged.

Most scholars think that the members of the Constitutional Convention intended the Court to exert this power. They point to various remarks during the convention debates—and during the ratification conventions in the states—as indicating that many members of the convention simply assumed that the Supreme Court would have this power.

Most enduring of the arguments of this early period are those set out by Alexander Hamilton in *The Federalist Papers*. Hamilton reasoned that this function of the Court was essential to the existence of a limited constitutional government. The federal courts, he said, would serve as "bulwarks of a limited Constitution."[11]

After his often-quoted description of the judicial branch as "incontestably . . . beyond comparison the weakest of the three departments of power," Hamilton continued:

The complete independence of the courts of justice is peculiarly essential in a limited Constitution. By a limited Constitution, I understand one which contains certain specified exceptions to the legislative authority; such, for instance, as that it shall pass no bills of attainder, no ex post facto laws, and the like. Limitations of this kind can be preserved in practice no other way than through the medium of courts of justice, whose duty it must be to declare all acts contrary to the manifest tenor of the Constitution void. Without this, all the reservations of particular rights or privileges would amount to nothing.[12]

Hamilton rejected the argument that to allow the Court to declare acts of Congress invalid would elevate the "weakest branch" to a position superior to that of Congress:

. . . every act of a delegated authority, contrary to the tenor of the commission under which it is exercised, is void. No legislative act, therefore, contrary to the Constitution, can be valid. To deny this would be to affirm . . . that the representatives of the people are superior to the people themselves; that men acting by virtue of powers may do not only what their powers do not authorize, but what they forbid. . . .

. . . the courts were designed to be an intermediate body between the people and the legislature in order, among other things, to keep the latter within the limits assigned to their authority. The interpretation of the laws is the proper and peculiar province of the courts. A constitution is, in fact, and must be regarded by the judges as, a fundamental

"Where the will of the legislature . . . stands in opposition to that of the people, declared in the Constitution, the judges ought to be governed by the latter."

Alexander Hamilton, *The Federalist Papers*

law. It therefore belongs to them to ascertain its meaning as well as the meaning of any particular act proceeding from the legislative body. If there should happen to be an irreconcilable variance between the two, that which has the superior obligation and validity ought, of course, to be preferred; or, in other words, the Constitution ought to be preferred to the statute, the intention of the people to the intention of their agents.

Nor does this conclusion by any means suppose a superiority of the judicial to the legislative power. It only supposes that the power of the people is superior to both, and that where the will of the legislature, declared in its statutes, stands in opposition to that of the people, declared in the Constitution, the judges ought to be governed by the latter.[13]

A Slow Start: 1790–1800

On September 24, 1789, President George Washington signed the Judiciary Act into law and sent the Senate his nominations of six men to serve as the first members of the Supreme Court. One of the men so honored declined to accept a state post; another accepted but never attended a formal session; and John Jay, the first chief justice, spent much of his tenure abroad, engaged in diplomatic duties; he resigned after six years to become governor of New York.

Washington's original selections—all active participants in the founding of the new government—were:

• Chief Justice John Jay, age forty-four, of New York, coauthor with Hamilton and James Madison of *The Federalist Papers*.

• John Rutledge of South Carolina, fifty, a member of the Constitutional Convention.

• Robert Hanson Harrison of Maryland, forty-four, who declined the post to become chancellor of Maryland.

• John Blair of Virginia, fifty-seven, a member of the Constitutional Convention and a leader in the effort to obtain Virginia's ratification of the new national charter.

• James Wilson of Pennsylvania, forty-seven, signer of the Declaration of Independence, member of the Constitutional Convention, and a leader in obtaining ratification of the new charter by his state.

• William Cushing of Massachusetts, fifty-seven, a state judge and leader of the state ratification effort.

After Harrison's refusal, Washington selected James Iredell of North Carolina, thirty-eight, for the fifth associate justice's seat. Iredell had led the initially unsuccessful effort to win North Carolina's vote in favor of the new Constitution.

Confirmation of these first nominees came within two days, on September 26. Iredell was nominated early the next year, February 9, 1790, and confirmed the next day.

The tenure of five of these original members was brief. Jay resigned in 1795. Two other men followed him as chief justice within the Court's first decade. Rutledge resigned in 1791. He had never attended a formal session of the full Court. Blair, after several years of irregular attendance, resigned because of poor health in 1796. Wilson died in 1798. Iredell, the only member of the first Court to move his family to the new nation's capital, New York, resigned in 1799.[14] Cushing alone served into the nineteenth century, remaining on the Court for twenty-one years until his death in 1810.

FIRST TERMS

"The status of the federal judiciary in the 1790s," wrote political scientist Robert G. McCloskey, "was ambiguous and . . . comparatively minor. . . . The paramount governmental tasks were legislative and executive."[15]

The record of the Supreme Court's first decade bears out that statement. Only three of the six justices were present for the Court's opening session February 1, 1790. Jay, Wilson, and Cushing, wearing robes and, at least in Cushing's case, a wig, met briefly in the Royal Exchange Building in New York.

By February 2 Blair had arrived, making the quorum needed for transaction of business. But there was no business, aside from organizational matters, chief among which was the appointment of a clerk. After several days of admitting attorneys to practice before it, the Court adjourned its first term on February 10, 1790.

The second term lasted two days—August 2–3, 1790. Iredell, confirmed in February, was present.

In 1791 the capital and the Court moved to Philadelphia where the Court shared, with the mayor's court, a room in the new City Hall. No cases were decided by the Court in 1791 or 1792. The Court met in Philadelphia until 1800. Three times—in 1793, 1794, and 1797—it was forced by epidemics of yellow fever to cancel its August term.[16]

In 1791 Justice Rutledge resigned to take a state judgeship. Two of the men offered his seat declined, preferring to retain their seats in state legislatures.[17]

President Washington then selected Thomas Johnson of Maryland, at fifty-nine, one of the Court's oldest members. Johnson would hold the seat only fourteen months.

In 1792 Chief Justice Jay campaigned unsuccessfully from the bench for the post of governor of New York. He described his Court post as "intolerable."[18]

On February 18, 1793, the Court announced its decision in *Chisholm v. Georgia,* its first major case. Within five years, the country overturned that decision.

Reading Article III literally in *Chisholm,* the Court upheld the right of citizens of one state, South Carolina, to bring original suits in the Supreme Court against another state, Georgia. The vote of the Court was 5–1. Iredell dissented. Each justice announced his opinion orally.

The states were shocked, seeing in this decision the potential for their economic ruin. Early in 1798 the Eleventh Amendment was ratified. This amendment declared that states could not be sued, without their consent, in federal Courts by citizens of another state.

Despite the lack of many notable decisions during these first years, the justices found themselves quite busy—and rather unhappy—with the demands of their duty as circuit judges. For a full century, the justices worked to convince Congress to abolish this role, which fell to the justices because the Judiciary Act of 1789 provided no separate set of judges for the federal circuit courts. The act instead provided that Supreme Court justices would travel to hold circuit court where and when necessary.

This aspect of judicial duty, although onerous, served an important function in the new nation. Historian Charles Warren notes that "it was . . . almost entirely through their contact with the judges sitting in the circuit courts that the people of the country became acquainted with this new institution, the federal judiciary."[19]

But the distances the justices were required to travel were long, conditions were difficult, and questions were raised about the propriety of the justices participating in cases at the circuit level that were then reviewed by the Supreme Court. As early as 1790 Chief Justice Jay asked Congress to remove this burden. Congress responded with minor changes in 1793; the Judiciary Act of 1801 (which was quickly repealed) abolished the duty temporarily; but until late in the nineteenth century the requirement that justices fill this function remained on the statute books.[20]

COURT, CONGRESS, AND PRESIDENT

During its first decade, the Court made clear its character as a purely judicial branch, declining to perform nonjudicial functions assigned by Congress or to issue advisory opinions in re-

John Jay

Oliver Ellsworth

sponse to executive queries. "In other words," wrote Goebel in summarizing the Court's first years, "it left the formulation of policy to the branches of government where it conceived such belonged."[21]

In 1792 Congress gave circuit courts the duty of ruling upon claims of invalid pensioners. Justices Iredell, Blair, and Wilson, sitting as circuit judges, refused to carry out that duty, declaring that Congress had overstepped itself by requiring them to undertake such nonjudicial responsibilities. As a result of their protest, Congress amended the pension law.[22]

In 1793 President Washington asked the Court for advice on certain questions of foreign policy, neutrality, and treaty law. The justices politely declined, citing "the lines of separation, drawn by the Constitution between the three departments of the government" and "our being Judges of a Court in the last resort." Thereby, the Court established its policy of issuing no advisory opinions.[23]

Earlier that year Johnson had resigned. He was replaced by William Paterson of New Jersey, age forty-four, one of the two senators who had been primarily responsible for drafting and enacting the Judiciary Act of 1789. Paterson would serve until 1806.

During the February 1794 term the Court heard *Georgia v. Brailsford,* one of a handful of cases tried before it by a jury.[24] And in the last major case in which John Jay participated, the Court rejected the assertion that a foreign country had the right—independent of any treaty or other legal guarantee—to set up a prize court in the United States to decide the disposition of captured vessels.[25]

In April 1794 Jay accepted an appointment as special ambassador to England; he never returned to his seat on the Court. After concluding a treaty of "amity, commerce, and navigation" (the Jay treaty) with Britain, he resigned in June 1795 to become governor of New York.

John Rutledge of South Carolina, the absentee justice of the Court's first terms, was nominated by Washington—at Rutledge's own suggestion—to succeed Jay. Appointed while the Senate was in recess in 1795, Rutledge presided over the Court's August 1795 term but was refused confirmation by the Senate in December. The Senate acted upon reports of Rutledge's criticism of the Jay treaty and on rumors of his mental instability, rumors to which Rutledge gave new credibility by attempting suicide after his rejection by the Senate.

Washington, early in 1796, named Cushing, the senior justice, to lead the Court. Although he was confirmed, Cushing declined the post on the basis that at sixty-four he was too old. He would serve for fourteen more years.

President Washington next offered the post of chief justice to Sen. Oliver Ellsworth of Connecticut, who, with Paterson, had drafted the Judiciary Act. Ellsworth, fifty-one, was nominated March 3, 1796, confirmed the following day, and took his seat March 8.

TREATIES AND TAXES

Without Ellsworth, who was sworn in too late to take part in the decisions, the Court during the February 1796 term decided the two most significant cases of the decade—the treaty case of *Ware v. Hylton* and the tax case of *Hylton v. United States.* John

Marshall argued *Ware v. Hylton*, apparently his only appearance as an advocate before the tribunal he would lead for more than three decades. He lost the case.

In *Ware v. Hylton* the Court established the supremacy of federal treaty provisions over conflicting state laws. A Virginia law that allowed the confiscation, or payment in depreciated currency, of debts owed by Virginians to British subjects was invalid, held the justices, because it conflicted with provisions of the peace treaty with Britain, which ensured the collection of such debts.

Hylton v. United States brought to the Court the first clear challenge to an act of Congress as unconstitutional. There was no debate over the Court's power to rule on that point. Each of the sitting justices—while on circuit duty—had indicated his belief that federal courts were empowered to resolve such challenges.[26]

Congress had imposed a tax on carriages. The tax was challenged as a direct tax, which the Constitution required be apportioned among the states by population. The definition of "direct tax" was unclear, but the Court declared that the carriage tax was not a direct tax and thus was not subject to the apportionment requirement. The Court said that direct taxes were only those on land and on individuals, a definition that would stand for a century, until its repudiation by the Court in 1895.

A new member of the Court took part in these two decisions—Samuel Chase of Maryland. Chase, a political maverick, would be the only justice in history to be impeached and tried by the Senate. Chase was Washington's surprise choice to fill the seat left vacant by the resignation, in mid-1795, of Justice Blair. A signer of the Declaration of Independence, Chase had opposed ratification of the Constitution, arguing that it was an undemocratic document.

Nominated and confirmed in January 1796, he took his seat as the February 1796 term began—and voted with the majority in both the tax and the treaty cases. Chase and Ellsworth were the last of Washington's appointments to the Court. With Cushing and Paterson, Chase would serve well into the next century.

THE ADAMS YEARS

During the administration of John Adams, the Court issued one major decision, declaring in *Calder v. Bull* that the constitutional ban on ex post facto laws applied only to criminal, not civil, laws. Few other decisions of lasting significance were announced during the 1797–1801 terms.

With the deaths of Justices Wilson and Iredell, Adams had the opportunity to fill two seats on the Court. To succeed Wilson, Adams named Bushrod Washington of Virginia, thirty-five, President Washington's nephew. To succeed Iredell, he chose Alfred Moore, forty-four, of North Carolina. Washington would serve for more than three decades; Moore resigned in 1804 after barely five years on the bench.

The 1799 and 1800 terms of the Court were uneventful. The August 1800 term was the last to be held in Philadelphia. Only three justices attended—Paterson, Moore, and Washington.

Ellsworth, named ambassador to France in February 1799, was abroad—as he would be for the remainder of his time as chief justice. Cushing was ill. Chase was campaigning, unsuccessfully, for Adams's reelection.

In the election of 1800 the staunch nationalist position of the Court became a campaign issue, coupled with complaints about the ambassadorial service of Chief Justices Jay and Ellsworth, acting as agents of the Federalist administrations.

The Court's first decade was a cautious time. As Goebel concludes:

> Its posture toward acts of Congress, except for a few instances of individual critique, was one of respect. There were, indeed, occasions . . . that invited inquiry into the constitutional basis for congressional action where less deference would have been appropriate. These opportunities were not seized, nor was there succumbing to the temptation to a loose construction of statutory language sometimes advanced by counsel in argument.
>
> When the Court was constrained to explore the intendment of statutory language, it did so as a court of law in terms familiar to the profession and not by flights of fancy about the "spirit" of the Constitution.[27]

Establishment of Power: 1801–1835

With the year 1801 the new nation began a new century with a new president, Thomas Jefferson, and a new chief justice, John Marshall. Although Jefferson and Marshall shared a home state, they were life-long antagonists, and that personal tension further heightened the natural strains between the young nation's executive and judicial branches.

That same year the government moved to a permanent home, Washington, D.C. The Capitol was under construction as the home of Congress, a residence was planned for the president, but no one thought to provide a place for the Supreme Court to meet. At the last minute, it was allotted a small room in the unfinished Capitol. There it convened for its February 1801 term, the first of Marshall's thirty-four-year tenure.

Oliver Ellsworth, still in France on diplomatic assignment, resigned as chief justice in 1800. President Adams first named former chief justice Jay to the seat. Confirmation was immediate; so was Jay's letter declining the honor. Jay noted his failing health and the continuing responsibilities of the justices for holding circuit court. He wrote:

> . . . the efforts repeatedly made to place the Judicial Department on a proper footing have proved fruitless. I left the bench perfectly convinced that under a system so defective, it would not obtain the energy, weight and dignity which are essential to its affording due support to the National Government, nor acquire the public confidence and respect which, as the last resort of the justice of the nation, it should possess.[28]

Adams was a lame duck, defeated for reelection in 1800, but he was not about to relinquish this opportunity. On January 20, 1801, he named John Marshall chief justice. Marshall was then secretary of state, after having served for a time on diplomatic assignment and in the House of Representatives.

Thomas Jefferson

After a brief delay by Federalist advocates of Justice Paterson's elevation to the chief justiceship, the Senate confirmed Marshall January 27.

MARSHALL AND *MARBURY*

Chief Justice Marshall was sworn in February 4, 1801, the second day of the Court's first term in Washington. He was forty-five years old. He would serve thirty-four years, until his death in 1835.

On the day set for the opening of the term, February 2, only Justice Cushing was present. By February 4 four members were present—Cushing, Chase, Washington, and Marshall. No cases were reported as decided during the term.

But events outside the Court's makeshift chamber were moving quickly with broad implications for the Court and its new chief justice. In February the House broke the electoral deadlock between Aaron Burr and Jefferson, choosing Jefferson as the new president. He took office March 4, 1801.

Only a few days before Jefferson's selection, Congress enacted the Circuit Court Act of 1801. The act eliminated circuit duty for the justices, providing for a separate staff of circuit judges. It shifted the Court's schedule, providing for June and December terms, instead of February and August; and it reduced to five the number of seats on the Court.

The law was widely viewed as a Federalist plan to allow Adams to name a last group of Federalist judges and to protect the Supreme Court from any immediate change through Jefferson's appointments. Adams filled the new judgeships with Federalist loyalists, confirming Jefferson's view that the federal judiciary would indeed remain a "strong fortress in the possession of the enemy."[29]

Another late-session law produced the situation that brought the case of *Marbury v. Madison* to the Court. This law created a number of justice-of-the-peace positions for the District of Columbia. On March 2 outgoing president Adams appointed men to fill those posts; they were confirmed the following day. Their commissions were made out and signed. But still-acting secretary of state John Marshall (also by now the sitting chief justice) failed to deliver all the commissions to all the nominees before the end of the Adams administration at midnight March 3.

President Jefferson appointed a number of these people to their sought-after posts, but not William Marbury, who came to the Supreme Court late in 1801, asking the justices to order Secretary of State James Madison to deliver him his commission. Marbury filed an original suit with the Court, asking that the justices use the authority granted them by the Judiciary Act of 1789 and issue a writ of mandamus to Madison.

The Court was already pursuing a path quite independent of the Jefferson administration. In August the justices demurred when Jefferson offered to give them his views on how to apply a law at issue in a pending case. The president's position, the Court indicated, was not relevant. Then, in December, the Court agreed to hear Marbury's case, setting arguments for the June 1802 term.

Jefferson was convinced that the Court would use *Marbury* as a vehicle for interfering in executive branch business. That view—and the Jeffersonians' distaste for the 1801 Circuit Court Act—sparked the law's repeal early in 1802. Circuit court duty was reinstated for the justices, and a single annual term was set for the Court, beginning each year in February.

Because the change in schedule was enacted after February 1802, this last provision delayed for fourteen months the term at which *Marbury v. Madison* would be argued. The Court did not meet from December 1801 until February 1803.

Two major decisions were announced in the 1803 term. In both their coupling and their resolution the skilled leadership of John Marshall was evident. Marshall's legal training was meager; he had little experience in the practice of law and none as a judge. Before his appointment as chief justice, he had been a politician and a diplomat. The skills gained from those posts characterized his tenure on the Court. For three decades his personality dominated the Court and the men who served with him.

More than at any other time in the Court's history, the personal characteristics of the chief justice were of considerably more importance than his legal talents. The Court operated as a family firm, not a federal institution. The justices, most of whom came to Washington for only a few months each year, leaving their wives and families at home, lived together in a boardinghouse. After their dinners together, they often, over wine, discussed and resolved the cases brought before them.[30]

These men, under the leadership of John Marshall, shaped

the Court and the federal judiciary, act by act and decision by decision. As Alexander M. Bickel described it:

Congress was created very nearly full blown by the Constitution itself. The vast possibilities of the presidency were relatively easy to perceive and soon, inevitably, materialized. But the institution of the judiciary needed to be summoned up out of the constitutional vapors, shaped and maintained; and the Great Chief Justice, John Marshall—not singlehanded, but first and foremost—was there to do it and did.[31]

The most famous example of Marshall's effect on the shaping of the court's role came just two years after he became chief justice. *Marbury v. Madison* was decided February 24, 1803. With that ruling, the Court at once claimed, exercised, and justified its power to review and nullify acts of Congress it found in conflict with the Constitution. And in so doing it neatly avoided an expected collision with Jefferson, although it did rebuke him for not delivering Marbury's commission.

Marbury was due his commission, the Court held: it should be delivered to him. But the Court also held that it was powerless to order the delivery, that the section of the Judiciary Act authorizing it to issue such orders was unconstitutional and void, an impermissible expansion of its original jurisdiction.

This decision "became authority . . . for the proposition— which had already been adopted in a majority of the states and which was destined to form a distinct feature of the whole political system of the United States—that a constitution is a fundamental law, that legislative and executive powers are limited by the terms of this fundamental law, and that the courts as interpreters of the law are expected to preserve and defend constitutions as inviolable acts, to be changed only by the people through the amending process."[32]

During congressional debate over repeal of the 1801 Circuit Court Act, the possibility was raised that the Court might declare the repeal unconstitutional, an improper effort by Congress to encroach on the independence of the Court. One week after *Marbury,* the Court made clear that it would exercise its newly affirmed power with care. The Court upheld the Repeal Act of 1802.[33]

It would be more than fifty years before the Court again declared void an act of Congress.

THE CHASE IMPEACHMENT

The business before the Court steadily increased during the first decade of the nineteenth century, but few of its decisions were of as much significance as some of the extrajudicial matters affecting the Court. Most notable of these was the impeachment, trial, and acquittal of Justice Samuel Chase.

Chase, a maverick at the time of his selection, continued to make enemies. He actively campaigned for President Adams in 1800. He strongly supported the hated Sedition Act of 1798— and presided as the judge in the trials of a number of persons charged with violating it.

After a particularly partisan speech to a grand jury in Baltimore in May 1803, Chase became the object of an impeachment drive. The charges against him involved both his conduct during the Sedition Act trials and this particular charge to the Baltimore grand jury. On March 12, 1804, the House impeached Justice Chase by a vote of 73–32.

His trial in the Senate began early in 1805. Chase, who continued to participate in the Court's functions, appeared in the Senate with his attorneys. Presentation of the evidence and arguments consumed a month. On March 1, 1805, he was acquitted. More than a majority of the senators voted to find him guilty on three of the charges against him, but the vote fell short of the two-thirds required for conviction.

Chase's acquittal ended any rumored Republican plans to impeach all four remaining Federalist justices—Marshall, Cushing, Paterson, and Washington. Furthermore, wrote Charles Warren, the acquittal represented a rejection of the Republican argument that impeachment could be used as "a means of keeping the courts in reasonable harmony with the will of the nation, as expressed through Congress and the executive, and that a judicial decision declaring an Act of Congress unconstitutional would support an impeachment and the removal of a judge."[34]

REPORTING THE DECISIONS

At the end of the 1804 term, William Cranch, then chief justice of the circuit court in the District of Columbia, began publication of Cranch's *Reports* of the decisions of the Supreme Court.

Alexander J. Dallas, a noted attorney in Pennsylvania, had reported some of the Court's decisions during its terms in Philadelphia, along with those of other courts in the state. But after the Court moved to Washington, Dallas discontinued this service.

Cranch, who would perform this public service for a dozen years, first published a volume including the decisions from 1801 through 1804. Until that time, the Court's opinions were little known by the bar and less by the general public. The exception was *Marbury,* which had been widely reported and discussed in the newspapers.

In his preface to the first volume, Cranch expressed the hope that publication of the Court's decisions would eliminate "much of that uncertainty of the law, which is so frequently, and perhaps so justly, the subject of complaint in this country."

Furthermore, he wrote, making public a permanent record of the Court's decisions might also limit judicial discretion:

Every case decided is a check upon the judge. He cannot decide a similar case differently, without strong reasons, which, for his own justification, he will wish to make public. The avenues to corruption are thus obstructed, and the sources of litigation closed.[35]

Early in Marshall's tenure—undoubtedly with the encouragement of Cranch—the Court began to write down its decisions and opinions. In addition, Chief Justice Marshall exerted all his considerable personal influence to convince his fellow justices to speak with one voice in these decisions. He persuaded them to drop the practice of *seriatim* opinions, under which each justice wrote and read his own views, and to adopt the

William Johnson

"opinion of the Court" approach, usually allowing him to write that opinion.

Appropriately enough, however, William Johnson, the first Republican justice, who served for most of Marshall's tenure, provided a counterbalance to the chief justice's push for judicial unanimity. Johnson, known as the "father of dissent," was only thirty-two at the time of his appointment to the Supreme Court, but he nevertheless did not hesitate to voice his disagreement with the chief justice and the Court.

Jefferson filled two other seats on the Court during his two terms in office. In 1806 Justice Paterson died, and Jefferson named John Jay's brother-in-law, Brockholst Livingston of New York, forty-nine, as Paterson's successor. Livingston served on the Court for sixteen years.

In 1807 increases in territorial and judicial business spurred Congress to create a new circuit that took in Kentucky, Tennessee, and Ohio, thus raising to seven the number of seats on the Supreme Court. Jefferson, after polling the members of Congress from those three states, named Thomas Todd, Kentucky's chief justice, to the new seat. Todd, forty-one, was nominated and confirmed in 1807, seated at the 1808 term, missed the 1809 term, and issued his first opinion—a dissent—in 1810. He served until 1826 but, like Livingston, his judicial career was notable mainly for his steady support of Chief Justice Marshall.

THE BURR TRIAL

In 1807 the Jefferson administration charged former vice president Aaron Burr with treason. The charge was related to Burr's alleged efforts to encourage an uprising in and a movement for the independence of the western states from the United States. The actions of the Supreme Court and its chief justice in this affair further heightened the animosity felt by the president for the Court.

Early in 1807 the Supreme Court, affirming its power to issue a writ of habeas corpus to challenge the detention of an individual by federal officials, held that there was insufficient evidence for the government to prosecute two of Burr's accomplices for treason.[36]

Jefferson, wrote Charles Warren, regarded this ruling as "another deliberate attack by the Court upon his executive authority" while the Federalists viewed it as "a noble example of the judicial safeguards to individual liberty."[37]

After the Supreme Court's term ended, Chief Justice Marshall traveled to Richmond to preside personally as circuit judge over the trial of Burr. His rulings that the government's evidence was insufficient to support a charge of treason were seen as directly contributing to Burr's acquittal later in the year. Jefferson, irate at the rulings and the outcome, suggested that the Constitution be amended to provide other means than impeachment for removing justices from the bench. The amendment was not approved.

Jefferson's feelings toward the Court were exacerbated during the national resistance to his administration's Embargo Act imposed during the conflict with Britain. Justice Johnson—one of Jefferson's appointees to the Court—declared illegal and void the president's effort to instruct customs officials to detain all vessels thought to be intending to evade the embargo.[38]

CONTRACTS AND CONFLICTS

In 1810 the Supreme Court for the first time exercised its power to strike down a state law as unconstitutional.

In *Fletcher v. Peck* the Court invalidated a law passed by Georgia's legislature in 1796 to repeal a 1795 land grant law obtained through bribery of the members of the 1795 legislature. The repeal was challenged by the innocent third parties who had acquired land under the 1795 grant and who now found their titles null and void. They argued that the legislative nullification was unconstitutional, a clear violation of the Constitution's language, which forbids states to impair the obligation of contracts.

The case was argued twice, in 1809 and 1810. One of the attorneys for the property owners bringing the challenge was thirty-two-year-old Joseph Story of Massachusetts.

On April 16, 1810, the Court—for whom Chief Justice Marshall spoke—held unconstitutional the legislative repeal of the land grant law and the nullification of the titles granted under it.

Story won his case, and the following year he was appointed to the Supreme Court.

In September 1810 Justice Cushing died—the last of the original six justices named to the Court in 1790; he had outlived all his original colleagues by a decade or more.

The interest that attended the search for Cushing's successor on the bench provided some indication of the status the Court had attained in its first decades. The Court was then evenly divided between Federalists (Marshall, Washington, Chase) and Republicans (Johnson, Todd, and Livingston).

President Madison received much advice on the selection of a nominee, including some from his predecessor, Thomas Jefferson. Despite all the advice—or perhaps because of it—Madison required four tries to fill Cushing's seat.

His first selection was Levi Lincoln, who had served as attorney general to Jefferson. Lincoln declined, but Madison nominated him anyway. The Senate confirmed the nomination, and Lincoln again declined, early in 1811.

In February Madison named Alexander Wolcott, a Republican leader in Connecticut, to the seat. Criticized as unqualified, Wolcott was rejected by the Senate: only nine votes were cast in favor of his confirmation. Madison subsequently nominated John Quincy Adams, then ambassador to Russia; Adams was confirmed but declined the appointment.

Madison then waited for most of 1811 before making another choice. The 1811 term—for which there was neither a quorum of justices present nor any business—passed virtually unnoticed.

At midyear Justice Chase died, creating a second vacancy. In November Madison nominated Gabriel Duvall of Maryland, comptroller of the treasury for almost a decade, to fill the Chase seat; he named Story to the Cushing seat. Both were confirmed and would serve long terms—Duvall, twenty-three years and Story, thirty-four.

For the next several years, the conflict with England—the War of 1812—was a dominant factor in the work of the Court. After the Capitol was burned by the British in August 1814, the Court met in temporary quarters for the next four terms, even holding some sessions in a tavern.

The cases before the Court largely involved wartime issues—neutral rights, ship seizures, and foreign affairs. The Court made clear in these rulings that violations of neutral rights were to be resolved diplomatically, not judicially. And it affirmed broad power for the federal government over the person and property of enemies during wartime.

One result of *Fletcher v. Peck* was considerable state resistance to the Court's exercise of its power to invalidate state actions. States began to question whether in fact Congress could authorize the Court to curtail state power in such a final manner. In 1816 the Court itself considered that question. The case presenting it was *Martin v. Hunter's Lessee,* a long-running dispute over the ownership of a large parcel of land in Virginia. Chief Justice Marshall did not participate in the Court's consideration of the case because of his own ties to the matter.

In 1813 the Court had ruled on the substance of the case, deciding in favor of the British claim to the land, rejecting the Virginian's claim. But the Virginia courts refused to obey the decision, ruling that the Supreme Court could not constitutionally tell a state court what to do.

This direct challenge to its authority returned to the Court in 1816. On March 20, 1816, it was firmly rebuffed. Justice Story wrote the Court's opinion, upholding the power of Congress to grant the Supreme Court appellate jurisdiction over all matters involving federal laws, treaties, and the U.S. Constitution—regardless of the court in which such cases had first been heard. This opinion, declared Charles Warren, "has ever since been the keystone of the whole arch of federal judicial power."[39]

In another 1816 ruling, however, the Court left the large and controversial area of criminal law almost entirely to state courts. In *United States v. Hudson and Goodwin* the justices declared that federal courts had no jurisdiction over criminal activity—except for matters that Congress had specifically declared to be federal crimes.

Warren described the end of the 1816 term as the end of an era. With the end of the War of 1812, he wrote, the attention of the people turned toward industrial and manufacturing endeavors, transportation, communication, and economic change. Questions of war, prize vessels, and embargo acts—which had taken so much of the Court's attention during the first years of the century—faded from the docket, replaced by questions of contract obligations, commerce regulation, and state powers.

Also at the end of this term, Cranch ended his work as unofficial reporter of the Court's work, and an official reporter, Henry Wheaton, was appointed. Congress authorized him a salary of $1,000 a year. He would hold that post for eleven years.

In their history of the Court, George L. Haskins and Herbert A. Johnson characterized the period 1801–1815 as one in which the Court, both in its dealings with the executive and Congress and in its internal development, established the foundations of the judicial power it would exercise with increasing visibility in the remaining decades of the Marshall era. With *Martin v. Hunter's Lessee,* Haskins and Johnson explained, the Court reinforced its power and the supremacy of the still-new federal government, and it did so even though the only Federalist still on the Court—Chief Justice Marshall—took no part in the ruling. That decision, they concluded, was "a victory for his [Marshall's] efforts to extricate the Court from partisan politics, and to establish a rule of law in the United States. The foundations of judicial power had been fixed firmly in place."[40]

1819: A REMARKABLE TERM

Three major constitutional decisions were announced by the Court in the term that convened February 2, 1819. This term, which brought the Court's rulings in *Dartmouth College v. Woodward, Sturges v. Crowninshield,* and *McCulloch v. Maryland,* was one of the most notable in history. With those decisions, the Court dramatically illustrated its view that the Constitution imposed far more stringent limitations on state actions than on the actions of Congress.

The Court was back in its permanent quarters in the rebuilt courtroom under the Senate chamber. Here the Court would meet until the Civil War.

The *Dartmouth College* decision was announced on the opening day of the term. Argued for three days in the preceding term, the case had drawn little attention in the nation's press. The dispute between a small college in New Hampshire and that state's legislature hardly seemed notable. But the issue was of major significance for the nation's economic development: Did the Constitution's contract clause protect private corporate charters—as well as public grants—against impairment by the state? "Yes, indeed!" responded the Court with only Justice Duvall dissenting. Not only did the decision protect Dartmouth College from a legislature that wished to reshape its structure and purpose; it also promised embryonic American corporations that they were secure against such tampering with charters.

Two weeks later the states received another blow. On February 17 the Court held invalid New York's insolvency law—enacted to ease the difficulties of debtors in default. The Court held that it violated the ban on state action impairing the obligation of contracts because it allowed the discharge of debts contracted before its passage.

The day before, the *National Intelligencer* of Washington, D.C., became the first newspaper in the country to begin printing daily announcements of the actions of the Supreme Court. Even so, the insolvency decision, *Sturges v. Crowninshield,* was misreported and misunderstood. Until a second ruling in 1827, it was generally thought that the states lacked any power to afford debtors this sort of relief.[41]

After these two rulings, the Court heard arguments—for nine days in late February and early March 1819—in *McCulloch v. Maryland.* Daniel Webster, a young member of Congress from Massachusetts who had argued successfully for Dartmouth College, argued for the Bank of the United States in this case. Again, he won.

McCulloch v. Maryland posed two questions: Could Congress charter a national bank? Could states tax its operations? The Court announced its decision on Saturday, March 6. Congress won and the states lost. The Court, with Chief Justice Marshall as its spokesman, was unanimous. Congress, Marshall declared, has broad power under the "necessary and proper" clause to decide the means by which it implements its powers. "Let the end be legitimate, let it be within the scope of the Constitution," he wrote, "and all means which are appropriate . . . which are not prohibited . . . are constitutional."[42] The bank was a useful fiscal instrument for national economic stability, so Congress might properly decide to incorporate it.

Furthermore, states could not hamper the exercise of this power. They could not tax the bank, for by taxing it, they could destroy it and frustrate the congressional purpose in chartering it. This decision aroused intense opposition, especially in the South and the West where the bank was particularly hated.

McCulloch v. Maryland, wrote Robert McCloskey, "is by almost any reckoning the greatest decision John Marshall ever handed down." In upholding the constitutionality of the bank's incorporation, Marshall "set down the classic statement of the doctrine of national authority. The argument he advanced was not new; its main outlines had been endlessly debated since the first Congress. . . . But Marshall deserves the credit for stamping

"Let the end be legitimate, let it be within the scope of the Constitution, and all means which are appropriate . . . which are not prohibited . . . are constitutional."

Chief Justice John Marshall, *McCulloch v. Maryland,* 1819

it with the die of his memorable rhetoric and converting it from a political theory into the master doctrine of American constitutional law."[43]

REVIEW AND REACTION

With its 1821 decision in *Cohens v. Virginia,* the Court for the second time reaffirmed its power to review state court decisions. *Cohens,* like *Martin v. Hunter's Lessee,* presented the Court with a basic challenge to its power under Section 25 of the Judiciary Act.

With great firmness, Chief Justice Marshall reiterated the points Justice Story had made in the 1816 ruling. When a state court held that state action did not conflict with the U.S. Constitution, federal law, or U.S. treaties, it was the constitutional obligation of the U.S. Supreme Court to review that decision.

Those who approved the decision considered it "one of the chief bulwarks of American unity." Critics—still led by former president Jefferson—saw it as one more blow to state sovereignty. Jefferson complained that the Court was "working like gravity . . . to press us at last into one consolidated mass."[44]

By 1825 the Court had nullified as unconstitutional at least one law from each of ten states. These rulings set off an effort to remove or at least restrict this power. Advocates of such a restriction considered repealing Section 25, amending the Constitution to have the Senate, not the Court, review all cases involving a state, and passing a law to require that five—or all seven—justices concur in holding a state law invalid.

Jefferson proposed that each justice be required to issue a separate opinion—as in the pre-Marshall days. He suggested that Congress then denounce the views of those with whom it disagreed—and impeach the justices who did not change their views. None of these proposals was approved by both chambers of Congress.

The years from 1811 until 1823 were remarkably stable at the Court. There was no change in the Court's membership. Then in March 1823 Justice Livingston died. President James Monroe chose Secretary of War Smith Thompson, also of New York and related by marriage to the Livingston clan, to fill the seat. Confirmed late in the year, Thompson took his seat in the February 1824 term. The most important case of his twenty-year-tenure would be the commerce power case of *Gibbons v. Ogden,* decided in his first term. But because of Thompson's close relationship to the Livingston family—to whom the contested steamboat monopoly involved in the case had been granted—Thompson would not participate in that landmark ruling.

CONGRESS AND COMMERCE

From the first day of its existence, Congress had—by constitutional grant—the power to regulate interstate and foreign commerce, but it scarcely exercised this power until well into the nineteenth century.

In contrast, the states had passed a variety of laws regulating commerce and transportation within their borders. In 1824, with its decision in *Gibbons v. Ogden,* the Court began the long process of defining the reach of federal commerce power and the limits it imposed on state power.

Gibbons v. Ogden was a challenge to New York's grant of a steamboat monopoly giving the Fulton-Livingston partnership exclusive rights to run steamships on New York waterways. The monopoly provoked considerable interstate animosity threatening to destroy both the national peace and any sort of incipient national commercial network.

The monopoly, challengers argued, interfered with federal power to regulate interstate commerce because it excluded from New York waterways vessels licensed under the federal coasting law, the most notable early law passed by Congress to implement its commerce power.

The case divided Republican against Federalist. It was argued for five days in February 1824. Daniel Webster represented the challengers. On March 3, 1824, Chief Justice Marshall announced the Court's opinion. Commerce, he explained, was not merely buying and selling of goods; it embraced "intercourse" of all sorts, including navigation. Congress had licensed vessels in the coasting trade. The state monopoly conflicted with the free operation of those federally licensed vessels and so must be held invalid.

Gibbons v. Ogden ranks with *McCulloch v. Maryland* as one of the two major rulings of the Marshall era establishing national power and national supremacy. Furthermore, *Gibbons v. Ogden* served as the "emancipation proclamation of American com-

merce,"[45] giving impetus to the development of the port of New York, the railroads, and a national system of commerce.

A few weeks after *Gibbons,* the Court approved further extension of federal authority at the expense of state prerogatives—holding in *Osborn v. Bank of the United States* that the bank could sue state officials in federal court even if the state did not consent. The Court declared that a state official who acted in reliance upon an unconstitutional state law—or exceeded his proper authority—was not immune from being sued in federal court for his actions. The justices thus began to narrow the effect of the Eleventh Amendment.

In response to the Court's steadily increasing workload, Congress lengthened the Court's term. Beginning in 1827, the Court convened its term a month earlier, on the second Monday in January.

When the 1827 term began, the Court had a new member. Justice Todd had died in 1826, and President John Quincy Adams named federal judge Robert Trimble of Kentucky as his successor. Trimble would serve only two terms before his death in 1828.

The 1827 term was a busy one. The Court resolved 77 cases during the two-month session, leaving 109 for resolution in the next term.[46]

With the January 1828 term a new reporter, Richard Peters Jr., took over publishing the Court's opinions. He would fill that post for fifteen years.

STATE POWERS

With federal supremacy firmly established by *Marbury, McCulloch,* and *Gibbons,* the Court in 1827 recognized that in some areas states could act concurrently with the federal government.

In *Ogden v. Saunders* the Court clarified the power of states to enact laws to help debtors. By an unusually close 4–3 vote, the justices upheld New York's revised insolvency law, which—as amended after the 1819 ruling in *Sturges v. Crowninshield*—applied only to debts contracted after its passage. For the first and only time in his career, Chief Justice Marshall was on the losing side in a constitutional case. Emphasizing the deference the Court owed to the decision of state legislators, Justice Washington wrote the majority opinion. Justices Duvall and Story joined Marshall in dissent.

Later in the term, the Court upheld a state's power to abolish the penalty of imprisonment for debtors. This change did not impair the obligation of a contracted debt, held the Court in *Mason v. Haile;* it simply modified the remedy for defaulting on that obligation.

Advocates of state powers did lose a major case. *Brown v. Maryland* posed the question of state power to tax imported goods. The state's advocate was Roger B. Taney, who would follow Marshall as Chief Justice. As Marshall had lost *Ware v. Hylton,* so Taney came out on the losing end of *Brown.*

States, the Court held in *Brown,* could not tax persons who sold imported goods; that tax interfered with the federal regulation of imports. So long as imported goods remained in their original package, held the Court, they could not be taxed by the state.

In 1828 Justice Trimble, the Court's junior member, died. Defeated for reelection, President Adams nonetheless named John J. Crittenden of Kentucky to fill the Trimble seat. The Senate refused to consider the nomination.

A week after his inauguration, President Andrew Jackson named John McLean of Ohio, Adams's postmaster general, to the empty seat. McLean, who would be a perennial presidential candidate during his thirty-one years as a justice, had already served in the House, run unsuccessfully for the Senate, and expanded the Post Office into the largest department in the executive branch. One of the most political of all the justices, McLean never hesitated to use his judicial opinions for political ends.

There was at least one other unsettling member of the Court during this period, wrote G. Edward White in *The Marshall Court and Cultural Change.* "If McLean's political concerns sometimes made him a distracted presence on the Court, Henry Baldwin's presence was surely a distracting one."[47]

Baldwin was President Jackson's choice to fill the seat left vacant in 1829 when Justice Washington died after thirty-two years on the Court. A Pennsylvanian, Baldwin was one of the most eccentric men ever to serve on the Court. His fourteen years as a justice were characterized by bouts of mental illness, vociferous quarrels with his colleagues, and bizarre constitutional writings.

Four times in the 1829 term, the Court spoke to questions of state power. The effect of three of the rulings was to restrict state authority. In *Providence Bank v. Billings* the Court held that a state that intended to grant a corporation a tax exemption must expressly include that privilege in the corporation's charter. In *Weston v. City of Charleston* the Court held that cities and states could not tax U.S. stock, finding such a tax an impermissible interference with the federal borrowing power. And in *Craig v. Missouri* the Court held that the constitutional ban on state bills of credit prohibited states from issuing loan certificates.

States, however, did win a ruling in *Willson v. Blackbird Creek Marsh Co.,* in which the Court upheld state power to regulate waterways and navigation thereupon, as long as Congress had not done so.

A slavery case was considered in the 1829 term. In *Boyce v. Anderson* the justices held that a slave who drowned in a steamboat accident was a passenger, not freight. Slave owners were disappointed; their recovery would have been greater had the slave been considered freight.

THE CHEROKEE CRISIS

Georgia and the Supreme Court collided in the waning years of the Marshall era over the state's effort to exert its authority over the Cherokee Indians by enacting stringent laws affecting the Indians and their land. The Cherokees asked the Supreme Court to order Georgia to stop enforcing these laws. While their request was pending before the Court late in 1830, Georgia ig-

nored a Court-ordered stay of execution for a Cherokee convicted of murder under the challenged laws and executed the man.

In 1831 the U.S. House of Representatives refused again to repeal the statute authorizing the Supreme Court to review state court rulings. In March the Court held that the Cherokees' case, brought as an original suit, could not proceed in that fashion because the tribe was not a separate nation in the eyes of federal law.

A second case arose quickly. Georgia had charged and convicted two missionaries, Samuel Worcester and Elizur Butler, for violating the state law that forbade white persons to live in Indian territory without a state license. Worcester and Butler took their case to the Supreme Court, arguing that the state lacked the power to impose or enforce such a requirement.

On March 3, 1832, Chief Justice Marshall announced that the Court found the state law unconstitutional, a usurpation of exclusive federal jurisdiction over Indian matters. The missionaries' conviction was reversed, and they should be released, the Court declared.

Georgia refused to comply. President Jackson openly sympathized with the state, allegedly remarking, "Well, John Marshall has made his decision, now let him enforce it."

For eight months the confrontation persisted. Worcester and Butler remained in jail. Jackson was reelected. Chief Justice Marshall was most depressed, writing to Justice Story that he doubted the Union would survive in the face of such rebellion by state authority.

But late in 1832 South Carolina's legislature, unhappy with a protectionist federal tariff, adopted a declaration "nullifying" the new tariff with which it had refused to comply. This placed Jackson in a highly contradictory position. He was supporting Georgia's resistance to the Supreme Court's decision while labeling South Carolina's resistance to the tariff as treason. Jackson made his choice and asked Congress to increase the power of federal courts to enforce federal laws in the face of such nullification.

It was clear to Georgia that its resistance to the Supreme Court's order would no longer have presidential support. The governor pardoned the missionaries, and the case ended. In 1833 Congress approved Jackson's request for expanded federal judicial power.

END OF AN ERA

Marshall's last major constitutional opinion was the 1833 ruling in *Barron v. Baltimore* that the Bill of Rights limited only federal, not state, action. "It is a striking fact," wrote Charles Warren, "that this last of Marshall's opinions on this branch of law should have been delivered in limitation of the operations of the Constitution whose undue extension he had been so long charged with seeking."[48]

As a result of *Barron v. Baltimore,* it was a full century before the Court addressed itself at length to questions of the rights of individuals rather than of institutions. And this decision made

Andrew Jackson

Roger B. Taney

In January 1835 the aged Duvall resigned. Jackson named Roger B. Taney, former attorney general and Treasury secretary, to succeed him. Taney had played a major role in Jackson's war on the Bank of the United States, implementing the president's order to remove U.S. funds from the bank. In that post he had made many enemies. Whig opposition to the nomination convinced the Senate, on the last day of its 1835 session, to postpone consideration of the Taney nomination. The vote was 24–21. The Duvall seat remained empty.

Then, on July 6, 1835, Chief Justice John Marshall died. The Court's great center chair was vacant.

Eulogies were numerous and elaborate. But perhaps the most objective assessment of his accomplishment as chief justice came from abroad. After traveling through the United States in the last years of the Marshall era, Alexis de Tocqueville wrote of the Supreme Court:

The peace, the prosperity, and the very existence of the Union are vested in the hands of the seven Federal judges. Without them the Constitution would be a dead letter: the executive appeals to them for assistance against the encroachments of the legislative power; the legislature demands their protection against the assaults of the executive; they defend the Union from the disobedience of the states, the states from the exaggerated claims of the Union, the public interest against private interests, and the conservative spirit of stability against the fickleness of the democracy. Their power is enormous, but it is the power of public opinion.[49]

No one had done more than John Marshall to establish that enormous power or to win the essential public respect for the still-young Supreme Court of the United States.

States' Rights: 1836–1860

Perhaps it indicates how infrequently presidential nominees to the Supreme Court adhere to the views of their patron, but the Court has rarely been known by the name of a president, even if he named all or most of its members. Washington select-

necessary the enactment of the Fourteenth Amendment, which would eventually, in the twentieth century, extend the guarantees of the Bill of Rights against state action and thus serve as the basis for an expansion of federal judicial power comparable to that of the Marshall era.

Three major cases were argued in the early 1830s but carried over to later terms because the Court was unable to resolve the questions they posed. They were *Charles River Bridge v. Warren Bridge, Briscoe v. Bank of the Commonwealth of Kentucky,* and *New York v. Miln.*

The Court's pace had slowed: Marshall was nearing eighty, and Johnson and Duvall were ill and absent much of the time.

An era was ending. In August 1834 Justice Johnson, the independent soul who fathered the Court's tradition of dissent, died. To succeed him, Jackson named James M. Wayne of Georgia. Wayne would serve for thirty-three years, until 1867.

Daniel Webster

Joseph Story

ed the entire original Court; it was never referred to as the "Washington Court."

The next president to name more than half the tribunal's members was Andrew Jackson. Of the six he named in eight years, four served for more than a quarter of a century, well into the Civil War years. McLean, Baldwin, and Wayne were Jackson's first three nominees. The fourth was Taney.

After consideration of Taney's nomination as an associate justice was postponed by the Senate early in 1835, Chief Justice Marshall's death created another vacancy on the Court. When Congress returned to town late in 1835, Jackson sent it a second Taney nomination. This time he named Taney chief justice.

To fill the other vacant seat Jackson chose Philip P. Barbour of Virginia, who had argued the state's case in *Cohens v. Virginia* (1821), in which the Court reaffirmed its power to review state court rulings denying federal claims. Barbour had served several terms in the House, during which he had advocated requiring five of seven justices to concur in holding a statute unconstitutional. He also had served as a state and a federal judge. Barbour would have the briefest tenure of all the Jackson appointees. He died in 1841 after five years on the Court.

The same political opposition that delayed action on Taney's first nomination to the Court delayed confirmation of him as chief justice until March 15, 1836. Leading the opposition were two of the foremost Supreme Court advocates of the era, Daniel Webster and Henry Clay. Nevertheless, the Senate confirmed Taney's nomination by a 29–15 vote.

While the Senate considered the nomination, the Court met without a chief justice for its 1836 term. Story, the senior sitting justice, presided.

CONTRACTS, CREDIT, AND COMMERCE

During Taney's first term, the 1837 term, the Court decided three major constitutional cases that had been pending throughout the last years of the Marshall era—*Charles River Bridge v. Warren Bridge, New York v. Miln,* and *Briscoe v. Bank of the Commonwealth of Kentucky.* All three went in favor of the states, and many saw the cases as evidence that the Taney Court would favor the rights of the states, which had been consistently curtailed by the Court under Chief Justice Marshall.

A more balanced assessment is provided by Carl B. Swisher, who wrote:

The work of the 1837 term . . . marked the beginning of a new order. The transition was not a sharp one, and those who saw it as such were mistaken. In spite of the radical doctrines sponsored by some Jacksonians of the time, the Court was careful to adhere to traditional patterns. . . . The change was limited . . . and yet it was there. There was a greater tendency to look to items of local welfare and to emphasize the rights of the states, a greater concern with living democracy in a rapidly changing society.[50]

First and most famous of these decisions is the case of Boston's Charles River Bridge, first argued before the Court in 1831. At issue was the constitutional ban on state action impairing the obligation of contracts. The Charles River Bridge Company, chartered by Massachusetts to build a bridge for pedestrian traffic across the Charles River, challenged a subsequent state decision allowing a second bridge. Daniel Webster argued for the original company that implicit in its charter was the exclusive privilege to carry such traffic. After five days of argument in January 1837, the Court announced its opinion in February. Chief Justice Taney wrote the Court's decision.

The Court did not undercut its earlier rulings protecting contracts, but it ruled against the Charles River Bridge Company. A charter, Taney explained, would not be construed to be more favorable to its corporate recipient, at public expense, than it explicitly required. In the absence of an explicit grant of monopoly privilege, the state had not infringed the first charter by granting a second to another company.

A few days later, the Court held that a state could require shipowners to report all passengers on ships arriving in its ports. This reporting requirement had been challenged in *New York v. Miln* as an infringement of the federal power to regulate foreign commerce. But the Court held the requirement a legitimate exercise of the state police power.

The term's third major ruling came in *Briscoe v. Bank of the Commonwealth of Kentucky,* which, like *Miln,* was first argued in the 1834 term. In it the Court upheld a state law that authorized a state-chartered bank to issue bank notes. Henry Clay had argued for the victorious bank.

This law, like that struck down seven years earlier in *Craig v. Missouri,* had been challenged as infringing the constitutional ban on state bills of credit. But where the Marshall Court had struck down the law in *Craig,* the Taney Court upheld that in *Briscoe.* Justice Story dissented, as he had in *Miln* and *Charles River Bridge,* saying that Chief Justice Marshall would have disagreed too.

On the last day of President Jackson's term, Congress expanded the Court to nine seats. Jackson immediately nominated John Catron of Tennessee and William Smith of Alabama to fill the two new seats.

Catron, the Tennessee campaign manager for the newly elected president, Martin Van Buren, was confirmed and served until 1865. Smith declined the second seat. Van Buren then named Alabama senator-elect John McKinley to the seat. He was confirmed and served fifteen years, although illness curtailed his participation for half that period.

During Taney's tenure, the Court continued to assert its own power and that of lower federal courts to resolve the increasingly frequent questions of the allocation of governmental authority. The decision reached in *Dred Scott v. Sandford* (1857) provides a dramatic example of the extreme to which this point could be carried. But unlike that ruling, most of the Court's pronouncements in this area simply consolidated and reinforced the position the Court already had assumed in earlier years.

In 1838 Rhode Island asked the justices to resolve a boundary dispute with Massachusetts, the first such case to come to the Court. Massachusetts moved to dismiss the case, arguing that the Court lacked the power to hear it. Over the dissent of the chief justice, the Court rejected the motion and proceeded with the case, which finally was resolved in favor of Massachusetts in 1846.

Also in the 1838 term the Court decided the case of *Kendall v. United States,* upholding the power of a federal court to issue an order directing an executive branch official to perform certain "ministerial" duties—even if the court order directly conflicted with presidential instructions. Such orders, held the Court, did not breach the separation of powers.

The increase in the number of corporations in the United States brought questions of corporate rights to the Court, and in 1839 the Court held that states could forbid out-of-state companies to do business within their borders. But in the same case the Court effectively moderated that holding; it declared that without clear evidence that a state intended to exercise this power, it would be assumed to consent to the operations of such "foreign" corporations.[51]

Five years later, the Court opened the doors of the federal courts to corporate litigation by modifying the strict view of a corporation's "residence" adopted early in the Marshall era. The new rule allowed more cases involving corporations to be heard in federal courts, rather than state courts, on the basis that the corporation and the opposing party were residents of different states.[52]

SLAVERY AND THE STATES

The early victories of the Taney era for advocates of state sovereignty were followed by a number of defeats in the 1840s. In *Holmes v. Jennison,* in 1840, the Court held that states had no power to engage in foreign affairs.

Two years later it held that federal courts were not bound by state judges' interpretations of state laws. In another case the Court held that states could not tax the income of federal officials.[53]

By this time virtually all questions of states' rights were linked to the increasingly sensitive issue of slavery. The Court had carefully avoided addressing this issue in any but peripheral ways, but in 1841, Swisher wrote, "the Court found itself in the thick of the slavery discussion, from which it did not actually escape until the close of the Civil War period, even though there were intervening years in which no such cases were actually decided."[54]

Thus, even when the issue was commerce in general, with no evident tie to slavery, the Court's opinions were closely perused and construed for their effect on state power to deal with slavery.

The double-edged nature of the issue—and all judicial efforts to deal with it—was evident in the 1841 and 1842 rulings of the Court and their public reception.

In 1841 the Court decided *Groves v. Slaughter* on a point other than the slavery questions presented. But Justice McLean's opinion, declaring the right of a state to exclude slavery, was interpreted by some southerners as upholding the right of a state to exclude free blacks as well.

The following year the Court decided *Prigg v. Pennsylvania,* striking down a Pennsylvania law setting up procedures for determining whether a black person was a sought-after fugitive before he or she was taken out of the state. Federal power over fugitive slaves was exclusive, leaving states no opportunity to pass such laws, held the Court. But, wrote Swisher, while upholding the power of the federal government to provide for the return of fugitive slaves, it nullified the obligations and seemed to nullify the power of the states to aid in the process, [and] it at once gave incentive to abolitionist activities and led the South to demand enactment of a Fugitive Slave Act which could be effectively administered without the aid of the states. Thereby it added to the furor of sectional conflict and the hysteria of competing parties.[55]

The Court's efforts to deal with increasingly difficult issues were hampered by the illness and disability of some of its members and then by long-vacant seats, the product of political turmoil outside the courtroom.

One of these vacancies was the longest in Supreme Court history. After the death of the eccentric Justice Baldwin, his seat remained empty for more than two years. This situation resulted from the political disaffection that marred the relationship between President John C. Tyler and Congress. Tyler had more nominations to the Court rejected than any other president. Of his six nominations, only one was confirmed.

Before Tyler took office, another new justice filled a seat. Justice Barbour died during the 1841 term. The lame-duck president, Van Buren, nominated—and the Senate confirmed—Peter V. Daniel of Virginia, a federal judge, to Barbour's seat. Daniel served until 1860.

Tyler had his first chance to name a justice when Justice Smith Thompson died in 1843. He chose Secretary of the Treasury John Spencer, who was rejected by the Senate in January 1844. Tyler next nominated Reuben Walworth of New York, state chancellor. Before its midyear adjournment, the Senate tabled that nomination.

In April, Justice Baldwin died. Tyler nominated Philadelphia lawyer James Edward King for that seat. The King nomination was also tabled by the Senate. Both nominations finally were withdrawn.

Early in 1845, Tyler, now a lame duck in addition to his other political disabilities, sent two more names to the Senate. To fill the Thompson seat he chose Samuel Nelson, a New York judge. Nelson, a well-respected figure, was quickly confirmed; he would serve on the Court for twenty-seven years, until 1872. But Tyler's selection of John M. Read as Baldwin's successor was ignored by the Senate. That seat remained empty for another full year.

Early in James Polk's administration, Justice Story died. He had served thirty-four years—longer than any other justice up to that time. Late in 1845 Polk nominated George W. Woodward of Pennsylvania to fill the Baldwin seat—and Sen. Levi Woodbury of New Hampshire to fill Story's chair. Woodbury—Taney's successor as secretary of the Treasury—was confirmed early in 1846; he would serve only six years before his death in 1851. Woodward, his nomination opposed by one of his state's senators, was rejected.

Finally, in August, Polk named Pennsylvania judge Robert C. Grier to the Baldwin seat. Grier's confirmation ended the twenty-eight-month vacancy on the Court. He served for twenty-four years, until his resignation in 1870.

For the next five years, the Court's membership was complete and stable.

CONFUSION AND CHANGE

Despite stability of membership, the Court's performance on the interlocking issues of commerce and slavery was confusing, to say the least. In the December 1846 term, the Court upheld the federal fugitive slave law.[56]

But in the same term, it backed state power to regulate commerce in intoxicating liquor. The diversity of reasoning among the justices in these latter cases—known as the *License Cases*—from Massachusetts, Rhode Island, and New Hampshire reflected the Court's increasing division over the proper allocation of state and federal power over commerce. Six justices wrote nine opinions.

In 1849 this uncertainty flowered into complete confusion with the Court's ruling in the so-called *Passenger Cases*. These two cases, from New York and Boston, involved challenges to state laws that required masters of vessels to post bonds and to pay a tax for each immigrant landed in the state. The laws were challenged as infringing upon federal power to regulate foreign commerce. They were defended as a proper exercise of the state's police power to protect its public health and welfare.

After hearing each case argued three times, the Court found these laws unconstitutional as in conflict with federal power over foreign commerce. But beyond that point the Court splintered, with eight justices writing separate opinions that took seven hours to read from the bench. The justices could not agree on whether the federal power over foreign commerce was exclusive, leaving no room for state regulation, or whether there might be such room if Congress had not exercised its power in a particular area.

There was no opinion of the Court in these cases, and Reporter Benjamin C. Howard, exercising considerable wisdom, declined to summarize the ruling beyond the fact that it struck down the challenged laws. For details and reasoning, he simply referred the reader to the "opinions of the judges."

In the 1829 case of *Foster v. Neilson*, the Court had refused to resolve an international boundary dispute because it said such a disagreement presented a "political question" that should be resolved by the more political branches of the government. Twenty years later the Court applied this doctrine in *Luther v. Borden* and refused to decide which of two competing factions was the legitimate government of Rhode Island. This too was a political question, held the Court, suitable for resolution by Congress, not the Court.

In 1844 Congress responded to the Court's increasing workload by once again lengthening its term. Opening day was moved back from January to the first Monday in December.

Other procedural changes during this time reflected the end of the days when the Court considered only a few cases and did so at a leisurely pace that allowed time for lengthy arguments and required less record keeping. In 1839 the Court required that all motions to it be filed in writing with the clerk. In 1849 the

Court limited the time for arguments, giving counsel for each side two hours to present his case, but no more, without special leave.

In 1843 Richard Peters, for fifteen years the Court's reporter, was fired by four of the justices acting in the absence of the chief justice and their other colleagues. Peters had fallen out of favor with several of the justices as a result of differences over the inclusion of their opinions in the reports. Peters was replaced by Benjamin Howard of Maryland, a former member of Congress and a college friend of Justice Wayne. Howard would serve until 1861.

CONFIDENCE AND CLARITY

Despite the personnel changes and philosophical difficulties endured by the Court during the 1840s, public confidence in it continued to grow. Charles Warren noted that public esteem for the Supreme Court was at a peak in the last years of that decade: "While there were extremists and radicals in both parties who inveighed against it and its decisions, yet the general mass of the public and the Bar had faith in its impartiality and its ability."[57]

The first decisions of the next decade appeared to bear out this confidence. The Court exercised restraint in dealing with the slavery issue—and appeared to be clarifying its position on commerce matters.

In the December 1850 term the Court heard arguments in *Strader v. Graham.* The basic question would arise again in *Scott v. Sandford* a few years later: Were slaves still slaves after they had worked for a time in a free state but then returned to a slave state?

The Court held that this matter should be resolved by the laws of the state in which the slaves were residing. This was not a matter for federal courts to resolve, held the justices.

In 1851 Justice Woodbury died. As his successor, President Millard Fillmore chose Benjamin R. Curtis, forty-one, a noted Boston attorney. Confirmed in December 1851, Curtis would serve only six terms, but in that brief tenure he would leave his mark on history.

During his first term, the Court decided *Cooley v. Board of Wardens of the Port of Philadelphia,* a commerce clause challenge to a Philadelphia ordinance regulating the use of pilots in its harbor. The Court upheld the ordinance, with Curtis as its spokesman. There are two categories of interstate and foreign commerce, he explained. One was essentially local and could be regulated locally, at least so long as it was not regulated by Congress; the other was essentially national and needed a uniform rule if it was to be regulated at all. This category could never be regulated by the states.

In one sense, Curtis' opinion was no more than "an eloquent statement of indefiniteness," wrote Swisher a century later, but "with the statement the indefiniteness came to seem in some way manageable, by contrast with the confusion of multiple opinions in the *License Cases* and the *Passenger Cases.* The opinion promised to give a more pragmatic, less conceptual and cat-

John A. Campbell

egorical direction to the Court's thinking concerning state regulation of commerce."[58]

This term brought two other commerce and navigation decisions of importance. In *Pennsylvania v. Wheeling & Belmont Bridge Co.,* the Court held that a bridge built by the state of Virginia across the Ohio River was too low and thus obstructed interstate commerce. The Court ordered the bridge torn down. But Congress in 1852 passed a law that declared the bridge did not obstruct interstate commerce, allowing the bridge to stand. This was the first example of Congress overturning a Court decision by legislation.

Also that term, the Court responded to the growing network of national commerce and transportation, substantially enlarging the federal government's admiralty jurisdiction to include all the nation's navigable waterways, not just those subject to the ebb and flow of tides.[59]

In July 1852 Justice McKinley died. To fill his place, President Fillmore chose Edward Bradford of Louisiana, who failed to win Senate confirmation. Fillmore next named Sen. George E. Badger of North Carolina, whose nomination was effectively killed when the Senate, in an unusual breach of tradition, postponed consideration of it, by a one-vote margin, early in 1853. In the last week of his term, Fillmore sent still a third name to the Senate, that of Louisianan William C. Micou—but the Senate refused to confirm him.

The new president, Franklin Pierce, chose John A. Campbell of Alabama, forty-one, well known both for his scholarship and for his advocacy before the Supreme Court. Campbell was confirmed and served until the outbreak of the Civil War.

Benjamin R. Curtis

In 1856 the Court began the long process of defining due process. In *Murray's Lessee v. Hoboken Land & Improvement Co.,* the Court held that the Fifth Amendment guarantee of due process applied to the actions of Congress, as well as to those of the executive and judicial branches.

And Justice Curtis, writing for the Court, defined due process as procedures that did not conflict with specific written provisions of the Constitution or with the established practice in England at the time of the settlement of the New World.

SCOTT V. SANDFORD

In 1856 the Court heard arguments in the case involving Dred Scott, a Missouri slave who claimed that he was free as a result of a sojourn in Illinois and other territories that were "free states" under the Missouri Compromise of 1820. Scott's case was first argued February 11. In May the Court ordered the case argued again. Reargument took place early in the December 1856 term. Justice Curtis's brother was one of the attorneys appearing in the case.

Chief Justice Taney was aging. This factor, along with health and family problems of other members of the Court, slowed its operations. Not until February 1857—a year after the first arguments—was *Scott v. Sandford* discussed at conference.

The Court agreed the decision would follow that in *Strader v. Graham* a few years earlier—holding that Scott's status should be resolved under state law. The majority agreed not to consider the larger issue—whether Congress had the power to exclude slavery from some territories, as it had done in the now-repealed Missouri Compromise. Justice Nelson was assigned to write the majority opinion.

But Justices McLean and Curtis, both adamant abolitionists, dissented and announced their intention to declare that the Missouri Compromise was proper, that Congress indeed had the power to ban slavery from the territories. The majority was compelled to revise its plan. Nelson's assignment was withdrawn, and Chief Justice Taney assumed the task of writing the majority's opinion.

Taney's illness delayed its announcement until March 6, 1857, just after President James Buchanan was inaugurated. Each justice wrote a separate opinion in this case; the reading of the opinions in Court took two days. The majority declared black people forever disabled from attaining citizenship, the Missouri Compromise unconstitutional, and Congress powerless to halt the spread of slavery.

The Court had overreached its power in setting such limits to the hopes of blacks and the powers of Congress. It forced the issue of slavery out of the courtroom and the legislative chambers and onto the battlefield. This was also the first of the "self-inflicted wounds" of the Court. One scholar summarized its impact:

During neither the Civil War nor the period of Reconstruction did the Supreme Court play anything like its role of supervision, with the result that during the one period the military powers of the President underwent undue expansion, and during the other, the legislative powers of Congress. The Court itself was conscious of its weakness. . . . [A]t no time since Jefferson's first administration has its independence been in greater jeopardy than between 1860 and 1870.[60]

The *Scott* decision was endorsed by southern Democrats and denounced by northern Democrats, dividing the party and enabling the Republican Party to win the White House in 1860. Of this development, Charles Warren wrote, "It may fairly be said that Chief Justice Taney elected Abraham Lincoln to the presidency."[61]

Another result of that decision was Justice Curtis's decision to resign after only six years on the Court. His philosophical disagreement with his colleagues and his general lack of confidence in the Court, compounded by an acrimonious exchange with Chief Justice Taney over access to the *Scott* opinions, spurred him to leave the bench and return to his more lucrative practice of law. He resigned in September 1857. He would argue more than fifty cases before the Court in subsequent years, including the first of the *Legal Tender Cases,* which he lost.

To replace Curtis in the "New England" seat President Buchanan nominated former attorney general Nathan Clifford. Clifford, considered a party hack by some in the Senate, was confirmed early in 1858 by a three-vote margin. He served until his death in 1881.

Although Chief Justice Taney's name became almost synonymous with his opinion in *Scott v. Sandford*—and the damage it did to the nation and the Court—his last major prewar opinion was both far more eloquent and more enduring in its impact.

Two years after the Scott ruling, the Court decided *Ableman v. Booth.* In speaking for the Court, Chief Justice Taney delivered a ringing reaffirmation of federal judicial power.

Ableman v. Booth involved an abolitionist in Wisconsin who was tried and convicted of violating the federal Fugitive Slave Act. Both before his trial and after his conviction, state judges ordered federal officials to release him, using the writ of habeas corpus and declaring his detention improper.

The case came before the Supreme Court in January 1859. The state did not send anyone to argue its side. On March 7, 1859, the unanimous Supreme Court declared that state judges lacked the power to interfere in such a manner in federal judicial proceedings. To allow such interference, wrote Taney, "would subvert the very foundations of this Government." As long as the Constitution endured, he continued, "this tribunal must exist with it, deciding in the peaceful forms of judicial proceedings the angry and irritating controversies between sovereignties, which in other countries have been determined by the arbitrament of force."[62]

The *Scott* case and the conflict that followed so colored historians' view of the Taney Court that only after a century had passed was an objective assessment of its accomplishments attempted.

In the concluding chapter of his history of the Taney era, Swisher described the Court's decisions and operations during this period:

By contrast with the work of the same tribunal in various other periods, the essence of its contribution was seldom focused in eloquent philosophical statement from the bench. The Taney Court was peculiarly unphilosophical. . . . [I]t tended to be assumed that the federal constitutional system was now generally understood so that the earlier forms of judicial explanation were unnecessary. The government was no longer experimental but was a going concern. . . .

The Taney Court fell upon evil times not because of Jacksonianism or even because of lack of ability on the part of its members, but because it was caught in the grinding pressures of sectional conflict. A Court committed to the application of the law was bound to crash into difficulties when the nation itself divided over whether there was indeed a surviving body of constitutional law binding on all the states and all the people.[63]

War and Recovery: 1861–1872

The Civil War decade brought the Supreme Court to a new low in public esteem. It was, Swisher explained,

not merely because it had handed down the *Scott* decision but because the rule of law as interpreted by the judiciary had given way to a rage for unrestricted exercise of power—which seemed to flare with even greater violence once the battlefields were stilled. There could be a restoration of the prestige of the judiciary only with restoration of respect for the rule of law.[64]

During the last years of Chief Justice Taney and the tenure of his successor, Chief Justice Salmon P. Chase, the Court underwent considerable change.

It moved into a new courtroom, grew to ten members and then shrank to eight, gained five new members—including the new chief justice—and found itself facing extremely sensitive questions of executive power.

In mid-1860 Justice Daniel died. His seat remained empty for

almost two years. Late in his term, President Buchanan named his former attorney general and secretary of state, Jeremiah S. Black, to fill Daniel's seat. But in February 1861 political opposition within both parties brought the rejection of Black's nomination by a vote of 25–26.

The Civil War broke out in April. That month Justice McLean died, and Justice Campbell resigned when his home state, Alabama, seceded. The Court's other southern members, Wayne and Catron, continued to hold their seats through the war.

President Abraham Lincoln thus had three seats to fill as soon as he arrived at the White House. In January 1862 he selected Noah H. Swayne, an Ohio attorney, fifty-seven, to fill the McLean seat. Swayne would serve nineteen years. In July 1862 Lincoln filled the empty Daniel seat by naming Samuel Freeman Miller of Iowa, forty-six, the only justice trained in medicine as well as law. Miller would serve for twenty-eight years, until 1890, writing 616 opinions.[65]

To the third seat Lincoln named his close friend and political adviser David Davis of Illinois, forty-seven. Davis would serve fourteen years, until he resigned to take a Senate seat.

In March 1863 Congress added a tenth seat to the Court, giving Lincoln a fourth appointment. To that new seat he named Stephen J. Field, chief justice of the California Supreme Court, who would serve almost thirty-five years and be the only justice ever the target of an assassination attempt as a result of his rulings. When Field was appointed he had to travel to Washington by steamship and railroad across Panama—the transcontinental railroad was not completed until 1869.

When the Court met for its December 1860 term, it met in a new courtroom. After four decades in the basement room under the Senate chamber, the Court moved upstairs. The new wings of the Capitol housing the Senate and House had been completed; the old Senate chamber had been refurbished for the Court at a cost of $25,000. The Court would meet in this room for the next seventy-five years, until it moved into its own building.

The Court had a new reporter in 1861. Benjamin Howard resigned to run a losing race for governor of Maryland. He was followed by Jeremiah Black, Buchanan's unsuccessful nominee for the Daniel seat. Black served for only two years, resigning in 1863 to resume his private law practice. He was succeeded in 1864 by John William Wallace of Pennsylvania, who held the post until 1875.

PRESIDENTIAL WAR POWERS

The Civil War began in April 1861. Congress was not in session and did not meet until midsummer. In the interim President Lincoln called for troops, imposed a blockade on southern ports, and in some circumstances authorized military commanders to suspend the writ of habeas corpus. These actions were the most dramatic expansion of executive power in the nation's history to that point and, not surprisingly, they were challenged as exceeding the president's constitutional authority.

Chief Justice Taney was among the first to declare Lincoln's actions unconstitutional. In May, the month after war had bro-

THE COURT IN 1865
From left: Court Clerk Daniel W. Middleton, Justices David Davis, Noah H. Swayne, Robert C. Grier, James M. Wayne, Chief Justice Salmon P. Chase, Justices Samuel Nelson, Nathan Clifford, Samuel F. Miller, Stephen J. Field

ken out, a military commander in Baltimore refused to comply with Taney's order—issued as a circuit judge, not a Supreme Court justice—to produce in court one John Merryman, a civilian imprisoned by the Union army for his anti-Union activities.

The commander cited, as grounds for his refusal, Lincoln's instructions allowing him to suspend the privilege of the writ of habeas corpus, the instrument used to inquire into the reasons justifying an individual's detention by government authority. Taney responded with an opinion, which he sent to Lincoln himself, declaring that only Congress could suspend this privilege and that Lincoln's actions were unconstitutional. If such authority can be "usurped by the military power . . . the people of the United States are no longer living under a government of laws, but every citizen holds his life, liberty, and property at the will and pleasure of the army officer in whose military district he may happen to be found."[66]

Lincoln, undeterred, continued to insist that emergency conditions required the exercise of extraordinary power. Five years later, after both Taney and Lincoln were dead, the Supreme Court in *Ex parte Milligan* confirmed Taney's position.

The legality of Lincoln's blockade of southern ports was the major war issue resolved by the Court during the war years. These *Prize Cases* were decided in favor of presidential power, although only by a vote of 5–4.

Had the vote tipped the other way, all of Lincoln's wartime actions would have been called into question, seriously undermining his ability to lead the nation in the conflict. The majori-

ty upheld the president's power to institute the blockade even before Congress officially had authorized such an action. The vote made clear the importance of Lincoln's appointments to the Court. The majority consisted of his first three nominees—Swayne, Miller, and Davis—and Wayne and Grier, who wrote the majority opinion. Dissenting were Taney, Nelson, Catron, and Clifford.

Having resolved that critical question, the Court retreated to a position of restraint in dealing with issues of war. In the December 1863 term, Taney's last, the Court held that it lacked jurisdiction to hear a challenge to the use of paper money as legal tender (necessary to finance the war),[67] or over a petition of habeas corpus ordering military officials to justify their detention of a civilian.[68] Within six years, the Court would reverse both holdings.

In October 1864, as the war neared its end, Chief Justice Taney died. He was eighty-seven years old and had served the nation as its chief justice for twenty-eight years.

President Lincoln wished to name a man who would back the administration on the critical issues of emancipation—another exercise of extraordinary presidential powers that lacked any clear base in the Constitution—and legal tender. Congress had passed laws making paper money legal tender in place of gold to enable the Union to finance its war effort.

Lincoln chose Salmon P. Chase, a potential political rival who had, nevertheless, served until mid-1864 as secretary of the Treasury. After his reelection in 1864, Lincoln nominated Chase as chief justice. He was confirmed and seated as the Court began its December 1864 term. Chase was fifty-six, three years younger than Taney when he had assumed the post, yet he would serve only nine years before his death in 1873.

"Never again would there be a term wherein so few questions of importance were answered as in that of 1864–65," wrote historian Charles Fairman.[69]

But the following term brought another facet of the *Merryman* issue that had confronted Chief Justice Taney five years earlier: Can a president in wartime replace the nation's civilian courts with courts-martial, to which civilians as well as military personnel are subject?

In April 1866 the Supreme Court answered this question with an emphatic no—just as Taney had. The justices were unanimous in holding that Lincoln had acted illegally when he instituted trial by military commission for civilians in nonwar areas where the civil courts continued to function.

The Court divided 5–4 on whether Congress and the president acting together could replace civilian justice with courts-martial in such areas.

The Court's full opinions in *Ex parte Milligan* were not released until December 1866—eight months later. The majority opinion was written by Lincoln's personal friend, Justice Davis, who warned as Taney had that suspension of constitutional guarantees during wartime would lead to despotism.

These opinions and this ruling provoked violent criticism in Congress, where they were viewed as evidence that the Court would—at its first opportunity—hold unconstitutional the military regimes imposed by Congress upon the defeated South as its Reconstruction program.

Congressional criticism took a variety of forms—proposals for impeachment of the justices in the majority, "reorganization" of the Court through the addition of new seats, curtailment of the Court's appellate jurisdiction, and the requirement that the Court be unanimous on constitutional rulings.

In fact, the Court did undergo some reorganization at this point, due, however, more to the unpopularity of President Andrew Johnson than to the Court's own rulings. In May 1865 Justice Catron died after twenty-eight years on the Court, the last of which he had spent in virtual exile from his southern home. Johnson's April 1866 nomination of his close friend, Attorney General Henry Stanbery, died after the Senate abolished the vacant seat and reduced the size of the Court to eight by providing that both Catron's seat and the next one becoming vacant not be filled.

In mid-1867 Justice Wayne, the Court's other southern member, died after thirty-two years on the bench. He was the last of the Jackson justices; his service had spanned the Taney era. His seat was not filled; the Court was now eight members.

RECONSTRUCTION AND REVIEW

The apprehensiveness of Reconstruction architects about the Court was heightened early in 1867. The Court struck down an act of Congress requiring persons wishing to practice law before the federal courts to take a "test oath" affirming their loyalty, past and present, to the Union.

Augustus H. Garland, a noted Supreme Court advocate who had served in the Confederate government, challenged this requirement. A similar state law also was challenged.

In *Ex parte Garland* and *Cummings v. Missouri,* the Court in 1867 held both state and federal oaths unconstitutional, in violation of the bans on ex post facto laws and bills of attainder. The only Lincoln justice voting with the majority against the oaths was Field, who apparently was persuaded by the arguments of his brother, David Dudley Field, who had argued one of the cases before the Court.

After *Milligan* and the *Test Oath Cases,* however, the Supreme Court showed no stomach for battle with Congress on the overall issue of Reconstruction.

In the 1867 term—only months after the *Garland* case—the Court unanimously refused Mississippi's request that it order President Johnson to stop enforcing the Reconstruction Acts. Such an order, the Court held in *Mississippi v. Johnson,* was outside its power and its jurisdiction.

In 1868, however, a southern editor named McCardle asked the Court to order his release through a writ of habeas corpus to military authorities in Mississippi. This case brought to a peak the concern of Reconstruction advocates in Congress.

McCardle was being held for trial by a military commission on charges that his anti-Reconstruction articles were impeding the process of "reconstructing" the South. The Court heard arguments the first week of March 1868, just as the Senate opened its impeachment trial of President Johnson. Three days after the Court had taken *McCardle* under advisement, Congress revoked its jurisdiction over such cases. Johnson vetoed the bill. It was immediately repassed over his veto.

The Court then considered a new issue, the impact of the repeal of its jurisdiction on the pending case. In May the Senate acquitted President Johnson. In April 1869 the Court dismissed the *McCardle* case, finding unanimously that once Congress revoked its jurisdiction over a category of cases, all it could do was dismiss all pending cases of that type.

The same day, in *Texas v. White,* the Court majority endorsed the view that as a matter of law the seceding states never had left the Union—that states had no power to secede—a moot point in 1869. Justices Swayne, Grier, and Miller objected that the majority was endorsing a legal fiction and ignoring political reality.

GOLD OR GREENBACKS

To finance the war, Congress had passed the Legal Tender Acts, allowing the use of paper money to pay debts. These laws, which resulted in drastic change in the nation's economic system, repeatedly were challenged in federal courts.

In the December 1867 term, the Supreme Court heard a challenge in the case of *Hepburn v. Griswold*. A second round of arguments took place in December 1868; one of the attorneys arguing for the acts was former justice Benjamin R. Curtis. The Court was expected to uphold the acts. After all, Chief Justice

Chase had been Treasury secretary when they were approved. But no decision was announced during the December 1868 term.

The justices apparently did not reach a decision until November 1869—and then their efforts were hampered by the vacillations of the aged justice Grier, who voted in conference first to uphold the acts, then to strike them down.[70] The final vote was 5–3 against the Legal Tender Acts. The majority was Chase, Nelson, Clifford, Field, and Grier.

Congress in 1869 provided that a justice might retire and continue to receive half his salary. In December—before the Court announced its decision in *Hepburn v. Griswold*—Justice Grier, seventy-six, was persuaded to retire, effective February 1, 1870. Six days after his resignation, on February 7, 1870, the Court announced that by a 4–3 vote it found the statutes unconstitutional. They were inappropriate means for the exercise of the war powers, held the majority, and, as applied to debts contracted before the passage of the laws, they were a clear impairment of contract obligations. The dissenters were Justices Miller, Swayne, and Davis.

Even as Chase was reading the opinion, the most effective Court packing in the nation's history was under way—or at least the best-timed appointments.

After Ulysses S. Grant's election as president in 1868, Congress increased the size of the Court to nine, giving Grant a new seat to fill. Grier's decision to retire opened a second vacancy. Grant first chose Attorney General Ebenezer Hoar of Massachusetts for the new seat, but personal and political opposition developed to block his nomination in the Senate. To smooth the way for Hoar's confirmation, Grant nominated former secretary of war Edwin M. Stanton—the choice of most members of Congress—for the Grier seat. Stanton was confirmed immediately, but died four days later. Hoar's nomination was rejected in February 1870; the vote was 24–33.

And so on February 7, 1870, Grant sent two more nominations to the Senate—Joseph P. Bradley of New Jersey, fifty-seven, a railroad attorney, and Grier's personal choice; and William Strong of Pennsylvania, a state judge. Bradley and Strong were confirmed and seated in March 1870.

Within weeks of their seating the Court announced it would rehear the constitutional challenge to the Legal Tender Acts. The second of these cases, *Knox v. Lee,* was argued in the December 1870 term.

On May 1, 1871, fifteen months after *Hepburn v. Griswold,* the Court overruled itself. By a 5–4 vote, the Court reversed the 4–3 vote in the earlier case. The majority upheld the Legal Tender Acts as a proper exercise of the power of Congress. Justice Strong, who with Bradley converted the dissenters in *Hepburn* into the majority in *Knox,* wrote the opinion. The full opinions were not released until January of the following year.

This abrupt about-face—so clearly the result of a change in the Court's membership—damaged the public confidence the Court had been slowly regaining after the *Scott* ruling and the war decade. It was, in the words of Charles Evans Hughes, the second of the Court's self-inflicted wounds. Hughes declared that "there was no ground for attacking the honesty of the judges or for the suggestion that President Grant had attempted to pack the court." But he added, "Stability in judicial opinions is of no little importance in maintaining respect for the court's work."[71]

The Balance of Power: 1873–1888

The Union had been preserved. Indeed, in *Texas v. White* a majority of the Supreme Court endorsed the legal fiction that it never had been disrupted. Now as the war issues faded from its docket, the Court set about restoring the state-federal balance of power.

Concern for the states as effective functioning units of the federal system was paramount in the minds of the justices. And so, to enhance state power, the Court curtailed federal authority.

The Court's power of judicial review of acts of Congress was wielded with new vigor. Between *Marbury* in 1803 and the *Slaughterhouse Cases* in 1873, the Court held unconstitutional ten acts of Congress. Six of the ten were struck down between 1870 and 1873.

Another sign of the Court's sensitivity to the claims of states was its decision in 1871 that, even as the salaries of federal officials were not subject to state taxes, so state officials' salaries were immune from federal taxes.[72]

THE FOURTEENTH AMENDMENT

No better example of the Court's view of the proper balance between state and federal power can be found than its rulings interpreting the Civil War Amendments, in particular the Fourteenth Amendment.

In 1865 the Thirteenth Amendment formally abolished slavery. In 1868 the Fourteenth Amendment gave added protection to the rights and liberties of persons threatened by state action. And in 1870 the Fifteenth Amendment guaranteed blacks the right to vote.

Intended as instruments of radical change in the nation's social fabric, these amendments were so narrowly construed by the Court in the decades immediately after their adoption that they lay virtually useless for most of the ensuing century.

The effect of these rulings was to preserve state power over the rights of individuals by denying any expansion of federal authority in that area.

The Court's first ruling on the scope of the Fourteenth Amendment came in the 1873 *Slaughterhouse Cases*. It was indicative of the direction in which Fourteenth Amendment protections would first be extended that these cases were brought by butchers seeking to protect their businesses rather than by blacks seeking to assert their newly granted civil rights.

Louisiana had granted one company a monopoly on the slaughtering business in New Orleans. That grant was challenged by other butchers as denying them the right to practice their trade. They argued that this right was protected by the Fourteenth Amendment's guarantee of the privileges and im-

THE COURT IN 1876

From left: Justices Joseph P. Bradley, Stephen J. Field, Samuel F. Miller, Nathan Clifford, Chief Justice Morrison R. Waite, Justices Noah H. Swayne, David Davis, William Strong, Ward Hunt

munities of U.S. citizenship, of equal protection of the laws, and of due process.

The *Slaughterhouse Cases* were first argued in January 1872, just before the Court's opinions in the second *Legal Tender Case* were read. But those arguments were before an eight-man Court. Justice Nelson, now eighty, was absent. The Court apparently was evenly divided and ordered the cases reargued in the following term.

Before the December 1872 term began, Nelson resigned after twenty-seven years of service. President Grant named Ward Hunt, a New York judge—as Nelson had been—to the seat. Hunt was seated in December 1872.

The *Slaughterhouse Cases* were reargued over a three-day period in February 1873. Attorney for the butchers was former justice John Campbell. The Court announced its decision April 14, 1873. By 5–4, the Court held that Louisiana had not violated the Fourteenth Amendment by its grant of a slaughtering monopoly.

Writing for the Court, Justice Samuel Miller stated that the amendment did not increase the number of rights an individual possessed, but only extended new protection to those few rights, privileges, and immunities that had their source in one's federal, rather than state, citizenship. The right to do business did not derive from one's U.S. citizenship, held the majority.

Any other decision, wrote Miller, would convert the Court into "a perpetual censor upon all legislation of the States on the civil rights of their own citizens."[73]

Chief Justice Chase dissented, as did Justices Swayne, Field, and Bradley. The next day, over Chase's lone dissent, the Court held that a state did not deny a woman the privileges or immunities of U.S. citizenship when it refused, because of her sex, to license her to practice law in its courts.[74]

Within the month, Chief Justice Chase was dead of a sudden stroke. His seat remained vacant for most of the following year.

President Grant tried unsuccessfully to place two of his personal friends in the seat, naming first George Williams, attorney general of Oregon, and then Caleb Cushing, a former attorney general of Massachusetts. Finally, he chose a little-known Ohio attorney, Morrison R. Waite, fifty-eight. Waite, who never had argued a case before the Supreme Court and who had no judicial experience, was confirmed. He was seated in March 1874.

The term in which Waite began his fourteen years as chief justice was the first to begin in October. Early in 1873 Congress had provided that the Court's term would begin the second Monday in October rather than in December as it had since 1844.

Unlike Chief Justice Chase, Waite agreed fully with the Court's narrow view of the privileges and immunities of federal citizenship. In 1875 he wrote the Court's opinion reinforcing its decision in the *Slaughterhouse Cases,* holding that the right to vote was not a privilege of U.S. citizenship.[75]

The Court remained reluctant to acknowledge either that the Civil War Amendments had expanded federal power to enforce individual rights or that the amendments had expanded the list of federally protected rights.

Illustrating that view, the Court in 1876 voided portions of laws Congress intended to ensure the Fifteenth Amendment's guarantee of the right to vote and the Thirteenth Amendment's abolition of slavery. Again, Waite spoke for the Court to declare that Congress had overreached itself in enacting a broad statute penalizing persons who used violence to deny blacks the right to vote. That right, the Court reiterated, came from the states; only the right to be free of racial discrimination in voting came from the U.S. Constitution. These rulings left Congress powerless to protect the newly enfranchised black Americans.[76]

The disputed presidential election of 1876 drew the Court directly into political controversy when five of its members—Bradley, Miller, Strong, Field, and Clifford—served on the commission that resolved the dispute over electoral votes and paved the way for the election of Republican Rutherford B. Hayes. Hayes subsequently placed Stanley Matthews—the man who had helped negotiate the compromise that elected him—on the Supreme Court.

STATE POWER

Not surprisingly, the Court of the 1870s, which refused to acknowledge a broadening federal power to enforce the rights of individuals, was quite hospitable to state claims of a far-reaching police power operative in ever-widening fields.

As large manufacturing and transportation companies grew rapidly after the Civil War, their customers organized to use state regulation to curtail the power of those businesses over individual consumers. Among the most successful were farm groups, including the Grange, which in some states obtained the passage of "Granger laws" limiting how much railroads and grain elevator companies could charge for hauling or storing farm products.

Despite the failure of the butchers to win Fourteenth Amendment protection of their right to do business in the *Slaughterhouse Cases,* the railroad and grain storage operators mounted a similar challenge to these Granger laws. They argued that the state, in passing these laws, deprived them of their liberty and property without due process of law.

In a group of cases known as the *Granger Cases,* and by the title of one of them, *Munn v. Illinois,* the Court in 1877 rejected this challenge to state regulatory laws. Upholding the laws, Chief Justice Waite explained that some private property, by virtue of its use, was so invested with a public interest that states could properly exercise their police power to regulate it. Justices Field and Strong dissented.

The majority also rejected the idea that federal courts should review such laws to determine if they were reasonable. Waite acknowledged that the state might abuse this power, but found that insufficient argument "against its existence. For protection against abuses by Legislatures the people must resort to the polls," he concluded, "not to the courts."[77]

Three years later, the Court found in the state police power a substantial qualification of the Constitution's ban on state impairment of contract obligations. In *Stone v. Mississippi* the Court held that a legislature could never by contract place a subject outside the reach of this power. It upheld a decision of the Mississippi legislature to ban lotteries, even though this de-

THE COURT IN 1882
Seated from left: Justices Joseph P. Bradley, Samuel F. Miller, Chief Justice Morrison R. Waite, Justices Stephen J. Field, Stanley Matthews. *Standing from left:* Justices William B. Woods, Horace Gray, John Marshall Harlan, Samuel Blatchford

cision nullified the charter of a lottery corporation granted by a previous legislature.

A week after *Munn v. Illinois,* Justice Davis resigned to take a Senate seat. As his replacement President Hayes chose John Marshall Harlan, a forty-four-year-old lawyer and a namesake of the fourth chief justice. Harlan's own namesake also would sit on the Court. Harlan would serve well into the twentieth century, his thirty-four-year tenure characterized by a long line of opinions dissenting from the Court's narrow view of the Fourteenth Amendment.

At the turn of the decade, the Court's personnel underwent further change. By 1881 only three of the justices who participated in the 1873 *Slaughterhouse* decision remained on the bench: Miller from the majority and Field and Bradley from the dissent.

By 1880 the Court was operating with three members who were no longer able to fill their proper roles. Swayne, now seventy-five, had been in failing mental health for three years.[78] Hunt suffered a stroke in 1879 and never returned to the bench. Clifford had been disabled for some time but refused to resign until a Democratic president could choose his successor.

But the first departure from the Court of the 1880s was none of these but Justice Strong, who, although in his seventies, still was at the peak of his abilities. President Hayes chose William B. Woods of Georgia as Strong's successor. Woods, a federal circuit judge, was the first southerner named to the Court since Justice Campbell was selected in 1853. Although just fifty-six at the time of his appointment, he served only six years before his death.

In January 1881, shortly after Woods was confirmed, Swayne resigned. To succeed him, Hayes selected Sen. Stanley Matthews, fifty-six, also of Ohio. Matthews had been instrumental in the compromise that placed Hayes in the White House in 1877. Nominated first by Hayes and then by incoming President James J. Garfield, Matthews was confirmed by the narrow margin of one vote, 24–23. He served on the Court for seven years, until his death in 1889.

Later in 1881 Justice Clifford died. To replace him President Chester A. Arthur selected Horace Gray, chief justice of the Massachusetts Supreme Court. Gray, fifty-three at the time, served for twenty years.

Finally in 1882, after three years of absence from the bench, Justice Hunt resigned. After Arthur's first choice, Roscoe Conkling, declined, Arthur chose federal judge Samuel Blatchford of New York to fill the seat. He served for eleven years.

PERSONAL RIGHTS

The Fourteenth Amendment, ratified in 1868, eventually became a mother lode of litigation. In the fifteen years between the *Slaughterhouse Cases,* the Court's first Fourteenth Amendment decision, and the end of Chief Justice Waite's term in 1888, the Court decided some 70 cases on the basis of that amendment. In the ensuing thirty years there would be ten times as many— some 725 Fourteenth Amendment cases.[79]

In general, individuals who sought to invoke the protection of the Fourteenth Amendment had little success. The Court was generally unresponsive to "social" legislation or to claims of individual rights. In 1878, for example, the Court struck down a state law that required equal access for black and white passengers to railroads operating in the state. The law was impermissible state interference with interstate commerce, held the Court in *Hall v. De Cuir.*

In 1880 the Court used the Fourteenth Amendment to deny states the freedom to restrict jury service to white persons. But three years later, in the *Civil Rights Cases,* the Court made clear that it would condone use of the amendment only to reach clearly discriminatory state action.

In the *Civil Rights Cases* the Court declared Congress powerless to reach acts of private discrimination against black persons. With Justice Bradley writing the majority opinion, the Court struck down the far-reaching Civil Rights Act of 1875, enacted to implement the guarantees of the Civil War Amendments.

The Fourteenth Amendment, the Court declared, did not give Congress the power to regulate matters that traditionally had been left to state control. Congress could act only to correct—not to prevent—discrimination by the state.

In 1884, however, the Court upheld the power of Congress to provide for the punishment of persons who beat up a black man to keep him from voting in a federal election.[80]

But the same day, the Court reaffirmed the view, first set out by Chief Justice John Marshall in *Barron v. Baltimore,* that the Bill of Rights did not apply against state action, even though there was clear evidence that the authors of the Fourteenth Amendment intended it to change the *Barron* view. Joseph Hurtado was convicted of murder under California law, which did not provide for a grand jury indictment in serious crimes. Citing the Fifth Amendment guarantee of charge by indictment for serious federal crimes, Hurtado challenged his conviction as a violation of the Fourteenth Amendment's due process guarantee. That guarantee, he argued, applied the indictment provision to the states.

The Court rejected Hurtado's argument. The Fifth Amendment, it reiterated, applies only against federal, not state, action. The Fourteenth Amendment, held the Court, did not extend the right to an indictment to persons charged with state crimes. Justice Harlan dissented from this ruling in *Hurtado v. California.*

In its first major ruling interpreting the guarantees of the Fourth and Fifth Amendments against *federal* authority, however, the Court just two years later read those provisions to give broad protection to the individual.

The Court's decision in *Boyd v. United States,* decided in 1886, was a ringing defense of individual privacy against the threat of governmental invasion. Justice Bradley, for the Court, declared that "constitutional provisions for the security of person and property should be liberally construed. A close and literal construction deprives them of half their efficacy and leads to gradual depreciation of the right."[81]

And later that year, in one of the first successful equal protec-

THE COURT IN 1888
Seated from left: Justices Joseph P. Bradley, Samuel F. Miller, Chief Justice Melville W. Fuller, Justices Stephen J. Field, Lucius Q. C. Lamar. *Standing from left:* Justices Stanley Matthews, Horace Gray, John Marshall Harlan, Samuel Blatchford

tion cases brought by an individual, the Court held that the equal protection guarantee extended to all persons, not just citizens, and meant that city officials could not deny Chinese applicants the right to operate laundries.[82]

PROPERTY RIGHTS

In the 1870s—most notably in the *Slaughterhouse* and *Grange* cases—the Court steadfastly had rejected the efforts of businessmen to use the Fourteenth Amendment as a shield against government regulation. But in the 1880s that stance began to weaken.

In 1869 the Court had held that corporations were not *citizens* and so could not invoke the Amendment's privileges and immunities clause.[83] Seventeen years later, in 1886, Chief Justice Waite simply announced—before the Court heard arguments in *Santa Clara County v. Southern Pacific Railway*—that there was no need for the arguing attorneys to discuss whether corporations were *persons* under the protection of the Amendment's equal protection clause: the Court had decided they were.

That same year the Court limited state power over railroad rates. In *Wabash, St. Louis and Pacific Railway Co. v. Illinois,* the Court held that states could not set rates for railroads that were part of an interstate network without infringing federal power over interstate commerce. This ruling cut back sharply the power the Court had granted the states just nine years earlier in *Munn v. Illinois.*

Yet in other areas the Court continued to support the exercise of state police power. It upheld state laws regulating intoxicating liquors and colored oleomargarine, refusing to find them in violation of due process or the commerce clause.[84]

In 1887 Justice Woods died. President Grover Cleveland filled this "southern seat" with Lucius Quintus Cincinnatus Lamar of Mississippi. Lamar, sixty-two, had served both in the House and the Senate and was secretary of interior at the time of his selection to the Court. He was the first Democrat placed on the Court in twenty-five years. Although the Republican-dominated Senate Judiciary Committee opposed him, he was confirmed, 32–28. He served only five years, until his death in 1893.

In March 1888 Chief Justice Waite, seventy-two, died of pneumonia.

President Cleveland selected Melville W. Fuller to be the new chief justice. Fuller was a successful Chicago attorney whose clients included several major railroads. He had argued a number of cases before the Court and was fifty-five years old at the time of his selection. Nominated in May 1888, he was confirmed in July by a vote of 41–20. He would lead the Court for twenty-two years, until his death in 1910.

By the end of its first century, the Court had become more institutional and less personal in its operations. No longer did the justices live, as well as work, together. That practice had ended soon after the Civil War. And after Reporter Wallace left that post in 1875, the volumes of the Court's decisions were no longer cited by the name of the reporter but by the impersonal "U.S." designation.

NOTES

1. *McCulloch v. Maryland,* 4 Wheat. 316 at 407 (1819).

2. Samuel F. Miller, *Lectures on the Constitution of the United States* (New York and Albany: Banks & Brothers, 1891), 71, 73–74.

3. *McCulloch v. Maryland,* 4 Wheat. 316 at 407 (1819).

4. Charles Grove Haines, *The American Doctrine of Judicial Supremacy* (Berkeley: University of California Press, 1932; reprint ed., New York: Da Capo Press, 1973), 23.

5. Robert H. Jackson, *The Supreme Court in the American System of Government* (Cambridge: Harvard University Press, 1955), 61.

6. Julius Goebel Jr., *History of the Supreme Court of the United States,* Vol. 1, *Antecedents and Beginnings to 1801* (New York: Macmillan, 1971), 206.

7. Quoted in ibid., 280.

8. Charles Warren, *Congress, the Constitution and the Supreme Court* (Boston: Little, Brown, 1925), 23.

9. James Madison, Alexander Hamilton, and John Jay, *The Federalist Papers.* Introduction by Clinton Rossiter (New York: New American Library, Mentor Books, 1961), No. 78, 465.

10. Ibid., No. 79, 474.

11. Ibid., No. 78, 469.

12. Ibid., 466.

13. Ibid., 467–468.

14. Goebel, *Antecedents and Beginnings,* 554.

15. Robert G. McCloskey, "James Wilson" in *The Justices of the United States Supreme Court, 1789–1969: Their Lives and Major Opinions,* 4 vols., ed. Leon Friedman and Fred L. Israel (New York: Chelsea House Publishers in association with R. R. Bowker, 1969), I: 93.

16. Charles Warren, *The Supreme Court in United States History,* rev. ed., 2 vols. (Boston: Little, Brown, 1922, 1926), I: 102.

17. Ibid., 57.

18. Ibid., 89.

19. Ibid., 58.

20. Goebel, *Antecedents and Beginnings,* 556–559, 566–569.

21. Ibid., 792.

22. Ibid., 560–565; Warren, *Supreme Court in U.S. History,* I: 70–82.

23. Warren, *Supreme Court in U.S. History,* I: 108–111.

24. Ibid., 104, note 2.

25. *Glass v. The Sloop Betsey,* 3 Dall. 6 (1794).

26. Goebel, *Antecedents and Beginnings,* 589–592.

27. Ibid., 792.

28. Warren, *Supreme Court in U.S. History,* I: 173.

29. Ibid., 194.

30. Ibid., 791–792.

31. Alexander M. Bickel, *The Least Dangerous Branch* (Indianapolis: Bobbs-Merrill, 1962), 1.

32. Haines, *Judicial Supremacy,* 202–203.

33. *Stuart v. Laird,* 1 Cr. 299 (1803).

34. Warren, *Supreme Court in U.S. History,* I: 293.

35. William Cranch, Preface to Vol. 1 of *Reports of Cases Argued and Adjudged in the Supreme Court of the United States in August and December Terms, 1801, and February Term, 1803.*

36. *Ex parte Bollman,* 4 Cr. 75 (1807).

37. Warren, *Supreme Court in U.S. History,* I: 307.

38. Ibid., 326.

39. Ibid., 339.

40. George L. Haskins and Herbert A. Johnson, *History of the Supreme Court of the United States,* Vol. 2, *Foundations of Power: John Marshall, 1801–1815* (New York: Macmillan, 1981), 365.

41. Ibid., 494.

42. *McCulloch v. Maryland,* 4 Wheat. 316 at 421 (1819).

43. Robert G. McCloskey and Sanford Levinson, *The Modern Supreme Court,* 2d ed. (Chicago: University of Chicago Press, 1994), 43.

44. Warren, *Supreme Court in U.S. History,* I: 550.

45. Ibid., 616.

46. Ibid., 699.

47. G. Edward White, *History of the Supreme Court of the United States,* Vols. 3–4, *The Marshall Court and Cultural Change, 1815–1835* (New York: Macmillan, 1988), 298.

48. Warren, *Supreme Court in U.S. History,* I: 780–781.

49. Alexis de Tocqueville, *Democracy in America* (New York: Alfred A. Knopf and Random House, Vintage Books, 1945), 156–157.

50. Carl B. Swisher, *History of the Supreme Court of the United States,* Vol. 5, *The Taney Period, 1836–1864* (New York: Macmillan, 1974), 97.

51. *Bank of Augusta v. Earle,* 13 Pet. 519 (1839).

52. *Louisville Railroad v. Letson,* 2 How. 497 (1844).

53. *Swift v. Tyson,* 16 Pet. 1 (1842); *Dobbins v. Erie County,* 16 Pet. 435 (1842).

54. Swisher, *The Taney Period,* 535.

55. Ibid., 546.

56. *Jones v. Van Zandt,* 5 How. 215 (1847).

57. Warren, *Supreme Court in U.S. History,* II: 207.

58. Swisher, *The Taney Period,* 407.

59. *Propeller Genesee Chief v. Fitzhugh,* 12 How. 443 (1851).

60. Edward S. Corwin, "The *Dred Scott* Decision in the Light of Contemporary Legal Doctrine," *American Historical Review* 17 (1911), quoted in Warren, *Supreme Court in U.S. History,* II: 316–317.

61. Warren, *Supreme Court in U.S. History,* II: 356.

62. *Ableman v. Booth,* 21 How. 506 at 525, 521 (1859).

63. Swisher, *The Taney Period,* 973–974.

64. Ibid., 974–975.

65. William Gillette, "Samuel Miller" in Friedman and Israel, *Justices of the Supreme Court,* II: 1023.

66. *Ex parte Merryman,* Federal Cases 9487, 152.

67. *Roosevelt v. Meyer,* 1 Wall. 512 (1863).

68. *Ex parte Vallandigham,* 1 Wall. 243 (1864).

69. Charles Fairman, *History of the Supreme Court of the United States,* Vol. 4, *Reconstruction and Reunion, 1864–1888* (New York: Macmillan, 1971), 32.

70. Frank Otto Gatell, "Robert C. Grier" in Friedman and Israel, *Justices of the Supreme Court,* II: 883.

71. Charles Evans Hughes, *The Supreme Court of the United States* (New York: Columbia University Press, 1928), 53.

72. *Collector v. Day,* 11 Wall. 113 (1871).

73. *The Slaughterhouse Cases,* 16 Wall. 36 at 78 (1873).

74. *Bradwell v. Illinois,* 16 Wall. 130 (1873).

75. *Minor v. Happersett,* 21 Wall. 162 (1875).

76. *United States v. Reese, United States v. Cruikshank,* 92 U.S. 214, 542 (1876).

77. *Munn v. Illinois,* 94 U.S. 113 at 134 (1877).

78. William Gillette, "Noah H. Swayne" in Friedman and Israel, *Justices of the Supreme Court,* II: 998.

79. Warren, *Supreme Court in U.S. History,* II: 599.

80. *Ex parte Yarbrough,* 110 U.S. 651 (1884).

81. *Boyd v. United States,* 116 U.S. 616 at 635 (1886).

82. *Yick Wo v. Hopkins,* 118 U.S. 356 (1886).

83. *Paul v. Virginia,* 8 Wall. 168 (1869).

84. *Mugler v. Kansas,* 123 U.S. 623 (1887); *Powell v. Pennsylvania,* 127 U.S. 678 (1888).

CHAPTER 2

The Second Century: Court and Controversy

MELVILLE W. FULLER became chief justice as the Court's first century ended. His tenure spanned the chronological, political, and social transition to the world of the twentieth century. Vast changes occurred during this period, changes that brought new challenges to the Supreme Court. William Swindler explained:

The passing of the frontier, the rise of an interstate industrialism, the shift from a rural to an urban distribution of population, the breakdown of nineteenth-century capitalism and the efforts to construct in its stead a twentieth-century capitalism, the breakthrough in science and technology, the change in the society of nations brought about by global wars and the militant dialectic of totalitarianism—the constitutional posture of the American people had to be readjusted in response to each of these.

Fuller's court stood upon the watershed, with a powerful pull of ideological gravity toward the past. At least three of his colleagues when he came onto the bench dated from the constitutional golden age: Justices Bradley, Field and Miller all had begun their careers under men who in turn had known John Marshall and Joseph Story. From these venerated predecessors, who interpreted the Constitution with reference to a pioneer economy and an ante-bellum concept of the Federal function, Fuller and his intimate associates undertook to derive a jurisprudence to apply to issues never imagined by the early Federalist jurists.[1]

Four other new justices joined the Court within Fuller's first five years there. All were chosen by President Benjamin Harrison; all were men of conservative bent.

The first of Harrison's selections was the most notable. Justice Matthews died in March 1889. As his successor, Harrison chose federal circuit judge David J. Brewer of Kansas, Justice Field's nephew. Brewer, fifty-two, was confirmed late in the year. During his twenty years on the Court he would be one of its most articulate members.

On March 3, 1890, Justice Brewer delivered his first major opinion for the Court. In *Louisville, New Orleans and Texas Railway Co. v. Mississippi*, the majority upheld a state law requiring railroads to provide separate accommodations for black and white passengers on trips within the state. Justices Harlan and Bradley dissented.

Accepting the state court's view that the state law applied only to intrastate trips, the Supreme Court majority held that it did not burden interstate commerce. This ruling distinctly foreshadowed the Court's acceptance, six years later in *Plessy v. Ferguson*, of the "separate but equal" doctrine, an action that established the racial segregation of U.S. society well past the midpoint of the next century.

Three weeks after the *Mississippi* ruling, on March 24, 1890, the era of "substantive due process" began. For the first time the Court endorsed the belief that the due process clause of the Fifth and the Fourteenth Amendments gives federal courts the power to review the *substance* of legislation, not just the *procedures* it sets up. At issue in the case of *Chicago, Milwaukee & St. Paul Railway Co. v. Minnesota* was a Minnesota law that prescribed the rates that the railroad could charge—and did not provide for judicial review of the reasonableness of these rates. The Court held that this law denied the businessmen their right to due process, declaring by its action that it would no longer defer to legislative judgment in rate setting, as it had in *Munn v. Illinois*. Now it assumed for itself and other courts the power to review the wisdom of these economic decisions.

This ruling extended the protection of the Fourteenth Amendment to business, adopting a view the Court had rejected in the *Slaughterhouse Cases*. Six months later, Justice Miller, author of the *Slaughterhouse* opinion, died after twenty-eight years on the bench. Harrison chose federal judge Henry B. Brown, a Yale classmate of Brewer's, to succeed Miller. Brown, from Michigan, would serve for fifteen years.

For the nation's first century, the Supreme Court was essentially the only federal court of appeals, the only court that heard appeals from the decisions of other federal courts. As a result of increasing litigation, its workload mushroomed. From the end of the Civil War until 1891 it was not at all uncommon for a case to wait two or three years after being docketed before it was argued before the Court.

The Court made various changes in its operations to promote more expeditious handling of cases, but all its efforts were of little avail to deal with the increasing volume of business.

Finally, in 1891, Congress eliminated the justices' obligation to ride circuit. It set up a system of federal appeals courts between the old district and circuit courts, on the one hand, and the Supreme Court on the other. The decisions of these new circuit courts of appeals were final in many cases. When a decision was appealed from one of these new courts, the Supreme Court had complete discretion in deciding whether to review it. The result, at least for a time, was a reduction in the press of business at the Court.

Early in 1892 the Supreme Court decided *Counselman v. Hitchcock*, one of its rare nineteenth-century rulings interpreting the Bill of Rights. And, as in *Boyd v. United States* six years earlier, the Court gave individuals broad protection against federal authority. The immunity provisions of the Interstate Commerce Act were constitutionally insufficient, the Court held. The Fifth Amendment, said the unanimous Court, required that a witness could be compelled to testify and give evidence against himself only if the government promised not to use that evidence in any way against him.

Within days of *Counselman*, Justice Bradley died. As his successor, President Harrison chose George Shiras Jr., a Pennsylvania lawyer whose clients included the great iron and steel companies of Pittsburgh and the Baltimore & Ohio Railroad. Despite opposition from his home state senators, Shiras was unanimously confirmed. He served for a decade.

In January of the following year, 1893, Justice Lamar died. To succeed him, Harrison chose a friend from his Senate days, Howell Jackson of Tennessee, a federal circuit judge. Jackson, however, became ill within a year of his appointment and died a year later.

In mid-1893 Justice Blatchford, the author of *Counselman*, died. The seat he had filled had been held by a New Yorker since 1806. With his death this tradition ended. President Cleveland tried twice, without success, to place another New York attorney in the seat, but the opposition of the senators from New York blocked the nominations of both William Hornblower and Wheeler Peckham.

Finally, in February 1894, Cleveland nominated Sen. Edward D. White of Louisiana, forty-eight, to the seat. He was confirmed the same day. White would serve on the Court twenty-seven years. After seventeen years as an associate justice, he would become the first sitting justice promoted to chief justice, a post in which he would serve for a decade more.

Business at the Court: 1889–1919

The conservative character of the Court of the 1890s was demonstrated with stunning force in the October 1894 term, one of the most notable single terms in Court history. With three landmark decisions, the Court placed itself firmly on the side of business, defending the interest of property against federal power and organized labor.

On January 21, 1895, the Court, 8–1, held that the Sherman Antitrust Act did not outlaw manufacturing monopolies. The Court reasoned that manufacturing was not commerce and so was not reachable under the federal commerce power, upon which the Sherman Act was based.

Chief Justice Fuller wrote the majority opinion in *United States v. E. C. Knight & Co.*, agreeing with the argument of the "sugar trust"—the sugar refining monopoly—that the United States could not challenge its concentrated power. The monopoly remained intact, and the antitrust law lay virtually useless.

On May 20, 1895, the Court struck down the act of Congress imposing the nation's first general peacetime tax on personal income. The decision came in the twice-argued case of *Pollock v. Farmers' Loan and Trust Co.* By a 5–4 vote, the Court overturned a century-old precedent and declared the income tax a direct tax, subject to—and, in this case, in conflict with—the constitu-

tional requirement that direct taxes be apportioned among the states according to population. Again Chief Justice Fuller wrote the majority opinion. Dissenting were Justices Harlan, Brown, Jackson, and White.

The ruling, which Justice Brown described as "nothing less than a surrender of the taxing power to the moneyed class,"[2] resulted in the Sixteenth Amendment, added to the Constitution in 1913, which lifted the apportionment requirement for income taxes.

It had fended off assaults upon property from trustbusters and the tax laws, but the Court was not yet finished. A week after *Pollock*, the Court gave federal judges the power to stop strikes.

In *In re Debs* the Court unanimously upheld the contempt conviction of labor leader Eugene V. Debs for disobeying a court order to call off a Pullman strike that halted rail traffic. Justice Brewer wrote the Court's opinion. As a result of this ruling, such court orders were frequently used by employers against labor unions. In the thirty-seven years between *Debs* and passage of a law forbidding judges to use injunctions in this way, they were sought in more than 120 major labor cases.[3]

In August 1895 Justice Jackson died. President Cleveland in December chose Rufus W. Peckham of New York—brother of his earlier unsuccessful nominee—for the seat. Peckham, fifty-seven, and a state judge, was quickly confirmed. During his thirteen years on the Court, he would serve as its spokesman in some of its most notable rulings defending property rights.

SEPARATE AND EQUAL

The social views of the Court of the 1890s were no more liberal than its economic beliefs. *Plessy v. Ferguson*, decided May 18, 1896, made that point clear: The Court, 8–1, upheld a Louisiana law requiring railroads operating in the state to provide separate cars for white and black passengers. This law was not in violation of the Fourteenth Amendment's equal protection clause, declared Justice Brown for the majority. It was a reasonable exercise of the state police power to preserve the public peace and public order.

Reflecting the view that laws are inadequate social instruments, Brown wrote that social equality of the races could not be accomplished by laws that conflicted with general community sentiment. The government can secure its citizens equal legal rights and equal opportunities, but it can and should go no further. "Legislation is powerless to eradicate racial instincts or to abolish distinctions based upon physical differences, and the attempt to do so can only result in accentuating the difficulties of the present situation. If the civil and political rights of both races be equal one cannot be inferior to the other civilly or politically. If one race be inferior to the other socially, the Constitution of the United States cannot put them upon the same plane."[4]

In lonely if prophetic dissent, Justice Harlan warned that this decision would "in time, prove to be quite as pernicious as the decision made by this tribunal in the *Dred Scott* case."[5] He continued:

THE COURT IN 1897

From left: Justices Edward D. White, Henry B. Brown, Horace Gray, Stephen J. Field, Chief Justice Melville W. Fuller, Justices John Marshall Harlan, David J. Brewer, George Shiras Jr., Rufus W. Peckham

If evils will result from the commingling of the two races upon public highways . . . they will be infinitely less than those that will surely come from state legislation regulating the enjoyment of civil rights upon the basis of race.[6]

This law, Harlan concluded, "is inconsistent with the personal liberty of citizens, white and black . . . and hostile to both the spirit and letter of the Constitution."[7]

Abraham Lincoln had nominated Justice Stephen Field of California to the Court in 1863 to hold the new "western" seat. In 1897 Field was eighty-one years old, his health was failing, and his irritability growing. Justice Harlan was selected by his colleagues to suggest that Field consider retirement. His reminder that Field had made such a suggestion to Justice Grier twenty-five years earlier was met with an angry rejoinder. But after thirty-four years and nine months—the longest service of any man in the Court's history, and a record unsurpassed for another seventy-five years—Field resigned in October 1897.

To succeed him President William McKinley named Attorney General Joseph McKenna of California, fifty-five, a political protégé of railroad magnate Leland Stanford, then a U.S. senator. McKenna, a former member of Congress, was confirmed, was seated early in 1898, and served on the Court well into the next century.

After McKenna filled Field's seat, there was no change in the Court's membership for the next four years.

FREEDOM OF CONTRACT

With its last decisions of the nineteenth century, the Court discovered a new aspect of the liberty protected by the Constitution, a freedom of contract that provided additional doctrinal foundation for rulings protecting property rights, rather than individual rights, against governmental power.

On March 1, 1897, the Court in *Allgeyer v. Louisiana* declared that the liberty protected by the Fourteenth Amendment included "the right of the citizen . . . to earn his livelihood by any lawful calling; to pursue any livelihood or avocation, and for that purpose to enter into all contracts which may be proper, necessary and essential" to those ends.[8]

This doctrine provided the Court, for forty years, with one of its most potent weapons against state laws intended to protect individual workers by setting the maximum hours they might work and the minimum wage they should be paid.

In a second ruling announced that day, *Chicago, Burlington & Quincy Railway Co. v. Chicago,* the Court in a business context acknowledged that some of the guarantees of the Bill of Rights might be of such a nature as to be included in the Fourteenth Amendment's guarantee of due process.

With Justice Harlan writing for the Court, the justices upheld state police power to require railroads to maintain certain safety measures. In so doing, it stated that due process required the government to compensate the owner of private property for property "taken" for use in the public interest.

Despite its new freedom-of-contract doctrine, the Court in 1898 upheld the first state maximum-hour law challenged as violating that freedom. In *Holden v. Hardy* the justices found that a law limiting the hours persons could spend working in underground mines was a proper exercise of the state's power to protect the health of its citizens.

The following week, however, the Court in *Smyth v. Ames* reaffirmed the judicial role in reviewing such state laws. When states set the rates that railroads could charge, wrote Justice Harlan, those rates must be set high enough to ensure the railways a fair return on their investment. And the courts will decide what return is fair.

In 1898 the Court also demonstrated its continuing willingness to leave to the states regulation of the suffrage, even if the states effectively denied blacks that right. In *Williams v. Mississippi* the Court found no constitutional flaw in a law that required voters to pass a literacy test before being allowed to cast their ballot. Justice McKenna wrote the Court's opinion, one of his first.

THE TURN OF THE CENTURY

What were the privileges and immunities of U.S. citizenship protected against state action by the Fourteenth Amendment? In 1873 the Court had held that the right to do business was not one of these. In later rulings it held that the right to vote was not such a privilege either.

But what about the guarantees of the Bill of Rights that protected U.S. citizens against federal action? In one of its first rulings of the twentieth century, the Court answered that these were not privileges or immunities of federal citizenship either. That ruling came in *Maxwell v. Dow,* decided in 1900. Justice Peckham, for the Court, rejected the argument that the Fourteenth Amendment required states to provide twelve-person juries to try persons accused of crimes. Justice Harlan dissented.

In 1901 the Court showed similar reluctance to extend constitutional protections to any new groups of persons. In the *Insular Cases* the Court held that it was up to Congress to decide whether the Constitution and its guarantees applied to persons residing in territory newly acquired by the United States.

Late in 1902 Justice Gray resigned. As his successor President Theodore Roosevelt chose Oliver Wendell Holmes Jr., sixty-one, chief justice of the Massachusetts Supreme Judicial Court. Holmes served on the Court for more than twenty-nine years, through the terms of three chief justices and into a fourth. He was, by all measures, one of the nation's greatest justices. Like Harlan, he was often in dissent from the rulings of the conservative Court; also like Harlan, many of his dissents later became the prevailing view of the modern Court.

The following year Justice Shiras resigned. Roosevelt chose Judge William R. Day, of the federal circuit court of appeals, as Shiras's successor. Day, fifty-three, a successful railroad lawyer and McKinley's secretary of state before moving to the bench, would serve for nineteen years.

The first few years of Holmes's service saw the Court give a broader reading to the federal commerce power than it had been willing to give earlier. In 1903 the Court recognized the existence of a federal police power, upholding in *Champion v. Ames* an act of Congress forbidding the use of the mails for transmitting lottery tickets. But the vote was close—5–4. Justice Harlan wrote the majority opinion; the dissenters were Chief Justice Fuller and Justices Brewer, Peckham, and Shiras.

The following year the Court enlarged on that ruling as it upheld a "police" use of the federal tax power to discourage the marketing of colored oleomargarine, holding that it would not inquire into the purposes of such a tax.[9]

In 1904 the Court began to revive the usefulness of the Sherman Antitrust Act, ruling for the government in *Northern Securities Co. v. United States.* Four of the justices, for whom Justice Harlan again spoke, read the Sherman Antitrust Act literally—forbidding all restraints of trade. The four dissenting justices—White, Holmes, Peckham, and Chief Justice Fuller—argued that the law forbade only unreasonable restraints of trade. The Harlan group became the majority through the concurrence of Justice Brewer and ruled in this case that the securities company was so powerful that it imposed an unreasonable restraint on trade.

In a separate dissenting opinion, Justice Holmes set out one of his most often-quoted epigrams:

Great cases, like hard cases, make bad law. . . . For great cases are called great, not by reason of their real importance in shaping the law of the future, but because of some accident of immediate overwhelming interest which appeals to the feelings and distorts the judgment.[10]

Holmes's comment appeared to be aimed directly at the man who had placed him on the bench—Theodore Roosevelt—whose intense interest in the success of the government's trust-busting effort, and this case, was well known. Roosevelt disregarded his appointee's comment and hailed the decision as a reversal of the 1895 holding in the sugar trust case.

In 1905 the Court unanimously backed the government's prosecution of the beef trust. Justice Holmes wrote the opinion in *Swift & Co. v. United States,* basing the ruling on a broad concept of commerce as a "current" among the states, a "stream" of which meatpacking was a part—and so was within the reach of the antitrust laws.

Although the Court was still willing to support the exercise of the state police power over a subject such as the public health, in 1905 its decision in *Lochner v. New York* signaled its distaste for state efforts to interfere with wage and hour bargaining between employer and employee.

In February 1905 the Court upheld state power to compel its citizens to be vaccinated against smallpox. This requirement, wrote Harlan, was a proper use of the police power.[11] Six weeks later, the Court—over the dissent of Harlan, Holmes, Day, and White—ruled in *Lochner* that New York's law setting an eight-hour maximum work day for bakery employees interfered with the freedom of contract.

Justice Peckham wrote the majority opinion declaring "that there is a limit to the valid exercise of the police power by the state." This law overstepped that limit: "Clean and wholesome bread does not depend upon whether the baker works but ten hours per day or only sixty hours a week."[12]

In 1906 Justice Brown resigned. President Roosevelt named his attorney general and close friend, William Moody, fifty-two, as Brown's successor. Only four years later, Moody would retire, disabled by acute rheumatism. Congress passed a bill allowing him to retire with special benefits.

LABOR AND THE COURT

With its unsympathetic ruling in the 1895 case of Eugene Debs and the Pullman strike, the Supreme Court expressed a profound distaste for the arguments and the tactics of the workers' labor movement. In 1908, it reaffirmed that view.

On January 6, 1908, the Court struck down an act of Congress enlarging the liability of railroads for injuries to their employees. By 5–4 the Court held that the law was invalid because it applied to intrastate aspects of interstate commerce.[13]

Three weeks later, the Court invalidated another law that outlawed "yellow-dog" contracts, which railroads used to make their employees promise, as a condition of keeping their jobs, not to join labor unions. Justice Harlan wrote the opinion of the Court in *Adair v. United States,* finding this federal law an undue restriction on freedom of contract. Holmes and McKenna dissented.

On February 3, 1908, the Court unanimously agreed that the Sherman Antitrust Act forbade secondary boycotts by labor unions; Chief Justice Fuller wrote the Court's opinion in *Loewe v. Lawlor,* known as the *Danbury Hatters* case.

This term did bring workers one major victory, a victory in which a Boston lawyer named Louis D. Brandeis played a significant role. Oregon law set the maximum hours that women should work in laundries. The law was challenged, on the basis of *Lochner,* as a violation of the liberty of contract. The state engaged Brandeis as its counsel. He submitted a brief full of factual data supporting the argument that long hours of hard labor had a harmful effect upon women, and thus, through mothers, upon their children.

Brandeis won a unanimous decision in favor of Oregon's law, modifying *Lochner* by finding some state interference with freedom of contract justified to protect the public health. Justice Brewer wrote the opinion in *Muller v. Oregon.* And the term "Brandeis brief" came to be used to refer to briefs filled with factual, as well as legal, arguments.

Throughout the early years of the new century, the Court continued to hold a narrow view of the Constitution's protection for individual rights. In May 1908—over the dissent of Justices Day and Harlan—the majority upheld a state law that required Kentucky's Berea College to separate black and white students in classes.[14]

And in November 1908 the Court reaffirmed its point made in *Maxwell v. Dow,* that the Fourteenth Amendment did not automatically extend the guarantees of the Bill of Rights to state defendants. In *Twining v. New Jersey* the Court refused to hold that a defendant was denied his constitutional rights when the judge in his case commented on his failure to testify in his own defense. The Fifth Amendment guarantee against self-incrimination, the Court held, did not apply in state trials. Justice Moody wrote the opinion; Justice Harlan dissented alone.

THE TAFT JUSTICES

William Howard Taft always wanted to be chief justice. But on March 4, 1909, he was sworn in as president instead. During his term he appointed six members of the Court, the greatest number named by a single president since George Washington. A dozen years later, he finally did become chief justice.

In 1909 Justice Peckham died. To succeed him Taft chose Horace H. Lurton, sixty-five, with whom he had served on the Court of Appeals for the Sixth Circuit. Lurton served only four years before his death in 1914.

In 1910 Taft placed three more new members on the Court and elevated Justice White to the seat of chief justice. Justice Brewer died in March after twenty years of service. Taft chose Charles Evans Hughes, forty-eight, governor of New York, as his successor. Hughes would serve six years before resigning to run unsuccessfully for president in 1916. He would return to the Court in 1930, Taft's successor as chief justice.

In July 1910 Chief Justice Fuller died after twenty-two years in his post. Taft broke precedent and named Justice White as the Court's new chief. White was immediately confirmed and served for more than ten years in his new seat.

To replace White, Taft chose Joseph R. Lamar, fifty-three, a Georgia attorney, whom he had met playing golf in Augusta. Lamar died after only five years on the Court.

In November 1910 Justice Moody resigned. Taft named to the seat Willis Van Devanter of Wyoming, fifty-one, a member of the Court of Appeals for the Eighth Circuit. Van Devanter would serve for twenty-six years, Taft's longest serving appointee.

In October 1911 Justice Harlan died after a long and distinguished, if often lonely, career on the Court. As his successor, Taft chose Mahlon Pitney of New Jersey, fifty-four, a member of that state's supreme court. Pitney served until 1922. With Harlan's death, only two members remained from the Court of the 1890s—White and McKenna.

TRUSTS AND TAXES

For a few years after White had replaced Fuller as chief justice, the Court relaxed its conservative stance.

In Harlan's last term the Court adopted the "rule of reason" for applying the Sherman Antitrust Act against restraints of trade, the rule that Harlan had so vigorously rejected in the *Northern Securities* case seven years earlier. By an 8–1 vote in mid-May 1911 the Court declared that the antitrust act outlawed only unreasonable restraints of trade, not all restraints of trade. The majority ordered the breakup of the Standard Oil trust, which they found to be an unreasonable restraint. Chief Justice White wrote the majority opinion, declaring reasonableness the standard, which the courts would apply. Justice Harlan dissented.[15]

Two weeks later the Court ordered the dissolution of the tobacco trust. Again Harlan dissented, arguing that the Court was acting as a legislature, rewriting the law by adding the rule of reason.[16]

Nevertheless, the rule of reason would stand through most of the twentieth century as the standard by which the federal antitrust laws would be applied against combinations charged with restraint of trade.

THE COURT IN 1914

Seated from left: Justices William R. Day, Joseph McKenna, Chief Justice Edward D. White, Justices Oliver Wendell Holmes Jr., Charles Evans Hughes.
Standing from left: Justices Mahlon Pitney, Willis Van Devanter, Joseph R. Lamar, James C. McReynolds

The federal police power continued to win backing at the Court, which upheld the Pure Food and Drug Act in 1911, a revised employers' liability act in 1912, and the White Slave Act in 1913.[17]

Other aspects of the federal commerce power were broadly construed as well. In the *Shreveport Rate Case* of 1914, the Court held that in some situations Congress, through the Interstate Commerce Commission, could set rates for railroads operating entirely within a state.

With the antitrust rulings culminating in the oil and tobacco trust decisions, the Court had resuscitated the Sherman Antitrust Act, which its sugar trust ruling of 1895 had seemed to leave useless.

Congress and the states overrode the second of those landmark 1895 rulings—the income tax decision. In 1913 Congress and the states added to the Constitution the Sixteenth Amendment, which declared that a federal income tax was not subject to the Constitution's apportionment requirement. Congress enacted a statute taxing incomes of more than $3,000 and $4,000 for single and married persons, respectively.

In the 1916 case of *Brushaber v. Union Pacific Railroad Co.*, the Court upheld the act as constitutional. Chief Justice White wrote the opinion for the Court, acknowledging that the clear intent of the new amendment was to overturn the Court's reasoning in the 1895 *Pollock* case.

RIGHTS AND REMEDIES

In 1914 the Court adopted the "exclusionary rule" to enforce the Fourth Amendment promise of personal security against unreasonable searches and seizures by federal agents. In *Weeks v. United States* the unanimous Court held that persons whose rights were violated by such searches could demand that any evidence so obtained against them be excluded from use in federal courts. Half a century later, when the Court applied this rule against state action as well, it would become one of the most controversial of the Court's rulings.

In 1915 the Court applied the Fifteenth Amendment to strike down Oklahoma's grandfather clause, which made it difficult for blacks to register to vote in the state. This decision in *Guinn v. United States,* however, did not settle the matter. Twenty-four years later, in *Lane v. Wilson,* the Court struck down a similarly discriminatory law Oklahoma adopted in place of the grandfather clause.

President Woodrow Wilson named three men to the Court, one of whom refused to speak to the other two for most of their tenure.

In 1914 Justice Lurton died. To succeed him, Wilson nominated his attorney general, James C. McReynolds, fifty-two, of Tennessee. McReynolds, one of the most conservative men to serve on the Court in the twentieth century, also was one of the most difficult. He went out of his way to avoid dealing with Justices Louis Brandeis and Benjamin Cardozo—both Jewish—and he refused to speak to Justice John H. Clarke, whom he considered unintelligent.[18]

Brandeis was Wilson's second nominee to the Court, chosen to fill the seat left vacant by Justice Lamar's death in 1916. The nomination of Brandeis, fifty-nine, was opposed by a number of leaders of the American bar, including former president Taft, who considered him a dangerous radical. After lengthy and contentious hearings, he was confirmed in June 1916 by a vote of 49–22. He served on the Court for twenty-three years.

As soon as Brandeis was confirmed, Justice Hughes resigned to run unsuccessfully against Wilson for the White House. Federal judge John Clarke of Ohio, fifty-eight, was Wilson's choice to fill this seat. Clarke resigned after six years on the bench to work for U.S. entrance into the League of Nations. He lived for thirty-three more years, dying in 1945. After Clarke joined the Court, there were no other changes in its membership until 1921.

By 1917 the Court appeared to have silently overruled *Lochner v. New York.* In two decisions early in the year, the Court upheld maximum-hour statutes. In *Wilson v. New* it approved a federal law setting an eight-hour work day on interstate railroads, and in *Bunting v. Oregon,* a state law setting maximum hours for all industrial workers. The law upheld in *Bunting* also set minimum wages for women and child workers; by implication the Court sustained those provisions as well.

But the votes were close. Day, Pitney, Van Devanter, and McReynolds dissented from *Wilson. Bunting,* decided by only eight justices, found White, Van Devanter, and McReynolds in disagreement with the majority.

CONSERVATISM CONFIRMED

The years in which the nation fought World War I ended the Court's liberal interlude.

In 1918 the Court abruptly halted the steady expansion of federal police power striking down, 5–4, a 1916 act of Congress intended to outlaw child labor by barring from interstate commerce goods produced by child workers.

Justice Day wrote the Court's opinion in *Hammer v. Dagenhart,* returning to the distinction between manufacturing and commerce set out in 1895. This child labor law attempted to regulate manufacturing and so overreached the commerce power. Child labor was a subject left to state regulation, Day proclaimed. The Court's most senior members, McKenna and Holmes, and its most junior ones, Brandeis and Clarke, dissented.

World War I also brought the Selective Service Act and the military draft. In June 1917, 9.5 million men were registered for military service.[19] The law was immediately challenged, and in January 1918, it was unanimously upheld by the Court in its decisions in the *Selective Draft Law Cases.*

Wartime also brought enactment of an espionage act and a sedition act, the most repressive legislation since the Alien and Sedition Acts of 1798. But unlike their predecessors—which were not challenged before the Court—the World War I legislation was contested as violating the freedom of speech protected by the First Amendment.

In 1919 the Court unanimously sustained the espionage act in *Schenck v. United States.* Justice Holmes wrote the Court's opinion, setting out the famous—if little-used—"clear and present danger" test for determining when government might permissibly curtail an individual's freedom of speech.

The First Amendment, Holmes wrote, would "not protect a man . . . [who] falsely shout[ed] fire in a theater and caus[ed] a panic." The question to be asked, he continued, "is whether the words are used in such circumstances and are of such a nature as to create a clear and present danger that they will bring about the substantive evils that Congress has a right to prevent. It is a question of proximity and degree."[20]

Schenck was quickly followed by decisions upholding convictions under these challenged wartime statutes. The Court soon divided over the use of the clear and present danger test—but *Schenck* remains notable for its declaration that the First Amendment does not provide an absolute protection for free speech and as the first step in the Court's effort to find and define the standards for deciding when government may permissibly curtail free speech.

New Times, Old Court: 1920–1937

In May 1921 Chief Justice White died suddenly. Former president William Howard Taft, who had made no secret of his long-held ambition to be chief justice, was chosen by President Warren G. Harding as the tenth man to hold that post. Taft was confirmed in June 1921. He would serve for nine years, during which he would play a pivotal role in winning passage of the Judiciary Act of 1925, giving the Court more control over its workload, and in initiating work on the Court's own building.

Under Taft the Court's conservatism intensified even further. It revived the *Lochner* doctrine of freedom of contract and used it vigorously to restrain state efforts to regulate economic matters. And it curtailed federal authority, persisting in the view that Congress could not regulate matters such as agricultural production and manufacturing, and converting the seldom-invoked Tenth Amendment into a potent instrument for protecting state sovereignty and business matters from federal power.

During the Taft era the Court accelerated its use of its power of judicial review. While the Court had struck down only two acts of Congress in the years between the nation's founding and the Civil War, it struck down twenty-two federal laws in the period between 1920 and 1932.[21]

Despite such clearly conservative views, it was this same Court that set the nation on its course toward the "due process revolution" of the 1960s.

RESTRAINT OF REGULATION

Three acts of Congress struck down by the Taft Court in its first years exemplify the Court's tendency to put certain subjects outside the reach of federal power.

In 1921 the Court, in *Newberry v. United States,* held that Congress could not regulate spending in primary elections. Federal regulatory power reached only to general election campaigns for federal office; all other aspects of the electoral process were left to the states. One effect of this decision, which invalidated part of the 1911 Federal Corrupt Practices Act, was to leave the way open for states to exclude black voters from the electoral process, by hindering or blocking their participation in the primary elections. The successful attorney in this case was former justice Charles Evans Hughes.

In 1904 the Court, in *McCray v. United States,* declared that so long as a subject taxed by Congress was properly within federal power, the justices would not look behind the tax to ascertain its purpose. With this assurance, Congress responded to the Court's 1918 ruling striking down its commerce-based effort to outlaw child labor by using its tax power to achieve that same end. The result: the Child Labor Tax Act—placing a high tax on products made by industries that employed children. The Court in 1919 had upheld a similar tax measure intended to outlaw narcotics.[22]

But the Taft Court found a new tool to wield against federal regulation: the Tenth Amendment. Part of the original Bill of

Rights added to the Constitution in 1791, the amendment states that "the powers not delegated to the United States by the Constitution, nor prohibited by it to the States, are reserved to the States respectively, or to the people."

In May 1922 the Court invoked this amendment to strike down the 1918 child labor tax law. Chief Justice Taft wrote the majority opinion in *Bailey v. Drexel Furniture Co.* By using the tax power to ban child labor, Congress was infringing upon the reserved rights of the states to regulate such topics, held the Court. Justice Clarke was the only dissenter.

The same day, with the same Tenth Amendment argument, the Court invalidated a 1921 law in which Congress had used its tax power to regulate the commodities futures trade. This too was a matter reserved to state control, wrote Chief Justice Taft.

If this sort of law were upheld, Taft wrote,

all that Congress would need to do hereafter, in seeking to take over to its control any one of the great number of subjects of public interest, jurisdiction of which the states have never parted with and which are reserved to them by the Tenth Amendment, would be to enact a detailed measure of complete regulation of the subject and enforce it by a so-called tax. . . . To give such magic to the word "tax" would be to break down all constitutional limitation of the powers of Congress and completely wipe out the sovereignty of the states.

THE COURT IN 1925
Seated from left: Justices James C. McReynolds, Oliver Wendell Holmes Jr., Chief Justice William Howard Taft, Justices Willis Van Devanter, Louis D. Brandeis. *Standing from left:* Justices Edward T. Sanford, George Sutherland, Pierce Butler, Harlan Fiske Stone

(Congress then passed a new grain futures regulatory law based on the commerce power; the Court upheld it in 1923.)[23]

Continuing to evidence an antilabor bias, the Court during these years made it even easier for management to use the antitrust laws against labor union efforts to organize and improve the conditions of workers.

Responding to earlier Court decisions, Congress in 1914 had included in the Clayton Act specific language exempting labor unions from the reach of the antitrust laws. But in the 1921 decisions—*Duplex Printing Press v. Deering* and *American Steel Foundries v. Trades Council*—the Court interpreted this exemption into uselessness. It was ten more years before Congress finally and effectively forbade the use of federal injunctions in labor disputes.

After the close of Taft's first term, three justices resigned: first Clarke in September 1922, followed by Day and Pitney, who had suffered a stroke several months earlier. To fill the empty seats President Harding chose former Utah senator George Sutherland, sixty; Minnesota corporate attorney Pierce Butler, fifty-six; and federal judge Edward T. Sanford of Tennessee, fifty-seven. Sutherland would serve for sixteen years, Butler, seventeen, and Sanford, seven.

Early in 1925 Justice McKenna—the last of the nineteenth-century justices—resigned after twenty-six years on the Court; he was eighty-two years old.

President Calvin Coolidge named Attorney General Harlan Fiske Stone to that seat. Stone, fifty-three at the time of his appointment, had been a law professor at Columbia Law School for fifteen years before entering government. He would serve for sixteen years as an associate justice before becoming chief justice in 1941, a post he held until his death five years later. After Stone's confirmation, there were no further changes in the Court's membership until Taft's death in 1930.

Taft's second term brought a surprise to those who assumed that the Court's rulings upholding state maximum-hour laws reflected the Court's abandonment of the *Lochner* principle that a state violated the Fourteenth Amendment guarantee of due process when it interfered with this "freedom of contract." In April 1923 *Lochner* was revived. In *Adkins v. Children's Hospital* the Court, 5–3, struck down as invalid a minimum-wage law for women workers in the District of Columbia.

With Justice Sutherland writing one of his first and most important opinions, the Court held that such a law unconstitutionally infringed on the freedom of contract of employer and employee. Chief Justice Taft and Justices Sanford and Holmes dissented; Brandeis did not participate in the case.

The same year brought two other notable decisions. In *Frothingham v. Mellon* the Court found that a federal taxpayer lacked sufficient personal interest in the use of tax moneys to justify a federal suit challenging the way Congress raised and spent money. For forty-five years this decision protected federal spending from taxpayer challenges.

Foreshadowing the role that federal courts would assume later in the century—of insisting that state procedures adhered to fundamental standards of fairness—the Court in *Moore v. Dempsey* approved the intervention of a federal judge to vindicate the rights of persons convicted in state courts dominated by a mob. In that situation, wrote Justice Holmes, where "the whole proceeding is a mask—that counsel, judge and jury were swept to the fatal end by an irresistible wave of public passion, and . . . the state courts failed to correct the wrong," the federal courts must act.[24]

DUE PROCESS AND FREE SPEECH

The Court's role as balance wheel can give its work a paradoxical character. So it was in 1925 when the conservative Court ignited the spark that eventually would flare into the "due process revolution" of the 1960s.

Benjamin Gitlow, a socialist, did not convince the Court to overturn his conviction for violating New York's criminal anarchy law by distributing a pamphlet calling for the overthrow of the government. Gitlow had challenged his conviction as violating the First Amendment, which, he contended, the Fourteenth Amendment extended to protect individual rights against state, as well as federal, action.

But although the Court in *Gitlow v. New York* upheld Gitlow's conviction, it accepted this argument. Almost in passing, Justice Sanford stated that the Court now assumed "that freedom of speech and of the press . . . are among the fundamental personal rights and 'liberties' protected by the due process clause of the Fourteenth Amendment from impairment by the states."[25]

During the 1930s this declaration would form the foundation for the Court's first decisions striking down state laws as encroaching upon First Amendment freedoms.

Federal law enforcement practices, however, survived constitutional challenge in two significant cases during the 1920s. The Court upheld routine searches, without search warrants, of cars that agents suspected were used in violating a law; and it upheld federal use of wiretaps, again without warrants, to obtain evidence. Neither practice, held the Court in *Carroll v. United States* and *Olmstead v. United States,* violated the individual's right to be secure from unreasonable search and seizure. *Carroll* remains in effect; *Olmstead* protected electronic surveillance from constitutional challenge until it was overturned in 1967.

The Court's first decision overturning a state conviction because it was obtained in violation of the Fourteenth Amendment's due process guarantee came in 1927. In *Tumey v. Ohio* the Court held that due process meant that a person charged with a violation of the law be tried before an impartial judge. It overturned the conviction of a person tried before a city court, where the judge was the mayor and the fines collected went into the city treasury.

The Court's definition of the liberty protected by the Fourteenth Amendment was slowly beginning to expand in the area of personal rights, even as it had expanded earlier in the area of property rights.

In 1923 the Court had struck down a state law forbidding a

teacher to use any language other than English.[26] The Fourteenth Amendment protected the right of teachers to teach a foreign language—and of parents to engage teachers to teach their children another language, held the Court.

In 1925 the Court in *Pierce v. Society of Sisters* invalidated a state law that required all children to attend public schools. Again, the Court found that parental freedom to choose private schools was within the protected area of personal liberty.

Black citizens, however, continued to meet with little success in asserting their rights under this amendment. In 1926 the Court in *Corrigan v. Buckley* clung to its nineteenth-century view that the Fourteenth Amendment did not reach private discrimination and so left unaffected the use of restrictive covenants limiting the sale of real estate to blacks.

When state action was involved, however, the Court was willing to exercise the power of the Civil War Amendments. In 1927 the Court in *Nixon v. Herndon,* the first in a long line of "white primary" cases, struck down Texas's efforts to exclude blacks from participating in the all-important Democratic primary elections.

THE ALLOCATION OF POWER

Local government won strong affirmation from the Court in 1926 of its power to control the use of its land through zoning. In *Euclid v. Ambler Realty Co.* the Court upheld such regulation as a legitimate use of the police power. The following year, in *Buck v. Bell,* the Court went even further, approving the use of the state's police power to sterilize some mentally defective state residents.

But when a state asserted its power over economic transactions, it again collided with the Court's insistence upon the freedom of contract. *Adkins* (1923) was followed by *Burns Baking Co. v. Bryan* (1924), which struck down a state law regulating the weight of loaves of bread sold to the public. In 1927 the Court held that states could not regulate the resale of theater tickets, and the following year it placed employment agency practices beyond state reach as well.[27]

The power of the chief executive was twice challenged and twice upheld. Confirming a virtually unlimited power of the president to remove appointees from office, the Court in the 1926 case of *Myers v. United States* held that Congress could not deny the president the power to remove postmasters without its consent. The power to remove was a necessary corollary of the power to appoint, held Taft in the majority opinion. Congress could not require a president to retain subordinates whom he wished to remove.

Two years later, in *Hampton v. United States,* the Court upheld Congress's delegation of power to the president to adjust tariff rates in response to the competitive conditions.

In February 1930 Chief Justice Taft resigned, a dying man. President Hoover selected Charles Evans Hughes, sixty-one, to return to the Court as chief justice. Hughes would serve through the turbulent decade of the New Deal, resigning in 1941.

Taft died March 8, 1930. So did Justice Sanford. To replace Sanford Hoover chose federal judge John J. Parker of North Carolina. But opposition to the nomination from labor and black groups resulted in Senate rejection of Parker's nomination in May. The vote was 39–41. It was the first time in the twentieth century that the Senate had refused to confirm a presidential nominee to the Court and the first such occurrence since Cleveland's New York nominees were blocked in 1894 by Senator Hill.

Hoover then chose Owen J. Roberts of Pennsylvania to fill the Sanford seat. Roberts, fifty-five, was a Philadelphia lawyer who had served as one of the two government prosecutors in the Teapot Dome scandal. He would serve on the Court for fifteen years.

In 1931 Justice Holmes was ninety, the oldest man to serve on the Court in its history. Hughes was the fourth chief justice with whom Holmes had served in his twenty-eight years on the Court. Age had slowed Holmes, and Chief Justice Hughes gently suggested to him that the time for retirement had come. On January 12, 1932, Holmes resigned. He died, at ninety-three, in 1935, leaving his estate to the nation; it eventually would be used to fund a history of the Court.

To replace Justice Holmes, Hoover selected New York judge Benjamin Cardozo, sixty-two, who had been almost unanimously proposed as Holmes's successor by leaders all over the nation. Cardozo's selection clearly represented the victory of merit over more mundane geographic or ethnic criteria. At the time there were two New Yorkers already on the Court—Hughes and Stone—and there was already a Jewish justice. Cardozo served only six years before his death in 1938.

After Cardozo took his seat on the Court in early 1932, there were no further changes in the Court personnel for more than five years.

FREEDOM, FAIRNESS, AND THE STATES

The first years of the 1930s were quiet at the Supreme Court. A nation devastated by the economic crash of 1929 and the resulting depression was preoccupied with survival and had little time for litigation.

In 1931 the Court for the first time struck down a state law because it infringed upon the freedoms protected by the First Amendment. In *Stromberg v. California* the Court divided 7–2 to strike down California's law forbidding citizens to display a red flag as a symbol of opposition to organized government. Chief Justice Hughes wrote the opinion, declaring that the opportunity for free political discussion was a fundamental principle of the U.S. constitutional system, both in itself and as a means of achieving lawful change and responsive government. Justices Butler and McReynolds dissented.

Two weeks after *Stromberg,* the Court struck down a second state law on similar grounds. In *Near v. Minnesota* the Court, 5–4, found that a state law penalizing newspapers for criticizing public officials violated the guarantee of a free press. Joining Butler and McReynolds in dissent were Sutherland and Van Devanter. Hughes again wrote the majority opinion.

Twice in the first half of the 1930s the Court considered constitutional questions arising from the case of the "Scottsboro boys," several young black men arrested in Alabama, away from their homes, and charged with raping two white women.

In 1932 *Powell v. Alabama* came to the Court. At issue was the right of these defendants, who were tried in state court, to have the effective aid of a lawyer in preparing a defense. This right is guaranteed defendants in federal trials by the Sixth Amendment, but the Court had not yet read the Fourteenth Amendment guarantee of due process as extending this right to state defendants.

In November 1932 the Court, 7–2, held that these black men, represented only at the last minute by a local lawyer, had been denied their constitutional right to due process. In these particular circumstances, wrote Justice Sutherland for the Court, the Constitution guaranteed these defendants the effective aid of an attorney. Justices Butler and McReynolds dissented.

Three years later—in the busy term of 1935—the second Scottsboro case came to the Court. In *Norris v. Alabama* the issue was not the right to counsel but the right to trial by a fairly chosen jury.

On April 1, 1935, a unanimous Court held that the Scottsboro defendants were denied their Fourteenth Amendment rights when they were indicted and tried by all-white juries, the result of the state's consistent practice of excluding blacks from jury duty. Chief Justice Hughes wrote the Court's opinion.

On the same day as *Norris v. Alabama*, the Court decided *Grovey v. Townsend*, the third of its rulings concerning Texas's persistent effort to keep blacks from voting in primary elections, the only significant elections in the Democratic-dominated South.

After the Court in *Nixon v. Herndon* (1927) struck down a state law barring blacks from voting in primary elections, the state handed over to state political parties the task of determining who could vote in its primary. In *Nixon v. Condon* (1932) the Supreme Court held that this delegation denied black voters equal protection. The state took no further action, but the Texas Democratic party barred all blacks from membership. In *Grovey v. Townsend* the Court held that the party's exclusion of blacks was beyond the reach of the Fourteenth Amendment. The party's action, it reasoned, was not state action. The Court was unanimous; Justice Roberts wrote the opinion.

In 1934 the Court lifted one long-standing restriction on state power to regulate business—and loosened another. The Court abandoned the view, first set out in *Munn v. Illinois* fifty-seven years earlier, that the only businesses states could regulate

THE COURT IN 1932
Seated from left: Justices Louis D. Brandeis, Willis Van Devanter, Chief Justice Charles Evans Hughes, Justices James C. McReynolds, George Sutherland.
Standing from left: Justices Owen J. Roberts, Pierce Butler, Harlan Fiske Stone, Benjamin N. Cardozo

were those "affected with a public interest." In its new case of *Nebbia v. New York* the Court, 5–4, upheld a New York law setting milk prices and declared that any business was subject to reasonable regulation. Roberts wrote the Court's opinion; McReynolds, Butler, Sutherland, and Van Devanter dissented. This decision was followed by rulings overturning the Taft Court's decisions nullifying state regulation of bread weights, ticket sales, and employment agencies.[28]

The Court also upheld a state mortgage moratorium law against a challenge that it violated the Constitution's contract clause. Again the vote was 5–4; the dissenters were the same as in *Nebbia*. Chief Justice Hughes wrote the opinion, finding the law a reasonable means of responding to the economic emergency of the Great Depression.[29]

THE COURT AND THE NEW DEAL

"The Court is almost never a really contemporary institution. The operation of life tenure in the judicial department, as against elections at short intervals of the Congress, usually keeps the average viewpoint of the two institutions a generation apart. The judiciary is thus the check of a preceding generation on the present one; a check of conservative legal philosophy upon a dynamic people, and nearly always the check of a rejected regime on the one in being." The man who wrote those words in 1941 was Attorney General Robert H. Jackson, an active participant in the New Deal battles between the Court and the president, and later a member of the Court.[30]

Never was Jackson's point more dramatically made than by the events of 1935, 1936, and 1937. A Court made up of men born in the mid-nineteenth century, and appointed to their seats by Presidents Wilson, Harding, Coolidge, and Hoover, looked with distaste upon radical legislative measures espoused by President Franklin D. Roosevelt and the Congress elected in the midst of national economic depression.

The Old Court

The Court of 1935 was five septuagenarians and four men only a few years their junior. Roberts, sixty, was the Court's youngest member. President Roosevelt was only fifty-three.

The Court's first decision on a New Deal measure came the first week of January 1935. Part of the National Industrial Recovery Act (NIRA) was invalidated, because in it Congress delegated power to the executive without setting specific standards for its use. The vote in *Panama Refining Co. v. Ryan* was 8–1. Chief Justice Hughes wrote the opinion; only Cardozo dissented.

Six weeks later, in mid-February 1935, the Court in the three *Gold Clause Cases* upheld the power of Congress to shift the nation away from the use of gold as its standard currency. The vote was 5–4: Hughes wrote the opinion; Sutherland, McReynolds, Butler, and Van Devanter dissented. McReynolds, distressed by the rulings, added to his dissenting opinion the extemporaneous lament: "As for the Constitution, it does not seem too much to say that it is gone. Shame and humiliation are upon us now!"[31]

But the *Gold Clause Cases* would be the administration's solitary victory before the Court in this October 1934 term. On May 6, 1935, the dissenters in the gold cases were joined by Justice Roberts to strike down the comprehensive retirement system Congress had set up for railroad employees. In *Railroad Retirement Board v. Alton Railway Co.*, the Court held that the commerce power did not provide a sufficient basis for such a system.

This decision was a harbinger of "Black Monday," three weeks later. On May 27 a unanimous Court handed Roosevelt three major defeats. In *Schechter Poultry Corp. v. United States*, the Court held invalid other major provisions of the NIRA, finding them an unconstitutional delegation of power from Congress to the president.

The Court also held the Federal Farm Bankruptcy Act in violation of the due process guarantee, and in a third decision the justices sharply limited the president's removal power, which it had envisioned as virtually unlimited only nine years earlier when it decided the *Myers* case.[32]

The 1936 Term

When the Court began its next term, in early October 1935, it met for the first time in its own building. Chief Justice Taft had persuaded Congress to approve the idea in 1929; the cornerstone had been laid by Chief Justice Hughes in October 1932; and the Court moved into the handsome marble building across from the Capitol for its 1936 term.

It was clear this would be a crucial term. Several cases testing the validity of New Deal legislation were pending; and the justices—even before they addressed these cases—were clearly divided. As historian Arthur M. Schlesinger Jr. described it:

They were already forming into distinct personal as well as constitutional blocs. The four conservatives used to ride to and from the Court together every day of argument and conference. To offset these riding caucuses, Stone and Cardozo began to go to Brandeis' apartment in the late afternoon on Fridays before conferences. Each group went over cases together and tried to agree on their positions.[33]

Hughes and Roberts were the two "swing men" between these two blocs. On January 6, 1936, they joined Sutherland, Van Devanter, Butler, and McReynolds to strike down the Agricultural Adjustment Act, which adopted crop controls and price subsidies as measures to stabilize the agricultural produce market. By 6–3 the Court held that Congress in this legislation intruded upon areas reserved by the Tenth Amendment for state regulation. Justice Roberts wrote the opinion in *United States v. Butler*.

On May 18 the Court by the same division struck down the Bituminous Coal Conservation Act. In *Carter v. Carter Coal Co.* the Court nullified a law designed to control working conditions of coal miners and to fix prices for the sale of coal. Coal mining was not commerce and so was outside the reach of federal authority, held the Court. The same day, the Court, 5–4, struck down the Municipal Bankruptcy Act.[34]

The administration claimed just one victory in the spring of

1936: the Court upheld—as a proper exercise of the commerce power—the creation of the Tennessee Valley Authority.[35]

As the term ended, Justice Stone commented:

I suppose no intelligent person likes very well the way the New Deal does things, but that ought not to make us forget that ours is a nation which should have the powers ordinarily possessed by governments, and that the framers of the Constitution intended that it should have. . . . We finished the term of Court yesterday, I think in many ways one of the most disastrous in its history.[36]

In this same term, so devastating in its impact on the effort of federal authority to deal with the nation's economic difficulties, the Court once again wielded the due process guarantee to strike down a state minimum-wage law. In *Morehead v. New York ex rel. Tipaldo* the same conservative majority that struck down the bankruptcy act struck down New York's law setting the minimum wage to be paid women workers. Such a law, wrote Butler for the Court, impaired the liberty of contract. Dissenting were Hughes, Stone, Brandeis, and Cardozo.

Almost overlooked amid the New Deal controversy, the Court in February 1936 took one more step toward imposing constitutional requirements on state criminal procedures. In *Brown v. Mississippi* the unanimous Court held that the Fourteenth Amendment guarantee of due process denied states the power to use as evidence against individuals any confession wrung from them by torture.

In December 1936 the Court, which held such a dim view of the president's efforts to deal with domestic crises, endorsed virtually unlimited power for the president in foreign affairs. In *United States v. Curtiss-Wright Export Corp.* the justices declared the president to be the sole negotiator of U.S. foreign policy. Justice Sutherland, author also of the opinions curtailing the removal power and striking down the coal act, described this aspect of presidential power as "plenary and exclusive."

PACKING THE COURT

Frustrated by the Court's adamant opposition to his efforts to lead the nation toward economic recovery, President Roosevelt began to look for a way to change the Court's views. His entire first term had passed without a vacancy there, despite the age and length of service of many of the justices. In part this state of affairs may have been due to the fierce opposition of the conservative justices to Roosevelt's New Deal, but it also was due to much more practical considerations.

In 1936 there was no "retirement" system for justices; they could withdraw from full-time active service only by resigning. Upon resignation the largest pension a justice could draw was $10,000. Chief Justice Hughes later would say that he felt that both Van Devanter and Sutherland would have retired earlier had the provisions for retirement income been more generous.[37]

Roosevelt decided to create vacancies by convincing Congress that the Court's functioning was hampered by the advanced age of its members. Early in February, just after his second inauguration, Roosevelt sent Congress a "judicial reform" proposal, quickly labeled his "Court packing" plan. He asked Congress to authorize him to appoint an additional member of the Supreme Court for each justice over age seventy who did not resign. This plan would have enabled Roosevelt immediately to appoint six new justices (Butler had turned seventy in 1936), and in all likelihood, assured him a majority in favor of the New Deal.

The reaction to the proposal was adverse on all sides, yet Congress began formal consideration of it. In a move that would prove crucial, Congress immediately separated out and passed a new Supreme Court Retirement Act on March 1. It provided that Supreme Court justices could retire and continue to receive their salary, just as other federal judges already were able to do.

The Senate Judiciary Committee then turned to consideration of the proposal's more controversial items.

THE TURNABOUT

Unknown to any but the justices themselves, however, the Court already had begun to abandon its conservative effort to protect business from state and federal regulation. Signaling this change was its decision, reached before the Court-packing proposal was made known, to abandon the *Lochner-Adkins* line of reasoning and uphold state minimum-wage laws.

Implicit in this reversal was the willingness of a majority of the Court to accept government authority to act to protect the general welfare of society—and to withdraw the Court from any role as the censor of economic legislation.

On March 29, 1937, while the Senate committee was still considering the Roosevelt plan, the Court announced its decision in *West Coast Hotel Co. v. Parrish*. By 5–4, the Court upheld Washington State's minimum-wage law, overruling *Adkins* and effectively reversing the previous year's ruling in *Morehead v. New York*. Justice Roberts, who had voted to strike down the New York law, now voted to uphold the Washington law. His changed position was popularly described at the time as "the switch in time that saved the Nine." Chief Justice Hughes wrote the majority opinion; Sutherland, Butler, McReynolds, and Van Devanter dissented.

In his opinion, Chief Justice Hughes interred the doctrine of freedom of contract. No such freedom was mentioned in the Constitution, he pointed out. The "liberty" protected by the due process clauses of the Fifth and Fourteenth Amendments, he continued, was not liberty of contract, but instead "liberty in a social organization which requires the protection of the law against the evils which menace the health, safety, morals and welfare of the people."[38] That liberty was protected by the minimum-wage law, which thus was fully constitutional.

The same day the Court unanimously upheld two New Deal statutes—a second Federal Farm Bankruptcy Act, virtually identical to the one struck down on Black Monday, and a provision of the Railway Labor Act encouraging collective bargaining.[39]

Two weeks later, on April 12, the Court—by the same 5–4 vote as in *Parrish*—upheld the National Labor Relations Act. Writing the majority opinion in *National Labor Relations Board v. Jones & Laughlin Steel Corp.*, Chief Justice Hughes declared that the right to organize for collective bargaining was a fundamental right well within the scope of Congress's power over commerce.

On May 18 the Senate Judiciary Committee reported Roosevelt's legislation adversely, recommending against its enactment.

Almost simultaneously, Justice Van Devanter, age seventy-eight, informed President Roosevelt that he intended to retire at the end of the current term.

Less than a week later, on May 24, the Court confirmed the completeness of its turnabout. In *Steward Machine Co. v. Davis* and *Helvering v. Davis*, the Court by votes of 5–4 and 7–2 upheld the unemployment compensation and old-age benefits programs set up by the Social Security Act. The Court upheld the first as a proper use of the taxing power and the second as an appropriate means of acting to protect the general welfare. Justice Cardozo wrote the majority opinions in both cases.

To replace Van Devanter, Roosevelt chose Alabama senator Hugo L. Black as his first nominee to the Court. Black, fifty-one, was confirmed in August 1937. He would serve on the Court until a week before his death in 1971.

In December 1937, soon after Black took his seat, the Court announced its decision in *Palko v. Connecticut*. With Cardozo writing for the majority, the Court firmly declined to rule that the due process clause of the Fourteenth Amendment automatically extended all the guarantees of the Bill of Rights against state, as well as federal action.

Only those rights essential to a scheme of ordered liberty were binding upon the states through the due process guarantee, stated Cardozo. In Black's thirty-four years on the Court, the justices would, one by one, place almost all of the guarantees of the Bill of Rights in this "essential" category.

The Court, Civil Rights, and Society: 1938–1968

On October 4, 1937, Justice Hugo Black took his seat as the Supreme Court's most junior justice, ushering in a new era. President Roosevelt's Court-packing bill had been deflated into a judicial procedure bill, signed into law in August 1937. Van Devanter, one of the conservative quartet of justices so staunchly opposed to the New Deal approach, had left the bench; the others would follow shortly. The Court had resigned as arbiter of the wisdom of economic legislation; it would now turn its attention to questions of individual rights and liberties.

Over the next six years Roosevelt would name eight justices and elevate a ninth to chief justice. The men he would place on the Court were young enough to be the sons of the men they succeeded, and the views of the Court would change accordingly.

A few months after Black was seated, Justice Sutherland, seventy-five, retired. To succeed him, Roosevelt named Solicitor General Stanley F. Reed, fifty-four. Reed served nineteen years until he retired in 1957.

In mid-1938 Justice Cardozo died. In his place Roosevelt chose his close friend and adviser, Felix Frankfurter, fifty-six, a Harvard law professor. Seated early in 1939, Frankfurter served for twenty-three years on the Court.

Soon after Frankfurter took his seat, Justice Brandeis resigned. He was eighty-two years old and had served on the Court twenty-three years. He was succeeded by a man literally half his age; William O. Douglas, the forty-year-old chairman of the Securities and Exchange Commission, would serve for thirty-six and one-half years—longer than any man in the Court's history.

Late in 1939 Justice Butler died at seventy-three. He was replaced by Attorney General Frank Murphy, fifty, who served until his death in 1949. With Murphy's arrival in January 1940, Roosevelt nominees became a majority of the Court. Of the four staunch conservatives who had blocked Roosevelt's New Deal plans, only McReynolds remained.

FROM COMMERCE TO CIVIL RIGHTS

The philosophical shift evident in the decisions of 1937 was reinforced by the rulings of the succeeding terms. Not only did the Court redirect its efforts away from matters of property rights and toward issues of personal rights, but also it began to evolve different standards for the two types of cases.

The change was illustrated in *United States v. Carolene Products Co.*, decided April 25, 1938. Over McReynolds's lone dissent, the Court upheld a federal law barring the interstate transportation of certain milk products.

In the majority opinion, Justice Stone tentatively set out a double standard for constitutional cases. When a law was challenged as impinging upon economic rights, he said, the Court would presume the law to be valid, unless the challenger could prove otherwise. But if a law was challenged as impinging upon personal liberties protected by the Bill of Rights, the Court might be less inclined to assume the law's validity. As Stone worded it, "there may be narrower scope for operation of the presumption of constitutionality when legislation appears on its face to be within a specific prohibition of the Constitution, such as those of the first ten amendments."[40]

The reasoning behind such a double standard, Stone explained, was based upon the relationship of economic rights and personal rights to the political processes. Laws infringing upon the individual rights guaranteed by the Bill of Rights restricted the operation of the very processes that could be expected to produce the repeal of repressive legislation. Laws operating to curtail economic freedom, on the other hand, did not hinder the political processes that therefore could be used to repeal or modify the offending laws.

This new set of standards—plus the extension of the guarantees of the Bill of Rights to the states, begun with *Gitlow*—provided the doctrinal underpinnings for the civil rights revolution to come. One observer calls the *Carolene Products* standard, set out in a footnote, "the manifesto in a footnote."[41]

In a steady line of decisions beginning with those announced on March 29, 1937, the Court upheld revised versions of virtually all the major New Deal legislation it had struck down in 1935 and 1936.[42]

Abandoning its restrictive view of the relationship between states' rights and federal power, the Court overturned its earlier decisions granting the incomes of federal officials immunity from state taxes and granting those of state officials similar immunity from federal taxation.[43]

This line of rulings—in which the Court also renounced many of the doctrines it had invoked to curtail state and federal power over economic matters—culminated on February 3, 1941. By a unanimous vote the Court upheld the Fair Labor Standards Act of 1938, which prohibited child labor and set a maximum forty-hour workweek and a minimum wage of forty cents an hour for workers in interstate commerce.

This decision, in *United States v. Darby Lumber Co.*, specifically overruled *Hammer v. Dagenhart*, the 1918 ruling placing child labor beyond the reach of the federal commerce power. The Court implicitly reaffirmed Hughes's earlier statement discarding the "freedom of contract" doctrine and declared the Tenth Amendment of no relevance to questions of federal power. Writing for the Court, Justice Stone explained that the justices viewed that amendment as "but a truism [stating] that all is retained which has not been surrendered."[44]

With this decision, legal scholar William F. Swindler wrote, the Court returned to Marshall's view of the broad commerce power:

[A]fter half a century of backing and filling, the Court had come unequivocally to acknowledge that a plenary power over interstate commerce was vested in Congress, and that Congress was the sole judge of the appropriate use of this power. The new constitutionalism, in this, was returning to the concept enunciated by John Marshall a century before, that the commerce power "is complete in itself, may be exercised to its utmost extent, and acknowledges no limitations other than are prescribed in the Constitution."[45]

Later this term, in May, the Court reversed another precedent and extended federal power in another direction. In *United States v. Classic* the Court acknowledged that Congress could regulate primary elections when they were an integral part of the process of selecting members of Congress. This decision overturned the Court's holding to the contrary in *Newberry v. United States,* decided twenty years earlier. Chief Justice Hughes, the attorney who had won the *Newberry* ruling, did not participate in the *Classic* decision.

Already in Black's first term questions of civil rights and individual freedom were beginning to occupy more of the Court's attention.

In March 1938 the Court unanimously held in *Lovell v. Griffin* that the First Amendment guarantee of freedom of religion was abridged when a city required Jehovah's Witnesses to be licensed before they could distribute religious literature to city residents.

THE COURT IN 1940
Seated from left: Justices Owen J. Roberts, James C. McReynolds, Chief Justice Charles Evans Hughes, Justices Harlan Fiske Stone, Hugo L. Black.
Standing from left: Justices William O. Douglas, Stanley F. Reed, Felix Frankfurter, Frank Murphy

In May the Court confirmed the broad scope of the Sixth Amendment right to counsel for federal defendants. The justices in *Johnson v. Zerbst* held that federal courts were constitutionally bound to provide defendants with legal counsel unless they waived that right.

And in December the Court began seriously to test the constitutional validity of the "separate but equal" doctrine, which had made possible the pervasive racial segregation of American life.

In *Missouri ex rel. Gaines v. Canada* the Court held that the Constitution required a state providing white residents the opportunity for higher education to offer it to blacks as well. This promise of equal protection, wrote Chief Justice Hughes, was not fulfilled by a state's offering to pay the tuition for a black student to attend law school in another state.

The following term the Court decided *Hague v. CIO*, striking down a city ordinance used to prevent union organizers from meeting and discussing labor union membership and related subjects. The First Amendment guarantee of free speech and assembly forbids such official restrictions, held the Court. And in 1940 the Court in *Thornhill v. Alabama* extended this rationale to strike down a state law forbidding labor picketing.[46]

Also in 1940 the Court in *Cantwell v. Connecticut* held that a state could not, without offending the First Amendment guarantees, convict persons for breach of the peace simply as a result of their making provocative statements about religion.

WAR AND PATRIOTISM

The war in Europe encouraged a resurgence of patriotic display in the United States. In 1940 the Court's emerging views on state power and religious freedom were tested by *Minersville School District v. Gobitis*. State efforts to inculcate patriotism prevailed, at least temporarily, over religious freedom. By 8–1 the Court upheld a state's right to require public school students to recite daily the national Pledge of Allegiance to the flag, even if the recitation conflicted with their religious beliefs. Justice Frankfurter wrote the majority opinion; only Justice Stone dissented.

Early in 1941 Justice McReynolds resigned after twenty-six years on the Court. He was seventy-eight years old, the last of the conservative foursome of the New Deal to leave the bench. At the end of the 1941 term, Chief Justice Hughes retired.

Roosevelt chose Justice Harlan Fiske Stone, a Republican who had sat on the Court as an associate justice for sixteen years, to move to the center chair. Stone, then sixty-nine, served in that post until his death in 1946.

To fill McReynolds's seat, Roosevelt chose Sen. James F. Byrnes of South Carolina, sixty-two. Byrnes did not find the post a satisfying one and resigned after one term, in October 1942, to take a more active role in the Roosevelt administration's war effort.

As Byrnes's successor Roosevelt chose federal judge Wiley B. Rutledge, forty-eight. Rutledge took his seat in February 1943 and served until his death six years later.

To fill the seat Stone left vacant upon becoming chief justice, Roosevelt in 1941 chose Attorney General Robert H. Jackson, forty-nine, who served for thirteen years.

The United States was forcibly brought into World War II early in Stone's first term as chief justice. War issues of personal liberty and governmental power dominated the Court's work during his tenure in that post.

After his first term, a special session was called in July 1942 so that the Court might consider the constitutional challenge brought by Nazi saboteurs, arrested in the United States, to Roosevelt's decision to have them tried by a military commission, not civilian courts. In *Ex parte Quirin* the Court upheld the president's actions as within the scope of the authority delegated to him by Congress.

In three later decisions in 1943 and 1944, the Court also upheld against constitutional challenge the actions of the president and Congress restricting the liberty of persons of Japanese descent living on the West Coast through a program of curfews and removal from the coast to inland camps. The Court conceded the odious nature of ethnic distinctions, but found them justified in this particular wartime situation.[47]

In one of these cases, however, *Korematsu v. United States,* the Court for the first time declared that "all legal restrictions which curtail the civil rights of a single racial group are immediately suspect . . . the Courts must subject them to the most rigid scrutiny."[48] Thus, even in condoning severe infringements of personal liberty and individual rights in the war years, the Court laid the foundation for later decisions expanding those rights.

A primary characteristic of the Court in the early 1940s, unlike its immediate predecessor, was its experimental approach to constitutional law, its "readiness to change new landmarks as well as old" ones.[49]

This readiness was amply demonstrated in the term that began in October 1942. In that term the Court reversed two of its own recent rulings concerning the First Amendment rights of Jehovah's Witnesses, a sect whose particular beliefs and evangelistic fervor brought its members into frequent collision with state and local authority.

In the 1940 *Gobitis* case the Court had upheld Pennsylvania's rule that schoolchildren participate in the Pledge of Allegiance to the U.S. flag each day.

In 1942 the Court had upheld, in *Jones v. Opelika*, a city ordinance requiring street vendors—including Jehovah's Witnesses passing out religious material—to obtain city licenses for their activity.[50] The vote was 5–4. Justice Reed wrote the majority opinion.

But three of the dissenters in *Opelika*—members of the majority in *Gobitis*—announced that they were ready to reverse the flag salute case. This unusual public confession of error came from Justices Black, Murphy, and Douglas.

Eleven months later, on May 3, 1943, the Court reversed *Jones v. Opelika,* returning to the view set out initially in *Lovell v. Griffin* that licenses could not be required of religious pamphleteers.

THE COURT IN 1943

Seated from left: Justices Stanley Reed, Owen R. Roberts, Chief Justice Harlan Fiske Stone, Justices Hugo L. Black, Felix Frankfurter.
Standing from left: Justices Robert H. Jackson, William O. Douglas, Frank Murphy, Wiley Blount Rutledge

By 5–4 the Court in *Murdock v. Pennsylvania* struck down licensing requirements similar to those upheld in *Opelika,* finding that they burdened the free exercise of religion when they were applied to the Jehovah's Witnesses. Justices Frankfurter, Reed, Roberts, and Jackson dissented.

Six weeks after *Murdock* the Court reversed *Gobitis.* The vote in *West Virginia Board of Education v. Barnette* was 6–3. The majority was composed of Stone, the lone dissenter in *Gobitis,* now joined by Black, Douglas, and Murphy, and two new justices— Jackson and Rutledge. Dissenting were Frankfurter, Reed, and Roberts.

The new majority's view was eloquently stated by Jackson:

If there is any fixed star in our constitutional constellation, it is that no official, high or petty, can prescribe what shall be orthodox in politics, nationalism, religion, or other matters of opinion or force citizens to confess by word or act their faith therein.[51]

In 1941 the Court refused to hold that the Fourteenth Amendment required states to provide all criminal defendants the aid of an attorney. Justices Black, Douglas, and Murphy dissented from the ruling in *Betts v. Brady;* twenty-two years later, Black would write the opinion overruling it.

In 1944 the Court in *Smith v. Allwright* expanded its definition of state action to strike down, once again, Texas's effort to maintain its "white primary." Relying on *United States v. Classic,* the Court effectively nullified *Grovey v. Townsend* (1935) by holding that when a primary election is an integral part of the electoral process, exclusion of black voters by a political party is state action within the reach of the Fourteenth Amendment.

THE POSTWAR COURT

In mid-1945 Justice Roberts resigned. President Harry S. Truman selected a friend, Republican senator Harold Burton of Ohio, fifty-seven, to fill the seat. Burton, the first Republican justice named by a Democratic president, served on the Court for thirteen years.

Despite the addition of Justice Burton, the Court operated for its October 1945 term with only eight members present. Justice Robert Jackson was absent for the term, acting as prosecutor at the Nuremberg trials of German war criminals.

On April 22, 1946, the Court, over dissenting votes by Stone, Reed, and Frankfurter, overruled several earlier decisions to permit conscientious objectors to become naturalized citizens, even if they were unwilling to bear arms in the defense of their adopted country. As Stone spoke from the bench to register his dissent in *Girouard v. United States,* his voice faltered. He had to be helped from the bench. He died that evening.

"The bench Stone headed was the most frequently divided, the most openly quarrelsome in history," wrote an observer.[52] That point was quickly borne out by events following his death. A long-distance feud erupted between Jackson, still absent in Europe, and Justice Black, now the Court's senior member. Many assumed that Truman would elevate Jackson to the post of chief justice; rumors flew that two other justices had said they would resign if he were appointed.

Hoping to smooth over these differences, Truman chose Secretary of the Treasury Fred M. Vinson to head the Court. Vinson, fifty-six, served for seven years, until his death in 1953.

After Stone's death, the Court—now with only seven participating members—announced its decision to strike down state laws requiring separate seating for black and white passengers on interstate buses. In *Morgan v. Virginia* the Court held such a rule a burden on interstate commerce. Seating rules for interstate vehicles was a matter for uniform national regulation, said the Court. This decision effectively reversed *Louisville, New Orleans and Texas Railway Co. v. Mississippi,* the Court's 1890 ruling upholding such requirements.

Also late in the October 1945 term, the Court by 4–3 in *Colegrove v. Green* declined to enter the "political thicket" of electoral malapportionment.

Questions of individual freedom came before the Court in increasing numbers during the postwar years. In its first rulings on the application of the First Amendment's establishment clause to state action, the Court in 1947 began a long effort to determine when and in what manner a state may provide aid to parochial schools or students at such schools without infringing on the amendment's guarantee.

In 1947 the Court reaffirmed its view that the due process clause of the Fourteenth Amendment did not require states to abide by all the provisions of the Bill of Rights. In that same term, however, the Court simply assumed that the Eighth Amendment ban on cruel and unusual punishment applied to state action.[53]

In 1949 the Court in *Wolf v. Colorado* declared that the states, like the federal government, were bound by the Fourth Amendment guarantee of security against unreasonable searches and seizures. But the Court rendered this declaration of little practical effect by refusing to require state judges to exclude evidence obtained in violation of the guarantee.

In 1948 the Court had effectively curtailed the use of restrictive covenants to perpetuate housing segregation. In *Shelley v. Kraemer* the Court held that although the Fourteenth Amendment did not reach the covenant itself, an agreement between private individuals, it did reach—and forbid—state court action enforcing those agreements.

In mid-1949 Justice Murphy died. President Truman selected Attorney General Tom C. Clark to fill the seat. Clark, forty-nine, served on the Court for eighteen years. Almost as soon as Clark was confirmed, Justice Rutledge died. Truman named Sherman Minton, fifty-nine, a colleague from his days as a senator, to that seat. Minton, who had become a federal judge, served on the Court for seven years.

SUBVERSION, SEGREGATION, AND STEEL SEIZURE

Cold war issues and the emerging civil rights movement dominated the work of the Supreme Court during most of the 1950s. Intense national concern over the threat of world communism produced a variety of laws and programs intended to prevent domestic subversion. Many of these antisubversive efforts were challenged as infringing on freedoms of belief and expression protected by the First Amendment.

In May 1950 the Court ruled on the first of these challenges. In *American Communications Association v. Douds* the Court upheld the Taft-Hartley Act's requirement that all labor union officers swear they were not members of the Communist Party. Chief Justice Vinson explained that Congress, under its commerce power, had the authority to impose such a requirement to avoid politically based strikes impeding the flow of interstate commerce. Justice Black in dissent argued that the commerce clause did not restrict "the right to think."

The following year the Court in *Dennis v. United States* upheld the Smith Act, which made it unlawful to advocate or teach the violent overthrow of government in the United States or to belong to an organization dedicated to the accomplishment of these ends. The Court upheld the convictions of eleven leaders of the U.S. Communist Party under the act. Chief Justice Vinson wrote the opinion; Justices Black and Douglas dissented.

During this term the Supreme Court also upheld the power of the attorney general to prepare a list of organizations considered subversive—and backed state power to require public employees to take an oath denying membership in the Communist Party.[54]

In a special term called in the summer of 1953, the Court considered a stay of execution granted by Justice Douglas for Julius and Ethel Rosenberg, convicted under the Espionage Act of 1917 of passing atomic secrets to the Soviet Union. The Court—over the dissents of Black and Douglas—lifted the stay, allowing the Rosenbergs to be executed.[55] Douglas's action in granting the stay sparked the first of several unsuccessful impeachment attempts against him.

By 1950 President Truman had named four justices, including the chief justice. Thus, when he found himself before the Court in May 1952, defending his decision to seize the nation's major steel companies to avoid a strike and disruption of steel production during the Korean conflict, he might have expected a favorable decision.

Instead, on June 2, 1952, the Court rebuked Truman, ruling that he had acted illegally and without constitutional authority. The vote was 6–3. In an opinion by Justice Black, the majority upheld a lower court's order blocking the seizure. Justices Burton and Clark voted against Truman; Chief Justice Vinson and Justice Minton voted for him.

The decision in *Youngstown Sheet & Tube Co. v. Sawyer* marked one of the rare instances where the Supreme Court flatly told the president he had overreached the limits of his constitutional power. And it was a mark of the Court's power that President Truman, fuming, complied.

In June 1951 the Court announced two unanimous decisions that called further into question the continuing validity of the "separate but equal" doctrine it had espoused in *Plessy v. Ferguson,* fifty-five years earlier.

In *Sweatt v. Painter* the Court ordered the University of Texas law school to admit a black student. The Court found the educational opportunity provided by a newly created "black" law school in the state in no way equal to that at the university law

THE COURT IN 1950
Seated from left: Justices Felix Frankfurter, Hugo L. Black, Chief Justice Frederick M. Vinson, Justices Stanley F. Reed, William O. Douglas.
Standing from left: Justices Tom C. Clark, Robert H. Jackson, Harold H. Burton, Sherman Minton

school. Therefore, the state did not fulfill the promise of equal protection under the Fourteenth Amendment by providing a separate black law school, held the Court in an opinion written by Chief Justice Vinson. In *McLaurin v. Oklahoma State Regents* the Court rebuffed the effort of the University of Oklahoma, forced by court order to accept a black student, to segregate that student in all phases of campus life.

A year and a half later, in December 1952, the Court heard arguments in a group of five cases challenging the segregation of public elementary and secondary schools. The cases are known by the title of one—*Brown v. Board of Education of Topeka.* In June 1953 the Court ordered reargument in the October 1953 term. Before the reargument took place, however, the Court had a new chief justice.

CHIEF JUSTICE WARREN

Chief Justice Vinson's last years were difficult ones. In addition to sensitive questions of antisubversive legislation, the face-off with Truman over the steel seizure and the tense special session considering the Rosenberg case confirmed Holmes's description of the Court as the quiet center of national storms.

In September 1953, less than three months after the Rosenberg decision, Vinson died. President Dwight D. Eisenhower then had the task of selecting a new chief justice within his first year of taking office. He looked to California, and chose that state's governor, Earl Warren.

Dwight D. Eisenhower

Earl Warren

Warren, a Republican, had run unsuccessfully for vice president on Thomas Dewey's ticket in 1948. As governor during World War II he had supported the relocation of residents of Japanese ancestry. He had just announced that he would not run for a fourth gubernatorial term when Vinson died. Explaining his choice, President Eisenhower said that he had selected Warren, then sixty-two, for his "integrity, honesty, middle-of-the-road philosophy."[56]

Warren received a recess appointment and began serving as the October 1953 term opened. He was confirmed in March 1954. He served for sixteen years, retiring in June 1969.

Brown v. Board of Education

When the *Brown* cases were reargued in December 1953, Warren presided over the Court. When they were decided on May 17, 1954, Warren spoke for the Court. In his brief opinion, the unanimous Supreme Court reversed *Plessy v. Ferguson*, decided fifty-eight years earlier when Earl Warren was five years old.

Concluding this, his first major opinion, Warren said:

We conclude that in the field of public education the doctrine of "separate but equal" has no place. Separate educational facilities are inherently unequal.[57]

Richard Kluger, twenty years later, assessed the impact of *Brown* this way:

Having proclaimed the equality of all men in the preamble to the Declaration of Independence, the nation's founders had then elected, out of deference to the slave-holding South, to omit that definition of equalitarian democracy from the Constitution. It took a terrible civil war to correct that omission. But the Civil War amendments were soon drained of their original intention to lift the black man to meaningful membership in American society. The Court itself would do much to assist in that process, and *Plessy* was its most brutal blow. Congress passed no civil rights laws after the Court-eviscerated one of 1875, and those that remained on the books were largely ignored by the states and unenforced by federal administration. . . .

It was into this moral void that the Supreme Court under Earl Warren now stepped. Its opinion in Brown v. Board of Education, for all its economy, represented nothing short of a reconsecration of American ideals.[58]

In April 1955 rearguments were held on the question of implementing the *Brown* decision. In May 1955 *Brown II* set out the standard—the states should proceed to end segregation in public schools with "all deliberate speed." Again the Court was unanimous; again Warren was its spokesman.

Although the Court had carefully limited its opinion to the subject of schools, "it became almost immediately clear that *Brown* had in effect wiped out all forms of state-sanctioned segregation."[59]

The impact of *Brown* was so fundamental—and public reaction to it so broad and deep—that it tends to dominate all descriptions of the Court's work during the 1950s. Yet with the exception of its 1958 ruling in *Cooper v. Aaron*, rebuking Gov. Orval Faubus of Arkansas for his resistance to desegregation, the Court did not hand down another major civil rights decision until the 1960s.

In case after case challenging various forms of segregation, the Court did not hear arguments but simply told lower courts to reconsider them in light of *Brown*. Resistance to these rulings was fierce, and was soon felt in Congress. The period from 1954 to 1960, writes William Swindler, was one of "tension between the high tribunal and Congress unparalleled even by the early years of the 1930s."[60] But now the roles were reversed: the Court was the vanguard of change—and Congress the bulwark of reaction.

The tension between Congress and the Court created by the school desegregation decisions was further heightened by subsequent decisions invalidating federal and state antisubversive programs and imposing new due process requirements upon police practices.

In 1956 the Court struck down a state sedition law, holding in *Pennsylvania v. Nelson* that Congress in passing the Smith Act had preempted state power to punish efforts to overthrow the federal government. The same term, the Court in *Slochower v. Board of Education* held that a state could not automatically dismiss employees simply because they invoked their Fifth Amendment right to remain silent when questioned by congressional committees.

And in the same term the Court applied the equal protection guarantee to require that a state provide an indigent defendant

THE COURT IN 1954

Seated from left: Justices Felix Frankfurter, Hugo L. Black, Chief Justice Earl Warren, Justices Stanley F. Reed, William O. Douglas.
Standing from left: Justices Tom C. Clark, Robert H. Jackson, Harold H. Burton, Sherman Minton

with a free transcript of his trial so that he might appeal his conviction. In *Griffin v. Illinois,* as in *Slochower,* Burton, Minton, Reed, and John Marshall Harlan, the newest justice, dissented.

The Eisenhower Justices

Just as the October 1954 term opened, Justice Jackson died. As his second nominee to the Court, President Eisenhower chose John Marshall Harlan, grandson and namesake of the famous dissenting justice whose career spanned the turn of the century. Harlan, a distinguished New York attorney, was fifty-five when he was appointed to the Supreme Court. He was confirmed in March 1955 and served for sixteen years.

Two years later, in October 1956, Justice Minton retired. As his successor, Eisenhower named William Joseph Brennan Jr., fifty, a judge on the New Jersey Supreme Court. Brennan was the first member of the Court born in the twentieth century. He would become a key strategist of Warren Court liberalism and serve thirty-four years before stepping down in 1990.

Early in 1957 Justice Reed retired after almost two decades on the bench. Eisenhower nominated federal judge Charles Whittaker, fifty-six, of Kansas. Whittaker would serve only five years before resigning in 1962.

In October 1958 Justice Burton retired, giving Eisenhower his fifth and last vacancy to fill. Eisenhower chose Potter Stewart of Ohio, a forty-three-year-old federal judge. Seated in the fall of

1958 as a recess appointment (as were Harlan and Brennan), Stewart was confirmed in May 1959. He served until 1981.

CASES AND CONTROVERSY

Criticism already aroused by *Brown* and some of the Court's other decisions during Warren's early years intensified in reaction to several lines of decisions in the late 1950s.

In 1951 the Court in *Dennis v. United States* had upheld the Smith Act, under which the leaders of the U.S. Communist Party were prosecuted for advocating the violent overthrow of the federal government. On June 17, 1957, the Court in *Yates v. United States* set such a strict standard for convictions under the Smith Act that it made successful prosecutions under the law almost impossible. Justice Harlan wrote the Court's opinion, making clear that only advocacy of subversive *activity* could be penalized without infringing on the First Amendment. The same day the Court in *Watkins v. United States* reversed the contempt citation of a witness who had refused to answer questions from the House Un-American Activities Committee about the Communist Party membership of other persons.

These opinions and two others announced that day led conservative critics to label June 17, 1957, "Red Monday"—as May 27, 1935, had been "Black Monday" and March 29, 1937, "White Monday" for supporters of the New Deal.[61]

Public and political criticism of the Court was intense. Legislation was proposed to reverse or circumvent the June 17 decisions and to withdraw the Court's jurisdiction over all matters of loyalty and subversion. Southerners critical of *Brown* joined others unhappy over the antisubversive rulings to raise congressional hostility toward the Court to a point unprecedented in the twentieth century.[62]

A week after Red Monday the Court in *Mallory v. United States* overturned a young man's conviction for rape because he had been interrogated too long without being informed of his rights and held too long between arrest and arraignment. The Court was unanimous in this ruling; the criticism was almost as unified.

The same day the Court in *Roth v. United States* made clear that obscene material did not have First Amendment protection, embarking on the long and difficult process of describing what is and what is not obscene.

In a special session in July 1957, the Court cleared the way for Japanese courts to try an American soldier for killing a Japanese woman on an Army rifle range, another ruling that won the Court few friends.[63]

In 1958 the Court began to give full constitutional recognition to the freedom of association—striking down Alabama's efforts to force the National Association for the Advancement of Colored People (NAACP) to disclose its membership lists.[64]

A second special session was called late in the summer of 1958 to consider the Little Rock, Arkansas, desegregation case. The Court in *Cooper v. Aaron* unanimously rejected city officials' request for delay in implementing the desegregation plan for the city's schools.

THE REAPPORTIONMENT REVOLUTION

In *Brown v. Board of Education* the Supreme Court set off a long overdue revolution in civil rights. But after *Brown* the Court played only a secondary role in the accelerating civil rights movement, leaving Congress to implement, at last, the guarantees of the Civil War Amendments through effective legislation. The Court's role was crucial but secondary. When civil rights legislation was challenged, as it had been during Reconstruction, the Court upheld it as constitutional.

But in the area of voting rights, the Court—unexpectedly—took the lead. In 1946 the Court had rebuffed a constitutional challenge to maldistribution of voters among electoral districts, declaring such a matter a political question beyond its purview.

In 1962 the Court abandoned that cautious stance and held that constitutional challenges to such malapportionment of political power were indeed questions the Courts might decide. This ruling was foreshadowed in the 1960 decision in *Gomillion v. Lightfoot,* in which the Court unanimously agreed that a state, in gerrymandering a district to exclude all blacks, had clearly violated the Fifteenth Amendment. Because such state action violated a specific constitutional guarantee, held the Court, it was properly a matter for federal judicial consideration.

It was from that ruling only a short step to *Baker v. Carr,* announced March 26, 1962. Tennessee's failure to redistrict for most of the twentieth century had produced electoral districts for the state legislature of grossly unequal population. This maldistribution of electoral power was challenged as violating the Fourteenth Amendment guarantee of equal protection. Abandoning the "political thicket" view of *Colegrove v. Green,* the majority held that this was clearly a constitutional case within the jurisdiction of the federal courts.

Later in 1962 Justices Whittaker and Frankfurter retired. President John F. Kennedy named Deputy Attorney General Byron R. White, forty-four, and Secretary of Labor Arthur Goldberg, fifty-four, to fill the empty seats. White took his seat in April 1962; Goldberg was seated at the beginning of the October 1962 term. Although Goldberg would serve only three years, White remained on the bench for more than three decades.

In March 1963 the Court set out the standard for constitutionally valid reapportionment plans. In *Gray v. Sanders* Justice Douglas wrote for the Court that the promise of political equality, contained in the nation's most basic documents, meant "one person, one vote." A year later, in February 1964, the Court applied that rule to congressional redistricting in *Wesberry v. Sanders.* Four months later in the June 1964 ruling in *Reynolds v. Sims,* the justices held that the same standard applied to the electoral districts for the members of both houses of the states' legislatures.

The result of these rulings, which Warren considered the most important of his tenure, was the redistribution of political power in Congress and every state legislature. In 1969 the Court in *Kirkpatrick v. Preisler* reaffirmed its commitment to this standard, requiring congressional districts within a state to be mathematically equal in population.

THE DUE PROCESS REVOLUTION

Involving itself in still another area traditionally left to state control, the Court in the 1960s accelerated the step-by-step application of due process requirements to state law enforcement and criminal procedures. By 1969 the Court had required states to abide by virtually every major provision of the Bill of Rights.

The first major ruling in this "due process revolution" came on June 19, 1961. By a 5–4 vote the Court held in *Mapp v. Ohio* that evidence obtained in violation of the Fourth Amendment guarantee of security against unreasonable search and seizure must be excluded from use in state, as well as federal, courts. Justice Clark wrote the opinion; Justices Stewart, Harlan, Frankfurter, and Whittaker dissented.

A year later the Court for the first time applied the Eighth Amendment ban on cruel and unusual punishment to strike down a state law. In *Robinson v. California* the Court held that a state could not make narcotics addiction a crime.

In 1963 the Court declared in *Gideon v. Wainwright* that states must provide legal assistance for all defendants charged with serious crimes. If defendants are unable to pay for an attorney, the state must provide one for them, wrote Justice Black for the unanimous Court, overruling the Court's 1941 refusal, in *Betts v. Brady,* to extend this right to state defendants.

On June 15, 1964, the same day it decided *Reynolds v. Sims,* the Court held that states must observe the Fifth Amendment privilege against compelled self-incrimination. The vote in *Malloy v. Hogan* was 5–4; Brennan wrote the opinion; Harlan, Clark, Stewart, and White dissented.

A week later, by the same vote, the Court held, in *Escobedo v. Illinois,* that suspects have a right to legal assistance as soon as they are the focus of a police investigation.

In April 1965 the Supreme Court overruled *Twining v. New Jersey* (1908) and held that state judges and prosecutors may not comment adversely upon the failure of defendants to testify in their own defense. Such comment infringes upon the Fifth Amendment right to remain silent, declared the Court in *Griffin v. California.*

The most controversial single Warren Court criminal law ruling came the following term, on June 13, 1966. In *Miranda v. Arizona* the Court held 5–4 that police may not interrogate suspects in custody unless they have informed them of their right to remain silent, of the fact that their words may be used against them, and of their right to have the aid of a lawyer. If suspects wish to remain silent or to contact an attorney, interrogation must cease until they wish to speak or until their attorney is present. Statements obtained in violation of this rule may not be used in court. Chief Justice Warren wrote the majority opinion; dissenting were Harlan, Clark, Stewart, and White.

The next term, as criticism of the Court mounted in Congress and in statehouses across the nation, the Court extended to state defendants the right to a speedy trial, enlarged the due process guarantees for juvenile defendants, and brought wiretapping and electronic surveillance under the strictures of the Fourth Amendment warrant requirement.[65]

This step-by-step process of applying the Bill of Rights against state, as well as federal, action was completed with the 1968 ruling in *Duncan v. Louisiana* and the 1969 ruling in *Benton v. Maryland.* In *Duncan* the Court announced that it was extending the right to a jury trial to state defendants. On Warren's last day as chief justice, the Court announced *Benton,* extending the guarantee against double jeopardy to states.

CIVIL RIGHTS, PERSONAL LIBERTY

Questions of freedom of belief and association, arising from the antisubversive measures of the 1950s, were still before the Court during the 1960s. Generally, the Court scrutinized these restrictive measures closely, and often it found some constitutional flaw.

In 1961 the Court upheld the constitutionality of the Subversive Activities Control Act of 1950, under which the Communist Party was required to register with the Justice Department. But this ruling in *Communist Party v. Subversive Activities Control Board (SACB)* came by a 5–4 vote. Four years later a unanimous Court held in *Albertson v. SACB* that individuals could not be compelled to register under the law without violating the Fifth Amendment protection against self-incrimination.

In 1966 the Court closely circumscribed the use of state loyalty oaths, and in 1967 it struck down the portion of the Subversive Activities Control Act that made it a criminal offense for a member of a "subversive" group to hold a job in the defense industry.[66]

In 1964 Congress at last reasserted its long-dormant power to implement the promises of the Civil War Amendments through legislation. Passage of the comprehensive 1964 Civil Rights Act was followed in 1965 by the Voting Rights Act and in 1968 by the Fair Housing Act. The modern Supreme Court, unlike the Court of the 1870s and 1880s, reinforced congressional action, finding these revolutionary statutes clearly constitutional.

In late 1964 the Court upheld the contested public accommodations provisions of the 1964 act in *Heart of Atlanta Motel v. United States.* Justice Clark wrote the opinion for a unanimous Court.

In 1966 the Court rebuffed a broad challenge to the Voting Rights Act of 1965 as violating states' rights. In *South Carolina v. Katzenbach* the Court, with only Justice Black dissenting in part, upheld the sweeping statute as within the power of Congress to enforce the Fifteenth Amendment guarantee against racial discrimination in voting. And even as Congress was debating the modern Fair Housing Act, the Court in *Jones v. Mayer* reinterpreted the Civil Rights Act of 1866 to prohibit racial discrimination in the sale of real estate.

Throughout the 1960s the Court exercised a supervisory role over the desegregation efforts of school systems across the country. In its first major school ruling since 1954, the Court in the 1964 case of *Griffin v. County School Board of Prince Edward County* said that a state could not avoid the obligation of desegregating its public schools by closing them down.

Four years later, in *Green v. County School Board of New Kent County,* the Court declared that "freedom of choice" desegregation plans were acceptable only when they were effective in desegregating a school system. The Court made clear that, in its view, there had been entirely too much deliberation and not enough speed in the nation's effort to implement *Brown.*

The Court during this decade also substantially expanded constitutional protection for the exercise of personal rights to choose a course of individual action.

In 1965 the Court in *Griswold v. Connecticut* struck down as unconstitutional a state law that forbade all use of contraceptives, even by married couples. The justices could not agree on the exact constitutional basis for this ruling, but they did agree there were some areas so private that the Constitution protected them from state interference. Two years later the Court, using similar reasoning in *Loving v. Virginia,* held it unconstitutional for a state to forbid a person of one race to marry a member of another race.

The criticism the Warren Court engendered by its rulings on security programs, segregation, and criminal procedures reached a new crescendo after the Court's "school prayer" decisions. On the basis of the First Amendment's ban on state action "establishing" religion, the Court in 1962 held that a state may not prescribe a prayer or other religious statement for use in public schools. This ruling in *Engel v. Vitale* was followed in 1963 by a second ruling denying a state power to require Bible reading as a daily religious exercise in public schools.[67]

The Supreme Court also expanded the meaning of other First Amendment provisions. In the landmark libel case of *New York Times v. Sullivan,* decided in March 1964, the Court enlarged the protection the First Amendment provided the press by stating that public officials and public figures could recover damages for libelous statements made by the news media only if they could prove the statements were published with "actual malice."

And early in 1969 the Court held that the First Amendment's protection for symbolic speech guaranteed students the right to engage in peaceful nondisruptive protest of the war in Vietnam, through the wearing of black armbands to school.[68]

Also during the 1960s, in decisions that drew far less public attention, the Court made it easier for state prisoners, federal taxpayers, and persons threatened by state action to come into federal court for assistance.

On March 18, 1963, the same day it announced its decisions in *Gray v. Sanders* and *Gideon v. Wainwright,* the Court in *Fay v. Noia* relaxed the requirements placed upon state prisoners who wished to challenge their detention in federal courts. Two years later, in *Dombrowski v. Pfister,* the Court indicated that federal judges should not hesitate to intervene and halt ongoing state proceedings under a law challenged as violating the First Amendment.

And in 1968 the Court in *Flast v. Cohen* substantially modified its 1923 bar against federal taxpayer suits challenging the use of tax moneys.

Impatient to place a man of his own choosing on the Supreme Court, President Lyndon B. Johnson in 1965 persuaded Justice Goldberg to leave the Court for the post of ambassador to the United Nations. In the empty seat Johnson placed Washington attorney Abe Fortas, his close friend and adviser and the successful advocate in *Gideon v. Wainwright.* Fortas, fifty-five, was seated just before the October 1965 term began.

Two years later, when his son, Ramsey Clark, became attorney general, Justice Tom Clark retired. To fill Clark's seat, Johnson nominated the nation's first black justice, Thurgood Marshall, who had argued the *Brown* cases for the NAACP Legal Defense Fund. Marshall, fifty-nine, began his service just before the opening of the October 1967 term. He would serve on the high Court for twenty-four years.

At the end of that term, in 1968, Chief Justice Warren informed President Johnson that he intended to retire as soon as a successor to him was confirmed. Johnson promptly nominated Justice Fortas chief justice.

Johnson was a lame duck; he had announced in March 1968 that he would not run for reelection. The Republicans had hopes of winning the White House and wished to have their candidate, Richard Nixon, select the new chief justice. These hopes were given added significance by the fact that the Court itself was a major campaign issue. Nixon criticized the Court for

"coddling criminals" and promised to appoint justices who would turn a more receptive ear to the arguments of the police and prosecutors.

Charges of cronyism—related to Fortas's continued unofficial role as adviser to Johnson—and conflict of interest further compounded the difficulties of his nomination as chief justice. After a filibuster stymied the nomination in October 1968, Johnson withdrew it at Fortas's request. Simultaneously, Johnson withdrew his nomination of federal judge Homer Thornberry of Texas to succeed Fortas as associate justice.

The following May, Fortas resigned his seat under threat of impeachment, the result of a magazine article charging him with unethical behavior. Fortas asserted his innocence in his letter of resignation and said he left the Court to avoid placing it under unnecessary stress.

The Court in Transition: 1969–1989

On June 23, 1969, Chief Justice Warren retired. He left behind a Court and a country dramatically changed since 1953, changed in significant part by the decisions of the Supreme Court during his sixteen years there. Many of those decisions were still hotly controversial, as was the strain of judicial activism which they had encouraged in lower federal courts across the country. Under Warren's leadership, the Court had exerted a strong liberalizing force on American life. Its rulings had initiated and accelerated the civil rights movement, ignited a reapportionment revolution, reformed police procedures, and curtailed state powers over controversial matters such as birth control and school prayer.

For twenty years after Warren's retirement, two presidents, Richard Nixon and Ronald Reagan, worked hard to undo his legacy, to return the Court—and the country—to a more conservative stance. Their appointments and their arguments moved the Court into an extended period of transition as it completed its second century.

CHIEF JUSTICE BURGER

Warren's successor, Warren Earl Burger of Minnesota, the nation's fifteenth chief justice, was sworn in June 23, 1969. President Nixon had chosen Burger, he said, to reverse the "liberal activism" of the Warren era. As an appeals judge, Burger had earned a reputation as a "strict constructionist" of the Constitution and federal laws. He usually sided with the state in criminal law cases and had publicly criticized the Warren Court for rulings showing leniency toward defendants. But Burger was more moderate on civil rights issues. Sixty-one at the time of his nomination, he was easily confirmed by the Senate.

Fortas's seat would remain vacant for a full year, however, as Nixon's effort to appoint a successor ran into unexpected difficulties. Three months after Fortas resigned, Nixon nominated a conservative South Carolinian, appeals court judge Clement F. Haynsworth Jr. In November a liberal backlash to the Fortas affair generated charges of conflict of interest against Haynsworth and denied him confirmation by a vote of 45–55. It was the first time since 1930 that a presidential nominee to the Court had been rejected.

Early in 1970 Nixon named G. Harrold Carswell of Florida, another appeals court judge, to the empty seat. Carswell, whose qualifications were mediocre at best, was rejected, 45–51, in April 1970. His nomination had drawn opposition from a wide variety of groups because of his views on racial issues and his undistinguished career.

Soon after the Carswell defeat, Nixon selected Harry A. Blackmun, an appeals court judge from Minnesota and a long-time friend of Chief Justice Burger, as his third choice for the seat. Blackmun, sixty-one, was confirmed unanimously, and he joined the Court in June 1970. He would serve as a justice for twenty-four years.

CONSERVATIVE CHOICES

President Nixon had promised to appoint justices who would give the Court a more conservative character. During his first term he named four justices, and some of the Court's rulings in the 1970s did lessen the impact of some of the landmarks of the Warren era. But none of those landmarks was overturned—and the Burger Court established a few more important rulings of its own on the liberal landscape.

The October 1970 term was an eventful one. In *Swann v. Charlotte-Mecklenburg County Board of Education* the Court made clear that it had no intention of retreating from its *Brown* ruling that racial segregation of public schools was unconstitutional. With Burger writing the opinion, it unanimously upheld the use of controversial methods such as busing, racial balance ratios, and gerrymandered school districts to remedy school segregation.

During this term the Court for the first time held invalid a state law discriminating against women and ushered in a line of decisions that would bring increasing pressure on laws that treated the sexes differently. The Court also declared alienage, like race, to be a suspect classification or category when used by lawmakers. It said statutes relating to alienage deserve the highest judicial scrutiny.[69]

In *Harris v. New York* the justices allowed limited in-court use of statements obtained from suspects who were not given their *Miranda* warnings. And in a set of cases known as *Younger v. Harris* the Court curtailed the power of federal judges to halt enforcement of state laws challenged as infringing the First Amendment.

The most dramatic ruling of the term came June 30, 1971. The Court resoundingly rejected the Nixon administration's effort to halt publication of newspaper articles based upon the classified "Pentagon Papers."[70]

Just two weeks before the opening of the October 1971 term, Justices Black and Harlan, in failing health, resigned. Black, eighty-five, had served thirty-four years; Harlan, seventy-two, had served almost seventeen.

Nixon chose Lewis F. Powell Jr., a former president of the American Bar Association and a successful Virginia attorney, to fill Black's seat, and William H. Rehnquist of Arizona, an assistant attorney general, to fill Harlan's. Powell, sixty-four, and Rehnquist, forty-seven, were confirmed in December 1971. Not since Warren Harding had one president in his first term placed four men on the Court.

Although these justices were picked by President Nixon for their conservative views, the Court's decisions continued to move in the liberal direction set by the Warren Court. In 1972—the first term in which all four Nixon nominees participated, the Court struck down all existing death penalty laws, expanded the right to counsel, and refused to allow the administration to use electronic surveillance without a warrant, even in cases involving the nation's security.[71]

The most controversial decision of the decade came early the following year. President Nixon opposed abortion rights. Yet in January 1973, in the same week as his second inaugural, the Supreme Court, 7–2, legalized abortion. Justice Blackmun wrote the Court's opinion. Only Justices Rehnquist and White dissented from the Court's ruling in the case of *Roe v. Wade*.

Also in that term, the Court rejected a constitutional challenge to the property-tax system for financing public schools, told nonsouthern schools they too must desegregate, formulated a new definition of obscenity, and held that state legislative districts need not always meet the standard of strict equality applied to congressional districts.[72]

The last and most stunning decision of the Court during the Nixon administration was a peculiarly personal blow for President Nixon. The Watergate scandal had set off full-scale investigations on Capitol Hill, as well as by a special prosecutor. In the course of his investigation, the special prosecutor subpoenaed the president for certain taped recordings of White House conversations that could be used as evidence in the trial of former White House aides charged with obstruction of justice.

Nixon refused to comply, asserting executive privilege—the president's privilege to refuse with impunity to obey such an order when that refusal was necessary to protect the confidentiality of conversations with his aides. In June 1974 the case came to the Supreme Court. *United States v. Nixon* was argued in a special late-term session in July. On July 24 the Court, 8–0, ruled that Nixon must comply with the subpoena and turn over the tapes. Rehnquist did not participate; the opinion was delivered by Chief Justice Burger.

With this ruling the Court reasserted the power first claimed for it by Chief Justice John Marshall: to say what the law is. In doing so, the Court flatly denied the president of the United States the right to operate outside the law.

Nixon said he would comply. Because of the contents of those tapes, he resigned the presidency, two weeks later, after the House Judiciary Committee had approved articles of impeachment against him.

DISABILITY, DEATH, AND DISCRIMINATION

In 1973 Justice William O. Douglas surpassed Justice Stephen Field's record to become the country's longest-serving justice.

Two years later he was disabled by a stroke and retired from the bench in November 1975. He had served on the Court thirty-six and one-half years since his appointment by President Roosevelt in 1939. He was seventy-seven years old.

To succeed him, President Gerald R. Ford—who as House minority leader had once led an effort to impeach Douglas—selected John Paul Stevens, fifty-five, a federal appeals court judge from Chicago. Stevens was sworn in December 19, 1975.

Stevens's first term was a busy one. In January 1976 the Court held invalid several major portions of the 1974 Federal Election Campaign Act Amendments intended to regulate campaign spending. In *Buckley v. Valeo* the Court invalidated spending limits, ruling that limits diminished political expression in violation of the First Amendment.

Also in 1976 the Court appeared ready to roll back the clock on the division of authority between the federal government and the states. For the first time in almost forty years, it used the Tenth Amendment to limit the power of Congress over interstate commerce. In *National League of Cities v. Usery* the Court, 5–4, nullified the 1974 act of Congress that required states and cities to pay their employees in line with federal minimum wage and overtime laws. Such matters, wrote Justice Rehnquist, are for state, not federal authority, to resolve.

Ten days later the Court cleared the way for executions of convicted murderers to resume in the United States after a four-year hiatus, as it upheld certain carefully drafted death penalty laws enacted by states in the wake of its 1972 ruling striking down all capital punishment statutes. But the Court also declared that states could not make death the mandatory penalty for first-degree murder. On this point the Court again divided 5–4.[73]

The justices also made it more difficult for state prisoners to challenge their convictions in federal court. The Court ruled that if their challenge was based on the argument that illegally obtained evidence was used to convict, it could succeed only if the state had failed to give them an opportunity to make that claim earlier.[74]

The most publicized decisions of the late 1970s involved "reverse discrimination"—claims by white men that they were denied fair treatment as a result of the efforts of schools and employers to implement affirmative action programs to remedy past discrimination against women, blacks, and other minority group members.

The Court was as divided as the country on that issue. In 1978 the Court in *University of California Regents v. Bakke* held, on the one hand, 5–4, that racial "quotas" were invalid—but, on the other, also 5–4, that moderate affirmative action policies were permissible. A majority refused to hold all consideration of race unconstitutional in school admissions decisions. Justice Powell—who would more and more often in succeeding years be the pivotal vote on close cases—was the swing vote on this issue.

The following year the Court in *United Steelworkers v. Weber* held, 5–2, that private corporations were free to adopt voluntary affirmative action programs to eliminate clear racial imbalances in certain job areas. In 1980, in *Fullilove v. Klutznick,* the Court

THE COURT IN 1979
Seated from left: Justices Byron R. White, William J. Brennan Jr., Chief Justice Warren E. Burger, Justices Potter Stewart, Thurgood Marshall.
Standing from left: Justices William H. Rehnquist, Harry A. Blackmun, Lewis F. Powell Jr., John Paul Stevens

upheld, 6–3, congressional power to set aside a certain percentage of federal funds under the 1977 Public Works Employment Act for contracts with minority-owned businesses.

CAMPAIGN FOR CHANGE

In 1981 Ronald Reagan became president, convinced that he had a mandate from the American people to change the way government related to the governed. The Supreme Court was a major focus of his campaign for change throughout his eight years in the White House.

Reagan disagreed with the substance of many of the modern Court's liberal decisions—and with the judicial activism that informed them. He believed that federal judges were intruding into controversial matters that, in a democracy, should be left to elected officials. The phrase *judicial restraint* was his administration's shorthand for the belief that courts should leave most major controversies to legislatures and elected officials to resolve.

Reagan used his appointments and his administration's power of argument to move the court in this direction.

The Reagan Appointments

President Jimmy Carter, Reagan's predecessor, had the unhappy distinction of being the only full-term president to enter and leave the White House without having the chance to name a member of the Supreme Court. There was no change in the Court from December 1975, when Justice Stevens took Justice Douglas's seat, until June 1981.

At that point, just five months into the Reagan presidency,

Sandra Day O'Connor

Justice Potter Stewart announced that he was retiring, after twenty-three years on the Court. Three weeks later, President Reagan made history by announcing that he would send to the Senate the name of a woman—Sandra Day O'Connor, fifty-one, an appeals court judge from Arizona—as Stewart's successor.

O'Connor, who had served in all three branches of Arizona government before her nomination, was easily confirmed, 99–0, in September. She was sworn in September 25, 1981, the 102d justice and the first woman member of the nation's highest court. She soon proved to be a reliable conservative vote and an articulate conservative voice on many issues before the Court.

Several years passed before another vacancy occurred. By 1984 the Court was one of the oldest in history: the average age of the justices was seventy; O'Connor was the only justice under sixty.

In March 1986 Justice Brennan turned eighty; he had served on the Court thirty years. As the liberal spokesman in a time of conservative resurgence, his continued presence on the Court was a focus of considerable speculation. But a happy second marriage after the death of his first wife and his continuing energy and enthusiasm for his job made his departure from the Court an unlikely prospect, heartening to liberals and discouraging to conservatives.

In June 1986 Chief Justice Burger, about to celebrate his seventy-ninth birthday, announced that he would retire. Three days after Burger's announcement, Reagan named Justice Rehnquist, then sixty-one, as Burger's successor. He selected Antonin

Ronald Reagan

William H. Rehnquist

Scalia, fifty, a member of the U.S. Court of Appeals for the District of Columbia Circuit, to take Rehnquist's seat.

Rehnquist's confirmation came with more difficulty than the White House had anticipated. Liberal criticism focused less on his opinions as a justice and more on allegations of discriminatory conduct years before he had come to the bench. Civil rights groups mounted an all-out fight to deny him confirmation. But he was confirmed September 17, 65–33. Scalia was confirmed the same day, 98–0.

The Court that presided over the October 1986 term was unique. The nine justices who sat together from late September of 1986 until July of 1987 did so for only those nine months. As the term ended, Justice Powell, seventy-nine, announced that he was retiring from the Court.

Public attention focused on the selection of Powell's successor with an intensity unlike that accorded the earlier three Reagan appointments, primarily because of Powell's pivotal position on several important issues. A reserved, courtly, and inherently conservative man, Powell had nonetheless cast several critical votes against school prayer, for freedom of choice in abortion, and for permitting the continued use of affirmative action. The person who took his seat would inherit the opportunity to swing the Court's position on those and other issues that divided the sitting justices.

President Reagan first nominated Robert H. Bork, sixty, a colleague of Scalia's on the Court of Appeals for the District of Columbia Circuit. Bork was well known for the strength of his intellect and his conservative views—and for the role he had

played in 1974 as solicitor general, when it fell to him to fire Special Prosecutor Archibald Cox during the Watergate tapes controversy. Bork's nomination was highly controversial, and in October 1987 the Senate denied him confirmation, 42–58.

Reagan moved quickly, announcing he would name another member of that same appeals bench, Douglas H. Ginsburg, forty-one, to the empty seat. His proposed nomination was short-lived; within two weeks, before it was officially sent to Capitol Hill, the nomination was withdrawn in the wake of Ginsburg's admission that he had used marijuana during his years as a student and professor at Harvard Law School.

Four days later, on November 11, Reagan named Anthony M. Kennedy of California, as his nominee to fill Powell's seat. Kennedy, fifty-one, was a member of the U.S. Court of Appeals for the Ninth Circuit. Kennedy's nomination created no controversy and he was confirmed by the Senate February 3, 1988, by a vote of 97 to 0.

The Reagan Arguments

Through his solicitors general, President Reagan for eight years argued his policy views consistently to the Court—on abortion, civil rights, and church and state. He was not successful in convincing the Court to change its mind on these issues during his time in the White House.

Twice the administration suggested to the justices that it was time to overturn *Roe v. Wade,* the landmark ruling legalizing abortion—and leave that decision to the states instead. Twice, in 1983 and in 1986, the Court rejected that suggestion and reaffirmed *Roe v. Wade.* But the margin was narrowing. In 1973 seven justices formed the majority in *Roe v. Wade,* with White and Rehnquist dissenting. Ten years later, the Court's 1983 ruling in a case from Akron, Ohio, came by a 6–3 vote as Justice O'Connor joined the dissenters with an opinion strongly critical of the logic of the *Roe* ruling.[75] When the Court revisited the issue in 1986, the margin had shrunk to one vote—that of Justice Powell. The reaffirmation of *Roe* came that year, 5–4; Powell then retired.[76]

The administration met with some limited success in its battle against affirmative action. In Reagan's first term, the Court held that affirmative action should not apply to override the traditional rule for layoffs—last hired, first fired.[77] But the administration's effort to stretch that ruling into a broad ban on affirmative action crumbled in 1986 and 1987, when the Court ruled decisively in four separate cases that, carefully applied, affirmative action was an appropriate and constitutional remedy for documented discrimination.[78]

The Court initially seemed receptive to Reagan's arguments urging it to relax its view that the First Amendment required strict separation of church and state. In 1984 the Court, 5–4, upheld a city's decision to include in its holiday display a nativity scene. The majority, in the words of Chief Justice Burger, declared that the Constitution "affirmatively mandates accommodation, not merely tolerance, of all religions, and forbids hostility toward any."[79]

Encouraged, the administration backed Alabama's bid in the next term for approval of its "moment of silence" law, permitting teachers to set aside a period in each public school classroom each day for quiet meditative activity.[80] But the theory of accommodation did not stretch that far and the Court, 6–3, held Alabama's law unconstitutional. A few weeks later, the Court told Grand Rapids, Michigan, and New York City that they too were in violation of the First Amendment for supplying remedial and enrichment services to disadvantaged children who attended parochial schools.[81]

SEPARATION OF POWERS

The doctrine of separated powers is implicit in the federal government set up by the Constitution. It allocates powers among the judicial, legislative, and executive branches so that they act as a check upon each other. As the federal government adapted to the increasingly complex demands of modern life, it experimented with new devices for governing—the legislative veto, a new budget-deficit-reduction mechanism, and the independent prosecutor. In the 1980s each was challenged before the Supreme Court as violating the separation of powers. Two fell to that challenge; one survived.

For half a century, Congress had found it useful to include in various laws—more than two hundred by 1983—a legislative veto provision requiring or permitting certain administrative actions implementing the law to return to Congress for approval before taking effect. The executive branch had long criticized this device as encroaching on its functions, and in 1983 the Court agreed. Not since the New Deal collisions had Congress felt so keenly the power of the Court to curtail its actions. The Court's ruling in *Immigration and Naturalization Service v. Chadha* invalidated parts of more federal laws than the Court had struck down up to that time in its entire history.[82]

Three years later the executive branch won another separation of powers victory, when the Court held unconstitutional a new mechanism that Congress had devised for forcing the president to reduce the ever-growing budget deficit. In *Bowsher v. Synar* the Court held that the comptroller general, head of the General Accounting Office, which the Court said was an arm of Congress, could not be given authority to dictate budget cuts to the president.

But Congress won the last big separation of powers argument with the Reagan administration when the Court, in 1988, upheld as appropriate the law that gave a special three-judge court the authority to appoint an independent counsel, a special prosecutor outside the Justice Department, to investigate alleged wrongdoing by high government officials. Written by Chief Justice Rehnquist, the Court's 7–1 opinion in *Morrison v. Olson* was decisive in upholding the power of Congress to grant this authority to the special court. The ruling had particular sting for President Reagan, for it left standing the convictions of two of his close former White House aides, both obtained by independent counsel.

REVERSALS AND EXCEPTIONS

In 1985 the Court reversed its 1976 ruling in *National League of Cities v. Usery,* which had revived the Tenth Amendment as a means for keeping certain state prerogatives from the reach of federal power. States, delighted with its promise, had tried repeatedly to convince the Court to apply the principle in other areas, without success. Its demise was anticipated. Justice Blackmun, who had voted with the five-man majority in *Usery,* changed his mind to cast the critical fifth vote to reverse it nine years later. The Tenth Amendment sank back into constitutional oblivion.[83] Three years later states suffered another blow, in *South Carolina v. Baker,* when the Court abandoned a position taken almost a century earlier in the *Pollock* ruling of 1895 and declared that nothing in the Constitution forbade Congress to tax the interest earned on municipal bonds.

For the first time, the Court in 1984 approved a clear exception to the exclusionary rule forbidding the use of illegally obtained evidence in court and a narrow but definite exception to the *Miranda* rule that suspects must first be warned of their rights before being questioned by police.[84]

In *Davis v. Bandemer* (1986), a decision akin to *Baker v. Carr,* decided twenty-four years earlier, the Court opened the doors of federal courthouses to constitutional challenges to political gerrymandering.

Also in 1986 the Court ruled 7–2 that prosecutors may not use peremptory challenges to exclude African Americans from serving on juries. The justices said in *Batson v. Kentucky* that rejecting someone on the basis of race violated the guarantee of equal protection of the laws.

Finally, in one of the most difficult cases of the term, the Court, 5–4, said that the Constitution's guarantees of personal liberty and privacy do not protect private consensual homosexual conduct between adults. Written by Justice White, *Bowers v. Hardwick* upheld Georgia's law against sodomy. Justice Powell, who was in the majority, would later state publicly that he regretted his vote. It would be nearly a decade before the Court decided another case involving gay rights.

A CONSERVATIVE CONCLUSION

For eight years President Ronald Reagan worked to bring about a change of direction in the Supreme Court. Despite four appointments and innumerable arguments, that change did not take place until he left the White House.

The October 1987 term, the last full term of the Court during Reagan's presidency, was a holding action. For more than half of it, the Court operated with only eight members. Reagan's last nominee, Justice Kennedy, did not join the Court until February 1988.

But the October 1988 term brought Reagan's campaign for change closer to fruition. Kennedy proved a powerful conservative force, allied with Scalia, O'Connor, White, and Rehnquist, who showed an increasing mastery of the power of the chief. By the end of the term, even the most cautious observers were call-

THE COURT IN 1989

Seated from left: Justices Thurgood Marshall, William J. Brennan Jr., Chief Justice William H. Rehnquist, Justices Byron R. White, Harry A. Blackmun.
Standing from left: Justices Antonin Scalia, John Paul Stevens, Sandra Day O'Connor, Anthony Kennedy

ing it a watershed in the Court's history. "Rarely has a single Supreme Court term had such an unsettling effect on the political landscape," declared the *New York Times*.[85]

The first signal of the Court's conservative shift came in January 1989, when the justices struck down a Richmond, Virginia, minority set-aside plan. The city's plan required that 30 percent of city funds granted for construction projects go to firms with black owners. The Court, 6–3, said that the set-aside, challenged by a white contractor, was too rigid and that the city had not sufficiently justified it with specific findings of past discrimination.[86]

The Court moved away from its usual emphasis on concern for the victims of discrimination. It returned to a more neutral stance, balancing the needs of employer and worker, minority and majority.[87]

On questions of criminal law, the Court took a tough stand, refusing to find it unconstitutional for a state to execute criminals who were juveniles at the time of their crime—or to execute a mentally retarded criminal.[88] In addition, two federal drug testing programs won the Court's approval, despite its acknowledgment that obligatory urine tests for drug use fell within the meaning of the constitutional promise of security against unreasonable searches. In these cases—the testing of railroad workers after accidents and the mandatory testing of customs officials involved in drug interdiction—the public interest out-

weighed the private right, the Court held. Justice Kennedy wrote both opinions.[89]

The single notable liberal ruling of the October 1988 term was a highly controversial one. In line with its precedents from the Vietnam era, the Court held in the case of *Texas v. Johnson* that Texas could not punish an individual who burned an American flag in protest. The Court said that the law violated the First Amendment's protection for freedom of expression. Not only did this ruling align the Court in unusual ways—Justice Kennedy joined the Court's liberal members in the majority and Stevens found himself in dissent with Rehnquist, White, and O'Connor—but it also set off calls for a constitutional amendment to reverse the ruling.[90]

In the most closely watched case of the term, the Court gave states power to regulate abortions more thoroughly than the states had for sixteen years. Although it did not reverse *Roe v. Wade* outright—the Court's willingness to uphold a ban on abortions in publicly funded hospitals and tests for fetal viability was widely viewed at the time as a step toward repudiation of *Roe.*

The vote in *Webster v. Reproductive Health Services* was 5–4. Chief Justice Rehnquist wrote the opinion without mentioning the right of privacy, which he previously had stated he had never located in the Constitution. Joining him in the majority were White, his fellow dissenter from *Roe,* Scalia, Kennedy, and

O'Connor. In bitter dissent were Brennan, Marshall, Stevens, and Blackmun, the author of *Roe.*[91]

As the Court's second century ended, it appeared likely that the most controversial decision of its latter decades—*Roe v. Wade*—would soon be reversed and discarded as precedent. The Court's rulings upholding increased state regulation of abortions, narrowing the reach of federal antidiscrimination laws, and strengthening the prosecutor's hand in criminal cases all indicated a clear conservative trend.

But the sweep of history now stretching back two hundred years bore testimony to the difficulty of predicting the Court's future path: Was the conservative coalescence of 1988–1989 merely a temporary deviation from the more liberal path of the second half of the Court's second century? Or was it evidence of a strong new force that would control the first years of the Court's third century?

NOTES

1. William F. Swindler, *Court and Constitution in the 20th Century: The Old Legality, 1889–1932* (Indianapolis: Bobbs-Merrill, 1969), 1–2.

2. *Pollock v. Farmers' Loan and Trust Co.*, 158 U.S. 601 at 695 (1895).

3. Swindler, *Court and Constitution: 1889–1932*, 60.

4. *Plessy v. Ferguson*, 163 U.S. 537 at 551–552 (1896).

5. Id. at 559.

6. Id. at 562.

7. Id. at 563.

8. *Allgeyer v. Louisiana*, 165 U.S. 578 at 589 (1897).

9. *McCray v. United States*, 195 U.S. 27 (1904).

10. *Northern Securities Co. v. United States*, 193 U.S. 197 at 400 (1904).

11. *Jacobson v. Massachusetts*, 197 U.S. 11 (1905).

12. *Lochner v. New York*, 198 U.S. 45 at 57 (1905).

13. *First Employers Liability Case*, 207 U.S. 463 (1908).

14. *Berea College v. Kentucky*, 211 U.S. 45 (1908).

15. *Standard Oil Co. v. United States*, 221 U.S. 1 (1911).

16. *United States v. American Tobacco Co.*, 221 U.S. 106 (1911).

17. *Hipolite Egg Co. v. United States*, 220 U.S. 45 (1911); *Second Employers Liability Case*, 223 U.S. 1 (1912); *Hoke v. United States*, 227 U.S. 308 (1913).

18. David Burner, "James C. McReynolds" in *The Justices of the United States Supreme Court, 1789–1969: Their Lives and Major Opinions*, ed. Leon Friedman and Fred L. Israel (New York: Chelsea House Publishers in association with R. R. Bowker, 1969), III: 2023.

19. Swindler, *Court and Constitution, 1889–1932*, 197.

20. *Schenck v. United States*, 249 U.S. 47 at 52 (1919).

21. Arthur M. Schlesinger Jr., *The Politics of Upheaval* (Cambridge, Mass.: Houghton Mifflin, 1960), 455.

22. *United States v. Doremus*, 249 U.S. 86 (1919).

23. *Hill v. Wallace*, 259 U.S. 44 at 67–68 (1922); *Chicago Board of Trade v. Olsen*, 262 U.S. 1 (1923).

24. *Moore v. Dempsey*, 261 U.S. 86 at 91 (1923).

25. *Gitlow v. New York*, 268 U.S. 652 at 666 (1925).

26. *Meyer v. Nebraska*, 262 U.S. 390 (1923).

27. *Burns Baking Co. v. Bryan*, 264 U.S. 504 (1924); *Tyson & Bro. v. Banton*, 273 U.S. 418 (1927); *Ribnik v. McBride*, 277 U.S. 350 (1928).

28. *Petersen Baking Co. v. Burns*, 290 U.S. 570 (1934); *Olsen v. Nebraska*, 313 U.S. 236 (1941).

29. *Home Building & Loan Association v. Blaisdell*, 290 U.S. 398 (1934).

30. Robert H. Jackson, *The Struggle for Judicial Supremacy* (New York: Knopf, 1941), 315.

31. Quoted in William F. Swindler, *Court and Constitution in the 20th Century: The New Legality, 1932–1968* (Indianapolis: Bobbs-Merrill, 1970), 37.

32. *Louisville Joint Stock Land Bank v. Radford*, 295 U.S. 555 (1935); *Humphrey's Executor v. United States*, 295 U.S. 602 (1935).

33. Schlesinger, *Politics of Upheaval*, 468.

34. *Ashton v. Cameron County District Court*, 298 U.S. 513 (1936).

35. *Ashwander v. TVA*, 297 U.S. 288 (1936).

36. Quoted in Schlesinger, *Politics of Upheaval*, 483.

37. Swindler, *Court and Constitution: 1932–1968*, 5.

38. *West Coast Hotel Co. v. Parrish*, 300 U.S. 379 at 391 (1937).

39. *Wright v. Vinton Branch*, 300 U.S. 440 (1937); *Virginia Railway Co. v. System Federation*, 300 U.S. 515 (1937).

40. *United States v. Carolene Products Co.*, 304 U.S. 144 at 152 (1938).

41. Leo Pfeffer, *This Honorable Court: A History of the United States Supreme Court* (Boston: Beacon Press, 1965), 342.

42. *NLRB v. Jones & Laughlin Steel Corp.*, 301 U.S. 1 (1937); *Steward Machine Co. v. Davis*, 301 U.S. 548 (1937); *Helvering v. Davis*, 301 U.S. 619 (1937); *Alabama Power Co. v. Ickes*, 302 U.S. 464 (1938); *United States v. Bekins*, 304 U.S. 27 (1938); *Mulford v. Smith*, 307 U.S. 38 (1939); *United States v. Rock Royal Cooperative*, 307 U.S. 533 (1939); *Chicot County Drainage District v. Baxter State Bank*, 308 U.S. 371 (1940); *Sunshine Coal Co. v. Adkins*, 310 U.S. 381 (1940).

43. *Helvering v. Gerhardt*, 304 U.S. 405 (1938); *Graves v. New York ex rel. O'Keefe*, 306 U.S. 466 (1939).

44. *United States v. Darby Lumber Co.*, 312 U.S. 100 (1941) at 124.

45. Swindler, *Court and Constitution: 1932–1968*, 104.

46. *Thornhill v. Alabama*, 310 U.S. 88 (1940).

47. *Hirabayashi v. United States*, 320 U.S. 81 (1943); *Korematsu v. United States*, 323 U.S. 214 (1944); *Ex parte Endo*, 323 U.S. 283 (1944).

48. *Korematsu v. United States*, 323 U.S. 214 at 216 (1944).

49. Swindler, *Court and Constitution: 1932–1968*, 139.

50. *Jones v. Opelika*, 316 U.S. 584 (1942).

51. *West Virginia Board of Education v. Barnette*, 319 U.S. 624 at 642 (1943).

52. Alpheus T. Mason, *The Supreme Court from Taft to Warren* (Baton Rouge: Louisiana State University, 1958), 154.

53. *Louisiana ex rel. Francis v. Resweber*, 329 U.S. 459 (1947).

54. *Joint Anti-Fascist Refugee Committee v. McGrath*, 341 U.S. 123 (1951); *Garner v. Board of Public Works*, 341 U.S. 716 (1951).

55. *Rosenberg v. United States*, 346 U.S. 273 (1953).

56. Anthony Lewis, "Earl Warren" in Friedman and Israel, *Justices of the Supreme Court*, IV: 2728.

57. *Brown v. Board of Education*, 347 U.S. 483 at 495 (1954); see also Richard Kluger, *Simple Justice* (New York: Knopf, 1976), 707.

58. Kluger, *Simple Justice*, 709–710.

59. Ibid., 758.

60. Swindler, *Court and Constitution: 1932–1968*, 235.

61. Ibid., 243.

62. Ibid., 246.

63. *Wilson v. Girard*, 354 U.S. 524 (1957).

64. *NAACP v. Alabama ex rel. Patterson*, 357 U.S. 449 (1958).

65. *Klopfer v. North Carolina*, 386 U.S. 213 (1967); *In re Gault*, 387 U.S. 1 (1967); *Katz v. United States*, 389 U.S. 347 (1967).

66. *Elfbrandt v. Russell*, 384 U.S. 11 (1966); *United States v. Robel*, 389 U.S. 258 (1967).

67. *Abington School District v. Schempp*, 374 U.S. 203 (1963).

68. *Tinker v. Des Moines Independent Community School District*, 393 U.S. 503 (1969).

69. *Reed v. Reed*, 404 U.S. 71 (1971); *Graham v. Richardson*, 403 U.S. 365 (1971).

70. *New York Times Co. v. United States, United States v. The Washington Post*, 403 U.S. 713 (1971).

71. *Furman v. Georgia*, 408 U.S. 238 (1972); *Argersinger v. Hamlin*, 407 U.S. 25 (1972); *United States v. U.S. District Court, Eastern Michigan*, 407 U.S. 297 (1972).

72. *San Antonio Independent School District v. Rodriguez*, 411 U.S. 1

(1973); *Keyes v. Denver School District No. 1*, 413 U.S. 921 (1973); *Miller v. California*, 413 U.S. 15 (1973); *Mahan v. Howell*, 410 U.S. 315 (1973).

73. *Gregg v. Georgia, Proffitt v. Florida, Jurek v. Texas*, 428 U.S. 153, 242, 262 (1976); *Woodson v. North Carolina, Roberts v. Louisiana*, 428 U.S. 280, 325 (1976).

74. *Stone v. Powell, Wolff v. Rice*, 428 U.S. 465 (1976).

75. *City of Akron v. Akron Center for Reproductive Health Inc.*, 462 U.S. 416 (1983).

76. *Thornburgh v. American College of Obstetricians and Gynecologists*, 476 U.S. 747 (1986).

77. *Firefighters Local #1784 v. Stotts*, 467 U.S. 561 (1984); see also *Wygant v. Jackson Board of Education*, 476 U.S. 267 (1986).

78. *Local #28 of the Sheet Metal Workers' International v. Equal Employment Opportunity Commission*, 478 U.S. 421 (1986); *Local #93, International Association of Firefighters v. City of Cleveland and Cleveland Vanguards*, 478 U.S. 501 (1986); *United States v. Paradise*, 480 U.S. 149 (1987); *Johnson v. Transportation Agency of Santa Clara County*, 480 U.S. 616 (1987).

79. *Lynch v. Donnelly*, 465 U.S. 668 (1984).

80. *Wallace v. Jaffree*, 472 U.S. 38 (1985).

81. *Aguilar v. Felton*, 473 U.S. 402 (1985); *Grand Rapids School District v. Ball*, 473 U.S. 373 (1985).

82. *Immigration and Naturalization Service v. Chadha*, 462 U.S. 919 (1983); see in particular Justice White's dissenting opinion for list of affected laws.

83. *Garcia v. San Antonio Metropolitan Transit Authority*, 469 U.S. 528 (1985).

84. *United States v. Leon*, 468 U.S. 897 (1984); *New York v. Quarles*, 467 U.S. 649 (1984); *Nix v. Williams*, 467 U.S. 431 (1984).

85. Linda Greenhouse, "The Year the Court Turned to the Right," *New York Times*, July 7, 1989, A1.

86. *City of Richmond v. J. A. Croson Co.*, 488 U.S. 469 (1989).

87. *Wards Cove Packing Co. v. Atonio*, 490 U.S. 642 (1989).

88. *Stanford v. Kentucky*, 492 U.S. 361 (1989); *Penry v. Lynaugh*, 492 U.S. 302 (1989).

89. *Skinner v. Railway Labor Executives' Association*, 489 U.S. 602 (1989); *National Treasury Employees Union v. Von Raab*, 489 U.S. 656 (1989).

90. *Texas v. Johnson*, 491 U.S. 397 (1989).

91. *Webster v. Reproductive Health Services*, 492 U.S. 490 (1989). *Allegheny County v. American Civil Liberties Union, Greater Pittsburgh Chapter*, 492 U.S. 573 (1989).

CHAPTER 3

The Third Century: New Challenges

THE SUPREME COURT began its third century speaking in a decidedly conservative voice. Two decades of pressure from three Republican presidents and an increasingly conservative Congress at last had their impact. Led by Chief Justice Rehnquist, the Court adopted a narrow view both of affirmative action and other remedies for race discrimination and, in many cases, of federal governmental power itself.

But during these same years, the Court affirmed *Roe v. Wade,* which had made abortion legal nationwide, endorsed earlier rulings against sex discrimination, and sanctioned equal rights for lesbians and gay men. These rulings drew considerable public notice, both because of their substance and their divergence from the contemporary Court's overall conservative direction.

Within the first five years of the Court's third century, its four senior members—including the three most liberal justices—retired. William J. Brennan Jr., Thurgood Marshall, and Byron R. White, the lone conservative of this group, had served since the days of Chief Justice Earl Warren. The fourth retiree and third liberal, Harry A. Blackmun, was the author of *Roe v. Wade.* Once the voices and votes of Brennan, Marshall, and Blackmun were no longer part of the Court's discussions, the conservative justices took control.

Brennan left the Court in 1990 and Marshall in 1991. One of Marshall's final dissents proclaimed a mournful epitaph for the liberal precedents he saw discarded: "Power, not reason, is the new currency of this Court's decisionmaking."[1] Brennan and Marshall were succeeded by David H. Souter and Clarence Thomas, conservative jurists selected by President George Bush from the federal appellate bench.

White and Blackmun retired in 1993 and 1994, respectively. As their successors, President Bill Clinton named Ruth Bader Ginsburg and Stephen G. Breyer, federal appeals court judges

THE COURT IN 1995
Seated from left: Justices Antonin Scalia, John Paul Stevens, Chief Justice William H. Rehnquist, Justices Sandra Day O'Connor, Anthony Kennedy.
Standing from left: Justices Ruth Bader Ginsburg, David H. Souter, Clarence Thomas, Stephen G. Breyer

with reputations for pragmatic moderation. They were expected to strengthen the Court's middle and reverse the conservative trend.

But on the most fractious issues, that did not happen.

Ginsburg and Breyer tended to be more centrist than liberal, and their choice of the court's middle ground coincided with moves by Justices Sandra Day O'Connor and Anthony M. Kennedy away from the center to a more conservative posture. The result was a Court characterized by a new fervor to check government's race-conscious decision making, to curb the reach of the federal government, and to shore up state sovereignty.

After decades of approving the uninterrupted expansion of the power of Congress to regulate interstate commerce, the Court in 1995 held that Congress had exceeded its commerce power when lawmakers banned the possession of guns near local schools.

The following term, in 1996, the Court significantly reduced the authority of Congress to subject states to lawsuits for failure to enforce federal rights. Both cases were decided by a majority led by Rehnquist, and made up of the three Reagan appointees (O'Connor, Kennedy, Antonin Scalia) and Bush-appointee Thomas.

Rehnquist had argued for the curtailment of federal power from the time he joined the Court a quarter-century earlier, but his views had been no more than dissenting opinions for most of that time. The passing of the liberal era finally gave him a majority as the Court returned to fundamental questions of the balance of power between the central government and the states.

But if the liberal stalwarts were no longer on the bench, the difficult social problems of prior decades remained central to the docket. The issue of school desegregation, which Marshall had argued as a young civil rights advocate and Brennan had helped decide a quarter-century earlier, was back before the Court in 1995. School prayer, first decided soon after White arrived on the Court in 1962, was the topic of one of the major cases of his last term in 1992.[2] These three justices, joined by Blackmun, also had voted together in the first affirmative action case in 1978, to permit consideration of race as a positive factor in school admissions. With all four gone by 1995, one of the major decisions that year set in place a far stricter standard for affirmative action in federal contracting.

Review of voting rights issues, begun in the 1960s, continued to be a staple of court business through the 1990s. But there was a modern-day twist. Instead of scrutinizing poll taxes and other government practices that had disadvantaged racial minorities, the Court heard challenges by white voters to electoral districts drawn to include a majority of racial minorities and boost their chances of electing one of their own. Over a series of cases from 1993 to 1996, the justices struck down several such districts. Justice O'Connor, who became the voice of the Court in this area, said, "Racial gerrymandering, even for remedial purposes, may balkanize us into competing racial factions; it threatens to carry us further from the goal of a political system in which race no longer matters—a goal that the Fourteenth and Fifteenth Amendments embody, and to which the Nation continues to aspire."[3]

The Contemporary Court: 1989–1996

The first term of the Court's new century, which began in October 1989, provided evidence of the growing conservatism and deep divisions within the Court. In two separate cases, the Court allowed states to require that parents be notified when a teenaged daughter seeks an abortion. Illustrative of their wrenching disunity on the questions of personal privacy, the justices issued nine separate opinions in the two cases.[4]

The Court also confronted the issue of withdrawing artificial life support from a comatose patient. Although the justices ruled against withdrawal from a patient who had not made it clear earlier that she would have chosen to end her life under such circumstances, the Court for the first time said that the Constitution protects an individual's right to make such a decision.[5]

In one notable, if short-lived, victory for liberals, the Court, 5–4, upheld preferential treatment of minorities seeking federal broadcast licenses. The Court said "benign race-conscious measures" are constitutional if they further important government objectives. The ruling in *Metro Broadcasting v. Federal Communications Commission* marked the first time the Court had upheld an affirmative action program that was not devised to relieve the effects of past discrimination.

THE LAST LIBERALS

This affirmative action decision turned out to be the last hurrah for Brennan, a champion for individual rights and liberties who had tried—and succeeded to a remarkable extent—to keep alive the activism of the Warren era. Brennan retired July 20, 1990, after suffering a minor stroke. His departure gave President Bush the opportunity to appoint his first justice. Bush chose David H. Souter, a dry-witted, twelve-year-veteran of New Hampshire state courts. Souter, a newly appointed judge on the U.S. Court of Appeals for the First Circuit, was fifty-one when he took his seat in October 1990.

During his first term, Souter helped carry out Bush's law-and-order agenda. With his vote, a five-justice majority reversed precedent to hold that a coerced confession used at trial does not automatically taint a verdict. The Court also ruled that a death row prisoner has only one chance to challenge the constitutionality of his state conviction and sentence in federal court, absent extraordinary circumstances. And it allowed evidence of a victim's character and the effect of a crime on her family to be used against a defendant at sentencing.[6]

Souter also voted with the majority to uphold administration regulations barring abortion counseling in publicly funded clinics. In a separate decision involving reproductive rights, the

Clarence Thomas, President Bush's 1991 appointee, became the second African-American justice in Court history.

For his first Supreme Court nomination, President Clinton selected Ruth Bader Ginsburg. She became the Court's second woman justice.

Court ruled unanimously that companies—in this case, a battery manufacturer—may not exclude women from jobs that might harm a developing fetus.[7]

At the end of the term, Justice Marshall, whose six-decade legal career had shaped the country's civil rights laws, retired. As Marshall's successor, Bush chose Clarence Thomas, forty-three, the second black man named to the Court. Opposition to his conservative views and highly public (but unproven) charges by a former employee that he had sexually harassed her made Thomas's confirmation the closest of the twentieth century. The Senate approved his appointment by a four-vote margin, 52–48.

The October 1991 term saw O'Connor, Kennedy, and Souter emerge as the Court's center, exerting a steadying influence born out of concern for the Court's institutional stability. Their effectiveness was most notable in the abortion case that was the single most visible decision of the term. In an unusual joint opinion they emphasized the importance of precedent and the need to preserve the integrity of the Court. In *Planned Parenthood of Southeastern Pennsylvania v. Casey,* the Court essentially affirmed the central ruling of *Roe v. Wade,* which established a constitutional right to end a pregnancy.

In the opinion, O'Connor, Kennedy, and Souter said *Roe* could not be discarded without serious social repercussions, because for nearly twenty years people had lived with the idea that abortion is available if contraception fails. But the Court made it somewhat easier for states to impose restrictions on the exer-

cise of this right as long as the regulation did not put an "undue burden" on a woman seeking an abortion.

The following term was a conservative reprise. On its final day, the Court signaled an end to its traditionally broad interpretation of the Voting Rights Act, allowing white voters to bring constitutional challenges to congressional districts that appeared to have been drawn solely on racial lines. "We believe that reapportionment is one area in which appearances do matter," said Justice O'Connor in *Shaw v. Reno.* "A reapportionment plan that includes in one district individuals . . . who may have little in common with one another but the color of their skin bears an uncomfortable resemblance to political apartheid."[8]

White retired in the summer of 1993, concluding a thirty-one-year career on the bench. As his first nominee, President Clinton chose the Court's second female justice, Ruth Ginsburg, age sixty, a federal appeals judge in Washington. The first successful Democratic nominee since Lyndon Johnson named Marshall in 1967, Ginsburg was easily confirmed by the Senate.

In her first term, Ginsburg, a legal strategist in the women's rights movement of the 1960s and 1970s, joined the majority to prohibit lawyers from using their peremptory challenges to exclude people from a jury pool based on sex and stereotypes of how men and women decide cases.[9] The Court also upheld the use of "buffer zones" around abortion clinics to protect them from antiabortion demonstrations. Chief Justice Rehnquist, a consistent opponent of abortion rights, wrote the opinion in

Madsen v. Women's Health Center. He stressed that judges have the authority to protect public safety and order with narrowly tailored injunctions.

At the end of the 1993–1994 term, Justice Blackmun retired at the age of eighty-six. Blackmun's evolution as a justice reflected the changes that had taken place in the Court during his twenty-four-year tenure. When he took his seat in 1970, an appointee of President Richard Nixon, Blackmun was an addition to the Court's conservative bloc. By the time he retired in 1994, he was its liberal pole. Blackmun was succeeded by President Clinton's second appointee, Stephen Breyer, fifty-seven, a judge on the U.S. Court of Appeals for the First Circuit in Boston. He was easily confirmed.

CONSERVATIVE CONSOLIDATION

For most of its existence, the Court has been slow to change. Rarely has a new majority emerged dramatically in a single term. But the October 1994 term, Breyer's first, was such a term. With Blackmun's departure, a bold conservative majority took control. Its members were Rehnquist, the Nixon appointee who had been elevated to chief justice in 1986 by Reagan; O'Connor, Kennedy, and Scalia, also Reagan appointees; and Thomas, named by Bush.

Voting together, they set a strict new legal standard for affirmative action programs and set in motion a new round of challenges to "majority minority" congressional districts. In both rulings, they criticized government decisions made on the basis of race. "Government may treat people differently because of their race only for the most compelling reasons," Justice O'Connor wrote for the majority in *Adarand Constructors Inc. v. Peña*. She said the Constitution's guarantee of equal protection of the laws protects "persons, not groups." "It follows from that principle that all governmental action based on race . . . should be subjected to detailed judicial inquiry to ensure that the personal right to equal protection of the laws has not been infringed."[10]

Similar reasoning was adopted when the Court struck down a black-majority voting district in Georgia.[11] The justices said that courts should apply "strict scrutiny" to the constitutionality of redistricting maps when the race of voters was the predominant factor in deciding how to draw the boundaries. The decision threw into doubt numerous voting districts that had produced a doubling of African American and Hispanic representation in Congress since the 1990 redistricting.

Taken with its school desegregation decision restricting the ability of a federal judge to order remedies to integrate a school district, the Court seemed to say that the time had come for the nation to stop seeking remedies for its history of segregation and put race aside.[12]

A similar retrenchment on a different front came in the Court's opinion striking down a federal ban on guns near schools. For the first time since the New Deal, the Court set a limit on Congress's power to regulate interstate commerce. Emphasizing the Framers' belief in limited congressional powers,

Chief Justice Rehnquist wrote that upholding the gun ban "would convert congressional authority under the commerce clause to a general police power of the sort retained by the states."[13]

The only notable victory for the more liberal justices, Souter, Ginsburg, Breyer, and John Paul Stevens, was the Court's rejection of state-imposed term limits for members of Congress. Joined by Kennedy in the majority, those justices declared that the only qualifications for persons seeking to be U.S. senators and members of the U.S. House of Representatives are those explicitly set out in the Constitution, relating to age, residency, and citizenship.[14]

Throughout the first years of its new century, the Court continued to wrestle with the issues of religious freedom and of separation of church and state.[15] By the end of the watershed 1994–1995 term, there was a new attitude of tolerance for government involvement with religion and a new ability for church groups to express their messages in the public arena.[16]

The 1995–1996 term echoed the Court's earlier actions invalidating minority voting districts and hemming in federal power. The Court struck down three more majority black and one majority Hispanic voting districts, emphasizing that voters are "more than mere racial statistics."[17]

The justices also restricted congressional authority to allow individuals to sue states to enforce federal rights. The Court struck down as a violation of the Eleventh Amendment the Indian Gaming Regulatory Act, which allowed tribes to sue states that had not negotiated in good faith toward a gaming contract.[18] The voting rights and Indian gambling cases were decided by the same five-justice majority: Rehnquist, Scalia, O'Connor, Kennedy, and Thomas. Dissenting were Stevens, Souter, Ginsburg, and Breyer.

In the blockbuster ruling of the term, the Court nullified an amendment to the Colorado constitution that barred localities from protecting homosexuals from discrimination. The justices said the amendment violated the federal Constitution's guarantee of equal protection.[19]

Justices O'Connor and Kennedy made the difference in the outcome. Their votes and Kennedy's opinion for the majority, asserting that "a state cannot so deem a class of persons a stranger to its laws," reflected their belief that government should not single out minorities, whether for preferential treatment as in the situation of federal contracting preferences, or for disfavored treatment as occurred in Colorado.

And so the Court began its third century—still nine controversial, independent individuals, working to maintain the great balances of order and freedom, still the balance wheel of the national system.

NOTES

1. *Payne v. Tennessee*, 501 U.S. 808 (1991).
2. *Lee v. Weisman*, 505 U.S. 577 (1992).

3. *Shaw v. Reno*, 509 U.S. 630 (1993).

4. *Hodgson v. Minnesota*, 497 U.S. 417 (1990), *Ohio v. Akron Center for Reproductive Health*, 497 U.S. 502 (1990).

5. *Cruzan v. Director, Missouri Department of Health*, 497 U.S. 261 (1990).

6. *Arizona v. Fulminante*, 499 U.S. 279 (1991); *McCleskey v. Zant*, 499 U.S. 467 (1991); *Payne v. Tennessee*, 501 U.S. 808 (1991).

7. *Rust v. Sullivan*, 500 U.S. 173 (1991); *International Union, United Automobile, Aerospace & Agricultural Implement Workers of America, UAW v. Johnson Controls*, 499 U.S. 187 (1991).

8. *Shaw v. Reno*, 509 U.S. 630 (1993).

9. *J. E. B. v. Alabama ex rel. T. B.*, 114 S. Ct. 1419 (1994).

10. *Adarand Constructors Inc. v. Peña*, 115 S. Ct. 2097 (1995).

11. *Miller v. Johnson*, 115 S. Ct. 2475 (1995).

12. *Missouri v. Jenkins*, 115 S. Ct. 2038 (1995).

13. *United States v. Lopez*, ____ U.S. ____ (1995).

14. *U.S. Term Limits v. Thornton*, 115 S. Ct. 1842 (1995).

15. *Lee v. Weisman*, 505 U.S. 577 (1992); *Board of Education of Kiryas Joel Village School District v. Grumet*, 512 U.S. ____ (1994).

16. *Board of Education of the Westside Community Schools (Dist. 66) v. Mergens*, 496 U.S. 226 (1990); *Lamb's Chapel v. Center Moriches Union Free School District*, 508 U.S. 384 (1993); *Zobrest v. Catalina Foothills School District*, 509 U.S. 1 (1993); *Rosenberger v. Rector and Visitors of University of Virginia*, 115 S. Ct. 2510 (1995); *Capitol Square Review and Advisory Board v. Pinette*, 115 S. Ct. 2440 (1995).

17. *Bush v. Vera*, ____ U.S. ____ (1996).

18. *Seminole Tribe of Florida v. Florida*, ____ U.S. ____ (1996).

19. *Romer v. Evans*, ____ U.S. ____ (1996).

CHAPTER 4

Operations and Traditions of the Court

CONSTITUTIONALLY and politically, the Supreme Court is at the helm of a branch of the federal government coequal with Congress and the executive. In some ways the judiciary appears the most powerful: the Court can declare the actions of the president illegal and acts of Congress unconstitutional.

Organizationally, however, the Supreme Court is dwarfed by the sprawling bureaucracies of the other branches. The Court is, after all, only nine people, housed within a single building at One First Street Northeast in the nation's capital. Its budget is but a fraction of the size of those required to fund Congress and the executive branch.

Nevertheless, the Court is hardly aloof from the problems of management, procedure, maintenance, and personnel faced by any other institution. Like Congress—or the local department store, for that matter—it must be administered, budgeted, staffed, and locked up after work each day. Moreover, it is the apex of a substantial federal judicial system that includes ninety-four district courts, thirteen courts of appeal, and two special courts, along with their judges and attendant staff.

The administrative aspects of the Court's operations are considerable, even if they do not rival those that have spawned the huge bureaucracies that serve the executive branch and Congress. Chief justices from John Jay to William H. Rehnquist have wrestled with the problems of ensuring the smooth functioning of the Court's managerial machinery to allow the judges to concentrate on dispassionate consideration of matters of law.

The ideal tableau of the Court—and certainly the image that it has sought to perpetuate over the years—is of nine wise, just, and serene jurists sitting to render, with irreproachable integrity, decisions crucial to the conduct of national life.

That this image has been maintained so well for more than two centuries testifies, to a remarkable degree, to its accuracy. The high standards necessary both to effective judicial performance and public trust have indeed been consistently maintained by a succession of mostly able jurists who were also individuals of exemplary personal demeanor. There have been few scandals involving the justices, and any embarrassments the Court has suffered have been resolved openly and expeditiously. With some notable exceptions, the political affinities of the justices have been more implicit than overt.

But to some extent the Court's sacrosanct image is also more apparent than real. The Court has no public relations mechanism as such, but the long-standing internal traditions of the institution effectively serve that function. The secrecy of its deliberations, in particular, protects the justices from disclosure of any of the fractiousness or ineptitude that certainly must occur from time to time. The elaborate courtesy and obeisance to seniority on the Court also serve its image as an august deliberative body aloof from contentious bickering and disharmony. Its imposing headquarters, the "marble palace," has erased the memory of the many years during which the justices were shunted from one "mean and dingy" makeshift office to another.

The image notwithstanding, the Court as a bureaucracy and administrative body continues to face many workaday challenges. These challenges involve matters much more pressing than the mere operation and upkeep of the Court itself. Most important, the Court must select which cases to review, and between 1975 and 1995, the number of new cases filed in federal district courts rose from 160,602 to 294,123. It is from this mountain of work that the Supreme Court is expected to cull the legal issues most worthy of its judgment. The Court's own docket also has been steadily climbing for the past quarter century. By 1996 about 7,000 petitions for review were coming to the Court each year.

So the august tribunal of justices is also, by necessity, a beleaguered bureaucracy that must decide how to allocate its resources. The former chief justice, Warren E. Burger, was a forceful, if unsuccessful, advocate urging a solution to the problem of the Court's mushrooming workload. In remarks to the sixtieth annual meeting of the American Law Institute in May 1983, Burger recalled that

in the 1920s, one of the Justices wrote . . . that he dreaded the thought of returning to the Court and having to cope with the weeks' burden of argued cases and in addition as many as 12 or 14 petitions for certiorari. . . . I wonder what that worthy gentleman would have thought of a conference list which every week contains more than 100 items! When we look at these Supreme Court figures . . . the increase in the docket . . . one must be forgiven for being puzzled by the irrational, unreasoning resistance we encounter to making any change in the system. We remember the tale of the farm boy who had acquired a new pony and . . . vowed he would increase his own strength by lifting that pony every morning. He did so for a long time, but obviously there came a day when the boy could no longer carry out his promise. Lifting a horse of 1,000 or 2,000 pounds . . . presents an unmanageable problem. Just when the bar and Congress will discover what the little boy discovered remains to be seen.

Chief Justice Rehnquist voiced similar concerns in 1996 about the steady stream of laws federalizing crimes long thought to be matters of concern only to the states. In a speech to an audience at American University's centennial celebration of its law school, Rehnquist recalled:

Forty-some years ago when I began the practice of law in Arizona, there were not many federal criminal statutes on the books. There were some very esoteric crimes, but the staple of the criminal business of federal courts outside of the metropolitan areas was confined to prosecutions for transporting a stolen car in interstate commerce, using the mails for interstate communications to commit fraud, and a very few other similar crimes. But that landscape has entirely changed in the last forty years. Congress, understandably concerned with the increasing trafficking of drugs and the violence resulting from the use of guns, has legislated again and again to make what once were only state crimes federal offenses. The same sort of dissatisfaction with state treatment of the cases in this area of the law has obtained as obtained earlier with welfare legislation and civil rights laws.

The result, lamented the chief justice, is an ever-increasing wave of litigation before the Supreme Court and federal courts of appeals.

The Constitution makes the Supreme Court the final arbiter in "cases" and "controversies" arising under the Constitution or the laws of the United States. As the interpreter of the law, the Court is often viewed as the least mutable and most tradition-bound of the three branches of the federal government.

Yet as the Supreme Court takes the first steps into its third century, it has undergone innumerable changes. A few of these changes have been mandated by law. Almost all of them, however, were made because members of the Court felt such changes would provide a more efficient or a more equitable way of dealing with the Court's responsibilities. Some of the changes are embodied in Court rules; others are informal adaptations to needs and circumstances.

The Schedule of the Term

The Court's annual schedule reflects both continuity and change. During its formal annual sessions, certain times are set aside for oral argument, for conferences, for the writing of opinions, and for the announcement of decisions. With the ever-increasing number of petitions that arrive at the Court each year, the justices are confronted with a tremendous—some say excessive—amount of work during the regular term, which now lasts nine months.

Their work does not end when the session is finished, however. During the summer recess, the justices receive new cases to consider. About a fourth of the applications for review filed during the term are read by the justices and their law clerks during the summer interim.

ANNUAL TERMS

By law, the Supreme Court begins its regular annual term on the first Monday in October.[1] The regular session, known as the October term, lasts nine months. The summer recess, which is not determined by statute or Court rules, generally begins in late June or early July of the following year, when the Court has

taken action on the last case argued before it during the term. The Court's increasing caseload has resulted in longer terms. For example, in 1955 the Court began its summer recess on June 6, while in the mid-1990s, it did not recess until the last week of June each term.

Until 1979 the Court actually adjourned its session when the summer recess began. The adjournment occurred when the chief justice announced in open court, "All cases submitted and all business before the Court at this term in readiness for disposition having been disposed of, it is ordered by this Court that all cases on the docket be, and they are hereby, continued to the next term." Since 1979, however, the Court has been in continuous session throughout the year, marked by periodic recesses; the October 1994 term, for example, did not adjourn until the first Monday in October 1995 when the new term began. This system makes it unnecessary to convene a special term to deal with matters arising in the summer.[2]

Over the years, the annual sessions of the Court have been changed a number of times. During the first decade of its existence, 1790–1801, the Court met twice a year, in February and August. The justices had few cases during these years, and the early sessions were devoted largely to organization and discussions of lawyers' qualifications. The first case did not reach the Court until 1791; the first formal opinion was not handed down until 1792, in the Court's third year.

Despite the dearth of casework during the early semiannual sessions, the chief justice and five associate justices had enough to do. The Judiciary Act of 1789, in addition to mandating the February and August sessions, required the justices to travel through the country to preside over the circuit courts—a time-consuming task that continued, except for a brief period, until circuit riding was finally abolished in 1891 and circuit courts of appeal were established.

The Judiciary Act of 1801 called for Court terms beginning in June and December. The Judiciary Act of 1802 restored the February term of the Court but not the August term, which resulted in a fourteen-month adjournment—from December 1801 until February 1803.

At the beginning of the 1827 term, Congress changed the opening day of the new term to the second Monday in January. This change was made to give the justices more time to ride their circuits.

The opening day of the term was changed to the second Monday in December by an act of June 17, 1844. By this statute, Charles Warren wrote, the justices "were relieved of holding more than one Term of the Circuit Court within any District of such Circuit, in any one year. The result of this provision was to enable the Court to sit later each spring in Washington; and in alternate years thereafter it made a practice of sitting through March, adjourning through April and sitting again in May."[3]

An act of January 24, 1873, moved the beginning of the term from the first Monday in December to the second Monday in October. Since 1917 terms have begun on the first Monday in October.

SPECIAL SESSIONS

The statute and rule covering the annual session of the Court also permit the justices to hold special terms after the regular session is over. Special sessions are called to deal with urgent matters that cannot be postponed until the next session.

There have been few special sessions in the Court's history; it has been far more common for the Court to consider important cases that arise toward the end of the term simply by delaying the end of the regular term until action is completed. Only four cases have been decided in special session:

• *Ex parte Quirin*. The Court convened a special term, July 29, 1942, heard arguments on July 29 and July 30 and, on July 31, upheld a military court's conviction of a group of Nazi saboteurs smuggled ashore from a German submarine. A formal opinion in the case was released October 29, 1942.

• *Rosenberg v. United States*. Three days after the end of the October 1952 term, the Supreme Court on June 18, 1953, convened a special term to consider a stay of execution ordered by Justice William O. Douglas for Ethel and Julius Rosenberg, convicted of divulging information about the atomic bomb to the Soviet Union. Arguments were heard June 18, and the Court vacated the stay June 19. The Rosenbergs were executed that day. The Court's opinion in the case was released July 16, 1953.

• *Cooper v. Aaron*. In a special session convened August 28, 1958, the Court unanimously upheld a lower court order enforcing a desegregation plan for Central High School in Little Rock, Arkansas. The order was opposed by state officials. The Court heard arguments on August 28 and September 11 and issued its decision September 12. City schools were to open in Little Rock September 15, but Gov. Orval Faubus closed them after the Court's decision. A formal opinion in the case was released September 29, 1958.

• *O'Brien v. Brown*. The Court convened a special session July 6, 1972, to consider the seating of delegates from California and Illinois at the Democratic National Convention, which was to open July 10. The Court decided, by a vote of 6–3 on July 7, 1972, to return the California and Illinois cases to the convention and to let the convention itself, rather than the Court, decide the matter.

Among the decisions made by the modern Court after postponing adjournment of the regular term, the most famous is *United States v. Nixon*. In that case the Court on July 24, 1974, unanimously denied President Richard Nixon's claim of absolute executive privilege to withhold documents requested by the Watergate special prosecutor.

Other important decisions delivered after delaying adjournment include *Wilson v. Girard*, handed down on July 11, 1957; *New York Times v. United States, United States v. Washington Post*, decided on June 30, 1971; and *Dames & Moore v. Regan*, decided on July 2, 1981. The first case involved an earlier stage of the Little Rock school desegregation case; the second rebuffed the effort by the Nixon administration to bar publication of the Pentagon Papers; and the third resolved a major challenge to the agreements with which President Jimmy Carter had won release of American hostages by Iran.[4]

OPENING DAY

Opening day ceremonies of the new term have changed considerably since the Court first met on February 1, 1790. Chief Justice Jay was forced to postpone the first formal session for a day because some of the justices were unable to reach New York City—at that time the nation's capital and home of the Court. It began proceedings the next day in a crowded courtroom but with an empty docket.

From 1917 to 1975, when the annual session began on the first Monday in October, the opening day and week were spent in conference. The justices discussed cases that had not been disposed of during the previous term and some of the petitions that had reached the Court during the summer recess. The decisions arrived at during this initial conference on which cases to accept for oral argument were announced on the second Monday of October.

At the beginning of the October 1975 term, this practice was changed. That year the justices reassembled for this initial conference during the last week in September. When the justices convened formally on Monday, October 6, 1975, oral arguments began.

SCHEDULE OF ARGUMENTS AND CONFERENCES

At least four justices must request that a case be argued before it can be approved for a hearing. Until 1955 the Court often heard oral arguments five days a week. Friday arguments were excluded when the Court's conference was moved to that day. Arguments are now heard on Monday, Tuesday, and Wednesday for seven two-week sessions, beginning in the first week in October and ending in the last week of April or the first week of May.

There usually are two consecutive weeks of oral arguments during this period, with two-week or longer recesses during which the justices consider the cases and deal with other Court business.

Since the early 1800s, when justices heard arguments from eleven a.m. until four or five p.m., the schedule for hearing arguments has been changed several times to achieve a more manageable daily calendar. The present schedule for oral arguments, ten a.m. to noon and one p.m. to three p.m., began during the 1969 term. Since most cases receive one hour apiece for argument, that means the Court can hear twelve cases a week. In the mid-1990s the Court was hearing about half that number, not because of time constraints but because the justices were granting fewer petitions for review.

The time provided for oral argument had been limited to two hours—one hour for each side—under a rule of the Court adopted March 12, 1849. Cases that the Court felt could be covered in a shorter period were placed on a "summary calendar," under which arguments were limited to a half hour for each side. That practice was revived during the 1940s, and one hour's argument became the current limit in 1970. Exceptions to the hour-per-case time limit must be sought and granted before arguments begin.

In the Court's early years, conferences often were held in the evenings or on weekends, sometimes in the common boarding-house the justices shared. The number of cases for which review was sought and the cases awaiting a final decision determined when and how often conferences were held. Later, Saturday was set aside as the regular conference day. Under a 1955 Court order that ended Friday oral arguments, Friday became conference day.

Until 1975 the Court held its first conferences during opening week, following its formal call to order on the first Monday in October. To streamline the procedure, the justices began meeting in the last week in September, before the official convening of the annual session. At its initial conference, the Court attempts to resolve leftover matters—appeals, petitions for certiorari, and so forth—from the previous session. The September conference allows the Court to announce its orders on these matters by opening day rather than a week after the formal convening.

In 1993 the justices began the practice of releasing the initial orders list of the term—announcing which cases they had accepted for oral argument—shortly after they completed their first conference in late September. The early start on the traditional opening of the term compensated for a drop in the number of cases the Court earlier had accepted for the 1993–1994 term and the justices' having several openings in their late fall calendar. In announcing the new petitions granted, the Court expedited the briefing schedule so that the new cases would fill open slots on the fall calendar.

In the October 1994 and October 1995 terms, the justices also made an early announcement of the initial batch of cases granted review. When the first Monday in October arrived in 1994 and 1995, the list of orders included only the cases that had been denied review.

During its term, the Court holds conferences each Friday during the weeks when arguments are heard, and on the Friday just before the two-week oral argument periods. To reduce the workload of its Friday sessions, the Court also holds Wednesday conferences during the weeks when oral arguments are scheduled.

The conferences are designed for consideration of cases heard in oral argument during the preceding week, and to resolve other business before the Court. Prior to each of the Friday conferences, the chief justice circulates a "discuss list"—a list of cases deemed important enough for discussion and a vote. Appeals (of which there are now only a small number) are placed on the discuss list almost automatically, but as many as three-quarters of the petitions for certiorari are summarily denied a place on the list and simply disappear. No case is denied review during conference, however, without an initial examination by the justices and their law clerks. Any one of the justices

can have a case placed on the Court's conference agenda for review. Most of the cases scheduled for the discuss list are also denied review in the end, but only after discussion by the justices during the conference.

Although the last oral arguments have been heard by late April or early May of each year, the Friday and Monday conferences of the justices continue until the end of the term to consider cases remaining on the Court's agenda.

All conferences are held in strict secrecy, with no legal assistants or staff present. The attendance of six justices constitutes a quorum. Conferences begin with handshakes all around. In discussing a case, the chief justice speaks first, followed by each justice in order of seniority.

DECISION DAYS

In the Court's earliest years, decisions were announced whenever they were ready, with no formal schedule for making them known. The tradition of announcing decisions on Monday—"Decision Monday"—began in 1857, apparently without any formal announcement or rule to that effect. This practice continued until the Court said on April 5, 1965, that "commencing the week of April 26, 1965, it will no longer adhere to the practice of reporting its decisions only at Monday sessions and that in the future they will be reported as they become ready for decision at any session of the Court."[5]

At present, opinions are released mostly on Tuesdays and Wednesdays during the weeks that the Court is hearing oral arguments; during other weeks, they are released on Mondays along with the orders.

Like the announcement of opinions, the day for release of the Court's "orders list"—the summary of the Court's action granting or denying review—has changed over the years. During the nineteenth century, the Court's summary orders were often announced on Friday, which was called "Motion Day." The practice of posting orders on Monday evolved gradually.

During the first three months of the 1971 term, orders were announced on Tuesday; but on January 10, 1972, Monday was reinstated as the day for posting orders. When urgent or important matters arise, the Court's summary orders may be announced on a day other than Monday. And when the last oral arguments of the term have been presented, the Court may release decisions and written opinions, as well as the orders list, on Mondays.

At present, the orders list is released at the beginning of the Monday session. It is not orally announced, but can be obtained from the clerk and the public information officer.

Unlike its orders, decisions of the Court are announced orally in open court. The justice who wrote the opinion announces the Court's decision, and justices writing concurring or dissenting opinions may state their views as well. When more than one decision is to be rendered, the justices who wrote the opinion make their announcements in reverse order of seniority.

It is rare for all or a large portion of the opinion to be read aloud. More often, the author will summarize the opinion or simply announce the result and state that a written opinion has been filed.

Reviewing Cases

In determining whether to accept a case for review, the Supreme Court has considerable discretion, subject only to the restraints imposed by the Constitution and Congress. Article III, Section 2, of the Constitution states, "In all Cases affecting Ambassadors, other public Ministers and Consuls, and those in which a State shall be Party, the Supreme Court shall have original jurisdiction. In all the other Cases . . . the Supreme Court shall have appellate Jurisdiction, both as to Law and Fact, with such Exceptions, and under such Regulations as the Congress shall make."

Original jurisdiction refers to the right of the Supreme Court to hear a case before any other court does. Appellate jurisdiction is the right to review the decision of a lower court. The vast majority of cases reaching the Supreme Court are appeals from rulings of the lower courts; generally only a handful of original jurisdiction cases are filed each term.

After enactment of the Judiciary Act of 1925, the Supreme Court had broad discretion to decide for itself what cases it would hear. Since Congress in 1988 virtually eliminated the Court's mandatory jurisdiction through which it was obliged to hear most appeals, that discretion has been nearly unlimited.[6]

METHODS OF APPEAL

Cases come to the Supreme Court in several ways. They may come through petitions for writs of certiorari, appeals, and requests for certification.

In petitioning for a writ of certiorari, a litigant who has lost a case in a lower court sets out the reasons why the Supreme Court should review his case. If it is granted, the Court requests a certified record of the case from the lower court.

Supreme Court rules provide that:

Whenever the Court grants a petition for a writ of certiorari, the Clerk will prepare, sign, and enter an order to that effect and will notify forthwith counsel of record and the court whose judgment is to be reviewed. The case then will be scheduled for briefing and oral argument. If the record has not previously been filed in this Court, the Clerk will request the clerk of the court having possession of the record to certify and transmit it. A formal writ will not issue unless specially directed.[7]

The main difference between the certiorari and appeal routes is that the Court has complete discretion to grant a request for a writ of certiorari, but is under an obligation to accept and decide a case that comes to it on appeal.

Most cases reach the Supreme Court by means of the writ of certiorari. In the relatively few cases to reach the Court by means of appeal, the appellant must file a jurisdictional statement explaining why his or her case qualifies for review and why the Court should grant it a hearing. With increasing frequency in recent years, the justices have been disposing of these cases by deciding them summarily, without oral argument or formal opinion.

Those whose petitions for certiorari have been granted by the Court must pay a $300 fee for docketing the case. The U.S. government does not have to pay this fee, nor do persons too poor to afford them. The latter may file *in forma pauperis* (in the character or manner of a pauper) petitions. The law governing *in forma pauperis* proceedings state:

[A]ny court of the United States may authorize the commencement, prosecution or defense of any suit, action or proceeding, civil or criminal, or appeal therein, without prepayment of fees and costs or security therefor, by a person who makes affidavit that he is unable to pay such costs or give security therefor. Such affidavit shall state the nature of the action, defense or appeal and affiant's belief that he is entitled to redress. . . . An appeal may not be taken in forma pauperis if the trial court certifies in writing that it is not taken in good faith.[8]

Another, but seldom used, method of appeal is certification, the request by a court of appeals for a final answer to questions of law in a particular case. The Supreme Court, after examining the certificate, may order the case argued before it.

PROCESS OF REVIEW

Each year the Court is asked to review about seven thousand cases. All petitions are examined by the clerk of the Court and his staff; those found to be in reasonably proper form are placed on the docket and given a number. Prior to 1970 there were two dockets: an appellate docket for petitions for certiorari and appeals in cases where the docketing fee was paid, and a miscellaneous docket for *in forma pauperis* petitions and appeals and other requests not qualifying for the appellate docket. When a case on the miscellaneous docket was accepted for review, it was transferred to the appellate docket and renumbered.

Since 1970 all cases except those falling within the Court's original jurisdiction are placed on a single docket, known simply as "the docket." Only in the numbering of the cases is a distinction made between prepaid and *in forma pauperis* cases on the docket. Beginning with the 1971 term, prepaid cases were labeled with the year and the number. The first case filed in 1995, for example, would be designated 95–1. *In forma pauperis* cases contain the year and begin with the number 5001. The second *in forma pauperis* case filed in 1995 would be number 95-5002.[9]

Cases on the original docket were unaffected by the 1970 revision. The original docket remains separate and distinct, but cases on it that are carried over to the next term are no longer renumbered; they retain the docket numbers assigned to them when they were filed.

Each justice, aided by his or her law clerks, is responsible for reviewing all cases on the dockets. Since the late 1970s, a number of justices have used a "cert pool" system in this review. Their clerks work together to examine cases, writing a pool memo on several petitions. The memo is then given to the justices who determine if more research is needed. (Some of the other justices have preferred to use a system in which they or their clerks review each petition themselves.)

Justice Douglas called the review of cases on the dockets "in many respects the most important and interesting of all our functions." Others apparently have found it time-consuming and tedious and support the cert pool as a mechanism to reduce the burden on the justices and their staffs. In 1996 Justice John Paul Stevens was the only one of the nine sitting justices who did not use the cert pool.

The delegation of review power to the justices' law clerks has raised a few eyebrows, as Chief Justice Rehnquist acknowledged in his 1987 book, *The Supreme Court: How It Was, How It Is:*

Recently I was asked whether or not the use of law clerks in a cert pool didn't represent the abandonment of the justices' responsibilities to a sort of internal bureaucracy. I certainly do not think so. The individual justices are of course quite free to disregard whatever recommendation the writer of the pool memo may have made, as well as the recommendation of his own law clerks, but this is not a complete answer to the criticism. It is one thing to do the work yourself, and it is another thing to simply approve the recommendation of another person who has done the work. But the decision as to whether to grant certiorari is a much more "channeled" decision than the decision as to how a case should be decided on the merits; there are really only two or three factors comprised in the certiorari decision—conflict with other courts, general importance, and perception that the decision is wrong in the light of Supreme Court precedent. Each of these factors is one that a well-trained law clerk is capable of evaluating, and the justices, of course, having been in the certiorari-granting business term after term, are quite familiar with many of the issues that come up.[10]

Petitions on the docket vary from elegantly printed and bound documents, of which multiple copies are submitted to the Court, to single sheets of prison stationery scribbled in pencil and filled with grammatical and spelling errors. All are considered by the justices, however, in the process of deciding which merit review.

TO GRANT OR DENY REVIEW: THE DISCUSS LIST AND THE ORDERS LIST

The decisions to grant or deny review of cases are made in conferences, which are held in the conference room adjacent to the chief justice's chambers. Justices are summoned to the conference room by a buzzer, usually between 9:30 and 10:00 a.m. They shake hands with each other, take their appointed seats, and the chief justice begins the discussion.

A few days before the conference convenes, the chief justice compiles a "discuss list"—a list of cases deemed important enough for discussion and a vote. As many as three-quarters of the petitions for certiorari are denied a place on the list and thus rejected without further consideration. Any justice can have a case placed on the discuss list simply by requesting that it be placed there.

Conferences are held in strict secrecy: only the justices attend, and no legal assistants or staff are present. The junior associate justice acts as doorkeeper and messenger, sending for reference material and receiving messages and data at the door. The secrecy has worked well; unlike other parts of the federal government, there have been very few leaks about what transpires during the conferences.

THE "RULE OF FOUR"

Congress in 1925 gave the Supreme Court broad discretion over the decision to review or deny review in most of the cases brought to its attention. The Court has adopted certain rules to guide the exercise of this discretion. One is the "Rule of Four"—a case is accepted for review only if four justices feel that it merits the Court's full consideration. That rule has since 1925 governed decisions to grant or deny review through use of the writ of certiorari.

More formal and official is the portion of the Rules of the Supreme Court of the United States that states:

Review on a writ of certiorari is not a matter of right, but of judicial discretion. A petition for writ of certiorari will be granted only for compelling reasons. The following, although neither controlling nor fully measuring the Court's discretion, indicate the character of the reasons the Court considers:

(a) a United States court of appeals has entered a decision in conflict with the decision of another United States court of appeals on the same important matter; has decided an important federal question in a way that conflicts with a decision by a state court of last resort; or has so far departed from the accepted and usual course of judicial proceedings, or sanctioned such a departure by a lower court, as to call for an exercise of this Court's supervisory power;

(b) a state court of last resort has decided an important federal question in a way that conflicts with the decision of another state court of last resort or of a United States court of appeals;

(c) a state court or United States court of appeals has decided an important question of federal law that has not been, but should be, settled by this Court, or has decided an important federal question in a way that conflicts with relevant decisions of this Court.

A petition for a writ of certiorari is rarely granted when the asserted error consists of erroneous factual findings or the misapplication of a properly stated rule of law.

SOURCE: Rule 10 of the Rules of the Supreme Court of the United States, adopted July 26, 1995; effective October 2, 1995.

At the start of the conference, the chief justice makes a brief statement outlining the facts of each case. Then each justice, beginning with the senior associate justice, comments on the case, usually indicating in the course of the comments how he or she intends to vote. A traditional but unwritten rule specifies that it takes four affirmative votes to have a case scheduled for oral argument.

Petitions for certiorari, appeal, and *in forma pauperis* that are approved for review or denied review during conference are placed on a certified orders list to be released the following Monday in open court.

Arguments

Once the Court announces it will hear a case, the clerk of the Court arranges the schedule for oral argument. Generally, cases are argued roughly in the order in which they were granted review, but that is subject to change, in the light of availability of appendices and other documents, extensions of time to file briefs, and other relevant factors. Cases generally are heard not sooner than three months after the Court has agreed to review them. Under special circumstances, the date scheduled for oral argument can be advanced or postponed.

Well before oral argument takes place, the justices receive the briefs and records from counsel in the case. The measure of attention the brief receives—from a thorough and exhaustive study to a cursory glance—depends both on the nature of the case and the work habits of the justice.

As one of the two public functions of the Court, oral arguments are viewed by some as very important. Others dispute their significance, contending that by the time a case is heard most of the justices have already made up their minds.

A number of justices have indicated that oral arguments serve a useful purpose. Chief Justice Charles Evans Hughes wrote that "the desirability . . . of a full exposition by oral argument in the highest court is not to be gainsaid" because it provides "a great saving of time of the court in the examination of extended records and briefs, to obtain the grasp of the case that is made possible by oral discussion and to be able more quickly to separate the wheat from the chaff."[11]

In 1967 Justice William J. Brennan Jr. said, "Oral argument is the absolute indispensable ingredient of appellate advocacy. . . . Often my whole notion of what a case is about crystallizes at oral argument. This happens even though I read the briefs before oral argument."[12]

Chief Justice Rehnquist has on occasion questioned the value of oral arguments, but he nevertheless has said, "I think that in a significant minority of the cases in which I have heard oral argument, I have left the bench feeling different about the case that I did when I came on the bench. The change is seldom a full one-hundred-and-eighty-degree swing, and I find that it is most likely to occur in cases involving areas of law with which I am least familiar."[13]

TIME LIMITS

Like many other aspects of the Court's operations, the time allotted for oral argument, as well as the atmosphere in which arguments were heard, have undergone considerable change over the years. In the early years of the Court, arguments in a single case often would continue for days.

For the spectators who crowded the courtroom, oral arguments provided high entertainment. In the nineteenth century women in Washington flocked to hear the popular and dashing Henry Clay argue before the Court. Arguments at least once were adjourned so that counsel could sober up. John P. Frank reported that one time a case was reargued so that a late-arriving woman could hear the part she had missed.[14]

The increasing number of cases heard by the Court made the continuation of such practices impossible. Under a rule the Court adopted March 12, 1849, counsel was allowed no more than two hours to present his argument. The two-hour allowance for oral argument continued until the early twentieth century.

In between his terms on the Court, Charles Evans Hughes wrote in 1928: "In the early period when cases were few, the Court could permit extended argument. At a more recent time, and until a few years ago, two hours was the regular allowance to each side and in very important cases, that time was extended. This allowance has been reduced to an hour, unless special permission is granted, and even in cases of great importance the Court has refused to hear arguments for more than an hour and a half on each side. This restriction is due to the crowded calendar of the Court."[15]

In 1970 the time allowed each side for oral argument was reduced from one hour to thirty minutes. The period for oral argument was reduced to save the Court's time. Since the time allotted must accommodate any questions the justices may wish to ask, the actual time for presentation may be considerably shorter than thirty minutes.

Under the current rules of the Court, as revised in 1995, only one counsel will be heard for each side, except by special permission when there are several parties on the same side and additional time has been granted. When cases were allowed one hour per party, the Court allowed two counsel to be heard for each side. Generally, the Court disfavors divided arguments.

An exception is made for an amicus curiae—a person who volunteers or is invited to take part in matters before a court but is not a party in the case. Counsel for an amicus curiae may participate in oral argument if the party supported by the amicus allows him or her to use part of its argument time or the Court grants a motion allowing argument by counsel for the "friend of the court." The motion must show, the rules state, that the amicus's argument "would provide assistance to the Court not otherwise available."[16]

Because the Court is reluctant to extend the time that each side is given for oral argument and because amicus curiae participation in oral argument would often necessitate such an extension, the Court is generally unreceptive to such motions. And counsel in a case is usually equally unreceptive to a request to give an amicus counsel any of the precious minutes allotted to argue the case.

Court rules provide advice to counsel appearing before the justices: "Oral argument should emphasize and clarify the written arguments in the briefs on the merits. Counsel should assume that all Justices have read the briefs before oral argument. Oral argument read from a prepared text is not favored."[17] On rare occasions, justices have been known to interrupt an attorney who was reading from a prepared text and called his attention to the rule. Most attorneys appearing before the Court use an outline or notes to make sure they cover the important points.

RECORDING THE ARGUMENT

The Supreme Court has tape-recorded oral arguments since 1955. In 1968 the Court, in addition to its own recording, began contracting with private firms to tape and transcribe all oral arguments. The contract stipulates that the transcript "shall include everything spoken in argument, by Court, counsel, or oth-

A CROWDED DOCKET, FEWER DECISIONS, AND A CONTINUING DEBATE

"Change is the law of life, in judicial systems as well as in other more lively areas of our affairs," Justice William H. Rehnquist declared a few months before he became chief justice in 1986. "And if the present difficulties in which the Supreme Court finds itself require additional change from its present role, such change should be regarded not as some strange anomaly, but instead as a very natural development following the path of other similar developments over a course of two centuries."[1]

Change had already come to the Court during Rehnquist's tenure there. When he was appointed in 1971, the Court's typical annual docket was about 4,000 cases. By the time he became chief justice, it was more than 5,000 cases a year. By 1996 some 8,000 cases were coming to the Court each term. The increased workload was one reason that the Court's first conference of the term was moved back from early October to the last week in September and that Wednesdays as well as Fridays became conference days.

A glance at the number of cases on the Court's docket over the years illustrates its growing burden. In 1803, thirteen years after the Court first convened, there were only fifty-one cases on the docket; seven years later, the number was ninety-eight. As the number of cases filed each year increased, Congress in 1837 created two additional circuits and added two justices to the seven then on the Supreme Court.

By 1845 there were 173 cases on the docket, and the number kept increasing. It grew to 253 cases in 1850, 310 in 1860, and 636 in 1870. A temporary increase in the number of justices to ten in 1863 and the creation of several more circuit judges in 1869 did little to stem the tide. In 1880 there were 1,212 cases on the docket and a decade later there were 1,816.

MORE AND MORE CASES

The Court of Appeals Act of 1891 had a dramatic impact on the caseload of the Supreme Court. The number of new cases dropped to 379 in 1891 and to 275 in 1892.

In the years that followed, however, Congress passed a spate of new laws creating opportunities for litigation, which consequently increased the Court's workload. There were 723 cases on the Court's docket in the 1900 term and 1,116 in the 1910 term.

Although the Judiciary Act of 1925 gave the Court considerable discretion in granting review and greatly reduced the number of cases meriting oral arguments, the number of cases on the docket continued to increase. There were 1,039 cases on the docket in 1930; 1,109 in 1940; 1,321 in 1950; 2,296 in 1960; 4,212 in 1970; 4,781 in 1980; 6,316 in 1990; and 7,922 in 1995.

The dramatic rise in the Court's caseload, particularly after 1960, was due primarily to the increase in *in forma pauperis* filings

and to congressional enactment of environmental, civil rights, consumer, safety, and social welfare legislation. Petitions *in forma pauperis* grew from 517 in 1951 to about 2,000 a year in the 1970s and 1980s, 4,000 in the early 1990s, and 5,422 in the October 1995 term.

Although the number of cases filed each year and the number on each term's docket have increased enormously, the number scheduled for oral argument has grown hardly at all. Indeed, between 1986 and 1996, the calendar shrank dramatically. As Rehnquist pointed out in 1986, the Court was hearing about 150 cases on the merits in 1935 and hearing about 150 cases on the merits in 1986. "The great difference," he noted, "is in the percentage of cases we are able to review as compared to those which we are asked to review. In 1935, there were roughly 800 petitions for certiorari, so that by granting and hearing 150 of them we reviewed somewhere between 15 and 20 percent of the cases . . . but for the past ten years, the petitions for certiorari have numbered more than 4,000; by granting review and deciding only 150 of those . . . we grant review in less than 5 percent of the cases in which it is asked."[2]

But when the number of cases dropped off in the next decade, Rehnquist said it was a natural byproduct of several factors. He noted that lower federal courts, which became dominated by appointees of Republican presidents Ronald Reagan and George Bush, were largely in accord with the Supreme Court, lessening the need to review many lower court rulings. Congress's removal in 1988 of virtually all mandatory jurisdiction also was a factor in the decrease, he said. The shrinking calendar was a topic of discussion among practitioners, Court scholars, and reporters. Rehnquist quipped in 1994 to a group of reporters that if the Court became concerned about the diminishing number of cases it heard, it had a solution: it would simply take more.[3]

FEWER AND FEWER CASES HEARD

The reduction in the number of cases granted review and resulting signed opinions was dramatic into the 1990s: in the October 1986 term the Court issued 145 opinions; in 1987, it issued 139; in 1988, 133; in 1989, 129; in 1990, 112; in 1991, 107; in 1992, 107; in 1993, 84; in 1994, 82; in 1995, 75.

Several of the justices have commented publicly about this decrease. Justices Sandra Day O'Connor and Ruth Bader Ginsburg both attributed the drop largely to the fact that the Court was no longer required to review certain categories of disputes. "The cutback in opinions doesn't mean that the Court is becoming a lazy lot," said Ginsburg in 1994.[4] At least two of the justices, O'Connor and Anthony Kennedy have expressed the view that the Court's caseload will level out at about 100 in future years.

ers, and nothing shall be omitted from the transcript unless the Chief Justice or Presiding Justice so directs." But "the names of Justices asking questions shall not be recorded or transcribed; questions shall be indicated by the letter 'Q.'"[18]

The marshal of the Court keeps the Court's tape during the term when oral arguments are presented. During that time use

of these tapes usually is limited to the justices and their law clerks. At the end of the term, the tapes are sent to the National Archives. Persons wishing to listen to the tape or buy a copy of the transcript can apply to the Archives for permission to do so. In 1993 the Court announced that the audio tapes would be available to the public on a generally unrestricted basis. Prior to

STUDYING THE PROBLEM

In the mid-1990s, the Court seemed content with the size of its calendar. But two decades earlier, there was concern that the gap between the number of cases on the docket and the number on which oral arguments are heard resulted in its neglecting many important cases.

Several study groups were established in the 1970s to investigate the matter. One, the Study Group on the Caseload of the Supreme Court, was set up by Chief Justice Warren E. Burger in the fall of 1971 and headed by Professor Paul A. Freund of Harvard Law School. Another, the Commission on Revision of the Appellate Court System, was set up by Congress in 1972 and headed by Sen. Roman L. Hruska, R-Neb.

The Court's study group issued its report in December 1972, declaring that "the pressures of the docket are incompatible with the appropriate fulfillment of [the Court's] historic and essential functions."[5]

To ease the burden, the study group recommended the creation of new court to be called the National Court of Appeals. This court would be headquartered in Washington and—except for cases involving original jurisdiction—be given jurisdiction to consider all cases now within the Supreme Court's jurisdiction. The National Court of Appeals would screen all cases coming to the Supreme Court, denying review in some, deciding some itself, and certifying the more important cases to the Supreme Court for disposition.

The Hruska commission likewise endorsed the creation of a new court of appeals in its 1975 report. But the function of the proposed new court had changed. Instead of sending cases on to the justices, this new body would decide cases of lesser importance referred to it by the Supreme Court.[6]

In 1982 Chief Justice Burger proposed a third alternative, the creation of a special but temporary panel of the then-new U.S. Court of Appeals for the Federal Circuit just to hear and resolve cases in which two of the other federal circuit courts of appeals disagreed. Like the earlier proposals, this idea met with mixed response—and no decisive action—from Congress. By the mid-1990s, as the Court had lessened its own workload, such proposals were no longer pressed.

1. William H. Rehnquist, "The Changing Role of the Supreme Court," Speech at Florida State University, February 6, 1986.

2. Ibid.

3. *Washington Post*, March 18, 1996.

4. *Washington Post*, August 21, 1994.

5. Report of the Study Group on the Caseload of the Supreme Court (Washington, D.C.: U.S. Government Printing Office, 1972).

6. Report of the Commission on Revision of the Appellate Court System (Washington, D.C.: U.S. Government Printing Office, 1975).

that, the oral argument tapes were available only to federal employees in connection with their official duties or to people doing "scholarly and legal research."

Transcripts made by the private firm can be acquired more quickly. These transcripts usually are available a week after arguments are heard. Those who purchase the transcripts from the firm must agree that they will not be photographically reproduced.[19] Transcripts usually run from forty to fifty pages for one hour of oral argument.

In recent years there have been many proposals that arguments should be taped for television and radio use. To date, the Court has shown little enthusiasm for these proposals.

USE OF BRIEFS

The Supreme Court rules state that "Counsel should assume that all Justices have read the briefs before oral argument."[20] The justices vary considerably in the attention they personally give to an attorney's briefs. In 1960 Justice Brennan wrote that "most of the members of the present Court follow the practice of reading the briefs before argument. Some of us, and I am one, often have a bench memorandum prepared before argument. This memorandum digests the facts and the arguments of both sides, highlighting the matters about which I may want to question counsel at the argument. Often I have an independent research made in advance of argument and incorporate the results in the bench memorandum."[21]

Nevertheless, an attorney cannot be sure that all the justices will devote such attention to their briefs. If the brief has been thoroughly digested by the justices, the attorney can use his or her arguments to highlight certain elements. But if it has merely been scanned—and perhaps largely forgotten—in the interval between the reading and the oral argument, the attorney will want to go into considerable detail about the nature of the case and the facts involved. Many lawyers therefore prepare their argument on the assumption that the justices know relatively little about their particular case but are well-acquainted with the general principles of relevant law.

The brief of the petitioner or appellant must be filed within forty-five days of the Court's announced decision to hear the case. Except for *in forma pauperis* cases, forty copies of the brief must be filed with the Court. For *in forma pauperis* proceedings, the party must file one typed copy with the clerk and send one typed copy to each of the other parties in the case. The opposing brief from the respondent or appellee is to be filed within thirty days of receipt of the brief of the petitioner or appellant. Either party may appeal to the clerk for an extension of time in filing the brief.

The form and organization of the brief are covered by Rule 33 and Rule 34 of the Court. The rules limit the number of pages in briefs, specifying that the major brief in a case, the brief on the merits, should not exceed fifty pages in length. Separately, Rule 24 gives general guidance on briefs, stating that they "shall be concise, logically arranged with proper headings, and free of irrelevant, immaterial, or scandalous matter. The Court may disregard or strike a brief that does not comply with this paragraph."[22]

In a 1974 case, for example, the Court declared that one party's brief did not comply with Court rules with respect to conciseness, statement of questions without unnecessary detail, and printing of appendices. Accordingly, the Court directed

Throughout much of the Court's history the justices have felt burdened by a heavy caseload, as depicted in this 1885 *Puck* cartoon.

counsel to file a brief complying with the rules within twenty days.[23]

Rule 24 sets forth the elements that a brief should contain. These are: the questions presented for review; a list of all parties to the proceeding; a table of contents and table of authorities; citations to the opinions and judgments delivered in the courts below; "a concise statement of the basis for jurisdiction in this Court"; constitutional provisions, treaties, statutes, ordinances, and regulations involved; "a concise statement of the case, setting out the facts material to the consideration of the questions presented"; a summary of argument; the argument, "exhibiting clearly the points of fact and of law being presented and citing the authorities and statutes relied on"; and a conclusion "specifying with particularity the relief the party seeks."

The rules also set out a color code for the covers of different kinds of briefs. Petitions are white; motions opposing them are orange. Petitioner's briefs on the merits are light blue, while those of respondents are to be light red. Reply briefs are yellow; amicus curiae, green; and documents filed by the United States, gray. All other documents should have a tan cover.

QUESTIONING

During oral argument the justices may interrupt with questions or remarks as often as they wish. In fact, in the 1990s justices' questions consumed much of a counsel's allotted half hour of argument. Unless counsel has been granted special permission extending the thirty-minute limit, he or she can continue talking after the time has expired only to complete a sentence.

The frequency of questioning, as well as the manner in which questions are asked, depends on the style of the justices and their interest in a particular case. Chief Justice Burger asked very few questions, as did Justice Brennan. Justice Clarence Thomas

has gone entire terms without asking more than one or two questions. At the other extreme, Justices Antonin Scalia, Ruth Bader Ginsburg, and Stephen G. Breyer have from their first days on the bench peppered attorneys with questions.

Questions from the justices may upset and unnerve counsel by interrupting a well-rehearsed argument and introducing an unexpected element. Nevertheless, questioning has several advantages. It serves to alert counsel about what aspects of the case need further elaboration or more information. For the Court, questions can bring out weak points in an argument—and sometimes strengthen it.

In 1928 Chief Justice Hughes wrote:

The judges of the Supreme Court are quite free in addressing questions to counsel during argument. The Bar is divided as to the wisdom of this practice in courts of last resort. Some think that as a rule the court will get at the case more quickly if counsel are permitted to present it in their own way. Well-prepared and experienced counsel, however, do not object to inquiries from the bench, if the time allowed for argument is not unduly curtailed, as they would much prefer to have the opportunity of knowing the difficulties in the minds of the court and of attempting to meet them rather than to have them concealed and presented in conference when counsel are not present. They prefer an open attack to a masked battery. From the standpoint of the bench, the desirability of questions is quite obvious as the judges are not there to listen to speeches but to decide the case. They have an irrepressible desire for immediate knowledge as to the points to be determined.[24]

It is politic for attorneys to answer the justices' questions immediately and directly. Several justices have made known their annoyance when informed by counsel that their inquiry will be answered later in the oral argument. Justice Robert H. Jackson advised in 1951, "never . . . postpone answer to a question, for that always gives an impression of evasion. It is better immediately to answer the question, even though you do so in short form and suggest that you expect to amplify and support your answer later."[25]

Anecdotes probably tell as much about the proceedings of the Court during oral argument as does any careful study of the rules and procedures. Perhaps the most famous story concerns Chief Justice Hughes, who was a stickler for observance of the time limit for oral argument. He is reported to have informed a leader of the New York Bar that his argument was over when the lawyer was in the middle of the word "if."[26] In the 1990s Chief Justice Rehnquist was equally concerned with punctuality, halting lawyers in midsentence when their time was up. When counsel would ask if he or she could complete the thought, the answer often was a firm "no."

Rehnquist's 1987 book, which characterizes the broad range of talent that appears before the Court daily, also relates his own experience at the lectern: "My adrenaline was up, and I sat like a greyhound in the slip waiting for my chance to begin. After the one argument I made before the Supreme Court of the United States when I was an assistant attorney general in the Justice Department, I was drenched with sweat."[27]

In the late nineteenth century when arguments went on for a full day, the justices occasionally left to have lunch behind a curtain in back of the bench when argument was particularly lengthy and inconsequential. Argument proceeded without the justices and amidst a clatter of china.[28] Justice Felix Frankfurter was renowned for treating counsel, as well as his fellow justices, much as he had his students when he was a professor. This annoyed many lawyers presenting arguments and was resented by other justices who complained about Frankfurter's professorial questioning and his pedantic, if erudite, lectures.[29] Justice Douglas was known to write opinions or articles during the presentation of oral argument.[30]

Conferences

Cases on which oral argument has been heard are discussed in conference. During the Wednesday afternoon conference, the cases that were argued the previous Monday are discussed and decided. At the Friday conference, the cases argued on the preceding Tuesday and Wednesday are discussed and decided. These conferences also consider new motions, appeals, and petitions.

Conferences are conducted in complete secrecy. No secretaries, clerks, stenographers, or messengers are allowed into the room. This practice began many years ago when the justices became convinced that there was a leak, a premature report of a decision. Suspicion focused on two page boys who waited upon the justices in the conference room. Despite the fact that the pages were later cleared when a member of the bar confessed that he had merely made an educated guess about the Court's decision in a particular case, conferences have henceforth been attended only by the justices themselves.

On Mondays and Wednesdays when the Court is in session, the justices meet in this conference room to discuss cases on which oral argument has been heard and to consider new motions, appeals, and petitions.

In 1979 the substance of an opinion—and even the identity of its author—were correctly reported in the press several days before its announcement. A typesetter assigned to the Court was then reassigned. *(See Inside the Conference Room, p. 86.)*

In the Court's early years conferences were held in the Washington boardinghouses in which the justices resided. The justices now meet in an elegant, oak-paneled, book-lined conference chamber adjacent to the chief justice's suite. There are nine chairs around the large rectangular table, each bearing the nameplate of the justice who sits there. The chief justice sits at the east end of the table, and the senior associate justice at the west end. The other justices take their places in order of seniority. The junior justice is charged with sending for and receiving documents or other information the Court needs. Justice Tom C. Clark, the junior justice from 1949 until 1954, once remarked: "For five years, I was the highest paid doorkeeper in the world."[31] Justice Stevens was the junior justice longer than any other member of the Court this century, having to wait from 1975 to 1981 for the arrival of a new justice.

On entering the conference room the justices shake hands with each other, a symbol of harmony that began in the 1880s. The chief justice begins the conference by calling the first case to be decided and discussing it. When the chief justice is finished, the senior associate justice speaks, followed by the other justices in order of seniority.

In theory, the justices can speak for as long as they wish. Even so, Chief Justice Hughes—impatient with long and occasionally irrelevant discourses during conference—convinced the other justices to limit the time they spent discussing a case. The record of the number of cases decided during Hughes's tenure as chief justice indicates that discussion and debate of the cases were considerably curtailed. As the number of cases considered during conference has grown, subsequent Courts have tended to follow Hughes's example.

Similarly, no one is supposed to interrupt the justice whose turn it is to speak during conference. But according to an often-repeated story, Justice Oliver Wendell Holmes Jr. did just that to Justice John Marshall Harlan early in this century. As Harlan was presenting his argument in a particular case, Holmes broke in with "That won't wash! That won't wash!" Chief Justice Melville W. Fuller allegedly relieved the tension with the remark: "Well, I'm scrubbing away, anyhow."[32]

Other than these procedural arrangements, little is known about what actually transpires in conference. Although discussions generally are said to be polite and orderly, they occasionally can be acrimonious. Likewise, consideration of the issues in a particular case may be full and probing, or perfunctory, leaving the real debate on the question to go on in the written drafts of opinions circulating up and down the Court's corridors between chambers.

Generally, it is clear—and often explicit—in the discussion of the case how a justice plans to vote on it. It takes a majority vote to decide a case—five votes if all nine justices are participating.

Opinions

After the justices have voted on a case, the writing of the opinion or opinions begins. An opinion is a reasoned argument explaining the legal issues in the case and the precedents on which the opinion is based.

Soon after a case is decided in conference, the task of writing the majority opinion is assigned. The chief justice assigns the task in cases in which he voted in the majority. In cases in which the chief justice was in the minority, the senior associate justice voting with the majority assigns the job of writing the majority opinion.

Any justice may decide to write a separate opinion. If he or she is in agreement with the Court's decision but disagrees with some of the reasoning in the majority opinion, he or she may write a concurring opinion giving the reasoning. If he or she disagrees with the majority, he or she may write a dissenting opinion or simply go on record as a dissenter without an opinion. More than one justice can sign a concurring or a dissenting opinion.

The amount of time consumed between the vote on a case and the announcement of the decision varies from case to case. In simple cases where few points of law are at issue, the opinion sometimes can be written and cleared by the other justices in two or three weeks. In more complex cases, especially those with several dissenting or concurring opinions, it can take six months or more. Some cases may have to be reargued or the initial decision reversed after the drafts of opinions have been circulated.

Writing opinions is often a long and tedious process but a highly important one. The way in which a majority opinion is written can have a tremendous impact on the lives of Americans. The impact of a particular opinion depends to some extent on who writes it, how it is written, and the extent of support of or dissent from the opinion by the other justices.

In 1993, when the papers of the late Justice Thurgood Marshall were unexpectedly made public at the Library of Congress, reporters gained access to numerous private memos and drafts of decisions. The *Washington Post* described the decision-making process revealed in the papers as "a continuing conversation among nine distinct individuals on dozens of issues simultaneously. The exchanges are serious, sometimes scholarly, occasionally brash and personalized, but generally well-reasoned and most often cast in understated, genteel language.... The months-long internal debate on a case often focuses on how much law to change or make. Sometimes, cases come right down to the wire.... In other cases, a majority of justices start down one path, only to reverse direction.... This is the kind of internal debate that the justices have argued should remain confidential, taking the position that only their final opinions have legal authority. They have expressed concern that premature disclosure of their private debates and doubts may undermine the court's credibility and inhibit their exchange of ideas."[33]

The assigning justice may consider the points made by majority justices during the conference discussion, the workload of the other justices, the need to avoid the more extreme opinions within the majority, and expertise in the particular area of law involved in a case. For example, the Court's landmark ruling on abortion was explained through a majority opinion written by Justice Harry A. Blackmun, who developed his expertise in medical law while in private practice, including work with the famous Mayo Clinic in Minnesota, his home state. Chief Justice Hughes sometimes assigned conservative opinions to liberal justices and liberal opinions to conservative justices to avoid giving any impression that the Court was divided along ideological lines.

The assignment of opinions can create morale problems among members of the Court. Justices have become annoyed and angered when not assigned to write opinions in cases of particular interest to them or directed to write them in routine, uninteresting cases. In 1898 Justice Harlan wrote to Chief Justice Fuller and complained: "Two Saturdays in succession you have not assigned to me any case but have assigned cases and important ones to Justice [Horace] Gray. I was in the majority in each case assigned to him."[34]

Rumors circulated about ill will between Chief Justice Burger and Justice Douglas. In a 1972 abortion case, Douglas was said to believe that Burger had abused his power by voting with the majority in order to assign the writing of the majority opinion, although, Douglas alleged, Burger's sympathies lay with the minority. Douglas threatened to file a scathing dissent on Burger's alleged misuse of the assignment powers but was dissuaded from doing so by his colleagues, who argued that the Court's reputation would suffer if the dissent were publicized.[35]

The style of writing a Court opinion—a majority opinion or a concurring or dissenting opinion—depends primarily on the individual justice. In some cases, the justice may prefer to write a restricted and limited opinion; in others, he or she may prefer a broader approach to the subject. The decision is likely to be influenced by the need to satisfy the other justices who voted with the writer.

The time spent to prepare an opinion varies from justice to justice. Justice Holmes was reportedly able to write an opinion over a weekend. Justices Hugo L. Black and Louis D. Brandeis were noted for reading widely on all aspects of a case before writing their opinions. Justice Frankfurter was a perfectionist who often prepared as many as thirty or more drafts for each opinion. On the contemporary Court, Justice Sandra Day O'Connor is known for her speed at producing opinions.

Justices use their law clerks to obtain and sift through the material needed to write an opinion. There has been speculation that some clerks actually ghostwrite a justice's opinion—or at least that justices sometimes tell a clerk what they want in an opinion and allow the clerk to write the first draft.

At the other extreme, Justice Douglas was said to give his clerks little or nothing to do in writing or organizing his written opinions. The traditional secrecy that surrounds each justice's office and work habits makes verification of such reports about the clerks' role in opinion writing very difficult.

CIRCULATION OF DRAFTS

The circulation of the drafts—whether computer-to-computer or on paper—provokes considerable discussion in many cases. Often the suggestions and criticisms require the author carefully to juggle opposing views. To retain a majority, the author of the draft opinion may have to make major emendations to oblige justices who are unhappy with the initial draft. Some opinions must be rewritten repeatedly before the majority is satisfied.

One illustration of the difficulty of writing a majority opinion is provided by Chief Justice Burger's problems in the case of the Nixon White House tapes. In mid-1974 the Court voted unanimously that the president must turn over the tapes sought as evidence in the Watergate "coverup" case, rejecting the argument that he could invoke executive privilege to withhold them.

After the decision had been reached, Burger assigned himself the opinion. To save time, he circulated the draft opinion piece by piece. The other justices were dissatisfied with what they were seeing. Many began writing their own version of the opinion. Burger, while annoyed, was forced to compromise. The final result, handed down on July 24, 1974, in *United States v. Nixon*,[36] was a rather unusual joint product, with a number of justices writing various parts of the final opinion. But, although a joint effort, the final opinion was issued in Burger's name.[37]

One reason for the secrecy surrounding the circulation of drafts is that one or more of the justices who voted with the majority may find the majority draft opinion so unpersuasive—or a dissenting draft so convincing—that votes may be switched.

If enough justices alter their votes, the majority may shift, so that what was a dissent becomes instead the majority opinion. When a new majority emerges from this process, the task of writing, printing, and the process of circulating a new majority draft begins again.

The papers of the late Thurgood Marshall reveal that in 1989, when Chief Justice Rehnquist was circulating drafts of his proposed majority opinion in an abortion case, *Webster v. Reproductive Health Services,* he was proceeding as if he held a majority (at least four other justices).[38] His draft opinion would have come close to overturning the landmark abortion rights decision *Roe v. Wade* (1973) and would have enhanced state legislatures' ability to pass laws restricting abortion. But shortly before the opinion was to be released, Justice O'Connor, who was the critical fifth vote, declined to agree with Rehnquist's attack on *Roe.* While the majority, including O'Connor, agreed to uphold the restrictive Missouri abortion law at issue, Rehnquist in the end lacked a majority for a major constitutional attack on abortion rights.

Similarly in 1989, Justice Brennan thought he had five votes in a racial harassment case that tested the breadth of a federal civil rights law. After the justices began exchanging draft opinions, however, Justice Anthony Kennedy decided he could not join Brennan's liberal view of the law and switched sides. Kennedy ended up writing the majority opinion concluding that racial harassment was not covered under the particular law at issue. The *Washington Post* reported of the exchange of memos found in Marshall's files:

The defeat did not sit well with Brennan. In an uncharacteristic display, he drafted a biting dissent attacking the Court: "The Court's fine phrases about our commitment to the eradication of racial discrimination . . . seem to count for little in practice."

Kennedy responded in kind, adding a footnote aimed at Brennan. Brennan, he said, "thinks it judicious to bolster his position by questioning the Court's understanding of the necessity to eradicate racial discrimination. The commitment to equality, fairness, and compassion is not a treasured monopoly of our colleagues in dissent."[39]

Those comments in draft opinions circulated among justices made it into Marshall's private papers but not into the final public version of the opinions.

When a justice is satisfied that the opinion he or she has written is conclusive or "unanswerable," it goes into print. In the past this process occurred at a print shop in the Court's basement, where the draft was printed under rigid security, with each copy numbered to prevent the removal of extra copies from the premises.

In the 1980s, however, new technology arrived at the Court; and the October 1982 term was the last in which the Court's opinions were set on hot-lead typesetters. Computerization of the Court's output began in 1973, when the Clerk's office began using a word processor for form letters. When an employee from the Clerk's office moved into Justice Lewis F. Powell's chambers in the mid-1970s, she convinced him to put in a similar word processor there. That was so successful that a pilot project was begun in 1978 to customize word processors to meet the Court's needs. In 1980 the first set of fifty-five terminals was installed for the drafting of opinions; soon some of the justices—Byron R. White and Stevens among them—were writing on computers. For the first year the system was used only for drafting opinions. But within several years, hot lead was dead and the draft opinions were circulated, revised, and printed on the computerized typesetting system.

THE TRADITION OF UNANIMOUS OPINIONS

Over the past few decades there has been considerable concern about the lack of unanimity in Court decisions and the frequent use of dissenting and concurring opinions. The chief argument in favor of greater unanimity is that it increases the authority of—and hence the respect for—the Court's decisions. Decades ago Judge Learned Hand wrote that "disunity cancels the impact of monolithic solidarity on which the authority of a bench of judges so largely depends."[40]

Such disunity actually has a long tradition, at odds with the relative harmony the Court likes to project. It was not until the fourth chief justice, John Marshall of Virginia, took his seat on the Court in 1801 that the aspiration toward unanimity became the norm. Before Marshall, each justice would announce his own independent opinion and the reason for it. These separate (or *seriatim*) opinions were the custom during the first decade of the Court's existence.

During Marshall's thirty-five years on the Court, the practice of *seriatim* opinions was largely abandoned. In his first four years as chief justice, Marshall delivered twenty-four opinions and the senior associate justice only two of the twenty-six handed down. The Court's ostensible unanimity was disturbed only once during these four years, by a one-sentence concurring opinion by Justice Samuel Chase in 1804.[41]

While Marshall's insistence on unanimity did much to dispel the early Court's image as a bickering and dissension-filled forum and to increase its respect and esteem by the public, it did not meet with universal approval. One of Marshall's strongest critics was President Thomas Jefferson, a Republican who often—and vociferously—expressed displeasure over the Court's decisions under Marshall, a Federalist.

In a letter to Thomas Richie, dated December 25, 1820, Jefferson wrote that he had long favored a return to "the sound practice of the primitive court" of delivering *seriatim* opinions. Of Marshall's changes, he wrote, "An opinion is huddled up in conclave, perhaps by a majority of one, delivered as if unanimous, and with the silent acquiescence of lazy or timid associates, by a crafty chief judge, who sophisticates the law to his own mind, by the turn of his own reasoning."[42]

THE TRADITION OF DISSENT

During the first decade of its existence, the Court followed the custom of the King's Bench of Great Britain in issuing *seriatim* opinions. Unlike the King's Bench, however, the Supreme Court delivered *seriatim* opinions in reverse order of seniority. The first case in which a full opinion was published was *State of Georgia v. Brailsford* (1792). The first opinion in the published record of that case was given by a justice who disagreed with the majority in the case.

The first real dissent, and most of the few other dissents to surface during Marshall's tenure, came from William Johnson of South Carolina, a Jefferson appointee. Soon after coming to the Court, Johnson delivered what amounted to a dissenting opinion in *Huidekoper's Lessee v. Douglass* (1805).

In a letter to Jefferson, dated December 10, 1822, Johnson complained about the adverse reaction to his concurring or dissenting opinions. "Some Case soon occurred in which I differed from my Brethren, and I felt it a thing of Course to deliver my Opinion. But, during the rest of the Session, I heard nothing but lectures on the Indecency of Judges cutting at each other."[43]

Under Marshall's successor, Chief Justice Roger B. Taney, dissent became more frequent. Unlike Marshall, Taney did not insist upon delivering the sole opinion for the Court and the use of *seriatim* opinions was even resumed.

Nevertheless, Marshall's tradition of unity continued for many years after his death. Until the early twentieth century, the

Court generally gave single opinions with only an occasional concurrence or dissent. Concurring or dissenting opinions were issued in only about a tenth of the cases decided in the middle and late nineteenth century.

While the increasing use of concurring and dissenting opinions after Marshall's death has been criticized, particularly during this century, it was, according to some observers, almost inevitable. Charles P. Curtis Jr., for example, has written that "if you require unanimity, you make compromise inevitable, in the Court as everywhere else. Compromise is as alien to the feelings of the judicial process as what Solomon offered to do with the baby was to the feelings of the mother."[44] Even Marshall, the high apostle of unanimity, filed nine dissents and one special concurrence during his thirty-five years as chief justice.

Dissenting opinions usually are defended by a recitation of cases in which a carefully reasoned dissent became, in time, the basis of a new majority opinion. But such turnabouts are infrequent. Justice Holmes, the "Great Dissenter," issued 173 formal dissents, but fewer than 10 percent of them had any impact on subsequent reversals of Court decisions.

A dissenting justice may hope that his dissent will convince a majority of the other justices that his opinion is the correct one or that a later Court will vindicate his views. A dissenting justice is able to avoid the process of revising and compromising his opinion that often faces the author of the majority opinion. The dissenter generally has only himself to please, a fact that makes many well-reasoned and well-written dissents more memorable or more enjoyable to read than the majority opinion.

The most frequently quoted defense of dissent on the Court was given by Chief Justice Hughes, who wrote, "A dissent in a court of last resort is an appeal to the brooding spirit of the law, to the intelligence of a future day, when a later decision may possibly correct the error into which the dissenting judge believes the court to have been betrayed."[45]

Hughes was by no means an unqualified advocate of dissent and is believed on a number of occasions to have yielded his dissent to join the majority without further argument. The words preceding his statement about "an appeal to the brooding spirit of the law" are probably more indicative of Hughes's feelings about dissent:

There are some who think it desirable that dissents should not be disclosed as they detract from the forces of the judgment. Undoubtedly, they do. When unanimity can be obtained without sacrifice or coercion, it strongly commends the decision to public confidence. But unanimity which is merely formal, which is recorded at the expense of strong conflicting views, is not desirable in a court of last resort, whatever may be the effect upon public opinion at the time. This is so because what must ultimately sustain the court in public confidence is the character and independence of the judges. They are not there simply to decide cases, but to decide them as they think they should be decided, and while it may be regrettable that they cannot always agree, it is better that their independence should be maintained and recognized than that unanimity should be secured through its sacrifice.[46]

A list of the "great dissenters" compiled by Karl M. Zobell includes those few who exercised dissent "in a manner which was—either because of a particular notable dissenting opinion, or because of the sheer weight of dissents filed—of historical or jurisprudential significance." According to Zobell, the great dissenters were:

• Justice William Johnson (1804–1834), who "did not choose to conceal his ideas when they differed from those of the majority." He wrote almost half of the seventy dissenting opinions filed while he served on the Court. Johnson differed with the majority most frequently in three areas: judicial versus legislative power, the sanctity of property, and the role of the states.

• Justice Benjamin R. Curtis (1851–1857), who "seldom dissented" during his six years on the Court. But his last opinion—a dissent in the case of *Dred Scott v. Sandford* (1857)—"was subsequently vindicated by the will of the people, and constitutional amendment; it is thus recalled as a landmark opinion in the history of American judicature."

• Justice John Marshall Harlan (1877–1911), a prodigious dissenter who delivered 380 dissents. He is most famous for his lone dissent against the "separate but equal" doctrine upheld in *Plessy v. Ferguson* (1896). "It was Harlan's lot to read the law differently from the majority of his brethren in numerous cases, only to have his views adopted by the legislature or by the Court years after his death," Zobell said.

• Justice Oliver Wendell Holmes Jr. (1902–1932), who "actually dissented less frequently during his tenure than did the average of his brethren—once in every 33 cases." But "Holmes' dissents had a way of later becoming correct expositions of the law, as defined by the court or as effected by the Legislature, not only more frequently, but sooner than did those of Harlan." The effect of Holmes on the use of dissent cannot be overestimated. During the so-called Holmes era, "Dissent became an instrument by which Justices asserted a personal, or individual, responsibility which they viewed as of a higher order than the institutional responsibility owed by each to the court, or by the court to the public."[47]

Other justices who almost certainly should be added to any list of great dissenters are Louis Brandeis (1916–1939), Benjamin N. Cardozo (1932–1938), Chief Justice Harlan Fiske Stone (1925–1946), Felix Frankfurter (1939–1962), William Brennan (1956–1990), and Thurgood Marshall (1967–1991). All served during a time of increasing Court division and dissension. Justice Stevens (1975–) has become a different kind of dissenter. Rather than standing apart from the others to protest their conservative or liberal ideology, Stevens often dissents because of his independent-minded, almost quirky, practical approach to cases. His opinion relies heavily on the facts of a situation, making Stevens over time one of the least predictable members of the Court.

CONCURRING OPINIONS

For those convinced that dissents damage the prestige of the Court and the impact of its decisions, concurring opinions are also distasteful. Concurrence is, in many ways, a variation on the *seriatim* opinions of the 1790s. A concurring opinion indicates that the justice who wrote it agrees in general with the majority opinion but has reservations about the way it was written, the reasoning behind it, or specific points in it.

During John Marshall's tenure as chief justice, dissents were often masked as concurring opinions. Justice William Johnson was a master at this, too, but he also wrote a number of concurring opinions supporting decisions of the Federalist majority but not the reasoning behind the decisions. In *Martin v. Hunter's Lessee,* for example, Johnson wrote in a concurring opinion: "I flatter myself that the full extent of the constitutional revisory power may be secured to the United States, and the benefits of it to the individual, without ever resorting to compulsory or restrictive process upon the state tribunals; a right which, I repeat again, Congress has not asserted; nor has this court asserted, nor does there appear any necessity for asserting."[48]

Modern day justices are more likely than their predecessors to write concurrences, explaining how their legal reasoning differs from the majority's approach. Such concurring opinions often are used to emphasize the limits of the majority's opinion or to address distinct concerns not embraced by other justices. As of 1994, Justice Stevens had written 265 concurring opinions, the highest number of any justice in history. Stevens, who was appointed in 1975 and still on the Court in 1996, also had the opportunity to add more separate opinions to his record.[49]

United States v. United Mine Workers, decided in 1947, provides one example of the problems and vexations accounting for and arising from the use of concurring opinions.[50] Chief Justice Fred M. Vinson and Justices Stanley F. Reed and Harold H. Burton voted against the United Mine Workers for two reasons. Justices Wiley B. Rutledge and Frank Murphy both dissented on the same grounds. Justices Frankfurter and Jackson agreed with Vinson, Reed, and Burton on one of the grounds but rejected the other. Justices Black and Douglas concurred with Vinson for the reason that Frankfurter and Jackson had rejected, but rejected the argument that Frankfurter had approved. The result was that five justices supported the decision for one reason, five justices supported it for another reason, and four justices were opposed for both reasons.

ISSUING THE OPINION

When the drafts of an opinion—including dissents and concurring views—have been written, circulated, discussed, and revised, if necessary, the final versions are printed.

Before computerization, final opinions were typed by the justices' secretaries and given to the printer in the Supreme Court building where they were kept under security. Now the whole process takes place internally in the Court's computer system, but security is still tight. Before the opinion is produced the reporter of decisions adds a "headnote" or syllabus summarizing the decision and a "lineup" at the end showing how each justice voted.

As the decision is announced in Court, the "bench opinion" is distributed to journalists and others in the public information office. Another copy, with any necessary corrections on it, is sent to the U.S. Government Printing Office, which prints "slip" opinions of which more than four thousand are distributed to federal and state courts and agencies. Copies of the slip opinions are available to the public free through the Public Information Office. The Government Printing Office also prints the opinion for inclusion in *United States Reports,* the official record of Supreme Court opinions.

The public announcement of opinions in Court is probably the Court's most dramatic function. It also may be the most expendable. Depending on who delivers the opinion and how, announcements can take a considerable amount of the Court's time. Opinions are simultaneously given to the public information officer for distribution.

Nevertheless, those who are in the courtroom to hear the announcement of a ruling are participating in a very old tradition. The actual delivery may be tedious or exciting, depending on the nature of the case and the eloquence of the opinion and the style of its oral delivery.

Differences between the opinion as actually spoken and its written counterpart, while of little legal or practical importance, can add a certain interest. Once, Justice James C. McReynolds allegedly became so agitated in delivering one dissent that he added, "The Constitution is gone."[51]

In this century, the Court has reduced the amount of time spent in delivering opinions. Before Hughes became chief justice in 1930, the Court generally read long opinions word for word. Early in the Court's history some opinions took days to announce. As the workload increased, this practice came to be regarded as a waste of the Court's time. Hughes encouraged the delivery of summaries of the opinion. The justice who has written the majority opinion now generally delivers only a summary, and dissenting justices often do the same with their opinions.

REPORTING OF DECISIONS

The importance—and difficulty—of adequately reporting Supreme Court decisions cannot be underestimated. Few people read the full Supreme Court opinions, and accounts in the news media often are superficial.

Justice Frankfurter was acutely aware of this problem. "The evolution of our constitutional law is the work of the initiate," he wrote in 1932. "But its ultimate sway depends upon its acceptance by the thought of the nation. The meaning of the Supreme Court decisions ought not therefore to be shrouded in esoteric mystery. It ought to be possible to make clear to lay understanding the exact scope of constitutional doctrines that underlie decisions."[52]

In a 1967 magazine article, Gilbert Cranberg of the Des Moines, Iowa, *Register and Tribune* quoted a columnist who described the Supreme Court as

the worst reported and the worst judged institution in the American system of government. . . .

The wholesale shunning of what the Court says leaves most of the country dependent on second-hand reports. It would be difficult to devise handicaps more devastating to an understanding of the Court than those that hobble news reporting of its rulings. . . . Where Congressmen, subordinate administrators and Presidents are frequently eager to explain and defend their policies, Justices of the Supreme Court emerge from isolation only to read their opinions. . . . No Justice is available to discuss or clarify the opinion he has written.[53]

Cranberg estimated that in 1967 "the total circulation of Supreme Court opinions is probably no more than 20,000. Most of the texts are located in forbidding legal libraries and inaccessible private law offices. . . . [E]ven many of the nation's attorneys do not actually read the court opinions."[54]

While total circulation of formal Court opinions is now considerably higher than it was in 1967, the psychological impediments to reading them are still there. As Cranberg noted, "poring over Supreme Court texts seemed about as inviting as an evening of wading through a technical manual. Indeed, the deadly, all-but-indigestible legalese I expected to find was there in abundance, but to my delighted surprise there was also a gold mine of information and often exciting, absorbing reading."[55]

Even as computerization has changed the way the opinions are drafted, polished, and produced, it has also made them much more accessible to interested persons across the nation. Several months used to elapse between the decision's release and its availability in the preliminary prints of the *United States Reports.* Today, opinions are available on legal databases, such as LEXIS and Westlaw, within hours of their release. In 1996 the Court was preparing to speed this process even more by electronically disseminating opinions. The system, which was scheduled to be in place in fall 1996, would make the Court's decisions available coast to coast within moments of their release from the bench. Copies of preliminary prints are sold by the U.S. Government Printing Office; the price of a bound volume depends on its length. Individual slip-sheet opinions are sold by GPO. Copies vary in price according to the length of the opinion. The opinions also are included in *The United States Law Week,* published by the Bureau of National Affairs, and *Supreme Court Bulletin,* published by Commerce Clearing House

News Media

Relatively few people make the effort or take the time to read the opinions of the Supreme Court, so most Americans must rely on the news media to learn what the Court has decided. Since the late eighteenth century, however, many—perhaps most—of the opinions handed down by the Court have not even been reported.

Efforts were made in the mid-twentieth century to improve media coverage of the Supreme Court. Justice Frankfurter played a considerable role in that improvement. As one of his biographers wrote:

Frankfurter's concern for public understanding of the Supreme Court took him into a long running fight with the *New York Times.* The press, Frankfurter believed, had a semipublic function and a semipublic responsibility. The *Times,* as the one documentary paper in the nation, should, he thought, furnish its readers the kind of competence in its reporting of the Supreme Court that it furnished in other fields. It should, Frankfurter was fond of saying, cover the Supreme Court at least as well as the World Series.

Beginning in 1933, Frankfurter barraged Arthur Hays Sulzberger, publisher of the *Times,* with letters in which he was outspokenly critical of its failings—and equally outspokenly congratulatory of its triumphs. Finally, in the mid-1950s, a young reporter and Pulitzer Prize winner named Anthony Lewis was sent to Harvard Law School for a year, then assigned to cover the Supreme Court. The *Times* expanded and deepened its Court coverage; a significant by-product of this development was the effect on other prominent newspapers which, encouraged by the *Times,* sought to improve their reporting of Court news and bring it up to World Series levels.[56]

Supreme Court justices long have felt that their opinions must speak for themselves and that efforts by the justices or by the Court's Public Information Office to explain or interpret the Court's opinions are unnecessary.

Nevertheless, the Court has taken a number of actions to make it easier for the news media to digest the written opinions in the limited time available.

These changes include:

• Announcement of opinions on days other than Monday so that the press would have a smaller list of cases to report on each day.

• The use of headnotes since 1970, which makes it easier for reporters to plow through hundreds of pages of written opinions.

• The availability of the *Preview of United States Supreme Court Cases,* a background analysis of the cases pending before the Court.

The *Preview* is published regularly, from September through April, by the Public Education Division of the American Bar Association. Prepared by law school professors and active practitioners of the law, it outlines the background, issues, and importance of all cases awaiting a final Court decision.

The Court's public information officer releases opinions to the news media shortly after they are announced. Many of the country's major newspapers and national news media have reporters on hand so that news in the Court opinions can be relayed quickly to their headquarters.

Other Channels

In addition to the formal and press reporting of Court opinions, there are a number of other, often impromptu, methods of publicizing its rulings. Various lobbying groups are not shy about speaking out on Court opinions that meet with their approval or provoke their disapproval. Decisions on issues such as school desegregation, prayer in the schools, capital punishment, and abortion always produce an avalanche of publicity from groups both supportive of and hostile to the opinions.

When Supreme Court justices were still riding circuit, they usually maintained strong contacts with people, particularly lawyers and local judges, in the communities they served. Through these contacts, they were able to inform community leaders about recent Court rulings and the legal principles on which those opinions were based.

In those days and at the present time, the legal fraternity also has provided a forum for discussing and clarifying Court opin-

SOURCES OF SUPREME COURT DECISIONS

PAPER SOURCES OF DECISIONS

The primary paper source for Supreme Court decisions is *United States Reports*, the official record of Supreme Court decisions and opinions published by the United States Government Printing Office.

This source can be supplemented by *United States Law Week*, published by the Bureau of National Affairs; *Supreme Court Reporter*, published by West Publishing Company; and *United States Supreme Court Reports, Lawyers' Edition*, published by Lawyers Cooperative Publishing Company.

ONLINE SOURCES OF DECISIONS

Using the Internet and bulletin board systems (BBSs), it is possible to read the full text of several Supreme Court decisions, listen to oral arguments from important historic cases, and receive alerts when new decisions are posted online. A number of Internet sites and BBSs offer Supreme Court information. Here are four:

U.S. Supreme Court BBS

Access method: BBS
Data: 202-554-2570

The U.S. Supreme Court BBS provides online users with opinions, calendars, order lists, an automated docket, and a booklet about the Court.

Opinions are available dating back to 1993, and the Court eventually plans to add opinions from 1992. They are available in both WordPerfect 5.1 and ASCII text formats.

The Supreme Court BBS posts opinions within five days after they are announced from the bench. The documents posted are the "slip" opinions, which contain page numbers so that users can cite them before they are formally published.

Cornell Law School Server

Access method: WWW
To access: http://www.law.cornell.edu
E-mail: lii@law.mail.cornell.edu

Although several Internet sites provide Supreme Court opinions, the Cornell Law School Server is a popular choice because it is so easy to use. It is operated by Cornell's Legal Information Institute.

Cornell offers the full text of all Supreme Court decisions from May 1990 to the present. Decisions are posted the same day they are released by the Court and can be accessed by using the name of the first party, the name of the second party, keyword, date, and other variables.

The site provides more than fifty historic Supreme Court decisions dating back to 1947. Some of the cases include *Regents of the University of California v. Bakke, Roe v. Wade, New York Times Co. v. United States, Tinker v. Des Moines Independent Community School District, Miranda v. Arizona, Griswold v. Connecticut, New York Times Co. v. Sullivan, Gideon v. Wainwright,* and *Brown v. Board of Education.*

The site also has the full text of the Supreme Court Rules, rule changes proposed by the Court, biographical data, and pictures of each current justice.

liibulletin

Access method: E-mail
To access: Send an e-mail message as described to listserv@lii.law.cornell.edu
E-mail (for questions): martin@law.mail.cornell.edu

The liibulletin is a free mailing list that alerts subscribers when new Supreme Court decisions are placed on the Internet. The list provides syllabi of new decisions, in addition to instructions about how to obtain the full text. It is operated by Cornell Law School's Legal Information Institute.

To subscribe, send an e-mail message to listserv@lii.law.cornell.edu and leave the subject line blank. In the message area type

subscribe liibulletin *your name, address, phone*

where *your name, address, phone* are replaced with your name, address, and telephone number.

Decisions can be requested by e-mail. To do so, it is necessary to note in liibulletin the docket number of the decision desired. Then an e-mail message should be sent to

liideliver@fatty.law.cornell.edu, leaving the subject line blank. In the message area type

request *96-161*

where *96-161* is replaced with the docket number of the decision desired.

Oyez Oyez Oyez: A Supreme Court WWW Resource

Access method: WWW
To access: http://oyez.at.nwu.edu/oyez.html
E-mail: j-goldman@nwu.edu

This site offers recordings of oral arguments from more than fifty historic Supreme Court cases dating back to 1961. The site is operated by Northwestern University, and the recordings are digitized from tapes in the National Archives.

To listen to the cases, one must have RealAudio software installed on a computer. Oyez offers a link to another Internet site where Real-Audio software can be downloaded for free.

Some of the Supreme Court cases available include *Planned Parenthood v. Casey, Hustler Magazine v. Falwell, Regents of the University of California v. Bakke, Roe v. Wade, Furman v. Georgia, Griswold v. Connecticut,* and *New York Times v. Sullivan.* The cases are indexed by date decided, party, and subject. For each case, the site provides recordings of oral arguments and text listing the attorneys who argued the case, the facts of the case, the constitutional question involved, the Supreme Court's conclusion, and how individual justices voted.

Eventually, the site plans to offer oral arguments from hundreds of Supreme Court cases.

SOURCE: Online sources are from Bruce Maxwell, *How to Access the Federal Government on the Internet 1997* (Washington, D.C.: Congressional Quarterly Inc., 1996).

ions through meetings of bar associations and publication of scholarly articles.

Traditions of the Court

Tradition plays a major role in the operations of the Supreme Court. The Court's insistence on the historic continuity of its procedures, and its strict adherence to conventions of secrecy and formal decorum, have yielded little to the changing moods and social patterns of the contemporary world outside its chambers.

At best, this overlapping network of traditions gives the Supreme Court an aura of substance, dignity, and caution that befits the nation's highest institution of law—and the public's confidence in the integrity, sobriety of purpose, and independence from outside pressure of its justices. But to some critics, much of the Court's tenacious adherence to its formal traditions of procedure and behavior reflect an anachronistic set of values that constrict the effective functioning of the modern Court.

Despite continuing efforts to streamline its procedures and find more efficient ways to cope with change, the Court remains the most traditional of the three major branches of government. Some traditional aspects of the Court seem merely quaint. The elevators in the Court building are operated by hand, and until the early 1990s, the justices employed a part-time seamstress to mend their robes. White quill pens are placed at each chair at the attorneys' tables in the courtroom on argument days, available for removal as mementos. While most lawyers no longer don frock coats and striped trousers to appear before the Court, male attorneys from the solicitor general's office still dress in the cutaways.

Other traditions are much more substantive and more controversial. Proposed changes in convention such as the mandatory retirement of justices or televising Court sessions continue to generate debate. No tape recorders are allowed in the chamber and visitors generally are not allowed to take notes of the oral arguments.

Even the more informal or irreverent of the justices have found the traditions of the Court of sufficient importance to observe and preserve them. Justice Frankfurter, for example, was a man who "brought a sense of informality and impish humor to the august tribunal. He would wave from the bench at friends among the spectators. He once escorted the child of a visiting Australian law school dean into the empty courtroom and let her sit on each of the justices' chairs.

When Mrs. Charles Fahy once came to court to hear her husband, the solicitor general, argue a case, Frankfurter teased her with this note scribbled from the bench: 'Anyhow—I'm for your hat!' He teased his own law clerks incessantly. He whistled in the marble halls, anything from 'The Stars and Stripes Forever' to the sextet from 'Lucia.'"

But "underneath the gaiety and banter there was a seriousness of purpose equal to anything Frankfurter had undertaken in his life. He approached the court with a kind of religious awe; he was indefatigable in guarding its traditions, and he felt, said Chief Justice Earl Warren, 'the burden of carrying on the traditions of the court more than any man.'"[57]

SECRECY

Among the Court's most important traditions is secrecy, which applies not only to formal deliberations but also to disclosure of personal disagreements and animosities among the justices. The unwritten code of secrecy has made the Court the most leakproof of Washington institutions. Nevertheless, there have been and continue to be occasional glimpses into its inner workings and conflicts.

The practice of allowing no one except the justices in the conference room began years ago with the mistaken impression that a page, secretary, clerk, or stenographer had leaked a decision. Subsequent leaks, including instances in 1973, 1977, and 1979, have moved the justices to take measures to prevent further premature disclosures or unwarranted gossip.

In addition to the rather infrequent revelations by an inquisitive press, justices and their law clerks have occasionally revealed something about the Court's inner workings and conflicts in their writings and speeches. Probably the three best-known examples were the use of the papers of Chief Justice Stone, Justice Brandeis, and Justice Thurgood Marshall.

When Stone died in 1946, his widow turned over all his files and papers to Alpheus T. Mason. In his biography of Stone, Mason revealed much of the Court's day-to-day operations, including feuds between liberal and conservative justices.[58] Alexander Bickel used Brandeis's papers to show the justice's contribution to Court solidarity, quoting Chief Justice William Howard Taft as saying of Brandeis, "He thinks much of the court and is anxious to have it consistent and strong, and he pulls his weight in the boat."[59]

Marshall's papers were made public by the Library of Congress within months of his death in 1993. The files covered Marshall's twenty-four years on the Court and showed the draft-by-draft evolution of opinions and the critical negotiations that occurred as individual justices—most of them still on the Court when the papers were made public—tried to win a majority in a particular case. A *Washington Post* series based on the previously secret information on the Court's deliberations prompted protest from Marshall's family and some of the sitting justices. They asserted that Marshall likely did not want his papers make available to the general public. But the Library of Congress maintained that the opening of the once-confidential files was part of an arrangement with him and refused to change the status of the papers.[60]

The justices believe they have good reason to maintain the veil of secrecy that surrounds their conference deliberations and their personal relations with other members of the Court. Widespread disclosure of what goes on in conference could reduce public esteem for the Court and its rulings. When leaks oc-

INSIDE THE CONFERENCE ROOM

An unusual and well-publicized leak from the Supreme Court occurred in 1979 when ABC-TV news reporter Tim O'Brien broadcast the results of two cases that had not yet been formally announced. On April 16 O'Brien revealed that Justice Byron R. White would deliver the majority opinion in an important libel case that would allow public figures offended by a report to inquire into the journalist's "state of mind."

Two days later the Court, with Justice White speaking for the majority, ruled that public figures could indeed look into the "state of mind" of a journalist and the editorial process when suing for allegedly libelous reporting. O'Brien also reported that during the conference discussion of the case, the justices became involved in an angry and vociferous shouting match about the decision.

On April 17 O'Brien reported that Chief Justice Warren E. Burger had written the opinion in a still unannounced case in which the Court ruled against the effort of prison inmates to expand their "due process" rights in parole hearings. After the two ABC-TV broadcasts, Burger was said by Court sources to have ordered an immediate investigation.

The Court made no public comment about the O'Brien reports, and O'Brien refused to reveal how or from whom he obtained the information. Within a week, however, it was reported that Chief Justice Burger had fired a typesetter from the Court's print shop. The typesetter, John Tucci, worked for the U.S. Government Printing Office in the Court's basement printing shop. Tucci, who would have had access to the opinion before it was released in Court, denied that he had leaked the information to O'Brien, but he was transferred to another job outside the Court.

Seven years later O'Brien once again broadcast the results of a decision *before* it was released by the Court. On Sunday, June 15, 1986, O'Brien reported on ABC News that the Court had voted 7–2 to strike down part of the Gramm-Rudman-Hollings deficit reduction law, and that the Court would issue its decision the following day.

The Court was expected to announce three decisions on June 16; only two were announced, and the Gramm-Rudman-Hollings decision was not one of them. It was three weeks before the decision in *Bowsher v. Synar* was announced, but the vote was 7–2, and the law was struck down.

a good idea to remind the justices that differences of opinion did not preclude overall harmony of purpose.[61] In court and in their written opinions, the justices traditionally addressed each other as "my brother" or "my dissenting brothers." On the contemporary Court, with two women justices, members refer to each other simply as "Justice." But the image of fraternal harmony is occasionally undermined by personal, ideological, and legal differences among justices with strong views and even stronger egos.

In his book on Justice Samuel F. Miller (1862–1890), Charles Fairman quoted Miller as having told a friend that Chief Justice Morrison R. Waite (1874–1888) was "mediocre" and that "I can't make a great Chief Justice out of a small man." Miller was equally critical of fellow justices Nathan Clifford, Noah Haynes Swayne, and David Davis. "I can't make Clifford and Swayne, who are too old, resign, or keep the Chief Justice from giving them cases to write opinions in which their garrulity is often mixed with mischief. I can't hinder Davis from governing every act of his life by his hope of the Presidency."[62]

More than a decade before his appointment as chief justice, President Taft indicated his distaste for some of the justices. "The condition of the Supreme Court is pitiable, and yet those old fools hold on with a tenacity that is most discouraging," Taft said in 1910. "Really, the Chief Justice Fuller is almost senile; Harlan does no work; Brewer is so deaf that he cannot hear and has got beyond the point of the commonest accuracy in writing his opinions; Brewer and Harlan sleep almost through all the arguments. I don't know what can be done. It is most discouraging to the active men on the bench."[63]

Once he became chief justice in 1921, Taft was far less publicly critical of the other justices. Still, Taft's efforts to control the disputes and acrimony among them "at times exhausted his supply of good nature, and he sometimes betrayed his own irritations by very sharp remarks in letters." One of these letters, written in 1929, when Justice Stone was being considered as Taft's successor, alleged that "Stone is not a leader and would have a good deal of difficulty in massing the Court." John Frank recounts how, when Stone was first appointed in 1925, "he was welcomed into the little extra-court meetings of the Taft bloc of conservative justices, and then, after a time, was dropped from those conventions when it appeared that he might be dangerously 'progressive.'"[64]

Perhaps the most publicized public airing of judicial antagonisms was the attack by Justice Jackson against Justice Black in 1946. Jackson had wanted and expected to become chief justice when Harlan Stone died. Instead, President Harry S. Truman nominated Fred Vinson; Jackson blamed Black for blocking his appointment as chief justice.

When Vinson was nominated, Jackson was serving as chief of a tribunal trying German war criminals in Nuremberg. Jackson responded to news of the appointment with a vitriolic letter to the Senate and House Judiciary Committees. In that letter, Jackson denounced Black for participating in a case in which, Jackson charged, Black should have disqualified himself. The case

cur, the Court refuses to confirm or deny their accuracy, and the justices are loath to reveal instances of infighting and conflict among themselves lest they demean the dignity of the Court and encourage further quarreling among the justices.

COURTESY

Both in and out of Court the justices seek to present an image of formality and courtesy. Before they go into the courtroom and at the beginning of their private conferences, the justices shake hands with each other. This practice began in the late nineteenth century when Chief Justice Fuller decided that it was involved the United Mine Workers, who were being represented by a former law partner of Black's, Crampton Harris. Unmentioned in the letter was the fact that Black and Harris had ceased being partners nineteen years earlier and had seen each other hardly at all since that time. Black did not reply to the charge, nor did he mention that he had disqualified himself in all cases involving the Federal Communications Commission because his brother-in-law was a member of the commission.

An earlier example of lack of judicial courtesy involved Chief Justice Taney and Justice Curtis in the *Scott v. Sandford* decision of 1857.[65] Nine separate opinions were filed in the case, with Taney speaking for the majority of the Court. Taney represented the southern point of view, and Curtis the northern, or abolitionist, side on the question of slavery in the territories. The chief justice made Curtis's dissent in the case far more difficult by allowing Curtis to see the other opinions before completing his dissent. Shortly after the opinions were released, Curtis resigned from the Court.

Justice McReynolds is often cited as a man whose lack of courtesy made life on the Court difficult for his fellow justices. McReynolds was appointed by President Woodrow Wilson in 1914 and served until 1941, but he was described by John Frank as "the total antithesis of everything Wilson stood for and . . . the most fanatic and hard-bitten conservative extremist ever to grace the Court."[66] McReynolds showed considerable antagonism to the more liberal members of the Court and particularly to the Jewish justices, Brandeis and Cardozo.

Frank noted that "far more striking than the Court's disputes over the years is the absence of personal friction among the judges, and the extent to which normal tendencies of irritability are controlled rather than exposed. When one considers how easily a bench of nine could march off in nine different directions, one's principal impression may well be not how often but how seldom this occurs. An instance of a McReynolds snarling in bare-toothed anti-Semitic hostility at his Jewish brothers on the Court is overbalanced by the real personal sympathy" among the justices. "This degree of respectful personal interrelations is by no means restricted to Justices who . . . were essentially like-minded."[67]

The desire of most justices to maintain these "respectful personal interrelations" has made outbursts like Justice Jackson's rare. Disagreements among justices are far more likely to be exhibited in subtler ways. A common method of criticizing another justice is to cite his or her words or previous opinions to prove the inconsistency of views on a particular issue or opinion. Jackson, for example, was fond of quoting the statements that Black had made when he was a senator from Alabama. Many of these criticisms are so subtle that they go unnoticed by everyone except those privy to the relationships between the justices.

On the modern Court, Justice Scalia is known for his brash style and confrontations with colleagues. Justice Powell's biographer wrote of Powell's reaction to Scalia when Scalia joined the bench in 1986:

Politically, Powell and Scalia were not so far apart, but personally they were like oil and water. Scalia's cheerful lack of deference rubbed his senior colleague the wrong way. His volubility struck Powell as bad manners. In Scalia's first oral argument he asked so many questions that Powell finally leaned over to Marshall and whispered, "Do you think he knows that the rest of us are here."[68]

Scalia is quick to take his colleagues to task for positions counter to his own, sometimes belittling their legal reasoning. When Justice O'Connor refused in a 1989 case to consider overturning *Roe v. Wade,* Scalia wrote, "Justice O'Connor's assertion that a 'fundamental rule of judicial restraint' requires us to avoid reconsidering *Roe* cannot be taken seriously" and deemed her approach in the case the "least responsible" of judicial options.[69]

SENIORITY

The system of seniority affects Supreme Court procedures such as conference discussion and voting, announcement of opinions, and seating in the courtroom. It is also a determining factor in assignment of office space. Only the chief justice is exempt from such traditional obeisance to seniority.

During conferences, discussion of cases begins with the chief justice and proceeds down the line of seniority to the junior associate justice. The junior justice has the task of sending for and receiving documents or other information the Court may need.

When opinions are announced in the courtroom, the justices who wrote the opinions announce them in reverse order of seniority. The chief justice is seated in the center of the winged mahogany table. The senior associate justice sits at his immediate right, and the second senior associate justice at his immediate left. In alternating order of seniority, the other justices take their places, with the junior associate justice at the far left of the bench and the second newest appointee at the far right.

Like the seating on the bench, the offices of the justices are assigned according to seniority. Because there were only six suites inside the so-called "golden gates"—the large bronze doors that seal the justices off from the public—the three junior justices usually occupy the offices on the corridor just outside. One exception to this rule was Justice Douglas who until 1962 chose to keep the office he had been assigned as the most junior justice when he came to the Court in 1939. Over the next twenty-three years, twelve justices with less seniority than Douglas moved to suites inside the door. In 1962, when Justice Frankfurter retired, Douglas at last decided to move inside the golden gates.

The suites were reconfigured early in the 1970s and now stretch entirely around the first floor of the Court. The offices occupied in 1996 by Justices O'Connor and Kennedy were originally offices for other purposes, converted into justices' chambers in a renovation during the 1970s. All the old chambers had working fireplaces, so fireplaces were added to these redesigned offices—but they do not work. When Justice Ginsburg joined the Court in 1993 she broke tradition and moved into an office on the second floor. She chose roomier, sunnier chambers so that all of her clerks could be nearby. She also said she was seeking a better atmosphere than she would have had in the smaller first-floor suite that was available.

CONTINUITY

Continuity is not merely an image that the Court seeks to perpetuate; it is inherent in the nature of the institution. The main factor in the continuity of the Court is that its justices are appointed for life, and for most members, that has been literally true. The majority of justices either have died while still on the bench or retired near the end of their lives.

Only 108 justices have been confirmed for Court service in little more than two centuries. (One—Edwin M. Stanton—died after confirmation before taking his seat on the bench.) None has been removed from the bench involuntarily, although several have resigned under pressure, and few have given up the prestige and accoutrements of the Court for another career. Just as change is central to Congress and the presidency through periodic elections, continuity is built into the Court through longevity of service. The average length of service of all justices of the Court, including sitting members, has been about fifteen years. More than half of them served for at least that long.

William Douglas served longer than any other justice in the Court's history. When he retired on November 12, 1975, he had been on the high bench for more than thirty-five years. Sen. Augustus H. Garland, D-Ark., reportedly told President Grover Cleveland, who wished to appoint him to the Court, that he thought himself unqualified because a justice should serve for at least twenty years and he doubted that he would live that long.

Turnover

The justices' long service on the Court is the most integral aspect of its continuity. With a new member added only every two years or so, successive Courts assume their own collective identity, as the same justices work together over the space of decades. Each new member, however different in ideology and temperament from his or her associates, can make only an incremental difference. A new member is influential as an instrument of change by a factor of only one-ninth—less so, in fact, given the deferential role imposed upon the newcomer by the tradition of seniority.

While it is customary to refer to influential Courts by the names of their chief justices—the "Marshall Court" or the "Warren Court"—such designations are somewhat misleading. Although the leadership and judicial ideology of each chief justice is without doubt a strong element in the direction "his" Court takes and the innovations it generates, the makeup of each Court is to a large degree fortuitous.

The chief justice, after all, usually inherits his associates when he takes office and does not himself choose replacements as vacancies occur—although his counsel may be covertly sought by a president. For the most part, a chief justice works with the associates he has been given, often nominated by a president and confirmed by a Congress of a different political persuasion from his own.

The Warren Court, for example, is considered the most liberal and activist of modern times. Yet its chief, Earl Warren, was a Republican appointee who took command of a bench manned entirely by eight veteran justices appointed by the liberal Democratic Roosevelt-Truman administrations. In subsequent years —although the Court absorbed four nominees of Warren's sponsor, Dwight Eisenhower—the Warren Court's membership also came to include four appointees of Democrats John F. Kennedy and Lyndon B. Johnson.

The direction of the Warren Court's successor—the clearly more conservative Burger Court—can easily be attributed to the judicial attitudes of its chief justice, Warren Burger, and the three justices named by President Richard Nixon. But it also encompassed three Eisenhower-Kennedy-Johnson holdovers and a moderate, Justice Stevens, appointed by Nixon's successor, Gerald R. Ford.

In other words, whether tending to be monolithic in its judgments or closely divided along liberal/conservative lines—or simply unpredictable—the membership of the Court is determined in large part by slowly evolving circumstances: by the political party in power as vacancies occur, by the length of time a Court has sat together, and finally by the durability of each justice, surviving changes in the Court and in the times.

Precedent

Another substantive factor in the Court's essential continuity is its reliance on precedent in arriving at decisions. Except in rare cases where there is no judicial opinion to be cited, any decision is based primarily on earlier relevant opinions of the Supreme Court or lower courts as interpreted in light of the case under consideration.

The most dramatic and far-reaching of the Court's decisions have been those in which a Court has arrived at a clear-cut reversal of an earlier Court's landmark opinion, especially where basic constitutional questions are involved. The 1954 decision in *Brown v. Board of Education* represented a watershed reversal of more than a century of earlier Court decisions in civil rights cases—decisions that the Warren Court, in effect, declared to have been unconstitutional.

But whatever the Court's decision—and it is far more common to uphold or modify an earlier Court's judgment than to reverse it outright—it is so rooted in precedent that it marks a further stage in a judicial continuum rather than an original judgment that stands on its own.

For some justices, precedent has been the only consideration. Justice Owen J. Roberts, for example, issued this scathing dissent in January 1944 when the Court overturned an admiralty case it had decided sixteen years earlier. "The evil resulting from overruling earlier considered decisions must be evident," Roberts contended. "The law becomes not a chart to govern conduct but a game of chance. . . . [T]he administration of justice will fall into disrepute. Respect for tribunals must fall when the bar and the public come to understand that nothing that has been said in prior adjudication has force in a current controversy."[70]

Justice Frankfurter joined in Roberts's dissent. Yet four years earlier, Frankfurter had this to say about reversing previous Court decisions: "We recognize that stare decisis [adherence to precedent] embodies an important social policy. It represents an element of continuity in law, and is rooted in the psychologic need to satisfy reasonable expectations. But stare decisis is a principle of policy and not a mechanical formula of adherence to the latest decision, however recent and questionable, when such adherence involves collision with a prior doctrine more embracing in its scope, intrinsically sounder, and verified by experience. . . . This Court, unlike the House of Lords, has from the beginning rejected a doctrine of disability at self-correction."[71]

NOTES

1. Supreme Court Rule 3.

2. Robert L. Stern, Eugene Gressman, Stephen M. Shapiro, and Kenneth S. Geller, *Supreme Court Practice,* 7th ed. (Washington, D.C.: Bureau of National Affairs, 1993), 3–4.

3. Charles Warren, *The Supreme Court in United States History,* rev. ed., 2 vols. (Boston: Little, Brown, 1922, 1926), II: 148.

4. *United States v. Nixon,* 418 U.S. 683 (1974); *Wilson v. Girard,* 354 U.S. 524 (1957); *New York Times Co. v. United States, United States v. Washington Post,* 403 U.S. 713 (1971); *Dames & Moore v. Regan,* 453 U.S. 654 (1981).

5. *Supreme Court Journal,* April 5, 1965, quoted by Stern et al. in *Supreme Court Practice,* 8.

6. John P. Frank, *Marble Palace: The Supreme Court in American Life* (New York: Alfred A. Knopf, 1958), 15. See also PL 100-352, passed in 1988, eliminating much of the Court's mandatory jurisdiction.

7. Supreme Court Rule 16.2.

8. 928 U.S.C. 1915.

9. Rules of the Supreme Court of the United States, adopted July 29, 1995.

10. William H. Rehnquist, *The Supreme Court: How It Was, How It Is* (New York: Quill, William Morrow, 1987), 265–266.

11. Charles Evans Hughes, *The Supreme Court of the United States* (New York: Columbia University Press, 1928), 62–63.

12. Quoted in Harvard Law School Occasional Pamphlet Number Nine (1967), 22.

13. Rehnquist, *The Supreme Court,* 276.

14. Frank, *Marble Palace,* 91–92.

15. Hughes, *The Supreme Court,* 61.

16. Supreme Court Rule 28.7

17. Supreme Court Rule 28.1.

18. Stern et al, *Supreme Court Practice,* 584.

19. Ibid., 585.

20. Supreme Court Rule 28.1.

21. William J. Brennan Jr., "State Court Decisions and the Supreme Court," *Pennsylvania Bar Association Quarterly* 31 (1960): 403–404.

22. Supreme Court Rule 24.6.

23. *Huffman v. Pursue, Ltd.,* 419 U.S. 892 (1974).

24. Hughes, *The Supreme Court,* 62.

25. Robert H. Jackson, "Advocacy Before the Supreme Court: Suggestions for Effective Case Presentations," *American Bar Association Journal* 101 (1951): 862.

26. Frank, *Marble Palace,* 92.

27. Rehnquist, *The Supreme Court,* 283.

28. Frank, *Marble Palace,* 93.

29. Ibid., 105.

30. Ibid.

31. Quoted by Richard L. Williams, "Justices Run 'Nine Little Law Firms' at Supreme Court," *Smithsonian,* February 1977.

32. Willard L. King, *Melville Weston Fuller* (New York: Macmillan, 1950), 290.

33. *Washington Post,* May 23, 1993, 1.

34. King, *Melville Weston Fuller,* 245. See also Bernard Schwartz, *Super Chief* (New York: New York University Press, 1983), 418.

35. Glen Elsasser and Jay Fuller, "The Hidden Face of the Supreme Court," *Chicago Tribune Magazine,* April 23, 1978, 50.

36. *United States v. Nixon,* 418 U.S. 683 (1974).

37. Elsasser and Fuller, "The Hidden Face," 50–57.

38. *Washington Post,* May 23, 1993, 1.

39. *Washington Post,* May 24, 1993, 1.

40. Learned Hand, *The Bill of Rights* (Cambridge: Harvard University Press, 1958), 72.

41. *Head & Amory v. Providence Ins. Co.,* 2 Cr. 127 (1804).

42. Quoted in Warren, *The Supreme Court in United States History,* I: 654.

43. Ibid., 655.

44. Charles P. Curtis Jr., *Lions Under the Throne* (Fairfield, N.J.: Kelley Press, 1947), 76.

45. Hughes, *The Supreme Court of the United States,* 68.

46. Ibid., 67–68.

47. Karl M. Zobell, "Division of Opinion in the Supreme Court: A History of Judicial Disintegration," *Cornell Law Quarterly* 44 (1959): 186–214.

48. *Martin v. Hunter's Lessee,* 1 Wheat. 304, 381 (1816).

49. Lee Epstein, Jeffrey A. Segal, Harold J. Spaeth, and Thomas G. Walker, *The Supreme Court Compendium: Data, Decisions, and Developments,* 2d ed. (Washington, D.C.: Congressional Quarterly, 1996), Table 6–10, 557.

50. *United States v. United Mine Workers,* 330 U.S. 258 (1947).

51. Frank, *Marble Palace,* 121.

52. *New York Times,* November 13, 1932.

53. Gilbert Cranberg, "What Did the Supreme Court Say?" *Saturday Review,* April 8, 1967.

54. Ibid.

55. Ibid.

56. Liva Baker, *Felix Frankfurter* (New York: Coward-McCann, 1969), 218.

57. Ibid., 216–217.

58. Alpheus T. Mason, *Harlan Fiske Stone* (New York: Viking Press, 1956).

59. Alexander Bickel, *The Unpublished Opinions of Justice Brandeis* (Cambridge: Harvard University Press, 1957), 203.

60. *Washington Post,* May 25, 1993, 1.

61. Mary Ann Harrell, *Equal Justice Under Law: The Supreme Court in American Life* (Washington, D.C.: The Foundation of the American Bar Association, with the cooperation of the National Geographic Society, 1975), 127.

62. Charles Fairman, *Mr. Justice Miller* (Cambridge: Harvard University Press, 1939), 373–374.

63. Henry F. Pringle, *Life and Times of William Howard Taft,* 2 vols. (New York: Farrar & Rinehart, 1939), I: 529–530.

64. Frank, *Marble Palace,* 76, 81, 264–265.

65. *Scott v. Sandford,* 19 How. 393 (1857).

66. Frank, *Marble Palace,* 45.

67. Ibid., 259.

68. John C. Jeffries Jr., *Justice Lewis F. Powell, Jr.: A Biography* (New York: Charles Scribner's Sons, 1994), 534.

69. *Webster v. Reproductive Health Services,* 492 U.S. 490 (1989).

70. *Mahnich v. Southern Steamship Co.,* 321 U.S. 96 at 112–113 (1944).

71. *Helvering v. Hallock,* 309 U.S. 106 at 119, 121 (1940).

CHAPTER 5

The People of the Court

Two hundred and seven years after the creation of the federal government, the Supreme Court is only nine people—the chief justice and eight associate justices. Even when the Court's supporting personnel are included, the numbers add up to hundreds, not thousands, of people.

The Court is not a bureaucracy, but an organization with well-defined jobs and responsibilities. That point remains valid even though the number of Court offices has grown. The clerk of the Court holds a position as old as the Court itself; the marshal's post is only half as old. The public information office has been a part of the Court for more than fifty years; the curator and the legal officer hold positions about two decades old.

The Chief Justice

The office of chief justice of the United States has developed in large part through the leadership, initiative, and inclinations of the men who have held the job. The Constitution mentions the title only once: "When the President of the United States is tried, the Chief Justice shall preside."[1]

The Judiciary Act of 1789 specifies only "That the supreme court of the United States shall consist of a chief justice and five associate justices."

Indeed, in the very early years of the Court, there was little indication that the title of chief justice would become so important and prestigious. As John P. Frank noted:

The great and yet intangible difference between the Chief and his Associates is the prestige that, rightly or wrongly, tradition attaches to the Chief Justiceship. Popular mythology makes the Chief Justiceship much of what it is, in part because there have been some very great Chief Justices whose personal glory has rubbed off on the office, and partly because of popular esteem for the very idea of "Chief."

Yet because of tradition, popular perception of the office, or other intangible factors, the chief justice is widely perceived as more than *primus inter pares,* or "first among equals." Although he casts only one vote in accepting and deciding cases, Frank pointed out,

his formal title is a trifle different: he is Chief Justice of the United States, and his fellows are Justices of the Supreme Court. He administers the oath of office to the President. He presides when the Court is in public session, and at its secret conferences. He also presides over the judicial conference of the judges of the lower courts, and he has the not inconsiderable duty of assigning the writing of most of the opinions of his brothers. He is the chief administrative officer of the Court.[2]

One of the five coathooks used by the justices when the Court occupied the basement of the U.S. Capitol Building (1810–1860).

FIRST AMONG EQUALS

The first three chief justices were not held in especially high esteem. The first, John Jay, came to the Court in 1789 and resigned six years later, on June 29, 1795, after concluding the peace treaty with England and being elected governor of New York.[3]

His successor, John Rutledge, had first been appointed to the Court in 1790 but resigned as a justice the next year to accept the post of chief justice of South Carolina. After Jay's election, Rutledge wrote to President George Washington that he would accept the chief justiceship "if you think me as fit as any other person and have not made choice of one to succeed him [Jay]."[4]

Washington immediately accepted the suggestion, and Rutledge was sworn in as chief justice on August 12, 1795. But before the Senate came back into session to confirm him, reports of

Rutledge's earlier criticism of the Jay Treaty provoked a storm of controversy. When the Senate returned in December, there were, in addition to that controversy, persistent rumors that the new chief justice was mentally unbalanced. Later that month, the Senate rejected the nomination, 14–10.

Washington next offered the chief justiceship to Henry Clay, but Clay declined the offer, as did Justice William Cushing. Washington then nominated Oliver Ellsworth, who served from 1796 until he resigned in 1800. President John Adams named Jay to succeed Ellsworth, but Jay refused to return to his old post, largely because of the onerous circuit duties imposed upon the justices. Adams then chose John Marshall.

John Marshall

John Marshall's great achievement was to increase public respect for the Supreme Court. When he became chief justice in 1801 the Court was held in low esteem, and its rulings, embodied in often unclear and confusing *seriatim* opinions, did little to enhance the prestige of the third branch of the government.

By his insistence on unanimity and the avoidance of dissenting and concurring opinions, Marshall—and, to a far lesser extent, his successor, Roger B. Taney (1836–1864)—gave the Court the prestige it needed to deal effectively with many of the conflicts and controversies facing the country. President Thomas Jefferson, who sought to break Federalist control of the Court, encouraged dissent but was successful only in his appointment of Jeffersonian loyalist William Johnson. Following the deaths of Justices William Cushing and Samuel Chase, Jefferson wrote to his successor, James Madison, in 1811 that "it will be difficult to find a character of firmness enough to preserve his independence on the same bench with Marshall."

According to Frank, a chief justice

must get his real eminence not from the office but from the qualities he brings to it. He must possess the mysterious quality of leadership. In this respect the outstanding Chief was Marshall, who for 35 years presided over a Court largely populated by Justices of an opposing political party. Moreover, his Court, because of the very newness of the Constitution it was expounding, dealt with some of the greatest questions of history. Nonetheless, Marshall dominated his Court as has no other Chief Justice. He wrote most of its important opinions, and his dissents are remarkable for their rarity. . . . More important, Marshall brought a first-class mind and a thoroughly engaging personality into second-class company. The Court when he came to it was lazy and quite willing to let him do the work.[5]

William Howard Taft

The only chief justice who had served as president (1909–1913), William Howard Taft came to the Court in 1921 and immediately embarked on efforts to modernize the U.S. judicial system. His greatest contributions to the Court came in his role as administrator rather than as judge or legal scholar.

Before winning the presidency and, later, joining the Supreme Court as chief justice, William Howard Taft *(right)* served as governor general of the Philippines and as secretary of war in the administration of President Theodore Roosevelt.

A year after his appointment, Taft succeeded in persuading Congress to establish the Judicial Conference of Circuit Court Judges—now the Judicial Conference of the United States—the governing body for the administration of the federal judicial system. *(See "U.S. Judicial Conference," p. 113.)*

More important to the Supreme Court was Taft's work in convincing Congress to enact the Judiciary Act of 1925. That law gave the Court—then suffering a severe backlog of cases—almost unlimited discretion in deciding which cases to accept for review. As a result, the caseload, at least for a time, became more manageable, and the Court was able to devote more time and energy to constitutional issues and important questions of federal law.

James F. Simon noted Taft's contribution as chief justice:

Some experts rate Chief Justice William Howard Taft as one of the Court greats, not because of his opinions, but because of his devoted efforts to reform an antiquated court system. . . . In his first year as Chief Justice Taft crisscrossed the country in a whistle stop campaign for reform of the courts. He spoke to bar associations, argued his case in legal periodicals and testified at length before the House and Senate judiciary committees. His efforts were handsomely rewarded the next year when Congress passed a judicial reform act that streamlined the federal judicial system by coordinating the activities of the far-flung federal districts and bringing them under surer executive control of the Chief Justice. That accomplished, Taft turned his attention to the problem of court congestion in the Supreme Court docket. "We made our preparations with care," he later said, "and it proved to be easier than we supposed." (Taft's reward was the Judges Bill of 1925. . . .) Before he was through, Chief Justice Taft's arm-twisting (he thought nothing of calling the chairman of the judiciary committee or even talking to the president about his reforms) had succeeded in winning the Court its first permanent home—the present Supreme Court building.[6]

Charles Evans Hughes

Another great chief justice, Charles Evans Hughes, called attention to the "personality and character" of the office before he assumed it in 1930:

The Chief Justice as the head of the Court has an outstanding position, but in a small body of able men with equal authority in the making of decisions, it is evident that his actual influence will depend upon the strength of his character and the demonstration of his ability in the intimate relations of the judges. It is safe to say that no member of the Supreme Court is under any illusion as to the mental equipment of his brethren. Constant and close association discloses the strength and exposes the weaknesses of each. Courage of conviction, sound learning, familiarity with precedents, exact knowledge due to painstaking study of the cases under consideration cannot fail to command that profound respect which is always yielded to intellectual power conscientiously applied. That influence can be exerted by any member of the Court, whatever his rank in order of precedence.[7]

Hughes served as an associate justice from 1910 to 1916 under the often indecisive, occasionally rambling Chief Justice Edward D. White. During those years, Hughes became acutely aware of the need for leadership by a chief justice in conference discussions and in the assignment of opinions. He also came to appreciate the value of harmony among the nine justices.

Years after Hughes's death, former justice Owen J. Roberts described Hughes as "the greatest of a great line of Chief Justices." During conferences, Roberts said, "his presentation of the facts of a case was full and impartial. His summary of the legal questions arising out of the facts was equally complete, dealing with opposing contentions so as to make them stand out clearly. . . . After the Chief Justice had finished his statement of the case and others took up the discussion, I have never known him to interrupt or to get into an argument with the Justice who was speaking. He would wait until the discussion had closed and then briefly and succinctly call attention to the matters developed in the discussion as to which he agreed or disagreed, giving his reasons."[8]

During oral argument and in assigning opinions, Hughes was said to show similar control and consideration. Counsel who were nervous or long-winded were often saved by a simple question from Hughes that sought to clarify or rephrase arguments they had presented poorly. "I know of no instance," Justice Roberts said, "where a lawyer had reason to feel rebuked or hurt by anything the Chief Justice said or did."[9]

Hughes described the assigning of opinions as "my most delicate task. . . . I endeavored to do this with due regard to the feelings of the senior Justices and to give each Justice the same proportion of important cases while at the same time equalizing so far as possible the burden of work. Of course, in making assignments I often had in mind the special fitness of a Justice for writing in the particular case."[10]

In assigning opinions, Hughes also tried to avoid extreme points of view and let the centrist view prevail. As Merlo Pusey pointed out in his study of Hughes, "When a Justice with a reputation as a liberal voted with the majority on the conservative side of a question, he usually got the opinion to write. The same was true in the case of a conservative voting on the liberal side. Hughes' constant effort was to enhance public confidence in the entire Court as an independent and impartial tribunal."[11]

Hughes also could be considerate in more personal ways. When he had voted with the majority at the Saturday conference, he usually had the opinion-writing assignment delivered to the appropriate justice that same night. Knowing that Justice Benjamin Cardozo, who had suffered a heart attack before coming to the Court in 1932, would begin work on an assignment immediately after getting it, Hughes delayed the delivery of Cardozo's assignments until Sunday. And—so that Cardozo would not be aware of this practice—he also delayed delivering the assignments to Justice Willis Van Devanter, who lived in the same apartment house as Cardozo. Similar tact was used when the other justices gave Hughes "the highly unpleasant duty" of asking for the resignation of the ninety-year-old Justice Oliver Wendell Holmes Jr.

Earl Warren

Chief Justice Earl Warren was nominated by President Dwight D. Eisenhower in October 1953 and confirmed unanimously by the Senate March 1, 1954. Three days after Warren's confirmation, columnist James Reston of the *New York Times* wrote that the new chief justice appeared to display "an ability to concentrate on the concrete; a capacity to do his homework; a

EARL WARREN AND THE *BROWN* DECISION

Chief Justice Earl Warren's personal qualities and his amiable relationship with the other justices played a major role in the Court's unanimous ruling in *Brown v. Board of Education.* That landmark decision, written by Warren and handed down May 17, 1954, declared racial segregation in public schools inherently discriminatory and therefore in contravention of the equal protection clause of the Fourteenth Amendment.

The *Brown* decision was a catalyst for the civil rights revolution of the late 1950s and 1960s. The opinion doubtless would have been far less important and far-reaching had it not been unanimous. Had there been dissenting or concurring opinions, the impact of the decision would have been reduced, and opponents of desegregation would have been given the opening to challenge the decision. Warren's achievement in securing unanimity was remarkable in itself. Equally remarkable was the fact that he had been chief justice only a few months when the decision was handed down.

In his book on the *Brown* decision, Richard Kluger wrote that

some time between late February and late March, the Court voted at one of its Saturday conferences on the school-segregation cases. The date is in doubt because the justices had agreed that the case was of such magnitude that no word ought to leak out before the decision was announced. . . . The vote was apparently eight to strike down segregation and one, Reed, to uphold it. But it was far from certain whether Jackson was going to file a separate concurrence or whether Frankfurter might or whether the two of them might agree on one. . . . Warren, of course, wished to avoid concurring opinions; the fewer voices with which the Court spoke, the better. And he did not give up his hope that Stanley Reed, in the end, would abandon his dissenting position. The Chief assigned himself the all-important task of writing the majority opinion.

On March 30 Justice Jackson suffered a serious heart attack. It was suspected that Jackson, along with Frankfurter, might issue a concurring opinion in the case.

Warren, who had been working on the majority opinion, did not circulate his draft until May 7. Justices Burton, Black, Douglas, Minton, and Clark responded quickly and enthusiastically, making only a few minor suggestions for change.

"It was with the three remaining members of the Court [Frankfurter, Jackson, Reed] that Warren could have anticipated problems: any of them might still choose to write his own opinion," Kluger wrote. But Frankfurter "had from the beginning been working for a unified Court. Nothing could have been worse, for the

Court or the nation itself, than a flurry of conflicting opinions that would confuse and anger the American people. So long as the Chief was willing to fashion his opinion in a frank, carefully modulated way, Frankfurter had intended to go along." Warren's draft apparently met with Frankfurter's approval.

"Warren personally delivered his draft opinions to Jackson's hospital room and left them for the ailing Justice to study." After having his clerk, Barrett Prettyman, read the draft, Jackson "was willing to settle for one whose principal virtue seemed to be its temperate tone." Prettyman was quoted by Kluger as saying that the "genius of the Warren opinion was that it was so simple and unobtrusive. [Warren] had come from political life and had a keen sense of what you could say in this opinion without getting everybody's back up. His opinion took the sting off the decision, it wasn't accusatory, and it didn't pretend that the Fourteenth Amendment was more helpful than the history suggested—he didn't equivocate on that point."

Justice Reed then remained the only holdout. According to Kluger, Reed's position on the *Brown* case "stemmed from a deeply held conviction that the nation had been taking big strides in race relations and that the Court's decision to outlaw separate schools threatened to impede that march, if not halt it altogether." Warren met many times with Reed and, according to Reed's clerk, George Mickum, had this to say in one of their last meetings: "Stan, you're all by yourself in this now. You've got to decide whether it's really the best thing for the country."

Warren, according to Mickum, "was not particularly eloquent and certainly not bombastic. Throughout, the chief justice was quite low-key and very sensitive to the problems that the decision would present to the South. He empathized with Justice Reed's concern. But he was quite firm on the Court's need for unanimity on a matter of this sensitivity." Mickum added that "I really think he [Reed] was really troubled by the possible consequences of his position. Because he was a Southerner, even a lone dissent by him would give a lot of people a lot of grist for making trouble. For the good of the country, he put aside his own basis for dissent." At a conference on May 15, the justices at last accepted—unanimously—Warren's opinion in the *Brown* case.

SOURCES: Richard Kluger, *Simple Justice: Brown v. Board of Education and Black America's Struggle for Equality* (New York: Alfred A. Knopf, 1976); Bernard Schwartz, *Super Chief: Earl Warren and His Supreme Court, A Judicial Biography* (New York: New York University Press, 1983), chap. 3.

sensitive, friendly manner, wholly devoid of pretense, and a self-command and natural dignity so useful in presiding over the court."[12]

Warren's affability and low-key persuasiveness—as much as the liberal affinities of the associate justices he inherited from Democratic presidents—were responsible for leading the Supreme Court into a revolutionary era of ideological decision making. *Brown v. Board of Education*[13] and other opinions of the Warren era were catalysts of social reform. They also unleashed a storm of protest from those who feared expanding the rights of blacks, the poor, criminals, and the underprivileged.

Despite his amiable relationships with his fellow justices, Warren could show a gritty leadership. On two occasions in early 1961, Warren publicly rebuked senior justice Felix Frankfurter for expanding his written opinion as he announced it in open court and for lecturing the other justices when he delivered a dissenting opinion.

Such rebukes were only the superficial signals of the deep differences between Warren and Frankfurter concerning the proper posture for the Court. Warren espoused an activist role; Frankfurter a restrained one.

Upon his retirement, Warren cited the Court's 1962 decision

in *Baker v. Carr* as the most significant of his tenure; Frankfurter wrote one of his most often quoted dissents in that case, which was announced just two weeks before a stroke ended his judicial career.

Marshall, Hughes, and Warren are generally considered the three greatest chief justices in American history. In his study of the office, Robert J. Steamer pointed out that despite dissimilar backgrounds and temperaments, these three men shared certain traits, chief among them a willingness "to stretch judging—in different degrees—to accommodate their own convictions."

"They were serious men who did not take themselves seriously," Steamer continued, but "perhaps most important, all were straightforward, moral men, personally, professionally, and publicly uncorruptible. . . . None of them was a scheming, petty politician; none was an aggressive office seeker."[14]

"Warren," Steamer wrote, "was neither scholar nor lawyer preeminent, but no matter; he created an ambiance that was to give the Court a unique and exciting character. . . . Under Earl Warren's leadership the Supreme Court became the refuge for those who had been ignored by the president, the Congress, and by governors and state legislatures, with mixed consequences both for the future of constitutional law and for the future of the nation."[15]

HEAD OF THE JUDICIAL SYSTEM

In addition to duties on the Supreme Court, the chief justice serves as chairman of the Judicial Conference of the United States and of the Board of the Federal Judicial Center and supervises the Administrative Office of the United States Courts. Chief Justice Burger estimated that he spent about a third of his time on administrative tasks that did not directly involve the other justices.

The Judicial Conference of the United States, the body that governs administration of the federal judicial system, was set up in 1922 by Chief Justice Taft. A former lower court judge as well as a former president, Taft felt the federal judiciary needed a forum for coordination.

The conference consists of the chief justice, its chairman, and twenty-six members—the thirteen chief judges of the U.S. courts of appeal, a district court judge elected by his or her peers in each of the twelve geographic circuits, and the chief judge of the Court of International Trade.

The Federal Judicial Center was created by Congress in 1967 as a research, training, and planning arm of the federal judiciary. Headquartered in Washington, D.C., its seven-member board meets four times a year. It was in his capacity as chairman of the Federal Judicial Center that Chief Justice Burger established the Study Group on the Caseload of the Supreme Court in 1972. (*See "Federal Judicial Center," pp. 113–114.*)

The Administrative Office of the U.S. Courts serves as the "housekeeper" and statistician for the federal court system. It was established by Congress in 1939 to take over the administrative duties that had been performed by the attorney general's office.

EXTRAJUDICIAL ROLES

The Constitution gives justices of the Supreme Court no other duty than to serve as justices and the chief justice no other duty than to preside over Senate impeachment proceedings. Congress, however, has given chief justices numerous additional tasks. For example, Congress has made the chief justice a member of the Board of Regents of the Smithsonian Institution and a member of the Board of Trustees of the National Gallery of Art and of the Joseph H. Hirshhorn Museum and Sculpture Garden, in addition to heading the Supreme Court and the federal judicial system. In addition, some chief justices have voluntarily assumed nonjudicial roles that have engendered some controversy.

Political Involvement

One reason why chief justices have taken on nonjudicial tasks may be that so many of them were prominent in politics and retained an activist political temperament upon assuming command of the High Court. John Marshall, Roger Taney, Salmon P. Chase, Charles Evans Hughes, Harlan Fiske Stone, and Fred M. Vinson had been cabinet members. Taft had been president. Edward White had been a U.S. senator. Earl Warren had been governor of California. In fact, only two chief justices have come essentially from the bar: Morrison R. Waite (1874–1888) and Melville W. Fuller (1888–1910).

Advising the President

During his first term, President Washington, without judicial advisers of his own, sent the Court twenty-nine questions on international law and treaties. At the time Washington was trying to keep the new country out of the war between Britain and France. The Court refused to give advice, maintaining that the Constitution gave them no authority to share executive power or to issue advisory opinions to a president. Nevertheless, as Chief Justice Burger pointed out, "Although the members of the first Supreme Court wisely resisted President Washington's request for advisory opinions and declined to perform other functions which they deemed to be executive in nature, there is little doubt that Chief Justice Jay gave advice to Washington over the dinner table and even in writing."[16]

Diplomatic Missions

Jay did more for President Washington than just that. During his first six months as chief justice, he also served as secretary of state. At the president's request, Jay undertook a successful diplomatic mission to Great Britain in 1794 to try to patch up quarrels over British troops in the American Northwest and private debts to British creditors.

The Jay Treaty, which the chief justice negotiated during the visit, may have prevented another war between Britain and the United States, but it involved Jay and the Court in partisan controversy. (So did Jay's subsequent decision to run for governor of New York while still chief justice.)

Although the Senate, 18–8, confirmed Jay's nomination as

envoy to Britain on April 19, 1794, there were strenuous objections to his accepting the post while serving as chief justice. During three days of Senate debate on the nomination, a resolution was offered that maintained that "to permit Judges of the Supreme Court to hold at the same time any other office of employment emanating from and holden at the pleasure of the Executive is contrary to the spirit of the Constitution and as tending to expose them to the influence of the Executive, is mischievous and impolitic."

Similar, but more subdued, criticism befell Jay's successor Oliver Ellsworth for accepting President John Adams's appointment as envoy to France in early 1799.

Chief Justice Stone referred to the impact on the Court of the Jay and Ellsworth missions in a letter to President Franklin D. Roosevelt on July 20, 1942. "We must not forget that it is the judgment of history that two of my predecessors, Jay and Ellsworth, failed in the obligation of their office and impaired their legitimate influence by participation in executive action in the negotiation of treaties," Stone wrote. "True, they repaired their mistake in part by resigning their commissions before resuming their judicial duties, but it is not by mere chance that every chief justice since has confined his activities strictly to the performance of his judicial duties."[17]

Investigatory Commissions

Stone's letter to Roosevelt was written in response to the president's suggestion that the chief justice conduct an investigation into the uses of rubber during World War II. Stone declined the offer, saying, "I cannot rightly yield to my desire to render for you a service which as a private citizen I should not only feel bound to do but one which I should undertake with zeal and enthusiasm."

Stone's main reason for rejecting the assignment was that "a judge and especially the Chief Justice cannot engage in political debate or make public defense of his acts. When his action is judicial he may always rely upon the support of the defined record upon which his action is based and of the opinion in which he and his associates unite as stating the grounds for decision. But when he participates in the action of the executive or legislative departments of government he is without those supports. He exposes himself to attack and indeed invites it, which because of his peculiar situation, inevitably impairs his value as a judge and the appropriate influence of his office."[18]

Chief Justice Warren proved more willing to accept a nonjudicial public duty after the assassination of President John F. Kennedy in 1963. But, for heading the Warren Commission, which investigated and reported upon the assassination, he was subjected to considerable criticism. Justice Frankfurter, who had retired in 1962, made little secret of his opposition to the chief justice's participation on the Warren Commission. Frankfurter predicted that as a result of Warren's participation in what was primarily a political investigation, the Court would suffer a considerable loss of public respect.[19]

PERQUISITES

The chief justice has a number of special perquisites. In addition to an annual salary of $171,500 (in 1996) and the attention and respect that surrounds the office, the chief justice also can have up to four law clerks, three secretaries, and a messenger. The chief justice is also provided with a car and driver, paid for by the government.

In 1972 Congress authorized the chief justice to "appoint an Administrative Assistant who shall serve at the pleasure of the Chief Justice and shall perform such duties as may be assigned to him by the Chief Justice." The statute authorizing the appointment of an administrative assistant says nothing about the functions and duties of such a position; it is left to the chief justice to determine how and in what areas he will work.

Both Burger and William H. Rehnquist had their administrative assistants operate in areas outside the chief justice's judicial functions. The administrative assistants provided research and analysis for the justices' speeches, monitored literature and developments in judicial administration, and helped with internal matters such as preparation of the court budget.

The Justices

From 1790 until 1996, only 108 individuals have served as Supreme Court justices. On average, a new justice joins the Court every twenty-two months. Every president who has served a full term or more, except Jimmy Carter, has made at least one appointment. That so few justices have served is due to the fact that justices are appointed for life; most of them are loath to give up a position of such prestige and influence.

Another factor in the low turnover has been the fact that the Court has remained the same size since 1869. In the Judiciary Act of 1789, Congress established the number of justices, including the chief justice, at six. The Circuit Court Act of 1801, enacted one month before President John Adams's term expired, reduced the number to five, to prevent the newly elected president, Thomas Jefferson, from filling any vacancies. Congress in 1802 repealed the 1801 law, bringing the number of Supreme Court justices back to six.

The Judiciary Act of 1807 increased the number to seven, primarily because of the increasing judicial work. In 1837 Congress added two new seats, bringing the number to nine, the size it has remained ever since, except during the Civil War period. The Judiciary Act of 1863 increased the number of justices to ten, but in 1866 Congress cut the Court's size down to seven to prevent President Andrew Johnson from filling vacancies with appointees who would reflect his views about the unconstitutionality of Reconstruction legislation.

The last adjustment in Court size came with the Judiciary Act of 1869, which increased it to nine seats. The act mandated "That the Supreme Court of the United States shall hereafter consist of the Chief Justice of the United States and eight associate justices, any six of whom shall constitute a quorum; and for

The Royal Exchange, New York City, first home of the U.S. Supreme Court

the purposes of this act there shall be appointed an additional associate justice of said court."

The last major effort to change the number of members on the Court was President Roosevelt's aborted "Court-packing" attempt in 1937 to add justices who ostensibly would be more sympathetic to his New Deal legislative proposals than were the sitting justices. In opposition to the plan, several justices argued "that a Court of nine is as large a court as is manageable. The Court could do its work, except for writing of the opinions, a good deal better if it were five rather than nine. Every man who is added to the Court adds another voice in counsel, and the most difficult work of the Court . . . is that that is done around the counsel table; and if you make the Court a convention instead of a small body of experts, you will simply confuse counsel. It will confuse counsel within the Court, and will cloud the work of the Court and deteriorate and degenerate it."[20]

Since the failure of Roosevelt's plan, there have been no further efforts to increase the number of justices, nor are there likely to be any in the foreseeable future. During the nineteenth century, the main reason for increasing the number of justices was the burden of circuit duty: as new circuits were added, more justices were needed to attend sessions of the courts in these circuits. Circuit-riding duties of the justices ended in 1891. (See box, Circuit Riding, p. 99.)

In the past, a Supreme Court justice usually was appointed from the circuit in which he was to serve. That has not been the case in the late twentieth century. Factors a president generally considers in nominating someone to the Court are the likelihood of the person winning Senate confirmation and the individual's ability, reputation, ideological position, and political affiliation and beliefs.

Throughout history, the Senate has formally rejected twenty-eight nominees to the Court. (The last was President Ronald Reagan's nominee Robert H. Bork in 1987.) In addition to the nominations the Senate has formally rejected, fifteen others have been denied confirmation without a vote.

A JUDICIAL "FAMILY"

Depending on shifting traditions and circumstances, members of the Court have sometimes behaved more like a close-knit, chummy family, at other times more like a group of dignitaries on their most scrupulously formal behavior.

In the early years of the Court, particularly after John Marshall became chief justice in 1801, the justices usually lived together during the term in the same boardinghouse and shared their meals together. During the Marshall years, when the Court was in session, the justices were together during oral arguments, usually from 11 A.M. until 4 P.M. each day, and during conference after 7 P.M. After the conferences, the justices often dined and socialized with each other.

About the justices of the early nineteenth century, Charles Warren has written, "The Judges of the Court appear to have been assiduous diners-out." John Quincy Adams, then secretary of state, wrote in his diary on March 8, 1821: "We had the Judiciary company to dine with us, this day. Chief Justice Marshall, the Judges Johnson, Story and Todd, the Attorney-General Wirt, and late District Attorney Walter Jones; also Messrs. Harper, Hopkinson, D. B. Ogden, J. Sergeant, Webster, Wheaton and Winder, all counsellors of the Court. . . . We had a very pleasant and convivial party."[21]

At this time, the justices "lived for the most part in the same lodgings," Warren continued, and "their intercourse was necessarily of the closest kind, off as well as on the bench."

Charles Sumner, later the radical Republican senator from Massachusetts and outspoken abolitionist, wrote in a letter of March 3, 1834:

All the judges board together, having rooms in the same house and taking their meals from the same table, except Judge McLean whose wife is with him, and who consequently has a separate table, though in the same house. I dined with them yesterday. . . . No conversation is forbidden, and nothing which goes to cause cheerfulness, if not hilarity. The world and all its things are talked of as much as on any other day.[22]

In a letter of March 8, 1812, Justice Joseph Story described the life of the justices in their common boardinghouse. "It is certainly true, that Judges here live with perfect harmony, and as agreeably as absence from friends and families could make our residence. Our intercourse is perfectly familiar and unrestrained, and our social hours, when undisturbed with the labors of the law, are passed in gay and frank conversation, which at once enlivens and instructs."[23]

Many of the justices continued to share a common boardinghouse until after the Civil War. In the late nineteenth century, however, as the terms of the Court grew longer, the justices abandoned the boardinghouses, moved their families to Washington, and set up their own households.

Some of the familial aspects of the earlier days remain. It is rare for one justice to allow his animosity toward another to come to public attention. Justices rarely criticize the views of their colleagues, except in their written opinions. And there have been repeated instances when the other justices have taken on extra work or exhibited extra kindness toward a justice who was physically or mentally unwell. Still, the secrecy and isolation of the Court tend to make the camaraderie of the boardinghouse days all but impossible today.

INDIVIDUALISM

History, tradition, and the nature of the Court's work limit the opportunities of its members to demonstrate their individual views and traits.

In the early years of the Court, several factors encouraged the growth of individualism. One was the practice of delivering *seriatim* opinions, resulting in the issuance of no single opinion of the Court. Chief Justice Marshall ended *seriatim* opinions, but, after his tenure, the increasing use of dissenting and concurring opinions had a similar effect.

Of judicial independence and individualism, Wesley McCune wrote:

Were it not for one institution, the dissenting opinion, anyone who accepted appointment to the Court would almost immediately lose his

individual identity, except for what he could retain in Washington society or during summer vacations. If justices wrote only majority opinions, blended to fit the views of five or more justices, the name on the opinion would mean little and the Court would become as impersonal as a big bank. But through dissents justices have asserted their personal views. Thus, each justice can build a reputation even after arriving on the Court, in addition, of course, to shaping future law by protesting that of the present.[24]

The justices' early circuit-riding responsibilities also encouraged individualism. While on the circuit, the justices operated not as a group but as individual judges with as much discretionary power as they wished to exert.

Another factor favoring independence was the lack of office space before the new Court building was completed in 1935. Until then, most of the justices worked in their own homes, seeing the other justices only when oral arguments were heard or conferences held.

Even after the Court had its own building, a number of justices continued their practice of working at home. Hugo Black was the first justice to move into his Court office and work there—in 1937, two years after the building was occupied. Justice Stone was already in the habit of working at home when he became chief justice in 1941 and continued to do so. Not until Fred Vinson became chief justice in 1946 did all nine justices work regularly in their court chambers.

Never again, however, has the Court approached the "old-boy" closeness of the boardinghouse days. After taking his seat on the Court in 1972, Justice Lewis F. Powell Jr. confessed:

I had thought of the Court as a collegial body in which the most characteristic activities would be consultation and cooperative deliberation, aided by a strong supportive staff. I was in for more than a little surprise. . . . The Court is perhaps one of the last citadels of jealously preserved individualism. . . . Indeed a justice may go through an entire term without being once in the chambers of all the other members of the Court.

Powell describes the justices and their staffs as "nine small independent law firms."[25]

RETIREMENT

Neither the Constitution nor the law states when or under what circumstances a justice should retire from service on the Supreme Court. Justices are appointed for life and "shall hold their Offices during good Behaviour," according to Article III, Section 1, of the Constitution.

Seventeen justices have resigned from the Court; one was impeached, tried, and acquitted; a few have been threatened with impeachment.

Forty-eight justices died while on the Court. Three who had announced their retirements died before their resignations took effect. Other reasons for resigning have included matters of conscience, the desire to do other work, and the threat of scandal or impeachment.

Thirty-one justices have retired. One, Charles Evans Hughes, resigned, served a second time, and then retired.

Until 1869, many older justices stayed on the job to keep drawing a salary, because a retired justice received no compen-

CIRCUIT-RIDING: BURDENS AND HAZARDS

Circuit-riding was a tremendous burden for most justices, and they frequently complained about the intolerable conditions that circuit duties imposed on them.

In a letter to the president on August 19, 1792, for example, the justices wrote:

We really, sir, find the burdens laid upon us so excessive that we cannot forbear representing them in strong and explicit terms. . . . That the task of holding twenty-seven Circuit Courts a year, in the different States, from New Hampshire to Georgia, besides two sessions of the Supreme Court at Philadelphia, in the two most severe seasons of the year, is a task which, considering the extent of the United States and the small number of Judges, is too burdensome. That to require of the Judges to pass the greater part of their days on the road, and at inns, and at a distance from their families, is a requisition which, in their opinion, should not be made unless in cases of necessity.

The president transmitted the letter to Congress, but Congress, then and for almost one hundred years thereafter, refused to abolish the circuit-riding duties. Therefore, the justices, many of them old and in ill health, faced days of difficult travel, inadequate lodgings, bad food, and epidemics and disease.

Many unsuccessful bills were introduced in Congress to free Supreme Court justices from this onerous task. In a speech on the Senate floor on January 12, 1819, Sen. Abner Lacock, D-Pa., summed up the major reasons for congressional defeat of the bills. If the justices were relieved of circuit duties, Lacock argued, they would become "completely cloistered within the City of Washington, and their decisions, instead of emanating from enlarged and liberalized minds, would assume a severe and local character." They might also become "another appendage of the Executive authority" and be subjected to the "dazzling splendors of the palace and the drawing room" and the "flattery and soothing attention of a designing Executive."

Congress finally ended the justices' circuit-riding duties when it approved the Circuit Court Act of 1891, which established intermediate—or circuit—courts between the district courts and the Supreme Court. That long-desired action came in the wake of the attempted murder of Justice Stephen Field by a litigant unhappy with one of Field's decisions as a circuit judge.

In 1888 Field, sitting as a circuit judge in California, his home state, held invalid a marriage contract between Sarah Althea Hill and William Sharon. Sharon, a wealthy mine owner and senator from Nevada (R, 1875–1881), had died by the time of the ruling. Hill, who had subsequently married David Terry, one of Justice Field's former colleagues on the California Supreme Court, was incensed at Field's ruling. As a result of their conduct in the courtroom when the ruling was announced, she and Terry were imprisoned for contempt of court.

The following year, Field returned to California to hold circuit court. Concerned for Field's safety, the attorney general authorized protection for him. David Neagle, an armed federal marshal, was to accompany him. As Field and Neagle were traveling by train to Los Angeles where Field was to hold court, the Terrys boarded the train. While Field was eating breakfast at a station restaurant, Terry accosted him and struck him. Neagle, thinking that Terry was reaching for a knife with the intent of attacking Field, shot and killed Terry.

Neagle was arrested and charged with murder by state officials. He contested his detention, arguing to the federal courts that the state could not hold him for actions taken in the performance of his duties under federal law.

The case came to the Supreme Court in 1890. Justice Field did not participate in the matter, but the Court agreed with Neagle's argument and ordered his release. (*In re Neagle*, 135 U.S. 1, 1890).

Although today's justices do not preside over circuit courts, they still have jurisdiction over one or more of the federal circuits and may issue injunctions, grant bail, or stay an execution in these circuits.

Requests for an injunction, bail, or a stay of execution go first to the presiding justice in that circuit. If denied, the application may then be made to one of the other justices.

---

sation. The Judiciary Statute of 1869 provided that any judge who had served on any federal court for at least ten years, and was seventy or older, could retire from the bench and continue to receive his regular salary until he died. The law now provides that a justice, if he wishes, may retire at age seventy after having served ten years or at age sixty-five after fifteen years of service, with compensation commensurate with his salary.

But despite old age or poor health, a number of justices have resisted leaving their seats until subjected to considerable pressure from their colleagues on the Court.

After the election of President Andrew Jackson in 1832, Chief Justice Marshall and Justice Gabriel Duvall (1811–1835), both in failing health, were reluctant to resign because they feared that the "radical" new president would choose equally "radical" new justices to take their places. Marshall remained on the Court until his death in 1835, and Duvall submitted his resignation the same year after learning that Jackson intended to nominate as his successor Roger Taney, of whom Duvall approved. (Taney was not confirmed by the Senate to Duvall's seat; after Marshall's death, Jackson named Taney chief justice, and Philip Barbour of Virginia took Duvall's chair.)

By 1869 it was apparent that Justice Robert C. Grier (1846–1870) was both physically and mentally unable to carry out his duties. Early the next year, all the other justices formed a committee to tell Grier that "it was their unanimous opinion that he ought to resign." Soon after meeting with the committee, Grier retired.

In his book on the Supreme Court, Hughes recounts the difficulties that certain justices had in convincing Justices Grier and Stephen J. Field (1863–1897) to retire.

Some justices have stayed too long on the bench. An unfortunate illustration was that of Justice Grier who had failed perceptibly at the time

Justices Oliver Wendell Holmes Jr. and Louis D. Brandeis. Holmes retired from the Court at age ninety after twenty-nine years of service.

of the first argument of the legal tender case. As the decision was delayed, he did not participate in it. A committee of the Court waited upon Justice Grier to advise him of the desirability of his retirement and the unfortunate consequences of his being in a position to cast a deciding vote in an important case when he was not able properly to address himself to it.

Justice Field tarried too long on the bench. . . . It occurred to the other members of the Court that Justice Field had served on a committee which waited upon Justice Grier to suggest his retirement, and it was thought that recalling that to his memory might aid him to decide to retire. Justice Harlan was deputed to make the suggestion. He went over to Justice Field, who was sitting alone on a settee in the robing room apparently oblivious of his surroundings, and after arousing him gradually approached the question, asking if he did not recall how anxious the Court had become with respect to Justice Grier's condition and the feeling of the other Justices that in his own interest and in that of the Court he should give up his work. Justice Harlan asked if Justice Field did not remember what had been said to Justice Grier on that occasion. The old man listened, gradually became alert and finally, with his eyes blazing with the old fire of youth, he burst out:

"Yes! And a dirtier day's work I never did in my life!"

That was the end of that effort of the brethren of the Court to induce Justice Field's retirement; he did resign not long after.[26]

In recounting the Grier and Field retirements, Hughes also described the "agreeable spectacle of Justice Holmes at eighty-

five doing his share of work, or even more, with the same energy and brilliance that he showed twenty years ago."[27] But in 1932 and after he had become chief justice, Hughes was obliged to suggest to Holmes, then ninety years old, that he retire. Holmes, doubtless recalling the Grier and Field cases, retired immediately.

At least three justices have resigned because of the dictates of conscience. Justice John A. Campbell (1853–1861) resigned soon after the outbreak of the Civil War to return to his native Alabama, even though he had opposed secession and had freed all of his own slaves.

Justice Benjamin R. Curtis (1851–1857) resigned after disagreeing with Chief Justice Taney over the Dred Scott decision; Curtis, a strong advocate of freedom for slaves once they were on free territory, felt he could no longer serve on a Court that had issued such a decision, and retired, for that and other reasons.

Justice Tom C. Clark (1949–1967) retired to avoid any possible charges of conflict of interest after his son, Ramsey Clark, was appointed attorney general.

A number of justices left the Court to run for elective office or to take other work. John Jay resigned in 1795 to become governor of New York. Five years later, he declined reappointment as chief justice because he felt that the Court lacked "the energy, weight and dignity which are essential to its affording due support to the national government."[28]

COMPULSORY RETIREMENT?

There have been repeated—if so far unsuccessful—suggestions that a constitutional amendment be enacted to require justices of the Supreme Court to retire at age seventy or seventy-five. Justice Owen J. Roberts expressed his support for such a proposal more than thirty years ago:

I believe it is a wise provision. First of all, it will forestall the basis of the last attack on the Court, the extreme age of the justices, and the fact that superannuated old gentlemen hung on there long after their usefulness had ceased. More than that, it tends to provide for each administration an opportunity to add new personnel to the Court, which, I think, is a good thing.[1]

Charles Fairman has written that "there are two distinct reasons for urging some scheme for compulsory retirement" of Supreme Court justices.

There is, first, the actual impairment of mental and physical powers. . . . A second reason for insuring renewal of the Court involves considerations of a different order. Rigidity of thought and obsolescence of social outlook, though more objective, may be no less real than the waning of bodily powers. When a majority of the Court cling to views of public policy no longer entertained by the community or shared by the political branches of government, a conflict arises which must be resolved.[2]

1. Speech to the Association of the Bar of the City of New York, December 11, 1948.

2. Charles Fairman, "The Retirement of Federal Judges," *Harvard Law Review* (January 1938): 397.

Justice Hughes resigned in 1916 to run unsuccessfully for the presidency. Fourteen years later he returned as chief justice. Arthur J. Goldberg resigned in 1965 when President Johnson asked him to become U.S. ambassador to the United Nations.

Abe Fortas, the only justice ever to resign amidst charges of judicial misconduct, submitted his resignation on May 14, 1969, a few weeks after *Life* magazine published reports that Fortas, during his first year on the Court, had received the first of what were to be annual fees of $20,000 from the Wolfson family foundation. Louis Wolfson was later convicted of violating federal securities laws. In submitting his resignation, Fortas denied any wrongdoing, saying that the fee in question had been returned and the relationship terminated. He was resigning nevertheless, he said, to quiet the controversy and enable the Court to "proceed with its work without the harassment of debate concerning one of its members."[29]

IMPEACHMENT ATTEMPTS

Only a few justices have faced impeachment. The first was Samuel Chase (1796–1811). Of the eight articles of impeachment the House voted against him in late 1804, six concerned his alleged arbitrary and improper actions at the treason and sedition trials of John Fries and James G. Callender in 1800. In its articles of impeachment, the House charged that his partisan behavior in and out of court amounted to "high Crimes and Misdemeanors" under the Constitution.

The Senate trial began on February 4, 1805. Although twenty-five of the thirty-four members of the Senate were Republicans, Chase, a Federalist, was acquitted on all counts on March 1. Soon after the acquittal, Chase's and Marshall's adversary, President Jefferson, acknowledged that the impeachment of justices was "a farce which will not be tried again."

Jefferson proved prophetic, except for several inchoate efforts to impeach Justice William O. Douglas (1939–1975) and Chief Justice Warren.

The first impeachment attempt against Douglas came after he stayed the execution of convicted spies Julius and Ethel Rosenberg in 1953. That resolution was tabled by the House Judiciary Committee after a one-day hearing. The second effort came on April 15, 1970, a week after the Senate's rejection of President Nixon's nomination of G. Harrold Carswell to the Supreme Court. In a speech on the House floor that day, Minority Leader Gerald R. Ford, R-Mich., charged that Douglas (1) had not disqualified himself from a 1970 Supreme Court case involving Ralph Ginzburg, publisher of *Eros* magazine, although Douglas had received $350 for a 1969 article in another magazine published by Ginzburg; (2) had allegedly sanctioned revolution in his book, *Points of Rebellion* (Random House, 1970); (3) was the author of an article entitled "Redress in Revolution" in the April 1970 issue of *Evergreen Review,* which contained a number of nude photographs; (4) practiced law in violation of federal statutes by assisting in the establishment of the Albert Parvin Foundation in 1960 and in giving the foundation legal advice; and (5) served as a consultant to the "leftish" Center for the Study of Democratic Institutions at a time when the center was the recipient of Parvin Foundation funds.

On December 3 a special House subcommittee created to investigate the charges against Douglas concluded that there were no grounds for impeachment.

The efforts to impeach Chief Justice Warren never got as far as those against Douglas. Most of the opposition to Warren came from right-wing groups angered over the Warren Court's expansion of individual, civil, and criminal rights. The demand for Warren's impeachment was confined, for the most part, to the fulminations of the John Birch Society and to a grassroots bumper-sticker campaign throughout the South.

EXTRAJUDICIAL ACTIVITIES

Supreme Court justices cannot be compelled to take any extrajudicial assignments but are free to engage in such activities if they wish. The use of this freedom has sparked considerable controversy both inside the Court and among its critics. It was Justice Douglas's extrajudicial activities that prompted the 1970 impeachment effort against him.

A Yen for Politics

The extrajudicial activities that cause most concern are those in which a political motive is suspected. Before 1900 the political activities of the justices involved a generally less-than-subtle quest for elective office or outright endorsement of or opposition to political candidates.

As Justice Owen Roberts pointed out in a 1948 speech, "every justice who has ever sat on that Court who was bitten by political ambition and has actively promoted his own candidacy for office has hurt his own career as a judge and has hurt the Court."[30]

The early justices did not hesitate to campaign openly for their party's candidates. Justices Samuel Chase and Bushrod Washington (1799–1829) campaigned actively for presidential candidates John Adams and Charles Pinckney, respectively, in 1800. Chase's campaigning was denounced by the anti-Federalist press, which complained, somewhat disingenuously, that he was neglecting his Court duties.

Other political-minded nineteenth-century justices included Smith Thompson (1823–1843), John McLean (1830–1861), Salmon Chase (the chief justice, 1864–1873, who presided over the Senate impeachment trial of President Andrew Johnson), David Davis (1862–1877), and Stephen Field (1863–1897). Like Chief Justice Jay before him, Justice Thompson, a Democrat, ran for governor of New York in 1828 but, unlike Jay, conducted an all-out campaign—which he lost.

Justice McLean, who before coming to the Court in 1830 had served in the cabinets of Presidents James Monroe and John Quincy Adams, sought and failed to receive his party's presidential nomination in 1836, 1848, 1852, and 1856. Referring to McLean specifically and to the tendency of justices during that period to become involved in politics, Alexander Bickel wrote "that the recurrence of justices with manifest political aspirations would in time destroy an institution whose strength derives from consent based on confidence." The conduct of justices acting upon their "manifest political aspirations," Bickel continued, "is awkward, unseemly and may give occasion for dire suspicions."[31]

Before his appointment as chief justice in 1864, Salmon Chase had been a U.S. senator, a governor, a cabinet member, and a presidential candidate. His political activities did not cease on the Court. From the bench in 1868 he unsuccessfully sought the presidential nomination of both parties.

Justice Davis accepted nomination as a minor party candidate for president in 1872 before resigning from the Court in 1877 to serve in the Senate. Justice Field periodically indicated his availability for the Democratic presidential nomination.

Far fewer justices have sought elective office in the twentieth century. Justice Robert H. Jackson (1941–1954) was approached to run for governor of New York, largely as a possible springboard for a run for the presidency. Franklin D. Roosevelt in 1944 and Harry S. Truman in 1948 both considered Justice Douglas as a running mate. After President Dwight D. Eisenhower suffered a heart attack, Chief Justice Warren was widely considered a possible Republican presidential nominee in 1956. Eisenhower recovered, ran again, and won.

1876 Electoral Commission

One ostensibly public-spirited activity on the part of five justices ended up involving the Court in one of its most serious political controversies. Justices Nathan Clifford (1858–1881), Samuel F. Miller (1862–1890), Stephen Field (1863–1897), William Strong (1870–1880), and Joseph P. Bradley (1870–1892) were appointed to serve on the electoral commission that resolved the disputed presidential election between Democratic candidate Samuel J. Tilden and Republican candidate Rutherford B. Hayes in 1876.

Congress set up the commission in January 1877 and specified that it be composed of fifteen members: three Republicans and two Democrats from the Senate, two Republicans and three Democrats from the House, and two Democrats and two Republicans from the Supreme Court. The Court itself was to choose a fifth justice. The Court finally selected Bradley, a Republican. Dexter Perkins and Glyndon G. Van Deusen wrote: "Justice Bradley, at first in favor of giving Florida's electoral vote to Tilden, changed his mind between midnight and the morning of the day the decision was announced; there is considerable evidence that he yielded to Republican pressure."[32] The commission's vote, announced February 10, 1877, favored Hayes, and Congress acquiesced on March 2, 1877.

Charles Warren pointed out that the justices' service on this commission did not enhance the Court's prestige. "The partisan excitement caused by this election and by the inauguration of Hayes led some newspapers to assert that public confidence in the judges had been weakened, and that the country would be the less willing to accept the doctrines laid down by the Court."[33]

"Public Service"

Some twentieth century justices have ignored the lesson of the Hayes-Tilden Electoral Commission that participation on supposedly nonpartisan commissions or investigative bodies can involve the Court in political controversy. Among these instances were the participation of Justice Joseph R. Lamar (1911–1916) in international arbitration cases; Justice Owen Roberts's role on the German-American Mixed Claims Commission and the Pearl Harbor Review Commission; and, the most controversial, Justice Robert Jackson's prosecution of Nazi war criminals at the Nuremberg trials and Chief Justice Earl Warren's role as head of a seven-member commission to investigate the assassination of President John Kennedy.

Jackson at Nuremberg. Several justices were troubled by Jackson's one-year absence from the Court because of his war-trial duties. Chief Justice Stone had opposed Jackson's acceptance of the assignment, and some of the other justices were angry about the extra work that Jackson's absence imposed on them. The situation became even worse after Stone's death in early 1946.

As John Frank wrote: "Taking a justice away from his primary duty can be done only at the expense of that duty. Stone's acute bitterness over the burdens placed upon the court by the absence of Jackson (who, Stone sputtered, was off running a lynching bee at Nuremberg) is understandable. Such extra-judicial work may also involve justices in controversies that lower the prestige so valuable to the court."[34]

But the fact that the Court did suffer some loss of prestige because of Jackson's role at Nuremberg had less to do with the workload burdens placed on the other justices than with Jackson's assault on Justice Hugo Black, issued from Nuremberg. According to Frank, "The most recent direct outbreak of one justice against another was Jackson's attack on Black at the time of the appointment of Chief Justice Vinson in 1946. Jackson, who was abroad at Nuremberg trying German war criminals at the time and who had deeply desired the place for himself, apparently felt that Black was in some way responsible for the appointment of Vinson. He issued a vitriolic public statement denouncing Black for having participated in a certain case in which Jackson felt that Black should have disqualified himself." Amidst the publicity that the statement received, Justice Black "maintained a complete silence."[35]

Somewhat surprisingly, Justice Frankfurter did not share his colleagues' resentment of Jackson's role in the Nuremberg trials. Years before his appointment to the Supreme Court in 1939 and after his retirement in 1962, Justice Frankfurter opposed the participation of justices in any public activities that were not strictly relevant to their judicial responsibilities.

In 1929, for example, Professor Frankfurter wrote: "In suggesting that judges engage in public activities off the bench, we are in danger of forgetting that it is the business of judges to be judges. . . . It is necessary for judges to be less worldly than others in order to be more judicial."[36] After his retirement from the

Court, Frankfurter also criticized Chief Justice Warren's decision to head the investigation of President Kennedy's assassination.

Although Frankfurter resigned immediately from the American Civil Liberties Union, the National Association for the Advancement of Colored People, and even the Harvard Club when named to the Court, he nevertheless served on several presidential and national commissions while a sitting justice.

The Warren Commission. To ascertain all the facts and circumstances relating to the assassination of President Kennedy, President Lyndon B. Johnson created a seven-man investigating commission on November 29, 1963. Chief Justice Warren agreed to head the commission, which also included Sens. Richard B. Russell, D-Ga., and John Sherman Cooper, R-Ky.; Reps. Hale Boggs, D-La., and Gerald Ford, R-Mich.; Allen W. Dulles, former director of the CIA; and John J. McCloy, former disarmament adviser to President Kennedy.

The Warren Commission released its findings on September 27, 1964, concluding that Lee Harvey Oswald, "acting alone and without advice or assistance," had shot President Kennedy. Before the report was released, critics of Warren's performance on the Court denounced the chief justice for neglecting his judicial duties and for participating in such a "political" undertaking. After the findings were released, those convinced that there had been a conspiracy to assassinate Kennedy joined in the criticism.

White House Advisers

Justice Frankfurter's continuing interest in political and other nonjudicial matters was particularly evident in his role as adviser to President Roosevelt on a variety of matters, foreign and domestic.

During the spring and summer of 1939, for example, Frankfurter sent almost three hundred notes to Roosevelt warning of the threat posed by Hitler and advising the president of the actions that should be taken to counter the German threat. These and subsequent actions led observers to label Frankfurter the "outside insider in the Roosevelt administration."[37]

Supreme Court justices have been giving advice to presidents and other elected officials since the time of John Jay. This informal relationship generally has resulted in criticism of the justices and the Court.

When President Roosevelt indicated at a press conference in September 1939 that he had discussed the situation in Europe with Justices Stone and Frankfurter, there was a storm of protest over the involvement of justices in the foreign policy deliberations and decisions of the executive branch. Stone thereafter refused all invitations to confer with the president. Frankfurter, however, continued advising Roosevelt and his successors.

In the 1960s Justice Fortas continued to advise President Johnson after his appointment to the Court. This role as advisor to Johnson was a major factor in Fortas's failure to win Senate confirmation as chief justice in 1968. It likely played some part in his resignation from the Court on May 14, 1969.

James Simon described the circumstances leading to Fortas's resignation. In the summer of 1968,

President Johnson named Associate Justice Abe Fortas to succeed Chief Justice Warren. At first, anti-Fortas forces, led by Republican Senator Robert P. Griffin of Michigan, opposed the nomination primarily because it had been made by a "lame duck" president. At the Senate's confirmation hearings, Fortas ran into deeper trouble. The chief justice-designate, it was learned, had counseled the president on national policy and had even done some behind-the-scenes lobbying on the president's behalf while sitting on the Supreme Court. Later, when Fortas admitted that he had received $15,000 for conducting a series of seminars at American University, his ethics as well as his politics were brought into question. As a result, his nomination as Chief Justice languished and was finally withdrawn by President Johnson.[38]

Fortas retained his seat as an associate justice. But in May 1969, *Life* magazine revealed that since becoming a justice Fortas had accepted—and then returned several months later—$20,000 from a charitable foundation controlled by the family of indicted stock manipulator Louis E. Wolfson. Shortly thereafter, Fortas resigned. In a letter to Chief Justice Warren on May 14, 1969, Fortas stated:

There has been no wrongdoing on my part. . . .

There has been no default in the performance of my judicial duties in accordance with the high standards of the office I hold. So far as I am concerned, the welfare and maximum effectiveness of the Court to perform its critical role in our system of government are factors that are paramount to all others. It is this consideration that prompts my resignation which, I hope, by terminating the public controversy, will permit the Court to proceed with its work without the harassment of debate concerning one of its members.[39]

PERQUISITES

The scandal surrounding Justice Fortas's acceptance of a fee from the Wolfson Foundation prompted Chief Justice Warren, shortly before his resignation, to urge adoption of a judicial code of ethics requiring judges to file an annual report on investments, assets, income, gifts, and liabilities and prohibiting them from accepting compensation other than their judicial salaries.

In 1973 the Judicial Conference, under Chief Justice Burger, adopted resolutions asking judges to report gifts of more than $100 and any income from outside work. Supreme Court justices today file annual financial disclosure reports of assets and income earned from activities off the bench.

In 1996 each associate justice was paid an annual salary of $164,100—the chief justice makes $171,500—so there was little need for a justice to seek outside sources of income. This was not always the case, however. Some of the early justices were so strapped for money and so badly reimbursed for their services on the Court that they were obliged to find ways to supplement their earnings. (*See box, Justices' Salaries, p. 122, in Chapter 6.*)

Justices have a number of perquisites. These include two secretaries, a messenger, and four law clerks. Like the chief justice, they also have their own offices, the services of a Court barber, for which they pay, and the use of the Court dining room, exercise room, and library. The Court maintains a small fleet of cars for the official use of the justices, but most of the justices drive themselves to and from work.

Supporting Personnel

Compared to the executive and legislative branches of the federal government, the Supreme Court employs few people and spends relatively little money. About 325 people work for the Court, and its annual budget in the mid-1990s was in the comparatively modest $30 million range.

The Court's statutory employees, the clerk, the marshal, the reporter of decisions, and the librarian, are appointed by the Court. The justices each select their clerks and other personal staff. All other support personnel are appointed by the chief justice. In addition, several other groups work with the Court but are not employees of it. These include the Federal Judicial Center, the Administrative Office of the U.S. Courts, the U.S. Judicial Conference, and the Supreme Court Historical Association.

The solicitor general and his staff, while closely involved with the work of the Court, are part of the executive branch, specifically the Department of Justice. The solicitor general and staff select which cases the government brings to the Court and advise the Court, when asked, on the government's view of various other cases. The Supreme Court bar, the attorneys who argue before the Court, are also independent yet important parts of the Court's support system.

CLERK OF THE COURT

The clerk of the Court is the Court's judicial business manager. The clerk ensures that the Court is able to carry on its constitutional duty, its judicial business, in orderly fashion. The office was established by the first formal rule of the Court, adopted in February 1790. Through the years, the clerk's duties have increased enormously. The clerk now has a staff of thirty people.

The responsibilities of the clerk of the Court include:

(a) the administration of the Court's dockets and argument calendars;

(b) the receipt and recording of all motions, petitions, jurisdictional statements, briefs, and other documents filed on the various dockets;

(c) the distribution of those various papers to the justices;

(d) the collection of filing fees and the assessment of costs;

(e) the preparation and maintenance of the Court's order list and journal, upon which are entered all the Court's formal judgments and mandates;

(f) the preparation of the Court's formal judgments and mandates;

(g) the notification to counsel and lower courts of all formal actions taken by the Court, including written opinions;

(h) the supervision of the printing of briefs and appendices after review has been granted in *in forma pauperis* cases;

(i) the requesting and securing of the certified record below upon the grant of review or other direction of the Court;

(j) the supervision of the admissions of attorneys to the

CLERKS OF THE COURT		
Name	Term	State of Origin
John Tucker	1790–1791	Massachusetts
Samuel Bayard	1791–1800	Pennsylvania
Elias B. Caldwell	1800–1825	New Jersey
William Griffith	1826–1827	New Jersey
William T. Carroll	1827–1863	Maryland
D. W. Middleton	1863–1880	D.C.
J. H. McKenney	1880–1913	Maryland
James D. Maher	1913–1921	New York
William R. Stansbury	1921–1927	D.C.
C. Elmore Cropley	1927–1952	D.C.
Harold B. Willey	1952–1956	Oregon
John T. Fey	1956–1958	Virginia
James R. Browning	1958–1961	Montana
John F. Davis	1961–1970	Maine
E. Robert Seaver	1970–1972	Missouri
Michael Rodak Jr.	1972–1981	West Virginia
Alexander Stevas	1981–1985	Virginia
Joseph F. Spaniol Jr.	1985–1991	Ohio
William K. Suter	1991–	Virginia

Supreme Court bar, as well as their occasional disbarments; and

(k) the constant giving of procedural advice, by telephone, mail, and in person, to those counsel and litigants who need assistance or assurance as to the Court's rules and procedures.

To help the clerk and his staff carry out these many functions, a computerized informational system was installed in 1976.[40]

To date, there have been only nineteen clerks of the Court. Four of them served for a quarter of a century or more: Elias B. Caldwell (1800–1825), William T. Carroll (1827–1863); J. H. McKenney (1880–1913), and C. Elmore Cropley (1927–1952). The first clerk, John Tucker, was selected on the third day of the Court's first session, February 3, 1790, to oversee the courtroom and library, manage subordinate employees, collect the salaries of the justices, and find them lodgings when necessary.

The 1790 rule that established the position of clerk prohibited him from practicing law before the Court while he was a clerk. In the early years the clerk performed many of the duties later taken over by the reporter and the marshal. So varied were the responsibilities of the early clerks that they were described as a combination business manager-errand boy for the justices and the lawyers who appeared before the Court.

The importance of the clerk was summed up nearly a century ago by a man who had had considerable experience with the clerk's office, Augustus H. Garland, former governor of Arkansas, former Democratic senator from that state, and former U.S. attorney general. Garland wrote:

It is well to note that it is quite important for lawyers practicing in that Court to see much of the Clerk's office and to know its workings. If any motion is to be had or proceedings asked in Court not specifically provided for by law or rule, it is wise to seek advice there beforehand. . . . Many useless and sometimes unpleasant collisions between the Court and counsel are avoided by this precaution. Even the oldest and most experienced attorneys are not ashamed to consult the Clerk's office and they do not hesitate to do so.[41]

Although the Office of the Clerk of the Court was established in 1790, no provision was made for a salary until nine years later. In 1799 Congress provided "That the compensation to the Clerk of the Supreme Court of the United States shall be as follows, to wit: for his attendance in Court, ten dollars per day, and for his other services, double the fees of the clerk of the Supreme Court of the state in which the Supreme Court of the United States shall be holden."[42]

For almost one hundred years the office of the clerk was self-supporting. It paid salaries and other expenses of its operations out of filing fees. The generous fees and other allowances gave some of the early clerks a handsome annual stipend. In 1881, for example, the clerk's net income was almost $30,000 a year— only slightly less than the president's and considerably more than the justices'.[43] Strict accountability for the Court's funds was not imposed until 1883. The filing fees now go to the U.S. Treasury, and Congress appropriates the money for the salaries and expenses of the clerk's office. The clerk in 1996 had an annual salary of about $118,000.

MARSHAL OF THE COURT

The Judiciary Act of 1867 gave the Court authority to appoint a marshal, to remove him, and to fix his compensation. Today, the marshal oversees the operations of the Court building. He is its general manager, its paymaster, and its chief security officer. Before the office was created, these duties were performed either by the clerk or the marshal of the district in which the Court was located. Between 1801 and 1867, for example, the twelve men who served as marshal of the District of Columbia also served, informally, as marshal of the Court.

Today, the marshal must attend all the Court's sessions, manage more than two hundred employees, supervise the federal property used by the Court, pay the justices and other employees, oversee telecommunications, order supplies, and pay the Court's bills.

The marshal, whose original duties were to keep order in the courtroom, also oversees the Supreme Court Police Force, which consists of a chief of police and about eighty officers. They police the building, grounds, and adjacent streets; they may make arrests and carry firearms. The marshal and his aides also receive visiting dignitaries and escort the justices to formal functions outside the Court.

During public sessions of the Court, the marshal (or his deputy) and the clerk—both dressed in morning coats or cutaways—station themselves at opposite ends of the bench. At exactly 10 A.M., on a signal from the chief justice, the marshal pounds the gavel and announces: "The Honorable, the Chief

MARSHALS OF THE COURT	
Name	*Term*
Richard C. Parsons	1867–1872
John C. Nicolay	1872–1887
John Montgomery Wright	1888–1915
Frank Key Green	1915–1938
Thomas E. Waggaman	1938–1952
T. Perry Lippitt	1952–1972
Frank M. Hepler	1972–1976
Alfred Wong	1976–1994
Dale E. Bosley	1994–

Justice and the Associate Justices of the Supreme Court of the United States." As the justices take their seats, he calls for silence by crying "Oyez" ("Hear ye") three times and announces: "All persons having business before the Honorable, the Supreme Court of the United States, are admonished to draw near and give their attention, for the Court is now sitting. God save the United States and this honorable Court." During oral argument, the marshal or his assistant flashes the white and red lights to warn counsel that the time for presenting arguments is about to expire.

Until recently, the marshal also was directed to "serve and execute all process and orders issued by the Court or a member thereof." The marshal would delegate the actual serving of papers—usually disbarment orders—to U.S. marshals. The only time this function drew attention came during the tenure of Marshal Frank Key Green (1915–1938). Green served a subpoena on business tycoon J. Pierpont Morgan Jr. when government officials were trying to regain possession of Martha Washington's will, which Morgan's father allegedly had stolen. Upon receiving the subpoena, Morgan returned the will. The process-and-orders function has passed to the clerk's office.

Like the other statutory officers of the Court—the clerk, the reporter, and the librarian—the marshal's salary in 1996 was about $118,000.

REPORTER OF DECISIONS

The reporter of decisions is responsible for editing the opinions of the Court and supervising their printing and publication in the official *United States Reports*. The reporter and his staff of nine check all citations after the opinions of the justices have been delivered, correct typographical and other errors in the opinions, and add the headnotes, the voting lineup of the justices, and the names of counsel that appear in the published version of the opinions.

The Court's orders and decisions are first circulated as "Preliminary Prints." Users of these preliminary prints are "requested to notify the reporter of decisions . . . of any typographical or other formal errors, in order that corrections may be made before the bound volume goes to press." The orders and decisions are printed under the auspices of the U.S. Government Printing Office and sold by the Superintendent of Documents.

The post of reporter of decisions had informal beginnings. The first reporter, Alexander J. Dallas (1790–1800), was self-appointed. Before the Supreme Court moved to Philadelphia, Dallas had published a volume on Pennsylvania court decisions. When the Court began meeting in Philadelphia in 1791, Dallas's book contained the cases of both the Pennsylvania court and the Supreme Court. Most accounts of the early Supreme Court indicate that Dallas, a lawyer, undertook the first reports as a labor of love and a public service. Dallas, who was also a journalist, editor, patron of the arts, and secretary of the Treasury (1814–1816), published four volumes of decisions covering the Supreme Court's first decade.

Dallas was succeeded unofficially by William Cranch in 1801. Like Dallas—who served as Treasury secretary while reporting on the Court's decisions—Cranch continued to sit as a judge and later chief justice of the circuit court in Washington, D.C.

During Cranch's service as reporter of decisions, the justices began supplementing their oral opinions with written texts in important cases. This was of immeasurable assistance to Cranch and subsequent reporters. Cranch, whose reports were highly praised for their accuracy and clarity, believed that public scrutiny of opinions was needed to keep the justices from making arbitrary decisions.

Cranch's successor, Henry Wheaton, was the first reporter formally appointed by the Court. In 1816 Congress provided for publication of Court decisions and, a year later, set the reporter's salary at $1,000 a year. The Judiciary Act of 1817 mandated that, for this salary, the reporter had to publish each opinion within six months of a decision and provide eighty copies to the secretary of state for distribution. The reports continued to be sold to the public, at $5 a volume, and the reporter was still able to share in the profits, such as they were.

After he retired in 1827 to become minister to Denmark, Wheaton and his successor, Richard Peters Jr., became involved themselves in a Supreme Court case.[44] Peters was determined to increase the meager sales of the reports and his own profits as well. He therefore decided to revise and streamline the earlier reports and publish them in "Peters' Condensed Reports" at a price of $36. Because the purchase of Peters's reports would make it unnecessary for the interested public to purchase Wheaton's reports, the former reporter of decisions sued Peters, charging a violation of copyright. The Court ruled, however, that Court opinions were in the public domain.

As Garland noted, "The office of the Reporter is not a . . . bed of roses. The work is constant, arduous and exacting. A failure to give full scope in the syllabus . . . to the utterances of a judge brings wrath upon him."[45] Reporters Benjamin C. Howard (1843–1861) and John W. Wallace (1863–1875) felt the wrath of several justices.

In 1855 Justice Peter V. Daniel (1842–1860) wrote to reporter Howard complaining that his name had not been inserted at the

REPORTERS OF DECISIONS	
Name	*Term*
Alexander J. Dallas	1790–1800
William Cranch	1801–1815
Henry Wheaton	1816–1827
Richard Peters Jr.	1828–1843
Benjamin C. Howard	1843–1861
Jeremiah S. Black	1861–1862
John W. Wallace	1863–1875
William T. Otto	1875–1883
J. C. Bancroft Davis	1883–1902
Charles Henry Butler	1902–1916
Ernest Knaebel	1916–1944
Walter Wyatt	1946–1963
Henry Putzel Jr.	1964–1979
Henry C. Lind	1979–1987
Frank D. Wagner	1987–

beginning of his dissenting opinion and that he was henceforth uncertain that he would allow his dissents to be published in the reports. Justices Swayne and Clifford complained that reporter Wallace failed to publish their opinions or butchered them.

Wallace was the last reporter to have his name on the cover of the Court's published reports. The first ninety volumes of the reports were titled Dall. 1–4; Cranch 1–15; Wheat. 1–12; Pet. 1–16; How. 1–24; Black 1–2, and Wall. 1–23. After 1874 the name of the reporter of decisions appeared only on the title page of the reports.

The reporter of decisions was paid an annual salary of about $118,000 in 1996. The first two reporters, Dallas and Cranch, were paid no salary at all and relied on the sale of their reports or on outside jobs for their income.

As was mentioned earlier, Congress in 1817 provided an annual stipend of $1,000. Reporters still found it necessary to rely on sales of the reports or to moonlight to supplement their meager incomes. Wheaton, for example, argued a number of cases before the Supreme Court and then reported them.

LIBRARIAN

The Supreme Court library, which contains more than 450,000 volumes in print, microform, and electronic formats, is located on the third floor of the Court building. (A private library for the justices, with 65,000 volumes, is on the second floor. There are also small core libraries in each chamber plus an offsite annex library containing 50,000 books.) The main Supreme Court library's use is limited to Court personnel, members of the Court bar, members of Congress, their legal staffs, and government attorneys. Usually, however, the library will grant access to its books to members of the public or press who specify a particular research interest.

LIBRARIANS OF THE COURT

Name	Term
Henry Deforest Clarke	1887–1900
Frank Key Green	1900–1915
Oscar Deforest Clarke	1915–1947
Helen C. Newman	1947–1965
Henry Charles Hallam Jr.	1965–1972
Edward G. Hudon	1972–1976
Betty H. Clowers (acting)	1976–1978
Roger F. Jacobs	1978–1985
Stephen G. Margeton	1985–1988
Shelley L. Dowling	1989–

Since 1887, when the post of librarian was created, there have been nine Court librarians. In 1996 the librarian's salary, like those of the clerk, the marshal, and the reporter, was about $118,000. The library has a staff of twenty-five, of whom twelve are professional librarians and some also are lawyers.

In the early years of the Court, the justices had no library of their own, and it was not until 1812 that Congress allowed the justices to use the Library of Congress. In 1832, after repeated refusals to give the Court its own library, Congress gave the justices the 2,011 law books in the Library of Congress but insisted that members of Congress retain the right to use them as well. Because the Court had no librarian at the time, the clerk of the Court was put in charge of the books. By 1863 the number of law books had increased to almost 16,000. In 1884 the marshal of the Court was given responsibility for the Court's collection of books. The post of librarian, created in 1887, remained in the marshal's department until Congress made it a separate office in 1948.

The library has the most complete available set of the printed briefs, records, and appendices of Court cases. It also contains all federal, state, and regional reports, federal and state statutory codes, legal periodicals, legal treatises, and digests and legislative and administrative source material. There are also special collections in international law, military law, British law, patent and trademark law, and Supreme Court history.

When the clerk was in charge of the library in the nineteenth century, lawyers and others allowed to use the library could borrow no more than three books at one time. The books had to be returned within a "reasonable" time. For books that were not returned within a reasonable time, the clerk imposed a fine of $1 a day on the borrower. If a book was lost, the borrower had to pay twice the value of the lost book. This rule was changed to protect the Court's collection. Books and other material now cannot be removed from the building, although members of the Supreme Court bar may request that material be sent to them when they are arguing a case.

PUBLIC INFORMATION OFFICER

The Court's public information office is responsible for answering questions from the public, facilitating competent coverage of the Court by the news media, and distributing information about the Court and the justices. The public information officer is the Court's public spokesperson on matters other than the interpretation of its opinions and orders. The justices believe that their opinions and orders must speak for themselves.

The public information office releases the opinions and orders of the Court to the press as soon as they are announced in open court, then serves as the public's source for these documents. The schedule of Court sessions and conferences, the activities of the justices, and changes in Court procedures are usually placed on a bulletin board in the press room adjoining the public information office. Special announcements about the Court or the justices are released by the office.

In 1982 the press room was modernized and expanded. It houses carrels for eighteen major news organizations covering the Court on a regular basis and facilities for other journalists. In addition, the major television and radio networks have separate broadcast booths on the ground floor where reporters tape record their news stories and then transmit them directly to their offices.

The public information office also maintains petitions, motions, briefs, responses, and jurisdictional statements on all current cases for the use of Court staff and the press. It supervises the assignment of Court press credentials and admission to the press section of the courtroom, and serves as liaison between the press and all other offices of the Court, including the chambers of the justices.

The public information office serves as the source of news and information within the Court, circulating news items and publishing an employee newsletter, *Oyez! Oyez!*, and an occasional features publication, *The Docket Sheet*.

The current public information officer, Toni House, is the fourth person to hold the post since it was established in 1935. Her predecessors were Ned Potter, Banning E. Whittington, and Barrett McGurn. House has held the office since 1982. The public information officer has a staff of four.

LEGAL OFFICE AND LAW CLERKS

As the number of cases has increased over the years, the justices have relied more and more on their law clerks. In 1996 there were thirty-five law clerks serving the nine justices—about twice the number employed in the mid-1960s. Most of the justices have four clerks each; Chief Justice Rehnquist has chosen to have only three. The clerks are hired by the individual justices, usually for one year. Some clerks stay longer than a year.

The justices have complete discretion in hiring the law clerks they want. The clerks are generally selected from candidates who were at the top of their classes in the country's most prestigious law schools. Many have previously clerked for a lower court judge. The nature and amount of a clerk's work depends on the work habits of his or her particular justice. Years ago, Justice Louis Brandeis once asked his clerk to check every page of every volume of *United States Reports* for information that Brandeis wanted. Justice Black insisted that some of his clerks play tennis with him. Chief Justice Stone liked his clerks to accompany him on his walks. On the contemporary Court, Justice Sandra Day O'Connor has been known to take her clerks whitewater rafting.

As John Frank, who clerked for Justice Black in the early 1950s, pointed out, "The tasks of the clerks are very much the product of the whims of their justices. In general, it is the job of the clerk to be eyes and legs for his judge, finding and bringing in useful materials."[46] The two major functions of the clerks are to read, analyze, and often prepare memoranda for the justices on the thousands of cases that reach the Court each year and to help otherwise in whatever way a justice expects in preparing the opinion that he or she will deliver.

It has been charged that law clerks have on occasion written the opinion issued in the name of the justices, but there has been no proof that any clerk actually has been the author of an opinion. How much of the preliminary writing a clerk may do is a well-guarded secret.

Three of the current justices served as law clerks: John Paul Stevens clerked for Wiley B. Rutledge in 1947 and 1948; Rehnquist clerked for Robert Jackson in 1952 and 1953; and Stephen G. Breyer clerked for Arthur Goldberg in 1964 and 1965.

All three tend to minimize the influence the clerks have on the justices and their opinions. Stevens has written that "an interesting loyalty develops between clerks and their Justices. It is much like a lawyer-client relationship, close and confidential. Like a lawyer, a clerk can't tell his client, the Justice, what to do. He can only suggest what can happen if he does or doesn't do something."[47]

Byron R. White (1962–1993), who was a law clerk for Chief Justice Vinson in 1946 and 1947, has said, "We couldn't get our work done without the clerks. But I don't think they influence the results here all that much. I like 'em around to hear their various views. When I served as a clerk, I don't think anything I ever did or said influenced my Justice. I felt I was doing Chief Justice Vinson a service by making sure that relevant considerations were placed before him, such as opinions from other courts, law journals, ideas of my own—things he wouldn't have time to dig up on his own."[48]

In 1957 Rehnquist described his activities as clerk to Justice Jackson:

On a couple of occasions each term, Justice Jackson would ask each clerk to draft an opinion for him along lines which he suggested. If the clerk were reasonably faithful to his instructions and reasonably diligent in his work, the Justice would be quite charitable with his black pencil and paste pot. The result reached in these opinions was no less the product of Justice Jackson than those he drafted himself; in literary style, these opinions generally suffered by comparison with those which he had drafted. . . . The specter of the law clerk as a legal Rasputin, exerting an important influence on the cases actually decided by the Court, may be discarded at once. No published biographical materials dealing with any of the Justices suggest any such influence. I certainly learned of none during the time I spent as Clerk.[49]

Thirty years later, when Rehnquist wrote a book about how the Court works, he noted that he always asks a law clerk to prepare a first draft of a Court opinion and said,

The practice of assigning the task of preparing first drafts of Court opinions to law clerks who are usually just one or two years out of law school may undoubtedly and with some reason cause raised eyebrows in the legal profession and outside of it. Here is the Supreme Court of the United States, picking and choosing with great care one hundred and fifty of the most significant cases out of the four or five thousand presented to it each year, and the opinion in the case is drafted by a law clerk! I think the practice is entirely proper: The justice must retain for himself control not merely of the outcome of the case, but the explanation for the outcome, and I do not believe this practice sacrifices either.[50]

Whatever the impact of the clerks on the justices and their opinions has been, they almost always remain in the shadows, inaccessible to the public and the press. The clerks talk among themselves about the views and personalities of their justices, but rarely has a clerk discussed clashes among the justices or leaked news about an opinion until it is announced. Such unwritten rules, as well as the clerks' loyalty to the justices they serve, account for the anonymity that surrounds the clerks during their time as staff members of the Court.

The first law clerk was hired by Justice Horace Gray in 1882. As early as 1850 the justices had sought congressional approval for the hiring of an "investigating clerk" to help each justice and to copy opinions. When that request was not granted, some of the justices used employees of the Court clerk's office to help them.

Justice Gray's law clerk, who had been the top graduate of Harvard Law School, served primarily as a servant and a barber, paid by the justice himself. It was not until 1886 that Congress provided $1,600 a year for a "stenographic clerk" for each justice. In the years that followed, clerks often served considerably longer than the one year they generally serve now. Chief Justices Hughes and Taft and Justice Frank Murphy employed law clerks who served for five years or more.

In 1973 the Court's legal office was established. It serves in part as "house counsel" on questions directly concerning the Court and its building and in part to provide permanent and specialized help to the justices in addition to the more transient assistance they receive from their law clerks.

The office consists of two attorneys (the Court counsel and staff counsel) and a legal assistant. The lawyers prepare memoranda for the justices' conference on a variety of matters, including petitions for extraordinary writs, issues related to original cases, Supreme Court Bar admissions and disbarment questions. They also advise the clerk of the Court and the justices' offices on requests that the Court expedite its consideration of a case. In addition, they provide legal services for Court officers on problems ranging from personnel grievances and contracts to proposed changes in the Court's rules. They work with outside counsel on legislation and litigation of concern to the Court.

CURATOR'S OFFICE

In 1973 the Court created another new office, that of curator. Its responsibilities include caring for the Court's historical papers and possessions, developing exhibits concerning the Court, offering educational programs for the public about the Court's history and its collections, and recording events at the Court for future researchers.

The Supreme Court's collections include antique furnishings; archives of documents, photographs, and cartoons; other memorabilia; and art. In 1994 the curator's staff installed a permanent exhibit portraying the architecture and construction of the Supreme Court building.

Nearly 800,000 people a year visit the Supreme Court building. The curator's office provides courtroom lectures and tours Monday through Friday. It also shows a continuously running twenty-three-minute film in the theater on the ground floor.

The first curator was Catherine Hetos Skefos, who served from 1973 to 1976; the second—and current—occupant of the post is Gail Galloway.

THE CHIEF JUSTICE'S ADMINISTRATIVE ASSISTANT

Since 1972 the chief justice of the United States has had an administrative assistant to help with the increasingly complex administrative duties that devolve upon the office in addition to its strictly judicial functions.

Under Chief Justice Rehnquist, the administrative assistant acts as a senior court manager, assisting the chief in the internal management of the Court with responsibilities for personnel, budget, information systems, public information, general organization policy, and other administrative matters. The assistant also helps the chief justice in his responsibilities involving the Judicial Conference of the United States, the Federal Judicial Center, the Administrative Office of the United States Courts, and the Smithsonian Institution. The assistant serves as a liaison with the executive branch, Congress, and the other state and private organizations involving the administration of justice.

The administrative assistant also oversees the judicial fellows program and the judicial internship program at the Court. The first administrative assistant was Mark Cannon; the second, Noel J. Augustyn; the third, Larry Averill; the fourth, Robb M. Jones; and the fifth, Harvey Rishikof. The current administrative assistant is James C. Duff.

Supreme Court Lawyers

The advocates—the lawyers who argue before the Supreme Court—do not work for the Court, but, without them, the Court would have no work. These lawyers counsel the clients, file the petitions, write the briefs, and argue the cases before the Court. They represent the federal government, the states, the individuals, and the businesses whose disputes come to the Court. Their skill—or lack of it—in presenting a client's claim and the issues it raises can make the Court's work easier or more difficult.

In 1879 Belva Lockwood became the first woman lawyer to be admitted to the Supreme Court bar. In 1906 she became the first woman to argue before the Court.

The Supreme Court bar is not an organized group, but its undisputed leader is the U.S. solicitor general. Because the U.S. government is involved in so many of the cases that come to the Court, the solicitor general and staff appear there more than any other "law firm" in the country. Indeed, the solicitor general is sometimes called the "tenth justice" and has a permanent office in the Court building.

SUPREME COURT BAR

When the Supreme Court first convened in February 1790, one of its first actions was to establish qualifications for lawyers who wished to practice before it. The current version of that rule says: "To qualify for admission to the Bar of this Court, an applicant must have been admitted to practice in the highest court of a State, Commonwealth, Territory or Possession, or the District of Columbia for a period of at least three years immediately before the date of application; must not have been the subject of any adverse disciplinary action pronounced or in effect during that three-year period; and must appear to the Court to be of good moral and professional character."[51]

The two requirements for admission to the Supreme Court bar—acceptable personal and professional character, and qualification to practice before a state's or territory's highest court—have remained the same since 1790. It is not known how many attorneys were admitted to the Supreme Court bar between 1790 and 1852. From 1853 to 1924, 25,097 were admitted. Since 1925 another 215,000 lawyers have been admitted, for a total of about 240,000 members since records began being kept. About 5,000 are now admitted each year.

The Supreme Court bar has been called "a heterogeneous collection of individual lawyers located in all parts of the nation. There is no permanent organization or formal leadership."[52] Although some lawyers seek admission to the Supreme Court bar merely for personal prestige, membership does have a real function. Except in limited circumstances, an attorney must be a member of the Supreme Court bar to file any legal document with the Court. All attorneys who argue cases before the Court are members of its bar. No attorney can by himself process any case to completion unless he is a member of the Supreme Court bar. A nonmember may work on a case, but at least one member of the bar must sponsor any case filed with the Court.

A lawyer who believes he or she meets the two requirements for admission to the bar must submit two documents to the clerk of the Court: (1) "a certificate from the presiding judge, clerk, or other authorized official of that court evidencing the applicant's admission to practice there and the applicant's current good standing, and (2) a completely executed copy of the form approved by this Court and furnished by the Clerk containing (a) the applicant's personal statement, and (b) the statement of two sponsors endorsing the correctness of the applicant's statement, stating that the applicant possesses all the qualifications required for admission, and affirming that the applicant is of good moral and professional character. Both sponsors must be members of the Bar of this Court who personally know, but are not related to, the applicant."[53]

Applications are screened by the clerk of the Court's office, and lawyers whose applications are in order are notified by the clerk. There is a $100 admission fee.

Since 1970 there have been two ways to gain formal admission to the bar. Previously, attorneys had only the route of an oral motion in open court. The attorney selects a day when the Court is in public session and notifies the clerk. The applicant then finds a standing member of the Supreme Court bar who is willing and able to appear in Court with the applicant. When the Court convenes, the chief justice announces that admissions will be entertained at that time. The clerk then calls the sponsor to the rostrum, the sponsor requests that the applicant be admitted to the bar, and the chief justice announces that the motion is granted.

After all the motions have been made and granted, the new members are welcomed by the chief justice, and the clerk of the Court administers the oath to the group. Each newly admitted member of the bar is asked to "solemnly swear that as an attorney and counselor of this Court, you will conduct yourself uprightly and according to law, and that you will support the Constitution of the United States. So help you God." The applicants reply in unison, "I do."

In 1970, largely as a result of the increasing amount of time being spent on the oral motions in open session, the Court began allowing applicants to submit written motions without making a formal appearance. These so-called mail-order admissions now constitute 80 percent or more of all admissions to the Supreme Court bar. Applicants choosing the written-motion form also must sign the oath of admission and have it notarized and send their checks to the clerk of the Court.

If all an applicant's papers are in order and the Court approves the admission, the clerk notifies the applicant and informs him or her that the certificate of admission will be mailed.

Attorneys can be disbarred from the Supreme Court bar, following disbarment in some jurisdiction or "conduct unbecoming a member of the Bar or for failure to comply with" the rules of the Court.[54] An attorney may also resign from the bar. No reason need be given.

To some observers, including John Frank, modern members of the Supreme Court bar lack the dramatic flair and oratorical genius of nineteenth century advocates like Daniel Webster, Henry Clay, John C. Calhoun, and Augustus Garland.

"In the 19th century, there was a Supreme Court bar, a group of lawyers in or about Washington . . . to whom other lawyers sent their cases in the same fashion that a New York lawyer today might send a piece of San Francisco business to a San Francisco lawyer," Frank wrote. But, he continued:

The ease of modern transportation coupled with the desire of individual lawyers to have the experience of appearing in the Supreme Court have almost totally destroyed the system of a Supreme Court bar, so that today a very small number of appearances makes a man an unusually experienced Supreme Court practitioner. The number of lawyers under the age of sixty engaged solely in private practice who have appeared before the court a substantial number of times could be quickly counted. Today the lawyer from Little Rock takes in his own case, whereas in 1880 he would have retained A. H. Garland, who as attorney general and private counsel argued 130 cases. Jeremiah Sullivan Black presented 16 cases between 1861 and 1865 and won 13, including eight reversals of lower courts. Today a very experienced private practitioner may have argued five cases in a lifetime.[55]

But in 1993 political scientist Kevin T. McGuire accurately documented a discrete, reemerging Supreme Court bar:

Who are these lawyers? They are former members of the solicitor general's staff who now utilize their enormous Supreme Court expertise in private practice. They are former clerks to the justices who have seen the Court from the inside. They are well-educated, talented litigators who work in some of the nation's largest, most prestigious law firms and who represent a sophisticated clientele in the Court. They are counsel to any number of organized interests that have established offices throughout the neighboring streets of the capital community and that use appellate litigation to further their policy goals. These lawyers position cases in lower courts for possible appeals. They file briefs at the agenda stage and argue cases on the merits. They strategize with amici curiae and consult with less experienced counsel. They are, in sum, central actors in the politics of the Supreme Court.[56]

Three attorneys in the twentieth century stood out as the most experienced Supreme Court advocates. John W. Davis, who was the solicitor general from 1913 to 1918, made 140 arguments before the Court both as the solicitor general and as a private attorney. Erwin N. Griswold, who was the solicitor general from 1967 to 1973, made 118 arguments as the solicitor general and as a private lawyer. Lawrence G. Wallace, an assistant solicitor general whose tenure began in 1968 and was continuing in the mid-1990s, had already made 133 arguments by early 1996.

SOLICITOR GENERAL

The solicitor general is appointed by the president to represent the U.S. government before the Supreme Court. It is the solicitor general, with an office staffed by about two dozen attorneys, who usually decides which cases the government should ask the Court to review and what the government's legal position on them will be. He and his staff prepare the government's briefs and argue the government's case before the Court. Often the solicitor general himself argues—in the mid-1990s, it was six

SOLICITORS GENERAL, 1870–1996

Name	Term	State of Origin	President
Benjamin H. Bristow	October 11, 1870–November 15, 1872	Kentucky	Grant
Samuel F. Phillips	November 15, 1872–May 3, 1885	North Carolina	Grant
John Goode	May 1, 1885–August 5, 1886	Virginia	Cleveland
George A. Jenks	July 30, 1886–May 29, 1889	Pennsylvania	Cleveland
Orlow W. Chapman	May 29, 1889–January 19, 1890	New York	B. Harrison
William Howard Taft	February 4, 1890–March 20, 1892	Ohio	B. Harrison
Charles H. Aldrich	March 21, 1892–May 28, 1893	Illinois	B. Harrison
Lawrence Maxwell Jr.	April 6, 1893–January 30, 1895	Ohio	Cleveland
Holmes Conrad	February 6, 1895–July 8, 1897	Virginia	Cleveland
John K. Richards	July 1, 1897–March 6, 1903	Ohio	McKinley
Henry M. Hoyt	February 25, 1903–March 31, 1909	Pennsylvania	T. Roosevelt
Lloyd Wheaton Bowers	April 1, 1909–September 9, 1910	Illinois	Taft
Frederick W. Lehman	December 12, 1910–July 15, 1912	Missouri	Taft
William Marshall Bullitt	July 16, 1912–March 11, 1913	Kentucky	Taft
John William Davis	August 30, 1913–November 26, 1918	West Virginia	Wilson
Alexander C. King	November 27, 1918–May 23, 1920	Georgia	Wilson
William L. Frierson	June 11, 1920–June 30, 1921	Tennessee	Wilson
James M. Beck	June 30, 1921–June 7, 1925	New Jersey	Harding
William D. Mitchell	June 4, 1925–April 5, 1929	Minnesota	Coolidge
Charles Evans Hughes Jr.	May 27, 1929–March 16, 1930	New York	Hoover
Thomas D. Thacher	March 22, 1930–May 4, 1933	New York	Hoover
James Crawford Biggs	May 4, 1933–March 24, 1935	North Carolina	F. Roosevelt
Stanley Reed	March 23, 1935–January 30, 1938	Kentucky	F. Roosevelt
Robert H. Jackson	March 5, 1938–January 17, 1940	New York	F. Roosevelt
Francis Biddle	January 22, 1940–September 4, 1941	Pennsylvania	F. Roosevelt
Charles Fahy	November 15, 1941–September 27, 1945	New Mexico	F. Roosevelt
J. Howard McGrath	October 4, 1945–October 7, 1946	Rhode Island	Truman
Philip B. Perlman	July 30, 1947–August 15, 1952	Maryland	Truman
Walter J. Cummings Jr.	December 2, 1952–March 1, 1953	Illinois	Truman
Simon E. Sobeloff	February. 10, 1954–July 19, 1956	Maryland	Eisenhower
J. Lee Rankin	August 4, 1956–January 23, 1961	Nebraska	Eisenhower
Archibald Cox	January 24, 1961–July 31, 1965	Massachusetts	Kennedy
Thurgood Marshall	August 11, 1965–August 30, 1967	New York	L. Johnson
Erwin N. Griswold	October 12, 1967–June 25, 1973	Massachusetts	L. Johnson
Robert H. Bork	June 19, 1973–January 20, 1977	Connecticut	Nixon
Wade Hampton McCree Jr.	March 28, 1977–August 5, 1981	Michigan	Carter
Rex E. Lee	August 6, 1981–May 31, 1985	Utah	Reagan
Charles Fried	October 25, 1985–January 20, 1989	Massachusetts	Reagan
Kenneth Starr	May 27, 1989–January 20, 1993	Virginia	Bush
Drew S. Days III	June 7, 1993–June 30, 1996	Florida	Clinton

Drew S. Days III

or seven times a term. The rest of the time he is represented by one of the lawyers on his staff. On rare occasions an important case may be argued by the attorney general, the solicitor general's superior.

One observer who spent many years in the Office of the Solicitor General wrote that the solicitor general "may not unfairly be described as the highest government official who acts primarily as a lawyer. He has few administrative responsibilities; he can devote his time to studying the legal problems which come before him. Moreover, he must stand on his own feet when he is presenting the most important government cases to the Supreme Court. . . . The solicitor general regards himself—and the Supreme Court regards him—not only as an officer of the executive branch but also as an officer of the Court."[57]

The principal duties of the solicitor general's office, which is part of the Department of Justice, are to review hundreds of briefs from government agencies, to decide which cases the government should appeal, and to argue the government's position to the Court. The briefs that are reviewed usually are amended and on occasion are totally rewritten. Most are revised and modified to some extent in collaboration with the author of the draft.

The Office of the Solicitor General has a heavy workload. During the October 1994 term, for example, the solicitor general participated in about two-thirds of all the cases fully considered by the Court. The solicitor general's office wins most of its cases; it has won slightly less than 70 percent of the cases it argued between 1943 and 1993.[58]

The solicitor general is under considerable pressure to limit the number of cases that he asks the Court to take. As Robert L. Stern noted, this pressure is "partly self-serving and partly not." On the more objective level, as Lincoln Caplan noted, the solicitor general

is aware of the necessity from the standpoint of the effective administration of the judicial system of restricting the number of cases taken to the Supreme Court to the number that the Court can hear. This alone permits the Court to give adequate consideration to the important matters which the highest tribunal in the land should decide. . . . A heavy additional burden would be imposed on the Court if the government, with its great volume of litigation, disregarded that policy and acted like the normal litigant who wants to take one more shot at reversing a decision which is obviously wrong because he lost.

The selfish reason for the Solicitor General's self-restraint in petitioning for certiorari is to give the Court confidence in government petitions. It is hoped and believed—although no one who has not been on the Court can be sure—that the Court will realize that the Solicitor General will not assert that an issue is of general importance unless it is—and that confidence in the Solicitor General's attempt to adhere to the Court's own standards will cause the Court to grant more government petitions.[59]

The post of solicitor general was created by Congress in 1870 when the Department of Justice was established. Before 1870 the functions of the solicitor general were carried out by the attorney general. Congress explained that its purpose in establishing the new office was to provide "a staff of law officers sufficiently numerous and of sufficient ability to transact this law business of the Government in all parts of the United States." The law also said that the solicitor general should be "a man of sufficient learning, ability and experience that he can be sent . . . into any court wherever the government has any interest in litigation, and there present the case of the United States as it should be presented."[60]

As far as the general public is concerned, solicitors general are fairly anonymous figures, although several—William Howard Taft, Stanley Reed, Robert Jackson, and Thurgood Marshall—later became justices of the Supreme Court. One exception was Robert H. Bork (1973–1977). Bork's notoriety, however, had nothing to do with his Court-related duties but with his role in the infamous "Saturday night massacre" following President Nixon's decision to fire special Watergate prosecutor Archibald Cox—himself a former solicitor general (1961–1965)—on October 20, 1973. Attorney General Elliot Richardson and Deputy Attorney General William Ruckelshaus resigned rather than obey Nixon's order to fire Cox, at which point Bork, as the highest-ranked official left in the Justice Department, took command and fired Cox.

President Reagan's aggressive push to convince the Court to change its views on major social issues—such as abortion, affirmative action, and school prayer—thrust the solicitor general back into the national limelight. Charles Fried, Reagan's second solicitor general, particularly drew much attention, and considerable criticism, as he carried the president's arguments on these questions to the Court.[61]

Supporting Organizations

Four other organizations have an impact directly or indirectly on how the Court operates, on its workload, and on the amount of public interest in the Court. These organizations are the Judicial Conference of the United States, the Administrative Office of the U.S. Courts, the Federal Judicial Center, and the Supreme Court Historical Society. The first three organizations were created by Congress and, with the chief justice, are involved in the administration of the federal courts. They are located in the Thurgood Marshall Federal Judiciary Center just a few blocks north of the Supreme Court building.

JUDICIAL CONFERENCE

The Judicial Conference of the United States is the policy-making body for the administration of the federal judicial system, the system's "board of trustees" or "board of directors." The conference is composed of the chief judges of the thirteen courts of appeals, a district court judge from each of the twelve geographic (or regional) circuits, and the chief judge of the Court of International Trade. The chief justice serves as the presiding officer. By law, the conference is charged with carrying on "a continuous study of . . . the general rules of practice and procedure" and recommending "such changes in and addition to those rules as the Conference may deem desirable to promote simplicity in procedure, fairness in administration, the just determination of litigation and the elimination of unjustifiable expense and delay."[62]

In 1996 the conference had committees on the Administrative Office, automation and technology, bankruptcy, budget, codes of conduct, court administration, criminal law, defender services, federal-state jurisdiction, financial disclosure, intercircuit assignments, international judicial relations, the judicial branch, judicial resources, long-range planning, magistrates, circuit council conduct and disability orders, rules of practice and procedure, and space and facilities.

The conference was created by Congress, at the urging of Chief Justice Taft, in 1922. It was then called the Judicial Conference of Senior Circuit Judges. It originally consisted of the chief justice of the United States, the chief judges of the nine circuit courts of appeal, and the attorney general, who was at that time responsible for the administrative affairs of the courts.

Until 1940 the reports of the conference were included in the annual reports of the attorney general. When the Administrative Office of the United States Courts was created in 1939, administrative responsibility over the courts was transferred from the attorney general to the new office. The administrative office has operated under the supervision and direction of the judicial conference ever since.

The number of members on the conference has more than doubled since 1922. In the 1950s a district court judge representing each regional circuit joined the judicial conference. In late 1986 the chief judge of the U.S. Court of International Trade was added. The conference has no separate budget of its own, and whatever staff assistance is needed is provided by the Administrative Office of the U.S. Courts.

ADMINISTRATIVE OFFICE

As its name indicates, the Administrative Office of the U.S. Courts performs many of the support functions needed for the federal court system. The duties and functions of the office have expanded considerably since it was created in 1939.

The office prepares and submits to Congress the budget and legislative agenda for the courts. It provides administrative assistance to the clerical staffs of the courts, the probation officers, bankruptcy judges, magistrate judges, and other court staff. It also audits and disburses funds for the operation of the courts.

The administrative office provides support to the committees of the Judicial Conference of the United States. It compiles and publishes statistics on the work and workloads of the federal courts. It conducts various studies of the courts as directed by the conference, and maintains liaison with various groups, including Congress and the executive branch. The director and deputy director are appointed by the chief justice in consultation with the Judicial Conference.

Since its creation nearly sixty years ago, the Administrative Office of the U.S. Courts has operated under the direction of the Judicial Conference. The director submits a report about the activities of the office, the situation of the federal courts, and any recommendations for improvement to the annual meeting of the judicial conference, to Congress, and to the attorney general. In 1996 nearly seven hundred people worked in the administrative office. In fiscal year 1996 the office had a budget of $47.5 million.

FEDERAL JUDICIAL CENTER

The Federal Judicial Center was created by Congress in 1967 "to further the development and adoption of improved judicial administration in the courts of the United States." The center serves as the research, training, and development arm of the federal judiciary. Its seven-member board, headed by the chief justice, includes two judges from the U.S. circuit courts, three from the U.S. district courts, and the director of the Administrative Office of the U.S. Courts. The board meets four times a year, and the center's policy decisions are made at these meetings.

The center provides a two-week orientation to new federal judges and offers continuing education programs on topics ranging from docket management to criminal sentencing. It provides training to improve the management practices of the 25,000 supporting personnel of the courts, helps clerks' offices process cases and teaches probation officers techniques for supervising defendants and preparing bail and sentencing recommendations.

The results of the center's research projects are often passed on to the U.S. Judicial Conference to assist it in making recommendations for improvement in the federal court system. The center's staff is made up of about 140 lawyers, educators, and social scientists. The center's annual budget in 1996 was $18 million.

HISTORICAL SOCIETY

The Supreme Court Historical Society was founded in November 1974 as a nonprofit group to increase public interest in and knowledge about the Supreme Court and the federal court system. The society collects and preserves data and memorabilia related to the Court's history. It supports historical research, publishing the results of that research in scholarly works and publications for the general public.

The society is funded through membership contributions from its five thousand members as well as from gifts, grants, and sales of Court-related books and memorabilia in a gift shop it operates on the Court's ground floor. Regular membership dues are $50 per year; life memberships begin at $5,000. Students pay $25 a year. The society has an active volunteer structure with committees on acquisitions, programs, development, publications, and membership, among others. It publishes a quarterly newsletter, an annual journal, and various books and pamphlets.

The society has cosponsored with the Court *The Documentary History of the Supreme Court of the United States, 1789–1800,* a comprehensive documentary collection of material relating to the first decade of the Court's history.

NOTES

1. Article I, Section 3, Clause 6.

2. John P. Frank, *Marble Palace: The Supreme Court in American Life* (New York: Alfred A. Knopf, 1958), 71.

3. Charles Warren, *The Supreme Court in United States History,* rev. ed., 2 vols. (Boston: Little, Brown, 1922, 1926), I: 124.

4. Quoted in ibid., I: 127.

5. Frank, *Marble Palace,* 78–79.

6. James F. Simon, *In His Own Image: The Supreme Court in Richard Nixon's America* (New York: David McKay, 1973), 92–93.

7. Charles Evans Hughes, *The Supreme Court of the United States* (New York: Columbia University Press, 1928), 57.

8. Address to the Association of the Bar of the City of New York, December 12, 1948.

9. Ibid.

10. Merlo Pusey, *Charles Evans Hughes,* 2 vols. (New York: Columbia University Press, 1963), II: 678.

11. Ibid., 679.

12. *New York Times,* March 4, 1954.

13. *Brown v. Board of Education,* 347 U.S. 483 (1954).

14. Robert J. Steamer, *Chief Justice: Leadership and the Supreme Court* (Columbia: University of South Carolina Press, 1986), 36–38.

15. Ibid., 50.

16. Address to the National Archives, September 21, 1978.

17. Letter to Franklin D. Roosevelt, July 20, 1942.

18. Ibid.

19. Bruce Allen Murphy, *The Brandeis/Frankfurter Connection: The Secret Political Activities of Two Supreme Court Justices* (New York: Oxford University Press, 1982), 340.

20. Charles Evans Hughes, Letter to Congress, March 21, 1937.

21. Charles Warren, *The Supreme Court in United States History,* I: 87, 471.

22. Ibid., 792.

23. Ibid., 473.

24. Wesley McCune, *The Nine Young Men* (New York: Harper & Brothers, 1947), 238.

25. Quoted by Richard L. Williams, "Justices Run 'Nine Little Law Firms' at Supreme Court," *Smithsonian,* February 1977, 89.

26. Hughes, *The Supreme Court,* 75–76.

27. Ibid., 76.

28. Warren, *The Supreme Court in United States History,* I: 173.

29. Letter to Chief Justice Earl Warren, May 14, 1969.

30. Address to the Association of the Bar of the City of New York, December 11, 1948.

31. Alexander Bickel, *Politics and the Warren Court* (New York: Harper and Row, 1965), 137.

32. Dexter Perkins and Glyndon G. Van Deusen, *The United States of America,* 2 vols. (New York: Macmillan, 1962), II: 64. But see also Charles Fairman, *Five Justices and the Electoral Commission of 1877,* Supplement to Volume VII of the Oliver Wendell Holmes Devise *History of the Supreme Court of the United States,* (New York: Macmillan, 1988).

33. Warren, *The Supreme Court in United States History,* II: 583.

34. Frank, *Marble Palace,* 269.

35. Ibid., 258–259.

36. *Boston Herald,* November 15, 1929. But see also Murphy, *The Brandeis/Frankfurter Connection.*

37. Liva Baker, *Felix Frankfurter* (New York: Coward-McCann, 1969), 237. See also Joseph P. Lash, *From the Diaries of Felix Frankfurter* (New York: W. W. Norton, 1975).

38. Simon, *In His Own Image,* 102.

39. Letter to Chief Justice Earl Warren, May 14, 1969.

40. Robert L. Stern, Eugene Gressman, Stephen M. Shapiro, and Kenneth S. Geller, *Supreme Court Practice,* 7th ed. (Washington, D.C.: Bureau of National Affairs, 1993), 14.

41. Augustus H. Garland, *Experience in the Supreme Court of the United States, with Some Reflections and Suggestions as to That Tribunal* (Washington, D.C.: John Byrne, 1898), 12.

42. 1 Stat. 624, 625.

43. Charles Fairman, "The Retirement of Federal Judges," *Harvard Law Review* (January 1938): 417.

44. *Wheaton v. Peters,* 8 Pet. 591 (1834).

45. Garland, *Experience in the Supreme Court,* quoted in Supreme Court Information Office, "The Docket Sheet" 13 (Summer 1976): 4.

46. Frank, *The Marble Palace,* 116.

47. Quoted by Williams in "Justices Run 'Nine Little Law Firms,'" 88.

48. Ibid., 90–91.

49. William H. Rehnquist, "Who Writes Decisions of the Supreme Court?" *U.S. News & World Report,* December 13, 1957, 74.

50. William H. Rehnquist, *The Supreme Court: How It Was, How It Is* (New York: Quill, William Morrow, 1987), 299–300.

51. Supreme Court Rule 5.1.

52. Stern et al., *Supreme Court Practice,* 733.

53. Supreme Court Rule 5.2.

54. Supreme Court Rule 8.2.

55. Frank, *Marble Palace,* 93–94.

56. Kevin T. McGuire, *The Supreme Court Bar: Legal Elites in the Washington Community* (Charlottesville: University Press of Virginia, 1993), 21–22.

57. Robert L. Stern, "The Solicitor General and Administrative Agency Litigation," *The American Bar Association Journal* (February 1960): 154–155.

58. Lincoln Caplan, *The Tenth Justice: The Solicitor General and the Rule of Law* (New York: Alfred A. Knopf, 1987), 295. Updated with statistics provided by the solicitor general's office, April 1996.

59. Caplan, *The Tenth Justice,* 156.

60. 28 U.S.C. 505.

61. Caplan, *The Tenth Justice.*

62. 28 U.S.C. 331, as amended in 1961.

CHAPTER 6

Courtrooms and Costs

FOR THE FIRST 145 YEARS of its existence, the Supreme Court of the United States was a tenant in buildings intended for other purposes. The Court did not move into its own building until 1935. Today, more than sixty years later, the Court is still housed in a single building. In contrast to Congress, its neighbor on Capitol Hill, the Court has no additional buildings or wings.

The costs of the Court likewise are comparatively small. In fiscal 1996 the Supreme Court's budget was about $30 million, and the full federal judiciary's was $3.1 billion, out of a total U.S. budget of $1.6 trillion.

Housing the Court

Between its first meeting in New York City and its first session in its present building at One First Street, Northeast, in Washington, D.C., the Supreme Court convened in about a dozen different places. During the Court's first 145 years, the justices moved, on average, once every 12 years.

EARLY DAYS

Some of the early courtrooms were shared with other courts. After the Court moved to Washington in 1801, it held formal sessions in various rooms of the Capitol and, according to some sources, in two taverns as well.[1] Some of the premises provided for the Court in the Capitol have been described by commentators of that time as "mean and dingy" and "little better than a dungeon."[2] Their present headquarters, by contrast, has been called a "marble palace."[3]

New York City

The Supreme Court first met on February 1, 1790, in New York City, then the nation's temporary capital. The Court held session at the Royal Exchange Building at the intersection of Broad and Water Streets in what is now Manhattan's financial district. The courtroom occupied the second floor of the gambrel-roofed, cupola-topped building. There was an open-air market on the first floor of the building, and the courtroom on the second floor was a room 60 feet long with a vaulted ceiling.

The justices stayed in New York for two terms. The first lasted from February 1 to February 10, 1790, and the second for only two days, August 2 and 3, 1790. There were no cases on the Court's docket during these two terms, and the justices spent their time at duties such as appointing a Court crier and admitting lawyers to the bar.

Philadelphia

Congress voted on July 16, 1790, to move the capital from New York to Philadelphia. The Supreme Court joined the rest of the federal government there for its next session, which began on February 7, 1791, at Independence Hall, then known as the "State House." With no cases to attend to, the Court adjourned the next day.

When the Court moved to Philadelphia, it was understood that the justices would sit in City Hall, but that building was not completed until the summer of 1791, in time for the Court's August 1791 term. The justices met in the east wing of the new City Hall, which also housed the state and municipal court.

Those courts usually met at times different from the Supreme Court. In March 1796, however, the "Mayor's Court" was scheduled to hold a session in the same first-floor courtroom that the Supreme Court was using. As a result, the Supreme Court vacated the courtroom and held session in the chambers of the Common Council on the second floor of the building.

The Court remained in City Hall until the end of the August 1800 term. City Hall also housed the U.S. Congress, which occupied the west wing, and the Pennsylvania legislature, which met in the central part of the building. The records indicate that while in City Hall the justices often kept late hours to hear oral arguments and that there they began wearing robes for the first time.

Washington, D.C.

The act of July 16, 1790, that transferred the seat of the federal government from New York to Philadelphia, also provided for a subsequent and permanent move to Washington, D.C. The law specified that the final move would take place on the "first Monday in December, in the year one thousand eight hundred." By that time, enough of the Capitol and the White House had been completed for the government to move. Congress and the president were subjected to considerable criticism because the buildings they were to occupy were labeled too palatial and extravagant for a young democracy.

For the Supreme Court, however, there were no accommodations at all. A House committee in 1796 had pointed out that a "building for the Judiciary" was needed, and in 1798 Alexander White, a commissioner for the federal city, had suggested appropriating funds for it. But two weeks before the Court moved to Washington, it was still seeking a place to conduct its business.

COURTROOMS IN THE CAPITOL

Faced with the imminent convening of the homeless Supreme Court in Washington, Congress on January 23, 1801, passed a resolution providing that "leave be given to the Commissioners of the City of Washington to use one of the rooms on the first floor of the Capitol for holding the present session of the Supreme Court of the United States."

Because only the north wing of the Capitol was ready for occupancy at that time, Congress assigned the Court a small room—24 feet by 30 feet, 31 feet high, and rounded at the south end—in the east basement, or first floor, entrance hall. There, the Court held its first session in Washington on February 2, 1801. It was the first of a series of often makeshift, hand-me-down quarters assigned by Congress to the Court before the completion of its present building in 1935.

By 1807 the north wing of the Capitol was in need of renovation. In a letter to Chief Justice John Marshall on September 17, Benjamin Henry Latrobe, the architect of the Capitol and surveyor of public buildings, suggested that the Court move "for the next session into the Library formerly occupied by the House of Representatives."

There the Court remained for the February and summer 1808 terms. But as Latrobe indicated in a letter to President James Monroe on September 6, 1809, "the Library became so inconvenient and cold that the Supreme Court preferred to sit at Long's Tavern" during the February 1809 term. Long's Tavern, where the first inaugural ball was held, was located on First Street, Southeast, where the Library of Congress now stands.

On February 5, 1810, the Court returned to the Capitol and met in a courtroom especially designed for it. Located in the basement beneath the new Senate chamber, the courtroom was also used by the U.S. Circuit Court and probably by the Orphan's Court of the District of Columbia. The noted Philadelphia lawyer, Charles J. Ingersoll, provided this description of the new courtroom:

Under the Senate Chamber, is the Hall of Justice, the ceiling of which is not unfancifully formed by the arches that support the former. The Judges in their robes of solemn black are raised on seats of grave mahogany; and below them is the bar; and behind that an arcade, still higher, so contrived as to afford auditors double rows of terrace seats thrown in segments round the transverse arch under which the Judges sit. . . . When I went into the Court of Justice yesterday, one side of the fine forensic colonnade was occupied by a party of ladies, who, after loitering some time in the gallery of the Representatives, had sauntered into the hall, and, were, with their attendants, sacrificing some impatient moments to the inscrutable mysteries of pleading. On the opposite side was a group of Indians, who are here on a visit to the President in their native costume, their straight black hair hanging in plaits down their tawny shoulders, with mockassins [sic] on their feet, rings in their ears and noses, and large plates of silver on their arms and breasts.[4]

The Court remained in the new courtroom until the Capitol was burned by the British on August 24, 1814, during the War of 1812. The British are said to have used Supreme Court documents to start the fire. When the Capitol was burned, Congress moved to the temporary "Brick Capitol" at the site of the present Supreme Court building, and then, during the two years that the Capitol was being restored, to a house rented from Daniel Carroll. That house, which the Court used from February 6, 1815, until July 1, 1816, subsequently became Bell Tavern.

The Court returned to the Capitol for its February 1817 term and occupied an undestroyed section in the north wing until 1819. This is the room that was described as "mean and dingy" and "little better than a dungeon."[5] The Court remained there until the February 1819 term, when its regular courtroom beneath the Senate chamber was repaired.

The courtroom, which the justices were to occupy until 1860, was the object of both praise and criticism. It was on the Court's first day in the restored courtroom—February 2, 1819—that the decision in *Dartmouth College v. Woodward* was announced, a decision that made the Court headline news throughout the country.[6] On the same day that *Dartmouth College* was decided, the *National Intelligencer* reported:

We are highly pleased to find that the Court-room in the Capitol is in a state fit for the reception of the Supreme Court. . . . It is . . . considerably more agreeable than that which was produced on entering the same apartment, previous to the re-modification of it made necessary by the conflagration of the interior of the Capitol.[7]

Many observers saw the courtroom in a less favorable light. The *New York Statesman*, for example, described it as

not in a style which comports with the dignity of that body, or which wears a comparison with the other halls of the Capitol. In the first place, it is like going down cellar to reach it. The room is on the basement story in an obscure part of the north wing. In arriving at it, you pass a labyrinth, and almost need the clue of Ariadne to guide you to the sanctuary of the blind goddess. A stranger might traverse the dark avenues of the Capitol for a week, without finding the remote corner in which Justice is administered to the American Republic.[8]

Other critics noted that the chamber was so small that the justices had to put on their robes in full view of the spectators.

Whatever its shortcomings, the courtroom at least lent a new aura of stability and permanence to the previously peripatetic Court. The Court remained in its basement courtroom for forty-one years, surviving fires in 1851 and 1852. After the Court moved to new chambers in 1860, the courtroom became part of the law library of Congress.

In 1860, with the Civil War imminent, the Court moved from the basement to the old Senate chamber on the first floor of the Capitol. The new courtroom was located on the east side of the main corridor between the rotunda and the current Senate chamber. The large room, with a dozen anterooms for office space and storage, was by far the most commodious and imposing quarters the Court had occupied. The galleries had been removed when the Senate moved to its new chambers, giving the courtroom an aura of spaciousness.

The justices sat on a raised platform behind a balustrade. In back of the balustrade was an arched doorway topped by a gilded American eagle and flanked by ten marble columns. The justices faced a large semicircular colonnaded chamber. The area

The Supreme Court occupied this chamber in the U.S. Capitol from 1860 until it moved to its permanent home in 1935.

just in front of the bench was used for the presentation of arguments, and it was ringed by wooden benches for the spectators. There were red drapes and carpets, and busts of former chief justices lined the walls.

Despite the dignity and spaciousness of the courtroom, the adjoining office space was cramped and inadequate. There was no dining hall, for example, and the justices were forced to use the robing room for their meals. The conference room, where the justices met to discuss cases and render their decisions, also served as the Court's library. Because of the reluctance of some of the justices to having the conference room windows open, the room was frequently close and stuffy. The clerk's office was similarly close and cluttered.

None of the justices had individual office space in the Capitol; each had to provide for his own and his staff's working quarters at a time when spacious housing in Washington was difficult to find. Nevertheless, the justices held sessions in these quarters for seventy-five years, with two exceptions. An explosion of illuminating gas on November 6, 1898, forced the Court to hold the November 7 and November 14 sessions in the Senate District of Columbia Committee room. During reconstruction of the courtroom from October to December 9, 1901, sessions were held in the Senate Judiciary Committee room.

President William Howard Taft began promoting the idea of a separate building for the Supreme Court around 1912. He continued to advocate the construction of a Supreme Court building when he became chief justice in 1921. At Taft's persistent urg-

ing, Congress finally relented in 1929 and authorized funds for the construction of a permanent dwelling for the Court. During the construction of the new building, the Court continued to sit in the old Senate chamber. Its last major decision announced there, at the end of the 1934 term, was that of striking down President Franklin D. Roosevelt's National Industrial Recovery Act.

NEW COURT BUILDING

The Supreme Court held its first session in the new building at One First Street, Northeast, across the plaza from the Capitol, on October 7, 1935. One hundred and forty-five years after it first met in New York City, 134 years after it moved to Washington, and 6 years after Congress had appropriated $9,740,000 for a permanent residence, the nation's highest tribunal finally had a home of its own.

In laying the cornerstone for the new building on October 13, 1932, Chief Justice Charles Evans Hughes paid tribute to his predecessor, William Taft, who had died two years before. "This building," Hughes said, "is the result of his intelligent persistence." The site chosen for the Court was the location of the Brick Capitol, which had been used by Congress after the British burned the Capitol in 1814.

Architect Cass Gilbert was commissioned to design the building and, in May 1929, submitted a plan for "a building of dignity and importance suitable for its use as a permanent home of the Supreme Court of the United States." Gilbert died

A model of the Supreme Court building is inspected by Justices Louis D. Brandeis, Willis Van Devanter, Chief Justice William Howard Taft, Justices Oliver Wendell Holmes Jr., Pierce Butler, George Sutherland, and Harlan Fiske Stone. Taft died in 1930 before his plan for a separate building for the Court was fulfilled.

in 1934, and the project was continued under Chief Justice Hughes and architects Cass Gilbert Jr. and John R. Rockart, under the supervision of Architect of the Capitol David Lynn.

The architects chose the Corinthian style of Greek architecture, which would blend most harmoniously with the congressional buildings on Capitol Hill. The dimensions of the building

were 385 feet east and west, from front to back, and 304 feet north and south. At its height, the building rises four stories above ground level.

Marble was selected as the primary material to be used, and more than $3 million—almost a third of the building's cost—was spent on domestic and foreign marble. Vermont marble was used for the exterior of the building. A thousand freight cars were needed to haul the stone from Vermont. Georgia marble flecked with crystal was quarried for the four inner courts, while a creamy Alabama marble was used for most of the walls and floors of corridors and entrance halls.

For the Court's Great Hall—its showcase—and the courtroom at the end of the Great Hall, architect Gilbert insisted on Ivory Vein Marble from Spain for the walls and Light Sienna Old Convent marble from the Montarrenti quarry in Italy for the huge columns. The Italian marble was shipped to finishers in Knoxville, Tennessee, and they made the blocks into 30-foot columns and shipped them to Washington. Darker Italian and African marble was used for the floor.

Most of the floors are oak, and the doors and walls of most offices are American-quartered white oak. Bronze and mahogany were also used. The roof was made from cream-colored Roman tile set on bronze strips over lead-coated copper on a slab of watertight concrete. As Wesley McCune noted, the "Court might succumb to a political storm, but it will never be driven out by any kind of inclement weather."[9] The building includes two self-supporting marble spiral staircases from the garage to the top floor. The only other spiral staircases like those in the Court are in the Vatican and the Paris Opera.

Since its completion in 1935, the Supreme Court building has been a subject of both outspoken criticism and praise. It has been described as a "marble palace" and a "marble mausoleum."

VISITING THE COURT

The Supreme Court is open for visitors year-round, Monday through Friday from 9 A.M. to 4:30 P.M. Annually, about 800,000 people visit the Court. The Court is in session for oral arguments during two-week periods from the first Monday in October until late April or early May. Arguments are held from 10 A.M. to noon and from 1 to 3 P.M. Monday, Tuesday, and Wednesday. The afternoon sessions depend on the justices' having accepted a certain number of cases to fill those hours. In the 1980s the Court nearly always held afternoon arguments, but in 1996, as the Court had decreased the number of petitions granted and cases heard, afternoon sessions were rare.

During the weeks when the Court is not in session, lectures are presented regularly by the staff of the Curator's Office from 9:30 A.M. to 3:30 P.M. On the ground floor there are exhibits, portraits of all former justices, a gift shop, and a cafeteria. In addition, visitors can see a film about the Court in a ground floor room. In 1994 the Curator's office began organizing extensive, permanent exhibits open to the public; the first was on the building's form and function. The exhibit included a model and pictures of the private conference room where justices vote on cases and historical items such as a snuff box, inkwells, and the chair used by Chief Justice John Marshall (1801–1835).

Supreme Court building, completed in 1935.

Its admirers speak in terms of structural simplicity, austerity, beauty, and dignity. For them, it is a fitting monument epitomizing the words on the front entrance of the building, "Equal Justice Under Law."

Despite general public approval of the new building, it has had numerous critics. In the 1930s the authors of the Federal Writers' Project *Guide to Washington* wrote that "the building has a cold, abstract, almost anonymous beauty but is lacking in that power which comes from a more direct expression of purpose." Chief Justice Harlan Fiske Stone called it "almost bombastically pretentious" and "wholly inappropriate for a quiet group of old boys such as the Supreme Court." Another justice said that the Court would be "nine black beetles in the Temple of Karnak." Another asked: "What are we supposed to do, ride in on nine elephants?"[10]

The building was designed so that the justices need not enter public areas except when hearing oral arguments and announcing their opinions. A private elevator connects the underground garage with the corridor, closed to the public, where the justices' offices are located.

The basement of the Supreme Court building contains—in addition to the garage—the offices of the facilities manager and a staff of thirty-two electricians, plumbers, painters, air-conditioning and heating specialists, and groundskeepers. The basement also houses a carpentry shop, laundry, and police roll-call room.

The ground floor contains the public information office, the clerk's office, the publications unit, police "headquarters," and other administrative offices, in addition to the exhibit halls, the cafeteria, and the gift shop. This floor also is the location of a bronze larger-than-life statue of Justice John Marshall (1801–1835). The sculptor was William Wetmore Story, the son of Justice Joseph Story (1812–1845).

The first floor contains the courtroom, the conference room, and all of the justices' chambers except Ruth Bader Ginsburg's. She chose a roomier office on the second floor.

The second floor contains the justices' dining room and library, the office of the reporter of decisions, the legal office, and law clerks' offices.

On the third floor is the library, paneled in hand-carved oak, and on the fourth floor there is a gymnasium and storage area.

The public is allowed to see only the ground floor and part of the first floor.

When Congress in 1929 authorized $9,740,000 for the construction of the Supreme Court building, it was expected then that extra funds for necessary furnishings would have to be appropriated. The final and complete cost of the building, in addition to all the furnishings, was below the authorization, and $94,000 was returned to the U.S. Treasury.

On the steps to the main entrance of the building are a pair of huge marble candelabra with carved panels representing justice, holding sword and scales, and the "three fates," who are weaving the thread of life. On either side of the steps are two marble figures by sculptor James Earle Fraser. On the left side is a female—the contemplation of justice—and on the right is a male—the guardian or authority of law.

At the entrance of the building is a pediment filled with sculptures representing, at the center, "Liberty Enthroned," guarded by "Order" and "Authority." On either side are groups depicting "Council and Research" in the guise of modern figures: the three on the left are a reclining Chief Justice William Howard Taft (1921–1930), who is portrayed as a student at Yale University and represents "Research Present"; New York Republican senator Elihu Root (1909–1915), who sponsored legislation creating a fine arts commission; and building architect Cass Gilbert. The three figures grouped to the right of the truly alle-

Since the Supreme Court building opened in 1935, the courtroom has been renovated only once, in 1992. This photo was taken after the renovation.

gorical forms are Justice Charles Evans Hughes (1910–1916, 1930–1941), the pediment's sculptor Robert Aitken; and Chief Justice John Marshall (1801–1835), representing "Research Past."

Panels on the main door were sculptured by John Donnelly Jr. and depict scenes in the development of the law. Along both sides of the great hall are busts of former chief justices, heraldic devices, and medallion profiles of lawgivers.

From the great hall, oak doors open into the courtroom, or court chamber. Measuring 82 feet by 91 feet with a 44-foot ceiling, the room has twenty-four columns of Italian marble. Overhead, along all four sides of the room, are marble panels sculptured by Adolph A. Weinman. Directly above the bench are two figures, depicting "majesty of the law" and "power of government." Between these figures is a tableau of the Ten Commandments. At the far left is a group representing "safeguard of the rights of the people" and "genii of wisdom and statescraft." At the far right is the "defense of human rights."

On the wall to the right of incoming visitors are figures of historical lawmakers of the pre-Christian era—Menes, Hammurabi, Moses, Solomon, Lycurgus, Solon, Draco, Confucius, and Augustus. These are flanked by figures symbolizing "fame" and "history." To the left of visitors are lawmakers of the Christian era—Napoleon, Marshall, Blackstone, Grotius, Saint Louis, King John, Charlemagne, Mohammed, and Justinian. They are flanked by figures representing "liberty," "peace," and "philosophy."

Little has changed in the physical appearance of the Court building since 1935. The courtroom was renovated in 1992, the first time since the building was opened. The new gold-fringed deep-red draperies and red, gold, and black carpet replaced worn-out furnishings yet remained consistent with the original interior's style. Toni House, the public information officer, said the cost of renovation was $264,000, of which about $69,000 came from funds appropriated by Congress and the other $195,000 derived from Supreme Court bar membership fees. Justices Sandra Day O'Connor and Anthony M. Kennedy oversaw the refurbishing.

Cost of the Court

Compared to its two coequal branches of the government, the executive branch and Congress, the Supreme Court seems to operate on a shoestring. In fiscal year 1996, for example, the Court received about $30 million to pay the salaries of the nine justices and Court employees, and to cover operating costs including care of the building and grounds. For the same fiscal year, Congress had an appropriation of about $2 billion.

The Supreme Court budget for each fiscal year is drawn up in the Office of the Marshal of the Court. It is submitted by October 15—nearly a year in advance—to the Office of Management and Budget (OMB). (The fiscal year begins the following October 1.)

The OMB is prohibited by statute from making any changes in the proposed budget for the federal judiciary before submitting it—along with proposed executive and legislative budgets—to Congress in January.

The Court's requests in the President's Budget Document have been divided into two categories—salaries and expenses of the Supreme Court and care of buildings and grounds—since fiscal year 1977. Before that, there were five categories: salaries, printing, miscellaneous expenses, car for the chief justice, and books for the Supreme Court.

FEDERAL JUDICIARY BUDGET

For the ninety-four district courts and thirteen courts of appeals, the budget process before submission to Congress involves several steps that are not applicable to the Supreme Court. The budget of each lower court is sent to the Administrative Office of the U.S. Courts by the court's chief judge. It is consolidated into a national budget by the Administrative Office and then approved by the Judicial Conference of the United States, which has no jurisdiction over the Supreme Court's budget. The conference is composed of the chief judges of the thirteen courts of appeals, a district court judge from each of the twelve geographic (or regional) circuits, and the chief judge of the Court of International Trade. The chief justice serves as the presiding officer.

In the budget process, the chief judge of the twelve geographical circuit courts has been assisted since 1972 by a "circuit executive" whose duties include preparing the budgets. Like those of the district, bankruptcy, and special courts, the proposed budget for the circuits must be submitted to the administrative office by May 1.

Budget requests are evaluated by specialists on the basis of program and project needs, in May and June. The conclusions are reviewed by the director of the administrative office, then sent to committees of judges for review before they are delivered to the judicial conference for approval.

Committees of the judicial conference review the requests, make recommendations, and send them to the budget committee for evaluation and further recommendations.

The judicial conference, usually in September, meets to consider the committees' recommendations and prepare a final version of the requests. The administrative office submits the final versions to the Office of Management and Budget (OMB) by October 15.

The fiscal 1996 appropriation for the federal judiciary was $3.1 billion.

Before the president sends the budget to Congress, the Administrative Office of the U.S. Courts submits justifications for the funds requested to the subcommittees of the congressional appropriations committees that will first consider the requests—the Senate and House subcommittees on Commerce, Justice, State, the Judiciary, and Related Agencies. Subcommittee hearings on the proposed budget generally begin in the spring of each year.

The subcommittees hold public hearings at which a justice of the Supreme Court, the chairman of the Judicial Conference Budget Committee, the chief judges of the special courts, and the director of the Administrative Office of the U.S. Courts are called to justify the budget requests. When the hearings are over, the subcommittees vote on appropriations bills and send them to a vote by the full Senate and House Appropriations Committees, followed by a final vote on the floors of the House and Senate. The Judiciary's budget requests are often reduced by Congress, but not in ways that significantly differ from reductions applied to executive agencies.

The funds Congress appropriates for the Supreme Court now go directly to the Court and are spent by the marshal for salaries of the justices and other employees and for Court needs. Before 1935 Congress channeled money for the Supreme Court through the Justice Department. The allocation of funds for the other federal courts is handled by the office of finance and budget of the Administrative Office of the U.S. Courts. The division submits recommendations on the allocation to the director of the administrative office and the executive committee of the judicial conference, who make the final decision on how the money is disbursed.

SALARIES OF THE JUSTICES

The salary of the chief justice of the United States was $171,500 in 1996, and that of the associate justices was $164,100.

Service on the Supreme Court was not always so remunerative. On September 23, 1789, Congress set the salary of an associate justice at $3,500 a year and for the chief justice at $4,000 a year.

That salary was not increased until 1819. When Congress was urged to raise the salaries in 1816, Justice Joseph Story (1812–1845) prepared a memorandum complaining that "the necessaries and comforts of life, the manner of living and the habits of ordinary expenses, in the same rank of society, have, between 1789 and 1815, increased in price from one hundred to two hundred percent. The business of the Judges of the Supreme Court, both at the Law Term in February and on the Circuits, has during the same period increased in more than a quadruple ratio and is increasing annually."[11] Congress was unreceptive at that time to Story's and other pleas for a pay raise for the justices.

The failure of Congress in early 1989 to approve a recommended raise for federal judges and other high-level federal officeholders, including members of Congress, moved Chief Justice William H. Rehnquist to do some serious lobbying as head of the judicial system. Breaking precedent, he appeared before a congressional committee, met privately with congressional leaders, and held a press conference to urge Congress to increase the salaries of federal judges. When he appeared before the House Post Office and Civil Service Committee in May 1989, he was the first sitting chief justice to appear to testify before Congress. In 1990 the judges were given a raise.[12]

RETIREMENT SYSTEM

From the establishment of the Supreme Court and for almost a century, many justices were caught in a dilemma: low salaries and no retirement plan. Many solved the problem by leaving the bench to accept more lucrative employment elsewhere. Justice Story, for one, did not. In 1816, when Congress re-

JUSTICES' SALARIES

Years	Chief Justice	Associate Justices
1789–1819	$4,000	$3,500
1819–1855	5,000	4,500
1855–1871	6,500	6,000
1871–1873	8,500	8,000
1873–1903	10,500	10,000
1903–1911	13,000	12,500
1911–1926	15,000	14,500
1926–1946	20,500	20,000
1946–1955	25,500	25,000
1955–1964	35,500	35,000
1964–1969	40,000	39,500
1969–1975	62,500	60,000
1975	65,625	63,000
1976*	68,800	66,000
1977	75,000	72,000
1978*	79,100	76,000
1979*	84,700	81,300
1980*	92,400	88,700
1981*	96,800	93,000
1982–1983*	100,700	96,700
1984	104,700	100,600
1985–1986	108,400	104,100
1987	115,000	110,000
1990	124,000	118,600
1991	160,600	153,600
1992	166,200	159,000
1993–1996	171,500	164,100

*A cost of living adjustment equal to 5 percent of regular salary.

omission was subsequently remedied, and the U.S. Code now contains provisions for resignation or retirement for age and retirement for disability.

Before 1937 justices who left the Court for any reason had to resign rather than retire, which meant that their pensions were subject to fluctuating civil service guidelines. That policy was changed with the Supreme Court Retirement Act of 1937. (See "Retirement," p. 98, in Chapter 5.)

The law now provides that:

Any justice or judge of the United States appointed to hold office during good behavior may retire from the office after attaining the age and meeting the service requirements, whether continuous or otherwise, of [the law] and shall, during the remainder of his lifetime, receive an annuity equal to the salary he was receiving at the time he retired.[13]

The age and years-of-service requirements delineated in the law are sixty-five years of age and fifteen years of service. The years of service required decrease by one as a justice's age increases by one. At age seventy, a justice needs only ten years of service to retire.[14]

Any justice or judge of the United States appointed to hold office during good behavior who becomes permanently disabled from performing his duties may retire from regular active service, and the President shall, by the advice and consent of the Senate, appoint a successor. Any justice or judge of the United States desiring to retire under this section shall certify to the President his disability in writing.[15]

A justice of the Supreme Court who is unable to perform his duties cannot be forced to resign. Congress, however, has provided that other federal judges deemed to be "unable to discharge efficiently all the duties of his office by reason of permanent mental or physical disability" can be replaced by the president with Senate approval.[16]

NOTES

1. "The Supreme Court—Its Homes Past and Present," *American Bar Association Journal* 27 (1941): 283–289.

2. Charles Warren, *The Supreme Court in United States History*, rev. ed., 2 vols. (Boston: Little, Brown, 1922, 1926), I: 164.

3. John P. Frank, *Marble Palace: The Supreme Court in American Life* (New York: Knopf, 1958).

4. Quoted by Warren in *The Supreme Court in United States History*, I: 457–458.

5. Ibid., 459.

6. *Dartmouth College v. Woodward*, 4 Wheat. 518 (1819).

7. *National Intelligencer*, February 2, 1819, quoted by Warren in *The Supreme Court in United States History*, I: 460.

8. *New York Statesman*, February 7, 1824, quoted in ibid.

9. Wesley McCune, *The Nine Young Men* (New York: Harper & Brothers, 1947), 2.

10. Quoted by Mary Ann Harrell in *Equal Justice Under Law: The Supreme Court in American Life* (Washington, D.C.: The Foundation of the American Bar Association, with the cooperation of the National Geographic Society, 1975), 116.

11. William Waldo Story, ed., *Life and Letters of Joseph Story*, 2 vols. (Boston: Little, Brown, 1851), I: 302.

12. Congressional Quarterly, *Weekly Report*, June 3, 1989, 1325.

13. 28 U.S.C. 371 (a).

14. 28 U.S.C. 371 (c).

15. 28 U.S.C. 372 (a).

16. 28 U.S.C. 372 (b).

fused to increase his and the other associate justices' salaries from $3,500, Story declined an offer to take over Charles Pinckney's law practice in Baltimore. Had he accepted, he would have been assured of an income of at least $10,000 a year.

Until 1869 justices who were unable to carry out their duties because of age or disability often hesitated to submit their resignations because there were no retirement benefits. It was in large measure the incapacity of Justices Robert C. Grier (1846–1870) and Samuel Nelson (1845–1872) that prompted Congress to provide in the Judiciary Act of April 10, 1869, "That any judge of any court of the United States, who, having held his commission as such at least ten years, shall, after having attained the age of seventy years, resign his office, shall thereafter, during the residue of his natural life, receive the same salary which was by law payable to him at the time of his resignation."

The Judiciary Act of 1869 made no provisions for retirement benefits for a justice who became incapacitated before reaching age seventy or before ten years of service on the Court. That

CHAPTER 7

Members of the Court

SINCE ITS ESTABLISHMENT in 1789, the Supreme Court has had only 108 members, making it one of the most exclusive as well as enduring of the world's governing bodies. All but two have been men, and all but two have been white. Only sixteen were not Protestant.

But the Court *has* exhibited diversity in other ways—politically, geographically, and in the age, personality, and previous service of its individual members. There have been periodic breakthroughs when appointees with controversial views or different backgrounds first attained a seat on the Court. The first Roman Catholic was appointed in 1835, the first Jew in 1916, the first black in 1967, and the first woman in 1981.

There are no constitutional or statutory qualifications at all for serving on the Supreme Court. The Constitution's Article III simply states that "the judicial power of the United States shall be vested in one supreme Court" as well as any lower federal courts Congress may establish. Article II directs that the president "by and with the Advice and Consent of the Senate, shall appoint . . . Judges of the supreme Court." There is no age limitation, no requirement that judges be native-born citizens, nor even that appointees have a legal background.

Naturally, informal criteria for membership quickly developed. Every nominee to the Court has been a lawyer—although it was not until the twentieth century that most justices were law school graduates.

Over the years, many other factors have entered into the process of presidential selection. Some of them became long-lasting traditions with virtually the force of a formal requirement. Others were as fleeting as the personal friendship between an incumbent president and his nominee.

The President Shall Appoint . . .

George Washington, as the first president, had the responsibility of choosing the original six justices of the Supreme Court. The type of men he chose and the reasons he chose them foreshadowed the process of selection carried out by his successors.

In naming the first justices, Washington paid close attention to their politics, which at that time primarily meant loyalty to the new Constitution. Of the six original appointees, three had attended the Philadelphia convention that formulated the Constitution, and the other three had supported its adoption. John Jay, the first chief justice, was coauthor with Alexander Hamilton and James Madison of *The Federalist Papers,* a series of influential essays published in New York supporting ratification of the Constitution. During his two terms of office, Washington had occasion to make five additional Supreme Court appointments. All were staunch supporters of the Constitution and the new federal government.

Another of Washington's major considerations was geography. The new states were a disparate group that barely had held together during the fight for independence and the confederation government of the 1780s. To bind them more closely together, Washington consciously tried to represent each geographical area of the country in the nation's new supreme tribunal.

His first six appointees were three northerners—Chief Justice John Jay from New York and Associate Justices William Cushing of Massachusetts and James Wilson of Pennsylvania—and three southerners—John Blair of Virginia, James Iredell of North Carolina, and John Rutledge of South Carolina. The five later appointees were Oliver Ellsworth of Connecticut, Thomas Johnson and Samuel Chase of Maryland, William Paterson of New Jersey, and Rutledge, appointed a second time. By the time Washington left office, nine of the original thirteen states had achieved representation on the Supreme Court.

With a total of eleven, Washington still holds the record for the number of Supreme Court appointments made by any president. The second highest total—nine—belongs to President Franklin D. Roosevelt, the only president to serve more than two terms. Roosevelt also came closest since Washington to naming the entire membership of the Court—only two justices who served prior to the Roosevelt years were still on the Court at the time of his death. Roosevelt elevated one of them, Harlan Fiske Stone, from associate justice to chief justice.

With six each, Presidents Andrew Jackson (1829–1837) and William Howard Taft (1909–1913) had the next highest number of justices appointed. Taft holds the record for a one-term president. Next in order are Abraham Lincoln (1861–1865) and Dwight D. Eisenhower (1953–1961) with five each.

Four presidents, William Henry Harrison, Zachary Taylor, Andrew Johnson, and Jimmy Carter, made no appointments to the Supreme Court. Harrison (1841) and Taylor (1849–1850) both died in office before any vacancies occurred. Johnson (1865–1869), who served just six weeks short of a full term, had no chance to make a Court appointment because of his rancorous political battle with Congress over Reconstruction. So bitter did the struggle become that Congress in effect took away Johnson's power of appointment by passing legislation in 1866 to reduce the Court to seven members from ten as vacancies should occur.

EMPTY CHAIRS: VACANCIES ON THE COURT

Twice in the Court's history a seat has been vacant for more than two years. The longest vacancy lasted for two years, three months, and twenty-three days. During that period the Senate rejected four nominations by two presidents, and a future president, James Buchanan, declined three invitations to the seat.

When Justice Henry Baldwin died April 21, 1844, John Tyler was president. Elected vice president on the Whig ticket in 1840, Tyler had broken with the party after he became president following William Henry Harrison's death in 1841. From then on, he was a president without a party or personal popularity. At the time of Baldwin's death, one Tyler nomination to the Court had already been rejected, and a second was pending. Tyler first offered the Baldwin vacancy to Buchanan, who, like Baldwin, was a Pennsylvanian. When he declined, the president nominated Philadelphia attorney Edward King.

Followers of Henry Clay, however, who controlled the Senate, thought Clay would win the presidency in that year's election, and they voted in June 1844 to postpone consideration of both King's nomination and Tyler's pending appointment of Reuben H. Walworth to the second vacancy. Tyler resubmitted King's name in December. Again the Senate refused to act, and Tyler was forced to withdraw the appointment.

By this time, Tyler was a lame-duck president and Clay had lost the election to Democrat James K. Polk. Nonetheless, Tyler in February 1845 named John M. Read, a Philadelphia attorney who had support among the Democrats and the Clay Whigs in the Senate. But the Senate failed to act on the nomination before adjournment, and the vacancy was left for Polk to fill.

Polk had only slightly better luck. After six months in office he offered the position to Buchanan, who again refused it. Another few months passed before Polk formally nominated George W. Woodward to the Baldwin vacancy in December 1845. Woodward turned out to be a hapless choice. He was opposed by one of the senators from his home state, Pennsylvania, and his extreme "American nativist" views made him unpopular with many other senators. His nomination was rejected on a 20–29 vote in January 1846.

Polk asked Buchanan once again to take the seat. Buchanan accepted, but later changed his mind and declined a third time. The president then turned to Robert C. Grier, a district court judge from Pennsylvania who proved acceptable to almost every one. The Senate confirmed him August 4, 1846, the day following his nomination.

The second-longest vacancy lasted almost as long as the first—two years, one month, and sixteen days. It occurred when Justice Peter V. Daniel of Virginia died May 31, 1860. At this point four of the remaining justices were northerners; four were from the South. Naturally, the South wanted Buchanan, now the president, to replace Daniel with another southerner; the North urged a nomination from one of its states.

Buchanan took a long time making up his mind. In February 1861, nearly eight months after the vacancy occurred, he nominated Secretary of State Jeremiah S. Black, a former chief justice of the Pennsylvania Supreme Court and U.S. attorney general. Black might have proved acceptable to southern senators, but many of them had already resigned from the Senate to join the Confederacy. Although he supported the Union, Black was not an abolitionist, and his nomination drew criticism from the northern antislavery press. Black also was opposed by Democrat Stephen A. Douglas, who had just lost the presidential election to Abraham Lincoln. Finally, Republicans in the Senate were not anxious to help fill a vacancy that they could leave open for the incoming Republican president. Had Buchanan acted earlier, it is likely that Black would have been confirmed. As it was, the Senate rejected his nomination by a one-vote margin, 25–26.

Buchanan made no further attempt to fill the Daniel vacancy. Lincoln, who soon had two more seats on the Court to fill, did not name anyone to the Daniel seat until July 1862—more than a year after his inauguration. His choice was Samuel F. Miller, a well-respected Iowa attorney. Miller's nomination had been urged by a majority of both the House and Senate and by other politicians and members of the legal profession. The Senate confirmed his nomination within half an hour of receiving it July 16, 1862.

SOURCES: Henry J. Abraham, *Justices and Presidents: A Political History of Appointments to the Supreme Court*, 3d ed. (New York: Oxford University Press, 1992); and Charles Warren, *The Supreme Court in United States History*, rev. ed., 2 vols. (Boston: Little, Brown, 1922, 1926).

The legislation was occasioned by the death of Justice John Catron in 1865 and Johnson's nomination in 1866 of Henry Stanbery to replace him. The Senate took no action on Stanbery's nomination and instead passed the bill reducing the size of the Court. When Justice James Wayne died in 1867, the membership of the Court automatically dropped to eight.

In 1869, when the Republicans recaptured the White House, Congress passed legislation increasing the Court to nine seats, allowing President Ulysses S. Grant to make a nomination.

Jimmy Carter was the only full-term president who has been denied the opportunity to nominate a member of the Court. No deaths or resignations occurred on the Court during his term.

PARTY LINES

As political parties became an established fact of American political life, the major parties sought to have members appointed to the Supreme Court who would espouse their view of what the federal government should and should not do. As Washington had appointed supporters of the new Constitution, so most presidents have selected nominees with whom they were philosophically and politically in accord.

It is the exception when a president goes to the opposite political party to find a nominee. The first clear-cut instance of a president of one party appointing a member of the other to the Supreme Court was Republican Abraham Lincoln's selection of

Democrat Stephen J. Field of California in 1863. President John Tyler, who was elected vice president as a Whig in 1840, appointed Democrat Samuel Nelson to the Court in 1845. But by that time Tyler was no longer identified with either major political party.

After Lincoln's example, Republican presidents occasionally appointed Democrats to the Court. President Benjamin Harrison selected Howell Jackson of Tennessee in 1893; Warren G. Harding appointed Pierce Butler in 1922; Herbert Hoover appointed Benjamin Cardozo in 1932; Dwight D. Eisenhower appointed William J. Brennan Jr. in 1956; and Richard Nixon appointed Lewis F. Powell Jr. in 1971. Republican William Howard Taft was the only president to appoint more than one member of the opposite party to the Court. Three of his six nominees to the Court were Democrats—Edward D. White, whom he elevated from associate justice to chief justice, and Horace Lurton and Joseph R. Lamar, southern Democrats appointed in 1909 and 1910, respectively.

The only two Democrats ever to appoint Republicans to the Supreme Court were Franklin D. Roosevelt and Harry S. Truman. Roosevelt elevated Justice Stone, a Republican, to chief justice in 1941. Truman appointed Sen. Harold H. Burton, R-Ohio, an old friend and colleague from Truman's Senate days, in 1945.

SEEKING A SEAT

Before a president finally decides whom to nominate, a process of balancing and sifting usually goes on, sometimes involving many participants and sometimes only a few. But occasionally, a president's choice has all but been made by overwhelming pressure for a particular nominee.

One of the more dramatic instances of this process occurred in 1853, when President Franklin Pierce nominated John A. Campbell of Alabama for a seat on the Court. Campbell was a forty-one-year-old lawyer who had such a brilliant reputation that the justices decided they wanted him as a colleague. The entire membership of the Court wrote to Pierce requesting Campbell's nomination. To emphasize their point, two justices delivered the letters in person. Pierce complied, and Campbell was confirmed within four days.

In 1862 President Lincoln was looking for a new justice from the Midwest. The Iowa congressional delegation began pressing for the appointment of Samuel Miller, a doctor and lawyer who had helped form the Iowa Republican Party and who had a strong reputation for moral and intellectual integrity. The movement grew rapidly until 129 of 140 House members and all but four senators had signed a petition for Miller's nomination. With such massive and unprecedented congressional support, Miller received Lincoln's approval despite his lack of any judicial experience. He became the first justice from west of the Mississippi River.

In 1932 a strong national movement began for the appointment of Benjamin Cardozo, chief judge of the New York Court of Appeals, to the Supreme Court. Cardozo was a Democrat, while the president who was to make the appointment, Herbert Hoover, was a Republican. Furthermore, Cardozo was Jewish and there was already one Jew on the Court, Louis D. Brandeis. Under these circumstances, it was considered unlikely Hoover would make the nomination.

But Cardozo's record was so impressive that a groundswell of support arose for him. Deans and faculty members of the nation's leading law schools, chief judges of other state courts, labor and business leaders, and powerful senators all urged Hoover to choose Cardozo. Despite his desire to appoint a western Republican, Hoover finally yielded and nominated Cardozo, who was confirmed without opposition.

STATES OF ORIGIN

George Washington's weighing of geographical factors in appointing the first justices continued as a tradition for more than a century. It was reinforced by the justices' duty under the Judiciary Act of 1789 to ride and preside over circuit court sessions. Presidents not only strove for geographical balance in their appointments but also considered it important that each justice be a native of the circuit over which he presided.

The burdensome attendance requirement was curtailed by legislation during the nineteenth century until it became optional in 1891 and was abolished altogether in 1911. In the twentieth century, geography became a less important consideration in Supreme Court nominations, although as recently as 1970 President Nixon made an issue of it when the Senate refused to confirm two southerners—Clement Haynsworth Jr. and G. Harrold Carswell—to the Court. Nixon claimed the Senate would not confirm a conservative southerner and turned to Harry A. Blackmun of Minnesota instead.

In its heyday, the geographical factor was sometimes almost sacrosanct. The longest-lasting example, which endured from 1789 to 1932, was the so-called New England seat, usually occupied by an appointee from Massachusetts. There was also a seat for a New Yorker from 1806 to 1894 and a Maryland-Virginia seat from 1789 to 1860.

Geography had strong political ramifications as well, especially for the South. With the growth of sectional differences, particularly over the slavery issue before the Civil War, the South felt itself to be on the defensive. One of the ways it sought to protect its interests was to gain a majority on the Supreme Court. And, indeed, five of the nine justices in 1860 were from slaveholding states.

With the coming of the Civil War, the sectional balance of power shifted. Four of the five southern justices died between 1860 and 1867, and another—Justice John A. Campbell of Alabama—resigned to join the Confederate cause.

Not one of these justices was replaced by a southerner, and by 1870 every Supreme Court seat was held by a northerner or westerner. But with the gradual decline of bitterness over the war, southerners again began to appear on the Court. President Rutherford B. Hayes, who sought to reconcile relations between the North and South, made the first move by appointing

THE IMPORTANCE OF BEING EASTERN . . . OR SOUTHERN

Geography was a prime consideration in the appointment of Supreme Court justices throughout the nineteenth century. Presidents found it expedient to have each of the expanding nation's rival sections represented on the Court.

THE "NEW ENGLAND" SEAT

The most notable example of geographical continuity was the seat traditionally held by a New Englander. William Cushing of Massachusetts was appointed an associate justice by President George Washington in 1789. For the next 143 years, that seat was held by a New Englander.

When Cushing died, President James Madison selected Joseph Story of Massachusetts. Story served thirty-four years. When he died in 1845, President James K. Polk appointed Levi Woodbury of New Hampshire, a prominent Jacksonian who had served as governor, senator, secretary of the Navy, and secretary of the Treasury.

Woodbury's tenure lasted less than six years, and it fell to President Millard Fillmore to find a successor. He chose Benjamin Curtis, another Massachusetts native. Curtis resigned in 1857, and President James Buchanan chose Nathan Clifford of Maine, a former attorney general, to fill the seat.

Clifford served until his death in July 1881, shortly after President James A. Garfield was shot. When Garfield died in September, Chester Arthur chose Horace Gray, the chief justice of the Massachusetts Supreme Court. Gray served until 1902, when he was succeeded by another Massachusetts Supreme Court chief justice, Oliver Wendell Holmes Jr., appointed by President Theodore Roosevelt.

By the time of Holmes's appointment, however, the significance of geography had declined, and it was mostly accidental that Holmes came from Massachusetts. Nevertheless, his selection extended for another thirty years the tradition of the "New England" seat. After Holmes resigned in 1932, President Herbert Hoover chose as his successor Benjamin Cardozo, chief judge of New York State's highest court, and ended the Supreme Court's longest-lasting geographical tradition.

THE "NEW YORK" SEAT

The appointment of Justice Henry Brockholst Livingston by President Thomas Jefferson in 1806 began a tradition of a New York seat that continued for almost ninety years.

Livingston served until his death in 1823. President James Monroe then chose Smith Thompson of New York, his secretary of the Navy. Thompson served for twenty years. His death in 1843 came at an inopportune moment politically: President John Tyler was disliked by both Democrats and Whigs and had little political leverage. His attempts to choose a successor to Thompson met with repeated failure. Finally, just before leaving office in 1845, Tyler found a New Yorker acceptable to the Senate, Justice Samuel Nelson, who served until 1872. After Nelson's retirement, two more New Yorkers held the seat, Ward Hunt from 1873 to 1882 and Samuel Blatchford from 1882 to 1893. But then a bitter quarrel between New Yorkers ended the tradition.

The New York antagonists were President Grover Cleveland and Sen. David B. Hill, old political enemies. Cleveland twice nominated a New Yorker for the post, and twice Hill used senatorial courtesy to object to the nominees. In both cases, the Senate followed its tradition of honoring a senator's objection to a nominee of his own party from his home state and rejected Cleveland's choices. On his third try to fill the vacancy, Cleveland abandoned New York and chose Sen. Edward D. White of Louisiana, who was confirmed immediately by his colleagues.

THE "VIRGINIA-MARYLAND" SEAT

Virginia and Maryland shared representation on the Court from 1789 until the Civil War. John Blair of Virginia, appointed by Washington, was succeeded by Samuel Chase of Maryland. After Chase's death in 1811, another Marylander, Gabriel Duvall, was given the seat. He resigned in 1835, and the seat went back to Virginia, with Philip Barbour holding it from 1836 to 1841, and Peter V. Daniel from 1841 to 1860. The Maryland-Virginia tradition was ended when President Abraham Lincoln appointed Samuel Miller of Iowa as Daniel's successor.

William B. Woods of Georgia in 1880. Woods was not a native southerner; he had moved South after the Civil War. But despite this "carpetbagger" background, he was never identified with the corruption and profligacy associated with the Reconstruction era. As a federal judge for the Fifth Circuit, in the deep South, he gained the respect of his neighbors for his fairness and honesty.

The first native southerner appointed to the Court after the Civil War was Woods's successor, Lucius Q. C. Lamar of Mississippi, appointed by President Grover Cleveland in 1888. Lamar had personally drafted the ordinance of secession for Mississippi in 1861 and had served the Confederacy both as a military officer and as a diplomatic envoy to Europe. So his accession to the Court was an even more significant symbol of reconciliation than Woods's appointment eight years earlier.

Thirty-one states have contributed justices to the Supreme Court. New York has by far the highest total, with fourteen, two of whom, Charles Evans Hughes and Harlan Stone, served as both associate justice and chief justice, followed by Ohio with ten and Massachusetts and Virginia with eight. Several major states have had only one justice, including Texas, Indiana, and Missouri—as have less-populated states such as Utah, Maine, and Wyoming.

Nineteen states, mostly western states with small populations, have never had a native on the Court. Only six of the nineteen are east of the Mississippi River. The largest state never to have had a justice is Florida.

The lack of representation on the Court from some of the less densely populated states resulted in a controversy during the 1950s when North Dakota's outspoken maverick senator,

Republican William Langer, began opposing all non-North Dakotan Supreme Court nominees as a protest against big-state nominees. Langer was chairman of the Senate Judiciary Committee during the Eighty-third Congress (1953–1955). In 1954 he joined in delaying tactics against the nomination of Earl Warren as chief justice, managing to hold off confirmation for two months. He continued his struggle until his death in 1959.

Justices' Characteristics

All of President Washington's appointees were lawyers, and no president has deviated from this precedent. Legal education has changed radically over the years, however. Until the mid-nineteenth century, it was traditional for aspiring lawyers to study privately in a law office until they had learned the law sufficiently to pass the bar. There were no law schools as such in the early years, although some universities had courses in law. John Marshall, for example, attended a course of law lectures at William and Mary College in the 1770s. Two of the earliest justices, John Rutledge and John Blair, received their legal education in England, at the Inns of Court. A modern justice, Frank Murphy (1940–1949), also studied there. Three justices, Henry Baldwin, Levi Woodbury, and Ward Hunt, attended law lectures by Federalist judge Tapping Reeve in Lichtfield, Connecticut.

Of the sixty-one justices (including Rutledge and Blair) who attended law school, by far the largest number (sixteen) attended Harvard. Yale taught nine justices law, and Columbia six. The first justice to receive a law degree from an American university was Benjamin Curtis, who got his from Harvard in 1832.

It was not until 1957 that the Supreme Court was composed, for the first time, entirely of law school graduates. Before that, many had attended law school, but had not received degrees. The last justice never to have attended law school was James F. Byrnes, who served from 1941 to 1942. The son of poor Irish immigrants, Byrnes never even graduated from high school. He left school at the age of fourteen, worked as a law clerk, and eventually became a Court stenographer. Reading law in his spare time, Byrnes passed the bar at the age of twenty-four.

The last justice not to have a law degree was Stanley F. Reed, who served from 1938 to 1957. He attended both the University of Virginia and Columbia law schools, but received no law degree.

LIFE BEFORE THE COURT

Most justices were politicians or judges before coming to the Supreme Court. In fact, only one justice, George Shiras Jr., had never engaged in political or judicial activities before his appointment. A total of sixty-seven justices had some judicial experience—federal or state—before coming to the Supreme Court. Surprisingly, there have been more (forty-four) who had experience on the state level than on the federal level (thirty-one).

All except two of President Washington's appointees had state judicial experience. Washington believed such experience was important for justices of the new federal court. But not until 1826 was a federal judge appointed to the Court. Robert Trimble had served nine years as a U.S. district judge before being elevated to the Supreme Court.

Even after Trimble's appointment, judges with federal judicial experience continued to be a rarity on the Supreme Court. By 1880 only two other federal judges, Philip P. Barbour in 1836 and Peter V. Daniel in 1841, had made it to the high Court. After 1880, when federal circuit judge William B. Woods was appointed, the pace picked up, and federal judicial experience became an increasingly important criterion for appointment to the Supreme Court. By 1995, seven of the nine justices had served as federal judges before coming to the Court. An eighth had served as a state judge before her appointment.

Many justices had political careers, serving in Congress, as governors, or as members of a cabinet. One president, William Howard Taft, was later appointed to the Court, as chief justice, in 1921. As of 1995, a fourth of all justices, twenty-seven, had served in Congress before their elevation to the Court. An additional six justices sat in the Continental Congress in the 1770s or 1780s.

The first justice with congressional background was William Paterson, who had served in the Senate from 1789 to 1790. Chief Justice John Marshall was the first justice with cabinet experience, having held the post of secretary of state from 1800 to 1801. Only a few justices have come directly from Congress to the Court. Only one incumbent House member, James M. Wayne in 1835, has been named to the Court, and five incumbent senators: John McKinley in 1837, Levi Woodbury in 1846, Edward D. White in 1894, Hugo L. Black in 1937, and Harold H. Burton in 1945.

The Senate traditionally has confirmed its own members without much debate. But in January 1853, when lame-duck president Millard Fillmore nominated Whig senator George Badger of North Carolina to the Court, the Democratic Senate postponed the nomination until the close of the congressional session in March. Then the new Democratic president, Franklin Pierce, was able to nominate his own man. The postponement of Badger's nomination was a polite way of defeating a colleague's nomination, avoiding an outright rejection.

Senator White's nomination came about after a bitter quarrel between President Grover Cleveland and Sen. David B. Hill of New York resulted in the Senate's rejection of two Cleveland nominees from New York. Cleveland then turned to the Senate for one of its own members, and that body quickly approved him.

Hugo Black's 1937 nomination was surrounded by controversy. Sen. Joseph T. Robinson of Arkansas, the Senate majority leader who had led the fight for President Franklin D. Roosevelt's so-called Court-packing plan, was expected to get the nomination, but he died suddenly. Roosevelt picked Black, one of the few southern senators other than Robinson who had championed the president in the Court battle. Black's support of the controversial bill—plus what some felt was his general

CATHOLIC AND JEWISH JUSTICES

All but sixteen Supreme Court justices have been of Protestant background. The first break with Protestant tradition came in 1835, when President Andrew Jackson nominated Roger B. Taney, a Roman Catholic, as chief justice. Taney's religion caused no controversy at the time; however, his close alliance with Jackson, whom he served as attorney general and Treasury secretary, was an issue.

After Taney's death in 1864, it was thirty years before another Catholic was appointed. In that year, President Grover Cleveland chose Edward D. White of Louisiana as associate justice. Sixteen years later, President William Howard Taft made White chief justice. As with Taney, White's religion attracted no particular notice. Both Taney and White were from traditional Catholic areas of the country, and both had long been engaged in politics. In 1897 President William McKinley chose Joseph McKenna, his attorney general and a Catholic, as associate justice. In that appointment, geography was the overriding factor—McKenna came from California, the same state as his predecessor, Stephen J. Field.

Pierce Butler was the next Catholic appointee, named by Warren G. Harding in 1922. On Butler's death in late 1939, Franklin D. Roosevelt picked as his successor Frank Murphy, an Irish Catholic who had been mayor of Detroit, governor of Michigan, and was then serving as Roosevelt's attorney general. In 1949, when Murphy died, Harris S. Truman named a Protestant, Tom C. Clark. For the first time since 1894, there was no Catholic on the Court.

Of all Catholic appointments, that of William J. Brennan Jr. by President Dwight D. Eisenhower in 1956 attracted the most notice, although it was relatively noncontroversial. But it was an election year, and the Republicans were making a strong appeal to normally Democratic Catholic voters in the big cities. Some saw Brennan's appointment as part of that GOP strategy, although Eisenhower insisted it was an appointment made purely on merit.

President Ronald Reagan named two Catholics to the Court—Anthony M. Kennedy and Antonin Scalia. Their religious beliefs seemed significant only insofar as the Catholic church, like Reagan, steadfastly opposed abortion. The link between Catholicism and that particular position, however, is not indissoluble. Justice Brennan had steadily supported abortion rights.

Much more controversial than any of the Catholic nominees was Louis D. Brandeis, the first Jewish justice, named by Woodrow Wilson in 1916. Brandeis was already a figure of great controversy because of his views on social and economic matters. Conservatives bitterly fought his nomination, raising an element of anti-Semitism. When Brandeis took his seat on the Court, Justice James McReynolds refused to speak to him for three years and once refused to sit next to him for a Court picture-taking session.

Herbert Hoover's nomination of Benjamin Cardozo in 1932 established a so-called Jewish seat on the Supreme Court. Justice Felix Frankfurter replaced Cardozo in 1939. He in turn was replaced by Justice Arthur J. Goldberg in 1962. And when Goldberg resigned his Court position to become U.S. Ambassador to the United Nations, President Lyndon B. Johnson chose Abe Fortas to replace him. But with Justice Fortas's resignation in 1969, President Richard Nixon broke the tradition of a "Jewish" seat by choosing Harry A. Blackmun of Minnesota, a Protestant.

A quarter of a century then passed before the Court had another Jewish member and then, in quick succession, President Bill Clinton named two Jewish justices: Ruth Bader Ginsburg in 1993 and Stephen G. Breyer in 1994. Religion was not an issue for either of the nominees, both of whom were long-serving judges on lower federal courts.

Clarence Thomas was an Episcopalian when named to the Court in 1991, but in 1996 he announced that he had returned to Catholicism, the faith of his youth. That personal decision made history: for the first time, a majority of the justices were not Protestant. Thomas, Scalia, and Kennedy were Catholic; Breyer and Ginsburg, Jewish.

---

lack of qualifications for the Supreme Court—led to a brief but acrimonious fight over his nomination. After he was confirmed, publicity grew over his one-time membership in the Ku Klux Klan, and charges were made that he was still a member. In a nationwide radio address, Black denied having any racial or religious intolerance and defused the criticism.

The last Supreme Court appointee with any previous congressional service was Sherman Minton in 1949. He had served as a U.S. senator from Indiana from 1935 to 1941, then was appointed to a circuit court of appeals judgeship. Since the retirement of Justice Black in 1971, no Supreme Court member has had any congressional experience.

Since John Adams's secretary of state, John Marshall, was appointed to the Supreme Court, twenty-two other cabinet members have become justices, thirteen of them appointed while still serving in the cabinet. Heading the list of cabinet positions that led to Supreme Court seats is that of attorney general. Nine attorneys general, including seven incumbents, have been appointed to the Court. Next come secretaries of the Treasury (four), secretaries of state (three), and secretaries of the Navy (three). One postmaster general, one secretary of the interior, one secretary of war, and one secretary of labor have been appointed to the Court.

The appointment of incumbent attorneys general has been largely a twentieth-century phenomenon; six of the seven appointments occurred after 1900. The other occurred in 1897, when President William McKinley appointed his attorney general, Joseph McKenna. The twentieth-century incumbents named to the Court were William H. Moody, appointed by Theodore Roosevelt in 1906; James C. McReynolds (Wilson, 1914); Harlan Fiske Stone (Coolidge, 1925); Frank Murphy (Roosevelt, 1940); Robert H. Jackson (Roosevelt, 1941); and Tom C. Clark (Truman, 1949).

During the nineteenth century two men who had served as attorney general eventually were elevated to the Supreme Court, but in both cases appointment came after their cabinet service.

They were Roger B. Taney, appointed chief justice by President Andrew Jackson in 1835, after serving as Jackson's attorney general from 1831 to 1833, and Nathan Clifford, appointed to the Court by President James Buchanan in 1857 after service as James K. Polk's attorney general from 1846 to 1848. The last justice with cabinet experience was Clark, who served on the Court from 1949 to 1967.

Six men have been appointed to the Supreme Court after serving as governor of their state. The first was William Paterson, who served as governor of New Jersey from 1790 to 1793. The most recent—and the most famous—was California governor Earl Warren, appointed chief justice by President Eisenhower in 1953. Warren had a long political career behind him, having served as attorney general of California before winning three terms as governor. In 1948 he was the Republican nominee for vice president and ran a brief campaign for the presidential nomination in 1952.

Charles Evans Hughes of New York was appointed to the Court by President Taft in 1910. Hughes was a reform governor who had conducted investigations into fraudulent insurance practices in New York before being elected governor in 1906. He left the Court in 1916 to run for president on the Republican ticket, losing narrowly to Woodrow Wilson. Later he served as secretary of state under Harding and Coolidge and returned to the Court in 1930 as chief justice, appointed by President Hoover.

The three other former governors appointed to the Supreme Court were Levi Woodbury of New Hampshire in 1846 (governor, 1823–1824), Salmon P. Chase of Ohio in 1864 (governor, 1856–1860), and Frank Murphy of Michigan in 1940 (governor, 1937–1939). One chief justice, John Jay, left the Court to become governor of New York.

James Byrnes followed Jay's path, leaving the Court in 1942, after only sixteen months in the post, for other positions in federal and state government, the last of which was that of governor of South Carolina, an office he held from 1951 to 1955.

GENERATION GAPS

The age at which justices join the Court varies widely. Oldest at the time of his initial appointment was Horace H. Lurton, who was sixty-five when he went on the Court in 1910. Two chief justices were older than that when they achieved their office, but they had previously served on the Court: in 1941 Harlan Fiske Stone was sixty-eight; and in 1930 Charles Evans Hughes was sixty-seven.

Representing the younger generation, Justices William Johnson and Joseph Story were only thirty-two when they were appointed in 1804 and 1811, respectively. Story was younger than Johnson by about a month.

Only two other justices were under forty when appointed: Bushrod Washington, nephew of the president, who was thirty-six when appointed in 1798, and James Iredell, who was thirty-eight when appointed in 1790. Iredell also was the youngest justice to die on the Court—forty-eight when he died in 1799. The youngest twentieth-century justice was William O. Douglas, who was forty when appointed in 1939.

The oldest justice to serve was Oliver Wendell Holmes, who retired at ninety in 1932, the Court's only nonagenarian. The second oldest member, Chief Justice Roger Taney, was eighty-seven when he died in 1864. As of 1996, all the other justices who had served past the age of eighty retired from the bench and did not die in office. They were Harry Blackmun, eighty-five when he retired; William Brennan, eighty-four; Thurgood Marshall, eighty-three; Louis Brandeis and Gabriel Duvall, both eighty-two; Joseph McKenna and Stephen Field, both eighty-one; and Samuel Nelson, eighty.

The youngest member to leave the Court was Benjamin Curtis, who resigned in 1857 at forty-seven. Others who left the Court before the age of fifty were Justices Iredell, dead at forty-eight, Alfred Moore, who retired at forty-eight, and John Jay and John Campbell, who retired at forty-nine. Jay also holds the record for number of years survived after leaving the Court—thirty-four years. In modern times, James Byrnes lived twenty-nine years after resigning from the Court in 1942.

LENGTH OF SERVICE

Length of service on the Court also has varied greatly, from fifteen months to thirty-six years. Byrnes served the shortest time; he was confirmed by the Senate June 12, 1941, and resigned October 3, 1942, to become director of the World War II Office of Economic Stabilization. Justice Thomas Johnson, who served from 1791 to 1793, was on the Court only sixteen months. Although he retired because of ill health, he lived another twenty-six years, dying at the age of eighty-seven.

In January 1974 Justice Douglas broke the record for service on the Court, held since December 1897 by Stephen Field, who had served thirty-four years and nine months when he resigned. Douglas served until November 1975, when he resigned after thirty-six years and seven months on the Court. Chief Justice Marshall established the first longevity record by serving for thirty-four years and five months between 1801 and 1835. That record held until Field broke it in 1897.

Other justices who served thirty years or longer include Brennan (thirty-four years, nine months), Black (thirty-four years, one month), the first John Marshall Harlan and Joseph Story (thirty-three years each), James Wayne (thirty-two years), Byron R. White (thirty-one years, two months), John McLean (thirty-one years), and Bushrod Washington and William Johnson (thirty years each).

Four or five years is usually the longest the Court goes without a change in justices. The long terms of Black and Douglas spanned an era of such changing membership on the Court that they each served with more than a quarter of the Court's entire membership throughout its history. But there was one lengthy period—twelve years—when the Court's membership remained intact. That was from 1811, when Joseph Story was confirmed, to 1823, when Justice Henry Brockholst Livingston died.

Long service sometimes leads to questions of disability, as

SIX FOREIGN-BORN JUSTICES

The Constitution does not require that Supreme Court justices be native-born Americans, and so presidents are free to name foreign-born persons to the Court. In all, six Supreme Court justices have been born outside the United States, one the son of an American missionary abroad. Of the remaining five, four were born in the British Isles. Only one—Felix Frankfurter—was born in a non-English-speaking country, Austria.

President George Washington appointed three of the foreign-born justices. The others were selected by Presidents Benjamin Harrison, Warren G. Harding, and Franklin D. Roosevelt.

The six justices born outside the United States are:

• James Wilson, born September 14, 1742, in Caskardy, Scotland. Wilson grew up in Scotland and was educated at St. Andrews University in preparation for a career in the ministry. But in 1765 he sailed for America, where he studied law and became a land speculator. A signer of the Declaration of Independence, Wilson also was a member of the 1787 Constitutional Convention and its Committee of Detail, which was responsible for writing the first draft of the Constitution. In 1789 President Washington appointed Wilson one of the original members of the Supreme Court.

• James Iredell, born October 5, 1751, in Lewes, England. Iredell was born into an old English family allegedly descended from Oliver Cromwell's son-in-law. Through family connections, Iredell received an appointment as colonial comptroller of customs at Edenton, North Carolina, at age seventeen. After six years he was promoted to collector of the port of Edenton. But Iredell identified with the colonial cause and resigned his job as collector in 1776. While serving in his colonial offices, Iredell had studied law and began practice in 1770. By 1788 he had become a strong supporter of the new federal Constitution and worked for its ratification by North Carolina. President Washington appointed him a Supreme Court justice in 1790.

• William Paterson, born December 24, 1745, in County Antrim, Ireland. Paterson emigrated to America with his parents when he was only two years old. He received his education at the College of New Jersey (now Princeton University) and then read law, opening his own law practice in 1769. Paterson was active in New Jersey affairs during the Revolutionary and Confederation periods, and he served as a delegate to the Constitutional Convention in 1787. He was a member of the First Senate from 1789 to 1790 and, as a member of the Judiciary Committee, helped write the Judiciary Act of 1789. Later, he codified the laws of the state of New Jersey and, in association with Alexander Hamilton, laid out plans for the industrial city of Paterson. He was appointed to the Supreme Court by President Washington in 1793.

• David Brewer, born June 20, 1837, in Smyrna, Asia Minor, where his father was serving as a Congregational missionary. Brewer's mother was the sister of Justice Stephen J. Field (1863–1897) and Cyrus W. Field, promoter of the first Atlantic cable. The family returned to the United States soon after Brewer's birth. Brewer sought his fortune in Kansas and spent most of his career in the Kansas court system and lower federal courts. He was elevated to the Supreme Court by President Benjamin Harrison in 1890.

• George Sutherland, born March 25, 1862, in Buckinghamshire, England. Sutherland's father converted to Mormonism about the time of George's birth and moved his family to the Utah Territory. Although the senior Sutherland soon deserted the Mormons, the family remained in Utah, where George was educated at Brigham Young Academy (now Brigham Young University). When Utah entered the Union as a state in 1896, Sutherland was elected to the state legislature. In 1900 he won a seat in the U.S. House and served two terms in the U.S. Senate (1905–1917) before being defeated for reelection. While in the Senate, he formed a close friendship with a fellow senator, Warren G. Harding of Ohio. When Harding became president, he appointed Sutherland to the Supreme Court.

• Felix Frankfurter, born November 15, 1882, in Vienna, Austria. Frankfurter came to the United States with his parents in 1894 and grew up on the lower East Side of New York City. He had a brilliant academic record at City College and Harvard Law School, after which he practiced law for a time in New York City. In 1914 he joined the Harvard Law faculty and remained there, with time out for government service during World War I, until his appointment to the Supreme Court by President Franklin D. Roosevelt in 1939.

---

justices age and are no longer capable of carrying a full load of casework. By early 1870 Justice Robert C. Grier was nearly seventy-six. His mental and physical powers were obviously impaired, and often he seemed confused and feeble. Grier complied when a committee of his fellow justices finally approached him to urge his resignation. He died eight months later.

Justice Field was among those urging Grier's retirement. Ironically, a quarter of a century later, Field found himself in the same position as Grier. His powers had visibly declined, and he was frequently absent from the Court. The other justices finally began hinting strongly that Field resign. But Field insisted on staying on long enough to break Chief Justice Marshall's record for length of service.

In 1880 the Court was manned by an especially infirm set of justices; three of the nine, Ward Hunt, Nathan Clifford, and Noah Swayne, were incapacitated. Hunt had suffered a paralytic stroke in 1879 and took no further part in Court proceedings, but he refused to resign because he was not eligible for a full pension under the law then in effect. Finally, after three years, Congress passed a special law exempting Hunt from the terms of the pension law, granting him retirement at full pay if he would resign from the Court within thirty days of enactment of the exemption. Hunt resigned the same day.

Justice Clifford also had suffered a stroke that prevented him from participating in Court activities. But Clifford also refused to resign, hoping to live long enough for a Democratic president to name a successor. At the time, Clifford was the only Democrat left on the Court who had been named by a Democratic president. But he died while Republicans were still in power.

While Hunt and Clifford were both incapacitated, Justice Swayne's mental acuity was noticeably declining. He was finally persuaded to resign by President Hayes, with the promise that Swayne's friend and fellow Ohioan Stanley Matthews would be chosen as his successor.

The most recent case of a Court disability was that of Justice Douglas, who suffered a stroke in January 1975. At first, Douglas attempted to continue his duties, but in November 1975 he resigned, citing pain and physical disability.

Controversial Justices

Only once has a justice been driven from the Court by outside pressure. That occurred in 1969, when Justice Abe Fortas resigned. The resignation followed by less than eight months a successful Senate filibuster against President Lyndon B. Johnson's nomination of Fortas to be chief justice. Fortas's departure from the Court climaxed a furor brought on by the disclosure early in May 1969 that he had received and held for eleven months a $20,000 fee from the family foundation of a man later imprisoned for illegal stock manipulation.

A year after Fortas's resignation, an attempt was made to bring impeachment charges against Justice Douglas. General dissatisfaction with Douglas's liberal views and controversial lifestyle—combined with frustration over the Senate's rejection of two of President Nixon's conservative southern nominees—seemed to spark the action. House Republican leader Gerald R. Ford of Michigan, who led the attempt to impeach Douglas, charged among other things that the justice had practiced law in violation of federal law, had failed to disqualify himself in cases in which he had an interest, and had violated standards of good behavior by allegedly advocating revolution. A special House Judiciary subcommittee created to investigate the charges found no grounds for impeachment.

The only Supreme Court justice ever to be impeached was Samuel Chase. A staunch Federalist who had rankled Jeffersonians with his partisan political statements and his vigorous prosecution of the Alien and Sedition Act, Chase was impeached by the House in 1804. But his critics failed to achieve the necessary two-thirds majority in the Senate for conviction.

Other, less heralded cases of questionable behavior have occurred from time to time. In 1857, when the nation was awaiting the Court's decision in *Scott v. Sandford,* Justices Robert Grier and John Catron wrote privately to the incoming president, James Buchanan, detailing the Court's discussions and foretelling the final decision.

Buchanan was glad of the news and was able to say in his inaugural address that the decision was expected to come soon and that he and all Americans should acquiesce in it. But divulging the Court's decision before it is publicly announced is generally considered to be unethical.

Another controversy arose fourteen years later in the so-called *Legal Tender Cases.* The Court, with two vacancies, had found the Civil War legal tender acts unconstitutional. But then President Grant named two justices to fill the vacancies, and the Court voted to rehear the case. With the two new justices—William Strong and Joseph P. Bradley—voting with the majority, the Court now found the legal tender acts constitutional. It was charged that Grant had appointed the two knowing in advance that they would vote to reverse the Court's previous decision. Historians have no evidence of any explicit arrangements.

Although political activity by Supreme Court justices usually has been frowned upon, it has not been unknown, especially during the nineteenth century, when several justices manifested a hunger for their party's presidential nomination. Justice McLean entertained presidential ambitions throughout his long Supreme Court career (1829–1861) and flirted with several political parties at various stages. In 1856 he received 190 votes on an informal first ballot at the first Republican national convention. He also sought the Republican presidential nomination in 1860.

Chief Justice Chase had aspired to the presidency before going on the bench, losing the Republican nomination to Lincoln in 1860. In 1864, while serving as Lincoln's secretary of Treasury, he allowed himself to become the focus of an anti-Lincoln group within the Republican Party. During his service on the Court, in both 1868 and 1872, he made no secret of his still-burning presidential ambitions and allowed friends to maneuver politically for him.

In 1877 the Supreme Court was thrust into the election process when a dispute arose as to the outcome of the 1876 presidential election. To resolve the problem, Congress created a special electoral commission that included five Supreme Court justices. Each House of Congress also chose five members, the Democratic House selecting five Democrats, and the Republican Senate five Republicans.

The five justices were supposed to be divided evenly politi-cally—two Democrats, Clifford and Field; two Republicans, Miller and Strong; and independent David Davis. Davis, however, withdrew from consideration because he had been elected a U.S. senator from Illinois. Justice Bradley, a Republican, was substituted for Davis, making the overall lineup on the commission eight to seven in favor of the Republicans.

The three Republican justices loyally supported the claims of Republican presidential aspirant Rutherford Hayes on all questions, and the two Democratic justices backed Democratic nominee Samuel J. Tilden. The result was the election of Hayes. Justice Clifford, the chairman of the commission, was so contemptuous of the outcome that he called Hayes an illegitimate president and refused to enter the White House during his term.

CHAPTER 8
Brief Biographies

THE FOLLOWING PAGES include vital statistics and brief accounts of the lives and public careers of each of the 108 individuals who have served as justices of the Supreme Court of the United States to date. They are listed in order of their appointment to the Court; the dates beneath each of their names indicate the period of service on the Court, beginning with the year each took the judicial oath.

The material is organized as follows: name; years of service; date and place of birth; education (including private legal study and practice); public service; Supreme Court service; marriage and children; date and place of death; and a narrative biographical study.

In addition to biographies of the individual justices, including those contained in *The Justices of the United States Supreme Court 1789–1969: Their Lives and Major Opinions*, ed. Leon Friedman and Fred L. Israel (New York: R. R. Bowker, 1969); *The*

Supreme Court Justices: Illustrated Biographies, 1789–1995, 2d ed., ed. Clare Cushman (Washington, D.C.: Congressional Quarterly, 1995), and Lee Epstein, Jeffrey A. Segal, Harold J. Spaeth, and Thomas G. Walker, *The Supreme Court Compendium: Data, Decisions, and Developments,* 2d ed. (Washington, D.C.: Congressional Quarterly, 1996), the information about each justice was provided by standard reference works such as the *Dictionary of American Biography* (New York: Charles Scribner's Sons, 1928–1936); *Encyclopedia of American Biography,* ed. John A. Garraty (New York: Harper and Row, 1974); *Encyclopedia Americana* (New York: Americana, 1968); *Encyclopaedia Britannica* (Chicago: Encyclopaedia Britannica, 1973); *Who Was Who in America* (Chicago: Marquis-Who's Who, 1968); and several Supreme Court histories, chiefly Charles Warren, *The Supreme Court in United States History,* 2 vols. (Boston: Little, Brown, 1922, 1926).

John Jay
(1789–1795)

BIRTH: December 12, 1745, New York City.

EDUCATION: privately tutored; attended boarding school; graduated from King's College (later Columbia University), 1764; clerked in law office of Benjamin Kissam; admitted to the bar in 1768.

OFFICIAL POSITIONS: secretary, Royal Boundary Commission, 1773; member, New York Committee of 51, 1774; delegate, Continental Congress, 1774, 1775, 1777, president, 1778–1779; delegate, New York provincial congress, 1776–1777; chief justice, New York State, 1777–1778; minister to Spain, 1779; secretary of foreign affairs, 1784–1789; envoy to Great Britain, 1794–1795; governor, New York, 1795–1801.

SUPREME COURT SERVICE: nominated chief justice by President George Washington September 24, 1789; confirmed by the Senate September 26, 1789, by a voice vote; took judicial oath October 9, 1789; resigned June 29, 1795; replaced by Oliver Ellsworth, nominated by President Washington.

FAMILY: married Sarah Van Brugh Livingston, April 28, 1774; died 1802; five daughters, two sons.

DEATH: May 17, 1829, Bedford, New York.

John Jay, the first chief justice of the United States, was descended from two of New York's most prominent families. His mother, Mary Van Cortlandt Jay, was Dutch, and his father, Peter Jay, was a wealthy merchant descended from French Huguenots.

The youngest of eight children, Jay grew up on the family farm at Rye, New York. He was taught Latin by his mother and attended a boarding school in New Rochelle for three years. Following more private tutoring, he entered King's College and graduated at the age of nineteen. He was admitted to the bar four years later.

In 1774 Jay married Sarah Van Brugh Livingston, daughter of William Livingston, later governor of New Jersey during the Revolution. The couple had seven children, one of whom became a lawyer and active abolitionist. John Jay, Jay's grandson, served as minister to Austria in the early 1870s.

In retirement, Jay pursued an interest in agriculture and devoted time to the Episcopal church. He was one of the founders of the American Bible Society and was elected its president in 1821. He opposed the War of 1812.

During his many years of public service, Jay developed a reputation for fairness and honesty. Prior to the presidential election of 1800, Alexander Hamilton urged Governor Jay to call a special session of the New York legislature and change the state's election laws to ensure that New York would deliver Federalist votes. Although a strong Federalist, Jay refused, writing to Hamilton that he would be "proposing a measure for party purposes which I think it would not become me to adopt."

Jay represented his state at both the first and second Continental Congresses. Although he was not present for the signing of the Declaration of Independence, he worked for its ratification in New York. At this time he also helped to draft the new state constitution.

In December 1778 Jay was elected president of the Continental Congress. The following September, he was sent to Spain in an attempt to win diplomatic recognition and large amounts of economic aid. Although the mission was at best only a modest success, it provided Jay with important diplomatic experience. In 1783 Jay helped negotiate the Treaty of Paris, which formally ended the Revolutionary War.

Although he was not a member of the Constitutional Convention in 1787, Jay recognized the need for a stronger union while serving as secretary of foreign affairs. He contributed five essays to *The Federalist Papers* urging support of the new Constitution. In the presidential election of 1789 Jay received nine electoral votes.

While organizing his first administration, George Washington first offered Jay the position of secretary of state. When Jay declined, the president named him chief justice of the new Supreme Court. In this position, Jay helped pave the way for a strong, independent national judiciary.

In 1794 Jay, while still chief justice, was sent to England in an effort to ease growing hostilities between that country and the United States. The result was the controversial Jay Treaty, which outraged many at home who felt it surrendered too many American rights.

When he returned from the treaty negotiations Jay discovered he had been elected governor of New York, a position he had run for and lost in 1792. He promptly resigned as chief justice and served as governor for two three-year terms.

During his tenure Jay supported the gradual freeing of slaves and instituted a revision of the state criminal code. He became interested in prisoner welfare and recommended the construction of a model penitentiary. He also reduced the number of crimes carrying the death penalty.

Following the resignation of Oliver Ellsworth, President Adams, in December 1800, nominated Jay for a second term as chief justice. Although he was immediately confirmed by the Senate, Jay refused the office for health reasons and, as he wrote Adams, because the Court lacked "the energy, weight, and dignity which are essential to its affording due support to the national government."

Jay lived in retirement on his eight hundred-acre estate in Westchester County, New York, for twenty-eight years until his death at eighty-three in 1829.

THE OATHS OF OFFICE

As he or she is sworn into office, every justice of the U.S. Supreme Court has taken two oaths, the Constitutional Oath and the Judicial Oath.

Article VI of the Constitution requires of all federal employees to pledge to support the Constitution. The oath reads: "I, ————, do solemnly swear that I will support and defend the Constitution of the United States against all enemies, foreign and domestic; that I will bear true faith and allegiance to the same; that I take this obligation freely, without any mental reservation or purpose of evasion; and that I will well and faithfully discharge the duties of the office on which I am about to enter. So help me God."

The Judicial Oath is required by Section 8 of the Judiciary Act of 1789. The original oath included the phrase: "according to the best of my abilities and understanding, agreeably to the constitution." The oath was amended in 1990 to say, "under the Constitution."

The oath reads: "I, ————, do solemnly swear (or affirm) that I will administer justice without respect to persons, and do equal right to the poor and to the rich, and that I will faithfully and impartially discharge and perform all the duties incumbent upon me as ———— under the Constitution and laws of the United States. So help me God."

John Rutledge
(1790–1791, 1795)

BIRTH: September 1739, Charleston, South Carolina.

EDUCATION: privately tutored; studied law at the Middle Temple in England; called to the English bar February 9, 1760.

OFFICIAL POSITIONS: member, South Carolina Commons House of Assembly, 1761–1776; South Carolina attorney general pro item, 1764–1765; delegate, Stamp Act Congress, 1765; member, Continental Congress, 1774–1776, 1782–1783; president, South Carolina General Assembly, 1776–1778; governor, South Carolina, 1779–1782; judge of the Court of Chancery of South Carolina, 1784–1791; chief, South Carolina delegation to the

John Rutledge

Constitutional Convention, 1787; member, South Carolina convention to ratify U.S. Constitution, 1788; chief justice, South Carolina Supreme Court, 1791–1795; member, South Carolina Assembly, 1798–1799.

SUPREME COURT SERVICE: nominated associate justice by President George Washington September 24, 1789; confirmed by the Senate September 26, 1789, by a voice vote; took judicial oath February 15, 1790; resigned March 5, 1791; replaced by Thomas Johnson, nominated by President Washington. Later sworn in by virtue of recess appointment as chief justice August 12, 1795; appointment not confirmed, and service terminated December 15, 1795.

FAMILY: married Elizabeth Grimke, May 1, 1763; died 1792; ten children.

DEATH: July 18, 1800, Charleston, South Carolina.

Sarah Hext Rutledge was only fifteen years old when she gave birth to her first son, John. When her husband, Dr. John Rutledge, died in 1750, she was left a wealthy twenty-six-year-old widow with seven children.

As a youth, John Rutledge studied law in the office of his uncle, Andrew Rutledge, Speaker of the South Carolina Commons House of Assembly. Later he read for two years under Charleston lawyer James Parsons and then sailed for England, where he studied at the Inns of Court in London.

The wealthy Rutledge family, together with the Pinckneys, exerted great influence over South Carolina politics toward the end of the eighteenth century. John Rutledge's brother Edward, a law partner of Thomas Pinckney, was a signer of the Declaration of Independence and a delegate to the Constitutional Convention in Philadelphia; he was elected governor of South Carolina in 1798. Hugh Rutledge, another brother, also was a member of the South Carolina bar.

In 1763 Rutledge married Elizabeth Grimke, a member of an old Charleston family and aunt of Angelina and Sarah Moore Grimke, two of South Carolina's most famous abolitionists and reformers. One of Rutledge's children, John Jr., became a member of the U.S. House of Representatives.

Almost immediately upon his return to South Carolina from England in 1761, Rutledge became a leading member of the local bar. He had been home only three months when he was elected to the provincial legislature. In 1764 he was appointed attorney general by the king's governor in an attempt to win his support in a power struggle between the Crown and the assembly. Rutledge held the position for ten months but did not take sides against the assembly.

At the age of twenty-five Rutledge was the youngest delegate to the Stamp Act Congress in New York in 1765. There he served as chairman of the committee that drafted a petition to the king demanding repeal of the Stamp Act. The demand was met the following year.

In 1774 Rutledge headed the South Carolina delegation to the Continental Congress, which included his brother Edward and Edward's father-in-law, Henry Middleton. At the Congress in Philadelphia, Rutledge allied with other conservatives in supporting colonial rights but opposing separation from the mother country. When the Congress proposed an economic boycott against Britain, he convinced them to allow one product to continue to be traded—South Carolina's principal export, rice.

Rutledge continued to serve in the Continental Congress in 1775 but returned to South Carolina in December of that year to help form a new state government. A new constitution was written, calling for the formation of a new state assembly. Rutledge was elected president of the assembly in March 1776. In 1778 he resigned rather than accept a new, more liberal and democratic state constitution. In the face of a British invasion the following year, however, he was made governor by the assembly and given broad emergency powers.

South Carolina fell to the British in the summer of 1780. After the British army moved to Virginia in 1781, Rutledge returned to South Carolina to help restore civil authority. In 1784 he was appointed chief judge of the new state court of chancery.

At the Constitutional Convention in 1787 Rutledge served on the select committee that produced the first draft of the Constitution. He is responsible for writing the supremacy clause, which states that the Constitution and laws of the United States "shall be the supreme Law of the Land."

Most of his attention, however, was directed toward protecting wealthy, antidemocratic interests. He successfully opposed, for example, an immediate ban on the slave trade. In 1789 South Carolina's electors cast their vice-presidential votes for Rutledge, in recognition of his service to the state.

Rutledge accepted President Washington's offer to become an associate justice of the Supreme Court in 1789. Although he participated in circuit court duties, he never sat as a justice due to personal illness and the inactivity of the Court. In February 1791 Rutledge resigned to accept what he considered to be a more prestigious position—chief justice of the Supreme Court of South Carolina.

The importance of the U.S. Supreme Court was gradually increasing, however, and in 1795 Rutledge wrote Washington of his desire to succeed John Jay as chief justice. He presided unofficially over the August term of the Court, but his nomination as chief justice was rejected by the Senate in December 1795 because of his public opposition to the Jay Treaty with England.

Rutledge attempted to drown himself after hearing news of his Senate rejection and suffered lapses of sanity until the end of his life. He died July 18, 1800, at the age of sixty.

William Cushing
(1790–1810)

BIRTH: March 1, 1732, Scituate, Massachusetts.

EDUCATION: graduated Harvard, 1751, honorary LL.D., 1785; honorary A.M., Yale, 1753; studied law under Jeremiah Gridley; admitted to the bar in 1755.

OFFICIAL POSITIONS: judge, probate court for Lincoln County, Massachusetts (now Maine), 1760–1761; judge, Superior Court of Massachusetts Bay province, 1772–1777; chief justice, Superior Court of the Commonwealth of Massachusetts, 1777–1780, Supreme Judicial Court, 1780–1789; member, Massachusetts Constitutional Convention, 1779; vice president, Massachusetts Convention, which ratified U.S. Constitution, 1788; delegate to electoral college, 1788.

SUPREME COURT SERVICE: nominated associate justice by President George Washington September 24, 1789; confirmed by the Senate September 26, 1789, by a voice vote; took judicial oath February 2, 1790; served until September 13, 1810;

MARGINS OF VICTORY

For most of the Court's history, the Senate's confirmation of a Supreme Court nominee has been a simple formality. Deference to the president who has selected the new justice usually has prevailed over any reservations senators may have. Indeed, seventy-three justices have been approved by voice vote with no recorded opposition; five of them subsequently declined the seat.

Six justices—including three of President Ronald Reagan's nominees—were confirmed by unanimous roll-call votes. In two other cases, the nominee was officially confirmed by voice vote, but each time one senator wanted his opposition recorded. Sen. Joseph McCarthy, R-Wis., opposed confirmation of Justice William J. Brennan Jr. in 1957, and Sen. Strom Thurmond, R-S.C., opposed the nomination of Arthur J. Goldberg in 1962.

There have been some very close votes on confirmation to the Court. Stanley Matthews won confirmation by the barest of margins—one vote—in 1881; the count was 24–23. Nathan Clifford was confirmed in 1858 by a 26–23 vote, and Lucius Q. Lamar squeaked by, 32–28, in 1888. In the twentieth century, Clarence Thomas won confirmation by the closest margin, 52–48.

The entire list of nominees who were confirmed over substantial opposition—more than ten votes—follows:

Chief Justice Roger B. Taney, 29–15, in 1836
Philip P. Barbour, 30–11, in 1836
William Smith, 23–18, in 1837 (he declined the seat)
John Catron, 28–15, in 1837
Edwin M. Stanton, 46–11, in 1869
Roscoe Conkling, 39–12, in 1882 (he declined the seat)

Chief Justice Melville W. Fuller, 41–20, in 1888
David J. Brewer, 53–11, in 1889
Mahlon Pitney, 50–26, in 1912
Louis D. Brandeis, 47–22, in 1916
Chief Justice Charles E. Hughes, 52–26, in 1930
Hugo L. Black, 63–16, in 1937
Sherman Minton, 48–16, in 1949
John M. Harlan, 71–11, in 1955
Potter Stewart, 70–17, in 1959
Thurgood Marshall, 69–11, in 1967
William H. Rehnquist, 68–26, in 1971, and as chief justice, 65–33, in 1986
Clarence Thomas, 52–48 in 1991

Some nominees were rejected by the barest of margins. Jeremiah S. Black was defeated by a single vote, 25–26, in 1861.

The entire list of those who came close to confirmation only to lose it were:

John Rutledge as chief justice, 10–14, in 1795
John C. Spencer, 21–26, in 1844
George W. Woodward, 20–29, in 1845
Ebenezer R. Hoar, 24–33, in 1870
Jeremiah S. Black, 25–26 in 1861.
William B. Hornblower, 24–30, in 1894
Wheeler H. Peckham, 32–41, in 1894
John J. Parker, 39–41, in 1930
Clement Haynsworth Jr., 45–55, in 1969

William Cushing

began preparing impeachment proceedings against him, he now began to be perceived as a supporter of the revolutionary cause. This belief was strengthened when he was denied a seat on the governor's council because of his stand.

In 1775 the new revolutionary government of Massachusetts reorganized the judicial system but retained Cushing as senior associate justice of the superior court. In 1777 he was elevated to chief justice.

Although Cushing played only a small role in the state constitutional convention of 1779, he actively supported ratification of the Constitution. He also served as vice president of the state convention that ratified the document in 1788.

Cushing was one of Washington's original appointees to the Supreme Court in 1789. In 1794 he was persuaded to run against Samuel Adams for governor of Massachusetts—while retaining his Court seat—but lost by a two-to-one margin. In 1795 he declined an offer from Washington to succeed John Jay as chief justice. As senior associate justice, however, he presided over the court when Chief Justice Ellsworth was absent.

Cushing remained on the bench until his death in 1810, the longest term of the original members of the Court.

replaced by Joseph Story, nominated by President James Madison.

FAMILY: married Hannah Phillips, 1774.
DEATH: September 13, 1810, Scituate, Massachusetts.

William Cushing, the son of Mary Cotton Cushing and John Cushing, was a member of one of the oldest and most prominent families of colonial Massachusetts. He was descended on his mother's side from John Cotton, the seventeenth-century Puritan minister. Both his father and grandfather served in the government of the Massachusetts Bay province.

Cushing graduated from Harvard in 1751. After teaching for a year in Roxbury, Massachusetts, he began studying law under Jeremiah Gridley in Boston. In 1755 he set up a private practice in his home town of Scituate.

In 1760 Cushing moved to what is now Dresden, Maine, to become justice of the peace and judge of probates. He was not an accomplished lawyer and seemed unable to make decisions. Before long, he had lost most of his corporate business to other lawyers. In 1774 Cushing married Hannah Phillips of Middletown, Connecticut.

Cushing is known as the last American judge to wear a full wig, a habit he did not abandon until 1790.

When Cushing's father, John Cushing, decided to retire from the provincial superior court in 1772, he insisted that his son succeed him as judge. Although William Cushing was not the colonial government's first choice, he nonetheless was appointed to the position that year.

In 1774 Cushing reluctantly allied himself with the colonials by refusing to accept his salary through the British government. Although his decision did not come until the state legislature

James Wilson
(1789–1798)

BIRTH: September 14, 1742, Caskardy, Scotland.
EDUCATION: attended University of St. Andrews (Scotland); read law in office of John Dickinson; admitted to the bar in 1767; honorary M.A., College of Philadelphia, 1776; honorary LL.D., 1790.

OFFICIAL POSITIONS: delegate, first Provincial Convention at Philadelphia, 1774; delegate, Continental Congress,

1775–1777, 1783, 1785–1787; delegate, U.S. Constitutional Convention, 1787; delegate, Pennsylvania convention to ratify U.S. Constitution, 1787.

SUPREME COURT SERVICE: nominated associate justice by President George Washington September 24, 1789; confirmed by the Senate September 26, 1789, by a voice vote; took judicial oath October 5, 1789; served until August 21, 1798; replaced by Bushrod Washington, nominated by President John Adams.

FAMILY: married Rachel Bird, November 5, 1771; died 1786; six children; married Hannah Gray, September 19, 1793; one son died in infancy.

DEATH: August 21, 1798, Edenton, North Carolina.

James Wilson was born in the Scottish Lowlands, the son of a Caskardy farmer, also named James. His mother was Alison Lansdale Wilson. Although the family had little money, his devout Calvinist parents were determined that James be educated for the ministry.

After study in local grammar schools, Wilson at fourteen won a scholarship to St. Andrews University and matriculated in the fall of 1757. During his fifth year, he entered the university's divinity school but was forced to leave for financial reasons when his father died.

To help support his family, he took a job as a private tutor but left the position to study accounting and bookkeeping in Edinburgh. In 1765 he decided against becoming a clerk and sailed for America.

After studying law in the new country, Wilson became one of its foremost legal scholars. Described as a man of extreme energy, he was driven by a desire for wealth and fame, constantly involved in various speculation schemes, primarily in land. He was part-owner of the Somerset Mills on the Delaware River and president of the Illinois and Wabash Company, which had vast western land holdings.

From 1777 to 1787 Wilson devoted most of his energy to developing new business interests. As his financial commitments built, he continued to seek new investments. But the credit cycle eventually caught up with Wilson. As an associate justice, he traveled the southern circuit in constant fear of being thrown in jail for bad debts.

Wilson arrived in Philadelphia in the fall of 1765 and immediately obtained a tutorship at the College of Philadelphia. Teaching tired him, however, and he saw a better opportunity in law. He soon began reading law in the office of John Dickinson, a prominent attorney who had studied at the Inns of Court.

In 1768 Wilson opened private practice in Reading, Pennsylvania. Two years later, he moved west to Carlisle, where his practice expanded rapidly. By 1774 he was practicing in seven counties, specializing in land law.

In 1775 Wilson was elected a delegate to the Continental Congress, where he served on several committees. He aligned himself with other members of the Pennsylvania delegation in opposing separation from England. In the end, however, he followed the state assembly's instructions and signed the Declaration of Independence.

Wilson's opposition to the Pennsylvania constitution of 1776 attracted criticism from state populists and earned him a reputation as a conservative aristocrat. That reputation grew when he developed an active practice in Philadelphia defending wealthy Tories and other rich businessmen. In 1779 he was forced to barricade his home against an armed attack by a riotous mob angered over high inflation and food shortages. He eventually had to go into hiding.

At the Constitutional Convention in 1787, Wilson was a member of the committee of detail, responsible for writing the first draft of the Constitution. Although his populist foes refused to believe it, Wilson was a fervent advocate of popular sovereignty and democracy who supported popular election of the president and members of both the Senate and House. One of the first to envision the principle of judicial review, Wilson fought for a strong national judiciary and a powerful presidency. He saw no conflict between the ideal of popular rule and a strong national government because, in his view, the national government existed only by virtue of the popular will. Wilson is credited with incorporating this idea of popular sovereignty into the Constitution.

As the new national government was being formed, Wilson hoped for federal office and offered his name to Washington as chief justice of the United States. Washington appointed John Jay instead and named Wilson an associate justice.

Of the original Washington appointees to the Supreme Court, Wilson was its most accomplished legal scholar. A pamphlet he had published in 1774 presaged the concept of "dominion status" that serves today as the official guiding principle of the British Commonwealth.

His defense of the Bank of North America in 1785 anticipated constitutional opinions delivered by Chief Justice Marshall at least twenty-five years later. In 1964 Associate Justice Hugo Black in *Wesberry v. Sanders* cited Wilson as a supporting source for the "one-man-one-vote" principle.

Around 1796 Wilson's investment schemes began to collapse around him. While riding circuit, he was chased by angry creditors who caught up with him at least once and had him jailed. He then sought refuge in Edenton, North Carolina—the hometown of fellow justice James Iredell—but was soon discovered and imprisoned again. Eventually released, he remained in Edenton in ill health. He died at fifty-five in a dingy inn next to the Edenton Court House.

John Blair Jr.

(1790–1796)

BIRTH: 1732, Williamsburg, Virginia.

EDUCATION: graduated with honors from College of William and Mary, 1754; studied law at Middle Temple, London, 1755–1756.

OFFICIAL POSITIONS: member, Virginia House of

John Blair Jr.

Burgesses, 1766–1770; clerk, Virginia Governor's Council, 1770–1775; delegate, Virginia Constitutional Convention, 1776; member, Virginia Governor's Council, 1776; judge, Virginia General Court, 1777–1778; chief justice, 1779; judge, first Virginia Court of Appeals, 1780–1789; delegate, U.S. Constitutional Convention, 1787; judge, Virginia Supreme Court of Appeals, 1789.

SUPREME COURT SERVICE: nominated associate justice by President George Washington September 24, 1789; confirmed by the Senate September 26, 1789, by a voice vote; took judicial oath February 2, 1790; resigned January 27, 1796; replaced by Samuel Chase, nominated by President Washington.

FAMILY: married Jean Blair, December 26, 1756; died 1792.

DEATH: August 31, 1800, Williamsburg, Virginia.

John Blair Jr. was the son of one of Virginia's most prominent colonial officials, a member of the House of Burgesses, and a member of the Governor's Council. He was also acting governor of the state in 1758 and 1768.

The family owned rich land holdings, and young John—one of ten children of John Blair Sr. and Mary Monro Blair—was given an excellent education. In 1754 he graduated from the College of William and Mary, which had been founded by his great-uncle James Blair. After studying law at the Middle Temple in London, he returned home to Williamsburg and began practicing law.

A slightly built man, six feet tall with thinning red hair, Blair toward the end of his life suffered from chronic headaches, possibly brought on by the rigors of riding circuit.

Blair entered the Virginia House of Burgesses in 1766 at the age of thirty-four. A conservative, he opposed the defiant resolutions of Patrick Henry condemning the Stamp Act, but joined with leading merchants in agreeing to boycott specific British imports.

In 1770 Blair resigned his seat to become clerk of the Governor's Council, the first of several state offices and judgeships. In 1782, while serving as a judge on the state's first court of appeals, he sided with the majority decision in *Commonwealth v. Caton* that the court could declare legislative acts unconstitutional.

Although not a leading participant in the Constitutional Convention of 1787, Blair firmly supported ratification and was one of three Virginia delegates who signed the new document. When the Virginia judicial system was reorganized in 1789, Blair sat on the new supreme court of appeals for three months until his appointment as one of the original justices of the U.S. Supreme Court. Because of his wife's illness and the relative inactivity of the Court, he did not attend all its sessions. He resigned in January 1796, four years after his wife's death.

In 1799 Blair wrote to his sister of being "struck with a strange disorder . . . depriving me of nearly all the powers of mind." He died August 31, 1800, at his home in Williamsburg.

RECESS APPOINTMENTS

Fifteen men have been nominated to the Supreme Court while the Senate was not in session and have received "recess" appointments to the Court. These appointments permit the individual to be sworn in and to take part in the Court's work even before the nomination is confirmed. Once the Senate returns, the president must then formally nominate the individual, who is then subject to confirmation. If confirmed, he or she is sworn in a second time.

Only five of the fifteen who received such appointments took their seats on the bench before confirmation. Four were eventually confirmed: Benjamin R. Curtis, appointed and confirmed in December 1851; Earl Warren, appointed as chief justice in September 1953 and confirmed in March 1954; William J. Brennan Jr., appointed in October 1956 and confirmed in March 1957; and Potter Stewart, appointed in October 1958 and confirmed in May 1959. The fifth was rejected by the Senate. John Rutledge, who had served as an associate justice from 1790 to 1791, was given a recess appointment as chief justice in the summer of 1795. He presided over the August 1795 term of the Court at which two cases were heard and decided. But, on December 15 the Senate refused, 10–14, to confirm him.

The ten who received recess appointments but waited to be seated until after confirmation were:

Thomas Johnson, confirmed in 1791
Bushrod Washington, 1798
Alfred Moore, 1799
Brockholst Livingston, 1806
Smith Thompson, 1823
John McKinley, 1837
Levi Woodbury, 1846
David Davis, 1862
John Marshall Harlan, 1877
Oliver Wendell Holmes Jr., 1902

James Iredell

(1790–1799)

BIRTH: October 5, 1751, Lewes, England.

EDUCATION: educated in England; read law under Samuel Johnston of North Carolina; licensed to practice, 1770–1771.

OFFICIAL POSITIONS: comptroller of customs, Edenton, North Carolina, 1768–1774; collector of customs, Port of North Carolina, 1774–1776; judge, Superior Court of North Carolina, 1778; attorney general, North Carolina, 1779–1781; member, North Carolina Council of State, 1787; delegate, North Carolina convention for ratification of federal Constitution, 1788.

SUPREME COURT SERVICE: nominated associate justice by President George Washington February 8, 1790; confirmed by the Senate February 10, 1790, by a voice vote; took judicial oath May 12, 1790; served until October 20, 1799; replaced by Alfred Moore, nominated by President John Adams.

FAMILY: married Hannah Johnston, July 18, 1773; two daughters, one son.

DEATH: October 20, 1799, Edenton, North Carolina.

James Iredell, the son of Francis Iredell and Margaret McCulloch Iredell, was born into an English family reputedly descended from Oliver Cromwell's son-in-law, Henry Ireton. The family was forced to change its name, so the story goes, following the return of Charles II to the throne.

When James's merchant father became ill in the early 1760s, James was able through his mother's family connections to acquire a position in America in 1768 as comptroller of the cus-

toms in Edenton, North Carolina. During his six years in that job he read law in the office of Samuel Johnston and began practice in December 1770. In 1773 he married his mentor's sister, Hannah Johnston.

Because of a slight lisp, Iredell was not effective as a public speaker but was a prolific writer of letters and essays. Many of these writings survive today and reveal a clear, candid style.

Although a new immigrant and an employee of the British, Iredell nevertheless soon found himself in support of the American revolutionary cause. In 1776 he resigned from his job as collector for the Crown at the port of Edenton.

Iredell then served on a commission to redraft North Carolina law in conformance with the state's new independent status. When a new state judicial court system was created the following year, he was chosen one of three Superior Court judges—a position he reluctantly accepted. But the rigors of traveling circuit were burdensome for him, and he resigned after a few months to return to private law practice.

From 1779 to 1781 Iredell served as state attorney general. In 1787 the legislature appointed him to collect and revise all state laws; the new code appeared in 1791.

After the war Iredell had aligned himself with conservative leaders who favored a strong government and adherence to the peace treaty terms of 1783. In 1786 he said that the state constitution had the power to limit the state legislature—a novel idea at the time.

Iredell's most influential work, written under the pen name Marcus, was his defense of the new federal Constitution. The tract, which appeared at the same time as the first issues of the Jefferson-Hamilton-Jay proconstitutional *Federalist Papers*, refuted George Mason's eleven objections to the document.

At the state ratification convention in 1788, Iredell served as floor leader of the Federalists, a position that brought him to the attention of George Washington. When Robert Harrison declined to serve on the Supreme Court in 1790, the president decided to appoint Iredell because, as Washington noted in his diary, "In addition to the reputation he sustains for abilities, legal knowledge and respectability of character, he is of a State of some importance in the Union that has given no character to a federal office."

Iredell served on the Court for nine years, riding the southern circuit, covering the eighteen hundred miles five times between 1790 and 1794. In dissent from *Chisholm v. Georgia*, he argued that a state could not be sued in federal court by a citizen from another state—a position later added to the Constitution by the Eleventh Amendment. In 1798 he set a precedent for *Marbury v. Madison* in arguing for the right of courts to declare laws unconstitutional (*Calder v. Bull*).

Iredell died in 1799 at the age of forty-eight at his home in Edenton.

Thomas Johnson

(1792–1793)

BIRTH: November 4, 1732, Calvert County, Maryland.

EDUCATION: educated at home; studied law under Stephen Bordley; admitted to the bar, 1760.

OFFICIAL POSITIONS: delegate, Maryland Provincial Assembly, 1762; delegate, Annapolis Convention of 1774; member, Continental Congress, 1774–1777; delegate, first constitutional convention of Maryland, 1776; first governor of Maryland, 1777–1779; member, Maryland House of Delegates, 1780, 1786, 1787; member, Maryland convention for ratification of the federal Constitution, 1788; chief judge, general court of Maryland, 1790–1791; member, board of commissioners of the Federal City, 1791–1794.

SUPREME COURT SERVICE: nominated associate justice by President George Washington November 1, 1791, to replace John Rutledge, who resigned; confirmed by the Senate November 7, 1791, by a voice vote; took judicial oath August 6, 1792; resigned February 1, 1793; replaced by William Paterson, nominated by President Washington.

FAMILY: married Ann Jennings, February 16, 1766; died 1794; three boys, five girls, one of whom died in infancy.

DEATH: October 26, 1819, Frederick, Maryland.

Born to Thomas and Dorcas Sedgwick Johnson, Thomas Johnson was one of twelve children. He received no formal education as a youth but trained in the office of Thomas Jennings, clerk of the Maryland provincial court in Annapolis. Following that apprenticeship, Johnson worked and studied in the office of Stephen Bordley, an Annapolis attorney. He was admitted to the bar in 1760.

During the Revolution Johnson served as first brigadier-general of the Maryland militia. In 1777 he was responsible for leading almost two thousand men from Frederick, Maryland, to General Washington's headquarters in New Jersey.

After the war Johnson revived a plan he had dreamed of as early as 1770—to improve navigation along the Potomac River and open a passageway to the west coast. To this end, he helped organize the state-chartered Potomac Company in 1785, with his good friend George Washington as its president. The company eventually proved unprofitable.

In 1766 Johnson married Ann Jennings, the daughter of his old employer in the provincial court. They were married for twenty-eight years, until her death in 1794.

Johnson began his career as a Maryland statesman in 1762 when he was chosen a delegate to the Maryland Provincial Assembly from Anne Arundel County. As a member of the first Continental Congress in Philadelphia, he served on the committee that drafted a petition of grievances to King George III. In 1775 Johnson placed the name of George Washington in nomination before the Congress for the position of commander in chief of the Continental Army.

Johnson was absent from Philadelphia the day the Declaration of Independence was signed. However, he thoroughly supported the document and voted for Maryland's independence on July 6, 1776. He also helped to write the new state constitution that year.

During the Revolution Johnson served three consecutive terms as governor of Maryland and played a major role in keeping Washington's army manned and equipped.

Declining to serve a fourth term as governor, Johnson entered the Maryland House of Delegates in 1780, where he helped prepare legislation determining the jurisdiction of the state admiralty court. As a member of the state ratification convention in 1788, he worked for approval of the new federal Constitution. Two years later he became chief judge of the Maryland general court.

Johnson was nominated associate justice of the Supreme Court in August 1791. Hesitant because of the rigors of riding circuit, he was assured by Chief Justice Jay that every attempt would be made to bring him relief. When assigned to the southern circuit, however, including all territory south of the Potomac, he was unable to persuade Jay to rotate assignments. Citing ill health, he resigned from the bench after serving little more than a year. He wrote only one opinion during his tenure.

Johnson, however, continued in public life as a member of the commission appointed by Washington to plan the new national capital on the Potomac. That commission selected the design submitted by Pierre L'Enfant and voted to name the new city "Washington." Johnson was present when the cornerstone of the new Capitol building was laid in September 1793.

In 1795 Johnson refused an offer from President Washington to serve as secretary of state. He retired to Frederick, Maryland, where he died at the age of eighty-six.

THOSE WHO DID NOT SERVE

Eight men were nominated and confirmed as Supreme Court justices, but did not serve. President Washington selected Robert H. Harrison to serve on the newly created Supreme Court in 1789, but Harrison refused. In 1796 Washington asked William Cushing to become the chief justice, and the Senate confirmed him. Cushing held the post for a week before he declined it, citing poor health. Nevertheless, he served as an associate justice until 1810. John Jay, the first chief justice, refused President John Adams's offer to serve on the Court a second time. Adams sent Jay's name to the Senate when Oliver Ellsworth resigned, but Jay declined the seat.

When Cushing's seat became available, President James Madison offered it to Levi Lincoln, Alexander Wolcott, and John Quincy Adams. Lincoln and Adams were confirmed by the Senate January 3, 1811, and February 22, 1811, respectively, but neither accepted the post. The Senate rejected Wolcott, 24–9.

In 1837 President Andrew Jackson named William Smith of Alabama to one of two new seats, but Smith turned it down.

Edwin M. Stanton, President Abraham Lincoln's fiery secretary of war, was named to the Court in 1869 by President Ulysses S. Grant. Stanton was in failing health at the time of the appointment and died in December, just four days after his confirmation. He never took his seat on the Court.

President Chester A. Arthur named Roscoe Conkling of New York to fill Ward Hunt's seat on the Court. Conkling, an influential Republican, had served in the U.S. House of Representatives and the U.S. Senate. Conkling was more interested in the presidency and therefore declined a place on the Court.

William Paterson

William Paterson

(1793–1806)

BIRTH: December 24, 1745, County Antrim, Ireland.

EDUCATION: graduated from College of New Jersey (Princeton), 1763; M.A., 1766; studied law under Richard Stockton; admitted to the bar, 1769.

OFFICIAL POSITIONS: member, New Jersey Provincial Congress, 1775–1776; delegate, New Jersey State Constitutional Convention, 1776; New Jersey attorney general, 1776–1783; delegate, U.S. Constitutional Convention, 1787; U.S. senator, 1789–1790; governor, New Jersey, 1790–1793.

SUPREME COURT SERVICE: nominated associate justice by President George Washington March 4, 1793, to replace Thomas Johnson, who resigned; confirmed by the Senate March 4, 1793, by a voice vote; took judicial oath March 11, 1793; served until September 9, 1806; replaced by Henry B. Livingston, nominated by President Thomas Jefferson.

FAMILY: married Cornelia Bell, February 9, 1779; died 1783; three children; married Euphemia White, 1785.

DEATH: September 9, 1806, Albany, New York.

Born in Ireland, William Paterson emigrated to America with his parents when he was two years old. The family lived in several places before settling in Princeton, New Jersey, where William's father, Richard, began manufacturing tin plate and selling general merchandise. He also made successful real estate investments, which helped to pay for William's education. Little is known about his mother, whose name was Mary.

At the college of New Jersey (Princeton), Paterson was a fellow student of Oliver Ellsworth, who would later become chief justice. With Ellsworth and others, Paterson founded the Well-Meaning Society (later the Cliosophic Club) as a forum for lively discussions on the political issues of the day.

In 1766 Paterson received a Master of Arts degree from Princeton and the same year began reading law in the office of Richard Stockton. In 1769 he opened his own practice in New Bromley, about thirty miles from Princeton. There was little demand for his services, however, and in 1772 he returned to the college town.

With his first wife, Cornelia Bell, Paterson lived on a farm on the Raritan River west of New Brunswick. She died in 1783 after the birth of their third child. Two years later Paterson married her close friend, Euphemia White.

Paterson was elected as a delegate from Somerset County to the First Provincial Congress of New Jersey in 1775, where he served as assistant secretary and later secretary. In 1776 he helped write the state constitution and was chosen attorney general. During this period Paterson also was a member of the state legislative council, an officer with the county minutemen, and a member of the council of safety.

In May 1787 Paterson was chosen a delegate to the Constitutional Convention in Philadelphia, where he was responsible for introducing the New Jersey Plan, proposing a unicameral legislature giving each state an equal vote. Despite failure of that plan, Paterson signed the Constitution and worked for its adoption in New Jersey.

As a member of the judiciary committee of the new U.S. Senate, Paterson was responsible, along with his old classmate Oliver Ellsworth, for writing the Judiciary Act of 1789. He left the Senate in 1790 when he was chosen governor and chancellor of the state of New Jersey.

In this capacity, Paterson codified the laws of the state and updated the procedural rules for the common-law and chancery courts. With the assistance of Alexander Hamilton, he laid plans for an industrial town on the Passaic River, to be named Paterson.

Appointed to the Supreme Court in 1793, Paterson—while riding circuit—tried several cases arising out of the Whiskey Rebellion in western Pennsylvania. He took the Federalist position in a number of sedition trials.

When Oliver Ellsworth resigned as chief justice in 1800, President Adams refused to elevate Paterson to the position because of his close alliance with Alexander Hamilton. In 1804 Paterson missed a session of the Court because of failing health and in 1806 decided to travel to Ballston Spa, New York, for treatment. He died at his daughter's home in Albany, on September 9.

Samuel Chase

(1796–1811)

BIRTH: April 17, 1741, Somerset County, Maryland.

EDUCATION: tutored by father; studied law in Annapolis law office; admitted to bar in 1761.

OFFICIAL POSITIONS: member, Maryland General Assembly, 1764–1784; delegate, Continental Congress, 1774–1778, 1784–1785; member, Maryland Committee of Correspondence, 1774; member, Maryland Convention and Council of Safety, 1775; judge, Baltimore Criminal Court, 1788–1796; chief judge, General Court of Maryland, 1791–1796.

SUPREME COURT SERVICE: nominated associate justice by President George Washington January 26, 1796, to replace John Blair, who resigned; confirmed by the Senate January 27, 1796, by a voice vote; took judicial oath February 4, 1796; served until June 19, 1811; replaced by Gabriel Duvall, nominated by President James Madison.

FAMILY: married Anne Baldwin May 21, 1762; seven children, three of whom died in infancy; married Hannah Kitty Giles, March 3, 1784; two daughters.

DEATH: June 19, 1811, Baltimore, Maryland.

Samuel Chase's mother, Martha Walker, died when he was still a child. His father, Thomas Chase, an Episcopal clergyman,

Samuel Chase

tutored him at home and gave him a foundation in the classics. At eighteen Chase began studying law in the office of Hammond and Hall in Annapolis. Two years later, in 1761, he was admitted to the bar and began practicing in the mayor's court of Annapolis. Chase lived in the state capital until 1786, when he moved to Baltimore.

During his lifetime Chase invested in several business schemes that later caused him embarrassment. In 1778, when his efforts to corner the flour market through speculation were discovered, he was dismissed as a member of the Maryland delegation to the Continental Congress for two years.

Chase also was involved in two war-supply partnerships and owned many iron and coal properties. These businesses were largely failures, and in 1789 he was forced to declare personal bankruptcy.

About six feet in height, Chase had a large head and brownish-red complexion that earned him the nickname "bacon face" among his law colleagues. He was a signer of the Declaration of Independence and a fervent patriot whose career was marked by turbulence and controversy.

When Chase entered the Maryland General Assembly in 1764 he immediately opposed the policies of the British-appointed governor of the colony. As a member of the "Sons of Liberty," he participated in riotous demonstrations, incurring the wrath of the Annapolis mayor and aldermen who called him a "busy, restless incendiary, a ringleader of mobs, a foul-mouthed and inflaming son of discord."

In 1778 Chase served on no fewer than thirty committees of the Continental Congress. As a delegate from Maryland, he urged that the colonies unite in an economic boycott of England. He served with Benjamin Franklin and Charles Carroll on a commission sent to Montreal to persuade Canada to join with the colonies against Great Britain. The mission failed.

Instrumental in achieving support in Maryland for the Declaration of Independence, Chase did not favor adoption of the new Constitution, arguing it would institute an elitist government and not a government of the people. He wrote a series of articles against ratification under the pen name Caution.

As a judge, his abusive and overbearing manner won him few friends. Displeased over the fact that Chase held two judgeships simultaneously, the Maryland Assembly at one point tried to strip from him all public offices, but the vote fell short.

By the time Chase reached the Supreme Court he had become a radical Federalist. As an associate justice, he took an active part in Federalist politics and campaigned hard for the Alien and Sedition Acts. Biased and dogmatic, he sought the indictment of Republican editors who sided against the Federalists.

Chase's greatest political impropriety came on May 2, 1803, when he gave an impassioned speech to a grand jury against democratic "mobocracy." He was impeached by the House on March 12, 1804. Although most senators agreed that Chase had acted poorly on the bench, there were not enough votes to convict him of "high crimes," and he kept his seat on the Court.

Following the trial, Chase sank into oblivion. He was often ill from gout and unable to attend the Court's sessions. He died in 1811.

Oliver Ellsworth
(1796–1800)

BIRTH: April 29, 1745, Windsor, Connecticut.

EDUCATION: A.B., Princeton, 1766; honorary LL.D., Yale (1790), Princeton (1790), Dartmouth (1797).

OFFICIAL POSITIONS: member, Connecticut General Assembly, 1773–1776; state's attorney, Hartford County, 1777–1785; delegate to Continental Congress, 1777–1784; member, Connecticut Council of Safety, 1779; member, Governor's Council, 1780–1785, 1801–1807; judge, Connecticut Superior Court, 1785–1789; delegate, Constitutional Convention, 1787; U.S. senator, 1789–1796; commissioner to France, 1799–1800.

SUPREME COURT SERVICE: nominated chief justice by President George Washington March 3, 1796, to replace John Jay, who had resigned; confirmed by the Senate March 4, 1796, by a 21–1 vote; took judicial oath March 8, 1796; resigned September 30, 1800; replaced by John Marshall, nominated by President John Adams.

FAMILY: married Abigail Wolcott, 1771; four sons, three daughters survived infancy.

DEATH: November 26, 1807, Windsor, Connecticut.

Oliver Ellsworth's great-grandfather emigrated in the middle of the seventeenth century from Yorkshire, England, to Wind-

Oliver Ellsworth

sor, Connecticut, where the future chief justice was born to Capt. David Ellsworth and Jemima Leavitt Ellsworth in 1745.

After studying under a Bethlehem, Connecticut, minister, Ellsworth entered Yale at seventeen. He left Yale at the end of his sophomore year and enrolled in Princeton, where he engaged in lively discussions about colonial politics and sharpened his debating skills.

After graduating from Princeton, Ellsworth began studying for the ministry at the urging of his father. Theology did not hold his interest long, however, and he soon turned to law. After four years of training he was admitted to the bar in 1777.

Ellsworth had little money in the early years of his practice. After marrying sixteen-year-old Abigail Wolcott, he settled on a farm that had belonged to his father and worked the land himself. When the Hartford court was in session, he walked to the town and back, a total of twenty miles.

Ellsworth's financial situation changed dramatically, however, as his practice grew. By 1780 he had become a leading member of the Connecticut bar and was well on his way toward acquiring a large fortune.

According to contemporary accounts, Ellsworth was a good conversationalist and elegant dresser who enjoyed frequent pinches of snuff. A tall, robust man, he was in the habit of talking to himself and was prone to obstinacy. Aaron Burr is said to have remarked: "If Ellsworth had happened to spell the name of the Deity with two d's, it would have taken the Senate three weeks to expunge the superfluous letter."

Deeply religious, Ellsworth was an active member of the Congregationalist church and returned to the study of theology after his retirement from the Court. He also advocated improved farming techniques for Connecticut and wrote a regular advice column on the subject.

Although his name is not among the signers of the Constitution, Ellsworth deserves to be included in any list of the nation's Founding Fathers. Principal author of the Judiciary Act of 1789 and coauthor of the Connecticut Compromise, Ellsworth originated the name for the new American government when he suggested the appellation "United States" in a resolution being considered by the Constitutional Convention.

Ellsworth's political career began in 1773 when he was elected to the Connecticut General Assembly. In 1775 he was appointed one of five members of the Committee of the Pay Table, which controlled the state's Revolutionary War expenditures. He also was a Connecticut delegate to the Continental Congress during the Revolution and served on many of its committees, including one that heard appeals from admiralty courts.

In 1787 Ellsworth was elected a member of the Connecticut delegation to the Constitutional Convention and helped devise the famous Connecticut Compromise that ended the dispute between large and small states over representation in the federal legislature.

Ellsworth had to leave the convention before it ended to attend to judicial business in Connecticut and was not present for the signing of the newly drafted Constitution. He worked hard for its ratification in Connecticut, however.

In 1789 Ellsworth became one of Connecticut's first two U.S. senators. His administrative skills were immediately put to use as he helped draft the first set of Senate rules and organize the army, a U.S. Post Office, and a census. Ellsworth engineered the conference report on the Bill of Rights and helped draft the measure that admitted North Carolina to the Union. It was Ellsworth's idea to force Rhode Island to join the federation by imposing an economic boycott.

A staunch supporter of Hamilton's monetary policies, Ellsworth had by this time become a strong Federalist. His most important work in the Senate came when he was chosen to head a committee to draft a bill organizing the federal judiciary. The bill, which provided for the Supreme Court, the district courts, and the circuit courts, became the Judiciary Act of 1789.

When John Jay resigned as chief justice in 1795, President Washington appointed John Rutledge as his successor. The Senate refused to confirm Rutledge, however, and Washington chose to elevate Associate Justice William Cushing. When Cushing declined, the nomination fell to Ellsworth.

Ellsworth had been on the Court only three years when President Adams sent him to France with two other envoys in an effort to soften hostilities between France and the United States. The mission, plagued by transportation difficulties and only partially successful, took its toll on Ellsworth's health.

Before returning home, Ellsworth notified Adams of his resignation as chief justice. He lived on his estate in Windsor until his death in 1807.

Bushrod Washington

(1799–1829)

BIRTH: June 5, 1762, Westmoreland County, Virginia.

EDUCATION: privately tutored; graduated College of William and Mary, 1778; read law under James Wilson; member, Virginia bar; honorary LL.D. degrees from Harvard, Princeton, and University of Pennsylvania.

OFFICIAL POSITIONS: member, Virginia House of Delegates, 1787; member, Virginia convention to ratify U.S. Constitution, 1788.

SUPREME COURT SERVICE: nominated associate justice by President John Adams December 19, 1798, to replace James Wilson, who had died; confirmed by the Senate December 20, 1798, by a voice vote; took judicial oath February 4, 1799; served until November 26, 1829; replaced by Henry Baldwin, nominated by President Andrew Jackson.

FAMILY: married Julia Ann Blackburn, 1785.

DEATH: November 26, 1829, in Philadelphia, Pennsylvania.

Bushrod Washington received his first name from his mother, Hannah Bushrod, a member of one of Virginia's oldest colonial families. His father, John Augustine Washington, was a brother of George Washington and served as a member of the Virginia legislature and magistrate of Westmoreland County, Virginia.

As a boy Bushrod was privately tutored. He graduated from the College of William and Mary at sixteen and was a founding member of Phi Beta Kappa, then a secret social club. He was a student in George Wythe's law course at the same time as John Marshall.

Toward the end of the Revolution, Washington enlisted as a private in the Continental Army. He was present when Cornwallis surrendered at Yorktown in October 1781. After the war, Washington studied law for two years under Philadelphia lawyer James Wilson, whom he would later succeed on the Supreme Court.

Washington was a confirmed user of snuff and an untidy dresser, blind in one eye. According to most accounts, he also was a diligent and methodical student of the law. In the words of his colleague, Justice Joseph Story, "His mind was solid, rather than brilliant; sagacious and searching, rather than quick or eager; slow, but not torpid."

In 1785 Washington married Julia Ann Blackburn, the daughter of an aide-de-camp to General Washington during the Revolution. She is said to have been at his side constantly, even when he made his rounds as a circuit judge. She was with him when he died in Philadelphia and died herself during the trip home to attend the funeral.

When George Washington died in 1799 with no children of his own, he left his Mount Vernon estate, including all his public and private papers, to his nephew Bushrod. The former president had provided that his slaves be freed when his wife Martha died. Bushrod Washington brought his own slaves to Mount Vernon, where his lack of farming experience pushed the estate into debt. In 1821 he sold more than half the Mount Vernon slaves, separating families in the process.

For this action he was bitterly attacked in several journals of the day. He dismissed the criticism by arguing the slaves were his property to do with as he saw fit. In 1816 Washington had been elected the first president of the American Colonization Society, established to transport free blacks to Africa, a movement that was criticized by abolitionists.

Washington began private law practice in Westmoreland County, Virginia, and later in Alexandria, Virginia, where he specialized in chancery cases. In 1787, with encouragement from his uncle, he ran for the Virginia House of Delegates and was elected. The following year he was sent as a delegate to the state ratification convention and successfully argued, along with Marshall and Madison, for state approval of the new federal Constitution.

Around 1790 Washington moved to Richmond, where he developed a successful law practice and trained many law students, including Henry Clay. During this period he also served as reporter for the court of appeals and spent much of his time writing two volumes of reports of cases argued before the court.

During his tenure on the Supreme Court, Washington was often allied with Chief Justice Marshall and Justice Story. Indeed, Justice William Johnson, another member of the Marshall Court, once complained that Marshall and Washington "are commonly estimated as a single judge." Washington disagreed with Marshall only three times during the twenty-nine years they were on the Court together.

He died November 26, 1829, while on circuit court business in Philadelphia. Julia Washington died while bringing her husband's body to Mount Vernon for burial.

Alfred Moore

(1800–1804)

BIRTH: May 21, 1755, New Hanover County, North Carolina.

EDUCATION: educated in Boston; studied law under his father; received law license, 1775.

OFFICIAL POSITIONS: member, North Carolina legislature, 1782, 1792; North Carolina attorney general, 1782–1791; trustee, University of North Carolina, 1789–1807; judge, North Carolina Superior Court, 1799.

SUPREME COURT SERVICE: nominated associate justice by President John Adams December 6, 1799, to replace James Iredell, who had died; confirmed by the Senate December 10, 1799, by a voice vote; took judicial oath April 21, 1800; resigned January 26, 1804; replaced by William Johnson, nominated by President Thomas Jefferson.

FAMILY: married Susanna Eagles.

DEATH: October 15, 1810, Bladen County, North Carolina.

Alfred Moore was the son of Maurice Moore, a North Carolina colonial judge, and Anne Grange Moore. He was descended from Roger Moore, a leader of the 1641 Irish Rebellion, and James Moore, governor of South Carolina in the early eighteenth century.

Following his mother's death and his father's remarriage, Moore was sent to school in Boston. His studies there completed, Moore returned home and read law under his father. At the age of twenty he was licensed to practice law.

During the Revolution Moore served as a captain in a Continental regiment commanded by his uncle, Col. James Moore. He saw action in several successful battles, but, after his father died in 1777, left the army and returned to the family plantation.

He continued his activities against the British by joining the local militia and participating in raids on troops stationed in Wilmington. The British plundered his property in retaliation.

Following brief service in the North Carolina legislature, Moore became state attorney general in 1782, succeeding James Iredell, his predecessor on the Supreme Court, and during that time became a leader of the state bar. In one major case, Moore argued in support of the North Carolina Confiscation Act, which allowed the state to confiscate all land that had been abandoned by Loyalists during the Revolution.

A strong Federalist, Moore lost election as a delegate to the state constitutional ratifying convention, but was instrumental in getting the state finally to approve in 1789.

Moore resigned as attorney general in 1791 when the state legislature created a new office of solicitor general, giving it the same powers and salary as the attorney general. Moore claimed the new office was unconstitutional.

In 1792 Moore was elected to the state legislature again, but three years later lost a race for the U.S. Senate by one vote in the legislature. In 1798 he was appointed by President John Adams as one of three commissioners to negotiate a treaty with the Cherokee Indians, but he withdrew from the discussions before the treaty was signed. In 1799 he served as a judge on the North Carolina Superior Court.

When Justice James Iredell died in 1799, Adams looked to North Carolina for a replacement. William R. Davie was apparently the first choice, but he had just been made a diplomatic agent to France, so the nomination went to Moore.

Moore exerted little influence during his five years on the Court and wrote only one opinion. He resigned in 1804, citing ill health, and returned home to work on the development of the University of North Carolina. He died in North Carolina on October 15, 1810, at the home of his son-in-law.

John Marshall

(1801–1835)

BIRTH: September 24, 1755, Germantown, Virginia.

EDUCATION: tutored at home; self-taught in law; attended one course of law lectures at College of William and Mary, 1780.

OFFICIAL POSITIONS: member, Virginia House of Delegates, 1782–1785, 1787–1790, 1795–1796; member, Executive Council of State, 1782–1784; recorder, Richmond City Hustings Court, 1785–1788; delegate, state convention for ratification of federal Constitution, 1788; minister to France, 1797–1798; U.S. representative, 1799–1800; U.S. secretary of state, 1800–1801; member, Virginia Constitutional Convention, 1829.

SUPREME COURT SERVICE: nominated chief justice by President John Adams January 20, 1801, to replace Oliver Ellsworth, who had resigned; confirmed by the Senate January 27, 1801, by a voice vote; took judicial oath February 4, 1801; served until July 6, 1835; replaced by Roger B. Taney, nominated by President Andrew Jackson.

John Marshall

FAMILY: Married Mary Willis Ambler, January 3, 1783; died December 25, 1831; ten children.

DEATH: July 6, 1835, Philadelphia, Pennsylvania.

The first of fifteen children, John Marshall was born in a log cabin on the Virginia frontier near Germantown. His father, Thomas Marshall, was descended from Welsh immigrants, was an assistant surveyor to George Washington and member of the Virginia House of Burgesses. His mother, Mary Randolph Keith Marshall, was the daughter of an educated Scottish clergyman.

As a youth, Marshall was tutored by two clergymen, but his primary teacher was his father, who introduced him to the study of English literature and Blackstone's *Commentaries*.

During the Revolutionary War, young Marshall participated in the siege of Norfolk as a member of the Culpeper Minute Men and was present at Brandywine, Monmouth, Stony Point, and Valley Forge as a member of the third Virginia Regiment. In 1779 he returned home to await another assignment but was never recalled. He left the Continental Army with the rank of captain in 1781.

Marshall's only formal instruction in the law came in 1780 when he attended George Wythe's course of law lectures at the College of William and Mary. He was admitted to Phi Beta Kappa, after returning to Fauquier County, to the Virginia bar. He gradually developed a lucrative practice, specializing in defending Virginians against their pre–Revolutionary War British creditors.

In January 1783 Marshall married Mary Willis Ambler, daughter of the Virginia state treasurer, and established a home in Richmond. The couple had ten children, only six of whom survived to maturity. Marshall spent many years attending to the needs of Polly, as his wife was called. She suffered from nervous disorders and chronic illness.

From 1796 until about 1806, Marshall's life was dominated by the pressures of meeting debts incurred by a land investment he had made in the northern neck of Virginia. It has been speculated that his need for money motivated him to write *The Life of George Washington,* which appeared in five volumes from 1804 to 1807. The book was written too quickly, and when Jefferson ordered federal postmasters not to take orders for it, the opportunity for large sales was lost.

The leisurely pace of the Supreme Court in its early days was well suited to Marshall, who had grown to enjoy relaxation and the outdoors as a boy. The chief justice enjoyed socializing in the clubs and saloons of Richmond and kept a fine supply of personal wines. He is said to have excelled at the game of quoits (similar to horseshoes), and was also known to take a turn at whist, backgammon, and tenpins.

Marshall was master of his Masonic lodge in Richmond and served as Masonic Grand Master of Virginia for several years. He was a member of the American Colonization Society, which worked toward the transfer of freed slaves to Africa, and belonged to the Washington Historical Monument Society and several literary societies.

Marshall was elected to the Virginia House of Delegates from Fauquier County in 1782 and 1784. He reentered the House in 1787 and was instrumental in Virginia's ratification of the new U.S. Constitution. At the state ratifying convention his primary attention was directed to the need for judicial review. By 1789 Marshall was considered to be a leading Federalist in the state.

Marshall refused many appointments in the Federalist administrations of Washington and Adams, including U.S. attorney general in 1795, associate justice of the Supreme Court in 1798, and secretary of war in 1800. In 1796 he refused an appointment by President Adams as minister to France, but the following year agreed to serve as one of three special envoys sent to smooth relations with that country. This mission, known as the XYZ Affair, failed when French diplomats demanded a bribe as a condition for negotiation. Congress, however, was greatly impressed by the stubborn resistance of the American emissaries, and Marshall received a generous grant as a reward for his participation.

In 1799 Marshall was persuaded by Washington to run for the U.S. House of Representatives as a Federalist from Richmond. His career in the House was brief, however, for in 1800 he became secretary of state under Adams. When Adams retired to his home in Massachusetts for a few months that year, Marshall served as the effective head of government.

Oliver Ellsworth resigned as chief justice in 1800, and Adams offered the position to John Jay, who had been the Court's first chief justice. Jay declined, and the Federalists urged Adams to elevate Associate Justice William Paterson. But Adams nominated Marshall instead.

As the primary founder of the American system of constitutional law, including the doctrine of judicial review, Marshall participated in more than one thousand Supreme Court decisions, writing more than five hundred of them himself. In 1807 he presided over the treason trial of Aaron Burr in the Richmond Circuit Court, locking horns with Jefferson, who sought an absolute conviction. Burr was acquitted.

In 1831, at age seventy-six, Marshall underwent successful surgery in Philadelphia for the removal of kidney stones. Three years later, he developed an enlarged liver, and his health declined rapidly. When Marshall died on July 6, 1835, three months short of his eightieth birthday, the Liberty Bell cracked as it tolled in mourning.

William Johnson

(1804–1834)

BIRTH: December 27, 1771, Charleston, South Carolina.

EDUCATION: graduated Princeton, 1790; studied law under Charles Cotesworth Pinckney; admitted to bar in 1793.

OFFICIAL POSITIONS: member, South Carolina House of Representatives, 1794–1798; Speaker, 1798; judge, Court of Common Pleas, 1799–1804.

SUPREME COURT SERVICE: nominated associate justice by President Thomas Jefferson March 22, 1804, to replace Alfred Moore, who had resigned; confirmed by the Senate March 24, 1804, by a voice vote; took judicial oath May 7, 1804; served until August 4, 1834; replaced by James M. Wayne, nominated by President Andrew Jackson.

FAMILY: married Sarah Bennett, March 20, 1794; eight children, six of whom died in childhood; two adopted children.

DEATH: August 4, 1834, Brooklyn, New York.

William Johnson's father, also named William, was a blacksmith, legislator, and Revolutionary patriot who moved from New York to South Carolina in the early 1760s. His mother was Sarah Nightingale Johnson. When the British captured Charleston during the war, the Johnson family was exiled from their home, and William's father sent to detention in Florida. After several months, the family was reunited in Philadelphia and returned to South Carolina together.

Young William graduated first in his class from Princeton in 1790. Returning to Charleston, he began reading law under Charles Cotesworth Pinckney, a prominent adviser to President Washington who had studied at the Inns of Court. Johnson joined the bar in 1793.

The following year, Johnson married Sarah Bennett, sister of Thomas Bennett, who later would become governor of South Carolina. The couple had eight children, but only two survived to maturity. They eventually adopted two refugee children from Santo Domingo.

A member of the American Philosophical Society, Johnson retained an interest in education and literature all his life. He was one of the primary founders of the University of South Carolina and in 1822 published a two-volume biography of Revolutionary War general Nathanael Greene. Johnson also published *Eulogy of Thomas Jefferson* in 1826.

Johnson's political career began in 1794 when he entered the South Carolina House of Representatives as a member of Jefferson's new Republican Party. Following service as Speaker in 1798, Johnson was chosen one of three judges to sit on the state's highest court, the Court of Common Pleas. Here, he gained experience riding circuit and dealing with the burgeoning judicial questions concerning federal-state relations. In 1804 Johnson became Jefferson's first Republican nominee to the Supreme Court.

At least until 1830, Johnson was the most independent of the justices on the Marshall Court, and he has been called "the first great Court dissenter." Fighting against the wishes of powerful—some would say dictatorial—Chief Justice John Marshall, Johnson succeeded in establishing the Court's tradition of dissenting opinions.

Johnson once wrote Jefferson that the Court was no "bed of roses," and in the first part of his career on the bench tried to obtain another appointment. He remained on the Court, however, until his death following surgery in 1834.

Henry Brockholst Livingston

(1807–1823)

BIRTH: November 25, 1757, New York City.

EDUCATION: graduated from College of New Jersey (Princeton), 1774; honorary LL.D., Harvard (1810), Princeton; studied law under Peter Yates; admitted to bar in 1783.

OFFICIAL POSITIONS: member, New York Assembly, Twelfth, Twenty-fourth, and Twenty-fifth sessions; judge, New York State Supreme Court, 1802–1807.

Henry Brockholst Livingston

SUPREME COURT SERVICE: nominated associate justice by President Thomas Jefferson December 13, 1806, to replace William Paterson, who had died; confirmed by the Senate December 17, 1806, by a voice vote; took judicial oath January 20, 1807; served until March 18, 1823; replaced by Smith Thompson, nominated by President James Monroe.

FAMILY: married Catharine Keteltas, five children; married Ann Ludlow, three children; married Catharine Kortright, three children.

DEATH: March 18, 1823, Washington, D.C.

As a member of the powerful Livingston family of New York, Brockholst Livingston was born into the colonial aristocracy. His father, William Livingston, was governor of New Jersey and a leader in the New York opposition to British colonial policies. His mother was Susanna French Livingston.

Young Livingston was graduated from Princeton in 1774, where he was a classmate of James Madison, and joined the Continental Army at the outbreak of the Revolution. As a commissioned major, he served under Generals Schuyler and St. Clair and participated in the siege of Ticonderoga. He was also an aide to Benedict Arnold during the Saratoga campaign and was present at Gen. John Burgoyne's surrender in 1777. Livingston left the army with the rank of lieutenant colonel.

After the war, Livingston traveled to Spain to serve as private secretary to his brother-in-law, John Jay, then serving as the American minister there. During this time, Livingston began to dislike Jay.

Although Livingston was considered an affable and genial man, there appears to have been a violent side to his personality.

He killed one man in a duel in 1798 and is believed to have fought several others. An assassination attempt was made on his life in 1785.

Livingston married three times and had a total of eleven children. A devotee of history, he was cofounder of the New York Historical Society and one of its vice presidents. He served as trustee and treasurer of Columbia University from 1784 until the end of his life and was instrumental in organizing the New York public school system. Livingston was an original member of the Society of the Cincinnati.

Livingston—who began using the middle name Brockholst, probably to avoid confusion with two cousins also named Henry—was elected to the New York Assembly in 1786. He also began practicing law at this time, working closely with Alexander Hamilton.

During these years, Livingston began a conversion, along with other members of his family, from Federalism to anti-Federalism. By 1792 he was bitterly attacking Jay's campaign for the New York governorship and succeeded in denying him a crucial bloc of votes. When Jay returned from negotiating a treaty with England in 1794, Livingston was at the forefront of voices critical of it.

As the New York anti-Federalist alliance of the Burr, Clinton, and Livingston factions reached its height around 1800, several Livingstons received high appointments. In 1802 Brockholst Livingston joined two of his relatives by marriage on the New York Supreme Court. He served for five years, specializing in commercial law.

In 1804 Livingston was considered seriously for an opening on the U.S. Supreme Court, but the position went instead to William Johnson. In 1806, however, Livingston was nominated by Jefferson to fill the vacancy created by the death of William Paterson.

Livingston died in 1823, after serving sixteen years on the high court.

Thomas Todd

(1807–1826)

BIRTH: January 23, 1765, King and Queen County, Virginia.

EDUCATION: graduated from Liberty Hall (now Washington and Lee University), Lexington, Virginia, 1783; read law under Harry Innes; admitted to bar in 1788.

OFFICIAL POSITIONS: clerk, federal district for Kentucky, 1792–1801; clerk, Kentucky House of Representatives, 1792–1801; clerk, Kentucky Court of Appeals (Supreme Court), 1799–1801; judge, Kentucky Court of Appeals, 1801–1806; chief justice, 1806–1807.

SUPREME COURT SERVICE: nominated associate justice by President Thomas Jefferson February 28, 1807, to fill a newly created seat; confirmed by the Senate March 3, 1807, by a voice vote; took judicial oath May 4, 1807; served until February 7, 1826; replaced by Robert Trimble, nominated by President John Quincy Adams.

Thomas Todd

FAMILY: married Elizabeth Harris, 1788; died 1811; five children; married Lucy Payne, 1812; three children.

DEATH: February 7, 1826, Frankfort, Kentucky.

Thomas Todd was only eighteen months old when his father, Richard Todd, died. His mother, Elizabeth Richards Todd, died when Thomas was eleven, and from then on he was raised by a guardian. The family owned large tracts of land handed down since the seventeenth century, but, because Thomas was not the oldest son, he was excluded from inheriting any of these holdings.

Todd's mother, Elizabeth, managed to leave her son money she had accumulated through her successful boarding house, and Thomas used it to acquire a solid education in the classics. Most of the inheritance, however, was eventually lost because of mismanagement by his guardian.

At age sixteen Todd served in the Revolutionary War for six months, returning home to attend Liberty Hall (now Washington and Lee University) in Lexington, Virginia. After graduation, he accepted an invitation from Harry Innes, a distant relative and respected member of the Virginia legislature, to tutor Innes's daughters in exchange for room, board, and law instruction.

In 1784, when Innes was asked to move to Danville, Kentucky, (then part of Virginia) to set up a district court in the area, Todd made the move with the family. It was at this time that the Kentucky area of Virginia held the first of five conventions seeking admission to the Union as a separate state. Through his friendship with Innes, Todd was able to act as clerk for each convention.

With his first wife, Elizabeth, Todd had five children, one of whom, Charles Stewart, became minister to Russia in 1841. Elizabeth died in 1811, and Todd married Dolley Madison's sister, Lucy Payne, in the East Room of the White House the following year. Todd lived in Danville until 1801 and then moved about forty miles north to Frankfort, Kentucky. During his lifetime, Todd accumulated more than 7,200 acres in Kentucky. He also owned stock in the Kentucky River Company, which promoted water navigation, and Kentucky Turnpike, one of the first public highways west of the Allegheny Mountains.

Todd joined the Virginia bar in 1788 and soon developed a specialty in land law. When Kentucky became a state in 1792, he served as secretary to the new Kentucky legislature. In 1799, when the state supreme court was created, Todd was chosen to be its chief clerk.

In 1801 Kentucky governor James Garrard appointed Todd to fill a newly created fourth seat on the state court. At the age of forty-one, Todd was named its chief justice. Most of the cases handled by the court during his tenure involved land title disputes, and the chief justice developed a reputation for being fair and honest in settling complicated land controversies.

In 1807 the federal Judiciary Act of 1789 was amended to create a new federal court circuit made up of Tennessee, Kentucky, and Ohio. On the recommendation of the members of Congress from those states, President Jefferson chose Todd to preside over this new circuit as the sixth associate justice on the Supreme Court.

During his years on the bench, Todd missed five entire Court sessions because of personal and health reasons. He delivered only fourteen opinions during his tenure, including one dissent.

He died in February 1826, leaving a considerable fortune.

Gabriel Duvall

(1811–1835)

BIRTH: December 6, 1752, Prince George's County, Maryland.

EDUCATION: classical preparatory schooling; studied law.

OFFICIAL POSITIONS: clerk, Maryland Convention, 1775–1777; clerk, Maryland House of Delegates, 1777–1787; member, Maryland State Council, 1782–1785; member, Maryland House of Delegates, 1787–1794; U.S. representative, 1794–1796; chief justice, General Court of Maryland, 1796–1802; presidential elector, 1796, 1800; first comptroller of the Treasury, 1802–1811.

SUPREME COURT SERVICE: nominated associate justice by President James Madison November 15, 1811, to replace Samuel Chase, who had died; confirmed by the Senate November 18, 1811, by a voice vote; took judicial oath November 23, 1811; resigned January 14, 1835; replaced by Philip Barbour, nominated by President Andrew Jackson.

FAMILY: married Mary Brice, July 24, 1787; died March 24, 1790; one son; married Jane Gibbon, May 5, 1795; died April 1834.

DEATH: March 6, 1844, Prince George's County, Maryland.

Gabriel Duvall

Descended from a family of French Huguenots, Gabriel Duvall was the sixth of ten children born to Benjamin and Susanna Tyler Duvall on the family plantation "Marietta." The farm land, located on the South River near Buena Vista, Maryland, had been assigned to Gabriel's great-grandfather by Lord Baltimore.

Duvall was active in the Revolutionary War, serving as mustermaster and commissary of stores for the Maryland troops, and later as a private in the Maryland militia. Toward the end of the war, he helped protect confiscated British property.

In 1787, at the age of thirty-five, Duvall married Mary Brice, daughter of Captain Robert Brice of Annapolis. She died three years later, after the birth of their son. In 1795 Duvall married Jane Gibbon, who died in 1834 shortly before Duvall resigned from the Supreme Court.

Duvall's first public appointment came in 1775 when he was made clerk of the Maryland Convention. When the Maryland state government was created in 1777, he was named clerk for the House of Delegates.

In 1787 Duvall was elected to the Maryland House of Delegates, where he served until 1794. He was also chosen to attend the Constitutional Convention in Philadelphia, but decided along with the four others elected from Maryland not to attend.

Duvall entered the Third Congress of the United States in 1794 as a Republican-Democrat. Two years later he resigned to become chief justice of the General Court of Maryland. As chief justice, Duvall also served as recorder of the mayor's court in Annapolis, and it was in this capacity that he heard Roger Taney deliver his first speech as a member of the bar.

Duvall was chosen by President Thomas Jefferson to be the first comptroller of the Treasury in 1802. Nine years later he was nominated by President James Madison to serve on the Supreme Court.

During his twenty-three years on the bench, Duvall generally voted with Chief Justice Marshall. His most notable dissent came in *Dartmouth College v. Woodward* (1819), although he wrote no formal opinion.

By the end of his tenure on the Court, Duvall was eighty-two years old. His deafness and frequent absences had become an embarrassment, and his resignation in 1835 came as a great relief. Duvall spent his last years working on his family history and devoting attention to his son and nieces and nephews. He died in 1844 at the age of ninety-one.

Joseph Story

(1812–1845)

BIRTH: September 18, 1779, Marblehead, Massachusetts.

EDUCATION: attended Marblehead Academy; graduated from Harvard, 1798; LL.D., 1821; read law under Samuel Sewall and Samuel Putnam; admitted to bar, 1801.

OFFICIAL POSITIONS: member, Massachusetts legislature, 1805–1808; Speaker of the House, 1811; U.S. representative, 1808–1809; delegate, Massachusetts Constitutional Convention, 1820.

SUPREME COURT SERVICE: nominated associate justice by President James Madison November 15, 1811, to replace William Cushing, who had died; confirmed by the Senate November 18, 1811, by a voice vote; took judicial oath February 3, 1812; served until September 10, 1845; replaced by Levi Woodbury, nominated by President James K. Polk.

FAMILY: married Mary Lynde Oliver, December 9, 1804;

died June 1805; married Sarah Waldo Wetmore, August 27, 1808; seven children.

DEATH: September 10, 1845, Cambridge, Massachusetts.

Joseph Story was descended on both sides from old New England families. His father, Elisha Story, was a participant in the Boston Tea Party in 1773. His mother was Mehitable Pedrick Story.

Following a disagreement with a fellow classmate, Joseph was forced to leave Marblehead Academy before completing his college preparatory studies. By constantly studying on his own through the fall of 1794, however, he was able to enroll in Harvard in time for the 1795 term. Such drive and diligence were to characterize much of Story's life.

After graduating (second in his class) from Harvard in 1798, Story began reading law, sometimes for fourteen hours a day, in the Marblehead office of Samuel Sewall, later chief justice of the Massachusetts Supreme Court. When Sewall was appointed to a judgeship, Story completed his studies under Samuel Putnam in Salem, Massachusetts.

Admitted to the bar in 1801, Story began practice in Salem. The county bar was dominated by the Federalist establishment, however, and Story, a Republican-Democrat, was exposed to a good deal of prejudice. In the beginning he considered moving to Baltimore, but as his practice grew in prestige and influence, he chose to remain in Salem.

Story was an ardent poetry lover throughout his life. He was known by his hometown friends as "the poet of Marblehead." In 1805 he published "The Power of Solitude," a long, effusive poem written in heroic couplets. When his father and his wife of only seven months both died that year, Story, in a fit of sorrow, burned all copies of the poem he could find. He experienced further tragedy losing five of his seven children by his second marriage.

An avid conversationalist, Story enjoyed music, drawing, and painting. Besides being a writer, Story was an able public speaker and eulogist. He delivered the annual Fourth of July oration in Salem in 1804 and in 1826 delivered the Phi Beta Kappa oration at Harvard.

Story served for three years in the Massachusetts legislature and then entered the U.S. Congress in 1808. During his one term of service in the House, he was blamed by Jefferson for the repeal of Jefferson's foreign trade embargo, and he lost more points with his party by calling for a plan to strengthen the U.S. Navy. In January 1811 Story returned to the Massachusetts legislature and was elected Speaker of the House. By November of that year he had become one of the two youngest men ever to sit on the Supreme Court. (The other was William Johnson.)

Only thirty-two years old and with no court experience, Story had not been Madison's first choice for the job, but Levi Lincoln and John Quincy Adams had both declined, and Alexander Wolcott had been rejected by the Senate. Although he had a few financial reservations about taking the job, Story accepted the position as a great honor.

A supporter of higher learning for women, Story retained an active interest in education for most of his life. In 1819 he was elected to the Harvard Board of Overseers and became a fellow of the Harvard Corporation six years later. In 1829 Story moved from Salem to Cambridge, Massachusetts, to become professor of law at his alma mater. He played a major role in the foundation of Harvard Law School. He is also credited, along with Chancellor James Kent of New York, with founding the equity system of jurisprudence as practiced in the United States today.

While at Harvard, Story wrote his famous nine *Commentaries* on the law. Each of these works went through many editions, and one—*Commentaries on the Constitution* (1833)—was published in French, Spanish, and German, enhancing Story's international reputation.

In addition to the *Commentaries,* Story wrote legal essays for the *North American Review* and the *American Law Review,* and contributed unsigned articles to the *Encyclopedia Americana.* His Court opinions, though often accused of being tedious, are seminal works in the history of American national law.

On the Court, Story rarely broke from the strong nationalism of Chief Justice Marshall. In fact, it was Story's opinion in *Martin v. Hunter's Lessee* (1816) that established the appellate supremacy of the Supreme Court over state courts in civil cases involving federal statutes and treaties.

When Marshall died in 1835, Story undoubtedly coveted the chief justiceship, and his colleagues generally agreed he should be appointed. But Story was anathema to Andrew Jackson (he once called Story the "most dangerous man in America") and Roger Taney received the nomination instead.

Story's nine years on the Taney Court were spent largely in dissent and by the beginning of the 1845 term he was prepared to resign. He refused to leave until he had attended to all his unfinished business, however. He died September 10, 1845, after a sudden illness.

Smith Thompson

(1823–1843)

BIRTH: January 17, 1768, Dutchess County, New York.

EDUCATION: graduated Princeton, 1788; read law under James Kent; admitted to the bar, 1792; honorary law doctorates from Yale, 1824; Princeton, 1824; and Harvard, 1835.

OFFICIAL POSITIONS: member, New York state legislature, 1800; member, New York Constitutional Convention, 1801; associate justice, New York Supreme Court, 1802–1814; appointed to New York State Board of Regents, 1813; chief justice, New York Supreme Court, 1814–1818; secretary of the Navy, 1819–1823.

SUPREME COURT SERVICE: nominated associate justice by President James Monroe December 8, 1823, to replace Brockholst Livingston, who had died; confirmed by the Senate December 19, 1823, by a voice vote; took judicial oath February 10, 1823; served until December 18, 1843; replaced by Samuel Nelson, nominated by President John Tyler.

FAMILY: married Sarah Livingston, 1794; died September

Smith Thompson

22, 1833; two sons, two daughters; married Eliza Livingston; two daughters, one son.

DEATH: December 18, 1843, Poughkeepsie, New York.

Smith Thompson's public career was inevitably shaped by his personal ties and social connections. His father, Ezra Thompson, was a successful New York farmer and a well-known Anti-Federalist in state politics. His mother was Rachel Smith Thompson. More important, however, was Thompson's link through marriage to the Livingston family, albeit to a less-prominent branch. The Livingstons were a powerful force in New York politics at the end of the eighteenth century.

Thompson was born in 1768 in Dutchess County, New York, between the Hudson River and the Connecticut border. After graduating from Princeton in 1788, he taught school and read law under James Kent, a well-respected jurist then working in Poughkeepsie. In 1793 Thompson joined the law practice of Kent and Gilbert Livingston, an old friend of his father.

Thompson married Livingston's daughter, Sarah, in 1794. When Sarah died in 1833, he married her first cousin, Eliza Livingston. By this time, however, the family's influence was on the decline.

Thompson's public career got off to a quick start in 1800 when he entered the state legislature as a member of the Livingston wing of the Anti-Federalist Republican party. The next year he attended the state constitutional convention and received an appointment as district attorney for the middle district of New York. Before he had a chance to assume those duties, however, he was appointed to the state supreme court and immediately assumed that position.

During his tenure on the state bench, Thompson served with two of his cousins by marriage. He replaced one of these men, Brockholst Livingston, on the U.S. Supreme Court. Thompson was also joined on the state court by James Kent, his old friend and mentor. When Kent stepped down as its chief justice in 1814 to become chancellor of New York, Thompson succeeded him.

Thompson became secretary of the Navy under President Monroe in 1819, probably through the influence of Martin Van Buren, a rising young New York politician and ally of Thompson. As Navy secretary, Thompson had few administrative duties and spent a good deal of his time dabbling in New York politics, working, at times, with Van Buren. He also made no secret of his presidential ambitions during this period.

When Brockholst Livingston died in 1823, Thompson was immediately thought of as a contender for the vacancy on the Supreme Court, along with Chancellor Kent. Thompson delayed expressing formal interest in the seat, however, hoping with Van Buren's help to mount a campaign drive for the 1824 presidential election. Van Buren outwitted him in the end, however, and Thompson accepted the Court appointment from Monroe. Thompson continued to foster political ambitions while on the Supreme Court and in 1828 decided to run for governor of New York. He lost to his old friend, Martin Van Buren, in a bitter and dramatic campaign.

While on the Court, Thompson became part of a group that began to pull away from the strong nationalism of Chief Justice John Marshall. In 1827 he voted with the majority against Marshall in *Ogden v. Saunders* supporting state bankruptcy laws. His most notable opinion came in *Kendall v. United States* (1838), in which he argued against President Jackson that the executive branch was not exempt from judicial control. The passage was later omitted from the printed opinion at the request of the U.S. attorney general.

Robert Trimble

(1826–1828)

BIRTH: November 17, 1776, Berkeley County, Virginia.

EDUCATION: Bourbon Academy; Kentucky Academy; read law under George Nicholas and James Brown; admitted to the bar in 1803.

OFFICIAL POSITIONS: Kentucky state representative, 1802; judge, Kentucky Court of Appeals, 1807–1809; U.S. district attorney for Kentucky, 1813–1817; U.S. district judge, 1817–1826.

SUPREME COURT SERVICE: nominated associate justice by President John Quincy Adams April 11, 1826, to replace Thomas Todd, who had died; confirmed May 9, 1826, by a 27–5 vote; took judicial oath June 16, 1826; served until August 25, 1828; replaced by John McLean, nominated by President Andrew Jackson.

FAMILY: married Nancy Timberlake, August 18, 1803; at least ten children.

DEATH: August 25, 1828, Paris, Kentucky.

Robert Trimble was the son of William Trimble, an early Kentucky pioneer who hunted game and scouted for Indians,

Robert Trimble

and Mary McMillan Trimble. It appears young Trimble studied at the Bourbon Academy in Kentucky and after teaching for a short time attended the Kentucky Academy (later Transylvania University) in Woodford County. Following his study at the Kentucky Academy, Trimble read law under George Nicholas, the first attorney general of Kentucky, and James Brown, who later became minister to France.

Trimble began private practice in Paris, Kentucky, in about 1800. In 1802 he entered the Kentucky House of Representatives and in 1807 was appointed justice of the Kentucky Court of Appeals. He resigned the judgeship in 1808, claiming the yearly salary of $1,000 was too low to support his growing family.

Trimble also refused the chief justiceship of Kentucky in 1810 for financial reasons and declined to run for the U.S. Senate in 1812. Although he twice refused to accept the law professorship at Transylvania University, he served as a trustee of the school for many years.

Trimble's decision to concentrate on his private law practice instead of public service proved profitable. By 1817 he had earned a sizable amount of money and owned a number of slaves. That year he decided to accept the nomination by President Madison to be the federal district judge for Kentucky. He served for eight years.

Trimble—John Quincy Adams's only appointment to the U.S. Supreme Court—was chosen for his belief in strong national power, a position that had not won him many friends in Kentucky. During his two years on the Supreme Court bench, he was a strong supporter of Chief Justice Marshall, but disagreed with him in *Ogden v. Saunders,* voting to sustain the power of the states to apply insolvency laws.

John McLean

(1830–1861)

BIRTH: March 11, 1785, Morris County, New Jersey.

EDUCATION: attended local school; privately tutored; read law with John S. Gano and Arthur St. Clair Jr.

OFFICIAL POSITIONS: examiner, U.S. Land Office, 1811–1812; U.S. representative, 1813–1816, chairman, Committee on Accounts; judge, Ohio Supreme Court, 1816–1822; commissioner, General Land Office, 1822–1823; U.S. postmaster general, 1823–1829.

SUPREME COURT SERVICE: nominated associate justice by President Andrew Jackson March 7, 1829, to replace Robert Trimble, who had died; confirmed by the Senate March 7, 1829, by a voice vote; took judicial oath January 11, 1830; served until April 3, 1861; replaced by Noah H. Swayne, nominated by President Abraham Lincoln.

FAMILY: married Rebecca Edwards, 1807; died 1840; four daughters, three sons; married Sarah Bella Ludlow Garrard, 1843; one son, died at birth.

DEATH: April 3, 1861, Cincinnati, Ohio.

John McLean's father, Fergus McLain, was a Scotch-Irish weaver who immigrated to New Jersey in 1775. After his marriage to Sophia Blackford of Middlesex County, New Jersey, and the birth of several children, Fergus moved his family first to western Virginia, then Kentucky; finally in 1797 they settled on a farm near Lebanon, Ohio, about forty miles north of Cincinnati. Young John attended the county school and later earned enough money as a farmhand to hire two Presbyterian ministers to tutor him.

In 1804 he began two years of work as an apprentice to the clerk of the Hamilton County Court of Common Pleas in Cincinnati. At the same time, he was able to study with John S. Gano and Arthur St. Clair, two respected Cincinnati lawyers.

Following his admission to the bar in 1807, McLean married Rebecca Edwards of Newport, Kentucky, and returned to Lebanon, where he opened a printing office. In a short time, he began publishing the Lebanon *Western Star* newspaper, a weekly journal supportive of Jeffersonian politics. In 1810, however, McLean relinquished the print shop to his brother, Nathaniel, and devoted all of his time to law practice.

McLean experienced a profound religious conversion in 1811 and remained a devout Methodist for the rest of his life. He participated actively in church affairs and was chosen honorary president of the American Sunday School Union in 1849.

McLean was elected to Congress in 1812. During his two terms in service, he supported the war measures of the Madison administration and opposed creation of a second Bank of the United States. In 1816 McLean resigned from the House and was elected to one of four judgeships on the Ohio Supreme Court, serving from 1816 to 1822.

McLean worked hard for the nomination and election of James Monroe to the presidency in 1816, and in 1822 Monroe returned the favor by appointing McLean commissioner of the General Land Office. A year later he was made postmaster general. McLean was well liked by the postal employees and proved to be a skilled administrator. The postal service greatly expanded under his leadership, and by 1828 the department was the largest agency in the executive branch.

By this time, McLean had become an astute politician. He managed to keep his job as postmaster general under John Quincy Adams while establishing ties with many of Andrew Jackson's men at the same time. When Jackson became president in 1829, Robert Trimble's seat on the Supreme Court was still vacant because of Senate political maneuverings, and McLean was nominated to fill it. His most famous opinion during his thirty-two years on the bench was his dissent in *Scott v. Sandford*, which was eventually reflected in the Fourteenth Amendment to the Constitution.

McLean entertained presidential ambitions throughout his Supreme Court career and flirted with several political parties at various stages. In 1856 he received 190 votes on an informal presidential ballot taken at the first Republican national convention in Philadelphia. Thaddeus Stevens pushed his candidacy four years later, but the effort was blocked by Ohio Republicans.

McLean died of pneumonia in 1861.

Henry Baldwin

(1830–1844)

BIRTH: January 14, 1780, New Haven, Connecticut.

EDUCATION: Hopkins Grammar School, 1793; Yale College, 1797, LL.D., 1830; attended the law lectures of Judge Tapping Reeve; clerked for Alexander James Dallas.

Henry Baldwin

OFFICIAL POSITIONS: U.S. representative; chairman, Committee on Domestic Manufactures.

SUPREME COURT SERVICE: nominated associate justice by President Andrew Jackson January 4, 1830, to replace Bushrod Washington, who had died; confirmed by the Senate January 6, 1830, by a 41–2 vote; took judicial oath January 18, 1830; served until April 21, 1844; replaced by Robert C. Grier, nominated by President James K. Polk.

FAMILY: married Marianna Norton, 1802; died 1803; one son; married Sally Ellicott, 1805.

DEATH: April 21, 1844, Philadelphia, Pennsylvania.

Baldwin was the product of a New England family dating back to the seventeenth century. His parents were Michael and Theodora Wolcott Baldwin. His half-brother, Abraham, was a representative to both the Continental Congress and the Constitutional Convention and a U.S. senator from Georgia.

As a boy, Henry lived on the family farm near New Haven, but moved to the city when he entered Yale College. Upon graduation in 1797, he attended law lectures at Judge Tapping Reeve's school in Litchfield, Connecticut. He clerked in the law office of Alexander James Dallas, a prominent Philadelphia attorney, and was soon admitted to the bar. Baldwin decided to settle in Pittsburgh, a young city that afforded opportunities for a beginning lawyer.

Baldwin settled easily and quickly into the Pittsburgh community, joining the county bar and making many friends. With Tarleton Bates and Walter Forward, he formed a successful law firm known as the "Great Triumvirate of Early Pittsburgh." During this period, Baldwin developed a reputation for his well-written law briefs, which he prepared in his large personal law library, considered to be one of the finest in the "West."

In only a short time, Baldwin and his law partners became known for their political leadership as well as their legal skill. Together, they published a newspaper called *The Tree of Liberty,* which supported a faction of the Republican Party in western Pennsylvania. Through his work in the party and in Pittsburgh civic affairs, Baldwin became a popular and prominent leader in the community by his mid-twenties. Before long, he was affectionately known as the "Idol of Pennsylvania" and the "Pride of Pittsburgh."

Despite his political and legal activities, Baldwin found time to involve himself in business affairs. He was part owner of at least three mills in Pennsylvania, in addition to a profitable woolen mill in Steubenville, Ohio.

Baldwin, the manufacturer, entered Congress in 1817 as a supporter of higher tariffs and as a spokesman for Pittsburgh's economic growth interests. He resigned from the House in 1822 for health reasons, but after two years of rest returned to his role as unofficial political leader of Allegheny County. In 1823 he urged Andrew Jackson to run for the presidency and throughout John Quincy Adams's administration was a close adviser to Jackson on western Pennsylvania politics.

When Justice Bushrod Washington died in 1829, President Jackson decided to nominate Baldwin to fill the seat, against the wishes of Vice President John C. Calhoun, who supported another candidate.

Baldwin's career on the bench has been characterized as erratic. In the beginning, he supported the liberal interpretations of Chief Justice Marshall, but later refused to embrace either strict or broad construction of the Constitution.

Baldwin is reported to have suffered temporary mental derangements toward the end of his life. Biographical sources do not elaborate on his illness except to say he did not get along well with other justices on the bench, and his closest friends were suspicious of his nonconforming and peculiar habits. As early as 1832, Roger Taney had advised President Jackson not to take legal action against the Bank of the United States because the case would be tried in Philadelphia and Baldwin would be unreliable as presiding judge. Baldwin, then fifty-two, had already begun to suffer lapses of reason.

Baldwin was said to be occasionally violent and ungovernable on the bench toward the end of his life. In 1844, when he died of paralysis, he was deeply in debt, and his friends had to take up a collection to pay his funeral expenses.

James Moore Wayne

(1835–1867)

BIRTH: 1790, Savannah, Georgia.

EDUCATION: College of New Jersey (Princeton University), 1808, honorary LL.B., 1849; read law under three lawyers including Judge Charles Chauncey of New Haven; admitted to the bar January 1811.

James Moore Wayne

OFFICIAL POSITIONS: member, Georgia House of Representatives, 1815–1816; mayor, Savannah, 1817–1819; judge, Savannah Court of Common Pleas, 1820–1822; Georgia Superior Court, 1822–1828; U.S. representative, 1829–1835; chairman, Committee on Foreign Relations.

SUPREME COURT SERVICE: nominated associate justice by President Andrew Jackson January 7, 1835, to replace William Johnson, who had died; confirmed by the Senate January 9, 1835 by a voice vote; took judicial oath January 14, 1835; served until July 5, 1867; replaced by Joseph Bradley, nominated by President Ulysses S. Grant.

FAMILY: married Mary Johnson Campbell, 1813; three children.

DEATH: July 5, 1867, Washington, D.C.

James Wayne was the son of Richard Wayne, a British army officer, and Elizabeth Clifford Wayne. He was the twelfth of their thirteen children. As a boy, James lived on the family rice plantation outside of Savannah and was educated by an Irish tutor. He progressed so quickly in his studies that he was ready to enter the College of New Jersey (now Princeton) at the age of fourteen. Shortly after his graduation in 1808, James's father died and his brother-in-law, Richard Stites, became his guardian.

Wayne had begun to study law under a prominent Savannah lawyer, John Y. Noel, and, after his father's death, he studied at Yale under Judge Charles Chauncey for almost two years. Upon returning to Savannah, he read in the office of his brother-in-law and in 1810 went into partnership with Samuel M. Bond.

During the War of 1812, Wayne served as an officer in a volunteer Georgia militia unit called the Chatham Light Dragoons.

In 1813 he married Mary Johnson Campbell of Richmond, Virginia. The couple had three children.

In 1815 Wayne was elected to the Georgia legislature, serving two years. At age twenty-seven he became mayor of Savannah, but resigned after two years to resume his law practice. At the end of 1819, he was elected to sit on the Savannah Court of Common Pleas and in 1822 was appointed to a superior court judgeship. The court provided him with much hard work and the opportunity for public recognition.

Wayne entered Congress in 1829 and served for three terms. During this period he became a strong ally of the Jackson administration. By 1835 he was considered a leading Unionist Democrat and was nominated to the Supreme Court by President Jackson.

Unlike his colleague, Justice Campbell of Alabama, Wayne refused to leave the bench when secession came and remained a strong Union supporter throughout the Civil War. It was an agonizing period for the justice, who was disowned by his home state and accused of being an enemy alien by a Confederate court.

At war's end, Wayne opposed the punitive Reconstruction measures taken against the South and refused to hold circuit court in states under military Reconstruction rule. He did not live to see the end of Reconstruction, dying of typhoid in 1867.

Roger Brooke Taney

(1836–1864)

BIRTH: March 17, 1777, Calvert County, Maryland.

EDUCATION: graduated from Dickinson College in Pennsylvania, 1795, honorary LL.D.; read law in office of Judge Jeremiah Chase in Annapolis.

OFFICIAL POSITIONS: member, Maryland House of Delegates, 1799–1800; Maryland state senator, 1816–1821; Maryland attorney general, 1827–1831; chairman, Jackson Central Committee for Maryland, 1827–1828; U.S. attorney general, 1831–1833; acting secretary of war, 1831; U.S. secretary of the Treasury, 1833–1834 (appointment rejected by Senate).

SUPREME COURT SERVICE: nominated chief justice by President Andrew Jackson December 28, 1835, to replace John Marshall, who had died; confirmed by Senate on March 15, 1836, by a 29–15 vote; took judicial oath March 28, 1836; served until October 12, 1864; replaced by Salmon P. Chase, nominated by President Abraham Lincoln.

FAMILY: married Anne Phoebe Carlton Key, January 7, 1806; died 1855; six daughters; one son, died in infancy.

DEATH: October 12, 1864, Washington, D.C.

Roger Taney was descended on both sides from prominent Maryland families. Monica Brooke Taney's family first arrived in the state in 1650, complete with fox hounds and other trappings of aristocracy. Michael Taney's forebear immigrated to America around 1660 as an indentured servant but eventually acquired a large amount of property and became a member of the landed Maryland tidewater gentry.

Taney was born in Calvert County, Maryland, on his father's tobacco plantation. He was educated in local rural schools and privately tutored by a Princeton student. In 1795, at the age of eighteen, he graduated first in his class from Dickinson College in Pennsylvania.

As his father's second son, Taney was not in line to inherit the family property and so decided on a career in law and politics. For three years, he was an apprentice lawyer in the office of Judge Jeremiah Chase of the Maryland General Court in Annapolis. He was admitted to the bar in 1799.

In 1806 Taney married Anne Key, daughter of a prominent farmer and the sister of Francis Scott Key. Because Taney was a devout Roman Catholic and his wife an Episcopalian, they agreed to raise their sons as Catholics and their daughters as Episcopalians. The couple had six daughters and a son who died in infancy. In 1855, the year *Scott v. Sandford* came before the Supreme Court, Taney's wife and youngest daughter died of yellow fever.

Taney began his political career as a member of the Federalist Party, serving one term in the Maryland legislature from 1799 to 1800. After being defeated for reelection, he moved from Calvert County to Frederick, where he began to develop a profitable law practice.

In 1803 Taney was beaten again in an attempt to return to the House of Delegates. Despite this setback, he began to achieve prominence in the Frederick community as a lawyer and politician. He lived there for twenty years.

In supporting the War of 1812, Taney split with the majority of his state's Federalists. But in 1816, as a result of shifting politi-

cal loyalties, he was elected to the Maryland Senate and became a dominant figure in party politics.

Taney's Senate term expired in 1821. In 1823 he settled in Baltimore, where he continued his successful law practice and political activities. By this time, the Federalist Party had virtually disintegrated, and Taney threw his support to the Jackson Democrats, leading Jackson's 1828 presidential campaign in Maryland. Taney served as the state's attorney general from 1827 until 1831 when he was named U.S. attorney general for the Jackson administration and left Baltimore for Washington.

Taney played a leading role in the controversy over the second Bank of the United States, helping to write Jackson's message in 1832 vetoing the bank's recharter. The next year, when Treasury Secretary William Duane refused to withdraw federal deposits from the bank, Duane was dismissed and replaced by Taney, who promptly carried out the action.

Taney held the Treasury job for nine months, presiding over a new system of state bank depositories called "pet banks." Jackson, who had delayed as long as he could, was eventually forced to submit Taney's nomination as Treasury secretary to the Senate. In June 1834 the Senate rejected Taney, and he was forced to resign.

In 1835 Jackson appointed Taney to replace aging Supreme Court justice Gabriel Duvall, but the nomination was indefinitely postponed by a close Senate vote. Ten months later, Jackson proposed Taney's name again, this time to fill the seat left vacant by the death of Chief Justice Marshall. To the horror of the Whigs, who considered him much too radical, Taney was confirmed as chief justice on March 15, 1836.

Taney's reputation rests almost entirely on his opinion in *Scott v. Sandford*, in which he held that slaves had no legal rights and could not become citizens. This decision hastened the Civil War and damaged the standing of the Court. But Taney is also responsible for a much earlier and more socially responsible decision in *Charles River Bridge v. Warren Bridge* (1837), in which the Court asserted that contracts made by a state legislature should benefit the public good.

Philip Pendleton Barbour

(1836–1841)

BIRTH: May 25, 1783, Orange County, Virginia.

EDUCATION: read law on his own; attended one session at College of William and Mary, 1801.

OFFICIAL POSITIONS: member, Virginia House of Delegates from Orange County, 1812–1814; U.S. representative, 1814–1825, 1827–1830; Speaker of the House, 1821–1823; state judge, General Court for the Eastern District of Virginia, 1825–1827; president, Virginia Constitutional Convention, 1829–1830; U.S. district judge, Court of Eastern Virginia, 1830–1836.

SUPREME COURT SERVICE: nominated associate justice by President Andrew Jackson February 28, 1835, to replace Gabriel Duvall, who had resigned; confirmed by the Senate,

Philip Barbour

March 15, 1836, by a 30–11 vote; took judicial oath May 12, 1836; served until February 25, 1841; replaced by Peter V. Daniel, nominated by President Martin Van Buren.

FAMILY: married Frances Todd Johnson, 1804; seven children.

DEATH: February 25, 1841, Washington, D.C.

Philip Barbour was a country gentleman from one of Virginia's oldest families. Descended from a Scottish merchant who settled in the state in the seventeenth century, Philip's father, Thomas Barbour, was a member of the Virginia House of Burgesses and an Orange County planter. His mother was Mary Pendleton Thomas Barbour, the daughter of a well-to-do farmer. James Barbour, Philip's older brother, was a Virginia governor, a U.S. senator, and secretary of war under President John Quincy Adams.

Because of his family's financial difficulties, Philip received his early education in the local schools, rather than the private schools attended by his social peers. He excelled in languages and classical literature. At the age of seventeen, he read law for a short time and then moved to Kentucky to begin practice. He soon returned to his home state, however, and borrowed money to enroll in the College of William and Mary. He attended only one session and left to resume his law practice. After two years, he had earned enough money to marry Frances Johnson, the daughter of an Orange County landowner. James Barbour had married Frances's sister twelve years earlier.

Philip Barbour was elected to the Virginia House of Delegates in 1812. Two years later he won a seat in the U.S. Congress

and, in a philosophical split with his brother, allied with a group of older Republicans who espoused strict construction and limited federal power.

Barbour served as Speaker of the House from 1821 until he was defeated by Henry Clay in 1823. In 1824 he chose not to run for reelection to his House seat.

After declining an offer from Thomas Jefferson to teach law at the University of Virginia, Barbour became a state judge on the General Court for the Eastern District of Virginia, serving for almost two years. In 1827 he returned to Congress and ran again for Speaker, losing this time to fellow Virginian Andrew Stevenson.

By this time Barbour was politically aligned with the Democratic forces of Andrew Jackson. After being passed over for a Jackson cabinet position in 1829, he was chosen president of the Virginia Constitutional Convention to replace the ailing James Monroe. In votes taken by the convention, he sided with the landed interests of the conservative eastern slaveholders against the claims of the westerners who later were to form a separate state, West Virginia.

In 1830 Barbour accepted an appointment as judge of the Federal District Court for Eastern Virginia. During the national election of 1832, he was touted as a vice-presidential candidate over Jackson's choice, Martin Van Buren. But party regulars, fearing the election might be thrown into the Senate, persuaded Barbour to withdraw his candidacy and support Van Buren as the nominee.

Barbour became an associate justice at the age of fifty-three. In his short term on the bench—only five years—he generally followed the Taney Court's drift toward a narrowing of corporate immunity and greater consideration of social and economic concerns.

Barbour became ill in early February 1841. By the end of the month, however, his health seemed to have improved, and on February 24 he attended a conference with other justices until ten o'clock at night. The next morning he was found dead of a heart attack.

John Catron

(1837–1865)

BIRTH: ca. 1786, Pennsylvania or Virginia.

EDUCATION: self-educated.

OFFICIAL POSITIONS: judge, Tennessee Supreme Court of Errors and Appeals, 1824–1831; first chief justice of Tennessee, 1831–1834.

SUPREME COURT SERVICE: nominated associate justice by President Andrew Jackson March 3, 1837, to fill a newly created seat; confirmed by the Senate March 8, 1837, by a 28–15 vote; took judicial oath May 1, 1837; served until May 30, 1865; seat abolished by Congress.

FAMILY: married Matilda Childress.

DEATH: May 30, 1865, Nashville, Tennessee.

John Catron

leave Nashville after Tennessee seceded from the Union. He returned home as soon as it was possible to resume his judicial duties, but by this time he was in failing health and died shortly thereafter.

John McKinley

(1838–1852)

BIRTH: May 1, 1780, Culpeper County, Virginia.

EDUCATION: read law on his own; admitted to the bar in 1800.

OFFICIAL POSITIONS: Alabama state representative, sessions of 1820, 1831, and 1836; U.S. senator, 1826–1831 and 1837; U.S. representative, 1833–1835.

SUPREME COURT SERVICE: nominated associate justice by President Martin Van Buren September 18, 1837, for a newly created Supreme Court seat; confirmed by the Senate September 25, 1837, by a voice vote; took judicial oath January 9, 1838; served until July 19, 1852; replaced by John A. Campbell, nominated by President Franklin Pierce.

FAMILY: married Juliana Bryan; married Elizabeth Armistead.

DEATH: July 19, 1852, Louisville, Kentucky.

Little is known about John Catron's early years. Born around 1786, of German ancestry, he is believed to have lived first in Virginia and then Kentucky. His father's name was Peter Catron. The family was poor, and young Catron probably had little if any formal education. In 1812 Catron moved to the Cumberland Mountain region of Tennessee and served under Andrew Jackson in the War of 1812. He joined the bar in 1815 and practiced in the Cumberland Mountain area until 1818, when he settled in Nashville and became an active member of the Davidson County bar. By this time he had developed a specialty in land law.

Catron was a successful businessman as well as a lawyer. With his brother George and a third partner, he owned and operated the profitable Buffalo Iron Works from 1827 until 1833 when he sold his interest in the business. He later reinvested in the company but kept himself out of its management.

In 1824 the Tennessee legislature created a new seat on the Supreme Court of Errors and Appeals—the state's highest court—and Catron was elected to fill the post. In 1831 he became the court's first chief justice but resigned in 1834 when the court was abolished by judicial reorganization.

After leaving the bench, Catron turned his attention to private practice and politics. In 1836 he directed Martin Van Buren's presidential campaign in Tennessee. As a result of his party loyalty and diligence, Catron was picked by Jackson, the outgoing president, in 1837 to fill one of two newly created seats on the Supreme Court. (The other was filled by John McKinley.) The appointment came on Jackson's final day in office.

On the Court, Catron supported states' rights and in 1857 sided with the "prosouthern" majority in *Scott v. Sandford*. He refused to support the Confederacy, however, and was forced to

Born in Virginia, McKinley at an early age moved to Lincoln County on the Kentucky frontier where his mother's family was prominent. His father, Andrew McKinley, was a physician. His mother's name was Mary Logan McKinley. Little is known about McKinley's early education; he read law on his own and was admitted to the bar in 1800.

After practicing in Frankfort, the state capital, and in Louisville, the state's main commercial center, McKinley set out for Alabama, a newly thriving territory about to be admitted to the Union. He settled in Huntsville and soon became a part of the so-called Georgia machine, a group of locally prominent lawyers, planters, and businessmen, mostly from Georgia, who dominated northern Alabama socially and politically.

Once settled in Huntsville, McKinley entered politics. He was elected to the Alabama legislature for the session of 1820. Then, in 1822, he missed election by the state legislature to the U.S. Senate by only one vote. Four years later, the seat opened up again with the death of the incumbent, and this time McKinley took it, by a margin of three votes.

During his term in the Senate, he stood for strict construction of the Constitution and a liberal reform of federal land policies, defending small landholders against speculators. McKinley was defeated for reelection to the Senate by Alabama governor Gabriel Moore in 1831.

During the 1820s McKinley had switched from support of Henry Clay to Andrew Jackson. Thereafter, he remained an ardent Jacksonian. In 1832 he was elected to the U.S. House and supported Jackson's campaign against the Bank of the United States. McKinley further proved his loyalty to Jackson by supporting Martin Van Buren, Jackson's choice for the vice presidency in 1832 and for the presidency in 1836.

Elected once again to the U.S. Senate in 1837, McKinley was picked for the Supreme Court by President Van Buren before the new Congress met, so he never got to serve his second Senate term. Congress had enacted a bill increasing the Court from seven members to nine in the waning days of Jackson's term. After William Smith of Alabama had turned down Jackson's nomination to one of the new seats, it fell to the newly inaugurated President Van Buren to pick another man. His choice was McKinley.

In his fifteen years on the bench, McKinley wrote only nineteen majority opinions, four dissents, and two concurrences. He suffered poor health during his last seven years on the Court, no doubt aggravated by the rigors of attending to the vast southern circuit. To the last, he stood by his states' rights and proslavery views.

Peter Vivian Daniel

(1841–1860)

BIRTH: April 24, 1784, Stafford County, Virginia.

EDUCATION: privately tutored; attended Princeton University, 1802–1803.

OFFICIAL POSITIONS: member, Virginia House of Delegates, 1809–1812; Virginia Privy Council, 1812–1835; lieutenant governor of Virginia, 1818–1835; U.S. district judge, Eastern District of Virginia, 1836–1841.

SUPREME COURT SERVICE: nominated associate justice by President Van Buren February 26, 1841, to replace Justice Philip Barbour, who had died; confirmed by the Senate March 2, 1841, by a 22–5 vote; took judicial oath January 10, 1842; served until May 31, 1860; replaced by Samuel F. Miller, nominated by President Abraham Lincoln.

Peter Vivian Daniel

FAMILY: married Lucy Randolph, 1809; died 1847; married Elizabeth Harris, 1853; two children.

DEATH: May 31, 1860, Richmond, Virginia.

Peter Daniel, the son of Travers and Frances Moncure Daniel, was a member of an old Virginia family which went back to the early days of the colony. It was a landed family, with a sizable estate, "Crow's Nest," where Daniel was born and brought up. His early education was by private tutors. He spent one year at Princeton, but returned to Virginia and moved to Richmond to study law in the office of Edmund Randolph.

Randolph had been both attorney general and secretary of state in George Washington's administration, and Daniel's association with him gained him access to the inner circle of Virginia political power. Daniel's marriage to Randolph's daughter Lucy further cemented the connection.

In 1809 Daniel was elected to the Virginia House of Delegates, where he served until elected to the Virginia Privy Council, an executive advisory and review body, in 1812. In 1818 he was chosen lieutenant governor of Virginia while continuing to serve on the Privy Council. He remained in both posts for the next seventeen years.

A loyal Jacksonian Democrat, Daniel supported President Andrew Jackson in his attack on the Bank of the United States. At one point, Jackson offered him the post of attorney general, but Daniel turned it down because of its inadequate salary. Because of his support of Jackson, Daniel was denied reelection in 1835 to his positions as privy councilor and lieutenant governor. The next year, Jackson appointed him federal district judge for the Eastern District of Virginia.

Daniel's elevation to the Supreme Court came suddenly. Justice Philip Barbour died February 24, 1841, only a week before President Martin Van Buren was to turn over his office to the new Whig administration of William Henry Harrison. To ensure that the Court seat remained in Democratic hands, Van Buren nominated Daniel only two days after Barbour's death, and the Democratic-controlled Senate confirmed the appointment on March 2, two days before adjournment.

Daniel remained on the Court for nineteen years, a vestige of the Jeffersonian school's advocacy of states' rights and a weak central government. He died on the eve of the Civil War and was not replaced on the Court for two years. The delay occurred because the Republicans took power and restructured the circuit court system to reduce the number of southern circuits and increase those in the Midwest and West.

Samuel Nelson

(1845–1872)

BIRTH: November 11, 1792, Hebron, New York.

EDUCATION: graduated, Middlebury College, 1813.

OFFICIAL POSITIONS: postmaster, Cortland, New York, 1820–1823; presidential elector, 1820; judge, Sixth Circuit of New York, 1823–1831; associate justice, New York Supreme Court, 1831–1837; chief justice, New York Supreme Court, 1837–1845; member, *Alabama* Claims Commission, 1871.

SUPREME COURT SERVICE: nominated associate justice by President John Tyler February 4, 1845, to replace Justice Smith Thompson, who had died; confirmed by the Senate February 14, 1845, by a voice vote; took judicial oath February 27,

1845; retired November 28, 1872; replaced by Ward Hunt, nominated by President Ulysses S. Grant.

FAMILY: married Pamela Woods, 1819; died 1822; one son; married Catherine Ann Russell, ca. 1825; two daughters, one son.

DEATH: December 13, 1873, Cooperstown, New York.

Samuel Nelson's grandparents were Scotch-Irish immigrants to America in the 1760s. His parents were John Rogers Nelson and Jean McCarter Nelson. Samuel spent his boyhood on farms in upstate New York. He attended local district schools, where his interest in his studies at first led him to plan a career in the ministry.

After graduation from Middlebury College in 1813, Nelson decided to study law instead. He clerked in a law office in Salem, New York, was admitted to the bar in 1817, and settled in Cortland, a small but thriving county seat in central New York. After establishing a successful law practice there, Nelson became involved in politics, identifying with the Democratic-Republicans and later with the Jackson-Van Buren wing of the Democratic Party.

In 1820 Nelson served as a presidential elector, voting for President James Monroe, and was appointed postmaster of Cortland, a position he held for three years. Also during that period, in 1821, Nelson was a delegate to the state constitutional convention, where he advocated the abolition of property qualifications for voting.

Beginning in 1823, Nelson embarked on a career in the judiciary which was to last for nearly fifty years. His first judicial position was as a judge of the Sixth Circuit of New York (1823–1831). In 1831 he was elevated to the state supreme court and in 1837 became chief justice. From there he went to the U.S. Supreme Court in 1845.

Nelson's nomination for the Supreme Court in the waning days of the Tyler administration came as a complete surprise. Two previous Tyler nominees had been turned down by the Senate, and several other prominent persons had declined offers of appointment. But Nelson's reputation as a careful and uncontroversial jurist, combined with his Democratic background, were received favorably, and the Democratic-controlled Senate confirmed him with little contention.

Most of Nelson's twenty-seven years on the Court were unspectacular. He achieved some brief notoriety in the secession crisis of 1860–1861 when he joined with Justice John A. Campbell to try to conciliate the North and South and avoid the Civil War. Nelson was also considered for the Democratic presidential nomination in 1860, but nothing came of it.

In 1871 President Grant appointed Nelson a member of the commission to settle the *Alabama* claims dispute against Great Britain. His hard work on the commission broke Nelson's health, and he retired from the Court the next year.

Levi Woodbury

(1845–1851)

BIRTH: December 22, 1789, Francestown, New Hampshire.

EDUCATION: Dartmouth College, graduated with honors, 1809; Tapping Reeve Law School, ca. 1810.

OFFICIAL POSITIONS: clerk, New Hampshire Senate, 1816; associate justice, New Hampshire Superior Court, 1817–1823; governor, New Hampshire, 1823–1824; Speaker, New Hampshire House, 1825; U.S. senator, 1825–1831, 1841–1845; secretary of the Navy, 1831–1834; secretary of the Treasury, 1834–1841.

SUPREME COURT SERVICE: nominated associate justice by President James K. Polk December 23, 1845, to replace Justice Joseph Story, who had died; confirmed by the Senate January 3, 1846, by voice vote; took judicial oath September 23, 1845; served until September 4, 1851; replaced by Benjamin R. Curtis, nominated by President Millard Fillmore.

FAMILY: married Elizabeth Williams Clapp, June 1819; four daughters, one son.

DEATH: September 4, 1851, Portsmouth, New Hampshire.

The second of ten children, Woodbury was born into an old New England family that traced its American roots back to 1630. Originally settled in Massachusetts, some of the family's descendants moved to New Hampshire in the late 1700s, where Woodbury was born in 1789. His parents were Peter and Mary Woodbury. His mother's maiden name was also Woodbury.

Woodbury graduated from Dartmouth College with honors in 1809 and then began the study of law. While he studied privately with practicing lawyers—as was then the custom—he also briefly attended a law school in Litchfield, Connecticut, making him one of the first Supreme Court justices to attend a law school.

After being admitted to the bar in 1812, Woodbury practiced in his native Francestown and in nearby Portsmouth, the main commercial center of the state, from 1812 to 1816. But his interests soon turned to politics, and he held some kind of political office almost constantly from 1816 until his appointment to the Supreme Court in 1845.

Woodbury started his climb up the political ladder in 1816 when he was appointed clerk of the state Senate. After serving a year, he was put on the New Hampshire Superior Court, where he remained until 1823, when he became a successful insurgent candidate for the governorship, beating the entrenched Democratic-Republican machine of Isaac Hill.

Woodbury was defeated for reelection in 1824, but came back the next year to win a seat in the state House and was elected Speaker. Shortly thereafter, the legislature elected him to the U.S. Senate, where he served from 1825 to 1831.

Woodbury was appointed secretary of the Navy in President Andrew Jackson's cabinet reorganization of 1831. He made little mark in that office, but in 1834 he was suddenly elevated to the crucial post of secretary of the Treasury in the midst of Jackson's war on the Bank of the United States. Jackson had gone through three Treasury secretaries in just over a year. Woodbury loyally cooperated with Jackson's policies, although with some reservations, and remained as head of the Treasury through the administration of Martin Van Buren (1837–1841).

Upon leaving the cabinet, Woodbury was chosen to serve once again in the U.S. Senate, where he was sitting when Polk used a recess appointment to place him on the Supreme Court just days after Justice Story's death. Woodbury' official nomination and confirmation came several months later.

He served for less than six years on the Court, dying in 1851. He was a contender for the Democratic presidential nomination in 1848, but lost to Lewis Cass.

Robert Cooper Grier

(1846–1870)

BIRTH: March 5, 1794, Cumberland County, Pennsylvania.

EDUCATION: Dickinson College, graduated 1812.

OFFICIAL POSITIONS: president judge, District Court of Allegheny County, Pennsylvania, 1833–1846.

SUPREME COURT SERVICE: nominated associate justice by President James K. Polk August 3, 1846, to replace Justice Henry Baldwin, who had died; confirmed by the Senate August 4, 1846, by a voice vote; took judicial oath August 10, 1846; retired January 31, 1870; replaced by William Strong, nominated by President Ulysses S. Grant.

FAMILY: married Isabella Rose, 1829.

DEATH: September 25, 1870, Philadelphia, Pennsylvania.

Robert Cooper Grier

The eldest of eleven children, Grier was born into a family of Presbyterian ministers. Both his father, Isaac Grier, and his maternal grandfather followed that vocation. His mother was Elizabeth Cooper Grier.

Grier was taught by his father until the age of seventeen, when he entered Dickinson College as a junior and finished in one year. He taught at Dickinson before becoming a teacher in the Northumberland Academy, his father's school, where he succeeded the elder Grier as principal in 1815.

But Grier's interests turned to the law, which he studied privately, passing the bar in 1817. He set up practice first in Bloomsburg, but soon moved to the county seat of Danville, where he became a prominent local attorney.

A solid Jacksonian Democrat, Grier came to the attention of the Democratic politicians in Harrisburg. As a result, he got a patronage appointment as president judge of the District Court of Allegheny County in 1833, a job he held for the next thirteen years, establishing a reputation as a thorough and knowledgeable judge.

In 1844 Supreme Court justice Henry Baldwin of Pennsylvania died, and a long effort began to fill his seat. It took more than two years for the spot to be filled finally by Grier. President Tyler had made two nominations; the first was withdrawn and the second got no action from the Democratic Senate. Tyler left office in March 1845, and the task of filling the vacancy fell to President Polk.

Polk also had difficulty finding a justice, first offering the position to future president James Buchanan. When Buchanan turned it down, Polk nominated George Woodward, but the Senate refused to confirm him. Finally, Polk selected Grier, who was confirmed.

Grier served on the Court for nearly a quarter of a century. He wrote the majority opinion in the *Prize Cases* (1863), upholding the legality of President Lincoln's blockade of southern ports. This action had taken place three months before Congress authorized the war. Grier stated that a formal declaration of war was unnecessary because a civil war is never "solemnly declared."

Toward the end of his service, his mental and physical powers waned to the point that he was barely functioning. Finally, a committee of his colleagues called on him to urge his retirement. He took their advice and retired in January 1870. He died seven months later.

Benjamin Robbins Curtis
(1851–1857)

BIRTH: November 4, 1809, Watertown, Massachusetts.

EDUCATION: Harvard University, graduated 1829 with highest honors; Harvard Law School, graduated 1832.

OFFICIAL POSITIONS: Massachusetts state representative, 1849–1851.

SUPREME COURT SERVICE: nominated associate justice by President Millard Fillmore December 11, 1851, to replace Justice Levi Woodbury, who had died; confirmed by the Senate December 20, 1851, by a voice vote; took judicial oath October 10, 1851; resigned September 30, 1857; replaced by Nathan Clifford, nominated by President James Buchanan.

FAMILY: married Eliza Maria Woodward, 1833; died 1844;

five children; married Anna Wroe Curtis, 1846; died 1860; three children; married Maria Malleville Allen, 1861; four children.

DEATH: September 15, 1874, Newport, Rhode Island.

Curtis was the son of a Massachusetts ship captain whose ancestors settled New England in the 1630s. His father, Benjamin Curtis III, died while on a voyage abroad when Curtis was a child. He was raised by his mother, Lois Robbins Curtis, with help from his half-uncle, George Ticknor, a Harvard professor and author.

When Curtis was ready to enter Harvard University in 1825, his mother moved to Cambridge and ran a boarding school for students there to support herself and her family. Curtis graduated from Harvard in 1829 and immediately entered Harvard Law School, from which he graduated in 1832 after taking a year off in 1831 to set up a law practice in Northfield, Massachusetts, a small town in the Connecticut River Valley.

In 1834 Curtis moved to Boston to join the law practice of his distant cousin, Charles Pelham Curtis. After the death of his first wife, Curtis married his law partner's daughter in 1846.

Curtis was elected to the Massachusetts House in 1849 and chaired a commission that designed a sweeping reform of judicial proceedings in the state. A conservative Whig, he was a strong supporter of Sen. Daniel Webster. He rallied behind Webster during the crisis of 1850 when the senator was working for compromise of the territorial and slave issues and was being denounced for his efforts by Massachusetts abolitionists.

In 1851, when President Fillmore was looking for a replacement for the late Justice Levi Woodbury, Webster, then serving as Fillmore's secretary of state, recommended Curtis. But Curtis found life in the capital uncomfortable and the salary, despite a raise of one-third in 1855, inadequate to support his large family. Adding to his difficulties was his perceived obligation to uphold the constitutionality of the Fugitive Slave Act of 1850, while he was on circuit duty in New England. The press attacked Curtis, labeling him "the slave-catcher judge," even though he was a strong abolitionist and abhorred slavery. Curtis's relations with his colleagues on the Court, especially with Chief Justice Taney, became so acrimonious during Court arguments over *Scott v. Sandford* and other pre–Civil War controversies that he decided to resign. Curtis and Justice John McLean were the only dissenters in *Scott*. Curtis pointed out that blacks were citizens and had voting rights in 1787. He left the Court on September 30, 1857.

Curtis devoted the remainder of his life to a lucrative law practice in Boston. He appeared before the Supreme Court on numerous occasions to argue for his clients. Politically, he remained a conservative, objecting to some of the emergency measures taken by President Abraham Lincoln, including the Emancipation Proclamation and the suspension of habeas corpus. He also opposed the radical Reconstruction policies of congressional Republicans during Andrew Johnson's administration. In 1868 he served as the leading counsel for President Johnson during the impeachment proceedings. Johnson offered Curtis the position of attorney general, but he declined.

John Archibald Campbell
(1853–1861)

BIRTH: June 24, 1811, Washington, Georgia.

EDUCATION: Franklin College (now the University of Georgia), graduated with first honors, 1825; attended U.S. Military Academy at West Point, 1825–1828.

OFFICIAL POSITIONS: Alabama state representative, sessions of 1837 and 1843; assistant secretary of war, Confederate States of America, 1862–1865.

SUPREME COURT SERVICE: nominated associate justice by President Franklin Pierce March 21, 1853, to replace Justice John McKinley, who had died; confirmed by the Senate March 25, 1853, by a voice vote; took judicial oath April 11, 1853; resigned April 30, 1861; replaced by David Davis, nominated by President Abraham Lincoln.

FAMILY: married Anna Esther Goldthwaite in the early 1830s; four daughters, one son.

DEATH: March 12, 1889, Baltimore, Maryland.

Born into a family of Scotch and Scotch-Irish descent, Campbell was the son of Duncan and Mary Williamson Campbell. A child prodigy, he entered college at the age of eleven, graduating at fourteen. He then attended West Point for three years before withdrawing to return home to support the family after the death of his father. A year later, at the age of eighteen, he was admitted to the bar by special act of the Georgia legislature.

In 1830 Campbell moved to Alabama to begin his legal career, settling first in Montgomery, where he met and married Anna Esther Goldthwaite, a New Hampshire native who had moved to the South with her brothers. The couple moved to Mobile in 1837, and Campbell was elected to the first of two terms in the state legislature.

Campbell quickly became one of the leading lawyers in Alabama, and before long his reputation spread nationally. Twice he declined appointment to the Alabama Supreme Court. He was a delegate to the Nashville convention of 1850, convened to protect southern rights in the face of what they saw as northern encroachment, especially on the slavery question. Campbell was a moderating influence at the convention, writing many of the resolutions that finally were adopted.

Campbell was selected for the Supreme Court after a Democratic Senate had refused to act on three choices nominated by Whig president Millard Fillmore. When Fillmore was replaced by Democrat Franklin Pierce in March 1853, Democrats were able to appoint one of their own to the Court. Campbell's selection was made in an unprecedented fashion. The Supreme Court justices wanted the new president to nominate Campbell and sent a delegation to Pierce to make their wish known. Pierce complied.

Campbell's service on the bench was cut short by the Civil War. He opposed secession and believed that slavery would slowly disappear if the South were left alone. He freed all his slaves upon his Supreme Court appointment and thereafter hired only free blacks as servants. During the secession crisis, he attempted to serve as a mediator between the seceding states and the new Lincoln administration.

But when the die was cast and hostilities broke out, he resigned his Court position and returned to the South, settling in New Orleans. In 1862 he was invited to join the Confederate government and accepted the position of assistant secretary of war in charge of administering the conscription law. He remained in that position until the fall of the Confederacy in 1865.

After a few months of detention by the Union, Campbell was freed and returned to New Orleans, where he built up a prosperous and prestigious law practice. He argued before the Supreme Court on numerous occasions in the quarter-century before his death.

Nathan Clifford

(1858–1881)

BIRTH: August 18, 1803, Rumney, New Hampshire.

EDUCATION: Haverhill Academy; studied law in office of Josiah Quincy in Rumney; admitted to New Hampshire bar, 1827.

OFFICIAL POSITIONS: Maine state representative, 1830–1834; attorney general of Maine, 1834–1838; U.S. representative, 1839–1843; U.S. attorney general, 1846–1848; minister to Mexico, 1848–1849.

SUPREME COURT SERVICE: nominated associate justice by President James Buchanan December 9, 1857, to replace Benjamin R. Curtis, who had resigned; confirmed by the Senate January 12, 1858, by a 26–23 vote; took judicial oath January 21,

Nathan Clifford

1858; served until July 25, 1881; replaced by Horace Gray, nominated by President Chester A. Arthur.

FAMILY: married Hannah Ayer, ca. 1828; six children.

DEATH: July 25, 1881, Cornish, Maine.

Nathan Clifford was the son of Lydia Simpson Clifford and Nathaniel Clifford, a New Hampshire farmer whose American roots went back three generations. His grandfather was an officer in the Revolutionary War.

Clifford attended the local academies for his early education, then studied law in the office of Josiah Quincy, a prominent attorney in Rumney, New Hampshire. Clifford was admitted to the bar in 1827 and moved to Newfield, Maine, to begin practice. There he met and married a local woman, Hannah Ayer.

He was a staunch Jacksonian Democrat, maintaining his early political beliefs throughout his long life and political career.

Clifford entered public life soon after beginning his law practice in Maine. In 1830, at the age of twenty-seven, he was elected to the lower house of the Maine legislature. He was reelected for three additional one-year terms and served the last two years as Speaker. He was then elected attorney general of the state by the legislature, serving four years. After that, he won two terms in the U.S. House, but was defeated for reelection to a third term.

Clifford's defeat in 1843 marked the end of the first phase of his political career. He then returned to law practice in Maine for three years. He had earned a reputation as a hard worker and received attention for the thoroughness of his preparation.

In 1846 President Polk chose Clifford as attorney general. Polk needed New England representation in his cabinet, and

Clifford supported his ideas. During his service in the Polk cabinet, Clifford played a major role in mediating the many disputes between Polk and his secretary of state, James Buchanan. Polk was vigorously pursuing his war with Mexico, while Buchanan advocated a more cautious policy. Buchanan liked and trusted Clifford.

In 1848 Polk entrusted Clifford with a diplomatic mission. He was sent to Mexico with the purpose of getting Mexico to ratify the peace treaty ending the war. Clifford did so and stayed on to become U.S. minister to the Mexican government from 1848 to 1849. With a new Whig administration in Washington in 1849, Clifford returned to Maine to resume law practice, this time in the more populous and prosperous city of Portland.

When a Supreme Court vacancy occurred in late 1857, President Buchanan chose Clifford to fill it. There was strong criticism against the nomination; Clifford was looked upon in the North as a "doughface"—a northern man with southern principles. Clifford had supported Buchanan policies that many northerners thought favored the South. But Clifford was confirmed in a close vote.

In 1877 Clifford—still on the Court—served as chairman of the electoral commission set up to decide the disputed presidential election of 1876. He voted with the Democrats for Tilden, but the Republican, Rutherford B. Hayes, won by one vote. Clifford always considered Hayes an illegitimate president and refused to enter the White House during his presidency.

In 1880 Clifford suffered a stroke, which prevented him from taking any further active role in Court proceedings. He refused to resign, however, hoping to live until a Democratic president could name his successor. But he died while the Republicans were still in power.

Noah Haynes Swayne

(1862–1881)

BIRTH: December 7, 1804, Frederick County, Virginia.

EDUCATION: studied law privately; admitted to the bar in Warrenton, Virginia, in 1823.

OFFICIAL POSITIONS: Coshocton County (Ohio) prosecuting attorney, 1826–1829; Ohio state representative, 1830 and 1836; U.S. attorney for Ohio, 1830–1841; Columbus city councilman, 1834.

SUPREME COURT SERVICE: nominated associate justice by President Abraham Lincoln January 21, 1862, to replace John McLean, who had died; confirmed by the Senate January 24, 1862, by a 38–1 vote; took judicial oath January 27, 1862; retired January 24, 1881; replaced by Stanley Matthews, nominated by President Rutherford B. Hayes and renominated by President James A. Garfield.

FAMILY: married Sarah Ann Wager, 1832; four sons, one daughter.

DEATH: June 8, 1884, New York City.

Although born in the slave-holding state of Virginia, Noah Swayne was the son of antislavery Quaker parents, Joshua and

Noah Haynes Swayne

Rebecca Smith Swayne, who came from Pennsylvania. Noah studied medicine as a youth, but after the death of his teacher he switched to law.

Following his admission to the bar, Swayne migrated to the free state of Ohio because of his opposition to slavery. During his long legal career in that state, he was involved in cases defending runaway slaves. When he married Sarah Ann Wager, a Virginian who owned slaves, she agreed to free them.

Shortly after settling in Ohio, Swayne became involved in politics as a Jacksonian Democrat. He was elected prosecuting attorney of Coshocton County in 1826 and to the Ohio legislature in 1829. In 1830 President Andrew Jackson appointed him U.S. attorney for Ohio, and he served throughout the rest of Jackson's administration as well as that of Martin Van Buren. During his service as U.S. attorney, he also developed a successful private law practice and served on the Columbus City Council and once again in the state legislature.

Swayne's political activity ebbed in the 1840s, but reemerged in the 1850s when the slavery issue began tearing the nation apart. Swayne's antislavery convictions drove him from the Democratic Party, and he supported the presidential candidate of the new Republican Party, John Charles Fremont, in 1856. Swayne also served in the 1850s as a member of a state committee overseeing Ohio's finances, which had fallen into disorder.

Although Swayne had no judicial experience and was not well known outside Ohio, Lincoln nevertheless made him his first appointment to the Supreme Court. The vacancy was caused by the death of Justice John McLean, a close friend of Swayne's, and McLean had let it be known that he wanted

Swayne to succeed him on the Court. In addition, Swayne was close to the governor of Ohio, William Dennison, who traveled to Washington to lobby for him. The Ohio congressional delegation also recommended him.

Swayne fulfilled Republican hopes that he would uphold the extraordinary Civil War measures of the national government, and he continued to take a generally nationalist stance in his decisions throughout his years on the Court. He also lobbied for passage of the Fifteenth Amendment, guaranteeing voting rights for blacks. His own state of Ohio was crucial to the ratification of the amendment, and Swayne used all his influence in his adopted state on behalf of approval.

Twice Swayne maneuvered for the chief justiceship—in 1864, when Roger B. Taney died, and again in 1873, when Salmon P. Chase died. But Swayne was disappointed both times. With his mental acuity noticeably declining by 1881, Swayne was persuaded by President Hayes to retire with the promise that his friend and fellow-Ohioan Stanley Matthews would be chosen as his successor.

Samuel Freeman Miller

(1862–1890)

BIRTH: April 5, 1816, Richmond, Kentucky.

EDUCATION: Transylvania University, M.D., 1838; studied law privately; admitted to the bar in 1847.

OFFICIAL POSITIONS: justice of the peace and member of the Knox County, Kentucky, court, an administrative body, in the 1840s.

SUPREME COURT SERVICE: nominated associate justice

by President Abraham Lincoln July 16, 1862, to replace Justice Peter V. Daniel, who had died; confirmed July 16, 1862, by a voice vote; took judicial oath July 21, 1862; served until October 13, 1890; replaced by Henry B. Brown, nominated by President Benjamin Harrison.

FAMILY: married Lucy Ballinger, November 8, 1842; died 1854; three children; married Elizabeth Winter Reeves, widow of his law partner, 1857; two children.

DEATH: October 13, 1890, Washington, D.C.

Samuel Miller was the eldest son of Frederick Miller, a Pennsylvania-German, and Patsy Freeman Miller, a North Carolinian, both of whom migrated to Kentucky at the turn of the nineteenth century. Young Miller began his career as a medical doctor. After graduating from the medical department of Transylvania University in 1838, he set up practice in Barboursville in Kentucky's small, mountainous Knox County.

Miller soon developed an interest in legal and political matters. He joined a debating society and studied law on the side, passing his bar exam in 1847. He favored gradual emancipation of slaves, and when the Kentucky constitutional convention of 1849 strengthened the position of slavery in the state, Miller freed his own slaves and moved west to Iowa, a free state.

In Iowa Miller abandoned medicine and set up a prosperous law practice in Keokuk. With political tensions rising in the 1850s, he joined the public arena and helped organize the Republican Party in Iowa, serving as chairman of the Keokuk County GOP organization.

By 1860 Miller was one of the leading Republican figures in the state and a strong backer of Abraham Lincoln for the party's presidential nomination. In 1861 Miller made a try for the Republican gubernatorial nomination but was defeated by incumbent governor Samuel J. Kirkwood.

Miller's appointment to the Supreme Court came despite his lack of judicial experience. With the creation of a new circuit west of the Mississippi, western members of Congress and politicians, including a unanimous Iowa delegation, pressed for Miller's appointment. Lincoln's agreement made Miller the first Supreme Court justice from west of the Mississippi. His best-known opinion came in the landmark *Slaughterhouse Cases* (1873), in which the Court decided that the right to do business did not derive from U.S. citizenship and therefore was not protected by the Fourteenth Amendment.

Miller was one of the five justices to serve on the electoral commission in 1877 to resolve the disputed presidential election of 1876 between Democrat Samuel J. Tilden and Republican Rutherford B. Hayes. Miller voted with his party to give the presidency to Hayes.

Twice Miller was considered for chief justice—in 1873 and 1888—but was passed over both times. His name was also mentioned for the presidency in 1880 and 1884, but no significant movement developed. Miller died October 13, 1890, just before the start of a new term.

David Davis

(1862–1877)

BIRTH: March 9, 1815, Cecil County, Maryland.

EDUCATION: graduated Kenyon College, 1832; Yale Law School, 1835.

OFFICIAL POSITIONS: Illinois state representative, 1845–1847; member, Illinois constitutional convention, 1847; Illinois state circuit judge, 1848–1862; U.S. senator, 1877–1883.

SUPREME COURT SERVICE: nominated associate justice by President Abraham Lincoln December 1, 1862, to replace John A. Campbell, who had resigned; confirmed by the Senate December 8, 1862, by a voice vote; took judicial oath December 10, 1862; resigned March 4, 1877; replaced by John Marshall Harlan, nominated by President Rutherford B. Hayes.

FAMILY: married Sarah Walker, October 30, 1838; died 1879; one son (two children died in infancy); married Adeline Burr, March 14, 1883; two daughters.

DEATH: June 26, 1886, Bloomington, Illinois.

David Davis was born in Maryland of Welsh ancestry and named for his father, a doctor, who had died before Davis was born. When his mother, Ann Mercer Davis, remarried, David went to live with an uncle in Annapolis. After studying law, he sought his fortune in the West.

Settling first in Pekin, Illinois, he moved within a year to Bloomington, which became his lifelong home. He was active in Whig politics, running a losing race for the state Senate in 1840 but winning a state House seat in 1844. During this period he became acquainted with Abraham Lincoln; this relationship deepened over the years and had a major effect on Davis's life.

After one term in the state legislature, Davis was chosen a member of the Illinois constitutional convention of 1847. At the convention, he fought for a popularly elected judiciary, replacing the system of election by the legislature. Davis's position prevailed, and in 1848 he was elected a judge of the Illinois Eighth Circuit, a position to which he was twice reelected and which he held until his appointment to the Supreme Court.

Among the prominent lawyers who practiced before Judge Davis in Illinois were Abraham Lincoln and Stephen Douglas. Davis became close to Lincoln in the 1850s and joined the new Republican Party with him when their Whig Party fell apart. Davis became Lincoln's campaign manager in 1860 and was perhaps the most important person in securing Lincoln the Republican presidential nomination that year.

Lincoln appointed Davis to the Supreme Court vacancy created by the resignation of Justice John A. Campbell, an Alabaman who withdrew to join the Confederate effort. Davis's opinion in *Ex parte Milligan* (1866) established that constitutional rights do not disappear during wartime and that military courts have no jurisdiction where civilian courts are operating.

Davis's interest in politics never faded. After Lincoln's death, he became disenchanted with the Republican Party. In 1872 he was nominated for president by the Labor Reform Party, a splinter group. Davis hoped to use this nomination to further his candidacy for the Liberal Republicans, a group opposing Grant. But when the Liberals chose Horace Greeley instead, Davis declined the Labor Reform nomination.

Tired of his career on the Supreme Court, Davis accepted his election in 1877 by the Illinois legislature to the U.S. Senate and resigned from the Court. Davis had been expected to be a member of the electoral commission set up to decide the disputed presidential election of 1876. Davis's political independence would have made him the swing vote on an otherwise evenly divided commission. His replacement was a Republican, Justice Joseph P. Bradley, who voted with the Republicans and gave the election to Republican Rutherford B. Hayes. At the time, it was thought that Davis might have voted with the Democrats on at least some of the disputed electoral votes, but he indicated later that he did not disagree with the commission's decisions.

Davis served one term in the Senate (1877–1883), voting independently, and then retired. From 1881 to 1883, he was president pro tem of the Senate, which under the succession law then in effect made him next in line for the presidency if anything had happened to President Chester A. Arthur.

Stephen Johnson Field

(1863–1897)

BIRTH: November 4, 1816, Haddam, Connecticut.

EDUCATION: graduated Williams College, 1837, class valedictorian; studied law in private firms; admitted to the bar in 1841.

OFFICIAL POSITIONS: Alcalde of Marysville, 1850; California state representative, 1850–1851; justice, California Supreme Court, 1857–1863.

Stephen Johnson Field

SUPREME COURT SERVICE: nominated associate justice by President Abraham Lincoln March 6, 1863, for a newly created seat; confirmed by the Senate March 10, 1863, by a voice vote; took judicial oath May 20, 1863; retired December 1, 1897; replaced by Joseph McKenna, nominated by President William McKinley.

FAMILY: married Sue Virginia Swearingen, June 2, 1859.

DEATH: April 9, 1899, in Washington, D.C.

The son of Submit Dickinson Field and David Dudley Field, a New England Congregational clergyman, Stephen Johnson Field was born into a family that produced several prominent people. His brothers included David Dudley Field, a noted New York lawyer and politician; Cyrus West Field, a promoter of the first Atlantic cable; and Henry Martyn Field, a leading clergyman and author. Field's nephew, David J. Brewer, was a Supreme Court justice (1889–1910) and served with Field for the last eight years of his uncle's term.

Field studied law with his brother Dudley and with John Van Buren, son of President Martin Van Buren. He was admitted to the New York bar in 1841 and for the next seven years practiced in partnership with his brother.

But in 1849, after a trip to Europe, he decided to strike out on his own and moved to California. Settling in Marysville, in the heart of the gold fields, Field lived the rough-and-tumble life of a frontier entrepreneur.

Field served in 1850 as Marysville's alcalde, the chief local administrative office under the old Spanish system. He quarreled with a local judge and was twice disbarred and once sent to jail for contempt of court.

Field was elected to the California Assembly, the lower house of the legislature, in 1850 and during his year of service was the chief drafter of the civil and criminal codes for the new state. After being defeated in a bid for the state Senate in 1851, he resumed his legal career for a time and then was elected to the California Supreme Court as a Democrat in 1857.

In 1863 Congress authorized an additional seat on the U.S. Supreme Court, partly to gain a new justice who would support the Civil War measures of the federal government, and partly because there was a need for a new circuit for the West Coast. Many cases concerning land and mineral issues were coming to the Court from California, and westerners wanted someone familiar with those issues.

Lincoln crossed party lines to appoint Field to the new seat. The California and Oregon congressional delegations unanimously recommended him, even though he was a Democrat. Field had staunchly supported the Union cause and was an acknowledged expert in land and mining issues.

It is rare for a Supreme Court justice to be involved in a case before the Court, but it happened to Field. David Neagle, a federal marshall assigned to protect Field shot and killed a would-be assassin—an old enemy of Field's—during a circuit court trip to California. The state charged Neagle with murder, but the Court ruled that California could not try him for actions carried out under federal law. Field did not participate in the case.

During his term on the Court, Field served, in 1877, on the electoral commission that decided the contested presidential election in favor of Republican Rutherford B. Hayes. Field voted on the losing Democratic side on all questions.

Field's name was mentioned for the Democratic presidential nomination in 1880 and 1884, but his candidacy did not advance very far. He aspired to be chief justice in 1888, when Morrison Waite died, but President Cleveland picked Melville W. Fuller instead.

In the 1890s Field's mental powers were visibly declining, and he was taking less and less part in Court proceedings. Finally, the other justices strongly hinted that he retire. Ironically, Field had been part of an effort to get an aging justice, Robert C. Grier, to retire in 1877. Field finally quit the Court in late 1897, but only after he had surpassed Chief Justice John Marshall's record of thirty-four years and five months of service.

Salmon Portland Chase

(1864–1873)

BIRTH: January 13, 1808, Cornish, New Hampshire.

EDUCATION: Dartmouth College, 1826.

OFFICIAL POSITIONS: U.S. senator, 1849–1855, 1861; governor of Ohio, 1856–1860; secretary of the Treasury, 1861–1864.

SUPREME COURT SERVICE: nominated chief justice by President Abraham Lincoln December 6, 1864, to replace Chief Justice Roger B. Taney, who had died; confirmed by the Senate December 6, 1864, by a voice vote; took judicial oath December

Salmon Portland Chase

15, 1864; served until May 7, 1873; replaced by Morrison R. Waite, appointed by President Ulysses S. Grant.

FAMILY: married Katherine Jane Garniss, March 4, 1834; died December 1, 1835; married Eliza Ann Smith, September 26, 1839; died September 29, 1845; one daughter; married Sara Belle Dunlop Ludlow, November 6, 1846; died January 13, 1852; one daughter.

DEATH: May 7, 1873, New York City.

Chase, the son of Ithamar and Janette Ralston Chase, was born in New Hampshire of a prominent family that traced its American roots back to 1640. An uncle, Dudley Chase, served as a U.S. senator for Vermont (1813–1817 and 1825–1831), and another uncle, Philander Chase, was the Protestant Episcopal Bishop of Ohio (1818–1831). Chase's father was a tavern-keeper who held various local political offices. Chase grew up and made his career in Ohio.

Upon his father's death in 1817, Chase went to live with his Uncle Philander in Ohio and was brought up under his stern discipline. Throughout his life, Chase retained a strong and righteous religious streak, inculcated in his early years by his uncle.

After graduation from Dartmouth, Chase went to Washington, D.C., opened a private school, and studied law under Attorney General William Wirt. He was admitted to the bar in 1829, then moved west to Cincinnati to begin his legal career.

Chase became involved early in the antislavery movement and took a prominent role in defending runaway slaves, arguing one case up to the Supreme Court. For his activities, he became known as the "attorney general for runaway Negroes."

Chase's opposition to slavery soon moved him into politics, and he became a leader of the antislavery Liberty Party in the 1840s. In 1848 he joined the Free Soilers and helped write part of the party's platform. The following year, when the Free Soilers held the balance of power in the Ohio legislature, they helped the Democrats organize the legislature in return for the Democrats' support in electing Chase to the U.S. Senate.

In the Senate Chase joined antislavery stalwarts such as William Seward and Benjamin Wade. When the old party system broke up, he helped to form the new Republican Party.

In 1855 Chase was elected governor of Ohio by a coalition headed by Republicans, and was reelected in 1857. He was mentioned for the Republican presidential nomination in both 1856 and 1860, but did not receive many votes. In 1861 he was elected once again to the U.S. Senate, but resigned after only two days to become secretary of the Treasury, a position he held during most of Lincoln's administration. Chase was responsible for financing the Civil War, first with large borrowings and then with the issue of paper money. He also devised a new federal banking system that became the cornerstone of American finance for the next half-century. He received high marks from political enemies as well as friends for his management of the Treasury during a time of national crisis.

But Chase was not happy with Lincoln's leadership and allowed himself to become the focus of an anti-Lincoln group within the Republican Party, which wanted to deny the president renomination in 1864. Twice that year, efforts were made to substitute Chase for Lincoln, but they were unsuccessful. Chase also had a number running disagreements with Lincoln over other matters and submitted his resignation several times. Lincoln finally accepted it in the summer of 1864.

When Chief Justice Taney died in October, Chase was Lincoln's first choice for the post. Despite their differences, Lincoln had high regard for Chase's abilities, and the Republicans wanted someone on the Court they believed would sustain the extraordinary measures taken by the federal government during the war and others contemplated for the postwar period.

Chase was probably the most politically involved chief justice in American history, both because of his own ambitions and because of the tumultuous state of the country. In the spring of 1865 he made a tour of the South to study conditions there and report to President Andrew Johnson. Later, in 1868, Chase presided at the impeachment trial of Johnson and fought with the radical Republicans for his rights as presiding officer of the trial.

In both 1868 and 1872, Chase made no secret of his still-burning presidential ambitions and allowed friends to maneuver politically for him. But, as in the past, he was disappointed in his hopes for the nation's highest elected office.

William Strong

(1870–1880)

BIRTH: May 6, 1808, Somers, Connecticut.

EDUCATION: Yale College, A.B., 1828; M.A., 1831.

OFFICIAL POSITIONS: U.S. representative, 1847–1851; Pennsylvania Supreme Court justice, 1857–1868.

SUPREME COURT SERVICE: nominated associate justice by President Ulysses S. Grant February 7, 1870, to replace Robert C. Grier, who had retired; confirmed by the Senate February 18, 1870, by a voice vote; took judicial oath March 14, 1870; retired December 14, 1880; replaced by William B. Woods, nominated by President Rutherford B. Hayes.

FAMILY: married Priscilla Lee Mallery, November 28, 1836; died 1844; two daughters, one son; married Rachel Davis Bull, a widow, November 22, 1849; two daughters, two sons.

DEATH: August 19, 1895, Lake Minnewaska, New York.

Strong was born into an old New England family that traced its ancestry in America back to 1630. He was the eldest of eleven children of Harriet Deming Strong and William Lighthouse Strong, a Presbyterian clergyman. After graduating from Yale in 1831, Strong taught school in New Jersey to pay his student debts. He studied with a local attorney before returning to Yale for a master's degree in law. He was admitted to the Connecticut and Pennsylvania bars in 1832. He began his practice in Reading, a thriving industrial town in the heart of the rich Pennsylvania-Dutch country. Since many of his clients did not speak English, Strong mastered the local German dialect and soon developed a thriving practice.

After establishing himself as a member of Reading's elite through his successful law career, Strong was elected to two terms in the U.S. House as an antislavery Democrat (1847–1851). In 1857 he was elected to a fifteen-year term on the Pennsylvania Supreme Court. With the coming of the Civil War, Strong joined the Republican Party.

In 1864, when Chief Justice Roger B. Taney died, Lincoln considered Strong as a potential replacement, but chose Salmon P. Chase instead. Strong resigned from the Pennsylvania court in 1868 to devote himself to making money, but in 1869 his name came up again for a Court vacancy, this time as an associate justice. Justice Grier had announced his retirement because of age and infirmity, and President Grant's advisers recommended Strong for the spot. But there was great sentiment in the country and the Congress for Edwin M. Stanton, the former secretary of war. Members of Congress circulated a petition for Stanton which was signed by a large majority of both houses; as a result Grant sent up Stanton's name instead of Strong's. Stanton was confirmed December 20, 1869, but died suddenly four days later, never having had a chance to participate in Court proceedings.

With Stanton's death, the way was clear for Strong's appointment. His selection was clouded by charges that Grant was trying to "pack" the Court to reverse a decision unfavorable to the Civil War legal tender acts.

During his Court service, Strong was known for his keen intellect and the forceful and articulate manner in which he presented his arguments. He was appointed a member of the electoral commission that in 1877 decided the disputed presidential election of 1876 in favor of Republican Rutherford B. Hayes. Strong supported Hayes on all the votes of the commission.

Strong retired from the Court at age seventy-two, while he was still in good health. He devoted himself to religious work, something he had begun while on the bench. From 1883 to 1895, he was president of the American Sunday School Union; he also served as vice president of the American Bible Society from 1871 to 1895, and was president of the American Tract Society from 1873 to 1895.

Joseph P. Bradley

(1870–1892)

BIRTH: March 14, 1813, Berne, New York.

EDUCATION: Rutgers University, graduated 1836.

OFFICIAL POSITIONS: none.

SUPREME COURT SERVICE: nominated associate justice by President Ulysses S. Grant February 7, 1870, succeeding James Wayne, who died in 1867 and whose seat remained vacant by act of Congress until 1870; confirmed by the Senate March 21, 1870, by a 46–9 vote; took judicial oath March 23, 1870; served until January 22, 1892; replaced by George Shiras Jr., nominated by President Benjamin Harrison.

FAMILY: married Mary Hornblower in 1844; seven children.

DEATH: January 22, 1892, Washington, D.C.

Bradley's life and career exemplify the traditional American "Horatio Alger" success story. The eldest of the twelve children

Joseph P. Bradley

with the radical wing of the Republican Party and ran unsuccessfully as a Grant presidential elector in 1868.

Grant nominated Bradley for a seat on the Court in February 1870, the same day he chose William Strong for another Court vacancy. The choices raised a storm later because they made possible the reversal of a crucial Court decision, *Hepburn v. Griswold*, involving the validity of the Civil War legal tender acts.

The other major controversy of Bradley's Court career came in 1877 when he served on the electoral commission established to determine the outcome of the disputed presidential election of 1876. With the commission divided seven-to-seven along partisan lines, Supreme Court justice David Davis, an independent, was to have been the fifteenth and deciding member. But Davis withdrew from the commission because the Illinois legislature had chosen him to be a U.S. senator, and Bradley was substituted as the next least partisan justice. He voted with the Republicans on all the issues, awarding all twenty disputed electoral votes to Republican Rutherford B. Hayes, making him president by one vote. Although he was excoriated in the Democratic press, Bradley always contended that he voted on the basis of the legal and constitutional questions and not on a partisan basis.

The rest of Bradley's career on the Court was quieter. He was known for careful research and thoughtful analysis. He worked until almost the day he died, January 22, 1892.

Ward Hunt
(1873–1882)

BIRTH: June 14, 1810, Utica, New York.

EDUCATION: graduated with honors from Union College, 1828; attended Tapping Reeve law school.

OFFICIAL POSITIONS: member, New York Assembly, 1839; mayor of Utica, 1844; member, New York Court of Appeals, 1866–1869; New York State commissioner of appeals, 1869–1873.

SUPREME COURT SERVICE: nominated associate justice by President Ulysses S. Grant December 3, 1872, to replace Samuel Nelson, who had retired; confirmed by the Senate December 11, 1872, by a voice vote; took judicial oath January 9, 1873; retired January 27, 1882; replaced by Samuel Blatchford, nominated by President Chester A. Arthur.

FAMILY: married Mary Ann Savage, 1837; died 1845; three children; married Marie Taylor, 1853.

DEATH: March 24, 1886, Washington, D.C.

of Philo and Mercy Gardiner Bradley, Joseph Bradley was raised on a small farm in penurious circumstances. But he showed an early aptitude for learning and after going to a country school, began teaching at the age of sixteen. A local minister took an interest in him and sponsored his entrance to Rutgers University, where he was graduated in 1836.

Bradley then studied law in the office of Archer Gifford, collector of the port of Newark, New Jersey, and passed the bar in 1839. His assiduous legal work soon paid off in a successful law practice. Specializing in patent, commercial, and corporate law, he became counsel for various railroads, the most important being the powerful Camden and Amboy Railroad. In 1844 he married Mary Hornblower, daughter of the chief justice of the New Jersey Supreme Court.

Bradley had a lifelong interest in mathematics and geology. He devised a perpetual calendar designed to determine the day of the week any date fell on throughout history. And he researched and wrote a treatise on the origins of the steam engine. Always an avid reader, Bradley had a library numbering sixteen thousand volumes.

The middle initial "P" did not stand for a name; Bradley adopted its use some time during his early life, perhaps after his father's name, Philo.

Bradley was a Whig before the Civil War, and went to Washington, D.C., in the winter of 1860–1861 to lobby for a compromise settlement of issues between the North and South. But once the war broke out, he supported the Union cause and the Lincoln administration unreservedly. He ran a losing race for the U.S. House as a Unionist in 1862. After the war, he identified

Hunt was born and made his career in the upstate New York city of Utica. His father, Montgomery Hunt, was a banker there and descended from early New England settlers. His mother was Elizabeth Stringham Hunt. After graduation from Union College, Hunt studied law, first at Tapping Reeve's academy in Litchfield, Connecticut, and then with a local Utica judge, Hiram Denio. After admission to the bar in 1831, he formed a partnership with Denio and built a lucrative practice.

While practicing law, Hunt became actively engaged in poli-

Ward Hunt

tics. He was elected to the New York Assembly as a Jacksonian Democrat in 1838, and served a one-year term. He served a year as mayor of Utica in 1844.

Hunt's ties with the Democratic Party began to loosen in the 1840s, when he opposed the annexation of Texas and the expansion of slavery. In 1848 he broke with the party to back Martin Van Buren's presidential bid on the antislavery Free Soil ticket.

In 1853 Hunt lost a bid for the state supreme court (the state court of original jurisdiction in New York) as a Democrat, partly because many Democrats refused to back him because of his disloyalty in 1848. With the slavery issue becoming more contentious, Hunt broke permanently with the Democrats and helped found the Republican Party in New York in 1855. During the process, he formed an alliance with fellow Utica native Roscoe Conkling, later the boss of New York Republican politics to whom Hunt was to owe his Supreme Court appointment.

In 1865 Hunt was elected to the New York Court of Appeals, the state's highest court, becoming its chief judge in 1868. Following a court reorganization in 1869, he became commissioner of appeals, a position he held until his Supreme Court appointment.

Several other more famous names were presented to President Grant for the vacancy created by Justice Nelson's retirement, but Conkling, Grant's close ally, prevailed on the president to choose Hunt. Hunt's service is considered one of the more inconspicuous in the Court's history, and he was responsible for few major opinions. In January 1879 he suffered a paralytic stroke that incapacitated him from further service, but he

did not retire for another three years. The law then in effect granted a full pension only to justices who had reached the age of seventy and had served on the Court for ten years.

Finally, with the Court in danger of becoming bogged down because of Hunt's illness and the increasing age of several other justices, Congress passed a special law exempting Hunt from the terms of the pension law, granting him retirement at full pay if he would retire from the Court within thirty days of enactment of the exemption. He retired the day the law went into effect and died four years later.

Morrison Remick Waite
(1874–1888)

BIRTH: November 27, 1816, Lyme, Connecticut.

EDUCATION: graduated from Yale College, 1837.

OFFICIAL POSITIONS: Ohio state representative, 1850–1852; representative to the Geneva Arbitration, 1871; president of the Ohio Constitutional Convention, 1873–1874.

SUPREME COURT SERVICE: nominated chief justice by President Ulysses S. Grant January 19, 1874, to replace Salmon P. Chase, who had died; confirmed by the Senate January 21, 1874, by a 63–0 vote; took judicial oath March 4, 1874; served until March 23, 1888; replaced by Melville W. Fuller, nominated by President Grover Cleveland.

FAMILY: married his second cousin, Amelia C. Warner, September 21, 1840; five children.

DEATH: March 23, 1888, Washington, D.C.

Morrison Remick Waite

Born into an old New England family, Waite counted among his forebears a chief justice of the Connecticut Supreme Court, a prominent Connecticut justice of the peace, and a Revolutionary War hero. He was the eldest son of Henry Matson Waite and Maria Selden Waite. He attended one of New England's most prestigious institutions of higher learning, Yale College, graduating in the class of 1837, which included Samuel J. Tilden, later governor of New York and Democratic presidential nominee in 1876; William Evarts, later secretary of state under President Hayes (1877–1881); and Edwards Pierrepont, later attorney general under President Grant (1875–1876).

Seeing greater opportunities in the frontier, Waite moved to northwest Ohio in 1838 and studied law with Samuel D. Young, a prominent attorney in Maumee City. Waite was admitted to the bar in 1839 and practiced in Maumee City until 1850, when he and his family moved to the booming city of Toledo on Lake Erie. There he made a name for himself as a specialist in railroad law and developed a large business clientele.

Although Waite came to the Supreme Court as one of the least experienced and least known chief justices—he had never held a judicial position nor practiced before the Supreme Court before his appointment—he nevertheless had been involved in public affairs on and off for almost thirty years. He ran for Congress from the northwest Ohio district encompassing Toledo, as a Whig in 1846 and as an independent Republican in 1862, but lost both times. He was elected to the Ohio General Assembly in 1849, serving one term. Throughout the Civil War, Waite was strongly pro-Union and, with his speeches and writing, attempted to rally the population to the Union cause.

Waite was offered a seat on the Ohio Supreme Court in 1863 but declined in favor of an informal advisory role to the governor. The major break that brought Waite to the attention of the national administration headed by President Grant occurred in 1871 when he was appointed a member of the U.S. delegation to the Geneva Arbitration, which was to settle the *Alabama* claims case. The United States was demanding compensation from Great Britain for allowing Confederate vessels to be fitted out in British ports and operate from them during the Civil War. Waite's hard work during the arbitration proceedings and the final award to the United States of $15.5 million brought him a measure of national attention and praise.

When he returned to the United States, Waite was elected to the Ohio Constitutional Convention in 1873 and unanimously chosen its president. While he was presiding over the convention, he received word that President Grant had nominated him as chief justice. The selection came as a complete surprise to both the nation and to Waite. Waite was Grant's fourth choice for the post—the first refused to accept the job and the next two withdrew under threat of rejection by the Senate.

At first, Waite was treated with some condescension by his fellow Court members because of his inexperience, but he soon asserted his authority. He issued 872 opinions in fourteen years, a remarkably high number. Among the better-known are *Minor v. Happersett* (1875), upholding a state's right to deny women the right to vote; *Reynolds v. United States* (1878), in which the Court said that the practice of polygamy was not protected by the First Amendment; and *Munn v. Illinois* (1877), in which the Court said that private property could be regulated for the public good. By the end of his service he received praise for his industriousness if not his imaginativeness.

Waite also made efforts to protect his post from being involved in national politics, as it had during the tenure of his predecessor, Salmon P. Chase. Waite refused to allow his name to be considered for the 1876 Republican presidential nomination. And he also declined to make himself available for service on the electoral commission formed in 1877 to determine the outcome of the disputed 1876 presidential contest.

Even while fulfilling his duties on the Court, Waite assumed an additional load of civic responsibilities. He served as trustee of the Peabody Education Fund from 1874 to 1888 and was a member of the Yale Corporation from 1882 to 1888.

John Marshall Harlan

(1877–1911)

BIRTH: June 1, 1833, Boyle County, Kentucky.

EDUCATION: Centre College, A.B., 1850; studied law at Transylvania University, 1851–1853.

OFFICIAL POSITIONS: adjutant general of Kentucky, 1851; judge, Franklin County, 1858; state attorney general, 1863–1867; member, Louisiana Reconstruction Commission, 1877; member, Bering Sea Tribunal of Arbitration, 1893.

SUPREME COURT SERVICE: nominated associate justice by President Rutherford B. Hayes October 17, 1877, to replace

David Davis, who had resigned; confirmed by the Senate November 29, 1877, by a voice vote; took judicial oath December 10, 1877; served until October 14, 1911; replaced by Mahlon Pitney, nominated by President William Howard Taft.

FAMILY: married Malvina F. Shanklin, December 23, 1856; six children.

DEATH: October 14, 1911, Washington, D.C.

Harlan was born into a prominent Kentucky political family. Both his ancestors and his descendants played important roles in public life. His mother was Eliza Davenport Harlan. His father, James Harlan, an admirer of Henry Clay's patriotism and John Marshall's leadership on the Court, was a U.S. representative from Kentucky (1835–1839) and also served as attorney general and secretary of state of Kentucky. Justice Harlan's son, John Maynard Harlan (1864–1934), became a prominent Chicago lawyer and was the unsuccessful Republican nominee for mayor of Chicago in 1897 and 1905. And his grandson and namesake John Marshall Harlan (1899–1971) was himself a Supreme Court justice (1955–1971).

Young Harlan studied law at Transylvania University, known as the "Harvard of the West," and then completed his legal education in his father's law office. He was admitted to the bar in 1853.

Harlan's only judicial experience before his appointment to the Supreme Court was his first office, Franklin County judge, from 1858 to 1859. After that one-year experience on the bench, Harlan turned to politics. He ran for the U.S. House in 1859 as the candidate of a coalition of anti-Democratic groups, including the Whigs and Know-Nothings, but lost by sixty-seven votes.

As a slaveholder and a member of the southern aristocracy, Harlan had difficulty following many of the nation's Whigs into the new Republican Party. In the presidential election of 1860, he backed the Constitutional Union Party, which stood for a compromise settlement of the increasingly bitter sectional conflict. But when the Civil War came, Harlan chose to stay loyal to the Union and served as an officer in the northern forces.

When his father died in 1863, Harlan resigned his commission and ran successfully for attorney general of Kentucky on the pro-Union ticket. Although opposed to many policies of the Lincoln administration—he supported Democrat George B. McClellan against Lincoln in 1864—and believing the postwar constitutional amendments ending slavery and attempting to guarantee the rights of blacks were a mistake, Harlan eventually gravitated into the Republican Party and was its nominee for governor of Kentucky in 1875. He was also prominently mentioned as a Republican vice-presidential candidate in 1872.

But the major impact Harlan had on the national political scene came in 1876, when he headed the Kentucky delegation to the Republican National Convention. At a critical moment during the deadlocked proceedings, Harlan swung the state's votes to Ohio governor Rutherford B. Hayes, helping to start a bandwagon moving in Hayes's direction. Hayes was nominated and

elected and acknowledged his debt to Harlan by considering him for appointment as attorney general.

Although other political considerations intervened so that no cabinet post was open for Harlan, Hayes kept him in mind. The new president appointed him to head a commission to settle the rival claims of two factions for control of Louisiana in the spring of 1877. Then, when Supreme Court Justice Davis resigned to enter the U.S. Senate, Hayes nominated Harlan to fill the vacancy.

Harlan's tenure—almost thirty-four years—was one of the longest in the Court's history, being exceeded by only four other justices. During his service on the Court, he was called on by President Benjamin Harrison in 1892 to serve as the U.S. representative in the arbitration of the Bering Sea controversy with Great Britain.

He had a lively temperament, often delivering his opinions extemporaneously, in the style of an old-fashioned Kentucky stump speech. His vigorous attacks on several famous majority decisions earned him the title of "great dissenter." Most notable was his eloquent dissent in *Plessy v. Ferguson* (1896), the case that upheld Louisiana's "separate but equal" law with respect to public accommodations.

William Burnham Woods

(1881–1887)

BIRTH: August 3, 1824, Newark, Ohio.

EDUCATION: attended Western Reserve College for three years; graduated from Yale University, 1845.

OFFICIAL POSITIONS: mayor of Newark, Ohio, 1856; Ohio

state representative, 1858–1862, Speaker in 1858–1860 and minority leader in 1860–1862; chancellor, middle chancery district of Alabama, 1868–1869; U.S. circuit judge for the Fifth Circuit, 1869–1880.

SUPREME COURT SERVICE: nominated associate justice by President Rutherford B. Hayes December 15, 1880, to replace William Strong, who had retired; confirmed by the Senate December 21, 1880, by a 39–8 vote; took judicial oath January 5, 1881; served until May 14, 1887; replaced by Lucius Q. C. Lamar, nominated by President Grover Cleveland.

FAMILY: married Anne E. Warner, June 21, 1855; one son, one daughter.

DEATH: May 14, 1887, Washington, D.C.

Woods was born in Newark in the central part of Ohio. His father, Ezekiel Woods, was a farmer and merchant from Kentucky. His mother, Sarah Burnham Woods, came from New England. Following his education at Western Reserve University and Yale, Woods studied law with S. D. King, a prominent lawyer in his home town of Newark. Woods passed the bar in 1847 and joined in partnership with his mentor, King, until the Civil War changed the course of his life.

Following a rise to local prominence through the practice of law in Newark, the county seat of Licking County, Ohio, Woods was chosen mayor of his native city in 1856. The following year, he was elected to the state legislature, and was chosen Speaker. An ardent Democrat, he opposed the rise of the newly established Republican Party. When the Democrats lost control of the state House in the 1859 elections, Woods became the minority leader.

At first, he opposed the war policy of President Lincoln, but as the conflict continued Woods became convinced of the necessity of victory over the South. He joined the Union army in 1862, seeing action in the battles of Shiloh and Vicksburg and marching with Sherman through Georgia. He rose to the rank of brigadier general in 1865 and was brevetted a major general just before being mustered out of service in February 1866. His brother, Charles Robert Woods (1827–1885), was a well-known officer in the Union army.

After the war, Woods settled in Alabama, engaging in cotton planting, investing in an iron works, and resuming the practice of law. His decision to reside in the South invited the charge of "carpetbagger," but his name was never linked to the corruption and profligacy associated with that term.

By this time, Woods had become a Republican and was elected chancellor of the middle chancery division of Alabama on his new party's ticket in 1868. When President Grant and the national Republican Party came to power the next year, Woods received an appointment as a circuit court judge for the Fifth Circuit (Florida, Georgia, Alabama, Mississippi, Louisiana, and Texas). Despite his northern origins and Union military background, he gained the respect of his southern neighbors and colleagues. To master his job he had to learn Louisiana law, which was based on the Napoleonic code. In 1877 Woods moved to Atlanta.

In 1880, when President Hayes was looking for a southerner to appoint to the Court, he decided on Woods. Hayes made a constant effort throughout his administration to bring southerners back into the federal government. Woods became the first Supreme Court justice appointed from a southern Confederate state since 1853.

Woods wrote 159 opinions during his six and a half years on the Court. He is best known for two. In *United States v. Harris* (1883) the Court struck down the federal statute known as the "Ku Klux Law," which was designed to protect blacks against terrorism in the South. In *Presser v. State of Illinois* (1886) the Court supported the right of state authorities alone to maintain militias and to determine the conditions for individuals to carry arms.

Woods was partially incapacitated by illness during the last months. The tradition of a new southern seat on the Court was continued when President Cleveland picked as Woods's successor Lucius Q. C. Lamar of Mississippi.

Stanley Matthews

(1881–1889)

BIRTH: July 21, 1824, Cincinnati, Ohio.

EDUCATION: Kenyon College, graduated with honors, 1840.

OFFICIAL POSITIONS: assistant prosecuting attorney, Hamilton County, 1845; clerk, Ohio House of Representatives, 1848–1849; judge, Hamilton County Court of Common Pleas, 1851–1853; member, Ohio Senate, 1855–1858; U.S. attorney for southern Ohio, 1858–1861; judge, Superior Court of Cincinnati,

1863–1865; counsel, Hayes-Tilden electoral commission, 1877; U.S. senator, 1877–1879.

SUPREME COURT SERVICE: nominated associate justice by President Rutherford B. Hayes January 26, 1881, to replace Noah Swayne, who had retired; no action by Senate; renominated by President James A. Garfield, March 14, 1881; confirmed by Senate May 12, 1881, by a 24–23 vote; took judicial oath May 17, 1881; served until March 22, 1889; replaced by David J. Brewer, nominated by President Benjamin Harrison.

FAMILY: married Mary Ann Black, February 1843; died 1885; eight children; married Mary Theaker, 1887.

DEATH: March 22, 1889, Washington, D.C.

Thomas Johnson and Isabella Brown Matthews's first child, born in Cincinnati in 1824, was named Thomas Stanley. He preferred to be called Stanley and dropped his first name when he became an adult. His maternal grandfather, Col. William Brown, was an Ohio pioneer who settled in Hamilton County in 1788. His father, a Virginian, served as Morrison professor of mathematics and natural history at Transylvania University in Lexington, Kentucky, for a number of years before becoming president of Cincinnati's Woodward High School, which his son attended.

Matthews entered Kenyon College as a junior and graduated in 1840. After reading law for two years in Cincinnati, he left Ohio because he was too young to take the bar exam there. He moved to Maury County, Tennessee, where he passed the bar at the age of eighteen and began his legal practice and the editorship of the *Tennessee Democrat,* a weekly paper supporting James K. Polk for president.

In 1844 Matthews married Mary Ann Black, the daughter of a prosperous Tennessee farmer. They had eight children. After her death in 1885 he married Mary Theaker of Washington, D.C.

Matthews left Tennessee when he was twenty and returned to Cincinnati. Within a year he was appointed assistant prosecuting attorney for Hamilton County and made editor of the *Cincinnati Morning Herald.* His strong stance against slavery won him election as clerk of the Ohio House of Representatives in 1848. Three years later he was elected one of three judges of the Hamilton County Court of Common Pleas. Matthews served in the Ohio Senate from 1855 to 1858 and as U.S. attorney for southern Ohio from 1858 to 1861, a post to which he was appointed by President Buchanan. Although personally opposed to slavery, as U.S. attorney Matthews upheld the Fugitive Slave Act and prosecuted W. B. Connelly, a reporter who had helped two slaves escape.

An officer in Ohio's Twenty-third and Fifty-first Regiment of volunteers, Matthews resigned his command in 1863 to accept election to the Cincinnati Superior Court. Two years later he returned to his private practice of railroad and corporate law. During Reconstruction Matthews was active in Republican politics as a presidential elector in 1864 and 1868, temporary chairman of the Liberal Republican Convention in 1872, and GOP congressional candidate in 1876. He was defeated in part because of the unpopularity of his prosecution of Connelly before the war.

Matthews campaigned for presidential candidate Rutherford B. Hayes and was one of the principal spokesmen on his behalf at the 1877 electoral commission. When Sen. John Sherman of Ohio was appointed secretary of Treasury in Hayes's cabinet, Matthews was elected by the legislature to fill Sherman's Senate seat. In January 1878 he introduced the "Matthews resolution" for the remonetization of silver.

Matthews's nomination to the Supreme Court by President Hayes upon the resignation of Justice Swayne of Ohio was not confirmed by the Senate. The appointment was criticized as merely a reward for Matthews's aid in Hayes's disputed victory over Samuel J. Tilden. The president was accused of cronyism—he and Matthews were fellow students at Kenyon College, lawyers in Cincinnati, and officers in the Twenty-third Ohio Infantry.

Matthews was renominated by President Garfield, Hayes's successor, but received continued opposition. Some feared Matthews's defense of large corporations and railroads during his legal practice would hinder his ability to dispense justice impartially on the Court. A vote on the nominee was finally taken on May 12, 1881; he was confirmed 24–23. One of his best-known opinions was that for a unanimous Court in *Yick Wo v. Hopkins* (1886). The Court struck down a city ordinance that, Matthews said, was fair on its face, but administered to discriminate against a particular group.

Matthews died in Washington, D.C., during his eighth year on the Court.

Horace Gray

(1882–1902)

BIRTH: March 24, 1828, Boston, Massachusetts.

EDUCATION: Harvard College, A.B., 1845; Harvard Law School, 1849.

OFFICIAL POSITIONS: reporter, Massachusetts Supreme Court, 1854–1864; associate justice, 1864–1873; chief justice, 1873–1881.

SUPREME COURT SERVICE: nominated associate justice by President Chester A. Arthur December 19, 1881, to replace Nathan Clifford, who had died; confirmed by Senate December 20, 1881, by a 51–5 vote; took judicial oath January 9, 1882; served until September 15, 1902; replaced by Oliver Wendell Holmes Jr., nominated by President Theodore Roosevelt.

FAMILY: married Jane Matthews, June 4, 1889.

DEATH: September 15, 1902, Nahant, Massachusetts.

Harriet Upham Gray gave birth to her first child March 24, 1828, and named him Horace after his father, a businessman in the iron industry. His grandfather, Lt.-Gov. William Gray, was the son of a poor New England shoemaker. He made his fortune as one of the first American merchants and shipowners to trade with Russia, India, and China. Horace Gray's uncle, Francis Calley Gray, was a Massachusetts legal historian and his younger

Horace Gray

half-brother, John Chipman Gray, a renowned professor at Harvard Law School.

Gray graduated from Harvard in 1845 and traveled abroad. Reversals in the family business forced him to return to Boston to choose a career. Although Gray's chief interest had always been natural history, he chose the law and studied industriously at Harvard Law School. Reading law with Judge John Lowell and clerking in the firm of Sohier and Welch completed Gray's preparation for the bar, which he passed in 1851. He practiced in Boston for thirteen years.

As a young Boston lawyer, Gray was a member of the Free Soil Party, which advocated free homesteads and opposed the expansion of slavery into the territories. Late in his life Gray married Jane Matthews, the daughter of Supreme Court Justice Stanley Matthews.

Gray's career in the Massachusetts judiciary began in 1854 as a reporter for the state supreme court. After six years as a reporter he ran for state attorney general but failed to obtain the nomination of the Republican Party, which he joined soon after its founding. Gov. John A. Andrews promoted Gray to the position of associate justice on August 23, 1864. Gray was thirty-six years old, the youngest appointee in the history of the Massachusetts Supreme Court. The death or resignation of senior justices elevated Gray to the chief justiceship in 1873.

During his seventeen years of service on the state court, Gray dissented only once and during his lifetime none of his decisions was overruled. Gray was respected for his careful historical research and knowledge of legal precedent. As chief justice he employed as his law clerk a bright young Harvard student named Louis D. Brandeis.

President James A. Garfield considered nominating Horace Gray to the Supreme Court after the death of Justice Nathan Clifford on July 25, 1881. But Garfield died prior to making the appointment. His successor, Chester Alan Arthur, appointed Gray associate justice on December 19, 1881. The Senate, anxious to fill Clifford's seat, which had been vacant for five months, confirmed Arthur's nominee the following day by a 51–5 vote.

On the Court Gray became known as a strong nationalist, partly because of his opinion in *Juilliard v. Greenman* (1884). In this case the Court affirmed the right of the federal government to issue currency, even in the form of paper money. Gray is also known for his opinion in *United States v. Wong Kim Ark* (1898), in which the Court ruled that all Chinese born in the United States were citizens.

On July 9, 1902, after twenty years of service, the seventy-four-year-old justice informed President Theodore Roosevelt of his intention to retire. He died in September, before his retirement became effective, in Nahant, Massachusetts.

Samuel Blatchford

(1882–1893)

BIRTH: March 9, 1820, New York City.

EDUCATION: Columbia College, A.B., 1837.

OFFICIAL POSITIONS: judge, Southern District of New York, 1867–1872; judge, Second Circuit of New York, 1872–1882.

Samuel Blatchford

SUPREME COURT SERVICE: nominated associate justice by President Chester Arthur March 13, 1882, to replace Ward Hunt, who had retired; confirmed by Senate March 27, 1882, by a voice vote; took judicial oath April 3, 1882; served until July 7, 1893; replaced by Edward D. White, nominated by President Grover Cleveland.

FAMILY: married Caroline Appleton, December 17, 1844.

DEATH: July 7, 1893, Newport, Rhode Island.

Samuel Blatchford was the son of the former Julia Ann Mumford, daughter of a well-known publicist, and Richard M. Blatchford, counsel for the Bank of England and the Bank of the United States and a Whig in the New York legislature. His paternal grandfather, a British clergyman and the father of seventeen children, immigrated to Lansingburg, New York, in 1795.

At the age of thirteen, Blatchford entered Columbia College and four years later graduated at the top of his class. From 1837 to 1841 he prepared for the bar as the private secretary of his father's friend, New York governor William H. Seward. Blatchford passed the bar in 1842, practiced law with his father for three years, and joined Seward's law firm in Auburn, New York. In 1844 he married Caroline Appleton of Lowell, Massachusetts.

After nine years as a partner with Seward and Morgan, Blatchford and Seward's nephew established the New York City firm Blatchford, Seward, and Griswold. He declined a seat on the New York Supreme Court in 1855 to devote himself to his admiralty and international law practice.

During his legal career Blatchford reported extensively on federal court decisions. *Blatchford's Circuit Court Reports* (1852) included cases from New York's Second Circuit since 1845 and *Blatchford's and Howland's Reports* (1855) contributed to the extant knowledge of admiralty cases in the Southern District. His extensive research into the state's judicial history as well as his expertise in admiralty law qualified Blatchford for the post of district judge for Southern New York to which he was appointed in 1867 and for his subsequent appointment to the Second Circuit Court in 1872.

After fifteen years in the federal judiciary, Blatchford was nominated to the Supreme Court by President Chester A. Arthur to fill the vacancy created by the retirement of Justice Ward Hunt of New York. Two other nominees had refused the post. Roscoe Conkling, a New York lawyer and politician, was the president's first choice. The Senate confirmed him, but Conkling declined. Arthur's second choice, Sen. George F. Edmunds of Vermont, also declined. Blatchford accepted, and the Senate readily confirmed him.

During Blatchford's tenure, a steady stream of admiralty and patent cases inundated the Court. His expertise in these areas proved invaluable, and Blatchford earned a reputation as a workhorse.

Blatchford served as trustee of Columbia University from 1867 until his death in 1893 in Newport, Rhode Island.

Lucius Quintus Cincinnatus Lamar

(1888–1893)

BIRTH: September 17, 1825, Eatonton, Georgia.

EDUCATION: Emory College, A.B., 1845.

OFFICIAL POSITIONS: member, Georgia House of Representatives, 1853; U.S. representative, 1857–1860, 1873–1877; U.S. senator, 1877–1885; secretary of interior, 1885–1888.

SUPREME COURT SERVICE: nominated associate justice by President Grover Cleveland December 6, 1887, to replace William Woods, who had died; confirmed by U.S. Senate January 16, 1888, by a 32–28 vote; took judicial oath January 18, 1888; served until January 23, 1893; replaced by Howell Edmunds Jackson, nominated by President Benjamin Harrison.

FAMILY: married Virginia Longstreet, July 15, 1847; died 1884; one son, three daughters; married Henrietta Dean Holt, January 5, 1887.

DEATH: January 23, 1893, Macon, Georgia.

Of French Huguenot ancestry, Lamar was born into the landed aristocracy of the pre–Civil War South in 1825. The fourth of Lucius Quintus Cincinnatus and Sarah Bird Lamar's eight children, he attended the Georgia Conference Manual Labor School, an institution that combined farm work with academics. Lamar graduated from Emory College in 1845 and two years later married its president's daughter, Virginia Longstreet.

Lamar read law in Macon, Georgia, passed the bar in 1847, and shortly thereafter followed his father-in-law to Oxford, Mississippi. The Reverend Augustus B. Longstreet became president of the University of Mississippi, and Lamar taught mathematics and practiced law. The two men were devoted to one another. Longstreet had lost his only son, and Lamar's father had committed suicide when Lamar was nine years old.

In 1852 Lamar returned to Georgia and established a successful legal practice in Covington. The following year he was elected to the state legislature. The dissolution of his law partnership and his failure to obtain the Democratic nomination to Congress prompted Lamar's return to Mississippi in 1855. He settled on a plantation and began practicing law and participating in state politics. A Jefferson Davis supporter and states' rights extremist, Lamar was elected to Congress in 1857 but resigned before his term expired. He personally drafted the state's ordinance of secession at the Mississippi Secession Convention of 1861.

Lamar served the Confederacy as colonel of the Eighteenth Mississippi Regiment until an attack of apoplexy, an ailment since childhood, forced him to retire from active duty in May 1862. As special envoy to Russia he attended diplomatic briefings in Europe in 1863, but never went to Russia. He spent the remainder of the war as a judge advocate for the Army of Northern Virginia.

When General Lee surrendered, Lamar was forty years old. Two of his brothers had died in battle; his friend Jefferson Davis was in prison; and he was in debt. Disqualified from public office, he returned to Mississippi to practice law and teach metaphysics at the university.

Although a partisan sectionalist before the war, Lamar publicly advocated reconciliation and cooperation during the difficult days of Reconstruction. Pardoned for his role in the Confederacy, he was reelected to Congress in 1872. His eulogy of Massachusetts Unionist Charles Sumner, heralded by the Boston *Advertiser* as the most significant and hopeful word from the South since the war, won Lamar national acclaim as the Great Pacificator. A representative of the new South, Lamar reached the Senate in 1877. His reputation as a politician guided by more than sectional interests was strengthened by his refusal to follow the directive of the Mississippi legislature to support a bill authorizing the free coinage of silver.

Anxious to demonstrate the South's desire to serve the entire nation, Lamar resigned from his second Senate term to accept a cabinet appointment. As Grover Cleveland's secretary of the interior, he directed the reclamation of thousands of acres of public lands and the establishment of a new Indian policy. While in office Lamar married Henrietta Dean Holt.

The death in 1887 of Justice William Woods, a Georgia Republican, created the first vacancy on the Supreme Court in six years. Although Lamar's appointment by President Cleveland was strongly opposed by many Republicans, Senators Stanford of California and Stewart of Nevada argued persuasively that Lamar's rejection would be interpreted as a ban against all Confederate veterans. The sixty-three-year-old nominee was narrowly confirmed by the Senate, 32–28.

Lamar served on the Court for five years, voting consistently to uphold the rights of business. In *Kidd v. Pearson* (1888), one of his best-known opinions, Lamar defined commerce to exclude manufacturing, which made it more difficult for Congress to regulate.

He died from apoplexy in his native Georgia on January 23, 1893.

Melville Weston Fuller
(1888–1910)

BIRTH: February 11, 1833, Augusta, Maine.

EDUCATION: Bowdoin College, A.B., 1853; studied at Harvard Law School and read law, 1853–1855.

OFFICIAL POSITIONS: member, Illinois House of Representatives, 1863–1864; member, Venezuela-British Guiana Border Commission, 1899; member, Permanent Court of Arbitration at the Hague, 1900–1910.

SUPREME COURT SERVICE: nominated chief justice by President Grover Cleveland April 30, 1888, to replace Morrison R. Waite, who had died; confirmed by Senate July 20, 1888, by a 41–20 vote; took judicial oath October 8, 1888; served until July 4, 1910; replaced as chief justice by Edward D. White, nominated by President William Howard Taft.

FAMILY: married Calista Ophelia Reynolds, June 28, 1858; died 1864; two daughters; married Mary Ellen Coolbaugh, May 30, 1866; eight children, seven of whom survived childhood.

DEATH: July 4, 1910, Sorrento, Maine.

Melville Weston Fuller was the second son of Frederick Augustus Fuller and Catherine Martin Weston. When he was two months old, his mother divorced his father on the grounds of adultery and took her sons to live with their grandfather, a judge on the Maine Supreme Court. Although she remarried when Fuller was eleven, he and his brother continued to live with Judge Weston in Augusta.

Fuller attended Bowdoin College, where he was active in politics and a prolific writer of verse. He graduated Phi Beta Kappa in 1853 and, like his father and both his grandfathers, chose the legal profession. Fuller read law in Bangor and after six months at Harvard Law School passed the bar. He began to practice in

Augusta at the age of twenty-two and the same year took an editorial position on *The Augusta Age,* a local Democratic paper owned by his father's brother. At the age of twenty-four he was elected president of the Common Council and appointed city solicitor.

Like many young men in the 1850s, Fuller was lured west by the promise of a better life on the frontier. He settled in the booming railroad town of Chicago and started practicing real estate and commercial law.

Fuller married twice. His first wife, Calista Ophelia Reynolds, died of tuberculosis six years after they were married. In 1866 he married Mary Ellen Coolbaugh, the daughter of the president of Chicago's Union National Bank. They had eight children, losing one during childhood. Fuller also had two daughters by his previous marriage.

In Chicago Fuller pursued a political as well as a legal career. He managed Stephen Douglas's senatorial campaign against Abraham Lincoln in 1858, attended the Illinois Constitutional Convention three years later, and served in the Illinois House of Representatives from 1863 to 1864.

Meanwhile, Fuller's legal practice and real estate investments on the North Shore prospered; his earnings by the 1880s reached an estimated $30,000 a year. Fuller acted as Chicago's counsel in litigation over the city's rights to Lake Michigan shore property. He also defended—in a nationally publicized case—the Reverend Charles E. Cheney, rector of Christ Church in Chicago, who was accused of canonical disobedience by an ecclesiastical tribunal because of his "low church" practices. A high Episcopalian himself, Fuller opened the way for the founding of the Reformed Protestant Episcopal Church in America.

Grover Cleveland met Melville Fuller during a western presidential tour and was impressed by his "sound money," low-tariff economic philosophy. Although Fuller had previously declined the positions of civil service chairman and solicitor general in Cleveland's administration, he accepted the appointment of chief justice on April 30, 1888. The Republican Senate soon voiced their objections to the Democratic nominee. Midwesterners were wary of his ties with big corporations. Northerners accused him of anti-Union sentiment and circulated the pamphlet "The War Record of Melville Fuller," which was discredited only after Robert T. Lincoln, son of the former president, attested to his loyalty. The Philadelphia *Press* claimed that Cleveland's nominee was the most obscure man ever appointed chief justice.

Although Fuller had never held federal office, his professional credentials were sound and his appointment geographically expedient. Moreover, the Seventh Circuit, comprising Illinois, Indiana, and Wisconsin, had been unrepresented on the bench since Justice David Davis's resignation in 1877. Fuller was confirmed by the Senate, 41–20, nearly three months after his appointment.

During his Court tenure, Fuller served on the Venezuela-British Guiana Border Commission and the Permanent Court of Arbitration in the Hague. An efficient and courteous leader of the Court for twenty-two years, he was well respected by his colleagues on the bench, particularly by Justice Oliver Wendell Holmes Jr.

Fuller's best-known opinions are *Pollock v. Farmers' Loan & Trust Co.* and *United States v. E. C. Knight,* both decided in 1895. In *Pollock* the Court invalidated a general income tax. This decision was overturned by passage and ratification of the Sixteenth Amendment. In *E. C. Knight* the Court ruled that the Sherman Antitrust Act did not apply to manufacturing, even though the company in question refined more than 90 percent of the sugar sold in the United States.

When Cleveland returned to the presidency he offered Fuller the position of secretary of state, but Fuller declined, believing his acceptance would lower the dignity of the Court in the mind of the public. He died of heart failure at the age of seventy-seven at his summer home in Sorrento, Maine.

David Josiah Brewer

(1890–1910)

BIRTH: June 20, 1837, Smyrna, Asia Minor.

EDUCATION: Wesleyan University, 1852–1853; Yale University, A.B., 1856; Albany Law School, LL.B., 1858.

OFFICIAL POSITIONS: commissioner, U.S. Circuit Court, Leavenworth, Kansas, 1861–1862; judge of probate and criminal courts, Leavenworth County, 1863–1864; judge, First District of Kansas, 1865–1869; Leavenworth city attorney, 1869–1870; justice, Kansas Supreme Court, 1870–1884; judge, Eighth Federal Circuit, 1884–1889; president, Venezuela-British Guiana Border Commission, 1895.

SUPREME COURT SERVICE: nominated associate justice by President Benjamin Harrison December 4, 1889, to replace Stanley Matthews, who had died; confirmed by Senate, December 18, 1889, by a 53–11 vote; took judicial oath January 6, 1890; served until March 28, 1910; replaced by Charles Evans Hughes, nominated by President William Howard Taft.

FAMILY: married Louise R. Landon, October 3, 1861; died 1898; married Emma Miner Mott, June 5, 1901.

DEATH: March 28, 1910, Washington, D.C.

Brewer was born in the part of Asia Minor that is now Izmir, Turkey, where his father was a Congregational missionary. With his infant son and wife Emilia Field Brewer, the daughter of a New England clergyman, Reverend Josiah Brewer returned to America to become chaplain of St. Francis Prison, in Wethersfield, Connecticut. Young Brewer had three notable uncles: David Dudley Field, a jurist; Cyrus W. Field, a financier and promoter of the trans-Atlantic telegraph cable; and Stephen J. Field, a Supreme Court justice from California (1863–1897).

Brewer attended Wesleyan University for two years before enrolling in his father's alma mater, Yale University, from which he graduated with honors in 1856. After reading law for a year in David Field's office, Brewer attended Albany Law School. He passed the New York bar in 1858 and, deciding to go west as his Uncle Stephen had done, the Kansas bar the following year.

When he was twenty-four Brewer married Louise R. Landon of Burlington, Vermont. She died after thirty-seven years of marriage, and Brewer, at the age of sixty-four, married Emma Miner Mott of Washington, D.C.

Brewer's first official position was administrative. He was appointed commissioner of the U.S. Circuit Court for the District of Kansas in Leavenworth in 1861. After two years he was nominated judge of probate and criminal courts. From 1865 to 1869 Brewer served as state district attorney and the following year as city attorney for Leavenworth until his election at the age of thirty-three to the Kansas Supreme Court. When Kansas passed a prohibition amendment in 1881, Judge Brewer sought to defend the rights of manufacturers against the confiscation of their property without compensation. Brewer's fourteen years of service on the state court ended in 1884 when he was appointed to the Eighth Federal Circuit by President Chester A. Arthur.

When Justice Stanley Matthews died, Republican senators Preston B. Plumb and John J. Ingalls of Kansas urged President Benjamin Harrison to appoint Brewer to the Supreme Court. During his consideration of the nomination, the president received a letter from Brewer recommending the appointment of Henry B. Brown, a Michigan district court judge who had been in his class at Yale. Impressed by these generous comments about Brown, Harrison nominated Brewer instead. Although his appointment was opposed by some prohibitionists, Brewer was confirmed by the Senate by a 53–11 vote.

During his twenty years on the Supreme Court, Brewer spoke out freely on the issues of the day. He advocated independence for the Philippines, suffrage for women, and residency rights for Chinese aliens in America. He may be best known for his opinion in *Muller v. Oregon* (1908), in which the Court decided that a state could limit women's working hours for health reasons.

Brewer was one of the original officers in the American Society of International Law and in 1895 presided over the congressional commission to oversee the disputed Venezuela-British Guiana boundary. A lecturer on American citizenship at Yale and corporate law at Columbian, now George Washington, University, Brewer also edited collections of the world's best orations and essays and wrote numerous books and articles. He was a lifelong member of the Congregational church and active in missionary work.

Brewer died suddenly on March 28, 1910, in Washington, D.C.

Henry Billings Brown
(1891–1906)

BIRTH: March 2, 1836, South Lee, Massachusetts.

EDUCATION: Yale University, A.B., 1856; studied briefly at Yale Law School and Harvard Law School.

OFFICIAL POSITIONS: U.S. deputy marshal for Detroit, 1861; assistant U.S. attorney, 1863–1868; circuit judge, Wayne County, Michigan, 1868; federal judge, Eastern District of Michigan, 1875–1890.

SUPREME COURT SERVICE: nominated associate justice by President Benjamin Harrison December 23, 1890, to replace Samuel Miller, who had died; confirmed by the Senate December 29, 1890, by a voice vote; took judicial oath January 5, 1891;

retired May 28, 1906; replaced by William H. Moody, nominated by President Theodore Roosevelt.

FAMILY: married Caroline Pitts, July 1864; died 1901; married Josephine E. Tyler, June 25, 1904.

DEATH: September 4, 1913, Bronxville, New York.

The son of a prosperous merchant, Brown was born in a small town and raised in a middle-class Protestant home. His parents, Billings and Mary Tyler Brown prepared their son for the legal career they had chosen for him with a private secondary school and Yale University education. A moderately good student, he graduated from Yale in 1856 and went abroad for a year.

Brown began his legal education as a law clerk in Ellington, Connecticut. After a few months he returned to Yale to attend lectures at the law school. Brown also studied briefly at Harvard Law School.

In 1859 the twenty-three-year-old law student moved to Detroit. Within a year he finished his legal apprenticeship and passed the bar. Wealthy enough to hire a substitute, Brown escaped military service in the Civil War and immediately began his private practice.

He married Caroline Pitts, a member of a prosperous Detroit family, in 1864. She died in 1901. Three years later, at the age of sixty-seven, Brown married Josephine E. Tyler from Crosswicks, New Jersey, the widow of a lieutenant in the U.S. Navy.

In the early days of the Lincoln administration, Brown was appointed deputy U.S. marshal for Detroit, his first official position. After two years he was promoted to assistant U.S. attorney for the Eastern District of Michigan. Detroit was a busy Great Lakes port, and Brown became an expert in admiralty law.

Republican governor Henry H. Crapo appointed Brown interim circuit judge for Wayne County in 1868. Defeated in his bid for election to a full term, Brown returned to private practice and formed a partnership with John S. Newberry and Ashley Pond that specialized in shipping cases. After an unsuccessful congressional campaign in 1872, he resumed his practice until President Grant appointed him district judge of Eastern Michigan.

During his fourteen years as district judge, Brown won a national reputation as an authority on admiralty law. Howell E. Jackson, a judge on the Sixth Federal Circuit Court, urged President Benjamin Harrison to appoint Brown to the Supreme Court after the death of Justice Samuel Miller. Harrison had served with Jackson in the Senate and followed the advice of his former colleague. Nominated associate justice December 23, 1890, Brown was confirmed by the Senate within the week. Three years later Justice Brown returned Jackson's favor by recommending his appointment to the Court.

Brown's best-known opinion for the Court is *Plessy v. Ferguson* (1896), which established the legality of "separate but equal" facilities. This decision was overturned in 1954 by *Brown v. Board of Education.*

Despite an attack of neuritis in 1890 that blinded him in one eye, Brown served on the Court for fifteen years. At the age of seventy, severely handicapped by his impaired vision, he retired. He lived in semiretirement in Bronxville, New York, until his death on September 14, 1913, at the age of seventy-seven.

George Shiras Jr.
(1892–1903)

BIRTH: January 26, 1832, Pittsburgh, Pennsylvania.

EDUCATION: Ohio University, 1849–1851; Yale University, B.A., 1853, honorary LL.D., 1883; studied law at Yale and privately; admitted to the bar in 1855.

OFFICIAL POSITIONS: none.

SUPREME COURT SERVICE: nominated associate justice by President Benjamin Harrison July 19, 1892, to replace Joseph P. Bradley, who had died; confirmed by the Senate July 26, 1892, by a voice vote; took judicial oath October 10, 1892; retired February 23, 1903; replaced by William R. Day, nominated by President Theodore Roosevelt.

FAMILY: married Lillie E. Kennedy, December 31, 1857; two sons.

DEATH: August 2, 1924, Pittsburgh, Pennsylvania.

George Shiras Jr. was born into a family that had been in America since the 1760s. His father, of Scotch ancestry, married a Presbyterian minister's daughter, Eliza Herron, and was successful enough in the family brewery business to retire in his early thirties to a farm near the Ohio River. Here young Shiras, with his two brothers, spent his early years helping in his father's orchards.

In 1849 he left to attend Ohio University at Athens, Ohio, but after two years transferred to Yale where he graduated in 1853. He then read law at Yale (without graduating) and in the Pittsburgh law office of Judge Hopewell Hepburn before being admitted to the Allegheny County bar in November 1855. Before settling down in Pittsburgh in 1858 to become Judge Hepburn's law partner, he spent several years practicing law in Dubuque, Iowa, with his brother, Oliver Perry Shiras, who later became a federal district judge in northern Iowa.

On December 31, 1857, he married a Pittsburgh manufacturer's daughter, Lillie E. Kennedy, with whom he had two sons. Both offspring followed him into the law profession, and one, George Shiras III, served as U.S. representative from Pennsylvania in the Fifty-eighth Congress from 1903 to 1905.

Judge Hepburn died in 1862, and Shiras carried on a successful practice until his appointment to the Supreme Court in 1892. The years Shiras practiced law in Pittsburgh were those when the iron and steel, coal, and railroad magnates were amassing their fortunes. In more than thirty years as a lawyer in his native city, Shiras maintained a reputation of absolute integrity, of moderation in politics and manner, of restraint and good judgment, and of dignity and wit. Despite his financial success, Shiras remained modest, unostentatious, and respected by his peers. In 1883 he received an honorary LL.D. degree from Yale, the first alumnus to do so.

To the end he preferred quiet living among family and friends and his pursuits as a naturalist rather than seeking the limelight. His moderation seemed to be reflected in both his professional and personal lives.

Shiras's professional life was centered mainly in the private sector; he held no public offices until his Supreme Court appointment. In 1881 he refused the Pennsylvania state legislature's offer of the U.S. Senate nomination. A moderate Republican, he remained aloof from party politics and the state political machine. In 1888 he served as a presidential elector.

In July 1892, at the age of sixty, he was nominated by President Benjamin Harrison to be an associate justice of the Supreme Court to replace Joseph P. Bradley of New Jersey, who had died in January. Although Shiras had the support of the Pennsylvania bar, of the iron and steel interests (including Andrew Carnegie's personal support), and of U.S. representative John Dalzell, the U.S. senators who headed the state Republican machine vigorously opposed his appointment. President Harrison had sent Shiras's name to the Senate without first consulting Senators James Donald Cameron and Matthew S. Quay as senatorial courtesy dictated. However, when the press and prominent persons, including former Yale classmates, came to his defense and the opposition was shown to be purely political, the matter was resolved and he was confirmed unanimously.

Respected for his analytical powers and as a legal technician, Shiras exhibited a quiet competence and bore his share of the workload during his ten years on the Court. Although he wrote 259 majority opinions, he may be best remembered for switching his vote when *Pollock v. Farmers' Loan & Trust Co.* (1895) was reargued, a change that resulted in the decision that struck down a general income tax. The decision was overturned by ratification of the Sixteenth Amendment in 1913.

He retired, as he had earlier resolved to do, at the age of seventy-one, and lived out the years of his retirement in quiet comfort, shuttling between homes in Florida and the Lake Superior region of northern Michigan until his death in 1924 at age ninety-two.

Howell Edmunds Jackson

(1893–1895)

BIRTH: April 8, 1832, Paris, Tennessee.

EDUCATION: West Tennessee College, A.B., 1850; University of Virginia, 1851–1852; Cumberland University, 1856.

OFFICIAL POSITIONS: custodian of sequestered property for Confederate states, 1861–1865; judge, Court of Arbitration for Western Tennessee, 1875–1879; state legislature, 1880; U.S. senator, 1881–1886; judge, Sixth Federal Circuit Court, 1886–1891, U.S. Circuit Court of Appeals, 1891–1893.

SUPREME COURT SERVICE: nominated associate justice by President Benjamin Harrison February 2, 1893, to replace Lucius Q. C. Lamar, who had died; confirmed by the Senate February 18, 1893, by a voice vote; took judicial oath March 4, 1893; served until August 8, 1895; replaced by Rufus W. Peckham, nominated by President Grover Cleveland.

FAMILY: married Sophia Malloy in 1859; died 1873; six children, two died in infancy; married Mary E. Harding in April 1874; three children.

DEATH: August 8, 1895, Nashville, Tennessee.

In 1830 Alexander Jackson left his medical practice in Virginia and moved to Paris, Tennessee, with his wife Mary Hurt Jackson, the daughter of a Baptist minister. Two years later their eldest son, Howell Edmunds, was born. Howell grew up in Jackson, Tennessee, and studied classics at West Tennessee College, graduating at the age of eighteen. He continued his education at the University of Virginia from 1851 to 1852. After completing a year in the law school of Cumberland University in Lebanon, Tennessee, Jackson passed the bar and began practicing law in his hometown.

In 1859 Jackson moved to Memphis and formed the partnership Currin and Jackson, specializing in corporate, railroad, and banking cases, and he married a local woman, Sophia Malloy. After her death in 1873, Jackson wed Mary E. Harding, the daughter of General W. G. Harding, the owner of a three-thousand-acre thoroughbred stock farm near Nashville. The western part of the property, West Meade, became Jackson's home, where he lived with his second wife, their three children, and the four surviving children of his previous marriage.

Although opposed to secession, Jackson served the Confederacy as the receiver of confiscated property and after the Civil War was twice appointed to the Court of Arbitration of Western Tennessee. His younger brother, William Hicks Jackson—the husband of General Harding's daughter Selene, who inherited the Belle Meade plantation—was a famous brigadier general in the Confederate Army, known by his men as the "red fox."

In 1880 Jackson, a respected lawyer and antirepudiation Tennessean during Reconstruction, was elected to the state House of Representatives. Because of factions within the Democratic Party over the state debt, he was elected the following year to the U.S. Senate. A Whig before the war, Jackson had been able to win the needed support of Republicans and "state-credit" Democrats. In the Senate he served on the Post Office, Pensions, Claims, and Judiciary Committees and loyally defended President Grover Cleveland's tariff measures.

In 1886, at the president's request, Jackson reluctantly resigned before his Senate term expired to fill a vacancy on the Sixth Judicial Federal Circuit. When the U.S. Circuit Court of Appeals was established in 1891, Jackson became its first presiding judge.

In the Senate chamber, Jackson had been seated next to Benjamin Harrison, a Republican senator from Indiana. As president, Harrison remembered his former colleague and friend and nominated him to the Supreme Court on February 2, 1893, to fill the vacancy created by the death of Justice Lucius Q. C. Lamar. Grover Cleveland had been elected to a second term in November, and the lame-duck president realized Senate confirmation of a Republican nominee was unlikely. With the strong backing of Justice Henry B. Brown, who had known him on the Sixth Federal Circuit, Jackson was confirmed by the Senate February 18, 1893.

One year after his appointment, Jackson contracted a severe case of tuberculosis. Hoping to recuperate in the West, he took a leave from the Court in October 1894. But in May 1895 a full

Court was needed to hear a reargument of the case testing the constitutionality of income taxes because the eight active justices had been evenly divided on the question. Unwell but unwilling to resign, Jackson returned to Washington. Three months after his dissent from the Court's decision ruling income taxes unconstitutional, Jackson succumbed to tuberculosis at his home in Nashville.

Edward Douglass White
(1894–1910, 1910–1921)

BIRTH: November 3, 1845, Lafourche Parish, Louisiana.

EDUCATION: Mount St. Mary's College, Emmitsburg, Maryland, 1856; Georgetown College (University), Washington, D.C., 1857–1861; studied law at University of Louisiana (Tulane) and with Edward Bermudez; admitted to the bar in 1868.

OFFICIAL POSITIONS: Louisiana state senator, 1874; associate justice, Louisiana Supreme Court, 1878–1880; U.S. senator, 1891–1894.

SUPREME COURT SERVICE: nominated associate justice by President Grover Cleveland February 19, 1894, to replace Samuel Blatchford, who had died; confirmed by the Senate February 19, 1894, by a voice vote; took judicial oath March 12, 1894. Nominated chief justice of the United States by President William Howard Taft, December 12, 1910, to replace Melville Fuller, who had died; confirmed by the Senate December 12, 1910, by a voice vote; took judicial oath December 19, 1910; served until May 19, 1921; replaced as chief justice by former president Taft, appointed by President Warren G. Harding.

FAMILY: married Virginia Montgomery Kent, November 1894.

DEATH: May 19, 1921, in Washington, D.C.

White was born and raised in the deep South. His Irish-Catholic ancestors originally settled in Pennsylvania, but his peripatetic father, Edward White, moved his wife, Catherine Ringgold White, and their family farther into frontier country until they finally reached Louisiana. There they prospered on a large farm. White's father, a Whig, spent four years as a judge on the New Orleans city court and served five terms in the U.S. House of Representatives (1829–1834; 1839–1843) and one term as governor of Louisiana (1834–1838).

White received his early education at local Jesuit schools. In 1856 he enrolled for one year at Mount St. Mary's College in Emmitsburg, Maryland, and then entered Georgetown College (now University) in Washington, D.C. His academic career was interrupted by the Civil War. White left Georgetown in 1861, returned home, and joined the Confederate Army. He was captured in 1863 at Port Hudson, Louisiana, on the lower Mississippi River and spent the remainder of the war as a prisoner.

After the war, he began his legal career by reading law under the direction of Edward Bermudez, a successful New Orleans lawyer. Admitted to the Louisiana bar in 1868, White established a lucrative practice in New Orleans and became involved in Democratic politics. He was elected to the state Senate in 1874, and his support of Francis T. Nicholls in the 1877 gubernatorial election gained him, at age thirty-three, an appointment to the Louisiana Supreme Court the next year. Nicholls's successor, however, engineered White's removal from the court in 1880 through the passage of a law setting a minimum age requirement for justices that the youthful White failed to meet. Retribution came in 1888 when Nicholls was again elected governor and the state legislature gave one of Louisiana's U.S. Senate seats to Edward D. White.

White's short Senate career was marked by efforts to restrict the power of the federal government, except in matters protecting sugar farmers in the South from foreign competition. White himself farmed a large sugar-beet plantation. His unexpected appointment to the Supreme Court came in 1894. The beleaguered President Grover Cleveland had sought to replace Justice Samuel Blatchford, who had died July 7, 1893, with appointees from New York, Blatchford's home state. On two separate occasions, however, Cleveland's choices were rejected by the Senate in deference to the wishes of New York's senators, who were among his severest detractors. In frustration, Cleveland nominated White, who was approved immediately.

White's appointment to the chief justiceship was equally surprising. Chief Justice Melville Fuller died July 4, 1910, and President Taft, on December 12, 1910, elevated White to the post. He was the first associate justice successfully promoted to chief justice.

Historians tend to explain Taft's selection of White as chief justice in different ways. One side holds that Taft chose White, a southern Catholic, as a symbol of the president's desire to reduce lingering anti-South and anti-Catholic sentiments and to gain southern and Catholic support in the next election. The other, less sympathetic, view argues that Taft reckoned that he would have a better chance to become the chief justice himself (a lifelong ambition) after he left the White House if he appointed the aging White instead of the other contender for the post, the relatively young Charles Evans Hughes.

White's greatest legal contribution was his introduction of the "rule of reason" into the Court's interpretation of the Sherman Antitrust Act. The act outlawed all monopolies in restraint of trade, but White, from his earliest days on the Court, objected to a literal reading of the law; and he gradually persuaded his colleagues that only "unreasonable" restraints were prohibited.

In *Standard Oil v. United States* (1911) White wrote the opinion for a unanimous Court that broke up the oil company's monopoly on the grounds that it restricted free trade.

White wrote the opinion in *Guinn v. United States* (1915). In this case the Court struck down Oklahoma's "grandfather clause," a provision that exempted from a qualifying literacy test those whose ancestors had voted in the 1866 election. The law was intended to prevent blacks, who could not vote before ratification of the Fifteenth Amendment in 1870, from voting.

White was seventy-five years old and had been on the Court for twenty-six years, ten of them as chief justice, when he was taken ill May 13, 1921. He died May 19. His replacement was indeed William Howard Taft.

Rufus Wheeler Peckham

(1896–1909)

BIRTH: November 8, 1838, Albany, New York.

EDUCATION: Albany Boys' Academy; studied privately in Philadelphia.

OFFICIAL POSITIONS: district attorney, Albany County, 1869–1872; corporation counsel, City of Albany, 1881–1883; judge, New York Supreme Court, 1883–1886; judge, New York Court of Appeals, 1886–1895.

SUPREME COURT SERVICE: nominated associate justice by President Grover Cleveland December 3, 1895, to replace Howell E. Jackson, who had died; confirmed by Senate December 8, 1895, by a voice vote; took judicial oath January 6, 1896; served until October 24, 1909; replaced by Horace Harmon Lurton, nominated by President William Howard Taft.

FAMILY: married Harriette M. Arnold, November 14, 1866; two sons.

DEATH: October 24, 1909, Altamont, New York.

Rufus Wheeler Peckham was the son of Rufus Wheeler Peckham Sr. and Isabella Lacey Peckham, both members of old New York families. His father and his older brother, Wheeler Hazard Peckham, were both prominent lawyers and active in state Democratic politics. As district attorney for Albany County, the senior Rufus Peckham was elected to the U.S. House of Repre-

Rufus Wheeler Peckham

sentatives. He also served on the state supreme court and the New York Court of Appeals. During a vacation in 1873, Judge Peckham was lost at sea.

Young Rufus Peckham was educated at the Albany Boys' Academy and studied privately in Philadelphia. After a year in Europe with his brother, Rufus returned to Albany to read law in his father's firm, Peckham and Tremain. He joined the firm at the age of twenty-seven and in 1866 married Harriette M. Arnold, the daughter of a wealthy New York merchant.

Wheeler Peckham, a one-time president of the New York Bar Association, served as special counsel in the prosecution of the Tweed Ring in the city's political corruption trials.

Like his father before him, Peckham began his public career as district attorney for Albany County. In this post he gained recognition for his skillful prosecution and conviction of criminals involved in railroad express-car robberies. First as county attorney and then as corporation counsel for the city of Albany, 1881–1883, Peckham participated actively in upstate New York politics and became well acquainted with Gov. Grover Cleveland. Peckham's political connections, his legal reputation, and his respected name helped win him election to the state supreme court in 1883 and to the New York Court of Appeals three years later.

After Justice Howell E. Jackson's death, President Grover Cleveland nominated his friend associate justice of the Supreme Court. Peckham was confirmed without objection, although his brother's nomination two years earlier to fill Justice Blatchford's seat had been rejected due to political infighting. (Sen. David B.

Hill, D-N.Y., Wheeler's chief opponent, also succeeded in blocking the confirmation of William B. Hornblower, President Cleveland's earlier choice for the Blatchford seat.)

During his thirteen years on the bench, Peckham vigorously upheld the individual's right to contract and favored state regulation only when interstate commerce was directly and substantially affected. He wrote the Court's opinion in *Lochner v. New York* (1905), which struck down a state law limiting the hours bakers could work. Three years later, however, he voted to uphold an Oregon law regulating women's work hours.

Peckham died in Altamont, New York, on October 24, 1909, at the age of seventy.

Joseph McKenna

(1898–1925)

BIRTH: August 10, 1843, Philadelphia, Pennsylvania.

EDUCATION: Benicia Collegiate Institute, graduated in 1864; admitted to the bar in 1865.

OFFICIAL POSITIONS: district attorney, Solano County, California, 1866–1870; member, California Assembly, 1875–1876; U.S. representative, 1885–1892; judge, U.S. Ninth Judicial Circuit, 1892–1897; U.S. attorney general, 1897.

SUPREME COURT SERVICE: nominated associate justice by President William McKinley December 16, 1897, to replace Stephen J. Field, who had retired; confirmed by Senate January 21, 1898, by a voice vote; took judicial oath January 26, 1898; re-

Joseph McKenna

tired January 5, 1925; replaced by Harlan F. Stone, nominated by President Calvin Coolidge.

FAMILY: married Amanda Frances Bornemann, June 10, 1869; three daughters, one son.

DEATH: November 21, 1926, Washington, D.C.

Joseph McKenna, the first child of Irish immigrants John and Mary Ann Johnson McKenna, was born in the Irish quarter of Philadelphia. The growing popularity in Philadelphia of the staunchly anti-immigrant, anti-Catholic American Party contributed to the failure of John McKenna's bakery business. Hoping for success on the frontier, he took his family west, traveling third class on a Panamanian steamship to Benicia, California. In this small coastal town he succeeded in obtaining a better life for his family. He died when Joseph was fifteen years old.

Young McKenna attended public schools, graduated from the law department of the Benicia Collegiate Institute in 1864, and the following year was admitted to the California bar. The Republicans were becoming increasingly powerful in California and in 1861 elected railroad pioneer Leland Stanford the state's first Republican governor. McKenna switched his membership to the Republican Party, became acquainted with Stanford, and participated actively in political affairs. He was elected district attorney for Solano County in 1866. Three years later he married Amanda Frances Bornemann of San Francisco, his wife for fifty-five years.

For the ten years following his election to the state legislature in 1875, McKenna's political future was uphill. He was an unsuccessful candidate for the speakership of the California Assembly, from which he resigned after one term. Although twice nominated by his party for the U.S. Congress, he suffered two defeats prior to his election in 1885.

During four terms in the House, McKenna won passage of legislation extending railroad land grants, improving port facilities, and restricting the freedoms of Chinese workers. Considering his own immigrant parentage, McKenna's support for the latter is surprising, despite its popularity with his constituents.

As a member of the House Ways and Means Committee, McKenna became friends with its chairman, William McKinley. Another political ally in Congress was Sen. Leland Stanford. On Stanford's recommendation, President Benjamin Harrison appointed McKenna to California's Ninth Judicial Circuit. A circuit court judge for five years, McKenna was then promoted to attorney general. Within a year of assuming the post, he was nominated to the Supreme Court. When Justice Field resigned, President McKinley chose McKenna, another Californian and a trusted friend, to fill the vacancy. Over the objections of many to McKenna's ties with Stanford and western railroad interests, the Senate confirmed the appointment.

Realizing his own need for further legal training, McKenna studied for a few months at Columbia University Law School before taking office. Nevertheless, his early years on the bench proved difficult because of his lack of knowledge of the law and his inability to construct an opinion that expressed the convictions of his colleagues.

Scholars have pointed to McKenna's lack of judicial consistency, but in one area—the broad sweep of the commerce clause—he was consistent. In 1903 McKenna joined the majority in *Champion v. Ames,* a 5–4 decision upholding a federal law prohibiting the distribution of lottery tickets through the mail. In *Hipolite Egg Company v. United States* (1911) McKenna spoke for a unanimous Court in upholding the constitutionality of the Pure Food and Drug Act. In *Hoke v. United States* (1913) McKenna wrote the unanimous opinion upholding the Mann Act, which prohibited the interstate transportation of women for immoral purposes. All three of these cases were based on the federal government's ability to regulate interstate commerce.

McKenna served on the Court for twenty-six years. He was eighty-one years old and in failing health when Chief Justice Taft and the other members of the Court finally persuaded him to step down. The following year he died in his sleep at his home in Washington, D.C.

Oliver Wendell Holmes Jr.

(1902–1932)

BIRTH: March 8, 1841, Boston, Massachusetts.

EDUCATION: Harvard College, A.B., 1861; LL.B., 1866.

OFFICIAL POSITIONS: associate justice, Massachusetts Supreme Court, 1882–1899; chief justice, 1899–1902.

SUPREME COURT SERVICE: nominated associate justice by President Theodore Roosevelt December 2, 1902, to replace Horace Gray, who had died; confirmed by Senate December 4, 1902, by a voice vote; took judicial oath December 8, 1902; retired January 12, 1932, replaced by Benjamin N. Cardozo, nominated by President Herbert Hoover.

FAMILY: married Fanny Bowdich Dixwell, June 17, 1872.

DEATH: March 6, 1935; Washington, D.C.

Oliver Wendell Holmes Jr.'s father was a professor of anatomy at Harvard Medical School as well as a poet, essayist, and novelist in the New England literary circle that included Longfellow, Emerson, Lowell, and Whittier. Dr. Holmes's wife, Amelia Lee Jackson Holmes, was the third daughter of Justice Charles Jackson of the Massachusetts Supreme Court. Young Holmes attended a private school in Cambridge run by Epes Sargent Dixwell and received his undergraduate education at Harvard, graduating as class poet in 1861 as had his father thirty-two years before him.

Commissioned after graduation a second lieutenant in the Massachusetts Twentieth Volunteers, known as the Harvard Regiment, Holmes was wounded in three Civil War battles in three years. He was mustered out of the Army July 17, 1864, with the rank of captain in recognition of his bravery and gallant service. After the war, Holmes returned to Harvard to study law despite his father's conviction that "a lawyer can't be a great man."

He was admitted to the Massachusetts bar in 1867 and practiced in Boston for fifteen years, beginning with the firm of Chandler, Shattuck, and Thayer and later forming with Shattuck his own partnership. In 1872 Holmes married Fanny Bowdich Dixwell, the daughter of his former schoolmaster and a friend since childhood. They were married fifty-seven years.

During his legal career Holmes taught constitutional law at his alma mater, edited the *American Law Review,* and lectured on common law at the Lowell Institute. His twelve lectures were compiled in a volume entitled *The Common Law* and published shortly before his fortieth birthday after more than ten years of work. The London *Spectator* heralded Holmes's treatise as the most original work of legal speculation in decades. *The Common Law* was translated into German, Italian, and French.

In 1882 the governor of Massachusetts appointed Holmes—then a full professor at the Harvard Law School in a chair established by Boston lawyer Louis D. Brandeis—an associate justice of the Massachusetts Supreme Court. Holmes served on the state court for twenty years, the last three as chief justice, and wrote more than one thousand opinions, many of them involving labor disputes. Holmes's progressive labor views, criticized by railroad and corporate interests, were favorably considered by President Theodore Roosevelt during his search in 1902 for someone to fill the "Massachusetts seat" on the Supreme Court, vacated by the death of Horace Gray. Convinced of his compatibility with the administration's national policies, Roosevelt nominated Holmes, who was sixty-one years old. The Senate confirmed him without objection two days later.

Holmes's twenty-nine years of service on the Supreme Court spanned the tenures of Chief Justices Fuller, White, Taft, and Hughes and the administrations of Presidents Roosevelt, Taft, Wilson, Harding, Coolidge, and Hoover. For twenty-five years he never missed a session and walked daily the two and a half miles from his home to the Court. Like Justice Brandeis, Holmes voluntarily paid an income tax despite the majority's ruling that exempted federal judges. Unlike the idealistic and often moralistic Brandeis, with whom he is frequently compared, Holmes was pragmatic, approaching each case on its own set of facts without a preconceived notion of the proper result.

Although a lifelong Republican, on the Court Holmes did not fulfill Roosevelt's expectations as a loyal party man. Shortly after his appointment, he dissented from the Court's decision in 1904 to break up the railroad trust of the Northern Securities Company; his opinion surprised the nation and angered the president.

In his years on the Court, Holmes wrote 873 opinions and, although he is known as one of the great dissenters, he wrote proportionately fewer dissents than many other justices. His reputation rests on the clear writing and forcefulness of his dissents. In 1905 Holmes dissented in *Lochner v. New York.* Holmes argued for the right of a state to regulate working hours, in this case for bakers, some of whom were required to work one hundred hours per week.

Holmes is also known for the "clear and present danger" test for seditious speech in *Schenck v. United States* (1919). This unanimous decision upheld the conviction of a Socialist Party member who printed and distributed antidraft pamphlets at a time when the country was preparing for war. However, in *Abrams v. United States,* decided seven months later, Holmes dissented. In this case, the offensive material was a leaflet protesting American intervention in Russia. Holmes declared that the First Amendment protected speech unless it posed such a threat that an immediate response was necessary.

At the suggestion of Chief Justice Hughes and his colleagues on the bench, Holmes retired on January 12, 1932, at the age of ninety. A widower since 1929, he continued to spend his winters in Washington, D.C., and his summers in Beverly Farms, Massachusetts. He died at his Washington home two days before his ninety-fourth birthday.

William Rufus Day

(1903–1922)

BIRTH: April 17, 1849, Ravenna, Ohio.

EDUCATION: University of Michigan, A.B., 1870; University of Michigan Law School, 1871–1872.

OFFICIAL POSITIONS: judge, Court of Common Pleas, Canton, Ohio, 1886; first assistant U.S. secretary of state, 1897–1898; U.S. secretary of state, 1898; member, United States delegation, Paris Peace Conference, 1898–1899; judge, U.S. Court of Appeals for the Sixth Circuit, 1899–1903; umpire, Mixed Claims Commission, 1922–1923.

SUPREME COURT SERVICE: nominated associate justice by President Theodore Roosevelt February 19, 1903, to replace George Shiras Jr., who had resigned; confirmed by the Senate February 23, 1903, by a voice vote; took judicial oath March 2,

William Rufus Day

1903; resigned November 13, 1922; replaced by Pierce Butler, nominated by President Warren G. Harding.

FAMILY: married Mary Elizabeth Schaefer, 1875; four sons.
DEATH: July 9, 1923, Mackinac Island, Michigan.

William Day, the son of Luther Day and Emily Spalding Day, was raised in a family with a strong judicial background. His maternal great-grandfather, Zephania Swift, was the chief justice of Connecticut; his grandfather, Rufus Spalding, was a member of the Ohio Supreme Court; his father, Luther Day, served as chief justice of Ohio. It seemed predetermined, then, that William Day, after receiving his A.B. from the University of Michigan in 1870, should enter the law school at his alma mater, which he did after studying law for one year in his home town of Ravenna, Ohio. He attended law school for a year at the University of Michigan. He returned home to Ohio in 1872 and set up a law practice in Canton, about twenty-five miles from Ravenna.

Day established a solid reputation and a lucrative law practice in Canton, where he also became a good friend of another young attorney, William McKinley. Day and McKinley traveled in the same Republican circles, and McKinley soon came to rely on Day for help and counsel.

While McKinley's political fortunes took him to the U.S. House of Representatives (1877–1884; 1885–1891) and the governor's mansion (1892–1896), Day remained in Canton, married a local woman, and raised a family of four boys.

Day's popularity was so great in the Canton area that he was elected in 1886 judge of the Court of Common Pleas after receiving both the Democratic and Republican nominations.

Three years later he was appointed to the U.S. District Court by President Benjamin Harrison. However, his frail health prevented him from serving in that position.

When his friend McKinley was elected president, Day was named first assistant secretary of state. His job was to assist the aged and failing secretary of state, John Sherman, in performing the country's diplomatic chores. After the war between the United States and Spain over Cuba officially began April 11, 1898, Sherman was eased out of the State Department and replaced by Day, who had been closely involved in the events leading up to the outbreak of hostilities. Day served as secretary of state only from April 26, 1898 to August 26; during his brief tenure, however, he oversaw the delicate negotiations between the United States and Spain and was able to obtain assurances of neutrality and goodwill from the countries of Western Europe.

In August McKinley named Day to the U.S. commission to negotiate the terms of the peace with Spain. Day is credited with the plan to pay Spain $20 million for the Philippines instead of outright annexation.

His work on the peace commission finished, Day was named by McKinley in 1899 to the U.S. Court of Appeals for the Sixth Circuit, located in Cincinnati. Day enjoyed his four years on the bench—it was close to home, and his colleagues included William Howard Taft, the future president and Supreme Court chief justice, and Horace H. Lurton, a future associate justice.

Day was deeply shocked by the 1901 assassination of President McKinley. As a tribute to his longtime friend and patron, he began to mark McKinley's birthday with an annual memorial service. At one of these services, on January 29, 1903, Day first learned that McKinley's successor, Theodore Roosevelt, intended to name him to the Supreme Court. After Day introduced the president to the audience, Roosevelt surprised the crowd by referring to Day as "Mr. Justice Day." His appointment was announced officially February 19, 1903.

Day wrote the majority opinion in *Hammer v. Dagenhart* (1918), in which the Court overturned a federal law prohibiting the interstate shipment of goods made by child labor. However, he had ruled in a 1916 case that the federal government could regulate interstate commerce when moral and health hazards were involved.

Day retired from the Court November 13, 1922. He accepted an appointment from President Warren G. Harding to serve as an umpire on the Mixed Claims Commission, a board established to settle claims remaining from World War I. Day worked on the commission only until May 1923. He died July 9, 1923, at his summer home on Mackinac Island, Michigan.

William Henry Moody

(1906–1910)

BIRTH: December 23, 1853, Newbury, Massachusetts.
EDUCATION: Harvard College, A.B., cum laude, 1876; Harvard Law School, 1876–1877; read law with Richard Henry Dana.
OFFICIAL POSITIONS: city solicitor, Haverhill, 1888–1890;

William Henry Moody

district attorney, Eastern District of Massachusetts, 1890–1895; U.S. representative, 1895–1902; secretary of the Navy, 1902–1904; U.S. attorney general, 1904–1906.

SUPREME COURT SERVICE: nominated associate justice by President Theodore Roosevelt December 3, 1906, to replace Henry B. Brown, who had retired; confirmed by the Senate December 12, 1906, by a voice vote; took judicial oath December 17, 1906; retired November 20, 1910; replaced by Joseph R. Lamar, nominated by President William Howard Taft.

FAMILY: unmarried.

DEATH: July 2, 1917, Haverhill, Massachusetts.

William Moody was born to Henry L. Moody and Melissa A. Emerson Moody in a house that had been his family's home for more than two hundred years. He was raised in nearby Danvers, attended Phillips Academy in Andover, and, after a poor start at Harvard, graduated with honors in 1876. In the fall of that year he entered the Harvard School of Law but left in January 1877. To prepare for his entry to the bar he began an eighteen-month course of study in the law offices of Boston lawyer and author Richard Henry Dana. Although three years of study were normally required before an applicant was allowed to take the oral examination, an exception was made in Moody's case, and he passed easily.

Moody left Boston after his admittance to the bar in 1878 and established a private practice in Haverhill, Massachusetts. His clientele soon included most of the industries and manufacturers in the region. As his prestige grew, Moody became involved in Republican politics and in 1888 began his public career as city solicitor for Haverhill.

Two years later he was named district attorney for the Eastern District of Massachusetts. His most famous case (and that spread his name across the country) was the prosecution of Lizzie Borden, the alleged ax murderer of Fall River. Fall River was beyond Moody's venue, but he was called in to assist with the 1892 case, in which the defendant was acquitted by a sympathetic jury. Despite his loss, his adept handling of the state's case brought him to the attention of Massachusetts Republican Party leaders, notably Sen. Henry Cabot Lodge (1893–1924).

In 1895 Moody won a special election to fill the U.S. House seat in Massachusetts's Sixth Congressional District vacated by the death of Rep. William Cogswell (1887–1895). The same year, Moody met New York police commissioner Theodore Roosevelt, and the two men became close friends over the next few years.

In the House, Moody was respected for his mastery of details and facts. When Roosevelt became president after the assassination of William McKinley, Moody was one of the new president's first choices for his cabinet. As secretary of the Navy, Moody won increased congressional appropriations to enlarge and improve the U.S. fleet, which met with the hearty approval of President Roosevelt. He said of Moody, "We have never had as good a Secretary of the Navy."

Moody's next assignment in the Roosevelt administration was to replace Attorney General Philander Knox in 1904 and to continue the administration's prosecution of trusts. A dedicated progressive Republican, Moody personally argued for the government in the successful suit against the beef trust, *Swift and Company v. United States* (1905).

Moody's appointment to the Supreme Court was not without controversy; he was thought to be too radical. Opponents pointed to his eager prosecution of trusts and his enthusiasm for progressive reforms. Criticism notwithstanding, Moody was confirmed by the Senate December 12, 1906, to replace Justice Henry B. Brown.

Moody's Supreme Court career was shortened by the onslaught of a crippling form of arthritis that forced his retirement in 1910. In his brief career he wrote sixty-seven opinions, including five dissents. An important dissent came in *First Employers' Liability Case* (1908). Moody argued to uphold federal legislation designed make common carriers engaged in interstate commerce liable for deaths and injuries suffered by their employees on the job. Moody is also know for his opinion in *Twining v. New Jersey* (1908). In this case the Court refused to extend the Fifth Amendment protection against self-incrimination to state defendants.

Moody left the Court November 20, 1910. He returned home to Haverhill, where he died July 2, 1917.

Horace Harmon Lurton

(1910–1914)

BIRTH: February 26, 1844, Newport, Kentucky.

EDUCATION: Douglas University (University of Chicago), 1860; Cumberland Law School, L.B., 1867.

OFFICIAL POSITIONS: chancellor in equity, 1875–1878; judge, Tennessee Supreme Court, 1886–1893; judge, U.S. Court of Appeals for the Sixth Circuit, 1893–1909.

SUPREME COURT SERVICE: nominated associate justice by President William Howard Taft December 13, 1909, to replace Rufus W. Peckham, who had died; confirmed by Senate December 20, 1909, by a voice vote; took judicial oath January 3, 1910; served until July 12, 1914; replaced by James C. McReynolds, nominated by President Woodrow Wilson.

FAMILY: married Mary Francis Owen, September 1867; three sons, two daughters.

DEATH: July 12, 1914, Atlantic City, New Jersey.

Horace Harmon Lurton was born the same year Democrat James K. Polk defeated Whig Henry Clay for the presidency over the issue of annexation of the Republic of Texas. His parents, Sarah Ann Harmon Lurton and Dr. Lycurgus Leonidas Lurton, a physician who later became an Episcopal minister, moved the family to Clarksville, Tennessee, a town of fifteen thousand on the Cumberland River. When Lurton was sixteen the family moved again, this time to Chicago where he attended Douglas University until the outbreak of the Civil War.

Lurton served in the Confederate Army in both the Kentucky and Tennessee infantries before his capture during General Grant's siege of Fort Donelson. He escaped from Camp Chase in Columbus, Ohio, and joined General John Hunt Morgan's daredevil marauders, famous throughout the South for their surprise attacks on Union railroads, bridges, and telegraph stations. Lurton was captured again in July 1863. During his incarceration in one of the northernmost camps on Lake Erie he contracted tuberculosis. Fearing for her son's life, Sarah Ann Lurton went to Washington and succeeded in persuading President Lincoln to let her son return with her to Clarksville before the end of the war.

After his recuperation at home, Lurton attended law school at Cumberland University in Lebanon, Tennessee. He graduated in 1867, married Mary Francis Owen, the daughter of a local physician, and returned to Clarksville to practice law. Through his partner, James A. Bailey, who was elected to the U.S. Senate in 1877, Lurton became involved in Democratic politics. He was appointed by the governor to the Sixth Chancery Division of Tennessee, becoming at thirty-one the youngest chancellor in the state's history.

In 1878 Lurton returned to the practice of law in an eight-year partnership with ex-chancellor Charles G. Smith. During this period Lurton became a prosperous and well-respected Clarksville citizen as president of the Farmers' and Merchants' National Bank, vestryman of Trinity Episcopal Church, and trustee of the University of the South.

Lurton was elected to the Tennessee Supreme Court in 1886 and served for seven years. Immediately following his promotion to chief justice, he was appointed to the U.S. Court of Appeals for the Sixth Circuit by President Grover Cleveland. William Howard Taft was the presiding judge. Lurton succeeded him in office when Taft left to become governor general of the Philippines. In addition to his judicial responsibilities, Lurton taught constitutional law at Vanderbilt University from 1898 to 1905 and served as dean the following four years.

Close personal friendship as well as respect for his judicial ability prompted President Taft to make Lurton, then sixty-five, his first Supreme Court appointment. "There was nothing I had so much at heart in my whole administration," Taft said of his choice.

Lurton took a symbolic train ride northward to assume his new responsibilities. Explaining the personal significance of the trip he stated, "I felt that in appointing me, President Taft, aside from manifestations of his friendship, had a kindly heart for the South; that he wished to draw the South to him with cords of affection. So, being a southerner myself, I determined to go to Washington through the South—every foot of the way."

Lurton served only five years on the Court. He died of a heart attack July 12, 1914, in Atlantic City, New Jersey.

Charles Evans Hughes

(1910–1916, 1930–1941)

BIRTH: April 11, 1862, Glens Falls, New York.

EDUCATION: Madison College (now Colgate University), 1876–1878; Brown University, A.B., 1881, A.M., 1884; Columbia Law School, LL.B., 1884.

OFFICIAL POSITIONS: special counsel, New York state investigating commissions, 1905–1906; governor of New York, 1907–1910; U.S. secretary of state, 1921–1925; U.S. delegate, Washington Armament Conference, 1921; U.S. member, Permanent Court of Arbitration, 1926–1930; judge, Permanent Court of International Justice, 1928–1930.

SUPREME COURT SERVICE: nominated associate justice by President William Howard Taft April 25, 1910, to replace David J. Brewer, who had died; confirmed by Senate May 2, 1910, by a voice vote; took judicial oath October 10, 1910; resigned June 10, 1916, to become Republican presidential candidate; replaced by John H. Clarke, nominated by President Woodrow Wilson; nominated chief justice February 3, 1930, by President Herbert Hoover, to replace Chief Justice Taft, who had retired; confirmed by Senate February 13, 1930, by a 52–26 vote; took judicial oath February 24, 1930; retired July 1, 1941; replaced by Harlan F. Stone, nominated by President Franklin D. Roosevelt.

FAMILY: married Antoinette Carter, December 5, 1888; one son, three daughters.

DEATH: August 27, 1948, Osterville, Massachusetts.

Born during the Civil War, Charles Evans Hughes was the only child of David Charles Hughes, an abolitionist minister, and his wife Mary Catherine Connelly Hughes. When the Reverend Hughes became secretary of the American Bible Union in 1873, the family left the Adirondacks and moved to New York City. Charles was taught at home by his parents until age fourteen when he enrolled in Madison College (now Colgate University). Before his junior year he transferred to Brown University, chosen because of its Baptist tradition, which appealed to his parents, and its city location, which appealed to him. After graduation Hughes taught Greek, Latin, and algebra at the Delaware Academy in Delhi, New York, and clerked for the Wall Street firm Chamberlin, Carter, and Hornblower to earn money for law school. He graduated from Columbia in 1884 and passed the bar at age twenty-two with a score of ninety-nine and one-half.

Hughes then returned to Chamberlin, Carter, and Hornblower and married Antoinette Carter, the daughter of one of the partners. Two years later the firm became Carter, Hughes, and Cravath. Hughes's legal practice in New York City continued for twenty years, with an interim of three years teaching law at Cornell University.

In 1905 Hughes began investigating illegal rate-making practices and fraudulent insurance activities in New York as special counsel for the Stevens Gas Commission and the Armstrong Insurance Committee, established by the state legislature. His successful exposure of racketeering won him national recognition. Endorsed by President Theodore Roosevelt, Hughes defeated William Randolph Hearst in a 1906 race for governor and was reelected two years later.

When President William Howard Taft appointed Hughes to the Supreme Court to fill the vacancy left by Justice David Brewer's death in 1910, his nomination met with approval by the Court and the press. According to the liberal paper *The World*, "Mr. Taft could not have made a better or more popular selection." Justifying his acceptance of the seat on the Supreme Court to New York Republicans who envisioned for him a great political future, Hughes explained, "I had no right to refuse. A refusal on the ground that some time or other I might be a candidate for the Presidency . . . would have been absurd."

After six years on the Court, Hughes became a presidential candidate, endorsed by both the Republican Party and the Progressive Party. "Wilson with Peace and Honor or Hughes with Roosevelt and War?" was a popular slogan of the Democrats, critical of Hughes's advocacy of military preparedness against Germany. The former Supreme Court justice lost the 1916 election by only twenty-three electoral votes. He returned to the practice of law as senior partner in the New York firm Hughes, Rounds, Schurman, and Dwight.

When Warren G. Harding became president, he appointed Hughes secretary of state, a post he also held during the Coolidge administration. At the Washington Armament Conference in 1921 Hughes was instrumental in the agreement reached by the major powers to limit the naval race, end the Anglo-Japanese Alliance, and recognize China's open door diplomacy.

Unlike the general acclaim that greeted Hughes's Supreme Court appointment in 1910, his nomination as chief justice by President Herbert Hoover twenty years later met considerable opposition in the Senate. "No man in public life so exemplifies the influence of powerful combinations in the political and financial worlds as does Mr. Hughes," Sen. George W. Norris of Nebraska objected. Critics felt Hughes's representation of America's largest corporations after he left the State Department jeopardized his ability to defend the rights of the ordinary citizen on the Court. Supporters, on the other hand, pointed to his efforts on behalf of world peace during his legal career as a member of the Permanent Court of Arbitration in the Hague and the Permanent Court of International Justice. The Senate confirmed him February 13, 1930, by a 52–26 vote. His son, Charles Evans Hughes Jr., resigned the same day from his position as solicitor general.

Among Hughes's most important opinions as associate justice was the *Shreveport Rate Case* (1914). This opinion extended the federal government's regulation of rail rates to intrastate railroads, if the two were so intertwined that it would be impossible to regulate one without regulating the other. As chief justice, Hughes wrote the Court's opinion in several of the cases (that overturned New Deal legislation), including *Schechter Poultry Corp. v. United States* and *Panama Refining Co. v. Ryan*, both decided in 1935. But in *Home Building and Loan Assn. v. Blaisdell* (1934) Hughes upheld a state's emergency law designed to keep people from losing their homes during the Great Depression.

Hughes is also the author of the landmark freedom of the press case, *Near v. Minnesota* (1931). In *Near* the Court ruled, 5–4, that a law barring future publication of a newspaper that prints malicious or defamatory material is a prior restraint in violation of the First Amendment.

After eleven years of service as chief justice, Hughes informed President Franklin Roosevelt of his wish to retire due to "considerations of health and age." Justice Felix Frankfurter likened Hughes's ability to marshal the Court to "Toscanini lead[ing] an orchestra," and Justice William O. Douglas praised his "generosity, kindliness and forbearance."

In 1942, a year after his retirement, Hughes was awarded the American Bar Association medal for conspicuous service to jurisprudence. He died at his summer cottage on Cape Cod at the age of eighty-six.

Willis Van Devanter

(1911–1937)

BIRTH: April 17, 1859, Marion, Indiana.

EDUCATION: Indiana Asbury University, A.B., 1878; University of Cincinnati Law School, LL.B., 1881.

OFFICIAL POSITIONS: city attorney, Cheyenne, 1887–1888; member, Wyoming territorial legislature, 1888; chief justice, Wyoming Territory Supreme Court, 1889–1890; assistant attor-

Willis Van Devanter

ney general, Department of the Interior, 1897–1903; judge, U.S. Court of Appeals for the Eighth Circuit, 1903–1910.

SUPREME COURT SERVICE: nominated associate justice by President William Howard Taft December 12, 1910, to replace Edward D. White, who became chief justice; confirmed by U.S. Senate December 15, 1910, by a voice vote; took judicial oath January 3, 1911; retired June 2, 1937; replaced by Hugo L. Black, nominated by President Franklin D. Roosevelt.

FAMILY: married Dellice Burhans, October 10, 1883; two sons.

DEATH: February 8, 1941, in Washington, D.C.

Willis Van Devanter, the eldest of eight children of Isaac and Violetta Spencer Van Devanter, was born in Marion, Indiana. He attended Indiana Asbury (now DePauw) University and the University of Cincinnati Law School. After receiving his degree in 1881, Van Devanter joined his father's law firm in Marion. He married Dellice Burhans of Michigan, and in 1884 they moved to Cheyenne in the Wyoming Territory. There he established a practice and became involved in Republican politics by cultivating a close friendship with Gov. Francis E. Warren, who also became a U.S. senator. Warren served as head of the Republican Party in Wyoming and remained an influential friend.

Van Devanter served as city attorney in Cheyenne in 1887 and the following year was elected to the territorial legislature. He codified the territorial laws and statutes, which became the basis for the future state's constitution. In 1889, when Van Devanter was just thirty years old, President Benjamin Harrison named him chief justice of the Wyoming Territory Supreme

Court. He served for only one year before resigning to resume private practice.

Van Devanter enjoyed a thriving practice and remained active in Republican politics, serving as chairman of the Wyoming state committee (1892–1894) and as a member of the Republican National Committee (1896–1900). His service to the party was rewarded in 1897 when President William McKinley named him as assistant attorney general assigned to the Interior Department. There he relied on his years of experience in Wyoming to specialize in legal questions regarding public lands and Indian matters. He also found time to lecture at Columbian (now George Washington) University.

In 1903 President Theodore Roosevelt appointed Van Devanter to the U.S. Court of Appeals for the Eighth Circuit. His years on the bench were marked by a concern for jurisdictional questions, land claims, rights of railroads, and other complex technical areas.

President William Howard Taft December 12, 1910, named Van Devanter to the vacancy created by the promotion of Edward D. White to chief justice. Van Devanter's nomination was strongly opposed by several liberals, particularly William Jennings Bryan, who said that Van Devanter was "the judge that held that two railroads running parallel to each other for two thousand miles were not competing lines, one of the roads being that of Union Pacific," one of Van Devanter's former clients.

As one of the so-called Four Horsemen, the most consistently conservative members of the Court, Van Devanter voted to strike down several of President Roosevelt's measures aimed at stimulating the economy. He is also known for his opinion in *McGrain v. Daugherty* (1927), in which the Court affirmed Congress's subpoena power.

He retired from the Court June 2, 1937, and died February 8, 1941, in Washington, D.C.

Joseph Rucker Lamar

(1911–1916)

BIRTH: October 14, 1857, Elbert County, Georgia.

EDUCATION: University of Georgia, 1874–1875; Bethany College, A.B., 1877; Washington and Lee University, 1877.

OFFICIAL POSITIONS: member, Georgia legislature, 1886–1889; commissioner to codify Georgia laws, 1893; associate justice, Georgia Supreme Court, 1903–1905; member, mediation conference, Niagara Falls, Canada, 1914.

SUPREME COURT SERVICE: nominated associate justice by President William Howard Taft December 12, 1910, to replace William Henry Moody, who had retired; confirmed by the Senate December 15, 1910, by a voice vote; took judicial oath January 3, 1911; served until January 2, 1916; replaced by Louis D. Brandeis, nominated by President Woodrow Wilson.

FAMILY: married Clarinda Huntington Pendleton, January 30, 1879; two sons, one daughter.

DEATH: January 2, 1916, Washington, D.C.

Joseph Rucker Lamar

Joseph Rucker Lamar was named after his maternal grandfather on whose antebellum plantation, Cedar Grove in Ruckersville, Georgia, he was born and raised. Both the Ruckers and the Lamars were socially prominent Georgia families. Mary, the youngest daughter of Joseph Rucker, merchant, planter, banker, and founder of Ruckersville, married James Sanford Lamar of French Huguenot ancestry. Other notable family members were Mirabeau Buonaparte Lamar, president of the Republic of Texas from 1838 to 1841, and Lucius Quintus Cincinnatus Lamar, associate justice of the Supreme Court from 1888 to 1893.

After his mother's death when he was eight, Joseph Lamar left Cedar Grove and moved to Augusta, where his father became a minister in the Disciples of Christ church, a new Protestant denomination founded by Alexander Campbell, the president of Bethany College during James Lamar's attendance. Greatly influenced by Campbell, Joseph's father left his legal career to join the ministry. Woodrow Wilson's father was the minister of the leading Presbyterian church in Augusta, and the two boys became close friends.

Lamar attended Martin Institute and Richmond Academy in Georgia and the Penn Lucy Academy in Baltimore before enrolling in the University of Georgia. Consenting to his father's wishes, he transferred to Bethany College, from which he graduated in 1877. After reading law at Washington and Lee University and clerking for the well-known Augusta lawyer, Henry Clay Foster, Lamar passed the Georgia bar. He married Clarinda Huntington Pendleton, the daughter of the president of Bethany College, and they lived with her family for one year while he taught Latin at the college.

Lamar's legal practice began in 1880 when Foster asked him to become a partner. During their joint practice for more than ten years, Lamar served for two terms in the Georgia legislature. As elected representative for Richmond County, he continued studying the state's history of jurisprudence, his special field of interest, and wrote a number of essays. Lamar's research on Georgia's legal history was recognized in 1893 by the governor, who asked him to help rewrite Georgia's law codes.

During his legal practice, Lamar also served on the examining board for applicants to the Georgia bar. This experience helped prepare him for a seat on the Georgia Supreme Court, which he occupied from 1903 to 1905. Overworked and homesick for Augusta, Lamar resigned before his term expired and returned to private law practice, this time in a partnership specializing in railroad law with E. H. Callaway, a former superior court judge.

President William Howard Taft nominated Lamar associate justice of the Supreme Court December 12, 1910, much to the Georgian's surprise. He had become acquainted with the president during two brief vacations in Augusta. Lamar did not expect to be confirmed: not only was he little known outside of the South but also he was a Democrat. Only in the appointments of Justices Stephen J. Field, Howell E. Jackson, and Horace Lurton had party lines been crossed. But the Senate confirmed him five days after his nomination.

His best-known opinion came in *Gompers v. Bucks Stove and Range Company* (1911). In keeping with the times, the Court upheld the legality of an injunction against boycotts, one of the labor movement's most powerful weapons.

During his last term Justice Lamar overworked himself in the performance of his judicial responsibilities. He suffered a stroke in September 1916 and died three months later at fifty-eight after only five years on the bench.

"The whole country has reason to mourn," President Wilson telegraphed Clarinda Lamar. "It has lost an able and noble servant. I have lost in him one of my most loved friends."

Mahlon Pitney

(1912–1922)

BIRTH: February 5, 1858, Morristown, New Jersey.

EDUCATION: College of New Jersey (Princeton), A.B., 1879; A.M., 1882.

OFFICIAL POSITIONS: U.S. representative, 1895–1899; New Jersey State senator, 1899–1901; president, New Jersey Senate, 1901; associate justice, New Jersey Supreme Court, 1901–1908; chancellor of New Jersey, 1908–1912.

SUPREME COURT SERVICE: nominated associate justice by President William Howard Taft February 19, 1912, to replace John Marshall Harlan, who had died; confirmed by the Senate March 13, 1912, by a 50–26 vote; took judicial oath March 18, 1912; retired December 31, 1922; replaced by Edward T. Sanford, nominated by President Warren G. Harding.

Mahlon Pitney

FAMILY: married Florence T. Shelton, November 14, 1891; two sons, one daughter.

DEATH: December 9, 1924, Washington, D.C.

The second son of Henry Cooper Pitney and Sarah Louisa Halsted Pitney was born on his family's farm in Morristown, New Jersey. At least four of his forebears fought in the Revolutionary War, including his great-grandfather, for whom he was named. Pitney attended the College of New Jersey, now Princeton University, and graduated in 1879. Woodrow Wilson was a classmate. He received his legal education from his father, "a walking encyclopedia of law," and after passing the New Jersey bar in 1882 practiced for seven years in the industrial iron town of Dover. When his father was appointed vice-chancellor of New Jersey in 1889, Pitney moved back to Morristown to take over his legal practice. At the age of thirty-three he married Florence T. Shelton.

The popular choice among New Jersey Republicans, Pitney was elected to a Fourth District congressional seat in 1894. As a member of Congress, he endorsed conservative monetary policies and easily won a second term with the additional support of Democrats who favored gold-backed currency. Pitney resigned January 5, 1899, after his election to the New Jersey Senate.

Party leader William J. Sewall advised Pitney to remain in the legislature for a few years before running for governor, the political office to which he most aspired. When Republicans gained control of the New Jersey senate, Pitney was elected its president. Appointment to the New Jersey Supreme Court by Governor Foster M. Voorhees in 1901 altered his gubernatorial ambitions. For the next twenty years Pitney pursued a judicial career, the culmination of which was the position of chancellor of New Jersey. His father had been vice-chancellor nineteen years before.

Pitney was greatly surprised when, on February 19, 1912, President William Howard Taft named him to the U.S. Supreme Court. They had met just seven days before at a dinner party in Newark and discussed another associate justice of the New Jersey Supreme Court, Francis J. Swayze, who was being considered for the bench. After the Pitney nomination, Taft acknowledged, "I did consider with a good deal of care another lawyer from New Jersey."

Confirmation by the Senate followed in less than a month, although liberal senators and union leaders objected to him because of his antilabor record as a New Jersey judge. After the 50–26 vote in favor of confirmation, Pitney received a congratulatory telegram from New Jersey governor and former Princeton classmate Woodrow Wilson, who assured him "a better choice could not have been made."

His opposition to expanding the rights of workers continued during his tenure on the Court. He wrote the Court's opinion in *Coppage v. Kansas* (1915), which overturned a statute outlawing "yellow dog" contracts. Pitney wrote that a worker has no right to join a union and stay in the employ of a business that does not hire union members.

Mental and physical stress forced Pitney to resign at age sixty-four, after ten years of service. He suffered a stroke in August 1922 and retired in December. Pitney's death two years later in Washington, D.C., has been attributed to the strain of overwork while on the Court.

James Clark McReynolds

James Clark McReynolds

(1914–1941)

BIRTH: February 3, 1862, Elkton, Kentucky.

EDUCATION: Vanderbilt University, B.S., 1882; University of Virginia, LL.B., 1884.

OFFICIAL POSITIONS: assistant U.S. attorney, 1903–1907; U.S. attorney general, 1913–1914.

SUPREME COURT SERVICE: nominated associate justice by President Woodrow Wilson August 19, 1914, to replace Horace H. Lurton, who died; confirmed by the Senate August 29, 1914, by a 44–6 vote; took judicial oath October 12, 1914; retired January 31, 1941; replaced by James F. Byrnes, nominated by President Franklin D. Roosevelt.

FAMILY: unmarried.

DEATH: August 24, 1946, in Washington, D.C.

James McReynolds was born to John McReynolds, a noted surgeon, and Ellen Reeves McReynolds in a Kentucky community that exhibited considerable sympathy for the Confederacy during the Civil War. He was raised on a plantation by highly moral parents who were members of the fundamentalist Campbellite religious sect.

After receiving his B.S. from Vanderbilt University, where he was class valedictorian, McReynolds studied law at the University of Virginia. He received his LL.B. in 1884 and returned to Nashville to practice law. His legal business in Nashville went uninterrupted until 1903, except for two years as secretary to Sen. Howell E. Jackson, a Tennessee Democrat who later served on the Supreme Court. Representing primarily corporate clients, McReynolds gained a reputation as a meticulous lawyer, if a weak advocate. In 1900 he took a part-time position teaching commercial law at Vanderbilt University.

McReynolds ran for Congress in 1896 as a "Gold Democrat" with some Republican support, but his arrogant and standoffish manners while campaigning alienated a majority of the voters. His candidacy, however, provided him with a measure of prominence in the Democratic Party.

In 1903 he was appointed an assistant U.S. attorney in Theodore Roosevelt's administration. During his four years at the Justice Department, McReynolds handled several antitrust prosecutions, including the court battles with the anthracite coal trust and the tobacco trust. So involved was he in trustbusting that he once referred to the American Tobacco Company as a group of "commercial wolves and highwaymen."

He resigned from the U.S. attorney's office in 1907 and took up law practice in New York City. He continued, however, to assist the Justice Department with antitrust cases over the next several years. A Wilson supporter in the election of 1912, he was named U.S. attorney general in the new administration. Although he served in the post for little more than a year, McReynolds managed to anger several members of Congress and executive branch officials with his temper and haughtiness. To show his continued support for McReynolds and, at the same time, remove him from a political position, Wilson named him to the Supreme Court August 19, 1914. He replaced Justice Horace H. Lurton, also from Tennessee, who had died in July.

McReynolds was part of the voting bloc known as the Four Horsemen. They earned the nickname because of their unfailing opposition to President Franklin D. Roosevelt and the economic recovery legislation he had pushed through Congress. When the judicial tide began to turn against McReynolds, he retired from the Court January 31, 1941. He died August 24, 1946, in Washington, D.C.

Louis Dembitz Brandeis

(1916–1939)

BIRTH: November 13, 1856, Louisville, Kentucky.

EDUCATION: Harvard Law School, LL.B., 1877.

OFFICIAL POSITIONS: "people's attorney," Public Franchise League and Massachusetts State Board of Trade, 1897–1911; counsel, New England Policyholders' Protective Committee, 1905; special counsel, wage and hour cases in California, Illinois, Ohio, and Oregon, 1907–1914; counsel, Ballinger-Pinchot investigation, 1910; chairman, arbitration board, New York garment workers' labor disputes, 1910–1916.

SUPREME COURT SERVICE: nominated associate justice by President Woodrow Wilson January 28, 1916, to replace Joseph R. Lamar, who had died; confirmed by the Senate June 1, 1916, by a 47–22 vote; took judicial oath June 15, 1916; retired February 13, 1939; replaced by William O. Douglas, nominated by President Franklin D. Roosevelt.

FAMILY: married Alice Goldmark, March 23, 1891; two daughters.

DEATH: October 5, 1941, Washington, D.C.

Louis Dembitz Brandeis was the son of Adolph and Fredericka Dembitz Brandeis, Jews who emigrated from Bohemia after the unsuccessful democratic revolts of 1848. His father was a prosperous grain merchant who provided his family with comfort, education, and culture. Having completed two years of preparatory studies at the Annen-Realschule in Dresden, but without a college degree, Brandeis enrolled at Harvard Law School when he was eighteen years of age. He graduated in 1877 with the highest average in the law school's history. After eight months practicing law in St. Louis, Brandeis returned to Cambridge—for him "the world's center"—and with Bostonian Samuel D. Warren Jr., who ranked second in their law school class, opened a one-room office downtown.

Warren and Brandeis and the successor firm Brandeis, Dunbar, and Nutter handled a variety of cases and were highly successful. By the time he was thirty-five, Brandeis was earning more than $50,000 a year. He and his wife, Alice Goldmark of New York, preferred to live simply, however, and set a ceiling on their personal expenditures of $10,000 a year. As a young lawyer Brandeis devoted many hours to his alma mater. He helped raise funds for a teaching post for Oliver Wendell Holmes Jr. and was one of the founders of the *Harvard Law Review*.

The turn of the century marked the rapid growth in America of corporate monopolies—the "curse of bigness," as Brandeis described it. He chose to protect the rights not of special interest groups but of the general public, and usually without a fee for his services. Brandeis initiated sliding scale gas rates in Boston that lowered consumer costs while raising corporate dividends and instituted savings bank insurance policies, another reform later implemented in the rest of the country. He defended municipal control of Boston's subway system and opposed the monopolistic practices of the New Haven Railroad. He arbitrated labor disputes in New York's garment industry and established the constitutionality of state maximum hour and minimum wage statutes. For thirty-seven years Brandeis devoted his time, energy, and talents to a host of public causes. He called himself an "attorney for the situation," but the press adopted the popular title "people's attorney."

President Wilson respected Brandeis and often sought his opinion. He nominated him associate justice of the Supreme Court January 28, 1916, to fill the vacancy left by Justice Joseph Lamar's death. Vicious opposition to his appointment ensued. One particularly vituperative critic described Brandeis as a "business-baiter, stirrer up of strife, litigious lover of hate and unrest, destroyer of confidence, killer of values, commercial coyote, spoiler of pay envelopes."

Factory owners paying higher wages, New Haven Railroad stockholders, moguls in the Boston transit system, insurance and gas industries—in short, all the losers in court—united to voice their objections to the appointment. Among those seeking satisfaction for past injuries was William Howard Taft. His administration had been embarrassed by an investigation led in part by Brandeis of the conservation practices of Secretary of the Interior Richard A. Ballinger.

The former president, ambitious for a justiceship himself, described the nomination as "one of the deepest wounds that I have had as an American and a lover of the Constitution" and spoke of the "indelible stain" on the Wilson administration that confirmation would bring.

Another critic, Clarence W. Barron, editor and publisher of the *Wall Street Journal,* also felt the choice was unwise: "There is only one redeeming feature in the nomination and that is that it will assist to bury Mr. Wilson in the next Presidential election." The president viewed the political climate differently. He believed Brandeis was a smart choice who would attract the needed Progressive vote. Wilson could not count on a divided Republican Party to ensure his reelection.

During four months of acrimonious debate over his appointment, Brandeis quietly pursued his legal practice. He went to the office every day and did not resort to personal attacks against his opponents. "Your attitude while the wolves yelp is sublime," his young nephew wrote.

The hearings in the Senate Judiciary Committee turned up no valid grounds for rejection. According to Sen. Thomas J. Walsh, Brandeis's only "real crime" was that "he had not stood in awe of the majesty of wealth." One of his supporters from the Harvard Law School, Arthur Hill, attributed the opposition to the fact that "Mr. Brandeis is an outsider, successful and a Jew."

Brandeis was confirmed by the Senate on June 1, 1916, by a vote of 47–22, becoming the first Jewish justice.

His prolabor positions led to many dissents in cases favoring employers' rights over those of workers. A staunch believer in the rights of the individual, Brandeis also dissented when the Court upheld the government's right to wiretap. He said the Founding Fathers had included in the Constitution the "right to be let alone."

At eighty-two, Brandeis resigned from the Court but not from public service. After twenty-two years on the bench, he devoted the last two years of his life to the Zionist movement and a boycott of German products. As the *New York Times* noted upon his retirement in 1939, "the storm against him . . . seems almost incredible now."

John Hessin Clarke

(1916–1922)

BIRTH: September 18, 1857, Lisbon, Ohio.

EDUCATION: Western Reserve University, A.B., 1877, A.M., 1880.

OFFICIAL POSITIONS: federal judge, U.S. District Court for Northern District of Ohio, 1914–1916.

SUPREME COURT SERVICE: nominated associate justice by President Woodrow Wilson July 14, 1916, to replace Charles Evans Hughes, who had resigned; confirmed by the Senate July 24, 1916, by a voice vote; took judicial oath October 9, 1916;

John Hessin Clarke

resigned September 18, 1922; replaced by George Sutherland, nominated by President Warren G. Harding.

FAMILY: unmarried.

DEATH: March 22, 1945, San Diego, California.

John Hessin Clarke was the son of John and Melissa Hessin Clarke, Irish Protestants. His father had left Ireland in 1830 and settled in Lisbon, Ohio, the county seat, where he practiced law and participated in liberal Democratic politics. His son graduated Phi Beta Kappa from Western Reserve College in Hudson, Ohio, and returned to Lisbon to study law under his father's tutelage. He passed the bar with honors in 1878 and joined his father's practice.

In 1880 Clarke moved to Youngstown where his career in corporate law began. Under his ownership and direction, the town newspaper the *Vindicator* became a strong voice for progressive reform. A member of the Youngstown literary society, Clarke lectured on Shakespeare and James Russell Lowell. He was an honorary life trustee of the Youngstown Public Library and bequeathed the library $100,000 in his will.

Clarke left Youngstown and his legal practice of seventeen years to join the Cleveland firm of Williamson and Cushing in 1897. Although he represented corporate clients such as the Nickel Plate Railroad and the makers of Pullman railway cars, he remained true to his liberal politics and advocated antitrust and antirebate legislation. He even favored municipal ownership of street railways. A progressive reformer, Clarke supported suffrage for women, direct election of senators, and public disclosure of campaign expenditures.

In 1894 he ran for the U.S. Senate but was defeated by incumbent Calvin S. Brice. As chairman of the Ohio State Democratic Sound Money Convention, Clarke disagreed with William Jennings Bryan's free silver populism and split from the Democrats at the 1896 national convention over that issue. He ran for the Senate a second time in 1914 but withdrew when another Irishman, Timothy Hogan, announced his candidacy.

After more than thirty-five years in the legal profession and progressive politics, Clarke received his first federal post. In 1914 President Wilson appointed him federal judge for the Northern District of Ohio.

When Charles Evans Hughes resigned from the Court to run against Wilson, the president considered nominating Attorney General Tom Gregory or Republican senator Warren G. Harding to fill the vacancy. He decided instead on John Clarke because he wanted a decidedly progressive justice with an antitrust record on Chief Justice White's staid court.

After his nomination, Clarke was described by the *New York World* as "singularly like Brandeis in having been a successful corporation lawyer whose practice served only to quicken his sympathies and activities for the causes of political and social justice." Indeed, President Wilson had hoped that Clarke would join Brandeis "to restrain the court from the extreme reactionary course which it seem[ed] inclined to follow." He was therefore greatly disappointed when Clarke resigned from the Court to promote American participation in the League of Nations, even though the league was Wilson's own dream. Clarke informed the president he would "die happier" working for world peace rather than devoting his time "to determining whether a drunken Indian had been deprived of his land before he died or whether the digging of a ditch was constitutional or not."

From 1922 to 1930 Clarke presided over the League of Nations' Non-Partisan Association of the United States and—against the advice of his physician, who was concerned about his heart—spoke on its behalf across the country.

At the age of eighty, Clarke emerged unexpectedly from his retirement in San Diego to endorse over nationwide radio President Franklin D. Roosevelt's Court-packing plan. He died March 22, 1945, shortly before the convening of the San Francisco conference that created the United Nations.

William Howard Taft

(1921–1930)

BIRTH: September 15, 1857, Cincinnati, Ohio.

EDUCATION: Yale University, A.B., class salutatorian, 1878; Cincinnati Law School, LL.B., 1880.

OFFICIAL POSITIONS: assistant prosecuting attorney, Hamilton County, Ohio, 1881–1883; assistant county solicitor, Hamilton County, 1885–1887; judge, Ohio Superior Court, 1887–1890; U.S. solicitor general, 1890–1891; judge, U.S. District Court for the Sixth Circuit, 1892–1900; chairman, Philippine Commission, 1900–1901; governor general of the Philippines,

William Howard Taft

1901–1904; secretary of war, 1904–1908; president of the United States, 1909–1913; joint chairman, National War Labor Board, 1918–1919.

SUPREME COURT SERVICE: nominated chief justice by President Warren G. Harding June 30, 1921, to replace Chief Justice Edward D. White, who had died; confirmed by the Senate June 30, 1921, by a voice vote; took judicial oath July 11, 1921; retired February 3, 1930; replaced by Chief Justice Charles Evans Hughes, nominated by President Herbert Hoover.

FAMILY: married Helen Herron, June 19, 1886; two sons, one daughter.

DEATH: March 8, 1930, in Washington, D.C.

Public service was a tradition in the Taft family; William Howard Taft extended it to its limit during his lifetime. His grandfather, Peter Rawson Taft, was a judge on the probate and county courts in Windham County, Vermont. His father, Alphonso Taft, served two terms on the Ohio Superior Court before he was named secretary of war in the last months of the administration of Ulysses S. Grant. He also served briefly in the Grant administration as attorney general, and later was ambassador to Austria-Hungary and Russia under President Chester A. Arthur. Taft's mother, Louisa Maria Torrey Taft, was Alphonso's second wife. William's brother, Charles Phelps Taft, a Republican from Ohio, served a term in the U.S. House of Representatives, 1895–1897.

Born in Cincinnati, Taft received an A.B. in 1878 from Yale University, where he was the salutatorian of his graduating class. He entered Cincinnati Law School and took a job as a law reporter for the *Cincinnati Commercial*. He continued to report for the newspaper through 1880, the year in which he received his LL.B. and was admitted to the bar.

In 1886 he married Helen Herron. They had one daughter and two sons, one of whom, Robert A. Taft, served in the U.S. Senate, from 1939 until his death in 1953, and was one of its most powerful leaders. Taft's grandson, Robert Taft Jr., served several terms in the House of Representatives and the Senate from 1971 to 1976.

In 1881 Taft plunged into Republican politics and gave his support to a candidate for county prosecutor. After his candidate won, Taft was selected to be an assistant county prosecutor. He went back to private practice in 1883.

Taft was named to a two-year term as assistant county solicitor for Hamilton County in 1885 and, in 1887, when he was barely thirty years old, was appointed to the Ohio Superior Court.

He sat on the superior court bench until President Benjamin Harrison in 1890 named him solicitor general. In 1892, after Congress created additional judgeships for the federal circuit courts, Taft sought and received appointment to the Sixth Circuit.

Taft remained on the circuit court for eight years. He left reluctantly in 1900 when President William McKinley asked him to head a commission established to ensure the smooth transition from military to civilian government in the Philippines in the aftermath of the Spanish-American War. In 1901 he was made governor general of the Philippines, a position he held until President Theodore Roosevelt named him secretary of war to replace Elihu Root in 1904.

Once in the cabinet, Taft became one of Roosevelt's closest advisers; the president increasingly relied on Taft to handle important matters for the administration. As secretary of war Taft was in command of the Panama Canal project and made a goodwill tour of the site. He also was dispatched in 1906 to Cuba to investigate reports of revolutionary activity.

As Taft's prestige grew, so did his influence in the Republican Party. With Roosevelt's backing he won the party's nomination for president and the subsequent election in 1908. He was sworn in as the twenty-ninth president of the United States March 4, 1909.

The presidency was a post that Taft did not particularly covet—he would have preferred a seat on the Supreme Court as chief justice, but he ran at the urging of his wife and Republican Party regulars. His single term in office was not controversial. It saw the institution of the postal savings system and the Tariff Board, the intervention of American troops in the Dominican Republic, the ratification of the Sixteenth Amendment to the Constitution, and a continuation of the trustbusting begun under Theodore Roosevelt.

Taft also named six men to the Supreme Court, including a chief justice, Edward D. White. The others were Horace H. Lurton, Charles Evans Hughes (who resigned from the Court to run for president in 1916, lost, and was named chief justice in 1930 by President Herbert Hoover to replace Taft), Willis Van Devanter,

Joseph R. Lamar, and Mahlon Pitney. When Taft was named chief justice in 1921, only two of his appointees, Van Devanter and Pitney, were still on the bench.

Soon after he was elected president, Taft began to fall out of favor with former president Roosevelt. The two men came to represent opposing sides of a division within the Republican Party. When Taft was renominated in 1912, Roosevelt ran for president under the banner of the Bull Moose Party and effectively splintered the Republican vote. After the election, which was won by Democrat Woodrow Wilson, Taft described Roosevelt as "the most dangerous man that we have had in the country since its origin."

After leaving the White House, Taft taught constitutional law at Yale University, served a year as president of the American Bar Association, wrote magazine articles and was a frequent participant on the lecture circuit. He was elected president of the League to Enforce Peace in 1915. In 1916 he and four other former presidents of the American Bar Association joined with current president Elihu Root in writing to the U.S. Senate to register their disapproval of President Wilson's nomination of Louis D. Brandeis to the Supreme Court. During this period Taft also continued discreetly to publicize his desire to be named to the Court, especially as chief justice.

Taft served as the joint chairman of the National War Labor Board, 1918–1919. An enthusiastic advocate of the League of Nations, he embarked on a fifteen-state tour in an attempt to rally support for it. His greatest ambition was achieved when President Harding named him chief justice June 30, 1921, to replace Chief Justice White.

Taft can be credited with modernizing procedures at the Court and cutting down on its workload. He created the Judicial Conference of the United States, which fosters cooperation among the federal judiciary's many courts. He secured passage of the Judiciary Act of 1925, giving the Supreme Court greater power to decide which cases to hear. He also lobbied Congress to provide funds for the Supreme Court building, but he did not live to see it completed. The only person in U.S. history to hold both the presidency and the chief justiceship, Taft died March 8, 1930.

George Sutherland

(1922–1938)

BIRTH: March 25, 1862, Buckinghamshire, England.

EDUCATION: Brigham Young (University) Academy, 1879–1881; University of Michigan Law School, 1882.

OFFICIAL POSITIONS: Utah state senator, 1896–1900; U.S. representative, 1901–1903; U.S. senator, 1905–1917; chairman, advisory committee to the Washington Conference for the Limitation of Naval Armaments, 1921; U.S. counsel, Norway-United States arbitration, The Hague, 1921–1922.

SUPREME COURT SERVICE: nominated associate justice by President Warren G. Harding September 5, 1922, to replace Justice John H. Clarke, who had resigned; took judicial oath

George Sutherland

October 2, 1922; confirmed by the Senate September 5, 1922, by a voice vote; retired January 17, 1938; replaced by Stanley F. Reed, nominated by President Franklin D. Roosevelt.

FAMILY: married Rosamund Lee, June 18, 1883; two daughters, one son.

DEATH: July 18, 1942, Stockbridge, Massachusetts.

Sutherland was brought to the United States in 1863 by his parents, Alexander George Sutherland and Frances Slater Sutherland. His father, a recent convert to the Church of Jesus Christ of Latter-day Saints, settled his family in Springville in the Utah Territory. The senior Sutherland soon deserted the Mormons and moved the family to Montana. They returned to Utah in 1869, settling in Provo. George Sutherland learned the value of thrift and hard work in his childhood—he left school at age twelve to help support the family. By the time he was sixteen, however, he had saved enough money to enroll at Brigham Young Academy in Provo, where he stayed for three years. He then worked a year for the company building the Rio Grande Western Railroad and in 1882 entered the University of Michigan Law School. He studied law for only one year before passing the bars in Michigan and Utah. He started a law practice in Provo and married Rosamund Lee of Beaver, Utah.

After ten years in Provo, Sutherland in 1893 moved to Salt Lake City. The next year he helped found the Utah Bar Association. When the territory achieved statehood in 1896, Sutherland, running as a Republican, was elected to the first state senate. In 1900 he was elected to the U.S. House of Representatives. He declined to run for a second term in the House, but was elected in 1904 to the U.S. Senate.

During his first term in the Senate, Sutherland endorsed several reform measures, including the Pure Food and Drug Act (1906), the Postal Savings Act (1910), and a compensation bill for workers injured in interstate commerce (1911–1912). He also played a major role in the revision and codification of federal criminal statutes. Among the bills he opposed were statehood for Arizona and New Mexico (1912)—because their constitutions provided for recalls, initiatives, and referenda—the Federal Reserve Act (1913), the Sixteenth Amendment (1913), the Clayton Antitrust Act (1914), and the Federal Trade Commission Act (1914). He also opposed the nomination of Louis D. Brandeis to the Supreme Court.

In 1916 Sutherland failed in his attempt to be renominated by the Utah Republican Party. He stayed in Washington, D.C., practiced law, and remained in touch with his former Senate colleague, Warren Harding. Sutherland developed into one of Harding's closest advisers and worked on his successful presidential campaign in 1920. Soon thereafter Sutherland represented the Harding administration as chairman of the advisory committee to the Washington Conference for the Limitation of Naval Armaments in 1921 and as counsel in arbitration between Norway and the United States over matters of shipping.

President Harding named Sutherland to the Supreme Court when Justice John H. Clarke unexpectedly resigned to work for the cause of world peace. Sutherland joined Justices James McReynolds, Willis Van Devanter, and Pierce Butler (on the Court in 1923) to form a bloc known as the Four Horsemen. The bloc voted consistently to void regulatory and social legislation, which they saw as infringing the rights of individuals to make contracts. For example, in 1923 Sutherland wrote the opinion in *Adkins v. Children's Hospital*, in which the Court ruled unconstitutional the District of Columbia's minimum wage law for women.

Sutherland retired from the Court January 17, 1938, and died in Stockbridge, Massachusetts, July 18, 1942.

Pierce Butler

(1923–1939)

BIRTH: March 17, 1866, Pine Bend, Minnesota.

EDUCATION: Carleton College, A.B., B.S., 1887.

OFFICIAL POSITIONS: assistant county attorney, Ramsey County, Minnesota, 1891–1893; county attorney, 1893–1897.

SUPREME COURT SERVICE: nominated associate justice by President Warren G. Harding November 23, 1922, to replace William R. Day, who had retired; confirmed by Senate December 21, 1922, by a 61–8 vote; took judicial oath January 2, 1923; served until November 16, 1939; replaced by Frank Murphy, nominated by President Franklin D. Roosevelt.

FAMILY: married Annie M. Cronin, August 25, 1891; eight children.

DEATH: November 16, 1939, Washington, D.C.

Pierce Butler, born on St. Patrick's Day, was the sixth of Patrick and Mary Gaffney Butler's eight children. His parents,

Pierce Butler

minded by Taft of the political advantages of a Butler appointment: Taft, a Protestant, had replaced Chief Justice White, a Catholic, and another Catholic was needed on the bench.

Although Taft succeeded in convincing President Harding of Butler's merits, Senate liberals were not so easily persuaded. Their primary objection concerned Butler's defense of several railroads—the Northern Pacific, the Great Northern, and the Chicago, Burlington, and Quincy—during his legal practice. Also criticized were Butler's actions as regent of the University of Minnesota from 1907 to 1924. Faculty members whose economic or political views differed from his own had been dismissed or refused tenure. The liberal academics claimed he was a reactionary with no tolerance for dissent. Despite the opposition to Butler's appointment, only eight senators voted against his confirmation December 21, 1922.

As predicted, Pierce allied himself with the three most conservative members of the Court, completing the voting bloc known as the Four Horsemen. He maintained that government should not interfere in economic matters, even during the worst days of the Great Depression. He opposed social welfare legislation in all its forms, writing the Court's opinion in a 1936 case striking down a New York law that provided a minimum wage for women.

Butler died in Washington, D.C., during his seventeenth year of service on the Court.

Edward Terry Sanford
(1923–1930)

BIRTH: July 23, 1865, Knoxville, Tennessee.

EDUCATION: University of Tennessee, B.A. and Ph.B., 1883; Harvard, B.A., 1884, M.A., 1889; Harvard Law School, LL.B., 1889.

OFFICIAL POSITIONS: special assistant to the U.S. attorney general, 1906–1907; assistant U.S. attorney general, 1907–1908; federal judge, U.S. District Court for the Middle and Eastern Districts of Tennessee, 1908–1923.

SUPREME COURT SERVICE: nominated associate justice by President Warren G. Harding January 24, 1923, to replace Mahlon Pitney, who had retired; confirmed by the Senate January 29, 1923, by a voice vote; took judicial oath February 19, 1923; served until March 8, 1930; replaced by Owen J. Roberts, nominated by President Herbert Hoover.

FAMILY: married Lutie Mallory Woodruff, January 6, 1891; two daughters.

DEATH: March 8, 1930, Washington, D.C.

Born three months after the South had surrendered to the Union armies, Sanford grew up in one of the few Republican enclaves in the post–Civil War South. His father, Edward J. Sanford, had come to Tennessee in 1852 from Connecticut where his family had lived since 1634. In Tennessee he rose from poverty to make a fortune in the lumber and construction business and became a prominent member of the Republican Party. Sanford's

Roman Catholics, settled on a farm in Minnesota after emigrating from Ireland during the potato famine of the 1840s. With money earned at a nearby dairy, Pierce attended Carleton College in Northfield, graduating in 1887 with a bachelor of arts and a bachelor of science degree. He read law with a St. Paul firm, Pinch and Twohy, and was admitted to the bar in 1888 at age twenty-two.

Butler began his legal career practicing law with Stan Donnelly, the son of Ignatius Donnelly, a member of Congress from Minnesota and future vice-presidential candidate of the People's Party.

In 1891 Butler was elected assistant attorney of Ramsey County, which included St. Paul. While county attorney he formed the firm How, Butler, and Mitchell and later became senior partner of Butler, Mitchell, and Doherty. Attorney General George Wickersham chose Butler to represent the federal government in a number of antitrust cases around 1910. His skillful prosecution won him the attorney general's praise as the "foremost lawyer in his part of the country" and brought him to President Harding's attention.

When Justice William Day's resignation in 1922 left a vacancy on the Court, Butler was Chief Justice Taft's top choice for the seat. During arbitration in Canada the year before, Taft had been favorably impressed with Butler and recommended him to Harding. There were other reasons for Taft's strong preference, however. He wanted to obtain a conservative majority on the Court. Butler's conservative judicial past made Taft confident that if appointed he would align himself with Justices Van Devanter, McReynolds, and Sutherland. The president also was re-

Edward Terry Sanford

Justice Mahlon Pitney retired on December 31, 1922, giving Harding a fourth vacancy on the Court to fill during his term.

During his seven-year tenure, Sanford delivered the opinion of the Court in 130 cases. Among them was *Gitlow v. New York* (1925), in which the Court upheld the conviction of Benjamin Gitlow under a state criminal anarchy law. Even though the decision went against Gitlow, Sanford wrote that "freedom of speech and of the press . . . are among the . . . 'liberties' protected by the due process clause of the Fourteenth Amendment." The ruling was the first to extend the guarantees of the Bill of Rights to state action.

Sanford died suddenly March 8, 1930, only a few hours before the death of William Howard Taft.

Harlan Fiske Stone
(1925–1941, 1941–1946)

BIRTH: October 11, 1872, Chesterfield, New Hampshire.

EDUCATION: Amherst College, A.B., 1894, M.A., 1897, LL.D., 1913; Columbia University, LL.B., 1898.

OFFICIAL POSITIONS: U.S. attorney general, 1924–1925.

SUPREME COURT SERVICE: nominated associate justice by President Calvin Coolidge January 5, 1925, to replace Joseph McKenna, who had retired; confirmed by the Senate February 5, 1925, by a 71–6 vote; took judicial oath March 2, 1925; nominated chief justice by President Franklin D. Roosevelt June 12, 1941, to replace Chief Justice Hughes, who had retired; confirmed by the Senate June 27, 1941, by a voice vote; took judicial oath July 3, 1941; served until April 22, 1946; replaced by Fred M. Vinson, nominated by President Harry S. Truman.

mother, Emma Chavannes, was the daughter of French-Swiss parents, who had emigrated from Switzerland in 1848.

Following his education at the University of Tennessee and Harvard, where he was editor of the *Law Review,* Sanford studied in France and Germany for a year. He returned to Knoxville, settled into the practice of law, and married Lutie Mallory Woodruff.

Throughout his life, Sanford retained an interest in higher education. He served as trustee of the University of Tennessee from 1897 to 1923 and as trustee of the George Peabody College for Teachers from 1909 until his death in 1930. He also served as president of both the University of Tennessee and Harvard alumni associations.

Sanford's first official position came in 1905 at the age of forty-one when he accepted the post of special assistant to U.S. Attorney General William H. Moody (later appointed to the Supreme Court). Sanford's task—as one of President Theodore Roosevelt's "trustbusters"—was to prosecute the fertilizer trust under the Sherman Antitrust Act of 1890. In 1907 he became assistant attorney general. A year later Roosevelt nominated him as federal district judge for the Middle and Eastern Districts of Tennessee, a post Sanford held until his nomination to the Supreme Court in 1923.

After World War I, Sanford worked to mobilize support for the Treaty of Versailles and U.S. membership in the League of Nations. Although the treaty was defeated in the Senate, Sanford's efforts brought him to the attention of Chief Justice Taft—with whom he had become acquainted during his Justice Department service—and of Attorney General Harry M. Daugherty. They suggested his name to President Harding when

FAMILY: married Agnes Harvey, September 7, 1899; two sons.

DEATH: April 22, 1946, Washington, D.C.

Harlan Fiske Stone was the son of Frederick Lawson Stone, a New England farmer, and Ann Sophia Butler Stone. Phi Beta Kappa and president of his class at Amherst College, Stone graduated with an A.B. in 1894, one year before Calvin Coolidge, and with an M.A. three years later.

A Columbia University Law School graduate, Stone was admitted to the New York bar, married Agnes Harvey, whom he had known since childhood, and began his legal practice with the firm Sullivan and Cromwell in 1899. For the next twenty-five years he divided his time between his Wall Street practice and a career as professor of law and dean at Columbia.

In 1924 President Coolidge appointed his fellow Republican and Amherst alumnus to succeed the controversial Harry M. Daugherty as attorney general. Stone began a reorganization of the Justice Department and recommended J. Edgar Hoover to head the FBI. The Supreme Court resignation of Justice Joseph McKenna in 1925 gave Coolidge the opportunity to promote his old friend to the bench after only a year in his cabinet.

Despite reservations over Stone's moderate conservatism and ties to Wall Street wealth (five years before he had been J. P. Morgan's counsel), the Senate confirmed him February 5, 1925. A spokesman for judicial restraint on the Taft and Hughes Courts, Stone was nominated chief justice by President Franklin D. Roosevelt sixteen years later.

When the Agricultural Adjustment Act was declared unconstitutional by a 6–3 majority in 1936, Stone had sided with the president, declaring that the Court was not "the only agency of government that must be assumed to have the capacity to govern." Stone recognized the danger of the Court's becoming a "legislative Constitution-making body," and Roosevelt needed a chief justice who would not thwart his programs. Moreover, a Republican appointment, the president felt, would show him to be a nonpartisan leader. Favored by the press and bar, Stone's selection as chief justice was well received. Archibald MacLeish described the nomination as "the perfect word spoken at the perfect moment."

For Stone the appointment was not the culmination of a lifelong ambition: "I cannot say I had any thought of being a member of the Supreme Court or any other court," said Stone recalling his ambitions as a twenty-one-year-old college student, "for I believed then, as I do now, that the best insurance of a happy life and reasonable success in it is devotion to one's immediate job and happiness in doing it."

Stone achieved far more than "reasonable success." Progressing from the most junior to senior associate justice and finally to chief justice, he occupied consecutively, as none of his predecessors had done, every seat on the bench.

Stone may be the only member of the Court who is known for a famous footnote. In Footnote Four of *United States v. Carolene Products Corp.* (1938), Stone introduced the idea that statutes aimed at restricting fundamental rights would be regarded as suspect. Two years later, in *Minersville School District v. Gobitis,* Stone was the lone dissenter when the Court decided that the children of Seventh-day Adventists were required to salute the flag in school even though their religion forbade it. Three years later, the justices took his arguments to heart when they overruled the decision.

His twenty-one years of service on the Court ended suddenly. On April 22, 1946, while reading a dissent in a naturalization case, he was stricken and died later in the day.

Owen Josephus Roberts
(1930–1945)

BIRTH: May 2, 1875, Germantown, Pennsylvania.

EDUCATION: University of Pennsylvania, A.B. with honors, 1895; LL.B. cum laude, 1898.

OFFICIAL POSITIONS: assistant district attorney, 1903–1906; special deputy attorney general, Eastern District of Pennsylvania, 1918; special U.S. attorney, 1924–1930; umpire, Mixed Claims Commission, 1932; chairman, Pearl Harbor Inquiry Board, 1941–1942.

SUPREME COURT SERVICE: nominated associate justice by President Herbert Hoover May 9, 1930, to replace Edward Terry Sanford, who had died; confirmed by the Senate May 20, 1930, by a voice vote; took judicial oath June 2, 1930; resigned July 31, 1945; replaced by Harold H. Burton, nominated by President Harry S. Truman.

FAMILY: married Elizabeth Caldwell Rogers, 1904; one daughter.

DEATH: May 17, 1955, West Vincent Township, Pennsylvania.

Roberts's ancestors left Wales in 1808 and settled in southeastern Pennsylvania. His parents were Josephus and Emma Laferty Roberts. Owen Roberts was a quiet youngster who displayed a love for books and an aptitude for debating. He attended the University of Pennsylvania and graduated Phi Beta Kappa in 1895. He went on to the University of Pennsylvania Law School, where for two years he was the associate editor of the *American Law Register* (now the *University of Pennsylvania Law Review*). He graduated cum laude in 1898. In addition to starting private practice the same year, Roberts also taught at his former law school, rising from lecturer to full professor. He continued to teach part time at the university until 1919.

In 1903 Roberts was named assistant district attorney in Philadelphia. He returned to private practice in 1906 and built a prosperous business representing a large clientele, including several corporations.

Appointed a special deputy attorney general in 1918, Roberts prosecuted several cases in the Philadelphia area under the terms of the Espionage Act. In 1924 President Calvin Coolidge named him and former senator Atlee Pomerene, D-Ohio (1911–1923), as special U.S. attorneys to investigate the Teapot Dome Scandal of the Harding administration. Roberts uncovered a network of bribes to administration officials, several of whom were convicted but received relatively short prison sentences.

In May 1930 the Senate refused to confirm President Hoover's nomination of North Carolina judge John J. Parker to the Supreme Court because of Parker's rulings upholding "yellow dog" labor contracts and his derogatory comments on blacks. Roberts was Hoover's next choice, and the Senate confirmed him May 20.

Roberts joined a Court that was divided between a conservative group nicknamed the Four Horsemen and a more liberal group. As a swing vote, he could decide the outcome of a case. He is generally regarded as more conservative than liberal. For example, he wrote the 1936 opinion in *Butler v. United States,* which struck down one of the pillars of the New Deal, the Agricultural Adjustment Act. However, he also voted to uphold a Minnesota law that provided mortgage relief to homeowners suffering financial difficulties due to the depression. And in *Nebbia v. New York* (1934) he came out in favor of price regulation.

It is a popular myth that Roberts made the "switch in time that saved the Nine." Just months after President Franklin D. Roosevelt proposed adding more members to the Court, the story goes, Roberts changed his vote in a case involving a Washington State law providing a minimum wage for women. In truth, Roberts had voted before the "court-packing" plan became known.

In addition to his Court duties, Roberts oversaw an investigation of the attack on Pearl Harbor and headed the Commission for the Protection and Salvage of Artistic and Historic Monuments in Europe. The commission traced and catalogued art objects stolen or destroyed by the Germans during World War II.

After resigning from the Court, Roberts returned to his alma mater and served as dean of the University of Pennsylvania Law School from 1948 to 1951. He was involved in the world federalist movement and served in 1953 as the chairman of the Fund for the Advancement of Education. He died May 17, 1955, in Pennsylvania.

Benjamin Nathan Cardozo

(1932–1938)

BIRTH: May 24, 1870, New York City.

EDUCATION: Columbia University, A.B., 1889; A.M., 1891; Columbia Law School, 1891, no degree.

OFFICIAL POSITIONS: justice, New York Supreme Court, 1913; judge, New York State Court of Appeals, 1913–1932; chief judge, 1926–1932.

SUPREME COURT SERVICE: nominated associate justice by President Herbert Hoover February 15, 1932, to replace Oliver Wendell Holmes Jr., who had retired; confirmed by the Senate February 24, 1932, by a voice vote; took judicial oath March 14, 1932; served until July 9, 1938; replaced by Felix Frankfurter, nominated by President Franklin D. Roosevelt.

FAMILY: unmarried.

DEATH: July 9, 1938, Port Chester, New York.

Benjamin Nathan Cardozo and his twin sister Emily were the youngest children of Albert and Rebecca Nathan Cardozo, descendants of Sephardic Jews who had settled in New York in the mid-eighteenth century. A cousin, Emma Lazarus, wrote the verse at the base of the Statue of Liberty. Cardozo's childhood was spent in the aftermath of the Boss Tweed scandal, which implicated his father, a Tammany Hall judge, in the political corruption of the city government. Charged with graft, Albert Cardozo resigned rather than face impeachment.

At age fifteen Benjamin Cardozo was admitted to Columbia University. He graduated with honors in 1889 and completed his master's degree while also studying law. In 1891 he was admitted to the New York bar without a law degree—a not uncommon practice at that time—and began work in the law firm where his brother Albert was a partner. Cardozo remained a bachelor and drew his friends from among his legal colleagues. He was very fond of his older unmarried sister Ellen and lived with her until her death in 1929.

After years as a private lawyer, Cardozo ran against Tammany Hall in 1913 and was elected by a narrow margin to the New York Supreme Court, the state's trial bench. Shortly thereafter, Gov. Martin A. Glynn appointed him to a temporary position on the New York Court of Appeals, on which he was to serve until 1932. Elected to a full term as associate judge in 1917, he became chief judge in 1926 and won for the court its reputation as the leading state court in the country.

Cardozo's early judicial writings were used by lawyers as a handbook, and his lectures at Yale Law School on a number of topics were extended and published as *The Nature of the Judicial Process* in 1921, *The Growth of the Law* in 1924 and *The Paradoxes of Legal Science* four years later.

When ninety-year-old Justice Oliver Wendell Holmes Jr. announced his retirement, Sen. Robert F. Wagner, D-N.Y., presented Cardozo's name to President Hoover. University faculty, journalists, political leaders, and members of the bar all voiced their endorsement of the New York judge. Within ten days of Holmes's resignation, a tally of names received at the White House showed Cardozo a clear favorite. The *New York Times* described the unanimity of support for him as "quite without precedent."

Hoover was unconvinced, however. Two justices from New York, Hughes and Stone, and one Jew, Brandeis, were quite enough, he thought. Only after Stone offered his resignation (which was not accepted) on Cardozo's behalf did Hoover make his decision, appointing him February 15, 1932. Harvard professor Zechariah Chafee Jr. praised the nomination: the president's choice "ignored geography and made history."

In his six years as a liberal on a primarily conservative Court, Cardozo is well remembered for his dissents. But he also wrote more than one hundred opinions for the Court. In *Steward Machine Co. v. Davis* and *Helvering v. Davis*, both 1937, he affirmed the constitutionality of the Social Security Act. He wrote the opinion in *Palko v. Connecticut* (1937), in which the Court chose not to apply the Bill of Rights' prohibition against double jeopardy to the states.

Cardozo died in 1938 after a long illness. In *Nine Old Men*, columnists Drew Pearson and Robert S. Allen described the silver-haired justice as "the hermit philosopher." The Court, in its memorial testimony described "the strangely compelling power of that reticent, sensitive and almost mystical personality."

Hugo Lafayette Black

(1937–1971)

BIRTH: February 27, 1886, Harlan, Alabama.

EDUCATION: Birmingham Medical School, 1903–1904; University of Alabama Law School, LL.B., 1906.

OFFICIAL POSITIONS: police court judge, Birmingham, 1910–1911; county solicitor, Jefferson County, Alabama, 1914–1917; U.S. senator, 1927–1937.

SUPREME COURT SERVICE: nominated associate justice by President Franklin D. Roosevelt August 12, 1937, to replace Willis Van Devanter, who had retired; confirmed by the Senate August 17, 1937, by a 63–16 vote; took judicial oath August 19, 1937; retired September 17, 1971; replaced by Lewis F. Powell Jr., nominated by President Richard Nixon.

FAMILY: married Josephine Foster, February 1921; died 1951; two sons, one daughter; married Elizabeth Seay DeMerritte, September 11, 1957.

DEATH: September 25, 1971, Washington, D.C.

Hugo Black was the eighth child of William Lafayette Black, a Baptist storekeeper and farmer, and Martha Ardella Toland Black. He spent the first years of his life in the hill country near Harlan, Alabama. When he was still a youngster, his family moved to Ashland, a larger community where his father's business prospered.

Black attended the local schools in Ashland and after trying one year at Birmingham Medical School, decided to study law. At eighteen he entered the University of Alabama Law School at Tuscaloosa.

Graduating in 1906, Black returned to Ashland and set up his first law practice. The following year a fire destroyed his office and library, and Black moved to Birmingham. There he quickly established a relationship with labor by defending the United Mine Workers strikers in 1908. He also developed an expertise for arguing personal injury cases.

Black was named a part-time police court judge in Birmingham in 1911 and was elected county solicitor (public prosecutor) for Jefferson County in 1914. As solicitor, he gained a measure of local fame for his investigation of reports of the brutal means the police employed while questioning suspects at the notorious Bessemer jail.

When he left the solicitor's post to enter the army in World War I, Black had succeeded in emptying a docket that had once held as many as three thousand pending cases.

His brief military career kept him within the borders of the United States. He returned to practice in Birmingham in 1918, married the following year, and continued to expand his practice, still specializing in labor law and personal injury cases. In 1923 he joined the Ku Klux Klan, but resigned from the organization two years later just before announcing his intention to run for the Democratic nomination for the Senate. Campaigning as the poor man's candidate, Black won not only the party's endorsement but also the election. He entered the Senate in 1927 and immediately began to study history and the classics at the Library of Congress to compensate for his lack of formal education.

During his two terms in the Senate, Black used committee hearings to investigate several areas, including abuses of marine and airline subsidies and the activities of lobbying groups. In 1933 he introduced a bill to create a thirty-hour work week. This legislation, after several alterations, was finally passed in 1938 as the Fair Labor Standards Act. One of the Senate's strongest supporters of President Franklin D. Roosevelt, Black spoke out in favor of the 1937 Court-packing scheme and other New Deal programs. His support for the administration and his strong liberal instincts led the president to pick Black as his choice to fill the Supreme Court seat vacated by the retirement of Willis Van Devanter.

Black's previous affiliation with the Ku Klux Klan was widely reported in the national news media after his Senate confirmation. The furor quickly quieted, however, when the new justice admitted in a dramatic radio broadcast that he had indeed been a member of the Klan but added that he had resigned many years before and would comment no further.

Black is remembered for his reverence for the U.S. Constitution—he always carried a copy of it in his pocket. He believed the courts should protect the weak, minorities, and those who held unpopular view. He was passionate about the First Amendment, interpreting the language literally to mean that Congress shall pass *no law* abridging the freedoms the amendment guarantees.

He retired from the Court September 17, 1971, after suffering an impairing stroke. He died eight days later.

Stanley Forman Reed
(1938–1957)

BIRTH: December 31, 1884, Minerva, Kentucky.

EDUCATION: Kentucky Wesleyan University, A.B., 1902; Yale University, A.B., 1906; legal studies, University of Virginia and Columbia University (no degree); graduate studies, University of Paris, 1909–1910.

OFFICIAL POSITIONS: representative, Kentucky General Assembly, 1912–1916; general counsel, Federal Farm Board, 1929–1932; general counsel, Reconstruction Finance Corporation, 1932–1935; special assistant to attorney general, 1935; solicitor general, 1935–1938.

SUPREME COURT SERVICE: nominated associate justice by President Franklin D. Roosevelt January 15, 1938, to replace George Sutherland, who had retired; confirmed by Senate January 25, 1938, by a voice vote; took judicial oath January 31, 1938; retired February 25, 1957; replaced by Charles E. Whittaker, appointed by President Dwight D. Eisenhower.

FAMILY: married Winifred Elgin, May 11, 1908; two sons.

DEATH: April 2, 1980, New York City.

Stanley Forman Reed was born in tobacco-rich Mason County, Kentucky, to John A. Reed, a physician, and Frances Forman Reed. Reed received undergraduate degrees from Kentucky Wesleyan and Yale universities and studied law at the University of Virginia and Columbia University. He married Winifred Elgin from Maysville, Kentucky, May 11, 1908, and they left the following year for Paris where he took graduate courses in civil and international law at the Sorbonne.

Returning in 1910 to Maysville, Reed read law with a local attorney before passing the Kentucky bar. He set up a private practice, then closed it to serve in an army intelligence unit during World War I. Once his tour of duty was over, Reed joined a law firm and served in the Kentucky General Assembly for four years. Among the firm's clients were the Chesapeake and Ohio Railroad and the Burley Tobacco Growers Cooperative Association, which he helped organize.

In 1929 Reed's experience with the tobacco cooperative in market control through group sales became needed in Washington. Following the recommendation of Burley's president, James C. Stone, President Herbert Hoover appointed Reed general counsel for the Federal Farm Board, newly established to resell surpluses of American farm commodities abroad. After two years with the board, Reed was promoted to general counsel for the Reconstruction Finance Corporation, Hoover's loan-granting agency in the Great Depression to help banks, businesses, and agricultural enterprises.

When Franklin Roosevelt became president, one of his most controversial economic policies was to raise prices by reducing the gold content of the dollar. He appointed Reed special assistant to the attorney general with the unique task of defending the government's legal right to change the requirement of certain private companies for payment in gold. Reed argued the *Gold Clause Cases* before the Supreme Court in 1935; his success with this assignment made Roosevelt confident that as solicitor general Reed would be able to argue persuasively before the Supreme Court the constitutionality of his New Deal legislation. Despite defeats such as the Court's decision to invalidate the Agricultural Adjustment Act (AAA) in 1936, Solicitor General Reed succeeded in upholding the constitutionality of the National Labor Relations Act and other important measures of the Roosevelt era.

When Justice Sutherland retired in 1938, Roosevelt had the opportunity to choose his second justice. Reed's ten years of government experience under both Republican and Democratic administrations and seventeen years in private practice made him well qualified for the bench.

On the Court, Reed's opinions reflected his belief in social welfare and government regulation of the economy. He had the satisfaction of seeing the AAA upheld just three years after it was declared unconstitutional. He wrote the opinion in the landmark *Smith v. Allwright* (1944), in which the Court invalidated the white-only primary, a common practice in the southern states to keep blacks from running for elective office.

From 1939 to 1941 Justice Reed chaired President Roosevelt's Commission on Civil Service Improvement. After his resignation from the Court in 1957, he served as chairman of President Eisenhower's U.S. Civil Rights Commission. Reed left the commission because he felt his continued involvement with the federal judiciary disqualified him. Reed argued thirty-five cases before the Court of Claims and twenty-five cases before the Court of Appeals in the District of Columbia during his retirement. He maintained an office in the Supreme Court until his move to New York, where he died on April 2, 1980, twenty-three years after leaving the Supreme Court.

Felix Frankfurter

(1939–1962)

BIRTH: November 15, 1882, Vienna, Austria.

EDUCATION: College of the City of New York, A.B., 1902; Harvard Law School, LL.B., 1906.

OFFICIAL POSITIONS: assistant U.S. attorney, Southern District of New York, 1906–1909; law officer, Bureau of Insular Affairs, War Department, 1910–1914; assistant to the secretary of war, 1917; secretary and counsel, President's Mediation Commission, 1917; assistant to the secretary of labor, 1917–1918; chairman, War Labor Policies Board, 1918.

SUPREME COURT SERVICE: nominated associate justice by President Franklin D. Roosevelt January 5, 1939, to replace Benjamin Cardozo, who had died; confirmed by the Senate January 17, 1939, by a voice vote; took judicial oath January 30, 1939; retired August 28, 1962; replaced by Arthur Goldberg, nominated by President John F. Kennedy.

FAMILY: married Marion A. Denman, December 20, 1919.

DEATH: February 22, 1965, Washington, D.C.

An Austrian Jew, Felix Frankfurter came to the United States with his parents, Leopold and Emma Winter Frankfurter, in 1894 and was raised amidst the squalor of New York's Lower East Side. He attended City College and, after an impressive three years at the Harvard University School of Law, took a job with a New York law firm. He was soon recruited away by Henry L. Stimson, the U.S. attorney for the Southern District of New York.

Stimson had been appointed by President Theodore Roosevelt. At the end of the Roosevelt administration in 1909, Stimson went into private practice for a short time and brought

Frankfurter with him. After an unsuccessful bid for the governorship of New York, Stimson was named secretary of war under President William Howard Taft.

Frankfurter accompanied his mentor to Washington, D.C., and was appointed legal officer in the War Department's Bureau of Insular Affairs.

In 1913 Harvard University offered Frankfurter a teaching post in the law school, and he happily returned to his alma mater. Passionate about teaching, Frankfurter trained two generations of students devoted to the law and public service. He also became involved in the Zionist movement, argued a number of minimum and maximum wage cases for the National Consumers League, and helped found the *New Republic.*

Frankfurter returned to Washington in 1917 as an assistant to Secretary of War Newton D. Baker. That same year, President Woodrow Wilson named a mediation commission to handle the rash of strikes obstructing the defense industry; Frankfurter was named its secretary and counsel. While serving on the commission, Frankfurter investigated the handling of the case of Tom Mooney, the alleged Preparedness Day Parade bomber, and the Bisbee, Arizona, deportation case wherein approximately one thousand miners were taken roughly from their labor camps in Arizona and dropped in a deserted town in New Mexico. In both instances Frankfurter found that the rights of the individuals involved had been violated.

These cases, as well as his highly publicized arguments in defense of Sacco and Vanzetti, his work with the National Association for the Advancement of Colored People, and the fact that he was a founding member of the American Civil Liberties Union earned him a reputation as a die-hard liberal that would follow him throughout his career.

He also served as chairman of the War Labor Policies Board. This position first introduced him to Franklin Roosevelt who, as assistant secretary of the navy, sat on the board.

At war's end, Frankfurter attended the Paris Peace Conference as a representative of the American Zionist movement and then returned to Cambridge. In 1919 he married Marion A. Denman. The ceremony took place in Judge Learned Hand's chambers and was performed by Judge Benjamin Cardozo of the New York Court of Appeals, later Frankfurter's predecessor on the U.S. Supreme Court.

At Harvard, Frankfurter enjoyed a growing reputation as an expert on the Constitution and the Supreme Court. He was offered a seat on the Massachusetts Supreme Court in 1932, which he declined. His friendship with Roosevelt grew closer, and in 1933 the newly elected president asked him to be solicitor general, another post Frankfurter declined.

He remained, however, a close adviser to the president and recommended to him a number of Harvard graduates eager to work in the Roosevelt administration, including Thomas G. Corcoran, one of the most influential New Dealers.

Named to the Supreme Court in 1939 to replace Justice Cardozo, Frankfurter was Roosevelt's third appointment. Despite his support for liberal causes, Frankfurter's voting on the Court was considered conservative. He joined with the majority in *Korematsu v. United States* (1944), upholding the exclusion of Japanese Americans from the West Coast. He argued that the country was engaged in a world war against horrific foes, and he believed the claims of the nation were stronger than those of individuals. He dissented in *Board of Education v. Barnette* (1943), the case that overturned an earlier ruling that had said children could be expelled from school for declining to salute the flag for religious reasons. As an immigrant to the United States, Frankfurter felt it was important to show patriotism.

Frankfurter continued to advise the president on a number of issues until Roosevelt's death in 1945. Frankfurter remained on the Court until he suffered a debilitating stroke in 1962. He died in Washington, D.C., in 1965.

Frankfurter was the author of *The Case of Sacco and Vanzetti,* 1927; *The Business of the Supreme Court,* with James M. Landis, 1928; *The Labor Injunction,* with Nathan Greene, 1930; *The Public and Its Government,* 1930; *The Commerce Clause Under Marshall, Taney and Waite,* 1937; *Mr. Justice Holmes and the Supreme Court,* 1939; and the editor of several volumes on various areas of law.

William Orville Douglas
(1939–1975)

BIRTH: October 16, 1898, Maine, Minnesota.

EDUCATION: Whitman College, B.A., 1920; Columbia Law School, LL.B., 1925.

OFFICIAL POSITIONS: member, Securities and Exchange Commission, 1936–1939; chairman, 1937–1939.

SUPREME COURT SERVICE: nominated associate justice by President Franklin D. Roosevelt March 20, 1939, to replace Louis D. Brandeis, who had retired; confirmed by the Senate April 4, 1939, by a 62–4 vote; took judicial oath April 17, 1939; retired November 12, 1975; replaced by John Paul Stevens, nominated by President Gerald R. Ford.

FAMILY: married Mildred Riddle, August 16, 1923; divorced 1953; one son, one daughter; married Mercedes Hester Davison, December 14, 1954; divorced 1963; married Joan Martin, August 1963; divorced 1966; married Cathleen Ann Heffernan, July 1966.

DEATH: January 19, 1980, Washington D.C.

Born into an impoverished farm family in Minnesota shortly before the turn of the twentieth century, William Douglas was the son of Rev. William Douglas and Julia Bickford Douglas. He spent his early years in Yakima, Washington. A polio attack as a child sparked Douglas's lifelong passion for the outdoors, as he hiked the mountains near his home to build strength in his weakened legs.

After graduating Phi Beta Kappa from Whitman College in Walla Walla, Washington, in 1920, Douglas decided to pursue a law career. Despite his lack of funds, he decided to study law at Columbia University Law School. Douglas quickly became one of the school's top students and graduated second in his class in 1925.

Following law school, a two-year stint with a prestigious Wall Street law firm convinced Douglas that representing corporate clients was not to his liking. After a year back in Yakima, Douglas joined the law faculty of Columbia University. In 1929 he moved to New Haven, Connecticut, to teach law at Yale.

By the time the Great Depression struck in 1929, Douglas had already developed a reputation as one of the country's foremost financial law experts. So when President Franklin D. Roosevelt needed members for the newly formed Securities and Exchange Commission (SEC), created in 1934, he called on Douglas, who joined the commission in 1936 and became chairman the following year.

Douglas's 1939 Supreme Court nomination sailed through the Senate. Such easy relations with Congress, however, were not to mark his years in Washington. Three times he faced the threat of impeachment, although only in 1970 did the effort gain any real support.

Douglas's lifestyle and liberal political views—plus conservative resentment at the Senate's rejection of two of President Richard Nixon's Supreme Court nominees—were the main spur behind the 1970 impeachment attempt. The justice's relations with the Parvin Foundation, recipient of considerable income from gambling interests, were held up for scrutiny. Antiestablishment sentiments expressed in one of his many books further fueled the attack. His marital history also raised congressional eyebrows. But a special House Judiciary Subcommittee created to investigate the charges found no grounds for impeachment.

Although he voted with the Court in the Japanese exclusion cases, after World War II Douglas became known for his defense of civil liberties. He wrote the opinion in *Terminiello v. Chicago* (1949), in which the Court reversed a speaker's conviction for causing a near riot. He dissented in *Dennis v. United States* (1951), which upheld the convictions of American Communist Party members for conspiracy to overthrow the government. But Douglas may be best remembered for his opinion for the Court in *Griswold v. Connecticut* (1965). Finding an implicit right to privacy in the Constitution, Douglas overturned a state law prohibiting the sale of birth control devices to married people.

Douglas suffered a paralytic stroke in January 1975. He attempted to continue his work on the Court, but in November 1975 he retired, citing the pain and physical disability resulting from the stroke.

At the time of his retirement, he had served thirty-six years and seven months, longer than any other justice in history. He died four years and a few months later, in January 1980.

Francis William Murphy
(1940–1949)

BIRTH: April 13, 1890, Sand (now Harbor) Beach, Michigan.

EDUCATION: University of Michigan, A.B., 1912, LL.B., 1914; graduate study, Lincoln's Inn, London, and Trinity College, Dublin.

OFFICIAL POSITIONS: chief assistant U.S. attorney, Eastern District of Michigan, 1919–1920; judge, Recorder's Court, Detroit, 1924–1930; mayor of Detroit, 1930–1933; governor general of the Philippines, 1933–1935; U.S. high commissioner to the Philippines, 1935–1936; governor of Michigan, 1937–1939; U.S. attorney general, 1939–1940.

SUPREME COURT SERVICE: nominated associate justice by President Franklin D. Roosevelt January 4, 1940, to replace

Pierce Butler, who had died; confirmed by the Senate January 16, 1940, by a voice vote; took judicial oath February 5, 1940; served until July 19, 1949; replaced by Tom C. Clark, nominated by President Harry S. Truman.

FAMILY: unmarried.

DEATH: July 19, 1949, Detroit, Michigan.

Francis William Murphy, called Frank, was the third child of Irish Catholic parents, John T. Murphy, a country lawyer, and his wife Mary Brennan Murphy. As a young boy, Frank promised his mother he would never smoke or drink and he kept that promise until adulthood. He received his undergraduate and law degrees from the University of Michigan and after his admission to the bar in 1914 worked for the Detroit firm Monaghan and Monaghan for three years, teaching law at night school. During World War I Murphy served with the American Expeditionary Force in France and with the Army of Occupation in Germany. He did not return home immediately after the war but took graduate courses at Lincoln's Inn in London and Trinity College in Dublin.

Murphy began his career in Michigan as chief assistant U.S. attorney for the Eastern District. After practicing law in Detroit for three years, he became judge for the Recorder's Court, the principal criminal court in Detroit. In the midst of the Great Depression, Murphy, a prolabor Democrat and advocate of federal relief, was elected mayor of Detroit and served from 1930 to 1933.

Franklin Roosevelt was governor of New York during this period. Murphy supported Roosevelt's bid for the presidency in 1932 and, when Roosevelt was elected, wholeheartedly endorsed the Works Progress Administration (WPA).

In recognition of this support, Roosevelt named Murphy governor general of the Philippine Islands and in 1935, when commonwealth status was won, appointed him U.S. high commissioner. In the Far East as in the Midwest, Murphy enacted New Deal policies such as maximum hour and minimum wage laws. Once the independent government was working smoothly, he returned to Michigan, but his high regard for the people of the Philippines continued. The American and Philippine flags hung side by side in his Supreme Court office.

From 1937 to 1939 Murphy served as governor of Michigan. Immediately upon taking office, he was faced with a sit-down strike of 135,000 automotive workers. Murphy's refusal to call out the state troopers earned him many critics and cost him reelection in 1938.

Murphy aspired to be secretary of war in Roosevelt's cabinet. A bit of political juggling landed him the position of attorney general instead. Roosevelt had many people to please. To Solicitor General (later Supreme Court justice) Robert H. Jackson he wrote, "I want you for my attorney general, Bob, but I want to name Murphy immediately to something and since I can't name him to what he himself wants, it is desirable to use the attorney generalship temporarily for that purpose." During his one year in that office, Murphy indicted a number of Democratic politi-

cal bosses, most notably Tom Pendergast of Kansas City, brought suit against numerous trust companies, and established the first civil liberties unit in the Justice Department.

When Justice Butler died in 1939, President Roosevelt filled the vacancy in kind by appointing another Democrat and Catholic—Frank Murphy. Murphy did not want the job. To his parish priest he wrote, "I am not too happy about going on the court. A better choice could have been made." So anxious was he for involvement in the war effort that during Court recesses Murphy served as an infantry officer in Fort Benning, Georgia, much to the dismay of Chief Justice Stone.

On the Court, described by Murphy as the "Great Pulpit," he preached civil liberties, and his moralizing rhetoric gave birth to the phrase "justice tempered with Murphy." Murphy's Catholicism did not influence his decision making even where Jehovah's Witnesses, a strongly anti-Catholic sect, was concerned. He upheld their right to proselytize door to door and, in the Court's second flag-salute decision, voted with the majority to invalidate the salute as a compulsory requirement in schools.

Murphy continued to defend civil rights during World War II, arguing that for the Court to do otherwise would rob the war of its meaning. He concurred in *Hirabayashi v. United States* (1943), the case that upheld a wartime curfew for Japanese Americans living on the West Coast. The next year, however, he wrote a moving dissent in *Korematsu v. United States,* in which the Court agreed that the removal of Japanese Americans from the West Coast to relocation centers inland was within the war powers granted to the president and Congress. Murphy claimed the action went beyond constitutional power and fell into the "ugly abyss of racism."

Murphy died July 19, 1949, in Detroit, Michigan, at the age of fifty-nine. With the sudden deaths that year of Murphy and Wiley B. Rutledge, the Court lost two of its most consistently liberal spokesmen.

James Francis Byrnes

(1941–1942)

BIRTH: May 2, 1879, Charleston, South Carolina.

EDUCATION: St. Patrick's Parochial School (never graduated); studied law privately; admitted to the bar in 1903.

OFFICIAL POSITIONS: court reporter, Second Circuit of South Carolina, 1900–1908; solicitor, Second Circuit of South Carolina, 1908–1910; U.S. representative, 1911–1925; U.S. senator, 1931–1941; director, Office of Economic Stabilization, 1942–1943; director, Office of War Mobilization, 1943–1945; secretary of state, 1945–1947; governor of South Carolina, 1951–1955.

SUPREME COURT SERVICE: nominated associate justice by President Franklin D. Roosevelt June 12, 1941, to replace James McReynolds, who had retired; confirmed by the Senate June 12, 1941, by a voice vote; took judicial oath July 8, 1942; resigned October 3, 1942; replaced by Wiley B. Rutledge, appointed by President Roosevelt.

James Francis Byrnes

FAMILY: Married Maude Perkins Busch, May 2, 1906.
DEATH: April 9, 1972, Columbia, South Carolina.

The son of Irish immigrants, James Francis Byrnes was born in the Charleston of the post-Reconstruction South. He was named after his father, who had died shortly before his birth. Elisabeth E. McSweeney Byrnes supported the family as a dressmaker.

At age fourteen, Francis left school to work as a law clerk in a Charleston firm for $2 a week. With his mother's help he learned shorthand and won an exam for a court stenographer's job in Aiken, South Carolina, where he served as official court reporter for the Second Circuit for eight years, reading law in his spare time. Byrnes passed the bar in 1903, the same year he bought the Aiken newspaper, *Journal and Review,* and became its editor.

As solicitor, or district attorney, for South Carolina's Second Circuit, Byrnes unexpectedly won a seat in the U.S. House of Representatives in 1910. "I campaigned on nothing but gall, and gall won by fifty-seven votes," he later reminisced. During his second term, he became well acquainted with Franklin Roosevelt, Woodrow Wilson's assistant secretary of the Navy, who often appeared before Byrnes's House Appropriations Committee.

A speechwriter and political strategist for Roosevelt's campaign in 1932, he continued his loyal support of the administration during two terms in the Senate, despite his objections to certain New Deal labor and welfare policies. The president twice considered his friend as a running mate but decided in favor of

Henry Wallace in 1940 and Sen. Harry S. Truman four years later. Byrnes's failure to obtain the vice-presidential nomination was attributable in part to his unpopularity with northern liberals and, despite his conversion to the Episcopal faith, anti-Catholic sentiment.

Roosevelt rewarded Byrnes for his loyalty by nominating him to the Supreme Court in June 1941. However, so valuable was Byrnes to the president as a troubleshooter behind the scenes in the Senate that after Justice James McReynolds announced his retirement in January, Roosevelt kept Byrnes in the Senate for six months before naming him as McReynolds's successor.

Byrnes served only sixteen months on the Court, during which he wrote sixteen opinions. Best known is *Edwards v. California* (1941), in which the Court invalidated a California law that had made it illegal to transport indigents into California from other states. He based his opinion on the commerce clause, which, he said, guarantees free movement across state borders.

He was restless on the Court. "My country's at war and I want to be in it," he wrote. "I don't think I can stand the abstractions of jurisprudence at a time like this." Late in 1942 he resigned to take a more active part in the administration's war effort. Both as director of the Office of Economic Stabilization from 1942 to 1943 and as director of the Office of War Mobilization and Reconversion the following two years, Byrnes exercised great power in the administration. As the president stated when he called Byrnes from the Court to the White House, "I want you to act as a judge and I will let it be known that your decision is my decision and that there is no appeal. For all practical purposes, you will be assistant President." In 1945 Byrnes accompanied Roosevelt to the meeting in Yalta with Stalin and Churchill, and, as secretary of state in the Truman administration, he attended the Potsdam Conference.

Critical of the concentration of power in the Fair Deal government and criticized for his firm hand with the Soviets as secretary of state, Byrnes resigned from Truman's cabinet in 1947. For four years he practiced law in South Carolina and in Washington, D.C., with the firm Hogan and Hartson.

A proponent of states' rights and separate-but-equal schooling for blacks, Byrnes was elected governor of South Carolina in 1950, the last public office of his distinguished career. Few justices held so many positions of responsibility after leaving the bench.

Byrnes' autobiography, *All in a Lifetime* (1958), was written during his retirement. His first book, *Speaking Frankly,* published in 1947, described his firsthand experience with postwar diplomacy.

Byrnes died of a heart attack April 9, 1972, in Columbia, South Carolina.

Robert Houghwout Jackson

(1941–1954)

BIRTH: February 13, 1892, Spring Creek, Pennsylvania.

EDUCATION: Local schools in Frewsburg, New York; Albany Law School, 1912.

OFFICIAL POSITIONS: general counsel, Bureau of Internal Revenue, 1934–1936; assistant U.S. attorney general, 1936–1938; U.S. solicitor general, 1938–1939; U.S. attorney general, 1940–1941; chief U.S. prosecutor, Nuremberg war crimes trial, 1945–1946.

SUPREME COURT SERVICE: nominated associated justice by President Franklin D. Roosevelt June 12, 1941, to replace Harlan F. Stone, who was promoted to chief justice; confirmed by the Senate July 7, 1941, by a voice vote; took judicial oath July 11, 1941; served until October 9, 1954; replaced by John Marshall Harlan, nominated by President Dwight D. Eisenhower.

FAMILY: married Irene Alice Gerhardt, April 24, 1916; one daughter, one son.

DEATH: October 9, 1954, Washington, D.C.

A descendant of eighteenth-century settlers of Warren County, Pennsylvania, Robert Jackson was the son of William Eldred Jackson and Angelina Houghwout Jackson. He grew up across the border near Jamestown, New York, where at eighteen he apprenticed in a local law firm. After a year at Albany Law School, he was admitted to the New York bar in 1913. He then began his career in earnest, laying the foundation for a lucrative general practice.

Jackson entered politics at twenty-one when he was elected a Democratic state committeeman. His term as committeeman, marked by controversy over dispensing patronage posts, convinced Jackson that he preferred law to politics, and he refused to run for reelection. He said later that politics had "filled my office with people who came there asking political favors and waging political fights."

His early contact with Roosevelt and his growing reputation as a talented advocate brought Jackson to Washington in 1934 as the counsel to the Bureau of Internal Revenue, where he won a highly publicized $750,000 judgment in an income tax suit brought against Andrew W. Mellon, the fabulously wealthy former secretary of the Treasury. Jackson rose quickly in the Roosevelt administration: he was named assistant attorney general in 1936, solicitor general in 1938, and attorney general in 1940.

During that time, Jackson also became one of Roosevelt's closest advisers and supporters. He campaigned for the president's reelection in 1936 and was a chief assistant at the 1940 Democratic convention. He supported the president's Court-packing scheme. He devised the legal means for Roosevelt in 1940 to give destroyers to Great Britain in exchange for American bases on British territories in the Caribbean, the West Indies, and the North Atlantic.

Named in June 1941 to the Supreme Court seat vacated after Justice Stone was appointed chief justice, Jackson's opinions reflected his strong support for the rights of individuals. He wrote the majority opinion in *Board of Education v. Barnette* (1943), overturning an earlier decision that had compelled school children to salute the flag. "The very purpose of the Bill of Rights was to withdraw certain subjects from the vicissitudes of political controversy, to place them beyond the reach of majorities and officials and establish them as legal principles to be applied by courts," he wrote. In 1944 he dissented from the Court's decision in *Korematsu v. United States*. Expressing his disapproval of the government's removal of Japanese Americans from the West Coast, Jackson said it was a fundamental principle of the American system that guilt was personal and not inheritable.

Jackson also served as the chief U.S. prosecutor at the Nuremberg war crimes trial in 1945 and 1946. He originated the concept upon which the successful prosecution of the Nazi leaders was based: that it is a crime against international society to plan and wage an aggressive war. While Jackson was in Germany, growing dissension among the Supreme Court justices reached a climax; it was reported that, on the death of Chief Justice Stone, two justices had threatened to resign if Jackson was elevated to chief justice. Jackson exacerbated the controversy by releasing a letter he had written to President Truman castigating Justice Hugo L. Black for his participation in a case argued by Black's former law partner.

Jackson remained on the Court until his death. He was the author of *The Struggle for Judicial Supremacy*, 1941; *Full Faith and Credit: The Lawyer's Clause of the Constitution*, 1945; *The Case Against the Nazi War Criminals*, 1946; *The Nuremberg Case*, 1947; and *The Supreme Court in the American System of Government*, 1955.

Wiley Blount Rutledge

(1943–1949)

BIRTH: July 20, 1894, Cloverport, Kentucky.

EDUCATION: University of Wisconsin, A.B., 1914; University of Colorado, LL.B., 1922.

OFFICIAL POSITIONS: judge, U.S. Court of Appeals for the District of Columbia, 1939–1943.

SUPREME COURT SERVICE: nominated associate justice by President Franklin D. Roosevelt January 11, 1943, to replace James F. Byrnes, who had resigned; confirmed by the Senate February 8, 1943, by a voice vote; took judicial oath February 15, 1943; served until September 10, 1949; replaced by Sherman Minton, nominated by President Harry S. Truman.

FAMILY: married Annabel Person, August 28, 1917; two daughters, one son.

DEATH: September 10, 1949, York, Maine.

Wiley Blount Rutledge was the first son of Mary Lou Wiggington Rutledge, who named him for his father, a circuit-riding Baptist preacher. His mother's tuberculosis condition and his father's search for a pastorate caused the Rutledge family to move to Texas to Louisiana to North Carolina, finally settling in Asheville, where Pastor Rutledge found a position. When Wiley was nine years old, his mother died, whereupon his father took his three children and headed west again, settling in Maryville, Tennessee. Although raised in the conservative Christian tradition, Wiley later adopted the Unitarian faith.

An ancient languages major and debating team captain, Rutledge transferred his junior year from Maryville College to the University of Wisconsin, from which he graduated in 1914. Unable to afford legal studies there, he attended the Indiana University Law School part time, while supporting himself as a high school teacher in Bloomington.

Law school and teaching responsibilities proved too strenuous for Rutledge's health. He contracted a serious case of tuberculosis and went to recover in the mountains near Asheville, where his mother had died twelve years earlier. Two years later he married Annabel Person, a classmate at Maryville. They lived in New Mexico and Colorado, where he taught high school and continued to recuperate. Despite financial and physical setbacks, Rutledge was determined to become a lawyer. He resumed his legal studies full time at the University of Colorado and graduated in 1922, seven years after receiving his undergraduate degree. For the next two years Rutledge practiced law with the Boulder law firm Goss, Kimbrough, and Hutchinson before returning to academia. He served as a professor of law and dean for more than fifteen years.

Rutledge first came to Franklin Roosevelt's attention because of his outspoken support for the president's Court-packing plan as dean of the University of Iowa College of Law from 1935 to 1939. So unpopular was the proposed judicial reorganization in the Midwest that several Iowa state legislators threatened to withhold university salary increases to protest Dean Rutledge's unorthodox liberal stand. In a letter to his friend Irving Brant of the *St. Louis Star-Times* in 1936, Rutledge expressed confidence that Roosevelt would be able to gain control of the Court if re-elected: "I feel sure he will have the opportunity to make a sufficient number of liberal appointments to undo the major harm."

Recommended by Justice Frankfurter and Irving Brant, Rutledge was appointed to the Court seven years later. Although he had four years of federal judicial experience as a Roosevelt appointee to the Court of Appeals for the District of Columbia, some doubted his legal qualifications for the job. During Senate confirmation hearings Sen. William Langer of North Dakota challenged "the wisdom of the choice of this inexperienced member of the bar. . . . Second-best generals and admirals will not bring us victory and peace. Second-best justices or legal mediocrities will not insure justice in our land."

Judicial experience, however, was not the president's deciding criterion. As he explained to his eighth and last Supreme Court appointee, "Wiley, we had a number of candidates for the court who were highly qualified, but they didn't have geography—you have that."

Rutledge served only six years on the Court, during which he wrote 171 opinions, among them *Thomas v. Collins* (1945), invalidating a Texas law requiring a labor union to seek prior permission from a government official before soliciting members. Despite his sympathy for Jehovah's Witnesses and the discrimination they faced, Rutledge wrote the majority opinion in *Prince v. Massachusetts* (1944). He sustained the conviction of a woman who permitted her nine-year-old niece to sell religious literature on the street. Rutledge is also known for his dissents, especially in *Everson v. Board of Education* (1947) and *In re Yamashita* (1946).

He died suddenly on September 10, 1949.

Harold Hitz Burton

(1945–1958)

BIRTH: June 22, 1888, Jamaica Plain, Massachusetts.

EDUCATION: Bowdoin College, A.B., 1909; Harvard University LL.B., 1912.

OFFICIAL POSITIONS: member, Ohio House of Representatives, 1929; director of law, Cleveland, 1929–1932; acting mayor of Cleveland, November 9, 1931–February 20, 1932; mayor of Cleveland, 1935–1940; U.S. senator, 1941–1945.

SUPREME COURT SERVICE: nominated associate justice by President Harry S. Truman September 19, 1945, to replace Owen J. Roberts, who had resigned; confirmed by the Senate September 19, 1945, by a voice vote; took judicial oath October 1, 1945; retired October 13, 1958; replaced by Potter Stewart, appointed by President Dwight D. Eisenhower.

FAMILY: married Selma Florence Smith, June 15, 1912; two daughters, two sons.

DEATH: October 28, 1964, Washington, D.C.

Burton grew up in Jamaica Plain, a suburb of Boston, in a Republican Unitarian family. His father, Alfred E. Burton, was the dean of faculty at Massachusetts Institute of Technology. His mother, Gertrude Hitz Burton, was the granddaughter of a Swiss diplomat. Burton received a B.A. from Bowdoin College in Brunswick, Maine, in 1909, and an LL.B. from Harvard University in 1912. He married Selma Florence Smith of West Newton, Massachusetts, and together they headed to Ohio, where Burton believed it would be easier to establish a law practice than in the East.

During the next five years, Burton engaged in private practice in Ohio (1912–1914), worked for a Utah public utility (1914–1916), and was an attorney for an Idaho public utility (1917). When World War I began, he was assigned to the 361st Infantry, U.S. Army, where he rose to the rank of captain. After the war Burton returned to Cleveland and private practice.

Burton served a one-year term as a Republican representative to the Ohio state legislature in 1929 and that same year was named Cleveland's director of law, a position he held until 1932. After a brief term as acting mayor of Cleveland in 1931–1932, he won the 1935 mayoral election running as a reformer who would rid the city of gangsters. Twice reelected by the largest majorities in the city's history, he was then elected to the U.S. Senate in 1941. There he gained a reputation as an internationalist, particularly for his sponsorship of the "B²H²" resolution of 1943 that urged U.S. participation in a postwar international peace organization. (The resolution was named after its four sponsors, Senators Burton, Joseph Ball, R-Minn., Carl Hatch, D-N.M., and Joseph Lister Hill, D-Ala.) Burton was also a member of the "Truman Committee," which investigated fraudulent war claims against the government.

Justice Roberts's retirement from the Court July 31, 1945, gave President Truman his first opportunity to appoint a Supreme Court justice. The membership of the "New Deal" Court was heavily Democratic, with the single exception of Chief Justice Harlan Fiske Stone, who had been appointed an associate justice by Republican president Calvin Coolidge. He had been named chief justice, however, by President Roosevelt. Truman was under considerable pressure to name a Republican to the vacant seat. By naming Burton, the president not only improved his relationship with Republican congressional leaders but also gained a justice who, although he was a member of the opposition, was also a former colleague.

One of Burton's best-known opinions is his dissent in *Louisiana ex rel. Francis v. Resweber* (1947). In a 5–4 decision, the Court said it was neither double jeopardy nor cruel and unusual punishment to carry out an electrocution after a first attempt to do so failed. Burton pointed out that repeated attempts to electrocute a prisoner would certainly be considered cruel if the failures were intentional, so why should there be a distinction for an unintentional failure?

After thirteen years on the bench, Burton, suffering from debilitating Parkinson's disease, retired October 13, 1958. He died six years later in Washington, D.C.

Frederick Moore Vinson

(1946–1953)

BIRTH: January 22, 1890, Louisa, Kentucky.

EDUCATION: Kentucky Normal College, 1908; Centre College, A.B., 1909; LL.B., 1911.

OFFICIAL POSITIONS: commonwealth attorney, Thirty-second Judicial District of Kentucky, 1921–1924; U.S. representative, 1924–1929, 1931–1938; judge, U.S. Court of Appeals for the District of Columbia, 1938–1943; director, Office of Economic Stabilization, 1943–1945; administrator, Federal Loan Agency,

Frederick Moore Vinson

1945; director, Office of War Mobilization and Reconversion, 1945; secretary of the Treasury, 1945–1946.

SUPREME COURT SERVICE: nominated chief justice by President Harry S. Truman June 6, 1946, to replace Chief Justice Harlan F. Stone, who had died; confirmed by the Senate June 20, 1946, by a voice vote; took judicial oath June 24, 1946; served until September 8, 1953; replaced by Earl Warren, nominated by President Dwight D. Eisenhower.

FAMILY: married Roberta Dixson, January 24, 1923; two sons.

DEATH: September 8, 1953, Washington, D.C.

Frederick Moore Vinson was born in a small Kentucky town to James Vinson, the county jailer, and his wife, Virginia Ferguson Vinson. He worked his way through school, graduating with an A.B. from Centre College, Kentucky, in 1909 and from law school two years later. Passing the bar at age twenty-one, he began seventeen years of legal practice in the state.

Vinson's first official position came as commonwealth attorney for the Thirty-second Judicial District of Kentucky. When a vacancy occurred for the seat representing Kentucky's Ninth Congressional District, Vinson, a resident for thirty-three years and well known for his grocery, milling, and banking enterprises as well as for his legal practice, was elected. He served in the House from 1924 to 1929 and from 1931 to 1938 and spent the intervening years practicing law in Ashland, Kentucky. An influential member of the House Ways and Means Committee, Vinson worked for passage of President Franklin D. Roosevelt's tax and coal programs.

He resigned his seat in 1938 to become judge for the U.S.

Court of Appeals in the District of Columbia, a position to which he was appointed by Roosevelt in recognition of his New Deal support. After twelve years of legislative experience and five years in the federal judiciary, Vinson began his career in the executive branch as director of the Office of Economic Stabilization in the Roosevelt Administration. His knowledge of tax matters and his ties with Congress made him highly qualified for this position.

Vinson gained further administrative experience as federal loan administrator and director of the Office of War Mobilization and Reconversion, a post previously held by former member of Congress and Supreme Court justice James F. Byrnes.

When Harry Truman became president in 1945, he recognized his need for experienced advisers. Vinson's two years in the previous administration as a political organizer and congressional liaison made him valuable to Truman, who appointed him secretary of the Treasury. In this position Vinson administered the last of the war bond drives and recommended the Revenue Act of 1945 to raise taxes.

After the death of Harlan F. Stone, Truman appointed Vinson chief justice on June 6, 1946. Truman recognized in his friend and adviser someone who realized the need for strong government by the executive. As a member of Congress, Vinson had endorsed President Roosevelt's Court-packing plan. Truman had hoped that Vinson would bring calm leadership to a badly fractured Court, where disagreements among the justices had become public knowledge.

On the Court Vinson usually supported presidential authority. He dissented from the Court's opinion in *Youngstown Sheet & Tube Co. v. Sawyer* (1952), which struck down Truman's seizure of the nation's steel mills. The president was attempting to keep the mills operating while a labor dispute was settled.

Vinson wrote some of the Court's most important opinions concerning race relations and civil rights. In *Shelley v. Kraemer* (1948) the Court ruled that restrictive covenants in housing were unenforceable. In *McLaurin v. Oklahoma State Regents* (1950) the Court said that, once admitted to a state university, blacks may use all the facilities. And in *Sweatt v. Painter* (1950) the justices ruled that a state may not deny a black admission to law school, even if there is a "black" law school available. This case set the stage for *Brown v. Board of Education,* which in 1954 overturned the separate but equal principle that had kept schools segregated.

Vinson died of a heart attack September 8, 1953, ending seven years of service on the Court.

Tom C. Clark

(1949–1967)

BIRTH: September 23, 1899, Dallas, Texas.

EDUCATION: Virginia Military Institute, 1917–1918; University of Texas, A.B., 1921; LL.B., 1922.

OFFICIAL POSITIONS: assistant district attorney, Dallas County, 1927–1932; special assistant, Justice Department,

Tom C. Clark

1937–1943; assistant U.S. attorney general, 1943–1945; U.S. attorney general, 1945–1949; director, Federal Judicial Center, 1968–1970; judge, U.S. Court of Appeals, various circuits, by special arrangement, 1967–1977.

SUPREME COURT SERVICE: nominated associate justice by President Harry S. Truman August 2, 1949, to replace Frank Murphy, who had died; confirmed by the Senate August 18, 1949, by a 73–8 vote; took judicial oath August 24, 1949; retired June 12, 1967; replaced by Thurgood Marshall, nominated by President Lyndon B. Johnson.

FAMILY: Married Mary Jane Ramsey, November 8, 1924; one daughter, two sons.

DEATH: June 13, 1977, New York City.

Thomas Campbell Clark was the son of Virginia Falls Clark and William Clark, a prominent Dallas lawyer active in Democratic politics in Texas. Tom C. Clark, as he preferred to be known, maintained a close relationship with the Democratic Party throughout his life. During World War I Clark served in the national guard after the regular army rejected him. He entered the University of Texas, where he received his A.B. in 1921 and his LL.B. a year later. While a student he met Mary Jane Ramsey, the daughter of a Texas Supreme Court justice. They were married in 1924.

Clark practiced law with his father, whose connections to the Democratic Party helped him forge good relationships with the party's leaders, particularly Tom Connally (House 1917–1929, Senate 1929–1953). Clark was appointed an assistant district attorney for Dallas County in 1927. He returned to private practice in 1932.

With Connally's backing, Clark was named a special assistant in the Justice Department in 1937. He worked in antitrust matters, was the civilian coordinator of the program to evacuate Japanese-Americans from the West Coast, a task he later described as "the biggest mistake of my life." He also prosecuted fraudulent war claims, which brought him into contact with Sen. Harry Truman, D-Mo., head of the Senate War Investigating Committee. Clark was promoted to assistant attorney general in 1943 and the following year cultivated his friendship with Truman by supporting his vice-presidential bid at the Democratic convention. When Truman assumed the presidency after the death of Franklin Roosevelt in 1945, he chose Clark as his attorney general. During his four years at the Justice Department, Clark led the administration's effort to prosecute the American leaders of the Communist Party and other alleged subversives. The department also drafted the first attorney general's list of dangerous political organizations. Truman relied on these activities by the Justice Department to counter charges of being "soft" on communism in the 1948 presidential campaign.

Truman nominated Clark to the Supreme Court August 2, 1949, to replace Justice Frank Murphy, the only Roman Catholic then on the bench. The president was criticized for his choice of Clark, a Presbyterian, but Truman argued that religious considerations should not apply to the selection of Supreme Court justices.

On the Court, Clark showed his independence by voting against Truman's attempt to seize the nation's steel mills during the Korean War. Although he continued to side with the government in loyalty and national security cases, he also wrote some major opinions defending civil rights and civil liberties. In *Mapp v. Ohio* (1961) Clark ruled that evidence obtained through an illegal search could not be used at trial. In *Abington School District v. Schempp* (1963) the Court banned Bible reading and the recitation of prayers in public schools. He also wrote the Court's opinion in *Heart of Atlanta Motel v. United States* (1964), which outlawed segregation in hotels, motels, and restaurants that deal in interstate commerce.

To avoid any appearance of a conflict of interest, Clark resigned from the Court in 1967 when President Johnson named his son, William Ramsey Clark, attorney general.

Clark was a founder of the Federal Judicial Center, a unit within the judicial branch that studies ways to improve the administration of the courts, and he served as its first director, 1968–1970. Until his death in June 1977, he accepted assignments to sit on various circuits of the U.S. Court of Appeals to help ease the federal caseload.

Sherman Minton

(1949–1956)

BIRTH: October 20, 1890, Georgetown, Indiana.

EDUCATION: Indiana University, LL.B., 1915; Yale University, LL.M., 1917.

OFFICIAL POSITIONS: public counselor, Public Service

Sherman Minton

Democratic whip and forged friendships with the other freshman senators, particularly Harry Truman.

Beginning his third term as president, Franklin D. Roosevelt remembered Minton's Senate endorsement of his plan to pack the Court with justices of his choosing and his support for other New Deal policies. In 1941 the president asked Minton to join his staff as an adviser in charge of coordinating military agencies; in that capacity he backed Truman's efforts in the Senate to establish a new committee to investigate defense activities. Later that year Roosevelt appointed him to the U.S. Court of Appeals for the Seventh Circuit.

After Wiley Rutledge's death it took Truman only five days to name Minton, his friend of nearly fifteen years, to the Court. Although a liberal legislator, Minton proved to be a conservative justice. Most of his decisions favored the restrictive powers of the government over the civil liberties of the individual. For example, he wrote the majority opinion in *United States v. Rabinowitz* (1950). He found that it was not a violation of the Fourth Amendment's prohibition against unreasonable search and seizure for the police to conduct a warrantless search, during a lawful arrest, of the area within the suspect's control.

Pernicious anemia forced Minton to resign October 15, 1956, after seven years of service. His retirement announcement suggests that perhaps his career on the Court had not been as influential as he might have hoped. "There will be more interest in who will succeed me than in my passing," he wrote. "I'm an echo." He spent the last nine years of his life in retirement in New Albany, Indiana, where he died in 1965.

Commission, 1933–1934; U.S. senator, 1935–1941; assistant to president, 1941; judge, Seventh Circuit Court of Appeals, 1941–1949.

SUPREME COURT SERVICE: nominated associate justice by President Harry S. Truman September 15, 1949, to replace Wiley B. Rutledge, who had died; confirmed by the Senate October 4, 1949, by a 48–16 vote; took judicial oath October 12, 1949; retired October 15, 1956; replaced by William J. Brennan Jr., nominated by President Dwight D. Eisenhower.

FAMILY: married Gertrude Gurtz, August 11, 1917; two sons, one daughter.

DEATH: April 9, 1965 in New Albany, Indiana.

Sherman Minton, the son of John Evan and Emma Lyvers Minton, was born eight miles from New Albany, Indiana, which would be his home for much of his life. Tall and broad-shouldered, Shay, as he was called by his friends, attended Indiana University, where he excelled in football and basketball as well as his studies. In 1925 he graduated at the top of his class at the law college. His classmates included future GOP presidential candidate Wendell L. Willkie and Paul V. McNutt, who later became governor of Indiana. After graduation, Minton left the state with a $500 scholarship to attend Yale Law School for a year of graduate studies, where one of his teachers was William Howard Taft.

McNutt appointed his former classmate and fellow liberal Democrat to his first official position, as a public counselor, in 1933. The next year Minton successfully ran for the Senate on the New Deal ticket. "Sure I'm a New Dealer," he explained. "I'd be ashamed to be an old dealer." Minton became the assistant

Earl Warren

(1953–1969)

BIRTH: March 19, 1891, Los Angeles, California.

EDUCATION: University of California, B.L., 1912; J.D., 1914.

OFFICIAL POSITIONS: deputy city attorney, Oakland, California, 1919–1920; deputy district attorney, Alameda County, 1920–1925; district attorney, Alameda County, 1925–1939; California attorney general, 1939–1943; governor, 1943–1953.

SUPREME COURT SERVICE: nominated chief justice by President Dwight D. Eisenhower September 30, 1953, to replace Chief Justice Fred M. Vinson, who had died; confirmed March 1, 1954, by a voice vote; took judicial oath October 5, 1953; retired June 23, 1969; replaced by Warren E. Burger, nominated by President Richard Nixon.

FAMILY: married Nina P. Meyers, October 14, 1925; three sons, three daughters.

DEATH: July 9, 1974, Washington, D.C.

Earl Warren was the son of Scandinavian immigrant parents, Methias and Chrystal Hernlund Warren. Soon after his birth, the family moved to Bakersfield, where his father worked as a railroad car repairman. In 1938, after Warren had become active in politics, his father was bludgeoned to death in a crime that was never solved.

Earl Warren

Warren worked his way through college and law school at the University of California. After graduation, he worked in law offices in San Francisco and Oakland, the only time in his career that he engaged in private practice.

From 1919 until his resignation from the Supreme Court in 1969, Warren served without interruption in public office. His first post was deputy city attorney for Oakland. Then he was named a deputy district attorney for Alameda County, which embraces the cities of Oakland, Alameda, and Berkeley.

In 1925 Warren was appointed district attorney when the incumbent resigned. He won election to the post in his own right in 1926, 1930, and 1934. During his fourteen years as district attorney, Warren developed a reputation as a crime fighter, sending a city manager and several councilmen to jail on graft charges and smashing a crooked deal on garbage collection.

A Republican, Warren decided in 1938 to run for state attorney general. He cross-filed and won three primaries—his own party's, as well as the Democratic and Progressive Party contests.

In 1942 he ran for governor of California. Although at first rated an underdog, Warren wound up defeating the incumbent Democratic governor, Culbert Olson, by a margin of 342,000, winning 57.1 percent of the vote. He was reelected twice, winning the Democratic as well as the Republican nomination in 1946 and defeating Democrat James Roosevelt, son of President Franklin D. Roosevelt, by an almost two-to-one margin in 1950.

At first viewed as a conservative governor—he denounced "communistic radicals" and supported the wartime federal order to move all persons of Japanese ancestry away from the West Coast—Warren developed a progressive image after the war. In 1945 he proposed a state program of prepaid medical insurance and later championed liberal pension and welfare benefits.

Warren made two bids for national political office. In 1948 he ran for vice president on the Republican ticket with Gov. Thomas E. Dewey of New York. In 1952 he sought the Republican presidential nomination. But with little chance to win, he threw his support at a crucial moment behind Gen. Dwight D. Eisenhower, helping him win the battle with Sen. Robert A. Taft of Ohio for the nomination.

That support resulted in Eisenhower's political indebtedness to Warren, which the president repaid in 1953. After the death of Chief Justice Fred M. Vinson, Eisenhower nominated Warren to replace him. Reflecting on his choice years later in light of the Warren Court's liberal record, Eisenhower reportedly said that the appointment of Warren was the biggest mistake he made as president.

The Warren Court is credited with a large number of landmark decisions, many written by the chief justice. Best known is the Court's unanimous decision in *Brown v. Board of Education* (1954), which said that separate schools for blacks and whites were inherently unequal and violated the equal protection guarantee of the Fourteenth Amendment. Warren also wrote the majority opinion in *Miranda v. Arizona* (1966). Here the Court said that those held in police custody must be told of their constitutional rights before they can be questioned. But Warren said that the crowning achievement of his tenure was *Baker v. Carr*, a 1962 opinion written by Justice William Brennan. The decision in *Baker v. Carr* opened the federal courts to litigants who had been unable to convince their states to reapportion state legislative and congressional districts.

In addition to his work on the Court, Warren headed the commission that investigated the assassination of President John F. Kennedy.

In 1968 Warren submitted his resignation, conditional on confirmation of a successor. But the Senate got bogged down in the fight to confirm President Johnson's nomination of Associate Justice Abe Fortas to succeed him, so Warren agreed to serve another year. In 1969, when Richard Nixon assumed office, he chose Warren E. Burger as the new chief justice, and Warren stepped down.

John Marshall Harlan

(1955–1971)

BIRTH: May 20, 1899, Chicago, Illinois.

EDUCATION: Princeton University, B.A., 1920; Rhodes scholar, Oxford University, Balliol College, B.A. in jurisprudence, 1923; New York Law School, LL.B., 1924.

OFFICIAL POSITIONS: assistant U.S. attorney, Southern District of New York, 1925–1927; special assistant attorney general, New York, 1928–1930; chief counsel, New York State Crime Commission, 1951–1953; judge, U.S. Court of Appeals for the Second Circuit, 1954–1955.

SUPREME COURT SERVICE: nominated associate justice

John Marshall Harlan

by President Dwight D. Eisenhower November 8, 1954, to re-place Robert Jackson, who had died; confirmed by the Senate March 16, 1955, by a 71–11 vote; took judicial oath March 28, 1955; retired September 23, 1971; replaced by William H. Rehnquist, nominated by President Richard Nixon.

FAMILY: married Ethel Andrews, November 10, 1928; one daughter.

DEATH: December 29, 1971, Washington D.C.

The namesake and grandson of Justice John Marshall Harlan (Supreme Court, 1877–1911) was born in Chicago, where his father, John Maynard Harlan, was a prominent attorney. John Maynard Harlan was also engaged in politics, running two losing races for mayor of Chicago near the turn of the century. The future justice's mother was Elizabeth Palmer Flagg Harlan.

The younger Harlan, who went by John M. Harlan, to distinguish himself from his famous forebear, attended Princeton University, graduating in 1920. Awarded a Rhodes scholarship, he spent the next three years studying jurisprudence at Balliol College, Oxford. Returning to the United States, he earned his law degree in 1924 from New York Law School.

For the next twenty-five years Harlan was a member of a prominent Wall Street law firm, but he took periodic leaves to serve in various public positions. In 1925 he became an assistant U.S. attorney for the Southern District of New York. He returned to private practice but soon left again, this time to serve as one of the special prosecutors in a state investigation of municipal graft.

During World War II, Harlan served as head of the Opera-

tional Analysis Section of the Eighth Air Force, even though he was well past the usual age of service. After the war he returned to private practice, but was again called to public service. From 1951 to 1953 he was chief counsel to the New York State Crime Commission, which Gov. Thomas E. Dewey had appointed to investigate the relationship between organized crime and state government. During the same period, Harlan also became active in various professional organizations, serving as chairman of the committee on professional ethics of the Association of the Bar of the City of New York and later as chairman of its committee on the judiciary and as vice president of the association.

A lifelong Republican, Harlan was nominated in January 1954 by President Eisenhower to the U.S. Court of Appeals for the Second Circuit. Harlan had hardly begun his work there, however, when the president named him in November 1954 to the U.S. Supreme Court. The Senate, then in special session to consider the censure of Sen. Joseph R. McCarthy, postponed consideration of his nomination until the new Congress met in 1955. Harlan remained on the appeals court until confirmed by the Senate in March 1955.

Harlan did not share the activist views of the Warren Court. He allied himself with Felix Frankfurter—they agreed in more than 80 percent of the cases they heard together. But he was much more of a moderate than a doctrinaire conservative. And in the First Amendment area, his views were more liberal. In *NAACP v. Alabama ex rel. Patterson* (1958) he upheld the right of the organization to keep its membership lists private. In *Cohen v. California* (1971) he wrote the majority opinion, which extended to a rude message on the back of a jacket the constitutional protection afforded to speech.

Suffering from cancer of the spine, Harlan resigned from the Court in September 1971 and died December 29.

William Joseph Brennan Jr.

(1956–1990)

BIRTH: April 25, 1906, Newark, New Jersey.

EDUCATION: University of Pennsylvania, B.S., 1928; Harvard Law School, LL.B., 1931.

OFFICIAL POSITIONS: judge, New Jersey Superior Court, 1949–1950; judge, appellate division, New Jersey Superior Court, 1950–1952; associate judge, New Jersey Supreme Court, 1952–1956.

SUPREME COURT SERVICE: recess appointment as associate justice by President Dwight D. Eisenhower October 16, 1956, to replace Sherman Minton, who had resigned; nominated as associate justice by President Eisenhower January 14, 1957; confirmed by the Senate March 19, 1957 by a voice vote; took judicial oath October 16, 1956; retired July 20, 1990; replaced by David H. Souter, nominated by President George Bush.

FAMILY: married Marjorie Leonard, May 5, 1928, died 1982; two sons, one daughter; married Mary Fowler, March 9, 1983.

William Joseph Brennan Jr.

William J. Brennan Jr. was the second of eight children of Irish parents who immigrated to the United States in 1890. His mother was Agnes McDermott Brennan. William displayed impressive academic abilities early in life. He was an outstanding student in high school, an honors student at the University of Pennsylvania's Wharton School of Finance, and in the top 10 percent of his Harvard Law School class in 1931.

After law school Brennan returned to Newark, where he joined a prominent law firm. Following passage of the Wagner Labor Act in 1935, Brennan began to specialize in labor law. With the outbreak of World War II, Brennan entered the Army, serving as a manpower troubleshooter on the staff of the undersecretary of war, Robert B. Patterson. At the conclusion of the war, Brennan returned to his old law firm. But as his practice swelled, Brennan, a dedicated family man, began to resent the demands it placed on his time.

A desire to temper the pace of his work was one of the reasons Brennan accepted an appointment to the newly created New Jersey Superior Court in 1949. Because Brennan had been a leader in the movement to establish the court as part of a large program of judicial reform, it was not a surprise when Republican governor Alfred E. Driscoll selected him, even though he was a registered Democrat, to serve on it.

During his tenure on the superior court, Brennan's use of pretrial procedures to speed up the disposition of cases brought him to the attention of New Jersey Supreme Court justice Arthur T. Vanderbilt. It was reportedly at Vanderbilt's suggestion that Brennan was moved first in 1950 to the appellate division of the superior court and then in 1952 to the state supreme court. Late in 1956, when President Eisenhower was looking for

a justice to replace Sherman Minton, Vanderbilt and others strongly recommended Brennan for the post, and Eisenhower gave him a recess appointment in October. There was some criticism that Eisenhower was currying favor with voters by nominating a Roman Catholic Democrat to the bench so close to the election, but Brennan's established integrity and nonpolitical background minimized the impact of the charges.

In his time on the Court, thirty-four years and nine months, it was hard to find an area of American life that Brennan did not affect. Among his most important opinions is *Baker v. Carr* (1962). Ruling that federal courts could consider cases of disproportionate voting districts, he said that states that fail to reapportion may be in violation of the equal protection clause. In the area of free speech, Brennan ruled in *New York Times v. Sullivan* (1964) that to sue for libel public figures had to prove actual malice on the part of the media. Brennan also influenced thinking on the right to privacy. In *Eisenstadt v. Baird* (1972) Brennan wrote the opinion in which the Court expanded on its ruling in *Griswold v. Connecticut* (1965). *Eisenstadt* said that a ban on distribution of contraceptives to unmarried persons was unconstitutional.

Even after his many years on the Court, it was with reluctance that Brennan retired July 20, 1990. He had suffered a small stroke and was advised that the combination of his medical condition and his age, eighty-four at the time, would make it difficult to keep up his rigorous Court schedule. In the years immediately after his retirement, Brennan continued to go to his office every day. He kept busy with federal appeals court work, law school lectures, and speeches.

Charles Evans Whittaker

(1957–1962)

BIRTH: February 22, 1901, Troy, Kansas.

EDUCATION: University of Kansas City Law School, LL.B., 1924.

OFFICIAL POSITIONS: judge, U.S. District Court for Western District of Missouri, 1954–1956; judge, Eighth Circuit Court of Appeals, 1956–1957.

SUPREME COURT SERVICE: nominated associate justice by President Dwight D. Eisenhower March 2, 1957, to replace Stanley Reed, who had retired; confirmed by the Senate March 19, 1957, by a voice vote; took judicial oath March 25, 1957; retired March 31, 1962; replaced by Byron R. White, nominated by President John F. Kennedy.

FAMILY: married Winifred R. Pugh, July 7, 1928; three sons.

DEATH: November 26, 1973, Kansas City, Missouri.

Charles Evans Whittaker's beginnings were humble. The son of Charles and Ida Miller Whittaker, he was born in eastern Kansas and raised on his father's farm. After his nomination to the Supreme Court, Whittaker described to the Senate Judiciary Committee his early life: "I went to school in a little white school house on the corner of my father's farm through nine often had the unenviable task of breaking ties on a sharply divided Court. He tended to side with the liberals in cases dealing with individual liberties, such as *Green v. United States* (1957), which concerned double jeopardy, and *Moore v. Michigan* (1957), which dealt with the right to counsel. But he was on the side of the conservatives in two 1958 cases that upheld the convictions of defendants who claimed their confessions were coerced.

Exhausted from overwork, Whittaker suffered a nervous breakdown in 1962. He followed his doctor's advice and resigned from the Court at the age of sixty-one after only five years of service. Whittaker did not return to his former legal practice, nor was he active in public life. In 1965 he served on the legal staff of General Motors and the following year was asked by the Senate Committee on Standards and Conduct to help devise a code of senatorial ethics. The spread of civil disobedience in the 1960s particularly disturbed him, and he addressed the American Bar Association on various occasions concerning the need for "redress in the courts rather than in the streets."

He died November 26, 1973, in Kansas City.

Charles Evans Whittaker

grades and then I went to high school in Troy, Kansas, and rode a pony to school through six miles of mud night and morning for about a year and a half."

Whittaker quit school after his mother died on his sixteenth birthday. Four years later he applied to the University of Kansas City Law School and was accepted only after agreeing to private tutoring in the high school subjects he had missed. His education was financed from the sale of pelts of animals he trapped on the Kansas plains and from part-time work as an office boy in the law firm Watson, Gage, and Ess. In 1923 he passed the Missouri bar examination, a year before he graduated from law school.

Whittaker joined the law firm where he had been the office boy. He became a full partner in 1932. He represented many corporate clients including Union Pacific and Montgomery Ward. Another client was the *Kansas City Star*, a newspaper controlled by Roy Roberts. Whittaker and Roberts became friends. Roberts was also a friend and political supporter of Gen. Dwight D. Eisenhower. As president, Eisenhower appointed Whittaker to the U.S. District Court for the Western District of Missouri from 1954 to 1956 and on the U.S. Court of Appeals for the Eighth Circuit in 1956 and 1957.

Eisenhower considered previous judicial experience one of the most important criteria for a Supreme Court justice. Whittaker's outstanding qualifications as well as his ties to the Republican Party made him a likely choice to fill the vacancy left by Stanley Reed's retirement. On March 19, 1957, Charles Whittaker became the first Supreme Court justice born in Kansas and appointed from Missouri.

As the junior justice, who traditionally votes last, Whittaker

Potter Stewart

(1958–1981)

BIRTH: January 23, 1915, Jackson, Michigan.

EDUCATION: Yale College, B.A., cum laude, 1937; Yale Law School, LL.B., cum laude, 1941; fellow, Cambridge University, Cambridge, England, 1937–1938.

OFFICIAL POSITIONS: member, Cincinnati, Ohio, city council, 1950–1953; vice mayor of Cincinnati, 1952–1953; judge, Sixth Circuit Court of Appeals, 1954–1958.

SUPREME COURT SERVICE: received recess appointment as associate justice by President Dwight D. Eisenhower October 14, 1958, to replace Harold H. Burton, who had retired; nominated associate justice by President Eisenhower January 17, 1959; confirmed by the Senate May 5, 1959, by a 70–17 vote; took judicial oath October 14, 1958; retired July 3, 1981; replaced by Sandra Day O'Connor, nominated by President Ronald Reagan.

FAMILY: married Mary Ann Bertles, April 24, 1943; two sons, one daughter.

DEATH: December 7, 1985, Hanover, New Hampshire.

Stewart was the son of an established middle-class Cincinnati family with a strong tradition of public service and a respect for the benefits of a good education. His father, James Garfield Stewart, was mayor of Cincinnati from 1938 to 1947 and was the Republican nominee for governor of Ohio in 1944. He served on the Ohio Supreme Court from 1947 until his death in 1959. His mother, Harriet Potter Stewart, served as president of the League of Women Voters in Cincinnati.

Stewart attended two of the most prestigious eastern schools—Hotchkiss (preparatory) and Yale, where he received numerous academic honors and graduated Phi Beta Kappa in 1937. After completing his undergraduate work, he spent a year

Potter Stewart

doing postgraduate work at Cambridge University in England. He returned to the United States in 1938 and began law school at Yale. He graduated in 1941 and moved to New York, where he joined a Wall Street law firm. He had hardly begun work there, however, when World War II broke out, and he joined the Navy. Stewart served as a deck officer aboard oil tankers in the Atlantic and Mediterranean. He married Mary Ann Bertles April 24, 1943, while his ship was in port. The couple eventually had three children.

After the war, Stewart returned to his New York law practice but soon moved to his home town of Cincinnati, where he joined one of its leading law firms. In Cincinnati he took up the family's tradition of public service. He was twice elected to the city council and served one term as vice mayor. He was also involved in the 1948 and 1952 Republican presidential campaigns. In both years he supported the efforts of his friend, Sen. Robert A. Taft, to secure the Republican presidential nomination. When Eisenhower won the party's endorsement instead in 1952, Stewart actively supported him in the fall campaign.

Stewart's appointment in 1954 to the U.S. Court of Appeals for the Sixth Circuit ended his direct participation in politics. He was President Eisenhower's fifth and last appointment to the Supreme Court. He received a recess appointment in 1958, and Eisenhower sent his nomination to the new Congress early in 1959.

On the Court Stewart was described as a "swing justice," moving between the liberal and conservative factions. But he disliked the characterization of swing justice, saying that judges should be free of political, religious, and moral ideology when they make their decisions. He dissented from the Court's deci-

sion in *Griswold v. Connecticut* (1965), saying the statute in question, which prevented married couples from obtaining contraceptives, was "an uncommonly silly law," but not unconstitutional. He wrote more than six hundred opinions, many concerning the Fourth Amendment protection against unreasonable search and seizure—for example, the landmark *Katz v. United States* (1967), in which the Court extended such protection to the interception by police of telephone conversations.

Stewart retired July 3, 1981, after twenty-three years of service. He said he wanted to leave the Court while he was still relatively young and healthy enough to enjoy time with his family. He died four years later following a stroke in Hanover, New Hampshire December 7, 1985.

Byron Raymond White

(1962–1993)

BIRTH: June 8, 1917, Fort Collins, Colorado.

EDUCATION: University of Colorado, B.A., 1938; Rhodes Scholar, Oxford University, 1939; Yale Law School, LL.B., magna cum laude, 1946.

OFFICIAL POSITIONS: law clerk to Chief Justice Fred M. Vinson, 1946–1947; deputy U.S. attorney general, 1961–1962.

SUPREME COURT SERVICE: nominated associate justice by President John F. Kennedy March 30, 1962, to replace Charles E. Whittaker, who had retired; confirmed by the Senate April 11, 1962, by a voice vote; took judicial oath April 16, 1962; retired June 28, 1993; replaced by Ruth Bader Ginsburg, nominated by President Bill Clinton.

Byron Raymond White

FAMILY: married Marion Stearns, 1946; one son, one daughter.

White was born in Fort Collins, but grew up in Wellington, Colorado, a small town in the sugar beet area of the state. His father, Alpha Albert White, was in the lumber business and served as a Republican mayor of Wellington. His mother was Maude Burger White.

Ranking first in his high school class, White in 1934 won a scholarship to the University of Colorado, where he earned a reputation as an outstanding scholar-athlete. He was first in his class, a member of Phi Beta Kappa, and the winner of three varsity letters in football, four in basketball, and three in baseball. By the end of his college career in 1938 he had been dubbed "Whizzer" White for his prowess as a football player, a performance that earned him both a national reputation and a one-year contract with the old Pittsburgh Pirates professional football team.

But after a year as a professional football player, White sailed for England to attend Oxford University, where he had received a coveted Rhodes Scholarship. When World War II broke out in September 1939, White returned to the United States and enrolled in Yale Law School, alternating law study with playing professional football for the Detroit Lions.

When the United States entered the war, White joined the Navy, serving in the South Pacific. He returned to Yale after the war, earning his law degree magna cum laude.

White then served as law clerk to the new chief justice, Fred M. Vinson. In 1947 he returned to his native Colorado, where for the next fourteen years he practiced law with a prominent Denver law firm.

Several times during his adult life, White had crossed paths with John F. Kennedy. The two first met when White was studying at Oxford and Kennedy's father, Joseph, was ambassador to the Court of St. James's. They met again during White's wartime service in the South Pacific. And when White was clerking for Vinson, he renewed his acquaintance with Kennedy, then a freshman U.S. representative.

In 1960, when Kennedy decided to run for president, White joined the campaign and headed the preconvention Kennedy effort in Colorado. After Kennedy's nomination, White became chairman of the National Citizens for Kennedy organization, designed to attract independents and Republicans. President Kennedy named White to the post of deputy attorney general, a position White held until Kennedy named him to the Supreme Court in 1962.

Joining a Court with a solid liberal bloc, White quickly gained a reputation for strong dissents. Indeed, he dissented from some of the most influential decisions of the late twentieth century, among them *Escobedo v. Illinois* (1964) and *Miranda v. Arizona* (1966), in the criminal justice field, and *Roe v. Wade* (1973), which guarantees a woman's right to have an abortion. He wrote the majority opinion in *Bowers v. Hardwick* (1986), in which the Court upheld a state law prohibiting sodomy.

White retired from the Court June 28, 1993, after thirty-one years and two months of service. He was seventy-six years old at the time but in good health, still enjoying various athletic activities. "It has been an interesting and exciting experience to serve on the Court," he said, adding that he was retiring because it was time that "someone else be permitted to have a like experience."

Arthur Joseph Goldberg

(1962–1965)

BIRTH: August 8, 1908, Chicago, Illinois.

EDUCATION: Northwestern University, B.S.L., 1929; J.D., summa cum laude, 1930.

OFFICIAL POSITIONS: secretary of labor, 1961–1962; U.S. ambassador to the United Nations, 1965–1968.

SUPREME COURT SERVICE: nominated associate justice by President John F. Kennedy August 29, 1962, to replace Felix Frankfurter, who had retired; confirmed by the Senate September 25, 1962, by a voice vote; took judicial oath October 1, 1962; resigned July 25, 1965; replaced by Abe Fortas, nominated by President Lyndon B. Johnson.

FAMILY: married Dorothy Kurgans, July 18, 1931; one daughter, one son.

DEATH: January 19, 1990, Washington, D.C.

The youngest of eleven children born to his Russian Jewish parents, Joseph and Rebecca Perlstein Goldberg, Arthur Goldberg was admitted to the Illinois bar at age twenty. He first gained national attention as counsel to the Chicago Newspaper Guild during its 1938 strike. After serving as a special assistant in the Office of Strategic Services during World War II, Goldberg returned to the practice of labor law, representing both the Congress of Industrial Organizations (CIO) and the United Steelworkers of America. He played a major role in the 1955 merger of the CIO with the American Federation of Labor and worked as a special counsel to the new AFL-CIO until 1961.

Appointed secretary of labor in the first year of the Kennedy administration, Goldberg's tenure saw the passage of the Area Redevelopment Act of 1961, congressional approval of an increase in the minimum wage, and the reorganization of the Office of Manpower Administration (now the Employment and Training Administration).

President Kennedy's second Supreme Court appointment, Goldberg was named August 29, 1962, to replace Felix Frankfurter, who had held the "Jewish seat" since 1939. It had been occupied formerly by Justice Benjamin N. Cardozo, 1932–1938.

Although his service on the Court was brief, Goldberg wrote a number of significant majority opinions. Among the best known is *Escobedo v. Illinois* (1964), in which the Court overturned the conviction of a man for murder because he had not been informed of his right to remain silent and not incriminate himself.

President Johnson asked Goldberg to leave the Court and become U.S. ambassador to the United Nations July 20, 1965. Goldberg replaced Adlai Stevenson, who had died July 14 in London. He resigned the post in 1968. After an unsuccessful race for governor of New York against Republican incumbent Nelson Rockefeller in 1970, Goldberg returned to Washington, D.C., where he remained in private practice. A frequent guest instructor at universities and colleges, he was the author of *AFL-CIO Labor United*, 1956; *Defenses of Freedom*, 1966; and *Equal Justice: The Warren Era of the Supreme Court*, 1972.

Goldberg died January 19, 1990 in Washington, D.C.

Abe Fortas

(1965–1969)

BIRTH: June 19, 1910, Memphis, Tennessee.

EDUCATION: Southwestern College, A.B., 1930; Yale Law School, LL.B., 1933.

OFFICIAL POSITIONS: assistant director, corporate reorganization study, Securities and Exchange Commission, 1934–1937; assistant director, Public Utilities Division, Securities and Exchange Commission, 1938–1939; general counsel, Public Works Administration, 1939–1940, and counsel to the Bituminous Coal Division, 1939–1941; director, Division of Power, Department of the Interior, 1941–1942; undersecretary of the interior, 1942–1946.

SUPREME COURT SERVICE: nominated associate justice by President Lyndon B. Johnson July 28, 1965, to replace Arthur J. Goldberg, who had resigned; confirmed by the Senate August 11, 1965, by a voice vote; took judicial oath October 4, 1965; resigned May 14, 1969; replaced by Harry A. Blackmun, nominated by President Richard Nixon.

Abe Fortas

FAMILY: married Carolyn Eugenia Agger, July 9, 1935.

DEATH: April 5, 1982, in Washington, D.C.

Fortas was the youngest of five children born to Ray Berson Fortas and William Fortas, an English immigrant cabinetmaker. After working his way through Southwestern College in Memphis, from which he graduated first in his class in 1930, Fortas entered Yale Law School, where he met William O. Douglas, a young professor. Fortas served as editor of the school's law journal and graduated in 1933.

As a child Fortas had developed an interest in music and learned the violin, a skill he used to earn money while in school. Throughout his adult life he played in various string quartets. In 1935 he married Carolyn Eugenia Agger, who became a renowned tax lawyer.

Upon graduation, Fortas joined the faculty at Yale as an associate professor of law. But the excitement and activity generated by President Franklin D. Roosevelt's New Deal in Washington soon enticed the young lawyer away from academic pursuits and into public office.

During the 1930s Fortas held a series of jobs in the Roosevelt administration, mostly involving detailed legal work in newly created agencies such as the Securities and Exchange Commission (with Douglas) and the Public Works Administration. In 1942 he was appointed undersecretary of the interior, serving under the controversial and irascible Harold L. Ickes.

Following World War II, Fortas helped found the law firm of Arnold, Fortas, and Porter, which quickly became one of Washington's most prestigious legal institutions. The firm specialized in corporate law, but its members, including Fortas, found time to litigate some important civil and individual rights cases as well. He defended Owen Lattimore against charges of disloyalty and argued Clarence Earl Gideon's case before the Supreme Court.

In 1948 Fortas successfully defended a member of Congress from Texas—Lyndon B. Johnson—in a challenge to Johnson's election victory in the Texas Democratic senatorial primary. That defense was the basis for an enduring friendship between the two men, and Fortas became one of Johnson's most trusted advisers.

Preferring his role as confidential adviser, Fortas in 1964 declined Johnson's offer to name him attorney general. In 1965 Johnson persuaded Justice Arthur J. Goldberg to resign from the Supreme Court to become the U.S. Ambassador to the United Nations, which created a vacancy on the Court for Fortas. Johnson ignored Fortas's opposition and appointed him to the Court.

He is best known for two cases involving the rights of juveniles. In 1967 he held in *In re Gault* that the privilege against self-incrimination and the right to counsel extended to those accused in juvenile court. In *Tinker v. Des Moines Independent Community School District* (1969) Fortas said that the wearing of black armbands to school to protest the Vietnam War was "closely akin" to "pure speech" protected by the First Amendment.

When Chief Justice Earl Warren voiced his intention to resign in 1968, Johnson decided to elevate Fortas to the chief justiceship. But amid charges of "cronyism," events began to unfold that ultimately led to Fortas's undoing.

In the face of strong opposition from Republicans and conservative Democrats, Johnson was finally forced to withdraw the nomination, but not before it was revealed that Fortas had received $15,000 to teach a course at a local university.

Then, in May 1969, *Life* magazine revealed that since becoming a justice Fortas had accepted—and then returned several months later—$20,000 from a charitable foundation controlled by the family of an indicted stock manipulator. The allegations touched off talk of impeachment proceedings against Fortas. In mid-May, denying any "wrongdoing on my part," Fortas resigned from the Court. He then returned to private law practice in Washington in partnership with another attorney, a practice he maintained until his death in 1982.

Thurgood Marshall

(1967–1991)

BIRTH: July 2, 1908, Baltimore, Maryland.

EDUCATION: Lincoln University, A.B., cum laude, 1930; Howard University Law School, LL.B., 1933.

OFFICIAL POSITIONS: judge, Second Circuit Court of Appeals, 1961–1965; U.S. solicitor general, 1965–1967.

SUPREME COURT SERVICE: nominated associate justice by President Lyndon B. Johnson June 13, 1967, to replace Tom C. Clark, who had retired; confirmed by the Senate August 30,

Thurgood Marshall

1967, by a 69–11 vote; took judicial oath October 2, 1967; retired October 1, 1991; replaced by Clarence Thomas, nominated by President George Bush.

FAMILY: married Vivian Burey, September 4, 1929, died February 1955; married Cecilia Suyat, December 17, 1955; two sons.

DEATH: January 24, 1993, Bethesda, Maryland.

Marshall was the son of Norma Williams Marshall, a primary school teacher, and William Canfield Marshall, a club steward. In 1926 he left Baltimore to attend the all-black Lincoln University in Chester, Pennsylvania, where he developed a reputation as an outstanding debater. After graduating cum laude in 1930, Marshall decided to study law and entered Howard University in Washington, D.C.

While he was in college, Marshall developed a lifelong interest in civil rights. After graduating first in his law school class in 1933, he began a long and historic involvement with the National Association for the Advancement of Colored People (NAACP). In 1940 he became the head of the newly formed NAACP Legal Defense and Education Fund, a position he held for more than twenty years.

Over those two decades, Marshall coordinated the fund's attack on segregation in voting, housing, public accommodations, and education. The culmination of his career as a civil rights attorney came in 1954 as chief counsel in a series of cases grouped under the title *Brown v. Board of Education*. In that historic case, which Marshall argued before the Supreme Court, civil rights advocates convinced the Court to declare segregation in public schools unconstitutional.

In 1961 Marshall was appointed by President Kennedy to the

Second Circuit Court of Appeals, but because of heated opposition from southern Democratic senators, he was not confirmed for a year.

Four years after he was named to the appeals court, Marshall was chosen by President Lyndon B. Johnson to be the nation's first black solicitor general. During his years as the government's chief advocate before the Supreme Court, Marshall scored impressive victories in the areas of civil and constitutional rights. He won Supreme Court approval of the 1965 Voting Rights Act, voluntarily informed the Court that the government had used electronic eavesdropping devices in two cases, and joined in a suit that successfully overturned a California constitutional amendment that prohibited open housing legislation.

On June 13, 1967, President Johnson chose Marshall to become the first black justice of the Supreme Court. He is known for his majority opinion in *Stanley v. Georgia* (1969), which held that the Constitution protects a person's right to read anything he chooses in the privacy of his home. In *Benton v. Maryland* (1969) he wrote the opinion that applies the double jeopardy clause of the Constitution to state actions. Always opposed to the death penalty, Marshall joined his colleague William Brennan in dissenting in every case that upheld it.

After nearly a quarter century of service on the Court, Marshall retired October 1, 1991. When he announced he would be stepping down, he said his advancing age and worsening health prevented him from continuing on the bench. Marshall, who had championed civil rights and individual liberties, had become the bitter voice of dissent on a Court that was becoming more conservative. He died less than two years later, in January 1993.

Warren Earl Burger

(1969–1986)

BIRTH: September 17, 1907, St. Paul, Minnesota.

EDUCATION: attended the University of Minnesota, 1925–1927; St. Paul College of Law (now William Mitchell College of Law), LL.B., magna cum laude, 1931.

OFFICIAL POSITIONS: assistant U.S. attorney general, Civil Division, Justice Department, 1953–1956; judge, U.S. Court of Appeals for the District of Columbia, 1956–1969.

SUPREME COURT SERVICE: nominated chief justice by President Richard Nixon May 21, 1969, to replace Chief Justice Earl Warren, who had retired; confirmed by the Senate June 9, 1969, by a 74–3 vote; took judicial oath June 23, 1969; retired September 26, 1986; replaced as chief justice by William H. Rehnquist, named by President Ronald Reagan.

FAMILY: married Elvera Stromberg, November 8, 1933; one son, one daughter.

DEATH: June 25, 1995, Washington, D.C.

Burger was the fourth of seven children born to Charles J. Burger and Katharine Schnittger Burger. His Swiss-German-Austrian grandparents had come to the Middle West before the

Warren Earl Burger

Civil War. Financially unable to attend college full time, Burger spent the years following his 1925 graduation from high school attending college and law school evening classes—two years at the University of Minnesota and four at St. Paul College of Law, now William Mitchell College of Law. To support himself, Burger worked full time as an accountant for a life insurance company.

After graduating with honors from law school in 1931, Burger joined a respected law firm in Minnesota, where he practiced until 1953. He also taught part time at his alma mater from 1931 to 1948.

As a school boy Burger developed an interest in art and was an accomplished sculptor; as chief justice, he served as chairman of the board of the National Gallery of Art. He was an antiques buff and a connoisseur of fine wines. He also served as chancellor of the Smithsonian Institution.

Soon after beginning his law career in Minnesota, Burger became involved in Republican state politics. In 1938 he helped in the successful campaign of Harold E. Stassen for governor of Minnesota.

During Stassen's unsuccessful bid for the Republican presidential nomination ten years later, Burger first met a man who was to figure prominently in his future—Herbert Brownell, then campaign manager for GOP presidential nominee Thomas E. Dewey. Brownell, who became attorney general during the Eisenhower administration, brought Burger to Washington in 1953 to serve as assistant attorney general in charge of the Justice Department's Civil Division.

Burger's stint as assistant attorney general from 1953 to 1956 was not without controversy. His decision to defend the government's action in the dismissal of John F. Peters, a part-time federal employee, on grounds of disloyalty—after Solicitor General Simon E. Sobeloff had refused to do so on grounds of conscience—won Burger the enmity of many liberals.

But Burger's overall record as assistant attorney general apparently met with President Eisenhower's approval, and in 1956 the president appointed Burger to the U.S. Court of Appeals for the District of Columbia Circuit. As an appeals court judge, Burger developed a reputation as a conservative, especially in criminal justice cases.

Off the bench, Burger began to speak out in support of major administrative reform of the judicial system—a cause he continued to advocate as chief justice. Due in large part to Burger's efforts, the American Bar Association and other legal groups established the Institute of Court Management to train court executive officers, bring new management techniques to the courts, and relieve judges of paperwork. During Burger's years as chief justice, Congress also approved a number of measures to modernize the operations of the federal judiciary.

President Nixon's appointment of Burger as chief justice on May 21, 1969, caught most observers by surprise because, despite the nominee's years of service in the Justice Department and the court of appeals, he was little known outside the legal community. But Nixon apparently was impressed by Burger's consistent argument as an appeals judge that the Constitution should be read narrowly—a belief Nixon shared.

In an odd twist of fate, Burger announced the unanimous decision of the Court that led to Nixon's resignation. In *United States v. Nixon* (1974) the Court ruled that the president must surrender tapes of conversations recorded in the Oval Office. The tapes had been subpoenaed in a criminal conspiracy trial, the culmination of the Watergate scandal. Burger's opinion argued that a president's privileges and immunities were not absolute but depended on the circumstances. In this case the need for evidence to conduct a fair trial outweighed presidential privilege.

Burger served for seventeen years as chief justice, resigning in 1986 to devote full time to the chairmanship of the commission planning the Constitution's bicentennial celebration in 1987. He continued to write and speak about judicial administration and reform of the legal system until his death in Washington on June 25, 1995. Just a few months earlier, he had published a book entitled *It is So Ordered: A Constitution Unfolds*.

Harry Andrew Blackmun

(1970–1994)

BIRTH: November 12, 1908, Nashville, Illinois.

EDUCATION: Harvard College, B.A., summa cum laude, 1929; Harvard Law School, LL.B., 1932.

OFFICIAL POSITIONS: clerk, Eighth Circuit Court of Appeals, 1932–1933; judge, Eighth Circuit Court of Appeals, 1959–1970.

SUPREME COURT SERVICE: nominated associate justice

Harry Andrew Blackmun

by President Richard Nixon April 14, 1970, to replace Abe Fortas, who had resigned; confirmed by the Senate May 12, 1970, by a 94–0 vote; took judicial oath June 9, 1970; retired August 3, 1994; replaced by Stephen G. Breyer, nominated by President Bill Clinton.

FAMILY: married Dorothy E. Clark, June 21, 1941; three daughters.

Harry Blackmun was born in Nashville, Illinois, to Corwin Blackmun and Theo Reuter Blackmun. He spent most of his early years in the Minneapolis-St. Paul area. In grade school Blackmun began a lifelong friendship with Warren Burger, with whom he was later to serve on the Supreme Court.

Showing an early aptitude for mathematics, Blackmun went east after high school to attend Harvard College on a scholarship. At Harvard Blackmun majored in mathematics and thought briefly of becoming a physician, but chose the law instead. He graduated Phi Beta Kappa from Harvard in 1929 and entered Harvard Law School, from which he graduated in 1932. During his school years, Blackmun supported himself with a variety of odd jobs, including tutoring in math and driving the launch for the college crew team.

Blackmun returned to St. Paul, where he served for a year and a half as clerk to Judge John B. Sanborn, whom Blackmun was to succeed on the U.S. circuit court in 1959. He left the clerkship in 1933 to enter private practice with a Minneapolis law firm, where he remained for sixteen years. During that time he also taught at the St. Paul College of Law, Burger's alma mater, and at the University of Minnesota Law School.

In 1950 he accepted a post as counsel for the world-famous Mayo Clinic in Rochester, Minnesota. There, Blackmun quickly developed a reputation among his colleagues as a serious man totally engrossed in his profession.

This reputation followed him to the bench of the Eighth Circuit Court of Appeals, to which Blackmun was appointed by President Eisenhower in 1959. As an appeals court judge, Blackmun became known for his scholarly and thorough opinions.

Blackmun's nomination to the Supreme Court was President Nixon's third try to fill the seat vacated by Justice Abe Fortas's resignation. When the Senate refused to confirm Nixon's first two nominees—Clement F. Haynsworth Jr. of South Carolina and G. Harrold Carswell of Florida—Nixon said that he had concluded that the Senate "as it is presently constituted" would not confirm a southern nominee who was also a judicial conservative.

Nixon then turned to Chief Justice Burger's friend, Harry Blackmun, who was confirmed without opposition. During his first years on the Court, Blackmun was frequently linked with Burger as the "Minnesota Twins," who thought and voted alike, but, beginning with his authorship of the Court's 1973 ruling in *Roe v. Wade*, legalizing abortion, Blackmun moved in a steadily more liberal direction. Reinforcing his commitment to the concept of privacy, Blackmun dissented from *Bowers v. Hardwick* (1986), in which the majority upheld Georgia's law prohibiting sodomy. Blackmun declared that the case concerned not whether sodomy was constitutionally protected, but whether an individual has the right to be let alone.

Blackmun's liberal transformation continued into his last term on the Court when he surprised observers by announcing that he could no longer support capital punishment because it could not be fairly administered. By the time he retired in 1994, he was its most liberal member, a statement as revealing of the conservative transformation of the Court in the 1980s and early 1990s as of Blackmun's own shift to the liberal side.

Lewis Franklin Powell Jr.

(1972–1987)

BIRTH: September 19, 1907, Suffolk, Virginia.

EDUCATION: Washington and Lee University, B.S., 1929; Washington and Lee University Law School, LL.B., 1931; Harvard Law School, LL.M., 1932.

OFFICIAL POSITIONS: president of the Richmond School Board, 1952–1961; member, 1961–1969, and president, 1968–1969, Virginia State Board of Education; president of the American Bar Association, 1964–1965; president, American College of Trial Lawyers, 1968–1969.

SUPREME COURT SERVICE: nominated associate justice by President Richard Nixon October 22, 1971, to replace Hugo L. Black, who had retired; confirmed by the Senate December 6,

Lewis Franklin Powell Jr.

1971, by an 89–1 vote; took judicial oath January 6, 1972; retired June 26, 1987; replaced by Anthony Kennedy, nominated by President Ronald Reagan.

FAMILY: married Josephine M. Rucker, May 2, 1936; three daughters, one son.

Powell was born to Lewis F. Powell Sr. and Mary Gwathmey Powell in Suffolk, in Tidewater Virginia, but spent most of his life in Richmond. He attended Washington and Lee University in Lexington, Virginia, where he earned a B.S. and election to Phi Beta Kappa. He stayed at Washington and Lee for law school, graduating in two years instead of the usual three. He then obtained a master's degree from Harvard Law School in 1932.

Turning down an offer from a top New York law firm, Powell returned to Virginia and joined one of the state's oldest and most prestigious law firms, located in Richmond. After a two-year association, Powell joined another firm and eventually became a senior partner. Except for three years as an Air Force intelligence officer during World War II, Powell worked at this firm until his nomination to the Supreme Court.

Powell's practice included both corporate law and litigation experience. As attorney for a number of national corporations, he was no stranger to blue-chip boardrooms. He represented his profession on the national level as president of the American Bar Association and the American College of Trial Lawyers.

Powell's reputation as a moderate stemmed from his work as president of the Richmond School Board (1952–1961) and as a member and president of the Virginia State Board of Education. In the face of intense pressure for "massive" resistance to desegregation, Powell consistently advocated keeping the schools open.

A one-year stint from 1964 to 1965 as president of the American Bar Association provided Powell with a national platform from which to express his views on a variety of subjects and enhanced his reputation as a moderate. On the liberal side, Powell spoke out against inadequate legal services for the poor and worked to create the legal services program of the Office of Economic Opportunity. A more conservative tone characterized his view of social ills caused by parental permissiveness and his stern denunciations of civil disobedience and other forms of civil demonstrations. As a member in 1966 of President Lyndon B. Johnson's Crime Commission, Powell participated in a minority statement criticizing Supreme Court rulings upholding the right of criminal suspects to remain silent.

During Powell's sixteen years on the Court, it became more closely balanced between liberals and conservatives, and he became the single most important member, able to cast the deciding vote on a long list of issues, including abortion and affirmative action.

Powell retired on the last day of the October 1986 term. He said he had served longer than the decade he had originally intended and that a recent illness had made him aware of how the prolonged absence of one justice handicapped the Court. Powell's health improved after he stepped down, and he often volunteered to sit on federal appeals court cases. In the decade that followed, Powell frequently remarked that he wished he had not retired so soon.

William Hubbs Rehnquist

William Hubbs Rehnquist

(1972–1986, 1986–)

BIRTH: October 1, 1924, Milwaukee, Wisconsin.

EDUCATION: Stanford University, B.A., 1948, M.A., 1948; Harvard University, M.A., 1950; Stanford University Law School, LL.B., 1952.

OFFICIAL POSITIONS: law clerk to Supreme Court Justice Robert H. Jackson, 1952–1953; assistant U.S. attorney general, Office of Legal Counsel, 1969–1971.

SUPREME COURT SERVICE: nominated associate justice by President Richard Nixon October 21, 1971, to replace John Marshall Harlan, who had retired; confirmed by the Senate December 10, 1971, by a 68–26 vote; took judicial oath January 7, 1972; nominated chief justice by President Ronald Reagan June 20, 1986; confirmed by the Senate, 65–33, September 17, 1986; took judicial oath September 26, 1986; replaced as associate justice by Antonin Scalia, nominated by President Reagan.

FAMILY: married Natalie Cornell, August 29, 1953; died October 17, 1991; one son, two daughters.

William Rehnquist was born and grew up in Milwaukee. His mother was Margery Peck Rehnquist and his father was William

B. Rehnquist, a paper salesman. After World War II service in the Air Force, he attended Stanford University on the G.I. Bill and received both a B.A. and an M.A. in political science in 1948. He earned another M.A. in government at Harvard University (conferred in 1950) before returning to Stanford to attend law school. He graduated first in his class in 1952. One of his classmates was Sandra Day, who later joined him on the Supreme Court.

After finishing law school, Rehnquist clerked for Justice Robert H. Jackson. In 1952 he wrote a memorandum for Jackson that was much discussed during his Senate confirmation hearings. The memorandum favored separate but equal schools for blacks and whites. Asked about those views by the Senate Judiciary Committee in 1971, Rehnquist repudiated them, declaring that they were Justice Jackson's, not his own.

In 1953, following his clerkship, Rehnquist married Natalie Cornell, whom he had met at Stanford, and began his law practice in Phoenix, Arizona, He also became immersed in Republican state politics. From his earliest days in Arizona, Rehnquist was associated with the party's most conservative wing. A 1957 speech denouncing the liberalism of the Warren Court typified his views at the time.

During the 1964 presidential campaign, Rehnquist campaigned ardently for Barry Goldwater, the GOP candidate. He also met and worked with Richard G. Kleindienst, who, as President Nixon's deputy attorney general, would later appoint Rehnquist to head the Justice Department's Office of Legal Counsel.

Rehnquist quickly became one of the Nixon administration's chief spokesmen on Capitol Hill, commenting on issues ranging from wiretapping to rights of the accused. It was Rehnquist's job to review the legality of all presidential executive orders and other constitutional law questions in the executive branch. He frequently testified before congressional committees in support of the administration's policies—most of which matched his own conservative philosophy. So tightly reasoned and articulate was his testimony—backing controversial matters such as government surveillance of American citizens and tighter curbs on obscene materials—that members of Congress from both parties acknowledged his ability.

In 1971 President Nixon nominated him to the Supreme Court. As an associate justice, Rehnquist voted consistently in favor of law enforcement over the rights of suspects and for states' rights over the power of the federal government, votes that usually put him in the minority. After serving on the Court for fifteen years, he was promoted to chief justice by President Ronald Reagan, the third sitting associate justice in history to be elevated to chief justice.

Controversy surrounded his 1986 nomination. His views on civil rights were questioned, and he was accused of harassing black voters in Phoenix during the 1950s and early 1960s. He was approved by a vote of 65–33, which in 1986 was more opposition than any other successful Supreme Court nominee in the twentieth century had survived.

Since 1986 the Court has become more conservative, and Rehnquist's once-minority views have become the rule in several cases. He was the author of a 1995 opinion (*United States v. Lopez*) that struck down a federal ban on guns near local schools. Rehnquist said Congress had overstepped its power and encroached the states' domain. Rehnquist conceded that the Court had given "great deference" to Congress in the past. But unless it drew the line this time, he said, "there will never be a distinction between what is truly national and what is truly local."

Rehnquist is the author of two popular books on the Court: *The Supreme Court: How It Was, How It Is* (1988) and *Grand Inquests: The Historic Impeachments of Justice Samuel Chase and President Andrew Johnson* (1992).

John Paul Stevens
(1975–   )

BIRTH: April 20, 1920, Chicago, Illinois.

EDUCATION: University of Chicago, B.A., 1941; Northwestern University School of Law, J.D., magna cum laude, 1947.

OFFICIAL POSITIONS: law clerk to Justice Wiley B. Rutledge, 1947–1948; associate counsel, Subcommittee on the Study of Monopoly Power, House Judiciary Committee, 1951; member, U.S. Attorney General's National Committee to Study the Antitrust Laws, 1953–1955; judge, Seventh Circuit Court of Appeals, 1970–1975.

SUPREME COURT SERVICE: nominated associate justice by President Gerald R. Ford November 28, 1975, to replace

John Paul Stevens

William O. Douglas, who had retired; confirmed by the Senate December 17, 1975, by a 98–0 vote; took judicial oath December 19, 1975.

FAMILY: married Elizabeth Jane Sheeren, 1942, divorced 1979; one son, three daughters; married Maryan Mulholland Simon, 1980.

John Paul Stevens is the youngest of the four sons of Ernest James Stevens and Elizabeth Street Stevens. His family was prominent in Chicago. Stevens graduated Phi Beta Kappa from the University of Chicago in 1941. After a wartime stint in the Navy during which he earned the Bronze Star, he returned to Chicago to enter Northwestern University Law School, graduating in 1947. Stevens then served as a law clerk to Justice Wiley B. Rutledge. He left Washington to join a prominent Chicago law firm that specialized in antitrust law.

Stevens developed a reputation as a pre-eminent antitrust lawyer, and after three years formed his own law firm, Rothschild, Stevens, Barry, and Myers. He remained there, also teaching part time at Northwestern University and the University of Chicago law schools until his appointment by President Nixon in 1970 to the Seventh Circuit Court of Appeals.

Stevens for a time flew his own small airplane. He was also a nationally competitive bridge player and a golf and tennis enthusiast.

Stevens developed a reputation as a political moderate during his undergraduate days at the University of Chicago, then an overwhelmingly liberal campus. A registered Republican, he was never active in partisan politics. Nevertheless, Stevens served as

Republican counsel in 1951 to a House Judiciary subcommittee's study of monopoly power. He also served from 1953 to 1955, during the Eisenhower administration, as a member of the attorney general's National Committee to Study the Antitrust Laws.

When President Ford nominated Stevens to the Supreme Court seat vacated by veteran liberal William O. Douglas, observers struggled to pin an ideological label on the new nominee. But on the whole, they decided that he was neither a doctrinaire liberal nor a conservative, but a centrist whose well-crafted scholarly opinions made him a "judge's judge." He was unanimously confirmed.

On the Court, Stevens has proved the observations correct—he has been pragmatic and independent rather than ideological. For example, in writing the Court's opinion in *Federal Communications Commission v. Pacifica Foundation* (1978), Stevens chose to focus on the practical aspects of the case rather than freedom of speech in the abstract. He concluded that the FCC could regulate language that was broadcast at times when young children were likely to be listening.

With the conservative appointments of the Reagan and Bush years, Stevens, despite his lack of definitive ideology, is now considered one of the liberal justices. He wrote the Court's 1995 decision throwing out state term limits for members of Congress, saying that permitting such tenure restrictions would lead to a patchwork of state qualifications and undermine the uniformity and national character of the U.S. government.

Sandra Day O'Connor

Sandra Day O'Connor

(1981–)

BIRTH: March 26, 1930, El Paso, Texas.

EDUCATION: Stanford University, B.A., 1950, Stanford University Law School, LL.B., 1952.

OFFICIAL POSITIONS: deputy county attorney, San Mateo, California, 1952–1953; assistant attorney general, Arizona, 1965–1969; Arizona state senator, 1969–1975, majority leader, state Senate, 1973–1974; judge, Maricopa County Superior Court, 1975–1979; judge, Arizona Court of Appeals, 1979–1981.

SUPREME COURT SERVICE: nominated associate justice by President Ronald Reagan August 19, 1981 to replace Potter Stewart, who had retired; confirmed by the Senate by a 99–0 vote, September 21, 1981; took judicial oath September 26, 1981.

FAMILY: married John O'Connor, 1952; three sons.

Sandra Day, the daughter of Harry A. Day and Ada Mae Wilkey Day, was born a pioneer. She is the grandchild of a man who left Kansas in 1880 to take up farming in the desert Southwest. She was born in El Paso because her mother had gone there to stay with her parents, rather than give birth at the Lazy B Ranch, which was far from any hospital. Day grew up dividing her time between El Paso, where she lived with her grandmother and attended school, and summers on the 162,000-acre ranch that her grandfather had founded in southeastern Arizona.

After graduating from high school at sixteen, Day attended Stanford University, earning a degree in economics, magna cum laude, in 1950. She stayed at Stanford for her law degree, which she received in 1952. At law school, she met two men who would figure largely in her adult life—John J. O'Connor III, whom she married in December 1952, and William H. Rehnquist, whom she joined as a colleague on the U.S. Supreme Court in 1981.

Her law school record was outstanding. She was an editor of the *Stanford Law Review* and a member of Order of the Coif, a legal honorary society. But she was a woman in a field where women were oddities, and so it was difficult for her to find a job as an attorney. She applied, among other places, to the firm in which William French Smith was a partner, and was offered a job as a secretary. Smith, as U.S. attorney general, later played a part in her nomination to the U.S. Supreme Court.

O'Connor found a job as deputy county attorney for San Mateo County, California. When her husband finished school, he joined the Army, and the O'Connors moved to Germany where she worked as a civilian attorney for the U.S. Army.

The O'Connors returned to civilian life in 1957 and settled in Phoenix, Arizona. For eight years, O'Connor combined child rearing with volunteer work and some private practice of law and a number of miscellaneous legal tasks part time. She also became active in Republican politics.

In 1965 O'Connor became an assistant attorney general of Arizona, the first woman to hold the position. After four years, she was appointed to the state Senate, and the following year she won election to that body. During her six years as a state senator, she served for two years as majority leader—the first woman in the nation to hold such a post of legislative leadership.

Having served in the executive and legislative branches of state government, O'Connor rounded out her experience by moving to the bench in 1974, elected to the superior court of Maricopa County. Five years later, Gov. Bruce Babbitt—acting, some said, to remove a potential rival—appointed her to the Arizona Court of Appeals. A year earlier Arizona Republican leaders had pushed O'Connor to make a gubernatorial bid, but she had declined. It was from that state appeals court seat that President Reagan chose her as his first nominee to the Supreme Court. Once again, Sandra Day O'Connor was "the first woman"—this time, the first of her sex to sit on the U.S. Supreme Court.

On the Court, O'Connor was at first solidly in the conservative wing, voting in most cases with fellow Arizonian William H. Rehnquist. Over time she has moved to the center. In 1992 O'Connor joined David Souter and Anthony Kennedy in a plurality opinion that affirmed *Roe v. Wade* (1973), which guarantees a woman's right to have an abortion.

She has become a strong voice on the Court for strict judicial scrutiny of policies that benefit or penalize people based on race. O'Connor wrote in *Richmond v. J. A. Croson Co.* (1989) that government programs that set aside a fixed percentage of public contracts for minority-owned businesses violated the equal protection clause. In *Shaw v. Reno* (1993) she wrote for the majority that white voters could challenge racially drawn voting districts if the districts were "highly irregular" in shape and "lacked sufficient justification."

Antonin Scalia

(1986–   )

BIRTH: March 11, 1936, Trenton, New Jersey.

EDUCATION: Georgetown University, A.B., summa cum laude, 1957; Harvard Law School, LL.B., magna cum laude, 1960.

OFFICIAL POSITIONS: general counsel, White House Office of Telecommunications Policy, 1971–1972; chairman, Administrative Conference of the United States, 1972–1974; assistant attorney general, Office of Legal Counsel, 1974–1977; judge, U.S. Court of Appeals for the District of Columbia Circuit, 1982–1986.

SUPREME COURT SERVICE: nominated associate justice by President Ronald Reagan June 24, 1986, to replace William H. Rehnquist, who had been promoted to chief justice; confirmed by a 98–0 vote of the Senate, September 17, 1986; took judicial oath September 26, 1986.

FAMILY: married Maureen McCarthy, 1960; nine children.

Antonin Scalia was the first person of Italian ancestry to be appointed to the Supreme Court and the first Roman Catholic since William J. Brennan Jr. was named in 1956. Born in Trenton, New Jersey, Scalia was the only child of Eugene Scalia, a professor of Romance languages who had emigrated from Italy, and Catherine Panaro Scalia, a schoolteacher whose parents also had emigrated from Italy. Scalia grew up in Queens where he attended Jesuit schools.

Antonin Scalia

Scalia graduated from Georgetown University and Harvard Law School. The year he graduated from law school, he married Maureen McCarthy. Scalia spent seven years in private practice in Cleveland, Ohio, with the law firm of Jones, Day, Reavis, and Pogue, but left practice to teach law at the University of Virginia law school late in the 1960s. Early in his career, he developed a strong individual style marked by a keen legal intellect and a certain whimsicality. He made playful use of the language, would sometimes sing at public appearances, and liked to entertain friends with his piano playing.

Scalia was drawn to government service during the Nixon administration, which he joined in 1971 as general counsel of the White House Office of Telecommunications Policy. From that post, he became chairman of the Administrative Conference of the United States, and in 1974 he joined the Justice Department as assistant attorney general in charge of the Office of Legal Counsel, the same post William H. Rehnquist held from 1969 to 1971.

Scalia remained in that position through the Nixon and Ford administrations. He returned to teaching and held posts at Georgetown University Law School, the University of Chicago Law School, and Stanford University Law School. He was then named by President Reagan to the U.S. Court of Appeals for the District of Columbia Circuit in 1982.

Scalia developed a reputation as an outspoken conservative with very definite views of the law. He believed the power of the courts was limited. He also took a strong interest in the interpretation of statutes, arguing that the only legitimate guide for judges is the actual text of a statute and its related provisions. In 1986 Reagan promoted him to the U.S. Supreme Court.

True to his pattern on the appeals court, Scalia has established himself as one the most conservative members of the Supreme Court. He is not willing to acknowledge any individual right not clearly set forth in the language of the Constitution. In *Webster v. Reproductive Health Services* (1989) and *Cruzan v. Director, Missouri Department of Health* (1990), to cite two examples, Scalia rejected any constitutional basis for the right to an abortion or the right to refuse life-sustaining treatment. In 1996 he wrote an angry dissent in *Romer v. Evans*. He argued that Colorado voters had the right to amend their state constitution to ban any local ordinances attempting to protect homosexuals.

Anthony McLeod Kennedy

(1988–   )

BIRTH: July 23, 1936, Sacramento, California.

EDUCATION: Stanford University, A.B., 1958; London School of Economics, 1957–1958; Harvard Law School, J.D., 1961.

OFFICIAL POSITIONS: judge, U.S. Court of Appeals for the Ninth Circuit, 1976–1988.

SUPREME COURT SERVICE: nominated associate justice by President Ronald Reagan November 30, 1987, to replace Lewis F. Powell Jr., who had retired; confirmed by a 97–0 vote of the Senate, February 3, 1988; took judicial oath February 18, 1988.

FAMILY: married Mary Davis, 1963; three children.

Until called to serve as a justice of the U.S. Supreme Court, Anthony Kennedy's life centered around his hometown, Sacramento. His father, Anthony J. Kennedy, was a lawyer and lobbyist, well known in that state capitol. Kennedy, like his father, was both Catholic and Republican. Earl Warren, who would become a chief justice of the United States, was a family friend. Kennedy's mother was born Gladys McLeod.

Kennedy graduated from McClatchy High School in Sacramento and went on to Stanford, his mother's alma mater. He graduated in 1958 and was elected to Phi Beta Kappa. He spent his final undergraduate year at the London School of Economics before entering Harvard Law School, gaining his degree in 1961.

During his first year as a lawyer, he worked for a firm in San Francisco, but his father's sudden death brought him back to Sacramento. He took over his father's practice, including the lobbying activities, which he found less to his taste than the legal work. He also taught part time at the McGeorge School of Law at the University of the Pacific.

Kennedy's legal abilities brought him to the attention of the administration of Ronald Reagan, then governor of California. That connection won Kennedy a nomination by President Gerald R. Ford to a seat on the Ninth Circuit Court of Appeals in 1975. Easily confirmed, he took his seat in 1976 and remained on the court for a dozen years.

He earned a reputation as a conservative, diligent, and even-handed jurist. In one of his most controversial opinions as an appeals court judge, he invalidated a federal statute that allowed either house of Congress to cancel administration action on a deportation order. The Supreme Court in 1983 endorsed Kennedy's view when it rejected the one-house legislative veto in the important case of *Immigration and Naturalization Service v. Chadha*.

Kennedy became Ronald Reagan's choice for the Court in 1987 after the Senate had rejected the nomination of Robert H. Bork and Douglas Ginsburg's name was withdrawn.

Kennedy has taken conservative positions on many issues. In the area of search and seizure, he found constitutional the government's practice of testing railroad workers for drug and alcohol use after a major accident. He wrote the Court's opinion in *National Treasury Employees Union v. Von Raab* (1989), which upheld the U.S. Custom Service's requirement that employees undergo drug tests if they seek promotion to certain types of jobs.

A strong advocate of free speech, Kennedy joined the opinion of William J. Brennan Jr. to strike down the Texas law forbidding flag burning. The majority held that flag burning is symbolic speech protected by the First Amendment. One of Kennedy's most surprising votes came when he joined with David Souter and Sandra Day O'Connor to write the Court's opinion in *Planned Parenthood of Southeastern Pennsylvania v. Casey* in 1992, upholding the basic right to abortion while permitting certain state regulations.

David Hackett Souter

(1990–   )

BIRTH: September 17, 1939, Melrose, Massachusetts.

EDUCATION: Harvard College, B.A., 1961; Oxford University (Rhodes Scholar), 1961–1963; Harvard University Law School, LL.B., 1966.

OFFICIAL POSITIONS: assistant attorney general, New Hampshire, 1968–1971; deputy attorney general, New Hampshire, 1971–1976; attorney general, New Hampshire, 1976–1978; associate justice, New Hampshire Superior Court, 1978–1983; associate justice, New Hampshire Supreme Court, 1983–1990; judge, U.S. Court of Appeals for the First Circuit, 1990.

SUPREME COURT SERVICE: nominated associate justice by President George Bush July 23, 1990, to replace William J. Brennan Jr., who had retired; confirmed by the Senate, October 2, 1990, by a 90–9 vote; took judicial oath October 9, 1990.

FAMILY: Unmarried.

David Souter was born in Melrose, Massachusetts, the only child of Joseph A. Souter, a banker, and Helen Hackett Souter. He spent most summers at his maternal grandparents' farmhouse in Weare, New Hampshire. The family moved there when he was eleven years old. Except for his college years, Souter lived in Weare until 1990. He attended Harvard College where he majored in philosophy and wrote his senior honors thesis on the jurisprudence of Justice Oliver Wendell Holmes Jr. He was elected to Phi Beta Kappa and graduated magna cum laude in 1961. Souter attended Oxford University on a Rhodes scholarship from 1961 to 1963. He then attended Harvard Law School. He graduated in 1966 and worked for two years in a Concord law firm, Orr and Reno. Souter's practice included corporate law, real estate, and taxation.

In 1968 Souter became an assistant attorney general for the state's criminal division. He rose to deputy attorney general in 1971 and in 1976 was appointed attorney general. Under Gov. Meldrim Thomson Jr., Souter defended a number of controversial orders, including the lowering of state flags to half-staff on Good Friday to commemorate the death of Jesus. He prosecuted Jehovah's Witnesses who obscured the state motto "Live Free or Die" on their license plates. He also was responsible for the prosecution of protesters who took over the Seabrook nuclear power plant in 1977.

Souter served as attorney general until 1978, when he was named to the state's trial court. Five years later, Gov. John H. Sununu selected Souter for the state supreme court. Sununu later become President Bush's chief of staff and, when Bush had the opportunity to name a successor to retiring justice William J. Brennan Jr., Sununu suggested Souter's name. Just three months earlier, Bush had named Souter to the U.S. Court of Appeals for the First Circuit, but in July 1990 he nominated him to the U.S. Supreme Court. During Souter's confirmation hearings, he stressed that his years on state courts had taught him two lessons that he thought would help him as a justice. The first was that "at the end of our task some human being is going to be affected, some human life is going to be changed in some way by what we do." The second (and related) lesson: "We had better use every power of our minds and our hearts and our beings to get those rulings right."

On the Court Souter has shown a respect for precedent. He was one of the three authors (with Sandra Day O'Connor and Anthony M. Kennedy) of the Court's 1992 opinion in *Planned Parenthood of Southeastern Pennsylvania v. Casey* that upheld *Roe v. Wade* (1973).

Initially part of the conservative bloc, Souter has moved to the left of center on the modern conservative Court. During the 1994–1995 and 1995–1996 terms, he voted more often with Clinton appointees Ruth Bader Ginsburg and Stephen G. Breyer than with any of the conservative justices who formed the Court majority in the mid-1990s.

He dissented from *United States v. Lopez* (1995) when the Court overturned a law prohibiting the possession of firearms in or near school grounds. He dissented from *Rosenberger v. Rector and Visitors of the University of Virginia* (1995), in which the Court said that a state university that funds student publications out of a student activity fee cannot deny funding to religious publication solely because of its religious content.

When he dissented in the 1996 case of *Seminole Tribe of Florida v. Florida,* he took the extraordinary step of reading his opinion from the bench. He declared that the majority opinion, which said Congress exceeded its authority in trying to force state officials to negotiate gaming contracts with Indian tribes, "flies in the face of the Constitution's text."

Clarence Thomas

(1991–   )

BIRTH: June 23, 1948, Pin Point, Georgia.

EDUCATION: Immaculate Conception Seminary, 1967–1968; Holy Cross College, B.A., 1971; Yale University Law School, J.D., 1974.

OFFICIAL POSITIONS: assistant attorney general, Missouri, 1974–1977; assistant secretary of education for civil rights, 1981–1982; chairman, Equal Employment Opportunity Commission, 1982–1990; judge, U.S. Court of Appeals for the District of Columbia, 1990–1991.

SUPREME COURT SERVICE: nominated associate justice by President George Bush July 1, 1991, to replace Thurgood Marshall, who had retired; confirmed by the Senate, October 15, 1991, by a 52–48 vote; took judicial oath October 23, 1991.

FAMILY: married Kathy Grace Ambush, 1971; one son; divorced 1984; married Virginia Lamp, 1987.

Clarence Thomas, the son of Leola Williams and M. C. Thomas, was born in an enclave of five hundred inhabitants south of Savannah, Georgia. He overcame great odds to reach a seat on the U.S. Supreme Court. His father abandoned the family when Thomas was two years old, and his mother struggled to provide for her three children, working as a maid. After their house burned down, Thomas and his only brother were sent to live with their grandfather, Myers Anderson, in Savannah. Thomas has often spoken of his grandfather's lessons of hard work and determination. Thomas attended an all-black school run by white nuns, whom he credited with instilling in him a strong sense of the possibilities of life. Intending to become a priest, he enrolled in Immaculate Conception Seminary in northwestern Missouri in 1967. The prejudice of other students convinced him to leave the seminary, and in 1968 he transferred to Holy Cross College in Worcester, Massachusetts. Thomas graduated in 1971 with honors in English. In 1974 he graduated from Yale Law School.

Thomas joined the staff of John C. Danforth, Missouri's attorney general. Danforth, a Republican, became Thomas's political mentor. Following a three-year stint as an assistant attorney general, Thomas worked as a staff attorney for Monsanto Company from 1977 to 1979. He returned to public service to work from 1979 to 1981 as a legislative assistant to Danforth, who had been elected to the U.S. Senate. Thomas then accepted a position in the Reagan administration as assistant secretary for civil rights in the Department of Education. In 1982 Reagan named him chairman of the Equal Employment Opportunity Commission.

President Bush appointed Thomas to the Court of Appeals for the District of Columbia Circuit in 1990. Eighteen months later Bush selected Thomas, whose judicial record was notably conservative, for the Supreme Court. Thomas was critical of abortion rights and opposed affirmative action. Those positions and controversy over other substantive issues, however, were eclipsed during the confirmation hearings by allegations of Anita Hill, a former employee of Thomas, that he had sexually harassed her. The charges were never proved, but Thomas said the ordeal, shown on national television, dramatically changed him. The Senate's 52–48 vote on Thomas was the closest Supreme Court confirmation vote in more than a century. Thomas succeeded Thurgood Marshall, whose six-decade legal career had shaped the country's civil rights struggle. Marshall was the first black justice, and Thomas became the second.

On the Court Thomas was a member of the conservative bloc, opposing abortion rights and favoring law enforcement, states' rights, and a more accommodating approach to religion. He voted most often with Justice Antonin Scalia and Chief Justice William H. Rehnquist.

Thomas was one of four dissenters from *Lee v. Weisman* (1992), taking issue with the ruling that prayer at a public school graduation ceremony violated the constitutional requirement of separation of church and state. Thomas also dissented from the Court's opinion in *Board of Education of Kiryas Joel Village School District v. Grumet* (1994), striking down a New York law that had created a special school district to serve the disabled children of a Hasidic sect as violating the constitutional requirement of separation of church and state.

Thomas has been a strong voice against race-based remedies for past discrimination, such as affirmative action and "majority minority" voting districts. He wrote in a 1994 opinion, *Holder v. Hall,* that the Court's earlier cases upholding racially designated voting districts disserved the country: "In doing so we have collaborated in what may aptly be termed the racial balkanization of the Nation."

Thomas wrote the dissent to *U.S. Term Limits v. Thornton* (1995), in which the Court declared that states may not limit the number of terms their representatives serve in Congress. He said the Constitution is "simply silent" on term limits. So, under the Tenth Amendment, the states retained the authority to pre-scribe "eligibility requirements" for Congress.

Ruth Bader Ginsburg

(1993–   )

BIRTH: March 15, 1933, Brooklyn, New York.

EDUCATION: Cornell University, B.A., 1954; attended Har-vard University Law School, 1956–1958; graduated Columbia Law School, J.D., 1959.

OFFICIAL POSITIONS: judge, U.S. Court of Appeals for the District of Columbia, 1980–1993.

SUPREME COURT SERVICE: nominated associate justice by President Bill Clinton June 22, 1993, to replace Byron R. White, who had retired; confirmed by the Senate, August 3, 1993, by a 96–3 vote; took judicial oath August 10, 1993.

FAMILY: married Martin D. Ginsburg, 1954; one daughter, one son.

Born into a Jewish family of modest means in Brooklyn, Ruth Bader Ginsburg is the daughter of Nathan Bader and Celia Amster Bader. Ruth was greatly influenced by her mother, who imparted a love of learning and a determination to be independent. Celia Bader died of cancer on the eve of her daughter's high school graduation in 1948. Ruth Bader attended Cornell University, where she graduated first among the women in her class and was elected to Phi Beta Kappa. She also met her future husband, Martin Ginsburg.

At Harvard Law School Ruth Ginsburg made law review, cared for an infant daughter, and helped her husband complete his studies after he was diagnosed with cancer. Martin Ginsburg recovered, graduated, and got a job in New York, and she trans-ferred to Columbia for her final year of law school. Ginsburg was tied for first place in her class when she graduated. She won a two-year clerkship with a federal district court judge. She then accepted a research position at Columbia that took her to Swe-den, where she studied civil procedure. Ginsburg taught at Rut-gers University Law School in New Jersey from 1963 to 1972. She also worked for the American Civil Liberties Union (ACLU), where her caseload included several early sex discrimination complaints. In 1972 Ginsburg became the first woman to be named to a tenured position on the Columbia Law School fac-ulty. Then, as director of the national ACLU's newly established Women's Rights Project, she also handled the cases that over time led the Supreme Court to require heightened scrutiny of legal classifications based on sex. Ginsburg won five of the six cases she argued before the Court.

As an advocate, Ginsburg gained nationwide attention in the 1970s for developing the legal strategy that established constitu-tional principles against sex discrimination. In 1980 President Jimmy Carter named her to the U.S. Court of Appeals for the District of Columbia. She developed a moderate judicial record, following the letter of the law and believing that judging has its limits. "Measured motions seem to me right, in the main, for constitutional as well as common law adjudication," she wrote in an article that criticized the broad sweep of the Court's 1973 *Roe v. Wade* decision. In 1993 Ginsburg became President Bill Clinton's choice for the Supreme Court. Clinton said he was moved by her nontraditional life and predicted she would bring consensus to the Court. Ginsburg was the first Supreme Court justice appointed by a Democratic president in twenty-six years, since Lyndon Johnson appointed Thurgood Marshall in 1967.

The Court she joined was composed of eight justices, all of whom had been appointed by Republican presidents. She was the second woman to serve on the Court and its first Jewish member since the resignation of Justice Abe Fortas in 1969.

In one of her early cases, Ginsburg suggested that the Court may someday find that the Constitution guarantees as much protection for sexual equality as it does for racial equality.

She joined the full Court ruling in *Harris v. Forklift Systems Inc.* (1993) that an employee claiming job discrimination on the basis of sexual harassment need not prove she suffered serious psychological injury to win a case. Then Ginsburg, in her first written opinion as a justice, said in a concurring statement that "the critical issue is whether members of one sex are exposed to disadvantageous terms or conditions of employment to which members of the other sex are not exposed." And she added in a footnote that the Court has left unresolved whether government classifications that put one sex at an advantage over the other should be scrutinized as closely as racial classifications.

Stephen Gerald Breyer

(1994–   )

BIRTH: August 15, 1938, San Francisco, California.

EDUCATION: Stanford University, A.B., 1959; Oxford University, B.A., 1961; Harvard Law School, LL.B., 1964.

OFFICIAL POSITIONS: Law clerk to Justice Arthur J. Goldberg, 1964–1965; assistant to assistant attorney general, Antitrust Division, U.S. Justice Department, 1965–1967; assistant special prosecutor, Watergate Special Prosecution Force, 1973; special counsel, Senate Judiciary Committee, 1974–1975; chief counsel, Senate Judiciary Committee, 1979–1980; judge, U.S. Court of Appeals for the First Circuit, 1980–1994.

SUPREME COURT SERVICE: nominated associate justice by President Bill Clinton May 13, 1994, to replace Harry A. Blackmun, who had retired; confirmed by the Senate, July 29, 1994, by a 87–9 vote; took judicial oath August 3, 1994.

FAMILY: married Joanna Hare, 1967; two daughters, one son.

Stephen Breyer was born in 1938 in San Francisco, the first of two sons of Irving G. Breyer and Anne Roberts Breyer. Breyer's father was a lawyer for the San Francisco public school system, and his mother was active in local Democratic politics and community activities. They encouraged their son to do well academically but also, in his mother's words, to learn how "to work with other people." Breyer excelled at Lowell High School, especially in math and science, and was voted "most likely to succeed" when he graduated in 1955. He then graduated Phi Beta Kappa from Stanford University in 1959 and went to Oxford as a Mar-

shall Scholar, completing course work in 1961. Breyer graduated from Harvard Law School in 1964. While working in Washington, he met his wife, Joanna Hare, the daughter of a former high-ranking official in Britain's Conservative Party and heir to a wealthy media company. They were married in 1967. Breyer is a prolific author, avid bird watcher, bicyclist, and gourmet cook.

Breyer acquired early Supreme Court experience as a law clerk to Justice Arthur J. Goldberg during the 1964–1965 term. That term produced a decision establishing the right of married couples to use contraceptives, and Breyer helped draft Goldberg's influential concurring opinion finding a right of personal privacy in the Constitution. Breyer then served two years in the Justice Department's Antitrust Division. In 1967 he obtained a teaching position at Harvard Law School, beginning an association that would continue through his various tours in public service until he was named to the Supreme Court.

Breyer took leave from Harvard to serve as an assistant prosecutor in the Watergate investigation in 1973, to be a special counsel to the Judiciary Committee's Administrative Practices Subcommittee from 1974 to 1975, and to serve as the full Judiciary Committee's chief counsel, 1979 to 1980. He helped write major legislation to deregulate the airline industry in the mid-1970s and then to standardize federal criminal sentences in 1980.

Breyer worked for the Democratic committee chairman, Sen. Edward M. Kennedy of Massachusetts, but established good relationships with Republican committee members, too. Those ties proved beneficial when President Jimmy Carter nominated Breyer to be a judge on the U.S. Court of Appeals for the First Circuit in November 1980. Although Ronald Reagan had been elected president and would soon have the opportunity to name his own judges, Republican senators allowed a vote to confirm Breyer's nomination.

On the appeals court, Breyer continued to be interested in regulatory reform. His academic writings focused on government's failure to work out health and environmental problems. He asserted that federal regulation sometimes imposed millions of dollars in extra costs for only marginal health improvements. Breyer served as a member of the U.S. Sentencing Commission from 1985 to 1989.

In 1993 President Clinton considered Breyer for a Supreme Court vacancy, but at the last minute chose Ruth Bader Ginsburg. When Breyer was nominated the following year, his selection was embraced by both Democrats and Republicans, and he was easily confirmed, 87–9.

In his early years on the Court, Breyer proved himself a strong advocate for congressional authority, particularly when balanced against the powers of the states. He wrote the main dissenting opinion when a five-justice majority struck down a federal ban on guns near public schools. Breyer contended that the gun law "falls well within the scope of the commerce power as this Court has understood that power over the last half-century." The majority said the ban had nothing to do with commerce or any sort of economic enterprise.

Reference Materials

APPENDIX A Chronological Documents and Texts

Declaration of Independence

On June 11, 1776, the responsibility to "prepare a declaration" of independence was assigned by the Continental Congress, meeting in Philadelphia, to five members: John Adams, Benjamin Franklin, Thomas Jefferson, Robert Livingston, and Roger Sherman. Impressed by his talents as a writer, the committee asked Jefferson to compose a draft. After modifying Jefferson's draft the committee turned it over to Congress on June 28. On July 2 Congress voted to declare independence; on the evening of July 4, it approved the Declaration of Independence.

The declaration is best remembered for its ringing preamble, which affirms the "self-evident" truths that "all men are created equal, that they are endowed by their Creator with certain unalienable Rights, that among these are Life, Liberty, and the pursuit of Happiness." Besides asserting this natural law, the declaration also elevated the importance of public will: "Governments are instituted among Men, deriving their just powers from the consent of the governed." Many later Supreme Court decisions attempted to find a balance these two fundamental pillars of American democracy: unalienable rights and popular will.

In Congress, July 4, 1776,

THE UNANIMOUS DECLARATION OF THE THIRTEEN UNITED STATES OF AMERICA,

When in the Course of human events, it becomes necessary for one people to dissolve the political bands which have connected them with another, and to assume among the Powers of the earth, the separate and equal station to which the Laws of Nature and of Nature's God entitle them, a decent respect to the opinions of mankind requires that they should declare the causes which impel them to the separation.

We hold these truths to be self-evident, that all men are created equal, that they are endowed by their Creator with certain unalienable Rights, that among these are Life, Liberty and the pursuit of Happiness. That to secure these rights, Governments are instituted among Men, deriving their just powers from the consent of the governed. That whenever any form of Government becomes destructive of these ends, it is the Right of the People to alter or to abolish it, and to institute new Government, laying its foundation on such principles and organizing its powers in such form, as to them shall seem most likely to effect their Safety and Happiness. Prudence, indeed, will dictate that Government long established should not be changed for light and transient causes; and accordingly all experience hath shown, that mankind are more disposed to suffer, while evils are sufferable, than to right themselves by abolishing the forms to which they are accustomed. But when a long train of abuses and usurpations, pursuing invariably the same Object evinces a design to reduce them under absolute Despotism, it is their right, it is their duty, to throw off such Government, and to provide new Guards for their future security. — Such has been the patient sufferance of these Colonies; and such is now the necessity which constrains them to alter their former Systems of Government. The history of the present King of Great Britain is a history of repeated injuries and usurpations, all having in direct object the establishment of an absolute Tyranny over these States. To prove this, let Facts be submitted to a candid world.

He has refused his Assent to Laws, the most wholesome and necessary for the public good.

He has forbidden his Governors to pass Laws of immediate and pressing importance, unless suspended in their operation till his Assent should be obtained; and when so suspended, he has utterly neglected to attend to them.

He has refused to pass other Laws for the accommodation of large districts of people, unless those people would relinquish the right of Representation in the Legislature, a right inestimable to them and formidable to tyrants only.

He has called together legislative bodies at places unusual, uncomfortable, and distant from the depository of their Public Records, for the sole purpose of fatiguing them into compliance with his measures.

He has dissolved Representative Houses repeatedly, for opposing with manly firmness his invasions on the rights of the people.

He has refused for a long time, after such dissolutions, to cause others to be elected; whereby the Legislative Powers, incapable of Annihilation, have returned to the People at large for their exercise; the State remaining in the mean time exposed to all the dangers of invasion from without, and convulsions within.

He has endeavored to prevent the population of these States; for that purpose obstructing the Laws of Naturalization of Foreigners; refusing to pass others to encourage their migration hither, and raising the conditions of new Appropriations of Lands.

He has obstructed the Administration of Justice, by refusing his Assent to Laws for establishing Judiciary Powers.

He has made Judges dependent on his Will alone, for the tenure of their offices, and the amount and payment of their salaries.

He has erected a multitude of New Offices, and sent hither swarms of Officers to harass our People, and eat out their substance.

He has kept among us, in times of peace, Standing Armies without the Consent of our legislature.

He has affected to render the Military independent of and superior to the Civil Power.

He has combined with others to subject us to a jurisdiction foreign to our constitution, and unacknowledged by our laws; giving his Assent to their acts of pretended legislation:

For quartering large bodies of armed troops among us:

For protecting them, by a mock Trial, from Punishment for any Murders which they should commit on the Inhabitants of these States:

For cutting off our Trade with all parts of the world:

For imposing taxes on us without our Consent:

For depriving us in many cases, of the benefits of Trial by Jury:

For transporting us beyond Seas to be tried for pretended offences:

For abolishing the free System of English Laws in a neighbouring Province, establishing therein an Arbitrary government, and enlarging its Boundaries so as to render it at once an example and fit instrument for introducing the same absolute rule into these Colonies:

For taking away our Charters, abolishing our most valuable Laws, and altering fundamentally the Forms of our Governments:

For suspending our own Legislature, and declaring themselves invested with Power to legislate for us in all cases whatsoever.

He has abdicated Government here, by declaring us out of his Protection and waging War against us.

He has plundered our seas, ravaged our Coasts, burnt our towns, and destroyed the lives of our people.

He is at this time transporting large armies of foreign mercenaries to compleat the works of death, desolation and tyranny, already begun with circumstances of Cruelty & perfidy scarcely parallel in the most barbarous ages, and totally unworthy the Head of a civilized nation.

He has constrained our fellow Citizens taken Captive on the high Seas to bear Arms against their Country, to become the executioners of their friends and Brethren, or to fall themselves by their Hands.

He has excited domestic insurrections amongst us, and has endeavoured to bring on the inhabitants of our frontiers, the merciless Indian Savages, whose known rule of warfare, is an undistinguished destruction of all ages, sexes and conditions.

In every stage of these Oppressions We have Petitioned for Redress in the most humble terms: Our repeated Petitions have been answered only by repeated injury. A Prince, whose character is thus marked by every act which may define a Tyrant, is unfit to be the ruler of a free People.

Nor have We been wanting in attention to our British brethren. We have warned them from time to time of attempts by their legislature to extend an unwarrantable jurisdiction over us. We have reminded them of the circumstances of our emigration and settlement here. We have appealed to their native justice and magnanimity, and we have conjured them by the ties of our common kindred to disavow these usurpations, which would inevitably interrupt our connections and correspondence. They too have been deaf to the voice of justice and of consanguinity. We must, therefore, acquiesce in the necessity, which denounces our Separation, and hold them, as we hold the rest of mankind, Enemies in War, in Peace Friends.

We, therefore, the Representatives of the United States of America, in General Congress, Assembled, appealing to the Supreme Judge of the world for the rectitude of our intentions, do, in the Name, and by Authority of the good People of these Colonies, solemnly publish and declare, That these United Colonies are, and of Right ought to be Free and Independent States; that they are Absolved from all Allegiance to the British Crown, and that all political connection between them and the State of Great Britain, is and ought to be totally dissolved; and that as Free and Independent States, they have full Power to levy War, conclude Peace, contract Alliances, establish Commerce, and to do all other Acts and Things which Independent States may of right do. And for the support of this Declaration, with a firm reliance on the Protection of Divine Providence, we mutually pledge to each other our Lives, our Fortunes and our sacred Honor.

John Hancock.

New Hampshire:
Josiah Bartlett,
William Whipple,
Matthew Thornton.

Massachusetts-Bay:
Samuel Adams,
John Adams,
Robert Treat Paine,
Elbridge Gerry.

Rhode Island:
Stephen Hopkins,
William Ellery.

Connecticut:
Roger Sherman,
Samuel Huntington,
William Williams,
Oliver Wolcott.

New York:
William Floyd,
Philip Livingston,
Francis Lewis,
Lewis Morris.

Pennsylvania:
Robert Morris,
Benjamin Harris,

Benjamin Franklin,
John Morton,
George Clymer,
James Smith,
George Taylor,
James Wilson,
George Ross.

Delaware:
Caesar Rodney,
George Read,
Thomas McKean.

Georgia:
Button Gwinnett,
Lyman Hall,
George Walton.

Maryland:
Samuel Chase,
William Paca,
Thomas Stone,
Charles Carroll of
    Carrollton.

Virginia:
George Wythe,
Richard Henry Lee,
Thomas Jefferson,
Benjamin Harrison,

Thomas Nelson Jr.,
Francis Lightfoot
Lee,
Carter Braxton.

North Carolina:
William Hooper,
Joseph Hewes,
John Penn.

South Carolina:
Edward Rutledge,
Thomas Heyward
Jr.,
Thomas Lynch Jr.,
Arthur Middleton.

New Jersey:
Richard Stockton,
John Witherspoon,
Francis Hopkinson,
John Hart,
Abraham Clark.

Articles of Confederation

On June 11, 1776, the same day that it created a five-member committee to prepare the Declaration of Independence, the Continental Congress appointed a thirteen-member committee (one from each state) to draft a "plan of confederation." The two decisions were closely connected: a new and independent nation needed a government of some sort. The committee recommended the Articles of Confederation to Congress on July 12; Congress adopted the plan on November 15, 1777; and unanimous ratification by the states finally came on March 1, 1781.

The Articles of Confederation, which did not provide for a system of national courts, created a weak central government with no executive at all and made Congress the sole organ of the new national government. The Articles provided a barely adequate framework for fighting and winning the Revolutionary War: the presence of a common enemy fostered a certain amount of unity among the states. But when the British were defeated in 1783, the national government found it increasingly difficult to unite the country to confront the new challenges of peace. The lack of a federal court system also remained a major source of embarrassment for the young nation.

To all to whom these Presents shall come, we the undersigned Delegates of the States affixed to our Names send greeting. Whereas the Delegates of the United States of America in Congress assembled did on the fifteenth day of November in the Year of our Lord One Thousand Seven Hundred and Seventy seven, and in the Second Year of the Independence of America agree to certain articles of Confederation and perpetual Union between the States of Newhampshire, Massachusetts-bay, Rhodeisland and Providence Plantations, Connecticut, New York, New Jersey, Pennsylvania, Delaware, Maryland, Virginia, North-Carolina, South-Carolina and Georgia in the Words following, viz. "Articles of Confederation and perpetual Union between the states of Newhampshire, Massachusetts-bay, Rhodeisland and Providence Plantations, Connecticut, New-York, New-Jersey, Pennsylvania, Delaware, Maryland, Virginia, North-Carolina, South-Carolina and Georgia.

Article I. The Stile of this confederacy shall be "The United States of America."

Article II. Each state retains its sovereignty, freedom and independence, and every Power, Jurisdiction and Right, which is not by this confederation expressly delegated to the United States, in Congress assembled.

Article III. The said states hereby severally enter into a firm league of friendship with each other, for their common defence, the security of their Liberties, and their mutual and general welfare, binding themselves to assist each other, against all force offered to, or attacks made upon them, or any of them, on account of religion, sovereignty, trade, or any other pretence whatever.

Article IV. The better to secure the perpetuate mutual friendship and intercourse among the people of the different states in this union, the free inhabitants of each of these states, paupers, vagabonds and fugitives from Justice excepted, shall be entitled to all privileges and immunities of free citizens in the several states; and the people of each state shall have free ingress and regress to and from any other state, and shall enjoy therein all the privileges of trade and commerce, subject to the same duties, impositions and restrictions as the inhabitants thereof respectively, provided that such restriction shall not extend so far as to prevent the removal of property imported into any state, to any other state of which the Owner is an inhabitant; provided also that no imposition, duties or restriction shall be laid by any state, on the property of the united states, or either of them.

If any Person guilty of, or charged with treason, felony, or other high misdemeanor in any state, shall flee from Justice, and be found in any of the united states, he shall upon demand of the Governor or executive power, of the state from which he fled be delivered up and removed to the state having jurisdiction of his offence.

Full faith and credit shall be given in each of these states to the records, acts and judicial proceedings of the courts and magistrates of every other state.

Article V. For the more convenient management of the general interests of the united states, delegates shall be annually appointed in such manner as the legislature of each state shall direct, to meet in Congress on the first Monday in November, in every year, with a power reserved to each state, to recall its delegates, or any of them, at any time within the year, and to send others in their stead, for the remainder of the Year.

No state shall be represented in Congress by less than two, nor by more than seven Members; and no person shall be capable of being a delegate for more than three years in any term of six years; nor shall any person, being a delegate, be capable of holding any office under the united states, for which he, or another for his benefit receives any salary, fees or emolument of any kind.

Each state shall maintain its own delegates in a meeting of the states, and while they act as members of the committee of the states.

In determining questions in the united states, in Congress assembled, each state shall have one vote.

Freedom of speech and debate in Congress shall not be impeached or questioned in any Court, or place out of Congress, and the members of congress shall be protected in their persons from arrests and imprisonments, during the time of their going to and from, and attendance on congress, except for treason, felony, or breach of the peace.

Article VI. No state without the Consent of the united states in congress assembled, shall send any embassy to, or receive any embassy from, or enter into any conference, agreement, or alliance or treaty with any King, prince or state; nor shall any person holding any office of profit or trust under the united states, or any of them, accept of any present, emolument, office or title of any kind whatever from any king, prince or foreign state; nor shall the united states in congress assembled, or any of them, grant any title of nobility.

No two or more states shall enter into any treaty, confederation or alliance whatever between them, without the consent of the united states in congress assembled, specifying accurately the purposes for which the same is to be entered into, and how long it shall continue.

No state shall lay any imposts or duties, which may interfere with any stipulations in treaties, entered into by the united states in congress assembled, with any king, prince or state, in pursuance of any treaties already proposed by congress, to the courts of France and Spain.

No vessels of war shall be kept up in time of peace by any state, except such number only, as shall be deemed necessary by the united states in congress assembled, for the defence of such state, or its trade; nor shall any body of forces be kept up by any state, in time of peace, except such number only, as in the judgment of the united states, in congress assembled, shall be deemed requisite to garrison the forts necessary for the defence of such state; but every state shall always keep up a well regulated and disciplined militia, sufficiently armed and accoutred, and shall provide and constantly have ready for use, in public stores, a due number of field pieces and tents, and a proper quantity of arms, ammunition and camp equipage.

No state shall engage in any war without the consent of the united states in Congress assembled, unless such state be actually invaded by enemies, or shall have received certain advice of a resolution being formed by some nation of Indians to invade such state, and the danger is so imminent as not to admit of a delay, till the united states in congress assembled can be consulted: nor shall any state grant commissions to any ships or vessels of war, nor letters of marque or reprisal, except it be after a declaration of war by the united states in congress assembled, and then only against the kingdom or state and the subjects thereof, against which war has been so declared, and under such regulations as shall be established by the united states in congress assembled, unless such state be infested by pirates, in which case vessels of war may be fitted out for that occasion, and kept so long as the danger shall continue, or until the united states in congress assembled shall determine otherwise.

Article VII. When land-forces are raised by any state for the common defence, all officers of or under the rank of colonel, shall be appointed by the legislature of each state respectively by whom such forces shall be raised, or in such manner as such state shall direct, and all vacancies shall be filled up by the state which first made the appointment.

Article VIII. All charges of war, and all other expences that shall be incurred for the common defence or general welfare, and allowed by the united states in congress assembled, shall be defrayed out of a common treasury, which shall be supplied by the several states, in proportion to the value of all land within each state, granted to or surveyed for any Person, as such land and the buildings and improvements thereon shall be estimated according to such mode as the united states in congress assembled, shall from time to time direct and appoint. The taxes for paying that proportion shall be laid and levied by the authority and direction of the legislatures of the several states within the time agreed upon by the united states in congress assembled.

Article IX. The united states in congress assembled, shall have the sole and exclusive right and power of determining on peace and war, except in the cases mentioned in the sixth article—of sending and receiving ambassadors—entering into treaties and alliances, provided that no treaty of commerce shall be made whereby the legislative power of the respective states shall be restrained from imposing such imposts and duties on foreigners, as their own people are subjected to, or from prohibiting the exportation or importation of any species of goods or commodities whatsoever—of establishing rules for deciding in all cases, what capture on land or water shall be legal, and in what manner prizes taken by land or naval forces in the service of the united states shall be divided or appropriated—of granting letters of marque and reprisal in times of peace—appointing courts for the trial of piracies and felonies committed on the high seas and establishing courts for receiving and determining finally appeals in all cases of captures, provided that no member of congress shall be appointed a judge of any of the said courts.

The united states in congress assembled shall also be the last resort on appeal in all disputes and differences now subsisting or that hereafter may arise between two or more states concerning boundary, jurisdiction or any other cause whatever; which authority shall always be exercised in the manner following. Whenever the legislative or executive authority or lawful agent of any state in controversy with another shall present a petition to congress, stating the matter in question and praying for a hearing, notice thereof shall be given by order of congress to the legislative or executive authority of the other state in controversy, and a day assigned for the appearance of the parties by their lawful agents, who shall then be directed to appoint by joint consent, commissioners or judges to constitute a court for hearing and determining the matter in question: but if they cannot agree, congress shall name three persons out of each of the united states, and from the list of such persons each party shall alternately strike out one, the petitioners beginning, until the number shall be reduced to thirteen; and from that number not less than seven, nor more than nine names as congress shall direct, shall in the presence of congress be drawn out by lot, and the persons whose names shall be so drawn or any five of them, shall be commissioners or judges, to hear and finally determine the controversy, so always as a major part of the judges who shall hear the cause shall agree in the determination: and if either party shall neglect to attend at the day appointed, without shewing reasons, which congress shall judge sufficient, or being present shall refuse to strike, the congress shall proceed to nominate three persons out of each state, and the secretary of congress shall strike in behalf of such party absent or refusing; and the judgment and sentence of the court to be appointed, in the manner before prescribed, shall be final and conclusive; and if any of the parties shall refuse to submit to the authority of such court, or to appear to defend their claim or cause, the court shall nevertheless proceed to pronounce sentence, or judgment, which shall in like manner be final and decisive, the judgment or sentence and other proceedings being in either case transmitted to congress, and lodged among the acts of congress for the security of the parties concerned: provided that every commissioner, before he sits in judgment, shall take an oath to be administered by one of the judges of the supreme or superior court of the state, where the cause shall be tried, "well and truly to hear and determine the matter in question, according to the best of his judgment, without favour, affection or hope of reward:" provided also that no state shall be deprived of territory for the benefit of the united states.

All controversies concerning the private right of soil claimed under different grants of two or more states, whose jurisdictions as they may respect such lands, and the states which passed such grants are adjusted, the said grants or either of them being at the same time claimed to have originated antecedent to such settlement of jurisdiction, shall on the petition of either party to the congress of the united states, be finally determined as near as may be in the same manner as is before prescribed for deciding disputes respecting territorial jurisdiction between different states.

The united states in congress assembled shall also have the sole and exclusive right and power of regulating the alloy and value of coin struck by their own authority, or by that of the respective states—fixing the standard of weights and measures throughout the united states—regulating the trade and managing all affairs with the Indians, not members of any of the states, provided that the legislative right of any state within its own limits be not infringed or violated—establishing and regulating post-offices from one state to another, throughout all the united states, and exacting such postage on the papers passing thro' the same as may be requisite to defray the expences of the said office—appointing all officers of the land forces, in the service of the united states, excepting regimental officers—appointing all the officers of the naval forces, and commissioning all officers whatever in the service of the united states—making rules for the government and regulation of the said land and naval forces, and directing their operations.

The united states in congress assembled shall have authority to appoint a committee, to sit in the recess of congress, to be denominated "A Committee of the States," and to consist of one delegate from each state; and to appoint such other committees and civil officers as may be necessary for managing the general affairs of the united states under their direction—to appoint one of their number to preside, provided that no person be allowed to serve in the office of president more than one year in any term of three years; to ascertain the necessary sums of Money to be raised for the service of the united states, and to appropriate and apply the same for defraying the public expences—to borrow money, or emit bills on the credit of the united states, transmitting every half year to the respective states an account of the sums of money so borrowed or emitted,—to build and equip a navy—to agree upon the number of land forces, and to make requisitions from each state for its quota, in proportion to the number of white inhabitants in such state; which requisition shall be binding, and thereupon the legislature of each state shall appoint the regimental officers, raise the men and cloath, arm and equip them in a soldier like manner, at the expence of the united states, and the officers and men so cloathed, armed and equipped shall march to the place appointed, and within the time agreed on by the united states in congress assembled: But if the united states in congress assembled shall, on consideration of circumstances judge proper that any state should not raise men, or should raise a smaller number than its quota, and that any other state should raise a greater number of men than the quota thereof, such extra number shall be raised, officered, cloathed, armed and equipped in the same manner as the quota of such state, unless the legislature of such state shall judge that such extra number cannot be safely spared out of the same, in which case they shall raise, officer, cloath, arm and equip as many of such extra number as they judge can be safely spared. And the officers and men so cloathed, armed and equipped, shall march to the place appointed, and within the time agreed on by the united states in congress assembled.

The united states in congress assembled shall never engage in a war, nor grant letters of marque and reprisal in time of peace, nor enter into any treaties or alliances, nor coin money, nor regulate the value thereof, nor ascertain the sums and expences necessary for the defence and welfare of the united states, or any of them, nor emit bills, nor borrow money on the credit of the united states, nor appropriate money, nor agree upon the number of vessels of war, to be built or purchased, or the number of land or sea forces to be raised, nor appoint a commander in chief of the army or navy, unless nine states assent to the same: nor shall a question on any other point, except for adjourning from day to day be determined, unless by the votes of a majority of the united states in congress assembled.

The congress of the united states shall have power to adjourn to any time within the year, and to any place within the united states, so that no period of adjournment be for a longer duration than the space of six Months, and shall publish the Journal of their proceedings monthly, except such parts thereof relating to treaties, alliances or military operations as in their judgment require secresy; and the yeas and nays of the delegates of each state on any question shall be entered on the Journal, when it is desired by any delegate; and the delegates of a state, or any of them, at his or their request shall be furnished with a transcript of the said Journal, except such parts as are above excepted, to lay before the legislatures of the several states.

Article X. The committee of the states, or any nine of them, shall be authorised to execute, in the recess of congress, such of the powers of congress as the united states in congress assembled, by the consent of nine states, shall from time to time think expedient to vest them with; provided that no power be delegated to the said committee, for the exercise of which, by the articles of confederation, the voice of nine states in the congress of the united states assembled is requisite.

Article XI. Canada acceding to this confederation, and joining in the measures of the united states, shall be admitted into, and entitled to all the advantages of this union: but no other colony shall be admitted into the same, unless such admission be agreed to by nine states.

Article XII. All bills of credit emitted, monies borrowed and debts contracted by, or under the authority of congress, before the as-sembling of the united states, in pursuance of the present confederation, shall be deemed and considered as a charge against the united states, for payment and satisfaction whereof the said united states, and the public faith are hereby solemnly pledged.

Article XIII. Every state shall abide by the determinations of the united states in congress assembled, on all questions which by this confederation are submitted to them. And the Articles of this confederation shall be inviolably observed by every state, and the union shall be perpetual; nor shall any alteration at any time hereafter be made in any of them; unless such alteration be agreed to in a congress of the united states, and be afterwards confirmed by the legislatures of every state.

And Whereas it has pleased the Great Governor of the World to incline the hearts of the legislatures we respectively represent in congress, to approve of, and to authorize us to ratify the said articles of confederation and perpetual union. Know Ye that we the under-signed delegates, by virtue of the power and authority to us given for that purpose, do by these presents, in the name and in behalf of our respective constituents, fully and entirely ratify and confirm each and every of the said articles of confederation and perpetual union, and all and singular the matters and things therein contained: And we do further solemnly plight and engage the faith of our respective constituents, that they shall abide by the determinations of the united states in congress assembled, on all questions, which by the said confederation are submitted to them. And that the articles thereof shall be inviolably observed by the states we respectively represent, and that the union shall be perpetual. In Witness whereof we have hereunto set our hands in Congress. Done at Philadelphia in the state of Pennsylvania the ninth Day of July in the Year of our Lord one Thousand seven Hundred and Seventy-eight, and in the third year of the independence of America.

New Hampshire:
Josiah Bartlett,
John Wentworth Jr.

Massachusetts:
John Hancock,
Samuel Adams,
Elbridge Gerry,
Francis Dana,
James Lovell,
Samuel Holten.

Rhode Island:
William Ellery,
Henry Marchant,
John Collins.

Connecticut:
Roger Sherman,
Samuel Huntington,
Oliver Wolcott,
Titus Hosmer,
Andrew Adams.

New York:
James Duane,
Francis Lewis,
William Duer,
Gouverneur Morris.

New Jersey:
John Witherspoon,
Nathaniel Scudder.

Pennsylvania:
Robert Morris,
Daniel Roberdeau,
Jonathan Bayard
    Smith,
William Clingan,
Joseph Reed.

Delaware:
Thomas McKean,
John Dickinson,
Nicholas Van Dyke.

Maryland:
John Hanson,
Daniel Carroll.

Virginia:
Richard Henry
    Lee,
John Banister,
Thomas Adams,
John Harvie,
Francis Lightfoot
    Lee.

North Carolina:
John Penn,
Cornelius Harnett,
John Williams.

South Carolina:
Henry Laurens,
William Henry
    Drayton,
John Mathews,
Richard Hutson,
Thomas Heyward Jr.

Georgia:
John Walton,
Edward Telfair,
Edward Langworthy.

Constitution of the United States

The United States Constitution was written at a convention that Congress called on February 21, 1787, for the purpose of recommending amendments to the Articles of Confederation. Every state but Rhode Island sent delegates to Philadelphia, where the convention met that summer. The delegates decided to write an entirely new constitution, completing their labors on September 17. Nine states (the number the Constitution itself stipulated as sufficient) ratified by June 21, 1788.

The Framers of the Constitution included only six paragraphs on the Supreme Court. Article III, Section 1, created the Supreme Court and the federal system of courts. It provided that "[t]he judicial power of the United States, shall be vested in one supreme Court," and whatever inferior courts Congress "from time to time" saw fit to establish. Article III, Section 2, delineated the types of cases and controversies that should be considered by a federal—rather than a state—court. But beyond this, the Constitution left many of the particulars of the Supreme Court and the federal court system for Congress to decide in later years in judiciary acts.

We the People of the United States, in Order to form a more perfect Union, establish Justice, insure domestic Tranquility, provide for the common defence, promote the general Welfare, and secure the Blessings of Liberty to ourselves and our Posterity, do ordain and establish this Constitution for the United States of America.

ARTICLE I

Section 1. All legislative Powers herein granted shall be vested in a Congress of the United States, which shall consist of a Senate and House of Representatives.

Section 2. The House of Representatives shall be composed of Members chosen every second Year by the People of the several States, and the Electors in each State shall have the Qualifications requisite for Electors of the most numerous Branch of the State Legislature.

No Person shall be a Representative who shall not have attained to the age of twenty five Years, and been seven Years a Citizen of the United States, and who shall not, when elected, be an Inhabitant of that State in which he shall be chosen.

[Representatives and direct Taxes shall be apportioned among the several States which may be included within this Union, according to their respective Numbers, which shall be determined by adding to the whole Number of free Persons, including those bound to Service for a Term of Years, and excluding Indians not taxed, three fifths of all other Persons.][1] The actual Enumeration shall be made within three Years after the first Meeting of the Congress of the United States, and within every subsequent Term of ten Years, in such Manner as they shall by Law direct. The Number of Representatives shall not exceed one for every thirty Thousand, but each State shall have at Least one Representative; and until such enumeration shall be made, the State of New Hampshire shall be entitled to chuse three, Massachusetts eight, Rhode-Island and Providence Plantations one, Connecticut five, New-York six, New Jersey four, Pennsylvania eight, Delaware one, Maryland six, Virginia ten, North Carolina five, South Carolina five, and Georgia three.

When vacancies happen in the Representation from any State, the Executive Authority thereof shall issue Writs of Election to fill such Vacancies.

The House of Representatives shall chuse their Speaker and other Officers; and shall have the sole Power of Impeachment.

Section 3. The Senate of the United States shall be composed of two Senators from each State, [chosen by the Legislature thereof,][2] for six Years; and each Senator shall have one Vote.

Immediately after they shall be assembled in Consequence of the first Election, they shall be divided as equally as may be into three Classes. The Seats of the Senators of the first Class shall be vacated at the Expiration of the second Year, of the second Class at the Expiration of the fourth Year, and of the third Class at the Expiration of the sixth Year, so that one third may be chosen every second Year; [and if Vacancies happen by Resignation, or otherwise, during the Recess of the Legislature of any State, the Executive thereof may make temporary Appointments until the next Meeting of the Legislature, which shall then fill such Vacancies.][3]

No Person shall be a Senator who shall not have attained to the Age of thirty Years, and been nine Years a Citizen of the United States, and who shall not, when elected, be an Inhabitant of that State for which he shall be chosen.

The Vice President of the United States shall be President of the Senate, but shall have no Vote, unless they be equally divided.

The Senate shall chuse their other Officers, and also a President pro tempore, in the Absence of the Vice President, or when he shall exercise the Office of President of the United States.

The Senate shall have the sole Power to try all Impeachments. When sitting for that Purpose, they shall be on Oath or Affirmation. When the President of the United States is tried, the Chief Justice shall preside: And no Person shall be convicted without the Concurrence of two thirds of the Members present.

Judgment in Cases of Impeachment shall not extend further than to removal from Office, and disqualification to hold and enjoy any Office of honor, Trust or Profit under the United States: but the Party convicted shall nevertheless be liable and subject to Indictment, Trial, Judgment and Punishment, according to Law.

Section 4. The Times, Places and Manner of holding Elections for Senators and Representatives, shall be prescribed in each State by the Legislature thereof; but the Congress may at any time by Law make or alter such Regulations, except as to the Places of chusing Senators.

The Congress shall assemble at least once in every Year, and such Meeting shall [be on the first Monday in December],[4] unless they shall by Law appoint a different Day.

Section 5. Each House shall be the Judge of the Elections, Returns and Qualifications of its own Members, and a Majority of each shall constitute a Quorum to do Business; but a smaller Number may adjourn from day to day, and may be authorized to compel the Attendance of absent Members, in such Manner, and under such Penalties as each House may provide.

Each House may determine the Rules of its Proceedings, punish its Members for disorderly Behaviour, and, with the Concurrence of two thirds, expel a Member.

Each House shall keep a Journal of its Proceedings, and from time to time publish the same, excepting such Parts as may in their Judgment require Secrecy; and the Yeas and Nays of the Members of either House on any question shall, at the Desire of one fifth of those Present, be entered on the Journal.

Neither House, during the Session of Congress, shall, without the

Consent of the other, adjourn for more than three days, nor to any other Place than that in which the two Houses shall be sitting.

Section 6. The Senators and Representatives shall receive a Compensation for their Services, to be ascertained by Law, and paid out of the Treasury of the United States. They shall in all Cases, except Treason, Felony and Breach of the Peace, be privileged from Arrest during their Attendance at the Session of their respective Houses, and in going to and returning from the same; and for any Speech or Debate in either House, they shall not be questioned in any other Place.

No Senator or Representative shall, during the Time for which he was elected, be appointed to any civil Office under the Authority of the United States, which shall have been created, or the Emoluments whereof shall have been encreased during such time; and no Person holding any Office under the United States, shall be a Member of either House during his Continuance in Office.

Section 7. All Bills for raising Revenue shall originate in the House of Representatives; but the Senate may propose or concur with Amendments as on other Bills.

Every Bill which shall have passed the House of Representatives and the Senate, shall, before it become a Law, be presented to the President of the United States; If he approve he shall sign it, but if not he shall return it, with his Objections to that House in which it shall have originated, who shall enter the Objections at large on their Journal, and proceed to reconsider it. If after such Reconsideration two thirds of that House shall agree to pass the Bill, it shall be sent, together with the Objections, to the other House, by which it shall likewise be reconsidered, and if approved by two thirds of that House, it shall become a Law. But in all such Cases the Votes of both Houses shall be determined by yeas and Nays, and the Names of the Persons voting for and against the Bill shall be entered on the Journal of each House respectively. If any Bill shall not be returned by the President within ten Days (Sundays excepted) after it shall have been presented to him, the Same shall be a Law, in like Manner as if he had signed it, unless the Congress by their Adjournment prevent its Return, in which Case it shall not be a Law.

Every Order, Resolution, or Vote to which the Concurrence of the Senate and House of Representatives may be necessary (except on a question of Adjournment) shall be presented to the President of the United States; and before the Same shall take Effect, shall be approved by him, or being disapproved by him, shall be repassed by two thirds of the Senate and House of Representatives, according to the Rules and Limitations prescribed in the Case of a Bill.

Section 8. The Congress shall have Power To lay and collect Taxes, Duties, Imposts and Excises, to pay the Debts and provide for the common Defence and general Welfare of the United States; but all Duties, Imposts and Excises shall be uniform throughout the United States;

To borrow Money on the credit of the United States;

To regulate Commerce with foreign Nations, and among the several States, and with the Indian Tribes;

To establish an uniform Rule of Naturalization, and uniform Laws on the subject of Bankruptcies throughout the United States;

To coin Money, regulate the Value thereof, and of foreign Coin, and fix the Standard of Weights and Measures;

To provide for the Punishment of counterfeiting the Securities and current Coin of the United States;

To establish Post Offices and post Roads;

To promote the Progress of Science and useful Arts, by securing for limited Times to Authors and Inventors the exclusive Right to their respective Writings and Discoveries;

To constitute Tribunals inferior to the supreme Court;

To define and punish Piracies and Felonies committed on the high Seas, and Offences against the Law of Nations;

To declare War, grant Letters of Marque and Reprisal, and make Rules concerning Captures on Land and Water;

To raise and support Armies, but no Appropriation of Money to that Use shall be for a longer Term than two Years;

To provide and maintain a Navy;

To make Rules for the Government and Regulation of the land and naval Forces;

To provide for calling forth the Militia to execute the Laws of the Union, suppress Insurrections and repel Invasions;

To provide for organizing, arming, and disciplining, the Militia, and for governing such Part of them as may be employed in the Service of the United States, reserving to the States respectively, the Appointment of the Officers, and the Authority of training the Militia according to the discipline prescribed by Congress;

To exercise exclusive Legislation in all Cases whatsoever, over such District (not exceeding ten Miles square) as may, by Cession of particular States, and the Acceptance of Congress, become the Seat of the Government of the United States, and to exercise like Authority over all Places purchased by the Consent of the Legislature of the State in which the Same shall be, for the Erection of Forts, Magazines, Arsenals, dock-Yards, and other needful Buildings;—And

To make all Laws which shall be necessary and proper for carrying into Execution the foregoing Powers, and all other Powers vested by this Constitution in the Government of the United States, or in any Department or Officer thereof.

Section 9. The Migration or Importation of such Persons as any of the States now existing shall think proper to admit, shall not be prohibited by the Congress prior to the Year one thousand eight hundred and eight, but a Tax or duty may be imposed on such Importation, not exceeding ten dollars for each Person.

The Privilege of the Writ of Habeas Corpus shall not be suspended, unless when in Cases of Rebellion or Invasion the public Safety may require it.

No Bill of Attainder or ex post facto Law shall be passed.

No Capitation, or other direct, Tax shall be laid, unless in Proportion to the Census or Enumeration herein before directed to be taken.[5]

No Tax or Duty shall be laid on Articles exported from any State.

No Preference shall be given by any Regulation of Commerce or Revenue to the Ports of one State over those of another; nor shall Vessels bound to, or from, one State, be obliged to enter, clear, or pay Duties in another.

No Money shall be drawn from the Treasury, but in Consequence of Appropriations made by Law; and a regular Statement and Account of the Receipts and Expenditures of all public Money shall be published from time to time.

No Title of Nobility shall be granted by the United States: And no Person holding any Office of Profit or Trust under them, shall, without the Consent of the Congress, accept of any present, Emolument, Office, or Title, of any kind whatever, from any King, Prince, or foreign State.

Section 10. No State shall enter into any Treaty, Alliance, or Confederation; grant Letters of Marque and Reprisal; coin Money; emit Bills of Credit; make any Thing but gold and silver Coin a Tender in Payment of Debts; pass any Bill of Attainder, ex post facto Law, or Law impairing the Obligation of Contracts, or grant any Title of Nobility.

No State shall, without the Consent of the Congress, lay any Imposts or Duties on Imports or Exports, except what may be absolutely necessary for executing it's inspection Laws: and the net Produce of all Duties and Imposts, laid by any State on Imports or Exports, shall be for the Use of the Treasury of the United States; and all such Laws shall be subject to the Revision and Controul of the Congress.

No State shall, without the Consent of Congress, lay any Duty of Tonnage, keep Troops, or Ships of War in time of Peace, enter into any Agreement or Compact with another State, or with a foreign Power, or engage in War, unless actually invaded, or in such imminent Danger as will not admit of delay.

ARTICLE II

Section 1. The executive Power shall be vested in a President of the United States of America. He shall hold his Office during the Term of four Years, and, together with the Vice President, chosen for the same Term, be elected, as follows

Each State shall appoint, in such Manner as the Legislature thereof may direct, a Number of Electors, equal to the whole Number of Senators and Representatives to which the State may be entitled in the Congress: but no Senator or Representative, or Person holding an Office of Trust or Profit under the United States, shall be appointed an Elector.

[The Electors shall meet in their respective States, and vote by Ballot for two Persons, of whom one at least shall not be an Inhabitant of the same State with themselves. And they shall make a List of all the Persons voted for, and of the Number of Votes for each; which List they shall sign and certify, and transmit sealed to the Seat of the Government of the United States, directed to the President of the Senate. The President of the Senate shall, in the Presence of the Senate and House of Representatives, open all the Certificates, and the Votes shall then be counted. The Person having the greatest Number of Votes shall be the President, if such Number be a Majority of the whole Number of Electors appointed; and if there be more than one who have such Majority, and have an equal Number of Votes, then the House of Representatives shall immediately chuse by Ballot one of them for President; and if no Person have a Majority, then from the five highest on the list the said House shall in like Manner chuse the President. But in chusing the President, the Votes shall be taken by States, the Representation from each State having one Vote; A quorum for this Purpose shall consist of a Member or Members from two thirds of the States, and a Majority of all the States shall be necessary to a Choice. In every Case, after the Choice of the President, the Person having the greatest Number of Votes of the Electors shall be the Vice President. But if there should remain two or more who have equal Votes, the Senate shall chuse from them by Ballot the Vice President.][6]

The Congress may determine the Time of chusing the Electors, and the Day on which they shall give their Votes; which Day shall be the same throughout the United States.

No Person except a natural born Citizen, or a Citizen of the United States, at the time of the Adoption of this Constitution, shall be eligible to the Office of President; neither shall any Person be eligible to that Office who shall not have attained to the Age of thirty five Years, and been fourteen Years a Resident within the United States.

In Case of the Removal of the President from Office, or of his Death, Resignation, or Inability to discharge the Powers and Duties of the said Office,[7] the Same shall devolve on the Vice President, and the Congress may by Law provide for the Case of Removal, Death, Resignation or Inability, both of the President and Vice President, declaring what Officer shall then act as President, and such Officer shall act accordingly, until the Disability be removed, or a President shall be elected.

The President shall, at stated Times, receive for his Services, a Compensation, which shall neither be encreased nor diminished during the Period for which he shall have been elected, and he shall not receive within that Period any other Emolument from the United States, or any of them.

Before he enter on the Execution of his Office, he shall take the following Oath or Affirmation:—"I do solemnly swear (or affirm) that I will faithfully execute the Office of President of the United States, and will to the best of my Ability, preserve, protect and defend the Constitution of the United States."

Section 2. The President shall be Commander in Chief of the Army and Navy of the United States, and of the Militia of the several States, when called into the actual Service of the United States; he may require the Opinion, in writing, of the principal Officer in each of the executive Departments, upon any Subject relating to the Duties of their respective Offices, and he shall have Power to grant Reprieves and Pardons for Offences against the United States, except in Cases of Impeachment.

He shall have Power, by and with the Advice and Consent of the Senate, to make Treaties, provided two thirds of the Senators present concur; and he shall nominate, and by and with the Advice and Consent of the Senate, shall appoint Ambassadors, other public Ministers and Consuls, Judges of the supreme Court, and all other Officers of the United States, whose Appointments are not herein otherwise provided for, and which shall be established by Law: but the Congress may by Law vest the Appointment of such inferior Officers, as they think proper, in the President alone, in the Courts of Law, or in the Heads of Departments.

The President shall have Power to fill up all Vacancies that may happen during the Recess of the Senate, by granting Commissions which shall expire at the End of their next Session.

Section 3. He shall from time to time give to the Congress Information of the State of the Union, and recommend to their Consideration such Measures as he shall judge necessary and expedient; he may, on extraordinary Occasions, convene both Houses, or either of them, and in Case of Disagreement between them, with Respect to the Time of Adjournment, he may adjourn them to such Time as he shall think proper; he shall receive Ambassadors and other public Ministers; he shall take Care that the Laws be faithfully executed, and shall Commission all the Officers of the United States.

Section 4. The President, Vice President and all civil Officers of the United States, shall be removed from Office on Impeachment for, and Conviction of, Treason, Bribery, or other high Crimes and Misdemeanors.

ARTICLE III

Section 1. The judicial Power of the United States, shall be vested in one supreme Court, and in such inferior Courts as the Congress may from time to time ordain and establish. The Judges, both of the supreme and inferior Courts, shall hold their Offices during good Behaviour, and shall, at stated Times, receive for their Services, a Compensation, which shall not be diminished during their Continuance in Office.

Section 2. The judicial Power shall extend to all Cases, in Law and Equity, arising under this Constitution, the Laws of the United States, and Treaties made, or which shall be made, under their Authority; — to all Cases affecting Ambassadors, other public Ministers and Consuls; —to all Cases of admiralty and maritime Jurisdiction; —to Controversies to which the United States shall be a Party; —to Controversies between two or more States; —between a State and Citizens of another State;[8] —between Citizens of different States; —between Citizens of the same State claiming Lands under Grants of different States, and between a State, or the Citizens thereof, and foreign States, Citizens or Subjects.[8]

In all Cases affecting Ambassadors, other public Ministers and Consuls, and those in which a State shall be Party, the supreme Court shall have original Jurisdiction. In all the other Cases before mentioned, the supreme Court shall have appellate Jurisdiction, both as to Law and Fact, with such Exceptions, and under such Regulations as the Congress shall make.

The Trial of all Crimes, except in Cases of Impeachment, shall be by Jury; and such Trial shall be held in the State where the said Crimes shall have been committed; but when not committed within any State, the Trial shall be at such Place or Places as the Congress may by Law have directed.

Section 3. Treason against the United States, shall consist only in levying War against them, or in adhering to their Enemies, giving them Aid and Comfort. No Person shall be convicted of Treason unless on the Testimony of two Witnesses to the same overt Act, or on Confession in open Court.

The Congress shall have Power to declare the Punishment of Treason, but no Attainder of Treason shall work Corruption of Blood, or Forfeiture except during the Life of the Person attainted.

ARTICLE IV

Section 1. Full Faith and Credit shall be given in each State to the public Acts, Records, and judicial Proceedings of every other State. And the Congress may by general Laws prescribe the Manner in which such Acts, Records and Proceedings shall be proved, and the Effect thereof.

Section 2. The Citizens of each State shall be entitled to all Privileges and Immunities of Citizens in the several States.

A Person charged in any State with Treason, Felony, or other Crime, who shall flee from Justice, and be found in another State, shall on Demand of the executive Authority of the State from which he fled, be delivered up, to be removed to the State having Jurisdiction of the Crime.

[No Person held to Service or Labour in one State, under the Laws thereof, escaping into another, shall, in Consequence of any Law or Regulation therein, be discharged from such Service or Labour, but shall be delivered up on Claim of the Party to whom such Service or Labour may be due.]

Section 3. New States may be admitted by the Congress into this Union; but no new State shall be formed or erected within the Jurisdiction of any other State; nor any State be formed by the Junction of two or more States, or Parts of States, without the Consent of the Legislatures of the States concerned as well as of the Congress.

The Congress shall have Power to dispose of and make all needful Rules and Regulations respecting the Territory or other Property belonging to the United States; and nothing in this Constitution shall be so construed as to Prejudice any Claims of the United States, or of any particular State.

Section 4. The United States shall guarantee to every State in this Union a Republican Form of Government, and shall protect each of them against Invasion; and on Application of the Legislature, or of the Executive (when the Legislature cannot be convened) against domestic Violence.

ARTICLE V

The Congress, whenever two thirds of both Houses shall deem it necessary, shall propose Amendments to this Constitution, or, on the Application of the Legislatures of two thirds of the several States, shall call a Convention for proposing Amendments, which, in either Case, shall be valid to all Intents and Purposes, as Part of this Constitution, when ratified by the Legislatures of three fourths of the several States, or by Conventions in three fourths thereof, as the one or the other Mode of Ratification may be proposed by the Congress; Provided [that no Amendment which may be made prior to the Year One thousand eight hundred and eight shall in any Manner affect the first and fourth Clauses in the Ninth Section of the first Article; and][10]

that no State, without its Consent, shall be deprived of its equal Suffrage in the Senate.

ARTICLE VI

All Debts contracted and Engagements entered into, before the Adoption of this Constitution, shall be as valid against the United States under this Constitution, as under the Confederation.

This Constitution, and the Laws of the United States which shall be made in Pursuance thereof; and all Treaties made, or which shall be made, under the Authority of the United States, shall be the supreme Law of the Land; and the Judges in every State shall be bound thereby, any Thing in the Constitution or Laws of any State to the Contrary notwithstanding.

The Senators and Representatives before mentioned, and the Members of the several State Legislatures, and all executive and judicial Officers, both of the United States and of the several States, shall be bound by Oath or Affirmation, to support this Constitution; but no religious Test shall ever be required as a Qualification to any Office or public Trust under the United States.

ARTICLE VII

The Ratification of the Conventions of nine States, shall be sufficient for the Establishment of this Constitution between the States so ratifying the Same.

Done in Convention by the Unanimous Consent of the States present the Seventeenth Day of September in the Year of our Lord one thousand seven hundred and Eighty seven and of the Independence of the United States of America the Twelfth. IN WITNESS whereof We have hereunto subscribed our Names,

George Washington,
President and deputy from Virginia.

New Hampshire:
John Langdon,
Nicholas Gilman.

Massachusetts:
Nathaniel Gorham,
Rufus King.

Connecticut:
William Samuel Johnson,
Roger Sherman.

New York:
Alexander Hamilton.

New Jersey:
William Livingston,
David Brearley,
William Paterson,
Jonathan Dayton.

Pennsylvania:
Benjamin Franklin,
Thomas Mifflin,
Robert Morris,
George Clymer,
Thomas FitzSimons,
Jared Ingersoll,
James Wilson,
Gouverneur Morris.

Delaware:
George Read,
Gunning Bedford Jr.,
John Dickinson,
Richard Bassett,
Jacob Broom.

Maryland:
James McHenry,
Daniel of St. Thomas Jenifer,
Daniel Carroll.

Virginia:
John Blair,
James Madison Jr.

North Carolina:.
William Blount,
Richard Dobbs Spaight,
Hugh Williamson.

South Carolina:
John Rutledge,
Charles Cotesworth Pinckney,
Charles Pinckney,
Pierce Butler.

Georgia:
William Few,
Abraham Baldwin.

[The language of the original Constitution, not including the Amendments, was adopted by a convention of the states on September 17, 1787, and was subsequently ratified by the states on the following dates: Delaware, December 7, 1787; Pennsylvania, December 12, 1787; New Jersey, December 18, 1787; Georgia, January 2, 1788; Connecticut, January 9, 1788; Massachusetts, February 6, 1788; Maryland, April 28, 1788; South Carolina, May 23, 1788; New Hampshire, June 21, 1788.

Ratification was completed on June 21, 1788.

The Constitution subsequently was ratified by Virginia, June 25, 1788; New York, July 26, 1788; North Carolina, November 21, 1789; Rhode Island, May 29, 1790; and Vermont, January 10, 1791.]

AMENDMENTS

Amendment I

(First ten amendments ratified December 15, 1791.)

Congress shall make no law respecting an establishment of religion, or prohibiting the free exercise thereof; or abridging the freedom of speech, or of the press; or the right of the people peaceably to assemble, and to petition the Government for a redress of grievances.

Amendment II

A well regulated Militia, being necessary to the security of a free State, the right of the people to keep and bear Arms, shall not be infringed.

Amendment III

No Soldier shall, in time of peace be quartered in any house, without the consent of the Owner, nor in time of war, but in a manner to be prescribed by law.

Amendment IV

The right of the people to be secure in their persons, houses, papers, and effects, against unreasonable searches and seizures, shall not be violated, and no Warrants shall issue, but upon probable cause, supported by Oath or affirmation, and particularly describing the place to be searched, and the persons or things to be seized.

Amendment V

No person shall be held to answer for a capital, or otherwise infamous crime, unless on a presentment or indictment of a Grand Jury, except in cases arising in the land or naval forces, or in the Militia, when in actual service in time of War or public danger; nor shall any person be subject for the same offence to be twice put in jeopardy of life or limb; nor shall be compelled in any criminal case to be a witness against himself, nor be deprived of life, liberty, or property, without due process of law; nor shall private property be taken for public use, without just compensation.

Amendment VI

In all criminal prosecutions, the accused shall enjoy the right to a speedy and public trial, by an impartial jury of the State and district wherein the crime shall have been committed, which district shall have been previously ascertained by law, and to be informed of the nature and cause of the accusation; to be confronted with the witnesses against him; to have compulsory process for obtaining witnesses in his favor, and to have the Assistance of Counsel for his defence.

Amendment VII

In Suits at common law, where the value in controversy shall exceed twenty dollars, the right of trial by jury shall be preserved, and no fact tried by a jury, shall be otherwise re-examined in any Court of the United States, than according to the rules of the common law.

Amendment VIII

Excessive bail shall not be required, nor excessive fines imposed, nor cruel and unusual punishments inflicted.

Amendment IX

The enumeration in the Constitution, of certain rights, shall not be construed to deny or disparage others retained by the people.

Amendment X

The powers not delegated to the United States by the Constitution, nor prohibited by it to the States, are reserved to the States respectively, or to the people.

Amendment XI *(Ratified February 7, 1795)*

The Judicial power of the United States shall not be construed to extend to any suit in law or equity, commenced or prosecuted against one of the United States by Citizens of another State, or by Citizens or Subjects of any Foreign State.

Amendment XII *(Ratified June 15, 1804)*

The Electors shall meet in their respective states and vote by ballot for President and Vice-President, one of whom, at least, shall not be an inhabitant of the same state with themselves; they shall name in their ballots the person voted for as President, and in distinct ballots the person voted for as Vice-President, and they shall make distinct lists of all persons voted for as President, and of all persons voted for as Vice-President, and of the number of votes for each, which lists they shall sign and certify, and transmit sealed to the seat of the government of the United States, directed to the President of the Senate; — The President of the Senate shall, in the presence of the Senate and House of Representatives, open all the certificates and the votes shall then be counted; — The person having the greatest number of votes for President, shall be the President, if such number be a majority of the whole number of Electors appointed; and if no person have such majority, then from the persons having the highest numbers not exceeding three on the list of those voted for as President, the House of Representatives shall choose immediately, by ballot, the President. But in choosing the President, the votes shall be taken by states, the representation from each state having one vote; a quorum for this purpose shall consist of a member or members from two-thirds of the states, and a majority of all the states shall be necessary to a choice. [And if the House of Representatives shall not choose a President whenever the right of choice shall devolve upon them, before the fourth day of March next following, then the Vice-President shall act as President, as in the case of the death or other constitutional disability of the President. —][11] The person having the greatest number of votes as Vice-President, shall be the Vice-President, if such number be a majority of the whole number of Electors appointed, and if no person have a majority, then from the two highest numbers on the list, the Senate shall choose the Vice-President; a quorum for the purpose shall consist of two-thirds of the whole number of Senators, and a majority of the whole number shall be necessary to a choice. But no person constitutionally ineligible to the office of President shall be eligible to that of Vice-President of the United States.

Amendment XIII *(Ratified December 6, 1865)*

Section 1. Neither slavery nor involuntary servitude, except as a punishment for crime whereof the party shall have been duly convicted, shall exist within the United States, or any place subject to their jurisdiction.

Section 2. Congress shall have power to enforce this article by appropriate legislation.

Amendment XIV *(Ratified July 9, 1868)*

Section 1. All persons born or naturalized in the United States, and subject to the jurisdiction thereof, are citizens of the United States and of the State wherein they reside. No State shall make or enforce any law which shall abridge the privileges or immunities of citizens of the United States; nor shall any State deprive any person of life, liberty, or property, without due process of law; nor deny to any person within its jurisdiction the equal protection of the laws.

Section 2. Representatives shall be apportioned among the several States according to their respective numbers, counting the whole number of persons in each State, excluding Indians not taxed. But when the right to vote at any election for the choice of electors for President and Vice President of the United States, Representatives in Congress, the Executive and Judicial officers of a State, or the members of the Legislature thereof, is denied to any of the male inhabitants of such State, being twenty-one years of age,[12] and citizens of the United States, or in any way abridged, except for participation in rebellion, or other crime, the basis of representation therein shall be reduced in the proportion which the number of such male citizens shall bear to the whole number of male citizens twenty-one years of age in such State.

Section 3. No person shall be a Senator or Representative in Congress, or elector of President and Vice President, or hold any office, civil or military, under the United States, or under any State, who, having previously taken an oath, as a member of Congress, or as an officer of the United States, or as a member of any State legislature, or as an executive or judicial officer of any State, to support the Constitution of the United States, shall have engaged in insurrection or rebellion against the same, or given aid or comfort to the enemies thereof. But Congress may by a vote of two-thirds of each House, remove such disability.

Section 4. The validity of the public debt of the United States, authorized by law, including debts incurred for payment of pensions and bounties for services in suppressing insurrection or rebellion, shall not be questioned. But neither the United States nor any State shall assume or pay any debt or obligation incurred in aid of insurrection or rebellion against the United States, or any claim for the loss or emancipation of any slave; but all such debts, obligations and claims shall be held illegal and void.

Section 5. The Congress shall have power to enforce, by appropriate legislation, the provisions of this article.

Amendment XV *(Ratified February 3, 1870)*

Section 1. The right of citizens of the United States to vote shall not be denied or abridged by the United States or by any State on account of race, color, or previous condition of servitude.

Section 2. The Congress shall have power to enforce this article by appropriate legislation.

Amendment XVI *(Ratified February 3, 1913)*

The Congress shall have power to lay and collect taxes on incomes, from whatever source derived, without apportionment among the several States, and without regard to any census or enumeration.

Amendment XVII *(Ratified April 8, 1913)*

The Senate of the United States shall be composed of two Senators from each State, elected by the people thereof, for six years; and each Senator shall have one vote. The electors in each State shall have the qualifications requisite for electors of the most numerous branch of the State legislatures.

When vacancies happen in the representation of any State in the Senate, the executive authority of such State shall issue writs of election to fill such vacancies: *Provided,* That the legislature of any State may empower the executive thereof to make temporary appointments until the people fill the vacancies by election as the legislature may direct.

This amendment shall not be so construed as to affect the election or term of any Senator chosen before it becomes valid as part of the Constitution.

Amendment XVIII *(Ratified January 16, 1919)*

Section 1. After one year from the ratification of this article the manufacture, sale, or transportation of intoxicating liquors within, the importation thereof into, or the exportation thereof from the United States and all territory subject to the jurisdiction thereof for beverage purposes is hereby prohibited.

Section 2. The Congress and the several States shall have concurrent power to enforce this article by appropriate legislation.

Section 3. This article shall be inoperative unless it shall have been ratified as an amendment to the Constitution by the legislatures of the several States, as provided in the Constitution, within seven years from the date of the submission hereof to the States by the Congress.][13]

Amendment XIX *(Ratified August 18, 1920)*

The right of citizens of the United States to vote shall not be denied or abridged by the United States or by any State on account of sex.

Congress shall have power to enforce this article by appropriate legislation.

Amendment XX *(Ratified January 23, 1933)*

Section 1. The terms of the President and Vice President shall end at noon on the 20th day of January, and the terms of Senators and Representatives at noon on the 3d day of January, of the years in which such terms would have ended if this article had not been ratified; and the terms of their successors shall then begin.

Section 2. The Congress shall assemble at least once in every year, and such meeting shall begin at noon on the 3d day of January, unless they shall by law appoint a different day.

Section 3.[14] If, at the time fixed for the beginning of the term of the President, the President elect shall have died, the Vice President elect shall become President. If a President shall not have been chosen before the time fixed for the beginning of his term, or if the President elect shall have failed to qualify, then the Vice President elect shall act as President until a President shall have qualified; and the Congress may by law provide for the case wherein neither a President elect nor a Vice President elect shall have qualified, declaring who shall then act as President, or the manner in which one who is to act shall be selected, and such person shall act accordingly until a President or Vice President shall have qualified.

Section 4. The Congress may by law provide for the case of the death of any of the persons from whom the House of Representatives may choose a President whenever the right of choice shall have devolved upon them, and for the case of the death of any of the persons from whom the Senate may choose a Vice President whenever the right of choice shall have devolved upon them.

Section 5. Sections 1 and 2 shall take effect on the 15th day of October following the ratification of this article.

Section 6. This article shall be inoperative unless it shall have been ratified as an amendment to the Constitution by the legislatures of three-fourths of the several States within seven years from the date of its submission.

Amendment XXI *(Ratified December 5, 1933)*

Section 1. The eighteenth article of amendment to the Constitution of the United States is hereby repealed.

Section 2. The transportation or importation into any State, Territory, or possession of the United States for delivery or use therein of intoxicating liquors, in violation of the laws thereof, is hereby prohibited.

Section 3. This article shall be inoperative unless it shall have been ratified as an amendment to the Constitution by conventions in the several States, as provided in the Constitution, within seven years from the date of the submission hereof to the States by the Congress.

Amendment XXII *(Ratified February 27, 1951)*

Section 1. No person shall be elected to the office of the President more than twice, and no person who has held the office of President, or acted as President, for more than two years of a term to which some other person was elected President shall be elected to the office of the President more than once. But this Article shall not apply to any person holding the office of President when this Article was proposed by the Congress, and shall not prevent any person who may be holding the office of President, or acting as President, during the term within which this Article becomes operative from holding the office of President or acting as President during the remainder of such term.

Section 2. This article shall be inoperative unless it shall have been ratified as an amendment to the Constitution by the legislatures of three-fourths of the several States within seven years from the date of its submission to the States by the Congress.

Amendment XXIII *(Ratified March 29, 1961)*

Section 1. The District constituting the seat of Government of the United States shall appoint in such manner as the Congress may direct:

A number of electors of President and Vice President equal to the whole number of Senators and Representatives in Congress to which the District would be entitled if it were a State, but in no event more than the least populous State; they shall be in addition to those appointed by the States, but they shall be considered, for the purposes of the election of President and Vice President, to be electors appointed by a State; and they shall meet in the District and perform such duties as provided by the twelfth article of amendment.

Section 2. The Congress shall have power to enforce this article by appropriate legislation.

Amendment XXIV *(Ratified January 23, 1964)*

Section 1. The right of citizens of the United States to vote in any primary or other election for President or Vice President, for electors for President or Vice President, or for Senator or Representative in Congress, shall not be denied or abridged by the United States or any State by reason of failure to pay any poll tax or other tax.

Section 2. The Congress shall have power to enforce this article by appropriate legislation.

Amendment XXV *(Ratified February 10, 1967)*

Section 1. In case of the removal of the President from office or of his death or resignation, the Vice President shall become President.

Section 2. Whenever there is a vacancy in the office of the Vice President, the President shall nominate a Vice President who shall take office upon confirmation by a majority vote of both Houses of Congress.

Section 3. Whenever the President transmits to the President pro tempore of the Senate and the Speaker of the House of Representatives his written declaration that he is unable to discharge the powers and duties of his office, and until he transmits to them a written declaration to the contrary, such powers and duties shall be discharged by the Vice President as Acting President.

Section 4. Whenever the Vice President and a majority of either the principal officers of the executive departments or of such other body as Congress may by law provide, transmit to the President pro tempore of the Senate and the Speaker of the House of Representatives their written declaration that the President is unable to discharge the powers and duties of his office, the Vice President shall immediately assume the powers and duties of the office as Acting President.

Thereafter, when the President transmits to the President pro tempore of the Senate and the Speaker of the House of Representatives his written declaration that no inability exists, he shall resume the powers and duties of his office unless the Vice President and a majority of either the principal officers of the executive departments or of such other body as Congress may by law provide, transmit within four days to the President pro tempore of the Senate and the Speaker of the House of Representatives their written declaration that the President is unable to discharge the powers and duties of his office. Thereupon Congress shall decide the issue, assembling within forty-eight hours for that purpose if not in session. If the Congress, within twenty-one days after receipt of the latter written declaration, or, if Congress is not in session, within twenty-one days after Congress is required to assemble, determines by two-thirds vote of both Houses that the President is unable to discharge the powers and duties of his office, the Vice President shall continue to discharge the same as Acting President; otherwise, the President shall resume the powers and duties of his office.

Amendment XXVI *(Ratified July 1, 1971)*

Section 1. The right of citizens of the United States, who are eighteen years of age or older, to vote shall not be denied or abridged by the United States or by any State on account of age.

Section 2. The Congress shall have power to enforce this article by appropriate legislation.

Amendment XXVII *(Ratified May 7, 1992)*

No law varying the compensation for the services of the Senators and Representatives shall take effect, until an election of Representatives shall have intervened.

SOURCE: U.S. Congress, House, Committee on the Judiciary, *The Constitution of the United States of America, as Amended,* 100th Cong., 1st sess., 1987, H Doc 100–94.

NOTES: 1. The part in brackets was changed by section 2 of the Fourteenth Amendment.

2. The part in brackets was changed by the first paragraph of the Seventeenth Amendment.

3. The part in brackets was changed by the second paragraph of the Seventeenth Amendment.

4. The part in brackets was changed by section 2 of the Twentieth Amendment.

5. The Sixteenth Amendment gave Congress the power to tax incomes.

6. The material in brackets was superseded by the Twelfth Amendment.

7. This provision was affected by the Twenty-fifth Amendment.

8. These clauses were affected by the Eleventh Amendment.

9. This paragraph was superseded by the Thirteenth Amendment.

10. Obsolete.

11. The part in brackets was superseded by section 3 of the Twentieth Amendment.

12. See the Nineteenth and Twenty-sixth Amendments.

13. This amendment was repealed by section 1 of the Twenty-first Amendment.

14. See the Twenty-fifth Amendment.

Judiciary Act of 1789

Although the Constitution created the Supreme Court, it said much less about the Court than about Congress and the president. With the Judiciary Act of 1789, Congress set up a system of lower federal courts (district courts and circuit courts with limited jurisdiction), spelled out the appellate jurisdiction of the Supreme Court, and gave the Court the power to review and reverse or affirm state court rulings.

The act also set the number of Supreme Court justices at six: a chief justice and five associates. (Subsequent statutes changed the total number of justices successively to six, seven, nine, ten, seven, and nine.) In addition to establishing the size and jurisdiction of the Supreme Court, the act required the justices to "ride circuit"—a burdensome duty of traveling to and sitting on circuit courts around the country.

JUDICIARY ACT OF 1789

An Act to establish the Judicial Courts of the United States.

STATUTE I
Sept. 24, 1789.

Supreme court to consist of a chief justice, and five associates.
Two sessions annually.

Precedence.

SECTION 1. *Be it enacted by the Senate and House of Representatives of the United States of America in Congress assembled,* That the supreme court of the United States shall consist of a chief justice and five associate justices, any four of whom shall be a quorum, and shall hold annually at the seat of government two sessions, the one commencing the first Monday of February, and the other the first Monday of August. That the associate justices shall have precedence according to the data of their commissions, or when the commissions of two or more of them bear date on the same day, according to the respective ages.

Thirteen districts.

Maine.
N. Hampshire.

Massachusetts.

Connecticut.
New York.

New Jersey.

Pennsylvania.
Delaware.

Maryland.

Virginia.

Kentucky.

South Carolina.
Georgia.

SEC. 2. *And be it further enacted,* That the United States shall be, and they hereby are divided into thirteen districts, to be limited and called as follows, to wit: one to consist of that part of the State of Massachusetts which lies easterly of the State of New Hampshire, and to be called Maine District; one to consist of the State of New Hampshire, and to be called New Hampshire District; one to consist of the remaining part of the State of Massachusetts, and to be called Massachusetts district; one to consist of the State of Connecticut, and to be called Connecticut District; one to consist of the State of New York, and to be called New York District; one to consist of the State of New Jersey, and to be called New Jersey District; one to consist of the State of Pennsylvania, and to be called Pennsylvania District; one to consist of the State of Delaware, and to be called Delaware District; one to consist of the State of Maryland, and to be called Maryland District; one to consist of the State of Virginia, except that part called the District of Kentucky, and to be called Virginia District; one to consist of the remaining part of the State of Virginia, and to be called Kentucky District; one to consist of the State of South Carolina, and to be called South Carolina District; and one to consist of the State of Georgia, and to be called Georgia District.

A district court in each district.

SEC. 3. *And be it further enacted,* That there be a court called a District Court, in each of the aforementioned districts, to consist of one judge, who shall reside in the district for which he is appointed,

Four sessions annually in a district; and when held.

Special district courts.
Stated district courts; when holden.

Special courts, where held.

Where records kept.

and shall be called a District Judge, and shall hold annually four sessions, the first of which to commence as follows, to wit: in the districts of New York and of New Jersey on the first, in the district of Pennsylvania on the second, in the district of Connecticut on the third, and in the district of Delaware on the fourth, Tuesdays of November next; in the districts of Massachusetts, of Maine, and of Maryland, on the first, in the district of Georgia on the second, and in the districts of New Hampshire, of Virginia, and of Kentucky, on the third Tuesdays of December next; and the other three sessions progressively in the respective districts on the like Tuesdays of every third calendar month afterwards, and in the district of South Carolina, on the third Monday in March and September, the first Monday in July, and the second Monday in December of each and every year, commencing in December next; and that the District Judge shall have power to hold special courts at his discretion. That the stated District Court shall be held at the places following, to wit: in the district of Maine, at Portland and Pownalsborough alternately, beginning at the first; in the district of New Hampshire, at Exeter and Portsmouth alternately, beginning at the first; in the district of Massachusetts, at Boston and Salem alternately, beginning at the first; in the district of Connecticut, alternately at Hartford and New Haven, beginning at the first; in the district of Connecticut, alternately at Hartford and New Haven, beginning at the first; in the district of New York, at New York; in the district of New Jersey, alternately at New Brunswick and Burlington, beginning at the first; in the district of Pennsylvania, at Philadelphia and York Town alternately, beginning at the first; in the district of Delaware, alternately at Newcastle and Dover, beginning at the first; in the district of Maryland, alternately at Baltimore and Easton, beginning at the first; in the district of Virginia, alternately at Richmond and Williamsburgh, beginning at the first; in the district of Kentucky, at Harrodsburgh; in the district of South Carolina, at Charleston; and in the district of Georgia, alternately at Savannah and Augusta, beginning at the first; and that the special courts shall be held at the same place in each district as the stated courts, or in districts that have two, at either of them, in the discretion of the judge, or at such other place in the district, as the nature of the business and his discretion shall direct. And that in the districts that have but one place for holding the District Court, the records thereof shall be kept at that place; and in districts that have two, at that place in each district which the judge shall appoint.

Three circuits, and how divided.

SEC. 4. *And be it further enacted,* That the before mentioned districts, except those of Maine and Kentucky, shall be divided into three circuits, and be called the eastern, the middle, and the southern circuit. That the eastern circuit shall consist of the districts of New Hampshire, Massachusetts, Connecticut and New York; that the middle circuit shall consist of the districts of New Jersey, Pennsylvania, Delaware, Maryland and Virginia; and that the southern circuit shall consist of the districts of South Carolina and Georgia, and that there shall be held annually in each district of said circuits, two courts, which shall be called Circuit Courts, and shall consist of any two justices of the Supreme Court, and the district judge of such districts, any two of whom shall constitute a quorum: *Provided,* That no district judge shall give a vote in any case of appeal or error from his own decision; but may assign the reasons of such his decision.

First session of the circuit courts; when holden.

SEC. 5. *And be it further enacted,* That the first session of the said circuit court in the several districts shall commence at the times following, to wit: in New Jersey on the second, in New York on the fourth, in Pennsylvania on the eleventh, in Connecticut on the twenty-second, and in Delaware on the twenty-seventh, days of April next; in Massachusetts on the third, in Maryland on the seventh, in South Carolina on the twelfth, in New Hampshire on the twentieth, in Virginia on the twenty-second, and in Georgia on the twenty-eighth, days of May next, and the subsequent sessions in the respective districts on the like days of every sixth calendar month afterwards, except in South Carolina, where the session of the said court shall commence on the first, and in Georgia where it shall commence on the seventeenth day of October, and except when any of those days shall happen on a Sunday, and then the session shall commence on the next day following. And the sessions of the said circuit court

Where holden.

shall be held in the district of New Hampshire, at Portsmouth and Exeter alternately, beginning at the first; in the district of Massachusetts, at Boston; in the district of Connecticut, alternately at Hartford and New Haven, beginning at the last; in the district of New York, alternately at New York and Albany, beginning at the first; in the district of New Jersey, at Trenton; in the district of Pennsylvania, alternately at Philadelphia and Yorktown, beginning at the first; in the district of Delaware, alternately at New Castle and Dover, beginning at the first; in the district of Maryland, alternately at Annapolis and Easton, beginning at the first; in the district of Virginia, alternately at Charlottesville and Williamsburgh, beginning at the first; in the district of South Carolina, alternately at Columbia and Charleston, beginning at the first; and in the district of Georgia, alternately at Savannah and Augusta, beginning at the first. And

Circuit courts. Special sessions.

the circuit courts shall have power to hold special sessions for the trial of criminal causes at any other

time at their discretion, or at the discretion of the Supreme Court.

Supreme court adjourned by one or more justices; circuit courts adjourned.

District courts adjourned.

SEC. 6. *And be it further enacted,* That the Supreme Court may, by any one or more of its justices being present, be adjourned from day to day until a quorum be convened; and that a circuit court may also be adjourned from day to day by any one of its judges, or if none are present, by the marshal of the district until a quorum be convened; and that a district court, in case of the inability of the judge to attend at the commencement of a session, may by virtue of a written order from the said judge, directed to the marshal of the district, be adjourned by the said marshal to such day, antecedent to the next stated session of the said court, as in the said order shall be appointed; and in case of the death of the said judge, and his vacancy not being supplied, all process, pleadings and proceedings of what nature soever, pending before the said court, shall be continued of course until the next stated session after the appointment and acceptance of the office by his successor.

The courts have power to appoint clerks.

Their oath or affirmation.

SEC. 7. *And be it [further] enacted,* That the Supreme Court, and the district courts shall have power to appoint clerks for their respective courts, and that the clerk for each district court shall be clerk also of the circuit court in such district, and each of the said clerks shall, before he enters upon the execution of his office, take the following oath or affirmation, to wit: "I, A. B., being appointed clerk of _____, do solemnly swear, or affirm, that I will truly and faithfully enter and record all the orders, decrees, judgments and proceedings of the said court, and that I will faithfully and impartially discharge and perform all the duties of my said office, according to the best of my abilities and understanding. So help me God." Which words, so help me God, shall be omitted in all cases where an affirmation is admitted instead of an oath. And the said clerks shall also severally give bond, with sufficient sureties, (to be approved of by the Supreme and district courts respectively) to the United States, in the sum of two thousand dollars, faithfully to discharge the duties of his office, and seasonably to record the decrees, judgments and determinations of the court of which he is clerk.

Oath of justices of supreme court and judges of the district court.

SEC. 8. *And be it further enacted,* That the justices of the Supreme Court, and the district judges, before they proceed to execute the duties of their respective offices, shall take the following oath or affirmation, to wit: "I, A. B., do solemnly swear or affirm, that I will administer justice without respect to persons, and do equal right to the poor and to the rich, and that I will faithfully and impartially discharge and perform all the duties incumbent on me as _____, according to the best of my abilities and understanding, agreeably to the constitution and laws of the United States. So help me God."

District courts exclusive jurisdiction.

SEC. 9. *And be it further enacted,* That the district courts shall have, exclusively of the courts of the several States, cognizance of all crimes and offences that shall be cognizable under the authority of the United States, committed within their respective districts, or upon the high seas; where no other punishment than whipping, not exceeding thirty stripes, a fine not exceeding one hundred dollars, or a term of imprisonment not exceeding six months, is to be inflicted; and shall also have exclusive original cognizance of all civil causes of admiralty and maritime jurisdication, including all seizures under laws of impost, navigation or trade of the United States, where the seizures are made, on waters which are navigable from the sea by vessels of ten or more tons burthen, within their respective districts as well as upon the high seas; saving to suitors, in all cases, the right of a common law remedy, where the common law is competent to give it; and shall also have exclusive original cognizance of all seizures on land, or other waters than as aforesaid, made, and of all suits for penalties and forfeitures incurred, under the laws of the United States. And shall also have cognizance, concurrent with the courts of the several States, or the circuit courts, as the case may be, of all causes where an alien sues for a tort only in violation of the law of nations or a treaty of the United States. And shall also have cognizance, concurrent as last mentioned, of all suits at common law where the United States sue, and the matter in dispute amounts, exclusive of costs, to the sum or value of one hundred dollars. And shall also have jurisdiction exclusively of the courts of the several States, of all suits against consuls or vice-consuls, except for offences above the description aforesaid. And the trial of issues in fact, in the district courts, in all causes except civil causes of admiralty and maritime jurisdiction, shall be by jury.

Original cognizance in maritime causes and of seizure under the laws of the United States.

Concurrent jurisdiction.

Trial of fact by jury.

Kentucky district court.

SEC. 10. *And be it further enacted,* That the district court in Kentucky district shall, besides the jurisdiction aforesaid, have jurisdiction of all other causes, except of appeals and writs of error, hereinafter made cognizable in a circuit court, and shall proceed therein in the same manner as a circuit court, and writs of error and appeals shall lie from decisions therein to the Supreme Court in the same causes, as from a circuit court to the Supreme Court, and under the same regulations. And the district court in Maine district shall, besides the jurisdiction herein before granted, have jurisdiction of all causes, except of appeals and writs of error herein after made cognizable in a circuit court, and shall proceed therein in the same manner as a circuit court: And writs of error shall lie from decisions therein to the circuit court in the district of Massachusetts in the same manner as from other district courts to their respective circuit courts.

Maine district court.

Circuit courts original cognizance where the matter in dispute exceeds five hundred dollars.

SEC. 11. *And be it further enacted,* That the circuit courts shall have original cognizance, concurrent with the courts of the several States, of all suits of a civil nature at common law or in equity, where the matter in dispute exceeds, exclusive of costs, the sum or value of five hundred dollars, and the United States are plaintiffs, or petitioners; or an alien is a party, or the suit is between a citizen of the State where the suit is brought, and a citizen of another State. And shall have exclusive cognizance of all crimes and offences cognizable under the authority of the United States, except where this act otherwise provides, or the laws of the United States shall otherwise direct, and concurrent jurisdiction with the district courts of the crimes and offences cognizable therein. But no person shall be arrested in one district for trial in another, in any civil action before a circuit or district court. And no civil suit shall be brought before either of said courts against an inhabitant of the United States, by any original process in any other district than that whereof he is an inhabitant, or in which he shall be found at the time of serving the writ, nor shall any district or circuit court have cognizance of any suit to recover the contents of any promissory note or other chose in action in favour of an assignee, unless a suit might have been prosecuted in such court to recover the said contents if no assignment had been made, except in cases of foreign bills of exchange. And the circuit courts shall also have appellate jurisdiction from the district courts under the regulations and restrictions herein after provided.

Exclusive cognizance of crimes and offences cognizable under the laws of the United States.

No person to be arrested in one district for trial in another on any civil suit.

Limitation as to civil suits.

Actions on promissory notes.

Circuit courts shall also have appellate jurisdiction.

Matter in dispute above 500 dollars.

SEC. 12. *And be it further enacted,* That if a suit be commenced in any state court against an alien, or by a citizen of the state in which the suit is brought against a citizen of another state, and the matter in dispute exceeds the aforesaid sum or value of five hundred dollars, exclusive of costs, to be made to appear to the satisfaction of the court; and the defendant shall, at the time of entering his appearance in such state court, file a petition for the removal of the cause for trial into the next circuit court, to be held in the district where the suit is pending, or if in the district of Maine to the district court next to be holden therein, or if in Kentucky district to the district court next to be holden therein, and offer good and sufficient surety for his entering in such court, on the first day of its session, copies of said process against him, and also for his there appearing and entering special bail in the cause, if special bail was originally requisite therein, it shall then be the duty of the state court to accept the surety, and proceed no further in the cause, and any bail that may have been originally taken shall be discharged and the said copies being entered as aforesaid, in such court of the United States, the cause shall there proceed in the same manner as if it had been brought there by original process. And any attachment of the goods or estate of the defendant by the original process, shall hold the goods or estate so attached, to answer the final judgment in the same manner as by the laws of such state they would have been holden to answer final judgment, had it been rendered by the court in which the suit commenced. And if in any action commenced in a state court, the title of land be concerned, and the parties are citizens of the

Removal of causes from state courts.

Special bail.

Attachment of goods holden to final judgment.

Title of land where value exceeds 500 dollars.

same state, and the matter in dispute exceeds the sum or value of five hundred dollars, exclusive of costs, the sum or value being made to appear to the satisfaction of the court, either party, before the trial, shall state to the court and make affidavit if they require it, that he claims and shall rely upon a right or title to the land, under a grant from a state other than that in which the suit is pending, and produce the original grant or an exemplification of it, except where the loss of public records shall put it out of his power, and shall move that the adverse party inform the court, whether he claims a right or title to the land under a grant from the state in which the suit is pending; the said adverse [party] shall give such information, or otherwise not be allowed to plead such grant, or give it in evidence upon the trial, and if he informs that he does claim under such grant, the party claiming under the grant first mentioned may then, on motion, remove the cause for trial to the next circuit court to be holden in such district, or if in the district of Maine, to the court next to be holden therein; or if in Kentucky district, to the district court next to be holden therein; but if he is the defendant, shall do it under the same regulations as in the beforementioned case of the removal of a cause into such court by an alien; and neither party removing the cause, shall be allowed to plead or give evidence of any other title than that by him stated as aforesaid, as the ground of his claim; and the trial of issues in fact in the circuit courts shall, in all suits, except those of equity, and of admiralty, and maritime jurisdiction, be by jury.

If in Maine and Kentucky, where causes are removable.

Issues in fact by jury.

Supreme court exclusive jurisdiction.

SEC. 13. *And be it further enacted,* That the Supreme Court shall have exclusive jurisdiction of all controversies of a civil nature, where a state is a party, except between a state and its citizens; and except also between a state and citizens of other states, or aliens, in which latter case it shall have original but not exclusive jurisdiction. And shall have exclusively all such jurisdiction of suits or proceedings against ambassadors, or other public ministers, or their domestics, or domestic servants, as a court of law can have or exercise consistently with the law of nations; and original, but not exclusive jurisdiction of all suits brought by ambassadors, or other public ministers, or in which a consul, or vice consul, shall be a party. And the trial of issues in fact in the Supreme Court, in all actions at law against citizens of the United States, shall be by jury. The Supreme Court shall also have appellate jurisdiction from the circuit courts and courts of the several states, in the cases herein after specially provided for; and shall have power to issue writs of prohibition to the district courts, when proceeding as courts of admiralty and maritime jurisdiction, and writs of *mandamus,* in cases warranted by the principles and usages of law, to any courts appointed, or persons holding office, under the authority of the United States.

Proceedings against public ministers.

Sup. Court appellate jurisdiction.

Writs of Prohibition.

Of Mandamus.

Courts may issue writs scire facias, habeas corpus, &c.

SEC. 14. *And be it further enacted,* That all the before-mentioned courts of the United States, shall have power to issue writs of *scire facias, habeas cor-*

Limitation of writs of habeas corpus.

pus, and all other writs not specially provided for by statute, which may be necessary for the exercise of their respective jurisdictions, and agreeable to the principles and usages of law. And that either of the justices of the supreme court, as well as judges of the district courts, shall have power to grant writs of *habeas corpus* for the purpose of an inquiry into the cause of commitment — *Provided,* That writs of *habeas corpus* shall in no case extend to prisoners in gaol, unless where they are in custody, under or by colour of the authority of the United States, or are committed for trial before some court of the same, or are necessary to be brought into court to testify.

Parties shall produce books and writings.

SEC. 15. *And be it further enacted,* That all the said courts of the United States, shall have power in the trial of actions at law, on motion and due notice thereof being given, to require the parties to produce books or writings in their possession or power, which contain evidence pertinent to the issue, in cases and under circumstances where they might be compelled to produce the same by the ordinary rules of proceeding in chancery; and if a plaintiff shall fail to comply with such order, to produce books or writings, it shall be lawful for the courts respectively, on motion, to give the like judgment for the defendant as in cases of nonsuit; and if a defendant shall fail to comply with such order, to produce books or writings, it shall be lawful for the courts respectively on motion as aforesaid, to give judgment against him or her by default.

Suits in equity limited.

SEC. 16. *And be it further enacted,* That suits in equity shall not be sustained in either of the courts of the United States, in any case where plain, adequate and complete remedy may be had at law.

Courts may grant new trials.

SEC. 17. *And be it further enacted,* That all the said courts of the United States shall have power to grant new trials, in cases where there has been a trial by jury for reasons for which new trials have usually been granted in the courts of law; and shall have power to impose and administer all necessary oaths or affirmations, and to punish by fine or imprisonment, at the discretion of said courts, all contempts of authority in any cause or hearing before the same; and to make and establish all necessary rules for the orderly conducting business in the said courts, provided such rules are not repugnant to the laws of the United States.

Execution may be stayed on conditions.

SEC. 18. *And be it further enacted,* That when in a circuit court, judgment upon a verdict in a civil action shall be entered, execution may on motion of either party, at the discretion of the court, and on such conditions for the security of the adverse party as they may judge proper, be stayed forty-two days from the time of entering judgment, to give time to file in the clerk's office of said court, a petition for a new trial. And if such petition be there filed within said term of forty-two days, with a certificate thereon from either of the judges of such court, that he allows the same to be filed, which certificate he may make or refuse at his discretion, execution shall of course be further stayed to the next session of said court. And if a new trial be granted, the former judgment shall be thereby rendered void.

Facts to appear on record.

SEC. 19. *And be it further enacted,* That it shall be the duty of circuit courts, in causes in equity and of admiralty and maritime jurisdiction, to cause the facts on which they found their sentence or decree, fully to appear upon the record of either from the pleadings and decree itself, or a state of the case agreed by the parties, or their counsel, or if they disagree by a stating of the case by the court.

Costs not allowed unless 500 dollars recovered.

SEC. 20. *And be it further enacted,* That where in a circuit court, a plaintiff in an action, originally brought there, or a petitioner in equity, other than the United States, recovers less than the sum or value of five hundred dollars, or a libellant, upon his own appeal, less than the sum or value of three hundred dollars, he shall not be allowed, but at the discretion of the court, may be adjudged to pay costs.

Appeals from the district to the circuit court where matter in dispute exceeds 300 dolls.

SEC. 21. *And be it further enacted,* That from final decrees in a district court in causes of admiralty and maritime jurisdiction, where the matter in dispute exceeds the sum or value of three hundred dollars, exclusive of costs, an appeal shall be allowed to the next circuit court, to be held in such district. *Provided nevertheless,* That all such appeals from final decrees as aforesaid, from the district court of Maine, shall be made to the circuit court, next to be holden after each appeal in the district of Massachusetts.

Final decrees re-examined above 50 dollars.

Altered by the 2d section of the act of March 3, 1803, chap. 40.

SEC. 22. *And be it further enacted,* That final decrees and judgments in civil actions in a district court, where the matter in dispute exceeds the sum or value of fifty dollars, exclusive of costs, may be re-examined, and reversed or affirmed in a circuit court, holden in the same distict, upon a writ of error, whereto shall be annexed and returned therewith at the day and place therein mentioned, an authenticated transcript of the record, an assignment of errors, and prayer for reversal, with a citation to the adverse party, signed by the judge of such district court, or a justice of the Supreme Court, the adverse party having at least twenty days' notice. And upon a like process, may final judgments and decrees in civil actions, and suits in equity in a circuit court, brought there by original process, or removed there from courts of the several States, or removed there by appeal from a district court where the matter in dispute exceeds the sum or value of two thousand dollars, exclusive of costs, be re-examined and reversed or affirmed in the Supreme Court, the citation being in such case signed by a judge of such circuit court, or justice of the Supreme Court, and the adverse party having at least thirty days' notice. But there shall be no reversal in either court on such writ of error for error in ruling any plea in abatement, other than a plea to the jurisdiction of the court, or such plea to a petition or bill in equity, as is in the nature of a demurrer, or for any error in fact. And

And suits in equity, exceeding 2000 dollars in value.

Writs of error limited.

writs of error shall not be brought but within five years after rendering or passing the judgment or decree complained of, or in case the person entitled to such writ of error be an infant, *feme covert, non compos mentis,* or imprisoned, then within five years as aforesaid, exclusive of the time of such disability. And every justice or judge signing a citation on any writ of error as aforesaid, shall take good and sufficient security, that the plaintiff in error shall prosecute his writ to effect, and answer all damages and costs if he fail to make his plea good.

Plaintiff to give security.

Writ of error a supersedeas.

SEC. 23. *And be it further enacted,* That a writ of error as aforesaid shall be a supersedeas and stay execution in cases only where the writ of error is served, by a copy thereof being lodged for the adverse party in the clerk's office where the record remains, within ten days, Sundays exclusive, after rendering the judgment or passing the decree complained of. Until the expiration of which term of ten days, executions shall not issue in any case where a writ of error may be a supersedeas; and whereupon such writ of error the Supreme or a circuit court shall affirm a judgment or decree, they shall adjudge or decree to the respondent in error just damages for his delay, and single or double costs at their discretion.

Judgment or decree reversed.

SEC. 24. *And be it further enacted,* That when a judgment or decree shall be reversed in a circuit court, such court shall proceed to render such judgment or pass such decree as the district court should have rendered or passed; and the Supreme Court shall do the same on reversals therein, except where the reversal is in favor of the plaintiff, or petitioner in the original suit, and the damages to be assessed, or matter to be decreed, are uncertain, in which case they shall remand the cause for a final decision. And the Supreme Court shall not issue execution in causes that are removed before them by writs of error, but shall send a special mandate to the circuit court to award execution thereupon.

Supreme court not to issue execution but mandate.

Cases in which judgment and decrees of the highest court of a state may be examined by the supreme court, on writ of error.

SEC. 25. *And be it further enacted,* That a final judgment or decree in any suit, in the highest court of law or equity of a State in which a decision in the suit could be had, where is drawn in question the validity of a treaty or statute of, or an authority exercised under the United States, and the decision is against their validity; or where is drawn in question the validity of a statute of, or an authority exercised under any State, on the ground of their being repugnant to the constitution, treaties or laws of the United States, and the decision is in favour of such their validity, or where is drawn in question the construction of any clause of the constitution, or of a treaty, or statute of, or commission held under the United States, and the decision is against the title, right, privilege or exemption specially set up or claimed by either party, under such clause of the said Constitution, treaty, statute or commission, may be re-examined and reversed or affirmed in the Supreme Court of the United States upon a writ of error, the citation being signed by the chief justice, or judge or chancellor of the court rendering or passing the judgment or decree complained of, or by a justice of the Supreme Court of the United States, in the same manner and under the same regulations, and the writ shall have the same effect, as if the judgment or decree complained of had been rendered or passed in a circuit court, and the proceeding upon the reversal shall also be the same, except that the Supreme Court, instead of remanding the cause for a final decision as before provided, may at their discretion, if the cause shall have been once remanded before, proceed to a final decision of the same, and award execution. But no other error shall be assigned or regarded as a ground of reversal in any such case as aforesaid, than such as appears on the face of the record, and immediately respects the before mentioned questions of validity or construction of the said constitution, treaties, statutes, commissions, or authorities in dispute.

Proceedings on reversal.

No writs of error but as above mentioned.

In cases of forfeiture the courts may give judgment according to equity.

SEC. 26. *And be it further enacted,* That in all causes brought before either of the courts of the United States to recover the forfeiture annexed to any articles of agreement, covenant, bond, or other specialty, where the forfeiture, breach or non-performance shall appear, by the default or confession of the defendant, or upon demurrer, the court before whom the action is, shall render judgment therein for the plaintiff to recover so much as is due according to equity. And when the sum for which judgment should be rendered is uncertain, the same shall, if either of the parties request it, be assessed by a jury.

Jury to assess damages when the sum is uncertain.

Marshal to be appointed. Duration of office.

SEC. 27. *And be it further enacted,* That a marshal shall be appointed in and for each district for the term of four years, but shall be removable from office at pleasure, whose duty it shall be to attend the district and circuit courts when sitting therein, and also the Supreme Court in the district in which that court shall sit. And to execute throughout the district, all lawful precepts directed to him, and issued under the authority of the United States, and he shall have power to command all necessary assistance in the execution of his duty, and to appoint as there shall be occasion, one or more deputies, who shall be removable from office by the judge of the district court, or the circuit court sitting within the district, at the pleasure of either; and before he enters on the duties of his office, he shall become bound for the faithful performance of the same, by himself and by his deputies before the judge of the district court to the United States, jointly and severally, with two good and sufficient sureties, inhabitants and freeholders of such district, to be approved by the district judge, in the sum of twenty thousand dollars, and shall take before said judge, as shall also his deputies, before they enter on the duties of their appointment, the following oath of office: "I, A. B., do solemnly swear or affirm, that I will faithfully execute all lawful precepts directed to the marshal of the district of ____ under the authority of the United States, and true returns make, and in all things

Deputies removable by the district and circuit courts.

Sureties.

Oath of marshal, and of his deputies.

well and truly, and without malice or partiality, perform the duties of the office of marshal (or marshal's deputy, as the case may be) of the district of ____, during my continuance in said office, and take only my lawful fees. So help me God."

If marshal, or his deputy, a party to a suit, process to be directed to a person selected by the court.

SEC. 28. *And be it further enacted,* That in all causes wherein the marshal or his deputy shall be a party, the writs and precepts therein shall be directed to such disinterested person as the court, or any justice or judge thereof may appoint, and the person so appointed, is hereby authorized to execute and return the same. And in case of the death of any marshal, his deputy or deputies shall continue in office, unless otherwise specially removed; and shall execute the same in the name of the deceased, until another marshal shall be appointed and sworn: And the defaults or misfeasances in office of such deputy or deputies in the mean time, as well as before, shall be adjudged a breach of the condition of the bond given, as before directed, by the marshal who appointed them; and the executor or administrator of the deceased marshal shall have like remedy for the defaults and misfeasances in office of such deputy or deputies during such interval, as they would be entitled to if the marshal had continued in life and in the exercise of his said office, until his successor was appointed, and sworn or affirmed: And every marshal or his deputy when removed from office, or when the term for which the marshal is appointed shall expire, shall have power notwithstanding to execute all such precepts as may be in their hands respectively at the time of such removal or expiration of office; and the marshal shall be held answerable for the delivery to his successor of all prisoners which may be in his custody at the time of his removal, or when the term for which he is appointed shall expire, and for that purpose may retain such prisoners in his custody until his successor shall be appointed and qualified as the law directs.

Deputies to continue in office on the death of the marshal.

Defaults of deputies.

Powers of the executor or administrator of deceased marshals.

Marshal's power after removal.

Trial of cases punishable with death to be had in county.

SEC. 29. *And be it further enacted,* That in cases punishable with death, the trial shall be had in the county where the offence was committed, or where that cannot be done without great inconvenience, twelve petit jurors at least shall be summoned from thence. And jurors in all cases to serve in the courts of the United States shall be designated by lot or otherwise in each State respectively according to the mode of forming juries therein now practised, so far as the laws of the same shall render such designation practicable by the courts or marshals of the United States; and the jurors shall have the same qualifications as are requisite for jurors by the laws of the State of which they are citizens, to serve in the highest courts of law of such State, and shall be returned as there shall be occasion for them, from such parts of the district from time to time as the court shall direct, so as shall be most favourable to an impartial trial, and so as not to incur an unnecessary expense, or unduly to burthen the citizens of any part of the district with such services. And writs of *venire farias* when directed by the court shall issue from the

Jurors by lot.

Writs of venire facias from clerk's office.

clerk's office, and shall be served and returned by the marshal in his proper person, or by his deputy, or in case the marshal or his deputy is not an indifferent person, or is interested in the event of the cause, by such fit person as the court shall specially appoint for that purpose, to whom they shall administer an oath or affirmation that he will truly and impartially serve and return such writ. And when from challenges or otherwise there shall not be a jury to determine any civil or criminal cause, the marshal or his deputy shall, by order of the court where such defect of jurors shall happen, return jurymen *de talibus circumstantibus* sufficient to complete the pannel; and when the marshal or his deputy are disqualified as aforesaid, jurors may be returned by such disinterested person as the court shall appoint.

Juries de talibus, &c.

Mode of proof. SEC. 30. *And be it further enacted,* That the mode of proof by oral testimony and examination of witnesses in open court shall be the same in all the courts of the United States, as well in the trial of causes in equity and of admiralty and maritime jurisdiction, as of actions at common law. And when the testimony of any person shall be necessary in any civil cause depending in any district in any court of the United States, who shall live at a greater distance from the place of trial than one hundred miles, or is bound on a voyage to sea, or is about to go out of the United States, or out of such district, and to a greater distance from the place of trial than as aforesaid, before the time of trial, or is ancient or very infirm, the deposition of such person may be **Depositions de** taken *de bene esse* before any justice or judge of any **bene esse.** of the courts of the United States, or before any chancellor, justice or judge of a supreme or superior court, mayor or chief magistrate of a city, or judge of a county court or court of common pleas of any of the United States, not being of counsel or attorney to either of the parties, or interested in the event of the cause, provided that a notification from the magistrate before whom the deposition is to be taken to the adverse party, to be present at the taking of **Adverse party to** the same, and to put interrogatories, if he think fit, **be notified.** be first made out and served on the adverse party or his attorney as either may be nearest, if either is within one hundred miles of the place of such caption, allowing time for their attendance after notified, not less than at the rate of one day, Sundays ex- **Notice in admiralty** clusive, for every twenty miles travel. And in causes **and maritime causes.** of admiralty and maritime jurisdiction, or other cases of seizure when a libel shall be filed, in which an adverse party is not named, and depositions of persons circumstanced as aforesaid shall be taken before a claim be put in, the like notification as **Agent notified.** aforesaid shall be given to the person having the agency or possession of the property libelled at the time of the capture or seizure of the same, if known to the libellant. And every person deposing as aforesaid shall be carefully examined and cautioned, and sworn or affirmed to testify the whole truth, and shall subscribe the testimony by him or her given after the same shall be reduced to writing, which shall be done only by the magistrate taking the de-

Depositions retained. position, or by the deponent in his presence. And the depositions so taken shall be retained by such magistrate until he deliver the same with his own hand into the court for which they are taken, or shall, together with a certificate of the reasons as aforesaid of their being taken, and of the notice if any given to the adverse party, be by him the said magistrate sealed up and directed to such court, and remain under his seal until opened in court. **Persons may be** And any person may be compelled to appear and **compelled to appear** depose as aforesaid in the same manner as to ap- **and testify.** pear and testify in court. And in the trial of any cause of admiralty or maritime jurisdiction in a **Appeal allowed.** district court, the decree in which may be appealed from, if either party shall suggest to and satisfy the court that probably it will not be in his power to produce the witnesses there testifying before the circuit court should an appeal be had, and shall move that their testimony be taken down in writing, it shall be so done by the clerk of the court. And if an appeal be had, such testimony may be used on the trial of the same if it shall appear to the satisfaction of the court which shall try the appeal, that the witnesses are then dead or gone out of the United States, or to a greater distance than as aforesaid **Depositions used** from the place where the court is sitting, or that by **in case of sickness,** reason of age, sickness, bodily infirmity or impris- **death, &c.** onment, they are unable to travel and appear at court, but not otherwise. And unless the same shall be made to appear on the trial of any cause, with respect to witnesses whose depositions may have been taken therein, such depositions shall not be admitted or used in the cause. *Provided,* That nothing herein shall be construed to prevent any court **Dedimus potestatem** of the United States from granting a *dedimus potes-* **as usual.** *tatem* to take depositions according to common usage, when it may be necessary to prevent a failure or delay of justice, which power they shall severally possess, nor to extend to depositions taken in *perpetuam rei memoriam,* which if they relate to matters that may be cognizable in any court of the United States, a circuit court on application thereto made as a court of equity, may, according to the usages in chancery direct to be taken.

SEC. 31. *And be it [further] enacted,* That where any suit shall be depending in any court of the United States, and either of the parties shall die before final judgment, the executor or administrator of such **Executor or adminis-** deceased party who was plaintiff, petitioner, or de- **trator may prosecute** fendant, in case the cause of action doth by law sur- **and defend.** vive, shall have full power to prosecute or defend any such suit or action until final judgment; and the defendant or defendants are hereby obliged to answer thereto accordingly; and the court before whom such cause may be depending, is hereby empowered and directed to hear and determine the same, and to render judgment for or against the executor or administrator, as the case may require. **Neglect of executor** And if such executor or administrator having been **or administrator to** duly served with a *scire facias* from the office of the **become a party to the** clerk of the court where such suit is depending, **suit, judgment to be** twenty days beforehand, shall neglect or refuse to **rendered.**

become a party to the suit, the court may render judgment against the estate of the deceased party, in the same manner as if the executor or administrator had voluntarily made himself a party to the suit. And the executor or administrator who shall become a party as aforesaid, shall, upon motion to the court where the suit is depending, be entitled to a continuance of the same until the next term of the said court. And if there be two or more plaintiffs or defendants, and one or more of them shall die, if the cause of action shall survive to the surviving plaintiff or plaintiffs, or against the surviving defendant or defendants, the writ or action shall not be thereby abated; but such death being suggested upon the record, the action shall proceed at the suit of the surviving plaintiff or plaintiffs against the surviving defendant or defendants.

Executor and administrator may have continuance. Two plaintiffs. Surviving plaintiff may continue suit.

SEC. 32. *And be it further enacted,* That no summons, writ, declaration, return, process, judgment, or other proceedings in civil causes in any of the courts of the United States, shall be abated, arrested, quashed or reversed, for any defect or want of form, but the said courts respectively shall proceed and give judgment according as the right of the cause and matter in law shall appear unto them, without regarding any imperfections, defects, or want of form in such writ, declaration, or other pleading, return, process, judgment, or course of proceeding whatsoever, except those only in cases of demurrer, which the party demurring shall specially sit down and express together with his demurrer as the cause thereof. And the said courts respectively shall and may, by virtue of this act, from time to time, amend all and every such imperfections, defects and wants of form, other than those only which the party demurring shall express as aforesaid, and may at any time permit either of the parties to amend any defect in the process or pleadings, upon such conditions as the said courts respectively shall in their discretion, and by their rules prescribe.

Writs shall not abate for defect of form.

Exceptions.

Courts may amend imperfections.

SEC. 33. *And be it further enacted,* That for any crime or offence against the United States, the offender may, by any justice or judge of the United States, or by any justice of the peace, or other magistrate of any of the United States where he may be found agreeably to the usual mode of process against offenders in such state, and at the expense of the United States, be arrested, and imprisoned or bailed, as the case may be, for trial before such court of the United States as by this act has cognizance of the offence. And copies of the process shall be returned as speedily as may be into the clerk's office of such court, together with the recognizances of the witnesses for their appearance to testify in the case; which recognizances the magistrate before whom the examination shall be, may require on pain of imprisonment. And if such commitment of the offender, or the witnesses shall be in a district other than that in which the offence is to be tried, it shall be the duty of the judge of that district where the delinquent is imprisoned, seasonably to issue, and of the

Criminals against U.S. arrested by any justice of the peace.

Recognizance to be returned to the clerk's office.

Offender may be removed by warrant.

marshal of the same district to execute, a warrant for the removal of the offender, and the witnesses, or either of them, as the case may be, to the district in which the trial is to be had. And upon all arrests in criminal cases, bail shall be admitted, except where the punishment may be death, in which cases it shall not be admitted but by the supreme or a circuit court, or by a justice of the supreme court, or a judge of a district court, who shall exercise their discretion therein, regarding the nature and circumstances of the offence, and of the evidence, and the usages of law. And if a person committed by a justice of the supreme or a judge of a district court for an offence not punishable with death, shall afterwards procure bail, and there be no judge of the United States in the district to take the same, it may be taken by any judge of the supreme or superior court of law of such state.

Bail admitted.

Bail, how taken.

SEC. 34. *And be it further enacted,* That the laws of the several states, except where the constitution, treaties or statutes of the United States shall otherwise require or provide, shall be regarded as rules of decision in trials at common law in the courts of the United States in cases where they apply.

Laws of States rules of decision.

SEC. 35. *And be it further enacted,* That in all the courts of the United States, the parties may plead and manage their own causes personally or by the assistance of such counsel or attorneys at law as by the rules of the said courts respectively shall be permitted to manage and conduct causes therein. And there shall be appointed in each district a meet person learned in the law to act as attorney for the United States in such district, who shall be sworn or affirmed to the faithful execution of his office, whose duty it shall be to prosecute in such district all delinquents for crimes and offences, cognizable under the authority of the United States, and all civil actions in which the United States shall be concerned, except before the supreme court in the district in which that court shall be holden. And he shall receive as a compensation for his services such fees as shall be taxed therefore in the respective courts before which the suits or prosecutions shall be. And there shall also be appointed a meet person, learned in the law, to act as attorney-general for the United States, who shall be sworn or affirmed to a faithful execution of his office; whose duty it shall be to prosecute and conduct all suits in the Supreme Court in which the United States shall be concerned, and to give his advice and opinion upon questions of law when required by the President of the United States, or when requested by the heads of any of the departments, touching any matters that may concern their departments, and shall receive such compensation for his services as shall by law be provided.

Parties may manage their own cause.

Attorney of the U.S. for each district.

His duties.

Compensation.

Attorney General of the U.S.

Duties.

Compensation.

APPROVED, September 24, 1789.

SOURCE: *Public Statutes at Large of the United States of America,* Vol. I (Boston: Charles C. Little & James Brown, 1845).

Circuit Court of Appeals Act of 1891

In 1891 Congress passed the Circuit Court of Appeals Act, which established a new level of federal courts between the circuit and district courts and the Supreme Court. Relieving Supreme Court justices of the duty of sitting as circuit judges, the new circuit court of appeals was to hear all appeals from the decisions of the district and circuit courts.

Prior to the act, Supreme Court justices were required to ride circuit, a hardship for most justices. The justices were often required to travel long distances and deal with difficult conditions. Questions were also raised about the propriety of the justices participating in cases at the circuit level that were then reviewed by the Supreme Court.

The new circuit court of appeals would have final word in almost all diversity, admiralty, patent, revenue, and noncapital criminal cases. The Supreme Court would review such cases, after their decision by the appeals courts, only if the appeals court judges certified a case to the High Court—or if the Supreme Court decided to grant review through issue of a writ of certiorari. Cases involving constitutional questions, matters of treaty law, jurisdictional questions, capital crimes, and conflicting laws were still granted a right to appeal to the Supreme Court.

CIRCUIT COURT OF APPEALS ACT OF 1891

March 3, 1891

An act to establish circuit courts of appeals and to define and regulate in certain cases the jurisdiction of the courts of the United States, and for other purposes.

United States courts. Additional circuit judges to be appointed. Qualifications, etc.

Be it enacted by the Senate and House of Representatives of the United States of America in Congress assembled, That there shall be appointed by the President of the United States, by and with the advice and consent of the Senate, in each circuit an additional circuit judge, who shall have the same qualifications, and shall have the same power and jurisdiction therein that the circuit judges of the United States, within their respective circuits, now have under existing laws, and who shall be entitled to the same compensation as the circuit judges of the United States in their respective circuits now have.

Circuit court of appeals created. Composition.

General powers.

SEC. 2. That there is hereby created in each circuit a circuit court of appeals, which shall consist of three judges, of whom two shall constitute a quorum, and which shall be a court of record with appellate jurisdiction, as is hereafter limited and established. Such court shall prescribe the form and style of its seal and the form of writs and other process and procedure as may be conformable to the exercise of its jurisdiction as shall be conferred by law. It shall have

Marshal.

the appointment of the marshal of the court with the same duties and powers under the regulations of the court as are now provided for the marshal of the Supreme Court of the United States, so far as the same may be applicable. The court shall also appoint

Clerk.

a clerk, who shall perform and exercise the same duties and powers in regard to all matters within its jurisdiction as are now exercised and performed by the clerk of the Supreme Court of the United States, so far as the same may be applicable. The salary of the

Salaries.

marshal of the court shall be twenty-five hundred dollars a year, and the salary of the clerk of the court shall be three thousand dollars a year, to be paid in equal proportions quarterly. The costs and fees in

Costs, etc.

the Supreme Court now provided for by law shall be costs and fees in the circuit courts of appeals; and the same shall be expended, accounted for, and paid for, and paid over to the Treasury Department of the United States in the same manner as is provided in respect of the costs and fees in the Supreme Court.

Rules, etc.

The court shall have power to establish all rules

and regulations for the conduct of the business of the court within its jurisdiction as conferred by law.

Constitution of court.

SEC. 3. That the Chief-Justice and the associate justices of the Supreme Court assigned to each circuit, and the circuit judges within each circuit, and the several district judges within each circuit, shall be competent to sit as judges of the circuit court of appeals within their respective circuits in the manner hereinafter provided. In case the Chief-Justice or an

Precedence.

associate justice of the Supreme Court should attend at any session of the circuit court of appeals he shall preside, and the circuit judges in attendance upon the court in the absence of the Chief-Justice or associate justice of the Supreme Court shall preside in the order of the seniority of their repective commissions.

Service of district judges

In case the full court at any time shall not be made up by the attendance of the Chief-Justice or an associate justice of the Supreme Court and circuit judges, one or more district judges within the circuit shall be competent to sit in the court according to such order or provision among the district judges as either by general or particular assignment shall be designated by the court: *Provided,* That no

Proviso
No judge to sit on appeal from his court.

justice or judge before whom a cause or question may have been tried or heard in a district court, or existing circuit court, shall sit on the trial or hearing of such cause or question in the circuit court of appeals. A term shall be held annually by the circuit

Terms.

court of appeals in the several judicial circuits at the following places: In the first circuit, in the city of

Regular.

Boston; in the second circuit, in the city of New York; in the third circuit, in the city of Philadelphia; in the fourth circuit, in the city of Richmond; in the fifth circuit, in the city of New Orleans; in the sixth circuit, in the city of Cincinnati; in the seventh circuit, in the city of Chicago; in the eighth circuit, in the city of Saint Louis; in the ninth circuit in the city of San Francisco; and in such other places in each of

Additional.
First term.
Post, p. 1115.

the above circuits as said court may from time to time designate. The first terms of said courts shall be held on the second Monday in January, eighteen hundred and ninety-one, and thereafter at such times as may be fixed by said courts.

No appeal allowed from district to circuit courts.

SEC. 4. That no appeal, whether by writ of error or otherwise, shall hereafter be taken or allowed from the district court to the existing circuit courts, and no appellate jurisdiction shall hereafter be exercised or allowed by said existing circuit courts, but all appeals by writ of error otherwise, from said district courts shall only be subject to review in the Supreme Court of the United States or in the circuit court of appeals hereby established, as is hereinafter provided, and the review, by appeal, by writ of error, or otherwise, from the existing circuit courts shall be had only in the Supreme Court of the United States or in the circuit courts of appeals hereby established according to the provisions of this act regulating the same.

Appeals, etc., from circuit court.

SEC. 5. That appeals or writs of error may be taken from the district courts or from the existing circuit courts direct to the Supreme Court in the following cases:

Appeals allowed direct to Supreme Court.

In any case in which the jurisdiction of the court is in issue; in such cases the question of jurisdiction alone shall be certified to the Supreme Court from the court below for decision.

Jurisdiction questions.

From the final sentences and decrees in prize causes.

Prizes.

In cases of conviction of a capital or otherwise infamous crime.

Capital crimes.

In any case that involves the construction or application of the Constitution of the United States.

Constitutional questions.

In any case in which the constitutionality of any law of the United States, or the validity or construction of any treaty made under its authority, is drawn in question.

Construction of law, treaty, etc.

In any case in which the constitution or law of a State is claimed to be in contravention of the Constitution of the United States.

Conflict of laws.

Nothing in this act shall affect the jurisdiction of the Supreme Court in cases appealed from the highest court of a State, nor the construction of the statute providing for review of such cases.

Appeals from highest State court.

SEC. 6. That the circuit courts of appeals established by this act shall exercise appellate jurisdiction to review by appeal or by writ of error final decision in the district court and the existing circuit courts in all cases other than those provided for in the preceding section of this act, unless otherwise provided by law, and the judgments or decrees of the circuit courts of appeals shall be final in all cases in which the jurisdiction is dependent entirely upon the opposite parties to the suit or controversy, being aliens and citizens of the United States or citizens of different States; also in all cases arising under the patent laws, under the revenue laws, and under the criminal laws and in admiralty cases, excepting that in every such subject within its appellate jurisdiction the circuit court of appeals at any time may certify to the Supreme Court of the United States any questions or propositions of law concerning which it desires the instruction of that court for its proper decision. And thereupon the Supreme Court may either give its instruction on the questions and propositions certified to it, which shall be binding upon the

Jurisdiction of court of appeals.

Judgments final.

Certificate for instruction.

Proceedings in Supreme Court.

circuit courts of appeals in such case, or it may require that the whole record and cause may be sent up to it for its consideration, and thereupon shall decide the whole matter in controversy in the same manner as if it had been brought there for review by writ of error or appeal.

And excepting also that in any such case as is hereinbefore made final in the circuit court of appeals it shall be competent for the Supreme Court to require, by certiorari or otherwise, any such case to be certified to the Supreme Court for its review and determination with the same power and authority in the case as if it had been carried by appeal or writ of error to the Supreme Court.

Certiorari to Supreme Court.

In all cases not hereinbefore, in this section, made final there shall be of right an appeal or writ of error or review of the case by the Supreme Court of the United States where the matter in controversy shall exceed one thousand dollars besides costs. But no such appeal shall be taken or writ of error sued out unless within one year after the entry of the order, judgment, or decree sought to be reviewed.

Appeals and writs of error.

Limitation.

SEC. 7. That where, upon a hearing in equity in a district court, or in an existing circuit court, an injunction shall be granted or continued by an interlocutory order or decree, in a cause in which an appeal from a final decree may be taken under the provisions of this act to the circuit court of appeals, an appeal may be taken from such interlocutory order or decree granting or continuing such injunction to the circuit court of appeals: *Provided,* That the appeal must be taken within thirty days from the entry of such order or decree, and it shall take precedence in the appellate court; and the proceedings in other respects in the court below shall not be stayed unless otherwise ordered by that court during the pendency of such appeal.

Appeal in equity causes.

Proviso.

To be taken in 30 days.

SEC. 8. That any justice or judge, who, in pursuance of the provisions of this act, shall attend the circuit court of appeals held at any place other than where he resides shall, upon his written certificate, be paid by the marshal of the district in which the court shall be held his reasonable expenses for travel and attendance, not to exceed ten dollars per day, and such payments shall be allowed the marshal in the settlement of his accounts with the United States.

Expenses of attending judges.

SEC. 9. That the marshals of the several districts in which said circuit court of appeals may be held shall, under the direction of the Attorney-General of the United States, and with his approval, provide such rooms in the public buildings of the United States as may be necessary, and pay all incidental expenses of said court, including criers, bailiffs, and messengers: *Provided, however,* That in case proper rooms cannot be provided in such buildings, then the said marshals, with the approval of the Attorney-General of the United States, may, from time to time, lease such rooms as may be necessary for such

Court rooms in public buildings.

Expenses.

Proviso.

Rent.

Compensation
to officers.

courts. That the marshals, criers, clerks, bailiffs, and messengers shall be allowed the same compensation for their respective services as are allowed for similar services in the existing circuit courts.

Remanding causes
reviewed by Supreme
Court.

SEC. 10. That whenever an appeal or writ of error or otherwise a case coming directly from the district court or existing circuit court shall be reviewed and determined in the Supreme Court the cause shall be remanded to the proper district or circuit court for further proceedings to be taken in pursuance of such determination. And whenever on appeal or writ of error or otherwise a case coming from a circuit court of appeals shall be reviewed and determined in the Supreme Court the cause shall be remanded by the Supreme Court to the proper district or circuit court for further proceedings in pursuance of such determination. Whenever on appeal or writ or error or otherwise a case coming from a district or circuit court shall be reviewed and determined in the circuit court of appeals in a case in which the decision in the circuit court of appeals is final such cause shall be remanded to the said district or circuit court for further proceedings to be there taken in pursuance of such determination.

From circuit courts
of appeal.

Review in circuit
court of appeals.

Appeals, etc.,
to be brought in
six months.

SEC. 11. That no appeal or writ of error by which any order, judgment, or decree may be reviewed in the circuit courts of appeals under the provisions of this act shall be taken or sued out except within six months after the entry of the order, judgment, or decree sought to be reviewed: *Provided however,* That in all cases in which a lesser time is now by law limited for appeals or writs of error such limits of time shall apply to appeals or writs of error in such cases taken to or sued out from the circuit courts of appeals. And all provisions of law now in force regulating the methods and system of review, through appeals or writs of error, shall regulate the methods and system of appeals and writs of error provided for in this act in respect of the circuit courts of appeals, including all provisions for bonds or other securities to be required and taken on such appeals, in respect of cases brought or to be brought to that court, shall have the same powers and duties as to

Proviso.
Less time in
certain cases.

Rules and
regulations, etc.

Issue of writs.

the allowance of appeals or writs of error, and the conditions of such allowance, as now by law belong to the justices or judges in respect of the existing courts of the United States respectively.

R.S., sec. 716,
p. 136.

SEC. 12. That the circuit court of appeals shall have the powers specified in section seven hundred and sixteen of the Revised Statutes of the United States.

Appeals, etc.,
from Indian
Territory Court.

SEC. 13. Appeals and writs of error may be taken and prosecuted from the decisions of the United States court in the Indian Territory to the Supreme Court of the United States, or to the circuit court of appeals in the eighth circuit, in the same manner and under the same regulations as from the circuit or district courts of the United States, under this act.

Appeals to
Supreme Court.

R.S., sec. 691,
p. 128, repealed.

Vol. 18, p. 316,
repealed.

Inconsistent laws
repealed.

SEC. 14. That section six hundred and ninety-one of the Revised Statutes of the United States and section three of an act entitled "An act to facilitate the disposition of cases in the Supreme Court, and for other purposes," approved February sixteenth, eighteen hundred and seventy-five, be, and the same are hereby repealed. And all acts and parts of acts relating to appeals or writs of error inconsistent with the provisions for review by appeals or writs of error in the preceding sections five and six of this act are hereby repealed.

Jurisdiction in cases
from Territorial
supreme courts.

SEC. 15. That the circuit court of appeal in cases in which the judgments of the circuit courts of appeal are made final by this act shall have the same appellate jurisdiction, by writ of error or appeal, to review the judgments, orders, and decrees of the supreme courts of the several Territories as by this act they may have to review the judgments, orders, and decrees of the district court and circuit courts; and for that purpose the several Territories shall, by orders of the Supreme court, to be made from time to time, be assigned to particular circuits.

Approved, March 3, 1891.

SOURCE: *Public Statutes At Large of the United States of America,* Vol. XXVI (Washington, D.C.: U.S. Government Printing Office, 1891).

Judiciary Act of 1925

The Judiciary Act of 1925 established the jurisdictional rules that currently shape the Supreme Court's workload. The act gave the Court greater control of its docket by reducing the types of cases the Court was obliged to hear and by expanding its authority to select cases for review under a writ of certiorari—giving the Court virtually unlimited power in deciding which cases it would review.

Specifically, the act eliminated the right of appeal from appeals court rulings, except where the appeals court held a state law invalid under the Constitution, federal law, or treaties. A right of appeal from district court decisions remained, however, in cases under antitrust or interstate

commerce laws; appeals by the government in criminal cases; suits to halt enforcement of state law or other official state action; and suits designed to halt enforcement of Interstate Commerce Commission orders.

The act is also known as the "judges bill"—a reference to the fact that the original legislation was drafted by members of the Court. Chief Justice William Howard Taft was instrumental in lobbying Congress for its passage. Taft maintained that the Court was becoming severely backlogged with cases. The law gave the justices, at least for a time, a more manageable caseload.

JUDICIARY ACT OF 1925

February 13, 1925. [H.R. 8206.] [Public, No. 415.]

An Act To amend the Judicial Code, and to further define the jurisdiction of the circuit courts of appeals and of the Supreme Court, and for other purposes.

Judicial Code.

Be it enacted by the Senate and House of Representatives of the United States of America in Congress assembled, That sections 128, 129, 237, 238, 239, and 240 of the Judicial Code as now existing be, and they are severally, amended and reenacted to read as follows:

Circuit Courts of Appeals. Appeals or writs of error to. Vol. 38, p. 803, amended. In district courts. Exception. Hawaii and Porto Rico district courts. Alaska and Virgin Islands. Cases reviewable.

SEC. 128. (a) The circuit courts of appeal shall have appellate jurisdiction to review by appeal or writ of error final decisions —

"First. In the district courts, in all cases save where a direct review of the decision may be had in the Supreme Court under section 238.

"Second. In the United States district courts for Hawaii and for Porto Rico in all cases.

"Third. In the district courts for Alaska or any division thereof, and for the Virgin Islands, in all cases, civil and criminal, wherein the Constitution or a statute or treaty of the United States or any authority exercised thereunder is involved; in all other civil cases wherein the value in controversy, exclusive of interest and costs, exceeds $1,000; in all other criminal cases where the offense charged is punishable by imprisonment for a term exceeding one year or by death, and in all habeas corpus proceedings; and in the district court for the Canal Zone in the cases and mode prescribed in the Act approved September 21, 1922, amending prior laws relating to the Canal Zone.

Canal Zone. Vol. 42, p. 1006.

"Fourth. In the Supreme Courts of the Territory of Hawaii and of Porto Rico, in all civil cases, civil or criminal, wherein the Constitution or a statute or treaty of the United States or any authority exercised thereunder is involved; in all other civil cases wherein the value in controversy, exclusive of interest and costs, exceeds $5,000, and in all habeas corpus proceedings.

Hawaii and Porto Rico Supreme Courts. Cases reviewable.

United States Court for China. Other appellate jurisdiction.

"Fifth. In the United States Court for China, in all cases.

(b) The circuit court of appeals shall also have appellate jurisdiction—

Specified orders, etc., of district courts.

"First. To review the interlocutory orders or decrees of the district courts which are specified in section 129.

Awards of railway employees' controversies. Vol. 38, p. 107.

"Second. To review decisions of the district courts sustaining or overruling exceptions to awards in arbitrations, as provided in section 8 of an Act entitled 'An Act providing for mediation, conciliation, and arbitration in controversies between certain employers and their employees,' approved July 15, 1913.

Bankruptcy cases. Vol. 30, p. 553.

"(c) The circuit courts of appeal shall also have an appellate and supervisory jurisdiction under sections 24 and 25 of the Bankruptcy Act of July 1, 1898, over all proceedings, controversies, and cases had or brought in the district courts under that Act or any of its amendments, and shall exercise the same in the manner prescribed in those sections; and the jurisdiction of the Circuit Court of Appeals for the Ninth Circuit in this regard shall cover the courts of bankruptcy in Alaska and Hawaii, and that of the Circuit Court of Appeals for the First Circuit shall cover the court of bankruptcy in Porto Rico.

In Alaska and Hawaii.

In Porto Rico. Distribution to circuits.

"(d) The review under this section shall be in the following circuit courts of appeal: The decisions of a district court of the United States within a State in the circuit court of appeals for the circuit embracing such State; those of the District Court of Alaska or any division thereof, the United States district court, and the Supreme Court of Hawaii, and the United States Court for China, in the Circuit Court of Appeals for the Ninth Circuit; those of the United States district court and the Supreme Court of Porto Rico in the Circuit Court of Appeals for the First Circuit; those of the District Court of the Virgin Islands in the Circuit Court of Appeals for the Third Circuit; and those of the District Court of the Canal Zone in the Circuit Court of Appeals for the Fifth Circuit.

Further specified authority. Federal Trade Commission orders. Vol. 38, p. 720.

Orders of Interstate Commerce Commission, etc., under Clayton Act. Vol. 38, p. 735.

"(e) The circuit courts of appeal are further empowered to enforce, set aside, or modify orders of the Federal Trade Commission, as provided in section 5 of 'An Act to create a Federal Trade Commission, to define its powers and duties, and for other purposes,' approved September 26, 1914; and orders of the Interstate Commerce Commission, the Federal Reserve Board, and the Federal Trade Commission, as provided in section 11 of 'An Act to supplement existing laws against unlawful restraints and monopolies, and for other purposes,' approved October 15, 1914.

Appeals allowed from injunctions and interlocutory orders of district courts. Cases specified. Vol. 36, p. 1157, amended.

"SEC. 129. Where, upon a hearing in a district court, or by a judge thereof in vacation, an injunction is granted, continued, modified, refused, or dissolved by an interlocutory order or decree, or an application to dissolve or modify an injunction is refused, or an interlocutory order or decree is made appointing a receiver, or refusing an order to wind up a pending receivership or to take the appropriate steps to accomplish the purposes thereof, such as directing a sale or other disposal of property held thereunder, an appeal may be taken from such interlocutory order or decree to the circuit court of appeals; and sections 239 and 240 shall apply to such cases in the circuit courts of appeals as to other cases therein; *Provided,* That the appeal to the circuit court of appeals must be applied for within thirty days from the entry of such order or decree, and shall take precedence in the appellate court; and the proceedings in other respects in the district court shall not be stayed during the pendency of such appeal unless otherwise ordered by the court, or the appellate court, or a judge thereof: *Provided, however,* That the district court may, in its discretion, require an additional bond as a condition of the appeal."

Authority of Supreme Court.

Provisos. Precedence given.

Additional bond discretionary.

Supreme Court. Writ of error allowed from decision of State court against validity of treaty or statute of United States. If validity of State statute drawn in question as repugnant to Constitution, etc. Vol. 39, p. 726, amended.

SEC. 237. (a) A final judgment or decree in any suit in the highest court of a State in which a decision in the suit could be had, where is drawn in question the validity of a treaty or statute of the United States, and the decision is against its validity; or where is drawn in question the validity of a statute of any State, on the ground of its being repugnant to the Constitution, treaties, or laws of the United States, and the decision is in favor of its validity, may be reviewed by the Supreme Court upon a writ of error. The writ shall have the same effect as if the judgment or decree had been rendered or passed in a court of the United States. The Supreme Court may reverse, modify, or affirm the judgment or decree of such State court, and may, in its discretion, award execution or remand the cause to the court from which it was removed by the writ.

Authority of Supreme Court.

Certiorari to State court where validity of United States treaty or statute drawn in question.

State law as repugnant to the Constitution, etc.

Title, etc., set up under United States authority.

"(b) It shall be competent for the Supreme Court, by certiorari, to require that there be certified to it for review and determination, with the same power and authority and with like effect as if brought up by writ of error, any cause wherein a final judgment or decree has been rendered or passed by the highest court of a State in which a decision could be had where is drawn in question the validity of a treaty or statute of the United States; or where is drawn in question the validity of a statute of any State on the ground of its being repugnant to the Constitution, treaties, or laws of the United States; or where any title, right, privilege, or immunity is specially set up or claimed by either party under the Constitution, or any treaty or statute of, or commis-

Use of writ of error not hereby limited.

sion held or authority exercised under, the United States; and the power to review under this paragraph may be exercised as well where the Federal claim is sustained as where it is denied. Nothing in this paragraph shall be construed to limit or detract from the right to a review on a writ of error in a case where such a right is conferred by the preceding paragraph; nor shall the fact that a review on a writ of error might be obtained under the preceding paragraph be an obstacle to granting a review on certiorari under this paragraph.

Writ of error not dismissed if certiorari proper mode of review, etc.

"(c) If a writ of error be improvidently sought and allowed under this section in a case where the proper mode of invoking a review is by a petition for certiorari, this alone shall not be a ground for dismissal; but the papers whereon the writ of error was allowed shall be regarded and acted on as a petition for certiorari and as if duly presented to the Supreme Court at the time they were presented to the court or judge by whom the writ of error was allowed: *Provided,* That where in such a case there appears to be no reasonable ground for granting a petition for certiorari it shall be competent for the Supreme Court to adjudge to the respondent reasonable damages for his delay, and single or double costs, as provided in section 1010 of the Revised Statutes."

Proviso. Damages, etc., if no reasonable ground for certiorari.

R.S., sec. 1010, p. 189.

Direct review of action of district courts in specified Acts limited. Vol. 38, p. 804, amended. Expediting antitrust, etc., cases. Vol. 32, p. 823.

"SEC. 238. A direct review by the Supreme Court of an interlocutory or final judgment or decree of a district court may be had where it is so provided in the following Acts or parts of Acts, and not otherwise:

"(1) Section 2 of the Act of February 11, 1903, 'to expedite the hearing and determination' of certain suits brought by the United States under the antitrust or interstate commerce laws, and so forth.

Adverse decisions in criminal cases. Vol. 34, p. 1246.

"(2) The Act of March 2, 1907, 'providing for writs of error in certain instances in criminal cases' where the decision of the district court is adverse to the United States.

Restricting interlocutory injunctions against State laws, etc. Vol. 37, p. 1013, amended.

"(3) An Act restricting the issuance of interlocutory injunctions to suspend the enforcement of the statute of a State or of an order made by an administrative board or commission created by and acting under the statute of a State, approved March 4, 1913, which Act is hereby amended by adding at the end thereof, 'The requirement respecting the presence of three judges shall also apply to the final hearing in such suit in the district court; and a direct appeal to the Supreme Court may be taken from a final decree granting or denying a permanent injunction in such suit.'

Requirement for presence of three judges, etc.

Judgments, etc., on Interstate Commerce Commission orders. Vol. 38, p. 220.

"(4) So much of 'An Act making appropriations to supply urgent deficiencies in appropriations for the fiscal year 1913, and for other purposes,' approved October 22, 1913, as relates to the review of interlocutory and final judgments and decrees in suits to enforce, suspend, or set aside orders of the Interstate Commerce Commission other than for the payment of money.

Orders by Interstate

"(5) Section 316 of 'An Act to regulate interstate

Commerce Commission as to livestock, poultry, etc.
Vol. 42, p. 168.

and foreign commerce in livestock, livestock products, dairy products, poultry, poultry products, and eggs, and for other purposes' approved August 15, 1921."

Questions certified for instructions by courts of appeals.
Vol. 36, p. 1157, amended.

Authority of court.

"SEC. 239. In any case, civil or criminal, in a circuit court of appeals, or in the Court of Appeals of the District of Columbia, the court at any time may certify to the Supreme Court of the United States any questions or propositions of law concerning which instructions are desired for the proper decision of the cause; and thereupon the Supreme Court may either give binding instructions on the questions and propositions certified or may require that the entire record in the cause be sent up for its consideration, and thereupon shall decide the whole matter in controversy in the same manner as if it had been brought there by writ of error or appeal."

Allowance of certiorari to courts of appeals on petition of either party.
Vol. 36, p. 1157, amended.

SEC. 240. (a) In any case, civil or criminal, in a circuit court of appeals, or in the Court of Appeals of the District of Columbia, it shall be competent for the Supreme Court of the United States, upon the petition of any party thereto, whether Government or other litigant, to require by certiorari, either before or after a judgment or decree by such lower court, that the cause be certified to the Supreme Court for determination by it with the same power and authority, and with like effect, as if the cause had been brought there by unrestricted writ of error or appeal.

Writ of error or appeal allowed, where decision against validity of State law as repugnant to United States Constitution, etc.

Limitation.

(b) Any case in a circuit court of appeals where is drawn in question the validity of a statute of any State, on the ground of its being repugnant to the Constitution, treaties, or laws of the United States, and the decision is against its validity, may, at the election of the party relying on such State statute, be taken to the Supreme Court for review on writ of error or appeal; but in that event a review on certiorari shall not be allowed at the instance of such party, and the review on such writ of error or appeal shall be restricted to an examination and decision of the Federal questions presented in the case.

No other review by Supreme Court.

"(c) No judgment or decree of a circuit court of appeals or of the Court of Appeals of the District of Columbia shall be subject to review by the Supreme Court otherwise than as provided in this section."

Certiorari, etc., allowed.
Railway employees arbitrations.
Vol. 38, p. 107.
Trade Commission orders.
Vol. 38, p. 720.
Clayton Act enforcement.
Vol. 38, p. 735.

SEC. 2. That cases in a circuit court of appeals under section 8 of "An Act providing for mediation, conciliation, and arbitration in controversies between certain employers and their employees," approved July 15, 1913; under section 5 of "An Act to create a Federal Trade Commission, to define its powers and duties, and for other purposes," approved September 26, 1914; and under section 11 of "An Act to supplement existing laws against unlawful restraints and monopolies, and for other purposes," approved October 15, 1914, are included among the cases to which sections 239 and 240 of the Judicial Code shall apply.

Court of Claims.
May certify to Supreme Court questions of law for instruction.

SEC. 3. (a) That in any case in the court of Claims, including those begun under section 180 of the Judicial Code, that court at any time may certify to the Supreme Court any definite and distinct questions of law concerning which instructions are desired for the proper disposition of the cause; and thereupon the Supreme Court may give appropriate instructions on the questions certified and transmit the same to the Court of Claims for its guidance in the further progress of the cause.

Certiorari by either party of any cause for review and determination.

(b) In any case in the Court of Claims, including those begun under section 180 of the Judicial Code, it shall be competent for the Supreme Court, upon the petition of either party, whether Government or claimant, to require, by certiorari, that the cause, including the findings of fact and the judgment or decree, but omitting the evidence, be certified to it for review and determination with the same power and authority, and with like effect, as if the cause had been brought there by appeal.

No other review of judgments.

(c) All judgments and decrees of the Court of Claims shall be subject to review by the Supreme Court as provided in this section, and not otherwise.

Claims cases in district courts subject to like review as other judgments.

Ante, p. 938.

SEC. 4. That in cases in the district courts wherein they exercise concurrent jurisdiction with the Court of Claims or adjudicate claims against the United States the judgments shall be subject to review in the circuit courts of appeals like other judgments of the district courts; and sections 239 and 240 of the Judicial Code shall apply to such cases in the circuit courts of appeals as to other cases therein.

District of Columbia Court of Appeals.
Jurisdiction of, like circuit court of appeals.

SEC. 5. That the Court of Appeals of the District of Columbia shall have the same appellate and supervisory jurisdiction over proceedings, controversies, and cases in bankruptcy in the District of Columbia that a circuit court of appeals has over such proceedings, controversies, and cases within its circuit, and shall exercise that jurisdiction in the same manner as a circuit court of appeals is required to exercise it.

Habeas corpus.
Circuit courts of appeals to review final orders for.

SEC. 6. (a) In a proceeding in habeas corpus in a district court, or before a district judge or a circuit judge, the final order shall be subject to review, on appeal, by the circuit court of appeals of the circuit wherein the proceeding is had. A circuit judge shall have the same power to grant writs of habeas corpus within his circuit that a district judge has within his district; and the order of the circuit judge shall be entered in the records of the district court of the district wherein the restraint complained of is had.

By District of Columbia Court of Appeals.

(b) In such a proceeding in the Supreme Court of the District of Columbia, or before a justice thereof, the final order shall be subject to review, on appeal, by the Court of Appeals of that District.

Authority of Supreme Court.

(c) Sections 239 and 240 of the Judicial Code shall apply to habeas corpus cases in the circuit

Ante, p. 938.

Circuit courts of
appeals jurisdiction
in State court cases.
R.S., secs. 765,
766, p. 144.
Vol. 35, p. 40.

courts of appeals and in the Court of Appeals of the District of Columbia as to other cases therein.

(d) The provisions of sections 765 and 766 of the Revised Statutes, and the provisions of an Act entitled "An Act restricting in certain cases the right of appeal to the Supreme Court in habeas corpus proceedings," approved March 10, 1908, shall apply to appellate proceedings under this section as they heretofore have applied to direct appeals to the Supreme Court.

Philippine Islands.
Cases where certio-
rari from Supreme
Court allowed.

Vol. 36, p. 1158.

SEC. 7. That in any case in the Supreme Court of the Philippine Islands wherein the Constitution, or any statute or treaty of the United States is involved, or wherein the value in controversy exceeds $25,000, or wherein the title or possession of real estate exceeding in value the sum of $25,000 is involved or brought in question, it shall be competent for the Supreme Court of the United States, upon the petition of a party aggrieved by the final judgment or decree, to require, by certiorari, that the cause be certified to it for review and determination with the same power and authority, and with like effect, as if the cause had been brought before it on writ of error or appeal; and, except as provided in this section, the judgments and decrees of the Supreme Court of the Philippine Islands shall not be subject to appellate review.

No other appellate
review allowed.

Time limit for
bringing judgments
to Supreme Court
for review.

SEC. 8. (a) That no writ of error, appeal, or writ of certiorari, intended to bring any judgment or decree before the Supreme Court for review shall be allowed or entertained unless application therefor be duly made within three months after the entry of such judgment or decree, excepting that writs of certiorari to the Supreme Court of the Philippine Islands may be granted where application therefor is made within six months: *Provided,* That for good cause shown either of such periods for applying for a writ of certiorari may be extended not exceeding sixty days by a justice of the Supreme Court.

Proviso.
Extension
for cause.

Certiorari allowed
prior to hearing in
courts of appeals.

(b) Where an application for a writ of certiorari is made with the purpose of securing a removal of the case to the Supreme Court from a circuit court of appeals or the Court of Appeals of the District of Columbia before the court wherein the same is pending has given a judgment or decree the application may be made at any time prior to the hearing and submission in that court.

Time limit to apply
for review by circuit
courts of appeals.

(c) No writ of error or appeal intended to bring any judgment or decree before a circuit court of appeals for review shall be allowed unless application therefor be duly made within three months after the entry of such judgment or decree.

Judgments may be
stayed in cases sub-
ject to certiorari
from Supreme
Court.

(d) In any case in which the final judgment or decree of any court is subject to review by the Supreme Court on writ of certiorari, the execution and enforcement of such judgment or decree may be stayed for a reasonable time to enable the party aggrieved to apply for and to obtain a writ of certiorari from the Supreme Court. The stay may be granted by a judge of the court rendering the judgment or decree or by a justice of the Supreme Court, and may be conditioned on the giving of good and sufficient security, to be approved by such judge or justice, that if the aggrieved party fails to make application for such writ within the period allotted therefor, or fails to obtain an order granting his application, or fails to make his plea good in the Supreme Court, he shall answer for all damage and costs which the other party may sustain by reason of the stay.

Surety to be
given, etc.

Ascertainment of
value not disclosed
upon record, if
jurisdiction depends
on amount thereof.

SEC. 9. That in any case where the power to review, whether in the circuit courts of appeals or in the Supreme Court, depends upon the amount or value in controversy, such amount or value, if not otherwise satisfactorily disclosed upon the record, may be shown and ascertained by the oath of a party to the cause or by other competent evidence.

Appellate courts.
No case dismissed,
solely for mistake of
procedure.
Vol. 39, p. 727.

SEC. 10. That no court having power to review a judgment or decree of another shall dismiss a writ of error solely because an appeal should have been taken, or dismiss an appeal solely because a writ of error should have been sued out; but where such error occurs the same shall be disregarded and the court shall proceed as if in that regard its power to review were properly invoked.

Action if Federal,
etc.,officer dies
while suit pending.

SEC. 11. (a) That where, during the pendency of an action, suit, or other proceeding brought by or against an officer of the United States, or of the District of Columbia, or the Canal Zone, or of a county, city, or other governmental agency of such Territory or insular possession, and relating to the present or future discharge of his official duties, such officer dies, resigns, or otherwise ceases to hold such office, it shall be competent for the court wherein the action, suit, or proceeding is pending, whether the court be one of first instance or an appellate tribunal, to permit the cause to be continued and maintained by or against the successor in office of such officer, if within six months after his death or separation from the office it be satisfactorily shown to the court that there is a substantial need for so continuing and maintaining the cause and obtaining an adjudication of the questions involved.

Cause continued,
and successor substi-
tuted if substantial
need thereof.

Similar action
as to State,
etc., officer.

(b) Similar proceedings may be had and taken where an action, suit, or proceeding brought by or against an officer of a State, or of a county, city, or other governmental agency of a State, is pending in a court of the United States at the time of the officer's death or separation from the office.

Notice of proposed
substitution to be
given.

(c) Before a substitution under this section is made, the party or officer to be affected, unless expressly consenting thereto, must be given reasonable notice of the application therefor and accorded an opportunity to present any objection which he may have.

Federal incorporation not a ground for action in district courts.

SEC. 12. That no district court shall have jurisdiction of any action or suit by or against any corporation upon the ground that it was incorporated by or under an Act of Congress: *Provided,* That this section shall not apply to any suit, action, or proceeding brought by or against a corporation incorporated by or under an Act of Congress wherein the Government of the United States is the owner of more than one-half of its capital stock.

Proviso. Except if Government principal owner of stock.

Laws repealed.

SEC. 13. That the following statutes and parts of statutes be, and they are, repealed:

Judicial Code sections.

Sections 130, 131, 133, 134, 181, 182, 236, 241, 242, 243, 244, 245, 246, 247, 248, 249, 250, 251, and 252 of the Judicial Code.

Appellate jurisdiction, court of appeals to Supreme Court.
Vol. 38, pp. 803, 804
Writs of error to Supreme Court.
Vol. 39, p. 726

Sections 2, 4, and 5 of "An Act to amend an Act entitled 'An Act to codify, revise, and amend the laws relating to the judiciary,' approved March 3, 1911," approved January 28, 1915.

Sections 2, 3, 4, 5, and 6 of "An Act to amend the Judicial Code, to fix the time when the annual term of the Supreme Court shall commence, and further to define the jurisdiction of that court," approved September 6, 1916.

Judgments of Philippine Supreme Court.
Vol. 39, p. 555.

Section 27 of "An Act to declare the purpose of the people of the United States as to the future political status of the people of the Philippine Islands, and to provide a more autonomous government for those islands," approved August 29, 1916.

Review by Supreme Court of suits against the United States.
Vol. 24, pp. 506, 507.

So much of sections 4, 9, and 10 of "An Act to provide for the bringing of suits against the Government of the United States," approved March 3, 1887, as provides for a review by the Supreme Court on writ of error or appeal in the cases therein named.

Direct appeal in habeas corpus.
Vol. 35, p. 40.

So much of "An Act restricting in certain cases the right of appeal to the Supreme Court in habeas corpus proceedings," approved March 10, 1908, as permits a direct appeal to the Supreme Court.

Review of bankruptcy cases.
Vol. 30, p. 553.

So much of sections 24 and 25 of the Bankruptcy Act of July 1, 1898, as regulates the mode of review by the Supreme Court in the proceedings, controversies, and cases therein named.

Porto Rico courts.
Vol. 39, p. 966.

So much of "An Act to provide a civil government for Porto Rico, and for other purposes," approved March 2, 1917, as permits a direct review by the Supreme Court of cases in the courts of Porto Rico.

Hawaii courts.
Vol. 42, p. 120.

So much of the Hawaiian Organic Act, as amended by the Act of July 9, 1921, as permits a direct review by the Supreme Court of cases in the courts in Hawaii.

Canal Zone district courts.
Vol. 37, p. 566.

So much of section 9 of the Act of August 24, 1912, relating to the government of the Canal Zone as designates the cases in which, and the courts by which, the judgments and decrees of the district court of the Canal Zone may be reviewed.

Bankruptcy appeals.
R.S., secs. 763, 764, p. 143.
Vol. 23, p. 437.
Actions against Federal officers.
Vol. 30, p. 822.
Contracts repugnant to the Constitution.
Vol. 42, p. 366.
Transfers of appeals and writs of error.
Vol. 42, p. 837.
All other inconsistent Acts, etc.

Sections 763 and 764 of the Revised Statutes.

An Act entitled "An Act amending section 764 of the Revised Statutes," approved March 3, 1885.

An Act entitled "An Act to prevent the abatement of certain actions," approved February 8, 1899.

An Act entitled "An Act to amend section 237 of the Judicial Code," approved February 17, 1922.

An Act entitled "An Act to amend the Judicial Code in reference to appeals and writs of error," approved September 14, 1922.

All other Acts and parts of Acts in so far as they are embraced within and superseded by this Act or are inconsistent therewith.

Effective in three months. Pending cases in Supreme Court, etc., not affected.

SEC. 14. That this Act shall take effect three months after its approval; but it shall not affect cases then pending in the Supreme Court, nor shall it affect the right to a review, or the mode or time for exercising the same, as respects any judgment or decree entered prior to the date when it takes effect.

Approved, February 13, 1925.

SOURCE: *Public Statutes at Large of the United States of America,* Vol. XLIII, Part 1 (Washington, D.C.: U.S. Government Printing Office, 1925).

Roosevelt's 1937 Court Reform Plan

President Franklin D. Roosevelt's plan to increase the Supreme Court's membership in 1937 was an example of a president attempting to change the size of the Court's membership to achieve a judicial consensus more to his liking.

In 1935 and 1936 the Court struck down nearly every important measure of Roosevelt's New Deal program, which called for government spending and work projects to help farmers, labor, and business survive the Great Depression. Encouraged by his overwhelming reelection mandate of 1936, Roosevelt proposed his "Court reform" bill—permitting a president to add a justice to the Supreme Court for every justice over seventy who refused to retire, for a total of fifteen justices. The "Court-packing" plan—as it became known—was extremely unpopular in Congress, and it opened a serious rift in the Democratic Party.

But the potential political confrontation was averted. By the time the bill was unfavorably reported by the Senate Judiciary Committee, Roosevelt had begun to get more cooperation from a Court suddenly more amenable to his legislation. The bill never reached the Senate floor, and the scheme was allowed to die. Roosevelt eventually transformed the Court by making nine appointments to it as vacancies arose during the rest of his presidency.

LETTER OF ATTORNEY GENERAL

FEBRUARY 2, 1937

The President,
The White House.

MY DEAR MR. PRESIDENT: Delay in the administration of justice is the outstanding defect of our Federal judicial system. It has been a cause of concern to practically every one of my predecessors in office. It has exasperated the bench, the bar, the business community, and the public.

The litigant conceives the judge as one promoting justice through the mechanism of the courts. He assumes that the directing power of the judge is exercised over its officers from the time a case is filed with the clerk of the court. He is entitled to assume that the judge is pressing forward litigation in the full recognition of the principle that "justice delayed is justice denied." It is a mockery of justice to say to a person when he files suit that he may receive a decision years later. Under a properly ordered system rights should be determined promptly. The course of litigation should be measured in months and not in years.

Yet in some jurisdictions the delays in the administration of justice are so interminable that to institute suit is to embark on a lifelong adventure. Many persons submit to acts of injustice rather than resort to the courts. Inability to secure a prompt judicial adjudication leads to improvident and unjust settlements. Moreover, the time factor is an open invitation to those who are disposed to institute unwarranted litigation or interpose unfounded defenses in the hope of forcing an adjustment which could not be secured upon the merits. This situation frequently results in extreme hardships. The small businessman or the litigant of limited means labors under a grave and constantly increasing disadvantage because of his inability to pay the price of justice.

Statistical data indicate that in many districts a disheartening and unavoidable interval must elapse between the date that issue is joined in a pending case and the time when it can be reached for trial in due course. These computations do not take into account the delays that occur in the preliminary stages of litigation or the postponements after a case might normally be expected to be heard.

The evil is a growing one. The business of the courts is continually increasing in volume, importance, and complexity. The average case load borne by each judge has grown nearly 50 percent since 1913, when the district courts were first organized on their present basis. When the courts are working under such pressure it is inevitable that the character of their work must suffer.

The number of new cases offset those that are disposed of, so that the courts are unable to decrease the enormous backlog of undigested matters. More than 50,000 pending cases, exclusive of bankruptcy proceedings, overhang the Federal dockets—a constant menace to the orderly processes of justice. Whenever a single case requires a protracted trial the routine business of the court is further neglected. It is an intolerable situation and we should make shift to amend it.

Efforts have been made from time to time to alleviate some of the conditions that contribute to the slow rate of speed with which cases move through the courts. The Congress has recently conferred on the Supreme Court the authority to prescribe rules of procedure after verdict in criminal cases and the power to adopt and promulgate uniform rules of practice for civil actions at law in the district courts. It has provided terms of court in certain places at which Federal courts had not previously convened. A small number of judges have been added from time to time.

Despite these commendable accomplishments sufficient progress has not been made. Much remains to be done in developing procedure and administration, but this alone will not meet modern needs. The problem must be approached in a more comprehensive fashion if the United States is to have a judicial system worthy of the Nation. Reason and necessity require the appointment of a sufficient number of judges to handle the business of the Federal courts. These additional judges should be of a type and age which would warrant us in believing that they would vigorously attack their dockets rather than permit their dockets to overwhelm them.

The cost of additional personnel should not deter us. It must be borne in mind that the expense of maintaining the judicial system constitutes hardly three-tenths of 1 percent of the cost of maintaining the Federal establishment. While the estimates for the current fiscal year aggregate over $23,000,000 for the maintenance of the legislative branch of the Government, and over $2,100,000,000 for the permanent agencies of the executive branch, the estimated cost of maintaining the judiciary is only about $6,500,000. An increase in the judicial personnel, which I earnestly recommend, would result in a hardly perceptible percentage of increase in the total annual Budget.

This result should not be achieved, however, merely by creating new judicial positions in specific circuits or districts. The reform should be effectuated on the basis of a consistent system which would revitalize our whole judicial structure and assure the activity of judges at places where the accumulation of business is greatest. As congestion is a varying factor and cannot be foreseen, the system should be flexible and should permit the temporary assignment of judges to points where they appear to be most needed. The newly created personnel should constitute a mobile force, available for service in any part of the country at the assignment and direction of the Chief Justice. A functionary might well be created to be known as proctor, or by some other suitable title, to be appointed by the Supreme Court and to act under its direction, charged with the duty of continuously keeping informed as to the state of Federal judicial business throughout the United States and of assisting the Chief Justice in assigning judges to pressure areas.

I append hereto certain statistical information, which will give point to the suggestions I have made.

These suggestions are designed to carry forward the program for improving the processes of justice which we have discussed and worked upon since the beginning of your first administration.

The time has come when further legislation is essential.

To speed justice, to bring it within the reach of every citizen, to free it of unnecessary entanglements and delays are primary obligations of our Government.

Respectfully submitted.

HOMER CUMMINGS,
Attorney General.

ROOSEVELT'S MESSAGE TO CONGRESS

FEBRUARY 5

February 5, 1937.—Referred to the Committee on the Judiciary and ordered to be printed.

THE WHITE HOUSE, *February 5, 1937*

TO THE CONGRESS OF THE UNITED STATES:

I have recently called the attention of the Congress to the clear need for a comprehensive program to reorganize the administrative machinery of the executive branch of our Government. I now make a similar recommendation to the Congress in regard to the judicial branch of the Government, in order that it also may function in accord with modern necessities.

The Constitution provides that the President "shall from time to time give to the Congress information of the state of the Union, and recommend to their consideration such measures as he shall judge necessary and expedient." No one else is given a similar mandate. It is therefore the duty of the President to advise the Congress in regard to the judiciary whenever he deems such information or recommendation necessary.

I address you for the further reason that the Constitution vests in the Congress direct responsibility in the creation of courts and judicial offices and in the formulation of rules of practice and procedure. It is, therefore, one of the definite duties of the Congress constantly to maintain the effective functioning of the Federal judiciary.

The judiciary has often found itself handicapped by insufficient personnel with which to meet a growing and more complex business. It is true that the physical facilities of conducting the business of the courts have been greatly improved, in recent years, through the erection of suitable quarters, the provision of adequate libraries, and the addition of subordinate court officers. But in many ways these are merely the trappings of judicial office. They play a minor part in the processes of justice.

Since the earliest days of the Republic, the problem of the personnel of the courts has needed the attention of the Congress. For example, from the beginning, over repeated protests to President Washington, the Justices of the Supreme Court were required to "ride circuit" and, as circuit justices, to hold trials throughout the length and breadth of the land—a practice which endured over a century.

In almost every decade since 1789 changes have been made by the Congress whereby the numbers of judges and the duties of judges in Federal courts have been altered in one way or another. The Supreme Court was established with 6 members in 1789; it was reduced to 5 in 1801; it was increased to 7 in 1807; it was increased to 9 in 1837; it was increased to 10 in 1863; it was reduced to 7 in 1866; it was increased to 9 in 1869.

The simple fact is that today a new need for legislative action arises because the personnel of the Federal judiciary is insufficient to meet the business before them. A growing body of our citizens complain of the complexities, the delays, and the expense of litigation in United States courts.

A letter from the Attorney General, which I submit herewith, justifies by reasoning and statistics the common impression created by our overcrowded Federal dockets—and it proves the need for additional judges.

Delay in any court results in injustice.

It makes lawsuits a luxury available only to the few who can afford them or who have property interests to protect which are sufficiently large to repay the cost. Poorer litigants are compelled to abandon valuable rights or to accept inadequate or unjust settlements because of sheer inability to finance or to await the end of a long litigation. Only by speeding up the processes of the law and thereby reducing their cost, can we eradicate the growing impression that the courts are chiefly a haven for the well-to-do.

Delays in the determination of appeals have the same effect. Moreover, if trials of original actions are expedited and existing accumulations of cases are reduced, the volume of work imposed on the circuit courts of appeals will further increase.

The attainment of speedier justice in the courts below will enlarge the task of the Supreme Court itself. And still more work would be added by the recommendation which I make later in this message for the quicker determination of constitutional questions by the highest court.

Even at the present time the Supreme Court is laboring under a heavy burden. Its difficulties in this respect were superficially lightened some years ago by authorizing the Court, in its discretion, to refuse to hear appeals in many classes of cases. This discretion was so freely exercised that in the last fiscal year, although 867 petitions for review were presented to the Supreme Court, it declined to hear 717 cases. If petitions in behalf of the Government are excluded, it appears that the Court permitted private litigants to prosecute appeals in only 108 cases out of 803 applications. Many of the refusals were doubtless warranted. But can it be said that full justice is achieved when a court is forced by the sheer necessity of keeping up with its business to decline, without even an explanation, to hear 87 percent of the cases presented to it by private litigants?

It seems clear, therefore, that the necessity of relieving present congestion extends to the enlargement of the capacity of all the Federal courts.

A part of the problem of obtaining a sufficient number of judges to dispose of cases is the capacity of the judges themselves. This brings forward the question of aged or infirm judges—a subject of delicacy and yet one which requires frank discussion.

In the Federal courts there are in all 237 life tenure permanent judgeships. Twenty-five of them are now held by judges over 70 years of age and eligible to leave the bench on full pay. Originally no pension or retirement allowance was provided by the Congress. When after 80 years of our national history the Congress made provision for pensions, it found a well-entrenched tradition among judges to cling to their posts, in many instances far beyond their years of physical or mental capacity. Their salaries were small. As with other men, responsibilities and obligations accumulated. No alternative had been open to them except to attempt to perform the duties of their offices to the very edge of the grave.

In exceptional cases, of course, judges, like other men, retain to an advanced age full mental and physical vigor. Those not so fortunate are often unable to perceive their own infirmities. "They seem to be tenacious of the appearance of adequacy." The voluntary retirement law of 1869 provided, therefore, only a partial solution. That law, still in force, has not proved effective in inducing aged judges to retire on a pension.

This result had been foreseen in the debates when the measure was being considered. It was then proposed that when a judge refused to retire upon reaching the age of 70, an additional judge should be appointed to assist in the work of the court. The proposal passed the House but was eliminated in the Senate.

With the opening of the twentieth century, and the great increase of population and commerce, and the growth of a more complex type of litigation, similar proposals were introduced in the Congress. To meet the situation, in 1913, 1914, 1915, and 1916, the Attorneys General then in office recommended to the Congress that when a district or a circuit judge failed to retire at the age of 70, an additional judge be appointed in order that the affairs of the court might be promptly and adequately discharged.

In 1919 a law was finally passed providing that the President "may" appoint additional district and circuit judges, but only upon a finding that the incumbent judge over 70 "is unable to discharge efficiently all the duties of his office by reason of mental or physical disability of permanent character." The discretionary and indefinite nature of this legislation has rendered it ineffective. No President should be asked to determine the ability or disability of any particular judge.

The duty of a judge involves more than presiding or listening to testimony or arguments. It is well to remember that the mass of details involved in the average of law cases today is vastly greater and more complicated than even 20 years ago. Records and briefs must be read; statutes, decisions, and extensive material of a technical, scientific, statistical, and economic nature must be searched and studied; opinions must be formulated and written. The modern tasks of judges call for the use of full energies.

Modern complexities call also for a constant infusion of new blood in the courts, just as it is needed in executive functions of the Government and in private business. A lowered mental or physical vigor leads men to avoid an examination of complicated and changed conditions. Little by little, new facts become blurred through old glasses fitted, as it were, for the needs of another generation; older men, assuming that the scene is the same as it was in the past, cease to explore or inquire into the present or the future.

We have recognized this truth in the civil service of the Nation and of many States by compelling retirement on pay at the age of 70. We have recognized it in the Army and Navy by retiring officers at the age of 64. A number of States have recognized it by providing in their constitutions for compulsory retirement of aged judges.

Life tenure of judges, assured by the Constitution, was designed to place the courts beyond temptations or influences which might impair their judgments; it was not intended to create a static judiciary. A constant and systematic addition of younger blood will vitalize the courts and better equip them to recognize and apply the essential concepts of justice in the light of the needs and the facts of an ever changing world.

It is obvious, therefore, from both reason and experience, that some provision must be adopted which will operate automatically to supplement the work of older judges and accelerate the work of the court.

I, therefore, earnestly recommend that the necessity of an increase in the number of judges be supplied by legislation providing for the appointment of additional judges in all Federal courts, without exception, where there are incumbent judges of retirement age who do not choose to retire or to resign. If an elder judge is not in fact incapacitated, only good can come from the presence of an additional judge in the crowded state of the dockets; if the capacity of an elder judge is in fact impaired, the appointment of an additional judge is indispensable. This seems to be a truth which cannot be contradicted.

I also recommend that the Congress provide machinery for taking care of sudden or long-standing congestion in the lower courts. The Supreme Court should be given power to appoint an administrative assistant who may be called a proctor. He would be charged with the duty of watching the calendars and the business of all the courts in the Federal system. The Chief Justice thereupon should be authorized to make a temporary assignment of any circuit or district judge hereafter appointed in order that he may serve as long as needed in any circuit or district where the courts are in arrears.

I attach a carefully considered draft of a proposed bill, which, if enacted, would, I am confident, afford substantial relief. The proposed measure also contains a limit on the total number of judges who might thus be appointed and also a limit on the potential size of any one of our Federal courts.

These proposals do not raise any issue of constitutional law. They do not suggest any form of compulsory retirement for incumbent judges. Indeed, those who have reached the retirement age, but desire to continue their judicial work, would be able to do so under less physical and mental strain and would be able to play a useful part in relieving the growing congestion in the business of our courts. Among them are men of eminence and great ability whose services the Government would be loath to lose. If, on the other hand, any judge eligible for retirement should feel that his court would suffer because of an increase in its membership, he may retire or resign under already existing provisions of law if he wishes so to do. In this connection let me say that the pending proposal to extend to the Justices of the Supreme Court the same retirement privileges now available to other Federal judges, has my entire approval.

One further matter requires immediate attention. We have witnessed the spectacle of conflicting decisions in both trial and appellate courts on the constitutionality of every form of important legislation. Such a welter of uncomposed differences of judicial opinion has brought the law, the courts, and, indeed, the entire administration of justice dangerously near to disrepute.

A Federal statute is held legal by one judge in one district; it is simultaneously held illegal by another judge in another district. An act valid in one judicial circuit is invalid in another judicial circuit. Thus rights fully accorded to one group of citizens may be denied to others. As a practical matter this means that for periods running as long as 1 year or 2 years or 3 years—until final determination can be made by the Supreme Court—the law loses its most indispensable element—equality.

Moreover, during the long processes of preliminary motions, original trials, petitions for rehearings, appeals, reversals on technical grounds requiring retrials, motions before the Supreme Court, and the final hearing by the highest tribunal—during all this time labor, industry, agriculture, commerce, and the Government itself go through an unconscionable period of uncertainty and embarrassment. And it is well to remember that during these long processes the normal operations of society and government are handicapped in many cases by differing and divided opinions in the lower courts and by the lack of any clear guide for the dispatch of business. Thereby our legal system is fast losing another essential of justice—certainty.

Finally, we find the processes of government itself brought to a complete stop from time to time by injunctions issued almost automatically, sometimes even without notice to the Government, and not infrequently in clear violation of the principle of equity that injunctions should be granted only in those rare cases of manifest illegality and irreparable damage against which the ordinary course of the law offers no protection. Statutes which the Congress enacts are set aside or suspended for long periods of time, even in cases to which the Government is not a party.

In the uncertain state of the law, it is not difficult for the ingenious to devise novel reasons for attacking the validity of new legislation or its application. While these questions are laboriously brought to issue and debated through a series of courts, the Government must stand aside. It matters not that the Congress has enacted the law, that the Executive has signed it, and that the administrative machinery is waiting to function. Government by injunction lays a heavy hand upon normal processes; and no important statute can take effect—against any individual or organization with the means to employ lawyers and engaged in wide-flung litigation—until it has passed through the whole hierarchy of the courts. Thus the judiciary, by postponing the effective date of acts of the Congress, is assuming an additional function and is coming more and more to constitute a scattered, loosely organized, and slowly operating third house of the National Legislature.

This state of affairs has come upon the Nation gradually over a period of decades. In my annual message to this Congress I expressed some views and some hopes.

Now, as an immediate step, I recommend that the Congress provide that no decision, injunction, judgment, or decree on any constitutional question be promulgated by any Federal court without previous and ample notice to the Attorney General and an opportunity for the United States to present evidence and be heard. This is to prevent court action on the constitutionality of acts of the Congress in suits between private individuals, where the Government is not a party to the suit, without giving opportunity to the Government of the United States to defend the law of the land.

I also earnestly recommend that, in cases in which any court of first instance determines a question of constitutionality, the Congress provide that there shall be a direct and immediate appeal to the Supreme Court and that such cases take precedence over all other matters pending in that court. Such legislation will, I am convinced, go far to alleviate the inequality, uncertainty, and delay in the disposition of vital questions of constitutionality arising under our fundamental law.

My desire is to strengthen the administration of justice and to make it a more effective servant of public need. In the American ideal of government the courts find an essential and constitutional place. In striving to fulfill that ideal, not only the judges but the Congress and the Executive as well, must do all in their power to bring the judicial organization and personnel to the high standards of usefulness which sound and efficient government and modern conditions require.

This message has dealt with four present needs:

First, to eliminate congestion of calendars and to make the judiciary as a whole less static by the constant and systematic addition of new blood to its personnel; second, to make the judiciary more elastic by providing for temporary transfers of circuit and district judges to those places where Federal courts are most in arrears; third, to furnish the Supreme Court practical assistance in supervising the conduct of business in the lower courts; fourth, to eliminate inequality, uncertainty, and delay now existing in the determination of constitutional questions involving Federal statutes.

If we increase the personnel of the Federal courts so that cases may be promptly decided in the first instance, and may be given adequate and prompt hearing on all appeals; if we invigorate all the courts by the persistent infusion of new blood; if we grant to the Supreme Court further power and responsibility in maintaining the efficiency of the entire Federal judiciary; and if we assure Government participation in the speedier consideration and final determination of all constitutional questions, we shall go a long way toward our high objectives. If these measures achieve their aim, we may be relieved of the necessity of considering any fundamental changes in the powers of the courts or the Constitution of our Government—changes which involve consequences so far reaching as to cause uncertainty as to the wisdom of such course.

FRANKLIN D. ROOSEVELT

WHITE HOUSE BROADCAST
MARCH 9, 1937

Last Thursday I described in detail certain economic problems which everyone admits now face the Nation. For the many messages which have come to me after that speech, and which it is physically impossible to answer individually, I take this means of saying "thank you."

Tonight, sitting at my desk in the White House, I make my first radio report to the people in my second term of office.

I am reminded of that evening in March, four years ago, when I made my first radio report to you. We were then in the midst of the great banking crisis.

Soon after, with the authority of the Congress, we asked the Nation to turn over all of its privately held gold, dollar for dollar, to the Government of the United States.

Today's recovery proves how right that policy was.

But when, almost two years later, it came before the Supreme Court its constitutionality was upheld only by a five-to-four vote. The change of one vote would have thrown all the affairs of this great Nation back into hopeless chaos. In effect, four Justices ruled that the right under a private contract to exact a pound of flesh was more sacred than the main objectives of the Constitution to establish an enduring Nation.

In 1933 you and I knew that we must never let our economic system get completely out of joint again—that we could not afford to take the risk of another great depression.

We also became convinced that the only way to avoid a repetition of those dark days was to have a government with power to prevent and to cure the abuses and the inequalities which had thrown that system out of joint.

We then began a program of remedying those abuses and inequalities—to give balance and stability to our economic system—to make it bomb-proof against the causes of 1929.

Today we are only part-way through that program—and recovery is speeding up to a point where the dangers of 1929 are again becoming possible, not this week or month perhaps, but within a year or two.

National laws are needed to complete that program. Individual or local or state effort alone cannot protect us in 1937 any better than ten years ago.

It will take time—and plenty of time—to work out our remedies administratively even after legislation is passed. To complete our program of protection in time, therefore, we cannot delay one moment in making certain that our National Government has power to carry through.

Four years ago action did not come until the eleventh hour. It was almost too late.

If we learned anything from the depression we will not allow ourselves to run around in new circles of futile discussion and debate, always postponing the day of decision.

The American people have learned from the depression. For in the last three national elections an overwhelming majority of them voted a mandate that the Congress and the President begin the task of providing that protection—not after long years of debate, but now.

The Courts, however, have cast doubts on the ability of the elected Congress to protect us against catastrophe by meeting squarely our modern social and economic conditions.

We are at a crisis in our ability to proceed with that protection. It is a quiet crisis. There are no lines of depositors outside closed banks. But to the far-sighted it is far-reaching in its possibilities of injury to America.

I want to talk with you very simply about the need for present action in this crisis—the need to meet the unanswered challenge of one-third of a Nation ill-nourished, ill-clad, ill-housed.

Last Thursday I described the American form of Government as a three horse team provided by the Constitution to the American people so that their field might be plowed. The three horses are, of course, the three branches of government—the Congress, the Executive and the Courts. Two of the horses are pulling in unison today; the third is not. Those who have intimated that the President of the United States is trying to drive that team overlook the simple fact that the President, as Chief Executive, is himself one of the three horses.

It is the American people themselves who are in the driver's seat.

It is the American people themselves who want the furrow plowed.

It is the American people themselves who expect the third horse to pull in unison with the other two.

I hope that you have re-read the Constitution of the United States. Like the Bible, it ought to be read again and again.

It is an easy document to understand when you remember that it was called into being because the Articles of Confederation under which the original thirteen States tried to operate after the Revolution showed the need of a National Government with power enough to handle national problems. In its Preamble, the Constitution states that it was intended to form a more perfect Union and promote the general welfare; and the powers given to the Congress to carry out those purposes can be best described by saying that they were all the powers needed to meet each and every problem which then had a national character and which could not be met by merely local action.

But the framers went further. Having in mind that in succeeding generations many other problems then undreamed of would become national problems, they gave to the Congress the ample broad powers "to levy taxes . . . and provide for the common defense and general welfare of the United States."

That, my friends, is what I honestly believe to have been the clear and underlying purpose of the patriots who wrote a Federal Constitution to create a National Government with national power, intended as they said, "to form a more perfect union . . . for ourselves and our posterity."

For nearly twenty years there was no conflict between the Congress and the Court. Then, in 1803, Congress passed a statute which the Court said violated an express provision of the Constitution. The Court claimed the power to declare it unconstitutional and did so declare it. But a little later the Court itself admitted that it was an extraordinary power to exercise and through Mr. Justice Washington laid down this limitation upon it: "It is but a decent respect due to the wisdom, the integrity and the patriotism of the Legislative body, by which any law is passed, to presume in favor of its validity until its violation of the Constitution is proved beyond all reasonable doubt."

But since the rise of the modern movement for social and economic progress through legislation, the Court has more and more often and more and more boldly asserted a power to veto laws passed by the Congress and State Legislatures in complete disregard of this original limitation.

In the last four years the sound rule of giving statutes the benefit of all reasonable doubt has been cast aside. The Court has been acting not as a judicial body, but as a policy-making body.

When the Congress has sought to stabilize national agriculture, to improve the conditions of labor, to safeguard business against unfair competition, to protect our national resources, and in many other ways, to serve our clearly national needs, the majority of the Court has been assuming the power to pass on the wisdom of these Acts of the Congress—and to approve or disapprove the public policy written into these laws.

That is not only my accusation. It is the accusation of most distinguished Justices of the present Supreme Court. I have not the time to quote to you all the language used by dissenting Justices in many of these cases. But in the case holding the Railroad Retirement Act unconstitutional, for instance, Chief Justice Hughes said in a dissenting opinion that the majority opinion was "a departure from sound principles," and placed "an unwarranted limitation upon the commerce clause." And three other Justices agreed with him.

In the case holding the A.A.A. unconstitutional, Justice Stone said of the majority opinion that it was a "tortured construction of the Constitution." And two other Justices agreed with him.

In the case holding the New York Minimum Wage Law unconstitutional, Justice Stone said that the majority were actually reading into the Constitution their own "personal economic predilections," and that if the legislative power is not left free to choose the methods of solving the problems of poverty, subsistence and health of large numbers in the community, then "government is to be rendered impotent." And two other Justices agreed with him.

In the face of these dissenting opinions, there is no basis for the claim made by some members of the Court that something in the Constitution has compelled them regretfully to thwart the will of the people.

In the face of such dissenting opinions, it is perfectly clear, that as Chief Justice Hughes has said: "We are under a Constitution but the Constitution is what the Judges say it is."

The Court in addition to the proper use of its judicial functions has improperly set itself up as a third House of the Congress—a super-legislature, as one of the Justices has called it—reading into the Constitution words and implications which are not there, and which were never intended to be there.

We have, therefore, reached the point as a Nation where we must take action to save the Constitution from the Court and the Court from itself. We must find a way to take an appeal from the Supreme Court to the Constitution itself. We want a Supreme Court which will do justice under the Constitution—not over it. In our Courts we want a government of laws and not of men.

I want—as all Americans want—an independent judiciary as proposed by the framers of the Constitution. That means a Supreme Court that will enforce the Constitution as written—that will refuse to amend the Constitution by the arbitrary exercise of judicial power—amendment by judicial say-so. It does not mean a judiciary so independent that it can deny the existence of facts universally recognized.

How then could we proceed to perform the mandate given us? It was said in last year's Democratic platform "If these problems cannot be effectively solved within the Constitution, we shall seek such clarifying amendment as will assure the power to enact those laws, adequately to regulate commerce, protect public health and safety, and safeguard economic security." In other words, we said we would seek an amendment only if every other possible means by legislation were to fail.

When I commenced to review the situation with the problem squarely before me, I came by a process of elimination to the conclusion that short of amendments the only method which was clearly constitutional, and would at the same time carry out other much needed reforms, was to infuse new blood into all our Courts. We must have men worthy and equipped to carry out impartial justice. But, at the same time, we must have Judges who will bring to the Courts a present-day sense of the Constitution—Judges who will retain in the Courts the judicial functions of a court, and reject the legislative powers which the Courts have today assumed.

In forty-five out of the forty-eight States of the Union, Judges are chosen not for life but for a period of years. In many States Judges must retire at the age of seventy. Congress has provided financial security by offering life pensions at full pay for Federal Judges on all Courts who are willing to retire at seventy. In the case of Supreme Court Justices, that pension is $20,000 a year. But all Federal Judges, once appointed, can, if they choose, hold office for life, no matter how old they may get to be.

What is my proposal? It is simply this: whenever a Judge or Justice of any Federal Court has reached the age of seventy and does not avail himself of the opportunity to retire on a pension, a new member shall be appointed by the President then in office, with the approval, as required by the Constitution, of the Senate of the United States.

That plan has two chief purposes. By bringing into the Judicial system a steady and continuing stream of new and younger blood, I hope, first, to make the administration of all Federal justice speedier and, therefore, less costly; secondly, to bring to the decision of social and economic problems younger men who have had personal experience and contact with modern facts and circumstances under which average men have to live and work. This plan will save our national Constitution from hardening of the judicial arteries.

The number of Judges to be appointed would depend wholly on the decision of present Judges now over seventy, or those who would subsequently reach the age of seventy.

If, for instance, any one of the six Justices of the Supreme Court now over the age of seventy should retire as provided under the plan, no additional place would be created. Consequently, although there never can be more than fifteen, there may be only fourteen, or thirteen, or twelve. And there may be only nine.

There is nothing novel or radical about this idea. It seeks to maintain the Federal bench in full vigor. It has been discussed and approved by many persons of high authority ever since a similar proposal passed the House of Representatives in 1869.

Why was the age fixed at seventy? Because the laws of many States, the practice of the Civil Service, the regulations of the Army and Navy, and the rules of many of our Universities and of almost every great private business enterprise, commonly fix the retirement age at seventy years or less.

The statute would apply to all the Courts in the Federal system. There is general approval so far as the lower Federal courts are concerned. The plan has met opposition only so far as the Supreme Court of the United States itself is concerned. If such a plan is good for the lower courts it certainly ought to be equally good for the highest Court from which there is no appeal.

Those opposing this plan have sought to arouse prejudice and fear by crying that I am seeking to "pack" the Supreme Court and that a baneful precedent will be established.

What do they mean by the words "packing the Court"?

Let me answer this question with a bluntness that will end all *honest* misunderstanding of my purposes.

If by that phrase "packing the Court" it is charged that I wish to place on the bench spineless puppets who would disregard the law and would decide specific cases as I wished them to be decided, I make this answer—that no President fit for his office would appoint, and no Senate of honorable men fit for their office would confirm, that kind of appointees to the Supreme Court.

But if by that phrase the charge is made that I would appoint and the Senate would confirm Justices worthy to sit beside present members of the Court who understand those modern conditions—that I will appoint Justices who will not undertake to override the judgment of the Congress on legislative policy—that I will appoint Justices who will act as Justices and not as legislators—if the appointment of such Justices can be called "packing the Courts," then I say that I and with me the vast majority of the American people favor doing just that thing—now.

Is it a dangerous precedent for the Congress to change the number of the Justices? The Congress has always had, and will have, that power. The number of Justices has been changed several times before—in the Administrations of John Adams and Thomas Jefferson,—both signers of the Declaration of Independence—Andrew Jackson, Abraham Lincoln and Ulysses S. Grant.

I suggest only the addition of Justices to the bench in accordance with a clearly defined principle relating to a clearly defined age limit. Fundamentally, if in the future, America cannot trust the Congress it elects to refrain from abuse of our Constitutional usages, democracy will have failed far beyond the importance to it of any kind of precedent concerning the Judiciary.

We think it so much in the public interest to maintain a vigorous judiciary that we encourage the retirement of elderly Judges by offering them a life pension at full salary. Why then should we leave the fulfillment of this public policy to chance or make it dependent upon the desire or prejudice of any individual Justice?

It is the clear intention of our public policy to provide for a constant flow of new and younger blood into the Judiciary. Normally every President appoints a large number of District and Circuit Judges and a few members of the Supreme Court. Until my first term practically every President of the United States had appointed at least one member of the Supreme Court. President Taft appointed five members and named a Chief Justice—President Wilson three—President Harding four including a Chief Justice—President Coolidge one—President Hoover three including a Chief Justice.

Such a succession of appointments should have provided a Court well-balanced as to age. But chance and the disinclination of individuals to leave the Supreme bench have now given us a Court in which five Justices will be over seventy-five years of age before next June and one over seventy. Thus a sound public policy has been defeated.

I now propose that we establish by law an assurance against any such ill-balanced Court in the future. I propose that hereafter, when a Judge reaches the age of seventy, a new and younger Judge shall be added to the Court automatically. In this way I propose to enforce a sound public policy by law instead of leaving the composition of our Federal Courts, including the highest, to be determined by chance or the personal decision of individuals.

If such a law as I propose is regarded as establishing a new precedent—is it not a most desirable precedent?

Like all lawyers, like all Americans, I regret the necessity of this controversy. But the welfare of the United States, and indeed of the Constitution itself, is what we all must think about first. Our difficulty with the Court today rises not from the Court as an institution but from human beings within it. But we cannot yield our constitutional destiny to the personal judgment of a few men who, being fearful of the future, would deny us the necessary means of dealing with the present.

This plan of mine is no attack on the Court; it seeks to restore the Court to its rightful and historic place in our system of Constitutional Government and to have it resume its high task of building anew on the Constitution "a system of living law."

I have thus explained to you the reasons that lie behind our efforts to secure results by legislation within the Constitution. I hope that thereby the difficult process of constitutional amendment may be rendered unnecessary. But let us examine that process.

There are many types of amendment proposed. Each one is radically different from the other. There is no substantial group within the Congress or outside it who are agreed on any single amendment.

It would take months or years to get substantial agreement upon the type and language of an amendment. It would take months and years thereafter to get a two-thirds majority in favor of that amendment in *both* Houses of the Congress.

Then would come the long course of ratification by three-fourths of the States. No amendment which any powerful economic interests or the leaders of any powerful political party have had reason to oppose has ever been ratified within anything like a reasonable time. And thirteen States which contain only five percent of the voting population can block ratification even though the thirty-five States with ninety-five percent of the population are in favor of it.

A very large percentage of newspaper publishers, Chambers of Commerce, Bar Associations, Manufacturers' Associations, who are trying to give the impression that they really do want a constitutional amendment would be the first to exclaim as soon as an amendment was proposed "Oh! I was for an amendment all right, but this amendment that you have proposed is not the kind of an amendment that I was thinking about. I am, therefore, going to spend my time, my efforts and my money to block that amendment, although I would be awfully glad to help get some other kind of amendment ratified."

Two groups oppose my plan on the ground that they favor a constitutional amendment. The first includes those who fundamentally object to social and economic legislation along modern lines. This is the same group who during the campaign last Fall tried to block the mandate of the people.

Now they are making a last stand. And the strategy of that last stand is to suggest the time-consuming process of amendment in order to kill off by delay the legislation demanded by the mandate.

To them I say—I do not think you will be able long to fool the American people as to your purposes.

The other group is composed of those who honestly believe the amendment process is the best and who would be willing to support a reasonable amendment if they could agree on one.

To them I say—we cannot rely on an amendment as the immediate or only answer to our present difficulties. When the time comes for action, you will find that many of those who pretend to support you will sabotage any constructive amendment which is proposed. Look at these strange bed-fellows of yours. When before have you found them really at your side in your fights for progress?

And remember one thing more. Even if an amendment were passed, and even if in the years to come it were to be ratified, its meaning would depend upon the kind of Justices who would be sitting on the Supreme Court bench. An amendment like the rest of the Constitution is what the Justices say it is rather than what its framers or you might hope it is.

This proposal of mine will not infringe in the slightest upon the civil or religious liberties so dear to every American.

My record as Governor and as President proves my devotion to those liberties. You who know me can have no fear that I would tolerate the destruction by any branch of government of any part of our heritage of freedom.

The present attempt by those opposed to progress to play upon the fears of danger to personal liberty brings again to mind that crude and cruel strategy tried by the same opposition to frighten the workers of America in a pay-envelope propaganda against the Social Security Law. The workers were not fooled by that propaganda then. The people of America will not be fooled by such propaganda now.

I am in favor of action through legislation:

First, because I believe that it can be passed at this session of the Congress.

Second, because it will provide a reinvigorated, liberal-minded Judiciary necessary to furnish quicker and cheaper justice from bottom to top.

Third, because it will provide a series of Federal Courts willing to enforce the Constitution as written, and unwilling to assert legislative

powers by writing into it their own political and economic policies.

During the past half century the balance of power between the three great branches of the Federal Government, has been tipped out of balance by the Courts in direct contradiction of the high purposes of the framers of the Constitution. It is my purpose to restore that balance. You who know me will accept my solemn assurance that in a world in which democracy is under attack, I seek to make American democracy succeed.

LETTER OF CHIEF JUSTICE HUGHES
MARCH 21

SUPREME COURT OF THE UNITED STATES
Washington, D.C., March 21, 1937

HON. BURTON K. WHEELER,
United States Senate, Washington, D.C.

MY DEAR SENATOR WHEELER: In response to your inquiries, I have the honor to present the following statement with respect to the work of the Supreme Court:

1. The Supreme Court is fully abreast of its work. When we rose on March 15 (for the present recess) we had heard argument in cases in which certiorari had been granted only 4 weeks before—February 15.

During the current term, which began last October and which we call "October term, 1936", we have heard argument on the merits in 150 cases (180 numbers) and we have 28 cases (30 numbers) awaiting argument. We shall be able to hear all these cases, and such others as may come up for argument, before our adjournment for the term. There is no congestion of cases upon our calendar.

This gratifying condition has obtained for several years. We have been able for several terms to adjourn after disposing of all cases which are ready to be heard.

2. The cases on our docket are classified as original and appellate. Our original jurisdiction is defined by the Constitution and embraces cases to which States are parties. There are not many of these. At the present time they number 13 and are in various stages of progress to submission for determination.

Our appellate jurisdiction covers those cases in which appeal is allowed by statute as a matter of right and cases which come to us on writs of certiorari.

The following is a comparative statement of the cases on the dockets for the six terms preceding the current term:

For terms 1930–32

	1930	1931	1932
TOTAL CASES ON DOCKETS	1,039	1,023	1,037
Disposed of during term	900	884	910
Cases remaining on dockets	139	139	127
Distribution of cases:			
Cases disposed of:			
Original cases	8	1	4
Appellate, on merits	326	282	257
Petitions for certiorari	566	601	649
Remaining on dockets:			
Original cases	16	19	17
Appellate, on merits	76	60	56
Petitions for certiorari	47	60	54

For terms 1933–35

	1933	1934	1935
TOTAL CASES ON DOCKETS	1,132	1,040	1,092
Disposed of during term	1,029	931	990
Cases remaining on docket	103	109	102
Distribution of cases:			
Cases disposed of:			
Original cases	4	5	4
Appellate, on merits	293	256	269
Petitions for certiorari	732	670	717
Remaining on dockets:			
Original cases	15	13	12
Appellate, on merits	43	51	56
Petitions for certiorari	45	45	34

Further statistics for these terms, and those for earlier terms, are available if you desire them.

During the present term we have thus far disposed of 666 cases which include petitions for certiorari and cases which have been argued on the merits and already decided.

3. The statute relating to our appellate jurisdiction is the act of February 13, 1925 (43 Stat. 936). That act limits to certain cases the appeals which come to the Supreme Court as a matter of right. Review in other cases is made to depend upon the allowance by the Supreme Court of a writ of certiorari.

Where the appeal purports to lie as a matter of right, the rules of the Supreme Court (rule 12) require the appellant to submit a jurisdictional statement showing that the case falls within that class of appeals and that a substantial question is involved. We examine that statement, and the supporting and opposing briefs, and decide whether the Court had jurisdiction. As a result, many frivolous appeals are forthwith dismissed and the way is open for appeals which disclose substantial questions.

4. The act of 1925, limiting appeals as a matter of right and enlarging the provisions for review only through certiorari was most carefully considered by Congress. I call attention to the reports of the Judiciary Committees of the Senate and House of Representatives (68th Cong., 1st sess.). That legislation was deemed to be essential to enable the Supreme Court to perform its proper function. No single court of last resort, whatever the number of judges, could dispose of all the cases which arise in this vast country and which litigants would seek to bring up if the right of appeal were unrestricted. Hosts of litigants will take appeals so long as there is a tribunal accessible. In protracted litigation, the advantage is with those who command a long purse. Unmeritorious appeals cause intolerable delays. Such appeals clog the calendar and get in the way of those that have merit.

Under our Federal system, when litigants have had their cases heard in the courts of first instance, and the trier of the facts, jury or judge, as the case may require, has spoken and the case on the facts and law has been decided, and when the dissatisfied party has been accorded an appeal to the circuit court of appeals, the litigants, so far as mere private interests are concerned, have had their day in court. If further review is to be had by the Supreme Court it must be because of the public interest in the questions involved. That review, for example, should be for the purpose of resolving conflicts in judicial decisions between different circuit courts of appeals or between circuit courts of appeals and State courts where the question is one of State law; or for the purpose of determining constitutional questions or

settling the interpretation of statutes; or because of the importance of the questions of law that are involved. Review by the Supreme Court is thus in the interest of the law, its appropriate exposition and enforcement, not in the mere interest of the litigants.

It is obvious that if appeal as a matter of right is restricted to certain described cases, the question whether review should be allowed in other cases must necessarily be confided to some tribunal for determination, and, of course, with respect to review by the Supreme Court, that Court should decide.

5. Granting certiorari is not a matter of favor but of sound judicial discretion. It is not the importance of the parties or the amount of money involved that is in any sense controlling. The action of the Court is governed by its rules from which I quote the following (rule 38, par. 5):

"5. A review on writ of certiorari is not a matter of right, but of sound judicial discretion, and will be granted only where there are special and important reasons therefor. The following, while neither controlling nor full measuring the Court's discretion, indicate the character of reason which will be considered:

"(a) Where a State court has decided a Federal question of substance not therefore determined by this Court, or has decided it in a way probably not in accord with applicable decisions of this Court.

"(b) Where a circuit court of appeals has rendered a decision in conflict with the decision of another circuit court of appeals on the same matter; or has decided an important question of local law in a way probably in conflict with applicable local decisions; or has decided an important question of general law in a way probably untenable or in conflict with the weight of authority; or has decided an important question of Federal law which has not been, but should be, settled by this Court; or has decided a Federal question in a way probably in conflict with applicable decisions of this Court; or has so far departed from the accepted and usual course of judicial proceedings, or so far sanctions such a departure by a lower court, as to call for an exercise of this Court's power of supervision.

"(c) Where the United States Court of Appeals for the District of Columbia has decided a question of general importance, or a question of substance relating to the construction or application of the Constitution, or a treaty or statute, of the United States, which has not been, but should be, settled by this Court; or where that court has not given proper effect to an applicable decision of this Court."

These rules are impartially applied, as it is most important that they should be.

I should add that petitions of certiorari are not apportioned among the Justices. In all matters before the Court, except in the more routine of administration, all the Justices—unless for some reason a Justice is disqualified or unable to act in a particular case—participate in the decision. This applies to the grant or refusal of petitions for certiorari. Furthermore, petitions for certiorari are granted if four Justices think they should be. A vote by a majority is not required in such cases. Even if two or three of the Justices are strongly of the opinion that certiorari should be allowed, frequently the other Justices will acquiesce in their view, but the petition is always granted if four so vote.

6. The work of passing upon these applications for certiorari is laborious but the Court is able to perform it adequately. Observations have been made as to the vast number of pages of records and briefs that are submitted in the course of a term. The total is imposing but the suggested conclusion is hasty and rests on an illusory basis. Records are replete with testimony and evidence of facts. But the questions on certiorari are questions of law. So many cases turn on the facts, principles of law not being in controversy. It is only when

the facts are interwoven with the questions of law which we should review that the evidence must be examined and then only to the extent that it is necessary to decide the questions of law.

This at once disposes of a vast number of factual controversies where the parties have been fully heard in the courts below and have no right to burden the Supreme Court with the dispute which interests no one but themselves.

This is also true of controversies over contracts and documents of all sorts which involve only questions of concern to the immediate parties. The applicant for certiorari is required to state in his petition the grounds for his application and in a host of cases that disclosure itself disposes of his request. So that the number of pages of records and briefs afford no satisfactory criterion of the actual work involved. It must also be remembered that Justices who have been dealing with such matters for years have the aid of a long and varied experience in separating the chaff from the wheat.

I think that it is safe to say that about 60 percent of the applications for certiorari are wholly without merit and ought never to have been made. There are probably about 20 percent or so in addition which have a fair degree of plausibility but which fail to survive critical examination. The remainder, falling short, I believe, of 20 percent, show substantial grounds and are granted. I think that it is the view of the members of the Court that if any error is made in dealing with these applications it is on the side of liberality.

7. An increase in the number of Justices of the Supreme Court, apart from any question of policy, which I do not discuss, would not promote the efficiency of the Court. It is believed that it would impair that efficiency so long as the Court acts as a unit. There would be more judges to hear, more judges to confer, more judges to discuss, more judges to be convinced and to decide. The present number of Justices is thought to be large enough so far as the prompt, adequate, and efficient conduct of the work of the Court is concerned. As I have said, I do not speak of any other considerations in view of the appropriate attitude of the Court in relation to questions of policy.

I understand that it has been suggested that with more Justices the Court could hear cases in divisions. It is believed that such a plan would be impracticable. A large proportion of the cases we hear are important and a decision by a part of the Court would be unsatisfactory.

I may also call attention to the provisions of article III, section 1, of the Constitution that the judicial power of the United States shall be vested "in one Supreme Court" and in such inferior courts as the Congress may from time to time ordain and establish. The Constitution does not appear to authorize two or more Supreme Courts or two or more parts of a supreme court functioning in effect as separate courts.

On account of the shortness of time I have not been able to consult with the members of the Court generally with respect to the foregoing statement, but I am confident that it is in accord with the views of the Justices. I should say, however, that I have been able to consult with Mr. Justice Van Devanter and Mr. Justice Brandeis, and I am at liberty to say that the statement is approved by them.

I have the honor to remain,
Respectfully yours,

CHARLES E. HUGHES,
Chief Justice of the United States.

HON. BURTON K. WHEELER,
United States Senate, Washington, D.C.

SENATE JUDICIARY COMMITTEE REPORT
JUNE 7
June 7 (calendar day, June 14), 1937.—ordered to be printed
MR. McCARRAN (*for* MR. KING), *from the committee on the judiciary, submitted the following*

ADVERSE REPORT
[To accompany S. 1392]

The Committee on the Judiciary, to whom was referred the bill (S. 1392) to reorganize the judicial branch of the Government, after full consideration, having unanimously amended the measure, hereby report the bill adversely with the recommendation that it do not pass.

The amendment agreed to by unanimous consent, is as follows:
Page 3, lines 5, 8, and 9, strike out the words "hereafter appointed."

Summary of Proposed Measure
The bill, as thus amended, may be summarized in the following manner:

By section 1 (a) the President is directed to appoint an additional judge to any court of the United States when and only when three contingencies arise:

(a) That a sitting judge shall have attained the age of 70 years;

(b) That he shall have held a Federal judge's commission for at least 10 years;

(c) That he has neither resigned nor retired within 6 months after the happening of the two contingencies first named.

The happening of the three contingencies would not, however, necessarily result in requiring an appointment, for section 1 also contains a specific defeasance clause to the effect that no nomination shall be made in the case of a judge, although he is 70 years of age, has served at least 10 years and has neither resigned nor retired within 6 months after the happening of the first two contingencies, if, before the actual nomination of an additional judge, he dies, resigns, or retires. Moreover, section 6 of the bill provides that "it shall take effect on the 30th day after the date of its enactment."

Thus the bill does not with certainty provide for the expansion of any court or the appointment of any additional judges, for it will not come into operation with respect to any judge in whose case the described contingencies have happened, if such judge dies, resigns, or retires within 30 days after the enactment of the bill or before the President shall have had opportunity to send a nomination to the Senate.

By section 1 (b) it is provided that in event of the appointment of judges under the provisions of section 1 (a), then the size of the court to which such appointments are made is "permanently" increased by that number. But the number of appointments to be made is definitely limited by this paragraph. Regardless of the age or service of the members of the Federal judiciary, no more than 50 judges may be appointed in all; the Supreme Court may not be increased beyond 15 members; no circuit court of appeals, nor the Court of Claims, nor the Court of Customs and Patent Appeals, nor the Customs Court may be increased by more than 2 members; and finally, in the case of district courts, the number of judges now authorized to be appointed for any district or group of districts may not be more than doubled.

Section 1 (c) fixes the quorum of the Supreme Court, the Court of Appeals for the District of Columbia, the Court of Claims, and the Court of Customs and Patent Appeals.

Section 1 (d) provides that an additional judge shall not be appointed in the case of a judge whose office has been abolished by Congress.

Section 2 provides for the designation and assignment of judges to courts other than those in which they hold their commissions. As introduced, it applied only to judges to be appointed after the enactment of the bill. As amended, it applies to all judges regardless of the date of their appointment, but it still alters the present system in a striking manner, as will be more fully indicated later.

Circuit judges may be assigned by the Chief Justice for service in any circuit court of appeals. District judges may be similarly assigned by the Chief Justice to any district court, or by the senior circuit judge of his circuit (but subject to the authority of the Chief Justice) to any district court within the circuit.

After the assignment of a judge by the Chief Justice, the senior circuit judge of the district in which he is commissioned may certify to the Chief Justice any reason deemed sufficient by him to warrant the revocation or termination of the assignment, but the Chief Justice has full discretion whether or not to act upon any such certification. The senior circuit judge of the district to which such assignment will be made is not given similar authority to show why the assignment should not be made effective.

Section 3 gives the Supreme Court power to appoint a Proctor to investigate the volume, character, and status of litigation in the circuit and district courts, to recommend the assignment of judges authorized by section 2, and to make suggestions for expediting the disposition of pending cases. The salary of the Proctor is fixed at $10,000 per year and provision is made for the functions of the office.

Section 4 authorizes an appropriation of $100,000 for the purposes of the act.

Section 5 contains certain definitions.

Section 6, the last section, makes the act effective 30 days after enactment.

The Argument

The committee recommends that the measure be rejected for the following primary reasons:

I. The Bill does not accomplish any one of the objectives for which it was originally offered.

II. It applies force to the judiciary and in its initial and ultimate effect would undermine the independence of the courts.

III. It violates all precedents in the history of our Government and would in itself be a dangerous precedent for the future.

IV. The theory of the bill is in direct violation of the spirit of the American Constitution and its employment would permit alteration of the Constitution without the people's consent or approval; it undermines the protection our constitutional system gives to minorities and is subversive of the rights of individuals.

V. It tends to centralize the Federal district judiciary by the power of assigning judges from one district to another at will.

VI. It tends to expand political control over the judicial department by adding to the powers of the legislative and executive departments respecting the judiciary.

Bill Does Not Deal with Injunctions

This measure was sent to the Congress by the President on February 5, 1937, with a message . . . setting forth the objectives sought to be attained.

It should be pointed out here that a substantial portion of the message was devoted to a discussion of the evils of conflicting decisions by inferior courts on constitutional questions and to the alleged abuse of the power of injunction by some of the Federal courts. These matters, however, have no bearing on the bill before us, for it contains neither a line nor a sentence dealing with either of those problems.

Nothing in this measure attempts to control, regulate, or prohibit the power of any Federal court to pass upon the constitutionality of any law—State or National.

Nothing in this measure attempts to control, regulate, or prohibit the issuance of injunctions by any court, in any case, whether or not the Government is a party to it.

If it were to be conceded that there is need of reform in these respects, it must be understood that this bill does not deal with these problems.

Objectives as Originally Stated

As offered to the Congress, this bill was designed to effectuate only three objectives, described as follows in the President's message:

1. To increase the personnel of the Federal courts "so that cases may be promptly decided in the first instance, and may be given adequate and prompt hearing on all appeals";

2. To "invigorate all the courts by the permanent infusion of new blood";

3. To "grant to the Supreme Court further power and responsibility in maintaining the efficiency of the entire Federal judiciary."

The third of these purposes was to be accomplished by the provisions creating the office of the Proctor and dealing with the assignment of judges to courts other than those to which commissioned.

The first two objectives were to be attained by the provisions authorizing the appointment of not to exceed 50 additional judges when sitting judges of retirement age, as defined in the bill, failed to retire or resign. How totally inadequate the measure is to achieve either of the named objectives, the most cursory examination of the facts reveals.

Bill Fails of Its Purpose

In the first place, as already pointed out, the bill does not provide for any increase of personnel unless judges of retirement age fail to resign or retire. Whether or not there is to be an increase of the number of judges, and the extent of the increase if there is to be one, is dependent wholly upon the judges themselves and not at all upon the accumulation of litigation in any court. To state it another way the increase of the number of judges is to be provided, not in relation to the increase of work in any district or circuit, but in relation to the age of the judges and their unwillingness to retire.

In the second place, as pointed out in the President's message, only 25 of the 237 judges serving in the Federal courts on February 5, 1937, were over 70 years of age. Six of these were members of the Supreme Court at the time the bill was introduced. At the present time there are 24 judges 70 years of age or over distributed among the 10 circuit courts, the 84 district courts, and the 4 courts in the District of Columbia and that dealing with customs cases in New York. Of the 24, only 10 are serving in the 84 district courts, so that the remaining 14 are to be found in 5 special courts and in the 10 circuit courts. . . . Moreover, the facts indicate that the courts with the oldest judges have the best records in the disposition of business. It follows, therefore, that since there are comparatively few aged justices in service and these are among the most efficient on the bench, the age of sitting judges does not make necessary an increase of personnel to handle the business of the courts.

There was submitted with the President's message a report from the Attorney General to the effect that in recent years the number of cases has greatly increased and that delay in the administration of justice is interminable. It is manifest, however, that this condition cannot be remedied by the contingent appointment of new judges to sit beside the judges over 70 years of age, most of whom are either altogether equal to their duties or are commissioned in courts in which congestion of business does not exist. It must be obvious that the way to attack congestion and delay in the courts is directly by legislation which will increase the number of judges in those districts where the accumulation exists, not indirectly by the contingent appointment of new judges to courts where the need does not exist, but where it may happen that the sitting judge is over 70 years of age.

Local Justice Centrally Administered

Perhaps, it was the recognition of this fact that prompted the authors of the bill to draft section 2 providing for the assignment of judges "hereafter appointed" to districts other than those to which commissioned. Such a plan, it will not be overlooked, contemplates the appointment of a judge to the district of his residence and his assignment to duty in an altogether different jurisdiction. It thus creates a flying squadron of itinerant judges appointed for districts and circuits where they are not needed to be transferred to other parts of the country for judicial service. It may be doubted whether such a plan would be effective. Certainly it would be a violation of the salutary American custom that all public officials should be citizens of the jurisdiction in which they serve or which they represent.

Though this plan for the assignment of new judges to the trial of cases in any part of the country at the will of the Chief Justice was in all probability intended for no other purpose than to make it possible to send the new judges into districts where actual congestion exists, it should not be overlooked that most of the plan involves a possibility of real danger.

To a greater and a greater degree, under modern conditions, the Government is involved in civil litigation with its citizens. Are we then through the system devised in this bill to make possible the selection of particular judges to try particular cases?

Under the present system (U.S.C., title 28, sec. 17) the assignment of judges within the circuit is made by the senior circuit judge, or, in his absence, the circuit justice. An assignment of a judge from outside the district may be made only when the senior circuit judge or the circuit justice makes certificate of the need of the district to the Chief Justice. Thus is the principle of local self-government preserved by the present system.

This principle is destroyed by this bill which allows the Chief Justice, at the recommendation of the Proctor, to make assignments anywhere regardless of the needs of any district. Thus is the administration of justice to be centralized by the proposed system.

Measure Would Prolong Litigation

It has been urged that the plan would correct the law's delay, and the President's message contains the statement that "poorer litigants are compelled to abandon valuable rights or to accept inadequate or unjust settlements because of sheer inability to finance or to await the end of long litigation." Complaint is then made that the Supreme Court during the last fiscal year "permitted private litigants to prosecute appeals in only 108 cases out of 803 applications."

It can scarcely be contended that the consideration of 695 more cases in the Supreme Court would have contributed in any degree to curtailing the law's delay or to reducing the expense of litigation. If it be true that the postponement of final decision in cases is a burden on poorer litigants as the President's message contends, then it must be equally true that any change of the present system which would enable wealthy litigants to pursue their cases in the Supreme Court would result only in an added burden on the "poorer litigants" whose "sheer inability to finance or to await the end of long litigation" compels them "to abandon valuable rights or to accept inadequate or unjust settlements."

Of course, there is nothing in this bill to alter the provisions of the act of 1925 by which the Supreme Court was authorized "in its discretion to refuse to hear appeals in many classes of cases." The President has not recommended any change of that law, and the only amendment providing an alteration of the law that was presented to the committee was, on roll call, unanimously rejected by the committee.

It is appropriate, however, to point out here that one of the principal considerations for the enactment of the certiorari law was the belief of Congress that the interests of the poorer litigant would be served and the law's delay reduced if the Supreme Court were authorized to reject frivolous appeals. Congress recognized the fact that wealthy clients and powerful corporations were in a position to wear out poor litigants under the old law. Congress was convinced that, in a great majority of cases, a trial in a nisiprius court and a rehearing in a court of appeals would be ample to do substantial justice. Accordingly, it provided in effect that litigation should end with the court of appeals unless an appellant could show the Supreme Court on certiorari that a question of such importance was involved as to warrant another hearing by the Supreme Court. Few litigated cases were ever decided in which the defeated party thought that justice had been done and in which he would not have appealed from the Supreme Court to Heaven itself, if he thought that by doing so he would wear down his opponent.

The Constitution provides for one Supreme Court (sec. 1, art. III) and authorizes Congress to make such exceptions as it deems desirable to the appellate jurisdiction of the Supreme Court (sec. 2, art. III). One obvious purpose of this provision was to permit Congress to put an end to litigation in the lower courts except in cases of greatest importance, and, also, in the interest of the poorer citizen, to make it less easy for wealthy litigants to invoke delay to defeat justice.

No alteration of this law is suggested by the proponents of this measure, but the implication is made that the Supreme Court has improvidently refused to hear some cases. There is no evidence to maintain this contention. The Attorney General in his statement to the committee presented a mathematical calculation to show how much time would be consumed by the Justices in reading the entire record in each case presented on appeal. The members of the committee and, of course the Attorney General, are well aware of the fact that attorneys are officers of the Court, that it is their duty to summarize the records and the points of appeal, and that the full record is needed only when, after having examined the summary of the attorneys, the court is satisfied there should be a hearing on the merits.

The Chief Justice, in a letter presented to this committee (appendix C), made it clear that "even if two or three of the Justices are strongly of the opinion that certiorari should be allowed, frequently the other judges will acquiesce in their view, but the petition is always granted if four so vote."

It thus appears from the bill itself, from the message of the President, the statement of the Attorney General, and the letter of the Chief Justice that nothing of advantage to litigants is to be derived from this measure in the reduction of the law's delay.

Question of Age Not Solved

The next question is to determine to what extent "the persistent infusion of new blood" may be expected from this bill.

It will be observed that the bill before us does not and cannot compel the retirement of any judge, whether on the Supreme Court or any other court, when he becomes 70 years of age. It will be remembered that the mere attainment of three score and ten by a particular judge does not, under this bill, require the appointment of another. The man on the bench may be 80 years of age, but this bill will not authorize the President to appoint a new judge to sit beside him unless he has served as a judge for 10 years. In other words, age itself is not penalized; the penalty falls only when age is attended with experience.

No one should overlook the fact that under this bill the President, whoever he may be and whether or not he believes in the constant infusion of young blood in the courts, may nominate a man 69 years and 11 months of age to the Supreme Court, or to any court, and, if confirmed, such nominee, if he never had served as a judge, would continue to sit upon the bench unmolested by this law until he had attained the ripe age of 79 years and 11 months.

We are told that "modern complexities call also for a constant infusion of new blood in the courts, just as it is needed in executive functions of the Government and in private business." Does this bill provide for such? The answer is obviously no. As has been just demonstrated, the introduction of old and inexperienced blood into the courts is not prevented by this bill.

More than that, the measure, by its own terms, makes impossible the "constant" or "persistent" infusion of new blood. It is to be observed that the word is "new," not "young."

The Supreme Court may not be expanded to more than 15 members. No more than two additional members may be appointed to any circuit court of appeals, to the Court of Claims, to the Court of Customs and Patent Appeals, or to the Customs Court, and the number of judges now serving in any district or group of districts may not be more than doubled. There is, therefore, a specific limitation of appointment regardless of age. That is to say, this bill, ostensibly designed to provide for the infusion of new blood, sets up insuperable obstacles to the "constant" or "persistent" operation of that principle.

Take the Supreme Court as an example. As constituted at the time this bill was presented to the Congress, there were six members of that tribunal over 70 years of age. If all six failed to resign or retire within 30 days after the enactment of this bill, and none of the members died, resigned, or retired before the President had made a nomination, then the Supreme Court would consist of 15 members. These 15 would then serve, regardless of age, at their own will, during good behavior, in other words, for life. Though as a result we had a court of 15 members 70 years of age or over, nothing could be done about it under this bill, and there would be no way to infuse "new" blood or "young" blood except by a new law further expanding the Court, unless, indeed, Congress and the Executive should be willing to follow the course defined by the framers of the Constitution for such a contingency and submit to the people a constitutional amendment limiting the terms of Justices or making mandatory their retirement at a given age.

It thus appears that the bill before us does not with certainty provide for increasing the personnel of the Federal judiciary, does not remedy the law's delay, does not serve the interest of the "poorer litigant" and does not provide for the "constant" or "persistent infusion of new blood" into the judiciary. What, then, does it do?

The Bill Applies Force to the Judiciary

The answer is clear. It applies force to the judiciary. It is an attempt to impose upon the courts a course of action, a line of decision which, without that force, without that imposition, the judiciary might not adopt.

Can there be any doubt that this is the purpose of the bill? Increasing the personnel is not the object of this measure; infusing young blood is not the object; for if either one of these purposes had been in the minds of the proponents, the drafters would not have written the following clause to be found on page 2, lines 1 to 4, inclusive:

Provided, That no additional judge shall be appointed hereunder if the judge who is of retirement age dies, resigns, or retires prior to the nomination of such additional judge.

Let it also be borne in mind that the President's message submitting this measure contains the following sentence:

If, on the other hand, any judge eligible for retirement should feel that his Court would suffer because of an increase of its membership, he may retire or resign under already existing provisions of law if he wishes to do so.

Moreover, the Attorney General in testifying before the committee (hearings, pt. 1, p. 33) said:

If the Supreme Court feels that the addition of six judges would be harmful to that Court, it can avoid that result by resigning.

Three invitations to the members of the Supreme Court over 70 years of age to get out despite all the talk about increasing personnel to expedite the disposition of cases and remedy the law's delay. One by the bill. One by the President's message. One by the Attorney General.

Can reasonable men by any possibility differ about the constitutional impropriety of such a course?

Those of us who hold office in this Government, however humble or exalted it may be, are creatures of the Constitution. To it we owe all the power and authority we possess. Outside of it we have none. We are bound by it in every official act.

We know that this instrument, without which we would not be able to call ourselves presidents, judges, or legislators, was carefully planned and deliberately framed to establish three coordinate branches of government, every one of them to be independent of the others. For the protection of the people, for the preservation of the rights of the individual, for the maintenance of the liberties of minorities, for maintaining the checks and balances of our dual system, the three branches of the Government were so constituted that the independent expression of honest difference of opinion could never be restrained in the people's servants and no one branch could overawe or subjugate the others. That is the American system. It is immeasurably more important, immeasurably more sacred to the people of America, indeed, to the people of all the world than the immediate adoption of any legislation however beneficial.

That judges should hold office during good behavior is the prescription. It is founded upon historic experience of the utmost significance. Compensation at stated times, which compensation was not to be diminished during their tenure, was also ordained. Those comprehensible terms were the outgrowths of experience which was deepseated. Of the 55 men in the Constitutional Convention, nearly one-half had actually fought in the War for Independence. Eight of the men present had signed the Declaration of Independence, in which, giving their reasons for the act, they had said of their king: "He has made judges dependent upon his will alone for their tenure of office and the amount and payment of their salaries." They sought to correct an abuse and to prevent its recurrence. When these men wrote the Constitution of their new Government, they still sought to avoid such an abuse as had led to such a bloody war as the one through which they had just passed. So they created a judicial branch of government consisting of courts not conditionally but absolutely independent in the discharge of their functions, and they intended that entire and impartial independence should prevail. Interference with this independence was prohibited, not partially but totally. Behavior other than good was the sole and only cause for interference. This judicial system is the priceless heritage of every American.

By this bill another and wholly different cause is proposed for the intervention of executive influence, namely, age. Age and behavior have no connection; they are unrelated subjects. By this bill, judges who have reached 70 years of age may remain on the bench and have their judgment augmented if they agree with the new appointee, or vetoed if they disagree. This is far from the independence intended for the courts by the framers of the Constitution. This is an unwarranted influence accorded the appointing agency, contrary to the spirit of the Constitution. The bill sets up a plan which has as its stability the changing will or inclination of an agency not a part of the judicial system. Constitutionally, the bill can have no sanction. The effect of the bill, as stated by the Attorney General to the committee, and indeed by the President in both his message and speech, is in violation of the organic law.

Object of Plan Acknowledged

No amount of sophistry can cover up this fact. The effect of this bill is not to provide for an increase in the number of Justices composing the Supreme Court. The effect is to provide a forced retirement or, failing in this, to take from the Justices affected a free exercise of their independent judgment.

The President tells us in his address to the Nation of March 9 . . . Congressional Record, March 10, page 2650:

When the Congress has sought to stabilize national agriculture, to improve the conditions of labor, to safeguard business against unfair competition, to protect our national resources, and in many other ways, to serve our clearly national needs, the majority of the Court has been assuming the power to pass on the wisdom of these acts of the Congress and to approve or disapprove the public policy written into these laws. . . . We have, therefore, reached the point as a nation where we must take action to save the Constitution from the Court and the Court from itself. We must find a way to take an appeal from the Supreme Court to the Constitution itself. We want a Supreme Court which will do justice under the Constitution—not over it. In our courts we want a government of laws and not of men.

These words constitute a charge that the Supreme Court has exceeded the boundaries of its jurisdiction and invaded the field reserved by the Constitution to the legislative branch of the Government. At best the accusation is opinion only. It is not the conclusion of judicial process.

Here is the frank acknowledgement that neither speed nor "new blood" in the judiciary is the object of this legislation, but a change in the decisions of the Court—a subordination of the views of the judges to the views of the executive and legislative, a change to be brought about by forcing certain judges off the bench or increasing their number.

Let us, for the purpose of the argument, grant that the Court has been wrong, wrong not only in that it has rendered mistaken opinions but wrong in the far more serious sense that it has substituted its will for the congressional will in the matter of legislation. May we nevertheless safely punish the Court?

Today it may be the Court which is charged with forgetting its constitutional duties. Tomorrow it may be the Congress. The next day it may be the Executive. If we yield to temptation now to lay the lash upon the Court, we are only teaching others how to apply it to ourselves and to the people when the occasion seems to warrant. Manifestly, if we may force the hand of the Court to secure our interpretation of the Constitution, then some succeeding Congress may repeat the process to secure another and a different interpretation and one which may not sound so pleasant in our ears as that for which we now contend.

There is a remedy for usurpation or other judicial wrongdoing. If this bill be supported by the toilers of this country upon the ground that they want a Court which will sustain legislation limiting hours and providing minimum wages, they must remember that the procedure employed in the bill could be used in another administration to lengthen hours and to decrease wages. If farmers want agricultural relief and favor this bill upon the ground that it gives them a Court which will sustain legislation in their favor, they must remember that the procedure employed might some day be used to deprive them of every vestige of a farm relief.

When members of the Court usurp legislative powers or attempt to exercise political power, they lay themselves open to the charge of having lapsed from that "good behavior" which determines the period of their official life. But, if you say, the process of impeachment is difficult and uncertain, the answer is, the people made it so when they framed the Constitution. It is not for us, the servants of the people, to find a more easy way to do that which our masters made difficult.

But, if the fault of the judges is not so grievous as to warrant impeachment, if their offense is merely that they have grown old, and we feel, therefore, that there should be a "constant infusion of new blood", then obviously the way to achieve that result is by constitutional amendment fixing definite terms for the members of the judiciary or making mandatory their retirement at a given age. Such a provision would indeed provide for the constant infusion of new blood, not only now but at all times in the future. The plan before us is but a temporary expedient which operates once and then never again, leaving the Court as permanently expanded to become once more a court of old men, gradually year by year falling behind the times.

What Size the Supreme Court?

How much better to proceed according to the rule laid down by the Constitution itself than by indirection to achieve our purposes. The futility and absurdity of the devious rather than the direct method is illustrated by the effect upon the problem of the retirement of Justice Van Devanter.

According to the terms of the bill, it does not become effective until 30 days after enactment, so the number of new judges to be appointed depends not upon the bill itself, not upon the conditions as they exist now or as they might exist when the bill is enacted, but upon conditions as they exist 30 days thereafter. Because Justice Van Devanter's retirement was effective as of June 2, there were on that date only five rather than six Justices on the Supreme Court of retirement age. The maximum number of appointments, therefore, is now 5 rather than 6 and the size of the Court 14 rather than 15. Now, indeed, we have put an end to 5-to-4 decisions and we shall not be harassed by 8-to-7 decisions. Now instead of making one man on the Court all-powerful, we have rendered the whole Court impotent when it divides 7 to 7 and we have provided a system approving the lower court by default.

But we may have another vacancy, and then the expanded court will be 13 rather than 14. A court of 13 with decisions by a vote of 7 to 6 and the all-powerful one returned to his position of judicial majesty. Meanwhile, the passage of years carries the younger members onward to the age of retirement when, if they should not retire, additional appointments could be made until the final maximum of 15 was reached.

The membership of the Court, between 9 and 15, would not be fixed by the Congress nor would it be fixed by the President. It would not even be fixed by the Court as a court, but would be determined by the caprice or convenience of the Justices over 70 years of age. The size of the Court would be determined by the personal desires of the Justices, and if there be any public advantage in having a court of any certain size, that public advantage in the people's interest would be wholly lost. Is it of any importance to the country that the size of the Court should be definitely fixed? Or are we to shut our eyes to that factor just because we have determined to punish the Justices whose opinions we resent?

But, if you say the process of reform by amendment is difficult and uncertain, the answer is, the people made it so when they framed the Constitution, and it is not for us, the servants of the people, by indirection to evade their will, or by devious methods to secure reforms upon which they only in their popular capacity have the right to pass.

A Measure Without Precedent

This bill is an invasion of judicial power such as has never before been attempted in this country. It is true that in the closing days of the administration of John Adams, a bill was passed creating 16 new circuit judges while reducing by one the number of places on the Supreme Court. It was charged that this was a bill to use the judiciary for a political purpose by providing official positions for members of a defeated party. The repeal of that law was the first task of the Jefferson administration.

Neither the original act nor the repealer was an attempt to change the course of judicial decision. And never in the history of the country has there been such an act. The present bill comes to us, therefore, wholly without precedent.

It is true that the size of the Supreme Court has been changed from time to time, but in every instance after the Adams administration, save one, the changes were made for purely administrative purposes in aid of the Court, not to control it.

Because the argument has been offered that these changes justify the present proposal, it is important to review all of the instances.

They were seven in number.

The first was by the act of 1801 reducing the number of members from six, as originally constituted, to five. Under the Judiciary Act of 1789 the circuit courts were trial courts and the Justices of the Supreme Court sat in them. That onerous duty was removed by the act of 1801 which created new judgeships for the purpose of relieving the members of the Supreme Court of this task. Since the work of the Justices was thereby reduced, it was provided that the next vacancy should not be filled. Jeffersonians explained the provision by saying that it was intended merely to prevent Jefferson from making an appointment of a successor to Justice Cushing whose death was expected.

The next change was in 1802 when the Jefferson administration restored the membership to six.

In neither of these cases was the purpose to influence decisions.

The third change was in 1807 under Jefferson when, three new States having been admitted to the Union, a new judicial circuit had to be created, and since it would be impossible for any of the six sitting Justices of the Supreme Court to undertake the trial work in the new circuit (Ohio, Kentucky, and Tennessee), a seventh Justice was added because of the expansion of the country. Had Jefferson wanted to subjugate John Marshall this was his opportunity to multiply members of the Court and overwhelm him, but he did not do it. We have no precedent here.

Thirty years elapsed before the next change. The country had continued to expand. New States were coming in and the same considerations which caused the increase of 1807 moved the representatives of the new West in Congress to demand another expansion. In 1826 a bill adding three justices passed both Houses but did not survive the conference. Andrew Jackson, who was familiar with the needs of the new frontier States, several times urged the legislation. Finally, it was achieved in 1837 and the Court was increased from 7 to 9 members.

Here again the sole reason for the change was the need of a growing country for a larger Court. We are still without a precedent.

Changes During the Reconstruction Period

In 1863 the western frontiers had reached the Pacific. California had been a State since 1850 without representation on the Supreme Court. The exigencies of the war and the development of the coast region finally brought the fifth change when by the act of 1863 a Pacific circuit was created and consequently a tenth member of the High Court.

The course of judicial opinion had not the slightest bearing upon the change.

Seventy-five years of constitutional history and still no precedent for a legislative attack upon the judicial power.

Now we come to the dark days of the reconstruction era for the sixth and seventh alterations of the number of justices.

The congressional majority in Andrew Johnson's administration had slight regard for the rights of minorities and no confidence in the President. Accordingly, a law was passed in 1866, providing that no appointments should be made to the Court until its membership had been reduced from 10 to 7. Doubtless, Thaddeus Stevens feared that the appointees of President Johnson might not agree with reconstruction policies and, if a constitutional question should arise, might vote to hold unconstitutional an act of Congress. But whatever the motive, a reduction of members at the instance of the bitterest majority that ever held sway in Congress to prevent a President from influencing the Court is scarcely a precedent for the expansion of the Court now.

By the time General Grant had become President in March 1869 the Court had been reduced to 8 members by the operation of the law of 1866. Presidential appointments were no longer resented, so Congress passed a new law, this time fixing the membership at 9. This law was passed in April 1869, an important date to remember, for the *Legal Tender* decision had not yet been rendered. Grant was authorized to make the additional appointment in December. Before he could make it however, Justice Grier resigned, and there were thus two vacancies.

The charge has been made that by the appointment to fill these vacancies Grant packed the Court to affect its decision in the *Legal Tender case*. Now whatever Grant's purpose may have been in making the particular appointments, it is obvious that Congress did not create the vacancies for the purpose of affecting any decision, because the law was passed long before the Court had acted in *Hepburn v. Griswold* and Congress made only one vacancy, but two appointments were necessary to change the opinion.

It was on February 7, 1870, that the court handed down its judgment holding the Legal Tender Act invalid, a decision very much deplored by the administration. It was on the same date that Grant sent down the nomination of the two justices whose votes, on a reconsideration of the issue, caused a reversal of the decision. As it happens, Grant had made two other nominations first, that of his Attorney General, Ebenezer Hoar, who was rejected by the Senate, and Edwin Stanton, who died 4 days after having been confirmed. These appointments were made in December 1869, 2 months before the decision, and Stanton was named, according to Charles Warren, historian of the Supreme Court, not because Grant wanted him but because a large majority of the members of the Senate and the House urged it. So Grant must be acquitted of having packed the Court and Congress is still without a precedent for any act that will tend to impair the independence of the Court.

A Precedent of Loyalty to the Constitution

Shall we now, after 150 years of loyalty to the constitutional ideal of an untrammeled judiciary, duty bound to protect the constitutional rights of the humblest citizen even against the Government itself, create the vicious precedent which must necessarily undermine our system? The only argument for the increase which survives analysis is that Congress should enlarge the Court so as to make the policies of this administration effective.

We are told that a reactionary oligarchy defies the will of the majority, that this is a bill to "unpack" the Court and give effect to the desires of the majority; that is to say, a bill to increase the number of Justices for the express purpose of neutralizing the views of some of the present members. In justification we are told, but without authority, by those who would rationalize this program, that Congress was given the power to determine the size of the Court so that the legislative branch would be able to impose its will upon the judiciary. This amounts to nothing more than the declaration that when the Court stands in the way of a legislative enactment, the Congress may reverse the ruling by enlarging the Court. When such a principle is adopted, our constitutional system is overthrown!

This, then, is the dangerous precedent we are asked to establish. When proponents of the bill assert, as they have done, that Congress in the past has altered the number of Justices upon the Supreme Court and that this is reason enough for our doing it now, they show how important precedents are and prove that we should now refrain from any action that would seem to establish one which could be followed hereafter whenever a Congress and an executive should become dissatisfied with the decisions of the Supreme Court.

This is the first time in the history of our country that a proposal to alter the decisions of the court by enlarging its personnel has been so boldly made. Let us meet it. Let us now set a salutary precedent that will never be violated. Let us, of the Seventy-fifth Congress, in words that will never be disregarded by any succeeding Congress, declare that we would rather have an independent Court, a fearless Court, a Court that will dare to announce its honest opinions in what it believes to be the defense of the liberties of the people, than a Court that, out of fear or sense of obligation to the appointing power, or factional passion, approves any measure we may enact. We are not the judges of the judges. We are not above the Constitution.

Even if every charge brought against the so-called "reactionary" members of this Court be true, it is far better that we await orderly but inevitable change of personnel than that we impatiently overwhelm them with new members. Exhibiting this restraint, thus demonstrating our faith in the American system, we shall set an example that will protect the independent American judiciary from attack as long as this Government stands.

An Independent Judiciary Essential

It is essential to the continuance of our constitutional democracy that the judiciary be completely independent of both the executive and legislative branches of the Government, and we assert that independent courts are the last safeguard of the citizen, where his rights, reserved to him by the express and implied provisions of the Constitution, come in conflict with the power of governmental agencies. We assert that the language of John Marshall, then in his 76th year, in the Virginia Convention (1829–31), was and is prophetic:

Advert, sir, to the duties of a judge. He has to pass between the Government and the man whom the Government is prosecuting; between the most powerful individual in the community and the poorest and most unpopular. It is of the last importance that in the exercise of these duties he should observe the utmost fairness. Need I express the necessity of this? Does not every man feel that his own personal security and the security of his property depends on that fairness? The judicial department comes home in its effect to every man's fireside; it passes on his property, his reputation, his life, his all. Is it not, to the last degree, important that he should be rendered perfectly and completely independent, with nothing to influence or control him but God and his conscience?

The condition of the world abroad must of necessity cause us to hesitate at this time and to refuse to enact any law that would impair the independence of or destroy the people's confidence in an independent judicial branch of our Government. We unhesitatingly assert that any effort looking to the impairment of an independent judiciary of necessity operates toward centralization of power in the other branches of a tripartite form of government. We declare for the continuance and perpetuation of government and rule by law, as distinguished from government and rule by men, and in this we are but reasserting the principles basic to the Constitution of the United States. The converse of this would lead to and in fact accomplish the destruction of our form of government, where the written Constitution

with its history, its spirit, and its long line of judicial interpretation and construction, is looked to and relied upon by millions of our people. Reduction of the degree of the supremacy of law means an increasing enlargement of the degree of personal government.

Personal government, or government by an individual, means autocratic dominance, by whatever name it may be designated. Autocratic dominance was the very thing against which the American Colonies revolted, and to prevent which the Constitution was in every particular framed.

Courts and the judges thereof should be free from a subservient attitude of mind, and this must be true whether a question of constitutional construction or one of popular activity is involved. If the court of last resort is to be made to respond to a prevalent sentiment of a current hour, politically imposed, that Court must ultimately become subservient to the pressure of public opinion of the hour, which might at the moment embrace mob passion abhorrent to a more calm, lasting consideration.

True it is, that courts like Congresses, should take account of the advancing strides of civilization. True it is that the law, being a progressive science, must be pronounced progressively and liberally; but the milestones of liberal progress are made to be noted and counted with caution rather than merely to be encountered and passed. Progress is not a mad mob march; rather, it is a steady, invincible stride. There is ever-impelling truth in the lines of the great liberal jurist, Mr. Justice Holmes, in *Northern Securities v. The United States,* wherein he says:

Great cases like hard cases make bad law. For great cases are called great, not by reason of their real importance in shaping the law of the future, but because of some accident of immediate overwhelming interest which appeals to the feelings and distorts the judgment. These immediate interests exercise a kind of hydraulic pressure which makes what previously was clear, seem doubtful, and before which even well settled principles of law will bend.

If, under the "hydraulic pressure" of our present need for economic justice, we destroy the system under which our people have progressed to a higher degree of justice and prosperity than that ever enjoyed by any other people in all the history of the human race, then we shall destroy not only all opportunity for further advance but everything we have thus far achieved.

The whole bill prophesies and permits executive and legislative interferences with the independence of the Court, a prophecy and a permission which constitute an affront to the spirit of the Constitution.

The complete independence of the courts of justice is peculiarly essential in a limited Constitution. By a limited Constitution, I understand one which contains certain specified exceptions to the legislative authority; such, for instance, as that it shall pass no bills of attainder, no ex-post-facto laws, and the like. Limitations of this kind can be preserved in practice no other way than through the medium of courts of justice, whose duty it must be to declare all acts contrary to the manifest tenor of the Constitution void. Without this, all the reservations of particular rights or privileges would amount to nothing (The Federalist, vol. 2, p. 100, no. 78).

The spirit of the Constitution emphasizing the establishment of an independent judicial branch was reenunciated by Madison in Nos. 47 and 48 (The Federalist, vol. 1, pp. 329, 339) and by John Adams (Adams' Works, vol. 1, p. 186).

If interference with the judgment of an independent judiciary is to be countenanced in any degree, then it is permitted and sanctioned in all degrees. There is no constituted power to say where the degree ends or begins, and the political administration of the hour may apply the essential "concepts of justice" by equipping the courts with one strain of "new blood", while the political administration of another day may use a different light and a different blood test. Thus would influence run riot. Thus perpetuity, independence, and stability belonging to the judicial arm of the Government and relied on by lawyers and laity, are lost. Thus is confidence extinguished.

The President Gives Us Example

From the very beginning of our Government to this hour, the fundamental necessity of maintaining inviolate the independence of the three coordinate branches of government has been recognized by legislators, jurists, and presidents. James Wilson, one of the framers of the Constitution who later became a Justice of the Supreme Court, declared that the independence of each department recognizes that its proceedings "shall be free from the remotest influence, direct or indirect, of either of the other two branches." Thus it was at the beginning. Thus it is now. Thus it was recognized by the men who framed the Constitution and administered the Government under it. Thus it was declared and recognized by the present President of the United States who, on the 19th day of May 1937, in signing a veto message to the Congress of the United States of a measure which would have created a special commission to represent the Federal Government at the World's Fair in New York City in 1939, withheld his approval because he felt that the provision by which it gave certain administrative duties to certain Members of Congress amounted to a legislative interference with executive functions. In vetoing the bill, President Roosevelt submitted with approval the statement of the present Attorney General that:

In my opinion those provisions of the joint resolution establishing a commission composed largely of Members of the Congress and authorizing them to appoint a United States commissioner general and two assistant commissioners for the New York World's Fair, and also providing for the expenditure of the appropriation made by the resolution, and for the administration of the resolution generally, amount to an unconstitutional invasion of the province of the Executive.

The solicitude of the President to maintain the independence of the executive arm of the Government against invasion by the legislative authority should be an example to us in solicitude to preserve the independence of the judiciary from any danger of invasion by the legislative and executive branches combined.

Extent of the Judicial Power

The assertion has been indiscriminately made that the Court has arrogated to itself the right to declare acts of Congress invalid. The contention will not stand against investigation or reason.

Article III of the Federal Constitution provides that the judicial power "shall extend to all cases in law and equity arising under this Constitution, the laws of the United States and treaties made under their authority."

The words "under this Constitution" were inserted on the floor of the Constitutional Convention in circumstances that leave no doubt of their meaning. It is true that the Convention had refused to give the Supreme Court the power to sit as a council of revision over the acts of Congress or the power to veto such acts. That action, however, was merely the refusal to give the Court any legislative power. It was a decision wholly in harmony with the purpose of keeping the judiciary independent. But, while carefully refraining from giving the Court power to share in making laws, the Convention did give it judicial power to construe the Constitution in litigated cases.

After the various forms and powers of the new Government had been determined in principle, the Convention referred the whole matter to the Committee on Detail, the duty of which was to draft a tentative instrument. The report of this committee was then taken up section by section on the floor, debated and perfected, whereupon the instrument was referred to the Committee on Style which wrote the final draft.

When the Committee on Detail reported the provision defining the judicial power, it read as follows:

The jurisdiction of the Supreme Court shall extend to all cases arising under laws passed by the Legislature of the United States, etc. (Elliot's Debates, vol. 5, p. 380).

On August 27, 1787, when this sentence was under consideration of the full Convention, it was changed to read as follows on motion of Dr. Johnson:

The jurisdiction of the Supreme Court shall extend to all cases arising under this Constitution and the laws passed by the Legislature of the United States.

Madison in his notes (Elliot's Debates, vol. 5, p. 483) reports the incident in this language:

Dr. Johnson moved to insert the words, "this Constitution and the" before the word "laws."

Mr. Madison doubted whether it was not going too far, to extend the jurisdiction of the Court generally to cases arising under the Constitution, and whether it ought not to be limited to cases of a judiciary nature. The right of expounding the Constitution, in cases not of this nature, ought not to be given to that department.

The motion of Dr. Johnson was agreed to, nem. con., it being generally supposed that the jurisdiction given was constructively limited to cases of a judiciary nature.

In other words, the framers of the Constitution were not satisfied to give the Court power to pass only on cases arising under the laws but insisted on making it quite clear that the power extends to cases arising "under the Constitution." Moreover, Article VI of the Constitution, clause 2, provides:

This Constitution and the laws of the United States which shall be made in pursuance thereof ... shall be the supreme law of the land. ...

Language was never more clear. No doubt can remain. A pretended law which is not "in pursuance" of the Constitution is no law at all.

A citizen has the right to appeal to the Constitution from such a statute. He has the right to demand that Congress shall not pass any act in violation of that instrument, and, if Congress does pass such an act, he has the right to seek refuge in the courts and to expect the Supreme Court to strike down the act if it does in fact violate the Constitution. A written constitution would be valueless if it were otherwise.

The right and duty of the Court to construe the Constitution is thus made clear. The question may, however, be propounded whether in construing that instrument the Court has undertaken to "override the judgment of the Congress on legislative policy." It is not necessary for this committee to defend the Court from such a charge. An invasion of the legislative power by the judiciary would not, as has already been indicated, justify the invasion of judicial authority by the legislative power. The proper remedy against such an invasion is provided in the Constitution.

Very Few Laws Held Unconstitutional

We may, however, point out that neither in this administration nor in any previous administration has the Supreme Court held unconstitutional more than a minor fraction of the laws which have been enacted. In 148 years, from 1789 to 1937, only 64 acts of Congress have been declared unconstitutional—64 acts out of a total of approximately 58,000. ...

These 64 acts were held invalid in 76 cases, 30 of which were decided by the unanimous vote of all the justices, 9 by the agreement of all but one of the justices, 14 by the agreement of all but two, another

12 by agreement of all but three. In 11 cases only were there as many as four dissenting votes when the laws were struck down.

Only four statutes enacted by the present administration have been declared unconstitutional with three or more dissenting votes. And only 11 statutes, or parts thereof, bearing the approval of the present Chief Executive out of 2,699 signed by him during his first administration, have been invalidated. Of the 11, three—the Municipal Bankruptcy Act, the Farm Mortgage Act, and the Railroad Pension Act—were not what have been commonly denominated administration measures. When he attached his signature to the Railroad Pension Act, the President was quoted as having expressed his personal doubt as to the constitutionality of the measure. The Farm Mortgage Act was later rewritten by the Congress, reenacted, and in its new form sustained by the court which had previously held it void. Both the Farm Mortgage Act in its original form and the National Recovery Administration Act were held to be unconstitutional by a unanimous vote of all the justices. With this record of fact, it can scarcely be said with accuracy that the legislative power has suffered seriously at the hands of the Court.

But even if the case were far worse than it is alleged to be, it would still be no argument in favor of this bill to say that the courts and some judges have abused their power. The courts are not perfect, nor are the judges. The Congress is not perfect, nor are Senators and Representatives. The Executive is not perfect. These branches of government and the office under them are filled by human beings who for the most part strive to live up to the dignity and idealism of a system that was designed to achieve the greatest possible measure of justice and freedom for all the people. We shall destroy the system when we reduce it to the imperfect standards of the men who operate it. We shall strengthen it and ourselves, we shall make justice and liberty for all men more certain when, by patience and self-restraint, we maintain it on the high plane on which it was conceived.

Inconvenience and even delay in the enactment of legislation is not a heavy price to pay for our system. Constitutional democracy moves forward with certainty rather than with speed. The safety and the permanence of the progressive march of our civilization are far more important to us and to those who are to come after us than the enactment now of any particular law. The Constitution of the United States provides ample opportunity for the expression of popular will to bring about such reforms and changes as the people may deem essential to their present and future welfare. It is the people's charter of the powers granted those who govern them.

Guaranties of Individual Liberty Threatened

Let it be recognized that not only is the commerce clause of the Constitution and the clauses having to do with due process and general welfare involved in the consideration of this bill, but every line of the Constitution from the preamble to the last amendment is affected. Every declarative statement in those clauses which we choose to call the Bill of Rights is involved. Guaranties of individual human liberty and the limitation of the governing powers and processes are all reviewable.

During the period in which the writing and the adoption of the Constitution was being considered, it was Patrick Henry who said:

The Judiciary are the sole protection against a tyrannical execution of the laws. They (Congress) cannot depart from the Contitution; and their laws in opposition would be void.

Later, during the discussion of the Bill of Rights, James Madison declared:

If they (the rights specified in the Bill of Rights) were incorporated into the Constitution, independent tribunals of justice will consider themselves in a peculiar manner the guardians of those rights; they will be an impenetrable bulwark against every assumption of power

in the legislative or Executive; they will be naturally led to resist every encroachment upon rights stipulated in the Constitution by the Declaration of Rights.

These leaders, who were most deeply imbued with the duty of safeguarding human rights and who were most concerned to preserve the liberty lately won, never wavered in their belief that an independent judiciary and a Constitution defining with clarity the rights of the people, were the only safeguards of the citizen. Familiar with English history and the long struggle for human liberty, they held it to be an axiom of free government that there could be no security for the people against the encroachment of political power save a written Constitution and an uncontrolled judiciary.

This has now been demonstrated by 150 years of progressive American history. As a people, Americans love liberty. It may be with truth and pride also said that we have a sensitive regard for human rights. Notwithstanding these facts, during 150 years the citizen over and over again has been compelled to contend for the plain rights guaranteed in the Constitution. Free speech, a free press, the right of assemblage, the right of a trial by jury, freedom from arbitrary arrest, religious freedom—these are among the great underlying principles upon which our democracy rests. But for all these, there have been occasions when the citizen has had to appeal to the courts for protection as against those who would take them away. And the only place the citizen has been able to go in any of these instances, for protection against the abridgment of his rights, has been to an independent and uncontrolled and incorruptible judiciary. Our law reports are filled with decisions scattered throughout these long years, reassuring the citizen of his constitutional rights, restraining States, restraining the Congress, restraining the Executive, restraining majorities, and preserving the noblest in rights of individuals.

Minority political groups, no less than religious and racial groups, have never failed, when forced to appeal to the Supreme Court of the United States, to find in its opinions the reassurance and protection of their constitutional rights. No finer or more durable philosophy of free government is to be found in all the writings and practices of great statesmen than may be found in the decisions of the Supreme Court when dealing with great problems of free government touching human rights. This would not have been possible without an independent judiciary.

Court Has Protected Human Rights

No finer illustration of the vigilance of the Court in protecting human rights can be found than in a decision wherein was involved the rights of a Chinese person, wherein the Court said:

When we consider the nature and the theory of our institutions of government, the principles upon which they are supposed to rest, and review the history of their development, we are constrained to conclude that they do not mean to leave room for the play and action of purely personal and arbitrary power. . . . The fundamental rights to life, liberty, and the pursuit of happiness considered as individual possessions are secured by those maxims of constitutional law which are the monuments showing the victorious progress of the race in securing to men the blessings of civilization under the reign of just and equal laws, so that in the famous language of the Massachusetts Bill of Rights, the government of the Commonwealth "may be a government of laws and not of men." For the very idea that one man may be compelled to hold his life or the means of living or any material right essential to the enjoyment of life, at the mere will of another, seems to be intolerable in any country where freedom prevails, as being the essence of slavery itself. (*Yick Wo v. Hopkins,* 118 U.S. 356.)

In the case involving the title to the great Arlington estate of Lee, the Court said:

No man in this country is so high that he is above the law. No officer of the law may set that law at defiance, with impunity. All the officers of the Government, from the highest to the lowest, are creatures of the law and are bound to obey it. (*U.S. v. Lee,* 106 U.S. 196.)

In a noted case where several Negroes had been convicted of the crime of murder, the trial being held in the atmosphere of mob dominance, the Court set aside the conviction, saying:

The State is free to regulate the procedure of its courts in accordance with its own conceptions of policy, unless in so doing it "offends some principle of justice so rooted in the traditions and conscience of our people as to be ranked as fundamental." (*Snyder v. Mass.; Rogers v. Peck,* 199 U.S. 425, 434.)

The State may abolish trial by jury. It may dispense with indictment by a grand jury and substitute complaint or information. (*Walker v. Sauvinet,* 92 U.S. 90; *Hurtado v. California,* 110 U.S. 516; *Snyder v. Mass.,* supra.) But the freedom of the State in establishing its policy is the freedom of constitutional government and is limited by the requirement of due process of law. Because a State may dispense with a jury trial, it does not follow that it may substitute trial by ordeal. The rack and torture chamber may not be substituted for the witness stand. The State may not permit an accused to be hurried to conviction under mob domination—where the whole proceeding is but a mask—without supplying corrective process. . . .

Under a law enacted by a State legislature, it was made possible to censor and control the press through the power of injunction on the charge that the publication of malicious, scandalous, and defamatory matters against officials constituted a nuisance. The Supreme Court, holding the law void, said:

The administration of government has become more complex, the opportunities for malfeasance and corruption have multiplied, crime has grown to most serious proportions, and the danger of its protection by unfaithful officials and of the impairment of the fundamental security of life and property by criminal alliances and official neglect, emphasizes the primary need of a vigilant and courageous press, especially in great cities. The fact that the liberty of the press may be abused by miscreant purveyors of scandal does not make less necessary the immunity of the press from previous restraint in dealing with official misconduct.

Speaking of the rights of labor, the Supreme Court has said:

Labor unions are recognized by the Clayton Act as legal when instituted for mutual help and lawfully carrying out their legitimate objects. They have long been thus recognized by the courts. They were organized out of the necessities of the situation. A single employee was helpless in dealing with an employer. He was dependent ordinarily on his daily wage for the maintenance of himself and family. If the employer refused to pay him the wages that he thought fair, he was nevertheless unable to leave the employ and to resist arbitrary and unfair treatment. Union was essential to give laborers opportunity to deal on equality with their employer. They united to exert influence upon him and to leave him in a body in order by this inconvenience to induce him to make better terms with them. They were withholding their labor of economic value to make him pay what they thought it was worth. The right to combine for such a lawful purpose has in many years not been denied by any court. The strike became a lawful instrument in a lawful economic struggle or competition between employer and employees as to the share or division between them of the joint product of labor and capital (*American Foundries v. Tri City Council,* 257 U.S. 184).

In another instance where the rights of labor were involved, the Court said:

The legality of collective action on the part of employees in order to safeguard their property interests is not to be disputed. It has long been recognized that employees are entitled to organize for the pur-pose of securing the redress of grievances and to promote agreements with employers relating to rates of pay and conditions of work. Congress . . . could safeguard it and seek to make their appropriate collective action an instrument of peace rather than of strife. Such collective action would be a mockery if representation were made futile by interference with freedom of choice. Thus the prohibition by Congress of interference with the selection of representatives for the purpose of negotiation and conference between employers and employees, instead of being an invasion of the constitutional rights of either, was based on the recognition of the rights of both (*Texas & New Orleans Railway Co. v. Brotherhood of Railway & Steamship Clerks,* 281 U.S. 548).

By the philosophy behind the pending measure it is declared that the Bill of Rights would never be violated, that freedom of speech, freedom of assemblage, freedom of the press, security in life, liberty, and property would never be challenged. Law takes its greatest force and its most secure foundation when it rests on the forum of experience. And how has our court of last resort in the past been called upon to contribute to that great fortification of the law?

In *Cummings v. Missouri* the rights of the lowly citizen were protected in the spirit of the Constitution by declaring that "no State shall pass any bill of attender or ex post fact in law." In the *Milligan case,* in the midst of the frenzied wake of the Civil War, it was the Supreme Court which sustained a citizen against an act of Congress, suspending the right of trial by jury.

In the case of *Pierce v. The Society of Sisters,* it was the Supreme Court that pronounced the inalienable right of the fathers and mothers of America to guide the destiny of their own children, when that power was challenged by an unconstitutional act of a sovereign State.

Only a few months ago in the Scottsboro cases the rights of a Negro to have counsel were upheld by this Court under the due process clause of the Constitution. On March 26 of this year, in the *Herndon case,* the rights of freedom of speech and freedom of assembly were reenunciated. Only a few weeks ago the Supreme Court construed the Constitution to uphold the Wagner Labor Act.

It would extend this report beyond proper limits to pursue this subject and trace out the holdings of the Court on the many different phases of human rights upon which it has had to pass; but the record of the Court discloses, beyond peradventure of doubt, that in preserving and maintaining the rights of American citizens under the Constitution, it has been vigilant, able, and faithful.

If, at the time all these decisions were made, their making had been even remotely influenced by the possibility that such pronouncement would entail the appointment of a co-judge or co-judges to "apply the essential concepts of justice" in the light of what the then prevailing appointing power might believe to be the "needs of an ever-changing world" these landmarks of liberty of the lowly and humble might not today exist; nor would they exist tomorrow. However great the need for human progress and social uplift, their essentials are so interwoven and involved with the individual as to be inseparable.

The Constitution of the United States, courageously construed and upheld through 150 years of history, has been the bulwark of human liberty. It was bequeathed to us in a great hour of human destiny by one of the greatest characters civilization has produced—George Washington. It is in our hands now to preserve or to destroy. If ever there was a time when the people of America should heed the words of the Father of Their Country this is the hour. Listen to his solemn warning from the Farewell Address:

It is important, likewise, that the habits of thinking, in a free country, should inspire caution in those intrusted with its administration, to confine themselves within their respective constitutional spheres, avoiding, in the exercises of the powers of one department, to encroach upon another. The spirit of encroachment tends to consolidate the powers of all the departments in one, and thus to create, whatever the form of government, a real despotism. A first estimate of that love of power, and proneness to abuse it, which predominates in the human heart, is sufficient to satisfy us of the truth of this position. The necessity of reciprocal checks in the exercise of political power, by dividing and distributing it into different depositories, and constituting each the guardian of the public weal, against invasions by the others, has been evinced by experiment, ancient and modern; some of them in our own country, and under our own eyes. To preserve them must be as necessary as to institute them. If, in the opinion of the people, the distribution or modification of the constitutional powers be, in any particular, wrong, let it be corrected by an amendment in the way which the Constitution designates. But let there be no change by usurpation; for though this, in one instance, may be the instrument of good, it is the customary weapon by which free governments are destroyed. The precedent must always greatly overbalance, in permanent evil, any partial or transient benefit which the use can, at any time, yield.

Summary

We recommend the rejection of this bill as a needless, futile, and utterly dangerous abandonment of constitutional principle.

It was presented to the Congress in a most intricate form and for reasons that obscured its real purpose.

It would not banish age from the bench nor abolish divided decisions.

It would not affect the power of any court to hold laws unconstitutional nor withdraw from any judge the authority to issue injunctions.

It would not reduce the expense of litigation nor speed the decision of cases.

It is a proposal without precedent and without justification.

It would subjugate the courts to the will of Congress and the President and thereby destroy the independence of the judiciary, the only certain shield of individual rights.

It contains the germ of a system of centralized administration of law that would enable an executive so minded to send his judges into every judicial district in the land to sit in judgment on controversies between the Government and the citizen.

It points the way to the evasion of the Constitution and establishes the method whereby the people may be deprived of their right to pass upon all amendments of the fundamental law.

It stands now before the country, acknowledged by its proponents as a plan to force judicial interpretation of the Constitution, a proposal that violates every sacred tradition of American democracy.

Under the form of the Constitution it seeks to do that which is unconstitutional.

Its ultimate operation would be to make this Government one of men rather than one of law, and its practical operation would be to make the Constitution what the executive or legislative branches of the Government choose to say it is—an interpretation to be changed with each change of administration.

It is a measure which should be so emphatically rejected that its parallel will never again be presented to the free representatives of the free people of America.

WILLIAM H. KING.   TOM CONNALLY.

FREDERICK VAN NUYS.   JOSEPH C. O'MAHONEY.

PATRICK MCCARRAN.   WILLIAM E. BORAH.

CARL A. HATCH.   WARREN R. AUSTIN.

EDWARD R. BURKE.   FREDERICK STEIWER.

INDIVIDUAL VIEWS OF MR. HATCH

In filing this separate brief statement on S. 1392 it is not intended to depart in any degree from the recommendation of the majority report for the committee to the effect that S. 1392 should not pass. In that recommendation I join.

It should be noted that the recommendation and the arguments advanced by the majority are directed against the bill in its present form. It has been my thought that the principal objections set forth in the majority report can be met by proper amendments to the bill; that with sufficient safeguards, it can be made a constructive piece of legislation, not designed for the immediate present, but to provide a permanent plan for the gradual and orderly infusion of new blood into the courts. Such a plan, intended to aid in the better administration of justice and to enable the courts to discharge their judicial function more efficiently, but so safeguarded that it cannot be used to change or control judicial opinions, is within both the spirit and the letter of the constitution.

Intending to offer amendments which it is believed will accomplish this purpose, I desire to make this additional statement to accompany the majority report.

CARL A. HATCH.

PROPOSED BILL

JUNE 7

Be it enacted by the Senate and the House of Representatives of the United States of America in Congress assembled, That —

(a) When any judge of a court of the United States, appointed to hold his office during good behavior, has heretofore or hereafter attained the age of seventy years and has held a commission or commissions as judge of any such court or courts at least ten years, continuously or otherwise, and within six months thereafter has neither resigned nor retired, the President, for each such judge who has not so resigned or retired, shall nominate, and by and with the advice and consent of the Senate, shall appoint one additional judge to the court to which the former is commissioned: *Provided,* That no additional judge shall be appointed hereunder if the judge who is of retirement age dies, resigns, or retires prior to the nomination of such additional judge.

(b) The number of judges of any court shall be permanently increased by the number appointed thereto under the provisions of subsection (a) of this section. No more than fifty judges shall be appointed thereunder, nor shall any judge be so appointed if such appointment would result in (1) more than fifteen members of the Supreme Court of the United States, (2) more than two additional members so appointed to a circuit court of appeals, the Court of Claims, the United States Court of Customs and Patent Appeals, or the Customs Court, or (3) more than twice the number of judges now authorized to be appointed for any district or, in the case of judges appointed for more than one district, for any such group of districts.

(c) That number of judges which is at least two-thirds of the number of which the Supreme Court of the United States consists, or three-fifths of the number of which the United States Court of Appeals for the District of Columbia, the Court of Claims, or the United States Court of Customs and Patent Appeals consists, shall constitute a quorum of such court.

(d) An additional judge shall not be appointed under the provisions of this section when the judge who is of retirement age is commissioned to an office as to which Congress has provided that a vacancy shall not be filled.

Sec. 2 (a) Any circuit judge hereafter appointed may be designated and assigned from time to time by the Chief Justice of the United States for service in the circuit court of appeals for any circuit. Any district judge hereafter appointed may be designated and assigned from time to time by the Chief Justice of the United States for service in any district court, or, subject to the authority of the Chief Justice, by the senior circuit judge of his circuit for service in any district court within the circuit. A district judge designated and assigned to another district hereunder may hold court separately and at the same time as the district judge in such district. All designations and assignments made hereunder shall be filed in the office of the clerk and entered on the minutes of both the court from and to which a judge is designated and assigned, and thereafter the judge so designated and assigned shall be authorized to discharge all the judicial duties (except the power of appointment to a statutory position or of permanent designation of a newspaper or depository of funds) of a judge of the court to which he is designated and assigned. The designation and assignment of a judge shall not impair his authority to perform such judicial duties of the court to which he was commissioned as may be necessary or appropriate. The designation and assignment of any judge may be terminated at any time by order of the Chief Justice or the senior circuit judge, as the case may be.

(b) After the designation and assignment of a judge by the Chief Justice, the senior circuit judge of the circuit in which such judge is commissioned may certify to the Chief Justice any consideration which such senior circuit judge believes to make advisable that the designated judge remain in or return for service in the court to which he was commissioned. If the Chief Justice deems the reasons sufficient he shall revoke or designate the time of termination of such designation and assignment.

(c) In case a trial or hearing has been entered upon but has not been concluded before the expiration of the period of service of a district judge designated and assigned hereunder, the period of service shall, unless terminated under the provisions of subsection (a) of this section, be deemed to be extended until the trial or hearing has been concluded. Any designated and assigned district judge who has held court in another district than his own shall have power, notwithstanding his absence from such district and the expiration of any time limit in his designation, to decide all matters which have been submitted to him within such district, to decide motions for new trials, settle bills of exceptions, certify or authenticate narratives of testimony, or perform any other act required by law or the rules to be performed in order to prepare any case so tried by him for review in an appellate court; and his action thereon in writing filed with the clerk of the court where the trial or hearing was had shall be as valid as if such action had been taken by him within that district and within the period of his designation. Any designated and assigned circuit judge who has sat on another court than his own shall have power, notwithstanding the expiration of any time limit in his designation, to participate in the decision of all matters submitted to the court while he was sitting and to perform or participate in any act appropriate to the disposition or review of matters submitted while he was sitting on such court, and his action thereon shall be as valid as if it had been taken while sitting on such court and within the period of his designation.

Sec. 3. (a) The Supreme Court shall have power to appoint a proctor. It shall be his duty (1) to obtain and, if deemed by the Court to be desirable, to publish information as to the volume, character, and status of litigation in the district courts and circuit courts of appeals, and such other information as the Supreme Court may from time to time require by order, and it shall be the duty of any judge, clerk, or marshal of any court of the United States promptly to furnish such information as may be required by the proctor; (2) to investigate the need of assigning district and circuit judges to other courts and to make recommendations thereon to the Chief Justice; (3) to recommend, with the approval of the Chief Justice, to any court of the United States methods for expediting cases pending on its dockets; and (4) to perform such other duties consistent with his office as the Court shall direct.

(b) The proctor shall, by requisition upon the Public Printer, have any necessary printing and binding done at the Government Printing Office and authority is conferred upon the Public Printer to do such printing and binding.

(c) The salary of the proctor shall be $10,000 per annum, payable out of the Treasury in monthly installments, which shall be in full compensation for the services required by law. He shall also be allowed, in the discretion of the Chief Justice, stationery, supplies, travel expenses, equipment, necessary professional and clerical assistance, and miscellaneous expenses appropriate for performing the duties imposed by this section. The expenses in connection with the maintenance of his office shall be paid from the appropriation of the Supreme Court of the United States.

Sec. 4. There is hereby authorized to be appropriated, out of any money in the Treasury not otherwise appropriated, the sum of $100,000 for the salaries of additional judges and the other purposes of this Act during the fiscal year 1937.

Sec. 5. When used in this Act—

(a) The term "judge of retirement age" means a judge of a court of the United States, appointed to hold his office during good behavior, who has attained the age of seventy years and has held a commission or commissions as judge of any such court or courts at least ten years, continuously or otherwise, and within six months thereafter, whether or not he is eligible for retirement, has neither resigned nor retired.

(b) The term "circuit court of appeals" includes the United States Court of Appeals for the District of Columbia; the term "senior circuit judge" includes the Chief Justice of the United States Court of Appeals for the District of Columbia; and the term "circuit" includes the District of Columbia.

(c) The term "district court" includes the District Court of the District of Columbia but does not include the district court in any territory or insular possession.

(d) The term "judge" includes justice.

Sec. 6. This Act shall take effect on the thirtieth day after the date of its enactment.

SOURCE: U.S. Senate, Committee on the Judiciary, Reorganization of the Federal Judiciary, S. Rept. 711, *75th Congress*, 1st session, 1937.

Fortas Letter Explaining Resignation (1969)

In 1969 Abe Fortas became the first Supreme Court justice to resign under threat of impeachment. A prominent Washington, D.C., lawyer, Fortas was the winning counsel in Gideon v. Wainwright *in 1963 and later was a principal adviser to President Lyndon B. Johnson. In 1965 Johnson appointed him to the Court and in 1968 tried to elevate Fortas to chief justice. The nomination was blocked in the Senate when it became known that Fortas had remained a close adviser to Johnson while on the Court.*

In May 1969 Life *magazine reported that after becoming a justice in 1965 Fortas had accepted $20,000 for advising the family charitable foundation of Louis Wolfson. Fortas had returned the money later in 1966 after Wolfson was indicted for violating federal securities law. (Wolfson was later convicted.) Within days of the* Life *article, there were calls for his resignation and movement in the House for impeachment. Fortas resigned from the Court May 14, 1969.*

In his letter of resignation, Fortas maintained that he had done nothing wrong and that he decided to resign because he did not want the controversy to adversely affect the work and position of the Court.

FORTAS LETTER EXPLAINING RESIGNATION

The text of the May 14, 1969, letter of resignation from Justice Fortas to Chief Justice Earl Warren:

MY DEAR CHIEF JUSTICE:

I am filing with you this memorandum with respect to my association with the Wolfson Family Foundation, and a statement of the reasons which in my judgment indicate that I should resign in order that the Court may not continue to be subjected to extraneous stress which may adversely affect the performance of its important functions.

As you know, I have delayed issuing a detailed report or announcing my decision until it could first be communicated to the members of the Court. In my judgment, this was the only proper course open to me as an Associate Justice of this Court, because of the Court's position as a separate and independent branch of the government under the Constitution. Because of the Court's recess, this report was not possible until yesterday.

In the spring or summer of 1965, before I was nominated as Associate Justice of the Supreme Court, my law firm represented New York Shipbuilding Corporation, a company controlled by Mr. Louis E. Wolfson, with respect to various civil claims. Later in the summer of 1965, and also before my nomination, my firm was retained in connection with some securities problems of Merritt-Chapman and Scott Corporation, of which Mr. Wolfson was Chairman of the Board.

I became acquainted with Mr. Wolfson and he told me about the Wolfson Family Foundation and his hopes and plans for it. He knew that its program—the improvement of community relations and the promotion of racial and religious cooperation—concerned matters to which I had devoted much time and attention.

Mr. Wolfson stated that he intended to increase the Foundation's resources, and he hoped that the Foundation might expand its work so as to make unique and basic contributions in its field. As we proceeded in our discussions, Mr. Wolfson suggested that he would like me to participate in and help shape the Foundation's program and activities. I told him I was interested in these objectives and that I hoped we would continue our discussions.

I became a member of the Court in October 1965. Shortly thereafter, Mr. Wolfson was in Washington and again conferred with me about the Foundation's work and my possible association with it. I again indicated my interest in the Foundation's program and in expanding its scope, and we discussed the possibility of my participating in the project on a long-term basis. Because of the nature of the work, there was no conflict between it and my judicial duties. It was then my opinion that the work of the Court would leave me adequate time for the Foundation assignments.

The Board of the Foundation met in December 1965, and approved, by resolution, an agreement under which I was to perform services for the Foundation. It was understood between us that the program in question was a long-range one and that my association would be meaningful only if it were on a long-term basis. The agreement, therefore, contemplated that I would perform continuing services, and, instead of fixing variable compensation from time to time for work done, it provided that I would receive Twenty Thousand Dollars per year for my life with arrangements for payments to Mrs. Fortas in the event of my death.

In January 1966, I received a check for Twenty Thousand Dollars under the agreement, and began my association with the Foundation. In June of that year I attended and participated in a meeting of the Trustees of the Foundation at Jacksonville, Florida. It is my recollection that Mr. Wolfson did not attend the meeting. I went from Jacksonville to his farm at Ocala where I had an overnight visit, as I recall, with him and his family.

Later, in June 1966, I reached the decision that the continuing role in the Foundation's work which our agreement contemplated should be terminated. There were two reasons for this decision: My work for the Court was much heavier than I had anticipated and my idea of the amount of time I would have free for non-judicial work had been a substantial over-estimate. I had also learned shortly before informing the Foundation of my decision to terminate the arrangement, that the SEC had referred Mr. Wolfson's file to the Department of Justice for consideration as to criminal prosecution.

I therefore wrote a letter to the Foundation, addressed to its General Counsel, dated June 21, 1966, cancelling the agreement we had entered into, subject to completing the projects for the year. I recited as my reason only the burden of Court work.

In September and October of 1966, Mr. Louis E. Wolfson was indicted on separate charges stemming from stock transactions, and in December 1966, I returned to the Foundation, in its entirety, the sum of Twenty Thousand Dollars previously paid to me. I concluded that, because of the developments which had taken place, the services which I had performed should be treated as a contribution to the Foundation.

Since becoming a member of the Court, I have not, at any time, directly or indirectly, received any compensation from Mr. Wolfson or members of his family or any of his associates for advice, assistance or any reason whatever, except the Foundation fee which was returned.

Since I became a member of the Court, Mr. Wolfson on occasion would send me material relating to his problems, just as I think he did to many other people, and on several occasions he mentioned them to me, but I have not interceded or taken part in any legal, administrative or judicial matter affecting Mr. Wolfson or anyone associated with him.

It is my opinion, however, that the public controversy relating to my association with the Foundation is likely to continue and adversely affect the work and position of the Court, absent my resignation. In these circumstances, it seems clear to me that it is not my duty to remain on the Court, but rather to resign in the hope that this will enable the Court to proceed with its vital work free from extraneous stress.

There has been no wrongdoing on my part. There has been no default in the performance of my judicial duties in accordance with the high standards of the office I hold. So far as I am concerned, the welfare and maximum effectiveness of the Court to perform its critical role in our system of government are factors that are paramount to all others. It is this consideration that prompts my resignation which, I hope, by terminating the public controversy, will permit the Court to proceed with its work without the harassment of debate concerning one of its members.

I have written a letter asking President Nixon to accept my resignation, effective as of this date.

I leave the Court with the greatest respect and affection for you and my colleagues, and my thanks to all of you and to the staff of the Court for your unfailing helpfulness and friendship. I hope that as I return to private life, I shall find opportunities to continue to serve the Nation and the cause of justice which this Court so ably represents.

Sincerely,

ABE FORTAS

Rules of the Supreme Court (1995)

The Supreme Court, empowered by Title 28, section 2071 of the U.S. Code, sets its own rules covering the activities of the Court. These rules, first established in 1790, are revised from time to time, generally by a consensus of the justices. The current rules were adopted July 26, 1995, and went into effect October 2, 1995.

There are currently forty-eight rules governing the presentation of cases to the Court. These rules cover the activities of Court officers (Part I), the requirements for attorneys and counselors (Part II), the jurisdiction of the Court (Parts III and IV), procedures that must be followed in the presentation of cases (Parts V, VI, and VII), Court procedures and litigant requirements at the disposition of cases (Part VIII), and definitions and the effective date of the rules (Part IX).

The rules go into specific detail on many matters, such as the time allotted for oral argument, the preparation of documents, and the printing of appendices.

RULES OF THE SUPREME COURT OF THE UNITED STATES

Adopted July 26, 1995
Effective October 2, 1995

PART I. THE COURT

RULE 1. CLERK

1. The Clerk receives documents for filing with the Court and has authority to reject any submitted filing that does not comply with these Rules.

2. The Clerk maintains the Court's records and will not permit any of them to be removed from the Court building except as authorized by the Court. Any document filed with the Clerk and made a part of the Court's records may not thereafter be withdrawn from the official Court files. After the conclusion of proceedings in this Court, original records and documents transmitted to this Court by any other court will be returned to the court from which they were received.

3. Unless the Court or the Chief Justice orders otherwise, the Clerk's office is open from 9 A.M. to 5 P.M., Monday through Friday, except on federal legal holidays listed in 5 U.S.C. §6103.

RULE 2. LIBRARY

1. The Court's library is available for use by appropriate personnel of this Court, members of the Bar of this Court, Members of Congress and their legal staffs, and attorneys for the United States and for federal departments and agencies.

2. The library's hours are governed by regulations made by the Librarian with the approval of the Chief Justice or the Court.

3. Library books may not be removed from the Court building, except by a Justice or a member of a Justice's staff.

RULE 3. TERM

The Court holds a continuous annual Term commencing on the first Monday in October and ending on the day before the first Monday in October of the following year. See 28 U.S.C. §2. At the end of each Term, all cases pending on the docket are continued to the next Term.

RULE 4. SESSIONS AND QUORUM

1. Open sessions of the Court are held beginning at 10 A.M. on the first Monday in October of each year, and thereafter as announced by the Court. Unless it orders otherwise, the Court sits to hear arguments from 10 A.M. until noon and from 1 P.M. until 3 P.M.

2. Six Members of the Court constitute a quorum. See 28 U.S.C. §1. In the absence of a quorum on any day appointed for holding a session of the Court, the Justices attending, or if no Justice is present, the Clerk or a Deputy Clerk may announce that the Court will not meet until there is a quorum.

3. When appropriate, the Court will direct the Clerk or the Marshal to announce recesses.

PART II. ATTORNEYS AND COUNSELORS

RULE 5. ADMISSION TO THE BAR

1. To qualify for admission to the Bar of this Court, an applicant must have been admitted to practice in the highest court of a State, Commonwealth, Territory or Possession, or the District of Columbia for a period of at least three years immediately before the date of application; must not have been the subject of any adverse disciplinary action pronounced or in effect during that 3 year period; and must appear to the Court to be of good moral and professional character.

2. Each applicant shall file with the Clerk (1) a certificate from the presiding judge, clerk, or other authorized official of that court evidencing the applicant's admission to practice there and the applicant's current good standing, and (2) a completely executed copy of the form approved by this Court and furnished by the Clerk containing (a) the applicant's personal statement, and (b) the statement of two sponsors endorsing the correctness of the applicant's statement, stating that the applicant possesses all the qualifications required for admission, and affirming that the applicant is of good moral and professional character. Both sponsors must be members of the Bar of this Court who personally know, but are not related to, the applicant.

3. If the documents submitted demonstrate that the applicant possesses the necessary qualifications, and if the applicant has signed the oath or affirmation and paid the required fee, the Clerk will notify the applicant of acceptance by the Court as a member of the Bar and issue a certificate of admission. An applicant who so wishes may be admitted in open court on oral motion by a member of the Bar of this Court, provided that all other requirements for admission have been satisfied.

4. Each applicant shall sign the following oath or affirmation: I, _____, do solemnly swear (or affirm) that as an attorney and as a counselor of this Court, I will conduct myself uprightly and according to law, and that I will support the Constitution of the United States.

5. The fee for admission to the Bar and a certificate bearing the seal of the Court is $100, payable to the United States Supreme Court. The Marshal will deposit such fees in a separate fund to be disbursed by the Marshal at the direction of the Chief Justice for the costs of admissions, for the benefit of the Court and its Bar, and for related purposes.

6. The fee for a duplicate certificate of admission to the Bar bearing the seal of the Court is $15, payable to the United States Supreme Court. The proceeds will be maintained by the Marshal as provided in paragraph 5 of this Rule.

RULE 6. ARGUMENT *PRO HAC VICE*

1. An attorney not admitted to practice in the highest court of a State, Commonwealth, Territory or Possession, or the District of Co-

lumbia for the requisite three years, but otherwise eligible for admission to practice in this Court under Rule 5.1, may be permitted to argue *pro hac vice.*

2. An attorney qualified to practice in the courts of a foreign state may be permitted to argue *pro hac vice.*

3. Oral argument *pro hac vice* is allowed only on motion of the counsel of record for the party on whose behalf leave is requested. The motion shall state concisely the qualifications of the attorney who is to argue *pro hac vice.* It shall be filed with the Clerk, in the form required by Rule 21, no later than the date on which the respondent's or appellee's brief on the merits is due to be filed and it shall be accompanied by proof of service as required by Rule 29.

RULE 7. PROHIBITION AGAINST PRACTICE

No employee of this Court shall practice as an attorney or counselor in any court or before any agency of government while employed by the Court; nor shall any person after leaving such employment participate in any professional capacity in any case pending before this Court or in any case being considered for filing in this Court, until two years have elapsed after separation; nor shall a former employee ever participate in any professional capacity in any case that was pending in this Court during the employee's tenure.

RULE 8. DISBARMENT AND DISCIPLINARY ACTION

1. Whenever a member of the Bar of this Court has been disbarred or suspended from practice in any court of record, or has engaged in conduct unbecoming a member of the Bar of this Court, the Court will enter an order suspending that member from practice before this Court and affording the member an opportunity to show cause, within 40 days, why a disbarment order should not be entered. Upon response, or if no response is timely filed, the Court will enter an appropriate order.

2. After reasonable notice and an opportunity to show cause why disciplinary action should not be taken, and after a hearing if material facts are in dispute, the Court may take any appropriate disciplinary action against any attorney who is admitted to practice before it for conduct unbecoming a member of the Bar or for failure to comply with these Rules or any Rule or order of the Court.

RULE 9. APPEARANCE OF COUNSEL

1. An attorney seeking to file a document in this Court in a representative capacity must first be admitted to practice before this Court as provided in Rule 5, except that admission to the Bar of this Court is not required for an attorney appointed under the Criminal Justice Act of 1964, see 18 U.S.C. §3006A(d)(6), or under any other applicable federal statute. The attorney whose name, address, and telephone number appear on the cover of a document presented for filing is considered counsel of record, and a separate notice of appearance need not be filed. If the name of more than one attorney is shown on the cover of the document, the attorney who is counsel of record shall be clearly identified.

2. An attorney representing a party who will not be filing a document shall enter a separate notice of appearance as counsel of record indicating the name of the party represented. A separate notice of appearance shall also be entered whenever an attorney is substituted as counsel of record in a particular case.

PART III. JURISDICTION ON WRIT OF CERTIORARI

RULE 10. CONSIDERATIONS GOVERNING REVIEW ON WRIT OF CERTIORARI

Review on a writ of certiorari is not a matter of right, but of judicial discretion. A petition for a writ of certiorari will be granted only for compelling reasons. The following, although neither controlling nor fully measuring the Court's discretion, indicate the character of the reasons the Court considers:

(a) a United States court of appeals has entered a decision in conflict with the decision of another United States court of appeals on the same important matter; has decided an important federal question in a way that conflicts with a decision by a state court of last resort; or has so far departed from the accepted and usual course of judicial proceedings, or sanctioned such a departure by a lower court, as to call for an exercise of this Court's supervisory power;

(b) a state court of last resort has decided an important federal question in a way that conflicts with the decision of another state court of last resort or of a United States court of appeals;

(c) a state court or a United States court of appeals has decided an important question of federal law that has not been, but should be, settled by this Court, or has decided an important federal question in a way that conflicts with relevant decisions of this Court.

A petition for a writ of certiorari is rarely granted when the asserted error consists of erroneous factual findings or the misapplication of a properly stated rule of law.

RULE 11. CERTIORARI TO A UNITED STATES COURT OF APPEALS BEFORE JUDGMENT

A petition for a writ of certiorari to review a case pending in a United States court of appeals, before judgment is entered in that court, will be granted only upon a showing that the case is of such imperative public importance as to justify deviation from normal appellate practice and to require immediate determination in this Court. See 28 U.S.C. §2101(e).

RULE 12. REVIEW ON CERTIORARI: HOW SOUGHT; PARTIES

1. Except as provided in paragraph 2 on this Rule, the petitioner shall file 40 copies of a petition for a writ of certiorari, prepared as required by Rule 33.1, and shall pay the Rule 38(a) docket fee.

2. A petitioner proceeding *in forma pauperis* under Rule 39 shall file an original and 10 copies of a petition for a writ of certiorari prepared as required by Rule 33.2, together with an original and 10 copies of the motion for leave to proceed *in forma pauperis.* A copy of the motion shall precede and be attached to each copy of the petition, and shall preface and be attached to the petition for a writ of certiorari. An inmate confined in an institution, if proceeding *in forma pauperis* and is not represented by counsel, need file only an original petition and motion.

3. Whether prepared under to Rule 33.1 or Rule 33.2, the petition shall comply in all respects with Rule 14 and shall be submitted with proof of service as required by Rule 29. The case then will be placed on the docket. It is the petitioner's duty to notify all respondents promptly, on a form supplied by the Clerk, of the date of filing, the date the case was placed on the docket, and the docket number of the case. The notice shall be served as required by Rule 29.

4. Parties interested jointly, severally, or otherwise in a judgment may petition separately for a writ of certiorari; or any two or more may join in a petition. A party not shown on the petition as joined therein at the time the petition is filed may not later join in that peti-

tion. When two or more judgments are sought to be reviewed on a writ of certiorari to the same court and involve identical or closely related questions, a single petition for a writ of certiorari covering all the judgments suffices. A petition for a writ of certiorari may not be joined with any other pleading, except that any motion for leave to proceed *in forma pauperis* shall be attached.

5. No more than 30 days after a case has been placed on the docket, a respondent seeking to file a conditional cross-petition (*i.e.,* a cross-petition that otherwise would be untimely) shall file, with proof of service as required by Rule 29, 40 copies of the cross-petition prepared as required by Rule 33.1, except that a cross-petitioner proceeding *in forma pauperis* under Rule 39 shall comply with Rule 12.2. The cross-petition shall comply in all respects with this Rule and Rule 14, except that material already reproduced in the appendix to the opening petition need not be reproduced again. A cross-petitioning respondent shall pay the Rule 38(a) docket fee or submit a motion for leave to proceed *in forma pauperis*. The cover of the cross-petition shall indicate clearly that it is a conditional cross-petition. The cross-petition then will be placed on the docket, subject to the provisions of Rule 13.4. It is the cross-petitioner's duty to notify all cross-respondents promptly, on a form supplied by the Clerk, of the date of filing, the date the cross-petition was placed on the docket, and the docket number of the cross-petition. The notice shall be served as required by Rule 29. A cross-petition for a writ of certiorari may not be joined with any other pleading, except that any motion for leave to proceed *in forma pauperis* shall be attached. The time to file a cross-petition will not be extended.

6. All parties to the proceeding in the court whose judgment is sought to be reviewed are deemed parties entitled to file documents in this Court, unless the petitioner notifies the Clerk of this Court in writing of the petitioner's belief that one or more of the parties below have no interest in the outcome of the petition. A copy of such notice shall be served as required by Rule 29 on all parties to the proceeding below. A party noted as no longer interested may remain a party by notifying the Clerk promptly, with service on the other parties, of an intention to remain a party. All parties other than the petitioner are considered respondents, but any respondent who supports the position of a petitioner shall meet the petitioner's time schedule for filing documents, except that a response supporting the petition shall be filed within 20 days after the case is placed on the docket, and that time will not be extended. Parties who file no document will not qualify for any relief from this Court.

7. The clerk of the court having possession of the record shall keep it until notified by the Clerk of this Court to certify and transmit it. In any document filed with this Court, a party may cite or quote from the record, even if it has not been transmitted to this Court. When requested by the Clerk of this Court to certify and transmit the record, or any part of it, the clerk of the court having possession of the record shall number the documents to be certified and shall transmit therewith a numbered list specifically identifying each document transmitted. If the record, or stipulated portions, have been printed for the use of the court below, that printed record, plus the proceedings in the court below, may be certified as the record unless one of the parties or the Clerk of this Court requests otherwise. The record may consist of certified copies, but if the lower court is of the view that original documents of any kind should be seen by this Court, that court may provide by order for the transport, safekeeping, and return of such originals.

RULE 13. REVIEW ON CERTIORARI: TIME FOR PETITIONING

1. Unless otherwise provided by law, a petition for a writ of certiorari to review a judgment in any case, civil or criminal, entered by a state court of last resort or a United States court of appeals (including the United States Court of Appeals for the Armed Forces) is timely when it is filed with the Clerk of this Court within 90 days after entry of the judgment. A petition for a writ of certiorari seeking review of a judgment of a lower state court that is subject to discretionary review by the state court of last resort is timely when it is filed with the Clerk within 90 days after entry of the order denying discretionary review.

2. The Clerk will not file any petition for a writ of certiorari that is jurisdictionally out of time. See, *e.g.,* 28 U.S.C. §2101(c).

3. The time to file a petition for a writ of certiorari runs from the date of entry of the judgment or order sought to be reviewed, and not from the issuance date of the mandate (or its equivalent under local practice). But if a petition for rehearing is timely filed in the lower court by any party, the time to file the petition for a writ of certiorari for all parties (whether or not they requested rehearing or joined in the petition for rehearing) runs from the date of the denial of the petition for rehearing or, if the petition for rehearing is granted, the subsequent entry of judgment. A suggestion made to a United States court of appeals for a rehearing en banc is not a petition for rehearing within the meaning of this Rule unless so treated by the United States court of appeals.

4. A cross-petition for a writ of certiorari is timely when it is filed with the Clerk as provided in paragraphs 1, 3, and 5 of this Rule, or in Rule 12.5. However, a conditional cross-petition (which except for Rule 12.5 would be untimely) will not be granted unless another party's timely petition for a writ of certiorari is granted.

5. For good cause, a Justice may extend the time to file a petition for a writ of certiorari for a period not exceeding 60 days. An application to extend the time to file shall set out the basis for jurisdiction in this Court, identify the judgment sought to be reviewed, include a copy of the opinion and any order respecting rehearing, and set out specific reasons why an extension of time is justified. The application must be received by the Clerk at least 10 days before the date the petition is due, except in extraordinary circumstances. For the time and manner of presenting the application, see Rules 21, 22, 30, and 33.2. An application to extend the time to file a petition for a writ of certiorari is not favored.

RULE 14. CONTENT OF A PETITION FOR A WRIT OF CERTIORARI

1. A petition for a writ of certiorari shall contain, in the order indicated:

(a) The questions presented for review, expressed concisely in relation to the circumstances of the case, without unnecessary detail. The questions should be short and should not be argumentative or repetitive. If the petitioner or respondent is under a death sentence that may be affected by the disposition of the petition, the notation "capital case" shall precede the questions presented. The questions shall be set out on the first page following the cover, and no other information may appear on that page. The statement of any question presented is deemed to comprise every subsidiary question fairly included therein. Only the questions set out in the petition, or fairly included therein, will be considered by the Court.

(b) A list of all parties to the proceeding in the court whose judgment is sought to be reviewed (unless the caption of the case contains the names of all the parties), and a list of parent companies and nonwholly owned subsidiaries as required by Rule 29.6.

(c) If the petition exceeds five pages, a table of contents and a table of cited authorities.

(d) Citations of the official and unofficial reports of the opinions and orders entered in the case by courts or administrative agencies.

(e) A concise statement of the basis for jurisdiction in this Court, showing:

(i) the date the judgment or order sought to be reviewed was entered (and, if applicable, a statement that the petition is filed under this Court's Rule 11);

(ii) the date of any order respecting rehearing, and the date and terms of any order granting an extension of time to file the petition for a writ of certiorari;

(iii) express reliance on Rule 12.5, when a cross-petition for a writ of certiorari is filed under that Rule, and the date of docketing of the petition for a writ of certiorari in connection with which the cross-petition is filed;

(iv) the statutory provision believed to confer on this Court jurisdiction to review on a writ of certiorari the judgment or order in question; and

(v) if applicable, a statement that the notifications required by Rule 29.4(b) or (c) have been made.

(f) The constitutional provisions, treaties, statutes, ordinances, and regulations involved in the case, set out verbatim with appropriate citation. If the provisions involved are lengthy, their citation alone suffices at this point, and their pertinent text shall be set out in the appendix referred to in subparagraph 1(i).

(g) A concise statement of the case setting out the facts material to consideration of the questions presented, and also containing the following:

(i) If review of a state-court judgment is sought, specification of the stage in the proceedings, both in the court of first instance and in the appellate courts, when the federal questions sought to be reviewed were raised; the method or manner of raising them and the way in which they were passed on by those courts; and pertinent quotations of specific portions of the record or summary thereof, with specific reference to the places in the record where the matter appears (*e.g.,* court opinion, ruling on exception, portion of court's charge and exception thereto, assignment of error), so as to show that the federal question was timely and properly raised and that this Court has jurisdiction to review the judgment on a writ of certiorari. When the portions of the record relied on under this subparagraph are voluminous, they shall be included in the appendix referred to in subparagraph 1(i).

(ii) If review of a judgment of a United States court of appeals is sought, the basis for federal jurisdiction in the court of first instance.

(h) A direct and concise argument amplifying the reasons relied on for allowance of the writ. See Rule 10.

(i) An appendix containing, in the order indicated:

(i) the opinions, orders, findings of fact, and conclusions of law, whether written or orally given and transcribed, entered in conjunction with the judgment sought to be reviewed;

(ii) any other opinions, orders, findings of fact, and conclusions of law entered in the case by courts or administrative agencies, and, if reference thereto is necessary to ascertain the grounds of the judgment, of those in companion cases (each document shall include the caption showing the name of the issuing court or agency, the title and number of the case, and the date of entry);

(iii) any order on rehearing, including the caption showing the name of the issuing court, the title and number of the case, and the date of entry;

(iv) the judgment sought to be reviewed if the date of its entry is diVerent from the date of the opinion or order required in sub subparagraph (i) of this subparagraph;

(v) material required by subparagraphs 1(f) or 1(g)(i); and

(vi) any other material the petitioner believes essential to understand the petition.

If the material required by this subparagraph is voluminous, it may be presented in a separate volume or volumes with appropriate covers.

2. All contentions in support of a petition for a writ of certiorari

shall be set out in the body of the petition, as provided in subparagraph 1(h) of this Rule. No separate brief in support of a petition for a writ of certiorari may be filed, and the Clerk will not file any petition for a writ of certiorari to which any supporting brief is annexed or appended.

3. A petition for a writ of certiorari should be stated briefly and in plain terms and may not exceed the page limitations specified in Rule 33.

4. The failure of a petitioner to present with accuracy, brevity, and clarity whatever is essential to ready and adequate understanding of the points requiring consideration is sufficient reason for the Court to deny a petition.

5. If the Clerk determines that a petition submitted timely and in good faith is in a form that does not comply with this Rule or with Rule 33 or Rule 34, the Clerk will return it with a letter indicating the deficiency. A corrected petition received no more than 60 days after the date of the Clerk's letter will be deemed timely.

RULE 15. BRIEFS IN OPPOSITION; REPLY BRIEFS; SUPPLEMENTAL BRIEFS

1. A brief in opposition to the petition for a writ of certiorari may be filed by the respondent in any case, but is not mandatory except in a capital case, see Rule 14.1(a) or when ordered by the Court.

2. A brief in opposition should be stated briefly and in plain terms and may not exceed the page limitations specified in Rule 33. In addition to presenting other arguments for denying the petition, the brief in opposition should address any perceived misstatement of fact or law in the petition that bears on what issues properly would be before the Court if certiorari were granted. Counsel are admonished that they have an obligation to the Court to point out in the brief in opposition, and not later, any perceived misstatement made in the petition. Any objection to consideration of a question presented based on what occurred in the proceedings below, if the objection does not go to jurisdiction, may be deemed waived unless called to the Court's attention in the brief in opposition.

3. Any brief in opposition shall be filed within 30 days after the case is placed on the docket, unless the time is extended by the Court or a Justice, or by the Clerk under Rule 30.4. Forty copies shall be filed, except that a respondent proceeding *in forma pauperis* under Rule 39, including an inmate of an institution, shall file the number of copies required for a petition by such a person under Rule 12.2, together with a motion for leave to proceed *in forma pauperis,* a copy of which shall precede and be attached to each copy of the brief in opposition. If the petitioner is proceeding *in forma pauperis,* the respondent may file an original and 10 copies of a brief in opposition prepared as required by Rule 33.2. Whether prepared under Rule 33.1 or Rule 33.2, the brief in opposition shall comply with the requirements of Rule 24 governing a respondent's brief, except that no summary of the argument is required. A brief in opposition may not be joined with any other pleading, except that any motion for leave to proceed *in forma pauperis* shall be attached. The brief in opposition shall be served as required by Rule 29.

4. No motion by a respondent to dismiss a petition for a writ of certiorari may be filed. Any objections to the jurisdiction of the Court to grant a petition for a writ of certiorari shall be included in the brief in opposition.

5. The Clerk will distribute the petition to the Court for its consideration upon receiving an express waiver of the right to file a brief in opposition, or, if no waiver or brief in opposition is filed, upon the expiration of the time allowed for filing. If a brief in opposition is timely filed, the Clerk will distribute the petition, brief in opposition, and any reply brief to the Court for its consideration no less than 10 days after the brief in opposition is filed.

6. Any petitioner may file a reply brief addressed to new points raised in the brief in opposition, but distribution and consideration by the Court under paragraph 5 of this Rule will not be deferred pending its receipt. Forty copies shall be filed, except that petitioner proceeding *in forma pauperis* under Rule 39, including an inmate of an institution, shall file the number of copies required for a petition by such a person under Rule 12.2. The reply brief shall be served as required by Rule 29.

7. If a cross-petition for a writ of certiorari has been docketed, distribution of both petitions will be deferred until the cross-petition is due for distribution under this Rule.

8. Any party may file a supplemental brief at any time while a petition for a writ of certiorari is pending, calling attention to new cases, new legislation, or other intervening matter not available at the time of the party's last filing. A supplemental brief shall be restricted to new matter and shall follow, insofar as applicable, the form for a brief in opposition prescribed by this Rule. Forty copies shall be filed, except that a party proceeding *in forma pauperis* under Rule 39, including an inmate of an institution, shall file the number of copies required for a petition by such a person under Rule 12.2. The supplemental brief shall be served as required by Rule 29.

RULE 16. DISPOSITION OF A PETITION FOR A WRIT OF CERTIORARI

1. After considering the documents distributed under Rule 15, the Court will enter an appropriate order. The order may be a summary disposition on the merits.

2. Whenever the Court grants a petition for a writ of certiorari, the Clerk will prepare, sign, and enter an order to that effect and will notify forthwith counsel of record and the court whose judgment is to be reviewed. The case then will be scheduled for briefing and oral argument. If the record has not previously been filed in this Court, the Clerk will request the clerk of the court having possession of the record to certify and transmit it. A formal writ will not issue unless specially directed.

3. Whenever the Court denies a petition for a writ of certiorari, the Clerk will prepare, sign, and enter an order to that effect and will notify forthwith counsel of record and the court whose judgment was sought to be reviewed. The order of denial will not be suspended pending disposition of a petition for rehearing except by order of the Court or a Justice.

PART IV. OTHER JURISDICTION

RULE 17. PROCEDURE IN AN ORIGINAL ACTION

1. This Rule applies only to an action invoking the Court's original jurisdiction under Article III of the Constitution of the United States. See also 28 U.S.C. §1251 and U.S. Const., Amdt. 11. A petition for an extraordinary writ in aid of the Court's appellate jurisdiction shall be filed as provided in Rule 20.

2. The form of pleadings and motions prescribed by the Federal Rules of Civil Procedure is followed. In other respects, those Rules and the Federal Rules of Evidence may be taken as guides.

3. The initial pleading shall be preceded by a motion for leave to file, and may be accompanied by a brief in support of the motion. Forty copies of each document shall be filed, with proof of service. Service shall be as required by Rule 29, except that when an adverse party is a State, service shall be made on both the Governor and the Attorney General of that State.

4. The case will be placed on the docket when the motion for leave to file and the initial pleading are filed with the Clerk. The Rule 38(a) docket fee shall be paid at that time.

5. No more than 60 days after receiving the motion for leave to file and the initial pleading, an adverse party shall file 40 copies of any brief in opposition to the motion, with proof of service as required by Rule 29. The Clerk will distribute the filed documents to the Court for its consideration upon receiving an express waiver of the right to file a brief in opposition, or, if no waiver or brief is filed, upon the expiration of the time allowed for filing. If a brief in opposition is timely filed, the Clerk will distribute the filed documents to the Court for its consideration no less than 10 days after the brief in opposition is filed. A reply brief may be filed, but consideration of the case will not be deferred pending its receipt. The Court thereafter may grant or deny the motion, set it for oral argument, direct that additional documents be filed, or require that other proceedings be conducted.

6. A summons issued out of this Court shall be served on the defendant 60 days before the return day specified therein. If the defendant does not respond by the return day, the plaintiff may proceed *ex parte*.

7. Process against a State issued out of this Court shall be served on both the Governor and the Attorney General of that State.

RULE 18. APPEAL FROM A UNITED STATES DISTRICT COURT

1. When a direct appeal from a decision of a United States district court is authorized by law, the appeal is commenced by filing a notice of appeal with the clerk of the district court within the time provided by law after entry of the judgment sought to be reviewed. The time to file may not be extended. The notice of appeal shall specify the parties taking the appeal, designate the judgment, or part thereof, appealed from and the date of its entry, and specify the statute or statutes under which the appeal is taken. A copy of the notice of appeal shall be served on all parties to the proceeding as required by Rule 29, and proof of service shall be filed in the district court together with the notice of appeal.

2. All parties to the proceeding in the district court are deemed parties entitled to file documents in this Court, but a party having no interest in the outcome of the appeal may so notify the Clerk of this Court and shall serve a copy of the notice on all other parties. Parties interested jointly, severally, or otherwise in the judgment may appeal separately, or any two or more may join in an appeal. When two or more judgments involving identical or closely related questions are sought to be reviewed on appeal from the same court, a notice of appeal for each judgment shall be filed with the clerk of the district court, but a single jurisdictional statement covering all the judgments suffices. Parties who file no document will not qualify for any relief from this Court.

3. No more than 60 days after filing the notice of appeal in the district court, the appellant shall file 40 copies of a jurisdictional statement and shall pay the Rule 38 docket fee, except that an appellant proceeding *in forma pauperis* under Rule 39, including an inmate of an institution, shall file the number of copies required for a petition by such a person under Rule 12.2, together with a motion for leave to proceed *in forma pauperis*, a copy of which shall precede and be attached to each copy of the jurisdictional statement. The jurisdictional statement shall follow, insofar as applicable, the form for a petition for a writ of certiorari prescribed by Rule 14, and shall be served as required by Rule 29. The appendix shall include a copy of the notice of appeal showing the date it was filed in the district court. For good cause, a Justice may extend the time to file a jurisdictional statement for a period not exceeding 60 days. An application to extend the time to file a jurisdictional statement shall set out the basis for jurisdiction in this Court; identify the judgment sought to be reviewed; include a copy of the opinion, any order respecting rehearing, and the notice of

appeal; and set out specific reasons why an extension of time is justified. For the time and manner of presenting the application, see Rules 21, 22, and 30. An application to extend the time to file a jurisdictional statement is not favored.

4. No more than 30 days after a case has been placed on the docket, an appellee seeking to file a conditional cross-appeal (*i.e.*, a cross-appeal that otherwise would be untimely) shall file, with proof of service as required by Rule 29, a jurisdictional statement that complies in all respects (including number of copies filed) with paragraph 3 of this Rule, except that material already reproduced in the appendix to the opening jurisdictional statement need not be reproduced again. A cross-appealing appellee shall pay the Rule 38 docket fee or submit a motion for leave to proceed *in forma pauperis.* The cover of the cross-appeal shall indicate clearly that it is a conditional cross-appeal. The cross-appeal then will be placed on the docket. It is the cross-appellant's duty to notify all cross-appellees promptly, on a form supplied by the Clerk, of the date of filing, the date the cross-appeal was placed on the docket, and the docket number of the cross-appeal. The notice shall be served as required by Rule 29. A cross-appeal may not be joined with any other pleading, except that any motion for leave to proceed *in forma pauperis* shall be attached. The time to file a cross-appeal will not be extended.

5. After a notice of appeal has been filed in the district court, but before the case is placed on this Court's docket, the parties may dismiss the appeal by stipulation filed in the district court, or the district court may dismiss the appeal on the appellant's motion, with notice to all parties. If a notice of appeal has been filed, but the case has not been placed on this Court's docket within the time prescribed for docketing, the district court may dismiss the appeal on the appellee's motion, with notice to all parties, and may make any just order with respect to costs. If the district court has denied the appellee's motion to dismiss the appeal, the appellee may move this Court to docket and dismiss the appeal by filing an original and 10 copies of a motion presented in conformity with Rules 21 and 33.2. The motion shall be accompanied by proof of service as required by Rule 29, and by a certificate from the clerk of the district court, certifying that a notice of appeal was filed and that the appellee's motion to dismiss was denied. The appellant may not thereafter file a jurisdictional statement without special leave of the Court, and the Court may allow costs against the appellant.

6. Within 30 days after the case is placed on this Court's docket, the appellee may file a motion to dismiss, to affirm, or in the alternative to affirm or dismiss. Forty copies of the motion shall be filed, except that an appellee proceeding *in forma pauperis* under Rule 39, including an inmate of an institution, shall file the number of copies required for a petition by such a person under Rule 12.2, together with a motion for leave to proceed *in forma pauperis,* a copy of which shall precede and be attached to each copy of the motion to dismiss, to affirm, or in the alternative to affirm or dismiss. The motion shall follow, insofar as applicable, the form for a brief in opposition prescribed by Rule 15, and shall comply in all respects with Rule 21.

7. The Clerk will distribute the jurisdictional statement to the Court for its consideration upon receiving an express waiver of the right to file a motion to dismiss or to affirm or, if no waiver or motion is filed, upon the expiration of the time allowed for filing. If a motion to dismiss or to affirm is timely filed, the Clerk will distribute the jurisdictional statement, motion, and any brief opposing the motion to the Court for its consideration no less than 10 days after the motion is filed.

8. Any appellant may file a brief opposing a motion to dismiss or to affirm, but distribution and consideration by the Court under paragraph 7 of this Rule will not be deferred pending its receipt. Forty copies shall be filed, except that an appellant proceeding *in forma pauperis* under Rule 39, including an inmate of an institution, shall file the number of copies required for a petition by such a person under Rule 12.2. The brief shall be served as required by Rule 29.

9. If a cross-appeal has been docketed, distribution of both jurisdictional statements will be deferred until the cross-appeal is due for distribution under this Rule.

10. Any party may file a supplemental brief at any time while a jurisdictional statement is pending, calling attention to new cases, new legislation, or other intervening matter not available at the time of the party's last filing. A supplemental brief shall be restricted to new matter and shall follow, insofar as applicable, the form for a brief in opposition prescribed by Rule 15. Forty copies shall be filed, except that a party proceeding *in forma pauperis* under Rule 39, including an inmate of an institution, shall file the number of copies required for a petition by such a person under Rule 12.2. The supplemental brief shall be served as required by Rule 29.

11. The clerk of the district court shall retain possession of the record until notified by the Clerk of this Court to certify and transmit it. See Rule 12.7.

12. After considering the documents distributed under this Rule, the Court may dispose summarily of the appeal on the merits, note probable jurisdiction, or postpone consideration of jurisdiction until a hearing of the case on the merits. If not disposed of summarily, the case stands for briefing and oral argument on the merits. If consideration of jurisdiction is postponed, counsel, at the outset of their briefs and at oral argument, shall address the question of jurisdiction. If the record has not previously been filed in this Court, the Clerk of this Court will request the clerk of the court in possession of the record to certify and transmit it.

13. If the Clerk determines that a jurisdictional statement submitted timely and in good faith is in a form that does not comply with this Rule or with Rule 33 or Rule 34, the Clerk will return it with a letter indicating the deficiency. If a corrected jurisdictional statement is received no more than 60 days after the date of the Clerk's letter, its filing will be deemed timely.

RULE 19. PROCEDURE ON A CERTIFIED QUESTION

1. A United States court of appeals may certify to this Court a question or proposition of law on which it seeks instruction for the proper decision of a case. The certificate shall contain a statement of the nature of the case and the facts on which the question or proposition of law arises. Only questions or propositions of law may be certified, and they shall be stated separately and with precision. The certificate shall be prepared as required by Rule 33.2 and shall be signed by the clerk of the court of appeals.

2. When a question is certified by a United States court of appeals, this Court, on its own motion or that of a party, may consider and decide the entire matter in controversy. See 28 U.S.C. §1254(2).

3. When a question is certified, the Clerk will notify the parties and docket the case. Counsel shall then enter their appearances. After docketing, the Clerk will submit the certificate to the Court for a preliminary examination to determine whether the case should be briefed, set for argument, or dismissed. No brief may be filed until the preliminary examination of the certificate is completed.

4. If the Court orders the case briefed or set for argument, the parties will be notified and permitted to file briefs. The Clerk of this Court then will request the clerk of the court in possession of the record to certify and transmit it. Any portion of the record to which the parties wish to direct the Court's particular attention should be printed in a joint appendix, prepared in conformity with Rule 26 by

the appellant or petitioner in the court of appeals, but the fact that any part of the record has not been printed does not prevent the parties or the Court from relying on it.

5. A brief on the merits in a case involving a certified question shall comply with Rules 24, 25, and 33.1, except that the brief for the party who is the appellant or petitioner below shall be filed within 45 days of the order requiring briefs or setting the case for argument.

RULE 20. PROCEDURE ON A PETITION FOR AN EXTRAORDINARY WRIT

1. Issuance by the Court of an extraordinary writ authorized by 28 U.S.C. §1651(a) is not a matter of right, but of discretion sparingly exercised. To justify the granting of any such writ, the petition must show that the writ will be in aid of the Court's appellate jurisdiction, that exceptional circumstances warrant the exercise of the Court's discretionary powers, and that adequate relief cannot be obtained in any other form or from any other court.

2. A petition seeking a writ authorized by 28 U.S.C. §1651(a), §2241, or §2254(a) shall be prepared in all respects as required by Rules 33 and 34. The petition shall be captioned "*In re* [name of petitioner]" and shall follow, insofar as applicable, the form of a petition for a writ of certiorari prescribed by Rule 14. All contentions in support of the petition shall be included in the petition. The case will be placed on the docket when 40 copies of the petition are filed with the Clerk and the docket fee is paid, except that a petitioner proceeding *in forma pauperis* under Rule 39, including an inmate of an institution, shall file the number of copies required for a petition by such a person under Rule 12.2, together with a motion for leave to proceed *in forma pauperis,* a copy of which shall precede and be attached to each copy of the petition. The petition shall be served as required by Rule 29 (subject to subparagraph 4(b) of this Rule).

3. (a) A petition seeking a writ of prohibition, a writ of mandamus, or both in the alternative shall state the name and office or function of every person against whom relief is sought and shall set out with particularity why the relief sought is not available in any other court. A copy of the judgment with respect to which the writ is sought, including any related opinion, shall be appended to the petition together with any other document essential to understanding the petition.

(b) The petition shall be served on every party to the proceeding with respect to which relief is sought. Within 30 days after the petition is placed on the docket, a party shall file 40 copies of any brief or briefs in opposition thereto, which shall comply fully with Rule 15. If a party named as a respondent does not wish to respond to the petition, that party may so advise the Clerk and all other parties by letter. All persons served are deemed respondents for all purposes in the proceedings in this Court.

4. (a) A petition seeking a writ of habeas corpus shall comply with the requirements of 28 U.S.C. §§2241 and 2242, and in particular with the provision in the last paragraph of §2242, which requires a statement of the "reasons for not making application to the district court of the district in which the applicant is held." If the relief sought is from the judgment of a state court, the petition shall set out specifically how and where the petitioner has exhausted available remedies in the state courts or otherwise comes within the provisions of 28 U.S.C. §2254(b). To justify the granting of a writ of habeas corpus, the petitioner must show that exceptional circumstances warrant the exercise of the Court's discretionary powers, and that adequate relief cannot be obtained in any other form or from any other court. This writ is rarely granted.

(b) Habeas corpus proceedings are *ex parte,* unless the Court requires the respondent to show cause why the petition for a writ of habeas corpus should not be granted. A response, if ordered, shall comply fully with Rule 15. Neither the denial of the petition, without more, nor an order of transfer to a district court under the authority of 28 U.S.C. §2241(b), is an adjudication on the merits, and therefore does not preclude further application to another court for the relief sought.

5. The Clerk will distribute the documents to the Court for its consideration when a brief in opposition under subparagraph 3(b) of this Rule has been filed, when a response under subparagraph 4(b) has been ordered and filed, when the time to file has expired, or when the right to file has been expressly waived.

6. If the Court orders the case set for argument, the Clerk will notify the parties whether additional briefs are required, when they shall be filed, and, if the case involves a petition for a common-law writ of certiorari, that the parties shall prepare a joint appendix in accordance with Rule 26.

PART V. MOTIONS AND APPLICATIONS
RULE 21. MOTIONS TO THE COURT

1. Every motion to the Court shall clearly state its purpose and the facts on which it is based and may present legal argument in support thereof. No separate brief may be filed. A motion should be concise and shall comply with any applicable page limits. Rule 22 governs an application addressed to a single Justice.

2. (a) A motion in any action within the Court's original jurisdiction shall comply with Rule 17.3.

(b) A motion to dismiss as moot (or a suggestion of mootness), a motion for leave to file a brief as *amicus curiae,* and any motion the granting of which would dispose of the entire case or would affect the final judgment to be entered (other than a motion to docket and dismiss under Rule 18.5 or a motion for voluntary dismissal under Rule 46) shall be prepared as required by Rule 33.1, and 40 copies shall be filed, except that a movant proceeding *in forma pauperis* under Rule 39, including an inmate of an institution, shall file a motion prepared as required by Rule 33.2, and shall file the number of copies required for a petition by such a person under Rule 12.2. The motion shall be served as required by Rule 29.

(c) Any other motion to the Court shall be prepared as required by Rule 33.2; the moving party shall file an original and 10 copies. The Court subsequently may order the moving party to prepare the motion as required by Rule 33.1; in that event, the party shall file 40 copies.

3. A motion to the Court shall be filed with the Clerk and shall be accompanied by proof of service as required by Rule 29. No motion may be presented in open Court, other than a motion for admission to the Bar, except when the proceeding to which it refers is being argued. Oral argument on a motion will not be permitted unless the Court so directs.

4. Any response to a motion shall be filed as promptly as possible considering the nature of the relief sought and any asserted need for emergency action, and, in any event, within 10 days of receipt, unless the Court or a Justice, or the Clerk under Rule 30.4, orders otherwise. A response to a motion prepared as required by Rule 33.1 shall be prepared in the same manner if time permits. In an appropriate case, the Court may act on a motion without waiting for a response.

RULE 22. APPLICATIONS TO INDIVIDUAL JUSTICES

1. An application addressed to an individual Justice shall be filed with the Clerk, who will transmit it promptly to the Justice concerned if an individual Justice has authority to grant the sought relief.

2. The original and two copies of any application addressed to an individual Justice shall be prepared as required by Rule 33.2, and shall be accompanied by proof of service as required by Rule 29.

3. An application shall be addressed to the Justice allotted to the Circuit from which the case arises. When the Circuit Justice is unavailable for any reason, the application addressed to that Justice will be distributed to the Justice then available who is next junior to the Circuit Justice; the turn of the Chief Justice follows that of the most junior Justice.

4. A Justice denying an application will note the denial thereon. Thereafter, unless action thereon is restricted by law to the Circuit Justice or is untimely under Rule 30.2, the party making an application, except in the case of an application for an extension of time, may renew it to any other Justice, subject to the provisions of this Rule. Except when the denial is without prejudice, a renewed application is not favored. Renewed application is made by a letter to the Clerk, designating the Justice to whom the application is to be directed, and accompanied by 10 copies of the original application and proof of service as required by Rule 29.

5. A Justice to whom an application for a stay or for bail is submitted may refer it to the Court for determination.

6. The Clerk will advise all parties concerned, by appropriately speedy means, of the disposition made of an application.

RULE 23. STAYS

1. A stay may be granted by a Justice as permitted by law.

2. A party to a judgment sought to be reviewed may present to a Justice an application to stay the enforcement of that judgment. See 28 U.S.C. §2101(f).

3. An application for a stay shall set out with particularity why the relief sought is not available from any other court or judge. Except in the most extraordinary circumstances, an application for a stay will not be entertained unless the relief requested was first sought in the appropriate court or courts below or from a judge or judges thereof. An application for a stay shall identify the judgment sought to be reviewed and have appended thereto a copy of the order and opinion, if any, and a copy of the order, if any, of the court or judge below denying the relief sought, and shall set out specific reasons why a stay is justified. The form and content of an application for a stay are governed by Rules 22 and 33.2.

4. A judge, court, or Justice granting an application for a stay pending review by this Court may condition the stay on the filing of a supersedeas bond having an approved surety or sureties. The bond will be conditioned on the satisfaction of the judgment in full, together with any costs, interest, and damages for delay that may be awarded. If a part of the judgment sought to be reviewed has already been satisfied, or is otherwise secured, the bond may be conditioned on the satisfaction of the part of the judgment not otherwise secured or satisfied, together with costs, interest, and damages.

PART VI. BRIEFS ON THE MERITS AND ORAL ARGUMENT

RULE 24. BRIEFS ON THE MERITS: IN GENERAL

1. A brief on the merits for a petitioner or an appellant shall comply in all respects with Rules 33.1 and 34 and shall contain in the order here indicated:

(a) The questions presented for review under Rule 14.1(a). The questions shall be set out on the first page following the cover, and no other information may appear on that page. The phrasing of the questions presented need not be identical with that in the petition for a writ of certiorari or the jurisdictional statement, but the brief may not raise additional questions or change the substance of the questions already presented in those documents. At its option, however, the Court may consider a plain error not among the questions presented but evident from the record and otherwise within its jurisdiction to decide.

(b) A list of all parties to the proceeding in the court whose judgment is under review (unless the caption of the case in this Court contains the names of all parties). Any amended list of parent companies and nonwholly owned subsidiaries as required by Rule 29.6 shall be placed here.

(c) If the brief exceeds five pages, a table of contents and a table of cited authorities.

(d) Citations of the official and unofficial reports of the opinions and orders entered in the case by courts and administrative agencies.

(e) A concise statement of the basis for jurisdiction in this Court, including the statutory provisions and time factors on which jurisdiction rests.

(f) The constitutional provisions, treaties, statutes, ordinances, and regulations involved in the case, set out verbatim with appropriate citation. If the provisions involved are lengthy, their citation alone suffices at this point, and their pertinent text, if not already set out in the petition for a writ of certiorari, jurisdictional statement, or an appendix to either document, shall be set out in an appendix to the brief.

(g) A concise statement of the case, setting out the facts material to the consideration of the questions presented, with appropriate references to the joint appendix, e.g., App. 12, or to the record, e.g., Record 12.

(h) A summary of the argument, suitably paragraphed. The summary should be a clear and concise condensation of the argument made in the body of the brief; mere repetition of the headings under which the argument is arranged is not sufficient.

(i) The argument, exhibiting clearly the points of fact and of law presented and citing the authorities and statutes relied on.

(j) A conclusion specifying with particularity the relief the party seeks.

2. A brief on the merits for a respondent or an appellee shall conform to the foregoing requirements, except that items required by subparagraphs 1(a), (b), (d), (e), (f), and (g) of this Rule need not be included unless the respondent or appellee is dissatisfied with their presentation by the opposing party.

3. A brief on the merits may not exceed the page limitations specified in Rule 33.1(g). An appendix to a brief may include only relevant material, and counsel are cautioned not to include in an appendix arguments or citations that properly belong in the body of the brief.

4. A reply brief shall conform to those portions of this Rule applicable to the brief for a respondent or an appellee, but, if appropriately divided by topical headings, need not contain a summary of the argument.

5. A reference to the joint appendix or to the record set out in any brief shall indicate the appropriate page number. If the reference is to an exhibit, the page numbers at which the exhibit appears, at which it was offered in evidence, and at which it was ruled on by the judge shall be indicated, e.g., Pl. Exh. 14, Record 199, 2134.

6. A brief shall be concise, logically arranged with proper headings, and free of irrelevant, immaterial, or scandalous matter. The Court may disregard or strike a brief that does not comply with this paragraph.

RULE 25. BRIEFS ON THE MERITS: NUMBER OF COPIES AND TIME TO FILE

1. The petitioner or appellant shall file 40 copies of the brief on the merits within 45 days of the order granting the writ of certiorari, noting probable jurisdiction, or postponing consideration of jurisdiction.

2. The respondent or appellee shall file 40 copies of the brief on the merits within 30 days after receiving the brief for the petitioner or appellant.

3. The petitioner or appellant shall file 40 copies of the reply brief, if any, within 30 days after receiving the brief for the respondent or appellee, but any reply brief must actually be received by the Clerk no more than one week before the date of oral argument.

4. The time periods stated in paragraphs 1 and 2 of this Rule may be extended as provided in Rule 30. An application to extend the time to file a brief on the merits is not favored. If a case is advanced for hearing, the time to file briefs on the merits may be abridged as circumstances require pursuant to an order of the Court on its own motion or that of a party.

5. A party wishing to present late authorities, newly enacted legislation, or other intervening matter that was not available in time to be included in a brief may file 40 copies of a supplemental brief, restricted to such new matter and otherwise presented in conformity with these Rules, up to the time the case is called for oral argument or by leave of the Court thereafter.

6. After a case has been argued or submitted, the Clerk will not file any brief, except that of a party filed by leave of the Court.

7. The Clerk will not file any brief that is not accompanied by proof of service as required by Rule 29.

RULE 26. JOINT APPENDIX

1. Unless the Clerk has allowed the parties to use the deferred method described in paragraph 4 of this Rule, the petitioner or appellant, within 45 days after entry of the order granting the writ of certiorari, noting probable jurisdiction, or postponing consideration of jurisdiction, shall file 40 copies of a joint appendix, prepared as required by Rule 33.1. The joint appendix shall contain: (1) the relevant docket entries in all the courts below; (2) any relevant pleadings, jury instructions, findings, conclusions, or opinions; (3) the judgment, order, or decision under review; and (4) any other parts of the record that the parties particularly wish to bring to the Court's attention. Any of the foregoing items already reproduced in a petition for a writ of certiorari, jurisdictional statement, brief in opposition to a petition for a writ of certiorari, motion to dismiss or affirm, or any appendix to the foregoing, that was prepared as required by Rule 33.1, need not be reproduced again in the joint appendix. The petitioner or appellant shall serve three copies of the joint appendix on each of the other parties to the proceeding as required by Rule 29.

2. The parties are encouraged to agree on the contents of the joint appendix. In the absence of agreement, the petitioner or appellant, within 10 days after entry of the order granting the writ of certiorari, noting probable jurisdiction, or postponing consideration of jurisdiction, shall serve on the respondent or appellee a designation of parts of the record to be included in the joint appendix. Within 10 days after receiving the designation, a respondent or appellee who considers the parts of the record so designated insufficient shall serve on the petitioner or appellant a designation of additional parts to be included in the joint appendix, and the petitioner or appellant shall include the parts so designated. If the Court has permitted the respondent or appellee to proceed *in forma pauperis,* the petitioner or appellant may seek by motion to be excused from printing portions of the record the petitioner or appellant considers unnecessary. In making these designations, counsel should include only those materials the Court should examine; unnecessary designations should be avoided. The record is on file with the Clerk and available to the Justices, and counsel may refer in briefs and in oral argument to relevant portions of the record not included in the joint appendix.

3. When the joint appendix is filed, the petitioner or appellant immediately shall file with the Clerk a statement of the cost of printing 50 copies and shall serve a copy of the statement on each of the other parties as required by Rule 29. Unless the parties agree otherwise, the cost of producing the joint appendix shall be paid initially by the petitioner or appellant; but a petitioner or appellant who considers that parts of the record designated by the respondent or appellee are unnecessary for the determination of the issues presented may so advise the respondent or appellee, who then shall advance the cost of printing the additional parts, unless the Court or a Justice otherwise fixes the initial allocation of the costs. The cost of printing the joint appendix is taxed as a cost in the case, but if a party unnecessarily causes matter to be included in the joint appendix or prints excessive copies, the Court may impose these costs on that party.

4. (a) On the parties' request, the Clerk may allow preparation of the joint appendix to be deferred until after the briefs have been filed. In that event, the petitioner or appellant shall file the joint appendix no more than 14 days after receiving the brief for the respondent or appellee. The provisions of paragraphs 1, 2, and 3 of this Rule shall be followed, except that the designations referred to therein shall be made by each party when that party's brief is served. Deferral of the joint appendix is not favored.

(b) If the deferred method is used, the briefs on the merits may refer to the pages of the record. In that event, the joint appendix shall include in brackets on each page thereof the page number of the record where that material may be found. A party wishing to refer directly to the pages of the joint appendix may serve and file copies of its brief prepared as required by Rule 33.2 within the time provided by Rule 25, with appropriate references to the pages of the record. In that event, within 10 days after the joint appendix is filed, copies of the brief prepared as required by Rule 33.1 containing references to the pages of the joint appendix in place of, or in addition to, the initial references to the pages of the record, shall be served and filed. No other change may be made in the brief as initially served and filed, except that typographical errors may be corrected.

5. The joint appendix shall be prefaced by a table of contents showing the parts of the record that it contains, in the order in which the parts are set out, with references to the pages of the joint appendix at which each part begins. The relevant docket entries shall be set out after the table of contents, followed by the other parts of the record in chronological order. When testimony contained in the reporter's transcript of proceedings is set out in the joint appendix, the page of the transcript at which the testimony appears shall be indicated in brackets immediately before the statement that is set out. Omissions in the transcript or in any other document printed in the joint appendix shall be indicated by asterisks. Immaterial formal matters (*e.g.,* captions, subscriptions, acknowledgments) shall be omitted. A question and its answer may be contained in a single paragraph.

6. Exhibits designated for inclusion in the joint appendix may be contained in a separate volume or volumes suitably indexed. The transcript of a proceeding before an administrative agency, board, commission, or officer used in an action in a district court or court of appeals is regarded as an exhibit for the purposes of this paragraph.

7. The Court, on its own motion or that of a party, may dispense with the requirement of a joint appendix and may permit a case to be heard on the original record (with such copies of the record, or relevant parts thereof, as the Court may require) or on the appendix used

in the court below, if it conforms to the requirements of this Rule. 8. For good cause, the time limits specified in this Rule may be shortened or extended by the Court or a Justice, or by the Clerk under Rule 30.4.

RULE 27. THE CALENDAR

1. From time to time, the Clerk will prepare a calendar of cases ready for argument. A case ordinarily will not be called for argument less than two weeks after the brief on the merits for the respondent or appellee is due.

2. The Clerk will advise counsel when they are required to appear for oral argument and will publish a hearing list in advance of each argument session for the convenience of counsel and the information of the public.

3. The Court, on its own motion or that of a party, may order that two or more cases involving the same or related questions be argued together as one case or on such other terms as the Court may prescribe.

RULE 28. ORAL ARGUMENT

1. Oral argument should emphasize and clarify the written arguments in the briefs on the merits. Counsel should assume that all Justices have read the briefs before oral argument. Oral argument read from a prepared text is not favored.

2. The petitioner or appellant shall open and may conclude the argument. A cross writ of certiorari or cross-appeal will be argued with the initial writ of certiorari or appeal as one case in the time allowed for that one case, and the Court will advise the parties who shall open and close.

3. Unless the Court directs otherwise, each side is allowed one-half hour for argument. Counsel is not required to use all the allotted time. Any request for additional time to argue shall be presented by motion under Rule 21 no more than 15 days after the petitioner's or appellant's brief on the merits is filed, and shall set out specifically and concisely why the case cannot be presented within the half hour limitation. Additional time is rarely accorded.

4. Only one attorney will be heard for each side, except by leave of the Court on motion filed no more than 15 days after the respondent's or appellee's brief on the merits is filed. Any request for divided argument shall be presented by motion under Rule 21 and shall set out specifically and concisely why more than one attorney should be allowed to argue. Divided argument is not favored.

5. Regardless of the number of counsel participating in oral argument, counsel making the opening argument shall present the case fairly and completely and not reserve points of substance for rebuttal.

6. Oral argument will not be allowed on behalf of any party for whom a brief has not been filed.

7. By leave of the Court, and subject to paragraph 4 of this Rule, counsel for an *amicus curiae* whose brief has been filed as provided in Rule 37 may argue orally on the side of a party, with the consent of that party. In the absence of consent, counsel for an *amicus curiae* may seek leave of the Court to argue orally by a motion setting out specifically and concisely why oral argument would provide assistance to the Court not otherwise available. Such a motion will be granted only in the most extraordinary circumstances.

PART VII. PRACTICE AND PROCEDURE
RULE 29. FILING AND SERVICE OF DOCUMENTS SPECIAL NOTIFICATIONS; CORPORATE LISTING

1. Any document required or permitted to be presented to the Court or to a Justice shall be filed with the Clerk.

2. A document is timely filed if it is sent to the Clerk through the United States Postal Service by first-class mail (including express or priority mail), postage prepaid, and bears a postmark showing that the document was mailed on or before the last day for filing. Commercial postage meter labels alone are not acceptable. If submitted by an inmate confined in an institution, a document is timely filed if it is deposited in the institution's internal mail system on or before the last day for filing and is accompanied by a notarized statement or declaration in compliance with 28 U.S.C. §1746 setting out the date of deposit and stating that first-class postage has been prepaid. If the postmark is missing or not legible, the Clerk will require the person who mailed the document to submit a notarized statement or declaration in compliance with 28 U.S.C. §1746 setting out the details of the mailing and stating that the mailing took place on a particular date within the permitted time. A document also is timely filed if it is forwarded through a private delivery or courier service and is actually received by the Clerk within the time permitted for filing.

3. Any document required by these Rules to be served may be served personally or by mail on each party to the proceeding at or before the time of filing. If the document has been prepared as required by Rule 33.1, three copies shall be served on each other party separately represented in the proceeding. If the document has been prepared as required by Rule 33.2, service of a single copy on each other separately represented party suffices. If personal service is made, it shall consist of delivery at the office of the counsel of record, either to counsel or to an employee therein. If service is by mail, it shall consist of depositing the document with the United States Postal Service, with no less than first-class postage prepaid, addressed to counsel of record at the proper post office address. When a party is not represented by counsel, service shall be made on the party, personally or by mail.

4.(a) If the United States or any federal department, office, agency, officer, or employee is a party to be served, service shall be made on the Solicitor General of the United States, Room 5614, Department of Justice, 10th St. and Constitution Ave., N.W., Washington, DC 20530. When an agency of the United States that is a party is authorized by law to appear before this Court on its own behalf, or when an officer or employee of the United States is a party, the agency, officer, or employee shall be served in addition to the Solicitor General.

(b) In any proceeding in this Court in which the constitutionality of an Act of Congress is drawn into question, and neither the United States nor any federal department, office, agency, officer, or employee is a party, the initial document filed in this Court shall recite that 28 U.S.C. §2403(a) may apply and shall be served on the Solicitor General of the United States, Room 5614, Department of Justice, 10th St. and Constitution Ave., N.W., Washington, DC 20530. In such a proceeding from any court of the United States, as defined by 28 U.S.C. §451, the initial document also shall state whether that court, pursuant to 28 U.S.C. §2403(a), certified to the Attorney General the fact that the constitutionality of an Act of Congress was drawn into question. See Rule 14.1(e)(v).

(c) In any proceeding in this Court in which the constitutionality of any statute of a State is drawn into question, and neither the State nor any agency, officer, or employee thereof is a party, the initial document filed in this Court shall recite that 28 U.S.C. §2403(b) may apply and shall be served on the Attorney General of that State. In such a proceeding from any court of the United States, as defined by 28 U.S.C. §451, the initial document also shall state whether that court, pursuant to 28 U.S.C. §2403(b), certified to the State Attorney General the fact that the constitutionality of a statute of that State was drawn into question. See Rule 14.1(e)(v).

5. Proof of service, when required by these Rules, shall accompany

the document when it is presented to the Clerk for filing and shall be separate from it. Proof of service shall contain, or be accompanied by, a statement that all parties required to be served have been served, together with a list of the names, addresses, and telephone numbers of counsel indicating the name of the party or parties each counsel represents. It is not necessary that service on each party required to be served be made in the same manner or evidenced by the same proof. Proof of service may consist of any one of the following:

(a) an acknowledgment of service, signed by counsel of record for the party served;

(b) a certificate of service, reciting the facts and circumstances of service in compliance with the appropriate paragraph or paragraphs of this Rule, and signed by a member of the Bar of this Court representing the party on whose behalf service is made or by an attorney appointed to represent that party under the Criminal Justice Act of 1964, see 18 U.S.C. §3006A(d)(6), or under any other applicable federal statute; or

(c) a notarized affidavit or declaration in compliance with 28 U.S.C. §1746, reciting the facts and circumstances of service in accordance with the appropriate paragraph or paragraphs of this Rule, whenever service is made by any person not a member of the Bar of this Court and not an attorney appointed to represent a party under the Criminal Justice Act of 1964, see 18 U.S.C. §3006A(d)(6), or under any other applicable federal statute.

6. Every document, except a joint appendix or *amicus curiae* brief, filed by or on behalf of one or more corporations shall list all parent companies and nonwholly owned subsidiaries of each of the corporate filers. If there is no parent or subsidiary company to be listed, a notation to this effect shall be included in the document. If a list has been included in a document filed earlier in the case, reference may be made to the earlier document (except when the earlier list appeared in an application for an extension of time or for a stay), and only amendments to the list to make it current need be included in the document being filed.

RULE 30. COMPUTATION AND EXTENSION OF TIME

1. In the computation of any period of time prescribed or allowed by these Rules, by order of the Court, or by an applicable statute, the day of the act, event, or default from which the designated period begins to run is not included. The last day of the period shall be included, unless it is a Saturday, Sunday, federal legal holiday listed in 5 U.S.C. §6103, or day on which the Court building is closed by order of the Court or the Chief Justice, in which event the period shall extend until the end of the next day that is not a Saturday, Sunday, federal legal holiday, or day on which the Court building is closed.

2. Whenever a Justice or the Clerk is empowered by law or these Rules to extend the time to file any document, an application seeking an extension shall be filed within the period sought to be extended. An application to extend the time to file a petition for a writ of certiorari or to file a jurisdictional statement must be received by the Clerk at least 10 days before the specified final filing date as computed under these Rules; if received less than 10 days before the final filing date, such application will not be granted except in the most extraordinary circumstances.

3. An application to extend the time to file a petition for a writ of certiorari, to file a jurisdictional statement, to file a reply brief on the merits, or to file a petition for rehearing shall be made to an individual Justice and presented and served on all other parties as provided by Rule 22. Once denied, such an application may not be renewed.

4. An application to extend the time to file any document or paper other than those specified in paragraph 3 of this Rule may be present-ed in the form of a letter to the Clerk setting out specific reasons why an extension of time is justified. The letter shall be served on all other parties as required by Rule 29. The application may be acted on by the Clerk in the first instance, and any party aggrieved by the Clerk's action may request that the application be submitted to a Justice or to the Court. The Clerk will report action under this paragraph to the Court as instructed.

RULE 31. TRANSLATIONS

Whenever any record to be transmitted to this Court contains material written in a foreign language without a translation made under the authority of the lower court, or admitted to be correct, the clerk of the court transmitting the record shall advise the Clerk of this Court immediately so that this Court may order that a translation be supplied and, if necessary, printed as part of the joint appendix.

RULE 32. MODELS, DIAGRAMS, AND EXHIBITS

1. Models, diagrams, and exhibits of material forming part of the evidence taken in a case and brought to this Court for its inspection shall be placed in the custody of the Clerk at least two weeks before the case is to be heard or submitted.

2. All models, diagrams, and exhibits of material placed in the custody of the Clerk shall be removed by the parties no more than 40 days after the case is decided. If this is not done, the Clerk will notify counsel to remove the articles forthwith. If they are not removed within a reasonable time thereafter, the Clerk will destroy them or dispose of them in any other appropriate way.

RULE 33. DOCUMENT PREPARATION: BOOKLET FORMAT; 8½- BY 11-INCH PAPER FORMAT

1. Booklet Format:

(a) Except for a document expressly permitted by these Rules to be submitted on 8½- by 11-inch paper, see, *e.g.*, Rules 21, 22, and 39, every document filed with the Court shall be prepared using typesetting (*e.g.*, word-processing, electronic publishing, or image setting) and reproduced by offset printing, photocopying, or similar process. The process used must produce a clear, black image on white paper.

(b) The text of every document, including any appendix thereto, except a document permitted to be produced on 8½- by 11-inch paper, shall be typeset in standard 11 point or larger type with 2 point or more leading between lines. The type size and face shall be no smaller than that contained in the United States Reports beginning with Volume 453. Type size and face shall be consistent throughout. No attempt should be made to reduce, compress, or condense the typeface in a manner that would increase the content of a document. Quotations in excess of three lines shall be indented. Footnotes shall appear in print as standard 9 point or larger type with 2 point or more leading between lines. The text of the document must appear on both sides of the page.

(c) Every document, except one permitted to be produced on 8½- by 11-inch paper, shall be produced on paper that is opaque, unglazed, 6⅛ by 9¼ inches in size, and not less than 60 pounds in weight, and shall have margins of at least three fourths of an inch on all sides. The text field, including footnotes, should be approximately 4⅛ by 7⅛ inches. The document shall be bound firmly in at least two places along the left margin (saddle stitch or perfect binding preferred) so as to permit easy opening, and no part of the text should be obscured by the binding. Spiral, plastic, metal, and string bindings may not be used. Copies of patent documents, except opinions, may be duplicated in such size as is necessary in a separate appendix.

(d) Every document, except one permitted to be produced on 8½-

by 11-inch paper, shall comply with the page limits shown on the chart in subparagraph 1(g) of this Rule. The page limits do not include the pages containing the questions presented, the list of parties and corporate affiliates of the filing party, the table of contents, the table of cited authorities, or any appendix. Verbatim quotations required under Rule 14.1(f), if set out in the text of a brief rather than in the appendix, are also excluded. For good cause, the Court or a Justice may grant leave to file a document in excess of the page limits, but application for such leave is not favored. An application to exceed page limits shall comply with Rule 22 and must be received by the Clerk at least 15 days before the filing date of the document in question, except in the most extraordinary circumstances.

(e) Every document, except one permitted to be produced on 8½- by 11-inch paper, shall have a suitable cover consisting of 65-pound weight paper in the color indicated on the chart in subparagraph 1(g) of this Rule. If a separate appendix to any document is filed, the color of its cover shall be the same as that of the cover of the document it supports. The Clerk will furnish a color chart upon request. Counsel shall ensure that there is adequate contrast between the printing and the color of the cover. A document filed by the United States, or by any other federal party represented by the Solicitor General, shall have a gray cover. A joint appendix, answer to a bill of complaint, motion for leave to intervene, and any other document not listed in subparagraph 1(g) of this Rule shall have a tan cover.

(f) Forty copies of a document prepared under this paragraph shall be filed.

(g) Page limits and cover colors for booklet-format documents are as follows [see table below]:

2. 8½- by 11-Inch Paper Format:

(a) The text of every document, including any appendix thereto, expressly permitted by these Rules to be presented to the Court on 8½- by 11-inch paper shall appear double spaced, except for indented quotations, which shall be single spaced, on opaque, unglazed, white paper. The document shall be stapled or bound at the upper left hand corner. Copies, if required, shall be produced on the same type of paper and shall be legible. The original of any such document (except a motion to dismiss or affirm under Rule 18.6) shall be signed by the party proceeding *pro se* or by counsel of record who must be a member of the Bar of this Court or an attorney appointed under the Criminal Justice Act of 1964, see 18 U.S.C. §3006A(d)(6), or under any other applicable federal statute. Subparagraph 1(g) of this Rule does not apply to documents prepared under this paragraph.

(b) Page limits for documents presented on 8½- by 11-inch paper are: 40 pages for a petition for a writ of certiorari, jurisdictional statement, petition for an extraordinary writ, brief in opposition, or motion to dismiss or affirm; and 15 pages for a reply to a brief in opposition, brief opposing a motion to dismiss or affirm, supplemental brief, or petition for rehearing. The page exclusions specified in subparagraph 1(d) of this Rule apply.

RULE 34. DOCUMENT PREPARATION: GENERAL REQUIREMENTS

Every document, whether prepared under Rule 33.1 or Rule 33.2, shall comply with the following provisions:

1. Each document shall bear on its cover, in the order indicated, from the top of the page:

(a) the docket number of the case or, if there is none, a space for one;

(b) the name of this Court;

(c) the October Term in which the document is filed (see Rule 3);

(d) the caption of the case as appropriate in this Court;

(e) the nature of the proceeding and the name of the court from which the action is brought (*e.g.,* "On Petition for Writ of Certiorari to the United States Court of Appeals for the Fifth Circuit"; or, for a

Type of Document	Page Limits	Color of Cover
i. Petition for a Writ of Certiorari (Rule 14); Motion for Leave to file a Bill of Complaint and Brief in Support (Rule 17.3); Jurisdictional Statement (Rule 18.3); Petition for an Extraordinary Writ (Rule 20.2)	30	white
ii. Brief in Opposition (Rule 15.3); Brief in Opposition to Motion for Leave to file an Original Action (Rule 17.5); Motion to Dismiss or Affirm (Rule 18.6); Brief in Opposition to Mandamus or Prohibition (Rule 20.3 (b)); Response to a Petition for Habeas Corpus (Rule 20.4)	30	orange
iii. Reply to Brief in Opposition (Rules 15.6 and 17.5); Brief Opposing a Motion to Dismiss or Affirm (Rule 18.8)	10	tan
iv. Supplemental Brief (Rules 15.8, 17, 18.10, and 25.5)	10	tan
v. Brief on the Merits by Petitioner or Appellant (Rule 24); Exceptions by Plaintiff to Report of Special Master (Rule 17)	50	light blue
vi. Brief on the Merits by Respondent or Appellee (Rule 24.2); Brief on the Merits for Respondent	50	light red

Type of Document	Page Limits	Color of Cover
or Appellee Supporting Petitioner or Appellant (Rule 12.6); Exceptions by Party Other than Plaintiff to Report of Special Master (Rule 17)		
vii. Reply Brief on the Merits (Rule 24.4)	20	yellow
viii. Reply to Plaintiff's Exceptions to Report of Special Master (Rule 17)	50	orange
ix. Reply to Exceptions by Party Other Than Plaintiff to Report of Special Master (Rule 17)	50	yellow
x. Brief for an *Amicus Curiae* at the Petition Stage (Rule 37.2)	20	cream
xi. Brief for an *Amicus Curiae* in Support of the Plaintiff, Petitioner, or Appellant, or in Support of Neither Party, on the Merits, or in an Original Action at the Exceptions Stage (Rule 37.3)	30	light green
xii. Brief for an *Amicus Curiae* in Support of the Defendant, Respondent, or Appellee, on the Merits or in an Original Action at the Exceptions Stage (Rule 37.3)	30	dark green
xiii. Petition for Rehearing (Rule 44)	10	tan

merits brief, "On Writ of Certiorari to the United States Court of Appeals for the Fifth Circuit");

(f) the title of the document (*e.g.,* "Petition for Writ of Certiorari," "Brief for Respondent," "Joint Appendix");

(g) the name of the attorney who is counsel of record for the party concerned (who must be a member of the Bar of this Court except as provided in Rule 33.2), and on whom service is to be made, with a notation directly thereunder identifying the attorney as counsel of record and setting out counsel's office address and telephone number. Only one counsel of record may be noted on a single document. The names of other members of the Bar of this Court or of the bar of the highest court of a State acting as counsel, and, if desired, their addresses, may be added, but counsel of record shall be clearly identified. Names of persons other than attorneys admitted to a state bar may not be listed, unless the party is appearing *pro se,* in which case the party's name, address, and telephone number shall appear. The foregoing shall be displayed in an appropriate typographic manner and, except for the identification of counsel, may not be set in type smaller than standard 11 point, if the document is prepared as required by Rule 33.1.

2. Every document exceeding five pages (other than a joint appendix), whether prepared under Rule 33.1 or Rule 33.2, shall contain a table of contents and a table of cited authorities (*i.e.,* cases alphabetically arranged, constitutional provisions, statutes, treatises, and other materials) with references to the pages in the document where such authorities are cited.

3. The body of every document shall bear at its close the name of counsel of record and such other counsel, identified on the cover of the document in conformity with subparagraph 1(g) of this Rule, as may be desired.

RULE 35. DEATH, SUBSTITUTION, AND REVIVOR; PUBLIC OFFICERS

1. If a party dies after filing a petition for a writ of certiorari to this Court, or after filing a notice of appeal, the authorized representative of the deceased party may appear and, on motion, be substituted as a party. If the representative does not voluntarily become a party, any other party may suggest the death on the record and, on motion, seek an order requiring the representative to become a party within a designated time. If the representative then fails to become a party, the party so moving, if a respondent or appellee, is entitled to have the petition for a writ of certiorari or the appeal dismissed, and if a petitioner or appellant, is entitled to proceed as in any other case of nonappearance by a respondent or appellee. If the substitution of a representative of the deceased is not made within six months after the death of the party, the case shall abate.

2. Whenever a case cannot be revived in the court whose judgment is sought to be reviewed, because the deceased party's authorized representative is not subject to that court's jurisdiction, proceedings will be conducted as this Court may direct.

3. When a public officer who is a party to a proceeding in this Court in an official capacity dies, resigns, or otherwise ceases to hold office, the action does not abate and any successor in office is automatically substituted as a party. The parties shall notify the Clerk in writing of any such successions. Proceedings following the substitution shall be in the name of the substituted party, but any misnomer not affecting substantial rights of the parties will be disregarded.

4. A public officer who is a party to a proceeding in this Court in an official capacity may be described as a party by the officer's official title rather than by name, but the Court may require the name to be added.

RULE 36. CUSTODY OF PRISONERS IN HABEAS CORPUS PROCEEDINGS

1. Pending review in this Court of a decision in a habeas corpus proceeding commenced before a court, Justice, or judge of the United States, the person having custody of the prisoner may not transfer custody to another person unless the transfer is authorized under this Rule.

2. Upon application by a custodian, the court, Justice, or judge who entered the decision under review may authorize transfer and the substitution of a successor custodian as a party.

3.(a) Pending review of a decision failing or refusing to release a prisoner, the prisoner may be detained in the custody from which release is sought or in other appropriate custody or may be enlarged on personal recognizance or bail, as may appear appropriate to the court, Justice, or judge who entered the decision, or to the court of appeals, this Court, or a judge or Justice of either court.

(b) Pending review of a decision ordering release, the prisoner shall be enlarged on personal recognizance or bail, unless the court, Justice, or judge who entered the decision, or the court of appeals, this Court, or a judge or Justice of either court, orders otherwise.

4. An initial order respecting the custody or enlargement of the prisoner, and any recognizance or surety taken, shall continue in effect pending review in the court of appeals and in this Court unless for reasons shown to the court of appeals, this Court, or a judge or Justice of either court, the order is modified or an independent order respecting custody, enlargement, or surety is entered.

RULE 37. BRIEF FOR AN *AMICUS CURIAE*

1. An *amicus curiae* brief that brings to the attention of the Court relevant matter not already brought to its attention by the parties may be of considerable help to the Court. An *amicus curiae* brief that does not serve this purpose burdens the Court, and its filing is not favored.

2. (a) An *amicus curiae* brief submitted before the Court's consideration of a petition for a writ of certiorari, motion for leave to file a bill of complaint, jurisdictional statement, or petition for an extraordinary writ, may be filed if accompanied by the written consent of all parties, or if the Court grants leave to file under subparagraph 2(b) of this Rule. The brief shall be submitted within the time allowed for filing a brief in opposition or for filing a motion to dismiss or affirm. The *amicus curiae* brief shall specify whether consent was granted, and its cover shall identify the party supported.

(b) When a party to the case has withheld consent, a motion for leave to file an *amicus curiae* brief before the Court's consideration of a petition for a writ of certiorari, motion for leave to file a bill of complaint, jurisdictional statement, or petition for an extraordinary writ may be presented to the Court. The motion, prepared as required by Rule 33.1 and as one document with the brief sought to be filed, shall be submitted within the time allowed for filing an *amicus curiae* brief, and shall indicate the party or parties who have withheld consent and state the nature of the movant's interest. Such a motion is not favored.

3. (a) An *amicus curiae* brief in a case before the Court for oral argument may be filed if accompanied by the written consent of all parties, or if the Court grants leave to file under subparagraph 3(b) of this Rule. The brief shall be submitted within the time allowed for filing the brief for the party supported, or if in support of neither party, within the time allowed for filing the petitioner's or appellant's brief. The *amicus curiae* brief shall specify whether consent was granted, and its cover shall identify the party supported or indicate whether it suggests affirmance or reversal. The Clerk will not file a reply brief for

an *amicus curiae*, or a brief for an *amicus curiae* in support of, or in opposition to, a petition for rehearing.

(b) When a party to a case before the Court for oral argument has withheld consent, a motion for leave to file an *amicus curiae* brief may be presented to the Court. The motion, prepared as required by Rule 33.1 and as one document with the brief sought to be filed, shall be submitted within the time allowed for filing an *amicus curiae* brief, and shall indicate the party or parties who have withheld consent and state the nature of the movant's interest.

4. No motion for leave to file an *amicus curiae* brief is necessary if the brief is presented on behalf of the United States by the Solicitor General; on behalf of any agency of the United States allowed by law to appear before this Court when submitted by the agency's authorized legal representative; on behalf of a State, Commonwealth, Territory, or Possession when submitted by its Attorney General; or on behalf of a city, county, town, or similar entity when submitted by its authorized law officer.

5. A brief or motion filed under this Rule shall be accompanied by proof of service as required by Rule 29, and shall comply with the applicable provisions of Rules 21, 24, and 33.1 (except that it suffices to set out in the brief the interest of the *amicus curiae,* the summary of the argument, the argument, and the conclusion). A motion for leave to file may not exceed five pages. A party served with the motion may file an objection thereto, stating concisely the reasons for withholding consent; the objection shall be prepared as required by Rule 33.2.

RULE 38. FEES

Under 28 U.S.C. §1911, the fees charged by the Clerk are:

(a) for docketing a case on a petition for a writ of certiorari or on appeal or for docketing any other proceeding, except a certified question or a motion to docket and dismiss an appeal under Rule 18.5, $300;

(b) for filing a petition for rehearing or a motion for leave to file a petition for rehearing, $200;

(c) for reproducing and certifying any record or paper, $1 per page; and for comparing with the original thereof any photographic reproduction of any record or paper, when furnished by the person requesting its certification, $.50 per page;

(d) for a certificate bearing the seal of the Court, $10; and

(e) for a check paid to the Court, Clerk, or Marshal that is returned for lack of funds, $35.

RULE 39. PROCEEDINGS *IN FORMA PAUPERIS*

1. A party seeking to proceed *in forma pauperis* shall file a motion for leave to do so, together with the party's notarized affidavit or declaration (in compliance with 28 U.S.C. §1746) in the form prescribed by the Federal Rules of Appellate Procedure, Form 4. See 28 U.S.C. §1915. The motion shall state whether leave to proceed *in forma pauperis* was sought in any other court and, if so, whether leave was granted. If the United States district court or the United States court of appeals has appointed counsel under the Criminal Justice Act, see 18 U.S.C. §3006A, or under any other applicable federal statute, no affidavit or declaration is required, but the motion shall cite the statute under which counsel was appointed.

2. If leave to proceed *in forma pauperis* is sought for the purpose of filing a document, the motion, and affidavit or declaration if required, shall be filed with that document and shall comply in every respect with Rule 21. As provided in that rule, it suffices to file an original and 10 copies, unless the party is an inmate confined in an institution and is not represented by counsel, in which case the original, alone, suffices. A copy of the motion shall precede and be attached to each copy of the accompanying document.

3. Except when these Rules expressly provide that a document shall be prepared as required by Rule 33.1, every document presented by a party proceeding under this Rule shall be prepared as required by Rule 33.2 (unless such preparation is impossible). Every document shall be legible. While making due allowance for any case presented under this Rule by a person appearing *pro se,* the Clerk will not file any document if it does not comply with the substance of these Rules or is jurisdictionally out of time.

4. When the documents required by paragraphs 1 and 2 of this Rule are presented to the Clerk, accompanied by proof of service as required by Rule 29, they will be placed on the docket without the payment of a docket fee or any other fee.

5. The respondent or appellee in a case filed *in forma pauperis* shall respond in the same manner and within the same time as in any other case of the same nature, except that the filing of an original and 10 copies of a response prepared as required by Rule 33.2, with proof of service as required by Rule 29, suffices. The respondent or appellee may challenge the grounds for the motion for leave to proceed *in forma pauperis* in a separate document or in the response itself.

6. Whenever the Court appoints counsel for an indigent party in a case set for oral argument, the briefs on the merits submitted by that counsel, unless otherwise requested, shall be prepared under the Clerk's supervision. The Clerk also will reimburse appointed counsel for any necessary travel expenses to Washington, D. C., and return in connection with the argument.

7. In a case in which certiorari has been granted, probable jurisdiction noted, or consideration of jurisdiction postponed, this Court may appoint counsel to represent a party financially unable to afford an attorney to the extent authorized by the Criminal Justice Act of 1964, 18 U.S.C. §3006A, or by any other applicable federal statute.

8. If satisfied that a petition for a writ of certiorari, jurisdictional statement, or petition for an extraordinary writ is frivolous or malicious, the Court may deny leave to proceed *in forma pauperis.*

RULE 40. VETERANS, SEAMEN, AND MILITARY CASES

1. A veteran suing to establish reemployment rights under 38 U.S.C. §2022, or under any other provision of law exempting veterans from the payment of fees or court costs, may file a motion for leave to proceed on papers prepared as required by Rule 33.2. The motion shall ask leave to proceed as a veteran and be accompanied by an affidavit or declaration setting out the moving party's veteran status. A copy of the motion shall precede and be attached to each copy of the petition for a writ of certiorari or other substantive document filed by the veteran.

2. A seaman suing under 28 U.S.C. §1916 may proceed without prepayment of fees or costs or furnishing security therefor, but is not entitled to proceed under Rule 33.2, except as authorized by the Court on separate motion under Rule 39.

3. An accused person petitioning for a writ of certiorari to review a decision of the United States Court of Appeals for the Armed Forces under 28 U.S.C. §1259 may proceed without prepayment of fees or costs or furnishing security therefor and without filing an affidavit of indigency, but is not entitled to proceed on papers prepared as required by Rule 33.2, except as authorized by the Court on separate motion under Rule 39.

PART VIII. DISPOSITION OF CASES

RULE 41. OPINIONS OF THE COURT

Opinions of the Court will be released by the Clerk immediately upon their announcement from the bench, or as the Court otherwise directs. Thereafter, the Clerk will cause the opinions to be issued in slip form, and the Reporter of Decisions will prepare them for publication in the preliminary prints and bound volumes of the United States Reports.

RULE 42. INTEREST AND DAMAGES

1. If a judgment for money in a civil case is affirmed, any interest allowed by law is payable from the date the judgment under review was entered. If a judgment is modified or reversed with a direction that a judgment for money be entered below, the mandate will contain instructions with respect to the allowance of interest. Interest in cases arising in a state court is allowed at the same rate that similar judgments bear interest in the courts of the State in which judgment is directed to be entered. Interest in cases arising in a court of the United States is allowed at the interest rate authorized by law.

2. When a petition for a writ of certiorari, an appeal, or an application for other relief is frivolous, the Court may award the respondent or appellee just damages, and single or double costs under Rule 43. Damages or costs may be awarded against the petitioner, appellant, or applicant, against the party's counsel, or against both party and counsel.

RULE 43. COSTS

1. If the Court affirms a judgment, the petitioner or appellant shall pay costs unless the Court otherwise orders.

2. If the Court reverses or vacates a judgment, the respondent or appellee shall pay costs unless the Court otherwise orders.

3. The Clerk's fees and the cost of printing the joint appendix are the only taxable items in this Court. The cost of the transcript of the record from the court below is also a taxable item, but shall be taxable in that court as costs in the case. The expenses of printing briefs, motions, petitions, or jurisdictional statements are not taxable.

4. In a case involving a certified question, costs are equally divided unless the Court otherwise orders, except that if the Court decides the whole matter in controversy, as permitted by Rule 19.2, costs are allowed as provided in paragraphs 1 and 2 of this Rule.

5. To the extent permitted by 28 U.S.C. §2412, costs under this Rule are allowed for or against the United States or an officer or agent thereof, unless expressly waived or unless the Court otherwise orders.

6. When costs are allowed in this Court, the Clerk will insert an itemization of the costs in the body of the mandate or judgment sent to the court below. The prevailing side may not submit a bill of costs.

7. In extraordinary circumstances the Court may adjudge double costs.

RULE 44. REHEARING

1. Any petition for the rehearing of any judgment or decision of the Court on the merits shall be filed within 25 days after entry of the judgment or decision, unless the Court or a Justice shortens or extends the time. The petitioner shall file 40 copies of the rehearing petition and shall pay the filing fee prescribed by Rule 38(b), except that a petitioner proceeding *in forma pauperis* under Rule 39, including an inmate of an institution, shall file the number of copies required for a petition by such a person under Rule 12.2. The petition shall state its grounds briefly and distinctly and shall be served as required by Rule 29. The petition shall be presented together with certification of counsel (or of a party unrepresented by counsel) that it is presented in good faith and not for delay; one copy of the certificate shall bear the signature of counsel (or of a party unrepresented by counsel). A copy of the certificate shall follow and be attached to each copy of the petition. A petition for rehearing is not subject to oral argument and will not be granted except by a majority of the Court, at the instance of a Justice who concurred in the judgment or decision.

2. Any petition for the rehearing of an order denying a petition for a writ of certiorari or extraordinary writ shall be filed within 25 days after the date of the order of denial and shall comply with all the form and filing requirements of paragraph 1 of this Rule, including the payment of the filing fee if required, but its grounds shall be limited to intervening circumstances of a substantial or controlling effect or to other substantial grounds not previously presented. The petition shall be presented together with certification of counsel (or of a party unrepresented by counsel) that it is restricted to the grounds specified in this paragraph and that it is presented in good faith and not for delay; one copy of the certificate shall bear the signature of counsel (or of a party unrepresented by counsel). A copy of the certificate shall follow and be attached to each copy of the petition. The Clerk will not file a petition without a certificate. The petition is not subject to oral argument.

3. The Clerk will not file any response to a petition for rehearing unless the Court requests a response. In the absence of extraordinary circumstances, the Court will not grant a petition for rehearing without first requesting a response.

4. The Clerk will not file consecutive petitions and petitions that are out of time under this Rule.

5. The Clerk will not file any brief for an *amicus curiae* in support of, or in opposition to, a petition for rehearing.

RULE 45. PROCESS; MANDATES

1. All process of this Court issues in the name of the President of the United States.

2. In a case on review from a state court, the mandate issues 25 days after entry of the judgment, unless the Court or a Justice shortens or extends the time, or unless the parties stipulate that it issue sooner. The filing of a petition for rehearing stays the mandate until disposition of the petition, unless the Court orders otherwise. If the petition is denied, the mandate issues forthwith.

3. In a case on review from any court of the United States, as defined by 28 U.S.C. §451, a formal mandate does not issue unless specially directed; instead, the Clerk of this Court will send the clerk of the lower court a copy of the opinion or order of this Court and a certified copy of the judgment. The certified copy of the judgment, prepared and signed by this Court's Clerk, will provide for costs if any are awarded. In all other respects, the provisions of paragraph 2 of this Rule apply.

RULE 46. DISMISSING CASES

1. At any stage of the proceedings, whenever all parties file with the Clerk an agreement in writing that a case be dismissed, specifying the terms for payment of costs, and pay to the Clerk any fees then due, the Clerk, without further reference to the Court, will enter an order of dismissal.

2. (a) A petitioner or appellant may file a motion to dismiss the case, with proof of service as required by Rule 29, tendering to the Clerk any fees due and costs payable. No more than 15 days after service thereof, an adverse party may file an objection, limited to the amount of damages and costs in this Court alleged to be payable or to showing that the moving party does not represent all petitioners or appellants. The Clerk will not file any objection not so limited.

(b) When the objection asserts that the moving party does not represent all the petitioners or appellants, the party moving for dismissal may file a reply within 10 days, after which time the matter will be submitted to the Court for its determination.

(c) If no objection is filed, or if upon objection going only to the amount of damages and costs in this Court, the party moving for dismissal tenders the additional damages and costs in full within 10 days of the demand therefor, the Clerk, without further reference to the Court, will enter an order of dismissal. If, after objection as to the amount of damages and costs in this Court, the moving party does not respond by a tender within 10 days, the Clerk will report the matter to the Court for its determination.

3. No mandate or other process will issue on a dismissal under this Rule without an order of the Court.

PART IX. DEFINITIONS AND EFFECTIVE DATE

RULE 47. REFERENCE TO "STATE COURT" AND "STATE LAW"

The term "state court," when used in these Rules, includes the District of Columbia Court of Appeals and the Supreme Court of the Commonwealth of Puerto Rico. See 28 U.S.C. §§1257 and 1258. References in these Rules to the common law and statutes of a State include the common law and statutes of the District of Columbia and of the Commonwealth of Puerto Rico.

RULE 48. EFFECTIVE DATE OF RULES

1. These Rules, adopted July 26, 1995, will be effective October 2, 1995.

2. The Rules govern all proceedings after their effective date except to the extent that, in the opinion of the Court, their application to a pending matter would not be feasible or would work an injustice, in which event the former procedure applies.

APPENDIX B Tables, Lists, and Graphical Data

Natural Courts

Natural court[a]	Justices[b]	Dates	U.S. Reports[c]
Jay 1	Jay (*o* October 19, 1789), J. Rutledge (*o* February 15, 1790), Cushing (*o* February 2, 1790), Wilson (*o* October 5, 1789), Blair (*o* February 2, 1790)	October 5, 1789–May 12, 1790	2
Jay 2	Jay, Rutledge (*r* March 5, 1791), Cushing, Wilson, Blair, Iredell (*o* May 12, 1790)	May 12, 1790–August 6, 1792	2
Jay 3	Jay, Cushing, Wilson, Blair, Iredell, T. Johnson (*o* August 6, 1792; *r* January 16, 1793)	August 6, 1792–March 11, 1793	2
Jay 4	Jay (*r* June 29, 1795), Cushing, Wilson, Blair, Iredell, Paterson (*o* March 11, 1793)	March 11, 1793–August 12, 1795	2–3
Rutledge 1	J. Rutledge (*o* August 12, 1795; *rj* December 15, 1795), Cushing, Wilson, Blair (*r* January 27, 1796), Iredell, Paterson	August 12, 1795–February 4, 1796	3
No chief justice	Cushing, Wilson, Iredell, Paterson, S. Chase (*o* February 4, 1796)	February 4, 1796–March 8, 1796	3
Ellsworth 1	Ellsworth (*o* March 8, 1796), Cushing, Wilson (*d* August 21, 1798), Iredell, Paterson, S. Chase	March 8, 1796–February 4, 1799	3
Ellsworth 2	Ellsworth, Cushing, Iredell (*d* October 20, 1799), Paterson, S. Chase, Washington (*o* February 4, 1799)	February 4, 1799–April 21, 1800	3–4
Ellsworth 3	Ellsworth (*r* December 15, 1800), Cushing, Paterson, S. Chase, Washington, Moore (*o* April 21, 1800)	April 21, 1800–February 4, 1801	4
Marshall 1	Marshall (*o* February 4, 1801), Cushing, Paterson, S. Chase, Washington, Moore (*r* January 26, 1804)	February 4, 1801–May 7, 1804	5–6
Marshall 2	Marshall, Cushing, Paterson (*d* September 9, 1806), S. Chase, Washington, W. Johnson (*o* May 7, 1804)	May 7, 1804–January 20, 1807	6–7
Marshall 3	Marshall, Cushing, S. Chase, Washington, W. Johnson, Livingston (*o* January 20, 1807)	January 20, 1807–May 4, 1807	8
Marshall 4	Marshall, Cushing (*d* September 13, 1810), S. Chase (*d* June 19, 1811), Washington, W. Johnson, Livingston, Todd (*o* May 4, 1807)	May 4, 1807–November 23, 1811	8–10
Marshall 5	Marshall, Washington, W. Johnson, Livingston, Todd, Duvall (*o* November 23, 1811)	November 23,1811–February 3, 1812	11
Marshall 6	Marshall, Washington, W. Johnson, Livingston (*d* March 18, 1823), Todd, Duvall, Story (*o* February 3, 1812)	February 3, 1812–February 10, 1824	11–21
Marshall 7	Marshall, Washington, W. Johnson, Todd (*d* February 7, 1826), Duvall, Story, Thompson (*o* February 10, 1824)	February 10, 1824–June 16, 1826	22–24
Marshall 8	Marshall, Washington (*d* November 26, 1829), W. Johnson, Duvall, Story, Thompson, Trimble (*o* June 16, 1826; *d* August 25, 1828)	June 16, 1826–January 11, 1830	25–27
Marshall 9	Marshall, W. Johnson (*d* August 4, 1834), Duvall (*r* January 14, 1835), Story, Thompson, McLean (*o* January 11, 1830), Baldwin (*o* January 18, 1830)	January 11, 1830–January 14, 1835	28–33
Marshall 10	Marshall (*d* July 6, 1835), Story, Thompson, McLean, Baldwin, Wayne (*o* January 14, 1835)	January 14, 1835–March 28, 1836	34–35
Taney 1	Taney (*o* March 28, 1836), Story, Thompson, McLean, Baldwin, Wayne	March 28, 1836–May 12, 1836	35
Taney 2	Taney, Story, Thompson, McLean, Baldwin, Wayne, Barbour (*o* May 12, 1836)	May 12, 1836–May 1, 1837	35–36
Taney 3	Taney, Story, Thompson, McLean, Baldwin, Wayne, Barbour, Catron (*o* May 1, 1837)	May 1, 1837–January 9, 1838	36

Natural court[a]	Justices[b]	Dates	U.S. Reports[c]
Taney 4	Taney, Story, Thompson, McLean, Baldwin, Wayne, Barbour (d February 25, 1841), Catron, McKinley (o January 9, 1838)	January 9, 1838–January 10, 1842	37–40
Taney 5	Taney, Story, Thompson (d December 18, 1843), McLean, Baldwin (d April 21, 1844), Wayne, Catron, McKinley, Daniel (o January 10, 1842)	January 10, 1842–February 27, 1845	40–44
Taney 6	Taney, Story (d September 10, 1845), McLean, Wayne, Catron, McKinley, Daniel, Nelson (o February 27, 1845)	February 27, 1845–September 23, 1845	44
Taney 7	Taney, McLean, Wayne, Catron, McKinley, Daniel, Nelson, Woodbury (o September 23, 1845)	September 23,1845–August 10, 1846	44–45
Taney 8	Taney, McLean, Wayne, Catron, McKinley, Daniel, Nelson, Woodbury (d September 4, 1851), Grier (o August 10, 1846)	August 10, 1846–October 10, 1851	46–52
Taney 9	Taney, McLean, Wayne, Catron, McKinley (d July 19, 1852), Daniel, Nelson, Grier, Curtis (o October 10, 1851)	October 10, 1851–April 11, 1853	53–55
Taney 10	Taney, McLean, Wayne, Catron, Daniel, Nelson, Grier, Curtis (r September 30, 1857), Campbell (o April 11, 1853)	April 11, 1853–January 21, 1858	56–61
Taney 11	Taney, McLean (d April 4, 1861), Wayne, Catron, Daniel (d May 31, 1860), Nelson, Grier, Campbell (r April 30, 1861), Clifford (o January 21, 1858)	January 21, 1858–January 27, 1862	61–66
Taney 12	Taney, Wayne, Catron, Nelson, Grier, Clifford, Swayne (o January 27, 1862)	January 27, 1862–July 21, 1862	66
Taney 13	Taney, Wayne, Catron, Nelson, Grier, Clifford, Swayne, Miller (o July 21, 1862)	July 21, 1862–December 10, 1862	67
Taney 14	Taney, Wayne, Catron, Nelson, Grier, Clifford, Swayne, Miller, Davis (o December 10, 1862)	December 10, 1862–May 20, 1863	67
Taney 15	Taney (d October 12, 1864), Wayne, Catron, Nelson, Grier, Clifford, Swayne, Miller, Davis, Field (o May 20, 1863)	May 20, 1863–December 15, 1864	67–68
Chase 1	S. P. Chase (o December 15, 1864), Wayne (d July 5, 1867), Catron (d May 30, 1865), Nelson, Grier (r January 31, 1870), Clifford, Swayne, Miller, Davis, Field	December 15, 1864–March 14, 1870	69–76
Chase 2	S. P. Chase, Nelson (r November 28, 1872), Clifford, Swayne, Miller, Davis, Field, Strong (o March 14, 1870), Bradley (o March 23, 1870)	March 14, 1870–January 9, 1873	76–82
Chase 3	S. P. Chase (d May 7, 1873), Clifford, Swayne, Miller, Davis, Field, Strong, Bradley, Hunt (o January 9, 1873)	January 9, 1873–March 4, 1874	82–86
Waite 1	Waite (o March 4, 1874), Clifford, Swayne, Miller, Davis (r March 4, 1877), Field, Strong, Bradley, Hunt	March 4, 1874–December 10, 1877	86–95
Waite 2	Waite, Clifford, Swayne, Miller, Field, Strong (r December 14, 1880), Bradley, Hunt, Harlan I (o December 10, 1877)	December 10, 1877–January 5, 1881	95–103
Waite 3	Waite, Clifford, Swayne (r January 24, 1881), Miller, Field, Bradley, Hunt, Harlan I, Woods (o January 5, 1881)	January 5, 1881–May 17, 1881	103
Waite 4	Waite, Clifford (d July 25, 1881), Miller, Field, Bradley, Hunt, Harlan I, Woods, Matthews (o May 17, 1881)	May 17, 1881–January 9, 1882	103–104
Waite 5	Waite, Miller, Field, Bradley, Hunt (r January 27, 1882), Harlan I, Woods, Matthews, Gray (o January 9, 1882)	January 9, 1882–April 3, 1882	104–105
Waite 6	Waite, Miller, Field, Bradley, Harlan I, Woods (d May 14, 1887), Matthews, Gray, Blatchford (o April 3, 1882)	April 3, 1882–January 18, 1888	105–124
Waite 7	Waite (d March 23, 1888), Miller, Field, Bradley, Harlan I, Matthews, Gray, Blatchford, L. Lamar (o January 18, 1888)	January 18, 1888–October 8, 1888	124–127
Fuller 1	Fuller (o October 8, 1888), Miller, Field, Bradley, Harlan I, Matthews (d March 22, 1889), Gray, Blatchford, L. Lamar	October 8, 1888–January 6, 1890	128–132
Fuller 2	Fuller, Miller (d October 13, 1890), Field, Bradley, Harlan I, Gray, Blatchford, L. Lamar, Brewer (o January 6, 1890)	January 6, 1890–January 5, 1891	132–137

Natural court[a]	Justices[b]	Dates	U.S. Reports[c]
Fuller 3	Fuller, Field, Bradley (d January 22, 1892), Harlan I, Gray, Blatchford, L. Lamar, Brewer, Brown (o January 5, 1891)	January 5, 1891–October 10, 1892	137–145
Fuller 4	Fuller, Field, Harlan I, Gray, Blatchford, L. Lamar (d January 23, 1893), Brewer, Brown, Shiras (o October 10, 1892)	October 10, 1892–March 4, 1893	146–148
Fuller 5	Fuller, Field, Harlan I, Gray, Blatchford (d July 7, 1893), Brewer, Brown, Shiras, H. Jackson (o March 4, 1893)	March 4, 1893–March 12, 1894	148–151
Fuller 6	Fuller, Field, Harlan I, Gray, Brewer, Brown, Shiras, H. Jackson (d August 8, 1895), E. White (o March 12, 1894)	March 12, 1894–January 6, 1896	152–160
Fuller 7	Fuller, Field (r December 1, 1897), Harlan I, Gray, Brewer, Brown, Shiras, E. White, Peckham (o January 6, 1896)	January 6, 1896–January 26, 1898	160–169
Fuller 8	Fuller, Harlan I, Gray (d September 15, 1902), Brewer, Brown, Shiras, E. White, Peckham, McKenna (o January 26, 1898)	January 26, 1898–December 8, 1902	169–187
Fuller 9	Fuller, Harlan I, Brewer, Brown, Shiras (r February 23, 1903), E. White, Peckham, McKenna, Holmes (o December 8, 1902)	December 8, 1902–March 2, 1903	187–188
Fuller 10	Fuller, Harlan I, Brewer, Brown (r May 28, 1906), E. White, Peckham, McKenna, Holmes, Day (o March 2, 1903)	March 2, 1903–December 17, 1906	188–203
Fuller 11	Fuller, Harlan I, Brewer, E. White, Peckham (d October 24, 1909), McKenna, Holmes, Day, Moody (o December 17, 1906)	December 17, 1906–January 3, 1910	203–215
Fuller 12	Fuller (d July 4, 1910), Harlan I, Brewer (d March 28, 1910), E. White, McKenna, Holmes, Day, Moody, Lurton (o January 3, 1910)	January 3, 1910–October 10, 1910	215–217
No chief justice	Harlan I, E. White (p December 18, 1910), McKenna, Holmes, Day, Moody (r November 20, 1910), Lurton, Hughes (o October 10, 1910)	October 10, 1910–December 19, 1910	218
White 1	E. White (o December 19, 1910), Harlan I (d October 14, 1911), McKenna, Holmes, Day, Lurton, Hughes, Van Devanter (o January 3, 1911), J. Lamar (o January 3, 1911)	December 19, 1910–March 18, 1912	218–223
White 2	E. White, McKenna, Holmes, Day, Lurton (d July 12, 1914), Hughes, Van Devanter, J. Lamar, Pitney (o March 18, 1912)	March 18, 1912–October 12, 1914	223–234
White 3	E. White, McKenna, Holmes, Day, Hughes, Van Devanter, J. Lamar (d January 2, 1916), Pitney, McReynolds (o October 12, 1914)	October 12, 1914–June 5, 1916	235–241
White 4	E. White, McKenna, Holmes, Day, Hughes (r June 10, 1916), Van Devanter, Pitney, McReynolds, Brandeis (o June 5, 1916)	June 5, 1916–October 9, 1916	241
White 5	E. White (d May 19, 1921), McKenna, Holmes, Day, Van Devanter, Pitney, McReynolds, Brandeis, Clarke (o October 9, 1916)	October 9, 1916–July 11, 1921	242–256
Taft 1	Taft (o July 11, 1921), McKenna, Holmes, Day, Van Devanter, Pitney, McReynolds, Brandeis, Clarke (r September 18, 1922)	July 11, 1921–October 2, 1922	257–259
Taft 2	Taft, McKenna, Holmes, Day (r November 13, 1922), Van Devanter, Pitney (r December 31, 1922), McReynolds, Brandeis, Sutherland (o October 2, 1922)	October 2, 1922–January 2, 1923	260
Taft 3	Taft, McKenna, Holmes, Van Devanter, McReynolds, Brandeis, Sutherland, Butler (o January 2, 1923)	January 2, 1923–February 19, 1923	260
Taft 4	Taft, McKenna (r January 5, 1925), Holmes, Van Devanter, McReynolds, Brandeis, Sutherland, Butler, Sanford (o February 19, 1923)	February 19, 1923–March 2, 1925	260–267
Taft 5	Taft (r February 3, 1930), Holmes, Van Devanter, McReynolds, Brandeis, Sutherland, Butler, Sanford, Stone (o March 2, 1925)	March 2, 1925–February 24, 1930	267–280
Hughes 1	Hughes (o February 24, 1930), Holmes, Van Devanter, McReynolds, Brandeis, Sutherland, Butler, Sanford (d March 8, 1930), Stone	February 24, 1930–June 2, 1930	280–281
Hughes 2	Hughes, Holmes (r January 12, 1932), Van Devanter, McReynolds, Brandeis, Sutherland, Butler, Stone, Roberts (o June 2, 1930)	June 2, 1930–March 14, 1932	281–285

Natural court[a]	Justices[b]	Dates	U.S. Reports[c]
Hughes 3	Hughes, Van Devanter (r June 2, 1937), McReynolds, Brandeis, Sutherland, Butler, Stone, Roberts, Cardozo (o March 14, 1932)	March 14, 1932–August 19, 1937	285–301
Hughes 4	Hughes, McReynolds, Brandeis, Sutherland (r January 17, 1938), Butler, Stone, Roberts, Cardozo, Black (o August 19, 1937)	August 19, 1937 January 31, 1938	302–303
Hughes 5	Hughes, McReynolds, Brandeis, Butler, Stone, Roberts, Cardozo (d July 9, 1938), Black, Reed (o January 31, 1938)	January 31, 1938–January 30, 1939	303–305
Hughes 6	Hughes, McReynolds, Brandeis (r February 13, 1939), Butler, Stone, Roberts, Black, Reed, Frankfurter (o January 30, 1939)	January 30, 1939–April 17, 1939	306
Hughes 7	Hughes, McReynolds, Butler (d November 16, 1939), Stone, Roberts, Black, Reed, Frankfurter, Douglas (o April 17, 1939)	April 17, 1939–February 5, 1940	306–308
Hughes 8	Hughes (r July 1, 1941), McReynolds (r January 31, 1941), Stone (p July 2, 1941), Roberts, Black, Reed, Frankfurter, Douglas, Murphy (o February 5, 1940)	February 5, 1940–July 3, 1941	308–313
Stone 1	Stone (o July 3, 1941), Roberts, Black, Reed, Frankfurter, Douglas, Murphy, Byrnes (o July 8, 1941; r October 3, 1942), R. Jackson (o July 11, 1941)	July 3, 1941–February 15, 1943	314–318
Stone 2	Stone, Roberts (r July 31, 1945), Black, Reed, Frankfurter, Douglas, Murphy, R. Jackson, W. Rutledge (o February 15, 1943)	February 15, 1943–October 1, 1945	318–326
Stone 3	Stone (d April 22, 1946), Black, Reed, Frankfurter, Douglas, Murphy, R. Jackson, W. Rutledge, Burton (o October 1, 1945)	October 1, 1945–June 24, 1946	326–328
Vinson 1	Vinson (o June 24, 1946), Black, Reed, Frankfurter, Douglas, Murphy (d July 19, 1949), R. Jackson, W. Rutledge, Burton	June 24, 1946–August 24, 1949	329–338
Vinson 2	Vinson, Black, Reed, Frankfurter, Douglas, R. Jackson, W. Rutledge (d September 10, 1949), Burton, Clark (o August 24, 1949)	August 24, 1949–October 12, 1949	338
Vinson 3	Vinson (d September 8, 1953), Black, Reed, Frankfurter, Douglas, R. Jackson, Burton, Clark, Minton (o October 12, 1949)	October 12, 1949–October 5, 1953	338–346
Warren 1	Warren (o October 5, 1953), Black, Reed, Frankfurter, Douglas, R. Jackson (d October 9, 1954), Burton, Clark, Minton	October 5, 1953–March 28, 1955	346–348
Warren 2	Warren, Black, Reed, Frankfurter, Douglas, Burton, Clark, Minton (r October 15, 1956), Harlan II (o March 28, 1955)	March 28, 1955–October 16, 1956	348–352
Warren 3	Warren, Black, Reed (r February 25, 1957), Frankfurter, Douglas, Burton, Clark, Harlan II, Brennan (o October 16, 1956)	October 16, 1956–March 25, 1957	352
Warren 4	Warren, Black, Frankfurter, Douglas, Burton (r October 13, 1958), Clark, Harlan II, Brennan, Whittaker (o March 25, 1957)	March 25, 1957–October 14, 1958	352–358
Warren 5	Warren, Black, Frankfurter, Douglas, Clark, Harlan II, Brennan, Whittaker (r March 31, 1962), Stewart (o October 14, 1958)	October 14, 1958–April 16, 1962	358–369
Warren 6	Warren, Black, Frankfurter (r August 28, 1962), Douglas, Clark, Harlan II, Brennan, Stewart, B. White (o April 16, 1962)	April 16, 1962–October 1, 1962	369–370
Warren 7	Warren, Black, Douglas, Clark, Harlan II, Brennan, Stewart, B. White, Goldberg (o October 1, 1962; r July 25, 1965)	October 1, 1962–October 4, 1965	371–381
Warren 8	Warren, Black, Douglas, Clark (r June 12, 1967), Harlan II, Brennan, Stewart, B. White, Fortas (o October 4, 1965)	October 4, 1965–October 2, 1967	382–388
Warren 9	Warren (r June 23, 1969), Black, Douglas, Harlan II, Brennan, Stewart, B. White, Fortas (r May 14, 1969), T. Marshall (o October 2, 1967)	October 2, 1967–June 23, 1969	389–395
Burger 1	Burger (o June 23, 1969), Black, Douglas, Harlan II, Brennan, Stewart, B. White, T. Marshall	June 23, 1969–June 9, 1970	395–397
Burger 2	Burger, Black (r September 17, 1971), Douglas, Harlan II (r September 23, 1971), Brennan, Stewart, B. White, T. Marshall, Blackmun (o June 9, 1970)	June 9, 1970–January 7, 1972	397–404

Natural court[a]	Justices[b]	Dates	U.S. Reports[c]
Burger 3	Burger, Douglas (*r* November 12, 1975), Brennan, Stewart, B. White, T. Marshall, Blackmun, Powell (*o* January 7, 1972), Rehnquist (*o* January 7, 1972)	January 7, 1972–December 19, 1975	404–423
Burger 4	Burger, Brennan, Stewart (*r* July 3, 1981), B. White, T. Marshall, Blackmun, Powell, Rehnquist, Stevens (*o* December 19, 1975)	December 19, 1975–September 25, 1981	423–453
Burger 5	Burger (*r* September 26, 1986), Brennan, B. White, T. Marshall, Blackmun, Powell, Rehnquist (*p* September 26, 1986), Stevens, O'Connor (*o* September 25, 1981)	September 25, 1981–September 26, 1986	453–478
Rehnquist 1	Rehnquist (*o* September 26, 1986), Brennan, B. White, T. Marshall, Blackmun, Powell (*r* June 26, 1987), Stevens, O'Connor, Scalia (*o* September 26, 1986)	September 26, 1986–February 18, 1988	478–484
Rehnquist 2	Rehnquist, Brennan (*r* July 20, 1990), B. White, T. Marshall, Blackmun, Stevens, O'Connor, Scalia, Kennedy (*o* February 18, 1988)	February 18, 1988–October 9, 1990	484–498
Rehnquist 3	Rehnquist, B. White, T. Marshall (*r* October 1, 1991), Blackmun, Stevens, O'Connor, Scalia, Kennedy, Souter (*o* October 9, 1990)	October 9, 1990–October 23, 1991	498–
Rehnquist 4	Rehnquist, B. White (*r* July 1, 1993), Blackmun, Stevens, O'Connor, Scalia, Kennedy, Souter, Thomas (*o* October 23, 1991)	October 23, 1991–August 10, 1993	
Rehnquist 5	Rehnquist, Blackmun (*r* August 3, 1994), Stevens, O'Connor, Scalia, Kennedy, Souter, Thomas, Ginsburg (*o* August 10, 1993)	August 10, 1993–August 3, 1994	
Rehnquist 6	Rehnquist, Stevens, O'Connor, Scalia, Kennedy, Souter, Thomas, Ginsburg, Breyer (*o* August 3, 1994)	August 3, 1994	

SOURCE: Lee Epstein and Thomas G. Walker, *Constitutional Law for a Changing America: Institutional Powers and Constraints*, Second Edition (Washington, D.C.: CQ Press, 1995), 617.

a. The term *natural court* refers to a period of time during which the membership of the Court remains stable. There are a number of ways to determine the beginning and end of a natural court. Here a natural court begins when a new justice takes the oath of office and continues until the next new justice takes the oath. When two or more justices join the Court within a period of fifteen or fewer days, we treat it as the beginning of a single natural court (for example, Marshall 9, Chase 2, White 1, and Stone 1).

Natural courts in the table are numbered sequentially within the tenure of each chief justice.

b. The name of the chief justice appears first, with associate justices following in order of descending seniority. In addition, the date a justice left the Court, creating a vacancy for the next justice to be appointed, is given, as well as the date the new justice took the oath of office. *o*=oath of office taken, *d*=died, *r*=resigned or retired, *rj*=recess appointment rejected by Senate, *p*=promoted from associate justice to chief justice.

c. Volumes of *United States Reports* in which the actions of each natural court generally may be found. Because of the way decisions were published prior to the twentieth century, these volume numbers may not contain all of the decisions of a given natural court. They do, however, provide a general guide to the location of each natural court's published decisions. Natural courts of short duration may have little business published in the reports.

Supreme Court Nominations, 1789–1996

Name	State	Date of Birth	To Replace	Date of Appointment	Confirmation or Other Action *	Date Resigned	Date of Death	Years of Service
WASHINGTON								
John Jay	N.Y.	12/12/1745		9/24/1789	9/26/1789	6/29/1795	5/17/1829	6
John Rutledge	S.C.	9/1739		9/24/1789	9/26/1789	3/5/1791	7/18/1800	1
William Cushing	Mass.	3/1/1732		9/24/1789	9/26/1789		9/13/1810	21
Robert H. Harrison	Md.	1745		9/24/1789	9/26/1789 (D)		4/20/1790	
James Wilson	Pa.	9/14/1742		9/24/1789	9/26/1789		8/21/1798	9
John Blair	Va.	1732		9/24/1789	9/26/1789	1/27/1796	8/31/1800	6
James Iredell	N.C.	10/5/1751	Harrison	2/8/1790	2/10/1790		10/20/1799	9
Thomas Johnson	Md.	11/4/1732	Rutledge	11/1/1791	11/7/1791	3/4/1793	10/26/1819	1
William Paterson	N.J.	12/24/1745	Johnson	2/27/1793	2/28/1793 (W)			
William Paterson†			Johnson	3/4/1793	3/4/1793		9/9/1806	13
John Rutledge ‡			Jay	7/1/1795	12/15/1795 (R, 10–14)			
William Cushing ‡			Jay	1/26/1796	1/27/1796 (D)			
Samuel Chase	Md.	4/17/1741	Blair	1/26/1796	1/27/1796		6/19/1811	15
Oliver Ellsworth	Conn.	4/29/1745	Jay	3/3/1796	3/4/1796 (21–1)	12/15/1800	11/26/1807	4
ADAMS								
Bushrod Washington	Va.	6/5/1762	Wilson	12/19/1798	12/20/1798		11/26/1829	31
Alfred Moore	N.C.	5/21/1755	Iredell	12/6/1799	12/10/1799	1/26/1804	10/15/1810	4
John Jay ‡			Ellsworth	12/18/1800	12/19/1800 (D)			
John Marshall	Va.	9/24/1755	Ellsworth	1/20/1801	1/27/1801		7/6/1835	34
JEFFERSON								
William Johnson	S.C.	12/27/1771	Moore	3/22/1804	3/24/1804		8/4/1834	30
H. Brockholst Livingston	N.Y.	11/25/1757	Paterson	12/13/1806	2/17/1806		3/18/1823	16
Thomas Todd	Ky.	1/23/1765	New seat	2/28/1807	3/3/1807		2/7/1826	19
MADISON								
Levi Lincoln	Mass.	5/15/1749	Cushing	1/2/1811	1/3/1811 (D)		4/14/1820	
Alexander Wolcott	Conn.	9/15/1758	Cushing	2/4/1811	2/13/1811 (R, 9–24)		6/26/1828	
John Quincy Adams	Mass.	7/11/1767	Cushing	2/21/1811	2/22/1811 (D)		2/23/1848	
Joseph Story	Mass.	9/18/1779	Cushing	11/15/1811	11/18/1811		9/10/1845	34
Gabriel Duvall	Md.	12/6/1752	Chase	11/15/1811	11/18/1811	1/14/1835	3/6/1844	23
MONROE								
Smith Thompson	N.Y.	1/17/1768	Livingston	12/8/1823	12/19/1823		12/18/1843	20
J. Q. ADAMS								
Robert Trimble	Ky.	11/17/1776	Todd	4/11/1826	5/9/1826 (27–5)		8/25/1828	2
John J. Crittenden	Ky.	9/10/1787	Trimble	12/17/1828	2/12/1829 (P)		7/26/1863	
JACKSON								
John McLean	Ohio	3/11/1785	Trimble	3/6/1829	3/7/1829		4/4/1861	32
Henry Baldwin	Pa.	1/14/1780	Washington	1/4/1830	1/6/1830 (41–2)		4/21/1844	14
James M. Wayne	Ga.	1790	Johnson	1/7/1835	1/9/1835		7/5/1867	32
Roger B. Taney	Md.	3/17/1777	Duvall	1/15/1835	3/3/1835 (P)			
Roger B. Taney †			Marshall	12/28/1835	3/15/1836 (29–15)		10/12/1864	28
Philip P. Barbour	Va.	5/25/1783	Duvall	12/28/1835	3/15/1836 (30–11)		2/25/1841	5
William Smith	Ala.	1762	New seat	3/3/1837	3/8/1837 (23–18) (D)		6/10/1840	
John Catron	Tenn.	1786	New seat	3/3/1837	3/8/1837 (28–15)		5/30/1865	28
VAN BUREN								
John McKinley	Ala.	5/1/1780	New seat	9/18/1837	9/25/1837		7/19/1852	15
Peter V. Daniel	Va.	4/24/1784	Barbour	2/26/1841	3/2/1841 (22–5)		5/31/1860	19
TYLER								
John C. Spencer	N.Y.	1/8/1788	Thompson	1/9/1844	1/31/1844 (R, 21–26)		5/18/1855	
Reuben H. Walworth	N.Y.	10/26/1788	Thompson	3/13/1844	6/17/1844 (W)		11/27/1867	
Edward King	Pa.	1/31/1794	Baldwin	6/5/1844	6/15/1844 (P)			

Name	State	Date of Birth	To Replace	Date of Appointment	Confirmation or Other Action *	Date Resigned	Date of Death	Years of Service
TYLER *(Continued)*								
Edward King [†]			Baldwin	12/4/1844	2/7/1845 (W)		5/8/1873	
Samuel Nelson	N.Y.	11/10/1792	Thompson	2/4/1845	2/14/1845	11/28/1872	12/13/1873	27
John M. Read	Pa.	2/21/1797	Baldwin	2/7/1845	No action		11/29/1874	
POLK								
George W. Woodward	Pa.	3/26/1809	Baldwin	12/23/1845	1/22/1846 (R, 20–29)		5/10/1875	
Levi Woodbury	N.H.	12/22/1789	Story	12/23/1845	1/3/1846		9/4/1851	5
Robert C. Grier	Pa.	3/5/1794	Baldwin	8/3/1846	8/4/1846	1/31/1870	9/25/1870	23
FILLMORE								
Benjamin R. Curtis	Mass.	11/4/1809	Woodbury	12/11/1851	12/29/1851	9/30/1857	9/15/1874	5
Edward A. Bradford	La.	9/27/1813	McKinley	8/16/1852	No action`		11/22/1872	
George E. Badger	N.C.	4/13/1795	McKinley	1/10/1853	2/11/1853 (P)		5/11/1866	
William C. Micou	La.	1806	McKinley	2/24/1853	No action		4/16/1854	
PIERCE								
John A. Campbell	Ala.	6/24/1811	McKinley	3/22/1853	3/25/1853	4/30/1861	3/12/1889	8
BUCHANAN								
Nathan Clifford	Maine	8/18/1803	Curtis	12/9/1857	1/12/1858 (26–23)		7/25/1881	23
Jeremiah S. Black	Pa.	1/10/1810	Daniel	2/5/1861	2/21/1861 (R, 25–26)		8/19/1883	
LINCOLN								
Noah H. Swayne	Ohio	12/7/1804	McLean	1/21/1862	1/24/1862 (38–1)	1/24/1881	6/8/1884	19
Samuel F. Miller	Iowa	4/5/1816	Daniel	7/16/1862	7/16/1862		10/13/1890	28
David Davis	Ill.	3/9/1815	Campbell	12/1/1862	12/8/1862	3/4/1877	6/26/1886	14
Stephen J. Field	Calif.	11/4/1816	New seat	3/6/1863	3/10/1863	12/1/1897	4/9/1899	34
Salmon P. Chase	Ohio	1/13/1808	Taney	12/6/1864	12/6/1864		5/7/1873	8
JOHNSON								
Henry Stanbery	Ohio	2/20/1803	Catron	4/16/1866	No action		6/26/1881	
GRANT								
Ebenezer R. Hoar	Mass.	2/21/1816	New seat	12/15/1869	2/3/1870 (R, 24–33)		1/31/1895	
Edwin M. Stanton	Pa.	12/19/1814	Grier	12/20/1869	12/20/1869 (46–11)		12/24/1869	
William Strong	Pa.	5/6/1808	Grier	2/7/1870	2/18/1870	12/14/1880	8/19/1895	10
Joseph P. Bradley	N.J.	3/14/1813	New seat	2/7/1870	3/21/1870 (46–9)		1/22/1892	21
Ward Hunt	N.Y.	6/14/1810	Nelson	12/3/1872	12/11/1872	1/27/1882	3/24/1886	9
George H. Williams	Ore.	3/23/1823	Chase	12/1/1873	1/8/1874 (W)		4/4/1910	
Caleb Cushing	Mass.	1/17/1800	Chase	1/9/1874	1/13/1874 (W)		1/2/1879	
Morrison R. Waite	Ohio	11/29/1816	Chase	1/19/1874	1/21/1874 (63–0)		3/23/1888	14
HAYES								
John M. Harlan	Ky.	6/1/1833	Davis	10/17/1877	11/29/1877		10/14/1911	34
William B. Woods	Ga.	8/3/1824	Strong	12/15/1880	12/21/1880 (39–8)		5/14/1887	6
Stanley Matthews	Ohio	7/21/1824	Swayne	1/26/1881	No action			
GARFIELD								
Stanley Matthews [†]			Swayne	3/14/1881	5/12/1881 (24–23)		3/22/1889	7
ARTHUR								
Horace Gray	Mass.	3/24/1828	Clifford	12/19/1881	12/20/1881 (51–5)		9/15/1902	20
Roscoe Conkling	N.Y.	10/30/1829	Hunt	2/24/1882	3/2/1882 (39–12) (D)		4/18/1888	
Samuel Blatchford	N.Y.	3/9/1820	Hunt	3/13/1882	3/27/1882		7/7/1893	11
CLEVELAND								
Lucius Q. C. Lamar	Miss.	9/17/1825	Woods	12/6/1887	1/16/1888 (32–28)		1/23/1893	5
Melville W. Fuller	Ill.	2/11/1833	Waite	4/30/1888	7/20/1888 (41–20)		7/4/1910	22

Name	State	Date of Birth	To Replace	Date of Appointment	Confirmation or Other Action *	Date Resigned	Date of Death	Years of Service
HARRISON								
David J. Brewer	Kan.	6/20/1837	Matthews	12/4/1889	12/18/1889 (53–11)		3/28/1910	20
Henry B. Brown	Mich.	3/2/1836	Miller	12/23/1890	12/29/1890	5/28/1906	9/4/1913	15
George Shiras, Jr.	Pa.	1/26/1832	Bradley	7/19/1892	7/26/1892	2/23/1903	8/2/1924	10
Howell E. Jackson	Tenn.	4/8/1832	Lamar	2/2/1893	2/18/1893		8/8/1895	2
CLEVELAND								
William B. Hornblower	N.Y.	5/13/1851	Blatchford	9/19/1893	1/15/1894 (R, 24–30)		6/16/1914	
Wheeler H. Peckham	N.Y.	1/1/1833	Blatchford	1/22/1894	2/16/1894 (R, 32–41)		9/27/1905	
Edward D. White	La.	11/3/1845	Blatchford	2/19/1894	2/19/1894		5/19/1921	17
Rufus W. Peckham	N.Y.	11/8/1838	Jackson	12/3/1895	12/9/1895		10/24/1909	13
McKINLEY								
Joseph McKenna	Calif.	8/10/1843	Field	12/16/1897	1/21/1898	1/5/1925	11/21/1926	26
ROOSEVELT								
Oliver W. Holmes	Mass.	3/8/1841	Gray	12/2/1902	12/4/1902	1/12/1932	3/6/1935	29
William R. Day	Ohio	4/17/1849	Shiras	2/19/1903	2/23/1903	11/13/1922	7/9/1923	19
William H. Moody	Mass.	12/23/1853	Brown	12/3/1906	12/12/1906	11/20/1910	7/2/1917	3
TAFT								
Horace H. Lurton	Tenn.	2/26/1844	Peckham	12/13/1909	12/20/1909		7/12/1914	4
Charles E. Hughes	N.Y.	4/11/1862	Brewer	4/25/1910	5/2/1910	6/10/1916	8/27/1948	6
Edward D. White ‡			Fuller	12/12/1910	12/12/1910		5/19/1921	10‡
Willis Van Devanter	Wyo.	4/17/1859	White	12/12/1910	12/15/1910	6/2/1937	2/8/1941	26
Joseph R. Lamar	Ga.	10/14/1857	Moody	12/12/1910	12/15/1910		1/2/1916	5
Mahlon Pitney	N.J.	2/5/1858	Harlan	2/19/1912	3/13/1912 (50–26)	12/31/1922	12/9/1924	10
WILSON								
James C. McReynolds	Tenn.	2/3/1862	Lurton	8/19/1914	8/29/1914 (44–6)	1/31/1941	8/24/1946	26
Louis D. Brandeis	Mass.	11/13/1856	Lamar	1/28/1916	6/1/1916 (47–22)	2/13/1939	10/5/1941	22
John H. Clarke	Ohio	9/18/1857	Hughes	7/14/1916	7/24/1916	9/18/1922	3/22/1945	6
HARDING								
William H. Taft	Ohio	9/15/1857	White	6/30/1921	6/30/1921	2/3/1930	3/8/1930	8
George Sutherland	Utah	3/25/1862	Clarke	9/5/1922	9/5/1922	1/17/1938	7/18/1942	15
Pierce Butler	Minn.	3/17/1866	Day	11/23/1922	12/21/1922 (61–8)		11/16/1939	17
Edward T. Sanford	Tenn.	7/23/1865	Pitney	1/24/1923	1/29/1923		3/8/1930	7
COOLIDGE								
Harlan F. Stone	N.Y.	10/11/1872	McKenna	1/5/1925	2/5/1925 (71–6)		4/22/1946	16
HOOVER								
Charles E. Hughes ‡			Taft	2/3/1930	2/13/1930 (52–26)	7/1/1941	8/27/1948	11‡
John J. Parker	N.C.	11/20/1885	Sanford	3/21/1930	5/7/1930 (R, 39–41)		3/17/1958	
Owen J. Roberts	Pa.	5/2/1875	Sanford	5/9/1930	5/20/1930	7/31/1945	5/17/1955	15
Benjamin N. Cardozo	N.Y.	5/24/1870	Holmes	2/15/1932	2/24/1932		7/9/1938	6
ROOSEVELT								
Hugo L. Black	Ala.	2/27/1886	Van Devanter	8/12/1937	8/17/1937 (63–16)	9/17/1971	10/25/1971	34
Stanley F. Reed	Ky.	12/31/1884	Sutherland	1/15/1938	1/25/1938	2/25/1957	4/2/1980	19
Felix Frankfurter	Mass.	11/15/1882	Cardozo	1/5/1939	1/17/1939	8/28/1962	2/22/1965	23
William O. Douglas	Conn.	10/16/1898	Brandeis	3/20/1939	4/4/1939 (62–4)	11/12/1975	1/19/1980	36‡
Frank Murphy	Mich.	4/13/1890	Butler	1/4/1940	1/15/1940		7/19/1949	9
Harlan F. Stone ‡			Hughes	6/12/1941	6/27/1941		4/22/1946	5‡
James F. Byrnes	S.C.	5/2/1879	McReynolds	6/12/1941	6/12/1941	10/3/1942	4/9/1972	1
Robert H. Jackson	N.Y.	2/13/1892	Stone	6/12/1941	7/7/1941		10/9/1954	13
Wiley B. Rutledge	Iowa	7/20/1894	Byrnes	1/11/1943	2/8/1943		9/10/1949	6
TRUMAN								
Harold H. Burton	Ohio	6/22/1888	Roberts	9/19/1945	9/19/1945	10/13/1958	10/28/1964	13
Fred M. Vinson	Ky.	1/22/1890	Stone	6/6/1946	6/20/1946		9/8/1953	7

Name	State	Date of Birth	To Replace	Date of Appointment	Confirmation or Other Action *	Date Resigned	Date of Death	Years of Service
TRUMAN *(Continued)*								
Tom C. Clark	Texas	9/23/1899	Murphy	8/2/1949	8/18/1949 (73–8)	6/12/1967	6/13/1977	18
Sherman Minton	Ind.	10/20/1890	Rutledge	9/15/1949	10/4/1949 (48–16)	10/15/1956	4/9/1965	7
EISENHOWER								
Earl Warren	Calif.	3/19/1891	Vinson	9/30/1953	3/1/1954	6/23/1969	6/9/1974	15
John M. Harlan	N.Y.	5/20/1899	Jackson	1/10/1955	3/16/1955 (71–11)	9/23/1971	12/29/1971	16
William J. Brennan, Jr.	N.J.	4/25/1906	Minton	1/14/1957	3/19/1957	7/23/1990		33
Charles E. Whittaker	Mo.	2/22/1901	Reed	3/2/1957	3/19/1957	3/31/1962	11/26/1973	5
Potter Stewart	Ohio	1/23/1915	Burton	1/17/1959	5/5/1959 (70–17)	7/3/1981	12/7/1985	22
KENNEDY								
Byron R. White	Colo.	6/8/1917	Whittaker	3/30/1962	4/11/1962	6/28/1993		31
Arthur J. Goldberg	Ill.	8/8/1908	Frankfurter	8/29/1962	9/25/1962	7/25/1965	1/19/1990	3
JOHNSON								
Abe Fortas	Tenn.	6/19/1910	Goldberg	7/28/1965	8/11/1965	5/14/1969	4/5/1982	4
Thurgood Marshall	N.Y.	6/2/1908	Clark	6/13/1967	8/30/1967 (69–11)	10/1/1991	1/24/1993	24
Abe Fortas ‡			Warren	6/26/1968	10/4/1968 (W)			
Homer Thornberry	Texas	1/9/1909	Fortas	6/26/1968	No action			
NIXON								
Warren E. Burger	Minn.	9/17/1907	Warren	5/21/1969	6/9/1969 (74–3)	9/26/1986	6/25/95	17
Clement Haynsworth, Jr.	S.C.	10/30/1912	Fortas	8/18/1969	11/21/1969 (R, 45–55)		11/22/1989	
G. Harrold Carswell	Fla.	12/22/1919	Fortas	1/19/1970	4/8/1970 (R, 45–51)		7/31/1992	
Harry A. Blackmun	Minn.	11/12/1908	Fortas	4/14/1970	5/12/1970 (94–0)	8/3/1994		24
Lewis F. Powell, Jr.	Va.	9/19/1907	Black	10/21/1971	12/6/1971 (89–1)	6/26/1987		16
William H. Rehnquist	Ariz.	10/1/1924	Harlan	10/21/1971	12/10/1971 (68–26)			
FORD								
John Paul Stevens	Ill.	4/20/1920	Douglas	11/28/1975	12/17/1975 (98–0)			
REAGAN								
Sandra Day O'Connor	Ariz.	3/26/1930	Stewart	8/19/1981	9/21/1981 (99–0)			
William H. Rehnquist ††			Burger	6/20/1986	9/17/1986 (65–33)			
Antonin Scalia	Va.	3/11/1936	Rehnquist	6/24/1986	9/17/1986 (98–0)			
Robert H. Bork	D.C.	3/1/1927	Powell	7/1/1987	10/23/1987 (R, 42–58)			
Anthony M. Kennedy	Calif.	7/23/1936	Powell	11/30/1987	2/3/1988 (97–0)			
BUSH								
David Hackett Souter	N.H.	9/17/1939	Brennan	7/23/1990	10/2/1990 (90–9)			
Clarence Thomas	Ga.	6/23/1948	Marshall	7/1/1991	10/15/1991 (52–48)			
CLINTON								
Ruth Bader Ginsburg	N.Y.	3/15/1933	White	6/22/1993	8/3/1993 (96–3)			
Stephen G. Breyer	Mass.	8/15/1938	Blackmun	5/13/1994	7/29/1994 (87– 9)			

SOURCES: Leon Friedman and Fred L. Israel, eds., *The Justices of the United States Supreme Court, 1789–1969, Their Lives and Major Opinions*, 5 vols. (New York and London: Chelsea House Publishers, 1969–1978); U.S. Senate, *Executive Journal of the U.S. Senate, 1789–1975* (Washington, D.C.: Government Printing Office); Congressional Quarterly *Almanacs*, 1971, 1975, 1981, 1986, 1987 (Washington, D.C.: Congressional Quarterly, 1972, 1976, 1982, 1987, 1988); Clare Cushman, ed., *The Supreme Court Justices: Illustrated Biographies, 1789–1995*, 2d ed. (Washington, D.C.: Congressional Quarterly, 1995).

NOTE: Boldface—Chief justice; Italics—Did not serve; *—Where no vote is listed, confirmation was by voice or otherwise unrecorded; †—Earlier nomination not confirmed. See above; ††—Earlier court service. See above; W—Withdrawn; P—Postponed; R—Rejected; D—Declined.

Glossary of Common Legal Terms

Accessory. In criminal law, a person not present at the commission of an offense who commands, advises, instigates, or conceals the offense.

Acquittal. Discharge of a person from a charge of guilt. A person is acquitted when a jury returns a verdict of not guilty. A person may also be acquitted when a judge determines that there is insufficient evidence to convict him or that a violation of due process precludes a fair trial.

Adjudicate. To determine finally by the exercise of judicial authority to decide a case.

Affidavit. A voluntary written statement of facts or charges affirmed under oath.

A fortiori. With stronger force, with more reason.

Amicus curiae. A friend of the court, a person not a party to litigation, who volunteers or is invited by the court to give his views on a case.

Appeal. To take a case to a higher court for review. Generally, a party losing in a trial court may appeal once to an appellate court as a matter of right. If he loses in the appellate court, appeal to a higher court is within the discretion of the higher court. Most appeals to the U.S. Supreme Court are within the Court's discretion. However, when the highest court in a state rules that a U.S. statute is unconstitutional or upholds a state statute against the claim that it is unconstitutional, appeal to the Supreme Court is a matter of right.

Appellant. The party that appeals a lower court decision to a higher court.

Appellee. One who has an interest in upholding the decision of a lower court and is compelled to respond when the case is appealed to a higher court by the appellant.

Arraignment. The formal process of charging a person with a crime, reading him the charge, asking whether he pleads guilty or not guilty, and entering his plea.

Attainder, Bill of. A legislative act pronouncing a particular individual guilty of a crime without trial or conviction and imposing a sentence upon him.

Bail. The security, usually money, given as assurance of a prisoner's due appearance at a designated time and place (as in court) in order to procure in the interim his release from jail.

Bailiff. A minor officer of a court usually serving as an usher or a messenger.

Brief. A document prepared by counsel to serve as the basis for an argument in court, setting out the facts of and the legal arguments in support of his case.

Burden of proof. The need or duty of affirmatively proving a fact or facts that are disputed.

Case Law. The law as defined by previously decided cases, distinct from statutes and other sources of law.

Cause. A case, suit, litigation, or action, civil or criminal.

Certiorari, Writ of. A writ issued from the Supreme Court, at its discretion, to order a lower court to prepare the record of a case and send it to the Supreme Court for review.

Civil law. Body of law dealing with the private rights of individuals, as distinguished from criminal law.

Class action. A lawsuit brought by one person or group on behalf of all persons similarly situated.

Code. A collection of laws, arranged systematically.

Comity. Courtesy, respect; usually used in the legal sense to refer to the proper relationship between state and federal courts.

Common law. Collection of principles and rules of action, particularly from unwritten English law, which derive their authority from longstanding usage and custom or from courts recognizing and enforcing these customs. Sometimes used synonymously with case law.

Consent decree. A court-sanctioned agreement settling a legal dispute and entered into by the consent of the parties.

Contempt (civil and criminal). Civil contempt consists in the failure to do something that the party is ordered by the court to do for the benefit of another party. Criminal contempt occurs when a person willfully exhibits disrespect for the court or obstructs the administration of justice.

Conviction. Final judgment or sentence that the defendant is guilty as charged.

Criminal law. That branch of law which deals with the enforcement of laws and the punishment of persons who, by breaking laws, commit crimes.

Declaratory judgment. A court pronouncement declaring a legal right or interpretation but not ordering a specific action.

De facto. In fact, in reality.

Defendant. In a civil action, the party denying or defending itself against charges brought by a plaintiff. In a criminal action, the person indicted for commission of an offense.

De jure. As a result of law, as a result of official action.

Deposition. Oral testimony from a witness taken out of court in response to written or oral questions, committed to writing, and intended to be used in the preparation of a case.

Dicta. See Obiter dictum.

Dismissal. Order disposing of a case without a trial.

Docket. See Trial docket.

Due process. Fair and regular procedure. The Fifth and Fourteenth Amendments guarantee persons that they will not be deprived of life, liberty, or property by the government until fair and usual procedures have been followed.

Error, Writ of. A writ issued from an appeals court to a lower court requiring it to send to the appeals court the record of a case in which it has entered a final judgment and which the appeals court will now review for error.

Ex parte. Only from, or on, one side. Application to a court for some ruling or action on behalf of only one party.

Ex post facto. After the fact; an ex post facto law makes an action a crime after it has already been committed, or otherwise changes the legal consequences of some past action.

Ex rel. Upon information from; usually used to describe legal proceedings begun by an official in the name of the state, but at the instigation of, and with information from, a private individual interested in the matter.

Grand jury. Group of twelve to twenty-three persons impaneled to hear in private evidence presented by the state against persons accused of crime and to issue indictments when a majority of the jurors find probable cause to believe that the accused has committed a crime. Called a "grand" jury because it comprises a greater number of persons than a "petit" jury.

Grand jury report. A public report released by a grand jury after an investigation into activities of public officials that fall short of criminal actions. Grand jury reports are often called "presentments."

Guilty. A word used by a defendant in entering a plea or by a jury in returning a verdict, indicating that the defendant is legally responsible as charged for a crime or other wrongdoing.

Habeas corpus. Literally, "you have the body"; a writ issued to inquire whether a person is lawfully imprisoned or detained. The writ demands that the persons holding the prisoner justify his detention or release him.

Immunity. A grant of exemption from prosecution in return for evidence or testimony.

In camera. "In chambers." Refers to court hearings in private without spectators.

In forma pauperis. In the manner of a pauper, without liability for court costs.

In personam. Done or directed against a particular person.

In re. In the affair of, concerning. Frequent title of judicial proceedings in which there are no adversaries, but rather where the matter itself—as a bankrupt's estate—requires judicial action.

In rem. Done or directed against the thing, not the person.

Indictment. A formal written statement based on evidence presented by the prosecutor from a grand jury decided by a majority vote, charging one or more persons with specified offenses.

Information. A written set of accusations, similar to an indictment, but filed directly by a prosecutor.

Injunction. A court order prohibiting the person to whom it is directed from performing a particular act.

Interlocutory decree. A provisional decision of the court that temporarily settles an intervening matter before completion of a legal action.

Judgment. Official decision of a court based on the rights and claims of the parties to a case that was submitted for determination.

Jurisdiction. The power of a court to hear a case in question, which exists when the proper parties are present, and when the point to be decided is within the issues authorized to be handled by the particular court.

Juries. See Grand jury and Petit jury.

Magistrate. A judicial officer having jurisdiction to try minor criminal cases and conduct preliminary examinations of persons charged with serious crimes.

Mandamus. "We command." An order issued from a superior court directing a lower court or other authority to perform a particular act.

Moot. Unsettled, undecided. A moot question is also one that is no longer material; a moot case is one that has become hypothetical.

Motion. Written or oral application to a court or a judge to obtain a rule or an order.

Nolo contendere. "I will not contest it." A plea entered by a defendant at the discretion of the judge with the same legal effect as a plea of guilty, but it may not be cited in other proceedings as an admission of guilt.

Obiter dictum. Statement by a judge or justice expressing an opinion and included with, but not essential to, an opinion resolving a case before the court. Dicta are not necessarily binding in future cases.

Parole. A conditional release from imprisonment under conditions that if the prisoner abides by the law and other restrictions that may be placed upon him, he will not have to serve the remainder of his sentence. But if he does not abide by specified rules, he will be returned to prison.

Per curiam. "By the court." An unsigned opinion of the court or an opinion written by the whole court.

Petit jury. A trial jury, originally a panel of twelve persons who tried to reach a unanimous verdict on questions of fact in criminal and civil proceedings. Since 1970 the Supreme Court has upheld the legality of state juries with fewer than twelve persons. Because it comprises fewer persons than a "grand" jury, it is called a "petit" jury.

Petitioner. One who files a petition with a court seeking action or relief, including a plaintiff or an appellant. But a petitioner is also a person who files for other court action where charges are not necessarily made; for example, a party may petition the court for an order requiring another person or party to produce documents. The opposite party is called the respondent.

When a writ of certiorari is granted by the Supreme Court, the parties to the case are called petitioner and respondent in contrast to the appellant and appellee terms used in an appeal.

Plaintiff. A party who brings a civil action or sues to obtain a remedy for injury to his rights. The party against whom action is brought is termed the defendant.

Plea Bargaining. Negotiations between prosecutors and the defendant aimed at exchanging a plea of guilty from the defendant for concessions by the prosecutors, such as reduction of charges or a request for leniency.

Pleas. See Guilty and Nolo contendere.

Presentment. See Grand jury report.

Prima facie. At first sight; referring to a fact or other evidence presumably sufficient to establish a defense or a claim unless otherwise contradicted.

Probation. Process under which a person convicted of an offense, usually a first offense, receives a suspended sentence and is given his freedom, usually under the guardianship of a probation officer.

Quash. To overthrow, annul, or vacate; as to quash a subpoena.

Recognizance. An obligation entered into before a court or magistrate requiring the performance of a specified act—usually to appear in court at a later date. It is an alternative to bail for pretrial release.

Remand. To send back. In the event of a decision being remanded, it is sent back by a higher court to the court from which it came for further action.

Respondent. One who is compelled to answer the claims or questions posed in court by a petitioner. A defendant and an appellee may be called respondents, but the term also includes those parties who answer in court during actions where charges are not necessarily brought or where the Supreme Court has granted a writ of certiorari.

Seriatim. Separately, individually, one by one.

Stare Decisis. "Let the decision stand." The principle of adherence to settled cases, the doctrine that principles of law established in earlier judicial decisions should be accepted as authoritative in similar subsequent cases.

Statute. A written law enacted by a legislature. A collection of statutes for a particular governmental division is called a code.

Stay. To halt or suspend further judicial proceedings.

Subpoena. An order to present one's self before a grand jury, court, or legislative hearing.

Subpoena duces tecum. An order to produce specified documents or papers.

Tort. An injury or wrong to the person or property of another.

Transactional immunity. Protects a witness from prosecution for any offense mentioned in or related to his testimony, regardless of independent evidence against him.

Trial docket. A calendar prepared by the clerks of the court listing the cases set to be tried.

Use immunity. Protects a witness against the use of his own testimony against him in prosecution.

Vacate. To make void, annul, or rescind.

Writ. A written court order commanding the designated recipient to perform or not perform acts specified in the order.

Acts of Congress Held Unconstitutional

1. ACT OF SEPTEMBER 24, 1789 (1 STAT. 81, § 13, IN PART).

Provision that ". . . [the Supreme Court] shall have power to issue . . . writs of mandamus, in cases warranted by the principles and usages of law, to any . . . persons holding office, under authority of the United States" as applied to the issue of mandamus to the Secretary of State requiring him to deliver to plaintiff a commission (duly signed by the President) as justice of the peace in the District of Columbia *held* an attempt to enlarge the original jurisdiction of the Supreme Court, fixed by Article III, § 2.

Marbury v. Madison, 1 Cr. (5 U.S.) 137 (1803).

2. ACT OF FEBRUARY 20, 1812 (2 STAT. 677).

Provisions establishing board of revision to annul titles conferred many years previously by governors of the Northwest Territory were *held* violative of the due process clause of the Fifth Amendment.

Reichart v. Felps, 6 Wall. (73 U.S.) 160 (1868).

3. ACT OF MARCH 6, 1820 (3 STAT. 548, § 8, PROVISO).

The Missouri Compromise, prohibiting slavery within the Louisiana Territory north of 36° 30', except Missouri, *held* not warranted as a regulation of Territory belonging to the United States under Article IV, § 3, clause 2 (and *see* Fifth Amendment).

Scott v. Sandford, 19 How. (60 U.S.) 393 (1857).

4. ACT OF FEBRUARY 25, 1862 (12 STAT. 345, § 1); JULY 11, 1862 (12 STAT. 532, § 1); MARCH 3, 1863 (12 STAT. 711, § 3), EACH IN PART ONLY.

"Legal tender clauses," making noninterest-bearing United States notes legal tender in payment of "all debts, public and private," so far as applied to debts contracted before passage of the act, *held* not within express or implied powers of Congress under Article I, § 8, and inconsistent with Article I, § 10, and Fifth Amendment.

Hepburn v. Griswold, 8 Wall. (75 U.S.) 603 (1870); overruled in *Knox v. Lee (Legal Tender Cases),* 12 Wall. (79 U.S.) 457 (1871).

5. ACT OF MAY 20, 1862 (§ 35, 12 STAT.); ACT OF MAY 21, 1862 (12 STAT. 407); ACT OF JUNE 25, 1864 (13 STAT. 187); ACT OF JULY 23, 1866 (14 STAT. 216); REVISED STATUTES RELATING TO THE DISTRICT OF COLUMBIA, ACT OF JUNE 22, 1874 (§§ 281, 282, 294, 304, 18 STAT. PT. 2).

Provisions of law requiring, or construed to require, racial separation in the schools of the District of Columbia, *held* to violate the equal protection component of the due process clause of the Fifth Amendment.

Bolling v. Sharpe, 347 U.S. 497 (1954).

6. ACT OF MARCH 3, 1863 (12 STAT. 756, § 5).

"So much of the fifth section . . . as provides for the removal of a judgment in a State court, and in which the cause was tried by a jury to the circuit court of the United States for a retrial on the facts and law, is not in pursuance of the Constitution, and is void" under the Seventh Amendment.

The Justices v. Murray, 9 Wall. (76 U.S.) 274 (1870).

7. ACT OF MARCH 3, 1863 (12 STAT. 766, § 5).

Provision for an appeal from the Court of Claims to the Supreme Court—there being, at the time, a further provision (§ 14) requiring an estimate by the Secretary of the Treasury before payment of final judgment, *held* to contravene the judicial finality intended by the Constitution, Article III.

Gordon v. United States, 2 Wall. (69 U.S.) 561 (1865). (Case was dismissed without opinion; the grounds upon which this decision was made were stated in a posthumous opinion by Chief Justice Taney printed in the appendix to volume 117 U.S. 697.)

8. ACT OF JUNE 30, 1864 (13 STAT. 311, § 13).

Provision that "any prize cause now pending in any circuit court shall, on the application of all parties in interest . . . be transferred by that court to the Supreme Court. . . ," as applied in a case where no action had been taken in the Circuit Court on the appeal from the district court, *held* to propose an appeal procedure not within Article III, § 2.

The Alicia, 7 Wall. (74 U.S.) 571 (1869).

9. ACT OF JANUARY 24, 1865 (13 STAT. 424).

Requirement of a test oath (disavowing actions in hostility to the United States) before admission to appear as attorney in a federal court by virtue of any previous admission, *held* invalid as applied to an attorney who had been pardoned by the President for all offenses during the Rebellion—as *ex post facto* (Article I, § 9, clause 3) and an interference with the pardoning power (Article II, § 2, clause 1).

Ex parte Garland, 4 Wall. (71 U.S.) 333 (1867).

10. ACT OF MARCH 2, 1867 (14 STAT. 484, § 29).

General prohibition on sale of naphtha, etc., for illuminating purposes, if inflammable at less temperature than 110 F., *held* invalid "except so far as the section named operates within the United States, but without the limits of any State," as being a mere police regulation.

United States v. Dewitt, 9 Wall. (76 U.S.) 41 (1870).

11. REVISED STATUTES 5132, SUBDIVISION 9 (ACT OF MARCH 2, 1867, 14 STAT. 539).

Provision penalizing "any person respecting whom bankruptcy proceedings are commenced . . . who, within 3 months before the commencement of proceedings in bankruptcy, under the false color and pretense of carrying on business and dealing in the ordinary course of trade, obtains on credit from any person any goods or chattels with intent to defraud. . . ," *held* a police regulation not within the bankruptcy power (Article I, § 4, clause 4).

United States v. Fox, 95 U.S. 670 (1878).

12. ACT OF MAY 31, 1870 (16 STAT. 140, §§ 3, 4).

Provisions penalizing (1) refusal of local election official to permit voting by persons offering to qualify under State laws, applicable to any citizens; and (2) hindering of any person from qualifying or voting, *held* invalid under Fifteenth Amendment.

United States v. Reese, 92 U.S. 214 (1876).

13. REVISED STATUTES 5507 (ACT OF MAY 31, 1870, 16 STAT. 141, § 4).

Provision penalizing "every person who prevents, hinders, controls, or intimidates another from exercising . . . the right of suffrage, to whom that right is guaranteed by the Fifteenth Amendment to the Constitution of the United States, by means of bribery. . . ," *held* not authorized by the Fifteenth Amendment.

James v. Bowman, 190 U.S. 127 (1903).

14. REVISED STATUTES 1977 (ACT OF MAY 31, 1870, 16 STAT. 144).

Provision that "all persons within the jurisdiction of the United States shall have the same right in every State and Territory to make and enforce contracts . . . as is enjoyed by white citizens. . . ," *held* invalid under the Thirteenth Amendment.

Hodges v. United States, 203 U.S. 1 (1906), overruled in *Jones v. Alfred H. Mayer Co.,* 392 U.S. 409, 441-443 (1968).

15. REVISED STATUTES OF THE DISTRICT OF COLUMBIA, § 1064 (ACT OF JUNE 17, 1870, 16 STAT. 154 § 3).

Provision that "prosecutions in the police court [of the District of Columbia] shall be by information under oath, without indictment by grand jury or trial by petit jury," as applied to punishment for conspiracy *held* to contravene Article III, § 2, requiring jury trial of all crimes.

Callan v. Wilson, 127 U.S. 540 (1888).

16. REVISED STATUTES 4937-4947 (ACT OF JULY 8, 1870, 16 STAT. 210), AND ACT OF AUGUST 14, 1876 (19 STAT. 141).

Original trademark law, applying to marks "for exclusive use within the United States," and a penal act designed solely for the protection of rights defined in the earlier measure, *held* not supportable by Article I, § 8, clause 8 (copyright clause), nor Article I, § 8, clause 3, by reason of its application to intrastate as well as interstate commerce.

Trade-Mark Cases, 100 U.S. 82 (1879).

17. ACT OF JULY 12, 1870 (16 STAT. 235).

Provision making Presidential pardons inadmissible in evidence in Court of Claims, prohibiting their use by that court in deciding claims or appeals, and requiring dismissal of appeals by the Supreme Court in cases where proof of loyalty had been made otherwise than as prescribed by law, *held* an interference with judicial power under Article III, § 1, and with the pardoning power under Article II, § 2, clause 1.

United States v. Klein, 13 Wall. (80 U.S.) 128 (1872).

18. REVISED STATUTES 5519 (ACT OF APRIL 20, 1871, 17 STAT. 13, § 2).

Section providing punishment in case "two or more persons in any State . . . conspire . . . for the purpose of depriving . . . any person . . . of the equal protection of the laws . . . or for the purpose of preventing or hindering the constituted authorities of any State . . . from giving or securing to all persons within such State . . . the equal protection of the laws. . . ," *held* invalid as not being directed at state action proscribed by the Fourteenth Amendment.

United States v. Harris, 106 U.S. 629 (1883).

In *Baldwin v. Franks,* 120 U.S. 678 (1887), an attempt was made to distinguish the *Harris* case and to apply the statute to a conspiracy directed at aliens within a State, but the provision was *held* not enforceable in such limited manner.

19. ACT OF MARCH 3, 1873 (CH. 258 § 2, 17 STAT. 599, RECODIFIED IN 39 U.S.C. § 3001(E)(2)).

Comstock Act provision barring from the mails any unsolicited advertisement for contraceptives, as applied to circulars and flyers promoting prophylactics or containing information discussing the desirability and availability of prophylactics, violates the free speech clause of the First Amendment.

Bolger v. Youngs Drug Products Corp. 463 U.S. 60 (1983).

20. ACT OF JUNE 22, 1874 (18 STAT. 1878, § 4).

Provision authorizing federal courts, in suits for forfeitures under revenue and custom laws, to require production of documents, with allegations expected to be proved therein to be taken as proved on failure to produce such documents, was *held* violative of the search and seizure provision of the Fourth Amendment and the self-incrimination clause of the Fifth Amendment.

Boyd v. United States, 116 U.S. 616 (1886).

21. ACT OF MARCH 1, 1875 (18 STAT. 336, §§ 1, 2).

Provision "That all persons within the jurisdiction of the United States shall be entitled to the full and equal enjoyment of the accommodations . . . of inns, public conveyances on land or water, theaters, and other places of public amusement; subject only to the conditions and limitations established by law, and applicable alike to citizens of every race and color, regardless of any previous condition of servitude"—subject to penalty, *held* not to be supported by the Thirteenth or Fourteenth Amendments.

Civil Rights Cases, 109 U.S. 3 (1883), as to operation within States.

22. ACT OF MARCH 3, 1875 (18 STAT. 479, § 2).

Provision that "if the party [i.e., a person stealing property from the United States] has been convicted, then the judgment against him shall be conclusive evidence in the prosecution against [the] receiver that the property of the United States therein described has been embezzled, stolen, or purloined," *held* to contravene the Sixth Amendment.

Kirby v. United States, 174 U.S. 47 (1899).

23. ACT OF JULY 12, 1876 (19 STAT. 80, SEC. 6, IN PART).

Provision that "postmasters of the first, second, and third classes . . . may be removed by the President by and with the advice and consent of the Senate," *held* to infringe the executive power under Article II, § 1, clause 1.

Myers v. United States, 272 U.S. 52 (1926).

24. ACT OF AUGUST 11, 1888 (25 STAT. 411).

Clause, in a provision for the purchase or condemnation of a certain lock and dam in the Monongahela River, that ". . . in estimating the sum to be paid by the United States, the franchise of said corporation to collect tolls shall not be considered or estimated...," *held* to contravene the Fifth Amendment.

Monongahela Navigation Co. v. United States, 148 U.S. 312 (1893).

25. ACT OF MAY 5, 1892 (27 STAT. 25, § 4).

Provision of a Chinese exclusion act, that Chinese persons "convicted and adjudged to be not lawfully entitled to be or remain in the United States shall be imprisoned at hard labor for a period not exceeding 1 year and thereafter removed from the United States ... (such conviction and judgment being had before a justice, judge, or commissioner upon a summary hearing), *held* to contravene the Fifth and Sixth Amendments.

Wong Wing v. United States, 163 U.S. 228 (1896).

26. JOINT RESOLUTION OF AUGUST 4, 1894 (28 STAT. 1018, NO. 41).

Provision authorizing the Secretary of the Interior to approve a second lease of certain land by an Indian chief in Minnesota (granted to lessor's ancestor by art. 9 of a treaty with the Chippewa Indians), *held* an interference with judicial interpretation of treaties under Article III, § 2, clause 1 (and repugnant to the Fifth Amendment).

Jones v. Meehan, 175 U.S. 1 (1899).

27. ACT OF AUGUST 27, 1894 (28 STAT. 553–560, §§ 27–37).

Income tax provisions of the tariff act of 1894. "The tax imposed by §§ 27 and 37, inclusive ... so far as it falls on the income of real estate and of personal property, being a direct tax within the meaning of the Constitution, and, therefore, unconstitutional and void because not apportioned according to representation [Article I, § 2, clause 3], all those sections, constituting one entire scheme of taxation, are necessarily invalid" (158 U.S. 601, 637).

Pollock v. Farmers' Loan & Trust Co., 157 U.S. 429 (1895), and rehearing, 158 U.S. 601 (1895).

28. ACT OF JANUARY 30, 1897 (29 STAT. 506).

Prohibition on sale of liquor "... to any Indian to whom allotment of land has been made while the title to the same shall be held in trust by the Government...," *held* a police regulation infringing state powers, and not warranted by the commerce clause, Article I, § 8, clause 3.

Matter of Heff, 197 U.S. 488 (1905), overruled in *United States v. Nice,* 241 U.S. 591 (1916).

29. ACT OF JUNE 1, 1898 (30 STAT. 428).

Section 10, penalizing "any employer subject to the provisions of this act" who should "threaten any employee with loss of employment ... because of his membership in ... a labor corporation, association, or organization" (the act being applicable "to any common carrier ... engaged in the transportation of passengers or property ... from one State ... to another State...," etc.), *held* an infringement of the Fifth Amendment and not supported by the commerce clause.

Adair v. United States, 208 U.S. 161 (1908).

30. ACT OF JUNE 13, 1898 (30 STAT. 448, 459).

Stamp tax on foreign bills of lading, *held* a tax on exports in violation of Article I, § 9.

Fairbank v. United States, 181 U.S. 283 (1901).

31. SAME (30 STAT. 448, 460).

Tax on charter parties, as applied to shipments exclusively from ports in United States to foreign ports, *held* a tax on exports in violation of Article I, § 9.

United States v. Hvoslef, 237 U.S. 1 (1915).

32. SAME (30 STAT. 448, 461).

Stamp tax on policies of marine insurance on exports, *held* a tax on exports in violation of Article I, § 9.

Thames & Mersey Marine Ins. Co. v. United States, 237 U.S. 19 (1915).

33. ACT OF JUNE 6, 1900 (31 STAT. 359, § 171).

Section of the Alaska Code providing for a six-person jury in trials for misdemeanors, *held* repugnant to the Sixth Amendment, requiring "jury" trial of crimes.

Rassmussen v. United States, 197 U.S. 516 (1905).

34. ACT OF MARCH 3, 1901 (31 STAT. 1341, § 935).

Section of the District of Columbia Code granting the same right of appeal, in criminal cases, to the United States or the District of Columbia as to the defendant, but providing that a verdict was not to be set aside for error found in rulings during trial, *held* an attempt to take an advisory opinion, contrary to Article III, § 2.

United States v. Evans, 213 U.S. 297 (1909).

35. ACT OF JUNE 11, 1906 (34 STAT. 232).

Act providing that "every common carrier engaged in trade or commerce in the District of Columbia ... or between the several States ... shall be liable to any of its employees ... for all damages which may result from the negligence of any of its officers ... or by reason of any defect ... due to its negligence in its cars, engines ... roadbed," etc., *held* not supportable under Article I, § 8, clause 3 because it extended to intrastate as well as interstate commercial activities.

The Employers' Liability Cases, 207 U.S. 463 (1908). (The act was upheld as to the District of Columbia in *Hyde v. Southern R. Co.,* 31 App. D.C. 466 (1908); and as to the Territories, in *El Paso & N.E. Ry. v. Gutierrez,* 215 U.S. 87 (1909).)

36. ACT OF JUNE 16, 1906 (34 STAT. 269, § 2).

Provision of Oklahoma Enabling Act restricting relocation of the State capital prior to 1913, *held* not supportable by Article IV, § 3, authorizing admission of new States.

Coyle v. Smith, 221 U.S. 559 (1911).

37. ACT OF FEBRUARY 20, 1907 (34 STAT. 889, § 3).

Provision in the Immigration Act of 1907 penalizing "whoever ... shall keep, maintain, control, support, or harbor in any house or other place, for the purpose of prostitution ... any alien woman or girl, within 3 years after she shall have entered the United States," *held* an exercise of police power not within the control of Congress over immigration (whether drawn from the commerce clause or based on inherent sovereignty).

Keller v. United States, 213 U.S. 138 (1909).

38. ACT OF MARCH 1, 1907 (34 STAT. 1028).

Provisions authorizing certain Indians "to institute their suits in the Court of Claims to determine the validity of any acts of Congress passed since . . . 1902, insofar as said acts . . . attempt to increase or ex-tend the restrictions upon alienation . . . of allotments of lands of Cherokee citizens. . . ," and giving a right of appeal to the Supreme Court, *held* an attempt to enlarge the judicial power restricted by Article III, § 2, to cases and controversies.

Muskrat v. United States, 219 U.S. 346 (1911).

39. ACT OF MAY 27, 1908 (35 STAT. 313, § 4).

Provision making locally taxable "all land [of Indians of the Five Civilized Tribes] from which restrictions have been or shall be re-moved," *held* a violation of the Fifth Amendment, in view of the Ato-ka Agreement, embodied in the Curtis Act of June 28, 1898, providing tax-exemption for allotted lands while title in original allottee, not exceeding 21 years.

Choate v. Trapp, 224 U.S. 665 (1912).

40. ACT OF FEBRUARY 9, 1909, § 2, 35 STAT. 614, AS AMENDED.

Provision of Narcotic Drugs Import and Export Act creating a presumption that possessor of cocaine knew of its illegal importation into the United States, *held,* in light of the fact that more cocaine is produced domestically than is brought into the country and in ab-sence of any showing that defendant could have known his cocaine was imported, if it was, inapplicable to support conviction from mere possession of cocaine.

Turner v. United States, 396 U.S. 398 (1970).

41. ACT OF AUGUST 19, 1911 (37 STAT. 28).

A proviso in § 8 of the Federal Corrupt Practices Act fixing a max-imum authorized expenditure by a candidate for Senator "in any campaign for his nomination and election," as applied to a primary election, *held* not supported by Article I, § 4, giving Congress power to regulate the manner of holding elections for Senators and Repre-sentatives.

Newberry v. United States, 256 U.S. 232 (1921), overruled in *United States v. Classic,* 313 U.S. 299 (1941).

42. ACT OF JUNE 18, 1912 (37 STAT. 136, § 8).

Part of § 8 giving the Juvenile Court of the District of Columbia (proceeding upon information) concurrent jurisdiction of desertion cases (which were, by law, punishable by fine or imprisonment in the workhouse at hard labor for 1 year), *held* invalid under the Fifth Amendment which gives right to presentment by a grand jury in case of infamous crimes.

United States v. Moreland, 258 U.S. 433 (1922).

43. ACT OF MARCH 4, 1913 (37 STAT. 988, PART OF PAR. 64).

Provision of the District of Columbia Public Utility Commission Act authorizing appeal to the United States Supreme Court from de-crees of the District of Columbia Court of Appeals modifying valua-tion decisions of the Utilities Commission, *held* an attempt to extend the appellate jurisdiction of the Supreme Court to cases not strictly judicial within the meaning of Article III, § 2.

Keller v. Potomac Elec. Co., 261 U.S. 428 (1923).

44. ACT OF SEPTEMBER 1, 1916 (39 STAT. 675).

The original Child Labor Law, providing "that no producer . . . shall ship . . . in interstate commerce . . . any article or commodity the product of any mill . . . in which within 30 days prior to the removal of such product therefrom children under the age of 14 years have been employed or permitted to work more than 8 hours in any day or more than 6 days in any week. . . ," *held* not within the commerce power of Congress.

Hammer v. Dagenhart, 247 U.S. 251 (1918).

45. ACT OF SEPTEMBER 8, 1916 (39 TAT. 757, § 2(A), IN PART).

Provision of the income tax law of 1916, that a "stock dividend shall be considered income, to the amount of its cash value," *held* in-valid (in spite of the Sixteenth Amendment) as an attempt to tax something not actually income, without regard to apportionment under Article I, § 2, clause 3.

Eisner v. Macomber, 252 U.S. 189 (1920).

46. ACT OF OCTOBER 6, 1917 (40 STAT. 395).

The amendment of §§ 24 and 256 of the Judicial Code (which pre-scribe the jurisdiction of district courts) "saving . . . to claimants the rights and remedies under the workmen's compensation law of any State," *held* an attempt to transfer federal legislative powers to the States—the Constitution, by Article III, § 2, and Article I, § 8, having adopted rules of general maritime law.

Knickerbocker Ice Co. v. Stewart, 253 U.S. 149 (1920).

47. ACT OF SEPTEMBER 19, 1918 (40 STAT. 960).

Specifically, that part of the Minimum Wage Law of the District of Columbia which authorized the Wage Board "to ascertain and declare . . . (a) Standards of minimum wages for women in any occupation within the District of Columbia, and what wages are inadequate to supply the necessary cost of living to any such women workers to maintain them in good health and to protect their morals. . . ," *held* to interfere with freedom of contract under the Fifth Amendment.

Adkins v. Children's Hospital, 261 U.S. 525 (1923), overruled in *West Coast Hotel Co. v. Parrish,* 300 U.S. 379 (1937).

48. ACT OF FEBRUARY 24, 1919 (40 STAT. 1065, § 213, IN PART).

That part of § 213 of the Revenue Act of 1919 which provided that ". . . for the purposes of the title . . . the term 'gross income' . . . in-cludes gains, profits, and income derived from salaries, wages, or compensation for personal service (including in the case of . . . judges of the Supreme and inferior courts of the United States . . . the com-pensation received as such) . . ." as applied to a judge in office when the act was passed, *held* a violation of the guaranty of judges' salaries, in Article III, § 1.

Evans v. Gore, 253 U.S. 245 (1920).

Miles v. Graham, 268 U.S. 501 (1925), held it invalid as applied to a judge taking office subsequent to the date of the act. Both cases were overruled by *O'Malley v. Woodrough,* 307 U.S. 277 (1939).

49. ACT OF FEBRUARY 24, 1919 (40 STAT. 1097, § 402(C)).

That part of the estate tax law providing that "gross estate" of a decedent should include value of all property "to the extent of any in-terest therein of which the decedent has at any time made a transfer or with respect to which he had at any time created a trust, in con-templation of or intended to take effect in possession or enjoyment at or after his death (whether such transfer or trust is made or created before or after the passage of this act), except in case of a *bona fide* sale . . ." as applied to a transfer of property made prior to the act and intended to take effect "in possession or enjoyment" at death of grantor, but not in fact testamentary or designed to evade taxation, *held* confiscatory, contrary to Fifth Amendment.

Nicholds v. Coolidge, 274 U.S. 531 (1927).

50. ACT OF FEBRUARY 24, 1919, TITLE XII (40 STAT. 1138, ENTIRE TITLE).

The Child Labor Tax Act, providing that "every person . . . operating . . . any . . . factory . . . in which children under the age of 14 years have been employed or permitted to work . . . shall pay . . . in addition to all other taxes imposed by law, an excise tax equivalent to 10 percent of the entire net profits received . . . for such year from the sale . . . of the product of such . . . factory. . . ," *held* beyond the taxing power under Article I, § 8, clause 1, and an infringement of state authority.

Bailey v. Drexel Furniture Co. (Child Labor Tax Case), 259 U.S. 20 (1922).

51. ACT OF OCTOBER 22, 1919 (41 STAT. 298, § 2), AMENDING ACT OF AUGUST 10, 1917 (40 STAT. 277, § 4).

(a) § 4 of the Lever Act, providing in part "that it is hereby made unlawful for any persons willfully . . . to make any unjust or unreasonable rate or charge in handling or dealing in or with any necessaries . . ." and fixing a penalty, *held* invalid to support an indictment for charging an unreasonable price on sale—as not setting up an ascertainable standard of guilt within the requirement of the Sixth Amendment.

United States v. L. Cohen Grocery Co., 255 U.S. 81 (1921).

(b) That provision of § 4 making it unlawful "to conspire, combine, agree, or arrange with any other person to . . . exact excessive prices for any necessaries" and fixing a penalty, *held* invalid to support an indictment, on the reasoning of the *Cohen Grocery* case.

Weeds, Inc. v. United States, 255 U.S. 109 (1921).

52. ACT OF AUGUST 24, 1921 (42 STAT. 187, FUTURES TRADING ACT).

(a) § 4 (and interwoven regulations) providing a "tax of 20 cents a bushel on every bushel involved therein, upon each contract of sale of grain for future delivery, except . . . where such contracts are made by or through a member of a board of trade which has been designated by the Secretary of Agriculture as a 'contract market'. . . ," *held* not within the taxing power under Article I, § 8.

Hill v. Wallace, 259 U.S. 44 (1922).

(b) § 3, providing "That in addition to the taxes now imposed by law there is hereby levied a tax amounting to 20 cents per bushel on each bushel involved therein, whether the actual commodity is intended to be delivered or only nominally referred to, upon each . . . option for a contract either of purchase or sale of grain. . . ," *held* invalid on the same reasoning.

Trusler v. Crooks, 269 U.S. 475 (1926).

53. ACT OF NOVEMBER 23, 1921 (42 STAT. 261, § 245, IN PART).

Provision of Revenue Act of 1921 abating the deduction (4 percent of mean reserves) allowed from taxable income of life insurance companies in general by the amount of interest on their tax-exempts, and so according no relative advantage to the owners of the tax-exempt securities, *held* to destroy a guaranteed exemption.

National Life Ins. v. United States, 277 U.S. 508 (1928).

54. ACT OF JUNE 10, 1922 (42 STAT. 634).

A second attempt to amend §§ 24 and 256 of the Judicial Code, relating to jurisdiction of district courts, by saving "to claimants for compensation for injuries to or death of persons other than the master or members of the crew of a vessel, their rights and remedies under the workmen's compensation law of any State . . ." *held* invalid on authority of *Knickerbocker Ice Co. v. Stewart.*

Washington v. Dawson & Co., 264 U.S. 219 (1924).

55. ACT OF JUNE 2, 1924 (43 STAT. 313).

The gift tax provisions of the Revenue Act of 1924, applicable to gifts made during the calendar year, were *held* invalid under the Fifth Amendment insofar as they applied to gifts made before passage of the act.

Untermeyer v. Anderson, 276 U.S. 440 (1928).

56. ACT OF FEBRUARY 26, 1926 (44 STAT. 70, § 302, IN PART).

Stipulation creating a conclusive presumption that gifts made within two years prior to the death of the donor were made in contemplation of death of donor and requiring the value thereof to be included in computing the death transfer tax on decedent's estate was *held* to effect an invalid deprivation of property without due process.

Heiner v. Donnan, 285 U.S. 312 (1932).

57. ACT OF FEBRUARY 26, 1926 (44 STAT. 95, § 701).

Provision imposing a special excise tax of $1,000 on liquor dealers operating in States where such business is illegal, was *held* a penalty, without constitutional support following repeal of the Eighteenth Amendment.

United States v. Constantine, 296 U.S. 287 (1935).

58. ACT OF MARCH 20, 1933 (48 STAT. 11, § 17, IN PART).

Clause in the Economy Act of 1933 providing ". . . all laws granting or pertaining to yearly renewable term war risk insurance are hereby repealed," *held* invalid to abrogate an outstanding contract of insurance, which is a vested right protected by the Fifth Amendment.

Lynch v. United States, 292 U.S. 571 (1934).

59. ACT OF MAY 12, 1933 (48 STAT. 31).

Agricultural Adjustment Act providing for processing taxes on agricultural commodities and benefit payments therefor to farmers, *held* not within the taxing power under Article I, § 8, clause 1.

United States v. Butler, 297 U.S. 1 (1936).

60. ACT OF JOINT RESOLUTION OF JUNE 5, 1933 (48 STAT. 113, § 1).

Abrogation of gold clause in Government obligations, *held* a repudiation of the pledge implicit in the power to borrow money (Article 1, § 8, clause 2), and within the prohibition of the Fourteenth

Amendment, against questioning the validity of the public debt. (The majority of the Court, however, held plaintiff not entitled to recover under the circumstances.)

Perry v. United States, 294 U.S. 330 (1935).

61. ACT OF JUNE 16, 1933 (48 STAT. 195, THE NATIONAL INDUSTRIAL RECOVERY ACT).

(a) Title I, except § 9.

Provisions relating to codes of fair competition, authorized to be approved by the President in his discretion "to effectuate the policy" of the act, *held* invalid as a delegation of legislative power (Article I, § 1) and not within the commerce power (Article I, § 8, clause 3).

Schechter Poultry Corp. v. United States, 295 U.S. 495 (1935).

(b) § 9(c).

Clause of the oil regulation section authorizing the President "to prohibit the transportation in interstate . . . commerce of petroleum . . . produced or withdrawn from storage in excess of the amount permitted . . . by any State law . . ." and prescribing a penalty for violation of orders issued thereunder, *held* invalid as a delegation of legislative power.

Panama Refining Co. v. Ryan, 293 U.S. 388 (1935).

62. ACT OF JUNE 16, 1933 (48 STAT. 307, § 13).

Temporary reduction of 15 percent in retired pay of judges, retired from service but subject to performance of judicial duties under the Act of March 1, 1929 (45 Stat. 1422), was *held* a violation of the guaranty of judges' salaries in Article III, § 1.

Booth v. United States, 291 U.S. 339 (1934).

63. ACT OF APRIL 27, 1934 (48 STAT. 646, § 6) AMENDING § 5(I) OF HOME OWNERS LOAN ACT OF 1933.

Provision for conversion of state building and loan associations into federal associations, upon vote of 51 percent of the votes cast at a meeting of stockholders called to consider such action, *held* an encroachment on reserved powers of State.

Hopkins Savings Assn. v. Cleary, 296 U.S. 315 (1935).

64. ACT OF MAY 24, 1934 (48 STAT. 798).

Provision for readjustment of municipal indebtedness, though "adequately related" to the bankruptcy power, was *held* invalid as an interference with state sovereignty.

Ashton v. Cameron County Dist., 298 U.S. 513 (1936).

65. ACT OF JUNE 27, 1934 (48 STAT. 1283).

The Railroad Retirement Act, establishing a detailed compulsory retirement system for employees of carriers subject to the Interstate Commerce Act, *held* not a regulation of commerce within the meaning of Article I, § 8, clause 3, and violative of the due process clause (Fifth Amendment).

Railroad Retirement Board v. Alton R. Co., 295 U.S. 330 (1935).

66. ACT OF JUNE 28, 1934 (48 STAT. 1289, CH. 869).

The Frazier-Lemke Act, adding subsection (5) to § 75 of the Bankruptcy Act, designed to preserve to mortgagors the ownership and enjoyment of their farm property and providing specifically, in paragraph 7, that a bankrupt left in possession has the option at any time

within 5 years of buying at the appraised value—subject meanwhile to no monetary obligation other than payment of reasonable rental, *held* a violation of property rights, under the Fifth Amendment.

Louisville Bank v. Radford, 295 U.S. 555 (1935).

67. ACT OF AUGUST 24, 1935 (49 STAT. 750).

Amendments of Agricultural Adjustment Act *held* not within the taxing power.

Rickert Rice Mills v. Fontenot, 297 U.S. 110 (1936).

68. ACT OF AUGUST 29, 1935 (CH. 814 § 5(E), 49 STAT. 982, 27 U.S.C. § 205(E)).

The prohibition in section 5(e)(2) of the Federal Alcohol Administration Act of 1935 on the display of alcohol content on beer labels is inconsistent with the protections afforded to commercial speech by the First Amendment. The government's interest in curbing strength wars among brewers is substantial, but, given the "overall irrationality" of the regulatory scheme, the labeling prohibition does not directly and materially advance that interest.

Rubin v. Coors Brewing Co., 115 S. Ct. 1585 (1995).

69. ACT OF AUGUST 30, 1935 (49 STAT. 991).

Bituminous Coal Conservation Act of 1935, *held* to impose, not a tax within Article I, § 8, but a penalty not sustained by the commerce clause (Article I, § 8, clause 3).

Carter v. Carter Coal Co., 298 U.S. 238 (1936).

70. ACT OF FEBRUARY 15, 1938 (CH. 29, 52 STAT. 30).

District of Columbia Code § 22-1115, prohibiting the display of any sign within 500 feet of a foreign embassy if the sign tends to bring the foreign government into "public odium" or "public disrepute," violates the First Amendment.

Boos v. Barry, 312, (1988).

71. ACT OF JUNE 25, 1938 (52 STAT. 1040).

Federal Food, Drug, and Cosmetic Act of 1938, § 301(f), prohibiting the refusal to permit entry or inspection of premises by federal officers *held* void for vagueness and as violative of the due process clause of the Fifth Amendment.

United States v. Cardiff, 344 U.S. 174 (1952).

72. ACT OF JUNE 30, 1938 (52 STAT. 1251).

Federal Firearms Act, § 2(f), establishing a presumption of guilt based on a prior conviction and present possession of a firearm, *held* to violate the test of due process under the Fifth Amendment.

Tot v. United States, 319 U.S. 463 (1943).

73. ACT OF AUGUST 10, 1939 (§ 201(D), 53 STAT. 1362, AS AMENDED, 42 U.S.C. § 402(G)).

Provision of Social Security Act that grants survivors' benefits based on the earnings of a deceased husband and father covered by the Act to his widow and to the couple's children in her care but that grants benefits based on the earnings of a covered deceased wife and mother only to the minor children and not to the widower *held* violative of the right to equal protection secured by the Fifth Amendment's due process clause, since it unjustifiably discriminates against female wage earners required to pay social security taxes by affording them less protection for their survivors than is provided for male wage earners.

Weinberger v. Wiesenfeld, 420 U.S. 636 (1975).

74. ACT OF OCTOBER 14, 1940 (54 STAT. 1169, § 401(G)); AS AMENDED BY ACT OF JANUARY 20, 1944 (58 STAT. 4, § 1).

Provision of Aliens and Nationality Code (8 U.S.C. § 1481(a) (8)), derived from the Nationality Act of 1940, as amended, that citizenship shall be lost upon conviction by court martial and dishonorable discharge for deserting the armed services in time of war, *held* invalid as imposing a cruel and unusual punishment barred by the Eighth Amendment and not authorized by the war powers conferred by Article I, § 8, clauses 11 to 14.

Trop v. Dulles, 356 U.S. 86 (1958).

75. ACT OF NOVEMBER 15, 1943 (57 STAT. 450).

Urgent Deficiency Appropriation Act of 1943, § 304, providing that no salary should be paid to certain named federal employees out of moneys appropriated, *held* to violate Article I, § 9, clause 3, forbidding enactment of bill of attainder or *ex post facto* law.

United States v. Lovett, 328 U.S. 303 (1946).

76. ACT OF SEPTEMBER 27, 1944 (58 STAT. 746, § 401(J)); AND ACT OF JUNE 27, 1952 (66 STAT. 163, 267–268, § 349(A)(10)).

§ 401(J) of Immigration and Nationality Act of 1940, added in 1944, and § 49(a)(10) of the Immigration and Nationality Act of 1952 depriving one of citizenship, without the procedural safeguards guaranteed by the Fifth and Sixth Amendments, for the offense of leaving or remaining outside the country, in time of war or national emergency, to evade military service *held* invalid.

Kennedy v. Mendoza-Martinez, 372 U.S. 144 (1963).

77. ACT OF JULY 31, 1946 (CH. 707, § 7, 60 STAT. 719).

District court decision *holding* invalid under First and Fifth Amendments statute prohibiting parades or assemblages on United States Capitol grounds is summarily affirmed.

Chief of Capitol Police v. Jeannette Rankin Brigade, 409 U.S. 972 (1972).

78. ACT OF JUNE 25, 1948 (62 STAT. 760).

Provision of Lindbergh Kidnapping Act which provided for the imposition of the death penalty only if recommended by the jury *held* unconstitutional inasmuch as it penalized the assertion of a defendant's Sixth Amendment right to jury trial.

United States v. Jackson, 390 U.S. 570 (1968).

79. ACT OF AUGUST 18, 1949 (63 STAT. 617, 40 U.S.C. § 13K)

Provision, insofar as it applies to the public sidewalks surrounding the Supreme Court building, which bars the display of any flag, banner, or device designed to bring into public notice any party, organization, or movement *held* violative of the free speech clause of the First Amendment.

United States v. Grace, 461 U.S. 171 (1983)

80. ACT OF MAY 5, 1950 (64 STAT. 107).

Article 3(a) of the Uniform Code of Military Justice subjecting civilian ex-servicemen to court martial for crime committed while in military service *held* to violate Article III, § 2, and the Fifth and Sixth Amendments.

Toth v. Quarles, 350 U.S. 11 (1955).

81. ACT OF MAY 5, 1950 (64 STAT. 107).

Insofar as Article 2(11) of the Uniform Code of Military Justice subjects civilian dependents accompanying members of the armed forces overseas in time of peace to trial, in capital cases, by court martial, it is violative of Article III, § 2, and the Fifth and Sixth Amendments.

Reid v. Covert, 354 U.S. 1 (1957).

Insofar as the aforementioned provision is invoked in time of peace for the trial of noncapital offenses committed on land bases overseas by employees of the armed forces who have not been inducted or who have not voluntarily enlisted therein, it is violative of the Sixth Amendment.

McElroy v. United States, 361 U.S. 281 (1960).

Insofar as the aforementioned provision is invoked in time of peace for the trial of noncapital offenses committed by civilian dependents accompanying members of the armed forces overseas, it is violative of Article III, § 2, and the Fifth and Sixth Amendments.

Kinsella v. United States, 361 U.S. 234 (1960).

Insofar as the aforementioned provision is invoked in time of peace for the trial of a capital offense committed by a civilian employee of the armed forces overseas, it is violative of Article III, § 2, and the Fifth and Sixth Amendments.

Grisham v. Hagan, 361 U.S. 278 (1960).

82. ACT OF AUGUST 16, 1950 (64 STAT. 451, AS AMENDED).

Statutory scheme authorizing the Postmaster General to close the mails to distributors of obscene materials *held* unconstitutional in the absence of procedural provisions which would assure prompt judicial determination that protected materials were not being restrained.

Blount v. Rizzi, 400 U.S. 410 (1971).

83. ACT OF AUGUST 28, 1950 (§ 202(C)(1)(D), 64 STAT. 483, 42 U.S.C. § 402(C)(1)(C)).

District court decision *holding* invalid as a violation of the equal protection component of the Fifth Amendment's due process clause a Social Security provision entitling a husband to insurance benefits through his wife's benefits, provided he received at least one-half of his support from her at the time she became entitled, but requiring no such showing of support for the wife to qualify for benefits through her husband, is summarily affirmed.

Califano v. Silbowitz, 430 U.S. 934 (1977).

84. ACT OF AUGUST 28, 1950 § 202(F)(1)(E), 64 STAT. 485, 42 U.S.C. § 402(F)(1)(D)).

Social Security Act provision awarding survivors' benefits based on earnings of a deceased wife to widower only if he was receiving at least half of his support from her at the time of her death, whereas widow receives benefits regardless of dependency, *held* violative of equal protection element of Fifth Amendment's due process clause because of its impermissible gender classification.

Califano v. Goldfarb, 430 U.S. 199 (1977).

85. ACT OF SEPTEMBER 23, 1950 (TITLE 1, § 5, 64 STAT. 992).

Provision of Subversive Activities Control Act making it unlawful for member of Communist front organization to work in a defense plant *held* to be an overbroad infringement of the right of association protected by the First Amendment.

United States v. Robel, 389 U.S. 258 (1967).

86. ACT OF SEPTEMBER 23, 1950 (64 STAT. 993, § 6).

Subversive Activities Control Act of 1950, § 6, providing that any member of a Communist organization, which has registered or has been ordered to register, commits a crime if he attempts to obtain or use a passport, *held* violative of due process under the Fifth Amendment.

Aptheker v. Secretary of State, 378 U.S. 500 (1964).

87. ACT OF SEPTEMBER 28, 1950 (TITLE I, §§ 7, 8, 64 STAT. 993).

Provisions of Subversive Activities Control Act of 1950 requiring in lieu of registration by the Communist Party registration by Party members may not be applied to compel registration or to prosecute for refusal to register of alleged members who have asserted their privilege against self-incrimination inasmuch as registration would expose such persons to criminal prosecution under other laws.

Albertson v. Subversive Activities Control Board, 382 U.S. 70 (1965).

88. ACT OF OCTOBER 30, 1951 (§ 5(F)(II), 65 STAT. 683, 45 U.S.C. § 231A(C)(3)(II)).

Provision of Railroad Retirement Act similar to section voided in *Goldfarb.* (ns. 81).

Railroad Retirement Bd. v. Kalina, 431 U.S. 909 (1977).

89. ACT OF JUNE 27, 1952 (CH. 477, § 244(E)(2), 66 STAT. 214, 8 U.S.C. § 1254 (C)(2)).

Provision of the immigration law that permits either House of Congress to veto the decision of the Attorney General to suspend the deportation of certain aliens violates the bicameralism and presentation requirements of lawmaking imposed upon Congress by Article I, §§ 1 and 7.

INS v. Chadha, 462 U.S. 919 (1983).

90. ACT OF JUNE 27, 1952 (TITLE III, § 349, 66 STAT. 267).

Provision of Immigration and Nationality Act of 1952 providing for revocation of United States citizenship of one who votes in a foreign election *held* unconstitutional under § 1 of the Fourteenth Amendment.

Afroyim v. Rusk, 387 U.S. 253 (1967).

91. ACT OF JUNE 27, 1952 (66 STAT. 163, 269, § 352(A)(1)).

§ 352(a)(1) of the Immigration and Nationality Act of 1952 depriving a naturalized person of citizenship for "having a continuous residence for three years" in state of his birth or prior nationality *held* violative of the due process clause of the Fifth Amendment.

Schneider v. Rusk, 377 U.S. 163 (1964).

92. ACT OF AUG. 16, 1954 (CH. 736, 68A STAT. 521, 26 U.S.C. § 4371(1)).

A federal tax on insurance premiums paid to foreign insurers not subject to the federal income tax violates the Export Clause, Art. I, § 9, cl. 5, as applied to casualty insurance for losses incurred during the shipment of goods from locations within the United States to purchasers abroad.

United States v. IBM Corp., 116 S. Ct. 1793 (1996).

93. ACT OF AUGUST 16, 1954 (68A STAT. 525, INT. REV. CODE OF 1954, §§ 4401-4423).

Provisions of tax laws requiring gamblers to pay occupational and excise taxes may not be used over an assertion of one's privilege against self-incrimination either to compel extensive reporting of activities, leaving the registrant subject to prosecution under the laws of all the States with the possible exception of Nevada, or to prosecute for failure to register and report, because the scheme abridged the Fifth Amendment privilege.

Marchetti v. United States, 390 U.S. 39 (1968), and *Grosso v. United States,* 390 U.S. 62 (1968).

94. ACT OF AUGUST 16, 1954 (68A STAT. 560, MARIJUANA TAX ACT, §§ 4741, 4744, 4751, 4753).

Provisions of tax laws requiring possessors of marijuana to register and to pay a transfer tax may not be used over an assertion of the privilege against self-incrimination to compel registration or to prosecute for failure to register.

Leary v. United States, 395 U.S. 6 (1969).

95. ACT OF AUGUST 16, 1954 (68A STAT. 728, INT. REV. CODE OF 1954, §§ 5841, 5851).

Provisions of tax laws requiring the possessor of certain firearms, which it is made illegal to receive or to possess, to register with the Treasury Department may not be used over an assertion of the privilege against self-incrimination to prosecute one for failure to register or for possession of an unregistered firearm since the statutory scheme abridges the Fifth Amendment privilege.

Haynes v. United States, 390 U.S. 85 (1968).

96. ACT OF AUGUST 16, 1954 (68A STAT. 867, INT. REV. CODE OF 1954, § 7302).

Provision of tax laws providing for forfeiture of property used in violating internal revenue laws may not be constitutionally used in face of invocation of privilege against self-incrimination to condemn money in possession of gambler who had failed to comply with the registration and reporting scheme held void in *Marchetti v. United States,* 390 U.S. 39 (1968).

United States v. United States Coin & Currency, 401 U.S. 715 (1971).

97. ACT OF JULY 18, 1956 (§ 106, STAT. 570).

Provision of Narcotic Drugs Import and Export Act creating a presumption that possessor of marijuana knew of its illegal importation into the United States *held*, in absence of showing that all marijuana in United States was of foreign origin and that domestic users could know that their marijuana was more likely than not of foreign origin, unconstitutional under the due process clause of the Fifth Amendment.

Leary v. United States, 395 U.S. 6 (1969).

98. ACT OF AUGUST 10, 1956 (70A STAT. 35, § 772(F)).

Proviso of statute permitting the wearing of United States military apparel in theatrical productions only if the portrayal does not tend to discredit the armed force imposes an unconstitutional restraint upon First Amendment freedoms and precludes a prosecution under 18 U.S.C. § 702 for unauthorized wearing of uniform in a street skit disrespectful of the military.

Schacht v. United States, 398 U.S. 58 (1970).

99. ACT OF AUGUST 10, 1956 (70A STAT. 65, UNIFORM CODE OF MILITARY JUSTICE, ARTICLES 80, 130, 134).

Servicemen may not be charged under the Act and tried in military courts because of the commission of non-service connected crimes committed off-post and off-duty which are subject to civilian court jurisdiction where the guarantees of the Bill of Rights are applicable.

O'Callahan v. Parker, 395 U.S. 258 (1969).

100. ACT OF SEPTEMBER 2, 1958 (§ 5601(B)(1), 72 STAT. 1399).

Provision of Internal Revenue Code creating a presumption that one's presence at the site of an unregistered still shall be sufficient for conviction under a statute punishing possession, custody, or control of an unregistered still unless defendant otherwise explained his presence at the site to the jury *held* unconstitutional because the presumption is not a legitimate, rational, or reasonable inference that defendant was engaged in one of the specialized functions proscribed by the statute.

United States v. Romano, 382 U.S. 136 (1965).

101. ACT OF SEPTEMBER 2, 1958 (§ 1(25)(B), 72 STAT. 1446), AND ACT OF SEPTEMBER 7, 1962 (§ 401, 76 STAT. 469).

Federal statutes providing that spouses of female members of the Armed Forces must be dependent in fact in order to qualify for certain dependent's benefits, whereas spouses of male members are statutorily deemed dependent and automatically qualified for allowances, whatever their actual status, *held* an invalid sex classification under the equal protection principles of the Fifth Amendment's due process clause.

Frontiero v. Richardson, 411 U.S. 677 (1973).

102. ACT OF SEPTEMBER 2, 1958 (PUB. L. 85-921, § 1, 72 STAT. 1771, 18 U.S.C. § 504(1)).

Exemptions from ban on photographic reproduction of currency "for philatelic, numismatic, educational, historical, or newsworthy purposes" violates the First Amendment because it discriminates on the basis of the content of a publication.

Regan v. Time, Inc., 468 U.S. 641 (1984).

103. ACT OF SEPTEMBER 14, 1959 (§ 504, 73 STAT. 536).

Provision of Labor-Management Reporting and Disclosure Act of 1959 making it a crime for a member of the Communist Party to serve as an officer or, with the exception of clerical or custodial positions, as an employee of a labor union *held* to be a bill of attainder and unconstitutional.

United States v. Brown, 381 U.S. 437 (1965).

104. ACT OF OCTOBER 11, 1962 (§ 305, 76 STAT. 840).

Provision of Postal Services and Federal Employees Salary Act of 1962 authorizing Post Office Department to detain material determined to be "communist political propaganda" and to forward it to the addressee only if he requested it after notification by the Department, the material to be destroyed otherwise, *held* to impose on the addressee an affirmative obligation which amounted to an abridgment of First Amendment rights.

Lamont v. Postmaster General, 381 U.S. 301 (1965).

105. ACT OF OCTOBER 15, 1962 (76 STAT. 914).

Provision of District of Columbia laws requiring that a person to be eligible to receive welfare assistance must have resided in the District for at least one year impermissibly classified persons on the basis of an assertion of the right to travel interstate and therefore *held* to violate the due process clause of the Fifth Amendment.

Shapiro v. Thompson, 394 U.S. 618 (1969).

106. ACT OF DECEMBER 16, 1963 (77 STAT. 378, 20 U.S.C. § 754).

Provision of Higher Education Facilities Act of 1963 which in effect removed restriction against religious use of facilities constructed with federal funds after 20 years *held* to violate the establishment clause of the First Amendment inasmuch as the property will still be of considerable value at the end of the period and removal of the restriction would constitute a substantial governmental contribution to religion.

Tilton v. Richardson, 403 U.S. 672 (1971).

107. ACT OF JULY 30, 1965 (§ 339, 79 STAT. 409).

Section of Social Security Act qualifying certain illegitimate children for disability insurance benefits by presuming dependence but disqualifying other illegitimate children, regardless of dependency, if the disabled wage earner parent did not contribute to the child's support before the onset of the disability or if the child did not live with the parent before the onset of disability held to deny latter class of children equal protection as guaranteed by the due process clause of the Fifth Amendment.

Jimenez v. Weinberger, 417 U.S. 628 (1974).

108. ACT OF SEPTEMBER 3, 1966 (§ 102(B), 80 STAT. 831), AND ACT OF APRIL 8, 1974 (§§ 6(A)(1) AMENDING § 3(D) OF ACT, 6(A)(2) AMENDING § 3(E)(2)(C), 6(A)(5) AMENDING § 3(S)(5), AND 6(A)(6) AMENDING § 3(X)).

Those sections of the Fair Labor Standards Act extending wage and hour coverage to the employees of state and local governments *held* invalid because Congress lacks the authority under the commerce clause to regulate employee activities in areas of traditional governmental functions of the States.

National League of Cities v. Usery, 426 U.S. 833 (1976).

109. ACT OF NOVEMBER 7, 1967 (PUB. L. 90-129, § 201(8), 81 STAT. 368), AS AMENDED BY ACT OF AUGUST 13, 1981 (PUB. L. 97-35, § 1229, 95 STAT. 730, 47 U.S.C. § 399).

Communications Act provision banning noncommercial educational stations receiving grants from the Corporation for Public Broadcasting from engaging in editorializing violates the First Amendment.

FCC v. League of Women Voters, 468 U.S. 364 (1984).

110. ACT OF JANUARY 2, 1968 (§ 163(A)(2), 81 STAT. 872).

District court decisions *holding* unconstitutional under Fifth Amendment's due process clause section of Social Security Act that reduced, perhaps to zero, benefits coming to illegitimate children upon death of parent in order to satisfy the maximum payment due the wife and legitimate children are summarily affirmed.

Richardson v. Davis, 409 U.S. 1069 (1972).

111. ACT OF JANUARY 2, 1968 (§ 203, 81 STAT. 882).

Provision of Social Security Act extending benefits to families whose dependent children have been deprived of parental support because of the unemployment of the father but not giving benefits when the mother becomes unemployed *held* to impermissibly classify on the basis of sex and violate the Fifth Amendment's due process clause.

Califano v. Westcott, 443 U.S. 76 (1979).

112. ACT OF JUNE 22, 1970 (CH. III, 84 STAT. 318).

Provision of Voting Rights Act Amendments of 1970 which set a minimum voting age qualification of 18 in state and local elections *held* to be unconstitutional because beyond the powers of Congress to legislate.

Oregon v. Mitchell, 400 U.S. 112 (1970).

113. ACT OF DECEMBER 29, 1970 (§ 8(A), 84 STAT. 1598, 29 U.S.C. § 637 (A)).

Provision of Occupational Safety and Health Act authorizing inspections of covered work places in industry without warrants *held* to violate Fourth Amendment.

Marshall v. Barlow's, Inc., 436 U.S. 307 (1978).

114. ACT OF JANUARY 11, 1971 (§ 2, 84 STAT. 2048).

Provision of Food Stamp Act disqualifying from participation in program any household containing an individual unrelated by birth, marriage, or adoption to any other member of the household violates the due process clause of the Fifth Amendment.

Department of Agriculture v. Moreno, 413 U.S. 528 (1973).

115. ACT OF JANUARY 11, 1971 (§ 4, 84 STAT. 2049).

Provision of Food Stamp Act disqualifying from participation in program any household containing a person 18 years or older who had been claimed as a dependent child for income tax purposes in the present or preceding tax year by a taxpayer not a member of the household violates the due process clause of the Fifth Amendment.

Dept. of Agriculture v. Murry, 413 U.S. 508 (1973).

116. ACT OF DECEMBER 10, 1971 (PUB. L. 92-178, § 801, 85 STAT. 570, 26 U.S.C. § 9012(F)).

Provision of Presidential Election Campaign Fund Act limiting to $1,000 the amount that independent committees may expend to further the election of a presidential candidate financing his campaign with public funds is an impermissible limitation of freedom of speech and association protected by the First Amendment.

FEC v. National Conservative Political Action Comm., 470 U.S. 480 (1985).

117. FEDERAL ELECTION CAMPAIGN ACT OF FEBRUARY 7, 1972 (86 STAT. 3), AS AMENDED BY THE FEDERAL CAMPAIGN ACT AMENDMENTS OF 1974 (88 STAT. 1263), ADDING OR AMENDING 18 U.S.C. §§ 608(A), 608(E), AND 2 U.S.C. § 437(C).

Provisions of election law that forbid a candidate or the members of his immediate family from expending personal funds in excess of specified amounts, that limit to $1,000 the independent expenditures of any person relative to an identified candidate, and that forbid expenditures by candidates for federal office in excess of specified amounts violate the First Amendment speech guarantees; provisions of the law creating a commission to oversee enforcement of the Act are an invalid infringement of constitutional separation of powers in that they devolve responsibilities upon a commission four of whose six members are appointed by Congress and all six of whom are confirmed by the House of Representatives as well as by the Senate, not in compliance with the appointments clause.

Buckley v. Valeo, 424 U.S. 1 (1976).

118. ACT OF MAY 11, 1976 (PUB. L. 92-225, § 316, 90 STAT. 490, 2 U.S.C. § 441)(B)).

Provision of Federal Election Campaign Act requiring that independent corporate campaign expenditures be financed by voluntary contributions to a separate segregated fund violates the First Amendment as applied to a corporation organized to promote political ideas, having no stockholders, and not serving as a front for a business corporation or union.

FEC v. Massachusetts Citizens for Life, Inc., 479 U.S. 238 (1986).

119. ACT OF MAY 11, 1976 (PUB. L. 94-283, § 112(2), 90 STAT. 489, 2 U.S.C. § 441A(D)(3)).

The Party Expenditure Provision of the Federal Election Campaign Act, which limits expenditures by a political party "in connection with the general election campaign of a [congressional] candidate," violates the First Amendment when applied to expenditures that a political party makes independently, without coordination with the candidate.

Colo. Repub. Campaign Comm. v. FEC, 116 S. Ct. ___, 64 USLW 4663 (1996).

120. ACT OF OCTOBER 1, 1976 (TITLE II, 90 STAT. 1446); ACT OF OCTOBER 12, 1979 (101(C), 93 STAT. 657).

Provisions of appropriations laws rolling back automatic pay increases for federal officers and employees is unconstitutional as to Article III judges because, the increases having gone into effect, they violate the security of compensation clause of Article III, § 1.

United States v. Will, 449 U.S. 200 (1980).

121. ACT OF NOVEMBER 6, 1978 (§ 241(A), 92 STAT. 2668, 28 U.S.C. § 1471)

Assignment to judges who do not have tenure and guarantee of compensation protections afforded Article III judges of jurisdiction over all proceedings arising under or in the bankruptcy act and over all cases relating to proceedings under the bankruptcy act is invalid, inasmuch as judges without Article III protection may not receive at least some of this jurisdiction.

Northern Pipeline Const. Co. v. Marathon Pipe Line Co., 458 U.S. 50 (1982).

122. ACT OF NOVEMBER 9, 1978 (PUB. L. 95-621, § 202(C)(1), 92 STAT. 3372, 15 U.S.C. § 3342(C)(1)).

Decision of Court of Appeals holding unconstitutional provision giving either House of Congress power to veto rules of Federal Energy Regulatory Commission on certain natural gas pricing matters is summarily affirmed on the authority of *Chadha.*

Process Gas Consumers Group v. Consumer Energy Council, 463 U.S. 1216 (1983).

123. ACT OF MAY 30, 1980 (94 STAT. 399, 45 U.S.C. § 1001 ET. SEQ.) AS AMENDED BY THE ACT OF OCTOBER 14, 1980 (94 STAT. 1959).

Acts of Congress applying to bankruptcy reorganization of one railroad and guaranteeing employee benefits is repugnant to the requirement of Article I, § 8, cl. 4, that bankruptcy legislation be "uniform."

Railway Labor Executives' Assn. v. Gibbons, 455 U.S. 457 (1982).

124. ACT OF MAY 28, 1980 (PUB. L. 96-252, § 21(A), 94 STAT. 393, 15 U.S.C. § 57A-1(A)).

Decision of Court of Appeals holding unconstitutional provision of FTC Improvements Act giving Congress power by concurrent resolution to veto final rules of the FTC is summarily affirmed on the basis of *Chadha.*

United States Senate v. FTC, 463 U.S. 1216 (1983).

125. ACT OF JANUARY 12, 1983 (PUB. L. 97-459, § 207, 96 STAT. 2519, 25 U.S.C. § 2206).

Section of Indian Land Consolidation Act providing for escheat to tribe of fractionated interests in land representing less than 2% of a tract's total acreage violates the Fifth Amendment's takings clause by completely abrogating rights of intestacy and devise.

Hodel v. Irving, 481 U.S. 704, 107 S. Ct. 2076, 95 L.Ed.2d 668 (1987).

126. ACT OF JAN. 15, 1985 (PUB. L. 99-240, § 5(D)(2)(C), 99 STAT. 1842, 42 U.S.C. § 2021E(D)(2)(C)).

"Take-title" incentives contained in the Low-Level Radioactive Waste Policy Amendments Act of 1985, designed to encourage states to cooperate in the federal regulatory scheme, offend principles of federalism embodied in the Tenth Amendment. These incentives, which require that non-participating states take title to waste or become liable for generators' damages, cross the line distinguishing encouragement from coercion. Congress may not simply commandeer the legislative and regulatory processes of the states, nor may it force a transfer from generators to state governments. A required choice between two unconstitutionally coercive regulatory techniques is also impermissible.

New York v. United States, 112 S. Ct. 2408 (1992).

127. ACT OF DECEMBER 12, 1985 (PUB. L. 99-177, § 251, 99 STAT. 1063, 2 U.S.C. § 901).

That portion of the Balanced Budget and Emergency Deficit Control Act which authorizes the Comptroller General to determine the amount of spending reductions which must be accomplished each year to reach congressional targets and which authorizes him to report a figure to the President which the President must implement violates the constitutional separation of powers inasmuch as the Comptroller General is subject to congressional control (removal) and cannot be given a role in the execution of the laws.

Bowsher v. Synar, 478 U.S. 714 (1986).

128. ACT OF OCT. 30, 1986 (PUB. L. 99-591, TITLE VI, § 6007(F), 100 STAT. 3341, 49 U.S.C. APP. § 2456(F)).

The Metropolitan Washington Airports Act of 1986, which transferred operating control of two Washington, D.C., area airports from the Federal Government to a regional airports authority, violates separation of powers principles by conditioning that transfer on the establishment of a Board of Review, composed of Members of Congress and having veto authority over actions of the airports authority's board of directors.

Metropolitan Washington Airports Auth. v. Citizens for the Abatement of Aircraft Noise, 501 U.S. 252 (1991).

129. ACT OF APRIL 28, 1988 (PUB. L. 100-297, § 6101, 102 STAT. 424, 47 U.S.C. § 223(B)).

Provision insofar as it bans indecent as well as obscene commercial interstate telephone messages violates the speech clause of the First Amendment.

Sable Communications v. FCC, 109 S. Ct. 2829 (1989).

130. ACT OF OCT. 17, 1988 (PUB. L. 100-497, § 11(D)(7), 102 STAT. 2472, 25 U.S.C. § 2710(D)(7)).

A provision of the Indian Gaming Regulatory Act authorizing an Indian tribe to sue a State in federal court to compel performance of a duty to negotiate in good faith toward the formation of a compact violates the Eleventh Amendment. In exercise of its powers under Article I, Congress may not abrogate States' Eleventh Amendment immunity from suit in federal court. *Pennsylvania v. Union Gas Co.,* 491 U.S. 1 (1989), is overruled.

Seminole Tribe of Florida v. Florida, 116 S. Ct. 1114 (1996).

131. ACT OF OCT. 28, 1989 (PUB. L. 101-131, 103 STAT. 777, 18 U.S.C. § 700).

The Flag Protection Act of 1989, criminalizing burning and certain other forms of destruction of the United States flag, violates the

First Amendment. Most of the prohibited acts involve disrespectful treatment of the flag, and evidence a purpose to suppress expression out of concern for its likely communicative impact.

United States v. Eichman, 496 U.S. 310 (1990).

132. ACT OF NOV. 30, 1989 (PUB. L. 101-194, § 601, 103 STAT. 1760, 5 U.S.C. APP. § 501).

Section 501(b) of the Ethics in Government Act, as amended in 1989 to prohibit Members of Congress and federal employees from accepting honoraria, violates the First Amendment as applied to Executive Branch employees below grade GS-16. The ban is limited to expressive activity and does not include other outside income, and the "speculative benefits" of the ban do not justify its "crudely crafted burden" on expression.

United States v. National Treasury Employees Union, 115 S. Ct. 1003 (1995).

133. ACT OF NOV. 29, 1990 (PUB. L. 101-647, § 1702, 104 STAT. 4844, 18 U.S.C. § 922Q).

The Gun Free School Zones Act of 1990, which makes it a criminal offense to knowingly possess a firearm within a school zone, exceeds congressional power under the Commerce Clause. It is "a criminal statute that by its terms has nothing to do with 'commerce' or any sort of economic enterprise." Possession of a gun at or near a school "is in no sense an economic activity that might, through repetition elsewhere, substantially affect any sort of interstate commerce."

United States v. Lopez, 115 S. Ct. 1624 (1995).

134. ACT OF DEC. 19, 1991 (PUB. L. 102-242 § 476, 105 STAT. 2387, 15 U.S.C. § 78AA-1).

Section 27A(b) of the Securities Exchange Act of 1934, as added in 1991, requiring reinstatement of any section 10(b) actions that were dismissed as time barred subsequent to a 1991 Supreme Court decision, violates the Constitution's separation of powers to the extent that it requires federal courts to reopen final judgments in private civil actions. The provision violates a fundamental principle of Article III that the federal judicial power comprehends the power to render dispositive judgments.

Plaut v. Spendthrift Farm, Inc., 115 S. Ct. 1447 (1995).

135. ACT OF OCT. 5, 1992 (PUB. L. 102-385, §§ 10(B) AND 10(C), 106 STAT. 1487, 1503; 47 U.S.C. § 532(J) AND § 531 NOTE, RESPECTIVELY).

Section 10(b) of the Cable Television Consumer Protection and Competition Act of 1992, which requires cable operators to segregate and block indecent programming on leased access channels if they do not prohibit it, violates the First Amendment. Section 10(c) of the Act, which permits a cable operator to prevent transmission of "sexually explicit" programming on public access channels, also violates the First Amendment.

Denver Area Educ. Tel. Consortium v. FCC, 116 S. Ct. ___, 64 USLW 4706 (1996).

SOURCES: Compiled from Library of Congress, *The Constitution of the United States of America; Analysis and Interpretation*, S. Doc., 103-6, 1992; Library of Congress, Congressional Research Service.

Chronology of Major Decisions of the Court, 1790–1996

Every Supreme Court decision begins with a dispute between two people. The interests they assert and defend may be personal, corporate, or official, but they all arise from a fundamental clash between two points of view.

Early on, the Court made clear that it would adhere to the language of the Constitution in Article III, Section 2, and refuse to rule on theoretical situations or hypothetical cases. It would only resolve actual "cases and controversies" in which there were real collisions of rights and powers. To decide a hypothetical case, said the justices, would be to exceed their constitutional function.

The individuals who bring their complaints before the justices are as diverse as the nation. William Marbury wished to secure his appointment as a justice of the peace. Dred Scott sought his freedom. Linda Brown wanted to attend her neighborhood school. Clarence Gideon believed he should have a lawyer to defend him in court. Richard Nixon wanted to keep his White House tapes confidential. The Court resolved their cases, as it has done each case of the thousands that have arrived before it, on the basis of their particular facts.

The immediate impact of each is simply to answer the claims of Marbury, Scott, Brown, Gideon, or Nixon, settling one particular situation. Many of the Court's rulings have no further effect. But often—as in these cases—the decision has a larger significance, upholding or striking down similar laws or practices or claims, establishing the Court's authority in new areas, or finding that some areas lie outside its competence.

To the Supreme Court, wrote Richard Kluger in the foreword to *Simple Justice,*

the nation has increasingly brought its most vexing social and political problems. They come in the guise of private disputes between only the litigating parties, but everybody understands that this is a legal fiction and merely a convenient political device. American society thus reduces its most troubling controversies to the scope—and translates them into the language—of a lawsuit.

Although the progress of cases to the Supreme Court is slow, the body of issues before the Court in a particular period does reflect public concerns. "Virtually all important decisions of the Supreme Court are the beginnings of conversations between the Court and the people and their representatives," Alexander M. Bickel wrote in *The Supreme Court and the Idea of Progress.*

Most major cases decided by the Court from 1790 until 1860 involved the balance between state and federal power. Questions of war powers and policies came to the Court during the Civil War; matters of civil rights and state powers questions followed during the era of Reconstruction. As the nation's economy flourished and grew, cases concerning the relationship of government and business became everyday matters at the Court. For the contemporary Court, questions of individual rights and liberties dominate its work.

Following are summary descriptions of the Supreme Court's major rulings from the first, *Chisholm v. Georgia* in 1793, through those issued in the summer of 1996. The summaries consist of a general subject heading, the case name, its citation, the vote by which it was decided, the date it was announced, the justice writing the major opinion, the dissenting justices, and a summary statement of the ruling. (In some early cases, the vote or the exact date of its announcement is unavailable.)

HOW TO READ A COURT CITATION

The official version of each Supreme Court decision and opinion is contained in a series of volumes entitled *United States Reports,* published by the U.S. Government Printing Office.

While there are several unofficial compilations of Court opinions, including *United States Law Week,* published by the Bureau of National Affairs; *Supreme Court Reporter,* published by West Publishing Company; and *United States Supreme Court Reports, Lawyers' Edition,* published by Lawyers Cooperative Publishing Company, it is the official record that is generally cited. An unofficial version or the official slip opinion might be cited if a decision has not yet been officially reported.

A citation to a case includes, in order, the name of the parties to the case, the volume of *United States Reports* in which the decision appears, the page in the volume on which the opinion begins, the page from which any quoted material is taken, and the year of the decision.

For example, *Colegrove v. Green,* 328 U.S. 549 at 553 (1946) means that the Supreme Court decision in the case of Colegrove against Green can be found in volume 328 of *United States Reports* beginning on page 549. The specific quotation in question will be found on page 553. The case was decided in 1946.

Until 1875 the official reports of the Court were published under the names of the Court reporters, and it is their names, or abbreviated versions, that appear in cites for those years, although U.S. volume numbers have been assigned retroactively to them. A citation such as *Marbury v. Madison,* 1 Cranch 137 (1803) means that the opinion in the case of Marbury against Madison is in the first volume of reporter Cranch beginning on page 137. (Between 1875 and 1883 a Court reporter named William T. Otto compiled the decisions and opinions; his name appears on the volumes for those years as well as the *United States Reports* volume number, but Otto is seldom cited.)

The titles of the volumes to 1875, the full names of the reporters, and the corresponding *United States Reports* volumes are:

1–4 Dall.	Dallas	1–4 U.S.
1–9 Cranch or Cr.	Cranch	5–13 U.S.
1–12 Wheat.	Wheaton	14–25 U.S.
1–16 Pet.	Peters	26–41 U.S.
1–24 How.	Howard	42–65 U.S.
1–2 Black	Black	66–67 U.S.
1–23 Wall.	Wallace	68–90 U.S.

1790–1799

EX POST FACTO LAWS

Calder v. Bull, 3 Dall. 386, decided by a 4–0 vote, August 8, 1798. Chase wrote the Court's opinion.

The Constitution's ban on ex post facto laws does not forbid a state to nullify a man's title to certain property. The ban applies only to laws making certain actions criminal after they had been committed. It was not intended to protect property rights.

FEDERAL COURTS

Chisholm v. Georgia, 2 Dall. 419, decided by a 4–1 vote, February 18, 1793. Jay wrote the Court's major opinion; Iredell dissented.

Citizens of one state have the right to sue another state in federal court, without the consent of the defendant state.

Adoption of the Eleventh Amendment reversed this ruling, barring such suits from federal court unless the defendant state consented.

TAXES

Hylton v. United States, 3 Dall. 171, decided without dissent, March 8, 1796. The participating justices—Chase, Paterson, and Iredell—submitted opinions; Cushing, Wilson, and Ellsworth did not participate; Wilson filed an opinion.

The Court upheld Congress's power to tax carriages. It declared that the only "direct" taxes required by the Constitution to be apportioned among the states were head taxes and taxes on land.

This definition remained in force until 1895 when the Court held that income taxes were direct and must be apportioned. The addition of the Sixteenth Amendment to the Constitution overturned that ruling.

TREATIES

Ware v. Hylton, 3 Dall. 199, decided by a 4–0 vote, March 7, 1796. Chase delivered the major opinion for the Court; Iredell did not participate in the decision, but placed an opinion in the record.

Treaties made by the United States override conflicting state laws. The 1783 Treaty of Paris with Britain, ending the Revolutionary War, provided that neither Britain nor the United States would block the efforts of the other nation's citizens to secure repayment of debts in the other country. This provision rendered invalid Virginia's law allowing debts owed by Virginians to British creditors to be "paid off" through payments to the state.

1800–1809

FEDERAL COURTS

Bank of the United States v. Deveaux, 5 Cr. 61, decided without dissent, March 15, 1809. Marshall wrote the Court's opinion; Livingston did not participate.

The Court strictly interpreted the "diversity" requirement in federal cases—the rule that certain cases could be heard in federal, not state, courts simply because the two parties were residents of different states. Cases involving corporations, the Court held, could only come into federal courts for this reason if all the stockholders of the corporation lived in a state other than that of the opposing party. This strict rule resulted in very little corporate litigation in the federal courts until 1844 when it was revised.

JUDICIAL REVIEW

Marbury v. Madison, 1 Cr. 137, decided without dissent, February 24, 1803. Marshall wrote the Court's opinion.

Congress may not expand or contract the Supreme Court's original jurisdiction. Therefore, Congress exceeded its power when, in Section 13 of the Judiciary Act of 1789, it authorized the Supreme Court to issue writs of mandamus in original cases ordering federal officials to perform particular acts. Although William Marbury had a right to receive his commission as a justice of the peace—already signed and sealed, but not delivered—the Court lacked the power, under its original jurisdiction, to order its delivery.

The immediate effect of the decision was to absolve the Jefferson administration of the duty to install several of President Adams's last-minute appointments in such posts.

The more lasting significance was the establishment of the Court's power of judicial review, the power to review Acts of Congress and declare invalid those it found in conflict with the Constitution.

1810–1819

CONTRACTS

Fletcher v. Peck, 6 Cr. 87, decided without dissent, March 16, 1810. Marshall wrote the Court's opinion; Johnson filed a separate opinion.

The Constitution forbids a state to impair the obligation of contracts. This prohibition denies a state legislature the power to annul titles to land secured under a land grant approved by a previous session of the legislature.

Dartmouth College v. Woodward, 4 Wheat. 519, decided by a 5–1 vote, February 2, 1819. Marshall wrote the Court's opinion; Duvall dissented.

The Constitution's ban on state action impairing the obligation of contracts denies a state the power to alter or repeal private corporate charters, such as that between New Hampshire and the trustees of Dartmouth College establishing that institution.

Sturges v. Crowninshield, 4 Wheat. 122, decided without dissent, February 17, 1819. Marshall wrote the Court's opinion.

The Constitution's grant of power to Congress to enact a uniform bankruptcy law does not deny states the power to pass insolvency statutes, at least until Congress enacts a bankruptcy law.

However, the constitutional ban on state action impairing the obligation of contracts denies a state the power to enact a law freeing debtors from liability for debts contracted before the law's passage.

JUDICIAL REVIEW

Martin v. Hunter's Lessee, 1 Wheat. 304, decided without dissent, March 20, 1816. Story wrote the Court's opinion; Marshall did not participate.

The Court upheld as constitutional Section 25 of the Judiciary Act of 1789, which gave the Supreme Court the power to review the rejection, by state courts, of federally based challenges to a state law or state action.

POWERS OF CONGRESS

McCulloch v. Maryland, 4 Wheat. 316, decided without dissent, March 6, 1819. Marshall wrote the Court's opinion.

In a broad definition of the Constitution's grant to Congress of the power to enact all laws that are "necessary and proper" to execute the responsibilities given the legislative branch by the Constitution, the Court ruled that Congress had the authority to charter a national bank in the exercise of its fiscal and monetary powers.

The necessary and proper clause empowered Congress to adopt any appropriate and legitimate means for achieving a legislative goal; it was not confined to using only those means that were indispensable to reaching the desired end.

The Court also held that the national bank was immune to state taxation. Observing that the "power to tax involves the power to destroy," the Court began to develop the doctrine that one government may not tax certain holdings of another government.

1820–1829

COMMERCE

Gibbons v. Ogden, 9 Wheat. 1, decided without dissent, March 2, 1824. Marshall wrote the Court's opinion.

In its first definition of Congress's power over interstate commerce, the Court ruled that Congress could regulate all commerce affecting more than one state. The Court defined commerce as intercourse, including navigation and other modes of transportation, as well as commercial transactions. The Court also declared that the congressional authority to regulate commerce is superior to state power to regulate the same commerce.

This decision laid the foundation for the modern interpretation of the power that gives Congress virtually exclusive control over all business, even that which only indirectly affects interstate commerce.

Willson v. Blackbird Creek Marsh Co., 2 Pet. 245, decided without dissent, March 20, 1829. Marshall wrote the Court's opinion.

A state may exercise its police power to regulate matters affecting interstate commerce if Congress has not enacted conflicting legislation.

CONTRACTS

Ogden v. Saunders, 12 Wheat. 213, decided by a 4–3 vote, February 18, 1827. Washington wrote the Court's major opinion; Marshall, Story, and Duvall dissented.

The contract clause does not deny states the power to enact insolvency statutes that provide for the discharge of debts contracted after its passage.

Mason v. Haile, 12 Wheat. 370, decided by a 6–1 vote in the January 1827 term. Thompson wrote the Court's opinion; Washington dissented.

The contract clause does not prevent a state from abolishing imprisonment as a punishment for debtors who fail to pay their obligations. Modifying the remedy for defaulting on a contract does not inevitably impair the obligation incurred under the contract.

FEDERAL COURTS

Osborn v. Bank of the United States, 9 Wheat. 738, decided with one dissenting vote, March 18, 1824. Marshall wrote the Court's opinion; Johnson dissented.

The Court upheld the right of the Bank of the United States to sue state officials in federal court. It held that the Eleventh Amendment—allowing states to be sued in federal court by citizens of another state only with the consent of the defendant state—did not deny federal courts jurisdiction over a case brought against a state official for actions under an unconstitutional state law or in excess of his legal authority. (See *Chisholm v. Georgia,* above.)

Foster v. Neilson, 2 Pet. 253, decided without dissent in the January 1829 term. Marshall delivered the Court's opinion.

The Court refused to rule in a boundary dispute involving territory east of the Mississippi River claimed by both the United States and Spain. Marshall described the matter as a "political question" that was not the business of the judiciary to resolve.

JUDICIAL REVIEW

Cohens v. Virginia, 6 Wheat. 264, decided without dissent, March 3, 1821. Marshall delivered the Court's opinion.

For the second time, the Court reaffirmed the constitutionality of Section 25 of the Judiciary Act of 1789, under which the Supreme Court was empowered to review state court rulings denying federal claims. (See *Martin v. Hunter's Lessee,* above.)

POWERS OF CONGRESS

Wayman v. Southard, 10 Wheat. 1, decided without dissent, February 12, 15, 1825. Marshall wrote the Court's opinion.

The Court for the first time recognized the power of Congress to delegate portions of its legislative authority. In this case the Court sanctioned the right of Congress to set an objective and then authorize an administrator to promulgate rules and regulations to achieve that objective. The right to delegate such authority provides the basis for creation of the federal regulatory agencies.

POWERS OF THE PRESIDENT

Martin v. Mott, 12 Wheat. 19, decided without dissent, February 2, 1827. Story wrote the Court's opinion.

A president's decision to call out the militia is not subject to judicial review and is binding on state authorities. As a result of congressional delegation of power to the president, the decision to call out the militia, the Court said, "belongs exclusively to the President, and . . . his decision is conclusive upon all other persons."

TAXES

Brown v. Maryland, 12 Wheat. 419, decided by a 6–1 vote, March 12, 1827. Marshall wrote the Court's opinion; Thompson dissented.

The Court reinforced its broad interpretation of congressional power over commerce, ruling that a state unconstitutionally infringed on that power when it taxed imported goods still the property of the importer and in their original package.

Weston v. City Council of Charleston, 2 Pet. 449, decided by a 4–2 vote, March 18, 1829. Marshall wrote the Court's opinion; Johnson and Thompson dissented.

A city tax on United States stock impermissibly hinders the exercise of the federal power to borrow money.

1830–1839

BILLS OF CREDIT

Craig v. Missouri, 4 Pet. 410, decided by a 4–3 vote, March 12, 1830. Marshall wrote the Court's opinion; Johnson, Thompson, and McLean dissented.

The constitutional provision barring states from issuing bills of credit denies a state the power to issue state loan certificates.

Briscoe v. Bank of the Commonwealth of Kentucky, 11 Pet. 257, decided by a 6–1 vote, February 11, 1837. McLean wrote the Court's opinion; Story dissented.

The constitutional ban on state bills of credit is not violated by a state law authorizing issuance of notes by a state-chartered bank, in which the state owns all the stock.

COMMERCE

New York v. Miln, 11 Pet. 102, decided by a 6–1 vote, February 16, 1837. Barbour wrote the Court's opinion; Story dissented.

The Court upheld a New York statute, which required all ships arriving in New York to report lists of passengers, against a challenge that the statute interfered with federal power to regulate foreign commerce. The state law was a valid exercise of state police power to protect public welfare against an influx of paupers, the majority said.

CONTRACTS

Charles River Bridge v. Warren Bridge, 11 Pet. 420, decided by a 4–3 vote, February 12, 1837. Taney wrote the Court's opinion; Story, Thompson, and McLean dissented.

Charters granted by a state should never be assumed to limit the state's power of eminent domain. Absent an explicit grant of exclusive privilege, a corporate charter granted by the state should not be interpreted as granting such a privilege and thereby limiting the state's power to charter a competing corporation.

The Court rejected the claim of the owners of the Charles River Bridge that their charter implicitly granted them a monopoly of the foot passenger traffic across the river and was impaired by state action authorizing construction of a second bridge over that same river.

FEDERAL COURTS

Kendall v. United States ex rel. Stokes, 12 Pet. 524, decided by votes of 9–0 and 6–3, March 12, 1838. Thompson wrote the Court's opinion; Taney, Barbour, and Catron dissented in part.

Federal courts—if they have jurisdiction over a controversy—have the power to issue a writ of mandamus to an executive branch official ordering him to take some ministerial action, which he is required by law to perform. The Court distinguished between ministerial actions of executive officials, which are prescribed by law or regulation and about which there is little discretion, and policy or political actions of those officials, which are beyond the reach of the courts.

INDIVIDUAL RIGHTS

Barron v. Baltimore, 7 Pet. 243, decided without dissent, February 16, 1833. Marshall wrote the Court's opinion.

The Bill of Rights was added to the Constitution to protect persons only against the action of the federal, not state, government. The Court rejected the effort of a wharf owner to invoke the Fifth Amendment to compel the city of Baltimore to compensate him for the value of his wharf which, he claimed, was rendered useless as a result of city action.

STATE POWERS

Worcester v. Georgia, 6 Pet. 515, decided by a 5–1 vote, March 3, 1832. Marshall wrote the Court's opinion; Baldwin dissented; Johnson did not participate.

Federal jurisdiction over Indian affairs is exclusive, leaving no room for state authority. States lack any power to pass laws affecting Indians living in Indian territory within their borders. The Court reversed the conviction, under Georgia law, of two missionaries who had failed to comply with a state law requiring the licensing of all white persons living in Indian territory. (This case is one of a pair known as the *Cherokee Cases.*)

1840–1849

COMMERCE

Thurlow v. Massachusetts, Fletcher v. Rhode Island, Peirce v. New Hampshire (License Cases), 5 How. 504, decided without dissent, March 6, 1847. Taney, McLean, Catron, Daniel, Woodbury, and Grier wrote separate opinions.

States may require that all sales of intoxicating liquors within their borders be licensed, including imported liquor. This requirement is a valid exercise of state police power.

Smith v. Turner, Norris v. Boston (Passenger Cases), 7 How. 283, decided by a 5–4 vote, February 7, 1849. McLean wrote the Court's opinion; Taney, Daniel, Nelson, and Woodbury dissented.

In apparent contradiction of *New York v. Miln,* the Court struck down state laws that placed a head tax on each passenger brought into a U.S. port. The revenue was intended to support immigrant paupers, but the majority held that such laws conflicted with federal power to regulate interstate and foreign commerce—even though Congress had not acted in this area.

FEDERAL COURTS

Louisville Railroad Company v. Letson, 2 How. 497, decided without dissent, March 15, 1844. Wayne wrote the Court's opinion. Taney did not participate.

Effectively overruling *Bank of the United States v. Deveaux* (1809), the Court declared that a corporation would be assumed to be a citizen of the state in which it was chartered. This assumed citizenship, for purposes of diversity jurisdiction, facilitated the movement of corporate litigation into federal courts.

Luther v. Borden, 7 How. 1, decided by a 5–1 vote, January 3, 1849. Taney delivered the Court's opinion; Woodbury dissented; Catron, McKinley, and Daniel did not participate.

The guaranty clause of the Constitution—stating that the United States will guarantee to each state a republican form of government—is enforceable only through the political branches, not the judiciary.

The Court refused to resolve a dispute between two competing political groups, each of which asserted it was the lawful government of Rhode Island. This dispute was a "political question," held the Court, that it would leave to Congress.

FOREIGN AFFAIRS

Holmes v. Jennison, 14 Pet. 540, decided by a 4–4 vote, March 4, 1840. Taney wrote an opinion for himself, Story, McLean, and Wayne; Barbour, Baldwin, Catron, and Thompson filed separate opinions; McKinley did not participate.

A fugitive from Canada, detained in Vermont, sought release through a petition for a writ of habeas corpus. After the state supreme court denied his petition, he asked the U.S. Supreme Court to review that action. The Court divided 4–4 over whether it had jurisdiction in the case. Taney, Story, McLean, and Wayne held that the Court did have jurisdiction; Barbour, Baldwin, Catron, and Thompson disagreed.

The 4–4 vote meant that the Court dismissed the case. But its significance came in Taney's declaration that states were forbidden by the Constitution to take any independent role in foreign affairs, and therefore a state governor could not surrender a fugitive within his jurisdiction to a foreign country who sought the fugitive's return.

INTERSTATE BOUNDARIES

Rhode Island v. Massachusetts, 4 How. 591, decided by 8–0 and 7–1 votes in the January 1846 term. McLean wrote the Court's opinion; Taney dissented in part.

This decision was the Court's first resolving an interstate boundary dispute. The Court affirmed its jurisdiction over these matters, a point upon which Taney dissented, and then resolved the dispute in favor of Massachusetts, the state that had challenged the Court's jurisdiction to hear the case.

SLAVERY

Prigg v. Pennsylvania, 16 Pet. 539, decided by 8–1 and 5–4 votes, March 1, 1842. Story wrote the Court's opinion. McLean dissented; Taney, Thompson, and Daniel dissented in part.

The Court struck down a Pennsylvania law concerning procedures for the return of fugitive slaves to owners in other states, finding the law in conflict with the federal Fugitive Slave Act. McLean dissented on this point. Story declared that federal power over fugitive slaves was exclusive, denying states any power to enact any laws on that subject. On this point the three justices dissented.

TAXES

Dobbins v. Erie County, 16 Pet. 435, decided without dissent, March 4, 1842. Wayne wrote the Court's opinion.

Extending the principle adopted in *McCulloch v. Maryland* (1819) that the power to tax involves the power to destroy, the Court held that states could not tax the income of federal officials.

This decision, together with that in *Collector v. Day,* 11 Wall. 113, (1871), which held that the federal government could not tax the incomes of state officials, led to numerous intergovernmental tax immunities that were not removed until 1939 when *Dobbins* and *Collector* were overruled.

1850–1859

COMMERCE

Cooley v. Board of Wardens of Port of Philadelphia, 12 How. 299, decided by a 7–2 vote, March 2, 1852. Curtis wrote the Court's opinion; McLean and Wayne dissented.

Adopting the "selective exclusiveness doctrine," the majority ruled that Congress had exclusive power to regulate commerce that was national in nature and demanded uniform regulation. The states retained the authority to regulate commerce that was local in nature.

Pennsylvania v. Wheeling and Belmont Bridge, 13 How. 518, decided by a 7–2 vote, February 6, 1852. McLean wrote the Court's opinion; Taney and Daniel dissented.

A bridge built across the Ohio River was so low that it obstructed interstate commerce, the Court ruled, and so it must either be raised so that ships could pass under it or be taken down.

In its first legislative reversal of a Supreme Court decision, Congress passed a law declaring that the bridge did not interfere with interstate commerce and requiring ships to be refitted so that they could pass under the bridge. The Court upheld this statute in 1856.

CONTRACTS

Dodge v. Woolsey, 18 How. 331, decided by a 6–3 vote, April 8, 1856. Wayne wrote the majority opinion; Campbell, Catron, and Daniel dissented.

A state may not revoke a tax exemption included in a charter, grant, or contract. The Constitution's ban on state action impairing the obligation of contracts forbids revocation. With this ruling the Court declared unconstitutional part of the Ohio constitution, the first time it had nullified part of a state's constitution.

DUE PROCESS

Murray's Lessee v. Hoboken Land and Improvement Co., 18 How. 272, decided by a unanimous vote, February 19, 1856. Curtis wrote the Court's opinion.

The due process clause of the Fifth Amendment limits the legislature as well as the executive and the judiciary. The Fifth Amendment "cannot be construed as to leave Congress free to make any process 'due process of law' by its mere will."

With this decision the Court began to define due process, stating that any process in conflict with specific constitutional provisions or the "settled modes and usages" of proceedings in English and early American practice was not due process of law.

FEDERAL COURTS

Ableman v. Booth, United States v. Booth, 21 How. 506, decided by a unanimous Court, March 7, 1859. Taney wrote the Court's opinion.

State courts lack the power to issue writs of habeas corpus ordering federal courts or federal officers to release a prisoner whose detention they cannot justify.

The Court overturned state court action using the writ to order federal officials to release a man convicted in federal courts of violating the Federal Fugitive Slave Act.

SLAVERY

Scott v. Sandford, 19 How. 393, decided by a 7–2 vote, March 6, 1857. Each justice submitted a separate opinion. Taney's is considered the formal opinion of the Court; McLean and Curtis dissented.

In what many think the most ill-considered decision in Supreme Court history, the majority declared unconstitutional the already repealed Missouri Compromise of 1820. Congress, the Court declared, did not have the authority to prohibit slavery in the territories. The majority also held that blacks were not and could not become citizens of the United States and therefore were not entitled to its privileges and immunities. This part of the decision was overturned by ratification of the Fourteenth Amendment.

1860–1869

COMMERCE

Paul v. Virginia, 8 Wall. 168, decided by a unanimous vote, November 1, 1869. Field wrote the opinion.

Insurance is a local business, not interstate commerce. The states, not Congress, are responsible for regulating insurance practices, even though insurance transactions crossed state lines. The Court reversed this ruling in 1944, but Congress quickly returned authority to regulate insurance to the states.

EX POST FACTO LAWS

Cummings v. Missouri, 4 Wall. 277, ***Ex parte Garland,*** 4 Wall. 333, decided by votes of 5–4, January 14, 1867. Field wrote the majority opinion; Chase, Swayne, Davis, and Miller dissented.

Neither the states nor the federal government may constitutionally require persons who wish to practice certain professions or exercise certain civil rights to take a "test oath" affirming past as well as present loyalty to the United States.

The Court held invalid state and federal test oaths, enacted to exclude persons who had supported the Confederacy from certain offices and certain professions. These requirements, held the Court, violated the constitutional prohibitions on ex post facto laws and bills of attainder.

EXTRADITION

Kentucky v. Dennison, 24 How. 66, decided by a unanimous Court, March 14, 1861. Taney wrote the opinion.

The federal government lacks the power to enforce the constitutional provision that a "person charged in any state with treason, felony or other crime, who shall flee from justice, and be found in another state, shall, on demand of the executive authority of the state from which he fled, be delivered up, to be removed to the state having jurisdiction of the crime."

The Constitution imposes a moral obligation upon a governor to surrender a fugitive sought and requested by another governor, but that obligation cannot be enforced in the federal courts.

FEDERAL COURTS

Mississippi v. Johnson, 4 Wall. 475, decided by a unanimous Court, April 15, 1867. Chase wrote the opinion.

The Supreme Court lacks jurisdiction over the political acts of the president; it has no power to issue an order directing him to stop enforcing acts of Congress, even if those acts are challenged as unconstitutional.

Ex parte McCardle, 7 Wall. 506, decided by a unanimous vote, April 12, 1869. Chase wrote the opinion.

The Constitution authorizes Congress to make exceptions to the appellate jurisdiction of the Supreme Court. That grant includes the power to revoke the Court's appellate jurisdiction over cases already argued and awaiting decision before it. Without jurisdiction over a case, the Court can do nothing but dismiss it.

Congress had revoked the Court's jurisdiction over cases in which lower courts denied prisoners' petitions for release through a writ of habeas corpus. Congress did so because it feared that in this particular case, seeking release of a southern editor held by military authorities for "impeding" the Reconstruction effort, the Court would declare the Reconstruction Acts unconstitutional.

POWERS OF THE PRESIDENT

The Prize Cases, 2 Black 635, decided by a 5–4 vote, March 10, 1863. Grier wrote the majority opinion; Taney, Catron, Clifford, and Nelson dissented.

These cases arose out of the capture of four ships seized while trying to run the Union blockade of Confederate ports that Lincoln instituted in April and Congress sanctioned in July 1861.

The Court sustained the president's power to proclaim the blockade without a congressional declaration of war. A state of war already existed, the majority said, and the president was obligated "to meet it in the shape it presented itself, without waiting for Congress to baptize it with a name."

Ex parte Milligan, 4 Wall. 2, decided by 9–0 and 5–4 votes, April 3, 1866. Full opinions in the case were not announced until December 17, 1866. Davis wrote the majority opinion; Chase, Miller, Swayne, and Wayne dissented in part.

The president lacks the power to authorize military tribunals to try civilians in areas where civil courts are still functioning.

Five justices said that even Congress and the president acting together lacked this power.

STATE POWERS

Texas v. White, 7 Wall. 700, decided by a 5–3 vote, April 12, 1869. Chase wrote the majority opinion; Grier, Swayne, and Miller dissented in part.

States lack the power to secede from the Union. From a legal point of view, Texas and the other states that had approved ordinances of secession had never left the Union.

TAXES

Woodruff v. Parham, 8 Wall. 123, decided without dissent, November 8, 1869. Miller wrote the majority opinion.

States may tax goods "imported" from other states. The constitutional ban on state taxes on imports or exports applies only to goods coming from or going to foreign countries.

States may tax goods from other states, once interstate transportation of those goods has ended, even if they are still in their original packages.

Veazie Bank v. Fenno, 8 Wall. 533, decided by a 7–2 vote, December 31, 1869. Chase wrote the majority opinion; Nelson and Davis dissented.

Congress may use its power to tax as a regulatory tool to support or enforce exercise of another constitutional power, even if the tax is designed to eliminate the matter taxed.

The Court sustained a federal statute that placed a 10 percent tax on the circulation of state bank notes in order to give the untaxed national bank notes a competitive edge and drive the state notes out of the market. The Court said the tax was a legitimate means through which Congress could regulate currency.

1870–1879

CIVIL RIGHTS

Hall v. DeCuir, 95 U.S. 485, decided without dissent, January 14, 1878. Waite wrote the opinion.

A state law forbidding racial discrimination on common carriers operating in the state impermissibly infringes upon the federal power to regulate interstate commerce. Equal access to steamboat accommodations is a matter that requires national, uniform regulation and thus is outside the proper scope of state regulation.

COMMERCE

Henderson v. Wickham, Commissioners of Immigration v. The North German Lloyd, 92 U.S. 259, ***Chy Lung v. Freeman,*** 92 U.S. 275, decided without dissent, March 20, 1876. Miller wrote the opinion.

A state may not require shipowners to give bond for each alien their ships bring into its ports. Despite the argument that this requirement would reduce the potential burden that immigrants place upon state finances, this bond requirement impermissibly interferes with the federal power to regulate foreign commerce.

This ruling resulted in the first general federal immigration law in U.S. history, enacted in 1882.

CURRENCY

Hepburn v. Griswold (First Legal Tender Case), 8 Wall. 603, decided by a 4–3 vote, February 7, 1870. Chase wrote the majority opinion; Davis, Miller, and Swayne dissented.

The Court declared unconstitutional acts of Congress that substituted paper money for gold as legal tender for the payment of debts contracted prior to adoption of the first legal tender act in 1862.

The statute had been enacted to help the Union finance the Civil War, but the Court held it an improper exercise of Congress's implied powers under the "necessary and proper" clause.

Knox v. Lee, Parker v. Davis (Second Legal Tender Case), 12 Wall. 457, decided by a 5–4 vote, May 1, 1871. Strong wrote the majority opinion; Chase, Nelson, Clifford, and Field dissented.

Overturning *Hepburn v. Griswold,* the majority held that Congress had exercised its implied powers properly when it made paper money legal tender for the payment of debts. The fact that the two justices appointed to the Court since the first decision supported the reversal led to charges that the Court had been "packed."

FEDERAL COURTS

Bradley v. Fisher, 13 Wall. 335, decided by a 7–2 vote, April 8, 1872. Field wrote the majority opinion; Davis and Clifford dissented.

Setting out the doctrine of judicial immunity, the Court ruled that judges may not be sued for their official actions, no matter how erroneous or injurious those actions may be.

JURY TRIALS

Walker v. Sauvinet, 92 U.S. 90, decided by a 7–2 vote, April 24, 1876. Waite wrote the majority opinion; Clifford and Field dissented.

The Seventh Amendment guarantee of a jury trial in suits involving more than $20, affects only federal, not state, trials.

PRIVILEGES AND IMMUNITIES

The Butchers' Benevolent Association of New Orleans v. The Crescent City Livestock Landing and Slaughterhouse Co., Esteben v. Louisiana (Slaughterhouse Cases), 16 Wall. 36, decided by a 5–4 vote, April 14, 1873. Miller wrote the majority opinion; Chase, Field, Swayne, and Bradley dissented.

Louisiana did not violate the Fourteenth Amendment when it granted a monopoly on the slaughterhouse business to one company for all of New Orleans. The right of other butchers to do business is neither a "privilege and immunity" of U.S. citizenship protected by the Fourteenth Amendment nor an aspect of the "property" protected by the amendment's due process guarantee.

Bradwell v. Illinois, 16 Wall. 130, decided by an 8–1 vote, April 15, 1873. Miller wrote the majority opinion; Chase dissented.

A state does not violate the Fourteenth Amendment's guarantee of the privileges and immunities of U.S. citizenship when it refuses on the grounds of gender to license a woman to practice law in its courts. The right to practice law is not a privilege or immunity of U.S. citizenship.

Minor v. Happersett, 21 Wall. 162, decided by a unanimous vote, March 29, 1875. Waite wrote the opinion.

The privileges and immunities clause of the Fourteenth Amendment does not guarantee women the right to vote. A state therefore does not violate that amendment's guarantee when it denies a woman the right to vote. "[T]he Constitution of the United States does not confer the right of suffrage on anyone," the Court said.

STATE POWERS

Munn v. Illinois, 94 U.S. 113, decided by a 7–2 vote, March 1, 1877. Waite wrote the majority opinion; Field and Strong dissented.

The state police power includes the right of states to regulate private business. The Court sustained a state law setting the maximum rate that grain elevator operators could charge for grain storage. Private property dedicated to public use was subject to government regulation.

TAXES

Low v. Austin, 13 Wall. 29, decided by a unanimous vote, January 29, 1872. Field wrote the opinion.

The constitutional ban on state taxes on imports or exports prohibits state taxes on goods imported from foreign countries so long as those goods retain their character as imports.

VOTING RIGHTS

United States v. Reese, 92 U.S. 214, decided by an 8–1 vote, March 27, 1876. Waite wrote the majority opinion; Hunt dissented.

The Fifteenth Amendment, forbidding states to deny anyone the right to vote because of race, color, or previous condition of servitude, did not give anyone the right to vote. It simply guaranteed the right to be free from racial discrimination in the exercise of the right to vote—a right granted under state, not federal, laws.

Congress therefore exceeded its power to enforce the Fifteenth Amendment when it enacted laws that penalized state officials who denied blacks the right to vote, refused to count votes, or obstructed citizens from voting.

United States v. Cruikshank, 92 U.S. 542, decided by a unanimous vote, March 27, 1876. Waite wrote the Court's opinion.

The Court dismissed indictments brought against Louisiana citizens accused of using violence and fraud to prevent blacks from voting. Because the indictments did not charge that these actions were motivated by racial discrimination, they were not federal offenses.

"We may suspect," Waite wrote, "that race was the cause of the hostility but it is not so averred."

1880–1889

CIVIL RIGHTS

Civil Rights Cases, 109 U.S. 3, decided by an 8–1 vote, October 15, 1883. Bradley wrote the Court's opinion; Harlan dissented.

Neither the Thirteenth nor the Fourteenth Amendment empowers Congress to enact a law barring discrimination against blacks in privately owned public accommodations. The Fourteenth Amendment prohibits only state-sponsored discrimination, not private discriminatory acts, the Court held. Private discrimination does not violate the Thirteenth Amendment because "such an act of refusal has nothing to do with slavery or involuntary servitude."

The decision effectively blocked further attempts by Congress in the post–Civil War period to end private racial discrimination; not until 1964 did Congress enact and the Court sustain a federal law prohibiting discrimination in privately owned public accommodations.

COMMERCE

Wabash, St. Louis and Pacific Railway Co. v. Illinois, 118 U.S. 557, decided by a 6–3 vote, October 25, 1886. Miller wrote the majority opinion; Waite, Bradley, and Gray dissented.

States may not regulate the rates charged by railroads which form part of an interstate network, even if the state regulates only for the intrastate portion of a trip. Such state regulation infringes upon the federal power to regulate interstate commerce.

Kidd v. Pearson, 128 U.S. 1, decided without dissent, October 22, 1888. Lamar wrote the opinion.

The Court upheld a state law that forbade the manufacture of liquor in the state—even if it was for sale and consumption outside the state. This law did not infringe federal power to regulate interstate commerce, held the Court. Manufacture of goods is not commerce and cannot be regulated as interstate commerce.

CONTRACTS

Stone v. Mississippi, 101 U.S. 814, decided without dissent, May 10, 1880. Waite wrote the opinion.

A state may not permanently contract away any portion of its police power, its power to act to protect the general welfare. Mississippi therefore did not act in violation of the contract clause when it amended its constitution to ban lotteries. This state action had been challenged as impairing the earlier obligation of another legislature that chartered a state lottery corporation.

DUE PROCESS

Hurtado v. California, 110 U.S. 516, decided by a 7–1 vote, March 3, 1884. Matthews wrote the majority opinion; Harlan dissented; Field did not participate.

The due process clause of the Fourteenth Amendment does not require states to use grand jury indictments or presentments in capital offenses.

EQUAL PROTECTION

Yick Wo v. Hopkins, 118 U.S. 356, decided by a unanimous vote, May 10, 1886. Matthews wrote the Court's opinion.

The Fourteenth Amendment protects persons, not just citizens. Holding that a city's arbitrary enforcement of a fire hazard ordinance had discriminated against Chinese laundry owners in violation of the amendment's equal protection clause, the Court said that guarantee applied "to all persons within the territorial jurisdiction, without regard to any differences of race, of color, or of nationality."

Santa Clara County v. Southern Pacific Railroad Co., 118 U.S. 394, decided by a unanimous vote, May 10, 1886. Harlan wrote the opinion; Waite made a preliminary announcement.

Before the Court heard arguments in this case, involving a tax dispute between a county, a state, and a railroad, Waite announced that the equal protection clause of the Fourteenth Amendment applied to protect corporations as well as individuals. Corporations were established to be "persons" within the meaning of that amendment and able to invoke its protection.

FEDERAL COURTS

Wisconsin v. Pelican Insurance Company, 127 U.S. 265, decided without dissent, May 14, 1888. Gray wrote the opinion.

States may not invoke the original jurisdiction of the Supreme Court to enforce their criminal laws against nonresidents. The Supreme Court refused to enforce the order of a Wisconsin court against a Louisiana corporation for failing to comply with Wisconsin laws.

IMMIGRATION

Chae Chan Ping v. United States (Chinese Exclusion Case), 130 U.S. 581, decided by a unanimous vote, May 13, 1889. Field wrote the opinion.

The power of Congress over the entry of aliens, derived from the need to preserve the nation's sovereign status, is exclusive and absolute. The Court sustained an act of Congress that barred the entry of Chinese aliens into the United States.

POWERS OF CONGRESS

Kilbourn v. Thompson, 103 U.S. 168, decided by a unanimous vote, January 24, February 28, 1881. Miller wrote the opinion.

The power of Congress to investigate is not unlimited, nor is its power to punish witnesses who refuse to cooperate with such an investigation. Investigations must be confined to subject areas over which Congress has jurisdiction, their purpose must be enactment of legislation, and they may not merely inquire into the private affairs of citizens. Contempt citations issued against witnesses who refuse to cooperate in investigations that do not meet these standards are invalid.

This assertion was the first of the Court's authority to review the propriety of congressional investigations. The Court subsequently modified the standards laid out in this case, but its basic limitations on the power of Congress to investigate remain in effect.

SEARCH AND SEIZURE

Boyd v. United States, 116 U.S. 616, decided without dissent, February 1, 1886. Bradley wrote the opinion.

The Court held that a revenue statute compelling a defendant to produce in court his private papers was unconstitutional as an unreasonable search and seizure violating the Fourth Amendment and as compelled self-incrimination in violation of the Fifth Amendment.

STATE POWERS

Mugler v. Kansas, 123 U.S. 623, decided by an 8–1 vote, December 5, 1887. Harlan wrote the majority opinion; Field dissented.

The Court upheld a state law that forbade the manufacture and sale of intoxicating liquor in the state. Rejecting a challenge to this law as abridging the privileges and immunities of U.S. citizenship, as well as the due process guarantee of the Fourteenth Amendment, the Court held the law a proper exercise of the state police power to safeguard the public health and morals.

TAXES

Head Money Cases, 112 U.S. 580, decided by a unanimous vote, December 8, 1884. Miller wrote the opinion.

The constitutional requirement that indirect taxes be uniform is met if the tax operates the same upon all subjects being taxed; an indirect tax is not unconstitutional simply because the subject being taxed is not distributed uniformly throughout the United States.

VOTING RIGHTS

Ex parte Siebold, 100 U.S. 371, decided by a 7–2 vote, March 8, 1880. Bradley wrote the majority opinion; Field and Clifford dissented.

Confirming federal power to protect the electoral process in congressional elections in the states, the Court upheld federal laws making it a federal crime for state election officers to neglect their duty in congressional elections. The Court upheld the convictions of two state officials tried and convicted for stuffing the ballot box.

Ex parte Yarbrough, 110 U.S. 651, decided by a unanimous Court, March 3, 1884; Miller wrote the opinion.

The Court upheld as a valid exercise of congressional power to enforce the Fifteenth Amendment legislation penalizing persons who conspired to stop blacks from exercising their right to vote. The Court upheld the convictions of several members of the Ku Klux Klan for intimidating a black man to stop him from voting. In some cases, the Court held, the Fifteenth Amendment does confer the right to vote, as well as the right to be free of racial discrimination in voting, and Congress has the power to enforce that right.

1890–1899

CITIZENSHIP

United States v. Wong Kim Ark, 169 U.S. 649, decided by a 6–2 vote, March 28, 1898. Gray wrote the majority opinion; Fuller and Harlan dissented; McKenna did not participate.

Children born in the United States to resident alien parents are citizens of the United States even if their parents are barred from becoming citizens because of their race.

This decision was the Court's first interpreting the Fourteenth Amendment's clause that defines U.S. citizens as all persons born in the United States.

CIVIL RIGHTS

Louisville, New Orleans and Texas Railway Co. v. Mississippi, 133 U.S. 587, decided by a 7–2 vote, March 3, 1890. Brewer wrote the majority opinion; Harlan and Bradley dissented.

Mississippi does not infringe on the federal commerce power when it requires railroads doing business in the state to provide separate accommodations for black and white passengers. The state supreme court viewed this as applying solely to intrastate railroad operations. The Supreme Court accepted those findings and held the requirement no burden on interstate commerce.

Plessy v. Ferguson, 163 U.S. 537, decided by an 7–1 vote, May 18, 1896. Brown wrote the Court's opinion; Harlan dissented; Brewer did not participate.

A state law requiring trains to provide separate but equal facilities for black and white passengers does not infringe upon federal authority to regulate interstate commerce nor is it in violation of the Thirteenth or Fourteenth Amendments. The train was local; a legal distinction between the two races did not destroy the legal equality of the two races guaranteed by the Thirteenth Amendment, and the Fourteenth Amendment protected only political, not social, equality, the majority said.

In dissent, Harlan declared that the "Constitution is color-blind, and neither knows nor tolerates classes among citizens." The "separate but equal" doctrine remained in effect until *Brown v. Board of Education* (1954).

COMMERCE

United States v. E. C. Knight Co., 156 U.S. 1, decided by an 8–1 vote, January 21, 1895. Fuller wrote the majority opinion; Harlan dissented.

In its first interpretation of the Sherman Antitrust Act, the Court ruled that the act did not apply to a trust that refined more than 90 percent of the sugar sold in the country.

Congress had no constitutional power to regulate manufacture, the Court stated, even though much of the refined sugar was intended for sale in interstate commerce. Such sales would affect interstate commerce only indirectly. Congressional authority extended only to regulation of matters that directly affected interstate commerce.

This distinction between matters affecting interstate commerce directly or indirectly significantly modified the Court's decision in *Gibbons v. Ogden* (1824), which held that the Constitution gave Congress authority to regulate intrastate matters that affected other states.

The holding in *Knight* was gradually eroded by later decisions.

In re Debs, 158 U.S. 564, decided by a 9–0 vote, May 27, 1895. Brewer wrote the Court's opinion.

Eugene V. Debs and other leaders of the 1894 Pullman strike challenged their contempt convictions for violating a federal court injunction that was intended to break the strike. A lower court upheld the validity of the injunction under the Sherman Antitrust Act.

The Supreme Court affirmed the validity of the injunction—and Debs's conviction—but on the broader grounds of national sovereignty, which the Court said gave the federal government authority to remove obstructions to interstate commerce and transportation of the mails.

COMPACTS

Virginia v. Tennessee, 148 U.S. 503, decided without dissent, April 3, 1893. Field wrote the opinion.

A compact to resolve a boundary dispute between two states need not be approved formally by Congress in order to be permissible. The Constitution does declare that "no state shall, without the consent of Congress, . . . enter into any Agreement or Compact with another state," but this requirement of formal consent applies only to compacts tending to increase the political power of the states at the expense of national authority or the federal government.

DUE PROCESS

Chicago, Milwaukee & St. Paul Railway Co. v. Minnesota, 134 U.S. 418, decided by a 6–3 vote, March 24, 1890. Blatchford wrote the majority opinion; Bradley, Gray, and Lamar dissented.

If a state deprives a company of the power to charge reasonable rates without providing judicial review of those rate limitations, the state is depriving the company of its property without due process of law.

Courts have the power to decide on the reasonableness of rates set by states for companies to charge and due process requires that an opportunity for judicial review be provided.

Allgeyer v. Louisiana, 165 U.S. 578, decided without dissent, March 1, 1897. Peckham wrote the opinion.

The liberty protected by the due process clause of the Fourteenth Amendment against denial by states included the freedom to make a contract. The Court struck down a state law that forbade its citizens to obtain insurance from out-of-state companies.

This decision was the first recognition by the Court of the protect-ed "freedom of contract" that the justices would use subsequently to strike down minimum wage and maximum hour laws.

Chicago, Burlington & Quincy Railroad Company v. Chicago, 166 U.S. 226, decided by a 7–1 vote, March 1, 1897. Harlan wrote the majority opinion; Brewer dissented; Fuller did not participate.

The Fourteenth Amendment guarantee of due process requires a state, when it takes private property for public use, to provide just compensation to the property owner.

Holden v. Hardy, 169 U.S. 366, decided by a 7–2 vote, February 28, 1898. Brown wrote the majority opinion; Brewer and Peckham dissented.

The Court upheld, against a due process challenge, Utah's law that limited the number of hours that miners could work in underground mines. The "freedom of contract" is subject to certain limitations imposed by the state in the exercise of its police power to protect the health of workers in hazardous conditions.

Smyth v. Ames, 169 U.S. 466, decided by a 7–0 vote, March 7, 1898. Harlan wrote the opinion; Fuller and McKenna did not participate.

Corporations are persons within the protection of the Fourteenth Amendment's guarantee of due process. That guarantee requires states to set railroad rates sufficiently high to ensure the railroad companies a fair return on the value of the investment and just compensation for the use of their property. To ensure compliance with this standard, federal courts have the power to review the rates.

FEDERAL COURTS

United States v. Texas, 143 U.S. 621, decided by a 7–2 vote, February 29, 1892. Harlan wrote the majority opinion; Fuller and Lamar dissented.

By joining the Union, states acquiesce in the constitutional provision extending federal judicial power over all cases in which the United States is a party, including those brought by the United States against a state. The Court rejected Texas's argument that the Court lacked jurisdiction over such a case.

California v. Southern Pacific Railway Co., 157 U.S. 220, decided by a 7–2 vote, March 18, 1895. Fuller wrote the majority opinion; Harlan and Brewer dissented.

The Supreme Court does not have original jurisdiction over cases brought by a state against its own citizens; such suits are generally to be brought in state courts, not federal courts.

SELF-INCRIMINATION

Counselman v. Hitchcock, 142 U.S. 547, decided by a unanimous vote, January 11, 1892. Blatchford wrote the opinion.

Only a grant of complete and absolute immunity against prosecution for an offense revealed in compelled testimony is sufficient to justify waiver of the Fifth Amendment privilege against compelled self-incrimination.

The Court struck down as insufficient the existing federal immunity statute that protected a witness only against the actual use of his testimony as evidence against him, not against its indirect use to obtain other evidence against him.

TAXES

Pollock v. Farmers' Loan and Trust Co., 158 U.S. 601, decided by a 5–4 vote, May 20, 1895. Fuller wrote the majority opinion; Harlan, Jackson, Brown, and White dissented.

Taxes on income derived from real estate and personal property are direct taxes. They therefore must be apportioned among the states according to population. The Court struck down the first general income tax law enacted by Congress and overruled earlier decisions that defined head taxes and taxes on land as the only two forms of direct taxation.

The decision led to adoption and ratification in 1913 of the Sixteenth Amendment, which exempted income taxes from the Constitution's apportionment requirement.

TREATIES

Geofroy v. Riggs, 133 U.S. 258, decided by a unanimous vote, February 3, 1890. Field wrote the opinion.

It is within the scope of the treaty power of the United States to regulate the inheritance by aliens of land and other property in the United States. The Court declared that the treaty power was unlimited except by the Constitution. Field observed: "It would not be contended that it extends so far as to authorize what the Constitution forbids."

VOTING RIGHTS

Williams v. Mississippi, 170 U.S. 213, decided by a unanimous vote, April 25, 1898. McKenna delivered the opinion.

A state does not violate the equal protection clause of the Fourteenth Amendment when it requires eligible voters to be able to read, write, and interpret or understand any part of the Constitution.

1900–1905

COMMERCE

Champion v. Ames, 188 U.S. 321, decided by a 5–4 vote, February 23, 1903. Harlan wrote the majority opinion; Fuller, Brewer, Peckham, and Shiras dissented.

In its first recognition of a federal "police" power, the Court sustained a federal law banning the shipment of lottery tickets in interstate commerce. Just as states might regulate intrastate matters to protect the health, welfare, and morals of their residents, so might Congress exercise its authority to regulate interstate commerce for the same purposes.

Northern Securities Co. v. United States, 193 U.S. 197, decided by a 5–4 vote, March 14, 1904. Harlan wrote the majority opinion; Fuller, White, Holmes, and Peckham dissented.

A holding company formed solely to eliminate competition between two railroad lines was a combination in restraint of trade and therefore in violation of the federal antitrust act.

This was a major modification of the *Knight* decision (1895). The majority now held that although the holding company itself was not in interstate commerce, it sufficiently affected that commerce by restraining it and therefore came within the scope of the federal antitrust statute.

Swift and Co. v. United States, 196 U.S. 375, decided by a unanimous vote, January 30, 1905. Holmes wrote the opinion.

Congress can regulate local commerce that is part of an interstate current of commerce. This opinion was the first enunciation of the "stream-of-commerce" doctrine.

The Court held that meatpackers who combined to fix the price of livestock and meat bought and sold in Chicago stockyards were in violation of the federal antitrust act because the meatpacking operation was the middle part of an interstate transaction in which cattle were shipped from out of the state into Chicago for slaughter and packing and then shipped to other states for sale.

DUE PROCESS

Lochner v. New York, 198 U.S. 45, decided by a 5–4 vote, April 17, 1905. Peckham wrote the majority opinion for the Court; Day, Harlan, Holmes, and White dissented.

The Court struck down a New York law limiting the hours bakery employees could work. The majority found the law a denial of due process, infringing upon the freedom of contract. Because there was no sufficient health reason for the limit, it could not be justified as an exercise of the state's police power.

PRIVILEGES AND IMMUNITIES

Maxwell v. Dow, 176 U.S. 581, decided by an 8–1 vote, February 26, 1900. Peckham wrote the majority opinion; Harlan dissented.

The right to be tried by a jury of twelve persons is not one of the privileges and immunities of U.S. citizenship protected by the Fourteenth Amendment against violation by states.

The Court upheld a state court judgment reached by a jury composed of eight persons, instead of twelve as required in federal courts.

TAXES

Knowlton v. Moore, 178 U.S. 41, decided by a 5–3 vote, May 14, 1900. White wrote the majority opinion; Harlan and McKenna dissented; Brewer dissented in part; Peckham did not participate.

The constitutional requirement that indirect taxes be uniform does not require that the tax rate be uniform, only that the same rate be applied to the same class in the same manner throughout the United States.

McCray v. United States, 195 U.S. 27, decided by a 6–3 vote, May 31, 1904. White wrote the Court's opinion; Fuller, Brown, and Peckham dissented.

Congress may use its taxing power as a regulatory "police" power. So long as the tax produces some revenue, the Court will not examine the motivation for imposing the tax.

The Court upheld a federal statute that placed a high tax on oleomargarine colored yellow to resemble butter. That tax was obviously designed to eliminate the competition to butter, but it was lawful on its face. The Court had no power to "restrain the exercise of a lawful power on the assumption that a wrongful purpose or motive has caused the power to be exerted."

This ruling came little more than a year after the Court held that Congress could also use its interstate commerce power as a police power; the two decisions substantially increased congressional power to regulate commerce in the United States.

TERRITORIES

The Insular Cases, decided May 27, 1901.

DeLima v. Bidwell, 182 U.S. 1, decided by a 5–4 vote; Brown wrote the majority opinion; Gray, McKenna, Shiras, and White dissented.

Downes v. Bidwell, 182 U.S. 244, decided by a 5–4 vote; Brown wrote the majority opinion; Fuller, Harlan, Brewer, and Peckham dissented.

In these two cases the Court ruled that as a result of U.S. annexation of Puerto Rico, the island was no longer a foreign country, but neither was it a part of the United States included within the full protection of the Constitution. The Constitution applied automatically only to states, the Court held, and it was up to Congress, in the exercise of its power to govern territories, to determine whether the Constitution should apply in particular territories.

In a third case, *Dorr v. United States,* 195 U.S. 138 (1904), the Court adopted the "incorporation theory," still in effect, under which the Constitution automatically applies in territories that have been formally incorporated into the United States either through ratified treaty or act of Congress, but not to unincorporated territories.

1906–1910

COMMERCE

Adair v. United States, 208 U.S. 161, decided by a 6–2 vote, January 27, 1908. Harlan wrote the majority opinion; Holmes and McKenna dissented; Moody did not participate.

A federal law prohibiting contracts that required an employee to promise not to join a labor union as a condition of employment exceeded federal authority to regulate interstate commerce and violated the "freedom of contract."

This decision, later overruled, placed "yellow dog" contracts beyond the reach of federal power. It was one of several decisions of the early twentieth century in which the Court ruled against the interests of the labor movement.

Loewe v. Lawler (Danbury Hatters Case), 208 U.S. 274, decided by a unanimous vote, February 3, 1908. Fuller wrote the opinion.

A union attempting to organize workers in a factory in one state by boycotting stores elsewhere that sell its products (secondary boycotts) is a combination in restraint of trade and in violation of the federal antitrust law.

This decision led to adoption of provisions in the Clayton Antitrust Act of 1914 exempting labor unions from suits brought under the antitrust laws.

CRUEL AND UNUSUAL PUNISHMENT

Weems v. United States, 217 U.S. 349, decided by a 4–2 vote, May 2, 1910. McKenna wrote the majority opinion; White and Harlan dissented; Moody and Lurton did not participate.

A Philippine law providing for a punishment of twelve years at hard labor in chains for the crime of falsifying an official document was "cruel and unusual punishment" prohibited by the Eighth Amendment.

FEDERAL COURTS

Ex parte Young, 209 U.S. 123, decided by an 8–1 vote, March 23, 1908. Peckham wrote the majority opinion; Harlan dissented.

Federal judges may properly enjoin, temporarily, the enforcement of a state law challenged as unconstitutional. The injunction may remain in effect until the validity of the law is determined.

SELF-INCRIMINATION

Twining v. New Jersey, 211 U.S. 78, decided by an 8–1 vote, November 9, 1908. Moody delivered the majority opinion; Harlan dissented.

The Fourteenth Amendment does not automatically extend the Fifth Amendment privilege against compelled self-incrimination—or other provisions of the Bill of Rights—to state defendants. The constitutional rights of state defendants are not impaired when a judge or prosecutor comments adversely upon their failure to testify in their own defense.

STATE POWERS

Georgia v. Tennessee Copper Co., 206 U.S. 230, decided by a unanimous vote, May 13, 1907. Holmes wrote the opinion.

In one of the first environmental cases to come to the Court, the justices declared that a state could ask a federal judge to order a company in another state to cease polluting the air shared by the two states.

Muller v. Oregon, 208 U.S. 412, decided by a unanimous vote, February 24, 1908. Brewer wrote the opinion.

The Court upheld Oregon's law setting maximum hours for women working in laundries. The Court relied on the argument that longer working hours might impair the childbearing function of women. State limitation of those hours was therefore justified as a health measure, properly within the state police power.

1911–1915

COMMERCE

Standard Oil Co. v. United States, 221 U.S. 1, decided by an 8–1 vote, May 15, 1911. White wrote the majority opinion; Harlan dissented in part.

Only unreasonable combinations and undue restraints of trade are illegal under the federal antitrust act. In this decision, which resulted in the breakup of the Standard Oil monopoly, a majority of the Court for the first time adopted the so-called "rule of reason." Previously, the Court had held that any combination that restrained trade, whether "reasonable" or "unreasonable," was a violation of the federal statute.

Houston, East and West Texas Railway Co. v. United States; Texas and Pacific Railway Co. v. United States (Shreveport Rate Cases), 234 U.S. 342, decided by a 7–2 vote, June 8, 1914. Hughes wrote the majority opinion; Lurton and Pitney dissented.

Congress may regulate intrastate rail rates if they are so intertwined with interstate rail rates that it is impossible to regulate the one without regulating the other. This so-called "Shreveport Doctrine" was eventually expanded to allow regulation of other intrastate matters that affected interstate commerce.

CONTEMPT

Gompers v. Buck's Stove and Range Co., 221 U.S. 418, decided by a unanimous Court, May 15, 1911. Lamar wrote the opinion.

Civil contempt and criminal contempt are distinguished by the character and purpose of the penalty imposed for them. The purpose of a punishment for civil contempt is remedial—to convince a witness to testify, for example—while the purpose of punishment for criminal contempt is clearly punitive, to vindicate the authority of the court.

Civil contempt ends whenever the person held in contempt decides to comply with the court; criminal contempt is punished by a fixed sentence.

DUE PROCESS

Frank v. Mangum, 237 U.S. 309, decided by a 7–2 vote, April 12, 1915. Pitney wrote the majority opinion; Holmes and Hughes dissented.

The Court upheld a state conviction for murder although the trial court atmosphere was dominated by anti-Semitism and hostility. The majority reasoned that review of the conviction by Georgia's highest state court guaranteed the defendant due process.

FEDERAL COURTS

Muskrat v. United States, 219 U.S. 346, decided by a unanimous vote, January 23, 1911. Day wrote the opinion.

The Court dismissed a case that Congress had authorized certain Indians to bring in order to test the constitutionality of certain laws. No actual dispute or conflict of rights and interests existed here, the Court held, and therefore there was no "case or controversy" properly within its power to resolve.

INTERSTATE RELATIONS

Virginia v. West Virginia, 238 U.S. 202, decided by a unanimous vote, June 14, 1915. Hughes wrote the opinion.

In one of the longest-running disputes to come before the Court, the justices held in 1915 that West Virginia owed Virginia some $12 million—its share of the pre–Civil War state debts of Virginia, which West Virginia had agreed to assume upon its becoming a separate state.

SEARCH AND SEIZURE

Weeks v. United States, 232 U.S. 383, decided by a unanimous vote, February 24, 1914. Day wrote the opinion.

A person whose Fourth Amendment rights to be secure against unreasonable search and seizure are violated by federal agents has the right to require that evidence obtained in the search be excluded from use against him in federal courts.

This was the Court's first decision adopting the so-called exclusionary rule.

STATE POWERS

Coyle v. Smith, 221 U.S. 559, decided by a 7–2 vote, May 29, 1911. Lurton wrote the Court's opinion; McKenna and Holmes dissented.

States are admitted into the Union on an equal footing with all other states; Congress may not place any restrictions on matters wholly under the state's control as a condition of entry. This ruling invalidated a congressional requirement that Oklahoma's state capital remain in Guthrie for seven years after statehood was granted.

Hadacheck v. Los Angeles, 239 U.S. 394, decided by a unanimous vote, December 12, 1915. McKenna wrote the opinion.

Zoning power is part of the state police power, enabling the state to control the use to which certain lands are put. A city's use of this power to forbid brickmaking in a certain area is valid and does not deny due process to a brickmaker, even if it puts him out of business.

VOTING RIGHTS

Guinn v. United States, 238 U.S. 347, decided by an 8–0 vote, June 21, 1915. White wrote the opinion; McReynolds did not participate.

The Court declared an Oklahoma "grandfather clause" for voters an unconstitutional evasion of the Fifteenth Amendment guarantee that states would not deny citizens the right to vote because of their race. Oklahoma law imposed a literacy test upon potential voters, but exempted all persons whose ancestors voted in 1866. The Court said that although race, color, or previous servitude were not mentioned in the law, selection of a date prior to adoption of the Fifteenth Amendment was intended to disenfranchise blacks in "direct and positive disregard" of the amendment.

United States v. Mosley, 238 U.S. 383, decided by a 7–1 vote, June 21, 1915. Holmes wrote the opinion; Lamar dissented; McReynolds did not participate.

The Court upheld congressional power to regulate elections tainted with fraud and corruption, sustaining provisions of the 1870 Enforcement Act implementing the Fifteenth Amendment. In *Ex parte Yarbrough* (1884) the Court had backed congressional power to penalize persons who used violence and intimidation to prevent blacks from voting.

1916–1920

COMMERCE

Hammer v. Dagenhart, 247 U.S. 251, decided by a 5–4 vote, June 3, 1918. Day wrote the majority opinion; Holmes, McKenna, Brandeis, and Clarke dissented.

Narrowing the federal "police" power, the Court struck down a federal statute that prohibited the shipment in interstate commerce of any goods produced by child labor.

Labor was an aspect of manufacture, an intrastate matter not subject to federal control, the majority held. Furthermore, Congress could prohibit shipments in interstate commerce only of goods that were in themselves harmful. Because products made by children were not themselves harmful, Congress had no authority to forbid their shipment.

This decision and a 1922 ruling that Congress had used its taxing power unconstitutionally in a second law intended to bring an end to child labor were overruled in 1941. (See *United States v. Darby Lumber Co.*)

DUE PROCESS

Bunting v. Oregon, 243 U.S. 426, decided by a 5–3 vote, April 9, 1917. McKenna wrote the majority opinion; White, McReynolds, and Van Devanter dissented; Brandeis did not participate.

Extending its decision in *Muller v. Oregon* (1908), the Court upheld an Oregon law setting ten hours as the maximum permissible workday for all industrial workers.

Buchanan v. Warley, 245 U.S. 60, decided by a 9–0 vote, November 5, 1917. Day wrote the opinion.

City ordinances that segregate neighborhoods by restricting some blocks to white residents only and other blocks to black residents only violate the Fourteenth Amendment guarantee of due process.

This decision led to the growth of private restrictive covenants under which neighbors would agree to sell or rent their homes only to persons of the same race. The Court upheld such private covenants in *Corrigan v. Buckley,* 271 U.S. 323 (1926).

FREEDOM OF EXPRESSION

Schenck v. United States, 249 U.S. 47, decided by a 9–0 vote, March 3, 1919. Holmes wrote the opinion.

In its first decision dealing with the extent of the First Amendment's protection for speech, the Court sustained the Espionage Act of 1917 against a challenge that it violated the guarantees of freedom of speech and press.

The First Amendment is not an absolute guarantee, the Court said. Freedom of speech and press may be constrained if "the words used are used in such circumstances and are of such a nature as to create a clear and present danger that they will bring about the substantive evils that Congress has a right to prevent."

POWERS OF CONGRESS

Clark Distilling Co. v. Western Maryland Railway, 242 U.S. 311, decided by a 7–2 vote, January 8, 1917. White wrote the majority opinion; Holmes and Van Devanter dissented.

States have the power, under the federal Webb-Kenyon Act of 1913, to ban the entry of intoxicating liquor into their territory. The act had been challenged as an unconstitutional delegation of power, but the Court held it permissible because the statute established the precise conditions under which states might act.

Selective Draft Law Cases, 245 U.S. 366, decided by a 9–0 vote, January 7, 1918. White wrote the opinion.

Congress is authorized to institute a compulsory draft of persons into the armed forces under its power to raise armies and under the necessary and proper clause. Moreover, service in the military is one of the duties of a citizen in a "just government." Compulsory conscription is not involuntary servitude in violation of the Thirteenth Amendment.

TAXES

Brushaber v. Union Pacific Railroad Co., 240 U.S. 1, decided by a 7–2 vote, January 24, 1916. White wrote the majority opinion; McKenna and Pitney dissented.

With two other cases decided the same day, the Court sustained the 1913 general income tax law enacted after ratification of the Sixteenth Amendment. This decision completed the action necessary to nullify the Court's 1895 ruling that income taxes were direct taxes that must be apportioned among the states according to population. The

Sixteenth Amendment exempted income taxes from the apportionment requirement.

TREATIES

Missouri v. Holland, 252 U.S. 416, decided by a 7–2 vote, April 19, 1920. Holmes wrote the majority opinion; Van Devanter and Pitney dissented.

In order to implement a treaty, Congress may enact legislation that otherwise might be an unconstitutional invasion of state sovereignty.

After lower courts ruled an act of Congress protecting migratory birds an unconstitutional invasion of state powers, the U.S. government negotiated a treaty with Canada for the protection of the birds. After the Senate ratified it, Congress again enacted protective legislation to fulfill the terms of the treaty. Sustaining this second act, the Court wrote: "It is obvious that there may be matters of the sharpest exigency for the national well-being that an act of Congress could not deal with but that a treaty followed by such an act could."

1921–1925

COMMERCE

Duplex Printing Press Co. v. Deering, 254 U.S. 443, decided by a 6–3 vote, January 3, 1921. Pitney wrote the majority opinion. Brandeis, Holmes, and Clarke dissented.

Reading the Clayton Act narrowly, the majority held that federal courts were prohibited from issuing injunctions only against normal labor union operations. A secondary boycott was a combination in restraint of trade, which was illegal, and could therefore be the target of a federal court injunction.

DOUBLE JEOPARDY

United States v. Lanza, 260 U.S. 377, decided by an 8–0 vote, December 11, 1922. Taft delivered the opinion.

Where both federal and state law make the same act a crime, the double jeopardy guarantee of the Fifth Amendment does not prohibit a federal prosecution and a state prosecution of the same defendant for the same crime.

DUE PROCESS

Moore v. Dempsey, 261 U.S. 86, decided by a 6–2 vote, February 19, 1923. Holmes wrote the majority opinion; McReynolds and Sutherland dissented.

Mob domination of the atmosphere of a trial can deny a defendant his right to a fair trial guaranteed by the Sixth Amendment.

Adkins v. Children's Hospital, 261 U.S. 525, decided by a 5–3 vote, April 9, 1923. Sutherland wrote the majority opinion; Taft, Holmes, and Sanford dissented; Brandeis did not participate.

The Court struck down an act of Congress setting a minimum wage for women and children workers in the District of Columbia. The majority found this law a price-fixing measure, in violation of the freedom of contract protected by the Fifth Amendment against infringement by federal action.

FEDERAL COURTS

Massachusetts v. Mellon, Frothingham v. Mellon, 262 U.S. 447, decided by a unanimous Court, June 4, 1923. Sutherland wrote the opinion.

Rejecting state and taxpayer challenges to a federal grant-in-aid program as unconstitutional, the Court held that the taxpayer lacked "standing" to sue, because her share of the federal revenues expended in the challenged program was too minute to constitute the personal interest one must have in a matter in order to bring a challenge in federal court.

FREEDOM OF SPEECH

Gitlow v. New York, 268 U.S. 652, decided by a 7–2 vote, June 8, 1925. Sanford wrote the majority opinion; Holmes and Brandeis dissented.

The First Amendment prohibition against government abridgment of the freedom of speech applies to the states as well as to the federal government. The freedoms of speech and press "are among the fundamental personal rights and 'liberties' protected by the due process clause of the Fourteenth Amendment from impairment by the states," the Court asserted, even though it rejected Gitlow's free speech claim. This ruling was the first of a long line of rulings holding that the Fourteenth Amendment extended the guarantees of the Bill of Rights to state, as well as federal, action.

PERSONAL LIBERTY

Pierce v. Society of Sisters, 268 U.S. 510, decided by a unanimous vote, June 1, 1925. McReynolds wrote the Court's opinion.

A state law that requires all children in the first eight grades to attend public, rather than private or parochial, schools violates the Fourteenth Amendment due process guarantee of "personal liberty." Implicit in this liberty is the right of parents to choose the kind of education they want for their children.

POWERS OF CONGRESS

Newberry v. United States, 256 U.S. 232, decided by a 5–4 vote, May 2, 1921. McReynolds wrote the majority opinion; White, Pitney, Brandeis, and Clark dissented in part.

The Court reversed the conviction of Truman H. Newberry for violating a federal law limiting campaign expenditures in a primary election. Congress, the Court held, lacks power to regulate primary campaigns because a primary was "in no real sense part of the manner of holding the election."

Dillon v. Gloss, 256 U.S. 368, decided by a unanimous vote, May 16, 1921. Van Devanter wrote the opinion.

The power of Congress to designate the manner in which the states shall ratify proposed amendments to the Constitution includes the power to set a "reasonable" time period within which the states must act.

SEARCH AND SEIZURE

Carroll v. United States, 267 U.S. 132, decided by a 7–2 vote, March 2, 1925. Taft delivered the majority opinion; McReynolds and Sutherland dissented.

The Court enlarged the scope of permissible searches conducted without a warrant. Federal agents could make warrantless searches of automobiles when they had a reasonable suspicion of illegal actions.

STATE POWERS

Ponzi v. Fessenden, 258 U.S. 254, decided by a unanimous vote, March 27, 1922. Taft wrote the opinion.

With federal consent, a state court may issue a writ of habeas corpus to federal officials, directing them to present a federal prisoner to state court for trial.

TAXES

Bailey v. Drexel Furniture Co., 259 U.S. 20, decided by an 8–1 vote, May 15, 1922. Taft wrote the majority opinion; Clarke dissented.

In its second decision frustrating congressional efforts to end child labor, the Court invalidated a federal law that imposed a 10 percent tax on the net profits of any company that employed children under a certain age. The Court said the tax was an impermissible use of Congress's police power because Congress intended it as a penalty rather than a source of revenue. The Court overruled this decision and that in *Hammer v. Dagenhart* (1918) in *United States v. Darby Lumber Co.* in 1941.

1926–1930

CIVIL RIGHTS

Corrigan v. Buckley, 271 U.S. 323, decided by a unanimous vote, May 24, 1926. Sanford wrote the opinion.

Civil rights are not protected by the Fifth, Thirteenth, or Fourteenth Amendments against the discriminatory actions of private individuals. Therefore no constitutional protection exists for individuals who have been discriminated against by private restrictive covenants, under which residents of one race living in a neighborhood agree among themselves not to sell or rent their homes to members of another race.

DUE PROCESS

Tumey v. Ohio, 273 U.S. 510, decided by a unanimous vote, March 7, 1927. Taft wrote the opinion.

The Fourteenth Amendment due process guarantee assures a defendant a trial before an impartial judge. A state, therefore, may not allow a city's mayor to serve as judge in cases, when half the fines collected go into the city treasury. A defendant is denied due process when he is tried before a judge with a direct, personal, pecuniary interest in ruling against him.

Buck v. Bell, 274 U.S. 200, decided by an 8–1 vote, May 2, 1927. Holmes wrote the majority opinion; Butler dissented.

Virginia did not violate the Fourteenth Amendment's due process guarantee when it sterilized, without her consent, a mentally defective mother.

FREEDOM OF ASSOCIATION

Whitney v. California, 274 U.S. 357, decided by a unanimous vote, May 26, 1927. Sanford wrote the opinion.

The Court upheld a state law that made it a crime to organize and participate in a group that advocated the overthrow by force of the established political system. The law was challenged as a violation of the First Amendment freedoms of speech and assembly.

JURY TRIALS

Patton v. United States, 281 U.S. 276, decided by a 7–0 vote, April 14, 1930. Sutherland wrote the opinion; Hughes did not participate.

The three essential elements of a jury trial required in federal courts by the Sixth Amendment are a panel of twelve jurors, supervision by a judge, and a unanimous verdict.

POWERS OF THE PRESIDENT

Myers v. United States, 272 U.S. 52, decided by a 6–3 vote, October 25, 1926. Taft wrote the majority opinion; Holmes, Brandeis, and McReynolds dissented.

This decision upheld the president's power to remove certain postmasters from office without congressional consent. The Court held that the statute creating the positions—which also provided for removal only with congressional consent—was an unconstitutional incursion upon executive power. The Court implied that the removal power was virtually unlimited, extending even to members of independent regulatory agencies.

SEARCH AND SEIZURE

Olmstead v. United States, 277 U.S. 438, decided by a 5–4 vote, June 4, 1928. Taft wrote the majority opinion; Brandeis, Holmes, Butler, and Stone dissented.

Wiretaps do not violate the Fourth Amendment's prohibition against unreasonable searches and seizures where no entry of private premises occurred.

STATE POWERS

Euclid v. Ambler Realty Co., 272 U.S. 365, decided by a 6–3 vote, November 22, 1926. Sutherland wrote the majority opinion; Butler, McReynolds, and Van Devanter dissented.

A city's zoning ordinance excluding apartment houses from certain neighborhoods is an appropriate use of the police power and does not violate due process in denying an individual the right to use his property as he desires. If the classification of land use in a zoning ordinance is "fairly debatable," it will be upheld.

TAXES

J. W. Hampton Jr. & Co. v. United States, 276 U.S. 394, decided by a unanimous vote, April 9, 1928. Taft wrote the opinion.

Imposition of protective tariffs is a permissible exercise of the power to tax, a power that may be used to regulate as well as to raise revenue.

VOTING RIGHTS

Nixon v. Herndon, 273 U.S. 536, decided by a unanimous vote, March 7, 1927. Holmes wrote the opinion.

The Court invalidated a Texas law that excluded blacks from voting in primary elections of the Democratic Party. The Court declared the Texas "white primary" law unconstitutional as a violation of the equal protection clause of the Fourteenth Amendment.

1931–1934

CONTRACTS

Home Building and Loan Assn. v. Blaisdell, 290 U.S. 398, decided by a 5–4 vote, January 8, 1934. Hughes wrote the majority opinion; Sutherland, Van Devanter, Butler, and McReynolds dissented.

The Court upheld an emergency state mortgage moratorium law against challenge that it violated the constitutional ban on state action impairing the obligation of contracts.

FREEDOM OF SPEECH

Stromberg v. California, 283 U.S. 359, decided by a 7–2 vote, May 18, 1931. Hughes wrote the majority opinion; McReynolds and Butler dissented.

A state violates the First Amendment guarantee of free speech when it penalizes persons who raise a red flag as a symbol of opposition to organized government. The Court did not directly address the First Amendment issue in this case but held instead that the language of the statute was impermissibly vague. Although aimed at curbing symbolic speech that advocated the unlawful overthrow of the government, the statute's language conceivably permitted punishment for the flying of any banner symbolizing advocacy of a change in government, even through peaceful means.

FREEDOM OF THE PRESS

Near v. Minnesota, 283 U.S. 697, decided by a 5–4 vote, June 1, 1931. Hughes wrote the majority opinion; Butler, Van Devanter, McReynolds, and Sutherland dissented.

A state law that bars continued publication of a newspaper that prints malicious or defamatory articles is a prior restraint of the press in violation of the First Amendment.

This decision marked the first time the Court specifically enforced the First Amendment's guarantee of freedom of the press to strike down a state law because it infringed too far on that freedom.

RIGHT TO COUNSEL

Powell v. Alabama, 287 U.S. 45, decided by a 7–2 vote, November 7, 1932. Sutherland wrote the majority opinion; Butler and McReynolds dissented.

Under the particular circumstances of this, the "First Scottsboro Case," in which a number of young black men charged with raping two white women were tried in a hostile community atmosphere, the failure of the trial court to provide the defendants the effective aid of an attorney for their defense constituted a denial of due process.

STATE POWERS

Nebbia v. New York, 291 U.S. 502, decided by a 5–4 vote, March 5, 1934. Roberts wrote the majority opinion; McReynolds, Butler, Van Devanter, and Sutherland dissented.

The Court abandoned its "public interest" rationale for determining which areas of business were properly subject to state regulation—a line of cases begun in *Munn v. Illinois* (1877).

In this case the Court upheld a New York law that set an acceptable range of prices to be charged for milk. States could regulate almost any business in the interest of the public good, so long as the regulation was reasonable and effected through appropriate means, the Court said.

VOTING RIGHTS

Nixon v. Condon, 286 U.S. 73, decided by a 5–4 vote, May 2, 1932. Cardozo wrote the majority opinion; McReynolds, Butler, Sutherland, and Van Devanter dissented.

Exclusion of blacks from primary elections—as a result of action by the Democratic Party—denies them equal protection of the laws and is impermissible under the Fourteenth Amendment.

The political party, the Court held, acted as the agent of the state when it denied blacks the opportunity to participate in primary elections.

After the Court's decision in *Nixon v. Herndon* (1927), the Texas legislature authorized the state party executive committee to set voting qualifications for its primary, and the party excluded blacks. The Court held this action unconstitutional, saying that neither the state nor political parties could exclude blacks from primaries on the basis of race alone.

Wood v. Broom, 287 U.S. 1, decided by a 5–4 vote, October 18, 1932. Hughes wrote the majority opinion; Brandeis, Stone, Cardozo, and Roberts dissented.

When Congress in the Apportionment Act of 1929 omitted the requirement that electoral districts for congressional elections be contiguous, compact, and equal, it effectively repealed similar requirements in previous laws.

Lacking statutory authority, federal courts therefore could not act to correct malapportionment in state districts.

1935

COMMERCE

Railroad Retirement Board v. Alton Railroad Co., 295 U.S. 330, decided by a 5–4 vote, May 6, 1935. Roberts wrote the majority opinion; Hughes, Brandeis, Cardozo, and Stone dissented.

Congress exceeded its authority when it enacted the Railroad Retirement Act of 1934, which set up a comprehensive pension system for railroad workers, the Court held, invalidating the act. The pension plan was unrelated to interstate commerce, the majority said, and several parts of the act violated the guarantee of due process.

Schechter Poultry Corp. v. United States, 295 U.S. 495, decided by a unanimous vote, May 27, 1935. Hughes wrote the opinion.

Congress exceeded its powers to delegate legislative powers and to regulate interstate commerce when it enacted the National Industrial Recovery Act. The section of the statute that permitted the president to approve "fair competition" codes under certain conditions left the chief executive with too much discretionary power. Furthermore, the statute regulated matters that affected interstate commerce indirectly and so were not within federal power to regulate.

CURRENCY

Norman v. Baltimore and Ohio Railroad Co., 294 U.S. 240, *Nortz v. United States,* 294 U.S. 317, *Perry v. United States,* 294 U.S. 330 *(Gold Clause Cases),* decided by a 5–4 vote, February 18, 1935. Hughes wrote the majority opinion; McReynolds, Butler, Sutherland, and Van Devanter dissented.

The power of Congress to regulate the value of currency permits it to abrogate clauses in private contracts requiring payment in gold. But the federal power to borrow money "on the credit of the United States" prohibits Congress from abrogating such clauses contained in government bonds and other federal contracts.

JURY TRIALS

Norris v. Alabama, 294 U.S. 587, decided by an 8–0 vote, April 1, 1935. Hughes wrote the opinion; McReynolds did not participate.

In the "Second Scottsboro Case," the Court set aside the conviction of the black defendant because blacks had been consistently barred from service on both the grand jury and trial jury in this case.

POWERS OF CONGRESS

Panama Refining Co. v. Ryan, 293 U.S. 388, decided by an 8–1 vote, January 7, 1935. Hughes wrote the majority opinion; Cardozo dissented.

The Court declared invalid a provision of the National Industrial Recovery Act that authorized the president to prohibit from interstate commerce oil produced in violation of state regulations controlling the amount of production. The Court said this congressional delegation of power was unconstitutionally broad, leaving too much to the discretion of the president. This ruling was the first of the Court's decisions striking down New Deal legislation.

POWERS OF THE PRESIDENT

Humphrey's Executor v. United States, 295 U.S. 602, decided by a unanimous vote, May 27, 1935. Sutherland wrote the opinion.

The Court denied the president the power to remove members of independent regulatory agencies without the consent of Congress and limited sharply the executive removal power given such broad scope in *Myers v. United States* (1926).

VOTING RIGHTS

Grovey v. Townsend, 295 U.S. 45, decided by a unanimous vote, April 1, 1935. Roberts wrote the opinion.

The Texas Democratic Party did not violate the Fourteenth Amendment by deciding to confine membership in the party to white citizens. A political party was a private organization, the Court ruled, and the Fourteenth Amendment's guarantee did not reach private action. (See *Nixon v. Herndon,* 1927; *Nixon v. Condon,* 1932.)

1936

DUE PROCESS

Brown v. Mississippi, 297 U.S. 278, decided by a unanimous Court, February 17, 1936. Hughes wrote the opinion.

States may not use coerced confessions as evidence at the trial of persons from whom the confessions were obtained by torture. Use of a person's involuntary statements to convict him is a clear denial of due process of law.

Morehead v. New York ex rel. Tipaldo, 298 U.S. 587, decided by a 5–4 vote, June 1, 1936. Butler wrote the majority opinion; Hughes, Brandeis, Cardozo, and Stone dissented.

The Court struck down a New York minimum wage law for women and children workers, declaring all minimum wage laws a violation of due process. The decision was overruled the following year with *West Coast Hotel Co. v. Parrish.*

FREE PRESS

Grosjean v. American Press Co., 297 U.S. 233, decided by a unanimous vote, February 10, 1936. Sutherland wrote the opinion.

A state law that taxes the gross receipts of certain newspapers and not others is a prior restraint on the press in violation of the First Amendment. Although labeled a tax on the privilege of doing business, the law had actually been written so that the tax fell only on those newspapers that opposed the governor.

POWERS OF CONGRESS

Ashwander v. Tennessee Valley Authority, 297 U.S. 288, decided by votes of 8–1 and 5–4, February 17, 1936. Hughes wrote the majority opinion; McReynolds, Brandeis, Stone, Roberts, and Cardozo dissented in part.

The Court implicitly upheld the statute authorizing the establishment of the Tennessee Valley Authority. It sustained the authority of the TVA to enter into a contract for the sale of the excess energy generated by a TVA-operated dam. Construction of the dam was within the federal power to defend the nation and improve navigation, the Court said. The Constitution gave the federal government unfettered power to dispose of government property.

This statute was one of only two major early New Deal laws declared valid by the Court.

Carter v. Carter Coal Co., 298 U.S. 238, decided by a 6–3 vote, May 18, 1936. Sutherland wrote the majority opinion; Hughes wrote a separate opinion; Cardozo, Brandeis, and Stone dissented.

Striking down the Bituminous Coal Conservation Act of 1935, the Court found that Congress had unconstitutionally delegated its legislative powers to private parties in that statute when it allowed a majority of coal mine operators to set mandatory wage and hours standards for the entire coal industry.

The Court also held unconstitutional those provisions giving miners collective bargaining rights. Such labor relations were local in nature and not subject to regulation by Congress under its interstate commerce powers.

POWERS OF THE PRESIDENT

United States v. Curtiss-Wright Export Corp., 299 U.S. 304, decided by a 7–1 vote, December 21, 1936. Sutherland wrote the majority opinion; McReynolds dissented; Stone did not participate.

The Court upheld an act of Congress authorizing the president, at his discretion, to embargo arms shipments to foreign belligerents in a South American war.

The plenary nature of the federal government's power over foreign affairs permitted Congress greater latitude in delegating power to the president in international relations than in internal matters. Sutherland described the power of the president in foreign affairs as "plenary and exclusive." The president is "the sole organ of the federal government in the field of international relations."

SPENDING POWER

United States v. Butler, 297 U.S. 1, decided by a 6–3 vote, January 6, 1936. Roberts wrote the majority opinion; Stone, Brandeis, and Cardozo dissented.

In its first interpretation of Congress's power to spend for the general welfare, the Court held that Congress could not combine that power with the power to tax in order to regulate a matter that was outside the scope of federal authority—in this instance, agricultural production.

The ruling declared unconstitutional the Agricultural Adjustment Act of 1933, which sought to regulate agricultural production by taxing processors of basic food commodities and then using the revenue from that tax to pay benefits to farmers who reduced their production of those commodities.

1937

COMMERCE

National Labor Relations Board v. Jones & Laughlin Steel Corp., 301 U.S. 1, decided by a 5–4 vote, April 12, 1937. Hughes wrote the majority opinion; McReynolds, Butler, Sutherland, and Van Devanter dissented.

The federal power to regulate interstate commerce permits Congress to regulate intrastate matters that directly burden or obstruct interstate commerce. In this case, the Court found that a dispute between management and labor that threatened to close down a Pennsylvania steel factory directly affected interstate commerce because the factory was in a stream of commerce.

This decision, in which the Court finally abandoned its narrow view of the federal power to regulate interstate commerce, sustained the constitutionality of the National Labor Relations Act of 1935.

DUE PROCESS

West Coast Hotel Co. v. Parrish, 300 U.S. 379, decided by a 5–4 vote, March 29, 1937. Hughes wrote the majority opinion; Butler, McReynolds, Sutherland, and Van Devanter dissented.

The Court upheld Washington State's law setting minimum wages for women and children workers. The Court overruled *Adkins v. Children's Hospital* (1923) in which it had declared minimum wage laws to be in violation of freedom of contract, and *Morehead v. Tipaldo* (1936).

Palko v. Connecticut, 302 U.S. 319, decided by an 8–1 vote, December 6, 1937. Cardozo wrote the majority opinion; Butler dissented.

The due process clause of the Fourteenth Amendment does not require states to observe the double jeopardy guarantee of the Fifth Amendment. The promise that an individual will not be tried twice for the same crime is "not of the very essence of a scheme of ordered liberty," and therefore due process does not mandate its application to the states.

FREEDOM OF ASSEMBLY

DeJonge v. Oregon, 299 U.S. 353, decided by an 8–0 vote, January 4, 1937. Hughes wrote the opinion; Stone did not participate.

The First Amendment guarantee of the freedom of assembly prohibits a state from making it a crime to organize and participate in a meeting at which no illegal action was discussed, even if the meeting was held under the auspices of an association that had as its goal the forcible overthrow of the government.

For the first time, the Court recognized that the right of assembly was on an equal footing with the rights of free speech and free press and that the First Amendment guarantee of freedom of assembly was applicable to the states through the due process clause of the Fourteenth Amendment.

SPENDING POWER

Steward Machine Co. v. Davis, 301 U.S. 548, decided by a 5–4 vote, May 24, 1937. Cardozo wrote the majority opinion; McReynolds, Butler, Sutherland, and Van Devanter dissented.

A system to induce employers to participate in the federal unemployment compensation program by taxing them and then giving those who participate a tax credit is a valid exercise of the taxing and spending powers to regulate interstate commerce. While not in commerce, employment affects commerce and therefore falls within the reach of federal regulation.

Helvering v. Davis, 301 U.S. 619, decided by a 7–2 vote, May 24, 1937. Cardozo wrote the majority opinion; McReynolds and Butler dissented.

Effectively overturning its ruling in *United States v. Butler* (1936), the Court sustained the Social Security Act of 1935. This statute placed a tax on employees and employers, the revenue from which was used to pay benefits to retired employees. Such a program was an appropriate combination of the power to tax and the power to spend for the general welfare, the Court said.

VOTING RIGHTS

Breedlove v. Suttles, 302 U.S. 277, decided by a unanimous vote, December 6, 1937. Butler wrote the opinion.

The Court upheld a Georgia law that required all inhabitants of the state between the ages of twenty-one and sixty to pay an annual poll tax of $1.00. Under the state constitution payment of the tax was a prerequisite to voting in any election. The Court ruled that the tax did not constitute denial of equal protection in violation of the Fourteenth Amendment, nor did it violate the Fifteenth Amendment ban on racial discrimination in voting.

1938

CIVIL RIGHTS

Missouri ex rel. Gaines v. Canada, 305 U.S. 337, decided by a 6–2 vote, December 12, 1938. Hughes wrote the majority opinion; McReynolds and Butler dissented.

A state denies equal protection of the laws to a black student when it refuses him admission to its all-white law school, even though it volunteers to pay his tuition at any law school in an adjacent state. By providing a law school for whites but not for blacks the state has created a privilege for one race and denied it to another.

This decision was the first in a series that culminated in abandonment of the "separate but equal" doctrine of *Plessy v. Ferguson* (1896).

FREEDOM OF THE PRESS

Lovell v. City of Griffin, 303 U.S. 444, decided by an 8–0 vote, March 28, 1938. Hughes wrote the opinion; Cardozo did not participate.

A city ordinance that prohibits circulation on public streets of handbills or literature of any kind without written permission from the city manager is an unconstitutional prior restraint on freedom of the press. (In subsequent cases, the Court said that a city could regulate the manner of distributing handbills.)

RIGHT TO COUNSEL

Johnson v. Zerbst, 304 U.S. 458, decided by a 6–2 vote, May 23, 1938. Black wrote the majority opinion; McReynolds and Butler dissented; Cardozo did not participate.

The Sixth Amendment guarantee that in "all criminal prosecutions, the accused shall enjoy the right . . . to have the Assistance of Counsel for his defence" means that federal courts may not deprive anyone of liberty or life unless he has been provided the aid of an attorney at his trial or has explicitly waived his right to that aid.

1939

COMMERCE

Mulford v. Smith, 307 U.S. 38, decided by a 7–2 vote, April 17, 1939. Roberts wrote the majority opinion; Butler and McReynolds dissented.

Congress has authority to limit the amount of any commodity shipped in interstate commerce. The imposition of marketing quotas on certain agricultural commodities is valid; such quotas are at the "throat" of interstate commerce.

The Court sustained the validity of the second agricultural adjustment act against challenge that the marketing quotas limited production, an area which Congress had no authority to regulate.

FEDERAL COURTS

Coleman v. Miller, 307 U.S. 433, decided by a 7–2 vote, June 5, 1939. Hughes wrote the majority opinion; Butler and McReynolds dissented.

It is up to Congress, not the Court, to resolve political questions such as, what is a "reasonable" time period for the ratification by states of proposed constitutional amendments and whether a state that has rejected a constitutional amendment may later reverse itself and ratify the amendment.

FREEDOM OF ASSEMBLY

Hague v. Congress of Industrial Organizations, 307 U.S. 496, decided by a 5–2 vote, June 5, 1939. There was no Court opinion; Roberts, Stone, and Hughes wrote separate concurring opinions; McReynolds and Butler dissented; Frankfurter and Douglas did not participate.

The right to speak and assemble in public may not be arbitrarily prohibited by federal, state, or local governments. Three members of the majority found this right to be a privilege and immunity of national citizenship; two justices found it implicit in the personal liberty protected by the Fourteenth Amendment's due process clause. This latter, broader view, which secured the right to all persons, not just citizens, was eventually accepted by a majority of the Court's members.

TAXES

Graves v. New York ex rel. O'Keefe, 306 U.S. 466, decided by a 7–2 vote, March 27, 1939. Stone wrote the Court's opinion; Butler and McReynolds dissented.

The Court specifically overruled two earlier decisions, *Collector v. Day* (1871) and *Dobbins v. Erie County* (1842), that held that the income of state and federal government employees was immune from taxation by the nonemploying governing body. *Graves* led to the demise of most intergovernmental tax immunities.

VOTING RIGHTS

Lane v. Wilson, 307 U.S. 268, decided by a 6–2 vote, May 22, 1939. Frankfurter wrote the majority opinion; McReynolds and Butler dissented; Douglas did not participate.

In ***Guinn v. United States*** (1915) the Court had held unconstitutional an Oklahoma "grandfather clause" exemption to a literacy test requirement for voters. The state legislature then adopted a second voting registration law that exempted from registration all those who had voted in the 1914 election, conducted while the "grandfather clause" was still in effect. The new law required all other potential voters to register within a two-week period. The Supreme Court held the second law invalid as a violation of the Fifteenth Amendment ban on racial discrimination in voting.

1940

FREEDOM OF RELIGION

Cantwell v. Connecticut, 310 U.S. 296, decided by a unanimous vote, May 20, 1940. Roberts wrote the opinion.

States may limit the free exercise of religion only by statutes that are narrowly drawn and applied in a nondiscriminatory manner. Therefore, a state may not convict a sidewalk preacher for breach of the peace under a general ordinance which sweeps in "a great variety of conduct under a general and indefinite characterization" and leaves too much discretion to the officials applying it. Furthermore, such activity may not be penalized under a general breach of the peace statute if there is no evidence that this speech, although insulting to some religions, caused any disturbance or threatened any "clear and present menace to public peace."

Likewise, a state statute that requires persons who wish to solicit for religious causes to obtain permits, but allows state officials discretion in determining which causes are religious is arbitrary and therefore violates the First Amendment guarantee of the free exercise of religion.

This case was the first in which the Court specifically applied the First Amendment's guarantee of free exercise of religion against state action.

Minersville School District v. Gobitis, 310 U.S. 586, decided by an 8–1 vote, June 3, 1940. Frankfurter wrote the majority opinion; Stone dissented.

In this first "flag-salute" case, the Court sustained a state law requiring all school children to pledge allegiance to the U.S. flag. The requirement had been challenged by Jehovah's Witnesses, for whom the pledge conflicted with their religious beliefs. They argued that the compulsory pledge violated their First Amendment freedom of religion.

Religious liberty must give way to political authority so long as that authority is not used directly to promote or restrict religion, the Court said. The "mere possession of religious convictions . . . does not relieve the citizen from the discharge of political responsibilities."

In 1943 the Court reversed this decision with its ruling in *West Virginia State Board of Education v. Barnette.*

TAXES

Sunshine Anthracite Coal Co. v. Adkins, 310 U.S. 381, decided by an 8–1 vote, May 20, 1940. Douglas wrote the majority opinion; McReynolds dissented.

The use of the tax power as a penalty is an appropriate means for Congress to employ in regulating interstate commerce. The Court upheld the second coal conservation act, which placed a high tax on coal sold in interstate commerce but exempted from payment those producers who agreed to abide by industry price and competition regulations.

1941

COMMERCE

United States v. Darby Lumber Co., 312 U.S. 100, decided by a unanimous vote, February 3, 1941. Stone wrote the opinion.

Congress has authority to prohibit the shipment in interstate commerce of any goods manufactured in violation of federally established minimum wage and maximum hours standards. This decision overruled *Hammer v. Dagenhart* (1918), in which the Court held that

Congress had no power to prohibit the shipment in interstate commerce of goods made by children.

Edwards v. California, 314 U.S. 160, decided by a unanimous vote, November 24, 1941. Byrnes wrote the opinion.

A state impermissibly obstructs interstate commerce when it penalizes persons who bring indigent persons into the state to reside there. The Court in this ruling struck down California's "anti-Okie" law.

In a concurring opinion, four justices held the right to travel to be one of the privileges and immunities of national citizenship protected by the Fourteenth Amendment from abridgment by the states.

FREEDOM OF ASSEMBLY

Cox v. New Hampshire, 312 U.S. 569, decided by a unanimous vote, March 31, 1941. Hughes wrote the Court's opinion.

The First Amendment guarantees of free speech and assembly do not bar states from setting the time, place, and manner of parades on public streets so that they do not interfere unduly with other use of the streets. Such ordinances must be precisely drawn and applied in a nondiscriminatory fashion.

VOTING RIGHTS

United States v. Classic, 313 U.S. 299, decided by a 5–3 vote, May 26, 1941. Stone wrote the majority opinion; Black, Murphy, and Douglas dissented. Hughes did not participate.

Congress has the power to regulate primary elections when the primary is an integral part of the process of selecting candidates for federal office.

This decision overruled *Newberry v. United States* (1921), which had limited congressional regulation to general elections.

1942

COMMERCE

Wickard v. Filburn, 317 U.S. 111, decided by a unanimous vote, November 9, 1942. Jackson wrote the opinion.

The federal power to prevent burdens on interstate commerce permits the federal government to regulate matters that are neither interstate nor commerce. The Court made this point in sustaining a penalty levied against a farmer who had produced for his own consumption more wheat than he was allotted under the 1938 Agricultural Adjustment Act. The Court held that Congress had the power to prevent home-grown wheat from competing with wheat sold in interstate commerce.

This decision is regarded as the high point in the Court's broad interpretation of federal regulatory powers authorized under the interstate commerce clause of the Constitution.

EQUAL PROTECTION

Skinner v. Oklahoma, 316 U.S. 535, decided by a unanimous vote, June 1, 1942. Douglas wrote the opinion.

A state law that provides for involuntary sterilization of certain felons violates the equal protection clause of the Fourteenth Amendment because it does not treat all persons convicted of the same crime in the same manner.

This decision was the first recognition by the Court that individuals have certain constitutionally protected "fundamental interests"—in this case, procreation—with which a state may interfere only if it shows a compelling need.

FREEDOM OF SPEECH

Chaplinsky v. New Hampshire, 315 U.S. 568, decided by a unanimous vote, March 9, 1942. Murphy wrote the opinion.

A state does not violate the First Amendment by enacting a precisely drawn and narrowly applied law making it a crime to use, in public, "fighting words"—words so insulting as to provoke violence from the person to whom they are directed. Fighting words, the lewd and obscene, profanity, and libelous statements are among the classes of speech that have so little value in advancing thought or ideas that they fall outside the protection of the First Amendment guarantees of freedom of speech and press.

RIGHT TO COUNSEL

Betts v. Brady, 316 U.S. 455, decided by a 6–3 vote, June 1, 1942. Roberts wrote the majority opinion; Black, Douglas, and Murphy dissented.

The Fourteenth Amendment's due process clause does not require states to supply defense counsel to defendants too poor to employ their own attorney.

This decision was overturned by *Gideon v. Wainwright* in 1963.

WAR POWERS

Ex parte Quirin, 317 U.S. 1, decided by a unanimous vote, July 31, 1942. Stone wrote the opinion; Murphy did not participate.

The Supreme Court upheld the conviction of seven Nazi saboteurs by a presidentially established military commission, instead of by a civilian jury. Congress had already provided for the trial of spies by military commission, and the acts charged against the saboteurs were acts of war. The guarantee of jury trial under the Sixth Amendment applies to civilian—not military—courts.

This decision firmly established the power of civil courts to review the jurisdiction of presidential military commissions.

1943

DUE PROCESS

McNabb v. United States, 318 U.S. 332, decided by a 7–1 vote, March 1, 1943. Frankfurter wrote the majority opinion; Reed dissented; Rutledge did not participate.

A person accused of a federal crime must be taken before a judicial officer for arraignment without delay after arrest.

FREEDOM OF RELIGION

Murdock v. Pennsylvania, 319 U.S. 105, decided by a 5–4 vote, May 3, 1943. Douglas wrote the majority opinion; Reed, Frankfurter, Roberts, and Jackson dissented.

A city ordinance that requires licenses for all persons taking orders for or delivering goods door-to-door and imposes a daily tax of $1.50 on the privilege is unconstitutional when applied to Jehovah's Witnesses who go from house to house soliciting new members and selling religious literature. "A state may not impose a charge for the enjoyment of a right granted by the federal Constitution," the majority said.

This decision overruled that of the previous year in *Jones v. Opelika,* 316 U.S. 584 (1942), in which the Court upheld such license fees as applied to Jehovah's Witnesses on the grounds that these activities were primarily commercial and so outside the protection of the First Amendment.

West Virginia State Board of Education v. Barnette, 319 U.S. 624, decided by a 6–3 vote, June 14, 1943. Jackson wrote the majority opinion; Roberts, Reed, and Frankfurter dissented.

The First Amendment guarantee of the free exercise of religion protects the right of persons to remain silent and forbids the government to compel them to participate in a symbolic display of patriotic unity that conflicts with their religious beliefs.

The Court upheld the right of Jehovah's Witnesses' children to refuse to participate in compulsory flag salute ceremonies in public schools. The decision overruled *Minersville School District v. Gobitis* (1940).

WAR POWERS

Hirabayashi v. United States, 320 U.S. 81, decided by a unanimous vote, June 21, 1943. Stone wrote the Court's opinion.

The Court upheld the wartime curfew law placed on Japanese-Americans living on the West Coast as an appropriate exercise by the president and Congress of the federal war powers.

The curfew law, by making a classification based solely on race, did not violate the Fifth Amendment. In this instance, consideration of race was relevant to the national security.

1944

COMMERCE

United States v. South-Eastern Underwriters Assn., 322 U.S. 533, decided by a 4–3 vote, June 5, 1944. Black wrote the majority opinion; Stone and Frankfurter dissented; Jackson dissented in part; Roberts and Reed did not participate.

Insurance transactions are matters in interstate commerce subject to regulation under the federal antitrust act.

This ruling overturned a long line of decisions, beginning in 1869, that held that purely financial and contractual transactions, such as insurance, were not in commerce, even if they involved parties in different states, and were therefore not subject to federal regulation.

Because this ruling called into question the validity of all state insurance regulations, Congress quickly passed a statute permitting states to continue to regulate insurance. The Court upheld that statute in *Prudential Insurance Co. v. Benjamin,* 328 U.S. 408 (1946).

POWERS OF CONGRESS

Yakus v. United States, 321 U.S. 414, decided by a 6–3 vote, March 27, 1944. Stone wrote the majority opinion; Roberts, Murphy, and Rutledge dissented.

The Court sustained portions of the Emergency Price Control Act of 1942 giving the federal price administrator discretionary power to enforce the act, including the maximum prices set under it. The law was challenged as an unconstitutional delegation of legislative power. The Court held that the standards for decisions under the law were "sufficiently definite and precise" and said it was "unable to find in them an unauthorized delegation of legislative power."

VOTING RIGHTS

Smith v. Allwright, 321 U.S. 649, decided by an 8–1 vote, April 3, 1944. Reed wrote the majority opinion; Roberts dissented.

When party primaries are part of the machinery for choosing state and national officials, the action of any political party to exclude blacks from voting in primaries is "state action" within the prohibitions of the Fourteenth and Fifteenth Amendments. This ruling reversed *Grovey v. Townsend* (1935).

WAR POWERS

Korematsu v. United States, 323 U.S. 214, decided by a 6–3 vote, December 18, 1944. Black wrote the majority opinion; Roberts, Murphy, and Jackson dissented.

The Court upheld the removal of Japanese-Americans to relocation centers at inland camps away from the West Coast. It held that the removal program was within the combined war powers of the president and Congress.

In this case, for the first time, a majority of the Court said it would give classifications by race increased attention to ensure that racial antagonism did not lie at the base of the classification. In this instance, however, the Court held that military necessity warranted the racial classification.

1946

BILLS OF ATTAINDER

United States v. Lovett, 328 U.S. 303, decided by an 8–0 vote, June 3, 1946. Black wrote the Court's opinion; Jackson did not participate.

Congress violated the ban on bills of attainder by passing a section of an appropriations law that prohibited payment of salaries to three specifically named federal employees until they were reappointed and reconfirmed to their positions.

CIVIL RIGHTS

Morgan v. Virginia, 328 U.S. 373, decided by a 7–1 vote, June 3, 1946. Reed wrote the Court's opinion; Burton dissented; Jackson did not participate.

A state law requiring segregated seating on interstate buses is an unconstitutional burden on interstate commerce. Where interstate commerce is involved, bus seating requires uniform national rules; otherwise the constant shifting of seats and rearrangement demanded by various state laws will burden interstate commerce.

FREEDOM OF RELIGION

Girouard v. United States, 328 U.S. 61, decided by a 5–3 vote, April 22, 1946. Douglas wrote the majority opinion; Stone, Reed, and Frankfurter dissented; Jackson did not participate.

The oath that persons must swear to become naturalized citizens does not expressly require them to swear to bear arms in defense of the United States. Therefore, a person who meets all other qualifications for naturalization should not be barred from citizenship because he is unwilling to bear arms, an activity that conflicts with his religious beliefs.

This decision overturned three earlier rulings in which the Court had interpreted the naturalization oath to require a willingness to bear arms. The decisions had barred from citizenship two women, who would not have been required to serve in the armed forces in any event, and a fifty-four-year-old divinity school professor unlikely to be called for duty because of his age.

VOTING RIGHTS

Colegrove v. Green, 328 U.S. 549, decided by a 4–3 vote, June 10, 1946. Frankfurter wrote the majority opinion; Black, Douglas, and Murphy dissented; Jackson did not participate.

The Court declined to compel the rural-dominated Illinois legislature to redraw congressional districts. The districts had not been reconfigured since 1901, resulting in population disparities of as much as nine to one between rural and urban regions within the state. The Court said this matter was a political question beyond judicial power to resolve.

1947

CONTEMPT

United States v. United Mine Workers, 330 U.S. 258, decided by a divided Court, March 6, 1947. Vinson wrote the majority opinion; Murphy and Rutledge dissented; Black, Frankfurter, Douglas, and Jackson dissented in part.

The same action may constitute civil and criminal contempt. The justices upheld the conviction of the United Mine Workers of America and its president, John L. Lewis, for both types of contempt for failure to obey a court order forbidding a strike.

CRUEL AND UNUSUAL PUNISHMENT

Louisiana ex rel. Francis v. Resweber, 329 U.S. 459, decided by a 5–4 vote, January 13, 1947. Reed wrote the majority opinion; Burton, Douglas, Murphy, and Rutledge dissented.

Assuming without argument that the Eighth Amendment ban on cruel and unusual punishment applied to state as well as federal actions, the Court nevertheless held that this ban was not violated by the state's execution of a man whose first execution attempt failed because the electric chair did not work.

FREEDOM OF RELIGION

Everson v. Board of Education of Ewing Township, 330 U.S. 1, decided by a 5–4 vote, February 10, 1947. Black wrote the majority opinion; Jackson, Frankfurter, Rutledge, and Burton dissented.

State reimbursement of parents for the cost of transporting their children to parochial schools does not violate the First Amendment clause barring government establishment of religion. Such reimbursements aid parents and children, not the church-affiliated schools.

This decision was the first in which the Court specifically applied the First Amendment's establishment clause to state action.

JURY TRIALS

Fay v. New York, 332 U.S. 261, decided by a 5–4 vote, June 23, 1947. Jackson wrote the majority opinion; Murphy, Black, Douglas, and Rutledge dissented.

The Court upheld New York's "blue ribbon" jury system saying that panels of specially qualified jurors disproportionately representing upper economic and social strata were not deliberately discriminatory and did not violate the Constitution.

OFFSHORE LANDS

United States v. California, 332 U.S. 19, decided by a 6–2 vote, June 23, 1947. Black wrote the majority opinion; Frankfurter and Reed dissented; Jackson did not participate.

The federal government, not the states, owns the tidelands immediately adjacent to the states and the oil therein. The Court reaffirmed this ruling in two subsequent cases, but then sustained—as an exercise of Congress's unrestricted power to dispose of government property—an act of Congress giving coastal states rights to the tidelands oil (*Alabama v. Texas,* 347 U.S. 272, 1954).

POWERS OF CONGRESS

United Public Workers v. Mitchell, 330 U.S. 75, decided by a 4–3 vote, February 10, 1947. Reed wrote the majority opinion; Black, Douglas, and Rutledge dissented; Murphy and Jackson did not participate.

The Court sustained the 1939 Hatch Act, upholding the power of Congress to impose limitations on the political activity of government employees.

1948

EQUAL PROTECTION

Shelley v. Kraemer, 334 U.S. 1, decided by a 6–0 vote, May 3, 1948. Vinson wrote the opinion; Reed, Jackson, and Rutledge did not participate.

The Fourteenth Amendment does not bar private parties from entering into racially restrictive covenants, which exclude blacks from buying or renting homes in "covenanted" neighborhoods, but it does prohibit state courts from enforcing such covenants. Such enforcement constitutes state action denying equal protection of the laws.

FREEDOM OF RELIGION

Illinois ex rel. McCollum v. Board of Education, 333 U.S. 203, decided by an 8–1 vote, March 8, 1948. Black wrote the majority opinion; Reed dissented.

The First Amendment clause barring establishment of religion is violated by a voluntary "released time" program in which religious instruction is given to public school students in the public school during school time.

The Court in 1952 sustained a released time program in which students left the school premises to receive religious instruction (*Zorach v. Clauson,* 343 U.S. 306).

1949

FREEDOM OF SPEECH

Terminiello v. Chicago, 337 U.S. 1, decided by a 5–4 vote, May 16, 1949. Douglas wrote the majority opinion; Vinson, Frankfurter, Jackson, and Burton dissented.

The Court reversed the conviction, for breach of the peace, of a speaker whose remarks in a meeting hall provoked a near-riot among protesters gathered outside.

Without deciding whether the First Amendment guarantee of free speech protected such inciteful speech, the majority held that the trial court's definition of breach of the peace was so broad that it included speech that was clearly protected by the First Amendment.

SEARCH AND SEIZURE

Wolf v. Colorado, 338 U.S. 25, decided by a 6–3 vote, June 27, 1949. Frankfurter wrote the majority opinion; Douglas, Murphy, and Rutledge dissented.

The Fourth Amendment protection of individuals against unreasonable searches and seizures by government agents applies against searches by state, as well as federal, agents.

State judges, however, are not required to exclude from use evidence obtained by searches in violation of this guarantee.

1950

CIVIL RIGHTS

Sweatt v. Painter, 339 U.S. 629, decided by a unanimous vote, June 5, 1950. Vinson wrote the opinion.

A state may not deny admission to its law school to a black even if there is a "black" law school available. The Court found the facilities of the "black" school inferior to those provided by the "white" school, therefore violating the "separate but equal" doctrine.

McLaurin v. Oklahoma State Regents for Higher Education, 339 U.S. 637, decided by a unanimous vote, June 5, 1950. Vinson wrote the opinion.

Going beyond *Sweatt* and eroding the "separate but equal" doctrine even more, the Court ruled that once a black was admitted to a state university, the state could not deny him the right to use all its facilities, including the library, lunchroom, and classrooms.

FREEDOM OF ASSOCIATION

American Communications Assn. v. Douds, 339 U.S. 382, decided by a 5–1 vote, May 8, 1950. Vinson wrote the majority opinion; Black dissented. Douglas, Clark, and Minton did not participate.

The Taft-Hartley Act can properly require each officer of a labor union to file an affidavit swearing that he was not a member of or affiliated with the Communist Party. The Court held that Congress could properly impose this requirement as part of its power to prevent political strikes obstructing interstate commerce.

SEARCH AND SEIZURE

United States v. Rabinowitz, 339 U.S. 56, decided by a 5–3 vote, February 20, 1950. Minton wrote the majority opinion; Frankfurter, Jackson, and Black dissented; Douglas did not participate.

The Fourth Amendment guarantee of security against unreasonable searches permits a warrantless search, incident to a lawful arrest, of the person arrested and the premises where the arrest occurs.

1951

EXCESSIVE BAIL

Stack v. Boyle, 342 U.S. 1, decided by an 8–0 vote, November 5, 1951. Vinson wrote the opinion; Minton did not participate.

The amount of bail required of twelve Communist Party leaders prosecuted under the Smith Act of 1940 was excessive and violated the Eighth Amendment's prohibition of excessive bail.

FREEDOM OF ASSOCIATION

Joint Anti-Fascist Refugee Committee v. McGrath, 341 U.S. 123, decided by a 5–3 vote, April 30, 1951. Burton wrote the majority opinion; Vinson, Reed, and Minton dissented; Clark did not participate.

The attorney general has the power to prepare and distribute a list of subversive organizations to aid the work of the federal Loyalty Review Board. But, the Court ruled, to list an organization without affording it a hearing violated the organization's constitutional rights.

Garner v. Board of Public Works, 341 U.S. 716, decided by a 5–4 vote, June 4, 1951. Clark wrote the majority opinion; Burton, Frankfurter, Black, and Douglas dissented.

A loyalty oath for public employees was not a denial of due process or invalid as a bill of attainder or an ex post facto law.

FREEDOM OF SPEECH

Kunz v. New York, 340 U.S. 290, decided by an 8–1 vote, January 15, 1951. Vinson wrote the majority opinion; Jackson dissented.

A New York City ordinance that barred worship services on public streets without a permit is an unconstitutional prior restraint on the exercise of the First Amendment rights of free speech and free exercise of religion.

Feiner v. New York, 340 U.S. 315, decided by a 6–3 vote, January 15, 1951. Vinson wrote the majority opinion; Black, Douglas, and Minton dissented.

The First Amendment is not violated by the conviction, for breach of the peace, of a street speaker who refused to stop speaking after police asked him to desist. The police had acted not to suppress speech but to preserve public order, a legitimate reason for limiting speech.

This decision, read with the decisions in *Terminiello v. Chicago* (1949) and *Kunz v. New York* (1951) demonstrate the Court's difficulty in defining precisely the circumstances in which a state might properly curtail free speech.

Dennis v. United States, 341 U.S. 494, decided by a 6–2 vote, June 4, 1951. Vinson wrote the majority opinion; Black and Douglas dissented; Clark did not participate.

Convictions under the Smith Act of 1940 for speaking and teaching about communist theory advocating forcible overthrow of the government do not abridge First Amendment rights.

1952

EXCESSIVE BAIL

Carlson v. Landon, 342 U.S. 524, decided by a 5–4 vote, March 10, 1952. Reed wrote the majority opinion; Black, Frankfurter, Burton, and Douglas dissented.

Five alien members of the Communist Party could be detained without bail pending the outcome of deportation proceedings. Denial of bail was justified because deportation was not a criminal proceeding.

POWERS OF THE PRESIDENT

Youngstown Sheet and Tube Co. v. Sawyer (Steel Seizure Case), 343 U.S. 579, decided by a 6–3 vote, June 2, 1952. Black wrote the majority opinion; Vinson, Reed, and Minton dissented.

President Truman exceeded his power in seizing the nation's steel mills to prevent a strike. The president had based the seizure order on his general powers as commander in chief and chief executive. But the Court held he could not take such action without express authorization from Congress.

SEARCH AND SEIZURE

Rochin v. California, 342 U.S. 165, decided by an 8–0 vote, January 2, 1952. Frankfurter wrote the opinion; Minton did not participate.

State police officers who used a stomach pump to obtain evidence of drugs—which a suspect had swallowed in their presence—violated Fourth Amendment prohibitions against unreasonable searches and seizures.

1953

VOTING RIGHTS

Terry v. Adams, 345 U.S. 461, decided by an 8–1 vote, May 4, 1953. Black wrote the majority opinion; Minton dissented.

The all-white Texas Jaybird Party primary, held before the regular Democratic Party primary, whose winners usually then won the Democratic nomination and election to county offices, is unconstitutional. It was an integral part of the election process and the exclusion of blacks from this primary violated the Fifteenth Amendment.

WAR POWERS

Rosenberg v. United States, 346 U.S. 273, decided by a 6–3 vote, June 19, 1953. Vinson wrote the majority opinion; Frankfurter, Black, and Douglas dissented.

The Court, after meeting in special session, lifted a stay of execution for Julius and Ethel Rosenberg, convicted of violating the Espionage Act of 1917 and sentenced to death.

Justice Douglas had granted the stay so that lower courts might consider the argument of the Rosenbergs' attorney that the espionage act had been repealed by subsequent passage of the Atomic Energy Act of 1946. The Rosenbergs were convicted of having conveyed atomic secrets to the Soviet Union. They were executed as soon as the Court lifted the stay.

1954

CIVIL RIGHTS

Brown v. Board of Education of Topeka, 347 U.S. 483, decided by a unanimous vote, May 17, 1954. Warren wrote the opinion.

Separate public schools for black and white students are inherently unequal, and their existence violates the equal protection guarantee of the Fourteenth Amendment.

In the companion case of *Bolling v. Sharpe* (347 U.S. 497), the Court ruled that the congressionally mandated segregated public school system in the District of Columbia violated the Fifth Amendment's due process guarantee of personal liberty.

In *Brown* the Court specifically overruled the "separate but equal" doctrine first enunciated in *Plessy v. Ferguson* (1896) so far as it applied to public schools. The ruling also led to the abolition of state-sponsored segregation in other public facilities.

1955

CIVIL RIGHTS

Brown v. Board of Education of Topeka, 349 U.S. 294, decided by a unanimous vote, May 31, 1955. Warren wrote the opinion.

The Court laid out guidelines for ending segregation in public schools. The Court placed primary responsibility on local school officials, recognizing that local factors would call for different treatment and timing, but admonishing the boards to proceed toward desegregation "with all deliberate speed."

Federal district courts were to retain jurisdiction over school desegregation cases. They could grant school districts additional time to complete desegregation once the process was begun, but the school boards had the burden of justifying such delays.

1956

SELF-INCRIMINATION

Ullmann v. United States, 350 U.S. 422, decided by a 7–2 vote, March 26, 1956. Frankfurter wrote the majority opinion; Douglas and Black dissented.

The Court sustained the Immunity Act of 1950, which provided that witnesses cannot claim their privilege against self-incrimination if the government grants them immunity from prosecution.

Slochower v. Board of Education of New York City, 350 U.S. 551, decided by a 5–4 vote, April 9, 1956. Clark wrote the majority opinion; Reed, Burton, Harlan, and Minton dissented.

The provision of New York City's charter that provided for summary dismissal of employees who invoked the Fifth Amendment privilege against self-incrimination violated the due process guarantee of the Fourteenth Amendment.

STATE POWERS

Pennsylvania v. Nelson, 350 U.S. 497, decided by a 6–3 vote, April 2, 1956. Warren wrote the majority opinion; Reed, Minton, and Burton dissented.

States may not punish persons for seditious activity against the federal government.

Congress has preempted that field by passing federal legislation on that subject.

1957

DUE PROCESS

Mallory v. United States, 354 U.S. 449, decided by a unanimous vote, June 24, 1957. Frankfurter delivered the opinion.

The Court reversed the criminal conviction of a man interrogated without being informed of his constitutional rights and held for an unnecessarily long period between arrest and arraignment. Such practices deprived him of his liberty without due process of law.

FREEDOM OF SPEECH

Yates v. United States, 354 U.S. 298, decided by votes of 6–1 and 4–3, June 17, 1957. Harlan wrote the majority opinion; Clark dissented; Black and Douglas dissented in part; Brennan and Whittaker did not participate.

To prosecute persons for violating the Smith Act by advocating the forcible overthrow of the government, the United States must show active engagement on the part of the defendant—overt acts, not just abstract arguments. The decision made it much more difficult for the government to obtain convictions under the Smith Act.

OBSCENITY

Roth v. United States, Alberts v. California, 354 U.S. 476, decided by votes of 6–3 and 7–2, June 24, 1957. Brennan wrote the majority opinion; Harlan dissented in Roth, but concurred in Alberts; Black and Douglas dissented.

Obscene material is not protected by the First Amendment guarantees of freedom of speech and press. Material is obscene, the Court said, if the average person would consider that its dominant theme appealed to prurient interest.

This definition of obscenity was the first offered by the Court. It was modified in several subsequent decisions and finally replaced with another standard in *Miller v. California* (1973).

POWERS OF CONGRESS

Watkins v. United States, 354 U.S. 178, decided by a 6–1 vote, June 17, 1957. Warren wrote the majority opinion; Clark dissented; Burton and Whittaker did not participate.

Declaring that "there is no congressional power to expose for the sake of exposure," the Court held that congressional investigations may be undertaken only in aid of the legislative function. House and Senate instructions to their investigating committees must therefore fully spell out the investigating committee's purpose and jurisdiction.

Furthermore, a witness may refuse with impunity to answer questions if they are not pertinent to the investigation. "It is the duty of the investigative body, upon objection of the witness on grounds of pertinency, to state . . . the subject under inquiry at the time and the manner in which the propounded questions are pertinent thereto," the majority said.

This reversed the contempt conviction of a labor union officer who answered questions about his own association with the Communist Party but refused to answer similar questions about other people.

1958

CIVIL RIGHTS

Cooper v. Aaron, 358 U.S. 1, decided by a unanimous vote, September 12, 1958. Warren wrote the opinion; each justice personally signed it.

Standing firm against defiance of its 1954 and 1955 decisions declaring public school segregation unconstitutional, the Court refused a request by Little Rock, Arkansas, school officials for a delay in desegregation of their public schools. Local school officials had made the request after Gov. Orval Faubus called out the state national guard to block the entrance to a Little Rock high school to prevent entry by black students. Federal troops were eventually sent to the city to restore order and protect the black students, and the school board asked for delay of further desegregation efforts. The Court convened a special session in late summer of 1958 to hear the case.

In a sharp rebuke to Faubus and state legislators, the Court said that the rights of black children could "neither be nullified openly and directly by state legislators or state executive officials nor nullified indirectly by them by evasive schemes for segregation."

CRUEL AND UNUSUAL PUNISHMENT

Trop v. Dulles, 356 U.S. 86, decided by a 5–4 vote, March 31, 1958. Warren wrote the majority opinion; Frankfurter, Burton, Clark, and Harlan dissented.

The Eighth Amendment ban on cruel and unusual punishment prohibits the use of expatriation or denaturalization as punishment for persons found guilty of desertion from the armed forces in wartime.

FREEDOM OF ASSOCIATION

National Association for the Advancement of Colored People v. Alabama ex rel. Patterson, 357 U.S. 449, decided by a unanimous vote, June 30, 1958. Harlan wrote the opinion.

The freedom to associate with others is implicit in the freedoms of speech and assembly guaranteed by the First Amendment. The right to associate carries with it the right of privacy in that association.

A state court order requiring the NAACP to produce its membership lists is therefore an unconstitutional restraint on NAACP members' right of association. The state did not show a sufficient interest in the disclosure of the lists to justify the limitation such disclosure placed on freedom of association.

PERSONAL LIBERTY

Kent v. Dulles, 357 U.S. 116, decided by a 5–4 vote, June 16, 1958. Douglas wrote the majority opinion; Clark, Harlan, Burton, and Whittaker dissented.

The freedom to travel is part of the personal liberty protected by the due process guarantee of the Fifth and Fourteenth Amendments.

Congress has not authorized the secretary of state to withhold passports from citizens because of their beliefs or associations.

POWERS OF THE PRESIDENT

Wiener v. United States, 357 U.S. 349, decided by a unanimous vote, June 30, 1958. Frankfurter wrote the opinion.

This decision reinforced the "nature of the office" approach to the presidential removal power. The Court held that where the duties of the office included quasi-judicial functions, and, where there was no statutory provision for removal, the president lacked the power to remove an incumbent official from his post simply to replace him with a person of his own choice.

1959

POWERS OF CONGRESS

Barenblatt v. United States, 360 U.S. 109, decided by a 5–4 vote, June 8, 1959. Harlan wrote the majority opinion; Warren, Black, Brennan, and Douglas dissented.

Retreating from *Watkins,* the Court held that the First Amendment rights of witnesses appearing before congressional investigating committees may be limited when the public interest outweighs the private interest.

In this case, the federal government's interest in preserving itself against those who advocated the forceful overthrow of that government outweighed the right of the witness, a teacher, to conduct a classroom discussion on the theoretical nature of communism.

VOTING RIGHTS

Lassiter v. Northampton County Board of Elections, 360 U.S. 45, decided by a unanimous vote, June 8, 1959. Douglas delivered the opinion.

North Carolina can require that all persons must be able to read and write a section of the state constitution in English before being allowed to vote. Such a provision, applied in a nondiscriminatory way, did not violate the Fourteenth, Fifteenth, or Seventeenth Amendments, the Court held.

1960

SEARCH AND SEIZURE

Elkins v. United States, 364 U.S. 206, decided by a 5–4 vote, June 27, 1960. Stewart wrote the majority opinion; Frankfurter, Clark, Harlan, and Whittaker dissented.

The Court abandoned the "silver platter" doctrine that permitted use—in federal court—of evidence illegally seized by state authorities and handed over to federal authority. The Court held that such a practice violated the Fourth Amendment prohibition against unreasonable search and seizure.

VOTING RIGHTS

Gomillion v. Lightfoot, 364 U.S. 339, decided by a unanimous vote, November 14, 1960. Frankfurter wrote the opinion.

It is unconstitutional, a violation of the Fifteenth Amendment guarantee of the right to vote, for a state legislative districting plan to exclude almost all black voters from voting in city elections in Tuskegee, Alabama.

1961

EQUAL PROTECTION

Hoyt v. Florida, 368 U.S. 57, decided by a unanimous vote, November 20, 1961. Harlan wrote the opinion.

States do not violate the equal protection guarantee by generally excluding women from jury duty. The exclusion was rational in light of the state's interest in preventing interference with women's traditional functions as wives, homemakers, and mothers, the Court said.

FREEDOM OF ASSOCIATION

Communist Party v. Subversive Activities Control Board, 367 U.S. 1, decided by a 5–4 vote, June 5, 1961. Frankfurter wrote the majority opinion; Warren, Black, Douglas, and Brennan dissented.

The Court upheld provisions of the Subversive Activities Control Act of 1950 requiring the Communist Party to register with the Justice Department, list its officials, and file financial statements. The Court rejected the party's arguments that the registration provisions were unconstitutional as a bill of attainder and a violation of the First Amendment guarantees of freedom of speech and association.

Scales v. United States, 367 U.S. 203, *Noto v. United States,* 367 U.S. 290, decided by 5–4 votes, June 5, 1961. Harlan wrote the majority opinions; Warren, Black, Douglas, and Brennan dissented.

The First Amendment freedoms of speech and association are not violated by laws providing penalties for active membership in a group specifically intending to bring about the violent overthrow of the government. The Court upheld Scales's conviction, but reversed Noto's, finding insufficient evidence in the latter case to justify the conviction.

SEARCH AND SEIZURE

Mapp v. Ohio, 367 U.S. 643, decided by a 5–4 vote, June 19, 1961. Clark wrote the majority opinion; Stewart, Harlan, Frankfurter, and Whittaker dissented.

Evidence obtained in violation of the Fourth Amendment guarantee against unreasonable search and seizure must be excluded from use at state as well as federal trials. With this decision, the Court overruled *Wolf v. Colorado* (1949).

1962

CRUEL AND UNUSUAL PUNISHMENT

Robinson v. California, 370 U.S. 660, decided by a 6–2 vote, June 25, 1962. Stewart wrote the majority opinion; Clark and White dissented; Frankfurter did not participate.

It is a violation of the Eighth Amendment ban on cruel and unusual punishment for a state to make narcotics addiction a criminal offense.

FREEDOM OF RELIGION

Engel v. Vitale, 370 U.S. 421, decided by a 6–1 vote, June 25, 1962. Black wrote the majority opinion; Stewart dissented; Frankfurter and White did not participate.

Public school officials may not require pupils to recite a state-composed prayer at the beginning of each school day, even though the prayer is denominationally neutral and pupils who so desire may be excused from reciting it.

Official state-sanctioned prayers, the Court held, are unconstitutional attempts by government to establish religion.

VOTING RIGHTS

Baker v. Carr, 369 U.S. 186, decided by a 6–2 vote, March 26, 1962. Brennan wrote the majority opinion; Frankfurter and Harlan dissented; Whittaker did not participate.

The Court for the first time held that constitutional challenges to the maldistribution of voters among legislative districts might properly be resolved by federal courts. The Court rejected the doctrine set out in *Colgrove v. Green* (1946) that all such apportionment challenges were "political questions" beyond the proper reach of the federal courts.

1963

FEDERAL COURTS

Fay v. Noia, 372 U.S. 391, decided by a 6–3 vote, March 18, 1963. Brennan wrote the majority opinion; Harlan, Clark, and Stewart dissented.

In some circumstances, a state prisoner may challenge his imprisonment by obtaining a federal writ of habeas corpus even if he has not appealed his conviction through the state court system.

The requirement that a state prisoner "exhaust" all state remedies before challenging his conviction in federal courts simply means that a state prisoner must have tried all state remedies still available to him at the time he comes into federal court seeking the writ.

FREEDOM OF ASSOCIATION

National Association for the Advancement of Colored People v. Button, 371 U.S. 415, decided by a 6–3 vote, January 14, 1963. Brennan wrote the majority opinion; Harlan, Clark, and Stewart dissented.

A state law, directed against the NAACP, which forbids solicitation of clients by an agent of an organization that litigates cases in which it is not a party and has no pecuniary interest, impermissibly infringes on the First Amendment right of association. "Abstract discussion is not the only species of communication which the Constitution protects; the First Amendment also protects vigorous advocacy, certainly of lawful ends, against government intrusion," the Court wrote.

FREEDOM OF RELIGION

School District of Abington Township v. Schempp, 374 U.S. 203, decided by an 8–1 vote, June 17, 1963. Clark wrote the opinion; Stewart dissented.

State-ordered recitation of the Lord's Prayer and the reading of the Bible in the public school system as a devotional exercise violates the establishment clause.

FREEDOM OF SPEECH

Edwards v. South Carolina, 372 U.S. 229, decided by an 8–1 vote, February 25, 1963. Stewart wrote the majority opinion; Clark dissented.

The Court reversed the breach-of-the-peace convictions of student demonstrators who had marched peacefully to protest racial discrimination. The Court held that the breach-of-the-peace statute was unconstitutionally broad and had been used in this case to penalize the exercise of free speech, assembly, and petition for redress of grievances "in their most pristine and classic form," a clear violation of the First Amendment.

RIGHT TO COUNSEL

Gideon v. Wainwright, 372 U.S. 335, decided by a unanimous vote, March 18, 1963. Black delivered the Court's opinion.

The due process clause of the Fourteenth Amendment extends to state as well as federal defendants the Sixth Amendment guarantee that all persons charged with serious crimes will be provided the aid of an attorney. *Betts v. Brady* (1942) is overruled. States are required to appoint counsel for defendants who can not afford to pay their own attorneys' fees.

SEARCH AND SEIZURE

Ker v. California, 374 U.S. 23, decided by a 5–4 vote, June 10, 1963. Clark wrote the majority opinion; Warren, Brennan, Douglas, and Goldberg dissented in part.

The same standards apply to determine whether federal and state searches and seizures are reasonable and therefore permissible under the Fourth Amendment. (The justices disagreed over whether the warrantless search at issue in this case was reasonable.)

VOTING RIGHTS

Gray v. Sanders, 372 U.S. 368, decided by an 8–1 vote, March 18, 1963. Douglas wrote the majority opinion; Harlan dissented.

Georgia's "county unit" system of electing officers to state posts violates the equal protection guarantee of the Fourteenth Amendment by giving more weight to the votes of people in rural counties than urban counties. The idea of political equality, inherent in the U.S. system, held the Court, "can mean only one thing—one person, one vote."

1964

CIVIL RIGHTS

Griffin v. County School Board of Prince Edward County, 377 U.S. 218, decided by a 7–2 vote, May 25, 1964. Black wrote the majority opinion; Clark and Harlan dissented in part.

Losing patience with state defiance of its school desegregation decisions, the Court declared that there had been "entirely too much deliberation and not enough speed." It was unconstitutional, a violation of the Fourteenth Amendment's equal protection clause, for Prince Edward County, Virginia, to close its schools, to avoid the impact of desegregation.

Heart of Atlanta Motel v. United States, 379 U.S. 241, decided by a unanimous vote, December 14, 1964. Clark wrote the opinion.

The commerce power may be used to prohibit racial discrimination in privately owned public accommodations. This decision effectively overturned the Court's 1883 *Civil Rights Cases* and sustained Title II of the Civil Rights Act of 1964. That section prohibited discrimination, on the basis of race, religion, or national origin, in accommodations that catered to interstate travelers or that served food or provided entertainment, a substantial portion of which was shipped through interstate commerce.

FREEDOM OF ASSOCIATION

Aptheker v. Secretary of State, 378 U.S. 500, decided by a 6–3 vote, June 22, 1964. Goldberg wrote the majority opinion; Clark, Harlan, and White dissented.

The Court declared unconstitutional a section of the Subversive Activities Control Act of 1950 that denied passports—and thus the right to travel—to persons who belonged to organizations listed as subversive by the attorney general. The law was too broad; it failed to distinguish between persons who joined such organizations with the full knowledge of their subversive purpose and persons who joined with less knowledge.

FREEDOM OF THE PRESS

New York Times Co. v. Sullivan, 376 U.S. 254, decided by a unanimous vote, March 9, 1964. Brennan wrote the opinion.

The First Amendment guarantee of freedom of the press protects the press from libel suits for defamatory reports on public officials unless the officials prove that the reports were made with actual malice. Actual malice is defined as "with knowledge that it [the defamatory statement] was false or with reckless disregard of whether it was false or not."

Until this decision, libelous statements were not protected by the First Amendment.

RIGHT TO COUNSEL

Escobedo v. Illinois, 378 U.S. 478, decided by a 5–4 vote, June 22, 1964. Goldberg wrote the majority opinion; Harlan, Stewart, White, and Clark dissented.

The Court expanded a suspect's right to counsel under the Sixth Amendment, holding that confessions obtained by police who had not advised the suspect of his right to counsel—or acceded to his requests for counsel—were inadmissible as evidence.

SELF-INCRIMINATION

Malloy v. Hogan, 378 U.S. 1, decided by a 5–4 vote, June 15, 1964. Brennan wrote the majority opinion; Harlan, Clark, White, and Stewart dissented.

The Fifth Amendment protection against self-incrimination is extended to state defendants through the due process clause of the Fourteenth Amendment.

Murphy v. Waterfront Commission of New York, 378 U.S. 52, decided by a unanimous vote, June 15, 1964. Goldberg wrote the opinion.

The Fifth Amendment privilege against compelled self-incrimination protects witnesses immunized by either state or federal officials from prosecution in either jurisdiction based on their testimony.

VOTING RIGHTS

Wesberry v. Sanders, 376 U.S. 1, decided by a 6–3 vote, February 17, 1964. Black wrote the majority opinion; Clark dissented in part; Harlan and Stewart dissented.

Substantial disparity in the population of congressional districts within a state is unconstitutional, violating the provision for election of members of the House of Representatives "by the people of the several states." Congressional voting districts within a state must be as nearly equal in population as possible.

Reynolds v. Sims, 377 U.S. 533, decided by an 8–1 vote, June 15, 1964. Warren wrote the majority opinion; Harlan dissented.

The equal protection clause of the Fourteenth Amendment requires application of the "one person, one vote" apportionment rule to both houses of a state legislature.

1965

DUE PROCESS

Pointer v. Texas, 380 U.S. 400, decided by a unanimous vote, April 5, 1965. Black wrote the opinion.

The Sixth Amendment guarantee of the right to confront and cross-examine witnesses is applied to state defendants by the Fourteenth Amendment's due process clause.

FEDERAL COURTS

Dombrowski v. Pfister, 380 U.S. 479, decided by a 5–2 vote, April 26, 1965. Brennan wrote the majority opinion; Harlan and Clark dissented; Black and Stewart did not participate.

Federal courts need not abstain from ordering state officials to halt enforcement of a law justifiably attacked as in violation of the First Amendment, even if the person seeking the order has not yet exhausted all state procedures for challenging that law.

PERSONAL PRIVACY

Griswold v. Connecticut, 381 U.S. 479, decided by a 7–2 vote, June 7, 1965. Douglas wrote the majority opinion; Stewart and Black dissented.

A state unconstitutionally interferes with personal privacy when it prohibits anyone, including married couples, from using contraceptives. There is a right of personal privacy implicit in the Constitution, although there is disagreement on its exact source.

SELF-INCRIMINATION

Griffin v. California, 380 U.S. 609, decided by a 6–2 vote, April 28, 1965. Douglas wrote the majority opinion; Stewart and White dissented; Warren did not participate.

The Fifth Amendment privilege against compelled self-incrimination, as applied to the states through the due process guarantee of the Fourteenth Amendment, is infringed when a judge or prosecutor comments adversely during a trial upon a defendant's failure to testify in his own behalf.

Albertson v. Subversive Activities Control Board, 382 U.S. 70, decided by an 8–0 vote, November 15, 1965. Brennan wrote the opinion; White did not participate.

The Court overturned convictions of Communist Party members who were ordered to register personally with the attorney general by the Subversive Activities Control Act of 1950. The registration orders violated the Fifth Amendment privilege against self-incrimination.

VOTING RIGHTS

Harman v. Forssenius, 380 U.S. 528, decided by a unanimous vote, April 27, 1965. Warren wrote the opinion.

A Virginia law imposing special registration requirements on persons not paying the state's poll tax violates the Twenty-fourth Amendment's ban on poll taxes in federal elections.

1966

FREEDOM OF ASSOCIATION

Elfbrandt v. Russell, 384 U.S. 11, decided by a 5–4 vote, April 18, 1966. Douglas wrote the majority opinion; White, Clark, Harlan, and Stewart dissented.

An Arizona loyalty oath violates the First Amendment freedom of association by penalizing persons for membership in certain groups whether or not they joined the group with the specific intent of engaging in unlawful acts.

SELF-INCRIMINATION

Miranda v. Arizona, 384 U.S. 436, decided by a 5–4 vote, June 13, 1966. Warren wrote the majority opinion; Clark, Harlan, Stewart, and White dissented.

The due process guarantee requires that suspects in police custody be informed of their right to remain silent, that anything they say may be used against them, and that they have the right to counsel—before any interrogation can permissibly take place.

VOTING RIGHTS

South Carolina v. Katzenbach, 383 U.S. 301, decided by an 8–1 vote, March 7, 1966. Warren wrote the majority opinion; Black dissented.

The Voting Rights Act of 1965 is a proper exercise of congressional power to enforce the Fifteenth Amendment ban on racial discrimination in voting.

Harper v. Virginia State Board of Elections, 383 U.S. 663, decided by a 6–3 vote, March 24, 1966. Douglas wrote the majority opinion; Black, Harlan, and Stewart dissented.

State laws that condition the right to vote upon payment of a tax violate the equal protection clause of the Fourteenth Amendment.

1967

CIVIL RIGHTS

Loving v. Virginia, 388 U.S. 1, decided by a unanimous vote, June 12, 1967. Warren wrote the opinion.

A state law punishing persons who enter into interracial marriages violates both the equal protection and due process clauses of the Fourteenth Amendment. "Under our Constitution, the freedom to marry or not marry a person of another race resides with the individual and cannot be infringed by the state," the Court declared.

This decision was the first in which the Court explicitly held classifications by race "inherently suspect" and justifiable only by compelling reasons.

DUE PROCESS

Klopfer v. North Carolina, 386 U.S. 213, decided by a unanimous vote, March 13, 1967. Warren wrote the Court's opinion.

The Sixth Amendment right to a speedy trial applies in state, as well as federal, proceedings.

In re Gault, 387 U.S. 1, decided by a 7–2 vote, May 15, 1967. Fortas wrote the majority opinion; Harlan and Stewart dissented.

Juveniles have some—but not all—due process privileges in juvenile court proceedings. The privilege against self-incrimination and the right to counsel do apply.

Washington v. Texas, 388 U.S. 14, decided by a unanimous vote, June 12, 1967. Warren wrote the opinion.

Compulsory process to obtain witnesses in the defendant's favor is so fundamental to the Sixth Amendment guarantee of a fair trial that it is applicable to state trials through the Fourteenth Amendment.

FREEDOM OF ASSOCIATION

Keyishian v. Board of Regents, 385 U.S. 589, decided by a 5–4 vote, January 23, 1967. Brennan wrote the majority opinion; Clark, Harlan, Stewart, and White dissented.

New York State's teacher loyalty oath requirement is invalid as too vague and uncertain. Membership in the Communist Party alone is not sufficient reason to disqualify a teacher from public school employment.

United States v. Robel, 389 U.S. 258, decided by a 6–2 vote, December 11, 1967. Warren wrote the majority opinion; White and Harlan dissented; Marshall did not participate.

The Subversive Activities Control Act of 1950 violates the First Amendment freedom of association by forbidding a member of a group listed as subversive by the attorney general to take a job in a defense industry.

RIGHT TO COUNSEL

United States v. Wade, 388 U.S. 218, decided by a unanimous vote, June 12, 1967. Brennan wrote the opinion.

A police line-up identification of a suspect—made without the suspect's attorney present—is inadmissible as evidence at trial.

SEARCH AND SEIZURE

Warden v. Hayden, 387 U.S. 294, decided by an 8–1 vote, May 29, 1967. Brennan wrote the majority opinion; Douglas dissented.

Law enforcement searches for "mere evidence" are just as constitutional and reasonable as searches for implements and products of crime.

Katz v. United States, 389 U.S. 347, decided by a 7–1 vote, December 18, 1967. Stewart wrote the majority opinion for the Court; Black dissented; Marshall did not participate.

The Court abandoned its view, set out in *Olmstead v. United States* (1928), that electronic surveillance and wiretapping were not "searches and seizures" within the scope of the Fourth Amendment. The amendment protects people, not places; it protects what an individual seeks to preserve as private, even in a place accessible to the public.

1968

CIVIL RIGHTS

Green v. County School Board of New Kent County, 391 U.S. 430, decided by a unanimous vote, May 27, 1968. Brennan wrote the opinion.

Local school district officials have an affirmative duty to eliminate segregation "root and branch" from public schools, the Court said, striking down a "freedom-of-choice" plan that would have maintained segregated schools in New Kent County, Virginia. "The burden on a school board today is to come forward with a [desegregation] plan that promises realistically to work and . . . to work *now*," the Court declared.

Jones v. Alfred H. Mayer Co., 392 U.S. 409, decided by a 7–2 vote, June 17, 1968. Stewart wrote the majority opinion; Harlan and White dissented.

The 1866 Civil Rights Act bars private as well as state-backed discrimination on the basis of race in the sale and rental of housing.

This decision reinterpreted congressional authority to enforce the Thirteenth Amendment, which was intended to remove "the badges of slavery." In the *Civil Rights Cases* of 1883, the Court had held that Congress had no authority to enforce the guarantees of the Thirteenth Amendment against private acts of discrimination.

DUE PROCESS

Duncan v. Louisiana, 391 U.S. 145, decided by a 7–2 vote, May 20, 1968. White wrote the majority opinion; Harlan and Stewart dissented.

The Fourteenth Amendment's guarantee of due process requires states to provide trial by jury to persons accused of serious crimes.

FEDERAL COURTS

Flast v. Cohen, 392 U.S. 83, decided by an 8–1 vote, June 10, 1968. Warren wrote the majority opinion; Harlan dissented.

Modifying *Frothingham v. Mellon* (1923), the Court held that a federal taxpayer may have the requisite standing to bring a federal challenge to federal spending and taxing programs as unconstitutional.

To prove the necessary personal interest in such programs, the Court ruled, the taxpayer must establish a logical connection between his taxpayer status and the claim before the court. This connection or "nexus" must be shown so that the federal courts not become merely forums for the airing of generalized grievances about government programs and policies.

SEARCH AND SEIZURE

Terry v. Ohio, 392 U.S. 1, decided by an 8–1 vote, June 10, 1968. Warren wrote the majority opinion; Douglas dissented.

The Court upheld the police practice of "stop and frisk," saying that when a police officer observes unusual conduct and suspects a crime is about to be committed, he may "frisk" a suspect's outer clothing for dangerous weapons. Such searches do not violate the Fourth Amendment's prohibition against unreasonable searches and seizures.

1969

DUE PROCESS

Benton v. Maryland, 395 U.S. 784, decided by a 6–2 vote, June 23, 1969. Marshall wrote the opinion; Stewart and Harlan dissented.

Overruling *Palko v. Connecticut* (1937), the Court declared that the Fourteenth Amendment due process guarantee extends the double jeopardy guarantee of the Fifth Amendment against state, as well as federal, action.

FREEDOM OF SPEECH

Tinker v. Des Moines Independent Community School District, 393 U.S. 503, decided by a 7–2 vote, February 24, 1969. Fortas wrote the majority opinion; Harlan and Black dissented.

Students have the right to engage in peaceful nondisruptive protest, the Court said, recognizing that the First Amendment guarantee of freedom of speech protects symbolic as well as oral speech.

The wearing of black armbands to protest the Vietnam War is "closely akin" to the "pure speech" protected by the First Amendment, the majority said, and therefore a public school ban on this form of protest, which did not disrupt the school's work or offend the rights of others, violated these students' rights.

PERSONAL LIBERTY

Shapiro v. Thompson, Washington v. Legrant, Reynolds v. Smith, 394 U.S. 618, decided by a 6–3 vote, April 21, 1969. Brennan wrote the majority opinion; Warren, Black, and Harlan dissented.

The right to travel is constitutionally protected. State or federal requirements that a person reside within a jurisdiction for one year before becoming eligible for welfare assistance violate individual rights to due process and equal protection of the laws.

No compelling government interest was presented to justify this infringement on the right to travel.

POWERS OF CONGRESS

Powell v. McCormack, 395 U.S. 486, decided by a 7–1 vote, June 16, 1969. Warren wrote the opinion; Stewart dissented.

The House of Representatives lacks authority to exclude a duly elected representative who meets the constitutional qualifications of age, residence, and citizenship. The House acted unconstitutionally when it voted to exclude Rep. Adam Clayton Powell, D-N.Y., for misconduct and misuse of public funds.

The Court did not deny the interest of Congress in maintaining its own integrity, but said such interest could be maintained by the use of each chamber's power to punish and expel its members.

The Court rejected the argument that the case presented a "political question," holding that a determination of Powell's right to his seat required only the interpretation of the Constitution, the traditional function of the Court.

SEARCH AND SEIZURE

Chimel v. California, 395 U.S. 752, decided by a 6–2 vote, June 23, 1969. Stewart wrote the opinion; White and Black dissented.

Overruling *United States v. Rabinowitz* (1950), the Court narrowed the limits of permissible searches conducted without a warrant incident to lawful arrest to the immediate area around the suspect from which he could obtain a weapon or destroy evidence. A person's entire dwelling cannot be searched simply because he is arrested there.

VOTING RIGHTS

Kirkpatrick v. Preisler, 394 U.S. 526, decided by a 6–3 vote, April 7, 1969. Brennan wrote the majority opinion; Harlan, Stewart, and White dissented.

Congressional districts with population variances of 3.1 percent from mathematical equality are unconstitutional unless the state can show that such variations are unavoidable.

Gaston County v. U.S., 395 U.S. 285, decided by a 7–1 vote, June 2, 1969. Harlan wrote the majority opinion; Black dissented.

The Court denied a county's request—under provisions of the 1965 Voting Rights Act—to reinstate a literacy test for voters. The combination of such a test, the Court ruled, with previous deprivation of educational opportunity for blacks in the county, would abridge the right to vote on account of race.

1970

DUE PROCESS

In re Winship, 397 U.S. 358, decided by a 5–3 vote, March 31, 1970. Brennan wrote the majority opinion; Burger, Black, and Stewart dissented.

The Fourteenth Amendment guarantee of due process requires that juveniles, like adult defendants, be found guilty "beyond a reasonable doubt." The Supreme Court forbade states to use a lesser standard of proof in juvenile proceedings.

Williams v. Florida, 399 U.S. 78, decided by a 7–1 vote, June 22, 1970. White wrote the majority opinion; Marshall dissented; Blackmun did not participate.

A six-member jury in noncapital state cases is constitutional. The number twelve is a "historical accident"; a jury can perform just as well with six members as it can with twelve.

VOTING RIGHTS

Oregon v. Mitchell, Texas v. Mitchell, United States v. Idaho, United States v. Arizona, 400 U.S. 112, decided by a 5–4 vote on lowered voting age, by an 8–1 vote on residency requirements, and by a unanimous vote on literacy test ban, December 21, 1970.

Black wrote the opinion; Burger, Harlan, Stewart, and Blackmun dissented on the question of age; Harlan dissented on the residency issue.

Congress has the power to lower the voting age for federal—but not for state and local—elections, to restrict state residency requirements to thirty days for voters in presidential elections, and to ban literacy tests as voter qualification devices in any election.

1971

CIVIL RIGHTS

Griggs v. Duke Power Co., 401 U.S. 424, decided by an 8–0 vote, March 8, 1971. Burger wrote the opinion; Brennan did not participate.

In its first case implicitly upholding the right of Congress to bar employment discrimination based on race, the Court held that the Civil Rights Act of 1964 prohibits employers from requiring a high school diploma or score on a general intelligence test as a condition for employment or promotion if neither test is related to job skills and if both tend to disqualify more black than white applicants.

Swann v. Charlotte-Mecklenburg County Board of Education, 402 U.S. 1, decided by a unanimous vote, April 20, 1971. Burger wrote the opinion.

Busing, racial balance ratios, and gerrymandered school districts are all permissible interim methods of eliminating the vestiges of state-imposed segregation from southern schools.

There were limits to the remedies that might be used to eliminate the remnants of segregation, the Court said, but no fixed guidelines setting such limits could be established. The Court acknowledged that there might be valid objections to busing when so much time or distance is involved as to risk the children's health or to impinge significantly on the education process.

DUE PROCESS

McKeiver v. Pennsylvania, In re Burrus, 403 U.S. 528, decided by votes of 6–3 and 5–4, June 21, 1971. Blackmun wrote the majority opinion; Douglas, Black, and Marshall dissented, joined in *Burrus* by Brennan.

The Sixth Amendment right to trial by jury does not extend to juvenile defendants.

EQUAL PROTECTION

Graham v. Richardson, 403 U.S. 365, decided by a unanimous vote, June 14, 1971. Blackmun wrote the Court's opinion.

Extending the equal protection guarantee to aliens, the Court struck down an Arizona law denying welfare benefits to aliens who lived in the United States less than fifteen years and a Pennsylvania law denying benefits to all resident aliens. The Court held that all classification by alienage was "suspect," requiring especially close scrutiny to ensure compliance with the equal protection guarantee.

Reed v. Reed, 404 U.S. 71, decided by a 7–0 vote, November 22, 1971. Burger wrote the opinion.

The Fourteenth Amendment guarantee of equal protection invalidates a state law that automatically prefers a father over a mother as executor of a son's estate. "To give a mandatory preference to members of either sex over members of the other . . . is to make the very kind of arbitrary legislative choice forbidden by the equal protection clause," the Court said in its first opinion declaring a state law unconstitutional on the grounds that it discriminated against women.

FEDERAL COURTS

Younger v. Harris, 401 U.S. 37, decided by an 8–1 vote, February 23, 1971. Black wrote the majority opinion; Douglas dissented.

Federal judges should not normally issue orders to state officials to halt enforcement of a state law or ongoing state proceedings—at least without a showing that continued enforcement of the law threatens to do irreparable injury to the person seeking the order.

FREEDOM OF RELIGION

Lemon v. Kurtzman, 403 U.S. 602, decided by a unanimous vote, June 28, 1971. Burger wrote the opinion; Marshall did not participate.

In this case the Court established a three-part test to determine whether state aid to parochial schools violated the First Amendment's ban on government action "establishing" religion.

State aid is permissible, the Court said, if it is intended to achieve a secular legislative purpose, if its primary effect neither advances nor inhibits religion, and if it does not foster excessive government entanglement with religion.

Applying this test, the Court declared invalid a state law authorizing supplemental salary grants to certain parochial school teachers and another state law authorizing reimbursement to parochial schools for teachers' salaries, textbooks, and instructional materials; the Court found that both laws fostered an excessive entanglement between government and religion.

FREEDOM OF THE PRESS

New York Times Co. v. United States, United States v. The Washington Post, 403 U.S. 713, decided by a 6–3 vote, June 30, 1971. The opinion was unsigned; each justice wrote a separate opinion. Burger, Blackmun, and Harlan dissented.

The Court in its brief per curiam opinion denied the government's request for a court order barring continued publication in the *New York Times* and the *Washington Post* of articles based on classified documents detailing the history of U.S. involvement in Indochina, popularly known as the Pentagon Papers.

Any request for prior restraint of the press bears a "heavy presumption against its constitutional validity," the Court said, and the government had failed to show sufficient justification for imposing such restraint.

SELF-INCRIMINATION

Harris v. New York, 401 U.S. 222, decided by a 5–4 vote, February 24, 1971. Burger wrote the majority opinion; Black, Douglas, Brennan, and Marshall dissented.

Voluntary statements made by a defendant not properly warned of his constitutional rights may be used in court to impeach his credibility if he takes the witness stand in his own defense and contradicts the earlier statements.

1972

DUE PROCESS

Johnson v. Louisiana, 406 U.S. 356, Apodaca v. Oregon, 406 U.S. 404, decided by a 5–4 vote, May 22, 1972. White wrote the majority opinion; Douglas, Brennan, Stewart, and Marshall dissented.

The constitutional guarantee of a jury trial applied to state courts does not require that the jury's verdict be unanimous. Lack of unanimity on the question of guilt does not constitute evidence of a reasonable doubt of guilt.

Furman v. Georgia, Jackson v. Georgia, Branch v. Texas, 408 U.S. 238, decided by a 5–4 vote, June 29, 1972. The Court's opinion was unsigned; each justice filed a separate opinion. Burger, Blackmun, Powell, and Rehnquist dissented.

The Court nullified all death penalty statutes in the United States. It held that the procedures the statutes provided for judges and juries to follow in deciding when and whether to impose a sentence of death upon a defendant left so much discretion to the judge and jury that the result was arbitrary, irrational, and deprived defendants of due process of law.

FREEDOM OF THE PRESS

Branzburg v. Hayes, In re Pappas, United States v. Caldwell, 408 U.S. 665, decided by a 5–4 vote, June 29, 1972. White wrote the majority opinion; Douglas, Brennan, Stewart, and Marshall dissented.

The constitutional guarantee of freedom of the press does not privilege news reporters to refuse—without risking contempt charges—to provide information to grand juries concerning a crime or the sources of evidence concerning a crime.

OFFICIAL IMMUNITY

United States v. Brewster, 408 U.S. 501, decided by a 6–3 vote, June 29, 1972. Burger wrote the opinion; Brennan, Douglas, and White dissented.

The constitutional immunity conferred on members of Congress by the "speech or debate clause" does not protect them from prosecution for accepting a bribe to vote a certain way on a legislative matter.

The holding cleared the way for prosecution of former senator Daniel B. Brewster, D-Md., (1963–1969), who had been indicted in 1969 on charges of accepting $24,000 in bribes from the mail order firm of Spiegel Incorporated to influence his vote on changes in postal rates. Taking a bribe is illegal, the majority wrote, and is no part of the legislative process. It is therefore subject to prosecution and punishment in the nation's courts.

RIGHT TO COUNSEL

Argersinger v. Hamlin, 407 U.S. 25, decided by a unanimous vote, June 12, 1972. Douglas wrote the opinion.

The right of counsel applies in trials for all offenses, state and federal, where a jail sentence is a possible penalty.

SELF-INCRIMINATION

Kastigar v. United States, 406 U.S. 441, decided by a 5–2 vote, May 22, 1972. Powell wrote the opinion; Douglas and Marshall dissented; Rehnquist and Brennan did not participate.

The narrowed witness immunity provisions of the 1970 Organized Crime Control Act do not infringe upon the Fifth Amendment privilege against self-incrimination. In any subsequent prosecution of an immunized witness, the government must demonstrate that the evidence is derived from sources independent of testimony given under a grant of immunity.

1973

CIVIL RIGHTS

Keyes v. Denver School District No. 1, 413 U.S. 921, decided by a 7–1 vote, June 21, 1973. Brennan wrote the majority opinion; Rehnquist dissented; White did not participate.

This decision was the Court's first definition of the responsibility of school officials to act to desegregate public schools in a district where racial segregation had never been required by law (de jure).

The Court held that school officials were constitutionally obligated to desegregate a school system if the segregation there had resulted from intentional school board policies. In the case of racially segregated schools within a system, the burden of proof was on the school board to prove such segregation was not a result of intentional board actions.

EQUAL PROTECTION

San Antonio Independent School District v. Rodriguez, 411 U.S. 1, decided by a 5–4 vote, March 21, 1973. Powell wrote the majority opinion; Marshall, Douglas, Brennan, and White dissented.

The right to an education is not a fundamental right guaranteed by the Constitution. Wealth is not a suspect way of classifying persons. Therefore, the equal protection guarantee does not require that courts give the strictest scrutiny to state decisions to finance public schools from local property taxes, a decision resulting in wide disparities among districts in the amount spent per pupil.

States do not deny anyone the opportunity for an education by adopting this means of financing public education. Financing public schools from local property taxes rationally furthers a legitimate state purpose and so is upheld.

OBSCENITY

Miller v. California, 413 U.S. 15, decided by a 5–4 vote, June 21, 1973. Burger wrote the majority opinion; Brennan, Stewart, Marshall, and Douglas dissented.

States have the power, without violating the First Amendment, to regulate material that is obscene in its depiction or description of sexual conduct. Material is obscene if the average person, applying contemporary local community standards, would find that it appeals to the prurient interest, and if it depicts in a patently offensive way, sexual conduct specifically defined by the applicable state law, and if the work, taken as a whole, lacks serious literary, artistic, political, or scientific value.

This definition of obscenity was the first approved by of a majority of the justices since 1957; it was less stringent than the prevailing standard and consequently gave the states more control over obscene materials.

PERSONAL PRIVACY

Roe v. Wade, 410 U.S. 113, **Doe v. Bolton,** 410 U.S. 179, decided by 7–2 votes, January 22, 1973. Blackmun wrote the majority opinions; Rehnquist and White dissented.

The right to privacy, grounded in the Fourteenth Amendment's due process guarantee of personal liberty, encompasses and protects a woman's decision whether or not to bear a child. This right is impermissibly abridged by state laws that make abortion a crime.

During the first trimester of pregnancy, the decision to have an abortion should be left entirely to a woman and her physician. The state can forbid abortions by nonphysicians. During the second trimester, the state may regulate the abortion procedure in ways reasonably related to maternal health. And during the third trimester, the state may, if it wishes, forbid all abortions except those necessary to save the mother's life.

VOTING RIGHTS

Mahan v. Howell, City of Virginia Beach v. Howell, Weinberg v. Prichard, 410 U.S. 315, decided by a 5–3 vote, February 21, 1973. Rehnquist wrote the opinion; Brennan, Douglas, and Marshall dissented; Powell did not participate.

The Court's decision in this case relaxed the requirement that state legislative districts be as nearly equal as possible—holding that states may apply more flexible standards in drawing new state legislative districts than in congressional redistricting.

The decision approved a Virginia plan permitting a 16 percent variation between the largest and smallest population districts.

1974

CIVIL RIGHTS

Milliken v. Bradley, 418 U.S. 717, decided by a 5–4 vote, July 25, 1974. Burger wrote the majority opinion; Douglas, Brennan, Marshall, and White dissented.

A multidistrict remedy for school segregation, such as busing school children across district lines, can be ordered by a federal court only when there has been a finding that all the districts involved have been responsible for the segregation to be remedied.

The Court reversed a lower court's order directing busing across city, county, and district lines to desegregate the schools of Detroit, Michigan. The majority ordered the lower court to devise a remedy that would affect only the city schools.

EQUAL PROTECTION

Geduldig v. Aiello, 417 U.S. 484, decided by a 6–3 vote, June 17, 1974. Stewart wrote the majority opinion; Douglas, Brennan, and Marshall dissented.

California did not violate the constitutional guarantee of equal protection by excluding from its disability insurance program women unable to work because of pregnancy-related disabilities.

Women were not denied equal protection by this exclusion because, the majority said, "there is no risk from which men are protected and women are not." The decision to exclude the risk of pregnancy from the risks insured by the state plan was a rational one in light of the state interest in maintaining a low-cost, self-supporting insurance fund.

FEDERAL COURTS

Edelman v. Jordan, 415 U.S. 651, decided by a 5–4 vote, March 25, 1974. Rehnquist wrote the majority opinion; Brennan, Douglas, Marshall, and Blackmun dissented.

The Eleventh Amendment immunity of states from federal lawsuits brought by citizens without the state's consent protects a state from a federal court order directing it to spend money to remedy past abuses.

Federal judges may order a state to halt enforcement of a law that violates due process and equal protection, but that order may only reach future action—it may not require the state to remedy past damages inflicted under the invalid law.

In 1976 the Court substantially modified the reach of this decision, holding unanimously in *Fitzpatrick v. Bitzer, Bitzer v. Matthews,* 427 U.S. 445, that federal courts could order states to pay retroactive benefits to persons against whom the state had discriminated in violation of the Fourteenth Amendment.

POWERS OF THE PRESIDENT

United States v. Nixon, 418 U.S. 683, decided by an 8–0 vote, July 24, 1974. Burger wrote the opinion; Rehnquist did not participate.

Neither the separation of powers nor the need to preserve the confidentiality of presidential communications alone can justify an absolute executive privilege of immunity from judicial demands for evidence to be used in a criminal trial.

The Court held that President Richard Nixon must comply with a subpoena for tapes of certain White House conversations, sought for use as evidence against White House aides charged with obstruction of justice in regard to the investigation of the break-in at the Democratic National Headquarters in the Watergate Office Building in June 1972.

1975

CIVIL RIGHTS

Albemarle Paper Co. v. Moody, 422 U.S. 405, decided by a 7–1 vote, June 25, 1975. Stewart wrote the majority opinion; Burger dissented; Powell did not participate.

Back pay awards to victims of employment discrimination are the rule, not the exception, in cases won under Title VII of the 1964 Civil Rights Act. Back pay awards carry out the intent of Congress to make persons whole for injuries suffered on account of unlawful discrimination and should not be restricted to cases in which the employer is found to have acted in bad faith.

EQUAL PROTECTION

Weinberger v. Wiesenfeld, 420 U.S. 636, decided by an 8–0 vote, March 19, 1975. Brennan wrote the opinion; Douglas did not participate.

Social Security law that provides survivors' benefits for widows with small children, but not for widowers with small children, violates the guarantee of due process by providing working women with fewer benefits for their Social Security contributions than it provides to working men. "It is no less important for a child to be cared for by its sole surviving parent when that parent is male rather than female," wrote Brennan, pointing out that the intended purpose of this benefit was to allow a mother not to work, but to stay home and care for her children.

FREE SPEECH

Bigelow v. Virginia, 421 U.S. 809, decided by a 7–2 vote, June 16, 1975. Blackmun wrote the opinion; Rehnquist and White dissented.

Commercial advertising enjoys some First Amendment protection; *Valentine v. Chrestensen,* 316 U.S. 52 (1942), held that the manner in which such ads were distributed could be regulated—not advertising itself.

The Court reversed the conviction of a newspaper editor in Virginia for violating a state law against "encouraging" abortions by running an advertisement including information on legal abortions available in New York. This law was an improper effort by the state to control what its citizens could hear or read, the Court held.

JURY TRIALS

Taylor v. Louisiana, 419 U.S. 522, decided by an 8–1 vote, January 21, 1975. White wrote the opinion; Rehnquist dissented.

State laws generally exempting women from jury duty are unconstitutional because they violate the Sixth Amendment requirement that juries be drawn from a fair cross-section of the community.

The Court overruled its 1961 decision in *Hoyt v. Florida,* which upheld this general exclusion of women from jury duty as rational in light of the state's interest in preventing interference with women's traditional functions as wives, homemakers, and mothers.

1976

CIVIL RIGHTS

Washington v. Davis, 426 U.S. 229, decided by a 7–2 vote, June 7, 1976. White wrote the majority opinion; Brennan and Marshall dissented.

Job qualification tests are not unconstitutional simply because more black than white job applicants fail them. Some racially discriminatory purpose must be found in order for such a test to be in violation of the constitutional guarantees of due process and equal protection. "Disproportionate impact is not irrelevant, but it is not the sole touchstone of an invidious racial discrimination forbidden by the Constitution."

Runyon v. McCrary, Fairfax-Brewster School Inc. v. Gonzales, Southern Independent School Association v. McCrary, 427 U.S. 160, decided by a 7–2 vote, June 25, 1976. Stewart wrote the opinion; White and Rehnquist dissented.

Racially segregated private schools that refuse to admit black students violate the Civil Rights Act of 1866, which gave "all persons within the jurisdiction of the United States the same right . . . to make and enforce contracts . . . as is enjoyed by white citizens." That law bans this type of private discrimination.

Pasadena Board of Education v. Spangler, 427 U.S. 424, decided by a 6–2 vote, June 28, 1976. Rehnquist wrote the opinion; Brennan and Marshall dissented; Stevens did not participate.

Once a school board has implemented a racially neutral plan for assignment of students to city schools, it is not constitutionally required to continue juggling student assignments in order to maintain a certain racial balance in the student body of each school.

COMMERCE

National League of Cities v. Usery, California v. Usery, 426 U.S. 833, decided by a 5–4 vote, June 24, 1976. Rehnquist wrote the opinion; Brennan, White, Marshall, and Stevens dissented.

Congress exceeded its power to regulate interstate commerce when it extended federal minimum wage and overtime standards to cover state and local government employees by its 1974 amendments to the Fair Labor Standards Act. Determination of state government employees' wages and hours is one of the "attributes of sovereignty attaching to every state government, which may not be impaired by Congress."

CRUEL AND UNUSUAL PUNISHMENT

Gregg v. Georgia, 428 U.S. 153, *Proffitt v. Florida,* 428 U.S. 242, *Jurek v. Texas,* 428 U.S. 262, decided by 7–2 votes, July 2, 1976. Stewart wrote the opinion in *Gregg;* Stevens wrote the opinion in *Jurek;* Powell wrote the opinion in *Proffitt;* Brennan and Marshall dissented.

As a punishment for persons convicted of first degree murder, death is not in and of itself cruel and unusual punishment in violation of the Eighth Amendment.

The Eighth Amendment requires the sentencing judge or jury to consider the individual character of the offender and the circumstances of the particular crime before deciding whether to impose a death sentence. A two-part proceeding—one for the determination of guilt or innocence and a second for determining the sentence—provides an opportunity for such individualized consideration prior to sentencing.

Woodson v. North Carolina, 428 U.S. 280, *Roberts v. Louisiana,* 428 U.S. 325, decided by votes of 5–4, July 2, 1976. Stewart wrote the opinion in *Woodson;* Stevens wrote the opinion in *Roberts;* Burger, White, Rehnquist, and Blackmun dissented.

States may not make death the mandatory penalty for first degree murder. Such mandatory sentences fail to meet the constitutional requirement for consideration of the individual offender and offense prior to the decision to impose the death penalty.

EQUAL PROTECTION

Craig v. Boren, 429 U.S. 190, decided by a 7–2 vote, December 20, 1976. Brennan wrote the opinion; Burger and Rehnquist dissented.

A classification based on gender is invalid unless it is substantially related to the achievement of an important government objective.

Using this rule, the Court declared unconstitutional a state law that permitted the sale of 3.2 beer to women at age eighteen but not to men until age twenty-one. The law was not substantially related to the state's expressed goal of promoting traffic safety.

FEDERAL COURTS

Stone v. Powell, Wolff v. Rice, 428 U.S. 465, decided by a 6–3 vote, July 6, 1976. Powell wrote the opinion; Brennan, Marshall, and White dissented.

A state prisoner's claim that illegally obtained evidence was used to convict him cannot serve as a basis for a federal court order of his release through a writ of habeas corpus—unless the state failed to provide the prisoner an opportunity for full and fair hearing of his challenge to the evidence.

FREEDOM OF ASSOCIATION

Elrod v. Burns, 427 U.S. 347, decided by a 5–3 vote, June 28, 1976. Brennan wrote the opinion; Burger, Powell, and Rehnquist dissented; Stevens did not participate.

Patronage firing—the discharge by an official of the public employees who do not belong to his party—violates the First Amendment freedom of political association.

FREEDOM OF SPEECH

Buckley v. Valeo, 424 U.S. 1, decided by votes of 8–0, 7–1, and 6–2, January 31, 1976. The opinion was unsigned; Burger, Blackmun, Rehnquist, White, and Marshall all dissented in part; Stevens did not participate.

The First Amendment guarantee of freedom of expression is impermissibly infringed by the limits placed by the 1974 Federal Election Campaign Act Amendments on the amount a candidate for federal office may spend. The vote was 7–1; White dissented.

The majority did find limits permissible for candidates who accepted public financing of their campaigns for the presidency.

The Court upheld, 6–2, the law's limits on the amount individuals and political committees could contribute to candidates. The limit was only a marginal restriction on a contributor's First Amendment freedom, justified by the interest in preventing corruption, the majority said. Burger and Blackmun dissented.

The Court upheld, 6–2, the system of public financing set up for presidential campaigns and elections. Burger and Rehnquist dissented. Burger also dissented from the majority's decision to uphold the law's requirements for public disclosure of campaign contributions of more than $100 and campaign expenditures of more than $10.

The Court unanimously agreed that the Federal Election Commission, as set up by the 1974 law, was unconstitutional as a violation of the separation of powers.

FREEDOM OF THE PRESS

Nebraska Press Association v. Stuart, 427 U.S. 539, decided by a unanimous vote, June 30, 1976. Burger wrote the opinion.

A gag order severely limiting what the press can report about pretrial proceedings in a mass murder case violates the First Amendment guarantee of a free press.

If ever permissible, this sort of prior restraint of publication can be justified only by the most extreme circumstances. In most situations, judges concerned about preserving a defendant's right to a fair trial by an unbiased jury have many less drastic means of ensuring that potential jurors are not prejudiced by publicity.

TAXES

Michelin Tire Corp. v. Wages, 423 U.S. 276, decided by an 8–0 vote, January 14, 1976. Brennan wrote the opinion; Stevens did not participate.

The Court overruled *Low v. Austin* (1872), which forbade states to tax imported goods so long as those goods retained their character as imports.

The export-import clause of the Constitution, the Court held, did not bar a county from imposing a property tax on imported goods stored prior to sale, so long as the tax did not discriminate against imported goods.

1977

CIVIL RIGHTS

Village of Arlington Heights v. Metropolitan Housing Development Corporation, 429 U.S. 252, decided by a 5–3 vote, January 11, 1977. Powell wrote the opinion; White dissented; Brennan and Marshall dissented in part; Stevens did not participate.

Without any showing of discriminatory motive, the refusal of a village to rezone property to permit building of a housing development for low- and moderate-income persons of both races does not violate the Fourteenth Amendment guarantee of equal protection.

CRUEL AND UNUSUAL PUNISHMENT

Coker v. Georgia, 433 U.S. 584, decided by a 7–2 vote, June 29, 1977. White wrote the opinion; Burger and Rehnquist dissented.

A death sentence for the crime of rape is an excessive and disproportionate penalty forbidden by the Eighth Amendment ban on cruel and unusual punishments.

TAXES

Complete Auto Transit Inc. v. Brady, 430 U.S. 274, decided by a unanimous vote, March 8, 1977. Blackmun wrote the opinion.

The commerce clause—granting Congress the power to regulate interstate and foreign commerce—does not forbid a state to tax an interstate enterprise doing business within the state for the "privilege" of doing business there.

Such taxes are permissible so long as the taxed activity has a sufficient nexus with the taxing state, the tax does not discriminate against interstate commerce, is fairly apportioned, and is related to services provided by the state.

VOTING RIGHTS

United Jewish Organizations of Williamsburgh v. Carey, 430 U.S. 144, decided by a 7–1 vote, March 1, 1977. White wrote the opinion; Burger dissented; Marshall did not participate.

The Court upheld the use of racial criteria by the state of New York in its 1974 state legislative redistricting plan drawn to comply with the 1965 Voting Rights Act. Even if the result of the redistricting dilutes the vote of a white ethnic minority—in this case the Hasidic Jewish community of Brooklyn—the Constitution "does not prevent a state subject to the Voting Rights Act from deliberately creating or preserving black majorities in particular districts in order to ensure that its reapportionment plan" complies with the act.

1978

CIVIL RIGHTS

Regents of the University of California v. Bakke, 438 U.S. 265, decided by a 5–4 vote, June 28, 1978. Powell announced the judgment of the Court; Stevens and Brennan filed separate opinions; Stevens was joined by Burger, Rehnquist, and Stewart; Brennan was joined by Marshall, White, and Blackmun.

A special state medical school admissions program under which a certain number of slots were set aside for minority group members, and white applicants were denied the opportunity to compete for them, violates Title VI of the 1964 Civil Rights Act. Title VI forbids exclusion of anyone, because of race, from participation in a federally funded program.

Admissions programs that consider race as one of several factors involved in the decision to admit an applicant are not unconstitutional in and of themselves. "Government may take race into account when it acts not to demean or insult any racial group, but to remedy disadvantages cast on minorities by past racial prejudice, at least when appropriate findings have been made by judicial, legislative, or administrative bodies with competence to act in this area."

FEDERAL COURTS

Monell v. Department of Social Services, 436 U.S. 658, decided by a 7–2 vote, June 6, 1978. Brennan wrote the opinion; Burger and Rehnquist dissented.

City officials, municipalities, and municipal agencies are not immune from civil rights damage suits filed under the Civil Rights Act of 1871.

Cities may be held liable for damages if action pursuant to official policy violates someone's constitutional rights. Cities are not liable if their employees or agents infringe someone's rights in the course of their duties.

FREEDOM OF SPEECH

First National Bank of Boston v. Bellotti, 435 U.S. 765, decided by a 5–4 vote, April 26, 1978. Powell wrote the opinion; White, Brennan, Marshall, and Rehnquist dissented.

State law banning corporate expenditures relative to a referendum issue that does not materially affect corporate business impermissibly abridges political speech protected by the First Amendment. "If the speakers here were not corporations, no one would suggest that the state could silence their proposed speech. It is the type of speech indispensable to decisionmaking in a democracy, and this is no less true because the speech comes from a corporation rather than an individual," the majority said.

JURY TRIALS

Ballew v. Georgia, 435 U.S. 223, decided by a unanimous vote, March 21, 1978. Blackmun wrote the opinion.

In order to fulfill the constitutional guarantee of trial by jury, state juries must be composed of at least six members.

OFFICIAL IMMUNITY

Butz v. Economou, 438 U.S. 478, decided by a 5–4 vote, June 29, 1978. White wrote the opinion; Burger, Rehnquist, Stewart, and Stevens dissented.

Federal officials are not absolutely immune from damage suits based upon actions taken in the performance of their official duties. Even when carrying out directives from Congress, federal officials are subject to the restraints of the Constitution.

SEARCH AND SEIZURE

Zurcher v. The Stanford Daily, 436 U.S. 547, decided by a 5–3 vote, May 31, 1978. White wrote the opinion; Stewart, Marshall, and Stevens dissented; Brennan did not participate.

The Fourth Amendment does not preclude or limit the use of search warrants for searches of places owned or occupied by innocent third parties not suspected of any crime.

The First Amendment guarantee of freedom of the press does not require that information concerning a crime in the possession of a newspaper be sought by a subpoena rather than a search warrant.

1979

CIVIL RIGHTS

United Steelworkers of America v. Weber, Kaiser Aluminum v. Weber, United States v. Weber, 443 U.S. 193, decided by a 5–2 vote, June 27, 1979. Brennan wrote the opinion; Burger and Rehnquist dissented; Powell and Stevens did not participate.

Title VII of the 1964 Civil Rights Act forbids racial discrimination in employment but does not forbid employers to adopt voluntarily race-conscious affirmative action programs to encourage minority participation in areas of work in which they have traditionally been underrepresented.

Columbus Board of Education v. Penick, Dayton Board of Education v. Brinkman, 443 U.S. 449, decided by votes of 7 to 2 and 5 to 4, July 2, 1979. White wrote the opinion; Rehnquist and Powell dissented in both; Burger and Stewart dissented in *Dayton.*

School boards operating segregated school systems at the time of the 1954 decision in *Brown v. Board of Education* are under an affirmative duty to end that segregation—even if it was not imposed as a result of state law. The Court upheld systemwide busing orders for Dayton and Columbus, Ohio, where segregated schools had not been required by law since 1888.

DUE PROCESS

Davis v. Passman, 442 U.S. 228, decided by a 5–4 vote, June 5, 1979. Brennan wrote the opinion; Burger, Powell, Rehnquist, and Stewart dissented.

An individual denied due process and equal protection by federal action can bring a federal suit for damages based on the Fifth Amendment guarantee.

For the first time, the Court provided a constitutional basis for job discrimination charges by congressional employees, who are not protected by the guarantees of the federal civil rights laws.

EQUAL PROTECTION

Orr v. Orr, 440 U.S. 268, decided by a 6–3 vote, March 5, 1979. Brennan wrote the opinion; Powell, Rehnquist, and Burger dissented.

States violate the Fourteenth Amendment guarantee of equal protection when they allow women, but not men, to receive alimony as part of a divorce settlement.

JURY TRIAL

Burch v. Louisiana, 441 U.S. 130, decided by a unanimous vote, April 17, 1979. Rehnquist wrote the opinion.

A state deprives a defendant of his constitutional right to a jury trial when it allows him to be convicted by the nonunanimous vote of a six-person jury.

OFFICIAL IMMUNITY

United States v. Helstoski, 442 U.S. 477, decided by a 5–3 vote, June 18, 1979. Burger wrote the opinion, Brennan dissented; Stevens and Stewart dissented in part; Powell did not participate.

The Constitution's provision immunizing members of Congress from being questioned outside Congress "for any Speech or Debate in either House" forbids the government, in prosecuting a member for accepting a bribe in return for a legislative act, to introduce evidence of the legislative act. The constitutional provision was intended to preclude prosecution of members for legislative acts.

Hutchinson v. Proxmire, 443 U.S. 111, decided by a 7–2 vote, June 26, 1979. Burger wrote the opinion; Brennan dissented; Stewart dissented in part.

The Constitution's speech or debate clause does not protect a senator from being sued for libel as a result of statements made in press releases and newsletters.

An individual who does not seek to thrust himself into the public eye or otherwise draw public attention, but who is drawn into public notice by events outside his control, is not a public figure subject to the "actual malice" standard set out by the Supreme Court for libel suits brought by public officials.

RIGHT OF ACCESS

Gannett Co. Inc. v. DePasquale, 443 U.S. 368, decided by a 5–4 vote, July 2, 1979. Stewart wrote the opinion; Blackmun, Brennan, White, and Marshall dissented in part.

The Constitution's guarantee of the right to a public trial is intended for the benefit of the defendant, not the public. Members of the public cannot use that guarantee as the basis for their constitutional right to attend a criminal trial.

A judge may constitutionally exclude press and public from a pretrial hearing to avoid publicity prejudicial to the defendant and to protect his right to a fair trial.

1980

CIVIL RIGHTS

Fullilove v. Klutznick, 448 U.S. 448, decided by a 6–3 vote, July 2, 1980. Burger announced the Court's decision; Stewart, Rehnquist, and Stevens dissented.

Congress may make limited use of racial quotas to remedy past discrimination. The Court upheld as constitutional a provision in the 1977 Public Works Employment Act that set aside for minority businesses 10 percent of federal funds provided for local public works projects.

POWERS OF CONGRESS

Harris v. McRae, 448 U.S. 297, decided by a 5–4 vote, June 30, 1980. Stewart wrote the opinion; Brennan, Marshall, Blackmun, and Stevens dissented.

Congress did not act unconstitutionally when it restricted federal funding of medically necessary abortions. The Court upheld the so-called Hyde Amendment, which denies federal reimbursement for abortions under the Medicaid program except when the abortion is necessary to save the pregnant woman's life or to terminate a pregnancy caused by promptly reported rape or incest.

In a companion decision the same day, the Court upheld similar state restrictions on public funding of abortions, *Williams v. Zbaraz, Miller v. Zbaraz, United States v. Zbaraz,* 448 U.S. 358.

RIGHT OF ACCESS

Richmond Newspapers Inc. v. Virginia, 448 U.S. 555, decided by a 7–1 vote, July 2, 1980. Burger announced the Court's decision; Rehnquist dissented; Powell did not participate.

The First Amendment guarantees citizens and members of the press the right to attend criminal trials. In some situations, a judge may limit that access to protect the defendant's right to a fair trial, but such closure should be explained and limited.

RIGHT TO COUNSEL

Rhode Island v. Innis, 446 U.S. 291, decided by 9–0 and 6–3 votes, May 12, 1980. Stewart wrote the opinion; Marshall, Brennan, and Stevens dissented.

The Court defined "interrogation"—a critical word in *Miranda v. Arizona* (1966)—as meaning the direct questioning of a suspect *and* the use of other "techniques of persuasion." Interrogation, said the Court, includes "words or actions on the part of police officers that they *should have known* were reasonably likely to elicit an incriminating response." The Court was unanimous in that holding although it declined, 6–3, to find that interrogation had occurred in this particular case.

SEARCH AND SEIZURE

Payton v. New York, Riddick v. New York, 445 U.S. 573, decided by a 6–3 vote, April 15, 1980. Stevens wrote the opinion; Burger, White, and Rehnquist dissented.

Police may not enter a home to arrest its occupant without an arrest warrant or the consent of the occupant—unless an immediate arrest is imperative under emergency circumstances.

VOTING RIGHTS

Mobile v. Bolden, 446 U.S. 55, decided by a 6–3 vote, April 22, 1980. Stewart wrote the opinion; Brennan, White, and Marshall dissented.

The Mobile, Alabama, at-large system for electing city commissioners is constitutional unless it is shown to be intentionally discriminatory. Its effect—the fact that no black officials had been elected—is not enough to prove it unconstitutional.

1981

DUE PROCESS

Chandler v. Florida, 449 U.S. 560, decided by an 8–0 vote, January 26, 1981. Burger wrote the opinion; Stevens did not participate.

Nothing in the Constitution—neither the guarantee of due process nor the promise of a fair trial—forbids states from permitting television cameras in a courtroom to broadcast criminal trials.

EQUAL PROTECTION

Rostker v. Goldberg, 453 U.S. 57, decided by a 6–3 vote, June 25, 1981. Rehnquist wrote the opinion; White, Marshall, and Brennan dissented.

Congress did not violate the Constitution by excluding women from the military draft. Because they are barred by law and policy from combat, they are not "similarly situated" with men for purposes of draft registration, and therefore Congress may treat the sexes differently in this context.

PERSONAL PRIVACY

H. L. v. Matheson, 450 U.S. 398, decided by a 6–3 vote, March 23, 1981. Burger wrote the opinion; Marshall, Brennan, and Blackmun dissented.

A pregnant minor's right of privacy is not violated by a Utah law requiring a doctor to notify her parents before providing her with an abortion. The law does not give parents a veto, but does require that they be notified.

POWERS OF THE PRESIDENT

Dames & Moore v. Regan, 453 U.S. 654, decided by a 9–0 vote, July 2, 1981. Rehnquist wrote the opinion.

President Jimmy Carter acted within the scope of his authority over foreign affairs when he reached a financial agreement with Iran that resulted in the release of Americans held hostage in that country, including the agreement to nullify all federal court orders attaching Iranian assets in the United States and to transfer them back to Iran.

It was also within the president's power to agree that all pending claims against Iran be transferred to an international tribunal for resolution. Congress in the International Emergency Economic Powers Act of 1977, and a number of other earlier laws, gave the president powers broad enough to authorize these actions.

1982

CRUEL AND UNUSUAL PUNISHMENT

Enmund v. Florida, 458 U.S. 782, decided by a 5–4 vote, July 2, 1982. White wrote the Court's opinion; Burger, O'Connor, Powell, and Rehnquist dissented.

It is cruel and unusual punishment, disproportionate to the actions of the defendant, for the driver of a getaway car to be sentenced to death after he is convicted of first-degree murder for his role in killings he neither committed nor witnessed.

EQUAL PROTECTION

Plyler v. Doe, Texas v. Certain Named and Unnamed Undocumented Alien Children, 457 U.S. 202, decided by a 5–4 vote, June 15, 1982. Brennan wrote the opinion; Burger, Rehnquist, White, and O'Connor dissented.

Aliens in the United States are guaranteed the equal protection of the law by the Fourteenth Amendment, even if they have entered the country illegally. Texas may not deny illegal alien children a free public education; there is neither national policy nor sufficient state interest to justify this action.

Youngberg v. Romeo, 457 U.S. 307, decided by a 9–0 vote, June 18, 1982. Powell wrote the opinion.

Mentally retarded persons in state institutions have a constitutional right to safe conditions, freedom of movement, and sufficient training to enable them to move freely and safely within that institution.

FREEDOM OF EXPRESSION

Board of Education, Island Trees Union Free School District No. 26 v. Pico, 457 U.S. 853, decided by a 5–4 vote, June 25, 1982. Brennan announced the Court's decision; Burger, Powell, Rehnquist, and O'Connor dissented.

The First Amendment limits a local school board's power to remove certain books from public school libraries. It is impermissible for a board to remove a book because it contains unpopular ideas; it is permissible to remove vulgar and irrelevant books.

National Association for the Advancement of Colored People v. Claiborne Hardware Co., 458 U.S. 886, decided by an 8–0 vote, July 2, 1982. Stevens wrote the opinion; Marshall did not participate.

The First Amendment protection for speech and expressive conduct includes a nonviolent boycott by civil rights demonstrators of the stores of white merchants. Violence, however, is not protected, and a state court may assess damages against those responsible for violence in such a setting. But any liability for damages must be based on the individual's participation in violent activity, not simply on his membership in the boycotting group.

OFFICIAL IMMUNITY

Nixon v. Fitzgerald, 457 U.S. 731, decided by a 5–4 vote, June 24, 1982. Powell wrote the opinion; White, Brennan, Marshall, and Blackmun dissented.

Presidents are absolutely immune from civil damages suits for all official actions taken while in office. The electoral process and the impeachment mechanism provide sufficient remedy for presidential wrongdoing.

Harlow v. Fitzgerald, 457 U.S. 800, decided by an 8–1 vote, June 24, 1982. Powell wrote the Court's opinion; Burger dissented.

Presidential aides do not have absolute immunity from civil rights damage suits by individuals who claim to have been denied their rights by those aides acting in their official capacity. Like other executive officials, they enjoy qualified immunity from such damage suits. Immunity attaches when the challenged conduct does not violate clearly established statutory or constitutional rights of which a reasonable person would have known.

1983

CIVIL RIGHTS

Bob Jones University v. United States, Goldsboro Christian Schools v. United States, 461 U.S. 574, decided by an 8–1 vote, May 24, 1983. Burger wrote the opinion; Rehnquist dissented.

The Internal Revenue Service acted within its authority when it denied tax-exempt status to private schools that discriminate against blacks. In light of the clear national policy against racial discrimination in education, the IRS was correct in its 1970 declaration that it would no longer grant tax-exempt status to discriminatory private schools.

The national interest in eradicating racial discrimination in education "substantially outweighs whatever burden denial of tax benefits places" on the exercise of First Amendment freedom of religion.

CRUEL AND UNUSUAL PUNISHMENT

Solem v. Helm, 463 U.S. 277, decided by a 5–4 vote, June 28, 1983. Powell wrote the opinion; Burger, White, Rehnquist, and O'Connor dissented.

South Dakota violated the constitutional ban on cruel and unusual punishment when it imposed a life sentence without possibility of parole on a man convicted on seven separate occasions of nonviolent felonies. This was the first time the Court had used this constitutional provision to judge the relative severity of a prison sentence.

FREEDOM OF RELIGION

Mueller v. Allen, 463 U.S. 388, decided by a 5–4 vote, June 29, 1983. Rehnquist wrote the opinion; Marshall, Brennan, Blackmun, and Stevens dissented.

The First Amendment permits Minnesota to grant parents a state income tax deduction for the cost of tuition, textbooks, and transportation for their elementary and secondary school children. The deduction is available to public school patrons as well as private school patrons, and therefore any benefit to church-run schools is the result of individual choices, not state design.

PERSONAL PRIVACY

Akron v. Akron Center for Reproductive Health Inc., Akron Center for Reproductive Health Inc. v. Akron, 462 U.S. 416, decided by a 6–3 vote, June 15, 1983. Powell wrote the opinion; White, Rehnquist, and O'Connor dissented.

An Akron, Ohio, ordinance unconstitutionally required that all abortions after the first trimester be performed in full-service hospitals; that physicians obtain parental consent before performing an abortion on a patient younger than sixteen; that physicians recite to women seeking abortions certain information about fetal development, alternatives to abortion, and possible abortion complications; that the attending physician inform a patient of the risks associated with her own pregnancy or abortion; that there be a twenty-four-hour waiting period between the time consent is signed for an abortion and the time it is performed; and that fetal remains be given a "humane" disposal.

Planned Parenthood Association of Kansas City, Missouri v. Ashcroft, Ashcroft v. Planned Parenthood Association of Kansas City, Missouri, 462 U.S. 476, decided by 5–4 and 6–3 votes, June 15, 1983. Powell wrote the opinion; Blackmun, Brennan, Marshall, and Stevens dissented in part; O'Connor, White, and Rehnquist dissented in part.

Missouri law requiring "unemancipated" minors to have parental or judicial consent for abortion is permissible, because it provides an alternative to parental consent. It is also appropriate for the law to require pathological examination of tissue from an abortion and that a second physician be present at late-term abortions. But the law is unconstitutional in requiring that all abortions after the first trimester be performed in a hospital.

POWERS OF CONGRESS

Immigration and Naturalization Service v. Chadha, United States House of Representatives v. Chadha, United States Senate v.

Chadha, 462 U.S. 919, decided by a 7–2 vote, June 23, 1983. Burger wrote the opinion; White and Rehnquist dissented.

The one-house legislative veto, under which Congress claimed the power to review and veto executive branch decisions implementing laws, is unconstitutional. It violates the separation of powers between executive and legislative branches, and it runs counter to the "single, finely wrought and exhaustively considered procedure" the Constitution prescribes for the enactment of legislation: approval by both chambers and signature of the president.

With this decision, invalidating a device included in one form or another in more than two hundred laws enacted since 1932, the Court struck down at one time more provisions in more federal laws than it had invalidated in its entire history.

VOTING RIGHTS

Karcher v. Daggett, 462 U.S. 725, decided by a 5–4 vote, June 22, 1983. Brennan wrote the opinion; Burger, Powell, Rehnquist, and White dissented.

A state must adhere as closely as possible to the "one person, one vote" standard of reapportionment. When precise equality is not achieved, the state must prove the variations are necessary to achieve some other important state goal. New Jersey did not prove this for its congressional redistricting plan that had a variation of less than 1 percent between the least and most populous districts. Therefore, its plan was invalid.

Brown v. Thomson, 462 U.S. 835, decided by a 5–4 vote, June 22, 1983. Powell wrote the opinion; Brennan, White, Marshall, and Blackmun dissented.

Wyoming law, requiring that each county have at least one representative in the state House of Representatives, is constitutional even though there is an 89 percent population variance between the largest and smallest counties. That result is permissible because the state has a legitimate interest in assuring each county its own representative.

1984

CIVIL RIGHTS

Firefighters Local Union No. 1794 v. Stotts, 467 U.S. 561, decided by a 6–3 vote, June 11, 1984. White wrote the Court's opinion; Brennan, Marshall, and Stevens dissented.

Federal judges may not override valid seniority systems to preserve the jobs of black workers hired under an affirmative action plan. Such good-faith seniority systems are expressly immunized from challenge as discriminatory under the Civil Rights Act of 1964.

DUE PROCESS

Schall v. Martin, Abrams v. Martin, 467 U.S. 253, decided by a 6–3 vote, June 4, 1984. Rehnquist wrote the opinion; Brennan, Marshall, and Stevens dissented.

For the first time, the Court upheld as constitutional a law providing for the preventive pretrial detention of suspects. The Court held that New York's law permitting pretrial detention of juveniles, when there is a serious risk that the juvenile may commit a serious crime before trial, falls within the bounds set by the constitutional guarantee of due process.

EQUAL PROTECTION

Grove City College v. Bell, 465 U.S. 555, decided by a 6–3 vote, February 28, 1984. White wrote the opinion; Brennan, Marshall, and Stevens dissented.

Title IX of the 1972 Education Amendments—barring sex discrimination in any "program or activity" receiving federal aid, does not apply to every program at an institution—but only to the particular program receiving aid.

FREEDOM OF ASSOCIATION

Roberts v. U.S. Jaycees, 468 U.S. 609, decided by a 7–0 vote, July 3, 1984. Brennan wrote the opinion; Burger and Blackmun did not participate.

Minnesota may invoke its public accommodations law to require the Jaycees, a large, nonexclusive membership organization, to admit women as full members. The state's interest in equal treatment for women outweighs any First Amendment freedom the Jaycees might assert.

FREEDOM OF RELIGION

Lynch v. Donnelly, 465 U.S. 668, decided by a 5–4 vote, March 5, 1984. Burger wrote the opinion; Brennan, Marshall, Blackmun, and Stevens dissented.

The inclusion of a nativity scene in a city-sponsored holiday display does not violate the First Amendment ban on establishment of religion. The Constitution, held the Court, "affirmatively mandates accommodation, not merely tolerance, of all religions, and forbids hostility toward any."

RIGHT TO COUNSEL

Nix v. Williams, 467 U.S. 431, decided by a 7–2 vote, June 11, 1984. Burger wrote the opinion; Brennan and Marshall dissented.

The Court approved an "inevitable discovery" exception to the exclusionary rule, permitting the use of evidence taken illegally if the prosecution shows that it would ultimately have been discovered by lawful means.

SEARCH AND SEIZURE

United States v. Leon, 468 U.S. 897, decided by a 6–3 vote, July 5, 1984. White wrote the opinion; Brennan, Marshall, and Stevens dissented.

Illegally obtained evidence may be used by the prosecution at trial if the police who seized it had a search warrant and thought they were acting legally. This ruling was the Court's first adoption of a "good faith" exception to the exclusionary rule it had adopted seventy years earlier in *Weeks v. United States,* barring all use of such evidence at trial.

This decision was limited to a situation in which police had a warrant and executed a search in accord with it, only to have the warrant later found defective. In such a case, there was no deterrent effect to excluding the evidence, and exclusion exacted too high a price from society, the Court held.

SELF-INCRIMINATION

New York v. Quarles, 467 U.S. 649, decided by 5–4 and 6–3 votes, June 12, 1984. Rehnquist wrote the opinion; O'Connor, Stevens, Marshall, and Brennan dissented.

The Court recognized a "public safety" exception to the rule set out in *Miranda v. Arizona* (1966), which denies prosecutors use of evidence obtained from a suspect who was not advised first of his constitutional rights. This decision was the first exception to that rule.

The Court reasoned that in some situations, concern for the public safety dictates that police immediately ask a suspect a particular question, such as "Where's the gun?" In these cases, the suspect's reply and any evidence it leads to may be used against him.

1985

EQUAL PROTECTION

Cleburne v. Cleburne Living Center Inc., 473 U.S. 432, decided by 9–0 and 6–3 votes, July 1, 1985. White wrote the opinion; Brennan, Marshall, and Stevens dissented in part.

Laws that treat the mentally retarded differently from other citizens are constitutional so long as they are a rational means to a legitimate end. Using that test, the Court struck down a city's zoning ordinance-based denial of a permit for a group home for mentally retarded adults in a residential neighborhood. That requirement was based on an irrational prejudice against the retarded, an impermissible basis for a city's action.

FREEDOM OF EXPRESSION

Federal Election Commission v. National Conservative Political Action Committee, Democratic Party of the United States v. National Conservative Political Action Committee, 470 U.S. 480, decided by a 7–2 vote, March 18, 1985. Rehnquist wrote the opinion; Marshall and White dissented.

Congress cannot limit independent spending by political action committees in presidential campaigns. The First Amendment guarantee of free speech is violated by the $1,000 limit imposed by the Federal Election Campaign Act Amendments on independent expenditures by PACs to promote or prevent the election of publicly funded presidential candidates.

FREEDOM OF RELIGION

Wallace v. Jaffree, 472 U.S. 38, decided by a 6–3 vote, June 4, 1985. Stevens wrote the opinion; Burger, Rehnquist, and White dissented.

Moment-of-silence laws intended to restore prayer to the nation's public schools are unconstitutional. The Court struck down an Alabama law that permitted a moment of silence for prayer or meditation at the beginning of each school day. The history of the law made clear that it was intended as an endorsement of religion, to encourage students to pray. Such state endorsement of religion is a violation of the First Amendment's establishment clause.

Aguilar v. Felton, 473 U.S. 402, decided by a 5–4 vote, July 1, 1985. Brennan wrote the opinion; Burger, White, Rehnquist, and O'Connor dissented.

New York's system for providing remedial and counseling services to disadvantaged students who attend nonpublic schools violates the First Amendment because it uses federal funds to send teachers and other educational personnel into private and parochial schools to provide services to these students during the regular school day. Therefore, like the Grand Rapids system held unconstitutional the same day in *Grand Rapids School District v. Ball,* 473 U.S. 373, it practically and symbolically advances religion by providing services the private or parochial school would otherwise have to provide itself.

POWERS OF CONGRESS

Garcia v. San Antonio Metropolitan Transit Authority, 469 U.S. 528, decided by a 5–4 vote, February 19, 1985. Blackmun wrote the opinion; Burger, Powell, Rehnquist, and O'Connor dissented.

Neither the Tenth Amendment nor any other specific provision of the Constitution limits Congress when it exercises its power to regulate commerce in such a fashion as to curtail the power of the states. The federal minimum wage and overtime law, the Fair Labor Standards Act, applies to the employees of a city owned and operated transit system. The Court overruled its 1976 decision in *National League of Cities v. Usery,* which found that the Tenth Amendment forbade the application of this law to employees of state and local governments.

The Framers of the Constitution intended for the political process and the structure of the federal government to protect state prerogatives. States must use their political power to persuade Congress, not the courts, to change federal laws they find too burdensome.

RIGHT TO COUNSEL

Ake v. Oklahoma, 470 U.S. 68, decided by an 8–1 vote, February 26, 1985. Marshall wrote the opinion; Rehnquist dissented.

Indigents seeking to defend themselves with a claim of insanity are entitled to the aid of a court-appointed psychiatrist, paid for by the government. Defendants in capital cases must also be provided psychiatric counsel when their sentence depends in part upon a finding that they pose a future danger to the community.

SEARCH AND SEIZURE

Tennessee v. Garner, 471 U.S. 1, decided by a 6–3 vote, March 27, 1985. White wrote the opinion; O'Connor, Burger, and Rehnquist dissented.

Police may not use deadly force to stop a fleeing felon unless they have reason to believe that he might kill or seriously injure persons nearby. "A police officer may not seize an unarmed, nondangerous suspect by shooting him dead," declared the Court.

1986

CIVIL RIGHTS

Wygant v. Jackson Board of Education, 476 U.S. 267, decided by a 5–4 vote, May 19, 1986. Powell announced the decision; Brennan, Marshall, Stevens, and Blackmun dissented.

An affirmative action plan voluntarily adopted by a school board, under which white teachers with more seniority were laid off to preserve the jobs of newly hired black teachers, is unconstitutional, a denial to the white teachers of the equal protection of the law. The primary flaw was that the plan was adopted without any showing that the school board had previously discriminated against black teachers. In a separate opinion, O'Connor emphasized that affirmative action, carefully used, was an appropriate remedy for past or present discrimination by a public employer.

Local 28 of Sheet Metal Workers International Assn. v. Equal Employment Opportunity Commission, 478 U.S. 421, decided by a 5–4 vote, July 2, 1986. Brennan wrote the opinion; Burger, White, Rehnquist, and O'Connor dissented.

Court-ordered minority quotas for union admission do not violate Title VII of the 1964 Civil Rights Act, which bans discrimination in employment based on race, sex, religion, or national origin.

Local 93 of International Association of Firefighters v. City of Cleveland, 478 U.S. 501, decided by a 6–3 vote, July 2, 1986. Brennan wrote the opinion; Burger, White, and Rehnquist dissented.

Race-based promotions do not violate Title VII of the 1964 Civil Rights Act when they are part of a consent decree settling a job bias case against a city, and when the promotion plan is for a limited period of time.

CRUEL AND UNUSUAL PUNISHMENT

Lockhart v. McCree, 476 U.S. 162, decided by a 6–3 vote, May 5, 1986. Rehnquist wrote the opinion; Brennan, Marshall, and Stevens dissented.

Opponents of the death penalty may be excluded from juries in capital cases if they oppose capital punishment so strongly that they cannot objectively assess the evidence in the case. They may be excluded even if their exclusion increases the likelihood that the jury will convict the defendant.

Neither the requirement that a jury be drawn from a fair cross-section of the community nor the requirement that the jury be impartial is offended by excluding opponents of capital punishment. An impartial jury is simply one composed of jurors who will conscientiously apply the law and find the facts.

Ford v. Wainwright, 477 U.S. 399, decided by 7–2 and 5–4 votes, June 26, 1986. Marshall wrote the opinion; Rehnquist and Burger dissented; White and O'Connor dissented in part.

The Constitution forbids the execution of an insane prisoner, the Court ruled, 5–4. By a 7–2 vote, it also held inadequate Florida's procedures for deciding whether a death row inmate had lost the ability to understand the reason for his execution. Current procedures permitted that decision to be made entirely within the executive branch without any judicial participation.

EQUAL PROTECTION

Vasquez v. Hillery, 474 U.S. 254, decided by a 6–3 vote, January 14, 1986. Marshall wrote the Court's opinion; Burger, Powell, and Rehnquist dissented.

Anyone indicted by a grand jury selected in a racially discriminatory fashion has the right to a new trial, regardless of how long ago the indictment occurred.

Batson v. Kentucky, 476 U.S. 79, decided by a 7–2 vote, April 30, 1986. Powell wrote the opinion; Burger and Rehnquist dissented.

Prosecutors may not use peremptory challenges to exclude someone from jury service on the basis of race. The Court ruled that such action, when based on racial stereotypes, including the assumption that black jurors will not fairly consider the state's case against a black defendant, violates the right to a fair trial and equal right to jury service.

FREEDOM OF ASSOCIATION

Tashjian v. Republican Party of Connecticut, 479 U.S. 208, decided by a 5–4 vote, December 10, 1986. Marshall wrote the opinion; Rehnquist, Stevens, O'Connor, and Scalia dissented.

States violate the First Amendment guarantee of freedom of association by requiring political parties to hold "closed" primary elections in which only party members may vote. Parties themselves may make that decision, but they may not be required to do so by the states.

PERSONAL PRIVACY

Thornburgh v. American College of Obstetricians and Gynecologists, 476 U.S. 747, decided by a 5–4 vote, June 11, 1986. Blackmun wrote the opinion; White, Rehnquist, O'Connor, and Burger dissented.

Reaffirming *Roe v. Wade,* 1973, the Court struck down a Pennsylvania law designed to discourage women from having abortions. Among the provisions invalidated as unduly burdening a woman's private decision to have an abortion were those that set out specific methods for ensuring that a woman gave "informed consent," required physicians to report certain information about the abortion and to take special care to preserve the life of the fetus in abortions performed after a certain point in pregnancy.

Bowers v. Hardwick, 478 U.S. 186, decided by a 5–4 vote, June 30, 1986. White wrote the opinion; Blackmun, Brennan, Marshall, and Stevens dissented.

The Constitution's guarantees of personal liberty and privacy do not protect private consensual homosexual conduct between consenting adults. The Court upheld Georgia's law against sodomy, which banned oral and anal sex.

POWERS OF CONGRESS

Bowsher v. Synar, Senate v. Synar, O'Neill v. Synar, 478 U.S. 714, decided by a 7–2 vote, July 7, 1986. Burger wrote the opinion; White and Blackmun dissented.

Congress violated the constitutional separation of powers among the judicial, legislative, and executive branches when it included in the 1985 Gramm-Rudman-Hollings deficit reduction law a provision giving the comptroller general the power to tell the president what fixed-percentage cuts he must make in federal spending to meet the targets set by the bill. The comptroller general is removable from office only at the initiative of Congress, which places this position under congressional, not executive, control.

VOTING RIGHTS

Davis v. Bandemer, 478 U.S. 109, decided by 6–3 and 7–2 votes, June 30, 1986. White wrote the opinion; Burger, O'Connor, and Rehnquist dissented in part; Powell and Stevens dissented in part.

Political gerrymanders are subject to constitutional challenge and review by federal courts, even if the disputed districts meet the "one person, one vote" test, the Court held. But, 7–2, it upheld Indiana's 1981 reapportionment plan that heavily favored Republicans, saying that more than one election's results are necessary to prove a gerrymander unconstitutional.

1987

CIVIL RIGHTS

United States v. Paradise, 480 U.S. 149, decided by a 5–4 vote, February 25, 1987. Brennan wrote the opinion; Rehnquist, O'Connor, Scalia, and White dissented.

A federal judge acted constitutionally when he imposed a one-black-for-one-white promotion quota on Alabama's state police. The action was appropriate in light of the state agency's long resistance to efforts to remedy past discrimination against blacks.

Johnson v. Transportation Agency of Santa Clara County, 480 U.S. 616, decided by a 6–3 vote, March 25, 1987. Brennan wrote the opinion; Rehnquist, Scalia, and White dissented.

The Court upheld an affirmative action plan adopted voluntarily by a county agency that resulted in the promotion of a woman over a man who had scored somewhat higher during the qualifying process. Affirmative action, carefully used, does not violate Title VII of the 1964 Civil Rights Act or the Fourteenth Amendment.

CRUEL AND UNUSUAL PUNISHMENT

Tison v. Arizona, 481 U.S. 137, decided by a 5–4 vote, April 21, 1987. O'Connor wrote the opinion; Brennan, Marshall, Blackmun, and Stevens dissented.

It is not unconstitutional to execute persons convicted of being accomplices to murder if their participation in the crime was major and they displayed reckless indifference to the value of human life.

McCleskey v. Kemp, 481 U.S. 279, decided by a 5–4 vote, April 22, 1987. Powell wrote the opinion; Brennan, Marshall, Blackmun, and Stevens dissented.

Statistics showing that black defendants are more likely than white defendants to be sentenced to death are not enough to establish that a particular black defendant was denied equal protection when he was given the death penalty.

DUE PROCESS

United States v. Salerno, 481 U.S. 739, decided by a 6–3 vote, May 26, 1987. Rehnquist wrote the opinion; Brennan, Marshall, and Stevens dissented.

The preventive detention provisions of a 1984 federal anticrime statute are constitutional. It does not violate either due process or the ban on excessive bail for a judge to invoke the law to keep in jail, before trial, a suspect who is considered a danger to the community.

FREEDOM OF RELIGION

Edwards v. Aguillard, 482 U.S. 578, decided by a 7–2 vote, June 19, 1987. Brennan wrote the opinion; Rehnquist and Scalia dissented.

A Louisiana law requiring public schools that teach the theory of evolution also to teach "creation science," violates the establishment clause because the state legislature enacted it for the purpose of promoting religion.

1988

CRUEL AND UNUSUAL PUNISHMENT

Thompson v. Oklahoma, 487 U.S. 815, decided by a 5–3 vote, June 29, 1988. Stevens wrote the opinion; Rehnquist, White, and Scalia dissented; Kennedy did not participate.

It is unconstitutional for a state to execute a capital defendant who was younger than sixteen at the time of his offense, if his sentence was imposed under a law that does not set a minimum age at which defendants are subject to the death penalty.

FREEDOM OF ASSOCIATION

New York State Club Association v. City of New York, 487 U.S. 1, decided by a 9–0 vote, June 20, 1988. White wrote the opinion.

Cities can constitutionally forbid discrimination in any place of public accommodation, including large private clubs used by their members for business purposes.

POWERS OF CONGRESS

South Carolina v. Baker, 485 U.S. 505, decided by a 7–1 vote, April 20, 1988. Brennan wrote the opinion; O'Connor dissented; Kennedy did not participate.

Neither the Tenth Amendment nor the doctrine of intergovernmental tax immunity is violated by the decision of Congress, in the 1982 Tax Equity and Fiscal Responsibility Act, to deny a federal income tax exemption for interest earned on state and local government bonds issued in unregistered form.

Morrison v. Olson, 487 U.S. 654, decided by a 7–1 vote, June 29, 1988. Rehnquist wrote the opinion; Scalia dissented; Kennedy did not participate.

Congress did not violate the separation of powers or usurp executive power when it authorized, as part of the 1978 Ethics in Government Act, the appointment of independent counsels to investigate and prosecute high government officials. The Constitution permits Congress to vest the appointment power of such officials in the judicial branch.

1989

CIVIL RIGHTS

Richmond v. J. A. Croson Co. 488 U.S. 469, decided by a 6–3 vote, January 23, 1989. O'Connor wrote the opinion; Marshall, Brennan, and Blackmun dissented.

A minority set-aside plan adopted by Richmond, Virginia, to assure that 30 percent of city funds granted for construction projects went to minority-owned firms was too rigid and insufficiently justified by past findings of specific discrimination. The Court said a state or local government's affirmative action plan could survive constitutional scrutiny only if the government had a compelling interest in creating the program and it was narrowly tailored to that interest.

Wards Cove Packing Co. v. Atonio, 490 U.S. 642, decided by a 5–4 vote, June 5, 1989. White wrote the Court's opinion; Blackmun, Brennan, Marshall, and Stevens dissented.

Citing statistics that show a particular group is underrepresented in a particular workforce is not sufficient to demonstrate racial discrimination, the Court held. The decision made it more difficult for workers to prove discrimination and made it easier for employers to rebut charges by demonstrating that there is a reasonable business justification for their policies. Congress overturned parts of this decision by passing the Civil Rights Act of 1991.

CRUEL AND UNUSUAL PUNISHMENT

Stanford v. Kentucky, 492 U.S. 361, decided by a 5–4 vote, June 26, 1989. Scalia announced the Court's decision; Brennan, Marshall, Blackmun, and Stevens dissented.

Imposition of the death penalty upon a defendant convicted of a capital crime committed when he or she was only sixteen or seventeen years old does not violate the ban on cruel and unusual punishment simply because of the defendant's youth.

Penry v. Lynaugh, 492 U.S. 302, decided by a 5–4 vote, June 26, 1989. O'Connor announced the Court's decision; Stevens, Blackmun, Brennan, and Marshall dissented.

The constitutional ban on cruel and unusual punishment does not categorically deny a state the power to execute a mentally retarded person who was found competent to stand trial, whose defense of legal insanity was rejected, and who was properly convicted.

FREEDOM OF EXPRESSION

Texas v. Johnson, 491 U.S. 397, decided by a 5–4 vote, June 21, 1989. Brennan wrote the opinion; Rehnquist, White, O'Connor, and Stevens dissented.

The First Amendment guarantee of freedom of expression precludes a state from punishing someone for desecrating the American flag in the course of a peaceful political demonstration.

FREEDOM OF RELIGION

Allegheny County v. American Civil Liberties Union, Greater Pittsburgh Chapter, 492 U.S. 573, decided by votes of 5–4 and 6–3, July 3, 1989. Blackmun wrote the opinion; Brennan, Marshall, and Stevens dissented on one point; Kennedy, Rehnquist, White, and Scalia dissented on another.

Allegheny County violated the First Amendment's establishment clause when it placed a crèche in the center of its courthouse staircase with a banner declaring "Gloria in Excelsis Deo." The vote on this point was 5–4.

But it was not unconstitutional establishment of religion for the county to include a menorah as part of a display outside another government building along with a Christmas tree. The vote on this point was 6–3. Taken together, the rulings suggested that a display that includes secular holiday symbols along with religious items can legitimately be viewed as having a secular purpose and not endorsing religion.

PERSONAL PRIVACY

Webster v. Reproductive Health Services, 492 U.S. 490, decided by a 5–4 vote, July 3, 1989. Rehnquist announced the Court's decision; Blackmun, Brennan, Marshall, and Stevens dissented.

Without overturning *Roe v. Wade,* 1973, the Court upheld Missouri's law barring the use of public facilities or public employees to perform abortions and requiring physicians to test for the viability of any fetus believed to be more than twenty weeks old.

POWERS OF CONGRESS

Mistretta v. United States, 488 U.S. 361, decided by an 8–1 vote, January 18, 1989. Blackmun wrote the opinion; Scalia dissented.

Congress did not unconstitutionally delegate authority to the U.S. Sentencing Commission when it authorized it to set binding guidelines for sentencing federal defendants.

The delegation was specific and detailed. The constitutional separation of powers does not deny Congress the power to delegate this function to a body within the judicial branch, including judges, or to direct the president to select the members of the commission.

SEARCH AND SEIZURE

Skinner v. Railway Labor Executives Association, 489 U.S. 602, decided by a 7–2 vote, March 21, 1989. Kennedy wrote the opinion; Marshall and Brennan dissented.

The Court upheld the Federal Railroad Administration's requirement that railroad workers be subjected to tests for drug and alcohol use after major accidents and other safety violations.

Such tests are a search, but they are reasonable in light of the government's compelling interest in protecting public safety, and warrants are not required.

National Treasury Employees Union v. Von Raab, 489 U.S. 656, decided by a 5–4 vote, March 21, 1989. Kennedy wrote the opinion; Marshall, Brennan, Scalia, and Stevens dissented.

The Court upheld the mandatory drug testing required by the U.S. Customs Service for employees who apply for promotions to positions involving drug-interdiction duties or carrying firearms.

In light of the government's interest in the integrity of the law enforcement process, this "search" is reasonable and may be conducted without a warrant and without any particularized suspicion of an employee.

1990

CIVIL RIGHTS

Metro Broadcasting Inc. v. Federal Communications Commission, Astroline Communications Co. v. Shurberg Broadcasting of Hartford Inc., 497 U.S. 547, decided by a 5–4 vote, June 27, 1990. Brennan wrote the opinion; O'Connor, Rehnquist, Scalia, and Kennedy dissented.

Congress may order preferential treatment of blacks and other minorities to increase their ownership of broadcast licenses. Racial preferences, including those not specifically intended to compensate victims of past discrimination, are constitutional as long as they serve important government objectives.

The Court rejected an argument that the broadcast set-aside programs at issue violated the constitutional guarantee of equal protection of the laws. It stressed Congress's determination that race-based preferences are necessary for broadcast diversity. Distinguishing the case from a 1989 decision in *City of Richmond v. J. A. Croson Co.,* which struck down a city's set-aside program, the Court said the federal government has more power to legislate racial preferences than do state and local governments.

FREEDOM OF ASSOCIATION

Rutan v. Republican Party of Illinois, Frech v. Rutan, 497 U.S. 62, decided by a 5–4 vote, June 21, 1990. Brennan wrote the opinion; Scalia, Rehnquist, Kennedy, and O'Connor dissented.

It is unconstitutional to hire, promote, or transfer most public employees based on party affiliation. Such patronage infringes on the First Amendment rights of public employees unless party membership is an appropriate requirement for the job, for example, in a policy or confidential position. The ruling expanded a 1976 decision, *Elrod v. Burns,* that patronage firing violates the First Amendment right of free association.

FREEDOM OF EXPRESSION

United States v. Eichman, United States v. Haggerty, 496 U.S. 310, decided by a 5–4 vote, June 11, 1990. Brennan wrote the opinion;

Rehnquist, White, Stevens, and O'Connor dissented.

The federal Flag Protection Act making it a crime to burn, mutilate, or otherwise destroy a U.S. flag infringes on free speech rights. The First Amendment forbids government from stopping such political protest by asserting an interest in the physical integrity of the flag. This statute was passed by Congress in response to the Court's 1989 ruling in *Texas v. Johnson,* which invalidated a state statute making it illegal to burn a flag.

FREEDOM OF RELIGION

Employment Division, Department of Human Resources of Oregon v. Smith, 494 U.S. 872, decided by 6–3 and 5–4 votes, April 17, 1990. Scalia wrote the opinion; Blackmun, Brennan, and Marshall dissented; O'Connor dissented in part of the opinion.

States may outlaw the sacramental use of the drug peyote without violating the First Amendment guarantee of free exercise of religion. In so deciding, a five-justice majority said no constitutional violation occurs when a criminal law is applied generally to all people and it has only the incidental effect of infringing on religious exercise. The Court declined to invoke a test used in earlier cases that required a state to prove it had a "compelling interest" in enforcing a statute that infringed on religious freedom. Justice O'Connor sought to keep the stricter constitutional standard.

In 1993 Congress passed the Religious Freedom Restoration Act to counteract the effects of this decision and to reinstate the "compelling interest" test in cases involving free exercise of religion.

Board of Education of the Westside Community Schools (Dist. 66) v. Mergens, 496 U.S. 226, decided by a 8–1 vote, June 4, 1990. O'Connor wrote the opinion; Stevens dissented.

Student religious groups may meet in public high schools on the same basis as other extracurricular clubs. The Equal Access Act, a 1984 federal law, does not breach the Constitution's required separation of church and state.

The Equal Access Act prohibits schools that receive federal funds and that allow extracurricular groups to meet at school from discriminating against any group because of the subject it wants to discuss. The Court said that because the law grants equal access to both secular and religious speech, it was not intended to endorse or disapprove of religion.

PERSONAL PRIVACY

Cruzan v. Director, Missouri Department of Health, 497 U.S. 261, decided by a 5–4 vote, June 25, 1990. Rehnquist wrote the opinion; Brennan, Marshall, Blackmun, and Stevens dissented.

States may stop the family of a comatose patient from disconnecting life support systems unless the family shows clear and convincing evidence of the patient's previously expressed wish to die under such circumstances. Because the choice between life and death is a personal decision of overwhelming finality, the Court said, a state may require clear and convincing evidence of that personal choice.

The Court said for the first time that an individual has a constitutionally protected right to decline lifesaving food and water. All of the justices except Scalia agreed that the due process guarantee protects an interest in life as well as an interest in refusing life-sustaining treatment.

Hodgson v. Minnesota, Minnesota v. Hodgson, 497 U.S. 417, decided by separate 5–4 votes, June 25, 1990. Stevens wrote the opinion striking down a statute that required a teenage girl to notify both biological parents of her decision to have an abortion; Scalia, Kennedy, Rehnquist and White dissented. A separate majority found the statute ultimately constitutional because it provided the alternative of a judicial hearing for girls who did not want to tell their parents. Brennan, Blackmun, Marshall, and Stevens dissented.

States may compel an unmarried woman under age eighteen to tell both parents before obtaining an abortion as long as states provide a judicial hearing on her decision as an alternative to parental notice. The Minnesota statute said no abortion could be performed on a minor until at least forty-eight hours after both biological parents had been notified. Part of the statute said that if the law was ever suspended by a court, it would automatically be amended to allow a judicial hearing as an alternative to a young woman's telling both parents. The so-called judicial bypass is intended to allow a teenager to show either that she is mature enough and well-informed enough to make the abortion decision herself or that the abortion would be in her best interest.

The Court said a required notification of both parents, without exception, does not further legitimate state interests and noted that Minnesota made no exception for a divorced parent, parent without custody, or a biological parent who never married or lived with the pregnant woman's mother.

Ohio v. Akron Center for Reproductive Health, 497 U.S. 502, decided by a 6–3 vote, June 25, 1990. Kennedy wrote the opinion; Blackmun, Brennan, and Marshall dissented.

A state may require an unmarried woman under eighteen who seeks an abortion to notify at least one parent before having an abortion. The Court upheld an Ohio law that barred a physician from performing an abortion on a teenager without giving twenty-four hours' notice to one of the girl's parents or guardians. The law gave young women who did not wish to tell a parent the alternative of appearing before a judge.

The Court said the one-parent notification did not impose an undue or otherwise unconstitutional burden on a minor seeking an abortion. It did not address whether a judicial bypass is necessary in all notice statutes.

SEARCH AND SEIZURE

Michigan Department of State Police v. Sitz, 496 U.S. 444, decided by a 6–3 vote, June 14, 1990. Rehnquist wrote the opinion; Brennan, Marshall, and Stevens dissented.

Police may stop and examine drivers for signs of drunkenness at highway checkpoints. The sobriety checkpoints are not unreasonable "seizures" under the Fourth Amendment because states have a strong interest in deterring drunk driving and the intrusion on motorists stopped is slight.

1991

CIVIL RIGHTS

International Union, United Automobile, Aerospace & Agricultural Implement Workers of America, UAW v. Johnson Controls Inc., 499 U.S. 187, decided by 9–0 and 5–4 votes, March 20, 1991. Blackmun wrote the opinion; White, Rehnquist, Kennedy, and Scalia dissented from a portion of the opinion.

Companies may not exclude women from jobs that might harm a developing fetus, the Court ruled unanimously. The justices divided over how to interpret standards in federal antidiscrimination law. Five justices, led by Blackmun, said Congress had intended to forbid all hiring practices based on a worker's ability to have children. The four dissenting justices said situations could arise in which a company, because of personal injury liability and workplace costs, could lawfully exclude women based on hazards to the unborn.

CRUEL AND UNUSUAL PUNISHMENT

Payne v. Tennessee, 501 U.S. 808, decided by a 6–3 vote, June 27, 1991. Rehnquist wrote the opinion; Marshall, Blackmun, and Stevens dissented.

Evidence of a victim's character and the impact of a crime on the victim's family may be considered by the jury deciding upon the sentence of a convicted murderer who could be sentenced to die. The Eighth Amendment ban on cruel and unusual punishment does not bar a jury from considering such factors.

DUE PROCESS

Arizona v. Fulminante, 499 U.S. 279, decided by a 5–4 decision, March 26, 1991. White and Rehnquist wrote opinions for separate majorities; White, Marshall, Blackmun, and Stevens dissented.

Use of a coerced confession at trial does not automatically taint a conviction that results. If there is other evidence sufficient to convict the defendant, use of a compelled confession may be harmless error—and therefore not require a new trial. With this decision, the Court reversed a 1967 decision, *Chapman v. California,* establishing the rule that due process is always denied when a forced confession is used against a defendant.

FREEDOM OF EXPRESSION

Barnes v. Glen Theatre, 501 U.S. 560, decided by a 5–4 vote, June 21, 1991. Rehnquist wrote the opinion; White, Marshall, Blackmun, and Stevens dissented.

A state may outlaw nude dancing without violating the First Amendment's guarantee of freedom of expression. Although nude dancing may be entitled to some First Amendment protection as communication of an erotic message, other community interests in safety and morality are overriding.

FREEDOM OF THE PRESS

Masson v. New Yorker Magazine, 501 U.S. 496, decided by a 7–2 vote, June 20, 1991. Kennedy wrote the opinion; White and Scalia dissented.

Fabricated quotes may be libelous if they materially change the speaker's meaning. The question for a jury in a libel case is whether a writer acted with knowledge of falsity or reckless disregard for the truth of the passages in question.

Cohen v. Cowles Media Co., 501 U.S. 663, decided by a 5–4 vote, June 24, 1991. White wrote the opinion; Souter, Marshall, Blackmun, and O'Connor dissented.

The First Amendment does not shield the news media from lawsuits charging reporters with breaking promises of confidentiality to sources. State law may permit an individual to recover damages caused by publication of information.

Simon & Schuster v. Members of New York State Crime Victims Board, 502 U.S. 105, decided by an 8–0 vote, December 10, 1991. O'Connor wrote the opinion; Thomas did not participate.

A state law prohibiting publishers from paying criminals for their stories violates the First Amendment guarantees of free press and free speech. The Court said New York's "Son of Sam" law, which redirected criminals' book proceeds to a victims' fund, was too broadly worded. The law covered works on any subject that expressed an author's thoughts about his crime, however incidentally, and it applied to writers who admitted to crimes even if they never were charged or convicted.

FREEDOM OF SPEECH

Rust v. Sullivan, 500 U.S. 173, decided by a 5–4 vote, May 23, 1991. Rehnquist wrote the opinion; Blackmun, Marshall, Stevens, and O'Connor dissented.

Congress may forbid workers at publicly funded clinics from counseling pregnant women on abortion. The Court upheld the administration's interpretation of Title X of the Public Health Service Act of 1970 as barring not only abortions but abortion counseling. The Court said Congress may regulate the content of the speech it funds.

Rejecting a First Amendment challenge, the justices said the restriction on a clinic worker's speech accompanies a worker's decision to be employed in a project financed by the government. It observed that government is not required to subsidize abortions and said the regulations ensure that federal money is spent on services for which it has been granted.

VOTING RIGHTS

Chisom v. Roemer, United States v. Roemer, 501 U.S. 380, decided by a 6–3 vote, June 20, 1991. Stevens wrote the opinion; Scalia, Rehnquist, and Kennedy dissented.

The Voting Rights Act of 1965, as amended in 1982, applies to elections for judges. The law enacted in 1965 unquestionably applied to judicial elections, despite 1982 amendments that referred to the election of "representatives."

1992

CIVIL RIGHTS

United States v. Fordice, Ayers v. Fordice, 505 U.S. 717, decided by an 8–1 vote, June 26, 1992. White wrote the opinion; Scalia dissented.

A state has not fulfilled its constitutional obligation to desegregate a public university system if its seemingly race-neutral policies continue to foster racial discrimination. Judges assessing whether a state has made sufficient effort to desegregate its colleges and universities must ask whether the racial identity of a school stems from state policies and must examine a range of factors to determine whether the state has perpetuated segregation. The state must justify potentially discriminatory practices and explain why a high percentage of whites attend certain schools and a high percentage of blacks attend other schools.

FREEDOM OF RELIGION

Lee v. Weisman, 505 U.S. 577, decided by a 5–4 vote, June 24, 1992. Kennedy wrote the opinion; Scalia, Rehnquist, White, and Thomas dissented.

Prayer at a public school graduation ceremony violates the constitutional requirement of separation of church and state. Elementary and secondary students should not be made to feel coerced to be part of the prayer exercises. In pointing to the constitutional flaws in a Rhode Island school's graduation prayer, the justices stressed that school officials organized the prayer exercise and students were obliged to attend the graduation.

FREEDOM OF SPEECH

R. A. V. v. City of St. Paul, 505 U.S. 377, decided by 9–0 and 5–4 votes, June 22, 1992. Scalia wrote the opinion; White, Blackmun, O'Connor, and Stevens dissented in part.

A city's "hate crime" ordinance, which includes a ban on cross-burning and the display of swastikas, violates the First Amendment's free speech guarantee. The Court ruled that cities may not target "hate speech" tied to race, color, creed, religion, or gender.

The ruling striking down a St. Paul, Minnesota, ordinance was unanimous, but the justices split in their rationale. A five-justice majority said if a municipality wants to outlaw speech that would be considered "fighting words," it must outlaw all fighting words, not just race-, religion-, or gender-based epithets. It said the ordinance's content-based distinctions were impermissible.

PERSONAL PRIVACY

Planned Parenthood of Southeastern Pennsylvania v. Casey, 505 U.S. 833, decided by 5–4 and 7–2 votes, June 29, 1992. O'Connor, Kennedy, and Souter wrote the opinion; Rehnquist, White, Scalia, and Thomas dissented from the part of the opinion upholding a woman's right to an abortion; Blackmun and Stevens dissented from the part of the opinion allowing Pennsylvania abortion restrictions to stand.

The Court affirmed the central holding of *Roe v. Wade,* 1973, which established a constitutional right to abortion and said states may not prohibit abortions at least until a fetus becomes viable. But a plurality of justices instituted a new standard for testing whether state restrictions infringe on the abortion right and upheld Pennsylvania regulations that had earlier been found to conflict with the "fundamental" right to abortion.

The plurality said the standard should be whether a regulation puts an "undue burden" on a woman seeking an abortion. An undue burden exists when a regulation places substantial obstacles in the path of a woman seeking an abortion before the fetus is viable. The Court said a state may adopt regulations to further the health or safety or a woman seeking an abortion but may not impose unnecessary health regulations.

The Pennsylvania provisions that were upheld required a woman seeking an abortion to wait twenty-four hours after being given certain information about the medical procedure and alternatives; required minors to obtain permission from one parent or, alternatively, to go before a judge to get a waiver; imposed reporting requirements on facilities providing abortions; and defined a "medical emergency" that excused compliance with the foregoing requirements. The Court struck down a provision requiring that a woman seeking an abortion sign a statement that she has notified her husband.

1993

CIVIL RIGHTS

Harris v. Forklift Systems, 510 U.S. 17, decided by a 9–0 vote, November 9, 1993. O'Connor wrote the opinion.

A worker who claims sexual harassment must prove the existence of a hostile or abusive work environment but need not show that he or she suffered serious psychological injury as a result of the harassment. The Court said the prohibition on sex discrimination in Title VII of the Civil Rights Act of 1964 "comes into play before the harassing conduct leads to a nervous breakdown."

CRUEL AND UNUSUAL PUNISHMENT

Herrera v. Collins, 506 U.S. 390, decided by a 6–3 vote, January 25, 1993. Rehnquist wrote the opinion; Blackmun, Stevens, and Souter dissented.

A death row prisoner ordinarily is not entitled to federal review of his case based only on an assertion that he is innocent. To obtain a writ of habeas corpus, the inmate must make an independent claim that a constitutional error occurred in his trial or other state proceedings. Federal habeas courts sit not to correct errors of fact but to ensure that individuals are not imprisoned because of constitutional violations.

EXCESSIVE FINES

Austin v. United States, 509 U.S. 602, decided by a 9–0 vote, June 28, 1993. Blackmun wrote the opinion.

The government's power to seize the property of criminals in civil forfeiture proceedings is subject to the Eighth Amendment's prohibition against excessive fines. Confiscation arising from drug trafficking, racketeering, and other criminal allegations must stand in some proportion to the crime at issue, said the Court, but it left unanswered what standard should be used to determine when a forfeiture is "excessive."

FREEDOM OF RELIGION

Lamb's Chapel v. Center Moriches Union Free School District, 508 U.S. 384, decided by a 9–0 vote, June 7, 1993. White wrote the opinion.

A school district policy that denies a religious group access to school facilities after hours for a film presentation, but allows secular groups to use the premises for similar presentations, violates the First Amendment's free speech guarantee. The Court said government cannot deny a speaker the use of public facilities based on the speaker's identity or point of view. The Court rejected an argument that a neutral policy permitting religious groups as well as nonreligious groups to use school property as a meeting place is an unconstitutional establishment of religion.

Zobrest v. Catalina Foothills School District, 509 U.S. 1, decided by a 5–4 vote, June 18, 1993. Rehnquist wrote the opinion; Blackmun, Stevens, O'Connor, and Souter dissented.

The government does not violate the constitutional requirement of separation of church and state when it pays for a sign-language interpreter to accompany a deaf student who attends a parochial school. Providing an interpreter, the Court said, is permissible under the federal Individuals with Disabilities Education Act that distributes benefits neutrally to disabled children in both public and sectarian schools.

VOTING RIGHTS

Shaw v. Reno, 509 U.S. 630, decided by a 5–4 vote, June 28, 1993. O'Connor wrote the opinion; White, Blackmun, Stevens, and Souter dissented.

White voters may challenge black-majority congressional districts that are "highly irregular" in shape and lack "sufficient justification." While the race of voters may be a consideration in redistricting, the Court said, some districts could be so bizarrely drawn that they only can be understood as an effort to segregate voters by race and, therefore, violate the Fourteenth Amendment's guarantee of equal protection of the laws.

The Court said racial gerrymanders may exacerbate the racial bloc voting that "majority-minority" districts originally were intended to counteract. Governments may justify a minority district that is irregular in shape by showing it is narrowly tailored to serve a compelling government interest.

1994

DUE PROCESS

Dolan v. City of Tigard, 114 S. Ct. 2481, decided by a 5–4 vote, June 24, 1994. Rehnquist wrote the opinion; Stevens, Blackmun, Souter, and Ginsburg dissented.

Municipalities that require property owners to turn over some of their land for public use in return for permission to develop the land must show a connection and a "rough proportionality" between conditions exacted and any asserted public harm caused by the development. Without that showing, the actions of local governments could amount to an uncompensated taking of property in violation of the guarantee of due process.

EQUAL PROTECTION

J. E. B. v. Alabama ex rel. T. B., 114 S. Ct. 1419, decided by a 6–3 vote, April 19, 1994. Blackmun wrote the opinion; Scalia, Rehnquist, and Thomas dissented.

Lawyers may not exclude people from serving on juries solely because of their gender. The constitutional guarantee of equal protection of the laws prohibits sexual discrimination in jury selection. This ruling extended the reasoning of a line of cases beginning in 1986 that had barred lawyers from eliminating potential jurors on account of race.

FREEDOM OF EXPRESSION

Turner Broadcasting System Inc. v. Federal Communications Commission, 114 S. Ct. 2445, decided by 9–0 and 5–4 votes, June 27, 1994. Kennedy wrote the opinion; Stevens dissented in one part; O'Connor, Scalia, Thomas, and Ginsburg dissented in another part.

Cable television is entitled to First Amendment protections comparable to those enjoyed by newspapers and other print media rather than those protections afforded broadcasters. The reason that broadcasters have lesser protection and therefore stricter regulation—the scarcity of radio and television channels—does not apply to cable television. The Court said restrictions on cable television should be reviewed under an "intermediate scrutiny" standard, which would allow a regulation of speech if it is narrowly tailored to further an important government interest.

The Court left unresolved a constitutional challenge to the 1992 law requiring cable systems to carry local broadcast stations, voting 5–4 to order a lower court to hear more evidence in the case. The dissenting justices said "must carry" rules were an inappropriate restraint on the cable operator's editorial discretion and freedom of speech.

FREEDOM OF RELIGION

Board of Education of Kiryas Joel Village School District v. Grumet, 114 S. Ct. 2481, decided by a 6–3 vote, June 27, 1994. Souter wrote the opinion; Scalia, Rehnquist, and Thomas dissented.

A New York law creating a special school district to serve the disabled children of a Hasidic sect violates the constitutional requirement of separation of church and state. The law designated the village of Kiryas Joel, inhabited exclusively by the Satmar Hasidim, as a state school district. The Court said New York's action wrongly favored a single religious group and there was no assurance that the state would provide the same benefit equally to other religious and nonreligious groups.

FREEDOM OF SPEECH

Madsen v. Women's Health Center Inc., 512 U.S. ____, decided by a 6–3 vote, June 30, 1994. Rehnquist wrote the opinion; Scalia, Kennedy, and Thomas dissented.

Judges may establish "buffer zones" to prevent antiabortion protesters from getting too close to clinics where abortions are performed. But judges may not restrict "more speech than necessary" to protect access to clinics or other government interests. The Court upheld an injunction prohibiting demonstrations within thirty-six feet of a clinic because it was aimed at protesters who had violated an earlier court order by blocking access, not at their particular anti-abortion message, and because it curtailed no more speech than necessary.

VOTING RIGHTS

Holder v. Hall, 114 S. Ct. 2581, decided by a 5–4 vote, June 30, 1994. Kennedy wrote the opinion; Blackmun, Stevens, Souter, and Ginsburg dissented.

The size of a governing body—in this case a single county commissioner with executive and legislative authority—is not subject to challenge under the federal Voting Rights Act. The Court barred a lawsuit against the unusual government structure used in rural Bleckley County, Georgia. Blacks, who made up about 20 percent of the county's population, claimed the single-member commission violated the Voting Rights Act by "diluting" their opportunity to elect a black to the office.

1995

CIVIL RIGHTS

Adarand Constructors Inc. v. Peña, 115 S. Ct. 2097, decided by a 5–4 vote, June 12, 1995. O'Connor wrote the opinion; Stevens, Souter, Ginsburg, and Breyer dissented.

Federal affirmative action programs are unconstitutional unless they serve a compelling government interest and are narrowly tailored to address that interest. Federal policies based on race should undergo the strictest judicial scrutiny to ensure that an individual's right to equal protection of the laws has not been infringed.

The Court did not decide whether the particular affirmative action program before it—a federal highway contracting program that gave bonuses to companies that subcontracted with minority-owned firms—was constitutional or not, leaving that to lower courts to resolve based on its new, heightened standard of scrutiny. With this decision the Court overturned its 1990 ruling in *Metro Broadcasting Inc. v. Federal Communications Commission,* which said minority set-asides are constitutional as long as they serve important government objectives.

Missouri v. Jenkins, 115 S. Ct. 2038, decided by a 5–4 vote, June 12, 1995. Rehnquist wrote the opinion; Stevens, Souter, Ginsburg, and Breyer dissented.

A federal district judge overseeing a school desegregation plan exceeded his authority when he ordered extra public spending to make the district more attractive to students in other districts and to reverse the trend of "white flight." Desegregation remedies must be tailored to address specific constitutional violations within a district.

COMMERCE

United States v. Lopez, 115 S. Ct. 1624, decided by a 5–4 vote, April 26, 1995. Rehnquist wrote the opinion; Breyer, Stevens, Souter, and Ginsburg dissented.

Congress exceeded its authority to regulate interstate commerce when it passed a law banning guns within one thousand feet of a school. The Court said the statute had "nothing to do with commerce or any sort of economic enterprise." The simple possession of a gun in or near a school is an essentially local, noncommercial activity that does not have a substantial effect on interstate commerce, the Court said.

FREEDOM OF EXPRESSION

McIntyre v. Ohio Elections Commission, 115 S. Ct. 1511, decided by a 7–2 vote, April 19, 1995. Stevens wrote the opinion; Scalia and Rehnquist dissented.

States cannot prohibit the distribution of anonymous leaflets and other campaign literature without impinging the First Amendment. Anonymous pamphleteering is part of the nation's heritage, the Court said, and a way to ensure that the voices of the minority are protected from the majority.

Hurley v. Irish-American Gay, Lesbian and Bisexual Group of Boston, 115 S. Ct. 2338, decided by a 9–0 vote, June 19, 1995. Souter wrote the opinion.

The organizers of a parade cannot be required by state law to include participants with whom they disagree, in this case, marchers who wish to proclaim their homosexual identity. A parade is a form of private expression protected by the First Amendment's guarantee of free speech.

FREEDOM OF RELIGION

Rosenberger v. Rector and Visitors of University of Virginia, 115 S. Ct. 2510, decided by a 5–4 vote, June 29, 1995. Kennedy wrote the opinion; Stevens, Souter, Ginsburg, and Breyer dissented.

A university violated the First Amendment by refusing to provide funds for a student group's Christian magazine while at the same time subsidizing nonreligious student publications. The Court rejected an argument that the constitutional requirement of separation of church and state prohibits a university from providing funds for a religious group. A university that sets up a general policy for disbursing student activity funds must subsidize secular and religious publications on the same basis.

Capital Square Review and Advisory Board v. Pinette, ____U.S. ____, decided by a 7–2 vote, June 29, 1995. Scalia wrote the opinion; Stevens and Ginsburg dissented.

Government officials cannot exclude a privately sponsored religious message from a public forum so long as the forum is open to other privately sponsored messages. Ohio officials denied members of the Ku Klux Klan their free speech rights when they barred them from putting up a large wooden cross in front of the state capitol. Such exclusion was not required to preserve the separation of church and state, the Court said, reasoning that a privately erected cross in a public forum would not cause an observer to think that the state endorsed its message.

SEARCH AND SEIZURE

Vernonia School District 47J v. Acton, 115 S. Ct. 2386, decided by a 6–3 vote, June 26, 1995. Scalia wrote the opinion; O'Connor, Stevens, and Souter dissented.

Public schools may require all student participants in sports to undergo drug tests, regardless of whether any are suspected of drug use. A school district's urinalysis requirement does not violate the constitutional protection against unreasonable searches because children do not have the full fundamental rights of adults and can be subjected to more regulation by school officials, who act as substitute parents.

STATE POWERS

U.S. Term Limits v. Thornton, 115 S. Ct. 1842, decided by a 5–4 vote, May 22, 1995. Stevens wrote the opinion; Rehnquist, O'Connor, Scalia, and Thomas dissented.

States may not set a limit on the number of terms their representatives serve in Congress. The Constitution sets three qualifications for members of Congress: age, citizenship, and residency. To allow states to adopt term limits would create a patchwork of tenure qualifications and undermine the uniform national character of Congress sought by the Founders.

VOTING RIGHTS

Miller v. Johnson, 115 S. Ct. 2475, decided by a 5–4 vote, June 29, 1995. Kennedy wrote the opinion; Stevens, Souter, Ginsburg, and Breyer dissented.

A judge should strictly scrutinize any redistricting plan in which the race of voters has been a "predominant factor" in drawing boundaries. Strict scrutiny is required by the Constitution to ensure that "majority minority" districts do not violate white voters' right to equal protection. A state must prove that it has a compelling interest in drawing districts in which race was a predominant factor and that the districts have been narrowly tailored to meet that interest.

1996

CIVIL RIGHTS

Romer v. Evans, ____U.S. ____, decided by a 6–3 vote, May 20, 1996. Kennedy wrote the opinion; Scalia, Rehnquist, and Thomas dissented.

An amendment to the Colorado state constitution prohibiting local laws that protect homosexuals from discrimination violates the federal Constitution's guarantee of equal protection. The amendment, adopted by voters in 1992, barred any legislative, executive, or judicial action designed to protect Coloradans based on their "homosexual, lesbian or bisexual orientation, conduct, practices or relationships."

The Court said the amendment lacked a rational relationship to any legitimate state interest. Indeed, it "seems inexplicable by anything but animus toward the class that it affects," the majority said.

DUE PROCESS

Bennis v. Michigan, _____U.S. _____, decided by a 5–4 vote, March 4, 1996. Rehnquist wrote the opinion; Stevens, Souter, Breyer, and Kennedy dissented.

A state law that allows an innocent co-owner to forfeit property because of the other owner's criminal activity does not violate the Fourteenth Amendment's due process clause or the Fifth Amendment protection against takings. The case involved a woman whose car was seized after her husband was caught in the car engaging in a sex act with a prostitute. The wife protested the forfeiture, saying she did not know her husband would use the car to violate state law. But the Court said that a co-owner's lack of knowledge of the wrongdoing is not an adequate defense.

EQUAL PROTECTION

United States v. Virginia, _____U.S. _____, decided by a 7–1 vote, June 26, 1996. Ginsburg wrote the opinion; Scalia dissented; Thomas did not participate.

The exclusion of women from the state-funded Virginia Military Institute breaches the constitutional guarantee of equal protection. When government defends sex-based distinctions, it must demonstrate an "exceedingly persuasive justification" for them.

Emphasizing that government may not rely on stereotypes of the talents and preferences of men and women, the Court reinforced its view that a state policy that separates people by sex is constitutional only if it serves important governmental objectives and is substantially related to the achievement of those objectives.

FREEDOM OF EXPRESSION

O'Hare Truck Service v. Northlake, _____U.S. _____, decided by a 7–2 vote, June 28, 1996. Kennedy wrote the opinion; Scalia and Thomas dissented.

Government officials may not retaliate against a contractor for voting for a political opponent or otherwise refusing to pledge political allegiance. The Court extended to contractors First Amendment associational protections articulated in past cases to protect regular payroll employees from being fired because they declined to adopt the policies of the government for which they worked.

FREEDOM OF SPEECH

44 Liquormart v. Rhode Island, _____U.S. _____, decided 9–0, May 13, 1996. Stevens wrote the opinion.

A Rhode Island prohibition on the advertisement of retail liquor prices violates the First Amendment guarantee of free speech. While the justices splintered in their reasoning over four separate opinions, the majority offered broad protections for commercial speech and said advertising that is neither false nor misleading should be especially scrutinized. Regarding the law's regulation of liquor prices, Stevens, joined by three justices, said courts should be especially skeptical of regulations "that seek to keep people in the dark for . . . their own good."

Board of County Commissioners, Wabaunsee County v. Umbehr, _____U.S. _____, decided by a 7–2 vote, June 28, 1996. O'Connor wrote the opinion; Scalia and Thomas dissented.

The First Amendment protects independent contractors from being terminated for speaking out on public issues. The Court extended free speech protections similar to those enjoyed by regular payroll employees to independent contractors, finding that, although an individual's and the government's interests are typically less strong in an independent contractor case, contractors are similar in most relevant respects. The majority said lower courts should weigh the public employer's legitimate interests against the contractor's free speech rights.

HABEAS CORPUS

Felker v. Turpin, _____U.S. _____, decided 9–0, June 28, 1996. Rehnquist wrote the opinion.

A federal law limiting successive habeas corpus petitions, intended by Congress to eliminate protracted appeals from death row prisoners, is constitutional. The Court said that while Congress changed the standards for the justices' review of most second and successive petitions, lawmakers did not constrain the Court's ability to hear habeas petitions as an original matter (petitions made directly to the Supreme Court, rather than coming from lower courts) and therefore did not affect the Court's constitutional jurisdiction.

STATE SOVEREIGNTY

Seminole Tribe of Florida v. Florida, _____U.S. _____, decided by a 5–4 vote, March 27, 1996. Rehnquist wrote the opinion; Stevens, Souter, Ginsburg, and Breyer dissented.

The Eleventh Amendment prevents Congress from authorizing lawsuits by Indian tribes to enforce federal legislation relating to Indian gambling compacts. The Indian Gaming Regulatory Act allowed tribes to run commercial gambling operations under valid agreements with a state. The act required states to negotiate in good faith with a tribe toward a compact and said a tribe could sue a state in federal court to compel the negotiations.

The Court ruled that Congress infringed on state sovereignty in allowing states to be sued. Congress may abrogate state sovereign immunity only when it acts pursuant to a valid exercise of power; the Indian Commerce Clause does not provide such authority.

VOTING RIGHTS

Bush v. Vera, _____U.S. _____, decided by a 5–4 vote, June 13, 1996. O'Connor wrote the opinion; Stevens, Ginsburg, Breyer, and Souter dissented.

Two Texas majority-black congressional voting districts and one majority-Hispanic district violate the equal protection guarantee because residents' race was the predominant factor in drawing boundaries and state officials lacked a compelling reason for the emphasis on race. The Court adopted findings from a special three-judge panel that Texas had substantially neglected traditional districting criteria, such as compactness, and had been committed from the outset to creating minority districts.

Shaw v. Hunt, _____U.S. _____, decided by a 5–4 vote, June 13, 1996. Rehnquist wrote the opinion; Stevens, Ginsburg, Breyer, and Souter dissented.

A North Carolina majority-black congressional voting district is unconstitutional because race was the predominant factor in drawing the lines and the state lacked a compelling interest for the action. The Court rejected North Carolina's arguments that the majority black district was required under federal voting rights law to eliminate the lingering effects of discrimination.

SOURCES: *United States Reports* (Washington, D.C.: U.S. Government Printing Office); *United States Law Week* (Washington, D.C.: Bureau of National Affairs); *Supreme Court Reporter* (Saint Paul, Minn.: West Publishing Company); *United States Supreme Court Reports, Lawyers' Edition* (Rochester, N.Y.: Lawyers Cooperative Publishing Company; Paul A. Freund and Stanley N. Katz, gen. eds., *History of the Supreme Court of the United States*. vol. 1, *Antecedents and Beginnings to 1801*, by Julius Goebel Jr., 1971; vol. 2, *Foundations of Power: John Marshall, 1801–1815*, by George L. Haskins and Herbert A. Johnson, 1981; vols. 3–4, *The Marshall Court and Cultural Change, 1815–1835*, by G. Edward White, 1988; vol. 5, *The Taney Period, 1836–1864*, by Carl B. Swisher, 1974; vol. 6: *Reconstruction and Reunion, 1864–1888*, part one, by Charles Fairman, 1971; vol. 7, *Reconstruction and Reunion, 1864–1888*, part two, by Charles Fairman, 1987; Supplement to vol. 7, *Five Justices and the Electoral Commission of 1877*, by Charles Fairman, 1988; vol. 8, *Troubled Beginnings of the Modern State, 1888–1910*, by Owen M. Fiss, 1993; vol. 9, *The Judiciary and Responsible Government, 1910–1921*, by Alexander M. Bickel and Benno C. Schmidt Jr., 1984 (New York: Macmillan); and Charles Warren, *The Supreme Court in United States History*, rev. ed., 2 vols. (Boston: Little, Brown, 1922, 1926).

NOTE: Any discrepancy between the votes reported for decisions in this list and those reported by other sources may be explained by the fact that this chronology summarizes the most important point of a decision and reports the vote on that point. Votes on other issues resolved in that case may differ, especially in a highly contentious case.

The Federal Court System

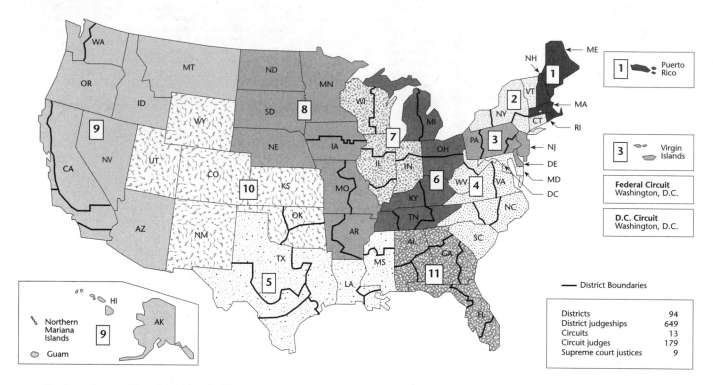

NOTE: Number and composition of circuits set forth by U.S.C. § 4. The large numerals indicate the Courts of Appeals.

SOURCES: Administrative Office of the United States Courts; Lee Epstein, Jeffrey A. Segal, Harold J. Spaeth, and Thomas G. Walker, *The Supreme Court Compendium: Data, Decisions, and Developments,* Second Edition (Washington, D.C.: Congressional Quarterly, 1996), 651.

Selected Bibliography

American Bar Association. "The Supreme Court—Its Homes Past and Present." *American Bar Association Journal* 27 (1941).

Baker, Liva. *Felix Frankfurter.* New York: Coward-McCann, 1969.

Bickel, Alexander M. *The Unpublished Opinions of Justice Brandeis.* Cambridge: Harvard University Press, 1957.

———. *The Least Dangerous Branch.* Indianapolis: Bobbs-Merrill, 1962.

———. *Politics and the Warren Court.* New York: Harper and Row, 1965.

———. *The Caseload of the Supreme Court.* Washington, D.C.: American Enterprise Institute for Public Policy Research, 1973.

Brennan, William J. Jr. "State Court Decisions and the Supreme Court." *Pennsylvania Bar Association Quarterly* 31 (1960).

Brenner, Saul, and Harold J. Spaeth. *Stare Indecisis: The Alteration of Precedent on the Supreme Court, 1946–1992.* Cambridge: Cambridge University Press, 1995.

Caplan, Lincoln. *The Tenth Justice: The Solicitor General and the Rule of Law.* New York: Knopf, 1987.

Cranberg, Gilbert. "What Did the Supreme Court Say?" *Saturday Review.* April 8, 1967.

Cranch, William. Preface to Vol. 1 of *Reports of Cases Argued and Adjudged in the Supreme Court of the United States in August and December Terms, 1801, and February Term, 1803.*

Curtis, Charles P. Jr. *Lions Under the Throne.* Boston: Houghton Mifflin, 1947.

Elsasser, Glenn, and Jack Fuller. "The Hidden Face of the Supreme Court." *Chicago Tribune Magazine,* April 23, 1978.

Fairman, Charles. *Mr. Justice Miller.* Cambridge: Harvard University Press, 1939.

Frank, John P. *Marble Palace: The Supreme Court in American Life.* New York: Knopf, 1961.

Freund, Paul A. *The Supreme Court of the United States.* Cleveland: World Publishing, 1961.

Freund, Paul A., and Stanley N. Katz, gen. eds., *History of the Supreme Court of the United States.* Vol. 1, *Antecedents and Beginnings to 1801,* by Julius Goebel Jr., 1971; Vol. 2, *Foundations of Power: John Marshall, 1801–1815,* by George L. Haskins and Herbert A. Johnson, 1981; Vols. 3–4, *The Marshall Court and Cultural Change, 1815–1835,* by G. Edward White, 1988; Vol. 5, *The Taney Period, 1836–1864,* by Carl B. Swisher, 1974; Vol. 6, *Reconstruction and Reunion, 1864–1888,* Part One, by Charles Fairman, 1971; Vol. 7, *Reconstruction and Reunion, 1864–1888,* Part Two, by Charles Fairman, 1987; Supplement to Vol. 7, *Five Justices and the Electoral Commission of 1877,* by Charles Fairman, 1988; Vol. 8, *Troubled Beginnings of the Modern State, 1888–1910,* by Owen M. Fiss, 1993; Vol. 9, *The Judiciary and Responsible Government, 1910–1921,* by Alexander M. Bickel and Benno C. Schmidt Jr., 1984. New York: Macmillan.

Friedman, Leon, and Fred L. Israel, eds. *Justices of the United States Supreme Court, 1789–1991.* 5 vols., rev. ed. New York: Chelsea House, 1992.

Greenhouse, Linda. "The Year the Court Turned to the Right." *New York Times,* July 7, 1989.

Haines, Charles G. *The American Doctrine of Judicial Supremacy.* 2d ed. Berkeley: University of California Press, 1932; reprint ed. New York: Da Capo Press, 1973.

Hand, Learned. *The Bill of Rights.* New York: Atheneum, 1964.

Harrell, Mary Ann. *Equal Justice Under Law: The Supreme Court in American Life.* 5th ed. Washington, D.C.: The Foundation of the Federal Bar Association, with the cooperation of the National Geographic Society, 1988.

Hughes, Charles Evans. *The Supreme Court of the United States: Its Foundations, Methods and Achievements, An Interpretation.* New York: Columbia University Press, 1928.

Jackson, Robert H. *The Struggle for Judicial Supremacy.* New York: Knopf, 1941.

———. "Advocacy Before the Supreme Court: Suggestions for Effective Case Presentations." *American Bar Association Journal* 101 (1951).

———. *The Supreme Court in the American System of Government.* Cambridge: Harvard University Press, 1955.

King, Willard L. *Melville Weston Fuller.* New York: Macmillan, 1950.

Kluger, Richard. *Simple Justice:* Brown v. Board of Education *and Black America's Struggle for Equality.* New York: Knopf, 1976.

Lash, Joseph P. *From the Diaries of Felix Frankfurter.* Norton, 1975.

Lasser, William. *The Limits of Judicial Power: The Supreme Court in American Politics.* Chapel Hill: University of North Carolina Press, 1988.

Lively, Donald E. *Foreshadows of the Law: Supreme Court Dissents and Constitutional Development.* Westport, Conn.: Praeger, 1993.

Madison, James, Alexander Hamilton, and John Jay. *The Federalist Papers.* Introduction by Clinton Rossiter. New York: New American Library, Mentor Books, 1961.

Mason, Alpheus T. *Harlan Fiske Stone: Pillar of the Law.* New York: Viking, 1956.

———. *The Supreme Court from Taft to Warren.* Baton Rouge: Louisiana State University, 1958.

McCloskey, Robert G., and Sanford Levinson. *The Modern Supreme Court.* 2d ed. Chicago: University of Chicago Press, 1994.

McCune, Wesley. *The Nine Young Men.* New York: Harper and Brothers, 1947.

McGuire, Kevin T. *The Supreme Court Bar: Legal Elites in the Washington Community.* Charlottesville: University of Virginia Press, 1993.

Miller, Samuel F. *Lectures on the Constitution of the United States.* New York and Albany: Banks & Brothers, 1891.

Murphy, Bruce Allen. *The Brandeis/Frankfurter Connection: The Secret Political Activities of Two Supreme Court Justices.* New York: Oxford University Press, 1982.

O'Brien, David M. *Storm Center: The Supreme Court in American Politics.* New York: Norton, 1986.

Perry, H. W. Jr. *Deciding to Decide: Agenda Setting in the United States Supreme Court.* Cambridge: Harvard University Press, 1992.

Pfeffer, Leo. *This Honorable Court: A History of the United States Supreme Court.* Boston: Beacon Press, 1965.

Pringle, Henry F. *Life and Times of William Howard Taft.* New York: Farrar and Rinehart, 1939.

Pusey, Merlo F. *Charles Evans Hughes.* New York: Columbia University Press, 1963.

Rehnquist, William H. *The Supreme Court: How It Was, How It Is.* New York: Morrow, 1987.

Schlesinger, Arthur M. Jr. *The Politics of Upheaval.* Cambridge, Mass.: Houghton Mifflin, 1960.

Schwartz, Bernard. *Super Chief: Earl Warren and His Supreme Court, A Judicial Biography.* New York: New York University Press, 1983.

Simon, James F. *In His Own Image: The Supreme Court in Richard Nixon's America.* New York: McKay, 1973.

Steamer, Robert J. *Chief Justice: Leadership and the Supreme Court.* Columbia: University of South Carolina Press, 1986.

Stern, Robert L., Eugene Gressman, Stephen M. Shapiro, and Kenneth S. Geller. *Supreme Court Practice.* 7th ed. Washington, D.C.: Bureau of National Affairs, 1993.

Swindler, William F. *Court and Constitution in the 20th Century: The Old Legality, 1889–1932.* Indianapolis: Bobbs-Merrill, 1969.

———. *Court and Constitution in the 20th Century: The New Legality, 1932–1968.* Indianapolis: Bobbs-Merrill, 1970.

Tocqueville, Alexis de. *Democracy in America.* New York: Knopf and Random House, Vintage Books, 1945.

Tribe, Laurence H. *God Save This Honorable Court.* New York: Random House, 1985.

Warren, Charles. *The Supreme Court in United States History.* rev. ed., 2 vols. Boston: Little, Brown, 1922, 1926.

———. *Congress, the Constitution and the Supreme Court.* Boston: Little, Brown, 1925.

Williams, Richard L. "Supreme Court of the United States: The Staff That Keeps It Operating." *Smithsonian,* January 1977.

———. "Justices Run 'Nine Little Law Firms' at Supreme Court." *Smithsonian,* February 1977.

Zobell, Karl M. "Division of Opinion in the Supreme Court: A History of Judicial Disintegration." *Cornell Law Quarterly* 44 (1959).

Illustration Credits and Acknowledgments

Subject Index

Case Index